This book is an introduction to syntactic theory and analysis which can be used for both introductory and advanced courses in theoretical syntax. Offering an alternative to the standard generative view of the subject, it deals with the major issues in syntax with which all theories are concerned. It presents syntactic phenomena from a wide range of languages and introduces students to the major typological issues that syntactic theories must address. A generous number of exercises is included, which provide practice with the concepts introduced in the text and in addition expose the student to in-depth analysis of data from many languages. Each chapter contains suggestions for further reading which encompass work from many theoretical perspectives.

CAMBRIDGE TEXTBOOKS IN LINGUISTICS

SYNTAX

In this series:

P. H. MATTHEWS *Morphology* Second edition
B. COMRIE *Aspect*
R. M. KEMPSON *Semantic theory*
T. BYNON *Historical linguistics*
J. ALLWOOD, L.-G. ANDERSON and Ö. DAHL *Logic in linguistics*
D. B. FRY *The physics of speech*
R. A. HUDSON *Sociolinguistics* Second edition
J. K. CHAMBERS and P. TRUDGILL *Dialectology*
A. J. ELLIOTT *Child language*
P. H. MATTHEWS *Syntax*
A. RADFORD *Transformational syntax*
L. BAUER *English Word-formation*
S. C. LEVINSON *Pragmatics*
G. BROWN and G. YULE *Discourse analysis*
R. HUDDLESTON *Introduction to the grammar of English*
R. LASS *Phonology*
B. COMRIE *Tense*
W. KLEIN *Second language acquisition*
A. CRUTTENDEN *Intonation*
A. J. WOODS, P. FLETCHER and A. HUGHES *Statistics in language studies*
D. A. CRUSE *Lexical semantics*
F. R. PALMER *Mood and modality*
A. RADFORD *Transformational grammar*
M. GARMAN *Psycholinguistics*
W. CROFT *Typology and universals*
G. G. CORBETT *Gender*
H. J. GIEGERICH *English phonology*
R. CANN *Formal semantics*
P. J. HOPPER and E. C. TRAUGOTT *Grammaticalization*
J. LAVER *Principles of phonetics*
F. R. PALMER *Grammatical roles and relations*
B. BLAKE *Case*
M. A. JONES *Foundations of French syntax*
A. RADFORD *Syntactic theory and the structure of English: a minimalist approach*
R. D. VAN VALIN, JR. and R. J. LAPOLLA *Syntax: structure, meaning and function*

SYNTAX

STRUCTURE, MEANING AND FUNCTION

ROBERT D. VAN VALIN, JR

STATE UNIVERSITY OF NEW YORK AT BUFFALO

RANDY J. LAPOLLA

CITY UNIVERSITY OF HONG KONG AND
ACADEMIA SINICA, TAIWAN

PUBLISHED BY THE PRESS SYNDICATE OF THE UNIVERSITY OF CAMBRIDGE
The Pitt Building, Trumpington Street, Cambridge CB2 1RP, United Kingdom

CAMBRIDGE UNIVERSITY PRESS
The Edinburgh Building, Cambridge CB2 2RU, United Kingdom
40 West 20th Street, New York, NY 10011–4211, USA
10 Stamford Road, Oakleigh, Melbourne 3166, Australia

First published 1997

Printed in the United Kingdom at the University Press, Cambridge

Typeset in 9/13pt Times Ten [GC]

A catalogue record for this book is available from the British Library

Library of Congress cataloguing in publication data

ISBN 0 521 49565 2 hardback
ISBN 0 521 49915 1 paperback

CONTENTS

FIGURES

TABLES

ACKNOWLEDGMENTS

This book began as transcripts of lectures given in a syntax course by the first author. They were used in courses at several universities over the years, and during that time many people, both students and faculty, gave suggestions, made comments and contributed to them in many ways. We would like to thank everyone who read and commented on the earliest versions of this text. In the past two years the transcripts have undergone an intense process of rethinking, rewriting, revising and expansion, and the resulting text owes a great deal to the many linguists who have read and commented on drafts, provided data and contributed in important ways. We would like to thank first and foremost our two editors from the Textbooks in Linguistics series, Bernard Comrie and Nigel Vincent, for their valuable comments and guidance. Jean-Pierre Koenig read the entire manuscript and provided many very helpful criticisms and suggestions. Balthasar Bickel, Knud Lambrecht and David Wilkins also contributed very useful comments and ideas on different parts of the text. We would also like to thank the following people for their valuable comments and suggestions: Keith Allan, Melissa Bowerman, R. M. W. Dixon, Yoko Hasegawa, Jeri Jaeger, Beth Levin, Wataru Nakamura, Dan Slobin, James Watters and Richard Weist.

A version of the manuscript was used in the first author's Syntax 2 course at SUNY Buffalo in spring semester, 1996, and we would like to thank the graduate students in the course for all of the invaluable input they gave us, especially Shingo Imai and Heechul Lee.

We would like to express our gratitude to the following people who provided us with data and shared their ideas and intuitions about it with us: Seydou S. Bengali (Bamanakan [Bambara]), Giulia Centineo (Italian), R. M. W. Dixon (Dyirbal), Yoko Hasegawa (Japanese), Shingo Imai (Japanese), Jean-Pierre Koenig (French), Aylin Kuntay (Turkish), Richard Lungstrum (Lakhota), Wataru Nakamura (Japanese), Suda Rangkupan (Thai), Eiríkur Rögnvaldsson (Icelandic), Sabine Stoll (Russian), Charles Walton (Sama), David Wilkins (Mparntwe Arrernte) and Milena Žic-Fuchs (Croatian).

The first author did a lot of writing on the book during two stints as a visitor in the Cognitive Anthropology Research Group at the Max-Planck-Institut für

Psycholinguistik in Nijmegen, the Netherlands. He would like to acknowledge the wonderful intellectual environment and to thank the members of the Cognitive Anthropology Group and the other scholars at the Institute for stimulating interactions on a variety of issues related to the book.

Finally, we would like to thank our families for their patience during the long writing process and for their encouragement and support.

NOTES FOR INSTRUCTORS

The purpose of this book is to provide an introduction to syntactic theory and analysis which can be used with both beginning and advanced students. The theoretical orientation of the presentation is laid out in chapter 1 and placed in the context of contemporary linguistic theories. There is more material in the book than could be easily covered in a single semester; accordingly, it has been organized in such a way as to facilitate breaking it up for introductory and more advanced courses.

If used as an introductory text, the book presupposes a standard introduction to the basic notions in syntax and morphology. The recommended sections for an introduction to syntactic theory course are:

chapter 1: all (optional)
chapter 2: all (section 2.4 optional)
chapter 3: all
chapter 4: sections 4.0–4.5
chapter 5: sections 5.0–5.4
chapter 6: all
chapter 7: sections 7.0–7.3 (section 7.3.2 optional)
chapter 8: sections 8.0–8.4
chapter 9: sections 9.0–9.2
Epilog: all (optional)

There are a number of options available when using the book for more advanced courses. First, if the introductory course were based on this book as well, then the sections listed above could be reviewed and then the more advanced material in the remaining sections could be worked through. Second, if the introductory course were based on GB or another generative theory, then presumably the material listed above could be covered more quickly, due to the students' familiarity with the major issues in syntactic theory. Many of the topics that are of particular concern to GB and related theories, e.g. binding, subjacency and quantifier scope, are dealt with in sections from chapters 5, 7 and 9 not listed above. Chapter 1 and the Epilog should definitely be included in such a course, since chapter 1 contrasts the orientation of this book with that of GB and the Epilog deals with the important issue of language acquisition.

The exercises at the end of each chapter are keyed to specific sections in the chapter. This is indicated by a section number in square brackets at the end of the text part of the problem, e.g. '[section 3.2.1]'. This means that the student should be able to do the exercise after having mastered the material in that section. This will allow the instructor to assign exercises that are appropriate for the material covered. Inquiries, comments and suggestions regarding the exercises are welcome; please direct them to VANVALIN@ACSU.BUFFALO.EDU. An instructor's guide, including solutions to all of the exercises, is available from the first author.

There are suggested readings at the end of each chapter, and they are not limited to work sharing the same theoretical orientation as the book; rather, they are intended to direct the student toward important work on a particular topic from a variety of theoretical perspectives. We have not included a glossary of terms used in syntactic theory and analysis; we recommend R. L. Trask's *A dictionary of grammatical terms in linguistics* (London: Routledge, 1993) as a companion to this volume, as it contains a comprehensive list of terms with definitions, exemplifications and references.

ABBREVIATIONS

A, ACT	Actor, actor of transitive verb
AAJ	Argument adjunct
ABS	Absolutive
ACC	Accusative
ACS	Accessible
ACV	Active, activated
Adj(P)	Adjective (phrase)
ADV	Adverb
AFD	Actual focus domain
AJT	Adjunct
ALL	Allative
AN(IM)	Animate
ANT	Anterior
ANTI	Antipassive
AOR	Aorist
APL	Applicative
ARG	Argument
AR/J	Argument or argument adjunct
ART	Article
ASC	Associative
ASP	Aspect
ATV	Active voice
AUG	Stem augment
AUX	Auxiliary
BEN	Benefactive
CatG	Categorial Grammar
CAUS	Causative
CD	Complement of degree
CL	Classifier
CL-A	Clausal actor
CL-U	Clausal undergoer

CLM	Clause linkage marker
CMPL	Complementizer
CMPV	Completive
CNTR	Contrastive
CogG	Cognitive Grammar
COM	Comitative
ConG	Construction Grammar
CONJ	Conjunction
CONT	Continuative
COP	Copula
DAT	Dative
DCA	Direct core argument
DCT	Direct
DEC	Declarative
DEF	Definite(ness)
DEIC	Deictic
DEM	Demonstrative pronoun
DEP	Dependent
DEPR	Deprecating
DES	Desiderative
DET	Determiner
DfP	Different pivot
DIM	Diminutive
DIR	Directional
dl	Dual
d.n.a.	does not apply
DO	Direct object
DP	Detached phrase
DS	Different subject
d-S	Derived intransitive subject
DT	Different topic
DUR	Durative
ECS	Extra-core slot
ERG	Ergative
EVID	Evidential
EX	Exclusive
EXCL	Exclamation
EXH	Exhortative
EXT	Extent of action
F, FEM	Feminine
FG	Functional Grammar

FIN	Finite
FOC	Focus
FUT	Future
GB	Government and Binding Theory
GEN	Genitive
GPSG	Generalized Phrase Structure Grammar
HAB	Habitual
HPSG	Head-Driven Phrase Structure Grammar
HS	Hearsay
IC	Immediate constituent
IF	Illocutionary force
IIF	Indirect information flow
IMM	Immediate past
IMP	Imperative
IMPER	Impersonal
IMPF	Imperfective
INA	Inactive
INAN	Inanimate
INC	Inclusive
IND(IC)	Indicative
INF	Infinitive
INGR	Ingressive
INES	Inessive
INST	Instrument, instrumental voice
INT	Interrogative
INTR	Intransitive
INTS	Intensive
INV	Inverse
IO	Indirect object
IRR	Irrealis
ISC	Invariable syntactic controller
LAD	Language acquisition device
LDP	Left-detached position
LFG	Lexical–Functional Grammar
LNK	Linker
LOC	Locative
LS	Logical structure
LSC	Layered structure of the clause
LSNP	Layered structure of the noun phrase
M, MASC	Masculine
MID	Middle voice

MOD	Modality
MOM	Momentaneous
NASP	Nominal aspect
NCBR	Non-clause-bounded reflexive
NEC	Necessity
NEG	Negative
N, NEUT	Neuter
NFIN	Non-finite
NM	Noun marker
NMZ	Nominalizer
NOM	Nominative
N(P)	Noun (phrase)
NPIP	NP-initial position
NPST	Non-past
nsg	Non-singular
NUC	Nucleus
NUM	Number
OBJ	Object
OBL	Oblique
OBLIG	Obligation
OBV	Obviative
OCA	Oblique core argument
OP	Operator
p	Person
P	Patient (object) of transitive verb
P&P	Principles and Parameters Theory
PART	Participle
PASS	Passive
P(A)ST	Past
PER	Periphery
PERF	Perfect
PFD	Potential focus domain
pl	Plural
PNCT	Punctual
PNM	Proper noun marker
PO	Primary object
PoCS	Postcore slot
POSS	Possessive
P(P)	Pre-/postposition (phrase)
PPP	Past participle passive
PrCS	Precore slot

PRDM	Predicate marker
PRED	Predicate
PRES	Present
PRFV	Perfective
PRO	Pronoun
PROG	Progressive
PROP	Proper noun
PROX	Proximate
PrP	Pragmatic pivot
PRPR	Proprietive case
PRT	Particle
PRTV	Partitive
PRV	Preradical vowel
PSA	Privileged syntactic argument(s)
PSBL	Possibility
PSTP	Past participle
PURP	Purposive
PVB	Preverb
Q	Question
QNT	Quantifier
QUOT	Quotation, quotative
RDP	Right-detached position
REAL	Realis
REC	Recent past
REF	Referential NP
REFL	Reflexive
REL	Relative clause marker
RelG	Relational Grammar
REPET	Repetitive
RRG	Role and Reference Grammar
S	Subject of intransitive verb
SBJ	Subjunctive
SEQ	Sequential conjunction
SFG	Systemic Functional Grammar
sg	Singular
SIM	Simultaneous action
SmC	Semantic controller
SMLF	Semelfactive aspect
SO	Secondary object
SP	Same pivot
SPEC	(Referential-)specific

S/R	Switch-reference marker
SS	Same subject
STA	Status
SUB	Subordinator
SUBJ	Subject
SUFF	Suffix
TEL	Telic
TM	Terminal marker
TNP	Transitive, non-past
TNS	Tense
TOP	Topic
TPAST	Past tense – earlier today
TRANS	Transitive
UG	Universal grammar
U, UND	Undergoer
V(P)	Verb (phrase)
VSP	Variable syntactic pivot
WG	Word Grammar
YPAST	Past tense – yesterday

Arabic numbers refer to Bantu noun class agreement markers or person in other examples. Roman numerals refer to Dyirbal noun classes.

1
The goals of linguistic theory

1.0 Introduction

This book is about some of the devices users of human languages employ to put meaningful elements together to form words, words together to form phrases, phrases together to form clauses, clauses together to form sentences, and sentences together to form texts. The emphasis here will be on the construction of units larger than words, in particular clauses and sentences. This has often been viewed primarily as the domain of **syntax**. 'The term "syntax" is from the Ancient Greek *sýntaxis*, a verbal noun which literally means "arrangement" or "setting out together". Traditionally, it refers to the branch of grammar dealing with the ways in which words, with or without appropriate inflections, are arranged to show connections of meaning within the sentence.' (Matthews 1982: 1). The expressions of a language involve a relationship between a sequence of sounds and a meaning, and this relationship is mediated by grammar, a core component of which is syntax. In English and many other languages, the arrangement of words is a vital factor in determining the meaning of an utterance, as illustrated in (1.1).

(1.1) a. The man saw the woman.
      b. The woman saw the man.

In Dyirbal (Australia; Dixon 1972) and many other languages, however, the order of words is irrelevant to the determination of the meaning of a sentence; it is, rather, the inflectional form of a phrase which is the crucial factor determining the interpretation of the sentence, as shown in (1.2). (The base forms of each noun are italicized.)

(1.2) a. Balan *ḍugumbil* baŋgul *yaɽa*-ŋgu buɽan.
      DET woman DET man see
      b. Baŋgul *yaɽa*-ŋgu balan *ḍugumbil* buɽan.
      DET man DET woman see
      'The man saw the woman.'
      c. Bayi *yaɽa* baŋgun *ḍugumbi*-ɽu buɽan.
      DET man DET woman see

d. Baŋgun *ḍugumbi*-ɽu bayi *yaɽa* buɽan.
DET woman DET man see
'The woman saw the man.'

Notice that the form of the noun phrases for 'the man' and 'the woman' differ in the second pair of sentences from the first, i.e. 'the woman' *balan ḍugumbil* in (a, b) → *baŋgun ḍugumbi-ɽu* in (c, d), and 'the man' *baŋgul yaɽa-ŋgu* in (a, b) → *bayi yaɽa* in (c, d), and it is this change in form, not the variation in position in the sentence, that signals the difference in meaning. Hence morphology can be used to express 'who is doing what to whom' in some languages, while word order does this in others, and accordingly the cross-linguistic study of syntax cannot be carried out without paying serious attention to morphology. In recognition of the functional overlap between syntax and morphology, the term 'morphosyntax' is used to capture the interrelatedness of these two central areas of grammar.

In this chapter we will lay out the theoretical background against which current work in syntax, both theoretical and descriptive, is carried out. In section 1.1, we will sketch the general goals of linguistic theory which most linguists would agree with, while in section 1.2 we will discuss the notion of 'explanation' in linguistics. In section 1.3 we will outline the two major perspectives on these goals that are most widely held in the field today.

1.1 Goals of linguistic theory

While it is probably impossible to draw up a list of goals for linguistic theory which every linguist would agree with, it is nevertheless possible to characterize a set of general goals which the majority of linguists would give assent to. They are: description of linguistic phenomena, explanation of linguistic phenomena, and understanding the cognitive basis of language. Each of these will be discussed in turn below.

1.1.1 Describing linguistic phenomena

Much of the work done in linguistics during the first half of the twentieth century was devoted to discovering and refining the basic tools of linguistic description. In phonology this meant Sapir, Swadesh, Trubetzkoy, Jakobson, Bloomfield and Bloch defining and redefining the phoneme, in order to ensure its methodological precision and validity. In morphology this meant Bloomfield and Harris, among others, working out the concepts of morph, morpheme and allomorph, and in addition there was the crucial problem of the interface between phonology and morphology, morphophonemics, and its implications for the analysis of the two levels. The fundamental constructs in syntactic analysis (constituent and immediate constituent, construction, and transformation, among others) were the result of Bloomfield's, Hockett's and Harris' efforts to extend the methods of structural analysis employed on the phonemic and morphemic levels to syntax, and of Jespersen's theorizing derived from his detailed study of English. Finally, important contributions to the study of syntax, especially in terms of the perspective to be adopted here, have come from the work of linguists in the Prague School, beginning with Mathesius in the third decade of this century.

Describing linguistic phenomena is one of the central goals in linguistics, and for many linguists it is their primary goal. This may include describing individual languages, describing what is common to all languages (language universals), or describing how languages differ from each other (language typology). And each of these endeavors can be carried out with respect to specific linguistic levels, e.g. phonology, syntax, narrative discourse structure. Linguistics in the United States grew out of anthropology, in particular out of the enterprise of describing the native cultures and languages of North America (see Boas 1911) and this descriptive tradition is still alive and well today. Linguistic description is vitally important, for two reasons. First, language is a major part of our common human heritage, and languages are vanishing as their last speakers die or they are supplanted by a socio-culturally dominant language, just as plant and animal species are becoming extinct. Documenting the diversity of human languages is a necessary and crucial aspect of linguistics. This directly relates to the second reason: all of the other goals presuppose this one. Developing serious explanatory theories of language is impossible in the absence of descriptions of the object of explanation. Understanding the cognitive basis of language is impossible in the absence of an adequate cross-linguistic characterization of linguistic behavior. We cannot explain or posit cognitive mechanisms for something unless it has first been described.

1.1.2 Explaining linguistic phenomena

The main impetus to the postulation of explanatory theories of linguistic phenomena came from Chomsky's early work in generative grammar. Chomsky (1957) argued that the proper role of linguistic theory is to provide criteria for selecting the most explanatory grammar from among a group of competing grammars. We will discuss what these criteria are in section 1.2; we will see in section 1.3 that different approaches have quite divergent views of what the appropriate criteria should be.

At a more basic level, what is there to be explained? That is, what is it that a linguistic theory should explain? There is in fact a wide range of candidates, and what a theory seeks to explain has profound consequences for the content and organization of the theory. A short, partial list of candidate topics is given in (1.3).

(1.3) *Candidates for what a linguistic theory should explain*
- a. how speakers use language in different social situations;
- b. why human languages have the structure that they do;
- c. what is common to all human languages;

d. why human languages vary structurally the way they do;
e. how human languages change over time;
f. how speakers produce and understand language in real time;
g. the nature of native speakers' knowledge of their language;
h. how children learn language.

There are many more questions one could come up with, but this list is sufficient for this discussion. Virtually all theories are interested in questions (b)–(d), and the issue is usually phrased, 'how are human languages different and how are they alike?' An important component of the answer a theory gives to the question of what is to be explained derives from the conception the theory has of what language is in the first place. If, for example, one holds that a language is simply a set of abstract formal objects representing the sentences of the language, then many of these questions will be excluded right away. In section 1.3 we will look at the definitions of language assumed by different theories and at what those theories seek to explain.

1.1.3 Understanding the cognitive basis of language

The last three topics listed in (1.3) refer to explicitly psychological questions about language, and many linguists, following Chomsky, maintain that cognitive issues are in fact the most important issues to be explained; they do not necessarily agree, however, on which questions are the most important and how they should be approached. The three questions in (1.4) highlight three major facets of the psychology of language:

(1.4) *Processing*: What cognitive processes are involved when human beings produce and understand language on line in real time? How specialized to language are these processes?
Knowledge: What constitutes knowledge of language? How is it organized? How is it represented? How is it employed in language processing? How does knowledge of language relate to knowledge in other cognitive domains?
Acquisition: How do human beings come to have knowledge of language? What is the nature of the acquisition process? Is coming to know language similar to or different from acquiring knowledge in other cognitive domains? Does it involve knowledge from other cognitive domains?

These questions have become fundamental ones in the cognitive sciences and are the driving force behind much of the research and theorizing in linguistics today.

1.2 Explanation in linguistics

Since explanation is an important goal in linguistic theory, it is necessary to clarify exactly what the explanatory criteria used by linguists are and what standards linguists set for their theories to meet.

1.2.1 Types of explanatory criteria

Philosophers of science typically divide theories into two basic types, **inductive** and **deductive**. Inductive theories derive generalizations from the observation of many exemplars of the phenomena under investigation; the hypotheses so generated are descriptive in nature. If one, for example, examined a large number of birds of various species and concluded 'all birds have wings', this would be an inductive generalization describing a property of birds. The generalizations of structural linguistics are inductive in nature, as are the language universals proposed in the work of Greenberg (e.g. Greenberg 1966). The relationship between data and theory with respect to inductive theories is **data → hypothesis**.

In deductive theories, on the other hand, hypotheses are formulated and then tested against data in order to ascertain their validity. Theories in the so-called 'hard' sciences, e.g. physics, are primarily of this kind. Typically, the hypotheses grow out of observations of phenomena but not directly as in inductive theories. For example, a physicist might examine the results of a series of experiments involving particle interactions and conclude that in order to account for them it is necessary to posit a type of particle which had not been previously observed. She would then formulate hypotheses which are intended to *explain* the observed facts and predict the results of additional experiments with respect to the postulated particle. The validity of the hypothesis would be determined relative to the accuracy of the predictions it made regarding the experimental results. Deductive theories are explanatory theories, and the relationship between data and theory is **hypothesis → data**.[1]

It is often the case that more than one set of hypotheses is proposed to account for a given observation or set of observations. How does one choose the best one among them? There are two types of criteria, empirical and theory-internal. The empirical criterion is the one mentioned above: is the theory in accord with the known facts or experimental results? If not, then it should be eliminated from consideration. But what happens when there is more than one theory that is empirically accurate? The answer is that there is a set of theory-internal criteria, which are given in (1.5).

(1.5) *Theory-internal explanatory criteria*

a. *Economy (Occam's Razor)*: Is it the simplest theory?

b. *Motivation*: Are the crucial explanatory constructs independently motivated or are they *ad hoc*?

c. *Predictiveness*: Do the hypotheses predict phenomena beyond those for which they were formulated?

While it is not always easy to come up with explicit criteria for simplicity in a particular theoretical domain, the intuition behind (1.5a) is straightforward: all other things being equal, the simplest theory is to be preferred. The second criterion, motivation, refers to the extent to which the hypotheses follow in a natural way from the preexisting theory and the extent to which the constructs invoked in the explanation are also required elsewhere in the theory. An account in which the explanatory constructs have no other function beyond dealing with the problem at hand is less highly valued than one in which they play a role in the explanation of other phenomena; in this case the constructs are said to be *independently motivated*, because they are required by the theory for phenomena other than the problem at hand. An example from linguistics would be the contrast between two hypothetical accounts of the contrasting pairs of sentences in (1.6).

(1.6) a. Who did Mary see?
a′. Mary saw who?
b. *Sandy* Robin doesn't like.
b′. Robin doesn't like Sandy.

In English a question word normally appears at the beginning of the sentence, as in (1.6a) and is interpreted as if it were in its 'usual' position, as in (a′). It is also possible for a noun phrase which is not a question word to occur initially before the subject, as in (b), and it too is interpreted as if it were in its usual position, as in (b′). Let us suppose further that there are two competing accounts of the relationship between the two (b) sentences, one which invokes the same rule which relates the two (a) sentences (call it 'displacement') and another one which applies just to the two (b) sentences (call it 'topicalization'). Assuming everything else to be equal (including that they are equally empirically accurate), the first solution is to be preferred, for two reasons: first, it is simpler (one rule vs. two rules); and second, the rule invoked to account for the (b) sentences in the first account is independently needed in the grammar to account for the (a) sentences, whereas in the second account the 'topicalization' rule applies only to sentences like those in (b) and nowhere else in the grammar. Hence the second account is not independently motivated, whereas the first one is.

With respect to the third criterion, hypotheses which make empirically testable predictions about other observed phenomena or phenomena not yet observed are more highly valued than those which do not. Continuing the example of the contrasting analyses of (1.6), let us say that the first account, the one which posits a single rule to handle both constructions, makes the following prediction: since both constructions are the result of a single rule of grammar, they are likely to cooccur across different languages. In particular, it may be the case that there is an implicational relationship between them, to the effect that if a language has the constructions in (1.6b–b′), it will also have the constructions in (1.6a–a′).[2] This predicts, then, that there will be no languages in which constructions of type (b) occur without there being constructions of type (a) in the language, but not vice versa. Whether this is correct or not can be determined by empirical investigation. The second account makes no such prediction; since each construction is the result of independent rules

Table 1.1 *Types of explanatory criteria*

Domain to be explained	*Theory-internal criteria*	*External criteria*	
		Language -internal	*Language-external*
SYNTAX	Economy Motivation Predictiveness	Phonology Semantics Pragmatics Processing	Reasoning Categorization Perception . . .

in the grammar, there is no reason to predict that they should or should not cooccur. Here again the first account, from which an empirically testable prediction follows, is more highly valued than the second.

As this example has shown, the theory-internal criteria in (1.5) play a central role in theoretical argumentation in linguistics. By referring to these criteria as 'theory-internal', we do not mean to imply that they are internal to any specific theory; rather, they are assumed by all linguistic theories. It is also possible to appeal to external phenomena in explanation, and this is a point of controversy among linguistic theories. An example of an external explanation would be an account of some syntactic pattern which makes crucial reference to semantics (i.e. the meaning of the pattern) and/or pragmatics (i.e. the context in which it occurs or the communicative function which it serves). A semantic explanation for a syntactic pattern would be an external explanation, on the standard (but not universally held) assumption that syntax and semantics are distinct from each other. In this instance we are dealing with external but language-internal explanations. It is also logically possible to appeal to language-external facts or principles in an explanation. For example, one could argue that some syntactic pattern holds in human languages because of the nature of human cognition or perception; such an appeal to non-linguistic aspects of cognition or perception would be an external explanation as well. These different explanatory criteria may be summarized as in table 1.1.

1.2.2 Levels of adequacy in linguistic theory

One of the most important arguments Chomsky made in *Syntactic structures* (1957), the monograph which introduced generative grammar to the field, was that linguistics should be considered a deductive, rather than an inductive, enterprise. Bloomfield had stated explicitly in his 1933 book, *Language*, that 'the only valid linguistic generalizations are inductive generalizations' (21), and one of Chomsky's main goals was to make linguistic theory explanatory and not simply descriptive. As part of this project, he proposed levels of adequacy that a grammar must meet in his 1965 book, *Aspects of the theory of syntax*. They are: (1) **observational adequacy**, i.e. the grammar correctly predicts which sentences in a language are well formed (grammatical) and which are not; (2) **descriptive adequacy**, i.e. the grammar is observationally adequate and it assigns structural descriptions to the sentences in the language that capture native speaker intuitions about the structure and meaning of the sentences; and (3) **explanatory adequacy**, i.e. the grammar is descriptively adequate and is part of a theory which provides an account of 'how these facts arise in the mind of the speaker–hearer' (Chomsky 1994: 386). For Chomsky, 'the fundamental empirical problem of linguistics is to explain how a person can acquire knowledge of language' (1977: 81). The last two levels of adequacy are explicitly cognitive in nature, as they refer to native speaker intuitions and to language acquisition. In terms of the criteria introduced in the previous section, observational adequacy is the criterion of empirical accuracy applied to the sentences of a language, whereas descriptive adequacy is also based on empirical accuracy, in this case applied to native speaker intuitions about sentences. It is at the level of explanatory adequacy that the theory-internal criteria in (1.5) come into play, and it is a point of disagreement among theories as to whether external criteria are relevant here or not. We will return to this issue in section 1.3.

Additional types of adequacy have been proposed. Dik (1978, 1991) proposes a broad notion of **psychological adequacy**, which states that a theory should be 'compatible with the results of psycholinguistic research on the acquisition, processing, production, interpretation and memorization of linguistic expressions' (1991: 248). This subsumes the criterion put forth in Kaplan and Bresnan (1982) that theories of linguistic structure should be directly relatable to testable theories of language production and comprehension. Dik also proposes two additional types of adequacy: **pragmatic adequacy**, i.e. 'the theory and the language descriptions based on it should be interpretable within a wider pragmatic theory of verbal communication' (1991: 247), and **typological adequacy**, i.e. the theory should 'formulate such rules and principles as can be applied to any type of language without "forcing", i.e. without adapting the language described to the theory already developed' (248). One of the issues to be explored in the next section is the types of adequacy that different theories assume.

1.3 Contrasting perspectives on the goals of linguistic theory

While the list of goals in section 1.1 is shared in some form by most linguists, there are sharply different points of view regarding their exact formulation and relative importance to each other. In this section we will sketch out two very general perspectives on these goals, each of which subsumes a variety of syntactic theories and approaches.

1.3.1 The syntactocentric perspective

In the syntactocentric view of language, laid out explicitly in Chomsky (1965), syntax is the central aspect of language. The phonological and semantic aspects of language are derivative of and secondary to syntactic structure. From Chomsky's point of view, language is an abstract object whose structure is to be studied independently of psycholinguistic, communicative, sociocultural and other considerations. Access to the object of study is primarily through the linguistic intuitions of native speakers of languages. Chomsky's own theories, Principles and Parameters Theory (P&P; 'the minimalist program' of Chomsky 1992, 1995), and its well-known predecessor, Government and Binding Theory (GB) (e.g. Chomsky 1986a), have dominated linguistic theory for many years.

Chomsky has explicitly denied that communication is a necessary or even important function of language (e.g. 1975: 56–7, 1980: 229–30). For him 'human language is a system for free expression of thought, essentially independent of stimulus control, need-satisfaction or instrumental purpose' (1980: 239) and 'a set of structural descriptions of sentences, where a full structural description determines (in particular) the sound and meaning of a linguistic expression' (Chomsky 1977: 81). In any case, it is not the use of language that generative theories are to investigate. Chomsky (1965) proposed a fundamental distinction between linguistic **competence** and linguistic **performance**: competence is a native speaker's knowledge of language, whereas performance is the actual use of language on particular occasions. For Chomsky the proper object of study for linguistics is competence only, and linguistic theory will have something to say about performance only insofar as a plausible theory of performance would of necessity incorporate a theory of competence. In his more recent work, e.g. (1986a), he has further distinguished between 'E[xternal]-language' and 'I[nternal]-language', where E-language corresponds roughly to the pretheoretical idea of what a language is and I-language is a speaker's internal grammar.

> The study of generative grammar in the modern sense . . . was marked by a significant shift in focus in the study of language. To put it briefly, the focus of attention was shifted from 'language' to 'grammar' . . . The shift of focus from language (an obscure and I believe ultimately unimportant notion) to grammar is essential if we are to proceed towards assimilating the study of language to the natural sciences. (Chomsky 1981a: 4, 7)

E-language consists of the overt phenomena of linguistic interaction in the sociocultural realm; on the other hand, I-language (the grammar) is an abstract object accessible only through native speaker intuitions, and in this view only I-language falls within the scope of linguistic inquiry. Thus linguistics, in this conception, is the science of grammar, not of language. Universals for Chomsky are generalizations about I-languages (properties of grammars e.g. 'all grammars make use of the syntactic categories NOUN and VERB'); he refers to them as 'linguistic universals'; they are not about E-languages (properties of languages, e.g. 'virtually all verb-initial languages have prepositions rather than postpositions').

Given Chomsky's postulation of explanatory adequacy (section 1.3.2), it might be assumed that he is very concerned with the psychological aspects of language and therefore his theories do not really consider language to be such an abstract object. However, the fundamentally 'abstract object' outlook of the theory is confirmed when the criteria relevant to explanatory adequacy are examined: they are *only* the theory-internal criteria in (1.5); no external and, in particular, no language-external criteria (see table 1.1) are invoked. Competing descriptively adequate grammars are to be evaluated solely with respect to economy, motivation and predictiveness. Dik's principle of psychological adequacy is not acceptable to Chomsky. This is reflected in Chomsky's overall theory of mind: language is a fully self-contained mental module, the inner workings of which are independent of and not accessible to other mental modules, e.g. reasoning, perception, vision, common sense, etc.

It might be suggested that interest in language acquisition must involve psycholinguistic research and therefore reflects a more psychological perspective. This does not follow, however. For Chomsky, language acquisition is a *logical* problem, not a psycholinguistic one, and therefore it requires no psycholinguistic research or even study of child language.[3] The logical problem may be formulated as follows: given an account of adult grammatical competence (what Chomsky calls the 'final state' of the organism), we may deduce the initial state of the language acquirer by factoring out what is supplied by experience. This may be represented graphically as in (1.7).

(1.7) Final knowledge state (= adult grammatical competence)
– Input from experience
= Initial knowledge state (= language acquisition device [LAD])

If there is some element of the final knowledge state which is not attributable to experience, then it must be part of the initial knowledge state or language acquisition device (LAD); this is known as 'the argument from the poverty of the stimulus'. It is assumed that the input to the child from experience is variable and degenerate and that it contains little or no information regarding the relevant grammatical principles. Hence it is claimed that the initial state, the LAD, is very rich and contains virtually all of the formal content of the final knowledge state. This claim has often been presented as a claim that 'language is innate', but this is in fact a misleading formulation. Chomsky's position is much stronger than the common-sense view that because humans alone possess true language, we must be genetically predetermined in some way to acquire it; language is innate in this sense, which is uncontroversial. Chomsky maintains that human beings are born with a generative grammar hard-wired into an autonomous language module in the mind; what enables humans to acquire language, the LAD, is specific to language and independent of all other cognitive capacities. Hence the real issue for Chomsky is the autonomy of the LAD, not whether it is innate.

Since a child can learn any human language, the LAD is in effect a theory of universal grammar (UG). UG contains universals of I-language, not E-language. What the child does in language acquisition is adapt the principles of the LAD/UG to fit the language to which she is exposed. In Chomsky's most recent work (e.g. 1995), he has claimed that the syntactic system in all languages is the same and that all differences among languages are attributable to differences in the properties of lexical items in different languages.

What, then, are the goals of linguistic theory from a Chomskyan perspective? Explanation is the highest goal. There are many theories which have adopted this general view of the goals of linguistic theory, including Generalized Phrase Structure Grammar (GPSG; Gazdar *et al.* 1985), Relational Grammar (RelG; e.g. Perlmutter 1980) and Categorial Grammar (CatG; e.g. Moortgaat 1991). With respect to the topics in (1.3), they are concerned with (c), (g) and (h), with the proviso that 'language' is understood as 'I-language' (grammar). They differ as to whether they are concerned with the cognitive issues in (1.4); Chomsky's own theory is concerned with the issues of knowledge and acquisition (but not processing), in the non-psychological way discussed above, while the other theories are basically agnostic on these issues. The explanatory criteria are either theory-internal only, as in P&P/GB, or both theory-internal and -external but still language-internal (usually semantics), as in some of the other theories.

1.3.2 The communication-and-cognition perspective

The second perspective we will call 'the communication-and-cognition perspective', and from this point of view, human language's role as a means of communication, its role in broader cognitive processes such as reasoning and conceptualization, and its relations with other cognitive systems such as perception and knowledge are all relevant to and indeed crucial to the study of language structure. Language is viewed as an abstract system, one which is nonetheless firmly grounded in human communication and cognition. Syntax is not the central aspect of language, in this view. Indeed, the status of syntax *vis-à-vis* semantics and pragmatics is an issue with respect to which theories within this perspective differ; some of the more radical practitioners argue that syntax does not exist or is reducible to discourse patterns (e.g. Hopper 1987), whereas the majority of linguists are interested in how syntax interacts with semantics and pragmatics. Access to the object of study is through a variety of means: native speaker intuitions, analysis of conversation, discourse and narrative, and the results of psycholinguistic experimentation, among others. Theories which reject the syntactocentric view and adopt this general perspective include Functional Grammar (FG; Dik 1978, 1991), Role and Reference Grammar (RRG; Van Valin 1993b), Systemic Functional Grammar (SFG; Halliday 1985, 1994, Matthiessen 1995), Tagmemics (Pike 1982), Lexical–Functional Grammar (LFG; Bresnan 1982a), Head-Driven Phrase Structure Grammar (HPSG; Pollard and Sag

1994), Construction Grammar (ConG; Fillmore 1988, Fillmore, Kay and O'Connor 1988), Autolexical Syntax (Sadock 1991), Word Grammar (WG; Hudson 1984), the St. Petersburg school of functional grammar (Bondarko 1991), Meaning–text theory (Mel'chuk 1979, 1987, Mel'chuk and Pertsov 1986), Cognitive Grammar (CogG; Langacker 1987, 1990; Lakoff 1987), Prague School Dependency Grammar (Sgall, Hajičová and Panevová 1986), and French functionalism (Martinet 1962, 1975). In addition, there are a number of individuals whose work has been very important in the development of this perspective but who are not associated with any of the above theories, in particular Michael Silverstein, Ray Jackendoff, Ellen Prince, T. Givón, Susumu Kuno, Leonard Talmy, Sandra Thompson and Anna Wierzbicka.

These approaches represent a great range of theoretical opinion, and by listing them together no claim is made that they are in agreement on all major issues. Rather, what they have in common is first, a rejection of the syntactocentric view of Chomsky, and second, an acknowledgment of the importance of communicative factors, cognitive factors or both in grammatical theory and analysis. Moreover, there is no individual analogous to Chomsky who defines the perspective. The theories can be placed along a continuum, according to whether they emphasize the communicative or cognitive aspects of language. SFG takes perhaps the most radical discourse-pragmatic view, a 'top–down' analytic model which starts with discourse and works 'down' to lower levels of grammatical structure. Halliday (1985) argues that the ultimate explanations for linguistic phenomena lie in language use.

> Language has evolved to satisfy human needs; and the way it is organized is functional with respect to these needs – it is not arbitrary. A functional grammar is essentially a 'natural' grammar, in the sense that everything in it can be explained, ultimately, by reference to how language is used. (1985: xiii) . . . The orientation is to language as a social rather than an individual phenomenon, and the origin and development of the theory have aligned it with the sociological rather than psychological modes of explanation. At the same time it has been used within a general cognitive framework. (1985: xxx)

At the other (cognitive) end of the spectrum, Langacker's CogG

> assumes that language is neither self-contained nor describable without essential reference to cognitive processing (regardless of whether one posits a special *faculté de langage*). Grammatical structures do not constitute an autonomous formal system or level of representation: they are claimed instead to be inherently symbolic, providing for the structuring and conventional symbolization of conceptual content. Lexicon, morphology, and syntax form a continuum of symbolic units, divided only arbitrarily into separate components; it is ultimately as pointless

> to analyze grammatical units without reference to their semantic value as to write a dictionary which omits the meanings of its lexical items. (Langacker 1990: 1)

CogG recognizes 'only three broad facets of linguistic structure – semantic, phonological and symbolic – represented in the grammar by the corresponding units' (Langacker 1990: 105), and Langacker specifically argues that the distinction between semantics and pragmatics is artificial and arbitrary.

Into the middle fall the remaining theories. Van Valin (1993b) characterizes the RRG view as follows:

> RRG takes language to be a system of communicative social action, and accordingly, analyzing the communicative functions of grammatical structures plays a vital role in grammatical description and theory from this perspective . . . Language is a system, and grammar is a system in the traditional structuralist sense; what distinguishes the RRG conception . . . is the conviction that grammatical structure can only be understood with reference to its semantic and communicative functions. Syntax is not autonomous. In terms of the abstract paradigmatic and syntagmatic relations that define a structural system, RRG is concerned not only with relations of cooccurrence and combination in strictly formal terms but also with semantic and pragmatic cooccurrence and combinatory relations. (1993b: 2)

Dik puts forth a similar view in FG.

> [A] language is considered in the first place as an instrument for communicative verbal interaction, and the basic assumption is that the various properties of natural languages should, wherever this is possible, be understood and explained in terms of the conditions imposed by their usage. The language system, therefore, is not considered as an autonomous set of rules and principles, the uses of which can only be considered in a secondary phase; rather it is assumed that the rules and principles composing the language system can only be adequately understood when they are analyzed in terms of conditions of use. In this sense the study of language use (pragmatics) precedes the study of the formal and semantic properties of linguistic expressions. (1991: 247)

Both theories are also concerned with the cognitive status of the grammars they propose and accept Dik's criterion of psychological adequacy. LFG but neither HPSG nor ConG would accept Dik's condition of psychological adequacy.

One of the striking things that these various approaches have in common is the acceptance of external criteria in explanation (see table 1.1), and this distinguishes them from the Chomskyan view. As is clear from the statements above, all acknowledge the central role of language-internal non-syntactic criteria in explanation; indeed, it seems clear that semantics and pragmatics are not truly external at all from this perspective, and accordingly Dik's notion of pragmatic adequacy could be applied to all of them. Language-external criteria are also accepted by most of these theories; in particular, all would recognize Dik's principle of psychological adequacy as a valid standard by which to evaluate competing theories.

Chomsky's level of explanatory adequacy is primarily concerned with explaining language acquisition, and there has been important research done in this area by psychologists and psycholinguists adopting this view of language, especially Bates, MacWhinney, Slobin, Bowerman, Braine, Tomasello and others. From a communication and cognition perspective, the object of study is not the acquisition of grammatical competence, but rather *communicative* competence (Hymes 1974, Halliday 1975, Ochs and Schieffelin 1979). Van Valin (1991a) argues that from this point of view what a child does in learning language is to *construct* a grammar, based on its inborn cognitive endowment (which is not assumed to be specific to language) and information from experience. Slobin's notion of a Basic Child Grammar (1985) is a concrete proposal regarding the kind of learning principles that could be involved, and Braine (1992) shows how a conception of clause structure very much like that to be introduced in chapter 2 could be constructed developmentally by the child. Tomasello (1992) employs CogG to illuminate children's early verb use, and Rispoli (1991a, b, 1994) shows how the lexical representations to be introduced in chapter 3 and the conception of grammatical relations to be presented in chapter 6 can be learned. Bowerman (1990) provides evidence in favor of the view that rules linking syntactic and semantic representations of the type to be introduced in chapter 7 are learned, and Van Valin (1994) puts forward an account of how some of the constraints on linking between syntactic and semantic representations in complex sentences of the type to be developed in chapter 9 could be learned. We return to these issues in the Epilog at the end of the book.

Dik also proposed the criterion of typological adequacy, and while all of these approaches would likely give assent to it in principle, they vary dramatically in terms of how typologically oriented they are. FG and RRG are the most explicitly typologically oriented theories; according to Van Valin (1995a), RRG grew out of an attempt to answer the question 'what would linguistic theory look like if it were based on the analysis of Lakhota, Tagalog and Dyirbal, rather than on the analysis of English?' (1995a: 461). Indeed, many of these approaches grew out of typological concerns and research on languages very different from English.

Typological questions invariably lead to the issue of universal grammar; what is UG from this point of view? While some linguists mentioned above adopt a Chomskyan perspective on UG (e.g. Jackendoff, Prince, Kuno), the majority of these linguists would take a theory of UG to be a theory of the notion of 'possible human linguistic communicative system', in which the features of particular languages are to be grounded but not rigidly or mechanically derived. To the extent that they would agree with the characterization of language acquisition sketched above, this theory of UG would not be a psychological model of the LAD.

The issues of typological adequacy and UG raise one of the major theoretical and methodological conflicts that linguists have faced in this century: namely, the balance between these two divergent perspectives. Until the early 1960s, most (but not all) American structuralist linguists eschewed formulating cross-linguistic generalizations in deference to the goal of producing a description of a language in terms that were appropriate for it. In contrast, Chomskyan generative grammar gave absolute priority to developing an explanatory theory of UG, and consequently within generative linguistics there has been little or no concern for language-particular issues except insofar as they impact on the theory of UG. For a theory to accept the criterion of typological adequacy as formulated by Dik means that it is concerned with being flexible enough to capture what Sapir (1921) called the 'structural genius' of the language, and yet to be part of a serious theory of UG it must make strong cross-linguistic claims. This is a very difficult task, but the rewards would be very great if it could be achieved.

What, then, are the goals of linguistic theory from the communication-and-cognition perspective? All of the theories mentioned above would agree on explanation as the highest goal, with description as a secondary but important goal. With respect to the topics in (1.3), as a group they are concerned with most of them, but the various theories differ with respect to which would be emphasized, e.g. only SFG and FG would take (a) as a major goal, while RRG is directly concerned with all but (a) and (e). They are all concerned to varying degrees with the cognitive issues in (1.4). The explanatory criteria adopted usually include external criteria.

1.4 Concluding remarks

In this chapter we have explored the goals of linguistic theory from two rather different perspectives. In the remainder of this book we will develop a framework for the analysis of syntax from the **communication-and-cognition** perspective. Our goal is two-fold: first, to present an explanatory theory of syntax which can address the major issues in contemporary syntactic theory; and second, to present a descriptive framework which can be used by field linguists for writing grammars. Most approaches concentrate on one of the goals to the exclusion of the other, and our intention is to present a theory which can satisfy the demands of both of these enterprises. The general skeleton of the framework will derive largely from RRG, but the content of the proposals will be drawn from the various theories and individuals' work that fall within this perspective; given the diversity of views that fall under this point of view, however, not all will be represented equally. There are numerous textbooks available which present the syntactocentric perspective; they include Radford (1988), Haegeman (1994), Cowper (1992) and Napoli (1993).

We will return to some of these general theoretical issues in the final chapter, after we have completed our investigation of syntactic phenomena and presented a theory in which to analyze and explain them.

Further reading

The term 'syntactocentric' comes from Jackendoff (1997). For background on the Prague School, see Toman (1995) and Luelsdorf (1994). For the original papers of the early Prague School, see Vachek (1964, 1983). See also Sgall, Hajičová and Panevová (1986) and Firbas (1992) for more recent work from the Prague School. See Hymes and Fought (1981), Dinneen and Koerner (1990) and Matthews (1993) on American structuralism, and Koerner and Asher (1995) for brief articles on different aspects of the history of linguistics. See Newmeyer (1980, 1986, 1988a, b), Crystal (1982) and Harris (1993) on some of the controversies in the later history of linguistics. For some representative works of the communication-and-cognition perspective not associated with the theories presented in this chapter, see Bates and MacWhinney (1982), Givón (1979a, 1984b, 1989, 1990), Prince (1981a, b), Silverstein (1976, 1977, 1987, 1993), Thompson (1987, 1988, 1989, to appear), Hopper and Thompson (1980, 1984, 1993), Matthiessen and Thompson (1988) and Wierzbicka (1980a, b, 1988, 1992). For a historical overview of the communication-and-cognition approach to language, see de Beaugrande (1985) and other papers from Dijk (1985).

2

Syntactic structure, I: simple clauses and noun phrases

2.0 Introduction

In this chapter we investigate the structure of phrases and clauses in simple sentences. There are two fundamental aspects of structure which every theory must deal with: relational and non-relational structure. As the names imply, relational structure deals with the relations that exist between one syntactic element and another, be they syntactic, semantic or pragmatic in nature, whereas non-relational structure expresses the hierarchical organization of phrases, clauses and sentences, however it may be conceptualized. Semantic relations are the focus of chapters 3 and 4, and pragmatic relations are the main subject of chapter 5. Syntactic relational structure is the main topic of chapter 6, which focuses on grammatical relations. We will concentrate on the non-relational structure in simple phrases and sentences in this chapter. The structure of complex noun phrases and sentences is discussed in chapter 8.

Before we begin, however, there are two general theoretical issues that need to be addressed: how many levels of syntactic representation are there in a grammar, and what aspects of clause structure are universal? These issues will be considered in the next section.

2.1 General theoretical issues

2.1.1 Levels of syntactic representation

One of the most important theoretical claims Chomsky made in his early work was that no theory of grammar could approach descriptive or explanatory adequacy if it recognized only a single level of syntactic representation, namely the overt or surface form. He argued that an additional, abstract level of syntactic representation is required. There are a number of phenomena which have been presented as justifying the postulation of multiple levels of syntactic representation. Among the most basic and important of these is what we may call 'non-local dependencies' involving case assignment and agreement. Simple examples of local and non-local assignment of case are given in (2.1).

(2.1) a. Pat sent them to us. Local
b. Whom did Pat send to us? Non-local
c. Whom did Pat send them to? Non-local

In English a direct object normally immediately follows the verb, and likewise the object of a preposition immediately follows its preposition. While English lacks the rich case morphology of languages like German and Dyirbal, for example, it can be said that the verb or preposition determines the case of its object when it is a pronoun, as in (2.1). The dependence between verb and object and preposition and object in (2.1a) is local, because the head and its dependent are adjacent to each other in the canonical pattern for English. In (b) and (c), on the other hand, the dependencies are not local, as the WH-word object of the verb in (b) or the object of the preposition in (c) is not in its canonical position but rather occurs clause-initially. There are two ways to handle case assignment in these three sentences. One is to postulate a rule which attempts to account for the local case assignment in (2.1a) and the non-local assignments in (2.1b, c). It must state not only that a governing head, such as a verb or preposition, assigns a particular case to the immediately following NP, but also that it can assign it to an NP in clause-initial position. The second part of this rule is complex and difficult to state in purely syntactic constituent structure terms, but let us assume that it is in fact formulable. The second approach is to write the relatively simple rule for the local dependence in (2.1a) and then to specify that it applies only in the canonical clause pattern. This canonical pattern is hypothesized as the abstract representation underlying the sentences with non-canonical patterns (2.1b, c), and these patterns are derived by applying a syntactic rule of WH-word fronting to this abstract structural representation, yielding the actual forms in these sentences. In this analysis case assignment is greatly simplified, since all instances of case assignment are reduced to the canonical local one, and the fronting rule can be independently motivated in the grammar of English. This may be represented as in figure 2.1 ('→' indicates the assignment of case).[1] Both of these accounts are observationally adequate, and the choice between these two alternative analyses revolves around the theory-internal criteria of simplicity and motivation. Chomsky has argued since his earliest work in generative grammar that the second solution is to be preferred. Accordingly, one of the strongest challenges for non-transformational theories is to account for non-local dependencies of this type. In Chomsky's terms, then, the actually occurring form of a sentence, the surface structure, constitutes the overt level of representation, and there is in addition a covert, abstract underlying level of representation, originally called the 'deep structure', which represents the elements in the clause in their canonical arrangement. There must, in addition, be rules to map the more abstract underlying representations into the less abstract representation closer to the actual form of the sentence; these were called 'transformational rules' in earlier

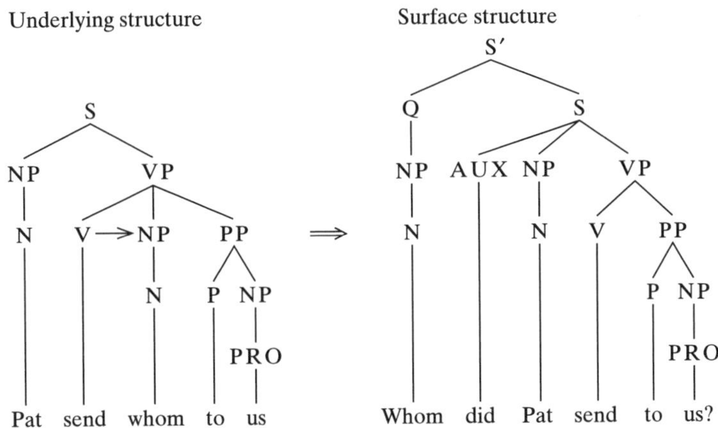

Figure 2.1 Transformational analysis of non-local case assignment

versions of the theory, while in current theory they are subsumed under the single rule of Move α.[2]

There are other phenomena with reference to which specific theoretical assumptions dictate a particular approach. In GB theory, certain rules like case assignment treat subjects and objects differently, and this is reflected in their distinct positions in the phrase structure tree: the subject NP (e.g. *Pat* in the left tree structure in figure 2.1) is the NP immediately dominated by the S(entence) node and is a sister to the verb phrase (VP) node, while the object NP (e.g. *whom* in the same example) is immediately dominated by the VP node and is a sister to the verb.[3] If the subject were a pronoun, it would have nominative case, while the object pronoun is in the accusative form; this follows from their different positions in the phrase structure tree, according to this analysis. Chomsky maintains that all languages have case assignment rules like this, and one of the consequences of this claim is that every language must have a VP in its clause structure in order for case assignment to work properly. Consider the following data from Dyirbal (Dixon 1972), an Aboriginal language of Australia.

(2.2) a. Ba-la-n ḍugumbil-∅ ba-ŋgu-l yaɽa-ŋgu buɽa-n.
DEIC-ABS-II woman-ABS DEIC-ERG-I man-ERG see-TNS[4]
b. Baŋgul yaɽaŋgu buɽan balan ḍugumbil.
c. Buɽan balan ḍugumbil baŋgul yaɽaŋgu.
d. Baŋgul yaɽaŋgu balan ḍugumbil buɽan.
e. Buɽan baŋgul yaɽaŋgu balan ḍugumbil.
f. Balan ḍugumbil buɽan baŋgul yaɽaŋgu.
'The man saw the woman.'

(2.3) Ba-yi yaɽa-∅ ba-ŋgu-n ḍugumbi-ɽu buɽa-n.
DEIC-ABS.I man-ABS DEIC-ERG-II woman-ERG see-TNS
'The woman saw the man.'

(2.4) a. Ba-la-n ḍugumbil-∅ wayɲḍi-n.
DEIC-ABS-II woman-ABS go.uphill-TNS
b. Wayɲḍin balan ḍugumbil.
'The woman went uphill.'

The major constituents in a Dyirbal clause can appear in any order, and if one wishes to change the meaning of the sentence to 'The woman saw the man', then the case marking of the NPs must be changed, as in (2.3). Of particular interest here are (2.2a, e) in which the 'object' NP *balan ḍugumbil* 'the woman' is separated from the verb *buɽan* 'see' by the 'subject' NP *baŋgul yaɽaŋgu* 'the man'.[5] These examples raise doubts that there is a VP in Dyirbal clause structure, because there is no evidence that the 'object' NP and the verb form any kind of unit. Since ergative case must be assigned to the 'subject' NP and absolutive to the 'object' in (2.2) and this assignment depends on one of them being immediately dominated by S and the other by VP, there is no easy formulation of case assignment (in Chomsky's terms) if we restrict ourselves to the forms in (2.2). There is a straightforward solution to this problem if we adopt an analysis like that in figure 2.1. In the underlying representation of Dyirbal clauses there is fixed word order and a VP, e.g. S[$_{VP}$V O], following Kayne's (1994) claim that all languages have SVO order in their underlying syntactic forms, and the case assignment rules apply to this abstract representation. Then there is an optional rule which scrambles the phrases in order to specify all of the possibilities given in (2.2) and (2.4). The important point about this situation is that the assumption of a structurally based account of case assignment, together with lack of overt evidence for a VP, forces the multilevel analysis. Even though the facts in (2.2)–(2.4) from Dyirbal are quite different from those in (2.1) from English, the analysis is the same: the canonical clause pattern is posited as the underlying form of the sentence, and a non-local dependence, i.e. the 'object' NP and the verb in (2.2a, e), is reduced to a local dependence. If, on the other hand, the theory assumed a non-structurally based account of case assignment, one based on grammatical relations or semantic relations, then the need for the abstract representation would be obviated. This highlights the fact that the justification for the abstract syntactic representation is entirely theory-internal.

There is no empirical fact in any human language that absolutely requires that a theory of syntax posit multiple levels of syntactic representation. Rather, the motivation for positing an abstract underlying syntactic level is theory-internal, in particular the argument that the potential complications of multiple syntactic levels are outweighed by the advantages of being able to treat all dependencies in terms of canonical local dependencies. Since the motivation for multiple levels of syntactic representation is entirely theory-internal, there is likewise no empirical fact in any human language that can disprove their existence. Arguments against them would generally have to be one of two kinds: (1) a demonstration that a certain phenomenon which has been asserted to require recourse to multiple levels, e.g. (2.1), can

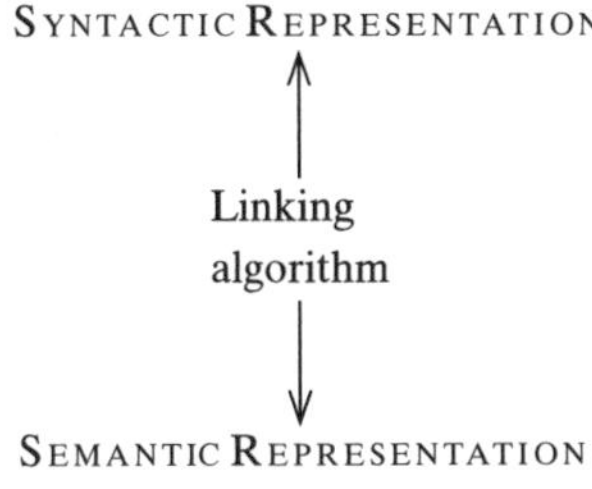

Figure 2.2 Organization of the theory of grammar to be presented

be handled equally well or better by a different analysis which posits only a single level of syntactic representation; or (2) a demonstration that multilevel syntactic analyses are unnecessarily complex and inelegant or entail a loss of significant generalizations.

At the present time, the idea of abstract underlying syntactic representations is highly controversial. Most contemporary theories do not posit any underlying level of syntactic representation; none of the theories discussed in section 1.3.2 does, and only two of the theories in section 1.3.1 (GB/P&P, RelG) do. All theories have a level of semantic representation, which is by definition abstract and distinct from the overt syntactic representation. The position assumed here is that *multiple levels of syntactic representation are **not** necessary*. Thus, the general structure of the RRG-based theory of grammar we will be presenting is as in figure 2.2. This picture will be elaborated as we proceed, but it makes clear that we are positing only a single level of syntactic representation for a sentence, which is mapped directly into the semantic representation of the sentence (and vice versa, hence the double-headed arrow). It is important to emphasize that the semantic representation, which will be developed in chapters 3 and 4, is not equivalent to the abstract syntactic representation of GB/P&P or earlier versions of transformational grammar. Theories like these have a semantic representation in addition to the abstract syntactic representations. There are no abstract syntactic representations mediating between the overt syntactic representation of a sentence and its semantic representation, be they derivationally related to the overt form, as in GB/P&P and earlier transformational theories, or non-derivationally related, as in the f(unctional)-structures of LFG. We are positing the minimal number of representations possible in order to capture the relationship between form and meaning in natural language.

No specific arguments against analyses assuming them will be made; rather the emphasis will be on showing how a single-level syntactic theory can account in a direct and elegant way for many of the phenomena which have been adduced as evidence in favor of multilevel syntactic analyses. In addition, the single morphosyntactic representation given to a sentence in a language should be concrete, not abstract, in the sense that it should represent the actual form of the sentence, including the linear sequence of its constituent elements and their morphological properties.[6]

2.1.2 Universal aspects of structure

We are presenting a single-level theory of syntactic structure that is part of a theory of universal grammar, and therefore it is imperative that we base it on notions that are universal. It makes no sense to postulate a conception of clause structure that is based on relations or categories that are demonstrably not universal. This would violate the principle of typological adequacy discussed in section 1.2.2.

What does it mean for something to be 'universal'? Let us take as a working hypothesis the idea that, in the strongest sense, this means that the concept, category or relation in question can be motivated in every human language; that is, evidence can be adduced in support of the existence of the construct in each language.[7] This is a very strong requirement, but it is consistent with the principle of typological adequacy. Moreover, let us impose an additional strong requirement on a universal theory of clause structure: comparable structures in different languages should be given comparable treatments by the theory. For example, the structural relationship between 'boy' and 'eat' in a sentence meaning 'The boy ate the apple' should be represented the same way in all languages, despite the obvious formal differences found in the wide variety of human languages. These two requirements are summarized in (2.5)

(2.5) *General considerations for a theory of clause structure*
  a. A theory of clause structure should capture all of the universal features without imposing features on languages in which there is no evidence for them.
  b. A theory should represent comparable structures in different languages in comparable ways.

These are very strong conditions, particularly in light of the requirement stated at the end of the previous section that the morphosyntactic representation of a sentence must be concrete and reflect the actual form of the sentence (ignoring morphophonology; see n. 6).

There is an important problem which we must raise here, even though there is no simple or easy solution to it. This is the problem of identifying correspondences, in particular corresponding structures, across languages. This is a problem which all theories concerned with cross-linguistic comparison face. Questions about the comparability of lexical and syntactic categories go back to the beginning of modern linguistics; Boas (1911) argued, for example, that specific definitions for terms like 'noun' and 'verb' should be restricted to closely related languages within a single family and that it was illegitimate to assume that what counts as, for example, a verb in Algonquian languages is the same as what counts as a verb in, say, Siouan languages, let alone in Indo-European languages. Most syntactic theories assume that noun, verb, adposition (i.e. preposition or postposition) and adjective are universally valid categories, but it is far from clear that adposition and adjective are universal categories (see section 2.2.1 below). The situation becomes much more complicated when one investigates phrasal categories, e.g. NP, VP, and syntactic constructions. The problem, in a nutshell, is this: similar forms in different languages can have very different meanings and/or functions within the overall grammatical system, and conversely, the same meaning or function within a grammatical system can be realized by formally quite different constructs in different languages. Hence in looking for comparable entities in different grammatical systems, neither form nor function is necessarily a reliable indicator of comparability. Having noted these difficulties, however, we will see that they are not insurmountable in practice. In chapter 6, for example, we will be specifically concerned with identifying grammatical relations like subject in different grammatical systems, and we will see that there are tests which permit this to be done.

The leading candidate for expressing hierarchical non-relational structure is immediate-constituent (IC) representations. These are traditional phrase structure representations of the type exemplified in figure 2.1. While the universality of VP is open to serious question, as we have seen, it is not a necessary component of an IC analysis *per se*, and therefore the problems that were raised with respect to VP as universal do not relate to the validity of IC structure as a universal means of representing non-relational structure. This means, however, that the structures assigned to a Dyirbal clause would be quite different from those assigned to an English clause, and this contrast is even more pronounced when it is recognized that in this Australian Aboriginal language there is no requirement that the modifiers of a noun occur adjacent to it. Thus not only are all of the sentences in (2.2) grammatical, but so are all of those in (2.6).

(2.6) a. Ba-ŋgu-l ba-la-n yaɽa-ŋgu buɽan ḍugumbil-∅.
DEIC-ERG-I DEIC-ABS-II man-ERG saw woman-ABS
b. ḍugumbil baŋgul buɽan balan yaɽaŋgu.
c. Yaɽaŋgu ḍugumbil balan baŋgul buɽan.
(all possible orders are grammatical)
'The man saw the woman.'

The structures that would be assigned to (2.6b) and its English translation are given in figure 2.3. It is not clear that the IC representations are capturing any similar features between the two languages, except for categorial information.

Another challenge for IC analysis is clause structure in what Nichols (1986) calls 'head-marking' languages. Dyirbal and English are 'dependent-marking' languages; that is, the syntactic relation between a head and its dependent(s) is coded morphologically on the dependent; in Dyirbal, this is exemplified by the case marking of the NP arguments of a verb. In a head-marking language, on the other hand, the relation between a head and its dependent(s) is coded morphologically on the head rather than on the dependents. This is illustrated in (2.7), from Lakhota, a Siouan language of North America.

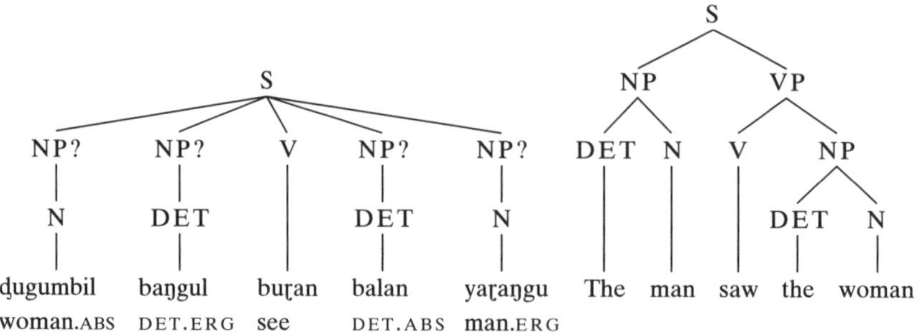

Figure 2.3 IC representation of Dyirbal and English clause structures

(2.7) a. Mathó ki hená wičhá-wa-kte.
bear the those them-I-kill
'I killed those bears.'
b. Wičhá-wa-kte.
them-I-kill
'I killed them.'

There is no case marking on NPs at all in this language; rather, the arguments are marked on the verb itself. This has the important consequence that the verb alone can constitute an entire sentence, as (2.7b) shows. While it would be possible to draw an IC representation of (2.7a), such a diagram of (2.7b) would be very unrevealing, and since the whole clause is a single phonological word, the S node would simply dominate V and nothing else. It is not possible in a syntactic IC structure for the representation to branch down into the internal structure of words. This is contrasted with the representation of the English translation in figure 2.4. Again, as in Dyirbal, an IC representation of this sentence is possible, but it fails to capture what is common to clause structure in English and Lakhota. It should be noted that there are ways for theories which assume IC structure to deal with these problems. In the case of Dyirbal, it was mentioned that positing multiple levels of syntactic

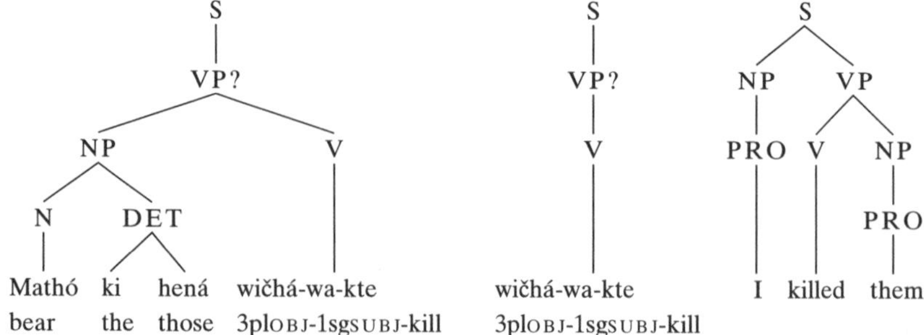

Figure 2.4 IC representation of Lakhota and English clause structures

representation with transformational-type rules can handle it. For Lakhota-type head-marking structures, it is possible to treat Lakhota as if it were a dependent-marking language, by claiming that the markers on the verb are simply agreement with phonological null pronouns in the argument positions in an English-like tree. This runs into some serious problems, however, as argued in Van Valin (1987a). Neither of these options is available in the framework we are developing here, since the first involves multiple levels of representation and the second violates the principle of typological adequacy. Therefore some other system of representing clause structure must be found. Thus, it would appear that there are serious problems with assuming an IC analysis as the basis for a universally valid representation of non-relational syntactic structure.

2.2 The layered structure of the clause in simple sentences

2.2.1 Universal distinctions in clause structure

The optimal representation of clause structure is one which reflects universal distinctions that every language makes. What might these distinctions be? Two which play a role in the syntax of every language are the contrasts between predicating elements and non-predicating elements, on the one hand, and between those NPs and adpositional phrases (prepositional or postpositional phrases) which are arguments of the predicate and those which are not. These contrasts are represented graphically in figure 2.5. The predicating element is normally a verb, but it need not be. English non-verbal predicates require the copula *be* or some kind of copular verb to be used. In other languages, however, a sentence like *John is a doctor* would have *doctor* as the predicate without any sort of copula, as in Russian *Ivan vrač* (John doctor-NOM). In Lakhota the word for 'boy' is *hokšíla* and the bound pronoun form for 'you' is *ni-*, and in order to say 'you are a boy', the pronoun is simply attached to the noun, yielding *nihókšila.* There are also nominal predicates which can take arguments and occur without a copula-type element, e.g. Mparntwe Arrernte *kaltye* 'know, be knowledgeable about', as in (2.8), from Wilkins (1989).

(2.8) Re kaltye Arrernte-ke.
3sgSUBJ know Arrernte-DAT
'She knows Arrernte.'

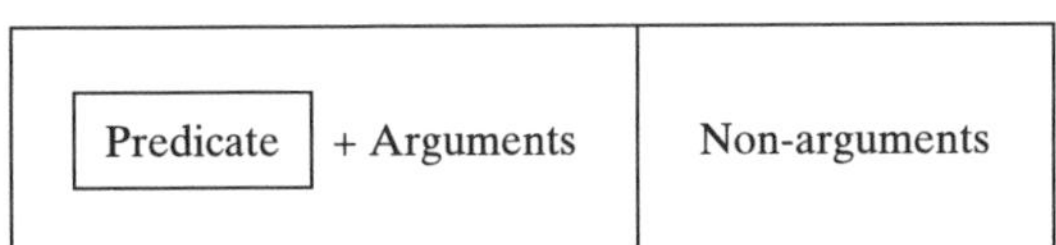

Figure 2.5 Universal oppositions underlying clause structure

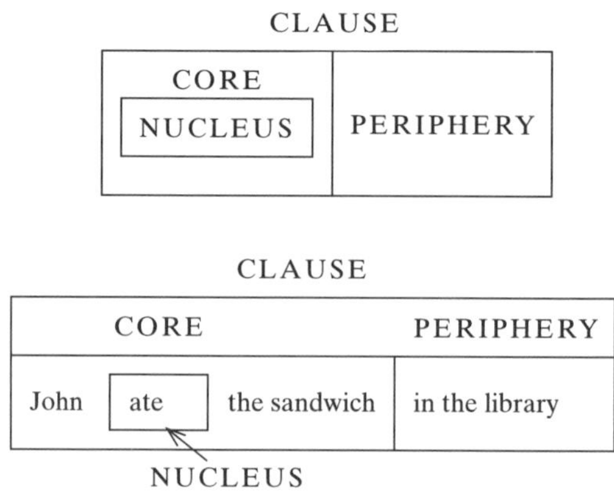

Figure 2.6 Components of the layered structure of the clause

A predicate, therefore, refers only to the predicating element, which is a verb, an adjective or a nominal of some sort. The predicate defines a syntactic unit in the structure of the clause, the **nucleus**.

In a clause containing a number of NPs (and PPs), some of them are semantic arguments of the predicate and some are not. It is, therefore, fundamentally important to distinguish those elements which are arguments of the predicate from those which are not. We may express this by positing a distinction between the **core** of the clause (the predicate + its arguments) and the **periphery** (those elements which are not arguments of the predicate). These distinctions, together with the notion of the nucleus, constitute what we will call the **layered structure of the clause** (LSC). In the English simple sentence *John ate the sandwich in the library*, *John ate the sandwich* is the core (with *ate* the nucleus and *John* and *the sandwich* the core arguments), and *in the library* is in the periphery, as in figure 2.6. If instead we had *John ate the sandwich yesterday in the library, John ate the sandwich* is still the core, but now *yesterday in the library* is in the periphery. The whole structure of *John ate the sandwich yesterday in the library* is the clause. Thus the core is defined as the nucleus plus the arguments of the predicate. So the first division in the clause is between a core and a periphery, and within the core a distinction is made between the nucleus (containing the predicating element, normally a verb) and its core arguments (NPs and PPs which are arguments of the predicate in the nucleus). *Core arguments are those arguments which are part of the semantic representation of the verb.* Hence a full account of which elements are core arguments and which are not cannot be given until we have presented the system of semantic representation for verbs and other predicating elements to be developed in chapter 3. However, an argument in the semantic representation of the verb may occur outside the core; as we will see in section 2.2.2.2 below, WH-words like *what* and *who* are normally arguments of the verb, and yet in a WH-question (e.g. *What did Pat buy?*) they

Table 2.1 *Semantic units underlying the syntactic units of the layered structure of the clause*

Semantic element(s)	*Syntactic unit*
Predicate	Nucleus
Argument in semantic representation of predicate	Core argument
Non-arguments	Periphery
Predicate + arguments	Core
Predicate + arguments + non-arguments	Clause (= core + periphery)

occur in a special position outside of the core called the 'precore slot'. Another way of looking at the periphery is that it contains the elements of the clause which are left out of the core. Non-arguments are often referred to as **adjuncts**. Time adverbials, such as *in five minutes* and *for five minutes* are part of the periphery, as are *yesterday* and *tomorrow*. Generally in English, elements which go into the periphery are either bare NP adverbials (*yesterday* and *tomorrow*), or they are locative and temporal PPs which are adverbial in nature (e.g. *after the party*). The distinctions between nucleus and core and between core and periphery are universal, as there is much cross-linguistic evidence for them from both clause-internal and complex sentence syntax. The relationships between the semantic and syntactic units are summarized in table 2.1.

This scheme is universal because every language makes a distinction between predicates and arguments, and every language distinguishes between NPs/PPs which are arguments of the predicate and those which are adjuncts. This has nothing to do with whether there is fixed or free word order, or whether or not there is a rigid hierarchical structure. This is completely independent of all those considerations. The distinctions among nucleus, core and periphery are fundamental to the clause structure of all human languages. It is important to keep in mind that the predicate–argument distinction is independent of the lexical distinctions that a language may make; that is, the claim is not that all languages distinguish nouns from verbs lexically, but rather that in structuring clauses at least some of the clauses in every language manifest predicate–argument structure, regardless of the lexical classes of the elements filling the predicate and argument slots. The existence of clause patterns in languages which fail to show predicate–argument structure, e.g. Lakhota *magážu* 'it is raining', is not evidence against this claim, since there are clause patterns in the language (in fact, the vast majority) which do show a clear predicate–argument bifurcation.

There is a systematic ambiguity in the way the term 'argument' is used in English; as can be seen in table 2.1, it can refer to an element in the semantic representation and also to a syntactic entity. This can be confusing at times, and consequently we will disambiguate them whenever necessary. In an expression like 'argument in the semantic representation', 'argument' clearly refers to semantic arguments, whereas the term 'core argument' is strictly syntactic in meaning. There are many instances where this distinction is crucial, and semantic arguments and syntactic arguments should not be confused.[8]

We have twice mentioned the issue of the universality of lexico-syntactic categories like noun and verb. Generative theories have taken these two categories to be basic and universal, and from them they have derived the other major categories: assuming two features [±V] and [±N], the four major syntactic categories are defined as [+V, –N] for verb, [–V, + N] for noun, [+V, +N] for adjective and [–V, –N] for adposition. As mentioned earlier, it is not at all clear that adjective and adposition are universally valid categories. Dyirbal, for example, lacks adpositions altogether; all nominals are case-marked (Dixon 1972). Lakhota, on the other hand, shows no evidence of having a syntactic category of adjective. There are, to be sure, words meaning 'tall', 'fat', 'red', etc., but syntactically they either function as predicates, as in *ixʔé ki thą́ke* (rock the big) 'the rock is big', or they are compounded with the noun they modify, as in *ixʔé-thąka ki* (rock-big the) 'the big rock'. Since verbs and nouns may be compounded in Lakhota, there is no reason to treat words of this class as belonging to a distinct syntactic category; they are, rather, a subclass of verb, in particular, a subclass of stative verbs. It has been suggested that there are languages which do not have noun and verb as distinct categories, e.g. Nootkan languages (Wakashan, North America), but Jacobsen (1979) has shown that even in these languages there are grounds for positing a categorial contrast between nouns and verbs. We will, therefore, assume that noun and verb are universally valid categories. This seems to be an intuitively reasonable assumption, but why should this be so? The answer given by a number of researchers working from a communication-and-cognition perspective (e.g. Hopper and Thompson 1984, Croft 1991, Langacker 1991) is that the universality of these two categories reflects the fact that each realizes one of the two fundamental functions of language, reference (nouns) and predication (verbs).

It is important to recognize that the nucleus, core, periphery and clause are *syntactic* units which are motivated by these semantic contrasts. The nucleus is the syntactic unit housing the predicate, but it is not identical with the predicate; this will be seen most clearly when we look at noun incorporation, in which there is both a verb and noun stem in the nucleus (see section 2.3.2). Similarly, the core is the unit containing the nucleus and the arguments in the semantic representation of the predicate in the nucleus (which will be developed in the next chapter), but there are instances in which the core contains a syntactic argument which is not a semantic argument of the predicate in its nucleus. This is the case, for example, in a 'raising' construction like *John seems to have eaten the sandwich*, in which *John* occurs in the core *John seems* but is not a semantic argument of *seem*; rather, it is a semantic argument of *eat*, the verb in the nucleus in the dependent core. This construction will be discussed in chapter 9. Hence, the notion of 'core' is motivated semantically, but it is not possible to determine it purely semantically. The periphery is a syntactic unit encompassing NPs/PPs which are either secondary participants or modifiers of the core. Finally, the clause is a syntactic unit composed of the core and periphery. The **sentence** is an even larger syntactic unit, which may contain multiple clauses in complex sentences, as we will see in chapter 8.

Languages typically code core arguments differently from adjuncts. The coding contrast between the two classes can only be understood in terms of the case-marking system of the language in question. In English and Icelandic, for example, NPs not marked by a preposition are normally core arguments,[9] but the converse does not hold. Examples of core arguments which are prepositionally marked include the *to*-phrase with *give* and the *from*-phrase with *take*. The NPs in these PPs are represented in the semantic representation of *give* and *take*, respectively. In Icelandic, the verb *skila* 'return, give back' takes three arguments which can be realized as either (2.9a) or (2.9b).

(2.9) a. Ég skila-ð-i henni pening-un-um.
1sgNOM return-PAST-1sg 3FsgDAT money-DEF-DAT
'I returned her the money.'
b. Ég skila-ð-i pening-un-um til hennar.
1sgNOM return-PAST-1sg money-DEF-DAT to 3FsgGEN
'I returned the money to her.'

Even though the non-subject NPs in these two sentences have different morphosyntactic codings, the semantic representation for *skila* 'give back' is the same in both sentences, just as the semantic representation for *give* is the same in both of its active-voice forms (i.e. *give x to y* and *give y x*). Consequently all of the NPs in these sentences are core arguments. Thus in English and Icelandic, if an argument is not marked by a preposition, it is a core argument, unless it is one of the bare NP adverbials mentioned in n. 9. Yet, just because an NP is marked by a preposition does not necessarily mean it is peripheral. It is necessary, therefore, to distinguish between **direct** core arguments, i.e. core arguments which are either unmarked, as in English, or marked by case alone, as in Icelandic, and **oblique** core arguments, i.e. core arguments which are adpositionally marked.[10] All of the NPs in (2.9a) are direct core arguments, as they are all case-marked only, whereas in (2.9b) *til hennar* is an oblique core argument because of the preposition *til* 'to'. Oblique core arguments differ from peripheral PPs in an important way syntactically. With verbs like *present* (e.g. *John presented the award* ***to Mary***), *award* and *supply*, the argument which is in the PP can also occur in a form without a preposition (e.g. *John presented* ***Mary*** *with the award*). Only core arguments, however, can do this in

English; peripheral PPs cannot become core arguments in English. Both *Mary* and *award* are core arguments, not only because they both would be represented in the semantic representation of *present*, but also because these prepositionally marked NPs have the possibility of appearing as direct core arguments. This is not an option that is available to peripheral PPs in English.[11] Other languages do have ways of making peripheral PPs core arguments, but it involves the addition of derivational markers to the verb; it is never a simple alternation like that with *present* in English or *skila* in Icelandic.[12]

In head-marking languages like Lakhota, verbs do not assign case to NPs; rather, they are cross-referenced by pronominal affixes on the verb. Peripheral elements are never cross-referenced and may be marked by adpositions. This is illustrated in the following example from Lakhota.[13]

(2.10) a. Wakpála ki aglágla lakhóta ki thathą́ka óta wą-wíčha-∅-yąka-pi.
creek the near Sioux the buffalo many stem-3plOBJ-3sSUBJ-see-pl
'The Indians (Siouxs) saw many buffalo near the creek.'

b. Wakpála ki aglágla lakhóta ki ixʔé óta wą-∅-∅-yą́ka-pi
creek the near Sioux the rock many stem-INAN-3sSUBJ-see-pl
/*wą-wíčha-∅-yáka-pi.
/*stem-3plOBJ-3sSUBJ-see-pl
'The Indians (Siouxs) saw many rocks near the creek.'

The core arguments, *lakhóta ki* 'the Indian(s)/Sioux(s)' and *thathą́ka óta* 'many buffalo' are cross-referenced by bound affixes on the verb, while the peripheral element *wakpála ki* 'the creek' is marked by the postposition *aglágla* 'along, near'. Lakhota is not entirely consistent in its treatment of core arguments; inanimate arguments are not cross-referenced on the verb in the same way as animate arguments, as illustrated in (2.10b). However, *ixʔé óta* 'many rocks' is not marked by a postposition, and this sets it off from peripheral elements like *wakpála ki aglágla*. With intransitive verbs that can take inanimate arguments, e.g. *hą́ska* 'tall', a plural subject is not signaled by the suffix *-pi*, as in (2.10), but rather by reduplication, e.g. *Čhą́ ki hená hą́ska-ska/*hą́ska-pi* (tree the those tall) 'Those trees are tall'. Plural inanimate objects are not cross-referenced by *-wičha-*, only by -∅-, as (2.10b) shows. Here again there is distinctive morphosyntactic treatment of core arguments which distinguishes them from peripheral elements.

A very important feature of the layered structure of the clause is that the distinctions among the layers are not dependent in any way on the linear order of elements in a clause. This can be seen in the following examples from Dyirbal, as illustrated in (2.11).

(2.11) a. Ba-yi bargan$_{CORE}$ ba-ŋgu-l yaɽa-ŋgu$_{CORE}$ ḍurga-ɲu$_{NUC}$
DEIC-ABS.I wallaby-ABS DEIC-ERG-I man-ERG spear-TNS
gambi-ɽa$_{PER}$.
mountains-LOC

b. Baŋgul yaɽaŋgu$_{CORE}$ gambiɽa$_{PER}$ bayi bargan$_{CORE}$ ɖurgaɲu$_{NUC}$.
   man mountains wallaby speared
c. ɖurgaɲu$_{NUC}$ gambiɽa$_{PER}$ bayi bargan$_{CORE}$ baŋgul yaɽaŋgu$_{CORE}$.
   speared mountains wallaby man
d. Bayi bargan$_{CORE}$ gambiɽa$_{PER}$ ɖurgaɲu$_{NUC}$ baŋgul yaɽaŋgu$_{CORE}$.
   wallaby mountains speared man
   'The man speared the wallaby in the mountains.'

The elements of the core, nucleus and periphery can in principle appear in any order in a clause, and because the definitions of each unit are independent of linear order or adjacency considerations, this variation is unproblematic.

2.2.2 Formal representation of the layered structure of the clause

Having introduced the fundamental units of clause structure, we need to have an explicit representation of them. After introducing it, we will present the non-universal features of the layered structure of the clause.

2.2.2.1 Representing the universal aspects of the layered structure of the clause

To represent the nucleus, core, periphery and clause, we will use a type of tree diagram which differs substantially from the constituent-structure trees discussed earlier. The abstract schema of the layered structure of the clause can be represented as in figure 2.7. The clause consists of the core with its arguments, and then the nucleus, which subsumes the predicate. At the very bottom are the actual syntactic categories which realize these units. Notice that there is no VP in the tree, for it is not a concept that plays a direct role in this conception of clause structure.[14] The periphery is represented on the margin, and the arrow there indicates that it is an adjunct; that is, it is an optional modifier of the core. Elements in the periphery are usually PPs or adverbials, but in languages like Dyirbal which lack PPs, case-marked NPs may be in it. The main structural line of the clause, which runs from

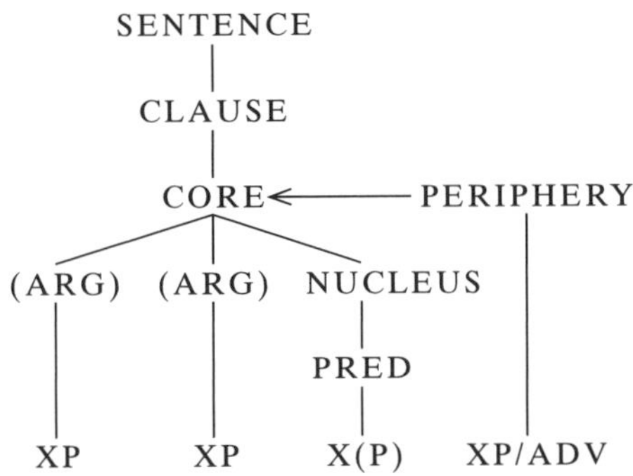

Figure 2.7 Formal representation of the layered structure of the clause

clause to core to nucleus, excludes the periphery. As noted in the previous section, the linear order of the core arguments and the predicate is irrelevant to the determination of whether an element is in the nucleus, core or periphery. This representational scheme will work for any linear order because none of these relationships depends upon linear order. Although these relations may happen to be coded by linear order in particular languages, there is nothing concerning the distinction between the nucleus and core arguments, or that between the core arguments and the peripheral elements, which is in any way directly related to linear order. An example of an English clause is given in figure 2.8 and an example from Japanese in figure 2.9. Both direct and oblique core arguments are labeled 'ARG' in these

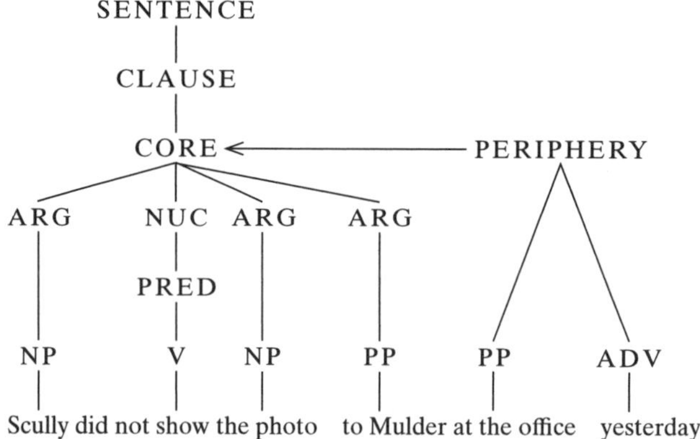

Figure 2.8 English LSC

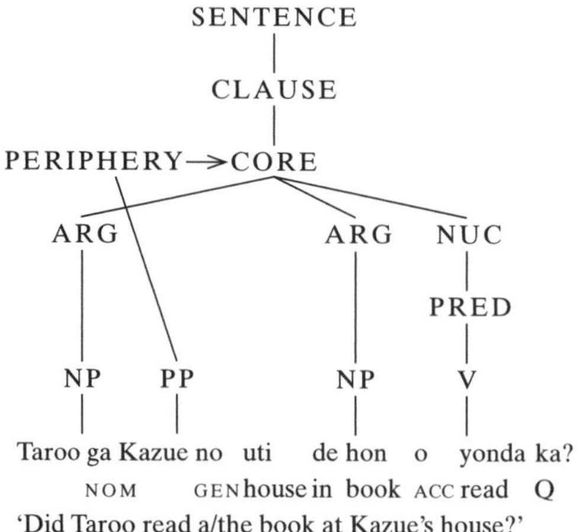

Figure 2.9 Japanese LSC

diagrams, e.g. the NPs *Scully* and *the photo* are direct core arguments and the NP *Mulder* in the PP *to Mulder* is an oblique core argument in figure 2.8.

It was argued at the end of section 2.1.2 that constituent structure representations of sentences in free-word-order and head-marking languages are unrevealing, because they fail to capture what is common to clauses in the different language types (see figures 2.3 and 2.4). The layered approach to clause structure does not suffer from the same shortcomings. For a language like Dyirbal, for example, the sentences in (2.11) would be represented as in figure 2.10. The lines linking the head nouns with their determiners will be discussed in the section on NP structure (section 2.3.2) below. The striking thing about these two structures is that they express the same structural relations among the elements in the clause, despite the obvious differences between the two languages. With respect to head-marking languages, Van Valin (1977, 1985, 1987a) argues that in languages like Lakhota the pronominal

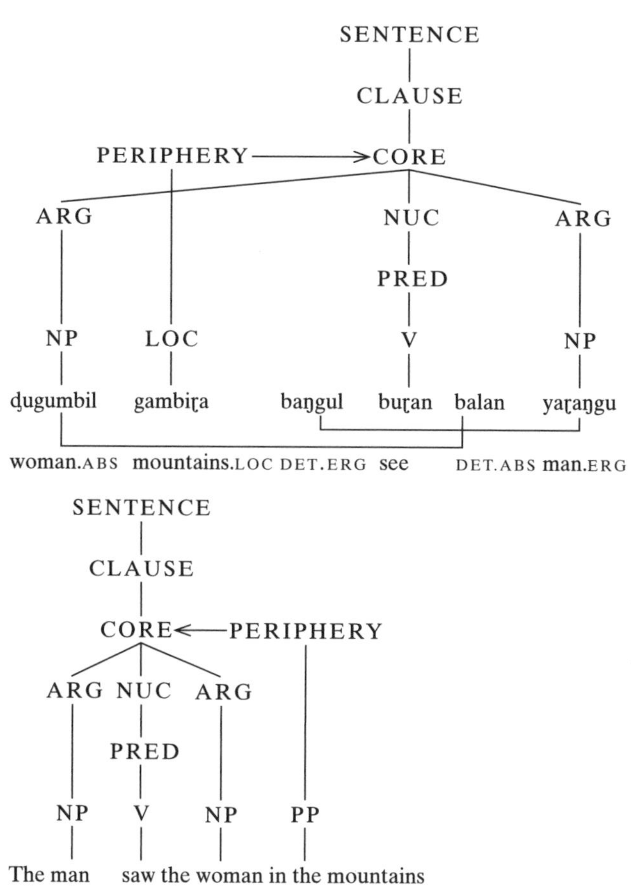

Figure 2.10 LSC of English and Dyirbal clauses

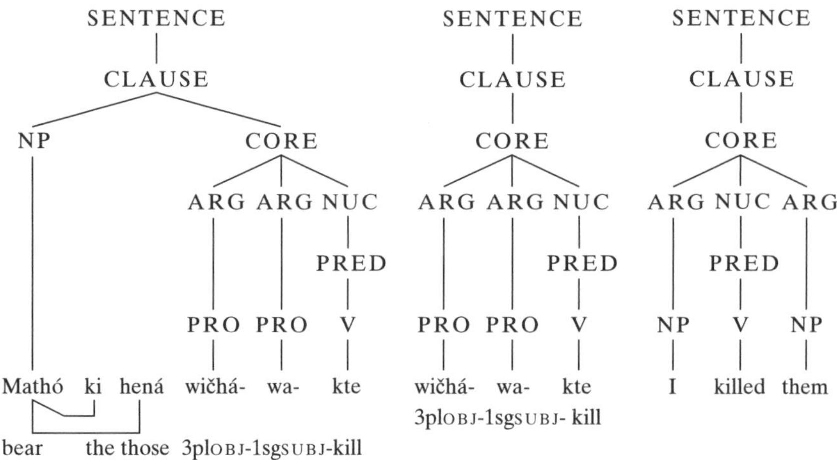

Figure 2.11 LSC of Lakhota and English clauses

affixes on the verb are the core arguments, not the independent NPs as in dependent-marking languages.[15] Thus in both (2.7a) and (2.7b) *wičha-* '3pl animate object' and *-wa-* '1sg subject' are the core arguments, with the independent NPs in (2.7a) being within the clause but not the core. Crucial evidence in support of this analysis comes from the fact that the syntactic rules of the language are sensitive to the arguments that are coded on the verb and apply in a clause regardless of whether the independent NPs are present or not. This may be represented as in figure 2.11. It is significant that 'I killed them' is assigned very similar representations in English and Lakhota, even though the pronouns are independent elements in English and bound morphemes in Lakhota. Contrast these with the representations in figure 2.4. Thus this approach to clause structure is not biased in favor of dependent-marking languages and is able to express the central similarities and differences in clause structure in the two types of languages. This also reemphasizes the point made at the beginning of chapter 1 that it is necessary to look at morphosyntax, not just syntax or just morphology, if we are to capture important cross-linguistic regularities.

The opposition between dependent-marking and head-marking languages is not absolute; there are dependent-marking languages with some head-marking features, and there are head-marking languages with some dependent-marking features. Italian, Spanish, Polish and Croatian, for example, are basically dependent-marking languages, but because they have verb agreement which expresses the person and number of the subject, no independent pronoun is necessary, unlike English. This is illustrated in the following examples from Croatian.

(2.12) a. Marij-a je kupi-l-a knjig-u.
Maria-FsgNOM be.3sg buy-PAST-Fsg book-FsgACC
'Maria bought the book.'

a′. Ona je kupi-l-a knjig-u.
3sgFEM be.3sg buy-PAST-Fsg book-FsgACC
'She bought the book.'

a″. Kupila je knjigu.
'She bought the book.'

b. Ja sam kupi-l-a knjig-u.
1sgNOM be.1sg buy-PAST-Fsg book-FsgACC
'I bought the book.' (female speaker)

b′. Kupila sam knjigu.
'I bought the book.'

Choctaw, a Muskogean language of North America (Heath 1977), exemplifies what Nichols (1986) calls a 'double-marking language', i.e. a head-marking language which also has NP case marking. This is illustrated in (2.13).

(2.13) a. Hattak at ∅-iya-h.
man DCT 3SUBJ-go-PRES
'The man goes.'

a′. ∅-iya-h.
'He/she goes.'

b. Hattak at oho:yoh (ã:) ∅-∅-pi:sa-h.
man DCT woman (OBL) 3SUBJ-3OBJ-see-PRES
'The man sees the woman.'

b′. ∅-∅-pi:sa-h.
'He/she sees him/her.'

Choctaw, like Lakhota, cross-references subject and object on the verb, but, unlike Lakhota, it has case marking for independent NPs. There are only two cases, which Heath (1977) labels 'direct' and 'oblique'; the subject receives the direct case, while non-subject core arguments receive the oblique case. Since Choctaw is basically head-marking, it would be assigned the same clause structures as Lakhota, with the independent NPs outside the core but inside the clause. In Croatian, on the other hand, sentences like (2.12a) would be analyzed as a purely dependent-marking structure with subject agreement, just like English and Icelandic, but in the structural representation of (a″) the subject would be the bound marker on the verb, while the object would be the independent case-marked NP. This yields a mixed representation, with the subject coded morphologically and the object syntactically. This is not surprising, however, given that Croatian is a dependent-marking language with a bit of head-marking in its grammar.

2.2.2.2 Non-universal aspects of the layered structure of the clause

There are additional elements in a sentence beyond the ones represented in figures 2.7–2.9, and, unlike the components of the layered structure of the clause, they are not universal. They are not universal, and linear order is relevant to the determination of these positions. Question words in languages like English appear in a clause-initial position which is distinct from the core-initial position that the subject occupies in English. It is also possible for a non-WH NP or PP to occur in this same position in sentences like ***That book*** *you put on the table,* ***This magazine*** *you put on the shelf*, or ***To Dana*** *Pat gave a new watch*. Neither this NP or PP nor a WH-word is separated from the rest of the sentence by a pause or intonation break. The position which these elements occupy is called the **precore slot**, and it is inside of the clause but outside of the core. In addition to a WH-word or NP/PP in the precore slot, it is also possible to have an initial phrase set off from the rest of the sentence by a pause or intonation break. Examples of this construction are given in (2.14).

(2.14) a. At the park, I talked to Leslie.
b. Yesterday, I walked on the beach with Kim.
c. As for Sam, I haven't seen him in two weeks.
d. As for Felipe, what did Maria get him for his birthday?

These initial phrases differ from the precore slot NPs in two important ways. First, as noted, they are normally set off from the following clause by a pause or intonation break, and second, if the NP in it functions as a semantic argument in the following clause, there must be a pronoun in the clause which refers to it. In *That book you put on the table*, there cannot be a pronoun referring to the precore slot NP, as the ungrammaticality of **That book you put it on the table* shows. Example (2.14d) shows that this initial phrase cannot be in the precore slot, because there is a WH-word in the precore slot in the sentence; hence the position of the initial phrase is distinct from the precore slot. This position, which will be termed the **left-detached position**, is outside of the clause but within the sentence. An example from English with all of these elements is given in figure 2.12.

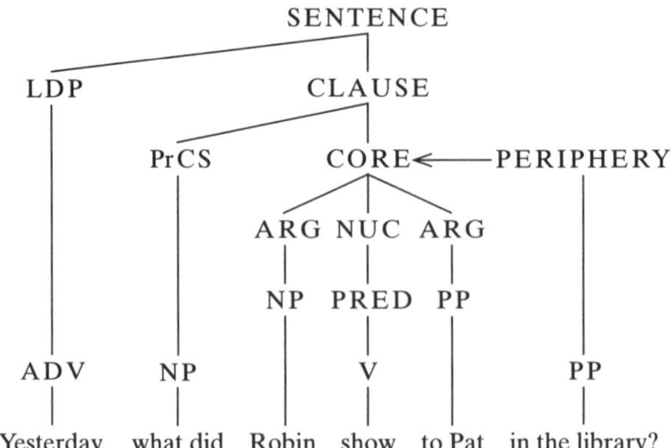

Figure 2.12 English sentence with precore slot and left-detached position

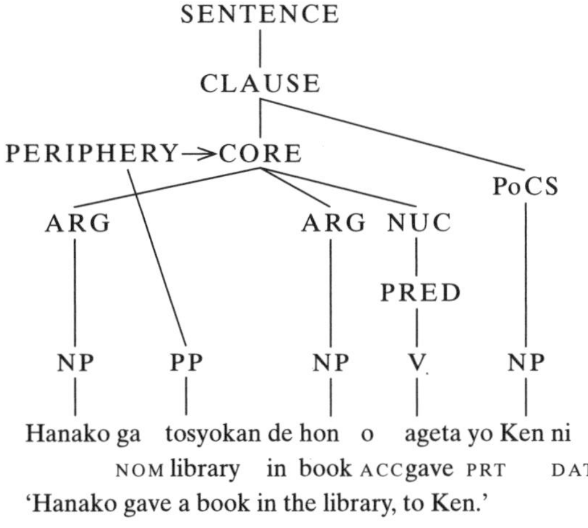

Figure 2.13 Postcore slot in Japanese

There are languages which have a *post*core slot as well, such as Japanese. The following examples are from Shimojo (1995), who demonstrates the existence of a postcore slot in Japanese.

(2.15) a. Hanako ga tosyokan de Ken ni hon o age-ta yo.
NOM library in DAT book ACC give-PAST PRT
'Hanako gave a book to Ken in the library.'
b. Hanako ga tosyokan de Ken ni age-ta yo hon o.
NOM library in DAT give-PAST PRT book ACC
c. Hanako ga tosyokan de hon o age-ta yo Ken ni.
NOM library in book ACC give-PAST PRT DAT
d. Hanako ga Ken ni hon o age-ta yo tosyokan de.
NOM DAT book ACC give-PAST PRT library in

The postcore slot NP, like the precore slot NP in a language like English, is not set off by a pause and is under the same intonation pattern as the main part of the sentence. The structure of (2.15c) is given in figure 2.13.

Detached phrases may in fact appear either before or after the clause, e.g. *I have not seen them in two weeks, the Smiths*, and therefore it is necessary to distinguish the two types of detached phrases, a left-detached position and a right-detached position. Hence position is relevant to the special position of WH-words, certain postposed elements and detached phrases, but it is not relevant to the more basic issue of determining core vs. peripheral elements. The abstract representation of the clause containing the pre- and postcore slots and the detached positions is given in figure 2.14; the periphery is omitted for simplicity of representation.

Both semantic arguments and non-arguments may occur in the precore slot; in figure 2.12, the precore slot NP is a semantic argument, whereas in a sentence

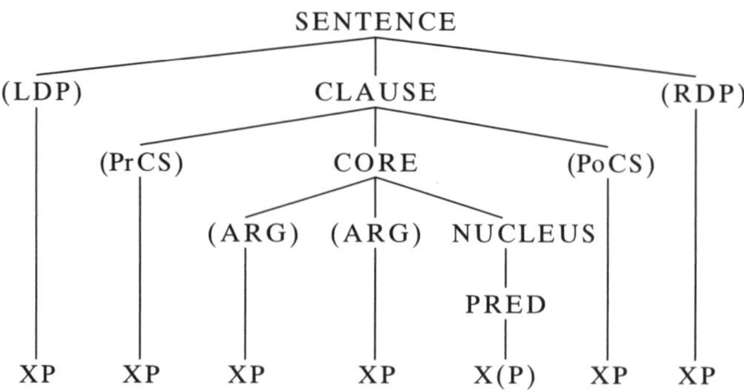

Figure 2.14 Abstract LSC including extra-core slots and detached positions

like *When did John show Mary the book?*, it is a non-argument. It was stated earlier that core arguments correspond to arguments in the semantic representation of the verb, and this needs to be modified slightly. Recall that 'core argument' is a syntactic, not a semantic, notion. In order for an element to appear in the core of the clause, it must be an argument in the semantic representation of the verb, but the converse does not hold: an argument in the semantic representation of the verb need not appear as a syntactic core argument but may appear in the pre- or postcore slot. Hence, 'semantic argument of the verb' and 'syntactic core argument' are not necessarily in a one-to-one relationship in languages in which NPs and PPs can appear both in the core and in the pre- or postcore slot. *What* in figure 2.12 is an argument, not an adjunct, but it is strictly speaking not a core argument; *what*, *John* and *Mary* are all syntactic (and semantic) arguments, but only *John* and *Mary* are core arguments. The direct vs. oblique syntactic argument contrast introduced in the previous section is relevant to precore slot elements; *what* in figure 2.12 is a direct argument, in terms of morphosyntactic coding, whereas in *To whom did John show the book?*, *to whom* is an oblique argument.

Evidence showing that the precore slot is clause-internal while the left-detached position is not can be found in Icelandic, a language in which the finite verb (or auxiliary) must be in second position in the clause in almost all main and subordinate clauses. This is illustrated in (2.16)–(2.18) from Maling and Zaenen (1981); in these examples the finite verb or auxiliary is in boldface, and the subject is italicized.

(2.16) a. *Henni* **hef-ur** alltaf þótt Ólaf-ur leiðinleg-ur.
3FsgDAT have-3sgPRES always think.PSTP Olaf-MsgNOM boring-MsgNOM
'She has always considered Olaf boring.'

b. Ólafur **hefur** *henni* alltaf þótt leiðinlegur.
'Olaf she has always considered boring.'

c. *Ólafur *henni* **hefur** alltaf þótt leiðinlegur.

(2.17) a. *Hún* **haf-ð-i** unn-ið að brúarsmíði í sumar.
3FsgNOM have-PAST-3sg work-PSTP at bridge.building in summer
'She worked at bridge-building in the summer.'
b. Í sumar **hafði** *hún* unnið að brúarsmíði.
'In the summer she worked at bridge-building.'
c. *Í sumar *hún* **hafði** unnið að brúarsmíði.
d. Hvenær **haf-ð-i** *hún* unn-ið að brúarsmíði?
when have-PAST-3sg 3FsgNOM work-PSTP at bridge.building
'When did she work at bridge-building?'
e. *Hvenær *hún* **hafði** unnið að brúarsmíði?

When a non-subject phrase appears in initial position in the clause, as in (2.16b, c) and (2.17b, c, d, e), the finite verb must immediately follow it, and the subject can no longer appear in its default position, as the ungrammaticality of (2.16c) and (2.17c, e) shows; it therefore appears immediately after the finite verb. The element in the precore slot is an NP in (2.16b, c), a PP in (2.17b, c) and a WH-word in (2.17d, e). These initial phrases are not set off from the rest of the sentence by a pause or intonation break, and there is no pronoun in the clause referring to the initial NP in any of the sentences of (2.16). The placement of the subject and finite verb in these constructions contrasts sharply with that in a sentence containing a left-detached phrase, as in (2.18).

(2.18) a. Smal-in-n, *ég* **held** að *tröll*
shepherd-DEF-MsgNOM 1sgNOM think.1sgPRES CMPL troll.NplNOM
muni taka hann á morgun.
will take.INF 3MsgACC tomorrow
'The shepherd, I think that trolls will take him tomorrow.'
b. *Smalinn, **held** *ég* að *tröll* **muni** taka hann á morgun.

Smalinn 'the shepherd' is a left-detached phrase separated from the rest of the sentence by an intonation break, and there is a pronoun in the sentence (*hann*) which refers to it. The important point about these examples is that the subject appears *before* the finite verb in (2.18a) in the main clause, showing that the finite verb is in second position in the clause, even though it is not in second position in the sentence. The ungrammaticality of (2.18b) shows that the initial NP is not in fact inside the clause. Thus these Icelandic facts demonstrate that there is a clear structural contrast between the precore slot and the left-detached position in a sentence.

There is an interesting difference between the universal and non-universal aspects of clause structure. The universal aspects (the nucleus, core, periphery and clause) are all semantically motivated, as shown in table 2.1. The non-universal aspects (the detached phrases, the extra-core slots) are not semantically motivated; rather, they seem to be pragmatically motivated (or at least are associated with constructions that have strong pragmatic conditions on their occurrence). We will find that this is a recurring pattern as we go through many grammatical phenomena: the more semantically motivated a phenomenon is, the less cross-linguistic variation we find, whereas the more pragmatically motivated a phenomenon is, the more cross-linguistic variation is evident.

2.2.3 Operators and their representation

In figures 2.8–2.10, elements like *did* and *not* in English and *ka* 'question marker' in Japanese are not attached to anything, and yet they are an important part of each sentence. These elements are in a whole domain of their own because they represent grammatical categories which are qualitatively different from predicates and their arguments. These categories are called **operators**, and they modify the clause and its parts. They include some familiar categories, like tense and aspect, and some perhaps unfamiliar, like evidentials. Often in English and other Indo-European languages operators are coded on or as auxiliary verbs. In other languages, they may be coded by a string of verbal affixes or clitics, without an independent auxiliary element to bear them. Nevertheless, they are quite different from predicates and their arguments. There are at least eight of these categories, and they are given a distinct representation from predicates and their arguments.

What are the categories? The first one is **tense**. Tense is a category which expresses a temporal relationship between the time of the described event and some reference time, which, in the unmarked case, is the speech time. In the simplest case, tense indicates the temporal relationship between the time of the event and the time of the utterance describing the event. In *John sang*, 'John' did his singing before the sentence was said. If we say *John is singing*, then 'John' is singing at the same time that we are speaking. And, of course, if we say *John will sing*, that means his singing is to be at some future time. Therefore, tense expresses a relationship between the time of the described event and some reference time. This reference time is normally the speech time, though it is not necessarily so.

Aspect, another category related to temporality, does not express this temporal relationship between event time and speech time. Instead, it tells us about the internal temporal structure of the event itself. In other words, is the event completed or not? Is it ongoing or recurring? Does it happen all in one moment, or is it extended in time? The main categories which we find in languages are notions like completed/non-completed (usually known by the terms 'perfective' and 'imperfective'), progressive (which is ongoing) and perfect (which is related to perfective but involves the additional notion of 'current relevance'). In English, the two major aspectual categories are perfect and progressive, but other Indo-European languages have different ones. In English there is past/present/future perfect and past/present/future progressive, in which two major aspectual categories interact with the three major tense categories.

Another category which should be relatively familiar is **negation**. It is instantiated in English by words like *not* and *never*, among others. The next one is **modality**, which is used in many different senses in the literature on verbal semantics. We will use it to refer to what is called the root, or deontic, sense of modal verbs. This category includes such things as strong obligation (*must* or *have to*), ability (*can* or *be able to*), permission (*may*) and weak obligation (*ought* or *should*). In other words, modality concerns the relationship between the referent of the subject NP and the action. Does the referent have the ability? Is the referent permitted to do the action? Does the referent have an obligation? The status of *will* is somewhat unclear. One of the interesting questions about the analysis of English is whether there are two tenses, past and non-past, and then a modal for intent (i.e. *will*), which also indicates future, or is it the case that there are three tenses, in which *will* is not really a modal, but rather an auxiliary verb? For our purposes, we will analyze it as expressing future tense.

Another operator, **status**, includes epistemic modality, external negation and categories like realis and irrealis. In English, deontic and epistemic modality share the same modal forms, but with a slightly different meaning. For instance, instead of obligation, *must* refers to necessity. Instead of ability or permission, *can*, *may* and *should* mean possibility. So the basic difference between epistemic and deontic modality is necessity and possibility versus obligation and ability. In the case of obligation, we can paraphrase root modals by substituting *is obliged to* for *must*, as in *John must/is obliged to win the race*. The paraphrase on the epistemic reading, however, would be *It is necessary for John to win the the race*, which does not necessarily place *John* under any obligation. It simply states that a certain state of affairs is necessary. Another alternation would be *It is possible for John to win the race* versus *John is able to win the race*. Therefore, the basic status opposition is between necessity and possibility. The term 'realis' is concerned with whether the event described is real or hypothetical. There is a semantic relation between realis and necessity, and irrealis and possibility. Indeed, one can think of status as covering a semantic continuum ranging from necessity (and realis) at one end to possibility (and irrealis) at the other. Many languages besides English use exactly the same forms for the two types of modality, but they exhibit different grammatical behavior.

Illocutionary force is an extremely important and universal operator; it refers to whether an utterance is an assertion, a question, a command or an expression of a wish. These are different types of illocutionary force, which means that we can talk about interrogative illocutionary force, imperative illocutionary force, optative illocutionary force and declarative illocutionary force. Every language must have illocutionary force as an operator, because it must be possible to make statements, ask questions and give commands in all languages. This follows from the very nature of language as a medium of verbal social interaction. With the exception of negation, which is central to human reasoning, none of the other operators need be universal. For any operator concept, except illocutionary force and negation, it is possible to find one or more languages which lack it as a formal operator category.

Languages use a variety of means for signaling illocutionary force. Many languages have particles or clitics which directly signal it, e.g. the sentence-final particles *he* 'interrogative', *yelo* 'declarative [male speaker]', and *ye* 'imperative [female speaker]' in Lakhota. English uses syntactic means: the position of tense in the (matrix) clause signals illocutionary force, with core-medial tense indicating declarative, core-initial tense signaling interrogative, and lack of tense signaling imperative. Prosody is also used to indicate illocutionary force in many languages, including English. It is important to distinguish speech act type from sentence type; that is, in many languages there are special sentence forms to express the different speech act types (English is a good example of this), but this is not a necessary feature of a language. It is entirely possible for a language to have a single basic sentence type and for speech act distinctions to be signaled either by prosody alone or by the addition of sentence-final particles, as in Lakhota.

Modality, status and illocutionary force are all conflated in traditional grammar under the term 'mood'. We will not use 'mood' as a theoretical term, however, because it is important to keep these concepts distinct. For instance, subjunctive mood is a combination of irrealis and particular illocutionary force notions, while indicative mood is declarative realis. Therefore, the indicative and subjunctive moods are combinations of these more basic categories, which need to be distinguished.

The categories which are probably less familiar are **directionals** and **evidentials**. Directionals, as the name implies, are markers which indicate direction. They can either indicate the direction of the action itself, as in *He shouted up* (where the direction of the shouting is up), or they can indicate the direction of motion of one of the core arguments. In German, for example, there are particles, *hin* and *her*, which can be put on verbs to indicate whether the motion is away from (*hin*) or toward (*her*) the speaker. The Tibeto-Burman language Qiang has a rich system of directionals, as illustrated in (2.19).

(2.19) *Qiang directional operators* (*ʁue* 'throw')
təʁů 'throw straight up'
ɦaʁů 'throw straight down'
səʁů 'throw down-river'
nəʁů 'throw up-river'
zəʁů 'throw toward the speaker'
daʁů 'throw away from the speaker'
əʁů 'throw inside'
haʁů 'throw outside'

Many languages, however, express these directional notions as distinct morphemes rather than lexicalizing them into verbs. In English verbs like *push* and *pull* involve induced movement in a specific direction, which is either toward the subject (*pull*), or away from the subject (*push*). In languages which keep these notions separate, e.g. Jakaltek,[16] a Mayan language (Craig 1979), there is a verb which means *to induce something to move,* upon which a prefix indicating direction is added, which then gives us *push* and *pull*. In English, though, many of these things are lexicalized into the verb so that speakers may not even be aware that there is a separate meaning component of directionality.

Evidentials refer to the sources of information which form the basis of what we are saying. Do we know what we are saying because we have witnessed it with our own eyes, or because we have heard it from someone? Did we deduce our information from some sort of evidence, or is it just generally true? Some languages make all of these distinctions, which means that nothing can be said without indicating how the information was obtained. In other words, we would have to use an evidential marker to say something like *Yes, I know that this is true because I saw it myself* or *I did not see it, but I think it is true because I deduced it from something*. The German first subjunctive, for example, is commonly used in broadcasting and periodicals in order to indicate that the speech is reported. Many languages mark these grammatical categories obligatorily, e.g. Quechua (Wölck 1987), whereas in English it is merely optional to mention how we know what we are saying.

We will now look at the expression of operators in a number of different languages. The first group of examples is from Kewa, a Papuan language (Franklin 1971).

(2.20)
a. Íra-paa-ru. — 'I finished cooking it.'
   cook-PRFV-1sgPAST — (V-ASPECT-TENSE)
b. Íra-waa-ru. — 'I cooked part of it.' (= wasn't finished)
   cook-IMPF-1sgPAST — (V-ASPECT-TENSE)
c. Íra-a-na. — 'He cooked it (seen).'
   cook-3sgPAST-seen — (V-TENSE-EVID)
d. Íra-a-ya. — 'He cooked it (hearsay, I didn't see it).'
   cook-3sgPAST-unseen — (V-TENSE-EVID)
e. Íra-pa-niaa-ru. — 'I burned it downward (as a hill).'
   cook-PRFV-down-1sgPAST — (V-ASPECT-DIR-TENSE)
f. Íra-pa-saa-ru. — 'I burned it upward (as a hill).'
   cook-PRFV-up-1sgPAST — (V-ASPECT-DIR-TENSE)

In (2.20a) *írapaaru* 'I finished cooking it', there is the verb stem for 'cook' and the perfective aspect marker, followed by a first singular past tense form. In all of these Kewa examples, tense and person are conflated together in one marker. Example (b) has the imperfective form of the same verb, while (c) *íraana* 'he cooked it', contains an evidential which indicates that the event was witnessed by the speaker. This can be compared with (d), in which the speaker did not actually see the event. Sentences (e) and (f) show directionals, which indicate the direction of the action as upward or downward. Further examples of evidentials come from Hixkaryana, a Carib language spoken in Brazil (Derbyshire 1985).

(2.21) a. Ton ha-tɨ Waraka.
3sg.go HEARSAY
'They say Waraka has gone', or 'It is reported that Waraka has gone.'

a′. Ton Waraka.
'Waraka has gone (I know from seeing it myself).'

b. Yaworo mɨkan ha-mɨ.
truly 2sg.say.3sg DEDUCTION
'It is evident that you are telling the truth', or 'I'm sure you are telling the truth.'

c. Kana yanɨmno ha-na.
fish 3sg.lift.3sg UNCERTAIN
'I don't know if he caught any fish', or 'I doubt he caught any fish', or 'Maybe he caught some fish.'

d. Awanaworo nomokyaha ha-mpɨnɨ.
tomorrow 3sg.come CERTAINTY
'It is certain he will come tomorrow', or 'I'm sure he will come tomorrow.'

All of the evidential markers are suffixed to an intensifier particle *ha-*. According to Derbyshire (1985), these particles 'function primarily to express the attitude or relationship of the speaker to what he is saying, including the degree of certainty and the authority for making the assertion' (127). He describes the meaning of *-tɨ* 'hearsay' as 'specifically signaling that the speaker was not an eyewitness of events he describes' (255), in contrast to zero marking, as in (2.21a′), which 'specifically marks "eyewitness" in contrast to "hearsay"' (*ibid.*). The marker in (b), *-mɨ*, indicates that 'the speaker has made a deduction from facts which he may or may not spell out' (*ibid.*). The other two markers, *-na* and *-mpɨnɨ*, signal the degree of certainty the speaker has about what is being asserted.

The following examples of operators come from Turkish (Watters 1993).

(2.22) a. Gel-miş-∅. 'I gather that he has come.'
come-INFER-3sg (V–EVID)

b. Gel-miş-ti-∅. 'He had come.'
come-PERF-PAST-3sg (V–ASPECT–TENSE)

c. Gel-iyor-du-m. 'I was coming.'
come-PROG-PAST-1sg (V–ASPECT–TENSE)

d. Gel-emi-yebil-ir-im. 'I may be unable to come.'
come-ABLE.NEG-PSBL-AORIST-1sg (V–MOD–NEG–STATUS–TENSE)

e. Ev-e gel-ince, yat-ma-ya git-ti mi?
home-DAT come-CMPL sleep-NMZ-DAT go-PAST Q
'Having come home, did he go to sleep?' (V–TENSE–IF)

Sentence (2.22a) has a past evidential marker which means 'I gather that he has come.' In (b), on the other hand, the same marker means 'perfect aspect'. In (c) there is a progressive aspect marker. Sentence (d) contains the morpheme which marks negation + ability and is followed by the marker of possibility, which is then followed by a marker of tense. In (e) the illocutionary force (IF) marker is the final operator. Finally, there are some examples from English in (2.23).

(2.23) a. He may be leaving soon. (IF/TENSE–STATUS–ASPECT–V)
b. She was able to see him. (IF/TENSE–MODALITY–V)
c. Will they have to be leaving? (IF/TENSE–MODALITY–ASPECT–V)

In all of these English examples, we are making the assumption that tense is the left-most element; that is, because it is a suffix morphologically, it does not appear phonetically as the left-most element, but the syntax treats it as if it were left-most. Thus, even though it attaches itself to the left-most auxiliary element as a suffix, grammatically it is the left-most operator; as noted earlier, it is the position of tense which signals illocutionary force in English. So in (2.23a), tense is followed by the status auxiliary *may* (which in this case indicates possibility), then aspect and then the verb. In (b) there is tense, modality (which is that she was *able* to see them) and then the verb. In (c), there is a question marker, tense, modal and aspect (*will have to be* + *-ing*) neatly strung together.

A crucial fact about operators is that different operators modify different layers of the clause: some only modify the nucleus, some only modify the core, and some modify the whole clause. Aspect is a nuclear modifier because it tells us about the internal temporal structure of the event itself, without reference to anything else (Jakobson 1957 [1971]). Some directionals are nuclear modifiers because they indicate the direction of the action without reference to the participants. Examples of this include *burn uphill*, as in (2.20f). On the other hand, some directionals are core in the sense that they indicate the direction of motion of one of the core arguments. So in German, we can add *hin* and *her* to verbs, yielding *hinkommen* and *herkommen*, and *hingehen* and *hergehen*, which shows that they express directional parameters independent of the basic meanings of *come* and *go*. Since these directionals orient the direction of motion of one of the core arguments, they are then expressing something about that core argument. Therefore, they are a kind of core operator. There are core operators which express relationships between the core arguments and the nucleus. We can paraphrase *John must leave* as *John is obliged to leave*, which shows the relationship of obligation between *John* and *leave*. Here, root modality codes a relationship between a core argument, the subject and the action.

Negation can be a nuclear operator, which is realized as a derivational negative like *un-* in ***un**happy* in English. More common is core negation, which is also known as narrow scope or internal negation. In *John did not read a book, he read a magazine*, neither *John* nor *read* is being negated. Rather, only the direct object is being negated, because the scope of negation is only on part of the core, not over the entire proposition. Propositional negation, on the other hand, can be paraphrased by 'it is not the case that', which is then followed by a proposition. This is external or clausal negation because it negates the entire proposition; it is a type of status operator. A sentence like *John did not buy books* is ambiguous out of context, for in English only stress distinguishes the meanings. Depending on stress, the meaning could be either that someone else besides John bought the books, or that John bought a magazine instead, or that none of it happened. One way to make a sentence less ambiguous, when dealing with narrow-scope negation, is to use a nominal negative like *He bought no books*, in which just the object is being negated, or a determiner such as *any*, which occurs with *not* to indicate the scope of negation, as in *John did not buy any books.* In German, on the other hand, these last two possibilities fall together in *Er hat keine Bücher gekauft* (he has no books bought) 'He did not buy any books', in which *kein* functions as the indicator of negation.

The basic principle of scope assignment governing operators is **clausal ⊃ core ⊃ nuclear**, where '⊃' means 'has scope over'. Among clausal operators, the scope relations are illocutionary force ⊃ evidentials ⊃ tense/status. There is no universal unique scope order between tense and status, as they are roughly equivalent in scope terms; some languages treat tense as the more outer operator, while others treat status as having scope over tense. Among core operators, the scope relations are modality/directionals ⊃ negation (see e.g. (2.22d)), while among nuclear operators, they are directionals/negation ⊃ aspect. In Qiang, for example, aspect is clearly the innermost operator, as in (2.24).

(2.24) ɦɑ-mə-tɕi-qɑ
down-not-ASP-go.1sg
'I haven't gone yet.'

The position of negation at the core level and directionals at the nuclear level is a function of the fact that they can also be the innermost operator at the next higher level; hence they in a sense overlap the layer boundaries (see table 2.2).

Both RRG and FG employ layered conceptions of clause structure; the FG notion (Hengeveld 1989) is primarily semantic in nature, whereas the RRG version has both syntactic and semantic aspects. Both theories posit operators modifying different clause layers, and the two approaches are summarized in table 2.2. One of the differences between the two systems is that FG takes the operators to be part of the layer, while RRG does not. Hence the FG utterance layer is the proposition plus the propositional operators. We will follow the RRG system, because it provides an explicit syntactic representation of clause layers and their operators.[17]

How are operators to be represented? Since they are qualitatively different from predicates and their arguments, they are represented in a distinct projection of the clause from predicates and arguments. The element common to both projections is the verb.[18] Operators are arranged in terms of ever wider scope with respect to the verb. This may be represented as in figure 2.15. This explicitly represents the fact

Table 2.2 *LSC with operators in RRG and FG*

Semantic unit	*RRG layer*	*RRG operator*	*FG layer*	*FG operator*
Predicate	Nucleus	Aspect Negation Directionals	Predicate	Perf/imp aspect Phasal aspect Negation
Predicate + argument(s)	Core	Directionals Modality (root) Negation	Predication	Quantif. aspect Modality, neg. Tense
Predicate + argument(s) + (Non-arg(s)) = proposition	Clause	Status, negation Tense Evidentials Illocut. force	Proposition	Epistemic modality Evidentials
Proposition + DP elements	Sentence	None	Utterance	IF, mode

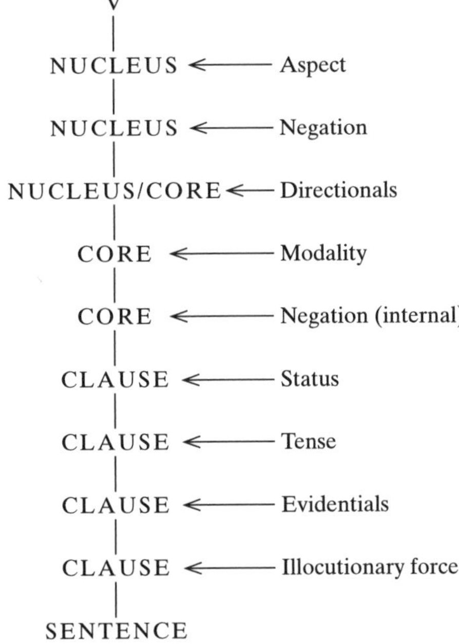

Figure 2.15 Operator projection in LSC

that aspect is nuclear, negation is any of the above (but mostly core or clausal) and directionals are nuclear or core. Tense, status, evidentials and illocutionary force are all clausal, which means that they modify the clause (proposition) as a whole, although they do so in different ways. Looking back at the epistemic readings of *must*, *can*, *may* and *should*, we can see explicitly in the syntax that the necessity meaning has the whole proposition in its scope. In a sentence like *It is possible that it will rain tomorrow*, it is clear that the scope of possibility is that it will rain tomorrow. We, however, cannot say **John is possible/necessary to leave tomorrow*, but rather *John is permitted/obliged/able to leave tomorrow*. Therefore, the syntax of English clearly indicates this difference, which then shows that status operators are clausal in scope. Tense, by definition, is also clausal in scope. Recall that the definition of tense is the relationship of the time of the utterance to the time of the event, which is a relationship between the entire proposition and some point in time. There is thus a significant difference between aspect and tense, for aspect is a nuclear operator while tense is a clausal operator. Evidentials are also clausal because they indicate how speakers know what they are saying, which is something that modifies the whole proposition. And again, with illocutionary force, the way in which a speaker expresses a proposition, whether it is a question, an assertion or whatever, concerns the whole clause. All of these operators at the bottom of the diagram are clausal, most of the directionals and modality are core, and some of the directionals and aspect are nuclear. The verb is the anchoring point of these operators, and it is no accident that these are recognized as verbal categories.

The operator projection in figure 2.15 may be combined with what we will call the 'constituent projection' in figure 2.7 to yield a more complete picture of the clause, as in figure 2.16; the periphery is omitted, since it can occur in a number of different positions. What we have here is two projections of the clause, one of which contains the predicate and its arguments (the constituent projection[19]), while the other contains the operators (the operator projection). They are both linked through the predicate, which may be a verb, NP, AdjP or PP, because it is the one crucial element common to both. The operator projection mirrors the constituent projection in terms of layering; hence 'nucleus' in the operator projection corresponds to 'nucleus' in the constituent projection, and so on. The multiple nucleus, core and clause nodes represent each of the individual operators at that level; the number of multiple nodes corresponds to the number of operators at that level present in the sentence. If there are no operators at a given level, a bare node will be given. As the 'bare skeleton' of the layered structure of the clause on the right makes clear, the two projections are indeed mirror images of each other, and this will become particularly important in representing the structure of complex sentences, as we will see in chapter 8. The English and Japanese examples from figures 2.8, 2.9 and 2.13 are given in figures 2.17–2.19 with the operator projection added; the second tree in figure 2.19 represents a copular construction. In the English

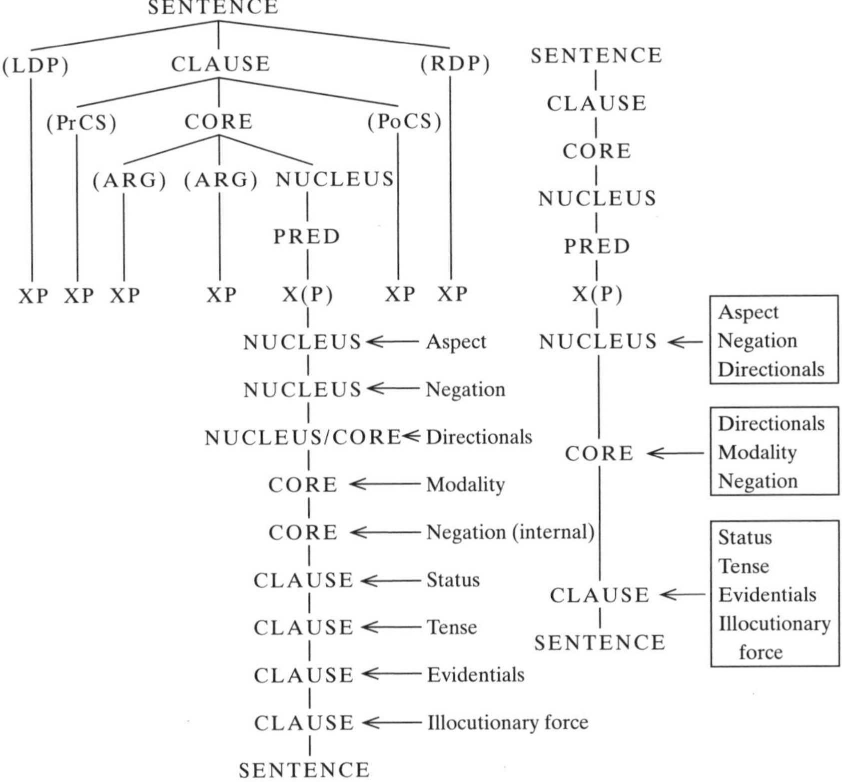

Figure 2.16 LSC with constituent and operator projections

representations, the tensed auxiliary (*did* or *is*) is labeled both 'TNS' and 'IF', because, as we mentioned earlier, the position of tense in the core signals illocutionary force in English. Hence it is labeled 'TNS' because of its inherent value as a tense operator, and it is also labeled 'IF' because its position is the indicator of that operator.[20]

One of the major motivations for this scheme is that operators virtually always occur in the same linear sequence with respect to the predicating element. When an ordering relationship can be established among operators, they are always ordered in the same way cross-linguistically, such that their linear order reflects their scope. This is a very significant point. Operators are ordered with respect to each other in terms of the scope principle discussed earlier, with the verb or other predicating element in the nucleus as the anchorpoint, and thus the ordering restrictions on the morphemes expressing the operators are universal.[21] Hence nuclear operators are closest to the nucleus, while clausal operators are farthest away from the nucleus. By looking at the linear order of operators in the English examples, and then comparing it with the comparable order of operators in the verb-final languages

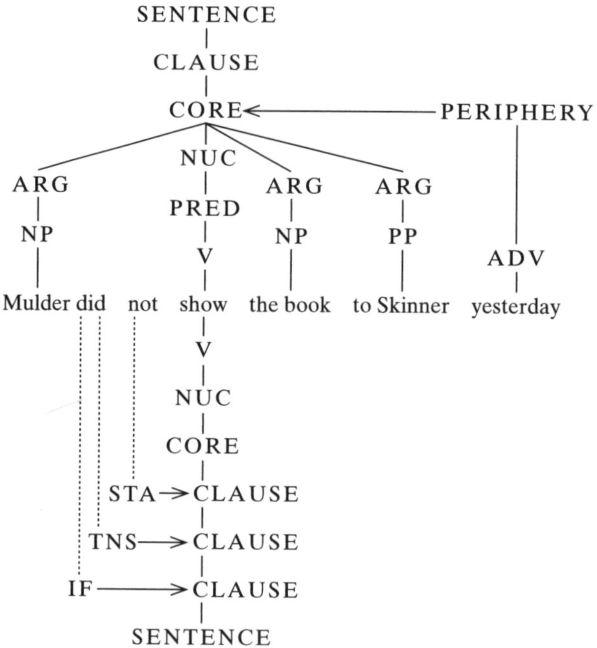

Figure 2.17 English LSC

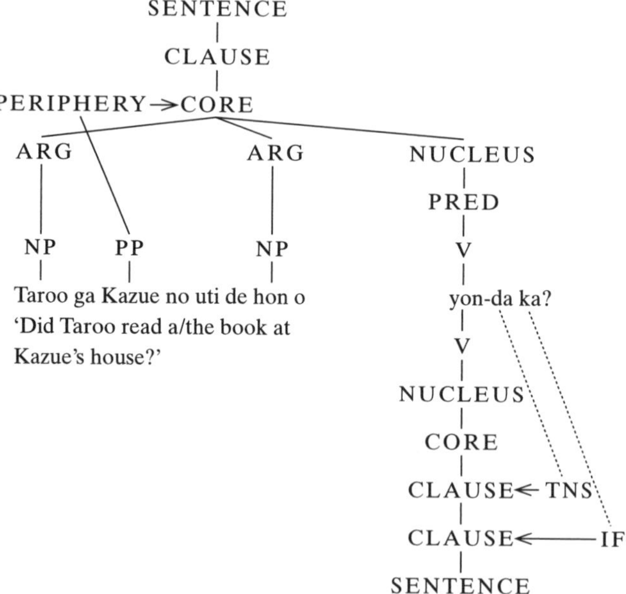

Figure 2.18 Japanese LSC

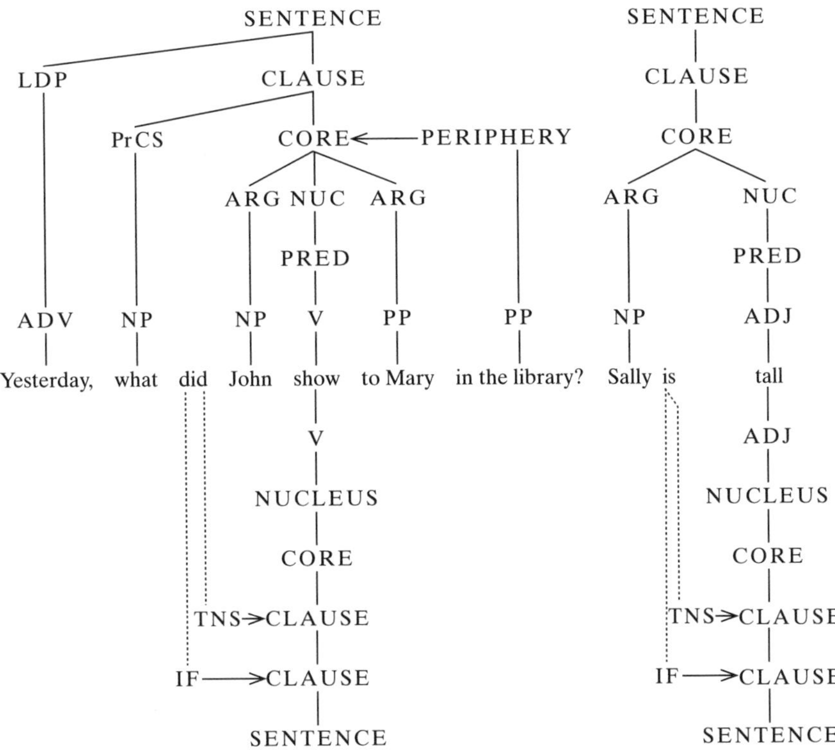

Figure 2.19 LSC of English sentences with verbal and adjectival predicates

(Kewa, Japanese, Turkish), we can see that they are just mirror images of each other. In other words, verb-final languages tend to order their operators as aspect, modality, tense and illocutionary force, whereas non-verb-final languages have these elements in the opposite order. There is some variation in ordering within a given layer; aspect and nuclear directionals occur in either order in different languages but always closer to the verb than the core and clausal operators. Similarly, tense and status vary in their position relative to each other in different languages, but they are always farther away from the verb than the nuclear and core operators but closer than evidentials and IF. There is no variation in the ordering between tense/status, on the one hand, and evidentials/illocutionary force, on the other, because the former are propositional modifiers, i.e. they modify the proposition expressed by the utterance, while evidentials and illocutionary force are utterance modifiers, i.e. evidentials express how the speaker came to have the information contained in the utterance, while the illocutionary force operator signals the speech act type of the utterance. What is not found is variation in ordering across layers. It is possible, however, for there to be no definable ordering among at least some operators in some cases. For instance, if tense were a prefix and aspect were a suffix in a language, then there is no definable ordering between them. If we look at Papuan languages like Kewa, which have all these operators strung out in a line, we can see that its sequence, and that of the English auxiliary, are exactly mirror images of each other, expressing identical scope relations. So the reason that English auxiliary elements line up the way they do is because that is the way operators always line up in every language that has them on the same side of the verb. And again, this simply follows from their definitions and their scopes. When representing the structure of sentences, we put the operators below the sentence, so that their relative scopes are expressed explicitly.

This approach expresses operators the same way, regardless of whether they are realized by bound morphemes, as in Kewa and Turkish, or by combinations of bound and free morphemes, as in English. By giving the operators their own projection, we can represent the fact that their ordering follows universal principles. In contrast, the ordering of the elements in the constituent projection varies considerably from language to language.

2.3 The layered structure of adpositional and noun phrases

Beginning at least with Harris' seminal paper 'From morpheme to utterance' (1946), many linguists have argued that there are strong structural parallels between clauses and noun phrases, e.g. Chomsky (1970) and Jackendoff (1977) in versions of transformational grammar, Langacker (1991) in CogG, Rijkhoff (1992) in FG and Nunes (1993) in RRG. In this section we explore the structural parallels among clauses, adpositional phrases and noun phrases, looking especially to see whether these types of phrase have a layered structure analogous to that of clauses.

2.3.1 Adpositional phrases

Adpositional phrases include prepositional phrases, e.g. *in the house*, and postpositional phrases, e.g. German *dem Haus gegenüber* (the.N.DAT house PostP) 'over across from the house'. Both types may be further classified in terms of whether they license the occurrence of an NP in the clause or not. The preposition *to* in a sentence like *Kim gave the book to Sandy* does not license the NP *Sandy* in the clause; the NP is a function of the meaning of the verb *give* and in fact can occur without *to*, as in *Kim gave Sandy the book.* The preposition *in* in *Robin read in the library* does make possible the occurrence of the NP *the library*; this NP is not related to the meaning of the verb *read* and is licensed by *in.* Prepositions like *to* with *give* which do not license their object will be referred to as **non-predicative** adpositions, whereas those like *in* in the above example which do function as predicates and license their object will be referred to as **predicative** adpositions, following the terminology in Bresnan (1982b). Adpositions in the periphery of the clause are always predicative, while non-predicative adpositions normally mark oblique core arguments.[22] A given adposition may function either predicatively or

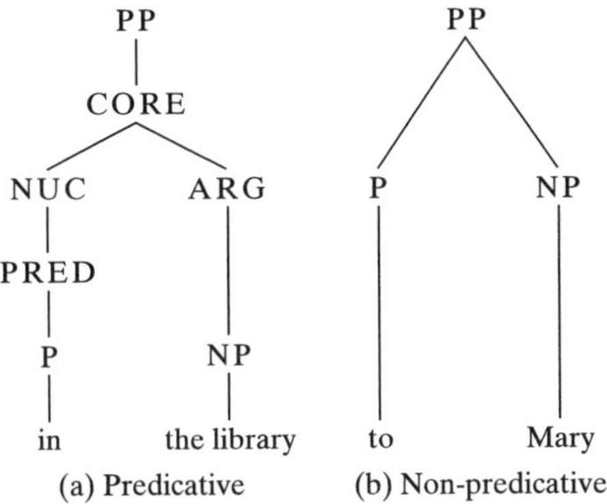

(a) Predicative (b) Non-predicative

Figure 2.20 Prepositional phrases

non-predicatively, depending upon which verb it appears with; for example, *from* is non-predicative when it occurs with a verb like *take*, which licenses a **source** argument, as in *Sally took the book from the boy*, whereas it is predicative with a verb like *die*, as in *She died from malaria.*[23]

Predicative and non-predicative PPs have different structural representations. Predicative adpositions function as predicates and therefore have a layered structure in which there is an adpositional predicate in the nucleus, and its semantic argument is treated as a core argument structurally. This is presented in figure 2.20a. Non-predicative PPs, on the other hand, are not predicates and therefore lack this structure; the adposition is essentially a case marker and nothing more. The structure of non-predicative PPs is given in figure 2.20b.

The examples in figure 2.20 are from a dependent-marking language, English. Not surprisingly, the structure of PPs in head-marking languages is not exactly the same as that as in dependent-marking languages, although the basic layered structure of predicative adpositions is the same. In Jakaltek (Craig 1977), the adposition bears a morpheme expressing its argument, e.g. *y-ul teʔ ŋah* (3ERG-in CL house) 'in the house' (lit. 'in-it$_i$ the house$_i$'). As with other head-marking structures, the NP object is optional, and when it is missing, the result is a grammatical PP, *y-ul*, with the meaning 'in it'. This is represented in figure 2.21.

2.3.2 Noun phrase structure

Noun phrases refer, while clauses predicate, and yet there are striking parallels between the structure of the two which have long been noted. For example, both can be said to have arguments; while this is obvious in the case of verbs in clauses, it is also clear that relational nouns like *father*, *friend* and *sister* can take what could be analyzed as arguments, e.g. *father of Sam*/*Sam's father*, *a friend of Bill*/*Bill's friend* and *the other sister of Mary*/*Mary's other sister*. Clauses sometimes have clauses within them as arguments, as in *Fred believed that pollution isn't a problem*, and

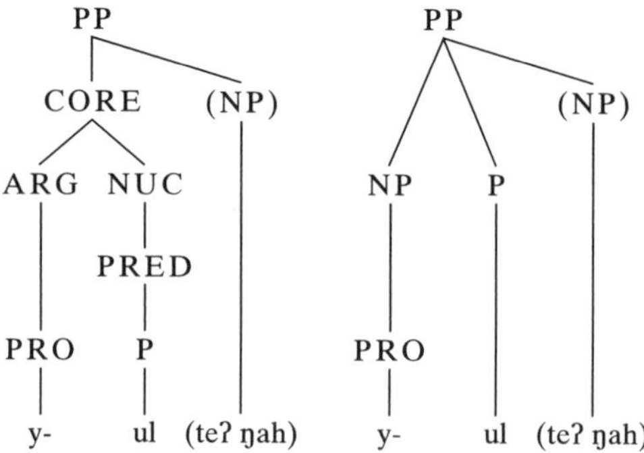

Figure 2.21 Head-marking predicative and non-predicative PP in Jakaltek

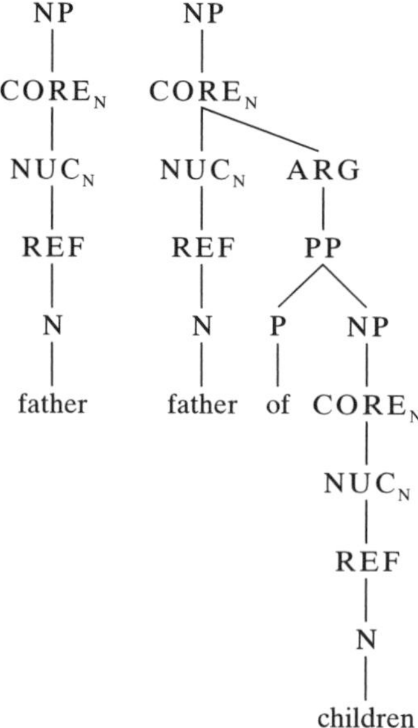

Figure 2.22 LSNP in English

the same is true of NPs, e.g. *Fred's belief that pollution isn't a problem.* Given these parallels, it would be appropriate to say that at least some nouns take arguments analogous to verbs taking arguments, and therefore it is also appropriate to posit a layered structure for NPs (LSNP) similar but not identical to that for clauses. One significant difference, relating to the fundamental functional difference between verbs and nouns, is that NUC_N dominates a REF (for 'reference') node, indicating that the unit in question refers, in contrast to the PRED (for 'predicate') node which appears in the nucleus of a clause. *Of* is non-predicative in this construction, because it does not license the argument; moreover, it is semantically empty, as it can occur with argument NPs having many different semantic functions.

Consider the range of semantic functions which the *of*-NPs have in the following examples.

(2.25) a. the attack of the killer bees — Agent[24]
b. the gift of a new car — Theme
c. the destruction of the city — Patient
d. the leg of the table — Possessor
e. the resupplying of the troops (with ammunition) — Recipient

Nunes (1993) shows that NPs have only a single direct core argument, and it is marked by *of*. This is consistent with the point made above that *of* does not mark any particular semantic relation, in much the same way that the direct grammatical functions, subject and direct object, are not restricted to particular semantic functions. Accordingly, the *of*-marked NP counts as the single direct syntactic argument of the nominal nucleus in the core of the NP. Predicative adpositions, by contrast, have well-defined semantic content, like other predicates.

The structure of NPs headed by deverbal nominals is represented in figure 2.23. The core$_N$–periphery$_N$ distinction in the layered structure of the noun phrase is illustrated here; the argument structure of deverbal nominals is directly related to the argument structure of the source verb (Nunes 1993; see section 4.7.2), and therefore *Bill* and *FBI agents* are core$_N$ arguments marked by non-predicative prepositions, while *in* is a predicative setting PP, just as in the corresponding clause *FBI agents arrested Bill in New York*. There is in addition, in some languages, a position before

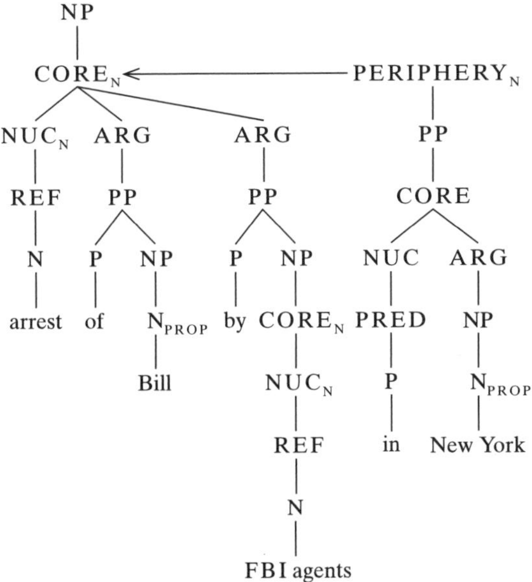

Figure 2.23 LSNP of English NP headed by deverbal nominal

the head in which possessors occur, e.g. *Pat's car*; this position is called simply the 'NP-initial position' (NPIP) and will be discussed in more detail below.

NPs headed by pronouns and proper nouns do *not* have a layered structure like those headed by common nouns. Neither takes any kind of argument or peripheral modifier. Hence there are no grounds for positing a structure like that given in figure 2.22. Consequently *Bill* and *New York*, both proper nouns in figure 2.23, lack 'CORE_N' and 'NUC_N' nodes as well as a 'REF' node; the latter is redundant, given that proper nouns are always referential. Pronouns can be classified into a number of subtypes: personal pronouns, including possessive pronouns (PRO), e.g. ***I** liked **her** book*; relative pronouns (PRO_{REL}), e.g. *the book **which** I bought*; demonstrative pronouns (PRO_{DEM}), e.g. ***That** pleased Mary*; WH-pronouns (PRO_{WH}), e.g. ***who** did Fred see?*; and expletive pronouns (PRO_{EXP}), e.g. ***it** rained.*

An important feature of the layered structure of the clause was the differential treatment given to operators like tense, aspect and illocutionary force, and the same contrast is a vital part of the layered structure of the noun phrase. NP operators include determiners (articles, demonstratives, deictics), quantifiers, negation and adjectival and nominal modifiers. Rijkhoff (1992) presents a typological study of NP structure from an FG perspective, and he proposes an FG-style layered structure for the noun phrase together with a theory of NP operators. Langacker (1991) explores what he calls the 'functional organization' of the NP and arrives at similar proposals. Table 2.3 summarizes Rijkhoff's theory and relates it to the theory of the NP structure being developed here. The overall structure of the layered structure of the NP with its operators is given in figure 2.24. As with the layered structure of the clause, the linear order of the elements in the constituent projection can vary, while the operators may precede or follow the head noun.

The quality operators signal, as the name implies, distinctive qualities of the referring expression. Nominal aspect refers to individuation, in particular to the fundamental mass/count distinction and further distinctions such as whether the referring

Table 2.3 *Operators in the LSNP*

Semantic unit	*Syntactic layer*	*FG layer*	*FG operator*
Referring Expression [REF]	Nucleus_N	Quality	Adj/Nom modifiers Nominal aspect
REF (+Argument(s) +Non-arg(s))	Core_N (+Periphery_N)	Quantity	Number Quantification Negation
REF (+Arg(s), Non-arg(s), NPIP)	NP	Locality	Deictics Definiteness

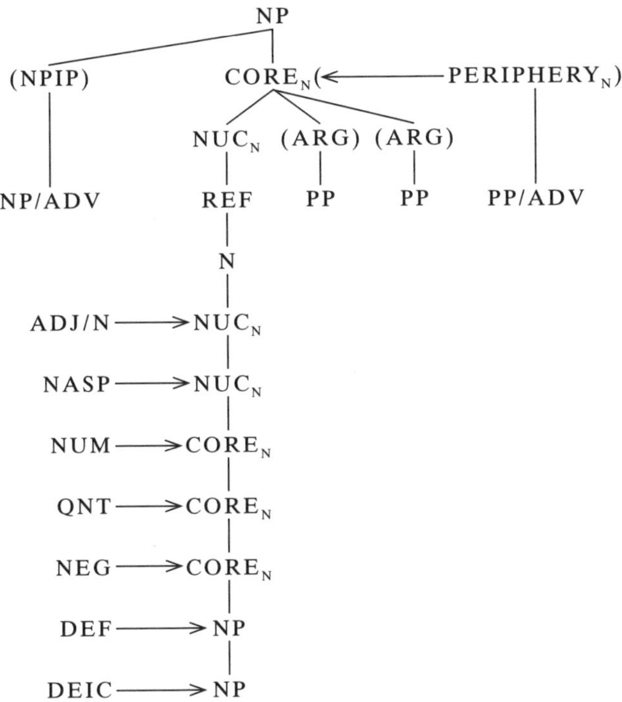

Figure 2.24 The general schema of the LSNP

expression denotes individuals or a collection of individuals. Rijkhoff notes the analogs between perfective (temporally bounded) and imperfective aspect (temporally unbounded) in verbs and the count/mass distinction in nouns. Jackendoff (1990) also discusses the parallels between the count/mass distinction in nouns and the bounded/unbounded distinction in verbs.

> It has often been observed that the bounded/unbounded (event/process, telic/atelic) distinction is strongly parallel to the count/mass distinction in NPs. An important criterion for the count/mass distinction has to do with the description of parts of an entity. For instance, a part of *an apple* (count) cannot itself be described as *an apple*; but any part of a body of *water* (mass) can itself be described as *water* . . . This same criterion applies to the event/process distinction: any part of *John ate the sandwich* (event) cannot itself be described as *John ate the sandwich*. By contrast, any part of *John ran toward the house* (process) can itself be described as *John ran toward the house* (unless the part gets smaller than a single stride) . . . It has also been observed that plurals behave in many respects like mass nouns and that repeated events behave like processes. (Talmy [1978] suggests the term *medium* to encompass them both.) (1990: 29)

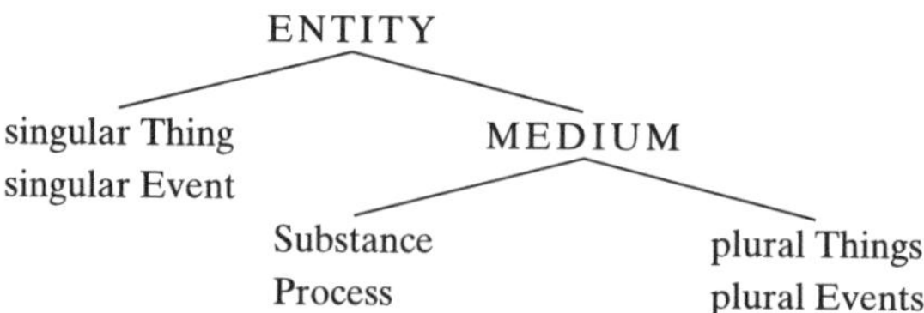

Figure 2.25 Parallels between events and things

Jackendoff summarizes these parallels in the diagram in figure 2.25.

The most common formal expression of nominal aspect is through noun classifiers, which are found in a wide range of languages. English has analogs of these in the constructions in which mass nouns are quantified, e.g. *one* ***sheet*** *of paper* (individual) vs. *one* ***ream*** *of paper* (collective), *two* ***glasses*** *of beer*, *three* ***head*** *of cattle*. A well-known example of a classifier language is Mandarin Chinese, in which nouns normally cooccur with a classifier when quantified or modified, e.g. *sān ge rén* (three CL person) 'three people', *nèi běn shū* (that CL book) 'that book', *yī bēi píjiǔ* (one CL beer) 'one glass of beer'.

Adjectival and nominal modifiers, e.g. ***tall*** *tree* and ***brick*** *house*, are also nuclear$_N$ operators, in that they express distinctive qualities of the referring expressions. Individuation operates over the modifier + N group, e.g. *one sheet of* [*blue paper*], *two glasses of* [*dark beer*], *nèi běn* [*dà shū*] 'that big book'.

The quantity operators modify the core$_N$ of the NP, and these are concerned with quantification and negation. Quantification is expressed through the grammatical category of number and lexical expressions like numerals and quantifiers, e.g. *three books*, *many dogs*, *few particles*, *every woman*. Negation may be expressed through a special negative form for NPs, e.g. English *no*, German *kein* (e.g. *keine Bücher* 'no books'), special determiners which interact with sentential negation, e.g. English *any* as in *Mary didn't buy any books*, and nouns and pronouns with an inherently negative meaning, e.g. German *nichts*, Russian *ničego*, French *rien* 'nothing'. Negation and quantification interact in intricate and complex ways, and this interaction is one of the major issues in formal semantics.

The locality operators modify the NP as a whole, and they are primarily concerned with expressing the location of the referent with respect to a reference point, usually the interlocutors (deictics), and with indicating the speaker's assumption about the identifiability of the referent by the hearer (definiteness).[25] The usual formal expressions of these operators are determiners, in particular, articles and demonstratives. They are the NP analogs of the illocutionary force indicators in clauses; they both have to do with the discourse-pragmatic properties of the NP or clause, and they are both the outermost operators. Examples from English and Mandarin with all three types of operator are given in figure 2.26; the Mandarin NP means 'those three big books'.

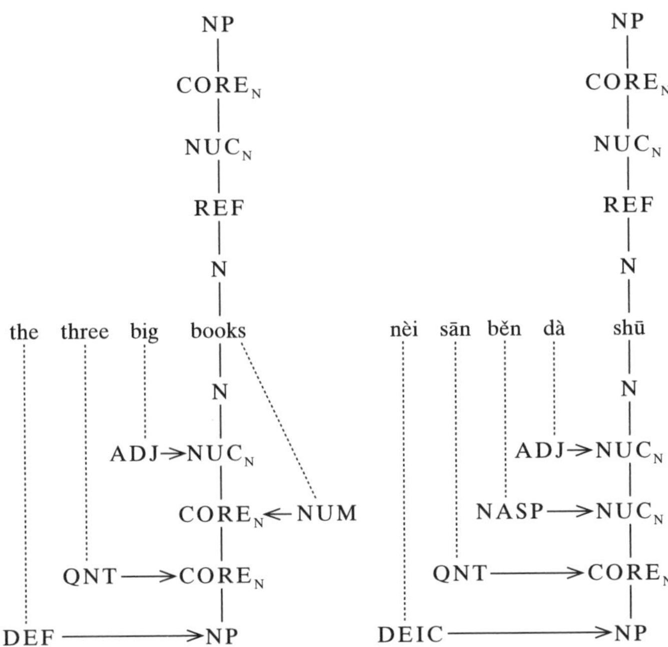

Figure 2.26 LSNP with operators in English and Mandarin Chinese

Like clausal operators, the ordering of NP operators generally adheres to the same scope principle discussed in section 2.2.3 with respect to operators in the clause, as the examples in this section have illustrated. Rijkhoff (1990, 1992) investigates this issue in detail and shows that the operator patterns within the NP reported in Greenberg (1966) and Hawkins (1983) conform to the layering of operators presented in table 2.3 and that apparent exceptions are shown to involve elements that are not an integral part of the NP.

It was stated earlier that NPs headed by pronouns and proper nouns lack a layered structure, but there are some instances in which they appear to take modifiers, which could be taken as evidence of a layered structure. When a name occurs with a modifier, e.g. *I didn't see* ***the tall Fred Jones****, I saw* ***the short Fred Jones***, it lacks a unique reference and is being used as a common noun, and therefore it has a layered structure. Names functioning as proper nouns in English can only take non-restrictive modifiers, e.g. *good old Barney*, ***A tired Clinton*** *arrived back at the White House*. There is some cross-linguistic variation with respect to proper nouns and pronouns taking modifiers. In Modern Greek, proper nouns cooccur with an article which, along with the noun, carries case, e.g. *o Yiorghos* 'the George [NOM]' vs. *ton Yiorgho* 'the George [ACC]'. Case-bearing articles may also accompany proper nouns in German, e.g. *Ich habe den Fritz gesehen* (I have the.ACC Fritz seen) 'I saw Fritz'. Mandarin Chinese allows modifiers with pronouns, e.g. *zuótiān* *de wǒmen* (yesterday GEN 1pl) 'the us of yesterday'. It appears, then, that in some languages proper nouns and pronouns may have a layered structure, at least with respect to modifiers.

English is quite unusual among languages in permitting the expression of two possessive NPs in an NP headed by a deverbal noun (one marked by genitive case and the other by the possessive preposition *of*), e.g. *the enemy's destruction of the city*, and the apparent similarities to the corresponding clause *The enemy destroyed the city* have been taken as support for the view that NPs and clauses have the same basic structure (Chomsky 1970, Jackendoff 1977), with the prenominal genitive NP being the 'subject' of the NP and the [*of* NP] being the 'object'. This has been put forward as a universal claim about NP structure, and yet, as Comrie (1976a) and Comrie and Thompson (1985) show, this construction is found in only a tiny fraction of the world's languages (with English being the primary example); what is commonly found across languages is constructions like *the destruction of the city by the enemy*, with only a single genitive NP. There is also some reason to doubt the analogy itself; as Nunes (1993) points out, it is possible to have adjuncts in the possessive phrase which would be impossible as subject in a sentence, e.g. *yesterday's shelling of Paris by unknown forces*. In the comparable sentence (i.e. *Yesterday unknown forces shelled Paris*), *yesterday* is an adjunct in the left-detached position, and this suggests that the NP-initial position is more analogous to the left-detached position in the clause than to a core argument position like subject, since either semantic arguments or non-arguments can appear in the left-detached position, but non-arguments (adjuncts) cannot appear in the core-internal subject position. It also bears some resemblance to the precore slot, as WH-words can appear in it, as in *which book*, but unlike the precore slot, it freely takes non-arguments like adjuncts and possessors. However, like a subject-type position and unlike a detached position, there are semantic restrictions on what elements can occur there. For example, while it is possible to say *Sally's knowledge of Shakespeare*, **Shakespeare's knowledge by Sally* is quite impossible, and the restriction holds across a large class of deverbal nominals. The conditions determining whether an element in an NP can or cannot occur in this position are quite complex, and involve both discourse-pragmatic (e.g. topicality) and semantic (e.g. affectedness) considerations, as Nunes (1993) shows in some detail. Since this position does not correspond exactly to the left-detached position, precore slot or core-internal subject position in a clause, we will label it simply the 'NP-initial position'. It is clearly $core_N$-external, since the nominal nucleus is initial in the $core_N$, but it corresponds structurally neither to the precore slot nor to the left-detached position, because there is no contrast within the NP corresponding to that between clause (which dominates the precore slot) and sentence (which dominates the left-detached position). The NP-initial position is dominated by the NP node.

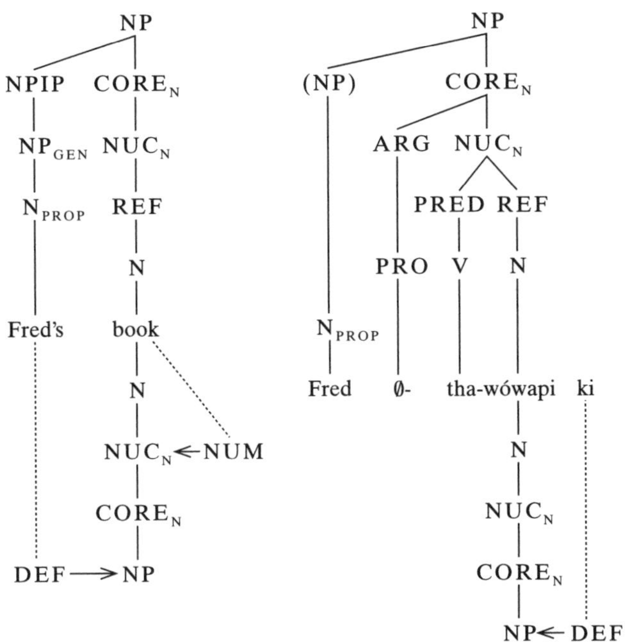

Figure 2.27 Possessive NP constructions in English and Lakhota

In English, the genitive NP in the NP-initial position cannot cooccur with a determiner; both **the* [*Fred's book*] and **the* [*the enemy's destruction of the city*] are ungrammatical. This restriction is not found in many languages; in Lakhota, for example, *Fred's book* would be *Fred ∅-tha-wówapi ki* (3sg-POSS-book the). English NPs containing a genitive NP in the NP-initial position are interpreted as definite, and therefore the possessor phrase does double duty; it is part of the constituent projection signaling possession and part of the operator projection signaling definiteness. If a possessed NP is indefinite, the possessor phrase occurs after the possessed noun, as in e.g. *a book of Fred's*. The structures of the English and Lakhota NP examples are given in figure 2.27. There are a number of interesting features of the Lakhota construction, which illustrates a head-marking possessive construction. First, *tha-*, glossed 'POSS', is in fact a reduced form of the possession verb *thawá*, and accordingly this form involves verb incorporation into a nominal head. The resulting form has a single core argument, the possessor, which is prefixed to *tha-* (cf. *mi-thá-wowapi ki* 'my book'). Second, because this is a head-marked construction, the NP *Fred* is only loosely associated with the NP *tha-wówapi ki*, which on its own means 'his book'; *Fred* is an optional element in this construction. This is in sharp contrast to the English expression *Fred's book*, in which *Fred's* is obligatory; without it, there would be no possessive construction. The contrasting

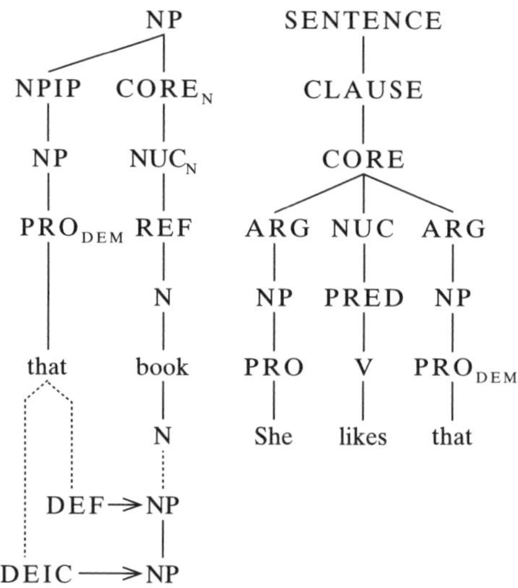

Figure 2.28 Representation of demonstrative pronouns

statuses of the NP *Fred* in the two constructions reflect the fundamental difference between head-marking and dependent-marking constructions.

It was mentioned earlier that English demonstratives like *this* and *that* are a subtype of pronoun, and when they occur as NP modifiers, they occur in the NP-initial position, just like possessive pronouns like *my* and *his*. Hence an NP like *that book* would have the same structure as the English NP in figure 2.27, with *that* replacing *Fred's*. Since demonstratives are pronominal in nature, unlike articles, they can occur as referring expressions on their own, as in ***That** irritates me*. In such a structure, *that* would function as the referring expression in the nominal nucleus. These two possibilities are presented in figure 2.28; the operator projection in the NP example is simplified, since there are no nuclear and core operators in the NP. One consequence of this analysis is that *this book* has a different structure from *the book* in English (cf. figure 2.26), due to the fact that *the* is an article, a 'pure' operator, while *that* is a pronominal demonstrative. In contrast, the demonstrative *nèi* 'that, those' in Mandarin in figure 2.26 is non-pronominal, because it cannot head an NP on its own (it requires a classifier), unlike true pronouns like *tā* '3sg'. Accordingly it occurs in the operator projection only. While distinguishing articles from demonstratives might seem odd from an English perspective, there is good cross-linguistic evidence for it. Even though in many languages demonstratives and articles cannot cooccur, in a few they can. The expression 'this dog' in Lakhota is *šų́ka ki lé* (dog the this), while in Mparntwe Arrernte it is *kngwelye nhenhe re* (dog this 3sgDEF). The order of the article and the demonstrative is different in the two languages, but in both languages they are the outermost operators within the NP. Hence we

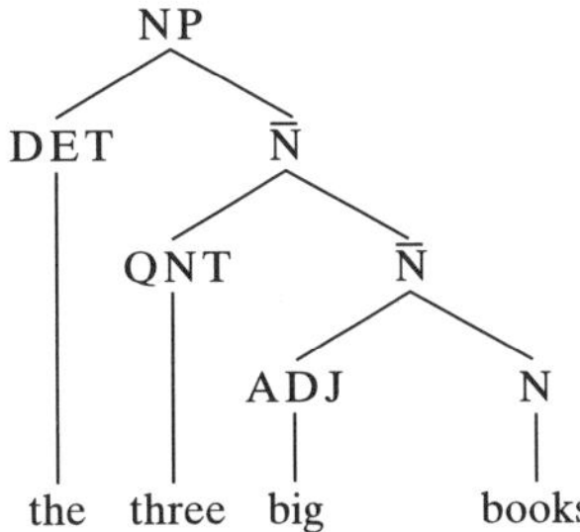

Figure 2.29 IC representation of English NP

see in the NP operator projection the same kind of cross-linguistic variation in the position of the operators within a single level that we saw with respect to e.g. tense and status in the operator projection in the clause. In Lakhota, demonstratives and articles are also subject to different ordering constraints, as demonstratives, but not articles, may either precede or follow the head noun, as the alternative form *le šų́ka ki* (this dog the) 'this dog' shows. Dryer (1992a) argues for them being members of distinct categories on the basis of their differential ordering behavior cross-linguistically. Hence treating articles and demonstratives as members of different categories and representing them differently in the layered structure of the NP has strong empirical support once we look beyond English.

These representations, especially the ones in figure 2.26, are virtually 'upside down' from the point of view of immediate-constituent (IC) representations, such as the one in figure 2.29. Are there any empirical grounds for preferring one style of representation over the other? While in most instances the two styles would be empirically equivalent, there are at least two instances where the layered structure of the noun phrase representation is to be preferred to the IC representation. The first concerns the Dyirbal examples in (2.6) and figures 2.3 and 2.10. It was argued above that an IC analysis is unrevealing and fails to capture what is similar between comparable English and Dyirbal clauses. Figure 2.30 is a more complete version of figure 2.10, showing the fully expanded NP structure with the operator projection. The translation of the Dyirbal sentence is 'The man saw the woman in the mountains.' In a language like English, demonstrative pronouns are located in the NP-initial position, analogous to the relationship between left-detached position elements and the following clause. In Dyirbal, on the other hand, noun markers are not structurally linked to the head noun of the NP structure. The Dyirbal NP has the same discontinuous, unordered structure as Dyirbal sentences. The pronominal nature of the noun markers is shown by the fact that they can be used independently as referring expressions, e.g. *gambiɽa baŋgul buɽan balan* (mountains-LOC NM-ERG saw NM-ABS) 'He saw her in the mountains.' Dyirbal is unusual in not requiring adjacency of the NP operators to the head and not imposing strict ordering requirements on them, either; English and most other languages have these

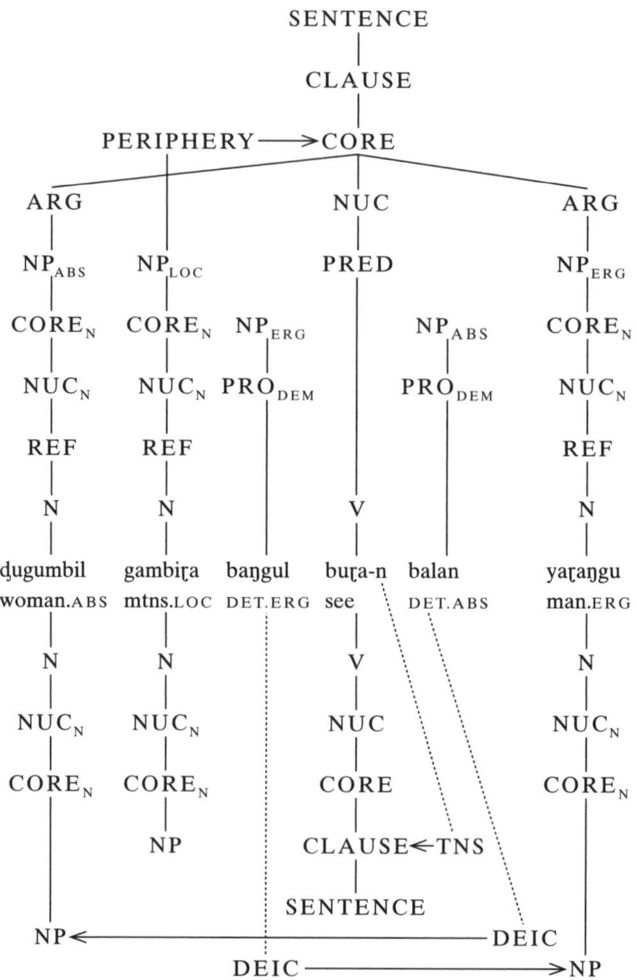

Figure 2.30 Dyirbal clause including LSNP with operators

requirements. With respect to languages with discontinuous NPs, such as Dyirbal, the double projection representation yields a simpler analysis which requires no special rules or abstract levels of representation.

The second case involves noun incorporation in Greenlandic Eskimo, which allows 'stranded modifiers' of the incorporated noun. This is shown in (2.26), from Sadock (1991).

(2.26) a. Ammassannik marlunnik nerivunga.
ammassak-nik marluk-nik neri-vunga
sardine-INSTpl two-INSTpl eat-1sgINDIC
'I ate two sardines.'

b. Marlunnik ammassattorpunga.
marluk-nik ammassak-tor-punga
two-INSTpl sardine-eat-1sgINDIC
'I ate two sardines.'

The object noun *ammassak-* 'sardine' is incorporated into the verb in (2.26b), leaving the stranded modifier *marlunnik* 'two'. Examples such as these have been presented as evidence for positing multiple levels of syntactic representation and transformational rules (in GB, e.g. Baker 1988). They can be accommodated in a natural way in the framework we are developing. The structures of the two sentences in (2.26) are given in figure 2.31. The incorporated NP is part of the nucleus,

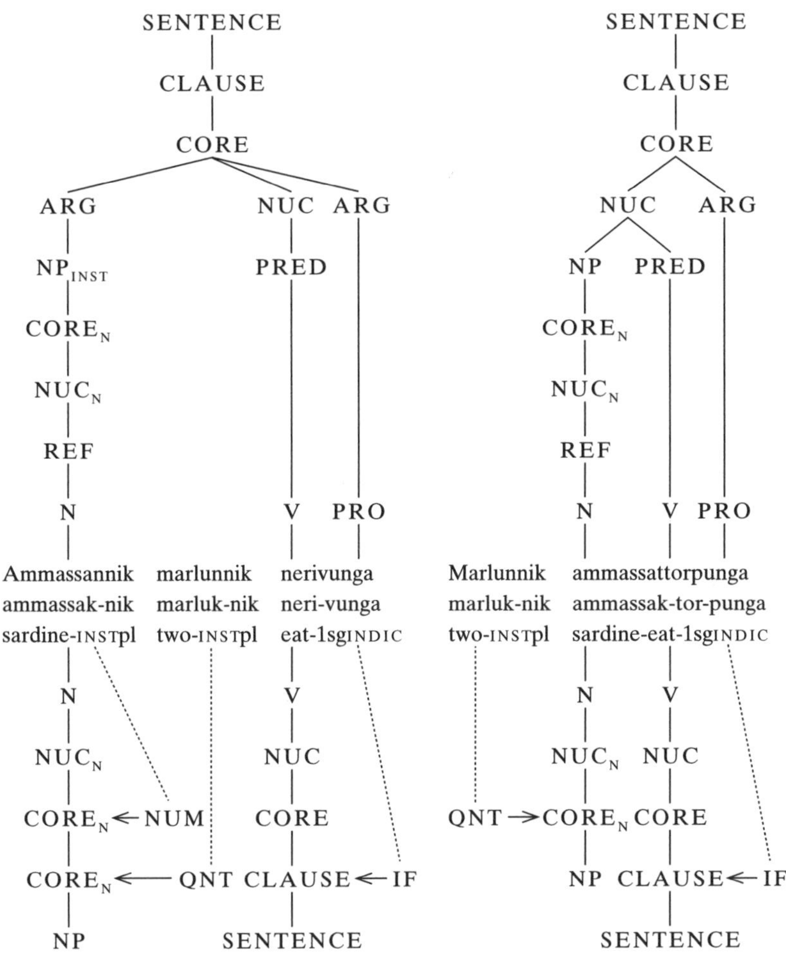

Figure 2.31 Greenlandic Eskimo clauses (±incorporation)

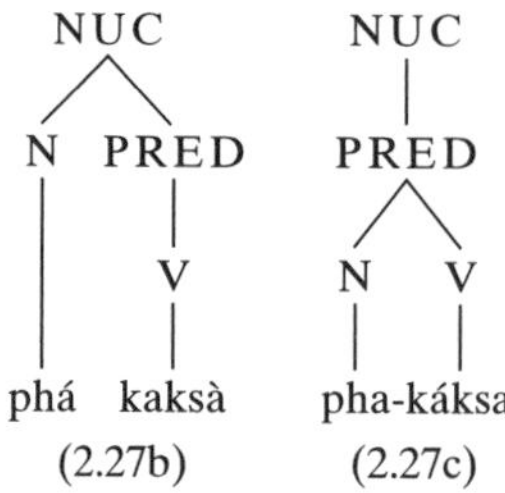

Figure 2.32 Lakhota noun incorporation structures

and the crucial thing is that it is a full NP: it is fully referential and retains its modifying lexical operators. Because it is now part of the same phonological word as the verb, it no longer bears its inflections (case and number), which, however, are realized on the independent quantifier *marluk-* 'two'. It would be impossible to express this directly if NP structure were represented as in figure 2.29; given the assumption that this type of hierarchical representation is correct, it has been necessary to resort to multiple syntactic representations (e.g. Baker 1988).[26] Given the layered structure of the noun phrase and the analysis of (2.26b) as NP incorporation, the facts follow. Constructions like this one contrast sharply with incorporation of a bare noun and with lexical compounding of a noun and verb; these two possibilities are illustrated from Lakhota (DeReuse 1994) in (2.27) and figure 2.32, in which only the nuclei are given.

(2.27) a. phá ki hé ka-ksá
head the that by.striking-sever
'cut off that head'
b. phá kaksà 'behead'
c. phakáksa 'behead'

In Lakhota, stress falls normally on the second syllable of a polysyllabic word, and stress is one of the crucial indicators of incorporation vs. compounding in the language. In the non-incorporated structure in (2.27a), both words receive full primary stress. In the incorporated N structure in (2.27b), the incorporated noun *pha* 'head' receives primary stress, while the verb has secondary stress on its second syllable. In the lexical noun–verb compound in (2.27c), there is a single primary stress on the second syllable of the compound, a syllable which does not receive stress in the other constructions.

The Lakhota constructions in (2.27b, c) do not allow stranded modifiers, e.g. **hé phá kaksà* or **hé phakáksa* (where *hé* 'that' is construed as a modifier of *phá* 'head'), and this follows from the fact that (2.27b) involves an incorporated noun, not a full NP as in Greenlandic Eskimo, and (2.27c) involves a lexical noun–verb compound. The fact that the NP in (2.26b) is fully referential while those in (2.27b, c) are not again follows, since only NPs (which may be a single word, as with a proper noun), not bare nouns, constitute referring expressions. Thus the layered structure of the noun phrase model of NP structure is able to capture both discontinuous NPs, as in Dyirbal, and the incorporation of an NP or noun, as in Greenlandic Eskimo and Lakhota, in a straightforward way without resorting to abstract representations of any kind.

2.4 Heads and headedness

Throughout this discussion we have often made reference to the notion of 'head', as in 'the noun is the head of the NP', and this traditional notion has been the focus of considerable interest in linguistic theory for the past decade or so. It is central to X-bar theory, in which all phrases are projections of their head, e.g. N → NP, P → PP, Adj → AdjP, etc. It is also crucial for the typological contrast between head-marking and dependent-marking languages discussed in this chapter. There has been considerable controversy regarding (1) the criteria for determining the head of a phrase, and (2) just exactly what the head of certain important constructions is. Zwicky (1985), Hudson (1987) and the papers in Corbett, Fraser and McGlashan (1993) are concerned with both of these issues. The two constructions with the most disagreement with respect to the choice of head are the clause and the NP. While it might be supposed that the verb is taken to be the head of the clause, this is not universally the case. In GPSG the verb is taken to be the head of the clause, and therefore the clause is a projection of V. In earlier versions of GB, on the other hand, the verb is not the head of the clause. Rather, the INFLection node, which contains the tense marker for the verb in finite clauses, is taken to be the head of the clause. On this view, a functional category, an operator in our terms, serves as head of the clause. One might wonder what the controversy about the head of an NP could be, but Abney (1987) argued that in a phrase like *the dog*, the primary head is the determiner *the*, which heads a determiner phrase (DetP). The NP, headed by *dog*, is a complement to the head of the DetP, the determiner, in Abney's analysis, as illustrated in figure 2.33. Here again a functional category, an NP operator in this case, is taken to be the head of the unit.

The principal reason why this kind of controversy can arise is that Chomskyan theory treats lexical and functional categories alike in terms of phrase structure

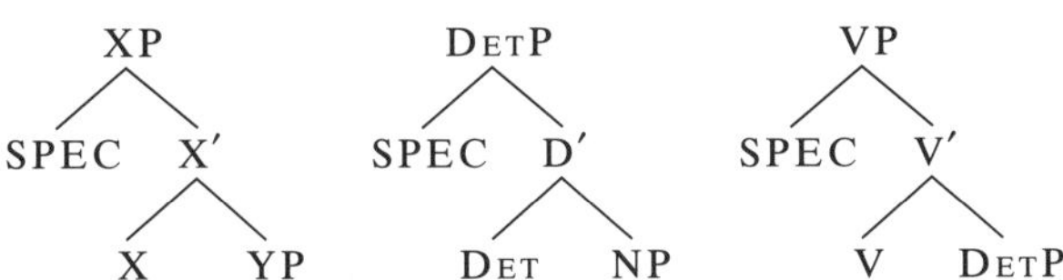

Figure 2.33 Syntactic projections headed by functional and lexical categories in GB/P&P

(X-bar theory). That is, both types of categories head full X-bar structures, as illustrated in figure 2.33 and in the figure in note 20. ('SPEC' stands for 'specifier'; 'YP' is another phrase which is a complement to the head.) There is no structural difference between the two types of projection, and therefore both types are candidates for heading a structure in which they occur.

The approach to syntactic representation we have employed treats lexical and functional (i.e. operator) categories quite differently, and consequently there is no possibility of an operator being taken to be the head of a lexical phrase like a PP, NP or clause. Each of these units is headed by a nucleus containing an adposition, a noun or a predicating element such as a verb, respectively.[27] As we will see in the next two chapters, these heads are the primary elements in the semantic representation of the PP, NP or clause. The elements functioning as nuclei of PPs and clauses are predicates in the semantic representation, while nominal nuclei are designated within the semantic representation of the NP. Thus the head of a phrase is a function of its semantics: an NP is headed by a nominal nucleus, a PP by an adpositional nucleus, and a clause by a predicating nucleus.

There is one interesting apparent exception to this that we have discussed, namely, non-predicative adpositions (see figure 2.20b). There is no adpositional nucleus, as with predicative adpositions. The reason for this is that these prepositions have no independent semantic representation within the semantic representation of the clause; that is, because they mark arguments of the verb, their occurrence is a function of the semantic representation of the verb and how its arguments are linked into the syntactic representation. We will discuss this briefly in section 4.4.1.1 and in detail in section 7.3.2. Thus the true head of a non-predicative PP is the nominal nucleus within the NP; as we mentioned in section 2.3.1, the adposition functions like a case marker. One may well wonder at this point why the phrase *to Skinner* in figure 2.17, for example, is labeled 'PP' rather than 'NP'. Indeed, these phrases have been considered to be NPs by some linguists, e.g. Ross (1967 [1986]). The reason for labeling them 'PP' is to distinguish between direct and oblique core arguments: NPs are direct core arguments, while PPs are oblique core arguments in languages like English and Icelandic. An equivalent notation would be to label NPs and non-predicative PPs as 'NPs' and then subscript them as 'direct' or 'oblique'. We will continue the traditional practice of labeling all adpositional phrases, predicative or non-predicative, as 'PPs'.

What about operators? Can they head phrases, too? Superficially it appears that they can, given expressions like *very big* (AdjP?) and *very few* (QP?). But are these full-fledged phrases of the type headed by adpositions, nouns, verbs and other predicates? There is no evidence that they are; rather, they are first and foremost modifiers that are themselves modified by an adverb. This can be seen most clearly when we contrast predicative vs. attributive adjectives. Predicative adjectives can have arguments, e.g. *Robin is (very) proud of Pat*, and therefore they have a full layered structure; attributive adjectives do not have a full layered structure and cannot take arguments, as the ungrammaticality of **the (very) proud of Pat teacher* shows. Hence elements functioning as operators in the operator projection of clauses or NPs do not head phrases with a layered structure; rather, they may be modified by one or more adverbs, forming what we may call an 'operator group', that is, an operator consisting of more than one item. We will reserve the term 'phrase' for units with a full layered structure.

2.5 Conclusion: the nature of morphosyntactic structure

In this chapter we have developed a notion of morphosyntactic structure that is very much semantically based. If we look back at table 2.1, we see that each of the basic units of the layered structure of the clause is motivated by a well-defined semantic concept. Indeed, the universal aspects of clause structure follow from two very basic principles which are grounded in lexical semantics: the contrast between predicating and non-predicating elements, and, among non-predicating elements, the contrast between those which are arguments of the predicating element and those which are not. Thus we may conclude that morphosyntactic structure is not radically arbitrary but rather is relatively motivated semantically, in Saussure's sense. That is, while syntactic structure is not identical with or completely reducible to semantic concepts, it is nevertheless derived and generalized from them.[28]

We have not addressed the question of how the structures proposed in this chapter are specified within a grammar. There are three general approaches to this: the first is to postulate a set of rewriting rules which will specify (generate) the structures; the second is to posit an inventory of constructional templates; and the third is to postulate a set of very general principles and attempt to derive construction-specific properties from their interaction. This third approach is associated with GB Theory, and we will have little to say about it, since a critical explication of it would require an extensive presentation of GB.[29] In the first view, a grammar contains a set of rules to generate structures and a lexicon in which words and morphemes, as well as larger fixed idiomatic chunks, are stored. This has been the approach assumed in many versions of transformational grammar and some varieties of phrase structure grammar. Following GPSG, we may divide these rules into two types: those that express dominance relations among elements in a structure (called 'immediate dominance' rules), and those that specify linear ordering relations among elements (called 'linear precedence' rules). The layered structure of the clause constituent projection for simple sentences in figures 2.7 and 2.13 can be generated by the following set of immediate-dominance rules.[30]

(2.28) a. SENTENCE → {(DP)}, CLAUSE
b. DP → XP/ADV
c. CLAUSE → {(ECS)}, CORE, (PERIPHERY), {NP*}
d. ECS → XP/ADV

e. PERIPHERY → XP/ADV
f. CORE → ARG*, NUC
g. NUC → PRED
h. PRED → V/XP
i. ARG → PRO/NP/PP

These immediate-dominance rules are universal; they describe the basic layered structure of the clause which is a feature of the grammar of every language. The only non-universal features are the detached positions and extra-core slots; their non-universal status is indicated by '{ }' in the rules. There is a Kleene star on ARG within the core rule because there are languages in which argumentless verbs may be a nucleus, e.g. Lakhota *magážu* 'it is raining'. Languages vary in two primary ways: first, with respect to whether the arguments are free phrases, as in dependent-marking languages, or bound morphemes, as in head-marking languages; and second, with respect to linear precedence rules. In head-marking languages only the core arguments are realized by bound pronominals, while full NPs are daughters of the CLAUSE node (see section 2.2.2); therefore that part of rule (2.28c) is not universal and is in curly brackets.

These immediate-dominance rules specify many possible structures in addition to the ones we have looked at in this chapter; they are relatively unconstrained. The primary constraint on them comes from semantics, in particular from the principles governing the linking of syntactic and semantic representations. In other words, the set of rules specifying possible syntactic structures is only one part of the story. These structures serve to express propositional content, the topic of the next two chapters, and only a small subset of the possible structures can be linked to the semantic representations of propositions. Hence the full picture will emerge only when we have developed a system of semantic representation (chapters 3 and 4) and principles for linking syntactic and semantic representations (chapters 7 and 9).

With respect to linear precedence rules, there are languages which lack them altogether, e.g. Dyirbal, and among languages which have them there is considerable variation. This variation has been the subject of intense investigation since it was presented in Greenberg (1966), and what has intrigued researchers is the fact that there are some very clear patterns in the variation, e.g. the order of verb + object seems to correlate with the order of adposition + object, such that VO languages tend strongly to be prepositional and OV languages postpositional. A number of proposals have been put forth to explain these correlations, e.g. Dik (1989), Hawkins (1983, 1994), Tomlin (1986). Dryer (1992a) argues convincingly that these correlations follow from the very strong tendency for languages to be consistently left-branching or right-branching. Branching directionality involves the placement of phrasal categories in relation to the non-phrasal or lexical categories they cooccur with, e.g. verb (non-phrasal) plus object (phrasal), adposition (non-phrasal) plus object (phrasal). English is a right-branching language, as can be seen clearly in figures 2.17, 2.22 and 2.23, while Japanese is a left-branching language, as shown in figure 2.18.[31] Dryer notes that elements that are not phrasal do not enter into these correlations, and prime examples of these non-phrasal elements are the operators that occur within the clause and the NP. We have already seen that the linear ordering of operators is subject to a basic scope principle (their ordering reflects their scope within the layered structure), and operators tend strongly to occur on the opposite side of the nucleus from the branching direction. Thus, it appears that elements in the constituent and operator projections are subject to different ordering principles: the constituent projection, which contains phrasal and non-phrasal categories, is subject to Dryer's branching directionality principle, whereas the operator projection is subject to the scope principle. This generalization is made possible in part by our treating operators and predicate–argument constituents separately in our representations, and as such it provides support for this treatment.

There are universal linear precedence rules with respect to detached phrases and the pre- and postcore slots which are valid in the languages which have these constituents. Examples of linear precedence rules for simple sentences are given in (2.29); in head-marking languages, they apply within the clause only, since the core is a single phonological word, whereas in dependent-marking languages they apply within the core and clause. ('>' means 'linearly precedes'.)

(2.29) a. *Universal linear precedence rules (for languages with DPs, ECS)*
1 LDP>CLAUSE
2 CLAUSE>RDP
3 PrCS>CORE
4 CORE>PoCS

b. *Language-specific clause-internal linear precedence rules*
1 Jakaltek (verb-initial)
(a) CORE>NP*
(b) NP*>PP*
2 Lakhota (verb-final): XP*>CORE
3 English (verb-medial):
(a) NP>NUC
(b) NUC>NP*>PP*
4 Dyirbal: None

The universal rules state simply that the left-detached position comes before the CLAUSE, while the RDP follows it, and that the precore slot comes before the CORE and the postcore slot follows it.[32] The Jakaltek rules specify that independent NPs follow the CORE and that if there are both NPs and PPs in a clause, the NPs will occur closer to the core than the PPs. Jakaltek has a precore slot in questions and topicalizations, and it follows universal rule (2.29a3). Lakhota has a simple system: the CORE must be the last element in the constituent projection of the clause, and NPs and PPs, if there are any, can occur in any order before it. English is a bit more complicated, since arguments occur on both sides of the nucleus. The rule in (2.29b3(a)) states that one NP precedes the NUCLEUS (the subject), while the second states that if there are NPs and PPs after the NUCLEUS, the NPs must occur between the NUCLEUS and the PPs (see Sadock 1995). Dyirbal lacks grammatical constraints on word order, but word order is pragmatically constrained. These are not the complete set of linear precedence rules for each language, but they define the basic word-order patterns in each. We return to the question of linearization in section 7.6.1.

The set of rules generating the operator projection is rather simpler than those specifying the constituent projection. They are given in (2.30). Each of the operators is represented by '←OP', as in the operator projection; the * is the Kleene star defined in n. 30 and indicates that there may be from zero to the maximum (four) operators modifying each layer.

(2.30) a. SENTENCE → CLAUSE←IF
b. CLAUSE←IF → CLAUSE←OP*
c. CLAUSE←OP → CORE(←OP*)
d. CORE(←OP) → NUC(←OP*)
e. NUC(←OP) → V/XP

The first rule is very important: it states that only a CLAUSE node immediately dominated by the SENTENCE node can have an illocutionary force operator. This excludes the possibility of independent illocutionary force marking in anything except a simple matrix CLAUSE or CLAUSEs in a coordinate construction. This is universally valid. The next rule states that there may be (but need not be) multiple CLAUSE nodes modified by different clausal operators in a sentence (see figure 2.16). The next rule states that a CLAUSE node modified by an operator (which may be illocutionary force, in the minimal case) dominates a CORE node, which may or may not have one or more core operator. The next rule, (d), provides for the transition from CORE to NUCLEAR operators, and the last rule anchors the operator projection in the predicating element, which may be a verb, adjective (phrase), NP or PP. The linear precedence rules for operators are much simpler than those for constituents: in the majority of languages they simply line up according to their scope on one side of the nucleus or the other. This is expressed in (2.31).

(2.31) a. *Universal operator linear precedence rule*
CLAUSAL ⊃ CORE ⊃ NUCLEAR
b. *Language-specific linear precedence rules*
1 OPs > NUC
2 NUC > OPs

Of course, there are languages in which operators occur on both sides of the nucleus; for example, in Jakaltek, the past and non-past tense markers are prefixes, while the future tense marker is a suffix. In such cases there will be more complex language-specific linear precedence rules for operators.

This first approach postulates two major components to a grammar: a rule component, containing the types of rules presented above, and a lexicon, containing the words and morphemes that appear in the structures generated by the rules. There is, however, another way to think about these structures. In ConG and RRG, it is proposed that grammatical structures are stored as *constructional templates*, each with a specific set of morphosyntactic, semantic and pragmatic properties, which may be combined with other templates to form more complex structures.[33] In ConG it is assumed that there is one structural store containing constructions, lexical items and morphemes. In the RRG approach to constructional templates, it is assumed that there is a set of syntactic templates representing the possible syntactic structures in the language, which are stored in the 'syntactic inventory', and that there is a separate lexicon containing lexical items, morphemes and other types of lexical entities. Since we have not talked about the lexicon yet (see chapter 4), we will deal only with the syntactic inventory here. As a simple example of what is meant here, consider figure 2.34. Each of the templates can be specified by the immediate-dominance rules given in (2.28); they are formally equivalent. They represent a part of the structure of a possible sentence in English. Advocates of ConG have argued that grammatical constructions are not reducible to simple rewriting rules; they have specific semantic and pragmatic properties that must be captured (Fillmore, Kay and O'Connor 1988). Hence in a full description a constructional template may carry quite specific semantic, pragmatic and other types of information. The syntactic templates in figure 2.34 represent only the syntactic structure of constructions. As we proceed and develop theories of semantic representation and information structure, we will see how different types of information can be integrated into constructional templates; all of this information will be presented in an integrated format in section 7.6. While syntactic templates have a universal basis in the layered structure of the clause, the templates in the syntactic inventory of any particular language will reflect the properties of clauses in that language. English syntactic templates, for example, reflect the fact that English has left- and right-detached positions, as well as a precore slot, and the restrictions on the ordering of the constituent projection summarized in (2.29a, b3). Dyirbal syntactic templates, by contrast, will lack representation of detached positions or extra-core slots, since they do not exist in the language, and moreover, the templates will be inherently unordered, reflecting (2.29b4).

In figure 2.34 we have five different core templates (arbitrarily labeled '1' through '5'), along with a precore slot template and a left-detached position template. Since we have not talked about semantics and pragmatics yet, the topics of the next three

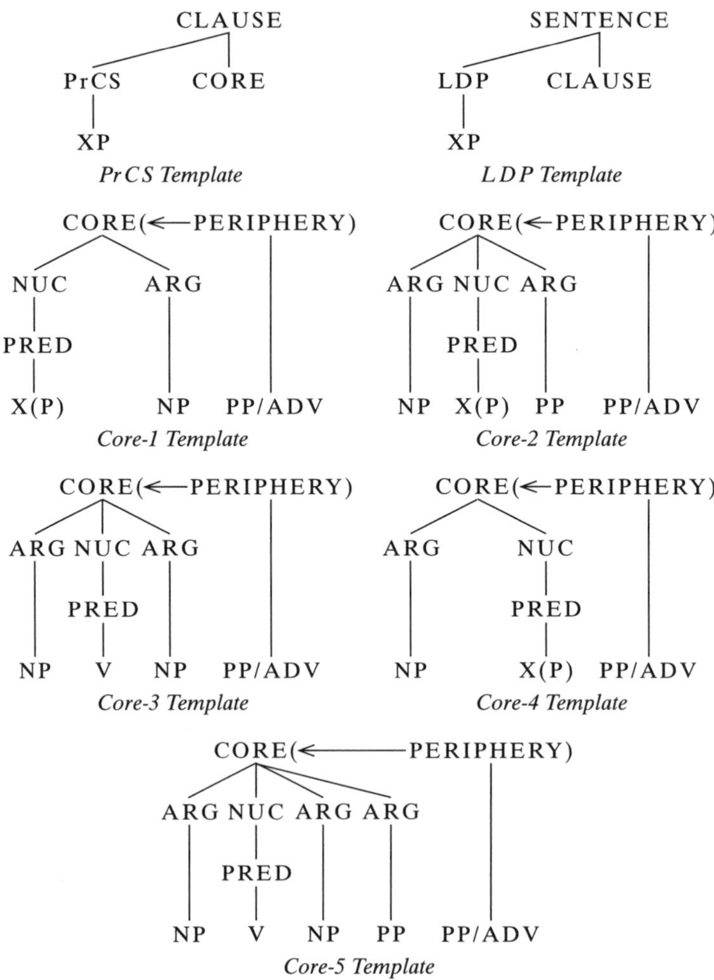

Figure 2.34 Examples of templates from the syntactic inventory

chapters, we will restrict our discussion to morphosyntactic properties. All of these core templates may be realized as simple sentences; Core-1 would be the structure of an imperative like *Close the window now!* Combined with the precore slot template, it would yield the structure of a WH-question like *Who kissed Sam yesterday?* or *What broke the window during the party?* Core-5 is the structure for sentences containing verbs like *give* or *put*, e.g. *Scully gave the files to Skinner* or *Max put the book on the table*, and combined with the left-detached position template it yields a sentence like *As for the book, Max put it on the table*. Core-2 by itself could be the structure of a sentence like *The book is lying on the table*, but when it is combined with the precore slot template, the result is a WH-question like *What did Robin give*

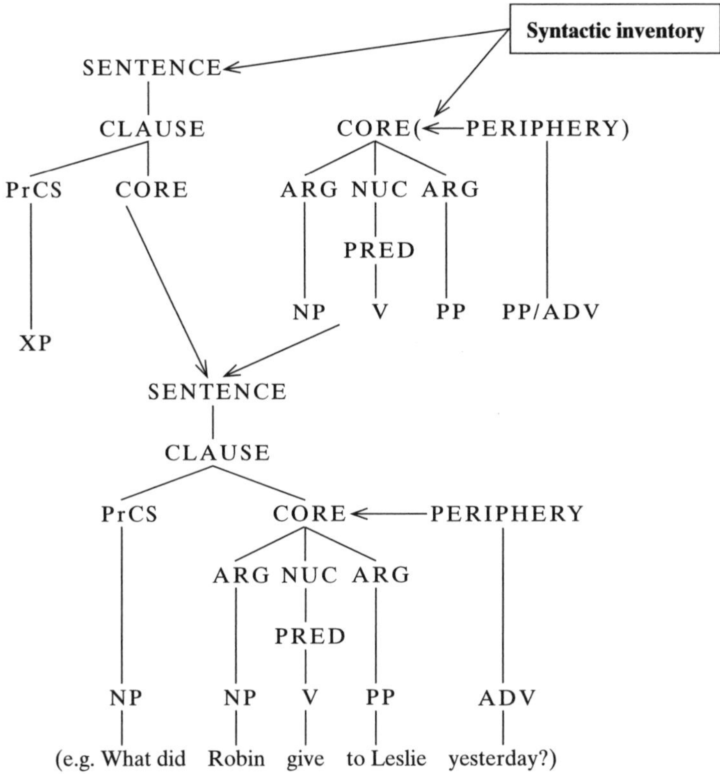

Figure 2.35 Combining templates

to Leslie yesterday? This is illustrated in figure 2.35. The core template fits into the core slot in the precore slot template. Syntactically speaking, templates combine to form more complex structures in a way that is formally equivalent to applying the various immediate-dominance rule options to create structures.[34] Template combining is also subject to the same semantic constraints as immediate-dominance rules, i.e. the resulting combinations must be able to be linked to a semantic representation by means of a set of very constrained linking principles; this will be the main topic of chapters 7 and 9. Once we have introduced semantic representations and focus structure representations, we will see how those properties of templates also combine in complex structures.

Further reading

On monostratal vs. multistratal representations of syntax, see Chomsky (1957, 1965, 1982), Perlmutter (1982), Bresnan (1978, 1982a), van Riemsdijk and Williams (1981), Koster and May (1981), van Riemsdijk (1982), Davies (1984), Van Valin (1990), Farrell, Marlett and Perlmutter (1991). For more on the structure of the noun phrase and its relationship to clauses, see Harris (1946), Chomsky (1970), Jackendoff (1977), Langacker (1991), Rijkhoff (1992) and Nunes (1993). On universals, see Chomsky (1965), Greenberg (1966), Comrie (1989b), Hawkins (1988), Croft (1990). For other approaches that involve a layered view of clause structure, see Nuyts (1993), Nuyts, Bolkenstein and Vet (1990). For a comparison of RRG, FG and SFG theories of clause structure, see Butler (1995). For discussion of head- vs. dependent-marking morphology and the significance of this distinction to grammatical theory, see Nichols (1986), Van Valin (1985, 1987a), Vincent (1993). For discussion of parts-of-speech systems, see Schachter (1985). For typological overviews of tense and aspect, see Comrie (1985a) and (1976b) respectively. On mood and modality, see Palmer (1986). On negation, see Payne (1985a). On evidentiality, see Chafe and Nichols (1986). For a philosophical discussion of speech acts and illocutionary force, see Austin (1962), Searle (1969). On the morphosyntactic manifestations of illocutionary force, see Sadock and Zwicky (1985).

Exercises

1 Draw a tree diagram of the layered structure of each sentence below, giving *only* the constituent projection. Don't worry about the internal structure of NPs or PPs. Assume that the verbs in the sentences from languages other than English have the same argument structure (intuitively determined, at this point) as their English counterparts. In particular, assume that only 'setting' locative PPs are peripheral and that other PPs are oblique core arguments. [**section 2.2.2.2**]

(1) a. Yesterday, Dana read two magazines at the library. (PP is not part of NP.)
b. Chris placed the notebook on the bench.
c. Who did Robin present with an award at the ceremony?
d. Robin presented an award to Pat at the ceremony.
e. After the party, Sandy went to a bar.

(2) Ég skila-ð-i pening-un-um til hennar. — Icelandic
1sgNOM return-PAST-1sg money-DEF-DAT to 3sgGEN
'I returned the money to her.'

(3) Wakpála ki aglágla lakhóta ki thathą́ka óta
creek the near Sioux the buffalo many
wičhá-∅-kte-pi. — Lakhota
3plOBJ-3sSUBJ-kill-pl
'The Siouxs killed many buffalo near the creek.'

(4) Hanako ga tosyokan de Ken ni hon o age-ta. — Japanese
NOM library in DAT book ACC give-PAST
'Hanako gave a book to Ken in the library.'

(5) Mac x-∅-aw-ila ewi? — Jakaltek
who TNS-3ABS-2sgERG-see yesterday
'Who did you see yesterday?'

(6) Chelsu-eykey-nun, nay-ka hakkyo-eyse chayk-ul
-DAT-TOP 1sg-NOM school-LOC book-ACC
cwu-ess-ta. Korean
give-PAST-DEC
'As for Chelsu, I gave a book [to him] at school.'

(7) Mangalean buku guru i tu imana. Toba Batak
give book teacher DET to 3sg (Indonesia)
'The teacher is giving a book to him.'

2 Explain why only some of the sequences of operators in the Thai sentences in (2) and (3) are possible. Does the syntactic theory proposed in the text predict these facts? Examples of each operator are given in (1). (Data from Suda Rangkupan.) [**section 2.2.3**]

(1) a. Khǎw càʔ kin khâaw.
3sg FUT eat rice
'He will eat rice', or 'He intends to eat rice.'
b. Khǎw tôang kin khâaw.
3sg OBLIG eat rice
'He has to eat rice.'
c. Khǎw khong kin khâaw.
3sg PSBL1 eat rice
'He might eat rice.' ('It is very possible that he eats rice.')
d. Khǎw khuan kin khâaw.
3sg NEC1 eat rice
'He should eat rice.' ('It ought to be the case that he eats rice.')
e. Khǎw nâa kin khâaw.
3sg NEC2 eat rice
'He should have eaten rice.' ('It ought to be the case that he ate rice, but he didn't.')
f. Khǎw ʔàat kin khâaw.
3sg PSBL2 eat rice
'He may eat rice.' ('It is possible but not likely that he eats rice.')

(2) a. Khǎw càʔ tôang kin khâaw.
3sg FUT OBLIG eat rice
'He will have to eat rice.'
a′. *Khǎw tôang càʔ kin khâaw.
b. Khǎw khong càʔ kin khâaw.
3sg PSBL1 FUT eat rice
'He might eat rice.' ('It is very possible that he will eat rice.')
b′. *Khǎw càʔ khong kin khâaw.
c. Khǎw khuan càʔ kin khâaw.
3sg NEC1 FUT eat rice
'He should eat rice.' ('It ought to be the case that he will eat rice.')

c′. ?*Khǎw càʔ khuan kin khâaw.
d. Khǎw nâa càʔ kin khâaw.
3sg NEC2 FUT eat rice
'He should have eaten rice.' ('It should have been the case that he will eat rice.')
d′. *Khǎw càʔ nâa kin khâaw.
e. Khǎw ʔàat càʔ kin khâaw.
3sg PSBL2 FUT eat rice
'He may eat rice.' ('It is possible but not likely that he will eat rice.')
e′. *Khǎw càʔ ʔàat kin khâaw.

(3) a. Khǎw khong càʔ tôang kin khâaw.
3sg PSBL1 FUT OBLIG eat rice
'It is very possible that he will have to eat rice.'
a′. *Khǎw tôang khong càʔ kin khâaw.
a″. *Khǎw càʔ khong tôang kin khâaw.
b. Khǎw khuan càʔ tôang kin khâaw.
3sg NEC1 FUT OBLIG eat rice
'It ought to be the case that he will have to eat rice.'
b′. *Khǎw tôang khuan càʔ kin khâaw.
b″. *Khǎw càʔ khuan tôang kin khâaw.
c. Khǎw nâa càʔ tôang kin khâaw.
3sg NEC2 FUT OBLIG eat rice
'It should have been the case that he would be obliged to eat rice (but the truth is he did not have to).'
c′. *Khǎw tôang nâa càʔ kin khâaw.
c″. *Khǎw càʔ nâa tôang kin khâaw.
d. Khǎw ʔàat càʔ tôang kin khâaw.
3sg PSBL2 FUT OBLIG eat rice
'It is possible but not likely that he will have to eat rice.'
d′. *Khǎw tôang ʔàat càʔ kin khâaw.
d″. *Khǎw càʔ ʔàat tôang kin khâaw.

3 Draw a tree diagram of the layered structure of each sentence below, giving *both* the constituent and operator projections. As in exercise 1, don't worry about the internal structure of NPs or PPs. Assume that the verbs in the sentences from languages other than English have the same argument structure (intuitively determined, at this point) as their English counterparts. In particular, assume that only 'setting' locative PPs are peripheral and that other PPs are oblique core arguments. Assume further that there is an illocutionary force operator in every example, which may be realized either by ∅ or by the position of the tense operator, as in English, Icelandic and German. In (1c), assume the passive auxiliary *be* to be part of the nucleus. **[section 2.2.3]**

(1) a. What did Robin present to Pat at the ceremony?
b. Who is Larry threatening now?
c. Max might have been being interrogated during the break.
d. Will they have to be leaving?
e. Sandy is in the house now.

(2) a. Hún haf-ð-i unnið að brúarsmíði
3FsgNOM have-PAST-3sg worked at bridge.building
í sumar. — Icelandic
in summer
'She worked at bridge-building in the summer.'
b. Í sumar haf-ð-i hún unnið að
in summer have-PAST-sg 3FsgNOM worked at
brúarsmíði.
bridge.building
'In the summer she worked at bridge-building.'

(3) Die Jäger werd-en viele Büffel neben dem Bach
the hunters FUT-3pl many buffalo next.to the creek
sehen können. — German
see can
'The hunters will be able to see many buffalo next to the creek.'

(4) Gel-emi-yebil-ir-im. — Turkish
come-ABLE.NOT-PSBL-TNS-1sg
'I may be unable to come.'

(5) Ipa sai ha ipa silaka ha sa kali-palo-ti
my house LOC my arrow LOC 1sg work-REPET-CONT
kule. — Sanuma (Brazil)
PRES
'I am working on my arrow at my house.'

(6) Dare ga kompyuutaa o tukatte imas-u ka? — Japanese
who SUBJ computer OBJ use PROG-TNS Q
'Who is using the computer?'

4 Draw the layered structure of the PPs given below. Do not give the internal structure of the NPs. Represent each PP twice, once as predicative and once as non-predicative. (Abkhaz data from Hewitt 1979.) **[section 2.3.1]**

(1) *Adpositional phrases: dependent marking*
zu dem Mann — German
to the.DAT man
'to the man'

(2) *Adpositional phrases: head marking*
a-jəyas a-q'nə Abkhaz
the-river 3sg-at
'at the river' (lit: 'the river$_i$ at-it$_i$')

5 Draw the layered structure of the NPs given below. Give the full layered structure of each NP, even NP-internal ones; include both constituent and operator projections. Also, represent the PPs as predicative or non-predicative, as appropriate. Treat the demonstratives in Tibetan and Mparntwe Arrernte as simple deictics and not as being pronominal like English demonstratives. [**section 2.3.2**]

(1) a. the capture of the fugitive by the police yesterday
b. the sister of Mary's tall neighbor
c. that new tall building

(2) das alte graue Gebäude in dem ehemaligen Ost-Berlin German
the old grey building in the former East-Berlin

(3) mar gsolpa rgyama rgu degyad Tibetan
butter fresh catty nine DEM
'those nine catties of fresh butter.'

(4) kere aherre kngerre urrpetye nhenhe itne Mparntwe Arrernte
CL:meat kangaroo big few/three DEM DEF
'these few/three big kangaroos (from the point of view of them being hunted as game for their meat)'

6 Give the complete layered structure of the clause, including the layered structure of the NPs, for one of the Warlpiri sentences in (1) (Hale 1973). Assume Warlpiri to be double-marking like Choctaw. [**section 2.3.2**]

(1) a. Wiri-ngki kapi-Ø-ji yarlki-mi maliki-rlu.
big-ERG FUT-3sgSUBJ-1sgOBJ bite-NPST dog-ERG
b. Maliki-rlu kapi-Ø-ji wiri-ngki yarlku-mi.
c. Wiri-ngki kapi-Ø-ji maliki-rlu yarlki-mi.
d. Maliki-rlu kapi-Ø-ji yarlki-mi wiri-ngki.
'The big dog will bite me.'

7 In Yagua, a language of the Amazon basin in Peru (Payne and Payne 1989), the elements which approximate definite articles in languages like English occur as enclitics on the preceding word. This is illustrated in the sentences below. [**section 2.3.2**]

(1) a. Siimyiy Alchíco-níí quiivą.
eat -DET fish
'Alchíco is eating the fish.'
b. Siimyiy Alchíco sinu-mu-níí quiivą.
eat land-LOC-DET fish
'Alchíco is eating the fish on land.'

(2) a. Sasąąy Alchíco-rà pą̊ą-níí sadeetu.
give -DET bread-DET his.daughter
'Alchíco gives the bread to his daughter.'

a′. Sasąąy Alchíco pą̊ą-níí sadeetu.
give bread-DET his.daughter
'Alchíco gives bread to his daughter.'

b. Sasąąy Alchíco-níí sadeetu-rà pą̊ą.
give -DET his.daughter-DET bread
'Alchíco gives his daughter the bread.'

How does the theory of clause and NP structure developed in this chapter handle this phenomenon? Give the layered structure of the clause, including the layered structure of the NPs, of either (2a) or (2b). For the clause, give only the constituent projection, and for the NPs, give both constituent and operator projections.

3

Semantic representation, I: verbs and arguments

3.0 Introduction

In the previous chapter we presented a theory of morphosyntactic structure which elucidated the structure of simple sentences and noun phrases. At many points in the discussion we made crucial reference to predicates and their arguments and to the semantic representation of sentences. Our task in this chapter and the next is to present a theory of just these things. We begin by presenting a classification of the kinds of events, actions and situations that sentences express and of the roles that the participants in these states of affairs may play. We then turn to the problem of representing the relevant semantic properties of verbs and other predicates that code these states of affairs; these representations will in turn form the basis of the semantic representations of clauses and sentences. From these we will derive the representation of the arguments of the verbs and other predicates, arguments which denote the participants in the states of affairs. In the next chapter we will present the notion of 'semantic macrorole' and investigate the semantic representation of adjuncts, operators and noun phrases.

3.1 A typology of states of affairs and their participants

In chapter 1 we pointed out that the general perspective from which this book is written maintains that the communicative functions of language are central to the analysis of its structure, and one (but not the only) function of language is reference and predication, that is, representing things that happen in the world (or a possible, fictional world) and the participants involved in those situations. Hence languages must have the means to depict or denote these participants and states of affairs, and it is usually the case that verbs and other predicating elements describe the situations, while noun phrases and other referring expressions denote the participants in them. In order to help us understand the semantic content of predicating elements and the syntagmatic relationships which hold between a predicate and its arguments, we will begin by setting up a typology of states of affairs and a list of the roles which participants may play in them.

We will use the term 'state of affairs' to refer to phenomena in the world, and, following a tradition dating back to Aristotle, we propose that there are four basic types of states of affairs:

(3.1) a. *Situations*: static, non-dynamic states of affairs which may involve the location of a participant (a book being on the table), the state or condition of a participant (Maria being tired), or an internal experience of a participant (Fred liking Alice).

b. *Events*: states of affairs which seem to happen instantly, e.g. balloons popping, a glass shattering, a building blowing up.

c. *Processes*: states of affairs which involve change and take place over time, e.g. a change in location (a book falling to the floor), in state or condition (ice melting, water freezing, clothes drying), or in the internal experience of a participant (Tanisha learning Swahili).

d. *Actions*: dynamic states of affairs in which a participant does something, e.g. Chris singing, the ball rolling, the sun shining, a fire crackling, Yolanda swimming, the ground shaking, Tyrone drinking beer.

These states of affairs can vary along a number of dimensions; among them are: (1) how many participants there are; (2) whether there is a terminal point; and (3) whether the state of affairs happens spontaneously or is induced. In all of the examples above there are states of affairs with one or more participants, and it is possible to have a large number of participants in complex states of affairs, e.g. Kim buying a book from Pat for Sandy with a ten-dollar bill. The question of a terminal point is whether a state of affairs *inherently* comes to a conclusion, for example, the state of affairs of drying necessarily involves a conclusion in which the entity in question is no longer wet and has become dry, whereas the state of affairs of rotating does not necessarily involve a conclusion in which the entity ceases to rotate (as, for example, the earth's rotating on its axis). Drying has an inherent terminal point, while rotating does not. Events, for example, have an inherent terminal point. However, it is often the case that a given event can happen over and over again, i.e. iteratively, and consequently the 'macroevent' will appear to lack a terminal point, e.g. balloons popping, firecrackers exploding. Situations, on the other hand, lack an inherent terminal point; there is nothing in the nature of, say, being on a table or knowing that 2 + 2 = 4 that implies that these situations should or could terminate. They can, of course, but they need not; this is the crucial point. Actions, too, are inherently unbounded; there is nothing in the nature of singing, crackling or swimming that implies that it must terminate in some way, unlike exploding or shattering. Like situations, actions may cease, but they need not, as in actions like the earth spinning on its axis or orbiting the sun. Processes, by contrast, do have inherent terminal points. After a certain amount of time, ice will have completed melting and turned into water, or clothes will have finished drying and be dry. Note that the result of the process may be a situation of some kind, e.g. clothes being dry.

All of these states of affairs may occur spontaneously or be induced or brought about in some way. Pairs of spontaneous and induced states of affairs are given in (3.2).

(3.2)		*Spontaneous*	*Induced*
	a. Situation	a boy being afraid	dogs frightening a boy
	b. Event	a balloon popping	a boy popping a balloon
	c. Process	snow melting	the sun melting snow
	d. Action	a ball rolling	a boy rolling a ball

Induced states of affairs are always complex, in that there is an initial state of affairs which induces or brings about the final state of affairs. With induced situations, for example, any state-of-affairs type can be the initial state of affairs, as (3.3) shows.

(3.3)		
	a. Situation → situation	Felipe's being morose frightening/annoying Juana
	b. Event → situation	a balloon's popping startling/frightening Dana
	c. Process → situation	the ice cream's melting pleasing/annoying Chris
	d. Action → situation	dogs' barking frightening/annoying Pat

Induced events, processes and actions typically have actions as the initial state of affairs, as in (a)–(c), but other combinations are possible, as illustrated in (d)–(i).

(3.4)		
	a. Action → event	a boy's pricking a balloon causing it to pop
	b. Action → process	the sun's radiating heat causing clothes to dry
	c. Action → action	Abdul's pushing on a boulder causing it to roll
	d. Event → process	lightning setting a tree on fire
	e. Event → action	an explosion causing a hillside to slide
	f. Event → event	sodium coming into contact with water causing an explosion
	g. Process → event	floodwaters flowing against a bridge support causing it to snap
	h. Process → action	melting snow causing a river to overflow
	i. Situation → action	Fred's beliefs leading him to join the clergy

Most states of affairs are complex ones composed of combinations of the four basic types.

There are participants in these states of affairs, as we have seen, and these participants have roles in the states of affairs, much the same way actors and props have roles in a play. We will refer to these roles as *participant roles* in states of affairs. These participant roles are a function of the state of affairs and do not exist independently of them. Consider the state of affairs of Juan cutting a rope with a knife and what roles the participants play in it. Juan is clearly the doer of the action, and this is often referred to as the *agent* of the action. The knife is being manipulated by Juan and does the actual cutting of the rope; it is often called an *instrument*. The rope is the participant most affected by the actions of Juan and the knife; it undergoes a change of condition (uncut → cut), and affected participants which undergo such a change of state or condition are often called *patients*. We may break down this complex state of affairs into its component states of affairs as in (3.5).

(3.5) a. *Initial situation*: rope (patient) being whole, uncut
b. *Action*: Juan (agent) cutting the rope (patient) using a knife (instrument)[1]
c. *Final situation*: rope (patient) being in two or more pieces

The participant role an entity has depends crucially on the state of affairs that the entity is involved in. In an action in which Felix sharpens a knife, the knife is undergoing a change of state or condition (dull → sharp) and hence is a patient in this state of affairs. Felix would be an agent in this state of affairs, akin to Juan in (3.5b), but if the state of affairs involved Felix seeing the knife only, then he could not be called an agent, since he is not doing anything. Rather, he would be experiencing something, in this case a perceptual experience, and therefore he would be an *experiencer* rather than an agent. A list of common participant roles is given below, where the participant with the role in question is in italics in the example state of affairs.

Commonly used participant roles in states of affairs

agent: a willful, purposeful instigator of an action or event, such as in *Leslie* breaking the glass on purpose.

effector: the doer of an action, which may or may not be willful or purposeful, as in *Max* breaking the clock accidentally, *a puppy* chewing up Maria's new shoes.

experiencer: sentient beings that experience internal states, such as perceivers, cognizers and emoters as in *Felipe* thinking about/remembering/disliking the question.

instrument: normally inanimate entities manipulated by an agent in the carrying out of an action, as in Juan breaking a window with *a rock*.

force: somewhat like instruments, but they cannot be manipulated. They can include things like tornados, storms and acts of God, as in *a flood* washing away a village.

patient: things that are in a state or condition, or undergo a change of state or condition, e.g. *Sue* being tall, sick or dying, or *a window* breaking.

theme: things which are located or are undergoing a change of location (motion), as in *a book* being on the table or Carl putting *a book* on the table.

benefactive: the participant for whose benefit some action is performed, e.g. Ned baking a cake for *Yvonne*, or picking up some dry cleaning for *Tanisha*.

recipient: someone who gets something (recipients are always animate or some kind of quasi-animate entity, e.g. an organization), as in Vidhu sending a card to *Hari*.

goal: destination, which is similar to recipient, except that it is often inanimate, as in Larry sending a package to *Baltimore*.

source: the point of origin of a state of affairs. It is used in a variety of cases, which can conflate the ambiguity between recipient and goal:

$$\text{source}\quad x \xrightarrow{\text{transfer}} y \xrightarrow{\text{recipient}} z$$
$$\qquad\qquad\quad \text{motion} \qquad\quad \text{goal}$$

x = initial position, y = object, and z = final position

If there is a transfer of *y* then *z* is a recipient. If *y* is in motion, then *z* is a goal. In either case, *x* is the source, and *y* is the theme. In the case of David giving a book to Kristen, *David* is both an agent and a source. Agent and recipient can also be the same participant, as in *Yolanda* buying the dog from Bill.

location: a place or a spatial locus of a state of affairs, as in the book being on *the table* or Bob eating a sandwich in *the kitchen*.

path: a route, as in Quentin jogging along *the creek* to the park.

This is not an exhaustive list, but it introduces the notions most relevant to our discussion. Again, it must be emphasized that the role an entity plays is crucially a function of the type of state of affairs in which it is involved. Put simply, it is possible to derive participant roles by analyzing states of affairs, but the converse is not possible, since participant roles cannot be defined without reference to states of affairs.

In communication, speakers construct sentences which depict the state(s) of affairs which they wish to make known to their interlocutor(s). As mentioned at the beginning of this section, verbs and other predicating elements typically code the type of state of affairs, and noun phrases and other referring expressions denote the participants therein. It is not the case, however, that language is a perfect mirror of reality, be it the real world or a fictional one. It is very important to distinguish what is in the state of affairs from what lexical items encode. Lexical items differ in the meanings they express, sometimes very subtly, and speakers always have a number of options with regard to which lexical items they choose to express a state of affairs. Consider the two states of affairs represented pictorially in figure 3.1. In both pictures there is a person (let's call him 'Fred'), an object (let's say it's a rock) and a window. In the first picture, Fred is holding the rock and hitting the window with it, thereby breaking it, whereas in the second, he has thrown the rock through the window, thereby causing it to break. There are a number of ways that the state of affairs in figure 3.1a could be expressed in English; a partial list is given in (3.6).

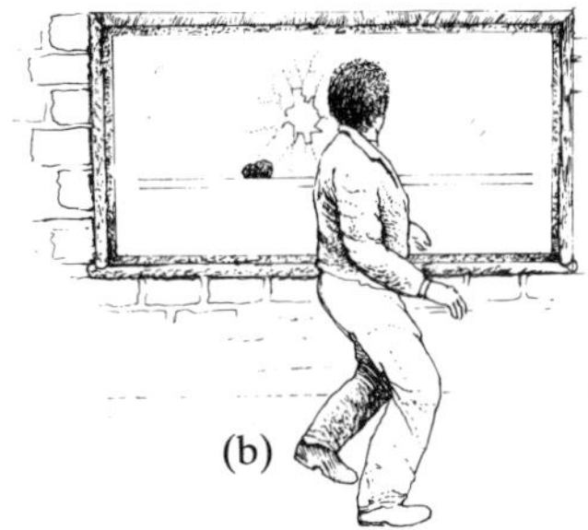

Figure 3.1 Two states of affairs

(3.6) a. Fred/Someone/A boy broke the window (with a rock).
b. Fred shattered the window (with a rock).
c. Fred smashed the window (with a rock).
d. Fred hit the window with a rock, breaking/shattering it.
e. A rock broke the window.
f. A rock shattered the window.
g. The window broke.
h. The window shattered.

All of the sentences in (3.6) are literally true, in that they all accurately characterize some aspect of the state of affairs depicted in figure 3.1a.[2] However, they all have different meanings, both in terms of the meanings of the lexical items chosen (*break* vs. *smash* vs. *shatter*) and in terms of which participants are mentioned. The first four sentences explicitly refer to all three participants, while the fifth and sixth refer only to the instrument and the patient; the last two refer only to a single participant, the patient (the window). Example (3.6d) explicitly mentions the manner in which the breaking was done. There are similar options with respect to figure 3.1b.

(3.7) a. Fred/Someone/A boy broke the window (with a rock).
b. Fred shattered the window (with a rock).
c. Fred smashed the window (with a rock).
d. Fred threw a rock through the window, breaking/shattering it.
e. A rock broke the window.
f. A rock shattered the window.
g. The window broke.
h. The window shattered.

The primary difference between the sentences in (3.7) and those in (3.6) is the specification of the manner of the action, in this case throwing instead of hitting. English allows speakers a variety of options for expressing a particular state of affairs, and no two mean exactly the same thing. Moreover, the language allows speakers to be as specific as they wish about the details; in particular, it allows them to leave out major participants and to gloss over differences in the nature of the action.

When we look at how other languages code states of affairs, we see even more clearly how important it is to distinguish between what is in the state of affairs and what lexical items encode. If a speaker of Lakhota were asked to describe figures 3.1a, b, a partial list of possible responses would include the sentences in (3.8) for figure 3.1a and those in (3.9) for 3.1b.

(3.8) a. Fred/Tuwá/Hokšíla wą (ixʔé wą ų́) ožą́žąglepi ki
/someone/boy a rock a with window the
ka-bléčhe/*wo-bléčhe.
by.striking-break/action.from.distance-break
'Fred/Someone/A boy broke the window (with a rock).'

b. *Ixʔé wą ožą́žąglepi ki ka-bléčhe.
rock a window the by.striking-break
'A rock broke the window.'

c. (Ixʔé wą ų́) ožą́žąglepi ki ka-bléčha-pi.
rock a with window the by.striking-break-3pl
'They [unspecified] broke the window (with a rock).'

(3.9) a. Fred/Tuwá/Hokšíla wą (ixʔé wą ų́) ožą́žąglepi ki
/someone/boy a rock a with window the
wo-bléčhe/*ka-bléčhe.
action.from.distance-break/by.striking-break
'Fred/Someone/A boy broke the window (with a rock).'

b. *Ixʔé wą ožą́žąglepi ki wo-bléčhe.
rock a window the action.from.distance-break
'A rock broke the window.'

c. (Ixʔé wą ų́) ožą́žąglepi ki wo-bléčha-pi.
rock a with window the action.from.distance-break-3pl
'They [unspecified] broke the window (with a rock).'

The first thing to notice about these sets of sentences is that the verb is not the same in each set and that they cannot be substituted for each other. Lakhota does not have a single verb corresponding to English *break*; rather, it has dozens of verbs for expressing states of affairs involving breaking. There are two primary considerations determining which verb will be chosen, because each verb consists of a verb stem plus an instrumental prefix. The first is the nature of the affected object, or patient. If it is a flat, brittle object, then the verb stem *-blečha* would be chosen. If, on the other hand, it were a long, thin object, like a pencil, then either *-ksa* or *-wega* would be chosen, depending upon the nature of the damage: if the pencil is broken completely in two, then *-ksa* would be chosen, whereas if it were cracked but not broken into two distinct pieces, then *-wega* would be used. Since we are dealing with a window in the two states of affairs in figure 3.1, *-blečha* would be selected. The contrast between *ka-* and *wo-* in the two verbs involves what are called instrumental prefixes; they specify the nature or manner of the action. *Ka-* signals that the action was done by striking, whereas *wo-* indicates action from a distance, as in shooting or throwing. Thus in Lakhota it is obligatory to express two aspects of the state of affairs that are only optionally and indirectly expressed in English: properties of the affected object, and the manner of the action.

The two languages also differ in terms of which participants must be expressed and how they can be expressed. In both languages it is not necessary to overtly code the instrument, a rock. However, in English it is possible to present the instrument participant as the subject of the sentence, as in (3.6e, f) and (3.7e, f), whereas this is impossible in Lakhota, as (3.8b) and (3.9b) show.[3] Moreover, it is not possible in Lakhota to express just the window's breaking without referring to any external cause in the states of affairs in figure 3.1. The expression *ožą́žąglepi ki nabléčhe* 'the window broke' (with instrumental prefix *na-* 'by internal force') can only be used when there is no external force acting on the window when it breaks, and this is not the case in these states of affairs. Accordingly, the closest that one can come to this is the (c) sentences, in which the verb is put in the third person plural form, which can be interpreted as meaning an unspecified breaker; but it clearly codes a force acting on the window in a specific way, causing it to break. Thus Lakhota offers its speakers a different set of options for expressing the states of affairs in figure 3.1 than English offers its speakers. Crucially, however, in both languages there is more than one option for each state of affairs, even if the set of possible options varies across the two languages.

In this section we have presented a classification of states of affairs (situations, events, processes and actions) and a (non-exhaustive) list of the roles which participants may have in them. The linguistic means for describing states of affairs typically consists of verbs and other predicating elements, which express the situation, event, process or action, and noun phrases and other referring expressions, which denote the participants. Hence what verbs mean must be in some way related to the state of affairs they express. Even though a speaker has considerable freedom with respect to the linguistic possibilities available for coding a state of affairs, these choices are nevertheless constrained by properties of the state of affairs. We have seen that languages lexicalize different aspects of a state of affairs and vary in what they require a speaker to code about it, e.g. Lakhota requires that the manner of the action of breaking be specified, while English does not.[4] The role that an entity plays in a state of affairs is always a function of the nature of the state of affairs, and it is nonsensical to separate participant roles from the states of affairs in which they occur. Thus it is states of affairs which are fundamental (i.e. basic), not participant roles (which are derived). In the next section we will present a theory of lexical representation for verbs and their arguments which will allow us to capture how linguistic expressions can code states of affairs.

3.2 The lexical representation of verbs and their arguments

Since verbs and other predicating elements express (aspects of) states of affairs, an adequate theory of lexical representation ought to represent explicitly the crucial distinctions which differentiate the different types of states of affairs, e.g. taking place over time, being dynamic or having a terminal point. Moreover, since the role of a participant is a function of the state of affairs it is involved in, the semantic function of an argument referring to a participant should follow from the representation of the verb or any other predicate coding the state of affairs. Hence our goal in this section is to develop a system of lexical representation for predicates and their arguments which will satisfy these conditions. Throughout this section we will use the term 'argument' to refer to the semantic arguments of predicates, unless otherwise noted.

The approach to the depiction of the lexical meaning of verbs which we will adopt is **lexical decomposition**, which involves paraphrasing verbs in terms of primitive elements in a well-defined semantic metalanguage.[5] As a simple example of the mechanism of lexical decomposition, *kill* can be paraphrased into something like 'cause to die', and then *die* can be broken down into 'become dead'. Thus the lexical representation of *kill* would be something like '*x* causes [*y* become dead]'. In Lakhota, for example, verbs of killing can be formed from the verb *t'a* 'die, be dead' by adding instrumental prefixes; the result is verbs like *ka-t'a* 'cause to die by striking' (*ka-* 'by striking'), *yu-t'a* 'strangle' (*yu-* 'with the hands'), *ya-t'a* 'bite to death' (*ya-* 'with the teeth') and *wo-t'a* 'shoot to death' (*wo-* 'by action from a distance'). The addition of the instrumental prefix causativizes the verb and codes a type of causing action; all of these verbs of killing are derived from a base verb meaning 'die' or 'be dead' via causativization. Another piece of evidence for this kind of analysis comes from intriguing morphological suppletion patterns found in some languages. In Georgian (Harris 1982), certain transitive verb stems supplete for the number of their objects. This means that if there is a singular object of the verb *kill*, for example, the verb stem has one form, e.g. *movk'ali* 'I killed it', and when the object is plural, the verb stem has a different form, e.g. *davxoce* 'I killed them' (*-v-* '1sg'). Interestingly, the same thing happens with some intransitive verbs, as they supplete for the number of their subject, e.g. *mok'vda* 'he died' vs. *daixoca* 'they died'. Thus 'die' suppletes for the number of its subject, and 'kill' for the number of its object. This seems like an odd relationship, until it is recognized that the subject of 'die' is semantically the same argument as the object of 'kill'. This can be seen explicitly in the decompositions of the two verbs: in both Georgian and English, *die* is '*y* becomes dead', and *kill* is '*x* causes [*y* become dead]'. The two verbs in Georgian supplete for the number of the *y* argument. This supports the semantic analysis of *kill* as something like 'cause to die'; the exact representation will be given below, and this provisional characterization should not be confused with the English expression *cause to die*.[6]

A system of lexical representation should include a way of expressing the fact that the subject of *die* and the object of *kill* are the same argument semantically. There are many verbs like this pair, and in many cases the relationship between them is overt. Examples include *sink*, as in *The boat sank* and *The torpedo sank the boat*, where *boat* is the subject of intransitive *sink* and the object of transitive *sink*. Another example is the predicate *cool*, which can take three forms, one adjectival and two verbal: *The soup is cool*, *The soup is cooling* and *The wind cooled the soup*. Thus, there seems to be a pattern of intransitive verbs whose subjects are identical to the objects of their transitive counterparts. There are cases, however, when the intransitive–transitive alternants do not have the same lexical form, as in *die* and *kill*, or *receive* and *give*.[7] An adequate theory of lexical representation should be able to capture these relationships, and lexical decomposition provides a promising method for doing it. There are many theories of lexical decomposition, which differ in terms of how fine-grained they are. It is necessary to find the right level of detail, one which allows the expression of certain important generalizations but which also has representations whose differences have morphosyntactic consequences. Thus, arriving at a decompositional system is a compromise between the demands of semantics (make all necessary distinctions relevant to meaning) and those of syntax (make syntactically relevant distinctions that permit the expression of significant generalizations). There is something akin to the law of diminishing returns at work here; at a certain point, the semantic distinctions being made cease to have significant syntactic consequences, and so from the point of view of syntactic theory the most desirable system of decomposition is one which is just fine-grained enough (and no more) to make the distinctions necessary for capturing linguistically significant generalizations about syntax, semantics and their interaction.

The semantic representation of the predicate in the nucleus is the heart of the semantic representation of the clause as a whole, and as such the two representations are obviously related. However, it is always necessary to distinguish the lexical meaning of the verb (which would be found in its lexical entry in the lexicon) from the meaning it has in a particular clause in which it occurs. In the next section, we will talk about both aspects of the meaning of verbs. We will first look at the classification of verbs themselves and then look at the issue of how they are interpreted in the context of a particular clause. The first determines how a verb will be represented in the lexicon, and the second determines the semantic representation of the core of a clause.

3.2.1 Verb classes

The system of lexical decomposition to be employed is based on the distinctions in *Aktionsart* (German for 'form of action') proposed originally in Vendler (1957 [1967]). He argued that verbs and other predicating elements could be classified in terms of their inherent temporal properties, and proposed four basic classes: states, achievements, accomplishments and activities. *Aktionsart*, then, is the term we use for the inherent temporal properties of verbs. States are non-dynamic and temporally unbounded. Activities are dynamic and temporally unbounded. Achievements code instantaneous changes, usually changes of state but also changes in activities as well; they have an inherent terminal point. Accomplishments are temporally extended (not instantaneous) changes of state leading to a terminal point. These classes are exemplified in (3.10).

(3.10) a. *States*: *be sick, be tall, be dead, love, know, believe, have*
b. *Achievements*: *pop, explode, collapse, shatter* (all intransitive)
c. *Accomplishments*: *melt, freeze, dry* (the intransitive versions); *recover from illness, learn*
d. *Activities*: *march, walk, roll* (the intransitive versions); *swim, think, rain, read, eat*

Each of these *Aktionsart* types corresponds to one of our basic state-of-affairs types.

(3.11)

State-of-affairs type	Aktionsart *type*
Situation	State
Event	Achievement
Process	Accomplishment
Action	Activity

This correspondence reveals the reason for the importance of the typology of states of affairs developed in the previous section: the distinctions among states of affairs are reflected to a striking degree in distinctions among *Aktionsart* types. That is, situations are expressed by state verbs or predicates, events by achievement verbs or predicates, processes by accomplishment verbs or predicates, and actions by activity verbs or predicates. It is important to distinguish properties of states of affairs from properties of verbs and other predicates; *Aktionsart* refers only to properties of linguistic predicates, not to properties of states of affairs.

In the previous section we pointed out that it is always necessary to distinguish the lexical meaning of the verb (which would be found in its entry in the lexicon) from the meaning it has in the particular clause in which it occurs. In *Aktionsart* terms, this means that verbs have a basic *Aktionsart* type, which is how they are represented in the lexicon. However, the addition of PPs or adverbials often results in a different *Aktionsart* interpretation for the verb in the context of the entire clause. Hence it is often the case that a given verb can be used with more than one *Aktionsart* interpretation. In this chapter we will first discuss verbs in terms of their basic *Aktionsart* classification, and then later in this chapter and in the next we will investigate how new interpretations arise in the context of whole sentences.

These four classes can be defined in terms of three features, [±static], [±punctual] and [±telic], which refers to whether the verb has an inherent terminal point or not. This is summarized in (3.12).

(3.12) a. State [+static], [–telic], [–punctual]
b. Activity [–static], [–telic], [–punctual]
c. Accomplishment [–static], [+telic], [–punctual]
d. Achievement [–static], [+telic], [+punctual]

Most fundamental is the distinction between static and non-static verbs, which distinguishes verbs which code a 'happening' from those which code a 'non-happening'. In other words, with reference to some state of affairs, one could ask 'what happened?' or 'what is happening?' If, for example, a sentence like *A deer ran through the room* could be the answer to this question, then the verb *run* is [–static]. On the other hand, a sentence like *John believes the world is round* could not be the answer to this question, because nothing is taking place. Hence *believe* is a [+static] verb. By this criterion activities, achievements and accomplishments are [–static]. States, however, are [+static]. The non-static nature of achievements can be seen in the fact that a sentence like *The window broke* could felicitously be the answer to the question 'what happened?'

The feature 'telic' has to do with whether a verb depicts a state of affairs with an inherent terminal point or not. States and activities lack inherent terminal points. For example, a sentence like *John is tall* makes no reference to a temporal boundary, and is therefore non-telic (atelic). In *John is running in the park*, for example, there is a reference to an activity, but running, like rotating, need not terminate. This is not a function of the progressive aspect; in *The clothes are drying on the line*, the verb *dry* entails that there is a terminal point at which the clothes will be dry. Therefore, *run* is [–telic], while the intransitive verb *dry* is [+telic]. Achievements also have terminal points; if a bomb explodes or a window shatters, the terminal point is the moment of the explosion or the shattering. Hence these verbs are [+telic] as well. Therefore, states and activities are unbounded (atelic), while achievements and accomplishments are bounded (telic). Tests to unambiguously determine whether a verb is [±telic] will be given below.

The final feature, [±punctual], distinguishes telic events with internal duration from those which lack it. The verbs *melt* and *pop* can both involve changes of state, as in *The ice melted* and *The balloon popped*, but they differ in that the former takes place over a time span, while the latter is instantaneous, for all practical purposes. Since states and activities are atelic, they must by definition involve temporal duration, and therefore they are always [–punctual].

How do we know which *Aktionsart* type a verb or other predicate is? The tests in table 3.1 will allow us to decide which class a verb belongs to.[8] The point of the tests is to uncover cooccurrence patterns which will reveal the *Aktionsart* class of a verb. Each of them is intended to isolate one or more semantic features of the class(es). The asterisks will be explained below. The tests are intended to have cross-linguistic validity, with some qualifications. It is possible to find valid tests which work only in the language being investigated. For example, one of the best tests for identifying a

Table 3.1 *Tests for determining* Aktionsart *type*

Criterion	*States*	*Achievements*	*Accomplishments*	*Activities*
1 Occurs with progressive	No	No	Yes	Yes
2 Occurs with adverbs like *vigorously*, *actively*, etc.	No	No	No	Yes
3 Occurs with adverbs like *quickly*, *slowly*, etc.	No	No*	Yes	Yes
4 Occurs with *X for an hour*, *spend an hour Xing*	Yes*	No	Irrelevant	Yes
5 Occurs with *X in an hour*	No	No*	Yes	No

state verb in English is the simple present test (Dowty 1979): if a verb can be used in the simple present form and has a present tense interpretation, then it is a state verb. For example, *Chris knows the answer* (*right now*) has a present tense interpretation, whereas *Dana sings the song* (**right now*) does not; it has only a habitual interpretation, hence the ungrammaticality of *right now* with it. This test would not work in other languages in which the morphological present tense has a present tense interpretation with all verbs.

Test 1 is useful only in languages like English, Spanish and Icelandic which have a progressive aspect; it may be interpreted as an indicator of [–static, –punctual], since it can occur with activity (3.13d) and accomplishment verbs (3.13b), but not with states (3.13a) or achievements (3.13c).[9]

(3.13) a. *Miriam is being tall/fat/a linguist.
a′. *Aisha is knowing the answer/believing that today is Wednesday.
b. The snow is melting.
c. *The balloon is popping.
d. Stan is dancing/singing/running/talking/crying/sleeping.

Verbs have their own inherent meaning, upon which are then added further temporal meanings through inflection. If one says *The balloon popped*, then one is merely stating the fact that it happened, but if one says *The balloons are popping*, there is a sequence of different balloons popping, i.e. there is an iterative interpretation. This is the result of adding the progressive to a [+punctual] verb. One could take an inherently bounded verb and add the progressive to it, which tends to mean that an action was working toward completion, but was as yet incomplete, as in (b); this can only be done with a [–punctual] verb. On the other hand, if one added the progressive to an inherently unbounded verb, it would refer to the middle of this unbounded action or process, as in (3.13d).[10]

Test 2 involves the ability to cooccur with adverbs that code dynamic action, e.g. *vigorously*, *actively*, *dynamically*, etc.

(3.14) a. *Max is vigorously tall/fat/a linguist.
a′. *Max vigorously knows the answer/believes that today is Wednesday.
b. *The snow is melting/melted vigorously.
b′. *The window shattered vigorously.
c. Mary is dancing/singing/running/talking/crying vigorously/actively.

Despite being [–static], achievement and accomplishment verbs are odd with these adverbs, since adverbs like *vigorously* and *dynamically* modify actions. This suggests that a further distinction is required among [–static] verbs, namely [±dynamic]. This test shows that activities are [+dynamic], while achievements and accomplishments are [–dynamic]. This feature does not apply to states, since they are [+static]. There is an important caution relevant to this test. It is crucial to avoid adverbs which require a controlling subject, e.g. *deliberately*, *carefully*. While they are incompatible with states and achievements, they are also incompatible with activity verbs which have subjects which refer to non-agent participants in the action, e.g. *shiver* as in *The dog shivered violently/*deliberately in the cold*, or *shake* as in *The house shook violently/*carefully during the earthquake*. Hence in selecting adverbs for this test, it is necessary to test their compatibility with involuntary verbs like *shiver* and with verbs like *shake* which can have an inanimate subject.

Test 3 applies only to [–static] verbs and distinguishes [–punctual] from [+punctual] verbs. Adverbs like *quickly*, *rapidly* and *slowly*, which we will call 'pace' adverbs, can occur with events involving temporal duration, regardless of whether they involve dynamic action, e.g. *The snow is melting slowly/ ??vigorously*, *John slowly/*vigorously realized his mistake*. The * on the 'No' in the achievement column of table 3.1 indicates that pace adverbs indicating very short temporal intervals are marginally acceptable with these verbs, e.g. *The bomb exploded instantly*. Hence with these verbs it is necessary to use pace adverbs which indicate a relatively slow process, e.g. *The bomb exploded *slowly/gradually*.

Tests 4 and 5 distinguish telic from non-telic verbs. When applied to other languages, they require one to determine which adposition indicates duration (the *for* test) and which indicates completion (the *in* test). Test 4 isolates the property of having duration in time; it shows that states, accomplishments and activities all have temporal duration, but achievements do not, and this supports the claim in (3.12) that achievements are [+punctual], the others all being [–punctual]. Test 5 focuses on terminal points. If something is done *in* ten minutes, then explicit reference is being made to the termination point of the event. In other words, the event started at a certain time and ended ten minutes later. But if something is done *for* ten minutes, the same event could still be going on at a later time. All the *for*-phrase indicates is that an event went on for a certain amount of time, without any information about when it began or when it ended. So in *He read the book in an hour*, the event began and ended in the space of one hour, with the subject having finished reading the book, whereas in *He read the book for an hour*, there is no indication of when the action began or ended, and the same event could still be going on at a later time. In general, states and activities readily take *for*-phrases, while achievements and accomplishments take *in*-phrases. Because achievements are punctual, they are only compatible with *in*-phrases referring to an exceedingly short period of time, e.g. *in the blink of an eye, in an instant, in a fraction of a second.* They are incompatible with *in*-phrases referring to temporal periods longer than this, e.g. *in ten seconds, in a minute* and *in an hour*, and accordingly they are marked 'No*' in table 3.1. Hence this test should also be used with temporal expressions of substantial duration.

(3.15) a. Max was tired/ill/happy for/*in an hour.
a′. Max liked Susan for/*in an hour.
b. The snow melted in/for an hour.
c. The window shattered in/*for a fraction of a second. (*The window shattered in an hour.)
d. Mary danced/sang/cried/talked/slept for/*in ten minutes.

State predicates which code inherent properties do not normally take *for*-phrases, e.g. **Sandy was tall/thin/short/fat for an hour*. Hence there is an asterisk on the 'Yes' indicating that this test is problematic for some state predicates. Some accomplishments can take *for*-phrases, e.g. *The clothes dried for ten minutes* or *The ice melted for five minutes*, which follows from their being non-punctual, which is the main point of test 3. Hence the occurrence of *for*-phrases with accomplishments is really redundant and tells us nothing new about accomplishments. So it is marked as 'irrelevant' in table 3.1. Finally, there is an additional cooccurrence which must be noted. Achievements and activities do cooccur with *in*-phrases, e.g. *The bomb will explode in one hour, Mary will sing in ten minutes*; these phrases refer to the time until the onset of the action or event, not to the temporal duration of the event itself and are therefore irrelevant to these tests. Thus, it is not sufficient simply to ascertain the type of temporal phrase that a verb can occur with; it is, rather, necessary to pay attention to the meaning of the sentence as well.

These tests are not perfect, but taken together they enable the analyst to distinguish the classes. As noted above, it is necessary to adapt the tests to the language being investigated, and not all of them are equally useful. If a language lacks a progressive aspect, for example, then test 1 is irrelevant. Finally, it is necessary to be sensitive to what we may call 'local cooccurrence effects' in interpreting the tests. For example, suppose we apply test 3 to the English verb *rush*, as in *She rushed across the room*, in order to determine whether this verb has temporal duration or not, yielding *She rushed quickly/swiftly/*slowly across the room.* Some but not all pace adverbs are possible here; what are we to conclude? The correct conclusion is that *rush* has temporal duration and therefore is either an accomplishment or an activity verb. But what about the incompatibility with *slowly*? This is an example of a local cooccurrence effect; because part of the inherent meaning of *rush* is to do something with some degree of rapidity, *slowly* conflicts with this aspect of the meaning of *rush*. This is not due to the verb not having temporal duration, as its cooccurrence with *quickly* and *swiftly* show. Rather, the incompatibility of *rush* and *slowly* is due to an aspect of the meaning of *rush* which is unrelated to what test 3 is testing for. In the same vein, it is possible that only one of the class of adverbs of the type mentioned in test 2 is compatible with a particular verb; that would be sufficient to show that the verb rates a 'Yes' for the test. Other factors irrelevant to the point of the test may cause the other adverbs to be ruled out. Thus one must be sensitive to these local cooccurrence effects in interpreting the results of the tests.

In the previous section we discussed how states of affairs may be either spontaneous or induced and how for each spontaneous type there is a corresponding induced type (see (3.2)–(3.4)). Thus far we have only talked about the *Aktionsart* classes corresponding to spontaneous states of affairs, and we now turn to the properties of verbs referring to induced states of affairs. For each of the basic *Aktionsart* classes there is a corresponding causative class, which corresponds to the induced state of affairs. This is exemplified in (3.16).

(3.16)	a.	State	The boy is afraid.
	a′.	Causative state	The dog frightens/scares the boy.
	b.	Achievement	The balloon popped.
	b′.	Causative achievement	The cat popped the balloon.
	c.	Accomplishment	The ice melted.
	c′.	Causative accomplishment	The hot water melted the ice.
	d.	Activity	The ball bounced around the room.
	d′.	Causative activity	The girl bounced the ball around the room.

The causative classes all respond to the tests in table 3.1 in the same way as the non-causative ones, and the causative classes can be distinguished from the non-causative ones by the existence of a causative paraphrase, as in (3.17).

(3.17) a. The dog caused the boy to fear/be afraid.
b. The cat caused the balloon to pop.
c. The hot water caused the ice to melt.
d. The girl caused the ball to bounce around the room.

It is important to make sure that the paraphrases have the same number of NPs as the original sentence being paraphrased; that is, 'Robin causes Kim to come to have the book' is an appropriate paraphrase of *Robin gives the book to Kim*, but 'Sandy causes Sandy/herself to run' is not a possible paraphrase of *Sandy runs*. This rules out using passive versions of the verbs in the paraphrases, since they do not have the same number of core arguments as the active verbs being tested. On the other hand, 'Mary caused the dog to run (around the block)' is a possible paraphrase of *Mary ran the dog (around the block)*. This means that this test cannot apply to single argument verbs, i.e. verbs that have one argument in their basic form, because it would be impossible to make a causative paraphrase with a single participant.

Some languages mark these verb classes overtly with some type of morphological marker, as exemplified in the following examples from Tepehua, a Totonacan language of Mexico (Watters 1988).

(3.18) a. *ʔaknu:-y* 'A is underground' → *ta:knu:-y* 'A goes underground' → *ma:knu:-y* 'B buries A'
b. *lakčahu-y* 'A is closed' → *talakčahu-y* 'A closes' → *ma:lakčahu-y* 'B closes A'
c. *paša-y* 'A is changed, different' → *tapaša-y* 'A changes' → *ma:paša-y* 'B changes A'
d. *laqɬtiʔa:-y* 'A is open' → *talaqɬtiʔa:-y* 'A opens' → *ma:laqɬtiʔa:-y* 'B opens A'

In Tepehua, many achievement and accomplishment verbs carry the inchoative prefix *ta-*, while many causative achievement and accomplishment verbs carry the causative prefix *ma:-*; states are unmarked. In Qiang, a Tibeto-Burman language, the relationship is even clearer: *ba* 'big' (state), *tə-ba* 'become big' (accomplishment), and *tə-ba-ʐ* 'cause to become big' (causative accomplishment). It is not always the case that state verbs are unmarked and the other classes are morphologically marked. In Russian, French and Yagua (Peru), for example, there are related forms in which the causative accomplishment verb is unmarked and the others are marked, e.g. French *briser* 'break' (causative accomplishment), *se briser* 'break' (accomplishment), [*être*] *brisé* 'broken' (state); Russian *razbit'* 'break' (causative accomplishment), *razbit'sja* 'break' (accomplishment), *razbityj* 'broken' (state); Yagua *-muta-* 'open' (causative accomplishment), *-muta-y-* 'open' (accomplishment) (Payne and Payne 1989). The accomplishments in French and Russian are indicated by the same morpheme which is used in reflexive constructions, *se* in French and *-sja* in Russian, while the states are an adjectival past participle (French) or a deverbal adjective (Russian); in Yagua the states are indicated by adding the perfect clitic *-maa* to the accomplishment form. In English, on the other hand, there is no consistent morphology marking these classes; in some cases they are all the same form, e.g. *cool*, *cool* and *cool*, and in others there is some indicator, albeit an inconsistent one, e.g. [*be*] *black* (state) vs. *blacken* (causative accomplishment), [*be*] *red* (state) vs. *redden* (accomplishment), [*be*] *sick* (state) vs. *sicken* (accomplishment) vs. *sicken* (causative accomplishment). In Tepehua, causative activities may also be derived with *ma:-*, e.g. *pu:pu-y* 'x boils' vs. *ma:pu:pu-y* 'y boils x', *soqo-y* 'x hurries' vs. *ma:soqo:-y* 'y hurries x'. In Lakhota, causative activities may be derived either with the instrumental prefix *yu-*, which is treated as a general causative prefix with activity verbs, or by the causative verb *-ya*, e.g. *čhéya* 'cry' vs. *yu-čhéya* 'make cry' vs. *čheyá-ya* 'make cry'. Causative states corresponding to (3.16a′) also involve the causative verb *-ya*, e.g. *iníhą* 'be scared, frightened, amazed, awed' vs. *iníhą-ya* 'scare, frighten, amaze, awe'. In Japanese, the same type of contrast holds between state and causative psych-verbs, with the latter marked by the causative morpheme -(*s*)*ase-*, e.g. *kowagaru* 'be terrified' vs. *kowagar-ase-ru* 'terrify', *okoru* 'be angry' vs. *okor-ase-ru* 'anger'. Barai, a language of Papua New Guinea (Olson 1981), makes a systematic contrast between state verbs of psychological and physical state, e.g. *doduae* 'be thirsty', *gare* 'be cool', *mae* 'be happy' and *visi* 'be sick', and causative verbs of induced psychological and physical state, e.g. *dodua-d-* 'make thirsty', *gara-d-* 'make cool', *ma-d-* 'please' and *visi-nam-* 'sicken'. No matter how these distinctions are indicated morphologically in a particular language, they are fundamental distinctions made in the verbal systems in all languages.

It was mentioned at the beginning of this section that verbs may have a different *Aktionsart* interpretation in the context of a particular sentence from what we may determine to be its basic or lexical *Aktionsart* interpretation. A very important alternation between classes is that between activities and accomplishments. *He walked in the park for ten minutes* is an activity, whereas *He walked to the park in ten minutes* is an accomplishment. If motion verbs have a definite goal, which provides a terminal point, then they behave like accomplishments; if they do not have a definite goal, then they behave like activities. This is a phenomenon which we find reflected in the grammar of different languages.[11] This contrast is significant cross-linguistically, as we will see.

Another important variation is that verbs which are normally thought of as accomplishments behave like activities if they have an object which is a mass noun or bare plural. So a sentence like *He ate a plate of spaghetti in ten minutes* is an accomplishment, but *He ate spaghetti for ten minutes* is an activity. Similarly, *He drank beer for an hour* is an activity, but *He drank a beer in an hour* is an accomplishment because there is a specified amount, which provides a delimitation of the event; that is, the terminal point is reached when all of the beer has been consumed. Therefore some verbs, basically those of consumption or creation (e.g. *write*, *paint*, *carve*), behave like activities if they have a non-specific, indefinite, generic or mass noun object, but they behave like accomplishments if they have a specific, quantified object which serves to delineate the action. The terminal point is reached when the entity is created or consumed. Cognate objects may also serve this function, e.g. *She sang a song*, *He drank a drink*. It must be emphasized that this alternation is not simply a function of whether the direct object has an article or not, as it appears from looking at English data only. In other languages, this contrast is coded on the verb itself, with no change in the coding of the direct object. For example, in Russian the activity and accomplishment forms of the verb *eat* are distinct: *est′* (*kašu*) 'eat (kasha)' vs. *s″est′ kašu* 'eat the/some kasha'. The verb *est′* does not require a direct object, whereas *s″est′* does require one. There is no change in the form of the direct object, although its interpretation changes from unspecified mass noun to a specific quantity with the change in the form of the verb. Similarly in Georgian, *c'er* 'write' is the activity form which contrasts with *dac'er* 'write', the accomplishment form. Here again the contrast is coded on the verb itself. A final example comes from Pirahã, a language spoken in the Amazon basin in Brazil, which has suffixes which Everett (1986) glosses as 'telic' and 'atelic', and with verbs like 'eat' they have the same effect seen in English, Georgian and Russian, e.g. *xápiso xaho-aí-* (bark eat-ATELIC) 'eat bark' vs. *xápiso xoho-áo-* (bark eat-TELIC) 'eat (the) bark'. Like Georgian and Russian, Pirahã lacks articles, and the contrast is coded on the verb and affects the interpretation of the NP. This alternation is found across languages, and it has interesting syntactic consequences, which will be discussed in sections 4.2 and 4.6. We will refer to the accomplishment uses of activity verbs as **active accomplishments**. There are causative active accomplishments, like transitive *march*, as in *The sergeant marched the troops to the barracks*.

We started out talking about four *Aktionsart* classes, and we have ended up with ten classes overall: the basic four classes (states, activities, achievements, accomplishments), active accomplishments, and a causative version of each of them. The tests in table 3.1 were meant to distinguish only the four basic classes, and accordingly we must repeat the table with all ten classes; this is given in table 3.2. The tests in table 3.1 are referred to by number; the causative paraphrase test is 'test 6'. The * for achievement and causative achievements with respect to tests 3 and 5 is the same as discussed above, as is the * for test 4 with state predicates. Causative states present some interesting complexities with respect to tests 1 and 2. Specifically, the more active the causing state of affairs is, the better the progressive and dynamic adverbs are with causative state predicates. Consider the following contrasts.

(3.19)
a. Your attitude upsets/?is upsetting me.
a′. Your boorish behavior upsets/is upsetting me.
b. Your clothes nauseate/?are nauseating me.
b′. The smell of your clothes nauseates/is nauseating me.
c. The clown's funny hair amuses/?is amusing the children.
c′. The clown's zany antics amuse/are amusing the children.

The first sentence in each pair presents a rather static situation as the cause of the state of affairs, while the second presents a more dynamic causing state of affairs.

Table 3.2 *Tests for determining predicate classes*

Class	*Test 1*	*Test 2*	*Test 3*	*Test 4*	*Test 5*	*Test 6*
State	No	No	No	Yes*	No	No
Activity	Yes	Yes	Yes	Yes	No	No
Achievement	No	No	No*	No	No*	No
Accomplishment	Yes	No	Yes	Irrelev.	Yes	No
Active accomplishment	Yes	Yes	Yes	Irrelev.	Yes	No
Causative state	Yes*	Yes*	No	Yes	No	Yes
Causative activity	Yes	Yes	Yes	Yes	No	Yes
Causative achievement	No	Yes*	No*	No	No*	Yes
Causative accomplishment	Yes	Yes*	Yes	Irrelev.	Yes	Yes
Causative active accomplishment	Yes	Yes	Yes	Irrelev.	Yes	Yes

While none of the combinations is impossible, the progressive is better with the more dynamic causing state of affairs and worse with the more static one. Dynamic adverbs also force a dynamic reading for the causing state of affairs. For example, the sentence *The clown actively amused the children* could only be a report about the state of affairs described by (3.19c′), not (3.19c).

The basic *Aktionsart* classes are non-causative, and their causative counterparts are obviously causative. What about active accomplishments? In Foley and Van Valin (1984), for example, it was argued that active accomplishments are causative, with a sentence like *Carl ran to the store* being analyzed as 'Carl's running caused him to arrive at the store.' This is problematic, for two reasons. First, it is not a valid causative paraphrase, because there are more NPs (three) in the paraphrase than in the sentence being paraphrased (two). A valid paraphrase would be 'Carl ran and arrived at the store'. Second, if these verbs were causative, one would reasonably expect that at least some languages would use causative morphology to signal the active accomplishment use of activity verbs, but to our knowledge, none do. Indeed, if one adds causative morphology to an activity verb, the inevitable result is a causative activity, not an active accomplishment. Hence it must be concluded that active accomplishments are not causative. As noted earlier, there are causative versions of active accomplishment verbs, e.g. intransitive *march*, as in *The soldiers marched to the barracks* (plain active accomplishment), vs. transitive *march*, as in *The sergeant marched the soldiers to the barracks* (causative active accomplishment).

The 'Yes' for test 2 for causative achievements and accomplishments reflects the fact than this type of adverb is not always acceptable with these verbs. It modifies the causing activity in the logical structure. Because they are sometimes acceptable, causative accomplishments differ little from causative active accomplishments in terms of these tests. But there are important differences. First, there should always be at least some dynamic adverbs which they are compatible with, and because there are two activity predicates in the logical structure, there may be ambiguity as to which one is being modified, something which is not the case with causative accomplishments. Second, causative accomplishments are derived from a state predicate, whereas causative active accomplishments are derived from an activity predicate. Hence, if the pattern of morphological derivation relates a telic, non-punctual causative verb to a state, then it must be a causative accomplishment, whereas if the pattern relates it to an activity, then it must be a causative active accomplishment. It should also be noted that causative accomplishments are much more common than causative active accomplishments, and therefore in unclear cases it is more likely that the verb would be a causative accomplishment rather than a causative active accomplishment.

3.2.2 Lexical representations for verbs

These distinctions among the four basic *Aktionsart* types may be represented formally as in table 3.3. These representations are called **logical structures**.[12] Following the conventions of formal semantics, constants (which are normally predicates) are presented in boldface followed by a prime, whereas variable elements are presented in normal typeface. The elements in boldface + prime are part of the vocabulary of the semantic metalanguage used in the decomposition; they are not words from any particular human language. Hence the same representations are used for all languages (where appropriate), e.g. the logical structure for Lakhota *t'á* and English *die* (intr.) would be BECOME **dead′** (x). The elements in all capitals, INGR and BECOME, are modifiers of the predicate in the logical structure; their function will be explained below. The variables are filled by lexical items from the language being analyzed; for example, the English sentence *The dog died* would have the logical structure BECOME **dead′** (dog), while the corresponding Lakhota sentence *Šų́ka ki t'é* 'The dog died' would have the logical structure BECOME **dead′** (šų́ka).

States are represented as simple predicates, e.g. **broken′** (x), **be-at′** (x, y), and **see′** (x, y). There is no special formal indicator that a predicate is stative. The logical structure, **be′** (x, [**pred′**]) is for identificational constructions, e.g. *Sam is a policeman*,

Table 3.3 *Lexical representations for the basic* Aktionsart *classes*

Verb class	*Logical structure*
State	**predicate′** (x) or (x, y)
Activity	**do′** (x, [**predicate′** (x) or (x, y)])
Achievement	INGR **predicate′** (x) or (x, y)
Accomplishment	BECOME **predicate′** (x) or (x, y)

and attributive constructions, e.g. *Mary is tall.* Schwartz (1993) has shown that these constructions behave differently from result state constructions, e.g. *The watch is broken*, in a variety of languages, and therefore these predicates require a different logical structure. In this logical structure the second argument is the attribute or identificational NP, e.g. **be′** (Mary, [**tall′**]), **be′** (Sam, [**policeman′**]). The primary criteria for distinguishing between attributive constructions and result state constructions is whether the attribute is inherent, e.g. *Coal is black* (**be′** (coal, [**black′**])), or whether it is the result of some kind of process, e.g. *The fire blackened the wood* (. . . BECOME **black′** (wood)). While English uses the same copular construction for both meanings, some languages systematically distinguish them. In Tagalog (Foley and Van Valin 1984), for example, the contrast is indicated by the prefixation of the state verb, e.g. *Ma-puti ang bulaklak* (*ma*-white DET flower) 'The flower is white (it faded)' vs. *Puti ang bulaklak* 'The flower is (naturally) white.' The bare stem is used for the attributive construction, and *ma-* is prefixed to it when the property is the result of some kind of process. Accordingly the logical structure for the first example would be **white′** (bulaklak) and for the second it would be **be′** (bulaklak, [**white′**]). Hence if the state predicate is not conceived of as being the result of a process, then the **be′** (x, [**pred′**]) logical structure should be used. **Be′** should not be confused with English *be* or copular verbs in other languages. It is used for logical structures with specific meanings, and its occurrence in a logical structure does not entail that the sentence realizing the logical structure should have a copula or the like. (See the Lakhota and Russian examples at the beginning of section 2.2.1.) The **pred′** element in the second argument position will constitute the nucleus in the clause (see section 2.2.1). The logical structure **feel′** (x, [**pred′**]) is used for internal sensations and transient emotional states, e.g. *I feel sad* (**feel′** (I, [**sad′**])), *She feels sick* (**feel′** (she, [**sick′**])). This is different from e.g. *she has gotten sick* (BECOME **sick′** (she)), which describes a physical state or condition, and not the internal sensations of the subject. It is, of course, possible to feel sick but not be sick, and vice versa. Some other languages also make this distinction explicitly. In Bonggi, a Western Austronesian language spoken in Malaysia (Boutin 1994), stative stems are affixed differently depending upon whether they are condition statives or experiential statives, e.g. the stem *ramig* 'cold' can appear as *me-ramig* if it is a condition stative with a meaning like 'cold to the touch' (e.g. *Sia me-ramig* [3sgNOM cold] 'it is cold') or as *rimig-adn* if it is an experiential stative with the meaning 'feel cold' (e.g. *Ou rimig-adn* [1sgNOM cold] 'I am/feel cold'). In the syntactic realization of such sentences in English, the nucleus will contain both *feel* and the **pred′** element, e.g. [$_{\text{NUC}}$ feel sad], [$_{\text{NUC}}$ feel sick].

All activity logical structures contain the generalized activity predicate **do′**, which serves as the marker of membership in this class, e.g. *sing* **do′** (x, [**sing′** (x)]), *run* **do′** (x, [**run′** (x)]), *eat* **do′** (x, [**eat′** (x, y)]). It should be noted that **sing′**, **run′** and **eat′** are not state predicates; they are activity predicates which always cooccur with **do′**, which is a two-argument predicate, i.e. **do′** (x, y), filling the second argument position. If the second argument position is left unspecified, i.e. **do′** (x, ∅), then this is the logical structure for an unspecified activity, as in English *Sally does/did.* It might seem odd to posit such a complex structure for simple verbs like *run* and *sing*, but in fact there are numerous languages which construct activity predications in just this way. Basque is a particularly good example of this. Almost all verbal expressions corresponding to intransitive activity verbs in languages like English are created by combining a noun with the verb *egin* 'do, make', as illustrated in (3.20) from Levin (1989).

(3.20) a. Ni-k lan-∅ egin d-u-t.
1sg-ERG work-ABS do 3sgABS-AUX-1sgERG
'I worked.' (lit. 'I did work')

b. Other combinations:

amets egin	'to dream'	*amets*	'dream'
barre egin	'to laugh'	*barre*	'laugh'
hitz egin	'to speak'	*hitz*	'word'
igeri egin	'to swim'	*igeri*	'swim'
lo egin	'to sleep'	*lo*	'sleep'
negar egin	'to cry'	*negar*	'tear'

Nouns like *lan* 'work' and *hitz* 'word' fill the second argument position in the logical structure of *egin*, which would be **do′** (x, y), to create activity predicates. Even English provides some evidence for this second argument position: first, it can be filled by a pronoun referring to a known state of affairs in the context, e.g. *Dana might do it*; and second, it can be filled by an interrogative WH-word in questions about actions, e.g. *What did they do*? States and activities are the most basic classes, semantically; they are the building blocks for all other classes.

Achievement and accomplishment verbs are composed of a state or activity predicate plus a symbol for change. 'INGR' is derived from 'ingressive' and encodes instantaneous changes; these may be changes of state or activity. Accomplishments are coded by BECOME, which codes change over some temporal span, plus a state predicate, e.g. *melt* (intr.) BECOME **melted′** (x), *sink* (intr.) BECOME **sunk′** (x). Examples of punctual changes of state include *explode* (intr.) INGR **exploded′** (x) and *shatter* (intr.) INGR **shattered′** (x). We have to look to other languages for good examples of inchoative or inceptive activities. Georgian (Holisky 1981a, b) has verbs of this type, e.g. *at'irdeba* 'he will begin to cry' (INGR **do′** (x, [**cry′** (x)])) vs. *t'iris* 'he is crying' (**do′** (x, [**cry′** (x)])), *ak'ank'aldeba* 'he will begin to tremble' (INGR **do′** (x, [**tremble′** (x)])) vs. *k'ank'alebs* 'he is trembling' (**do′** (x, [**tremble′** (x)])). Russian also has verbs of this kind: *govorit′* 'speak' (**do′** (x, [**speak′** (x)])) vs. *zagovorit′* 'start to speak' (BECOME **do′** (x, [**speak′** (x)])), *'plakat'* 'cry' vs. *zaplakat′* 'burst out crying' (INGR **do′** (x, [**cry′** (x)])). In Georgian and Russian an important clue as to whether the derived inceptives are punctual or not comes from their range of inflectional forms. According to Holisky, most derived inceptives in Georgian do not have imperfective forms, but a few do (all are derived from states rather than activities), e.g. *civa* 'it is cold' vs. *acivdeba* 'it will become cold'.[13] In Russian, *zagovorit'* 'start to talk' has an imperfective form, *zagovoryvat'* 'be starting to talk', whereas *zaplakat'* 'burst out crying' and *zasmejat'sja* 'burst out laughing' do not; hence *zaplakat'* and *zasmejat'sja* are punctual (achievements), while *zagovoryvat'* is non-punctual (accomplishment).[14] Hausa (Abdoulaye 1992) also has inceptive activity verbs, e.g. *ruugàa* 'start running'. Japanese has a suffix *-dasu* which derives inceptive activity verbs, e.g. *tabe-dasu* 'start to eat' (< *taberu* 'eat'), *hanasi-dasu* 'start to talk' (< *hanasu* 'talk') and *hasiri-dasu* 'start to run' (< *hasiru* 'run'). Pirahã (Everett 1986), has distinct inceptive markers for states and activities: *-hoi* for initiation of an action and *-hoag* for the beginning of a state, e.g. *xaitá-hóí* (sleep-*hoi*) 'go to sleep, fall asleep', *biioabá-hóág* (tired-*hoag*) 'get tired'.

Examples of some English verbs with their logical structures are given in (3.21).

(3.21) a. *States*

Leon is a fool.	**be'** (Leon, [**fool'**])
The window is shattered.	**shattered'** (window)
Fred is at the house.	**be-at'** (house, Fred)
John saw the picture.	**see'** (John, picture)

b. *Activities*

The children cried.	**do'** (children, [**cry'** (children)])
The wheel squeaks.	**do'** (wheel, [**squeak'** (wheel)])
John ate fish.	**do'** (John, [**eat'** (John, fish)])

c. *Achievements*

The window shattered.	INGR **shattered'** (window)
The balloon popped.	INGR **popped'** (balloon)
John glimpsed the picture.	INGR **see'** (John, picture)

d. *Accomplishments*

The snow melted.	BECOME **melted'** (snow)
The sky reddened.	BECOME **red'** (sky)
Mary learned French.	BECOME **know'** (Mary, French)

An important issue arises with respect to achievement and accomplishment verbs. Some verbs are necessarily punctual, e.g. *pop* or *shatter*, while others are necessarily temporally durative, e.g. *dry* or *grow*. In between these two groups there are many verbs which code states of affairs which may be virtually instantaneous but need not be, e.g. *break* (intr.). In the same way there are verbs coding states of affairs which are normally not instantaneous but could be under certain circumstances, e.g. freezing normally takes place over a period of time, but if one dipped something into a vat of liquid nitrogen, the freezing would be virtually instantaneous. Should, therefore, verbs like *freeze* be represented as both INGR **frozen'**

(x) and BECOME **frozen′** (x)? The answer is 'no', for the following reason. With respect to the feature [±punctual], achievements are the marked member of the opposition, i.e. they are [+punctual], while accomplishments are unmarked, i.e. they are [–punctual]. It is well established that the unmarked member of a privative opposition covers a much greater range than the marked member, which has a very specific property. Hence, a [+punctual] verb must code states of affairs which are always instantaneous (or very close to it), whereas a [–punctual] verb may code a state of affairs with a temporal duration ranging from very short (nearly instantaneous) to very long. Since the states of affairs expressed by *freeze* can cover this range of temporal possibilities, it should be considered an accomplishment with the logical structure BECOME **frozen′** (x). Among the non-punctual verbs, it is necessary to recognize that the default interpretation of a verb can fall in different places along the temporal range. For example, *arrive* is normally construed punctually, but it can, in the appropriate context, be construed non-punctually. *Freeze*, on the other hand, has a default interpretation at the other end of the range, as we noted above. *Break* seems to be neutral, and its interpretation is a function of the properties of the object broken; if it is brittle or hard, e.g. a window, then it is likely to have a punctual interpretation, whereas if it is non-brittle and somewhat soft, e.g. a green stick or tree branch, it is likely to have a more durative interpretation.

A change of state verb may be punctual in one language and non-punctual in another. A good example of this cross-linguistic variation is English *die* vs. Mandarin *sǐ*. Both have the result that the subject is dead, but they differ in that the Mandarin verb is punctual, while the English verb need not be. Accordingly, it is possible to say in English *He died quickly/slowly* and *He died suddenly*, while in Mandarin **Tā sǐ de kuài* 'He died quickly' is impossible. Hence the logical structure for English *die* would be BECOME **dead′** (x), an accomplishment, while the logical structure for Mandarin *sǐ* would be INGR **dead′** (x), an achievement. Another example of this is the contrast between the Japanese verbs *ik-* 'go' and *k-* 'come' and their English counterparts. Applying tests like those in table 3.1, Hasegawa (1992, 1996) shows that the Japanese verbs are *punctual* and therefore achievements. English *go* and *come*, on the other hand, are not punctual, are telic and cooccur with adverbs like *quickly* or *slowly* but not with ones like *vigorously* or *actively*; hence they are accomplishments. The same contrast holds between the verb *likma* in Belhare, a Tibeto-Burman language, and its English counterpart *enter*: the Belhare verb is punctual, while the English one is not (Bickel 1995). Here again it is clear that determining the *Aktionsart* of a verb is not a matter of looking at the state of affairs it depicts; rather, it is a *linguistic* property which can be determined only by means of *linguistic* tests like those in table 3.1.

It was mentioned in the previous section that each of these *Aktionsart* types has a corresponding causative type; the examples from (3.16) are repeated below.

(3.16) a. State — The boy is afraid.
a′. Causative state — The dog frightens/scares the boy.
b. Achievement — The balloon popped.
b′. Causative achievement — The cat popped the balloon.
c. Accomplishment — The ice melted.
c′. Causative accomplishment — The hot water melted the ice.
d. Activity — The ball bounced around the room.
d′. Causative activity — The girl bounced the ball around the room.

In order to represent the causative verbs, we will assume that their logical structure contains CAUSE, the second argument of which is the logical structure of the basic verb or predicate.[15] This is illustrated in (3.22).

(3.22) a. [. . .] CAUSE [**feel′** (boy, [**afraid′**])] = (3.16a′)
b. [. . .] CAUSE [INGR **popped′** (balloon)] = (3.16b′)
c. [. . .] CAUSE [BECOME **melted′** (ice)] = (3.16c′)
d. [. . .] CAUSE [**do′** (ball, [**bounce′** (ball)])] = (3.16d′)

What is '[. . .]', the first argument of CAUSE? Is it an individual or some kind of state of affairs? This is a point about which there is much disagreement among semanticists, both in philosophy and linguistics. If we look back briefly at the complex induced states of affairs in (3.3) and (3.4), we see that there are many instances in which one state of affairs brings about another, and therefore we will assume that what fills '[. . .]' in the causative logical structures may be the logical structure of a state, activity, achievement or accomplishment verb. This is illustrated in (3.23).

(3.23) a. Bill's owning a gun frightened Martha.
a′. [**have′** (Bill, gun)] CAUSE [**feel′** (Martha, [**afraid′**])]
b. The balloon's popping startled the baby.
b′. [INGR **popped′** (balloon)] CAUSE [INGR **startled′** (baby)]
c. The warming of the earth's atmosphere melted the arctic snowpack.
c′. [BECOME **warm′** (earth's atmosphere)] CAUSE [BECOME **melted′** (arctic snowpack)]
d. The dog's barking scared the boy.
d′. [**do′** (dog, [**bark′** (dog)])] CAUSE [**feel′** (boy, [**afraid′**])]

In all of these cases the nature of the cause is specified in the sentence, but in many instances it is not, e.g. *Max broke the window*. This sentence tells us that Max did the breaking and the window broke, but it does not specify exactly what Max did to break the window, as discussed in section 3.1. Such an unspecified action is represented in logical structure as '**do′** (x, ∅)', and accordingly the logical structure for *Max broke the window* would be as in (3.24).

(3.24) a. Max broke the window.
b. [**do′** (Max, ∅)] CAUSE [BECOME **broken′** (window)].

Further examples of causative constructions from English, French, Italian (Centineo 1995) and Mandarin (Hansell 1993) are given in (3.25). We will discuss the syntax of these examples in detail in chapter 8.

(3.25) a. Hakeem pushed open the door.
a′. [**do′** (Hakeem, [**push′** (Hakeem, door)])] CAUSE [BECOME **open′** (door)]
b. Pierre fer-a cour-ir Marie.
make-3sgFUT run-INF
'Pierre will make Marie run.'
b′. [**do′** (Pierre, ∅)] CAUSE [**do′** (Marie, [**run′** (Marie)])]
c. Tonino fece affonda-re la barca.
make.PAST.3sg sink-INF the.Fsg boat
'Tonino made the boat sink.'
c′. [**do′** (Tonino, ∅)] CAUSE [BECOME **sunk′** (barca)]
d. Tā qiāo pò le yī ge fànwǎn.
3sg hit break PRFV one CL bowl
'She broke (by hitting) a ricebowl.'
d′. [**do′** (3sg, [**hit′** (3sg, fànwǎn)])] CAUSE [BECOME **broken′** (fànwǎn)][16]

These constructions are illuminating, in that they show that what in some instances is coded by a single lexical verb, e.g. *sink*, *break* (trans.), can be expressed by a complex expression involving more than one verb. The Mandarin example is particularly interesting, since it involves a causing activity and an accomplishment (*pò* 'break' is always intransitive). It recalls the Lakhota forms discussed at the beginning of the chapter; they too were composed of a prefix signaling the nature of the causing activity and then a state predicate indicating the result state. These constructions, both morphological (Lakhota) and syntactic (Mandarin), show how the logical structure of causatives may be reflected more directly in the overt form of the sentence than in a language like English.

We may now restate the basic set of lexical representations, including causatives and active accomplishments (see table 3.4). Active accomplishments are included here, because some verbs have this as their basic *Aktionsart* type, e.g. Italian *andare* 'go', which always involves motion to a goal (Centineo 1986). There are two additional logical structure elements that must be introduced. The first is NOT, which occurs in the logical structure of verbs like *remove*, *drain* and *take* (as in *x took y from z*). This is illustrated in (3.26).

(3.26) a. Sally removed the book from the table.
a′. [**do′** (Sally, ∅)] CAUSE [BECOME NOT **be-on′** (table, book)][17]
b. Tom took the knife from the prisoner.
b′. [**do′** (Tom, ∅)] CAUSE [BECOME NOT **have′** (prisoner, knife)]

Table 3.4 *Lexical representations for* Aktionsart *classes (revised)*

Verb class	*Logical structure*
State	**predicate′** (x) or (x, y)
Activity	**do′** (x, [**predicate′** (x) or (x, y)])
Achievement	INGR **predicate′** (x) or (x, y), *or* INGR **do′** (x, [**predicate′** (x) or (x, y)])
Accomplishment	BECOME **predicate′** (x) or (x, y), *or* BECOME **do′** (x, [**predicate′** (x) or (x, y)])
Active accomplishment	**do′** (x, [**predicate$_1$′** (x, (y))]) & BECOME **predicate$_2$′** (z, x) or (y)
Causative	α CAUSE β, where α, β are LSs of any type

The second element is '&', meaning 'and then'. The logical structure in (3.26b′) does not tell the whole story of the state of affairs depicted by the sentence, since it entails that Tom ended up having the knife in his possession. In order to represent this, we need '&', as in (3.27).

(3.27) [**do′** (Tom, Ø)] CAUSE [BECOME NOT **have′** (prisoner, knife) & BECOME **have′** (Tom, knife)]

This should be read as meaning that Tom does something that causes (i) the prisoner to lose possession of the knife and (ii) Tom to come into possession of it. In general, '&' may be used to express the successive states of affairs involved in motion and transfers of possession, i.e. initial situation (location, possession) → subsequent situation (location, possession). '∧' may be used in the logical structure of verbs of transformation like *carve* in which there are simultaneous changes of state, as illustrated in (3.28).[18]

(3.28) a. The man carved the log into a canoe.
b. The man carved the canoe out of a log.
c. [**do′** (man, [**carve′** (man, log)])] CAUSE [BECOME NOT **exist′** (log) ∧ BECOME **exist′** (canoe)]

In this complex process, a log is acted upon by a man and, as it ceases to be a log, it becomes a canoe. Hence there are two simultaneous changes taking place, and this is expressed in the logical structure by 'BECOME NOT **exist′** (log) ∧ BECOME **exist′** (canoe).

This theory of lexical representation is extremely powerful yet highly constrained, and it is well supported by much cross-linguistic study. We have already seen examples from Lakhota, Qiang, Georgian, French, Russian, Tepehua and other languages of how languages may derive at least some of the verbs in one class from those in another class. The patterns found in these languages are summarized in (3.29).

(3.29)	a. State → accomplishment	Qiang, Tepehua, Pirahã
	b. Activity → accomplishment (i.e. 'start to V')	Georgian, Japanese, Russian, Pirahã
	c. Activity → active accomplishment	Georgian, Russian, Pirahã
	d. Accomplishment → causative accomplishment	Qiang, Lakhota
	e. State → causative accomplishment	Tepehua, Lakhota
	f. Causative accomplishment → accomplishment	French, Russian, Yagua
	g. Causative accomplishment → state	French, Russian
	h. Activity → causative activity	Tepehua, Lakhota
	i. State → causative state	Japanese, Lakhota, Barai

From a lexical semantic point of view, one of the advantages of this system of lexical decomposition is that it makes the task of representation more manageable, because detailed definitions need be formulated only for the primitive predicates. If there is an adequate semantic representation, for example, of *cool* as a state, one need not say anything more about the interpretation of *cool* as an accomplishment verb. It is necessary only to take the representation of the state predicate and add BECOME, which has a well-defined meaning attached to it, in order to derive the accomplishment form of the verb. In addition, its argument structure does not change in the transition from state to accomplishment. Hence nothing needs to be stated about the argument structure of the derived form. In other words, if there is an adequate definition of *be cool*, the meanings of both *cool* intransitive and *cool* transitive fall out from this because they are additions of a well-defined semantic modifier (BECOME) and a well-defined predicate-connective (CAUSE) to the basic lexical predicate. In a similar way, the lexical semantic theory does not need to have a representation for *kill*; it only needs a representation for *dead*, and then *kill* will fall out from this scheme because there are well-defined meanings for CAUSE and BECOME. It will be necessary to have an interpretation of **do′** (x, ∅), since there is no specification of the nature of the causing activity, but that is relatively straightforward. Because of this, there is no need to worry about the meaning of *kill* or the meaning of *die*. An investigation of possible decompositional schemes for the representation of the basic state and activity predicates in logical structures will not be undertaken here; the discussion will proceed with the representations in table 3.3, (3.21) and (3.23). Van Valin and Wilkins (1993) present a sketch of what a decompositional system for the state predicates would look like.

How should the accomplishment uses of activity verbs be represented in logical structure? To begin with, we note that these accomplishments are like plain accomplishments (e.g. *melt*, *freeze*) in that they are telic and take place over time; they differ from them in that they are more active and can cooccur with the dynamic adverbs like *actively*, *intensely*, etc. As we saw earlier, they are not causative. They fall generally into two types: verbs of motion and verbs of creation/consumption. For motion verbs, we need to represent the motion plus the change of location over time. This can be done as in (3.30).

(3.30) a. **do′** (x, [**run′** (x)]) — Activity
b. **do′** (x, [**run′** (x)]) & BECOME **be-at′** (y, x) — Active accomplishment
c. Paul ran to the store.
c′. **do′** (Paul, [**run′** (Paul)]) & BECOME **be-at′** (store, Paul)

This logical structure represents both the activity and accomplishment facets of the sentence. For verbs of creation, e.g. *write, paint, build*, etc., the result of the activity is the coming into being of some specific entity, e.g. *write a poem/letter/novel, paint a picture/portrait, build a house/model*, etc. This may be represented by adding an accomplishment logical structure expressing the coming into being of the entity.

(3.31) a. John wrote poetry. — Activity
a′. **do′** (John, [**write′** (John, poetry)])
b. John wrote a poem. — Active accomplishment
b′. **do′** (John, [**write′** (John, poem)]) & BECOME **exist′** (poem)

For verbs of consumption, e.g. *eat*, *drink*, *read*, the situation is similar, except that the result is that a preexisting entity has been consumed rather than created.

(3.32) a. Carl drank beer. — Activity
a′. **do′** (Carl, [**drink′** (Carl, beer)])
b. Carl drank a beer. — Active accomplishment
b′. **do′** (Carl, [**drink′** (Carl, beer)]) & BECOME **consumed′** (beer)

In these logical structures two related predicates appear, an activity predicate, e.g. **write′**, and a state predicate, e.g. **exist′**. This is because active accomplishments involve both an activity and a result state, and since the result state is a function of the activity, it seems reasonable to represent them in this way. These alternations may be summarized as in (3.33).

(3.33) a. *Motion verbs*
do′ (x, [**pred′** (x)]) ↔ **do′** (x, [**pred′** (x)]) & BECOME **be-LOC′** (y, x)
b. *Creation/consumption verbs*
do′ (x, [**pred′** (x, y)]) ↔ **do′** (x, [**pred′** (x, y)]) & BECOME **pred′** (y)

One of the questions that comes up here is whether an alternating verb like *eat* is really an activity or an active accomplishment; in other words, should it be represented in its lexical entry as an activity or an active accomplishment? Or should it be represented twice, once as an activity and once as an active accomplishment? With verbs like *run*, *eat* and *write*, the activity verb gives its name to the main semantic substance in the logical structure, and the accomplishment part is very general; in the case of consumption and creation verbs, the interpretation of the logical structure is dependent upon the semantic content of the activity part, as in the logical structures of *write* in (3.31b) and *drink* in (3.32b). In other words, the semantically general part in the active accomplishment structure which is not specific to particular verbs is in the accomplishment part, while the primary verb-specific lexical content is in the activity part. This suggests that these verbs are basically activities which may be used as accomplishments. Additional evidence for this analysis comes from their interpretation when used with bare plural or mass noun objects. When causative accomplishment verbs like *kill* or *break* are used with bare plural or mass noun objects, they pattern like activity verbs with respect to the *Aktionsart* tests, but they always have an iterative interpretation, e.g. *kill bears* or *break windows* always refers to multiple instances of killing or breaking, due to the fact that these verbs are necessarily telic. When verbs like *eat* and *drink* are used the same way, e.g. *eat peanuts*, they do not have to have an iterative interpretation; that is, it is possible to interpret *eat peanuts* as one single act of eating (non-iterative) or as a series of single acts of eating (iterative). This option is available because *eat* is not inherently telic, unlike *kill* and *break*; hence it must be analyzed as an activity verb, with an active accomplishment use. If we look at the Russian and Georgian verbs mentioned above, we see that the underived, base form of each verb is the activity form, not the active accomplishment form, and therefore we may conclude that in Russian 'eat' (*est'*) and Georgian 'write' (*c'er*) are basically activity verbs, with derived active accomplishment forms. Given how general the relationship between the two types of verbs is, as captured in (3.33), simply listing two forms of each verb in the lexicon would entail the loss of a linguistically significant generalization.

The crucial point to be emphasized again is that it is necessary to distinguish the basic lexical meaning of a verb, e.g. *eat* as an activity verb, from its meaning in a particular context, e.g. *eat a slice of pizza* as an active accomplishment predication. The former would be its representation in its lexical entry in the lexicon, whereas the latter would be the representation of the core of the clause in which *eat* appears. Moreover, a given logical structure is intended to represent a particular meaning or interpretation of a lexical item; it is not necessarily the case that there is a single logical structure underlying all of the uses of a particular verbal lexical item. For a polysemous verb each meaning would be associated with a different logical structure; for example, *take* in the sense of 'obtain' or 'get' (as in (3.27)) would have a different logical structure from *take* in the sense of 'carry'. There are other cases in which a verb is ambiguous between two related meanings, as with Lakhota *t'a*, which can mean either 'be dead' (state) or 'die' (accomplishment). This is a systematic ambiguity throughout the verbal system of Lakhota: many non-activity intransitive verbs can have either state or change-of-state readings. The simplest solution would be to posit '(BECOME) **dead'** (x)' as the logical structure for *t'a*, the parentheses indicating that BECOME is optional. This is different from the situation with *run*, *eat* or *write*, because a sentence like *Igmú ki t'é* (cat the *t'a*) is simply ambiguous between 'The cat is/was dead' and 'The cat dies/died.' Logical structures are associated fundamentally with the meanings which verbs express, not with the verbs themselves. We will discuss this issue further in section 4.6. We will discuss the composition of the semantic representation of whole clauses in section 4.8.

Having presented the system of lexical representation for verbs and other predicating elements, we now turn to the semantic interpretation of the arguments in the logical structures.

3.2.3 The semantics of predicate–argument relations

It was stated at the end of section 3.1 that the role that an entity plays in a state of affairs is a function of the nature of the state of affairs, and accordingly, it is also the case that the semantic interpretation of an argument is a function of the logical structure in which it is found. This is a fundamental point of great importance, and it cannot be emphasized strongly enough. The interpretation of an argument depends, first and foremost, on the verb or predicating element it occurs with. What is this interpretation? It is the semantic counterpart to the participant roles discussed in section 3.1. If Jack is the agent in an action, then the NP referring to him should be interpreted as the controlling and instigating argument of the verb. The semantic relations between a predicate and its arguments which express the participant roles in the state of affairs denoted by the verb are called **thematic relations**.[19] The labels usually used for thematic relations are basically the same as those used for participant roles on pages 85–6, and in order to avoid confusing the two types of roles, we will give participant roles in normal typeface and thematic relations in small capitals. Thus, 'patient' will refer to a participant role, while 'PATIENT' will refer to a thematic relation; the first refers to the role a participant plays in a state of affairs, whereas the second refers to the semantic interpretation of an argument in a logical structure and in a sentence. Thematic relations are linguistic entities, i.e. they are part of natural-language semantics, while participant roles are not; they are properties of states of affairs in the world. As we saw at the end of section 3.1, it is crucial to make this distinction and to motivate linguistic entities on linguistic grounds. It is not legitimate to argue that a verb needs to have a particular kind of argument solely because the state of affairs it denotes may have a specific kind of participant; as the discussion of (3.6)–(3.9) showed, verbs in different languages which may be used to refer to the same state of affairs may have quite different properties. The thematic relations associated with a verb must be justified on linguistic grounds first and foremost.

Following the proposal in Jackendoff (1976), thematic relations will be defined in terms of argument positions in logical structures. In the system we are developing here, only two types of predicate define thematic relations, states and activities; all of the other types are composed of these two basic types (see table 3.4). There are many subtypes of state and activity verbs, and only a small list of each will be discussed here. Levin (1993) presents a rich taxonomy of verb classes in English. Since all thematic relations are defined in terms of argument positions in state and activity predicates, it is necessary to look at the subclasses of these two types. There are at least ten subclasses of state predicates. 'State or condition' includes predicates like *being sick*, *being shattered* and *being broken*. State or condition verbs take one argument, as do predicates of existence, whereas all the others take two arguments (see section 3.2.3.4 below). There are no tests like those in table 3.2 to distinguish the various subtypes of state predicates, and accordingly it must be ascertained from the meaning alone whether a verb is a perception verb, as opposed to a cognition or possession verb. If the verb denotes a perceptual event of some kind, then we assume it is a perception verb; if it denotes a cognitive event, then it is a cognition verb, and so on. There are at least as many subtypes of activity predicates as there are of state predicates, and representing the distinctions among the state and activity predicates requires a more detailed decomposition than this schema provides. Based on these subtypes of activity and state predicates, a (non-exhaustive) list of possible thematic relations is given in table 3.5.

Each of the argument positions in the logical structures defines a thematic relation, and it is necessary to refer to the arguments as 'first argument' or 'second argument' when there is more than one. In table 3.5, 'first argument' refers to the *x* arguments in the logical structures, and 'second argument' refers to the *y* arguments. Role labels like 'EFFECTOR', 'COGNIZER', 'THEME' and 'PERFORMER' are merely mnemonics for argument positions in logical structure. Because there is as yet no adequate decompositional representation for the primitive state and activity predicates which are the building blocks of the system and carry the substantive semantic load, these labels are useful in that they designate the subclass of the predicate; hence 'EXPERIENCER' means 'first argument of a two-place state predicate of internal experience', 'POSSESSED' means 'second argument of a two-place state predicate of possession' and 'OBSERVER' means 'first argument of an activity predicate of directed perception', for example. Thus, the interpretation of an argument is a function of (1) the class or subclass of the predicate and (2) its position in the logical structure. For instance, if a verb is an accomplishment, it takes the appropriate state logical structure, and there is no change in the argument structure. In both *x is dry* and *x dried*, *x* is a PATIENT, and the logical structures are, respectively, **dry′** (x) and BECOME **dry′** (x). The thematic relation of *x* is not affected by the addition of

Table 3.5 *Definitions of thematic relations in terms of LS argument positions*

I *State verbs*		
A Single argument		
1 State or condition	**broken′** (x)	x = PATIENT
2 Existence	**exist′** (x)	x = ENTITY
B Two arguments		
1 Pure location	**be-**LOC′ (x, y)	x = LOCATION, y = THEME
2 Perception	**hear′** (x, y)	x = PERCEIVER, y = STIMULUS
3 Cognition	**know′** (x, y)	x = COGNIZER, y = CONTENT
4 Desire	**want′** (x, y)	x = WANTER, y = DESIRE
5 Propositional attitude	**consider′** (x, y)	x = JUDGER, y = JUDGMENT
6 Possession	**have′** (x, y)	x = POSSESSOR, y = POSSESSED
7 Internal experience	**feel′** (x, y)	x = EXPERIENCER, y = SENSATION
8 Emotion	**love′** (x, y)	x = EMOTER, y = TARGET
9 Attrib./identificational	**be′** (x, y)	x = ATTRIBUTANT, y = ATTRIBUTE
II *Activity verbs*		
A Single argument		
1 Unspecified action	**do′** (x, Ø)	x = EFFECTOR
2 Motion	**do′** (x, [**walk′** (x)])	x = MOVER
3 Static motion	**do′** (x, [**spin′** (x)])	x = ST-MOVER
4 Light emission	**do′** (x, [**shine′** (x)])	x = L-EMITTER
5 Sound emission	**do′** (x, [**gurgle′** (x)])	x = S-EMITTER
B One or two arguments		
1 Performance	**do′** (x, [**sing′** (x, (y))])	x = PERFORMER, y = PERFORMANCE
2 Consumption	**do′** (x, [**eat′** (x, (y))])	x = CONSUMER, y = CONSUMED
3 Creation	**do′** (x, [**write′** (x, (y))])	x = CREATOR, y = CREATION
4 Repetitive action	**do′** (x, [**tap′** (x, (y))])	x = EFFECTOR, y = LOCUS
5 Directed perception	**do′** (x, [**see′** (x, (y))])	x = OBSERVER, y = STIMULUS
6 Use	**do′** (x, [**use′** (x, y)])	x = USER, y = IMPLEMENT

BECOME. In the case of causative verbs, the argument structure is the sum of the arguments of the composite predicates.

The implications of this scheme for deriving thematic relations from logical structures are very important. If it is the case that the thematic relations which a verb takes are a function of the argument positions in its logical structure, and there is a system of lexical representation in which there are independent criteria for assigning logical structures to verbs, then there are independent criteria for assigning thematic relations to verbs. This is the case because the thematic relations are a function of the logical structure of a verb, and there are independent criteria for attributing a logical structure to a verb. Thematic relations cannot be assigned on an arbitrary basis, because logical structures cannot be assigned arbitrarily; rather, logical structures are determined on the basis of the tests in table 3.2. Thus the great advantage of this system of lexical representation is that there are tests which provide independent criteria for assigning a particular logical structure and hence a particular argument structure to a given verb.

This scheme also has important implications for how one actually goes about analyzing a language. In order to determine the argument structure of a verb, it is first necessary to ascertain its *Aktionsart* in the construction in which it occurs, using the tests in table 3.2. Having established that, its logical structure can be created, following table 3.4, and its argument structure follows from table 3.5. What is *not* appropriate in this system is to decide arbitrarily what thematic relations a verb should have and then to construct a logical structure which would yield those roles.

It is important to remember that in the system being developed, thematic relations play no direct role in lexical representation; the relevant semantic properties of the verbs are expressed by the decompositional logical structure representations, not by the thematic relations. We will continue to use these labels as mnemonics for argument positions in logical structure for the sake of convenience,[20] but it should be kept clearly in mind that these do not refer to independently meaningful thematic relations but rather to argument positions in the logical structure of predicates of a certain type.

In the next five sections, we will examine how certain groups of participant roles are expressed semantically through different logical structure combinations.

3.2.3.1 Verbs of saying and their arguments

Verbs of saying constitute an important subclass of activity verbs, but their complexity precludes a simple listing in table 3.5; Wierzbicka (1987), for example, lists thirty-eight subclasses of verbs of saying in English. We will be concerned here with *speak*, *say*, *talk*, *discuss* and *tell*, and it will be necessary to posit a more complex decomposition than we have done to this point, in order to capture important similarities among them; we will follow the general approach of Van Valin and Wilkins (1993). The problem verbs of saying raise for the decomposition we have been using is this: the second argument varies rather dramatically in its interpretation. With *talk*, for example, it is the addressee, whereas with *discuss* it is the topic of the conversation. Some verbs of saying take a metalinguistic noun, e.g. *word*, *syllable*, as in *say a few words*, while others take what we will call an 'utterance noun', e.g. *story*, *joke*, *rumor*, *statement*, as in *tell a story/joke about Frank*. Some can take indirect discourse complements (*that*-clauses), as in *say that it will rain*, *tell Sandy that it will rain*.

We propose to unite all of these different verbs of saying in a single, general logical structure, and the differences among them will fall out from the way the variables in the representation are interpreted. The general logical structure is given in (3.34).

(3.34) **do′** (x, [**express**(α)**.to.**(β)**.in.language.**(γ)**′** (x, y)])

The interpretation of the *x* argument is unproblematic; it defines the SPEAKER thematic relation for all verbs of saying. The new elements in the decomposition are the internal variables α, β and γ. They refer to the content of the utterance (α), which may be a metalinguistic noun, an utterance noun, a noun referring to a topic of the conversation, or an indirect discourse complement, the addressee (β), and the language used (γ). They are called *internal* variables because they are within the semantic representation of the verb, and they are variables because they represent a range of possibilities for that facet of the semantic content of the verb, e.g. the three possibilities for α mentioned above. One dimension along which speech act verbs may vary is which of these must or may be expressed and how they are expressed. The most minimal possible expression involves expression of *x* alone and none of the internal variables: *Sandy spoke. Speak* allows each of the three internal variables to be expressed as the *y* argument along with the SPEAKER, as in (3.35).

(3.35)	a. Sandy spoke but a few words.	$y=\alpha$
	b. Sandy spoke to Kim.	$y=\beta$
	c. Sandy spoke Telegu.	$y=\gamma$

We may summarize the selectional properties of these five verbs of saying as in (3.36).

(3.36)	a. *speak*	$y=\alpha$	$\alpha=$ metalinguistic noun	e.g. (3.35a)
		$y=\beta$		e.g. (3.35b)
		$y=\gamma$		e.g. (3.35c)
	b. *say*	$y=\alpha$	$\alpha=$ metalinguistic noun,	see above
			indirect discourse complement	see above
	c. *talk*	$y=\beta$		e.g. *talk to Kim*
		$y=\gamma$		e.g. *talk Cajun*
	d. *discuss*	$y=\alpha$	$\alpha=$ topic noun	e.g. *discuss the situation*
	e. *tell*	$y=\alpha$	$\alpha=$ utterance noun	e.g. *tell a joke*
		$y=\beta$		e.g. *tell Kim*

With some verbs it is also possible to realize the internal variables as oblique core arguments (PPs), as illustrated in (3.37).

(3.37) a. speak a few words to Sandy — *to* PP = β
b. speak to Sandy about Kim — *to* PP = β, *about* PP = α
c. say to Robin that . . . — *to* PP = β
d. talk to Pat about Sandy — *about* PP = α
e. tell a joke to Pat — *to* PP = β

The verb *tell* differs from the other four by virtue of its telicity; it is the only verb that can take an *in* PP (test 5) with the relevant meaning. The others are all activity verbs. It seems to be inherently causative, as the following paraphrase reveals: *Sandy told Kim that Robin would arrive soon* = 'Sandy's speaking made Kim become aware that Robin would arrive soon'. Accordingly, the logical structure for *tell* is that given in (3.38).

(3.38) [**do′** (x, [**express.(α).to.(β).in.language.(γ)′** (x, y)])] CAUSE [BECOME **aware.of′** (y, z)], where $y = \beta$, $z = \alpha$

Thus, the advantage of positing internal variables is that it allows us to see how the different verbs of saying realize different aspects of the basic representation in (3.34); otherwise, we would be forced to posit numerous homophonous verbs of saying, three just for *speak*, as (3.35) shows.

3.2.3.2 Agents, effectors, instruments and forces

Activity verbs raise a number of interesting issues. While the first argument of activity verbs receives a different thematic relation label with each subclass, the first arguments are all alike in that they are all doing something. As we saw in the *Aktionsart* tests in table 3.2, these verbs cooccur with adverbs like *vigorously* and *actively*, and these adverbs modify the action that the first argument is doing. There is a generalized activity verb in many languages, e.g. English *do*, Korean *ha*, Basque *egin* and Thai *thaam*, and the first argument of this verb is an EFFECTOR. This labels the participant that brings something about, but there is no implication of its being volitional or the original instigator. It is simply the effecting participant. It need not be animate. It would be appropriate to say that all of the other *x* arguments in part II of table 3.5 are subtypes of EFFECTOR. Thus, MOVERS are also EFFECTORS, but they occur with verbs of motion. Similarly, PERFORMERS are EFFECTORS that occur with performance verbs, just as SPEAKERS are EFFECTORS that occur with verbs of saying, and so on. The 'effectorhood' of these arguments is represented in the logical structures by the fact that all activity verb logical structures contain '**do′** (x, . . .' and the formal definition of EFFECTOR is the *x* argument in this logical structure configuration.

What about AGENTS? AGENTS are always a type of EFFECTOR semantically, and this means that AGENT is in effect an overlay over other, more basic thematic relations. AGENT is always associated with an activity logical structure, and therefore only verbs which have an activity predicate in their logical structure can have an AGENT argument. But how is AGENT to be represented in logical structure? It is not listed in table 3.5. For verbs which lexicalize agency, such as *murder*, we will represent them as 'DO (x, [**do′** (x, [. . .', following Ross (1972) and Dowty (1979), and the formal definition of AGENT is the *x* argument in this logical structure. Thus the minimal logical structure for *murder* would be DO (x, [**do′** (x, ∅)] CAUSE [BECOME **dead′** (y)]). This explicitly represents AGENT as an overlay over the more basic EFFECTOR, MOVER, CONSUMER, etc. roles.

What about the verb *kill*? Many analyses claim that it too takes an AGENT argument, but this is in fact questionable. For instance, it is perfectly correct to say both *John accidentally killed his neighbor's dog* and *John intentionally killed his neighbor's dog*. Moreover, *kill*, unlike *murder*, can take an inanimate subject, as in *Malaria killed/*murdered Fred*, and inanimate entities cannot intend anything. In Tsova-Tush (Bats; Holisky 1987), a language spoken in the Caucasus, some intransitive verbs take ergative (AGENT) marking while others take absolutive (PATIENT) marking, but most intransitive verbs can take either one depending upon the way it is used.[21] For instance, if one takes the verb meaning 'to lose one's footing and fall' and uses the ergative suffix, it means 'slide'. If, however, one uses the absolutive suffix, it means 'slip'. Sliding is controlled slipping; in other words, sliding is a controlled event, whereas slipping is not. Most intransitive verbs can use either prefix. The following example illustrates this for the verb for 'fall'.

(3.39) a. (As) vuiž-n-as
(1sgERG) fall-TNS-1sgERG
'I fell down (on purpose).'
b. (So) vož-en-sO[22]
(1sgABS) fall-TNS-1sgABS
'I fell down (accidentally).'

Examples like this, along with the variable interpretation of verbs like *kill*, show that most of the time agency is an implication of the way a particular verb is used in a sentence, and not an inherent lexical property of the verb. Consequently, putting DO (x, [**do′** . . . in every logical structure which can have an agentive interpretation is highly problematic, for it would mean that one would have to posit two verbs *kill* in English, one with it and one without, and the same analysis for 'fall' in Tsova-Tush.

Instead, it is preferable to have a theory in which an activity verb only takes DO (x, [**do′** . . . when its argument *must* be interpreted as an agent and has no such logical structure component when the agentive reading is merely possible. Thus, for verbs like *murder*, there is a DO (x, [**do′** . . . in logical structure, as we have seen, whereas with a verb like *kill* there is only [**do′** . . . Holisky argues that speakers tend to interpret a human EFFECTOR as an AGENT, unless there is information to the contrary in the sentence, e.g. the occurrence of an adverb like *unintentionally* or *inadvertently*. Hence DO (x, [**do′** . . . is part of the logical structure only if the argument must be interpreted as an AGENT; otherwise, the argument is simply an EFFECTOR ([**do′** . . .) which can under certain circumstances be construed as an AGENT. What are the criteria for determining whether agency is lexicalized with a verb or not? A simple test involves putting an adverb like *unintentionally or inadvertently* in the sentence and seeing if it yields a contradiction. If it is contradictory, then the verb lexicalizes agency, and if it is not a contradiction, the verb does not. *John unintentionally killed his neighbor's dog* is not a contradiction, while *John unintentionally murdered his neighbor* is; hence *kill* does not lexicalize agency, whereas *murder* does. Hence DO (x, [**do′** . . . appears only in the logical structures of those verbs which lexicalize agency.

Languages seem to vary strikingly with respect to how extensively agency is lexicalized in verbs. English and Tsova-Tush appear to have few verbs which have obligatory agentive arguments, whereas many Japanese verbs whose English counterparts are unmarked for agency do indeed require an AGENT argument, according to Kuno (1973) and Hasegawa (1992, 1995, 1996). The following examples from Hasegawa are all semantically anomalous.

(3.40) a. *Sensoo ga ookuno heesi o korosi-ta.
war SUBJ many soldiers OBJ kill-PAST
'The war killed many soldiers.'

b. *Zyoon ga guuzen ni tegami o sute-ta.
SUBJ accidentally letter OBJ throw.away-PAST
'Joan accidentally threw the letter away.'

c. *Zyoon wa ukkari-to megane o wat-ta.
SUBJ unintentionally glasses OBJ break-PAST
'Joan unintentionally broke the eye-glasses.'

Example (3.40a) is odd because of the inanimate abstract subject 'war', which is incapable of acting volitionally. In the (b) and (c) sentences the agency-canceling adverbs are incompatible with the requirements of these verbs for an agentive subject. Note that none of the English translations are semantically anomalous. In order to use these verbs with a non-agentive EFFECTOR, a special construction involving a nuclear juncture with the verb *simaw-* 'put' must be used. It is illustrated in (3.41), also from Hasegawa.

(3.41) a. Zyoon ga guuzen ni inu o korosi-te simat-ta.
SUBJ accidentally dog OBJ kill-LNK put-PAST
'Joan accidentally killed the dog.'

b. Zyoon ga guuzen ni tegami o sute-te simat-ta.
SUBJ accidentally letter OBJ throw.away-LNK put-PAST
'Joan accidentally threw the letter away.'

c. Zyoon wa ukkari-to megane o wat-te simat-ta.
SUBJ unintentionally glasses OBJ break-LNK put-PAST
'Joan unintentionally broke the eye-glasses.'

Thus, languages differ with respect to whether verbs like 'kill' and 'break' require an agentive EFFECTOR argument or not.

FORCE and INSTRUMENT thematic relations are not listed in table 3.5, because they can best be viewed as derivative of the more basic role of EFFECTOR, as argued in Van Valin and Wilkins (1996). FORCES are inanimate EFFECTORS that have two essential features in common with human and animate EFFECTORS: they can act and move independently, and they are not under the control of another EFFECTOR, animate or inanimate; in other words, they can serve as the instigators of an action, event or process. INSTRUMENTS, in contrast, are not capable of independent motion and action and are under the control of another EFFECTOR (see p. 85); they are not instigators. They are closely related semantically to the IMPLEMENT arguments of two-argument activity verbs like *use*. In the prototypical case of an INSTRUMENT, e.g. *Tom is cutting the bread with a knife*, an EFFECTOR, typically human, manipulates a knife and brings it into contact with the bread, whereupon the interaction of the knife with the bread brings about the result that the bread becomes cut. This may be represented as in (3.42). (The main CAUSE in the logical structure is italicized.)

(3.42) [**do′** (Tom, [**use′** (Tom, knife)])] *CAUSE* [[**do′** (knife, [**cut′** (knife, bread)])] CAUSE [BECOME **cut′** (bread)]]

The causing event in (3.42) is complex, and the INSTRUMENT argument appears three times in the logical structure: as the IMPLEMENT of **use′** and as the EFFECTOR of **do′** (x, [**cut′** (x, y)]). It is possible, if the first argument of the highest **do′** were left unspecified, to say *The knife cut the bread*, with the INSTRUMENT *knife* as actor. This contrasts with the occurrence of IMPLEMENTS with activity verbs like *eat* and *look at*; the corresponding examples with the human EFFECTOR unspecified are quite ungrammatical.

(3.43) a. Abdul ate the cereal with a spoon.
a′. *The spoon ate the cereal.
b. Tanisha looked at the comet with a telescope.
b′. *The telescope looked at the comet.

How is the difference between them to be captured? The crucial difference lies in the fact that the knife in the *cut* example is part of a causal chain, whereas in the examples with *eat* and *look at* there is no causal chain. The logical structures for (3.43a, b) are given in (3.44).

(3.44) a. **do′** (Abdul, [**eat′** (Abdul, cereal) ∧ **use′** (Abdul, spoon)])
b. **do′** (Tanisha, [**see′** (Tanisha, comet) ∧ **use′** (Tanisha, telescope)])

These logical structures reflect the fact that (3.43a, b) can be paraphrased as *Abdul ate the cereal, using a spoon* and *Tanisha looked at the comet, using a telescope*, respectively. The reason why *knife* can potentially function as actor whereas *spoon* and *telescope* cannot is now clear: *knife* is part of a causal chain and is the effector of *cut* in it, while *spoon* and *telescope* are not part of a causal chain and are not even directly arguments of *eat* or *look at*. Hence INSTRUMENTS are IMPLEMENTS in a causal chain which are also EFFECTORS. It should be noted that it is possible to leave most of the logical structure in (3.42) unspecified, yielding [**do′** (Tom, ∅)] CAUSE [BECOME **cut′** (bread)] and *Tom cut the bread*.

The formal definitions of FORCE and INSTRUMENT are given in (3.45).

(3.45) a. FORCE: Inanimate ‘x’ argument in LS configuration
b. INSTRUMENT: IMPLEMENT ‘y’ argument in LS configuration
[**do′** (x, [. . . .])] CAUSE [[. . . **do′** (y, [. . .])] CAUSE
[BECOME/INGR **pred′** (. . .)]]

If *x* were animate, it would be a candidate for the AGENT implicature. By saying that the *y* argument is an IMPLEMENT, we are in effect requiring that one of the higher activity predicates be **use′**.

3.2.3.3 The second argument of activity predicates

The second argument of some of the multiple argument activity predicates in II B in table 3.5 has unique properties among all of the argument types given there. These verbs behave in two ways, depending upon whether the second argument is referential or not. In the discussion of the alternation between activity and active accomplishment *Aktionsart* with verbs like *eat* in the previous section, it was pointed out that when *eat* has an activity interpretation, its second argument is necessarily *non-referential*; that is, it cannot be interpreted as having any specific reference. This can be seen most clearly when *eat* is used in the simple present with a generic or habitual interpretation: *Mario eats pizza* vs. ?*Mario eats a piece of pizza*. This suggests that the second argument of this type of activity verb is qualitatively different from all of the other arguments in table 3.5, which are normally referential, unless they occur within the scope of a reference-cancelling operator like negation. In *Mario ate pizza for an hour*, no specific pizza is referred to, as opposed to *Mario ate a slice of pizza in thirty seconds*, where reference to a specific piece of pizza is made. Given that the second argument of these verbs is non-referential, it is not surprising that it need not appear overtly, as in sentences like *Mary is eating/drinking*, and moreover the unrealized argument cannot be interpreted as having a discourse referent. That is, if someone asks, ‘Where is my sandwich?’, ‘Bill is eating’ is not an appropriate response if one means that Bill is eating the questioner’s sandwich (see Fillmore 1986). In a sentence like *Mary is eating*, it is understood that Mary is eating what one conventionally eats, namely food; it cannot be construed to mean she is eating poison, dirt, paper or the like. Many verbs in Mandarin Chinese normally take a non-referential argument when used as an activity, e.g. *chī fàn* ‘eat rice’, *chàng gē* 'sing song' (Li and Thompson 1981). Thus the second argument with an activity verb like *eat* will be called an INHERENT ARGUMENT, an argument which expresses an intrinsic facet of the meaning of the verb and does not refer specifically to any participants in an event denoted by the verb; it serves to characterize the nature of the action rather than to refer to any of the participants. It is not fixed, in that it can be used to characterize a number of different types of actions expressible by a particular verb, e.g. *drinking beer*, *drinking coffee*, *drinking tea*, *drinking milk*, etc. Inherent arguments are treated quite differently from normal, referential arguments. First, they can be freely omitted in English and many other languages, as noted above. Second, they are often incorporated into the verb. English is not usually thought of as a language with noun incorporation, but it is possible to have expressions like *beer drinking* as in *She's gone beer drinking*, where *beer* is the non-referential inherent argument. Other languages have more productive incorporation, and in many the inherent argument may or even must be realized as an incorporated noun. Examples from Lakhota and Tongan (Chung 1978) are given below.

(3.46) a. Wičháša ki čhą́ ki kaksá-he. Lakhota
man the wood the chop-CONT
'The man is chopping the wood.'
b. Wičháša ki čhą-káksa-he.
man the wood-chop-CONT
'The man is chopping wood', or 'The man is wood-chopping.'

(3.47) a. Na'e haka 'e he sianá 'a e ika. Tongan
PAST cook ERG DEF man ABS DEF fish
'The man cooked a/the fish.'
b. Na'e haka-ika 'a e sianá.
PAST cook-fish ABS DEF man
'The man cooked fish.'

The structure of Lakhota noun incorporation was discussed in chapter 2; see figure 2.32. Evidence that *čhą* 'wood' is incorporated in Lakhota comes from the fact that it lacks stress and that the stress has shifted to the first syllable in *kaksá* 'chop'; most multisyllabic words in Lakhota have second syllable stress, as can be seen in *kaksá* and *wičháša* 'man' in (3.46). Hence in languages like Lakhota the inherent argument appears as part of the verb and not as an independent constituent at all. The evidence for incorporation is even clearer in Tongan: *ika* 'fish' occurs compounded with the verb, and the subject appears in the absolutive case, the case of intransitive subjects, rather than in the ergative case, as in the canonical transitive construction in (3.47a). Thus, the non-referential second argument with two-argument activity verbs, the inherent argument, is qualitatively different from the other argument types listed in table 3.5.

Not all two-argument activity verbs treat their second argument in this way. If it is a fully referential NP, as with the verbs below, then it is realized as an oblique core argument, as in (3.48)–(3.51).

(3.48) a. The farmer plowed the field. — Active accomplishment
a′. The farmer plowed in the field. — Activity
b. The seamstress sewed the dress. — Active accomplishment
b′. The seamstress sewed on/at the dress. — Activity

(3.49) *Kabardian* (Catford 1975)
a. ħe-m q̣̓ʷɨpŝħe-r je-dzaq̣̓e. — Active accomplishment
dog-ERG bone-ABS TNS-bite
'The dog bites the bone (through to the marrow).'
b. ħe-r q̣̓ʷɨpŝħe-m je-w-dzaq̣̓e. — Activity
dog-ABS bone-ERG TNS-ANTI-bite
'The dog is gnawing on the bone.'

(3.50) *West Circassian* (Comrie 1978)
a. Piśaśa-m chəy-ər yadə. — Active accomplishment
girl-ERG cherkesska-ABS 3sg.sew.3sg.TRANS
'The girl is sewing the cherkesska.'
b. Piśaśa-r chəy-əm yada. — Activity
girl-ABS cherkesska-LOC 3sg.sew.INTR
'The girl is sewing away at the cherkesska.'

(3.51) *Tongan* (Clark 1973)
a. Na'e kai-'i 'a e ika 'e he tangata. — Active accomplishment
PAST eat-TRANS ABS DEF fish ERG DEF man
'The man ate the fish.'
b. Na'e kai 'a e tangata 'i he ika. — Activity
PAST eat ABS DEF man LOC DEF fish
'The man ate (some of/on) the fish.'

In all of these pairs, there is a transitive form with an active accomplishment reading and the second argument treated as a 'direct object' and an intransitive form with an activity reading in which the second argument is treated as an oblique core argument. The shift from transitive to intransitive is particularly striking in the three ergative languages, as the case marking on the subject shifts from ergative to absolutive. What is striking about activity verbs is that their second argument is not treated like the second argument of predicates of the other *Aktionsart* classes or the derived classes. We will discuss this further in section 4.2.

The second argument of two-argument activity verbs like *listen to* (directed perception) and *use* (use) behave like the second arguments of other classes. This is not surprising in the case of *look at*, since it is the activity version of a perception verb;

this is clearly reflected in its logical structure (**do´** (x, [**see´** (x, y)])). Like the other activity verbs discussed, the second argument is optional, as in *I'm listening/looking/watching*. *Use* seems to be somewhat unusual for this class, as it does not readily occur without a second argument. It is also unusual in that it normally occurs in a core juncture with purposive semantics, e.g. *She used the knife to cut the rope*, rather than in simple sentences (see chapter 8). The sentence *She used the knife* seems rather incomplete on its own out of context.

3.2.3.4 Two-place state predicates

Most of the state predicates in table 3.5 have two arguments, and they seem to define many thematic relations. Examples of verbs from these classes are given in (3.52).

(3.52) a. *Location*
The book is on the table. — **be-on′** (table, book), *table* = LOCATION, *book* = THEME

b. *Perception*
Mabel saw the accident. — **see′** (Mabel, accident), *Mabel* = PERCEIVER, *accident* = STIMULUS

c. *Cognition*
Dana knows the answer. — **know′** (Dana, answer), *Dana* = COGNIZER, *answer* = CONTENT

d. *Desire*
Sam wants a new car. — **want′** (Sam, car), *Sam* = WANTER, *car* = DESIRE

e. *Propositional attitude*
Max believes the rumor. — **believe′** (Max, rumor), *Max* = JUDGER, *rumor* = JUDGMENT

f. *Possession*
Tammy has a new car. — **have′** (Tammy, car), *Tammy* = POSSESSOR, *car* = POSSESSED

g. *Internal experience*
Diana feels sick. — **feel′** (Diana, [**sick′**]), *Diana* = EXPERIENCER, *sick* = SENSATION

h. *Emotion*
Charles hates his wife. — **hate′** (Charles, wife), *Charles* = EMOTER, *wife* = TARGET

i. *Attributive/identificational*
The building is tall. — **be′** (building, [**tall′**]), *building* = ATTRIBUTANT *tall* = ATTRIBUTE

The logical structures in (g) and (i) are somewhat unusual, in that the second argument position is filled by a predicate, rather than a referring expression, which is normally realized as the predicate or as part of the predicate in the nucleus. In traditional grammar, they are termed 'predicate adjectives'. The second position in an identificational logical structure can be filled by a nominal as in (3.21a) *Leon is a fool*; this is the traditional notion of a 'predicate nominal'.

It appears that there is a plethora of different thematic relations represented here, but upon closer inspection it turns out that there are fewer than meet the eye. There are two groups of thematic relations here, the first arguments and the second arguments of the state predicates, and a crucial fact about these two groups is that *the members of each group do not contrast with each other*. That is, no single predicate takes more than one argument from the group {LOCATIVE, PERCEIVER, COGNIZER, JUDGER, POSSESSOR, EXPERIENCER, EMOTER, ATTRIBUTANT}, more than one from the group {EFFECTOR, MOVER, ST-MOVER, L-EMITTER, S-EMITTER, PERFORMER, CONSUMER, CREATOR, SPEAKER, OBSERVER, USER}, or more than one from the group {THEME, ENTITY, STIMULUS, CONTENT, DESIRE, JUDGMENT, POSSESSED, SENSATION, TARGET, ATTRIBUTE, PERFORMANCE, CONSUMED, CREATION, LOCUS, IMPLEMENT}. Consequently, PERCEIVER never cooccurs with COGNIZER or EXPERIENCER, nor does THEME with CONTENT, STIMULUS or TARGET. Since these thematic relations never contrast with each other, only with roles from the other group, there are really only *two* basic thematic relations in (3.52), and what these role labels distinguish is the subclass of the state or activity predicate that the argument occurs with. This can be seen clearly if we set up a thematic relations continuum in terms of argument positions in logical structure. This yields the thematic relations continuum in figure 3.2. The continuum has AGENT and PATIENT as its anchor points, and the remaining groups of roles are ranked in terms of how AGENT-like and PATIENT-like they are. Since human EFFECTORS can be interpreted as AGENTS, 'first argument of **do′** . . .' would be the closest argument-type to AGENT. With respect to the two arguments of state '**predicate′** (x, y)', the first arguments of some of the classes clearly have things in common with the arguments in the first two columns. This is most obvious with OBSERVER and PERCEIVER, and there is a similar parallel between the COGNIZER of stative cognition predicates like *know* and activity cognition predicates like *think* (*about*/*over*). Similarly, a component of DO is wanting something to happen, and this is related to WANTER with desire verbs. Likewise, there seem to be connections between the second argument of these verbs and PATIENT. They denote entities which for the most part are not active and which are affected by the action of the verb in various ways. Hence it seems reasonable to place them closer to PATIENT than to EFFECTOR. There are really only three points, hence three distinct, contrasting thematic relations between AGENT and PATIENT.

3.2.3.5 Recipients, goals and sources

These participant roles were discussed on page 86, but they do not appear as thematic relations in the logical structures in table 3.5. The distinction between

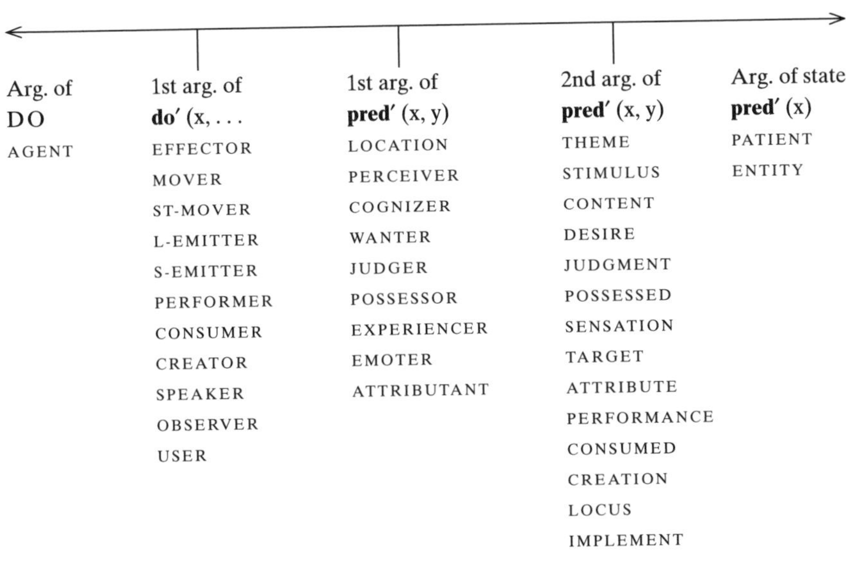

Figure 3.2 Thematic relations continuum in terms of LS argument positions

GOAL and RECIPIENT is important because RECIPIENT arguments behave differently from GOAL arguments. For instance, one can say *Send Mary the present* and *Send the present to Mary*, which shows that THEME and RECIPIENT can both be the direct object with *send*. On the other hand, it is possible to say *Send the package to Philadelphia* but not **Send Philadelphia the package*. This alternation is not possible between THEMES and GOALS. This is one of the reasons why it is desirable to have a GOAL role for motion separate from a RECIPIENT role for change of possession. The contrast between GOAL and RECIPIENT can be seen clearly in the logical structures for *put*, which takes a goal, and *give*, which takes a recipient; they are given in (3.53).

(3.53) a. *put*: [**do′** (x, ∅)] CAUSE [BECOME **be-LOC′** (y, z)]
b. *give*: [**do′** (x, ∅)] CAUSE [BECOME **have′** (y, z)]

In (3.53a) *x* is an EFFECTOR, *y* is a LOCATION and *z* is a THEME, while in (b) *x* is an EFFECTOR, *y* is a POSSESSOR and *z* is a POSSESSED. In a sentence like *The book is lying on the table* (**lie′** (y, z)), *y* is the LOCATION and *z* is the THEME. What, then, is the difference between LOCATION and GOAL? Similarly, in *Mary has a new car* (**have′** (y, z)), *y* is a POSSESSOR and *z* a POSSESSED. Here again, what is the difference between POSSESSOR and RECIPIENT? These contrasts are represented by the logical structure as a whole. The logical structures for *lie* and *have* are plain statives, while *put* uses BECOME **be-LOC′** and *give* BECOME **have′**. Therefore, it is BECOME which distinguishes pure POSSESSOR and LOCATION from RECIPIENT and GOAL. Simply because there is a semantic distinction, in this instance between POSSESSOR and RECIPIENT or between LOCATION and GOAL, it does not follow that it is necessary to create a new thematic relation in order to signal it. Hence it is the overall structure of the logical structure that gives the meaning of the argument. Thus the definitions of RECIPIENT and GOAL are as shown in (3.54).

(3.54) a. RECIPIENT: first argument in LS configuration '. . . BECOME/INGR **have′** (y, z)'
b. GOAL: first argument in LS configuration '. . . BECOME/INGR **be-LOC′** (y, z)'

SOURCE seems to have the same range of basic meanings as RECIPIENT and GOAL; that is, it is used in transfers of possession, i.e. *Mary took the book from Sam*, *Louise bought the watch from the jeweler*, and in changes of location, i.e. *Kim ran from the house to the barn*. The contrast with GOAL and RECIPIENT can be represented by adding NOT to the semantic representation, as suggested by Gruber (1965). Hence SOURCE can be defined as in (3.55).

(3.55) SOURCE: first argument in LS configuration '. . . BECOME/INGR NOT **have′/be-LOC′** (y, z)'

It is not really a distinct thematic relation from POSSESSOR or LOCATION; it is, rather, a POSSESSOR or LOCATION embedded under 'BECOME/INGR NOT' in logical structure.

In terms of the thematic relations continuum in figure 3.2, RECIPIENT, GOAL and SOURCE would fall in the third column under 'first argument of **pred′** (x, y)', along with LOCATION, POSSESSOR, etc.

3.3 Summary

It is important to emphasize again that in the system presented here, thematic relations play no direct role in lexical representation; the relevant semantic properties of the verbs are expressed by the decompositional logical structure representations, not by thematic relations. Thus even though we have used a large number of role labels like AGENT, COGNIZER, THEME and PATIENT, they are merely mnemonics for argument positions in logical structure. They have no independent status. Since there is as yet no adequate decompositional representation for the primitive state and activity predicates which are the argument-bearing components of the system and which carry the substantive semantic load, these labels are useful in that they indicate the subclass of the predicate; hence COGNIZER means 'first argument of a two-place state predicate of cognition', JUDGMENT means 'second argument of a two-place state predicate of propositional attitude' and THEME means 'second argument of a two-place state predicate of location', for example. We will continue to use these labels in this way (see n. 20), and it must be kept clearly in mind that these labels do not refer to independently meaningful relations but rather to argument positions in the logical structure of predicates of a certain type.

It is also worthwhile reiterating the consequences that follow from this approach for linguistic theory and practice. The theoretical implications of this system for deriving thematic relations from logical structures are very important. If it is the case that the thematic relations which a verb takes are a function of the argument positions in its logical structure, and there is a system of lexical representation in which there are independent criteria for assigning logical structures to verbs, then there are independent criteria for assigning thematic relations to verbs. This is the case because the thematic relations are a function of the logical structure of a verb, and there are independent criteria for attributing a logical structure to a verb. Thematic relations cannot be assigned on an arbitrary basis, because logical structures cannot be assigned arbitrarily; rather, logical structures are determined on the basis of the tests in table 3.2. Thus the great advantage of this system of lexical representation is that there are tests which provide independent criteria for assigning a particular logical structure and hence a particular argument structure to a given verb.

This system also has important implications for how one actually goes about analyzing a language. In order to determine the argument structure of a verb, it is first necessary to ascertain its *Aktionsart* in the construction in which it occurs, using the tests in table 3.2. Having established that, its logical structure can be created, following table 3.4, and its argument structure follows from table 3.5. Thus, it is necessary to ascertain the *Aktionsart* of the verb in the sentence, and from this its argument structure follows. What is *not* appropriate in this system is to decide arbitrarily what thematic relations a verb should have and then to construct a logical structure which would yield those roles.

Further reading

See Silverstein (1977) for an illuminating discussion of the place of reference and predication among the various functions language may serve. For alternative analyses of states of affairs and their linguistic encoding, see Dik (1989) and the papers in Seiler and Premper (1991). For discussions of *Aktionsart*, see Breu (1994), Dahl (1981), Holisky (1981b), Mourelatos (1981), Sasse (1991a, b), Voorst (1988), Verkuyl (1993). For other approaches to lexical decomposition, see Dowty (1979), Wierzbicka (1972, 1980a), Jackendoff (1976, 1990) and Pinker (1989), who presents a detailed analysis of a number of important English verb classes. Levin (1993) presents a general taxonomy of English verb classes. Fillmore (1968) and Gruber (1965) were the seminal works in the development of the concept of thematic relations (case roles); see also Van Valin and Wilkins (1996) for a discussion of a number of contemporary approaches. See Andrews (1985), Williams (1994) and Palmer (1994) for alternative approaches to thematic relations. See Talmy (1985, 1991) for extensive discussion of lexicalization patterns across languages.

Exercises

(*Note*: All exercises can be done after section 3.2.2.)

1 Determine the class of each of the following English verbs, using the tests in table 3.2. If a verb can be used in more than one way, classify each of its uses.

collapse
devour
dissolve
draw (in the sense of 'sketch', not 'pull')
doubt
irritate
perish

2 Determine the class of each of the following Mparntwe Arrernte verbs (Wilkins 1989). Use the tests in table 3.2; apply test 6 to the English translation, on the assumption that it accurately reflects whether a verb is causative or not. Discuss the evidence provided by each example sentence that led you to assign a given verb to a particular class. Give the logical structure for each verb. Comment on any patterns in the verbal morphology which correlate with the class of the verb. *Note*: the asterisk means that the sentence is impossible with the meaning specified; some of the sentences are fine with a different meaning, but that is irrelevant to this problem.

(1)	a.	The kngwelye areme.	'I see a dog.'
	b.	*The kngwelye arerleneme.	'I am seeing a dog.'
	c.	*The kngwelye tyepetyepele areme.	'I see a dog energetically.'
	d.	The kngwelye areke tine minitele.	'I saw a dog for ten minutes.'
	e.	*The kngwelye areke tine minitekekerte.	'I saw a dog in ten minutes.'
(2)	a.	Ayenge irrernte neme.	'I am cold.'
	b.	*Ayenge irrernte nerleneme.	'I am being cold.'
	c.	*Ayenge irrernte tyepeyepele neme.	'I am cold energetically.'
	d.	Ayenge irrernte neke arlte therrele.	'I was cold for three days.'
	e.	*Ayenge irrernte neke arlte therrekekerte.	'I was cold in three days.'
(3)	a.	Kwarte ateke.	'An egg exploded.'
	b.	*Kwarte aterleneke.	'An egg was exploding.'
	c.	*Kwarte iparrpele ateke.	'An egg exploded quickly.'
	d.	*Kwarte ateke minite nyente-le/kekerte.	'An egg exploded for/in one minute.'
(4)	a.	Ayenge alyelheme.	'I sing.'
	b.	Ayenge alyelherleneme.	'I am singing.'

	c. Ayenge tyepetyepele alyelherleneme.	'I am singing energetically.'
	d. Ayenge alyelheke tine minitele.	'I sang for ten minutes.'
	e. *Ayenge alyelheke tine minitekekerte.	'I sang in ten minutes.'
(5)	a. The Kwementyaye unthelhileke.	'I made Kwementyaye wander around.'
	b. The Kwementyaye unthe-lhilerleneke.	'I was making K wander around.'
	c. The Kwementyaye tyepetyepele unthelhileke.	'I made K wander around energetically', or 'I energetically made K wander around.'
	d. The Kwementyaye unthelhileke arlte therrele.	'I made K wander around for three days.'
	e. *The Kwementyaye unthelhileke arlte therrekekerte.	'I made K wander around in three days.'
(6)	a. Arntape urrperle neme.	'Some (tree) bark is black.'
	b. *Arntape urrperle nerleneme.	'Some bark is being black.'
	c. *Arntape urrperle arnterrele neme.	'Some bark is black intensely.'
	d. Arntape urrperle neke arlte therrele.	'Some bark was black for three days.'
	e. *Arntape urrperle neke arlte therrekekerte.	'Some bark was black in three days.'
(7)	a. Ayenge irrerntearleirreke. (cf. Ayenge irrerntirreke.	'I got cold.' 'I got cooler [but not to the point of being cold].')
	b. Ayenge irrerntearleirrerleneke.	'I was getting cold.'
	c. *Ayenge tyepetyepele irrerntearleirreke.	'I got cold energetically.'
	d. Ayenge irrerntearleirreke tine minitekekerte.	'I got cold in ten minutes.'
	e. *Ayenge irrerntearleirreke tine minitele.	'I got cold for ten minutes.'
(8)	a. Ayenge untheke.	'I wandered around.'
	b. Ayenge untherleneme.	'I am wandering around.'
	c. Ayenge tyepetyepele untheke.	'I wandered around energetically.'
	d. Ayenge untheke arlte therrele.	'I wandered around for three days.'
	e. *Ayenge untheke arlte therrekekerte.	'I wandered around in three days.'
(9)	a. Arntape urrperlearleirreke. (cf. Arntape urrperlirreke.	'Some bark became black.' 'Some bark became blacker, darker.')

b. Arntape urrperlearleirrerleneke. 'Some bark was getting black.'

c. *Arntape anterrele urrperlearleirreke. 'Some bark became black intensely.'

d. Arntape urrperlearleirreke tine minitekekerte. 'Some bark became black in ten minutes.'

e. *Arntape urrperlearleirreke tine minitele. 'Some bark became black for ten minutes.'

(10) a. Kwatyele ayenge irrerntearleirrelhileke. 'The water cooled me down [to the point that I was cold].'
(cf. Kwatyele ayenge irrerntirrelhileke 'The water made me cooler [but not to the point that I was cold].')

b. Kwatyele ayenge irrentearleirrelhilerleneke. 'The water was cooling me down.'

c. Kwatyele ayenge iparrpele irrentearleirrelhileke. 'The water quickly cooled me down.'

d. Kwatyele ayenge irrerntearleirrelhileke tine minitekekerte. 'The water cooled me down in ten minutes.'

e. *Kwatyele ayenge irrerntearleirelhileke tine minitele. 'The water cooled me down for ten minutes.'

(11) a. Kngwelye arreweke. 'A dog shivered.'

b. Kngwelye arrewerleneke. 'A dog was shivering.'

c. Kngwelye arnterrele arrewerleneke. 'A dog was shivering intensely.'

d. Kngwelye arreweke tine minitele. 'A dog shivered for ten minutes.'

e. *Kngwelye arreweke tine minitekekerte. 'A dog shivered in ten minutes.'

(12) a. Kwatyele ayenge irrerntearlelhileke. 'The water made/kept me cold.'

b. Kwatyele ayenge irrerntearlelhilerleneke. 'The water was making/keeping me cold.'

c. *Kwatyele ayenge iparrpele irrerntearlelhileke. 'The water quickly made/kept me cold.'

d. *Kwatyele ayenge irrerntearlelhileke tine minitekekerte. 'The water made/kept me cold in ten minutes.'

e. Kwatyele ayenge irrerntearlelhileke tine minitele. 'The water made/kept me cold for ten minutes.'

(13) a. The arntape urrperlearleirrelhileke. 'I blackened some bark, made some bark black.'

b. The arntape urrperlearleirrelhilerleneke. 'I was blackening some bark.'

c. The arntape tyepetyepele urrperlearleirrelhileke. 'I blackened some bark energetically.'

d. The arntape urrperlearleirrelhileke tine minitekekerte. 'I blackened some bark in ten minutes.'

e. The arntape urrperlearleirrelhileke tine minitele. 'I blackened some bark for ten minutes.'

3 Determine the class of each of the following Icelandic verbs. Use the tests in table 3.2; apply test 6 to the English translation, on the assumption that it accurately reflects whether a verb is causative or not. There are not examples for every test for every verb. Discuss the evidence provided by each example sentence that led you to assign a given verb to a particular class. Give the logical structure for each verb. Note: the asterisk means that the sentence is impossible with the meaning specified; some of the sentences are fine with a different meaning, but that is irrelevant to this problem.

(1) Strákurinn hljóp í garðinum í tíu mínútur/ — *hlaupa* 'run'
the boy ran in the park for ten minutes/
*á tíu mínútum.
*in ten minutes

(2) Ég er að hlaupa.
I am at run
'I am running.'

(3) Hún hljóp hægt/kröftuglega.
she ran slowly/vigorously

(4) Hann sá það í tíu mínútur/ *á tíu mínútum. — *sjá* 'see'
he saw it for ten minutes/ *in ten minutes

(5) *Ég er að sjá það.
I am at see it
*'I am seeing it.'

(6) *Ég sá það kröftuglega.
I saw it vigorously
*'I saw it vigorously.'

(7) Skipstjórinn sökkti skipinu (á tíu mínútum/ — *sökkva* 'sink'
the captain sank the ship (in ten minutes/
??í tíu mínútur).
for ten minutes)

(8) Ég er að sökkva skipinu.
I am at sink the ship
'I am sinking the ship.'

(9) Bátnum hvolfdi (á tíu mínútum). — *hvolfa* 'capsize'
'The boat capsized (in ten minutes).'

(10) Bátnum hvolfdi fljótt/*kröftuglega.
'The boat capsized quickly/*vigorously.'

(11) Ég er að skila henni peningunum. *skila* 'return, give back'
I am at return her the money
'I am giving her the money back.'

(12) Ég skilaði henni peningunum á tíu mínútum.
'I gave her back the money in ten minutes.'

(13) Hún dansaði kröftuglega í tíu mínútur/*á tíu mínútum. *dansa* 'dance'
'She danced vigorously for/*in ten minutes.'

(14) Ég er að dansa.
I am at dance
'I am dancing.'

(15) Snjórinn bráðnaði á tíu mínútum. *bráðna* 'melt'
'The snow melted in ten minutes.'

(16) Snjórinn bráðnaði fljótt/*kröftuglega.
'The snow melted quickly/*vigorously.'

(17) Mér þótti hann leiðinlegur í tíu mínútur/ *þykja* 'think, consider'
'I considered him boring for ten minutes/
*á tíu mínútum.
*in ten minutes.'

(18) *Mér var að þykja Ólafur leiðinlegur.
I was at consider Olaf boring
*'I was considering Olaf boring.'

(19) *Mér þótti hann leiðinlegur kröftuglega.'
*I thought him boring vigorously

4 Italian has two different auxiliary verbs that appear in the perfect tenses with intransitive verbs: *avere* 'have' and *essere* 'be'. Most verbs take one or the other, but some can take either one. Based on the following data (from Centineo 1986), what predicts which auxiliary a given intransitive verb will take?

(1) a. Angela ha parla-to per/*in un' ora.
have.3sgPRES talk-PSTP for/in an hour
'Angela talked for/*in an hour.'
b. Angela ha pian-to per/*in un' ora.
cry-PSTP
'Angela cried for/*in an hour.'
c. Angela ha balla-to per/*in un' ora.
dance-PSTP
'Angela danced for/*in an hour.'

d. Angela ha cammina-to per/*in un' ora.
   walk-PSTP
   'Angela walked for/*in an hour.'

(2) a. Angela è arriva-t-a in/*per un' ora.
   be.3sgPRES arrive-PSTP-3sgF in/for an hour
   'Angela arrived in an hour.'
b. Angela è annega-t-a in/*per un' ora.
   drown-PSTP-3sgF
   'Angela drowned in an hour.'
c. Angela è mor-t-a in/*per un' ora.
   die-PSTP-3sgF
   'Angela died in/*for an hour.'

(3) a. Luisa ha cor-so nel parco per/*in un' ora.
   have.3sgPRES run-PSTP in.the park
   'Luisa ran in the park for/*in an hour.'
a′. Luisa è cor-s-a a casa per/in un' ora.
   be.3sgPRES run-PSTP-3sgF to house
   'Luisa ran home for/in an hour.'

5 Intransitive verbs in Fijian (Dixon 1988) fall into two general classes, depending upon how they form transitive verbs when a transitivizing suffix is added. Based on the following sets of data, what appears to be the basic difference between the two types of intransitive verbs?

(1) *Type 1*
a. E la'o a marama.
   3sg go ART woman
   'The woman is going.'
a′. E la'o-va a suka a marama.
   3sg go-TRANS ART sugar ART woman
   'The woman is going for sugar.'
b. E 'ana a marama.
   3sg eat ART woman
   'The woman is eating.'
b′. E 'ani-a a dalo a marama.
   3sg eat-TRANS ART taro ART woman
   'The woman is eating the taro.'
c. E dree a cauravou.
   3sg pull ART youth
   'The youth is pulling.'
c′. E dre-ta a waqa a cauravou.
   3sg pull-TRANS ART boat ART youth
   'The youth is pulling a boat.'

(2) *Type 2*

a. E lo'i a kaukamea yai.
3sg bend ART metal this
'This (piece of) metal is bent.'

a′. E lo'i-a a kaukamea yai a cauravou.
3sg bend-TRANS ART metal this ART youth
'The youth is bending this (piece of) metal.'

b. E tawa a 'oro yai.
3sg inhabit ART village this
'This village is inhabited.'

b′. E tawa-na a 'oro yai a vuulagi.
3sg inhabit-TRANS ART village this ART stranger
'Strangers inhabit this village.'

c. E qaqi a dovu.
3sg crush ART sugar cane
'The sugar cane is crushed.'

c′. E qaqi-a a dovu a cauravou.
3sg crush-TRANS ART sugar cane ART youth
'The youth is crushing the sugar cane.'

6 What is the function of the morpheme *-so* and the function of the morpheme *-ma* in the verbal system of Sanuma, the language of the Yanomami in Brazil and Venezuela (Borgman 1989)? With respect to *-so*, explain its use in (2h). They are both glossed '??'; there is another morpheme *-ma*, a completive aspect marker glossed 'CMPV' which is not the focus of this problem. The examples in (1) do not contain either morpheme, while those in (2) contain *-so* and those in (3) contain *-ma*.

(1) a. Pilipoma a ku-a.
moon 3sg be-DUR
'There is a moon.'

b. (Ohi ohi te-nö) ulu te utiti.
hungry hungry 3sg-INST child 3sg weak
'The child is weak (from hunger).'

c. Pole a pata.
dog 3sg big
'The dog is big.'

d. Öla a pata ha sa kili.
jaguar 3sg big LOC1 1sg afraid
'I am afraid of the jaguar.'

e. Kau niha sa hĩso.
2sg LOC2 1sg angry
'I am angry at you.'

f. Pusopö a tiki-a kölö-a.
wife 3sg sit.off.ground-DUR there-DUR
'His wife sits (in the tree) down there.'

g. Pole ose wai niha a inamo-ma.
dog young DIM LOC2 3sg play-CMPV
'He played with the little puppy.'

h. Sa ami nini-a halu-ki.
1sg hand hurt-DUR at.night-SUFF
'My hand hurt during the night.'

i. Kanene sa te ta-pa kule.
killer 1sg 3sg see-EXT PRES
'I see the killer.'

j. Sama töpö se kite.
1plEX 3pl hit/kill FUT
'We will hit them.'

k. Pata töpö-nö wale kökö se-pa-lö-ma.
old 3pl-ERG peccary 3dl kill-EXT-GOAL-CMPV
'The old people killed the peccary.'

(2) a. Hi ulu te niha polakapi te inama ku-pa-so kite.
this child 3sg LOC2 two 3sg dry.season be-EXT-?? FUT
'This child will become two years old.'

b. Ohi ohi te-nö a utiti-a apö-pa-so-ma.
hungry hungry 3sg-INST 3sg weak-DUR INTS-EXT-??-CMPV
'He became very weak from hunger.'

c. Salaka-nö pole a pata-so-ma.
fish-INST dog 3sg big-??-CMPV
'The dog grew big with fish (diet).'

d. Ka pi ha wa kili-so ke?
what CL LOC1 2sg afraid-?? IMM
'What did you become afraid of?'

e. Sa hĩso opa halu-so kupi.
1sg angry INTS at.night-?? REC
'I got really angry at night.'

f. Moko te noma-so-ma.
young.woman 3sg dead-??-CMPV
'The young woman died.'

g. A nini-a apa-so kite.
3sg hurt-DUR INTS-?? FUT
'It will really start hurting.'

h. A se-pa-so-ma.
3sg hit/kill-EXT-??-CMPV
'He was hit,' or 'He got killed (accidentally by person with pole).'

(3) a. Pusopö a tiki-ma kölö.
wife 3sg sit.off.ground-?? there
'He makes his wife sit (in the tree) down there.'

b. Pole ose wai niha a inamo-ma-ma.
dog young DIM LOC2 3sg play-??-CMPV
'(She) made him play with the little puppy.'

c. Pumotomö a wani-nö alawali kökö-nö moko te
opossum 3sg DEPR-ERG magic.root 3dl-INST young.woman 3sg
noma-ma-nö-ma.
dead-??-GOAL-CMPV
'The opossum man killed the young woman with the magic root.'

d. Salaka niha pole wa pata-ma toti-ti-o-ma.
fish LOC2 dog 2sg big-?? good-CONT-PNCT-CMPV
'You made the dog really big with fish (diet).'

e. Hi a wani-nö wa hĩso-ma-ni kite.
this 3sg DEPR-ERG 2sg angry-??-GOAL FUT
'He will make you angry.'

f. Pata töpö-nö pole niha wale kökö se-ma-nö ke.
old 3pl-ERG dog LOC2 peccary 3dl kill-??-GOAL IMM
'The old people killed the peccary with the dogs.'

g. Kamisa-nö setenapi te niha manasi sa ta-ma-na-ni ke.
1sg-ERG non.Indian 3sg LOC2 guan.bird 1sg see-??-EXT-GOAL IMM
'I showed the guan bird to the non-Indian.'

4

Semantic representation, II: macroroles, the lexicon and noun phrases

4.0 Introduction

In the previous chapter we presented a system of lexical representation for verbs and other predicating elements and their arguments; the logical structures form the basis of the semantic representation for clauses and whole sentences. In this chapter we will fill in the remaining pieces that are needed for semantic representations, in particular the semantic representation of noun phrases and of clausal and NP operators. We will also discuss the lexicon, focusing on what kind of information needs to be represented in lexical entries and in lexical rules. We begin by continuing the discussion of the kinds of semantic relations that an argument can bear to its predicate.

4.1 Semantic macroroles

In this book we are presenting a framework for syntactic analysis which directly links the syntactic representation of a sentence, as developed in chapter 2, to the semantic representation, which was developed in chapter 3 (see figure 2.2). The aspects of grammar where these two interact is known as the **syntax–semantics interface**. The full linking system for simple and complex sentences will be the primary focus of chapters 7 and 9, but we need to introduce an important component of the linking system at this point, since it is tied in with important issues of lexical representation, argument structure and the content of lexical entries for verbs in the lexicon. This is the notion of **semantic macroroles**. Macroroles are generalizations across the argument-types found with particular verbs which have significant grammatical consequences; it is they, rather than specific arguments in logical structure, that grammatical rules refer to primarily.

We can see this by looking at the range of argument-types that can function as subject and object in English, as illustrated in (4.1) and (4.2).

(4.1)	a. *Fred* broke the window.	([**do′** (x, . . .)] . . .)
	b. *The bomb* destroyed the car.	(. . .[**do′** (x, . . .)] . . .)
	c. *Mary* received a parking ticket.	(BECOME **have′** (x, . . .))

d. *The farm animals* sensed the earthquake. (**sense′** (x, . . .))

(4.2) a. Max gave *the book* to the teacher. (. . . [BECOME **have′** (. . . , z)])
b. The tidal wave destroyed *the harbor*. (. . . [BECOME **destroyed′** (y)])
c. The rock hit *the wall*. (. . . [INGR **be-LOC′** (y, . . .)])
d. The mugger robbed *Tom* of $45.00. (. . . [BECOME NOT **have′** (y, . . .)])
e. Will presented *Sheila* with a bouquet. (. . . [BECOME **have′** (y, . . .)])

In (4.1) four different argument-types are being treated as subject, while in (4.2) five different argument-types are being treated as direct object. There is evidence, however, that what we are dealing with is not subject and direct object but a different type of relation. The evidence for this comes from passivization; if these conflations of argument-types are related to grammatical relations, which are different in active and passive forms of a sentence, then they would not be expected to hold in the passive form. However, in passive constructions these conflations are preserved, as shown in (4.3).

(4.3) a The window was broken by *Fred*.
b. The car was destroyed by *the bomb*.
c. The coming storm was sensed by *the farm animals*.
d. *The keys* were tossed to the policeman by Max.
e. *The village* was destroyed by the tidal wave.
f. *The door* was hit by the rock.

In all of these cases, the group of argument-types remained the same even though the syntactic relations have changed. Thus, this is not a question of *grammatical* functions, since the groups of arguments are acting the same way regardless of whether the sentence is active or passive; rather, these grouping of arguments constitute another, higher-level type of semantic relation. Each captures a grouping of semantic arguments which are treated alike in the grammar. There is a group of arguments indicating doers of an action in some general sense. There is also another group which seems to encompass the things affected by an action. For example, THEMES (e.g. . . . [INGR/BECOME **have′** (. . . , y)]) and PATIENTS (e.g. . . . [BECOME **destroyed′** (y)]) function alike for certain purposes in the grammar. One would, however, want to distinguish them because there are good reasons for doing so on semantic grounds and a variety of other grounds. But nevertheless, the grammar, for certain purposes, treats these roles as essentially the same, e.g. they can be both the direct object in an active sentence and the subject in a passive sentence. In fact, active and passive in English can be described in terms of these role lists. AGENT, EXPERIENCER, INSTRUMENT, RECIPIENT, SOURCE or FORCE, among others, can be subject of an active sentence; PATIENT, THEME, RECIPIENT, SOURCE or

LOCATION can be direct object. In the English passive, PATIENT, THEME, RECIPIENT, SOURCE or LOCATION can be subject, while AGENT, EXPERIENCER, INSTRUMENT, RECIPIENT, SOURCE or FORCE can be object of the preposition *by*. It appears that a significant generalization is being missed here, since there are long disjunctive lists of thematic relations in these statements. But in fact, it is not an accident that they seem to group together the way they do, and the obvious generalization can be captured in terms of generalized semantic roles: in an active construction, the generalized AGENT-type role is subject and the generalized PATIENT-type role is object, while in a passive construction the generalized PATIENT-type role is subject and the generalized AGENT-type role is object of the preposition *by*.

These generalized semantic roles are **semantic macroroles**. They are called 'macroroles' because each of them subsumes a number of specific argument-types (thematic relations). The generalized AGENT-type role will be termed **actor** and the generalized PATIENT-type role will be called **undergoer**. Accordingly, in an active sentence in English, the actor is the subject, which, with a certain kind of verb, would be an AGENT, and with another kind of verb would be an EXPERIENCER, and with yet another kind of verb would be a POSSESSOR, and so on. Similarly, the undergoer is the direct object in the English active, which would be a PATIENT with a verb like *kill*, but a THEME with *put*, a RECIPIENT with *present* (as in *present Mary with the award*) and so on. This may be represented as in figure 4.1. This shows that the specific semantic interpretation of an argument is a function of the semantics of each verb. In other words, the fact that the actor of *see* is a PERCEIVER is a function of the meaning of *see*, and the fact that *kill* takes a PATIENT for its undergoer is a function of the meaning of *kill* because it involves a participant that undergoes a change of state. On the other hand, *put* takes a THEME for its undergoer because it induces a change of location. In every case we can say that these *x*'s are the actors with these verbs, which shows us then that actor does not necessarily mean AGENT, but rather something much more general. Even a category such as 'doer of the action' is too restrictive for actor, because EXPERIENCERS and PERCEIVERS, for example, do not really do anything. The term actor is perfectly compatible with non-volitional things, such as in *The key opened the door*, where *key* is technically the actor, and certainly is inanimate and non-volitional. In *The tidal wave destroyed the*

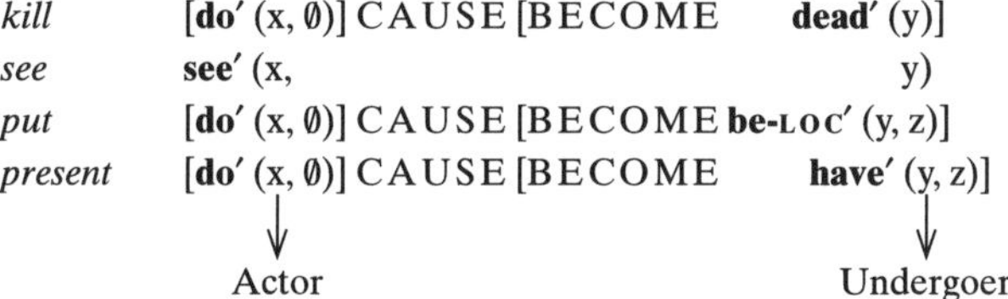

Figure 4.1 Macroroles as generalizations over specific thematic relations

village, the tidal wave is inanimate, but it is the actor. Similarly, we have PATIENT and THEME as the specific argument-types which are grouped together as undergoer. As the name implies, they are things which undergo something in a general sense. Keep in mind, however, that actor and undergoer are quite different from subject and object, because either the actor or the undergoer may be subject in English. So in a sentence like *y was killed by x*, the undergoer is the subject; whereas in *x killed y*, the actor is the subject. Therefore, these are distinct from grammatical relations. Actor and undergoer are generalizations across classes of specific argument positions in logical structure.

These generalizations are not unique to English; they are found in all languages, with some minor variation to be discussed below. The following examples illustrate these conflations of argument-types in Dyirbal (Dixon 1972); the arguments in question are in italics.

(4.4) a. Ba-yi ḏaban-∅ *ba-ŋgu-l*
DEIC-ABS.I eel-ABS DEIC-ERG-I
yaɽa-ŋgu ḏurga-ɲu. ([**do′** (x, . . .)] . . .)
man-ERG spear-TNS
'The man speared the eel.'

b. Ba-yi ḏaban-∅ *ba-ŋgu-n*
DEIC-ABS.I eel-ABS DEIC-ERG-II
ḏugumbi-ɽu buɽa-n. (**see′** (x, . . .))
woman-ERG see-TNS
'The woman saw the eel.'

(4.5) a. *Ba-la-∅* *yugu-∅* ba-ŋgu-l
DEIC-ABS-IV tree-ABS DEIC-ERG-I
yaɽa-ŋgu nudi-n. (. . . [BECOME **felled′** (y)])
man-ERG cut-TNS
'The man cut down the tree.'

b. *Bala* *yugu-∅* ba-ŋgu-l
DEIC-ABS-IV log-ABS DEIC-ERG-I
yaɽa-ŋgu ḏanayma-n. (. . . [**be-on′** (y, . . .)])
man-ERG stand.on-TNS
'The man is standing on the log.'

c. *Ba-la-m* *miraɲ-∅* ba-ŋgu-l
DEIC-ABS-III beans-ABS DEIC-ERG-I
yaɽa-ŋgu wuga-n ba-gu-n
man-ERG give-TNS DEIC-DAT-II
ḏugumbil-gu. (. . . [BECOME **have′** (. . . , z)])
woman- DAT
'The man gave beans to the woman.'

d. *Ba-la-n* *ḏugumbil-∅* ba-ŋgu-l
DEIC-ABS-II woman-ABS DEIC-ERG-I

yaɽa-ŋgu wuga-n ba-ŋgu-m
man-ERG give-TNS DEIC-INST-III
miraɲ-ḍu. (. . . [BECOME **have′** (y, . . .)])
beans-INST
'The man gave the woman beans.'

In Dyirbal the undergoer is the syntactic subject in the active voice, and yet the same types of argument conflations are found in (4.4)–(4.5). As in English, they occur in the marked voice form as well; this is the antipassive in Dyirbal, as in (4.6).

(4.6) a. Ba-la-n ḍugumbil-∅ ba-gu-l ḍaban-gu buɽal-ŋa-ɲu. (cf. (4.4b))
DEIC-ABS-II woman-ABS DEIC-DAT-I eel-DAT see-ANTI-TNS
'The woman saw the eel.'

b. Ba-yi yara-∅ ba-gu-n ḍugumbil-gu wugal-ŋa-ɲu
DEIC-ABS.I man-ABS DET-DAT woman-DAT give-ANTI-TNS
ba-ŋgu-m miraɲ-ḍu. (cf. (4.5d))
DEIC-INST-III beans-INST
'The man gave beans to the woman.'

In (4.6a) the actor *balan ḍugumbil* 'woman' is subject, while the undergoer *bagul ḍabangu* 'eel' is an oblique in the dative case, and the same pattern holds in (4.6b), analogous to the contrast between active and passive in English. (See chapter 6 for more detailed discussion of voice alternations.)

Languages vary narrowly with respect to the argument-types subsumed under actor or undergoer. Actor and undergoer are generalized semantic roles whose prototypes are the thematic relations AGENT and PATIENT, respectively. English happens to allow many argument-types in both the actor category and the undergoer category. Other languages, however, are much stricter. In Lakhota and Jakaltek (Craig 1977), for example, an INSTRUMENT cannot be actor, and therefore, INSTRUMENTS are always marked obliquely (cf. (3.8) and (3.9)). Only animate or quasi-animate entities, i.e. animate first arguments of **do′** or **pred′** (x, y) (see figure 3.2) can be actor in Lakhota and Jakaltek, unlike English, in which INSTRUMENTS can be actor. Thus, we are dealing with neutralizations of these argument-types which may vary in a limited way across languages (see section 7.4.1 for more detailed discussion).

One thing which is important to point out is that intransitive verbs can also take a wide range of different arguments. In *John is sick*, the subject, *John*, is a PATIENT, while in *The book is on the table, the book* is a THEME; in *Mary danced*, on the other hand, the subject is an EFFECTOR. In macrorole terms, the subject of *be sick* and *be on* is an undergoer, while the subject of *dance* is an actor. This shows that the single argument of an intransitive can be either actor or undergoer. The big difference between the notion of semantic macrorole and the notion of grammatical relation or grammatical function is that there is no semantic equivalent of intransitive subject; syntactically, there can be intransitive subject, transitive subject and transitive object, but semantically, there are only actor and undergoer. For English and many other languages, one can talk about a syntactic or a grammatical function of intransitive subject, but on the semantic level it is either an actor or an undergoer (see chapter 6).[1]

A very interesting situation arises with multiple-argument verbs. With verbs which take more than one argument, the choice of which argument will be actor and which will be undergoer is not random, and it is necessary to establish the principles which determine this. Recall that in English the actor is the subject of a clause with a transitive verb and the undergoer is the direct object. If a verb, for example, has a logical structure containing [**do′** (x, [. . . .])] CAUSE [[**do′** (y, [. . .])] CAUSE . . . (cf. (3.45)), how is it determined which role is going to be the actor? Similarly, if one looks at a range of verbs in English, it becomes clear that both THEMES and RECIPIENTS can be undergoer. The . . . [BECOME **have′** (. . . , z)] argument is the undergoer in a sentence like *John presented the plaque to Mary*, but the . . . [BECOME **have′** (y, . . .)] argument is undergoer in *John presented Mary with the book*; with *take* (in the sense of 'obtain', not in the sense of 'carry') only the THEME can be undergoer, as in *John took the book from Mary* (≠ *John took Mary the book*). With a verb which has more than one argument which could be undergoer, what criteria determine which one will be undergoer? In more general terms, what principles govern the interaction between arguments and macroroles?

A given verb may take more than one argument that is a potential actor or undergoer, and yet the choice, in the case of actors, is never random. In other words, there is only one possible actor with any given verb. The range of roles that can be actor includes AGENT, INSTRUMENT, PERCEIVER and RECIPIENT, as (4.1) shows. A verb like *break*, which is transitive, takes an EFFECTOR (the breaker; possibly an AGENT by implicature), an optional INSTRUMENT (the thing used to do the breaking) and a PATIENT (the thing broken, though right now we are not concerned about the patient). Either the INSTRUMENT or the AGENT–EFFECTOR can be the actor in English, as in ***The rock** broke the window* or ***John** broke the window.* If they both occur, there is no variation. Only *John broke the window with the rock* is possible, never **The rock broke the window by/with John.*

Therefore, when these two argument-types cooccur, there is an absolute priority of AGENT(-EFFECTOR) over INSTRUMENT for actor. In terms of the logical structure in (3.45), the *x* argument has absolute priority over the *y* argument for actorhood. Remember that the issue is not subject here, because in passives the same is true: *The window was broken by John with a rock*, not **The window was broken by a rock with John*. What about the first arguments of verbs of perception, cognition, propositional attitude and emotion? They tend not to cooccur with AGENTS or INSTRUMENTS, and therefore the kind of comparison that exists with AGENTS and INSTRUMENTS is not meaningful with AGENT or INSTRUMENT and PERCEIVER, COGNIZER, etc. There is no verb which allows variable actor choice in the sense of having two possible candidates, either of which could alternate as actor when both are present in the clause. In other words, if a speaker using *break* does not code the AGENT as actor but rather omits it, then the INSTRUMENT can be the actor. This lack of variability in actor selection is entirely reasonable, since the actor is the entity to which responsibility for the action or event is attributed, and normally there is only one such responsible entity encoded in a given verb. Where more than one possible responsible entity exists in a situation, then often there exists a pair of verbs, each of which lexicalizes one of the possibilities, e.g. *buy* vs. *sell.*

With undergoers, however, the situation is rather more complicated. It is possible, given certain actions with two non-actor arguments, to look at either argument as being the primary affected participant. For instance, if one says *load the hay onto the truck*, one can look at *the hay* as being affected because it is being relocated. Or one can say *load the truck with the hay*, in which case it is *the truck* which is getting filled up. A speaker can choose which argument he/she wants to focus on as being the one being primarily affected, and can therefore code it either way.

The undergoer, as the name implies, is the participant that the speaker is presenting as being most affected by the action. Therefore, if we have *load y on z*, the THEME is treated as being the primarily affected entity, as opposed to *load z with y*, where the LOCATION is the primarily affected entity. This, however, only applies when there is a choice, and there is not always a choice. For instance, patients never alternate with non-patients for undergoerhood. In a sentence like *John broke the cup against the glass*, the cup breaks, whereas in *John broke the glass with the cup*, the glass breaks. In both states of affairs, only the patient breaks, and there is no true alternation there. Hence with a verb like *break*, the PATIENT must be the undergoer. In causative achievement and accomplishment logical structures, the first and second arguments of the two-place state predicate, e.g. LOCATION and THEME, or POSSESSOR and POSSESSED, may alternate for undergoerhood, but PATIENTS never alternate with any other argument-type. In alternations between THEME and LOCATION for undergoerhood with *hit*, as in *hit the cane against the table* and *hit the table with the cane*, while both clauses involve contact and present different perspectives on it, *the cane* is the THEME (the entity moving) and *the table* the LOCATION (the place of contact) regardless of perspective. On the other hand, *break the cane against the table* and *break the table with the cane* do not mean the same thing (as in the former the cane breaks whereas in the latter the table breaks) and hence represent more than just different perspectives on the same event, and in each case, it is the PATIENT which is the undergoer.

As with actor, there is a ranking hierarchy for undergoerhood, with the prototype PATIENT (i.e. . . . **pred′** (x)) at the top, then the second argument of two-place state predicates (i.e. . . . **pred′** (. . . , y)), and then the first argument of two-place state predicates (i.e. . . . **pred′** (x, . . .)). The alternation between THEME- and LOCATIVE-type arguments is frequent with verbs which have ‘. . . BECOME/INGR

ACTOR				UNDERGOER
Arg. of DO	1st arg. of **do′** (x, . . .	1st arg. of **pred′** (x, y)	2nd arg. of **pred′** (x, y)	Arg. of state **pred′** (x)

[‘⟶’ = increasing markedness of realization of argument as macrorole]

Figure 4.2 The Actor–Undergoer Hierarchy

have′/be-LOC′/etc. (x, y)’ in their logical structure, but is not nearly as common with verbs which have ‘. . . BECOME/INGR NOT **have′/be-LOC′**/etc. (x, y)’ in their logical structure. For instance, it is possible to say *John gave the book to Mary* and *John gave Mary the book*, but not *John took the book from Fred* and **John took Fred of the book*. In order for this type of alternation to occur with verbs which take SOURCE arguments, two verbs are usually needed. For instance, with *rob* and *steal*, one can say *John robbed Fred of 50 dollars* and *John stole 50 dollars from Fred*. Therefore, those two verbs lexicalize this alternation, as there are very few verbs in English that allow this alternation. *Empty*, however, is one, as in *He emptied the water from the tank* and *He emptied the tank of its water*; another example is *drain*.[2] Thus, there are hierarchies of markedness for both actorhood and undergoerhood. This is summarized in the Actor–Undergoer Hierarchy in figure 4.2. When there is more than one argument of **do′**, as in the logical structure in (3.45), the argument of the first **do′** in the sequence has priority over arguments of subsequent **do′** predicates. Such a sequence represents what is often called a ‘causal chain’ (Langacker 1987, Croft 1991), i.e. a sequence of events in which the first causes the second, the second causes the third, etc. (cf. (3.5)), and it is the first EFFECTOR in such a causal chain which will be the actor.

What this hierarchy states is that ‘argument of DO’ (AGENT) is the unmarked choice for actor and ‘argument of **pred′** (x)’ (PATIENT) is the unmarked choice for undergoer. The arrows indicate increasing markedness of the occurrence of a particular argument-type as actor or undergoer. ‘Argument of DO’ is the least marked possibility for actor but the most marked possibility for undergoer. Conversely, ‘argument of **pred′** (x)’ is the least marked possibility for undergoer but the most marked possibility for actor. In fact, with a simple lexical verb it would be impossible for an AGENT to be undergoer or a PATIENT to be actor. With respect to actor, a marked choice is possible only if the higher-ranking arguments are not present in the clause. With respect to undergoer, on the other hand, a marked choice is possible if there is no PATIENT in the clause; with some verbs that have . . . BECOME/INGR (NOT) **have′/be-LOC′**/etc. (x, y) in their logical structure, either argument can be undergoer, and the occurrence of the *x* argument as undergoer does not change the meaning of the sentence.[3] Variable linking to undergoer will be discussed in chapter 7.

One last point needs to be made about macroroles: when macroroles occur as core arguments, they are always direct, never oblique. The only instance of an oblique macrorole is the actor in a passive construction, which may appear as a peripheral oblique element in some languages; in this case, however, it is not a core argument.

4.2 Valence, transitivity and macrorole assignment

We have been discussing issues of how many arguments a verb takes, and the general notion that covers this issue of how many arguments a verb takes is called **valence**. This notion was introduced independently in Tesnière (1953, 1959) and Hockett (1958). The syntactic valence of a verb is the number of overt morphosyntactically coded arguments it takes. One can talk about the semantic valence of the verb as well, where valence here refers to the number of semantic arguments that a particular verb can take. These two notions need not coincide. The two notions of valence are contrasted in table 4.1. *Rain* has no arguments semantically, but because all simple English clauses must have subjects, it has a syntactic valence of 1. *Eat* can have one argument, as in *Mary ate,* or two as in *Mary ate a sandwich. Put* can have three core arguments, as in *Dana put the files on the table*, or it can have only two, as in *Dana put the files away*. Some grammatical processes can also be described in terms of changing the valence of verbs. For example, passive is a syntactic valence-changing rule because in sentences like *John was killed* and *The sandwich was eaten* the syntactic valence of the verb is reduced from two to one. It is not necessary, however, for the semantic valence to change, as one can also say *John was killed* ***by the man*** and *The sandwich was eaten* ***by the boy***. The *by*-phrases are peripheral adjuncts and therefore do not count as part of the syntactic valence of the passive verb; but the actor NPs are semantic arguments of the verb. Syntactic valence-changing processes are an important part of grammar and will be discussed in chapter 6.

The discussion in the past several sections has been concerned with semantic valence, namely the number of arguments that a verb takes in its semantic representation or logical structure. We now turn to the question of syntactic valence.

Table 4.1 *Non-identity of semantic and syntactic valence*

	Semantic valence	*Syntactic valence*
rain	0	1
die	1	1
eat	2	1 or 2
put	3	3 or 2

Traditionally, syntactic valence has been equated with transitivity: verbs taking one core argument in the syntax are considered intransitive, verbs taking two are transitive, and verbs taking three (as in *Mary gave John the book*) are ditransitive. While there is manifestly some relationship between semantic and syntactic valence, as a glance at table 4.1 shows, the two are not identical, and it is necessary to determine if a predictive relationship can be uncovered; that is, is it possible to predict the syntactic valence of a verb from its semantic valence (logical structure)? Before attempting to answer this question, however, it is necessary to examine the important assumption mentioned above: is the syntactic valence of a verb the same as its transitivity?

To resolve this issue, it is necessary to find a case in which a verb with a certain number of arguments does not exhibit the syntactic behavior that would be predicted if its transitivity were assumed to be a direct function of its number of syntactic arguments. Such a case can be found with the verb *eat*, which appears to have variable transitivity: it can occur with only one argument, in which case it is intransitive, or it can appear with two, in which case it is transitive. Moreover, it also exhibits *Aktionsart* variation: its two-argument form can be either an activity or an active accomplishment, as we have seen. If transitivity is simply a function of the number of syntactic arguments that a verb takes, then it is to be expected that the two-argument form of *eat* should manifest consistent syntactic behavior. We will test this prediction by looking at the Italian verb *mangiare* 'eat', which is variably transitive like its English counterpart.

(4.7) a. Anna ha mangia-to spaghetti per/*in cinque minuti.
have.3sgPRES eat-PSTP for/in five minutes
'Anna ate spaghetti for five minutes.'
a′. Anna ha mangiato per cinque minuti.
'Anna ate for five minutes.'
b. **do′** (Anna, [**eat′** (Anna, spaghetti)])

(4.8) a. Anna ha mangia-to gli spaghetti *per/in cinque minuti.
have.3sgPRES eat-PSTP the
'Anna ate the spaghetti in five minutes.'
b. **do′** (Anna, [**eat′** (Anna, spaghetti)]) & BECOME **eaten′** (spaghetti)

In (4.7) and (4.8) *mangiare* 'eat' has two arguments, *Anna* and (*gli*) *spaghetti* '(the) spaghetti', and, as the temporal adverbials indicate, it is an activity in (4.7) and an active accomplishment in (4.8). Hence there are two uses of an apparently transitive verb with distinct *Aktionsarts*. Do the two versions of *mangiare* behave alike syntactically? We will look at two constructions, passive and participial absolutes (Rosen 1984). Italian, like English, has a very productive passive construction, and it would be expected that a transitive verb like *mangiare* would occur in it; this, however, is true only in part, as (4.9) shows.

(4.9) a. Gli spaghetti sono stat-i mangia-t-i da Anna in
the be.3plPRES be.PSTP-Mpl eat-PSTP-Mpl by in
cinque minuti.
five minutes
'The spaghetti was eaten by Anna in five minutes.'

b. *Spaghetti sono stati mangiati da Anna per cinque minuti.
are been eaten for
'Spaghetti was eaten by Anna for five minutes.'

b′. *Sono stati mangiati spaghetti da Anna per cinque minuti.

Surprisingly, only the active accomplishment form of *mangiare* can occur in a passive; the activity form cannot, regardless of whether *spaghetti* occurs preverbally or postverbally.[4] This is completely unexpected, if one assumes that having two arguments in the syntax is equivalent to being transitive. The second construction, participial absolutes, is illustrated in (4.10).

(4.10) a. Mangiati gli spaghetti, uscir-ono.
eat-PSTP-Mpl the went.out-3pl
'Having eaten the spaghetti, they went out.'

b. *Mangiati spaghetti, uscirono.
'Having eaten spaghetti, they went out.'

Here again there is no reason to expect that the two-argument activity form of *mangiare* should behave any differently from the active accomplishment form, and yet (4.10b) is impossible. The behavior of the active accomplishment version of *mangiare* in (4.9a) and (4.10a) is typical of canonical transitive verbs in Italian, and consequently because of the failure of the two-argument activity version of *mangiare* to manifest the same behavior, it must be concluded that the number of syntactic arguments alone does not correlate with transitivity.

What is the crucial difference between the two versions of *mangiare* that could explain their differential syntactic behavior? Active accomplishment *mangiare* has two syntactic arguments, and it also takes two macroroles, an actor and an undergoer. Likewise, activity *mangiare* has two syntactic arguments, but does it also have two macroroles? Recall from section 3.2.3.3 that the second argument in an activity logical structure is very different from all other arguments: if it is an inherent argument, as in (3.46)–(3.47), it is necessarily non-referential and serves to characterize the action rather than pick out any of the participants; if it is a referential argument, as in (3.48)–(3.51), then it is an oblique. In all of these examples the verb is intransitive. *Spaghetti* in (4.7a), (4.9b, b′) and (4.10b) is non-referential and therefore functions as an inherent argument. If it does not refer to any specific participant in a state of affairs, it cannot be an undergoer, because undergoer arguments refer to the participants which are viewed as primarily affected in the state of affairs; accordingly, undergoers must be referential. Consequently, the activity version of

Table 4.2 *Macrorole number and M-transitivity*

	Semantic valence	*Macrorole number*	*M-transitivity*
rain	0	0	Atransitive
die	1	1	Intransitive
eat [ACT]	1 or 2	1	Intransitive
eat [ACTACC]	2	2	Transitive
kill	2	2	Transitive
put	3	2	Transitive
give	3	2	Transitive

mangiare, unlike its active accomplishment counterpart, has only one macrorole argument, an actor. Having a single actor macrorole is a feature of canonical *in*-transitive activity verbs like *run*, *cry* and *fly*. Thus, two-argument activity verbs like *mangiare* and its English counterpart *eat* behave like intransitive, rather than transitive, verbs, despite having a syntactic valence of 2. This is perhaps clearest in ergative languages, in which the actor arguments of this type of multi-argument activity verb appear in the absolutive rather than the ergative case, absolutive being the case of intransitive subjects and ergative the case of transitive subjects; in the corresponding active accomplishment forms, they appear in the ergative case (cf. (3.49)–(3.51), section 6.4.3). With the vast majority of activity verbs, the second argument is realized either as an inherent argument (and incorporated in those languages with noun incorporation) or as an oblique core argument, as in (3.48)–(3.51).

Transitivity, then, cannot be characterized in terms of the number of syntactic arguments a verb takes (its syntactic valence) but must rather be defined in terms of the number of *macroroles* that it takes. We will, therefore, distinguish between **S-transitivity**, the number of syntactic arguments, and **M-transitivity**, the number of macroroles, following the proposal in Narasimhan (1995). In discussing transitivity hereafter, the default use of the term will refer to M-transitivity; whenever S-transitivity is intended, it will be specified explicitly. Given this definition, the facts regarding *mangiare* discussed above are to be expected, since activity verbs are normally intransitive, regardless of the number of syntactic arguments that appear with them. There are three transitivity possibilities in terms of macroroles: 0, 1 or 2. Zero macrorole verbs are terms 'M-atransitive'. This is represented in table 4.2.

The numbers in the 'semantic valence' column refer to the number of argument positions that a verb has in its logical structure. There is no notion of 'ditransitive' in terms of macroroles, since there are only two of them. Examples involving verbs of different transitivity are given in (4.11). ('∅' = not a macrorole, 'AJT' = adjunct.)

(4.11) a. It$_{\emptyset}$ rained.[5]
b. The horse$_{\text{UND}}$ died.
c. The bird$_{\text{ACTOR}}$ flew around in the room$_{\text{AJT}}$.
d. The boy$_{\text{ACTOR}}$ drank milk$_{\emptyset}$ for an hour$_{\text{AJT}}$.
e. The boy$_{\text{ACTOR}}$ drank the bottle of milk$_{\text{UND}}$ in twenty seconds$_{\text{AJT}}$.
f. The wolves$_{\text{ACTOR}}$ killed the deer$_{\text{UND}}$.
g. The deer$_{\text{UND}}$ was killed by the wolves$_{\text{ACTOR-AJT}}$.
h. Larry$_{\text{ACTOR}}$ put the watch$_{\text{UND}}$ on the table$_{\emptyset}$.
i. The nurse$_{\text{ACTOR}}$ handed the scalpel$_{\text{UND}}$ to the doctor$_{\emptyset}$.
j. The nurse$_{\text{ACTOR}}$ handed the doctor$_{\text{UND}}$ the scalpel$_{\emptyset}$.

These examples reinforce the point made in section 4.1 that macroroles are distinct from grammatical relations: actor is subject in (c)–(f) and (h)–(j) and an adjunct in (g), undergoer is subject in (b) and (g) and object in (e)–(f) and (h)–(j), and non-macrorole elements are subject in (a) and object in (d). They also highlight an important fact about the morphosyntactic realization of macrorole arguments: they are normally direct arguments of the verb, usually subject or object, and they are oblique *only* in voice constructions, e.g. the actor may be an adjunct in a passive, as in (4.11g).

Is there any systematic relationship between the number of arguments in logical structure and the transitivity of a verb? The answer is 'yes', and the basic principle is very simple: the number of macroroles that a verb has is less than or equal to the number of arguments in its logical structure. That is, a verb can have fewer macroroles than it has arguments, e.g. *give* and *put*; it can have the same number, e.g. *die*; but, not surprisingly, it cannot have more macroroles than it has arguments. For verbs that take 0 or 2 macroroles, the identity of the macroroles is unambiguous, but what about verbs that take 1? The macrorole can be either actor or undergoer. Does the identity of the macrorole with intransitive verbs follow from any sort of general principle? Again, the answer is 'yes', and the basic principle is very simple: the single macrorole with an intransitive verb is actor if the verb has an activity predicate in its logical structure; otherwise it is undergoer. We can see why this is true if we look at single-argument activity, achievement, accomplishment and state verbs. Verbs like *run*, *fly*, *dance*, *rotate*, *bounce* and *cry* all take EFFECTOR-type arguments, which are high on the actor end of the Actor–Undergoer Hierarchy in figure 4.2. Hence they would be actor arguments. Predicates like *be dead/broken/dry* (state) take PATIENT for their single argument, and their arguments are therefore undergoers. Adding BECOME or INGR to the logical structure to derive accomplishment and achievement verbs does not affect the argument structure, and therefore the arguments of these verbs would also be PATIENTS and undergoers. If, on the other hand, the language had single lexical verbs meaning 'start to cry', 'start to sing', 'start to run', etc., then by the same argument the addition of BECOME or INGR to the basic activity logical structure would not effect their argument structure, and therefore these arguments would be actors. It is on the basis of these facts that the general principle above was formulated. Note, however, that the same results could be captured if the principle were 'the single macrorole with an intransitive verb is undergoer if the verb has a state predicate in its logical structure; otherwise it is actor'. How can we choose between the two formulations? The crucial test is active accomplishment predications like *run to the store*; its logical structure from (3.30) is repeated below.

(4.12) a. **do′** (x, [**run′** (x)]) — Activity
b. **do′** (x, [**run′** (x)]) & BECOME **be-at′** (y, x)[6] — Active accomplishment
c. Paul ran to the store.
c′. **do′** (Paul, [**run′** (Paul)]) & BECOME **be-at′** (store, Paul)

Paul is both a subtype of EFFECTOR and also a THEME in the logical structure in (4.12b, c′); is it an actor or an undergoer? Strong evidence that it is an actor comes from the fact that it is subject to the agency inference discussed in section 3.2.3.2. That is, *run* is a verb whose first argument may or may not be construed agentively, as in *Paul inadvertently/intentionally ran into the dining room*, and this is possible *only* with actors, not with undergoers. This can be seen clearly in the contrast in (4.13).

(4.13) a. *The soldiers* marched to the mess hall (on purpose).
(AGENT interpretation possible)
b. The sergeant marched *the soldiers* to the mess hall (on purpose).
(AGENT interpretation impossible)

The NP *the soldiers* is an animate EFFECTOR-type argument in both (a) and (b), and the crucial difference between them is that it is actor in (a) but undergoer in (b). Since the AGENT interpretation is possible only in (a), this shows that this reading is possible only with animate EFFECTORS which are also actors. This becomes clear when *on purpose* is added; it may be construed as modifying the soldiers' actions in (a), but in (b) it cannot; it can only be interpreted as modifying the sergeant's actions. Hence the agent implicature is impossible when an animate EFFECTOR argument is undergoer, as in (4.13b). Since *Paul* in (4.12c) is available for the agent implicature, it must be an actor, not an undergoer. Since this logical structure contains both an activity predicate and a state predicate, only the first principle ('the single macrorole with an intransitive verb is actor if the verb has an activity predicate in its logical structure; otherwise it is undergoer') makes the correct prediction that *Paul* is an actor and therefore can be interpreted as an AGENT in (4.12c).

These principles are summarized in (4.14).

(4.14) *Default macrorole assignment principles*
a. Number: the number of macroroles a verb takes is less than or equal to the number of arguments in its logical structure,

1 If a verb has two or more arguments in its LS, it will take two macroroles.
2 If a verb has one argument in its LS, it will take one macrorole.

b. Nature: for verbs which take one macrorole,

1 If the verb has an activity predicate in its LS, the macrorole is actor.
2 If the verb has no activity predicate in its LS, the macrorole is undergoer.

There are some systematic exceptions to (4.14a1). First, the majority of activity verbs, regardless of how many arguments they have, take no more than one macrorole. Of the subclasses given in table 3.5, only activity verbs of directed perception and of use regularly take two macroroles, e.g. *watch* and *use.*[7] Since the directed perception verbs are derived from the stative perception verbs, which are transitive, they inherit the transitivity of the source verb. Aside from these two subclasses, activity verbs normally behave like intransitive verbs, regardless of the number of arguments. Which macrorole it is is correctly predicted by (4.14b): it is always actor. Second, verbs of location and change of location are normally M-intransitive in many languages, despite having two arguments (the moving entity and the location) in their logical structure, whereas in many others they are M-transitive. Talmy (1985, 1991) proposed a typological contrast between what he calls 'verb-framed' languages and 'satellite-framed' languages; it is illustrated in (4.15).

(4.15)	a. The girl ran into the room.	Satellite-framed
	b. The girl entered the room (running).	Verb-framed

One of the properties of a satellite-framed language is that verbs of motion typically encode motion + manner, and path or goal information is expressed by a satellite, such as a PP or adverbial; in (a), the verb *run* expresses motion + manner, and the goal is expressed by the PP *into the room*. In a verb-framed language, on the other hand, the verb encodes motion + path/goal, and manner is typically expressed by an adjunct of some kind; in (b) the verb *enter* expresses motion + goal, the goal being realized by its direct object, and manner can be expressed via an optional participial expression, *running*. Talmy argues that Romance and Slavic languages, as well as Japanese and Korean, are prototypical verb-framed languages, while Germanic languages, Mandarin Chinese and Lakhota are all examples of satellite-framed languages. English, as (4.15) shows, has both types of verb; note that *run* is a verb of Germanic origin, while *enter* is a borrowing from Romance. Thus in verb-framed languages, verbs of motion will tend strongly to be M-transitive, treating the goal as an undergoer, whereas in satellite-framed languages they will tend strongly to be M-intransitive, with the goal realized as an oblique core argument. Accordingly, verbs of motion in verb-framed languages would tend to follow (4.14a), while their analogs in satellite-framed languages would tend to violate (4.14a). It would make little sense, then, to mark most or all verbs of motion as having exceptional M-transitivity in a satellite-framed language; rather, in this type of language, M-intransitive verbs of motion should be treated as the norm and M-transitive ones as the exception. Hence in English, a Germanic language and therefore basically satellite-framed, *enter* is the exceptional verb, whereas in a verb-framed language *run* would be.

4.3 Lexical entries for verbs

We now turn to issues relating to the lexicon. Historically, the lexicon has been viewed as a list of irregularities, a mere appendage to the grammar (Bloomfield 1933), but over the last twenty-five years it has come to play a very important role in linguistic theory and analysis. The information contained in lexical entries is very important, as it consists of the crucial semantic, morphosyntactic and other properties which determine how a lexical item will behave grammatically. Theories differ with respect to the kind of information to be represented and on whether apparently related forms are to be represented separately as distinct lexical entries or derived one from the other by rules in the lexicon.

The logical structure of the verb is the heart of its lexical entry. There is no need to specify the thematic relations that the verb takes; they follow without stipulation from the logical structure, since they follow by definition from its structure. There is likewise no need to specify transitivity if the verb follows the principles in (4.14). The principles in (4.14) are general ones that operate across all entries for verbs in the lexicon; the information contained in them does not need to be stated in each lexical entry. But what about verbs that do not follow these principles? For verbs with exceptional M-transitivity, their logical structure will be augmented by a [MRα] feature, where 'MR' stands for 'macrorole'. [MR2] signals that the verb is M-transitive, i.e. takes two macroroles, [MR1] indicates that a verb is M-intransitive, and [MR0] records that the verb is M-atransitive, i.e. has no macroroles. An example of an [MR0] verb is *seem*; it is a propositional attitude verb, and its logical structure is **seem′** (x, y), where the first argument is an individual and the second a proposition. The curious property of *seem* is that neither of these arguments can appear as a direct argument in a core headed by *seem*: the first argument, if realized, must be in a prepositional phrase, and the second must occur as an extraposed clause, e.g. *It seems to me that Harry will win the race.* Since macroroles must be realized as direct arguments (subject or direct object) except in marked voice constructions (and there is no issue of voice here), neither of these arguments is a macrorole.[8] Hence *seem* is [MR0], and this would be indicated in its lexical entry. Another interesting example is the contrast between *own* and *belong to*; both are state possession predicates, but *own* is transitive and *belong* (*to*) intransitive. Hence the lexical entry for *belong* (*to*) will carry the [MR1] feature. We will return to the issue of determining the transitivity of verbs in chapter 7 as part of the discussion of case marking and agreement; as we will see, the *own–belong* (*to*) type of M-transitivity contrast is very common cross-linguistically. Examples of lexical entries for a number of English verbs are given in (4.16).

(4.16)	a.	*kill*	[**do′** (x, ∅)] CAUSE [BECOME **dead′** (y)]
	b.	*receive*	BECOME **have′** (x, y)
	c.	*own*	**have′** (x, y)
	d.	*belong* (*to*)	**have′** (x, y) [MR1]
	e.	*arrive*	BECOME **be-at′** (x, y)
	f.	*go*	**do′** (x, [**move.away.from.ref.point′** (x)]) & BECOME **be-LOC′** (y, x)
	g.	*seem*	**seem′** (x, y) [MR0]
	h.	*see*	**see′** (x, y)
	i.	*watch*	**do′** (x, [**see′** (x, y)])
	j.	*show*	[**do′** (w, ∅)] CAUSE [BECOME **see′** (x, y)]
	k.	*run*	**do′** (x, [**run′** (x)])
	l.	*drink*	**do′** (x, [**drink′** (x, y)])
	m.	*melt*	BECOME **melted′** (x)
	n.	*afraid*	**feel′** (x, [**afraid′** (y)])

Given a lexical entry like (4.16d) for *belong* (*to*), how is the choice of which argument will function as the macrorole argument determined? To answer this question, let's start by adding *Kim* and *book* to it, yielding **have′** (Kim, book) [MR1]. Since this verb is M-intransitive, as indicated by [MR1], it will have only a single macrorole argument. Which one? Following the principles in (4.14b), it must be undergoer, because this is a state predicate logical structure and lacks an activity predicate component. The next question is, which argument functions as undergoer? To answer this, we must look at the Actor–Undergoer Hierarchy in figure 4.2. *Kim* is the first argument of a two-place state predicate, and *book* is the second argument of a two-place state predicate, and with respect to the undergoer end of the hierarchy, *book* outranks *Kim* and therefore functions as undergoer. Since the single macrorole argument of intransitive verbs functions as subject in English, *book* will appear as subject, and *Kim* will appear as an oblique core argument, yielding *The book belongs to Kim.* If, on the other hand, the logical structure had been **have′** (Kim, book) for *own*, the result would have been very different. *Own* is M-transitive and therefore has two macrorole arguments, an actor and an undergoer. When we look at the Actor–Undergoer Hierarchy again, we see that *Kim* is the higher-ranking argument with respect to the actor end of the hierarchy and *book* is the higher-ranking with respect to the undergoer end (and conversely, each is the lower-ranking with respect to the other macrorole). Accordingly, *Kim* is the actor and *book* the undergoer, yielding *Kim owns the book* (assuming the default mapping of actor to subject and undergoer to direct object with transitive verbs in English).

Logical structures like **feel′** (Pat, [**angry.at′** (Kelly)]) for *Pat is angry at Kelly* and **be′** (Leslie, [**neurolinguist′**]) *Leslie is a neurolinguist* require brief comment in the context of determining macrorole assignments. The second argument in this type of logical structure is always a predicate, not a referring expression, and therefore it cannot function as an argument in the sentence; rather, it always appears as the predicate or part of the predicate in the nucleus (see section 3.2.2). Consequently, despite having two argument positions, these verbs are necessarily M-intransitive, and therefore need not be marked as such. Because they are states, their single macrorole is undergoer, and the one available argument will function as undergoer. Some of the internal sensation predicates can take an optional second argument, as in *be angry at* above. Since *Kelly* is an argument of the embedded predicate, it will always be outranked for undergoer by the matrix argument (*Pat*) in the logical structure and will appear as an oblique core argument.

Thus, given the principles in (4.14), the Actor–Undergoer Hierarchy in figure 4.2, and mapping principles relating macroroles to syntactic functions (see section 4.5, chapters 6 and 7), only minimal information needs to be specified in the lexical entries for verbs in most cases. In particular, it is not necessary to include what is called 'syntactic subcategorization' information in other theories, i.e. information about whether a verb takes a direct object, an indirect object, a PP, etc. This is a function of the M-transitivity of a verb, and for most verbs it follows from the principles in (4.14). It is also not necessary in most cases to specify which argument functions as which macrorole, since this follows from the Actor–Undergoer Hierarchy in figure 4.2 (but see below for some exceptions involving three-argument verbs). Finally, it is not necessary to specify which argument will function as subject, which as direct object, etc., since this follows from the macrorole assignments and the principles mapping macroroles into the syntax, as we saw in the examples involving *own* and *belong to* above.

There are three types of information that are not expressed directly in logical structures which in some cases must be indicated. The first is specific requirements that a verb imposes on one or more of its arguments; for example, the first argument of *see* (and by extension, the first argument of *look at* and the second argument of *show*) must be a sentient, animate entity, while the first argument of *receive* (and by extension, the second argument in the logical structure of *give* – see (3.44b)) must be either animate or some sort of institutional or organizational entity (see section 4.7). Many of these aspects of the meaning of a verb would be represented in a full decomposition, but given that no such representation exists at present, they will have to be stipulated for the time being. Given that this is not a feature of *see* alone but rather of the first argument of all perception, cognition, propositional attitude, emotion and internal experience verbs, one could formulate a very general lexical principle: the first argument in the logical structure of predicates of perception, cognition, propositional attitude, emotion and internal experience must be sentient. By stating this in terms of logical structure predicates instead of verbs, it covers both the state verbs and the related activities, achievements and accomplishments.

The second type of information is argument identity; that is, there are verbs in whose logical structure the same referent appears in more than one argument position. A simple example of this is found in activity verbs, where the first argument of **do′** is also the first argument of the embedded predicate in the second argument position of **do′**. This identity is signaled by using the same variable for both positions, as in (4.16i, l). A more complex example involves verbs like *take, buy, steal* and *get*, in which the effector is also the recipient; with all of these verbs, the effector undertakes some action which brings it about that he/she comes into possession of some entity. The general logical structure for this type of transfer is given in (4.17a), which contrasts with the *give*-type logical structure in (b).

(4.17) a. [**do′** (x, ∅)] CAUSE [BECOME NOT **have′** (y, z) & BECOME **have′** (x, z)]
a′. Bill_x took the book_z from Fred_y.
b. [**do′** (x, ∅)] CAUSE [BECOME **have′** (y, z)]
b′. Bill_x gave the book_z to Fred_y.

The logical structure in (4.17a) is significant for two reasons: first, it shows that a single participant (in this case, *Bill*) can be represented in more than one argument position, and the identity of the EFFECTOR and RECIPIENT is signaled by the use of the identical variable; second, it illustrates the representation of a complex event, one involving both loss of possession and coming into possession, which includes both SOURCE and RECIPIENT arguments. It would be possible to expand the logical structure in (b) to make explicit the SOURCE function of the *x* argument, i.e. [**do′** (x, ∅)] CAUSE [BECOME NOT **have′** (x, z) & BECOME **have′** (y, z)]. This makes the logical structure for *give* more parallel to that of *take*, with the only differences being the placement of the *x* and *y* arguments in the logical structures.

The third type of information refers to the possibility of variable undergoer choice with a verb with three or more arguments. Given the logical structure in (4.17b), it is possible for either *y* or *z* to be undergoer. But this is not the case with the logical structure in (4.17a); (4.17a′) is the only possible form, as **Bill took Fred of the book* is quite impossible. This lack of variable undergoer choice seems to be a general property of this type of change of possession verb; it is also impossible with *get, buy* and also *steal*, which has *rob* as the instantiation of the alternative linking possibility (*Bill stole $500 from the bank* vs. *Bill robbed the bank of $500*).[9] Hence for these verbs, unlike verbs like *give*, the linking to undergoer must be specified in the logical structure. Thus to the logical structure in (4.17a) the specification 'U = z' must be added. If it were the case that this restriction applied to whole classes of verbs, then it would be stated as a general constraint on the class, analogous to the way the requirement that the first argument of a number of verb classes be sentient was formulated above.

There are also instances of fixed undergoer choice with two-argument state verbs that must be indicated. As we saw in the discussion of *belong to* above, given a logical structure like **predicate′** (x, y) [MR1], the rules in (4.14) require that the single macrorole be an undergoer, and in terms of the Actor–Undergoer Hierarchy, the *y* argument should be the undergoer.[10] This is the norm, but there are verbs of this type with which the *x* argument is the undergoer. An example from Latin is the verb *memini* 'remember' as in *memini vivorum* (remember.1sgPRES living.GEN) 'I remember the living' (Michaelis 1993); the logical structure would be **remember′** (1sg, living).[11] These are both M-intransitive verbs and therefore take an undergoer as their single macrorole, but, contrary to the Actor–Undergoer Hierarchy, the *x* argument functions as undergoer. This is analogous to the lexicalized choice of undergoer with three-argument verbs discussed above. As in those cases, a specification like 'U = x' would have to appear in the lexical entries for these verbs.

The non-macrorole arguments in (4.17a′) and (b′) are marked by prepositions, and it is standardly assumed that these prepositions must be listed in the lexical entries of the verbs they occur with. However, it is normally not necessary to list them, because they can usually be predicted from the logical structure of a verb. This will be developed in detail in chapter 7, but the basic approach can be sketched out quickly here. In (4.17), *to* marks the first argument of BECOME **have′** when it is not undergoer, and *from* marks the first argument of BECOME NOT **have′** when it is not undergoer. This pattern is not restricted to arguments of the predicate **have′** in logical structure. In (4.16j), the first argument of **see′** in the logical structure for *show* is marked by *to* if it is not undergoer (*John showed the picture to Bill*), and in a sentence like *Sally removed the book from the shelf* ([**do′** (Sally, ∅)] CAUSE [BECOME NOT **be-on′** (shelf, book)]), the first argument of BECOME NOT **be-on′** is not undergoer and is marked by *from*. Thus there appears to be a general pattern here, which is summarized in (4.18).

(4.18) a. Assign *to* to non-MR *x* argument in LS segment: . . . BECOME/INGR **pred′** (x, y)
b. Assign *from* to non-MR *x* argument in LS segment: . . . BECOME/INGR NOT **pred′** (x, y)

Given general rules like these, it is not necessary to list *to* and *from* in the lexical entry of every verb they occur with. In languages with extensive case systems, it is likewise not necessary to specify in lexical entries for verbs which cases particular core arguments take, except in instances of extreme idiosyncrasy. We will return to the issue of case marking, including preposition assignment, in chapter 7.

4.4 The representation of adjuncts and operators

In the previous sections we have developed a system of lexical representation which yields a semantic representation for the core of the clause, i.e. for the predicate in the nucleus and its core arguments. We have as yet said nothing about how adjuncts, including peripheral constituents, and operators such as tense, aspect and modality (see section 2.2.3) are to be represented semantically. We will explore this issue in this section, beginning with adjuncts.

4.4.1 Adjuncts: adpositions and adverbs

There are two types of adjunct to be discussed: peripheral PPs and adverbs. We will examine their representation in both the semantic representation and the layered syntactic structure of the clause.

4.4.1.1 Adpositions

We start off with a typology of prepositions, following Jolly (1991, 1993). She posits three types of prepositions: (1) *argument-marking prepositions*; (2) *adjunct prepositions*, which are predicates in their own right, introduce an NP into the clause and head PPs which are peripheral (adjunct) modifiers of the core; and (3) *argument-adjunct prepositions*, which are predicates in their own right, introduce an argument into the clause and share it with the logical structure of the core, rather than taking the logical structure of the core as an argument.[12]

Argument-marking prepositions were discussed briefly at the end of section 4.3, and the rules for assigning *to* and *from* were given in (4.18). This type of adposition will be analyzed in more detail in section 7.3.2.1. The adpositions in peripheral PP adjuncts are always predicative by definition, since they do not mark arguments of the verb (see section 2.3.1). Since they modify the core as a whole, they take the logical structure of the verb of the clause as one of their arguments, as illustrated in (4.19).

(4.19) a. Sam baked a cake in the kitchen.
b. **be-in′** (kitchen, [[**do′** (Sam, ∅)] CAUSE [BECOME **baked′** (cake)]])

The same representation is given to temporal adjunct PPs, as in (4.20).

(4.20) a. Sam baked a cake after work.
b. **be-after′** (work, [[**do′**(Sam, ∅)] CAUSE [BECOME **baked′** (cake)]])

In both of these representations the logical structure of the event is treated as an entity being located with respect to a spatial or temporal reference point.

Argument-adjunct prepositions are predicates, but they introduce an argument rather than a modifier. We have already encountered one example of this type of preposition in chapter 3 in the alternation between *run* (activity) and *run to the store* (active accomplishment). The logical structures from (3.30) are repeated in (4.21).

(4.21) a. **do′** (x, [**run′** (x)]) — Activity
b. **do′** (x, [**run′** (x)]) & BECOME **be-at′** (y, x) — Active accomplishment
c. Paul ran to the store.
c′. **do′** (Paul, [**run′** (Paul)]) & BECOME **be-at′** (store, Paul)

To functions like a predicate here, with its own logical structure, and it introduces an argument, *the store*. It differs from argument-marking prepositions, in that the meaning of its argument is not derived from the logical structure of the verb, and from adjunct prepositions in that it does not take a logical structure as one of its arguments; rather, it shares an argument with the logical structure of the verb, in this example, *Paul*. It is this shared argument which is the defining feature of argument–adjunct prepositions.

Verbs like *put* and *place* present a slightly more complicated situation. They each can take a range of locative prepositions, as shown in (4.22a, b). The logical structures for these examples would include the components in (c)–(g).

(4.22) a. Robin placed the book on/under the shelf.
b. Robin put the book in/next to/behind the box.
c. . . . BECOME **be-on′** (shelf, book)
d. . . . BECOME **be-under′** (shelf, book)
e. . . . BECOME **be-in′** (box, book)
f. . . . BECOME **be-next.to′** (box, book)
g. . . . BECOME **be-behind′** (box, book)

Given these possibilities, it would be best to represent the logical structure of *put* and *place* as [**do′** (x, Ø)] CAUSE [BECOME **be-LOC′** ((y), z)], and in the actual semantic representation of a sentence **be-LOC′** would be replaced by the logical structure of a preposition such as those in (4.22c–g), all of which can function predicatively on their own. They must be considered argument-adjunct PPs in this use, despite being part of the derived logical structure of the verb, because they introduce an argument which is only indirectly an argument of *put* or *place*. In the logical structure for *put* the argument structure is incomplete, and the full argument structure is a function of the logical structure for *put* plus the logical structure for the preposition. This is important, because *put* does not always take three arguments; if it combines with an intransitive preposition, e.g. *down*, the result is a two-argument core, e.g. *Yolanda put the book down* ([**do′** (Yolanda, Ø)] CAUSE [BECOME **be-down′** (book)]), in which *Yolanda* and *the book* are the core arguments and *down* is an intransitive preposition, not an argument of *put*.

We now turn to the syntactic representation of PPs in clause structure. In section 2.3.1 we made a distinction between predicative prepositions, those that function as

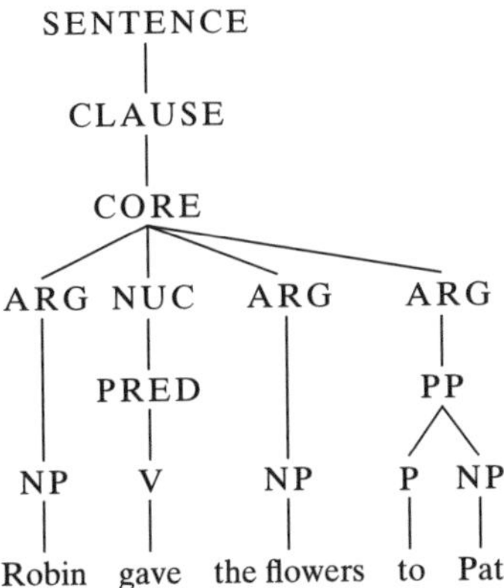

Figure 4.3 Syntactic representation of argument-marking non-predicative preposition

predicates, and non-predicative prepositions, those that function basically like a case marker. This distinction parallels the typology of PPs we have set up, since only non-predicative PPs can function as argument markers, and both argument-adjunct and adjunct PPs are always predicative.

The best example of an argument-marking preposition is *to* with *give*. The constituent projection of *Robin gave the flowers to Pat* is given in figure 4.3. As in figure 2.20b, the preposition *to* is not represented as a predicate but rather as simply marking the third argument of *give*. The semantics of its argument is entirely a function of the semantics of the verb in the nucleus.

Argument-adjunct prepositions present the interesting intermediate case between argument-marking and adjunct prepositions; they are always predicative. Their logical structure introduces an argument into the core, and they either share an argument with the logical structure of the main predicate or occur as a subpart of the verb's logical structure, as with *put.* Their argument is only indirectly at best an argument of the verb in the nucleus. Because they do not take the whole logical structure of the core as an argument and introduce a modifier, they do not occur in the periphery. Hence they are part of the core of the clause, and we need to distinguish them from the arguments of the main predicate in the nucleus. In order to do this, we introduce the label 'AAJ' for 'argument-adjunct'. The syntactic representations of *Sam ran to the store* (see (4.21)) and *Yolanda put the book in the box* are given in figure 4.4.

There can be more than one argument-adjunct PP with some verbs; for example, in *Sam ran from his office to the store*, both *from his office* and *to the store* are argument-adjunct PPs. This raises the question of how freely argument-adjunct PPs can be added to clauses. There appear to be three basic situations in which the logical structure of the verb may be so augmented as to allow the occurrence of these PPs.

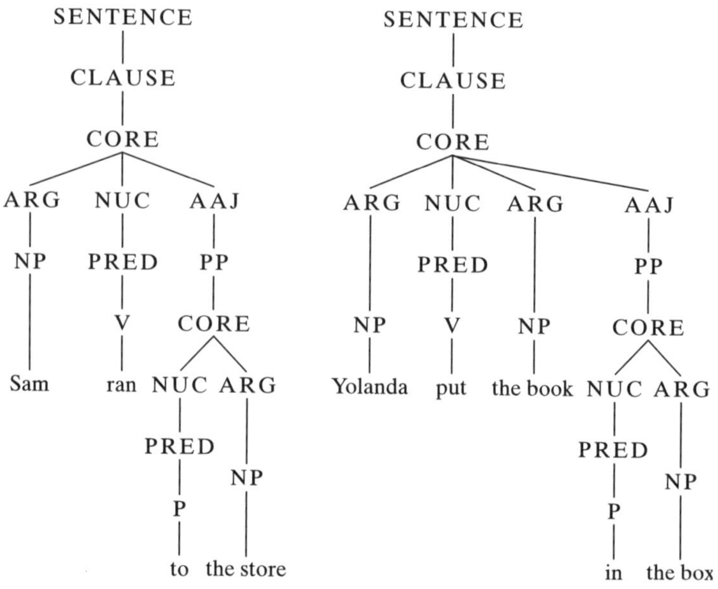

Figure 4.4 Syntactic representation of argument-adjunct predicative prepositions

They are: (1) specifying the range of motion with a verb of motion (e.g. *run*, *walk*) or induced motion (e.g. *push, pull, move*), which includes specification of a SOURCE, a PATH and/or a GOAL; (2) specifying an IMPLEMENT with certain types of activity verbs, e.g. *eat, look at, sew, fight, write*; and (3) specifying a beneficiary of some kind with *for.* We will discuss prepositions further in section 7.2.3.

Adjunct PPs occur in the periphery and are always predicative. A representation of *Robin saw Pat after the concert* is given in figure 4.5.

4.4.1.2 Adverbs

Adverbs are not restricted to the periphery and may modify any layer of the clause. Semantically, we will treat them as one-place predicates which take a logical structure or subpart of a logical structure as their argument, following the approach of Jackendoff (1972) and others. Peripheral bare NP adverbs like *tomorrow* and *yesterday* take the logical structure of the core as their argument.

(4.23) a. Sam baked a cake yesterday.
b. **yesterday′** ([**do′** (Sam, ∅)] CAUSE [BECOME **baked′** (cake)])

If there are multiple peripheral adjuncts, they are layered, with the last one represented as the highest predicate, as in (4.24).

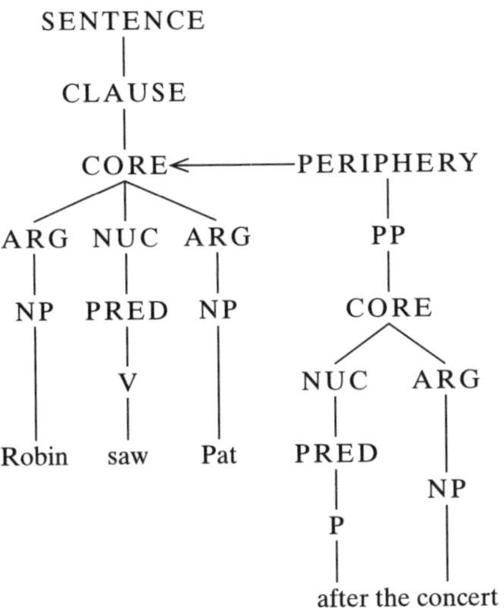

Figure 4.5 Syntactic representation of adjunct predicative preposition

(4.24) a. Sam baked a cake in the kitchen yesterday.
b. **yesterday′** (**be-in′** (kitchen, [[**do′** (Sam, ∅)] CAUSE [BECOME **baked′** (cake)]]))

In addition to temporal adverbs, epistemic and evidential adverbs may also take a core in their scope.

(4.25) a. Evidently, Sam baked a cake in the kitchen yesterday. Evidential
a′. **evident′** (**yesterday′** (**be-in′** (kitchen, [[**do′** (Sam, ∅)] CAUSE [BECOME **baked′** (cake)]])))
b. Probably, Sam will bake a cake tomorrow. Epistemic
b′. **probable′** (**tomorrow′** ([**do′** (Sam, ∅)] CAUSE [BECOME **baked′** (cake)]))

An important consideration is that these same epistemic and evidential adverbs have adjectival forms which can function as complement-taking predicates, as in (4.26).

(4.26) a. It is evident that Sam baked a cake in the kitchen yesterday.
b. It is probable that Sam will bake a cake tomorrow.

It is reasonable to propose that the same semantic representations underlie both forms, i.e. (4.25a′) for both (4.25a) and (4.26a), and (4.25b′) for both (4.25b) and (4.26b).[13]

Manner, pace and aspectual adverbs are also represented as one-place predicates taking a subpart of a logical structure as its argument. Manner adverbs typically modify activity logical structures, given their meaning (see section 3.2.1, test 2 for *Aktionsart* class in table 3.1). Examples are given in (4.27).

(4.27) a. The house shook vigorously during the earthquake.
a′. **during′** (earthquake, [**vigorous′** (**do′** (house, [**shake′** (house)]))])
b. Hamid crushed the box violently/Hamid violently crushed the box.
b′. [**violent′** (**do′** (Hamid, ∅))] CAUSE [BECOME **crushed′** (box)]

Pace adverbs, e.g. *slowly*, *quickly*, can modify any durative or dynamic logical structure.

(4.28) a. The door closed slowly/The door slowly closed.
a′. **slow′** (BECOME **closed′** (door))
b. The rabbit ran into the garden quickly/The rabbit quickly ran into the garden.
b′. **do′** (rabbit, [**run′** (rabbit)]) & **quick′** (BECOME **be-in′** (garden, rabbit))
b″. **quick′** (**do′** (rabbit, [**run′** (rabbit)])) & BECOME **be-in′** (garden, rabbit)
c. The boy closed the door slowly/The boy slowly closed the door.
c′. [**do′** (boy, ∅)] CAUSE [**slow′** (BECOME **closed′** (door))]
c″. [**slow′** (**do′** (boy, ∅))] CAUSE [BECOME **closed′** (door)]

Note that with an active accomplishment, as in (4.28b), and a causative accomplishment, as in (4.28c), the position of the pace adverb can lead to different interpretations, as indicated in the logical structures; the sentence-final position in (b) and (c) seems to be readily compatible with both interpretations, while preverbal placement favors the (b″) and (c″) readings. Variable positioning of the adverb in a sentence with a simple accomplishment logical structure, as in (a), has no such effect. Finally, aspectual adverbs like *completely* or *continuously* are modifiers of the basic state or activity predicates themselves.

(4.29) a. The ice melted completely/The ice completely melted.
a′. BECOME [**complete′** (**melted′** (ice))]
b. He talked continuously during the class.
b′. **during′** (class, [**continuous′** (**do′** (he, (**talk′** (he)])])
c. Hamid crushed the box completely/Hamid completely crushed the box.
c′. [**do′** (Hamid, ∅)] CAUSE [BECOME [**complete′** (**crushed′** (box))]]

Unlike pace adverbs, variation in the position of aspectual adverbs does not affect their interpretation in a causative accomplishment logical structure.

In chapter 2 we did not discuss the position of non-peripheral adverbs in the layered structure of the clause. Like peripheral adverbs, they are not operators but they are modifiers which are sensitive to the layered structure of the clause, in particular to the operator projection. Aspectual adverbs modify the predicate in the nucleus (analogous to aspect as a nuclear operator), while pace and manner adverbs are core-internal modifiers (analogous to modality as a core operator). Hence they will be represented in both constituent and operator projections; in the constituent projection, they will be treated as constituents of the appropriate level, unless they occupy one of the special syntactic positions, e.g. the left-detached position or precore slot, and their scope of modification will be represented in the operator projection.

Thus a manner adverb like *skillfully* would be represented as a constituent of the core in the constituent projection and as a modifier of the core in the operator projection. Manner and pace adverbs interact in an important way with the tense operator; those which occur before the tense operator can be construed as clausal modifiers, while those occurring after tense cannot be, as McConnell-Ginet (1982) has pointed out. This is illustrated in (4.30).

(4.30) a. Ruth cleverly hid the cash.
b. Ruth hid the cash cleverly.
b′. [**clever′** (**do′** (Ruth, ∅))] CAUSE [BECOME **hidden′** (cash)]
c. Cleverly, Ruth hid the cash.
c′. **clever′** ([**do′** (Ruth, ∅)] CAUSE [BECOME **hidden′** (cash)])

The first sentence is ambiguous between two readings; the first is that the manner in which she hid the cash was clever (= (4.30b, b′)), and the second is that the fact that she hid the cash was clever (= (4.30c, c′)). The other two sentences are each unambiguous. What all of these examples of adverb placement have shown is that the position of an adverb in a sentence is only indirectly related to its possible interpretation(s); some positions are unambiguous, but others are not.

When there are multiple adverbs in a sentence, they are constrained by the layers of the operator projection, in that adverbs related to more outer operators occur outside of adverbs related to more inner operators. In the simplest case, 'outside of' means 'farther from the verb'. This is illustrated below; ordering constraints of this kind were first noticed by Jackendoff (1972).

(4.31) a. Evidently, Leslie has slowly been completely immersing herself in the new language.
a′. Leslie has evidently been slowly immersing herself in the new language completely.
b. *evidently* [evidential: clausal] > *slowly* [pace: core] > *completely* [aspectual: nuclear]
c. *Evidently, Leslie has completely been slowly immersing herself in the new language.
d. *Slowly, Leslie has evidently been completely immersing herself in the new language.
e. *Slowly, Leslie has completely been evidently immersing herself in the new language.
f. *Completely, Leslie has evidently been slowly immersing herself in the new language.
g. *Completely, Leslie has slowly been evidently immersing herself in the new language.

(4.32) a. Leslie has been immersing herself completely in the new language slowly, evidently.
a′. Leslie has been completely immersing herself slowly in the new language, evidently.

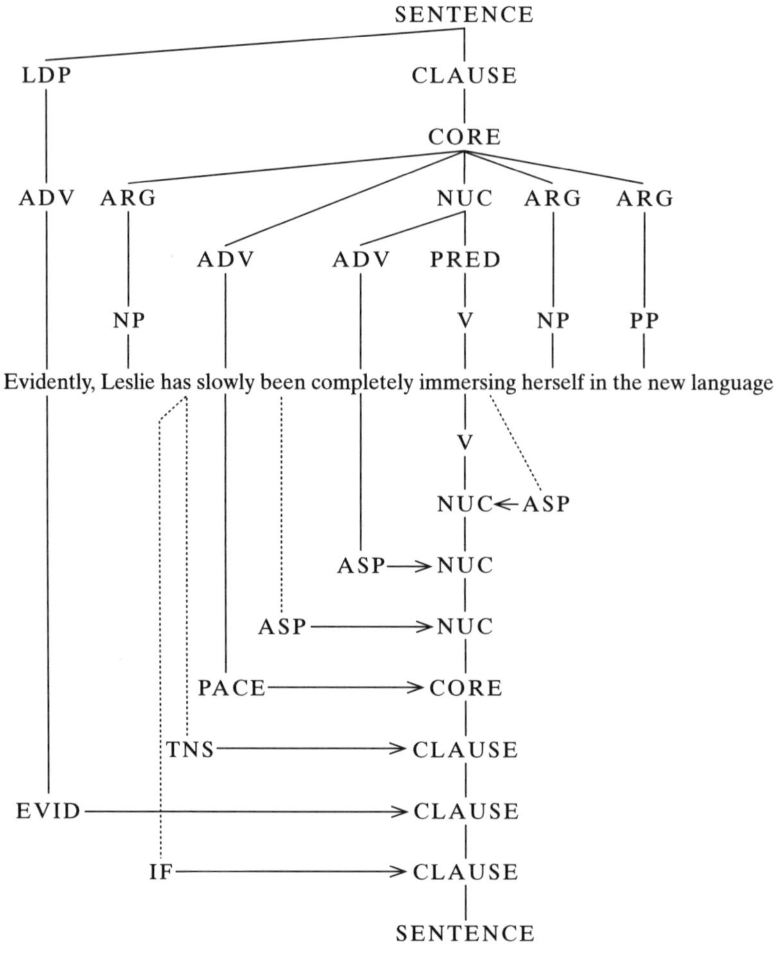

Figure 4.6 Syntactic representations for (4.31a) and (4.32a)

b. *completely* [aspectual: nuclear] < *slowly* [pace: core] < *evidently* [evidential: clausal].
c. *Leslie has been immersing herself slowly in the new language completely, evidently.
d. *Leslie has been immersing herself completely in the new language evidently, slowly.
e. *Leslie has been immersing herself evidently in the new language completely, slowly.
f. *Leslie has been immersing herself slowly in the new language evidently, completely.
g. *Leslie has been immersing herself evidently in the new language slowly, completely.

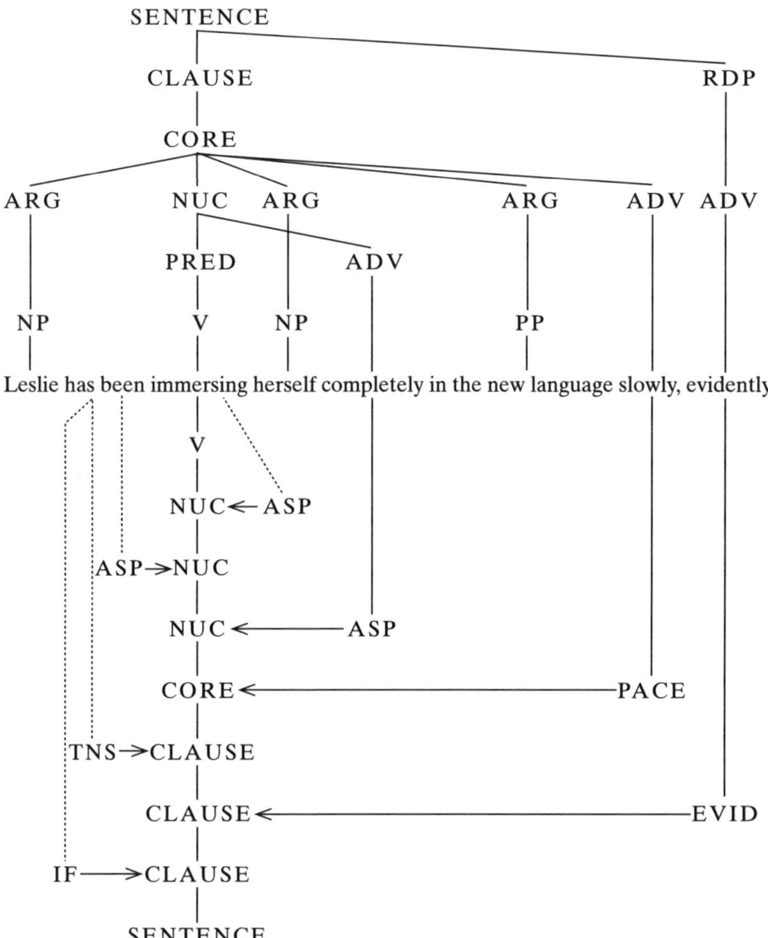

(4.33) **evident′** ([**slow′** (**do′** (x, ∅))] CAUSE [BECOME [**complete′** (**immersed′** (y, x)]])

These examples show clearly that the occurrence of multiple adverbs is constrained by the layered structure of the clause. What is particularly striking about the sentences in (4.31) and (4.32), which are derived from the logical structure in (4.33), is that the constraint is much subtler than the linearization constraint governing operators which we saw in section 2.2.3. That constraint is absolute; there is no variation in the ordering of operators within a language. With respect to adverbs, however, the situation is much more complex. First, as (4.31a, a′) and (4.32a, a′) clearly show, the constraint permits variable linearization, as long as the basic layering in (4.31b) and (4.32b), respectively, is respected. The syntactic representations for (4.31a) and

(4.32a) are given in figure 4.6.[14] The parallel layerings of operators and adverbs is clearer in the second representation, since they are on opposite sides of the verb.

It was emphasized in chapter 2 that the universal distinctions in the layered structure of the clause are not strictly dependent upon linear order, and this is manifest in the additional possibilities in (4.34).

(4.34) a. Leslie has evidently been completely immersing herself in the new language slowly.
b. Leslie has slowly been immersing herself completely in the new language, evidently.

These two sentences do not follow the ordering restrictions in (4.31b) and (4.32b), but they do obey the layering, unlike the (c)–(g) examples. The aspectual adverb *completely* occurs in a potential nucleus-internal position, the pace adverb *slowly* occurs in the core and the evidential adverb occurs in a clause-level position.

Single adverbs are sensitive to operators as well, especially when they occur preverbally among auxiliary elements. This is illustrated with nuclear, core and clausal adverbs below.

(4.35) a. *Completely, Leslie has been immersing herself in the new language.
b. *Leslie completely has been immersing herself in the new language.
c. *Leslie has completely been immersing herself in the new language.
d. Leslie has been completely immersing herself in the new language.
e. Leslie has been immersing herself completely in the new language.
f. Leslie has been immersing herself in the new language completely.
g. *Leslie has been immersing herself in the new language, completely.

(4.36) a. ?Slowly, Leslie has been immersing herself in the new language.
b. *Leslie slowly has been immersing herself in the new language.
c. Leslie has slowly been immersing herself in the new language.
d. Leslie has been slowly immersing herself in the new language.
e. Leslie has been immersing herself slowly in the new language.
f. Leslie has been immersing herself in the new language slowly.
g. *Leslie has been immersing herself in the new language, slowly.

(4.37) a. Evidently, Leslie has been immersing herself in the new language.
b. Leslie evidently has been immersing herself in the new language.
c. Leslie has evidently been immersing herself in the new language.
d. *Leslie has been evidently immersing herself in the new language.
e. *Leslie has been immersing herself evidently in the new language.
f. *Leslie has been immersing herself in the new language evidently.
g. Leslie has been immersing herself in the new language, evidently.

Each of the types of adverb shows a different distribution with respect to the positions in a sentence in which it can occur. The aspectual adverb *completely*, a nuclear modifier, has the most restricted distribution; it must occur within the core and, if preverbal, inside of the aspect operator. It cannot occur in the clause-external positions like the left- and right-detached positions (examples (4.35a) and (4.35g)), or in the periphery, as in (4.38a).

(4.38) a. *Leslie immersed herself in the new language last year completely.
b. *Leslie immersed herself in the new language last year slowly.
c. *Leslie immersed herself in the new language last year evidently.

Last year is a peripheral temporal adverbial, and since *completely* cannot follow it, it must be in the periphery. *Slowly* in (4.36) is a pace adverb, a core modifier, and it can occur in a slightly wider range of environments than *completely*; it must, however, occur within the core, as (4.36a, g) and (4.38b) show. It cannot occur outside of the core, as (4.36b) shows, in which it occurs after the peripheral adverb *last year*. Finally, the evidential adverb *evidently* is a clausal modifier, and it has the widest range of occurrence. If preverbal, it must occur outside of or adjacent to the tense operator, and if postverbal, it is better if it occurs in the right-detached position rather than in the periphery, as in (4.38c). No doubt different choices of operators and adverbs would yield slightly different cooccurrence patterns, but nonetheless it is clear that there is an important interaction between type of adverb and operators in determining their distribution in sentences. Thus, adverbs are like operators, in that they modify different layers of the clause and in some cases express semantic notions closely related to those expressed by operators, but they differ from them in having considerably greater freedom of occurrence.

This analysis has implications for the representation of adverbials in the periphery. In the figures in chapter 2 they were represented in the constituent projection only, but it is now clear that they must also be represented in the operator projection as well, in order to indicate their scope with respect to operators and other adverbials. Hence the syntactic representation for a sentence like *John did not show the book to Mary yesterday* would be as in figure 4.7, revised from figure 2.17.

The question might immediately be raised as to why the temporal adverb *yesterday* is treated as a core modifier rather than a clausal modifier, especially since tense, the related operator, is a clausal operator. There are two reasons for this, and they serve again to highlight the differences between adverbs and operators. The first is the structural parallel between the two projections: peripheral adverbials are core modifiers in the syntax and hence should be represented as such in the operator projection. Second, crucial evidence that peripheral temporal adverbs are core rather than clausal modifiers comes from the type of complex construction called a core juncture; it will be discussed in detail in chapter 8, but we may provisionally characterize it as a clause made up of two cores; in (4.39a) the two cores are, roughly, *Sam decided* and *Sam leave tomorrow.* In such a construction, the linked core may be modified by a temporal adverbial but may not have a tense operator. (The Turkish example is from Watters 1993.)

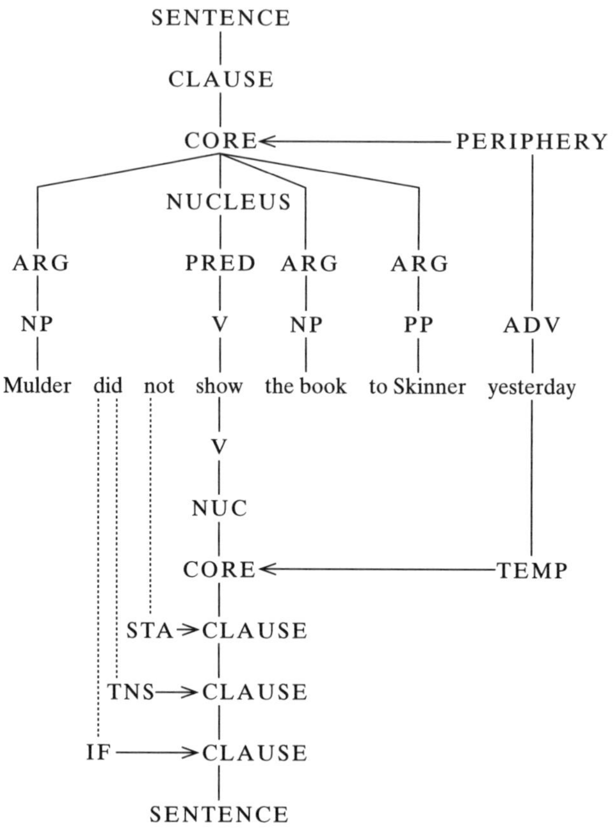

Figure 4.7 English clause with peripheral adverbial

(4.39) a. Sam decided to leave tomorrow.
b. Akşam-lar-ı televizyon seyret-mek ist-iyor-um.
evening-pl-DAT television watch-INF want-PROG-1sg
'I want to watch television in the evenings.'

In both of these sentences, the peripheral temporal adverb, *tomorrow* in English and *akşamları* 'in the evenings' in Turkish, is part of the linked core and modifies it alone; note the incompatibility between the initial core tense and the temporal adverb in (4.39a). Hence it must be a core, not a clausal, modifier, because it clearly does not modify the clause in these examples. Here again we have clear evidence that adverbs are distinct from operators. If a temporal adverb occurs in the left-detached position, then it is a clausal modifier, as in (4.40a) and this predicts the ungrammaticality of (4.40b).

(4.40) a. Yesterday, John did not show the book to Mary.
b. *Tomorrow, Sam decided to leave.

Thus all adverbs, regardless of whether they appear in the periphery, left-detached position, right-detached position or precore slot, will be represented in both constituent and operator projections.

4.4.2 Operators

Operators like tense, aspect, modality and illocutionary force are very complex semantically, and we will not attempt to present a substantive semantic representation for them. Rather, we will merely provide a place for them in the semantic representations, so that we can show how they interact with other elements of the representations. In order to distinguish them from the other elements in semantic representations, they will be represented in italicized capitals inside of angled brackets indicating their scope in logical structure. The general schema is summarized in (4.41). There is a range of values for each operator, which depends on the operator system in the language in question; for example, in a language with a past/non-past tense system, there are two values for the tense operator, whereas in a language with a past/present/future system, there are three values.

(4.41) $\langle_{\text{IF}}\mathit{DEC}\langle_{\text{EVID}}\mathit{HS}\langle_{\text{TNS}}\mathit{PAST}\langle_{\text{STA}}\mathit{REAL}\langle_{\text{NEG}}\emptyset\langle_{\text{MOD}}\mathit{OBLG}\langle_{\text{DIR}}\emptyset\langle_{\text{ASP}}\mathit{PERFPROG}\langle\text{LS}\rangle\rangle\rangle\rangle\rangle\rangle\rangle\rangle\rangle$

The full logical structure for *Has Joshua been singing?* would be as in (4.42). (Operators with no specification will be omitted for ease of presentation.)

(4.42) $\langle_{\text{IF}}\mathit{INT}\langle_{\text{TNS}}\mathit{PRES}\langle_{\text{ASP}}\mathit{PERF\ PROG}\langle\mathbf{do'}\,(\text{Joshua}, [\mathbf{sing'}\,(\text{Joshua}, \emptyset)])\rangle\rangle\rangle\rangle$

Two sorts of complications arise in this representation. First, as we saw in the previous section, adverbs interact in important ways with operators, and this should be reflected in the semantic representation. Hence operators and adverbs should be ordered appropriately in terms of their scope. This is illustrated in (4.43).

(4.43) a. Joshua evidently has been singing slowly.
b. $\langle_{\text{IF}}\mathit{DCL}(\mathbf{evident'}\,\langle_{\text{TNS}}\mathit{PRES}\,(\mathbf{slow'}\,\langle_{\text{ASP}}\mathit{PERF\ PROG}\langle\mathbf{do'}\,(\text{Joshua}, [\mathbf{sing'}\,(\text{Joshua})])\rangle\rangle\rangle\rangle\rangle\rangle\rangle$

The second complication arises with complex logical structures like those for causatives and for active accomplishments. Operators, especially nuclear operators like aspect, may differentially affect parts of such complex logical structures. This can be seen clearly in the following examples from Tepehua (Watters 1988). Tepehua has four aspects (progressive, imperfective, perfective and perfect), and what is of interest here is the interpretation of the perfect with activity verbs, on the one hand, and with achievement and accomplishment verbs, on the other. With activity verbs, the perfect has the standard interpretation of 'a past situation which has present relevance' (Comrie 1976b: 12), whereas with achievement and accomplishment verbs, it indicates that the result state still holds. This is illustrated in (4.44), in which the perfect and perfective are contrasted with the two types of verb.

(4.44) a. *Activity verbs*
  (i) *cihi-ta ni c'aɬ* (laugh-PERF the boy) 'The boy has laughed.'
  (ii) *cihi-ɬ ni c'aɬ* (laugh-PRFV the boy) 'The boy laughed.'
 b. *Achievement/accomplishment verbs*
  (i) *skaka-ta ni c'aɬ* (get.hot-PERF the boy) 'The boy is hot.'
  (ii) *skaka-ɬ ni c'aɬ* (get.hot-PRFV the boy) 'The boy got hot.' (but may not be hot now)

Causative accomplishment verbs contain an activity predicate and an accomplishment predicate in their logical structure; when the perfect is added to a causative accomplishment verb in Tepehua, does it mean that the action occurred and is still relevant, as with an activity verb, or does it mean that the result state continues, as with an accomplishment verb? The answer is given in (4.45).

(4.45) a. *ma:-skaka* 'heat up' [**do′** (x, ∅)] CAUSE [BECOME **hot′** (y)]
 b. *ma:-skaka-ta* (CAUS-get.hot-PERF) '*x* has heated *y*' (i.e. sometime prior to the moment of speaking, though *y* may no longer be hot)

The perfect with a causative accomplishment verb does not imply that the result state continues, only that the action happened at some time prior to the moment of speaking, and therefore it has the activity verb interpretation, not the accomplishment verb interpretation. This suggests strongly that the scope of the aspectual operator is only over the activity part of the logical structure, and accordingly a more complete logical structure for (4.45b) would be as in (4.46).

(4.46) . . . $\langle_{ASP}$*PERF* [**do′** (x, ∅)]$\rangle$ CAUSE [BECOME **hot′** (y)] . . .

These Tepehua facts also provide strong evidence for the decompositional approach to lexical representation. If these verbs were simply represented as something like '**heat-up′** (x, y)', it is difficult to see how this contrast in interpretation could be captured in a non-*ad hoc* way.

4.5 Linking syntactic and semantic representations (a brief introduction)

At the beginning of section 4.2, we raised the question of the relationship between syntactic valence information and semantic information. In particular, is it necessary to state for each verb what its syntactic arguments are (subject, direct object, etc.) in addition to the information in the lexical entries in (4.16)? We argued in section 4.3 that no such information is required in lexical entries in the approach we are presenting, for all of the relevant information is derivable from the logical structure of the verb plus information about its transitivity. This follows from the nature of the system linking syntactic and semantic representations; while it is the primary focus of chapters 7 and 9, we will present a brief introduction to it here, in order to show why no directly syntactic information need be listed in lexical entries.

There are two types of syntactic information that one might expect to be necessary in lexical entries. The first concerns the syntactic valence or S-transitivity of a verb: how many core argument positions are there in the core containing a particular verb or other predicating element? The second concerns grammatical relations of the elements that cooccur with the verb, which we have already discussed in part. We return to this issue below. With respect to the first issue, there is, fundamentally, a straightforward one-to-one relationship between the number of argument positions in the logical structure of the verb and the number of syntactic arguments and argument-adjuncts within the core. We may formulate this more precisely in (4.47).

(4.47) *Syntactic template selection principle*
The number of syntactic slots for arguments and argument-adjuncts within the core is equal to the number of distinct specified argument positions in the semantic representation of the core.

The phrase 'distinct specified argument positions' is important in two ways. First, it is possible to leave semantic argument positions unspecified, e.g. the logical structure for *Pedro is eating* is **do′** (Pedro, [**eat′** (Pedro, Ø)]), and unspecified semantic arguments require no syntactic argument position. Hence the core in which this logical structure would be realized must have only one syntactic argument position. Second, as in this logical structure and in (4.17a), it is possible for the same referent to occupy more than one argument position in the logical structure, i.e. *Pedro* occurs twice in this logical structure and *Bill* and *book* each occur twice in (4.17a). There are five argument variables in (4.17a), but only three distinct arguments: *Bill*, *Fred* and *book*. Consequently the core in which this logical structure will be instantiated should have three syntactic argument positions. It should be kept in mind that 'syntactic slot' in (4.47) refers simply to the 'ARG' and 'AAJ' nodes in the core, and these are not necessarily tied to linear order in any way. In head-marking languages these slots would be places for morphological argument markers on the verbal complex, rather than independent syntactic positions within the core.

The principle in (4.47) represents the universal default, and there are languages, e.g. Lakhota, in which it completely predicts all of the correct core types that go with the verbs in the language. English presents a much more complex situation, because it deviates from (4.47) in three ways. First, as mentioned at the beginning of section 4.2, all English verbs have a minimum syntactic valence of 1, so that even semantic-argument-less verbs like *rain* nevertheless occur with a syntactic argument slot, which is filled by the expletive pronoun *it*. Second, WH-questions lead to a reduction of core elements, when the WH-word is a semantic argument, since it occurs in the precore slot. Third, passives result in a reduction of core elements, since the actor is either omitted or appears as an adjunct in the periphery. These three

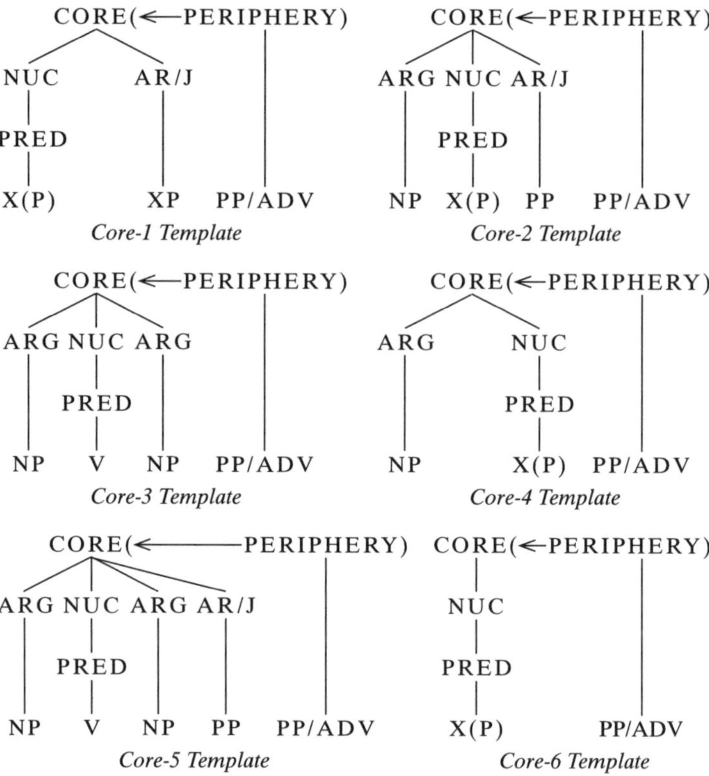

Figure 4.8 Examples of English core syntactic templates

qualifications are summarized in (4.48); they are language-specific in the sense that they are not universal and specific languages may manifest one or more of them.

(4.48) *Language-specific qualifications of the principle in (4.47)*
- a. All cores in the language have a minimum syntactic valence of 1.
- b. Passive constructions reduce the number of core slots by 1.
- c. The occurrence of a syntactic argument in the PrCS reduces the number of core slots by 1 (may override (a)).

Let's take some English verbs and the core templates from figure 2.34, repeated above with the addition of a sixth template, to see how these statements work. The major change from chapter 2 is the possibility of some of the PPs being argument-adjuncts rather than arguments. The English verbs and the sentences realizing them are given in (4.49) and (4.50).

(4.49)
- a. Manuel gave the envelope to the clerk. — Core-5
- a′. [**do′** (Manuel, ∅)] CAUSE [BECOME **have′** (clerk, envelope)]
- b. The envelope was given to the clerk (by Manuel). — Core-2

c. What did Manuel give to the clerk? Core-2
d. To whom did Manuel give the envelope? Core-3

(4.50) a. Chris broke the coffeepot. Core-3
a′. [**do′** (Chris, ∅)] CAUSE [BECOME **broken′** (coffeepot)]
b. The coffeepot was broken (by Chris). Core-4
c. Who broke the coffeepot? Core-1
d. What did Chris break? Core-4
e. What was broken (by Chris)? Core-6

The logical structure in (4.49a′) has three distinct specified arguments, and since the sentence in (a) is neither passive nor a WH-question, the default principle applies, selecting Core-5 as the appropriate template. The sentence in (4.49b) is a passive, and therefore the S-transitivity is reduced to two; accordingly, Core-2 is the appropriate template. The sentences in (c) and (d) are WH-questions, and accordingly if the WH-word is the undergoer, as in (c), then Core-2 is the correct template, whereas if the WH-phrase is the PP, then Core-3 is the appropriate template. The same considerations hold in (4.50). The last sentence is particularly interesting. There are two distinct specified arguments in the logical structure, but (e) is both a passive and a WH-question. This results in a core with no slots in it, as in Core-6. This template would combine with the precore slot template in figure 2.34 to yield the complete structure of the clause. Thus, the selection of the appropriate core template for a given logical structure is governed by the universal principle in (4.47) and the language-specific qualifications in (4.48).

We now return to the issue of the specification of the grammatical relations of the verb's arguments in its lexical entry. Chapter 6 is devoted to the presentation of the theory of grammatical relations; for the purposes of this section we will assume a traditional view of them. In every language with grammatical relations, there is a subject selection principle for multiple-argument verbs. In order to formulate these principles, we need to go back to the Actor–Undergoer Hierarchy in figure 4.2. With respect to subject selection, let us reinterpret it as a hierarchy with 'argument of DO' as the highest ranked argument and 'argument of **pred′** (x)' as the lowest ranked argument. This is given in (4.51).

(4.51) *Subject selection hierarchy*
arg. of DO > 1sg arg. of **do′** > 1st arg. of **pred′** (x, y) > 2nd arg. of **pred′** (x, y) > arg. of **pred′** (x)

In languages like English and German (which we will call 'syntactically accusative languages'), the subject selection principle is 'the highest-ranking core macrorole is the default choice for subject'. With a single macrorole argument verb, this means that it will be subject, but with a two macrorole verb, i.e. an M-transitive verb, it means that the actor is the default choice for subject; the other macrorole can only be subject in a passive construction. In languages like Dyirbal and Sama (Austronesian, Philippines; Walton 1986) (which we will call 'syntactically ergative languages'), on the other hand, the subject selection principle is 'the lowest-ranking core macrorole is the default choice for subject'. With an M-intransitive verb, the single macrorole will be subject regardless of its type, but with an M-transitive verb, this means that the undergoer is the default choice for subject. The other macrorole, in this case the actor, can only be subject in a voice construction like the antipassive construction exemplified in (4.6). Thus, in a syntactically accusative language the unmarked choice for syntactic subject of a transitive verb is the actor, with the undergoer being a marked choice possible only in a passive construction. On the other hand, in a syntactically ergative language, the unmarked choice for syntactic subject of a transitive verb is the undergoer, with the actor being a marked choice possible only in an antipassive construction. With an intransitive verb, the hierarchy is irrelevant, as the single macrorole functions as subject regardless of whether it is actor or undergoer. We will discuss this important typological contrast in detail in chapter 6.

The overall linking system is summarized in figure 4.9. The term 'privileged syntactic argument' (PSA) can be considered to be equivalent to 'syntactic subject' for this section. The notion of privileged syntactic argument will be developed and explicated in chapter 6. We have discussed logical structures, macroroles and the hierarchy linking them earlier in this chapter. This part of the system is universal, in that there is very little cross-linguistic variation. Where languages differ substantially is how macroroles and other arguments link into the syntax. The arrows are double-headed, because the linking system works both from semantics to syntax and from syntax to semantics.

Figure 4.10 illustrates the basics of the linking for a simple English sentence; the operator projection is omitted. Let's go through the semantics → syntax linking step by step. Where choices are possible, we will restrict ourselves to the defaults. The initial steps are to select the appropriate syntactic structure from the syntactic inventory, following the principles in (4.47) and (4.48), and the logical structure for the verb from the lexicon. The verb is *give*, and there is a temporal adverb *yesterday*; therefore the logical structure is **yesterday′** ([**do′** (x, ∅)] CAUSE [BECOME **have′** (y, z)]). We add the NPs for the participants in the state of affairs coded, yielding **yesterday′** ([**do′** (Sandy, ∅)] CAUSE [BECOME **have′** (Robin, what)]). We must now determine the macrorole assignments. *Sandy* is the highest-ranking argument in terms of the Actor–Undergoer Hierarchy and therefore is the actor. *Give* allows variable linking to undergoer, and therefore either *Robin* or *what* may function as undergoer. The default linking is for *what* to be undergoer, since as the second argument of a two-place state predicate it is closer to the undergoer end of the hierarchy than *Robin*, the first argument of a two-place state predicate. At this point we have completed the semantic phase of the linking. The next step is to map the

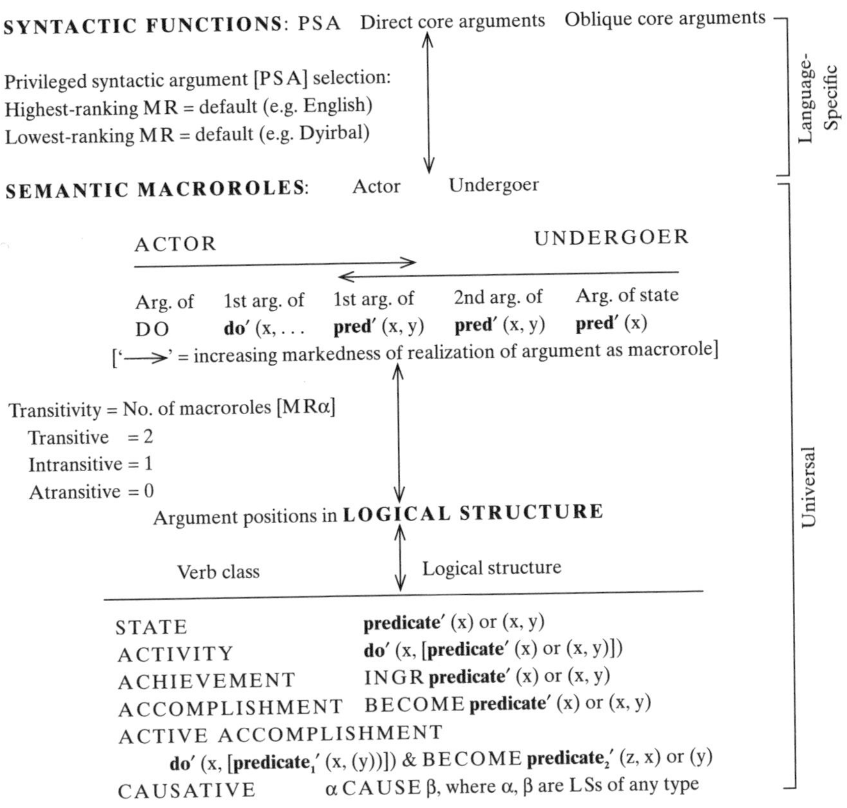

Figure 4.9 System linking semantic and syntactic representations

arguments into the syntactic representation. The default mapping in English is for actor to be subject, and therefore *Sandy* will appear in the core-initial subject position. Because the undergoer is a WH-word and the default for WH-words is that they occur in the precore slot, *what* will occur in the precore slot rather than the immediately postnuclear, core-internal position where undergoers in English normally occur. *Robin* is a non-macrorole core argument, and the conditions for the preposition assignment rule for *to* in (4.18a) are met; accordingly, *Robin* will appear as an oblique core argument marked by *to*. Finally, the adverb *yesterday* is linked to the periphery. The linking from syntax to semantics is somewhat more complex, and we will wait until section 7.2.3 to present it. The details of the linking algorithm for simple sentences will be presented in chapter 7, and those of the algorithm for complex sentences will be the main topic of chapter 9.

The subject selection principles obviate the need for listing any grammatical relations information in lexical entries. Given the transitivity of a verb, which is either

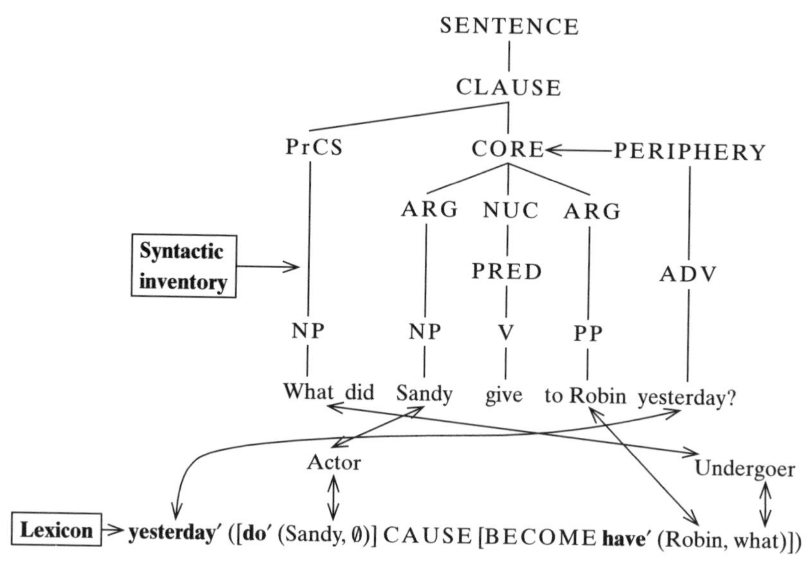

Figure 4.10 Linking of syntax and semantics in a simple sentence in English

determined by the principles in (4.14) or by the [MR] feature in the lexical entry, the possible realizations of the arguments in terms of grammatical relations follow from the general subject selection principle in the language. There are of course complications in some languages, and these will be discussed in chapter 7; but they do not require stipulating which argument will be subject, etc. in lexical entries.

4.6 Lexical rules

As noted at the beginning of section 4.3, the lexicon has come to play an ever-increasingly important role in linguistic theory in general and grammatical theory in particular, and a significant reason for this is that the development of rules which apply in the lexicon permits the capturing of important generalizations. Such rules are called 'lexical redundancy rules', and they have been assumed in most generative theories since they were initially proposed in Chomsky (1970) and further elaborated in Jackendoff (1975). The basic idea goes back to Harris' (1957) original notion of a transformation as a cooccurrence statement; in this case, however, the rules relate lexical entries to each other rather than syntactic patterns to each other, as in Harris' original formulation. In this section we will examine whether certain *Aktionsart* alternations are best captured in terms of lexical rules or separate lexical entries for the forms in question, and in section 4.7.2 we will briefly discuss deverbal nominals, which are related to their verbal sources by lexical rules.

In section 3.2.1 we discussed *Aktionsart* alternations with certain verbs, e.g. *break* as both an accomplishment and a causative accomplishment, or *eat* and *write* as an activity and an active accomplishment. An important question not addressed there is whether verbs like *break* and *eat* should be listed twice in the lexicon, once for each *Aktionsart* type, or whether there should be only one entry for each with lexical rules to derive the alternative form(s). There are three major considerations that figure in the answer to this question. First, how general is the alternation? Is it the case that there is a large number of verbs in the language which exhibit the alternation, or is it limited to a small number of verbs? Second, how predictable is the semantic information that would be added or subtracted by the putative lexical rule? Third, is there any morphological evidence to support such a derivation? We will examine each of these considerations separately.

The *break*-type causative alternation is very general in English and many other languages. Among the verbs involved in it are *shatter*, *crack*, *crumple*, *collapse*, *sink*, *melt*, *dry*, *freeze* and *harden*. The Georgian, French, Russian, Yagua, Lakhota and Tepehua examples discussed in sections 3.2 and 3.2.1 also illustrate this alternation. The causative alternation with activity verbs, e.g. *roll*, *walk* and *bounce*, is not as general as the *break*-type alternation (Levin 1993), but it appears to be quite general in Tepehua and Lakhota. The activity–active accomplishment alternation is also very general in English; Dowty (1979) noted that virtually any activity verb in English can be used as an active accomplishment with the addition of the right kind of NP or PP and that virtually any causative or active accomplishment verb can be used as an activity when it occurs with a bare plural or mass noun object. We have seen additional evidence of this alternation in Italian, Georgian, Pirahã and Russian in the earlier sections. Hence it too is sufficiently general to be a candidate for a lexical rule.

The second issue is the generality of the semantic information added or subtracted by the possible lexical rule. In the case of the causative alternation with achievements, accomplishments and activities, the information is very general, as represented in (4.52).

(4.52) a. BECOME/INGR **pred′** (y) ↔ [**do′** (x, ∅)] CAUSE [BECOME/INGR **pred′** (y)]
b. **do′** (y, [**pred′** (y)]) ↔ [**do′** (x, ∅)] CAUSE [**do′** (y, [**pred′** (y)])]

In both cases the relevant information is '[**do′** (x, ∅)] CAUSE' which is an expression of causality with an unspecified causing activity; the specific semantic information that distinguishes *break*, *sink*, *shatter* and *melt*, on the one hand, and *roll*, *walk* and *bounce*, on the other, is represented in the 'BECOME/INGR **pred′** (y)' or '**do′** (y, [**pred′** (y)])' part of the logical structure. The situation is a bit more complicated with the *eat*-type activity–active accomplishment alternation, because the semantic information added to the activity logical structure is a function of the subclass of the activity verb. In every instance, though, an atelic verb becomes telic. Consider the possible lexical rules in (4.53).

(4.53) a. Activity [motion] → active accomplishment: given an activity LS **do′** (x, [**pred′** (x)]), add '& BECOME **be-LOC′** (y, x)' to form an active accomplishment LS.

b. Activity [consumption] → active accomplishment: given an activity LS **do′** (x, [**pred′** (x, y)]), add '& BECOME **consumed′** (y)' to form an active accomplishment LS.

c. Activity [creation] → active accomplishment: given an activity LS **do′** (x, [**pred′** (x, y)]), add '& BECOME **exist′** (y)' to form an active accomplishment LS.

If the activity verb is a motion verb, e.g. *run*, then the part added will be a definite goal, e.g. BECOME **be-LOC′** (y, x). If the activity verb is one of consumption, e.g. *eat* or *drink*, then the part added will be BECOME **consumed′** (y). Finally, if it is a verb of creation (including verbs of performance), e.g. *write*, *paint*, *carve* or *sing*, then the part added will be BECOME **exist′** (y). Examples of verbs of each type are given in (4.54)–(4.57).

(4.54) a. Miriam ran.
a′. **do′** (x, [**run′** (Miriam)])
b. Miriam ran to the park.
b′. **do′** (x, [**run′** (Miriam)]) & BECOME **be-at′** (park, Miriam)

(4.55) a. Mario ate pizza.
a′. **do′** (x, [**eat′** (Mario, pizza)])
b. Mario ate the pizza.
b′. **do′** (x, [**eat′** (Mario, pizza)]) & BECOME **eaten′** (pizza)

(4.56) a. Ali sang.
a′. **do′** (x, [**sing′** (Ali, ∅)])
b. Ali sang the song.
b′. **do′** (x, [**sing′** (Ali, ∅)]) & BECOME **exist′** (song)

(4.57) a. Cleophus wrote poetry.
a′. **do′** (x, [**write′** (Cleophus, poetry)])
b. Cleophus wrote a poem.
b′. **do′** (x, [**write′** (Cleophus, poetry)]) & BECOME **exist′** (poem)

With verbs like *sing*, what comes into existence or is realized is the song as a performance, not as a group of musical notes on paper. With respect to all of these examples, it is clear that the semantic difference between the (a′) and (b′) logical structures is more varied than that between the two logical structures in (4.52). Nevertheless, since the differences are predictable from the type of activity verb, it would be possible to formulate general lexical rules for these alternations. It should be noted that the activity–active accomplishment alternation involving accomplishment verbs like *kill* and *crush* does not involve a change in the logical structure of the verb; as noted in section 3.2.1, these verbs remain telic even when used with a bare plural or mass noun object, as shown by their necessarily iterative interpretation.

The final consideration is whether there is any morphological evidence for the alternation. With respect to the causative achievement–accomplishment alternation, we saw in (3.18) that Tepehua overtly marks this alternation, as do Lakhota and Yagua; Tepehua and Lakhota also overtly mark the causative alternation with activity verbs. Lakhota probably presents the most general case; the vast majority of transitive causative accomplishment and achievement verbs in the language are derived from state/achievement/accomplishment roots via causativization involving instrumental prefixes (see section 3.2). It is clear that for Lakhota and Tepehua it would be appropriate to posit derivational rules to derive accomplishment verbs in the lexicon; such rules would resemble those in (4.58).

(4.58) a. *Lakhota*
state/achievement/accomplishment stem + instrumental prefix →
causative achievement/accomplishment
(BECOME/INGR) **pred′** (y) + *ka-/ya-/yu-. . . /na-* →
[**do′** (x, [. . .])] CAUSE [BECOME/INGR **pred′** (y)]
activity stem + instrumental prefix/causative suffix → causative activity
[**do′** (y, [**pred′** (y)]) + *yu-* or *-ya* → [**do′** (x, ∅)] CAUSE [**do′** (y, [**pred′** (y)])]

b. *Tepehua*
state + *ta-* → achievement/accomplishment, **pred′** (y) + *ta-* → BECOME/INGR **pred′** (y)
achievement/accomplishment + *ma-* → causative achievement/accomplishment
(*ta-* → ∅ / *ma:-*__) BECOME/INGR **pred′** (y) + *ma:-* → [**do′** (x, [. . .])] CAUSE [BECOME/INGR **pred′** (y)]
activity + *ma:-* → causative activity
[**do′** (y, [**pred′** (y)]) + *ma:-* → [**do′** (x, ∅)] CAUSE [**do′** (y, [**pred′** (y)])]

In the Lakhota rule, the activity part of the rule will vary, depending upon which instrumental prefix is involved; with respect to Tepehua, *ma-* can causativize underived achievement or accomplishment verbs as well, e.g. *'on* 'get fat' vs. *ma:'onu:* 'fatten'.

For languages like Yagua (Payne and Payne 1989; see section 3.2.1), on the other hand, some achievement and accomplishment verbs are clearly derived from their causative counterparts morphologically, and the lexical rule for this would be one like that in (4.59).

(4.59) *Yagua*
causative achievement/accomplishment + *-y* → achievement/ accomplishment
[**do′** (w, [. . .])] CAUSE [BECOME/INGR **pred′** (x)] + *-y* → BECOME/INGR **pred′** (x)

With respect to the activity–active accomplishment alternation, both Georgian and Russian code it morphologically with at least some verbs, e.g. Russian 'eat' *est′*

(activity) vs. *s″est′* (active accomplishment), Georgian 'write' *c'er* (activity) vs. *dac'er* (active accomplishment) (see section 3.2.1). Treating both Russian *s-* and Georgian *da-* as preverbs, we can posit the lexical rule in (4.60).

(4.60) *Georgian/Russian*
activity + preverb → active accomplishment
do′ (x, [. . .]) + preverb → **do′** (x, [**pred′** (x, y)]) & BECOME **pred′** (y)

There are a number of preverbs in each language, each of which cooccurs with different verbs; hence this rule is very schematic, as there would need to be a rule for each preverb, much like the rules for each instrumental prefix in Lakhota. Moreover, as noted above, the exact content of the added semantic component will be a function of the subtype of activity verb.

It is, thus, plausible to propose lexical rules for the causative alternation with achievement–accomplishment and activity verbs and the activity–active accomplishment alternations in those languages in which all three of these criteria are met. It is less clear that it is plausible to propose such rules for languages like English in which there is no overt morphological evidence for them. There are at least two possible analyses here, and in evaluating them we will use the theory-internal criteria introduced in section 1.2.1, namely, economy, motivation and predictiveness. Analysis 1 posits no derivational rules at all and has separate lexical entries for each *Aktionsart* form of a verb, i.e. separate lexical entries for *break* (accomplishment) and *break* (causative accomplishment), for *roll* (activity) and *roll* (causative activity), and for *eat* (activity) and *eat* (active accomplishment). Analysis 2 postulates that there is only one lexical entry for *break*, *roll* and *eat* and that there are rules akin to those in (4.58)–(4.60) to derive the alternative forms. Before we can compare them, however, we need to clarify certain aspects of analysis 2.

The primary questions with respect to analysis 2 is the direction of derivation; in other words, is the English rule for the causative alternation like the ones for Lakhota and Tepehua or the one for Yagua? Similarly, is the rule relating activities and active accomplishments like the one posited for Russian and Georgian in (4.60), or does it derive activities from active accomplishments? With respect to the activity–active accomplishment alternation, it was argued at the end of section 3.2.1 that verbs like *eat* are basically activities which have active accomplishment uses, and this requires that the derivational rule for English be activity → active accomplishment. Thus we may posit that English has a rule, like Russian and Georgian, which treats a verb's activity use as basic and derives the active accomplishment use from it by a derivational rule. As noted in section 3.2.1, causative accomplishment verbs which behave like activities do not have a different logical structure (since they are still telic and therefore have an iterative interpretation) and consequently would not be subject to a derivational rule of this kind; rather, their activity interpretation would be the result of a semantic interpretation rule. With respect to the causative alternation, there is no striking advantage to positing either rule; in both instances, there are verbs which have the appropriate input logical structure but which do not undergo the rule (see Pinker 1989). It appears (Levin 1993) that there are fewer intransitive achievement and accomplishment verbs which do not undergo causativization than there are causative verbs which do not undergo decausativization, and therefore we will assume that the rule for English follows the Lakhota and Tepehua pattern of deriving causatives from accomplishments, achievements and activities.

We are now in a position to compare the two approaches. With respect to the criterion of economy, analysis 1 leads to an enormous increase in the number of lexical entries in the lexicon, with multiple lexical entries for many verbs. Analysis 2, on the other hand, leads to a much leaner lexicon, and avoids multiple lexical entries for verbs, except in cases of true polysemy, e.g. *take* 'obtain' vs. *take* 'carry'. It does, however, involve the positing of two lexical rules, whereas analysis 1 avoids positing such rules. It might be suggested the analysis 1 is massively redundant, with a great deal of information about a verb repeated in its multiple entries. One possibility for avoiding this redundancy is, when there are multiple entries for a single verb, to state only that information which is distinctive for that form and have a rule which refers back to what we will call the 'root' entry where the information common to all of the entries is represented. This avoids the redundancy but at the cost of adding a new rule type to the system. Thus with respect to economy, analysis 2 would seem to be simpler, since it necessitates the positing of fewer verbal lexical entries, and both analyses require lexical rules of some type.

With respect to the criterion of motivation, both analyses can claim to be independently motivated in some way. Postulating multiple entries for a given verb is already required for cases of polysemy. Derivational rules are well motivated within the theory, as they are required for languages like Tepehua, Lakhota and many others. Within the grammar of English, derivational rules in the lexicon are also independently motivated, as there are numerous well-known derivational rules, e.g. ADJ + *-ize* → verb, ADJ + *-ness* → noun, N + *-y* → adjective, ADJ + *-ly* → adverb. Hence with respect to motivation, both analyses seem to be equivalent.

Finally, with respect to predictiveness, the two differ substantially. Analysis 1 makes no predictions at all. Analysis 2, on the other hand, makes a very interesting prediction. It is well established that as speakers learn a language they often overgeneralize the rules as they learn them; children, for example, often overregularize the regular past tense and plural endings to irregular verbs and nouns. Analysis 2 posits that part of learning English is learning the rule that derives causative accomplishments from accomplishments, and therefore it predicts that it, like other rules, could be overgeneralized during language learning, and this does in fact occur, as Bowerman (1974) and others have reported. Thus it is attested that some children have taken an accomplishment verb like *disappear*, which does not have an causative counterpart, and used it as a causative accomplishment in sentences like *He disappeared it*, i.e. 'He made it disappear'. Hence analysis 2 makes a correct prediction which does not follow from analysis 1.

In reviewing the three criteria, we see that analysis 2 is more economical and has greater predictiveness than analysis 1 and is therefore to be preferred. We may conclude, then, that it is reasonable to hypothesize that English does have a lexical rule deriving causative *break* from accomplishment *break* and therefore that *break* (and other verbs of its type) is represented only once in the lexicon with a logical structure of one of the basic four *Aktionsart* classes.

4.7 The semantic representation of nouns and noun phrases

Nouns may head nominal cores and take arguments, as we saw in section 2.3.2, and accordingly they require an appropriate semantic representation in the lexicon. In this section, we will discuss the semantic properties of non-derived nouns, deverbal derived nominals, possessive phrases and NP adjuncts, and NP operators.

4.7.1 Semantic properties of nouns

A non-derived noun like *dog* or *tree* does not have a logical structure like a verb or predicative preposition, but it does have semantic properties which contribute significantly to the interpretation of a sentence. Consider the following example.

(4.61) John started in on a new novel.

This sentence can normally be interpreted to mean that John either began to *read* a novel or to *write* a novel. Where does this interpretation come from? Why can't we interpret this to mean that he began to *eat* a novel, the way we can construe *Chris started in on a hamburger*? The answer obviously is that the interpretation derives from the different undergoers in the two sentences, *novel*, on the one hand, and *hamburger*, on the other. In order to capture these facts, Pustejovsky (1991, 1995) proposes a theory of nominal **qualia** to characterize the semantics of nominals. It is summarized in (4.62).

(4.62) *Qualia theory* (Pustejovsky 1991: 426–7)

a. *Constitutive role*: the relation between an object and its constituents, or proper parts
   1 material
   2 weight
   3 parts and component elements
b. *Formal role*: that which distinguishes the object within a larger domain
   1 orientation
   2 magnitude
   3 shape
   4 dimensionality

5 color
6 position

c. *Telic role*: purpose and function of the object
1 purpose that an agent has in performing an act
2 built-in function or aim that specifies certain activities

d. *Agentive role*: factors involved in the origin or 'bringing about' of an object
1 creator
2 artifact
3 natural kind
4 causal chain

Pustejovsky gives the following representation for *novel*.[15]

(4.63) **novel** (x)
a. Constitutive: **narrative′** (x)
b. Form: **book′** (x), **disk′** (x)
c. Telic: **do′** (y, [**read′** (y, x)])
d. Agentive: **artifact′** (x), **do′** (y, [**write′** (y, x)]) & BECOME **exist′** (x)

The source of the two interpretations for (4.61) is now clear: one reading is based on the telic role of *novel*, while the other is derived from the agentive role. Consider also the following sentences involving the noun *door*.

(4.64) a. Pat painted the door.
b. Pat walked through the door.
c. **door** ($x \vee y$)[16]
1 Constitutive: **obstruction′** (x), **aperture′** (y)
2 Form: **physical-object′** (x), **frame′** (y)
3 Telic: BECOME **closed′/open′** (x), **do′** (z, [**go.through′** (z, y)])
4 Agentive: **artifact′** ($x \vee y$)

A door is an aperture that one can pass through or a physical object that can fill the aperture. The sentence in (4.64a) refers to the physical object and (b) refers to the aperture. This is captured by having two variables for *door*, one referring to the opening and the other to the physical object which fills the opening.

Thus, the lexical entry for each noun will contain a set of qualia, $\{Q_C, Q_F, Q_T, Q_A\}$, which represent its primary semantic properties, much like a logical structure represents the primary semantic properties of a verb. Combining the two yields a more complete semantic representation for a clause, as in (4.65).

(4.65) a. The door opened.
b. BECOME **open′** ([**door** (x), $\{Q_C, Q_F, Q_T, Q_A\}$])

'**door** (x)' indicates that it is the *x*-variable in the lexical entry in (4.64c) which is selected, and therefore the relevant qualia properties are those containing it, e.g. **obstruction′** (x). In the case of (4.61), *John began a novel*, we would have the following logical structure.[17]

(4.66) BECOME **do′** ([**John** (x), {. . .}], [**verb′** ([**John** (x), {. . .}], [**novel** (y), {. . . ,Q_T[**do′** (x, [**read′** (x, y)])], Q_A[**do′** (x, [**write′** (x, y)])]}])])

Begin is treated semantically like a complement-taking predicate with an unspecified complement verb (the '**verb′**' in the logical structure), and the semantic content of the unspecified verb is supplied by the logical structure in the telic role in the qualia for the 'John began to read a novel' interpretation and in the agentive role in the qualia for the 'John began to write a novel' reading.[18]

4.7.2 Deverbal nominals

Many nouns are related to verbs, e.g. *arrest, destruction, investigation, student*, etc., and, as we saw in section 2.3.2, they may take arguments, as illustrated in (4.67).

(4.67) a. the arrest of Bill by FBI agents in New York City
b. the destruction of the city by the enemy
c. the investigation of the murders by Sherlock Holmes
d. the study of physics

Such constructions are found in many languages.

(4.68) a. *Tepehua* (Watters 1988)
'iš-puš-ka kafe
3GEN-pick-NMZ coffee
'the picking of coffee'
b. *Hausa* (Abdoulaye 1992)
kaamà kiifin Abdu
catch fish-of
'the catching of a fish by Abdu'
c. *Georgian* (Harris 1981)
c'erilis dac'era čems mier
letter-GEN writing me.GEN by
'the writing of the letter by me'
d. *Hebrew* (Berman 1978)
bniyat ha-báyit al ydey ha-soxnut
building the-house by the-agency
'the building of the house by the agency'

We will assume, following Nunes (1993), that deverbal nominals have the same logical structure in their lexical entry as the corresponding verb and that there are lexical redundancy rules which express the relationship between the verb and related derived nominal, e.g. [**do′** (x, Ø)] CAUSE [BECOME **destroyed′** (y)] → *destruction* (x, y). The prepositions marking the core_N arguments are predicted by the same rules that predict prepositions in clauses (see sections 4.3, 7.3.2). In the case of all of the examples in (4.67) and (4.68), the derived nominal corresponds to the verb, e.g. *destroy* ~ *destruction*, and the arguments of the verb are realized as arguments of the nominal nucleus. With respect to complement-taking nominals, e.g. *belief, claim*, the same will be true, as illustrated in (4.69).

(4.69) a. Max believes that the world is round.
b. Max's belief that the world is round
c. **believe′** (Max, [**be′** (world, [**round′**])])

The linking principles which govern the realization of these arguments are related to the linking principles for verbal arguments in clauses, which will be developed in chapter 7, but with some interesting variations which follow from the fundamental differences between nominal and verbal expressions. While there are action nominals like *running* and stative verbs like *know*, nominals are basically static in nature and verbs are basically non-static (see the features in (3.12)). Nunes (1993) argues that English deverbal nominals are inherently M-intransitive; that is, they never take more than one direct core_N argument, which is realized by the *of*-marked NP in the examples in (4.67) and (2.25) and the genitive case NPs in (4.68).[19] In section 4.2 we discussed the macrorole assignment principles for verbal predicates, and we compared two possible formulations for determining which macrorole M-intransitive verbal predicates would take, one which was sensitive to the presence of an activity predicate in the logical structure and the other which was sensitive to the presence of a state predicate in the logical structure. We concluded that for verbal predicates the principle sensitive to activity predicates makes the correct prediction, but Nunes (1993) shows that for nominals the opposite is true: a deverbal nominal takes an undergoer as its single macrorole if the verb from which it is derived contains a state predicate, otherwise an actor. This means that only deverbal nominals derived from activity verbs will take an actor as their single direct, *of*-marked core_N argument. This is illustrated in the following examples from Nunes (1993). (The subscripts 'CL-A' and 'CL-U' stand for 'clausal actor' and 'clausal undergoer', respectively.)

(4.70) *Deverbal nominals from state, achievement and accomplishment verbs (±causative)*

a.	Sara knows French.	State[20]
a′.	some knowledge of $\text{French}_{\text{CL-U}}$/*of $\text{Sara}_{\text{CL-A}}$	
b.	The balloon popped.	Achievement
b′.	the popping of the $\text{balloon}_{\text{CL-U}}$	
c.	The cat popped the balloon.	Causative achievement
c′.	the popping of the $\text{balloon}_{\text{CL-U}}$ by the $\text{cat}_{\text{CL-A}}$	
c″.	*the popping of the $\text{cat}_{\text{CL-A}}$ [must be interpreted as undergoer]	
d.	Chris died.	Accomplishment
d′.	the death of $\text{Chris}_{\text{CL-U}}$	
e.	The enemy destroyed the city.	Causative accomplishment
e′.	the destruction of the $\text{city}_{\text{CL-U}}$ by the $\text{enemy}_{\text{CL-A}}$	
e″.	*the destruction of the $\text{enemy}_{\text{CL-A}}$ [must be interpreted as undergoer]	

(4.71) *Deverbal nominals from activity verbs*

a. The dog barked.

a′. the barking of the $dog_{CL\text{-}A}$

b. The wheel is rotating.

b′. the rotation of the $wheel_{CL\text{-}A}$

With two-argument activity verbs, which can be both activities and active accomplishments, the actor argument can always be the direct $core_N$ argument of the derived nominal, and with some, the argument corresponding to the clausal undergoer can be the direct $core_N$ argument as well.

(4.72) *Deverbal nominals from activity/active accomplishment verbs*

a. The killer bees attacked the dog.

a′. the attack of the killer $bees_{CL\text{-}A}$ on the $dog_{CL\text{-}U}$

a″. the attack on/*of the $dog_{CL\text{-}U}$ by the killer $bees_{CL\text{-}A}$

b. Sherlock Holmes investigated the murder.

b′. the investigation of Sherlock $Holmes_{CL\text{-}A}$ into the $murder_{CL\text{-}U}$

b″. the investigation of the $murder_{CL\text{-}U}$ by Sherlock $Holmes_{CL\text{-}A}$

With *attack*, only the clausal actor can appear as a direct $core_N$ argument in the deverbal nominal, whereas with *investigate* both arguments can.

It is also the case that the result of nominalizing a verb may be a nominal referring to one of the arguments of the verb, rather than the state of affairs denoted by the verb. The simplest examples are agent nominalizations, e.g. *singer*, *dancer* and *talker*, which realize the *x* argument in the logical structure of these activity verbs, e.g. **do′** (x, [**sing′** (x, y)]). The general rule for agent nominalizations would look like (4.73).

(4.73) *verb* + *-er* → [$_N$ *verb* + *er*] 'x_i which *verbs*' ([$_{LS}$ . . . (x_i, . . .) . . .]), where 'x' is the actor argument in the logical structure

When transitive verbs are nominalized by this rule, there are two possible realizations of the undergoer argument. It may appear as a direct $core_N$ argument marked by *of*, as in *a drinker of beer*, *a painter of houses*, *a hunter of ducks* or *a killer of cops*, or it may be incorporated into the derived nominal, creating *beerdrinker*, *housepainter*, *duckhunter* or *copkiller*. Thus, expressions like *drinker of beer* and *beerdrinker* realize both of the primary arguments of the logical structure, the actor in the verb + *-er* derived nominal and the undergoer in the *of*-NP or the incorporated noun. There are some morphologically irregular outputs from the rule in (4.73); for example, if the input verb is *study*, the output NP is *student*, not **studier*. Hence the logical structure **do′** (x, [**study′** (x, physics)]) yields *student of physics* or *physics student* as the output of (4.73).

A somewhat extreme case of argument nominalization can be found with the Tepehua verb *č̌a'a:-* 'wash', which has eight derived nominal forms (Watters 1988, 1996). In order to see how these are formed, it is necessary to look at the logical structures this verb can have. The first thing to mention is that it is an activity verb which can also have an active accomplishment form. The second thing is that Tepehua has extensive valence-increasing verb morphology, and many of the derived forms are nominalizations of the added argument. There are three logical structures in (4.74): the basic activity logical structure in (a), the minimal active accomplishment logical structure in (b) and the expanded active accomplishment logical structure in (c), which is a crude approximation of what a detailed decomposition of **wash′** would be like.

(4.74) a. **do′** (x, [**wash′** (x, y)])
b. **do′** (x, [**wash′** (x, y)]) & [BECOME **washed′** (y)]
c. [**do′** (x, [**take.**(α).**put.**(α ∧ y).**in.**(β).**rub.**(y).**on.**(γ)′] & BECOME **washed′** (y)

The Greek variables represent potential arguments whose realization requires a valence-increasing affix on the verb. The first derived nominal is the agent nominalization formed by the addition of the suffix *-na:*, yielding *ča'a:na:* 'washer'. There is a comitative verb prefix *t'a-*, which, when added to *ča'a:na:*, results in a second agent nominalization *t'ača'a:na:* 'fellow washer'. There is a directional verb prefix *ɬi:-* 'to, toward', which is often used to give a sense of 'pointing toward' or a 'future orientation'. When it is added to *ča'a:-* and then the resulting verb is nominalized by *-ti*, the result is *ɬi:ča'a:ti* 'that which is to be washed' or 'dirty laundry'. This is the realization of the *y* argument in (4.74a) as a nominalization; since this is an activity logical structure, the action cannot have been completed, and therefore the *y* argument refers to what is to be washed. When the verb alone is nominalized, *ča'a:nti*, the result is ambiguous; it can refer either to the act of washing or to the result of washing, i.e. clean laundry. In this case it refers to the *y* variable in the active accomplishment logical structure in (b), since it refers to the result of the completed action. The passive nominal is *'is-ča'a:-ka* (3GEN-wash-PASS.NMZ) 'the washing of *y*' (see (4.68a)). The final three nominalizations are related to the Greek variable arguments in the logical structure in (c). When the prefix *ɬa:-* is added, the result is *ɬa:ča'a:n* 'soap' (the α variable); the prefix appears to be a reduced form of the verb *ɬa:'an* 'take'. The prefixes *pu:-* and *pa:-* both have locative senses: *pu:ča'a:n* 'washing trough' denotes the container in which the washing is done (the β variable), while *pa:ča'a:n* 'washboard' refers to the implement on which the clothes are rubbed as part of the process (the γ variable). Thus, it is possible for a range of arguments in the logical structure of a verb to be realized as nominalizations.

4.7.3 Possessive phrases and NP adjuncts

Possessive phrases obviously involve the notion of possession, which is essentially a predication relation (see section 3.2.3.4). Hence it makes sense to represent possession within NPs semantically the same way as it is represented semantically within clauses, i.e. in terms of the predicate **have′**. Accordingly, the clause *The man has a car* and the NP *the man's car* will both be related to the logical structure **have′** (man, car).[21] A very important difference between a clause and an NP is of course the nature of the head; the verb is the head of a clause, while a noun heads an NP. In order to indicate that we are dealing with a noun-headed construction, the head noun will be underlined in the logical structure for NPs. Thus, **have′** (man, car) is the logical structure of *the man has a car,* while **have′** (man, <u>car</u>) is a partial semantic representation of *the man's car.* **Have′** (man, car) is realized by a core in which *have* functions as the predicate in the nucleus; on the other hand, **have′** (man, <u>car</u>) is realized by a noun phrase in which *car* functions as the head in a nominal nucleus (see section 2.3.2). It is also possible to take the first argument in the logical structure as the head of the NP, i.e. **have′** (<u>man</u>, car), yielding *the man with the car.* This difference is termed 'profiling' in Langacker (1987); *the car* is profiled in *the man's car,* while *the man* is profiled in *the man with the car.* As we will see in chapter 7, the rules for preposition assignment in English correctly predict that *car* will be marked by *with* in this construction. In the discussion of headedness in section 2.4, we argued that the heads are the primary elements in the semantic representation of the phrase, and accordingly the underlined element in these semantic representations functions as both a semantic head, i.e. it is the primary element in the representation and the other elements are interpreted as modifiers of it, and as a syntactic head, i.e. it will function as the nucleus of the phrase in the syntactic representation.

There are important distinctions among alienable, inalienable and kin possession. Inalienable possession involves a part–whole relation between the possessor and the possessed, e.g. a table and its legs, a bird and its wings, a car and its wheels. As such, inalienable possession is related to the constitutive role of the nominal qualia (see (4.62a3)) and involves what we may call 'necessary' possession.[22] Alienable possession, on the other hand, is not based on a part–whole relation and is contingent possession, e.g. a man and his car, a boy and his toy, a woman and her jewelry. In order to distinguish these two types of possession, we will reserve **have′** for alienable possession and use the predicate **have.as.part′** for inalienable possession. Thus, *A car has wheels* would have the logical structure **have.as.part′** (car, wheels), and *the car's wheels* would have the logical structure **have.as.part′** (car, <u>wheels</u>). Kin possession is not a special category in languages like English, as most expressions of kinship are assimilated to the basic patterns of inalienable possession, e.g. *I have two children, Sam is my uncle, my daughter.* Kin and inalienable possessors share the property of not taking possessive inflection when they occur post-head, unlike alienable possessors, e.g. *Natasha's sister* vs. *sister of Natasha(*'s),* *the table's leg* vs. *leg of the table(*'s), Sam's car* vs. *car of Sam's/*Sam.* It was noted in section 2.3.2, however, that kinship nouns do have the property of taking arguments, e.g. *the oldest sister of Mary*, a property usually associated with deverbal nominals. Hence we referred to them there as relational nouns. We may represent these kin possession phrases semantically as **have.as.kin′** (x, y), where 'x' is the reference point and 'y' is the kin relation, e.g. **have.as.kin′** (3sg, <u>father</u>) 'his father'. Hence the logical structure for *Sam is my uncle* is **be′** (Sam, [**have.as.kin′** (1sg, <u>uncle</u>)]). In many languages, special constructions and forms exist for the expression of kin relations. In Mparntwe Arrernte (Wilkins 1989), as in many other Australian Aboriginal languages, there are special pronominal forms and constructions for expressing kin possession. They are illustrated in (4.75); the contrasting non-kin possessive forms for first and second person are given as well.

(4.75) a. Pronominal forms for kin possession
-atye '1sg kin possessor' e.g. *yay-atye* 'my sister' (cf. *atyenhe-* 'my')
-angkwe '2sg kin possessor' e.g. *me-angkwe* 'your mother' (cf. *ngkwinhe-* 'your')
-ikwe '3sg kin possessor' e.g. *altyerr-ikwe* 'his/her dreaming totem'
b. *Special dative of kin possession construction*
(i) atyenge akngeye
1sgDAT father
'my father'
(ii) Toby-ke alere
-DAT child
'Toby's child'

The logical structure for *yay-atye* 'my sister' would be **have.as.kin′** (1sg, <u>sister</u>). In Lakhota, for example, there is a special verbal construction for expressing that someone stands in a kinship relation to someone. This is illustrated in (4.76).

(4.76) a. Sam até-∅-wa-ye.
father-3sgU-1sgA-CAUS
'Sam is my father'
b. Wičhį́čala ki thožą́-wičha-ya-ye.
girl the niece-3plU-2sgA-CAUS
'The girls are your nieces.'

We may propose a predicate for the logical structure of verbs of kin possession, **have.as.kin**(α)′ (x, y), where 'α' is a variable representing the kin term. Hence for the Lakhota expression in (4.76a), the logical structure would be **have.as.father′** (1sg, Sam). For possessed kin terms, the inalienable possessor forms are used, e.g. *čhųkš* 'daughter', *mi-čhų́kši* 'my daughter', *ni-čhų́kši* 'your daughter' (Buechel 1939, Boas and Deloria 1941). There is one set of expressions in English that appear to pattern like the Lakhota kinship expressions, namely those involving royalty. Assuming a logical structure like **have.as.queen′** (England, Elizabeth II), this would be realized as *England has Elizabeth II as its Queen*. However, this is not the usual way of expressing this in English. The more common way would be to use an identificational logical structure like **be′** (Elizabeth II, [**queen′** (England)]), yielding

Elizabeth II is Queen of England/England's Queen, where **queen′** (x) is a one-place state predicate. The verbal expression is derived by replacing the variable 'α' in **have.as.royalty**(α)′ (y, z) with **queen′** (x), where the *x* argument of **queen′** (x) corresponds to the *y* argument in **have.as.royalty**(α)′ (x, y).

It might appear that possessive NPs involving alienable and inalienable possession are basically the same, but this is misleading. In the first place, there is an alternative realization of these NPs in which the possessor occurs in a non-predicative PP headed by *of*, but the two possibilities are not equally felicitous: *the wheels of the car* is fine, but *the car of the man* is somewhat odd in and of itself. Second, these judgments reverse when the possessor is selected as the head of the NP (**have.as.part.′** (<u>car</u>, wheels)): *the man with the car* is fine, as we saw above, but *the car with wheels* is odd without some additional semantic material, e.g. *the car with shiny/old/cool wheels* is fine. This would seem to follow from the fact that a car's having wheels is part of its inherent properties, and therefore *the car with wheels* by itself is not informative. Finally, it is possible to compound the possessor and possessed in inalienable possession, i.e. *the car wheels*, whereas this is ungrammatical with alienable possession, e.g. **the man car*.

In NPs like *the table in the bedroom*, the PP *in the bedroom* is a kind of adjunct, and there are other types of adjunct PPs possible in NPs, e.g. *the book on the shelf*, *the meeting after the interview*. The logical structures for these NPs are given in (4.77), following the logical structures for clausal adjuncts in section 4.4.1.

(4.77)	a.	**be-in′** (bedroom, <u>table</u>)	the table in the bedroom
	a′.	**be-in′** (<u>bedroom</u>, table)	the bedroom with the table in it
	b.	**be-on′** (shelf, <u>book</u>)	the book on the shelf
	b′.	**be-on′** (<u>shelf</u>, book)	the shelf with the book on it
	c.	**be-after′** (interview, <u>meeting</u>)	the meeting after the interview
	c′.	**be-after′** (<u>interview</u>, meeting)	the interview with the meeting after it

When the first argument is chosen as the head, a resumptive PP containing the preposition as a modifier of the head and a pronoun referring to it is required; this is because *with* PPs in NPs code possession, which is not the semantic relation of the prepositional predicate in these constructions, and therefore the resumptive PP expresses the semantic content of the prepositional predicate. Clausal logical structures containing possessive NPs and NPs containing adjuncts are given in (4.78).

(4.78) a. **see′** (I, [**be-in′** (bedroom, <u>table</u>)])
'I saw the table in the bedroom.'

b. [**do′** (baby, Ø)] CAUSE [BECOME **broken′** ([**have′** (Paul, <u>watch</u>)])]
'The baby broke Paul's watch.'

4.7.4 Pronouns and reflexives

Pronominal elements are present in the semantic representation of a sentence, as are the kind of independent reflexive elements found in languages like English,

German, Japanese and many others. Accordingly, the sentences in (4.79) would have the accompanying logical structures in their semantic representations.

(4.79) a. Chris saw Pat.
a′. **see′** (Chris, Pat)
b. He saw José.
b′. **see′** (3sgM, José)
c. Fatima saw herself.
c′. **see′** (Fatima, herself)

The pronoun in (b) is represented as '3sgM' because its actual form is determined by the outcome of the linking into the syntax; if an active linking occurs, then it will be realized as *he*, and if a passive linking occurs, it will be realized as *him*. The relevant case-marking rules will be presented in chapter 7. The conditions determining the possibilities of coreference and disjoint reference for pronouns will be presented in chapter 5, and the conditions governing the proper use of reflexives in simple sentences will be developed in chapter 7.

Most pronouns exhaustively fill an argument position in a logical structure, the way '3sgM' fills the first argument position in (4.79b′) and *herself* fills the second argument position in (c′). There is, however, an interesting exception to this generalization. It is *one*-pronominalization, as in (4.80).

(4.80) a. I bought one.
b. I saw the tall one with blond hair.

In (a) *one* functions as a complete core argument of *buy*, analogous to *he* in (4.79b) or *it* in *I bought it*. The interesting case is (b), in which *one* expresses a subpart of an argument. What does this subpart consist of? There are strong constraints on it, as the following examples show.

(4.81) a. the tall student of physics with blond hair
a′. *the tall one of physics with blond hair
a″. the one with blond hair
b. the present King of France
b′. *the present one of France
b″. the present one
c. the unexpected arrest of the mafia boss by the FBI
c′. *the unexpected one of the mafia boss by the FBI
c″. the unexpected one by the FBI
c‴. the unexpected one /the one by the FBI
d. the attack of the killer bees on the dog
d′. *the one of the killer bees on the dog
d″. the one on the dog
e. the attack on the dog by killer bees
e′. the one on the dog by killer bees

These examples show that *one* cannot replace just *student* in *student of physics*, *King* in *King of France*, *arrest* in *arrest of the mafia boss* and *attack* in *attack of the killer bees*. In every case it must replace the entire phrase. With respect to the deverbal nominals, *one* can replace the nucleus plus its single direct core$_N$ argument. In terms of the discussion of deverbal nominals in section 4.7.2, we can say that *one* minimally represents the deverbal nominal plus its primary argument: the undergoer with nominals derived from state, achievement and accomplishment verbs and the actor with nominals derived from activity verbs. With agent nominalizations like *student* and *hunter*, the primary argument is the second argument of the verb, which is normally realized either as an incorporated noun (e.g. *duckhunter*) or a direct core$_N$ argument (e.g. *student of physics*). Given that this second argument may occur incorporated in the agent nominalization, it is not surprising it is an obligatory part of the minimal unit which can be replaced by *one*. With respect to deverbal nominals, we may predict that if a derived nominal does not take a direct core$_N$ argument, then *one* may represent the head noun alone. The example in (e) is of particular interest here, since there is no direct core$_N$ argument in it, and, as predicted, *one* can appear in place of just the head noun *attack*. Generalizing across both kinds of nominalization, we see that the minimal semantic unit corresponding to *one* is a predicate plus its primary argument; the identity of the primary argument is a function of (1) the type of nominalization, and (2) the *Aktionsart* of the verb from which the nominal is derived.

Returning to the *King of France* example, we argued in section 4.7.3 that kin expressions like *Mary's sister/the sister of Mary* and *the Queen of England/England's Queen* have predicative structures in their semantic representation, and what *one* expresses is the predicate plus its primary argument(s). In the case of *the sister of Mary*, it expresses the whole logical structure **have.as.kin′** (Mary, sister), as in *I met Mary's tall sister, not the short one*, where the logical structures for the two NPs are **be′** ([**have.as.kin′** (Mary, <u>sister</u>)], [**tall′**]) and **be′** (<u>one</u>, [**short′**]). In the case of royalty, *one* replaces **king′** (France), not simply **king′**. Thus it appears that these constructions also follow the pattern seen for *one*-pronominalization in deverbal nominals and agent nominalizations described above.

4.7.5 NP operators

We introduced a set of NP operators in section 2.3.2, and as with operators in the layered structure of the clause we will not propose a substantive semantic representation for them. We will, accordingly, represent them in logical structure in much the same way as we represented clausal operators in section 4.4.2. The NP operators are summarized in (4.82).

(4.82) $\langle_{DEIC} PROX \langle_{DEF} + \langle_{NEG} \emptyset \langle_{QNT} \exists \langle_{NUM} SG \langle_{NASP} COUNT \langle \mathrm{LS} \rangle\rangle\rangle\rangle\rangle\rangle\rangle$

⟨IF *DCL* ⟨TNS *PAST* ⟨**yesterday**′ ([**gentle**′ (**do**′ (x, ∅))] CAUSE [BECOME **open**′ (y)])⟩⟩⟩

⟨DEF + ⟨QNT ∃ ⟨NUM *SG* ⟨NASP *COUNT* ⟨**be**′ (**dog** (x), [**big**′])⟩⟩⟩⟩⟩

⟨DEF + ⟨QNT ∃ ⟨NUM *SG* ⟨NASP *COUNT* ⟨[**be-in**′ (z, [**be**′ (**door** (y), [**green**′])])]⟩⟩⟩⟩⟩

⟨DEF + ⟨QNT ∃ ⟨NUM *SG* ⟨NASP *COUNT* ⟨(**kitchen** (z))⟩⟩⟩⟩⟩

Figure 4.11 Semantic representation of *The big dog gently opened the green door in the kitchen yesterday*

Adjectival and nominal modifiers are represented as predicates taking the head as an argument, much as in the possessive and adjunct constructions. The logical structure for *Larry's red house* would be as in (4.83).[23]

(4.83) ⟨DEF+⟨NEG∅⟨QNT∃⟨NUM*SG*⟨NASP*COUNT*⟨**have**′ (Larry, [**be**′ (house, [**red**′])])⟩⟩⟩⟩⟩⟩

There are important interactions among the elements in this representation. For example, it can be realized as *Larry's red house* only if the DEF operator is '+', since a possessor in the NP-initial position always signals a definite NP. If it were '–', then the only possible realization would be *a red house of Larry's.*

4.8 Summary

We are at last in a position to give a full semantic representation for a clause, including clausal adjuncts and operators as well as NP adjuncts and operators. The sentence *The big dog gently opened the green door in the kitchen yesterday* would have the semantic representation given in figure 4.11. It is obviously cumbersome to work with representations as complex as this one, and consequently in future chapters we will specify only those aspects of the semantic representation that are relevant to the issue at hand. Nevertheless, we have succeeded in developing a system of lexical representation which permits us to create rich semantic representations for sentences.

Further reading

For alternative approaches to macroroles, see A. E. Kibrik (1985), Dowty (1991), Palmer (1994). On valence and valence theory, see Allerton (1982), Abraham (1978). On lexical rules, see Chomsky (1970), Jackendoff (1975), Bresnan (1982a), Pinker (1989). For more on adpositions, see Bennett (1975), Cresswell (1978), Hawkins (1985), Gawron (1986), Jolly (1991, 1993), Rauh (1991). On adverbs, see Jackendoff (1972), Cresswell (1979), LoCasio (1986), McCawley (1979), McConnell-Ginet (1982), Nuyts (1994). For more on linking, see chapters 7 and 9, and the references given therein. For more detailed discussion of qualia theory, see Pustejovsky (1991, 1995). On deverbal nominals and lexicalization, see Talmy (1985), Nunes (1993), Comrie and Thompson (1985).

Exercises

1 In the following sentences, state which arguments are actors and which arguments are undergoers. [**section 4.2**]

(1) The house collapsed.
(2) The boy introduced his girlfriend to his mother.
(3) The salt dissolved quickly in the water.
(4) Sandy devoured the turkey sandwich.
(5) The students booed loudly at the politician.
(6) The cougar was captured by the game warden.
(7) Kim ran around the house for ten minutes.
(8) Pat executed a perfect crescent kick.
(9) The courier handed Robin the package.
(10) Sally laughed out loud.
(11) The hunter shot at the lion.
(12) It snowed heavily on Tuesday.
(13) The waiter placed the drink in front of Michael.
(14) The lawyer received a summons from the court.
(15) Sandy discussed Robin's request with Kim.

2 The data below are from Bambara, a Niger-Kordofanian language widely spoken in subsaharan West Africa (Bird and Shopen 1979).[24] Consider the alternation between the transitive and intransitive uses of the verbs in (1)–(6). How is the single argument of the intransitive verbs interpreted? How is the other possible intransitive meaning expressed? What implications does this second form have for the analysis of activity predications presented in section 3.2.2? [**section 4.2**]

(1)	a. Fanta bena daba ti.	'Fanta will break the hoe.'
	b. Daba bena ti.	'The hoe will break.'
	c. Fanta bena ti.	'Fanta will break.'/*'Fanta will break (something).'
(2)	a. Baba bena kini tobi.	'Baba will cook the rice.'
	b. Kini bena tobi.	'The rice will cook.'
	c. Baba bena tobi.	'Baba will [be] cook[ed].'/*'Baba will cook (something).'
(3)	a. Fanta be ji min.	'Fanta is drinking the water.'
	b. Ji be min.	'The water is being drunk.'
	c. *Fanta be min.	'Fanta is being drunk.'/*'Fanta is drinking (something).'

(4)	a.	Safura bena daba dila.	'Safura will repair the hoe.'
	b.	Daba bena dila.	'The hoe will be repaired.'
	c.	Safura bena dila.	'Safura will be repaired.'/*'Safura will repair (something).'
(5)	a.	U bena Baba fo.	'They will greet Baba.'
	b.	Baba bena fo.	'Baba will be greeted.'
	c.	U bena fo.	'They will be greeted.'/*'They will greet (someone).'
(6)	a.	An be sogo dumu.	'We are eating the meat.'
	b.	Sogo be dumu.	'The meat is being eaten.'
	c.	An be dumu.	'We are being eaten.'/*'We are eating (something).'
(7)	a.	Fanta bena tili ke.	'Fanta will break (something).'
	b.	Baba bena tobili ke.	'Baba will cook (something).'
	c.	Fanta be minli ke.	'Fanta is drinking.'
	d.	Safura bena dilali ke.	'Safura will repair (something).'
	e.	U bena foli ke.	'They will greet (someone).'
	f.	An be dumuli ke.	'We are eating.'
(8)	a.	Baba be mun ke?	'What is Baba doing?'
	b.	Baba be bara ke.	'Baba is working.'/'Baba is doing work.'
(9)	a.	Ne bena tobili ye.	'I will see the cooking.'
	b.	Tobili bena ye.	'The cooking will be seen.'
(10)	a.	U bena foli men.	'They will hear the greeting.'
	b.	Foli bena men.	'The greeting will be heard.'

3 Given the following logical structures, determine which argument will be actor and which will be undergoer, following the Actor–Undergoer Hierarchy in figure 4.2. If more than one assignment is possible, give all of them. Indicate how the non-macrorole arguments would be coded as well. [**section 4.3**]

(1)	*donate*	[**do′** (x, ∅)] CAUSE [BECOME **have′** (y, z)]
(2)	*drain*	[**do′** (x, ∅)] CAUSE [BECOME NOT **be-in′** (y, z)]
(3)	*hear*	**hear′** (x, y)
(4)	*persuade*	[**do′** (x, ∅)] CAUSE [BECOME **believe′** (y, z)]
(5)	*sit*	**be-on′** (x, y) [MR 1]
(6)	*set*	[**do′** (x, ∅)] CAUSE [BECOME **be-on′** (y, z)]
(7)	*run (to)*	[**do′** (x, [**run′** (x)])] & [BECOME **be-at′** (y, x)] [MR 1]
(8)	*show*	[**do′** (x, ∅)] CAUSE [BECOME **see′** (y, z)]
(9)	*fill*	[**do′** (x, ∅)] CAUSE [[BECOME **be-in′** (y, z)] CAUSE [BECOME **full′** (y)]]
(10)	*destroy*	[**do′** (x, ∅)] CAUSE [[**do′** (y, ∅)] CAUSE [BECOME **destroyed′** (z)]]

4 Give the semantic representation for the following sentences; include the logical structure of the verb and the semantic representation of adjuncts, adverbs and operators. Do not give a full semantic representation for the arguments; give them simply as 'John', 'book', etc. [**section 4.4**]

(1) The cougar was captured by the game warden next to a shopping mall.
(2) The house collapsed yesterday during the earthquake.
(3) Mary quickly showed Sally the plans.
(4) Robin is probably painting her room green.
(5) Evidently, Kim has not completely ruined the printer.

5 Give the syntactic representation of the following sentences, both constituent and operator projections. Specify the internal structure of the PPs but not that of the NPs. [**section 4.4**]

(1) Evidently, Sally put the letters in the mailbox yesterday.
(2) Robin ran to the store quickly.
(3) Chris has not written her essay yet.
(4) Latisha is still complaining about the traffic ticket.
(5) The waiter carefully placed a drink on the tray.

6 Diagram the linking from semantics to syntax in the sentences below, following the procedure outlined in section 4.5. Give the logical structure of the verb with arguments for the semantic representation and the constituent projection only for the syntactic representation, using the example in figure 4.10 as a model. [**section 4.5**]

(1) Sandy devoured the sandwich.
(2) The boy gave his girlfriend some flowers.
(3) What did Pat show to Kim?
(4) The cougar was captured by the game warden.

7 Give the semantic representation for the following NPs: include the semantic representation of the head noun, possessors, adjuncts and operators. [**section 4.7**]

(1) the two new red cars
(2) the sister of Kim's neighbor
(3) the bicycle's shiny wheel
(4) that loud guy in the kitchen
(5) a surprise party after the meeting

5
Information structure

5.0 Introduction

Whenever a sentence is uttered or written, it is done so in a particular communicative context, and for the addressee to correctly interpret the communicative intent of the speaker/writer,[1] the addressee must interpret the sentence in that same context. But as this context goes far beyond the immediate linguistic context to include assumptions of many different types, identification of the proper context by the addressee is not always possible, and so misunderstandings can take place. In order to decrease the chance of misunderstanding, the speaker, in creating the sentence, tailors the form of the sentence to allow the hearer to create the proper context for interpretation with minimal processing effort. For his part, the hearer assumes that the sentence will be tailored in just this way, and so takes the first proposition that comes to mind as the one the speaker intended to communicate, and the first associated set of contextual assumptions that come to his mind as the intended background assumptions. A crucial aspect of this tailoring is the distribution of information in the sentence, which we will call the 'information structure' of the sentence (similar to what the Prague School linguists called 'the functional sentence perspective'). To give one simple example, in the most common type of situation this generally means that the NP referring to the topic that is being spoken about will come first, and the expression of the comment being made about the topic will follow.[2]

The study of information structure goes back to the beginnings of modern linguistics, to the work of the Czech linguist Mathesius in the 1920s (Mathesius 1928, 1929). In recent years advances in understanding how information structure affects syntactic structure have been made by Kuno (1972a, 1972b, 1975), Sgall, Hajičová and Panevová (1986), Firbas (1964, 1966, 1992), Halliday (1967, 1985), Prince (1981a, b), Chafe (1976, 1987), Dryer (1996a), Lambrecht (1986, 1987, 1994), and others. It is largely Lambrecht's work which forms the basis of the conception of information structure developed in this chapter.

What is information? Lambrecht argues that there is 'a distinction . . . between (i) the *pragmatic states* of the denotata of individual sentence constituents in the minds of the speech participants, and (ii) the *pragmatic relations* established between these referents and the propositions in which they play the role of predicates or arguments. It is the establishment of such pragmatic relations that makes information possible' (1994: 49, emphasis in original).[3] For example, if someone says *It was John that left early*, the referent of the name *John* must already be known to the hearer; this is its identifiability status in the mind of the hearer. The proposition 'someone left early' must also be known to the hearer, and consequently the new information conveyed by this utterance is that John is the someone who left early. The pragmatic relations between the incomplete information (the 'open proposition') that someone left early (what we will be calling the 'presupposition') and the referent John (what we will be calling the 'focus') will be the main concern of this chapter. These pragmatic relations can be manifested in different ways in the information structure of a sentence. We will discuss each of the different types of information structure at length, but before doing that, we need to clarify some of the issues related to Lambrecht's first type of information structure category, 'the pragmatic states of the referents of individual sentence constituents in the minds of the speech participants'.

When a referent is introduced for the first time into the discourse, it is a 'new' referent, and in many languages will be coded as an indefinite NP.[4] A new referent may also be introduced 'anchored' to some more identifiable referent, as in *a guy I know from school*, and in these cases the language may often allow it to be used as a topic. Prince (1981b) uses the terms 'brand-new' **unanchored** referent and **anchored** referent to distinguish these two types of 'new' referent. In further mentions of a referent after its introduction it will of course be treated as identifiable.

If a referent is identifiable to the addressee, then it will be in one of three activation states: **active**, if it is the current focus of consciousness, **accessible**, if it is textually, situationally or inferentially available by means of its existence in the physical context or its relation to something in the physical or linguistic context but is not yet the current focus of consciousness, or **inactive**, if it is in the hearer's long-term memory, yet not in his short-term memory (i.e. not in either the focus or periphery of consciousness). These terms are from Chafe (1987).

A summary of the distinctions among the activation states of referents is given in figure 5.1 (from LaPolla 1995a: 305, based on Lambrecht 1994: 109).

Predicative NPs, such as *a lawyer* in *John is a lawyer*, are non-referential, in that they do not refer to an entity but rather simply characterize a referent already identified. Generics, such as *grapes* in *Grapes are good for you*, are non-specific, in that they are not individuated entities, yet generics are treated as accessible identifiable referents in most languages, and so can be topics, as in this example (see Givón 1984b: 413 for discussion). This is not the case for predicative NPs.

The particular form that the representation of a referent takes in a particular stretch of discourse is determined by a variety of factors involved in the total context, including activation status, information structure and certain language-specific

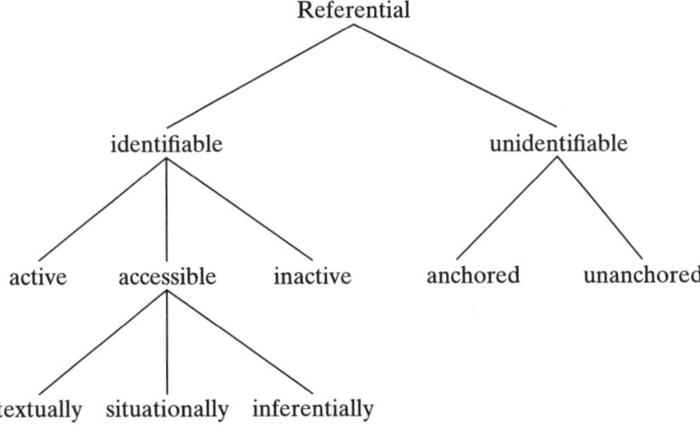

Figure 5.1 The cognitive states of referents in discourse

factors such as politeness strategies and tendency to use ellipsis; we will discuss this further below. Underlying all of these factors is the assumption on the part of the hearer mentioned earlier that the speaker will choose a form for the sentence that will allow the speaker to create the proper (i.e. most relevant) context of interpretation with the least amount of processing effort. Different types of coding can then be seen as guaranteeing different degrees of accessibility: zero marking guarantees that the referent intended is the most accessible one, generally an active referent, e.g. a current topic of conversation; use of a pronoun guarantees that the referent intended is either active (especially if unstressed) or at least accessible (if stressed); use of a definite NP guarantees that the referent intended is identifiable, and generally either inactive or accessible; use of an indefinite NP generally tells the hearer that the referent is not identifiable in the current context and hence is a new referent being introduced into the context.

5.1 Focus structure

In most communicative situations, when a speaker makes a statement, she makes what we will call a 'pragmatic assertion' or simply 'assertion'. This assertion is a piece of information, a proposition the speaker hopes the addressee will come to know or be aware of as a result of the sentence having been uttered. The assertion is a 'pragmatic assertion' because it is a pragmatically structured utterance, generally involving both 'old' information, such as the topic and the presuppositions associated with the topic, and 'new' information, such as the comment about the topic. All languages have some grammatical system for marking which type of information is which within the utterance; it may involve intonation, morphological marking, word order or some combination thereof. This association of a particular information structure with a particular morphosyntactic or intonational structure Lambrecht calls the 'focus structure' of the sentence. We used quote marks on the words 'old' and 'new' above because using the expressions 'old information' and 'new information' to refer to the different parts of the assertion is somewhat misleading. It is not the so-called 'new' information alone that is informative, but the relationship between the 'old' and 'new' information that makes the assertion informative. The 'old' information is the set of assumptions evoked by the utterance that make up the context necessary for understanding the utterance. We will now refer to this set of assumptions as the 'pragmatic presupposition' or just 'presupposition'. The part of the assertion which is not within the pragmatic presupposition we will call the 'focus' or 'focus of the assertion'; it is the part that is unpredictable or unrecoverable from the context.[5] What is informative about an assertion is not the information in the focus by itself, but the association of that information with the set of assumptions that constitute the pragmatic presupposition. For example, if I just say *John*, that is not in itself informative, but if I say *It was John that hit you*, or say *John* in response to the question *Who hit me?*, then the information in the focus ('John') completes the open proposition 'x hit the addressee' which is in the pragmatic presupposition, creating the informative assertion 'John hit the addressee.' That is, the information in the focus replaces 'someone' in the presupposition 'someone hit me' with the more specific referent 'John'.

Lambrecht (1994) gives the following definitions for the terms we have introduced so far:

> **Pragmatic assertion**: the proposition expressed by a sentence which the hearer is expected to know or believe or take for granted as a result of hearing the sentence uttered. (52)
>
> **Pragmatic presupposition**: the set of propositions lexico-grammatically evoked in an utterance which the speaker assumes the hearer already knows or believes or is ready to take for granted at the time of speech. (52)
>
> **Focus,** or **focus of the assertion**: the semantic component of a pragmatically structured proposition whereby the assertion differs from the presupposition. (213)
>
> **Focus structure**: the conventional association of a focus meaning [distribution of information] with a sentence form. (222)

As suggested by Lambrecht's definition of pragmatic presupposition, there is an awareness on the part of the speaker of what might be accessible information to the hearer, and awareness on the part of the addressee of what the speaker might assume to be accessible information to the hearer. The speaker believes that the knowledge the addressee needs to understand the utterance will be available to him at the time of utterance, either because it is stored in the addressee's memory, or because it is accessible from the context or through inference. It is important to emphasize that the set of assumptions in the pragmatic presupposition is not necessarily 'old' information. The addressee creates a particular context (puts together a particular set of assumptions) in which to process the sentence based on what is evoked by the form of the sentence and other factors. This can include creating what have been traditionally called 'presuppositions' when the interpretation of the sentence requires them. For example, if two people see a very nice car drive by and one says to the other, *I once drove a Bentley like that one*, the hearer may not have known what type of car it was, or may have thought it was a Rolls Royce, but in processing the speaker's utterance will create the presupposition that the car that just passed was a Bentley. In fact there are times when it is the creation of presuppositions, and not the overt assertion or question conveyed by the sentence that is the main communicative intention of the speaker, such as when a prosecutor asks a defendant *What did you do after you stole the money?*, when the defendant has not confessed to stealing the money, in order to cause the jury to create the presupposition that the defendant actually did steal the money!

The topic in a topic–comment construction is an entity within the pragmatic presupposition that has the function of naming the referent that the assertion is about. This definition differs somewhat from the traditional concept of topic, or 'theme' in the Prague School terminology, in that 'topic in a topic–comment construction' is a discourse-pragmatic function, not a structural position in the sentence or utterance. A topic is not an obligatory part of every utterance, though the most common types of utterance do have a topic. Lambrecht (1994) characterizes the nature of the topic and its relationship to the pragmatic presupposition as follows:

> **Topic expression**: a constituent is a topic expression if the proposition expressed by the clause with which it is associated is pragmatically construed as conveying information about the referent of the constituent. (131)
>
> Since the topic is the 'matter of current concern' about which new information is added in an utterance, for a proposition to be construable as being about a topic referent this referent must evidently be part of the pragmatic presupposition, i.e. it must already be 'under discussion' or otherwise available from the context. We can say that the proposition 'x is under discussion' . . . is evoked by the presuppositional structure of a sentence containing x as a topic. (150)

We will present examples of topic expressions and their coding from a number of languages in subsequent sections.

In much of the literature on information structure, topic is taken as synonymous with the 'given' or 'presupposed' part of an utterance, but for Lambrecht what is presupposed 'is not the topic itself, nor its referent, but the fact that the topic referent is expected to play a role in a given proposition, due to its status as a center of interest . . . One therefore ought not to say that a topic "is presupposed",

Table 5.1 *The Topic Acceptability Scale*

Active	Most acceptable
Accessible	↑
Inactive	
Brand-new anchored	↓
Brand-new unanchored	Least acceptable

but that, given its discourse status, it is presupposed to play a role in a given proposition' (1994: 151). There is a correlation, however, between the pragmatic state of the topic referent and its acceptability as a topic, as the more accessible the topic referent of an utterance is, the less processing effort will be required to properly interpret that utterance. An active referent makes the most acceptable topic, an accessible but not active topic makes a somewhat less acceptable topic, an inactive referent makes an even less acceptable topic, and an anchored brand-new referent makes one of the least acceptable topics. In the extreme case, where a topic is not identifiable (i.e. an unanchored brand-new referent), the utterance will require pragmatic accommodation ('going along with' the use of an unidentifiable referent as topic) in order to be interpreted correctly, or otherwise it may not be processable at all. Lambrecht (1994: 165) summarizes this scale of acceptability as the Topic Acceptability Scale (table 5.1).

In section 5.0 we discussed the fact that the pragmatic states of referents in the minds of the speech act participants and the pragmatic relations that we have been discussing as information structure are two different categories of information which often correlate with each other, but are not directly related. We also mentioned that the particular form that the representation of a referent takes can be seen as an instruction to the addressee to construe the referent as having a particular degree of accessibility, and that this guarantee is based on the assumption on the part of the hearer that the speaker will choose a form for the utterance that will allow the hearer to create the proper context of interpretation with the least amount of processing effort. In terms of the coding of the topic referent, this depends partly on the activation state of the topic referent and partly on the function of the topic. Topics either name a topic referent in the discourse, or they are simply involved in the expression of a semantic relation between a topic referent and a predication. This difference in function can influence the coding of the topic referent. Topics with the naming function are generally coded as lexical NPs, while those with the latter function are most often coded as zero or unstressed pronouns, as they are generally active referents. We saw in the Topic Acceptability Scale that topic referents that are not active, while possible, are less acceptable as topics. If we now combine the correlation between the activation state of a referent and its representation in discourse discussed in section 5.0, on the one hand, with the Topic

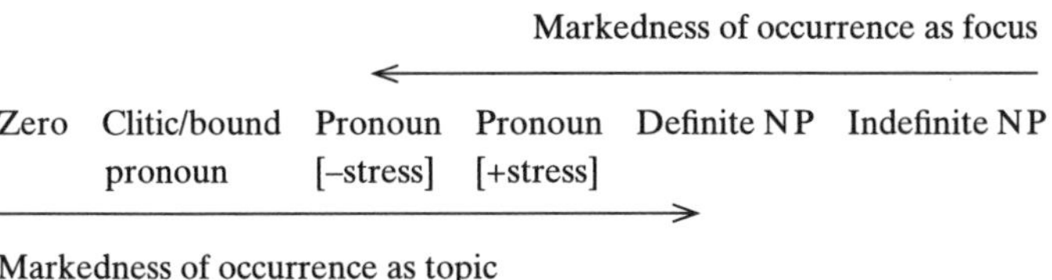

Figure 5.2 Coding of referents in terms of possible functions

Acceptability Scale, on the other, we come up with a scale of markedness relations between the form of a referring expression and its function as topic or focus, which is summarized in figure 5.2 (see Givón 1983, Levinson 1987, Gundel, Hedburg and Zacharski 1993, Ariel 1990 and Lambrecht 1994). Thus, zero coding is the least marked coding for a topic, while realization as an indefinite NP is the least marked coding for a focal element. While indefinite NPs can be topics under special contextual circumstances, it is impossible for a focal element to be zero.

While a non-active referent as topic is an anomaly, an active referent in a focus relation with an asserted proposition is not, as it requires no accommodation or extra processing effort. From these non-typical cases we can see that focus structure is not a question of identifiable vs. unidentifiable NPs; it is 'an indicator of a semantic **relation** holding on the level of the sentence or proposition as a whole, not . . . an expression of information properties of individual sentence constituents' (Lambrecht 1989: 3, emphasis in original). For example, if I say *Did you see John or Bill?*, and you answer *Bill*, the referent represented by the word *Bill* is already active, yet it is in a focus relation with the presupposition 'speaker saw x'. What is new is the proposition 'x = Bill', not the referent 'Bill'. In this case 'the speaker saw x' is the presupposition, 'x = Bill' is the assertion, the new information, and 'Bill' is the focus of the assertion, or we might say the focus of the new information.

It is necessary to distinguish between the focus of the assertion and the syntactic constituent in which it appears in the sentence (e.g. NP, core, clause). We will refer to the syntactic constituent in which focus occurs as the **focus domain**. As the focus must be an entity or state of affairs which when added to a presupposition will produce an assertion, it follows that focus domains must be phrasal rather than lexical categories, as entities and states of affairs are syntactically expressed only in phrasal categories. Lambrecht argues that 'focus domains cannot be lexical categories . . . because information structure is not concerned with words and their meanings, nor with the relations between the meanings of words and those of phrases or sentences, but with the pragmatic construal of the relations between entities and states of affairs in given discourse situations' (1994: 215). For example, if I ask *Did you put it in the box?*, and you want to say that you did not put it *in* the box but *on* the box, the presupposition involved in your answer is not 'speaker put it x the box' but 'speaker put it x', and the utterance must take the form of a whole prepositional phrase, e.g. *No,* ON *the box.* You cannot simply say *No, on*, as the preposition by itself cannot be the focus domain. Hence the minimal **information unit** corresponds to the minimal phrasal category in syntax.[6]

5.2 Focus types

Lambrecht presents a taxonomy of the different types of focus structure found in the world's languages, and discusses the morphosyntactic constructions used in representing them. There is a major contrast between narrow focus and broad focus, and a secondary contrast between two types of broad focus. **Narrow focus** is when a single constituent, such as an NP, is focused. **Broad focus** is when the focus includes more than one constituent. It may include all but the topic, as in the common 'topic–comment' construction, which Lambrecht calls **predicate focus**, or it may include the entire sentence, which Lambrecht calls **sentence focus**. These focus types correlate with three different communicative functions, i.e. identifying a referent, commenting on a topic and reporting an event or presenting a new discourse referent, respectively. We will discuss each of these types of focus structure individually.

5.2.1 Predicate focus

Predicate focus is the universally unmarked type of focus structure. In this type there is a topic within the pragmatic presupposition, while the predicate phrase expresses a comment about the topic. Here are some examples (Lambrecht 1994: 223):

(5.1)	Q: What happened to your car?	
	A: a. My car/It broke DOWN.	English
	b. (La mia macchina) si è ROTTA.	Italian
	c. (Ma voiture) elle est en PANNE.	French
	d. (Kuruma wa) KOSYOO-si-ta.	Japanese

In the answers to the question *What happened to your car?*, the presupposition evoked is that the speaker's car is a topic about which a comment can be made. The assertion is the establishment of an aboutness relationship between the topic and the particular state of affairs referred to by the predicate. The focus is the predicate *broke down*, and the focus domain is the core minus the subject–topic. The information structure of this example can be represented as follows (see Lambrecht 1994: 226):

(5.1′)	Sentence:	*My car broke* DOWN.
	Presupposition:	'speaker's car is available as a topic for comment x'
	Assertion:	'x = broke down'
	Focus:	'broke down'
	Focus domain:	verb plus remaining postverbal core constituents

As can be seen from these examples, the linguistic means for distinguishing the topic from the rest of the utterance and marking the state of affairs represented by the predicate as a comment about the topic can vary across languages. In the English and Italian examples it is the subject that is the topic, in the Japanese example it is the *wa*-marked NP, while in the (spoken) French example it is the left-detached NP. In these examples the topics are given as full lexical NPs for expository purposes, though in a predicate focus structure the topic is usually pronominalized or left unexpressed. In many sentences the topic coincides with the subject, but topics are not always subjects (see (5.2)); indeed, topics do not even have to have a direct relationship to the verb. All that is necessary is for there to be the aboutness relation that defines topichood.[7]

(5.2) a. As for José, I think he is a great guy.
b. Tulips, you have to plant new bulbs every year?
c. Sono okasi wa hutora-nai. — Japanese
those sweets TOP gain.weight-not
'Those sweets (even if one eats them, one) doesn't gain weight.'
d. Nèi xiē shù, shùshēn dà. — Mandarin
that few tree trunk big
'Those trees, the trunks are big.'

5.2.2 Sentence focus

In a sentence-focus construction the entire clause is within the focus domain, so there is no topic. No pragmatic presuppositions (other than non-distinctive presuppositions that would be involved in any focus type) are formally evoked by sentence-focus structures. Consider the following examples (Lambrecht 1994: 223):

(5.3) Q: What happened?
A: a. My CAR broke down. — English
b. Mi si è rotta la MACCHINA. — Italian
c. J'ai ma VOITURE qui est en PANNE. — French
d. KURUMA ga KOSYOO-si-ta. — Japanese

Here there is no presupposition, the assertion and the focus coincide and the focus domain is the clause:

(5.3′)		
	Sentence:	*My CAR broke down.*
	Presupposition:	none
	Assertion:	'speaker's car broke down'
	Focus:	'speaker's car broke down'
	Focus domain:	clause

Focus domains must be allowed to contain non-focal elements, such as *my* in *My CAR broke down* (see Lambrecht 1994, section 5.2.4). In this example, *my* is not focal and is topical, since it refers to the speaker. *My CAR*, on the other hand, is not the topic of the sentence, and this is one of the defining features of a sentence-focus construction: the subject is not the topic. As mentioned above, topichood is not so much the pragmatic status of the referent itself, but the relationship between the referent and the assertion being made. Sentence focus lacks a topic–comment relationship between the referent coded by the subject and the proposition expressed by the sentence; in other words, the utterance is not 'about' that referent. The absence of presupposition results in the assertion not exhibiting the type of binary relation that is involved in the other focus types (e.g. 'x = broken down'). That is, the construction is semantically non-binary, having neither a subject–predicate (topic–comment) nor a focus–presupposition bipartition.

Comparing these examples with those in (5.1), we see that Italian and French use a different word order for this type of pragmatic structure, Japanese uses a different morphological marking together with pitch prominence on both the subject NP and the predicate phrase, while English relies on stress on the subject alone to express the pragmatic difference. What the structures in all these languages have in common is the marking of the subject as a non-topic, and this lack of a subject–topic is one of the features that distinguishes marked focus structure (narrow- and sentence-focus structure) from unmarked focus structure (predicate-focus structure).

As mentioned above, sentence-focus structure is most often used in presentational situations, presenting either a new event/situation or a new referent, or both, as in the following examples:

(5.4) a. Once upon a time there was an OLD WOMAN (who lived in a SHOE).
b. (to the boss, on entering the office late) My CAR broke down.
c. There came a RIDER.
d. Oh m'God! A DUCK just flew into the LIVING room!

It is the non-binary nature of the sentence focus mentioned above that evokes this 'eventive' sense of these constructions. We can also see from these examples that in certain situations (e.g. (5.4a, c)) even English requires distinctive constructions for this particular pragmatic structure (similar to the French biclausal construction or Italian inversion construction – see the discussion below, section 5.3).

5.2.3 Narrow focus

In a narrow-focus structure, the focus domain is limited to a single constituent, and any constituent, be it subject, object, oblique NP or nucleus, can be the focused constituent.[8] Compare the following examples with those in (5.1) and (5.3):

(5.5) Q: I heard your motorcycle broke down.

A:	a. My CAR broke down.	English
	b. Si è rotta la mia MACCHINA./È la mia MACCHINA che si è rotta.	Italian (lit. 'broke down my car'/It's my car which broke down')

c. C'est ma VOITURE qui est en panne. French ('It is my car which broke down')

d. KURUMA ga kosyoo-si-ta. Japanese

In this structure the proposition 'something of the speaker's broke down' is part of the pragmatic presupposition, the assertion is that it is the speaker's car that broke down, the focus is 'car', and the focus domain is the whole NP. The focus domain is restricted to the single constituent. Since in this particular example the open proposition *x broke down* is active and the referent of *my car* is not, making the activation statuses of the two parts of the assertion in this example the reverse of the predicate-focus construction, this might lead one to think that it is this difference in activation status that is important. However, the same answer could have been given to the question *Was it your car or your motorcycle that broke down?*, where *my car* and the open proposition are both active. From this we can see that the 'new' information in the focus is not the constituent itself, but the establishment of a relationship between the referent and the presupposed proposition 'something of the speaker's broke down' in creating the 'new' information that it is the speaker's car that broke down. It is this relationship that makes a focus constituent informative, not the status of the referent as newly introduced or not. We can represent the information structure of this example as follows:

(5.5′) Sentence: *My CAR broke down.*
Presupposition: 'speaker's x broke down'
Assertion: x = 'car'
Focus: 'car'
Focus domain: NP

In Lambrecht (1994, section 5.6), a distinction is drawn between **marked** and **unmarked** narrow focus, and this is a very useful contrast. The difference lies in the position of the narrow-focused constituent. Many languages have a clearly defined unmarked focus position in the clause; in verb-final languages, it is normally the immediately preverbal position (Kim 1988), as in Korean (Kim 1988, Yang 1994) and Kaluli (Schieffelin 1985). In English, the unmarked focus position is the final position in the core, which may or may not be the final position in the clause. Unmarked narrow focus is that falling on an element in the unmarked focus position, whereas marked narrow focus is that falling on an element in a position in the clause other than the unmarked focus position. Consider the following English sentence with the different focal stress possibilities indicated.

(5.6) a. Chris gave the book to PAT yesterday.
b. Chris gave the book to Pat YESTERDAY.
c. Chris gave THE BOOK to Pat yesterday.
d. Chris GAVE the book to Pat yesterday.
e. CHRIS gave the book to Pat yesterday.

With focal stress falling on *Pat* in (5.6a), the result is ambiguous between a predicate-focus reading, in which *gave the book to Pat* is the actual focus domain, and a narrow-focus reading. Since the focused constituent is the last element in the core, the narrow-focus interpretation is an instance of unmarked narrow focus. All of the other examples represent marked narrow-focus possibilities. A WH-element in the precore slot is always unmarked narrow focus, whereas a non-WH-element in focus in the precore slot, e.g. *No,* THAT BOOK *Chris gave to Pat* (as a reply to *This book Chris gave to Pat*), it is a type of marked narrow focus. Non-WH NPs in the precore slot are sometimes referred to as 'contrastive topics', because they are in a clause-initial position associated with topics but have marked narrow focus, i.e. are contrastive. It should be noted, however, that not all non-WH NPs in the precore slot are focal. An example of a topical element in the precore slot is *Beans I can't stand*, with focal stress on the verb and the precore slot NP unstressed (see Gundel 1976, Prince 1981a).

5.3 The morphosyntactic coding of focus structure

Even closely related languages can vary greatly with respect to the extent to which focus structure influences syntactic structure, as the contrast between French and Italian in the previous section shows. All of the languages use intonation to some extent in marking the different focus structure constructions; they differ in terms of what other syntactic or morphological means they use in addition to intonation. In the English examples we saw that the same syntactic structure can be used for all three types of focus structure, with each type being differentiated only by differences in accentuation, as it is possible for the focal stress to fall on any constituent of the sentence in English. In a predicate-focus structure the accent is on the predicate phrase, and the subject NP is generally unaccented; in a sentence-focus structure and a marked narrow-focus structure the accent is on the focal NP and not on the predicate phrase. That the focus constituent in a narrow-focus structure is the only accented constituent in the sentence is true of all four of the languages under discussion. Thus there is an important correlation between intonation and focus structure, as has been often noted (see e.g. Kempson 1975, Selkirk 1984, Steedman 1991, Lambrecht 1994). In English, aside from accentuation, it is also possible to use marked word orders to express narrow- or sentence-focus structure, such as using the narrow-focus cleft construction in *It was Robin that hit you*, or the sentence-focus structures we saw in (5.4a) and (5.4c).

In the Japanese examples different focus structures are distinguished by a combination of intonation and morphological marking, essentially the use of different postpositions, either *wa* or *ga*. The particle *wa* marks a topic in a predicate-focus sentence such as example (5.1d), while *ga* may mark a sentence-focus structure, as in example (5.3d), if it is unstressed, or a narrow-focus structure, as in example (5.5d), if it is stressed; Kuno (1973) refers to these as 'neutral description *ga*' and 'exhaustive listing *ga*', respectively. In addition, if a topic occurs with an active proposition, i.e. both the topic NP and the proposition are active, then *ga* may mark the topic in this situation (Shimojo 1995). In Huallaga Quechua (Weber 1989) there is a suffix *-qa* which marks topical elements; like *wa* in Japanese, it may occur more than once in a clause. Evidential markers signal focus; that is, the normal placement of an evidential marker in a clause is on the focal element.

In both French and Italian there is a restriction on focal elements appearing preverbally, and therefore it is not possible to mark a sentence-focus or narrow-focus construction simply by accenting a preverbal NP, as in English. Syntactic means must be used to distinguish the different focus structures. We can see from the examples in (5.5) that both languages can use cleft constructions for narrow-focus structure, though in Italian the inverted structure is more natural in this situation. In the French narrow-focus structure a biclausal cleft construction is used to allow the focal NP to appear in the postverbal position (the usual focus position) of the first clause, even though it is the logical subject of the proposition 'my car broke down', with the main semantic content of the assertion appearing in a relative clause. The first clause then has the syntax and accentuation of a predicate-focus structure, while the second clause is not accented at all. In the French sentence-focus structure a similar syntactic structure is used (the *avoir*-cleft construction), though both clauses have normal predicate-focus accent on the predicate phrase. In Italian the situation is similar, though in Italian, unlike in French, it is more natural to use a type of simple inverted structure, where the focal subject simply appears in postverbal position, to mark both narrow- and sentence-focus structure.

The constraint that these two languages share against preverbal focal NPs is actually not uncommon in the languages of the world. In Mandarin Chinese (LaPolla 1995a), the NP representing the topic in a predicate-focus construction must appear in preverbal position, as in (5.7a). In a sentence-focus construction the logical subject will either appear in the postverbal position (if it involves a motion/location verb), as in (5.7b), or will appear after the first verb of a two-verb serial construction in which the first verb (*yǒu* 'to have/exist') simply serves the purpose of allowing a focal logical subject to appear in postverbal position, as in (5.8). In a narrow focus construction, though marked intonation alone can be used to signal this type of structure, more commonly a cleft construction, similar to the French *c'est* cleft construction, is used which allows the focal constituent to appear postverbally (after the copula), e.g. *tā laǒdà* 'her eldest [son]' in (5.9).

(5.7) a. Chē lái le.
vehicle come PRFV
'The car is here.'

b. Lái chē le.
come vehicle PRFV
'There is a car coming.'

(5.8) Yǒu rén xiǎng kàn nǐ.
exist person want see 2sg
'There is someone (here) who wants to see you.'

(5.9) Shì tā laǒdà gěi tā nàme-duō máfán.
COP 3sg old-big give 3sg that-much trouble
'It is her eldest (son) that gives her so much trouble.'

In Sesotho, one of the Sotho languages of southern Africa (Demuth 1989, 1990), there is an absolute constraint against focal elements appearing preverbally. This is an SVO language, and accordingly subjects must be 'highly topical, old, given information' (Demuth 1989). Since question words are always focal, they may not appear preverbally; in particular, they always appear either at the end of the sentence (in the unmarked form) or postverbally in a cleft construction. Consequently, it is not possible to have a question in which an interrogative pronoun (the focus) is the subject (see (5.10a)). Instead a passive construction, as in (5.10b), or a clefted form (5.10c, d) is used to put the interrogative pronoun in focus position (examples in (5.10) from Demuth 1989, 1990).[9]

(5.10) a. *Mang o-pheh-ile lijo?
who SUBJ-cook-PERF food
'Who cooked the food?'
b. Lijo li-pheh-li-o-e ke mang?
food SUBJ-cook-PERF-PASS-MOOD by who
'The food was cooked by who?' or 'Who cooked the food?'
c. Ea o-f-ile-ng ntja ke mang?
REL OBJ-give-PERF-REL dog COP who
'The one that gave you the dog is who?'
d. Ke mang ea o-f-ile-ng ntja?
COP who REL OBJ-give-PERF-REL dog
'It's who that gave you the dog?'

From these facts we can see that languages differ in terms of what we will call the **potential focus domain**, that is, the syntactic domain in which the focus element(s) may occur. What Lambrecht calls the 'focus domain', the actual part of the sentence in focus in the construction, we will refer to as the **actual focus domain**. In English, the focus can be anywhere in the clause, and so the potential focus domain is the entire clause, while in many other languages, such as Italian, French, Chinese and Sesotho, the potential focus domain is generally limited to the verb and postverbal positions within the clause. Among this latter group of languages there is also a difference in the scope of the potential focus domain between Sesotho and the other languages, as Sesotho does not allow interrogative pronouns to appear preverbally, while the other languages do allow interrogative pronouns to appear preverbally either *in situ* (Chinese) or in the precore slot (Italian). This difference involves whether the restriction on prenuclear focal material holds within the core, as in Italian, or within the clause, as in Sesotho. That is, if the restriction is only within the core, and not the whole clause, then interrogative pronouns can appear in the precore slot, while if the restriction holds for the whole clause, then interrogative pronouns will also not be able to appear there. We will see the importance of this distinction in the discussion of focus structure in complex sentences in chapters 8 and 9.

This discussion raises an interesting typological point. If we compare English and Italian, for example, we see that in English word order is very constrained and focus placement very flexible, whereas in Italian word order is very flexible and focus placement is very constrained. This contrast could be characterized in terms of how syntax and focus structure adapt to each other: in English, the focus structure adapts to the rigidity of the word order by allowing free focus placement (i.e. focus can fall on any constituent within a simple clause), whereas in Italian, the syntax adapts to the rigid focus structure (i.e. non-WH focal elements must be postnuclear) by having constructions which allow focal elements which would normally be prenuclear to occur in a postnuclear position. Hence it seems that one dimension along which languages could be characterized typologically is in terms of how syntax and focus structure interact. English, with its rigid word order, is the 'Dyirbal' of focus structure, allowing focus placement anywhere in a simple clause, whereas Dyirbal, with grammatically unconstrained word order, nevertheless has strong focus construction constraints on word order (see Dixon 1972; also section 7.5.1).

Allowing focus to fall on any constituent in a simple clause is not the only way a language with relatively rigid word order can deal with the demands of information structure. Toura, a Mande language spoken in the Ivory Coast in West Africa (Bearth 1992), has relatively strict SOV order and has a number of means for expressing focus distinctions. The basic predicate-focus form is given in (5.11a), while two different types of focus marking are exemplified in (b)–(c).

(5.11) a. Tìà ké gwɛ́ɛ́ lɔ̂'.
PRDM peanuts buy
'Tia BOUGHT PEANUTS.'

b. Q: Tìà-' mɛɛ lɔ̂' le?
-PRDM what buy TM
'WHAT did Tia buy?'

A: Tìà-' gwɛ́ɛ́-' lɔ̂' le.
-PRDM peanuts-FOC1 buy TM
'Tia bought PEANUTS.'

b′. Q: Waa gwɛ́ɛ́ lɔ̂' le?
who peanuts buy TM
'WHO bought peanuts?'

A: Tìà-' gwɛ́ɛ́ lɔ̂' le.
-FOC1 peanuts buy TM
'TIA bought peanuts.'

c. Tìà ké gwɛ́ɛ́-le lɔ̂'.
PRDM peanuts-FOC2 buy
'Tia bought PEANUTS.'

The focus marker in (b) is a tonal clitic (as is the predicate marker in many of these examples), while in (c) it is the same element that elsewhere is glossed 'TM'. The difference between the two types of focus seems to revolve around the presuppositions involved; the type in (b) is non-contrastive and is used in the answers to questions and introducing new elements into the discourse, while that in (c) seems to have a more contrastive function. In order to focus the verb, a special periphrastic construction is used, as in (5.12).

(5.12) Tìà-' gwɛ́ɛ́ lɔ̂-' wo' le.
-PRDM peanuts buy-FOC1 do TM
'Tia BOUGHT peanuts.'

As in English, there is a precore slot and a left-detached position in Toura; they are illustrated in (5.13).

(5.13) a. Gwɛ́ɛ́-' Tìà-' lɔ̂' le.
peanuts-FOC1 -PRDM buy TM
'PEANUTS Tia bought', or 'It is PEANUTS (not potatoes) that Tia bought.'

b. Gwɛ́ɛ́ (láà), Tìà ké à lɔ̂'.
peanuts (TOP) PRDM 3p buy
'As for peanuts, Tia bought them.'

The two positions differ in Toura just as they do in English and other languages that have them; there is no intonation break between the initial NP and the following material in (a), and there is no pronoun referring to the initial NP, whereas in (b) there is an intonation break between the initial NP and the following material and there is a resumptive pronoun referring to the initial NP. The NP in the precore slot in (a) carries a focus marker, while the NP in the left-detached position in (b) carries a topic marker. Thus, Toura presents an elaborated system of focus marking which employs both special positions (precore slot, left-detached position) as well as focus markers for core-internal elements.

5.4 The formal representation of focus structure

Just as the operator and constituent projections were represented separately in the representation of clause structure in chapter 2, we also represent focus structure as a separate projection. Though graphically separate, the focus structure projection is closely related to the constituent projection because of the influence of focus structure on constituent structure in many languages and because the constituents

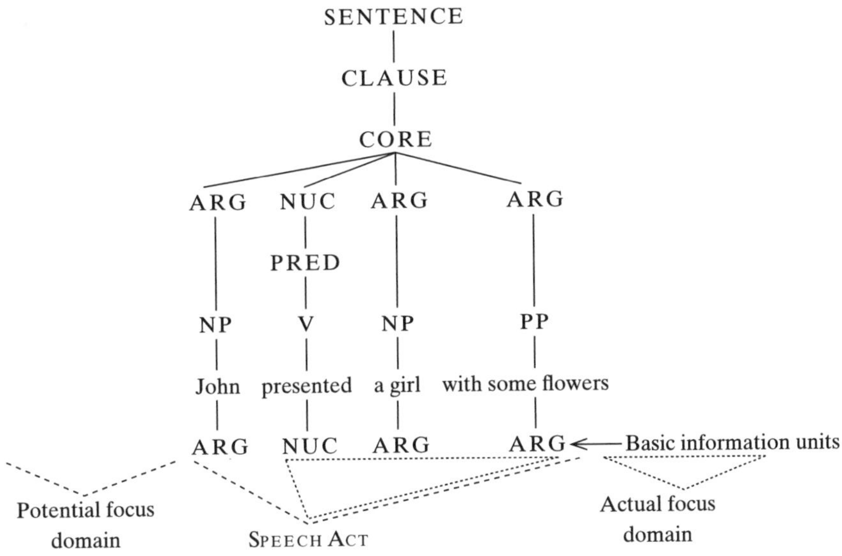

Figure 5.3 Predicate-focus construction

of the constituent projection define the focus domains. The focus structure projection is also closely related to the operator projection in that the potential focus domain must fall within the scope of the illocutionary force operator. The node anchoring the focus structure projection is labeled 'speech act', because the focus structure projection represents the division of the utterance, which is a speech act of some type (declarative, interrogative, etc.), into presupposed (non-focal) and non-presupposed (focal) parts. In these representations, the 'ARG,' 'NUC' and 'ADV' nodes are the basic information units in the focus structure projection (see section 5.1). The potential focus domain and actual focus domain will be represented as in the example of a predicate-focus structure in figure 5.3. Here the potential focus domain is the entire clause, and the actual focus domain is the nucleus plus the postnuclear arguments, with the sentence-initial NP as the topic of the sentence.[10] As discussed above, in English the main linguistic expression of focus is intonation, so we are assuming focus intonation on the phrase *presented a girl with some flowers*, and not on the NP *John*. In a narrow-focus structure we would have the focus accent on *John*, and the actual focus domain limited to that NP, as in figure 5.4 (note also the pronominalization of the postnuclear NPs in the English example). The first example, *John gave them to her*, has marked narrow focus on the subject, while the second example, *Lijo li-pheh-li-o-e ke mang?* 'The food was cooked by who?', is the structure of (5.10b) from Sesotho.[11]

In English the potential focus domain is the entire clause, with the actual focus domain being determined largely by intonation, unless there is an element in the

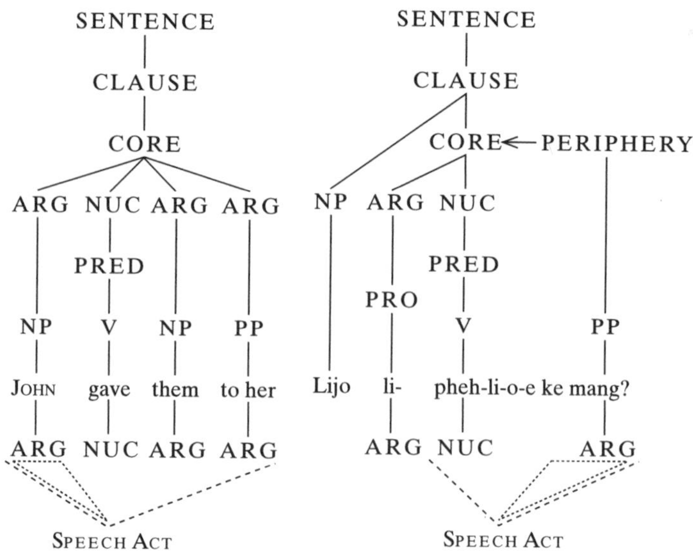

Figure 5.4 Narrow-focus constructions

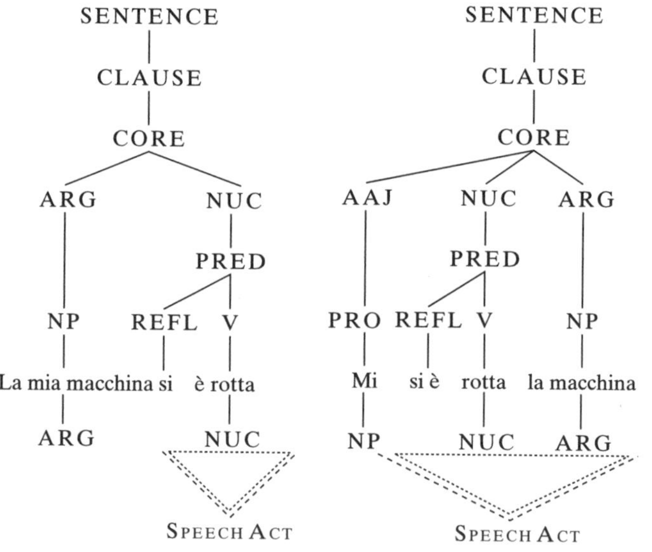

Figure 5.5 Italian predicate-focus and sentence-focus constructions

precore slot. In Sesotho and in Italian sentences that do not contain interrogative pronouns (which appear in the precore slot in Italian) the potential focus domain is always limited to the nuclear and postnuclear elements, as any prenuclear elements will always be interpreted as topical. In figure 5.5 are examples of predicate- and sentence-focus structures in Italian, from (5.1) and (5.3).[12]

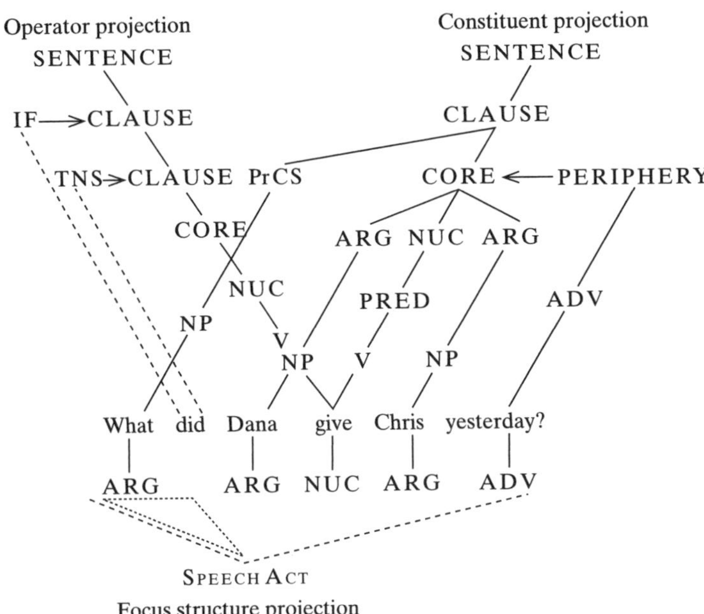

Figure 5.6 Clause structure with constituent, operator and focus structure projections

In the representations given above, only the constituent and focus structure projections are given. It is possible, however, to represent all three projections. This is illustrated in figure 5.6. There is an important difference between the relationship of the operator projection to the constituent projection and the relationship of the focus structure projection to the constituent projection. The operator projection has the same hierarchical structure as the constituent projection, and the operators modify the layers in this hierarchical structure. The focus structure projection, on the other hand, divides the linear string of elements in the constituent projection first into those elements within the potential focus domain and those outside of it and, second, within the potential focus domain, into those elements which are within the actual focus domain and those which are not. In chapter 8 we will investigate the important issue of the extent of the potential focus domain in complex sentences.

In the conception of clause structure developed in chapter 2, the layered structure of the clause, there is nothing corresponding to the traditional grouping of verb and object known as the verb phrase (VP), because cross-linguistic studies of sentence structure have not found this to be a universal feature of human languages (see section 2.1). What, then, is the source of this grouping in languages which manifest it? All languages have predicate-focus structures, which is universally the unmarked focus structure, and if we look at the example of predicate focus given above in figure 5.3, we can see that the actual focus domain includes exactly what would traditionally be considered the VP. Moreover, narrow-focus constructions with subject focus, as in the English example in figure 5.4, also isolate a VP-like grouping. It is reasonable to suppose, then, that the universal basis for the language-specific phrasal category VP is focus structure.

What is the theory-neutral evidence for the existence of a VP in English? The three strongest pieces of evidence come from so-called 'VP-anaphora', 'VP-fronting' and 'VP-deletion', as well as from conjoined clauses in which the subject in the second clause is omitted, as illustrated in (5.14).

(5.14) a. Q: Who gave the files to Dana?
A: Skinner did.
b. I expected to find someone mowing the lawn, and mowing the lawn was Fred.
c. Robin has been reading *War and Peace*, and Sandy has, too.
d. Kim left Buffalo this morning and will arrive in Miami tomorrow.

In the first three of these constructions, the verb phrase functions as a topical element. In (5.14a) it is replaced by the pro-verb *do*. In (b) it is preposed in the inverted construction in which the newly introduced and hence focal subject occurs after the finite auxiliary verb. In (c) it is omitted after the finite auxiliary under identity with the auxiliary plus 'VP' in the previous clause. In (d), on the other hand, there are conjoined predicate-focus constructions in which the topical subject of the second clause has been omitted under identity with the topical subject of the first clause; all that appears in the second clause is the actual focus domain (see figure 5.3). In English, then, the nucleus and non-subject core arguments function as a unit in these constructions. Where English differs from languages like Dyirbal and Lakhota that lack a VP is in its possession of constructions which refer to this grouping created by narrow focus on the subject or by the actual focus domain in a predicate-focus construction. All of the constructions in (5.14) have specific contextual restrictions on their occurrence, and 'VP-fronting' is really only possible in conjoined sentences in which the 'antecedent VP' occurs in the first clause. It is not necessary, however, to posit a VP in the constituent projection of the layered structure of the clause in English, because the relevant grouping is derived from the interaction of the constituent and focus structure projections. That is, there are 'VPs' in the English layered structure representations in figures 5.3 and 5.4 by virtue of the groupings imposed on the constituent structure projection by the focus structure projection. Thus, 'VPs' exist in English as a derivative of these two projections of the layered structure of the clause under specific contextual circumstances, and we assume this to be the case in other languages which exhibit the same 'VP' phenomena.

5.5 Focus structure and the scope of negation and quantification

Focus structure is crucially involved in the interpretation of negation and quantification. It has long been noted, going back to Russell (1905), that only the asserted part of an utterance can be interpreted as being negated, the presupposed part not being negated (see e.g. Jackendoff 1972, Givón 1984b). The part of the sentence that is interpreted as being negated is normally referred to as 'being in the scope of the negation', Thus, given a sentence like *John didn't talk to Mary*, the interpretation of what is being negated will be a function of the focus structure of the sentence (itself a function of the context) as reflected in intonation.

(5.15) a. JOHN didn't talk to Mary [Bill did].
b. John didn't TALK to Mary [he sent her e-mail].
c. John didn't talk to MARY [he talked to Susan].
d. John didn't TALK TO MARY [he had no contact with anyone].

The first three examples involve narrow focus, and in each instance the focus constituent is interpreted as being in the scope of the negation, the remainder of the sentence being presupposed. The final example is of a predicate-focus construction, and here the entire predicate phrase is negated.

In section 5.2 we saw that different languages use different morphological and syntactic means to express the focus structure contrasts that are expressed only prosodically in the above examples, and we therefore predict that the different scopes of negations should also be expressible by the same means, if scope of negation is tied to focus structure. This appears to be the case.

(5.16) a. La mia macchina non si è rotta. Italian
'My car didn't BREAK DOWN.' (*'MY CAR didn't break down.')
b. Non si è rotta la mia macchina.
'MY CAR didn't break down.' (*'My car didn't BREAK DOWN.')

(5.17) a. Chē méi lái. Mandarin
car NEG.PERF come
'The car did not COME.'
b. Méi lái shénme chē.
NEG.PERF come any car
'A CAR did not come', or 'NO CAR came.'

As we saw earlier in (5.3), (5.5) and (5.7), Italian and Mandarin put focal subject NPs after the verb, and therefore when it is the subject which is being negated, it must appear postverbally, as predicted.

Focus structure may also affect the interpretation of quantified NPs in a sentence. Given a sentence like (5.18a), with a universally quantified subject and an existentially quantified object, there are two interpretations for it, which are presented in (b).

(5.18) a. Every girl kissed a boy.
b. (i) Each girl kissed a different boy ('for each girl there is a boy such that the girl kissed the boy', i.e. [$\forall$x, $\exists$y (**kiss′** x, y), where x = girl and y = boy])
(ii) Each girl kissed the same boy ('there is a boy such that for each girl, the girl kissed the boy', i.e. [$\exists$y, $\forall$x (**kiss′** x, y), where x = girl and y = boy])
c. A boy was kissed by every girl. (= (b ii), (b i))

The (b i) reading is the unmarked one, in which the subject universal quantifier has wide scope over the object existential quantifier; the second reading, (b ii), involves giving the object existential quantifier wider scope than the subject universal quantifier. Note that when the sentence is passivized, the second reading becomes the primary reading, with the (b i) reading more difficult to get. Why should this be so? One answer could be that the linear order of the quantified NPs determines their interpretation: the first quantified NP has wider scope than the second. This account runs immediately into two problems. First, it incorrectly predicts that the (b ii) reading should be impossible in (5.18a) and the (b i) reading should be impossible with (5.18c). Second, there are languages with different word orders from English in which this principle would make incorrect predictions. For example, consider the examples from Malagasy (Keenan 1976a) and Tagalog, both VOS languages.

(5.19) a. Na-hita vorona ny mpianatra rehetra. Malagasy
PAST-see bird the student all
'All the students saw some birds.'
b. Ma-runong ng dalawa-ng wika ang lahat ng nandito. Tagalog
PRES-know OBJ two-LNK language SUBJ all LNK at-here
'Everyone here knows two languages.'

Keenan comments, 'subjects generally have wider scope than objects in the paradigm case of indefinite objects and universally quantified subjects. Thus [(5.19a)] is possibly true in a situation in which the students saw different birds' (1976a: 254). The same holds in the Tagalog example; the subject NP *ang lahat ng nandito* 'everyone here' has wider scope than the object NP *dalawa-ng wika* 'two languages'; hence the sentence can be true if it is the case that each person knows two languages which are different from the two languages known by the others. Here the default reading is the one in which the second quantified NP has wider scope than the first NP, the opposite of the situation in English. Ioup (1975) surveys quantifier scope interpretation phenomena in fourteen languages and shows conclusively that linear order is not the decisive factor in determining scope interpretation.

If we look at these examples in terms of focus structure, there is a simple generalization capturing the facts; it is given in (5.20).

(5.20) *Principle constraining the interpretation of quantified NPs*
Topical quantified NPs have scope over focal quantified NPs, i.e. topical Q ⊃ focal Q.

A similar observation is made in Sgall, Hajičová and Panevová (1986: 227). There are a number of other principles affecting the interpretation of quantifier scope, which interact with the general principle given here. These are the principles proposed by Ioup (1975) and Kuno (1991) which will be discussed below. In these examples we have attempted to construct sentences in which these other factors are neutralized, in order to illustrate the operation of the topical Q ⊃ focal Q principle.

Returning to the English, Malagasy and Tagalog examples, we may apply the principle in (5.20) as follows. Since predicate focus is the least-marked focus type, and since in English and Malagasy the subject is the unmarked topic, it follows that the default or favored interpretations in (5.18a) and (5.19) should be the ones where the subject quantified phrases have scope over the object phrases. The difference between English, on the one hand, and Malagasy and Tagalog, on the other, boils down to English having topic–comment as its least-marked focus structure ordering, while Malagasy and Tagalog have comment–topic as theirs. In order to get the (b ii) reading, it is necessary to have marked narrow focus on the subject and the object NP interpreted as the topic. The reason the (b i) reading is so difficult with (5.18c) has to do with the markedness of both the syntactic construction and the focus structure. In order to get that interpretation, it is necessary to combine a marked focus structure with a marked syntactic structure, passive (see chapter 6), in order to produce the same effect as the unmarked syntactic structure (active voice) together with the least-marked focus structure, predicate focus. Given that the default syntactic and focus structures will produce this interpretation, deriving it from a doubly marked combination of constructions is very difficult.

Now, consider the following examples involving quantifier scope from Mandarin, from Huang (1982) and Aoun and Li (1993).

(5.21) a. Měi ge rén dōu xǐhuān yī ge nyǔrén.
every CL person all like one CL woman
'Everyone likes a woman.' (= 'everyone likes a different woman', ≠ 'everyone likes the same woman')

b. Měi ge rén dōu bèi yī ge nyǔrén dǎsǐ-le.
every CL person all by one CL woman beat.die-PRFV
'Everyone was killed by a woman.' (= 'everyone was killed by a different woman', 'everyone was killed by the same woman')

These examples have been discussed extensively because they present a striking contrast to the English examples in (5.18): (5.21a), unlike its English counterpart, is *unambiguous*, while the passive sentence in (5.21b) is *ambiguous*. From a purely syntactic point of view, this is quite puzzling, since both Mandarin and English are SVO languages, with, one would assume, the same basic clause structure, and these interpretations are quite different from the ones found in English. However, given what we said about focus structure in Mandarin in section 5.3, these facts should not be surprising. As we saw in (5.7)–(5.9), Mandarin does not generally have non-WH focal elements in preverbal position; in this respect it is very similar to Italian. Thus preverbal quantifiers must have scope over postverbal quantifiers, since the marked narrow focus on the subject required for the other reading is precluded. Hence the principle in (5.20) correctly predicts the lack of ambiguity of (5.21a). It also correctly predicts the ambiguity of (5.21b). In the passive construction both quantified NPs are preverbal, and accordingly there is no topic–focus asymmetry between them; consequently, either may have scope over the other, as is the case. The explanation for the contrast between Mandarin and English does not lie in differences in syntactic structure alone, but rather in differences in the interaction of focus structure and syntactic structure.

Ioup (1975) argues for two sets of factors affecting the interpretation of quantifier scope in sentences with multiple quantifiers. They are given in table 5.2. Ioup omits *a* + NP_{sg} due to uncertainty as to its exact placement on the hierarchy; she speculates that it would be placed after *each* and *every*. She also omits *some* + NP_{sg}. Ioup argues that the semantic properties of the quantifiers themselves strongly affect their scope interpretation, and she speculates that *each*, being at the top of the hierarchy, would always have wide scope. Her hierarchy interacts with the principle in (5.20) in an interesting way. The quantifiers at the top of the hierarchy involve greater individuation and specificity of the NP; for example, *each boy* refers to every member of the group as an individual, whereas *many boys* or *several boys* refers to them as an aggregate or group as a whole and not to the individual members. The more specific the reference of an NP is, the better it is as a potential topic, and accordingly, the quantifiers at the top of the hierarchy would yield quantified NPs which would make better topics than those at the bottom. Given the principle

Table 5.2 *Factors affecting the interpretation of quantifier scope, from Ioup (1975)*

Quantifier Hierarchy

each > *every* > *all* > *most* > *many* > *several* > *some* (+NP_{pl}) > *a few*

Greatest inherent tendency ... Least inherent tendency toward wide scope

Greatest individuation, specificity ... Least individuation, specificity

Grammatical Function Hierarchy

Topic > Deep and Surface Subject > Deep Subject or Surface Subject > IO > PrepO > DO

Greatest tendency toward wide scope ... Least tendency toward wide scope in (5.20), this predicts that they should tend to have wide scope over NPs containing quantifiers at the bottom of the hierarchy. Thus, the ultimate explanation for the ranking of quantifiers in Ioup's hierarchy may lie in (5.20). She also argues that the grammatical functions of quantified NPs affects their interpretation. Under 'topic' she includes initial topic NPs in English in either the left-detached position or the precore slot, *wa*-marked NPs in Japanese and *ang*-marked NPs in Tagalog (see (5.19b)). Given what we have already discussed regarding subjects and topicality in many languages, either as a strong tendency or even as a correlation, as in the Sotho languages, and also the parallel relationship between object and focus, this hierarchy can also be seen as reflecting the more basic principle in (5.20).

Kuno (1991) also presents a number of factors affecting the interpretation of quantified NPs; he includes Ioup's hierarchy among them. Some of the other factors are listed below, and two of them, 'More discourse-linked Q > Less discourse-linked Q' and 'Topicalized Q > Non-topicalized Q', are clearly related to the principle in (5.20). By 'topicalized' Kuno means that the quantified NP appears in a special position at the beginning of the sentence, such as the left-detached position or the precore slot.

Factors affecting the interpretation of quantifier scope (from Kuno 1991)
Lefthand Q > Righthand Q
Subject Q > Non-subject Q
More discourse-linked Q > Less discourse-linked Q
More human Q > Less human Q
Topicalized Q > Non-topicalized Q

Thus, focus structure is crucially involved in the interpretation of the scope of negation and of quantified NPs. It is not, however, the only factor, as Ioup's and Kuno's contributions show.

5.6 Intrasentential pronominalization

An extremely important problem which all syntactic theories attempt to deal with is 'intrasentential pronominalization', that is, the issue of determining when a pronoun will have a coreferential or non-coreferential interpretation with a lexical NP within the same sentence. The pioneers in the development of information-structure-based explanations for intrasentential pronominalization are Kuno (1972a, b, 1975), Bickerton (1975) and Bolinger (1979). Though they differ in the terminology used and in the details of their analyses, they all essentially worked with the concepts of information structure that we introduced earlier. We will present the important conclusions of their work using Lambrecht's terminology.

Before one can describe the constraints on possible coreference in pronominalization, it is necessary to specify the structural domain in which intrasentential pronominalization is possible. It is not possible within the domain of obligatory reflexivization. The domain of obligatory reflexivization will be discussed in detail in chapter 7 in our analysis of reflexivization, but as a first approximation we will take it to be the core in English; languages differ with respect to what this domain is, e.g. core vs. clause vs. sentence. If the potential antecedent and the anaphoric element are both core arguments within the same core and they are coreferential, then reflexivization is obligatory, as in (5.22b); the exact conditions on reflexivization in English will be formulated in section 7.5.2. If they are not coreferential, then a non-reflexive pronoun must be used, as illustrated in (5.22a).

(5.22) a. Mary$_i$ saw her$_{j/*i}$.
b. Mary$_i$ saw herself$_{i/*j}$.

In (5.22a) the use of a pronoun signals disjoint reference or non-coreference, while the use of the reflexive form in (b) indicates coreference. Levinson (1987, 1991) presents an explanation for this in terms of Grice's (1975) theory of conversational cooperation. Within the domain of obligatory reflexivization, intrasentential pronominalization is impossible if the antecedent and anaphoric element are both core arguments, because the use of a pronoun in that environment automatically signals non-coreference with the potential antecedent.

Intrasentential pronominalization is only possible outside the domain of obligatory reflexivization, i.e. either when the lexical NP or the pronoun is not a core argument, e.g. a possessor, when both are non-core arguments, or when the lexical NP and the pronoun are in different cores within a single clause. This is illustrated in (5.23).

(5.23) a. Mary's$_i$ mother loves her$_{i/j}$.
b. Bill$_i$ asked Susan to help him$_{i/j}$.

The main principle that Bolinger, Bickerton and Kuno propose to explain when intrasentential coreference is possible between two elements not in the domain of obligatory reflexivization may be formulated as in (5.24).[13]

(5.24) *Principle governing intrasentential pronominalization (preliminary formulation)*
Coreference is possible between a lexical NP and a pronoun within the same sentence if and only if the lexical NP is outside of the actual focus domain.

In the prototypical cases, as in (5.23), intrasentential pronominalization goes **topic → focus** (assuming predicate focus in both sentences); in other words, the antecedent is outside of the actual focus domain and the pronoun is within it. This is the *opposite* of the situation in intersentential pronominalization, as illustrated in (5.25).

(5.25) In a house on a narrow lane lived an old woman$_i$. She$_i$ had two cats . . .

The focal NP in the first sentence serves as the antecedent for the topical pronoun in the second. We discuss intersentential pronominalization in the next section.

An important feature of the principle of intrasentential pronominalization is that it makes no direct reference to linear order. The irrelevance of linear order in some cases is illustrated by the following examples from Bickerton (1975: 26). In these examples, small capitals mark focal stress, and italics marks an item outside of the actual focus domain; the * indicates ungrammaticality with regard to the specified interpretation of coreference. All of the sentences are grammatical if non-coreference is assumed.

(5.26) a. My punching *Bill*$_i$ annoyed HIM$_i$.
b. *My punching *him*$_i$ annoyed BILL$_i$.
c. What annoyed *Bill*$_i$ was my punching HIM$_i$.
d. *What annoyed *him*$_i$ was my punching BILL$_i$.
e. *It was my punching BILL$_i$ that annoyed *him*$_i$.
f. It was my PUNCHING *Bill*$_i$ that annoyed *him*$_i$.
g. It was my punching HIM$_i$ that annoyed *Bill*$_i$.
h. It was my PUNCHING *him*$_i$ that annoyed *Bill*$_i$.

In each of the sentences which permit a coreferential interpretation, the lexical NP is outside of the actual focus domain, while the pronoun is either focal (5.26a, c, g) or also outside of it as well (5.26f, h). In (5.26b), (5.26d) and (5.26e), the lexical NP is focal, and the only interpretation possible is one of non-coreference. This principle is not the whole story, though, as there are some problematic cases where the pronoun precedes the lexical NP antecedent, as in (5.27).

(5.27) a. *HE$_i$ asked Susan to help *Bill*$_i$.
b. Her$_{i/j}$ mother loves Mary$_i$.

While (5.27a) satisfies the principle that the lexical NP must be outside of the actual focus domain for a coreference interpretation to be possible, it allows only a non-coreference interpretation. Note that the lexical NP (one of the least-marked focus forms for a referring expression – see figure 5.2) is in the unmarked focus position, and the pronoun (one of the least-marked topic forms for a referring expression) is in the unmarked topic position. This is, then, a maximally unmarked structure for the disjoint reference interpretation and conversely a highly marked structure for the coreference reading between the NP and the pronoun. The only vehicle for overriding these defaults is intonation, and its contribution to the interpretation is not strong enough to overcome the extreme markedness of the intended interpretation. In the case of (5.27b), there is again an unmarked topic form (a pronoun) in the unmarked position for a topic, and at the same time there is an unmarked focal form (a lexical noun) in the unmarked focus position. The actual interpretation depends upon the focus structure. If *Mary* is focal, then coreference is impossible. Coreference is only possible when there is narrow focus on *her mother* or on *loves*. Many speakers find the coreferential reading very difficult to get, and this is not surprising. As discussed earlier (figure 5.2), the different codings of referents are understood by the hearer as correlating with different degrees to which the speaker is guaranteeing the accessibility of the referent. The use of a lexical noun in focus position following a pronoun in topic position in the same clause implicates that the referent of the lexical noun is different from that of the pronoun. In both of these examples, focus structure, as expressed through intonation, is trying to block this default interpretation. The fact that intonation alone can make a coreference interpretation possible or block it with respect to the same syntactic structure, as in (5.26), and (5.27b), shows that the constraints on coreference are not purely syntactic in nature.

There are times, however, when a pronoun can precede a lexical NP and the coreference interpretation is still possible, as in (5.26g, h), and in the following examples ((b) and (c) are attested utterances from Carden 1982):

(5.28) a. Because he_i arrived late at the party, $Paul_i$ missed seeing Anna.
b. After his_i recent election as Republican national chairman, Bill $Brock_i$ said . . .
c. When she_i was five years old, a child of my $acquaintance_i$ announced a theory that she was inhabited by rabbits.

These examples are cases of what has been called 'backward pronominalization', as the pronoun precedes the first mention of the lexical NP in the discourse.

Is there any pattern here? In order to see what is going on, we first need to distinguish sentences in which the pronoun is in a syntactic argument position, as in (5.26g, h), (5.27a), and (5.28a, c), from those in which the pronoun is not in a syntactic argument position, as in (5.27b) and (5.28b). When the pronoun is in a syntactic argument position, backward pronominalization is possible *only* across a clause boundary; pronouns which are in non-argument positions are not subject to this restriction. This provides an additional reason why coreference in (5.27a) is impossible; it is a core juncture, i.e. a single clause made up of more than one core (see chapter 8), and accordingly there is only a single clause. Therefore the 'backward pronominalization is possible only across a clause boundary' condition is not met. In (5.26g, h), which are cleft constructions containing relative clauses, and in (5.28a, c), which contain a preposed adverbial clause, the backward pronominalization operates across a clause boundary. Sentences with backward pronominalization involving non-argument pronouns may or may not involve a clause boundary, but those with a clause boundary are much easier to interpret, as one would expect. Unlike in (5.27b), which involves clause-internal backward pronominalization, in (5.28b) the pronoun is in a PP in the left-detached position, which is outside the clause, and coreference is the preferred interpretation. We must therefore revise (5.24) as follows.

(5.29) *Principle governing intrasentential pronominalization (revised)*
Coreference is possible between a lexical NP and a pronoun within the same sentence if and only if
a. the lexical NP is outside of the actual focus domain, and
b. if the pronoun is in a syntactic argument position and precedes the lexical NP, there is a clause boundary between the pronoun and the lexical NP.

The reason for the clause boundary requirement in (5.29) is as follows. In a simple clause, the only way there could be a pronoun in an argument position followed by a lexical NP is either for the lexical NP to also occur in an argument position, in which the two are in the domain of obligatory reflexivization which precludes pronominalization, or for the lexical NP to occur as a possessor or other non-argument at the end of the clause, which is the normal position for focal elements. We have already seen how difficult it is to interpret a lexical NP as topical and a pronoun as focal when each occupies the default position for the opposite function (see (5.27)). It is easiest to interpret a lexical NP as topical in a clause when it is subject, but if this is the case, then it follows that the pronoun in an argument position cannot be in the same clause; it must be either in the left-detached position, as in (5.28b), or in a preposed adverbial clause, as in (5.28a, c). These are the only two structural possibilities available within the same sentence. Both of the conditions in (5.29) must be met for backward pronominalization to be possible, as (5.30) shows.

(5.30) a. *In his$_i$ house, Jane gave a plaque to Sam$_i$.
b. ?In his$_i$ house, Jane gave Sam$_i$ a plaque.

This sentence meets the clause boundary condition in (5.29b), but because the lexical NP is in the unmarked focus position, it is extremely difficult to interpret it as non-focal, which leads to a violation of the condition in (5.29a). Note that (b) seems to be much better than (a), and in it the lexical NP is not in the unmarked focus position but is in a position which is easier to interpret as more topical (Givón 1984a); hence the coreference reading is easier to get than in (a).

The following examples (from Kuno 1987, originally attributed to George Lakoff) appear to be a problem for this account.

(5.31) a. John$_i$ saw a snake near him$_i$.
b. Near him$_i$ John$_i$ saw a snake.
c. *He$_i$ saw a snake near John$_i$.
d. *Near John$_i$ he$_i$ saw a snake.

There are two striking things about these examples: the possibility of backward pronominalization in (5.31b) and the impossibility of 'regular' pronominalization in (d). Moreover, the examples in (5.32), also from Kuno (1987), which exhibit an at least superficially similar syntactic pattern, show a different pattern of possible coreference; in particular, in (5.32d) coreference is possible, whereas in (5.31d) it is not.

(5.32) a. John$_i$ saw a snake near the girl he$_i$ was talking with.
b. Near the girl he$_i$ was talking with, John$_i$ saw a snake.
c. *He$_i$ saw a snake near the girl John$_i$ was talking with.
d. Near the girl John$_i$ was talking with, he$_i$ saw a snake.

The first thing to be noted is that the NP or pronoun in the *near* PP is not an argument of *see*; these are argument-adjunct PPs (see section 4.4.1.1). Hence the presence or absence of a clause boundary is not relevant to solving this problem.

Our answer to this question begins with the recognition that the structures of (5.31d) and (5.32d) are not as parallel as they may seem, as the preposed elements in the two examples are actually quite different in nature. As we saw in chapter 2, there are in fact two different functionally distinct positions for preposed constituents in English. The two concepts introduced there are the left-detached position and the precore slot. The following are some examples with the two positions marked.

(5.33) a. What did John buy at the store?
PrCS
b. As for Sam, Jane met him at the airport.
LDP
c. At the airport, who did Jane meet?
LDP PrCS
d. Sam I've known for years.
PrCS

When an element appears in the precore slot, there is a corresponding gap in the following clause, as in (5.33d), unless it is an adjunct. In contrast, there is a corresponding (resumptive) pronoun in the following clause if the element in the left-detached position corresponds to a semantic argument of the verb. The default interpretation of elements in the precore slot is focal (obligatorily if they are WH-elements), while elements in the left-detached position are always topical; they are outside of the actual focus domain by definition, since they are outside of the clause and therewith outside of the potential focus domain. Between the precore slot and the following core there is no intonational break (pause), while there is generally such an intonational break between the left-detached position and the following clause.

What is important for our purposes here is that the two positions differ in terms of their coreference properties. Consider the following examples:

(5.34) a. In Sam$_i$'s hometown, he$_i$ is a big hero. LDP
a′. In his$_i$ hometown, Sam$_i$ is a big hero. LDP
b. *In Sam$_i$'s front hallway he$_i$ put a big vase. PrCS
b′. In his$_i$ front hallway Sam$_i$ put a big vase. PrCS
c. With Sam$_i$'s new job, he$_i$'ll make a lot of money. LDP
c′. *With Sam$_i$'s new boss he$_i$ has played golf many times. PrCS

ject NP in the following clause, whereas an NP in the precore slot will obligatorily be interpreted as non-coreferential with the subject NP in the following core. This is because an NP in the left-detached position must be outside the actual focus domain, whereas an NP in the precore slot in these constructions is focal. These NPs are focal because they occur in argument or argument-adjunct PPs which often introduce new and unpredictable information into the core; if they appeared in their usual position, they would be in the unmarked focus position in the core. This, combined with the default interpretation of precore slot elements as focal, strongly favors a focal interpretation. There is one additional factor, to be discussed below, which further reinforces the focal interpretation of these PPs. Setting (peripheral) adjunct PPs, by contrast, are normally presupposed, and when they are not, they represent marked narrow focus (see (5.6)).

The principle of coreference in (5.29) states that a lexical NP must be outside of the actual focus domain for there to be coreference. Therefore the non-coreference reading of (5.34b, c′) is due to the fact that the lexical NP is focal and thus within the actual focus domain, violating the principle of coreference. Looking again at the examples in (5.31b, d) and (5.32b, d), we see that the crucial difference is whether the preposed PP is in the precore slot or in the left-detached position. The preposed PPs in (5.31b, d) are in the precore slot, whereas those in (5.32b, d) are in the left-detached position. In (5.31b), *Near him John saw a snake*, coreference is possible because the lexical NP *John* is outside of the actual focus domain, thereby satisfying the coreference principle. In (5.31d), *Near John he saw a snake*, the potential lexical NP antecedent *John* in the PP is focal, and thus within the actual focus domain, thereby violating the coreference principle and making coreference impossible. In (5.32b, d), in contrast, the preposed PP is in the left-detached position and therefore is outside of the actual focus domain, as is the subject of the following clause. Hence the lexical NP antecedent *John* in (5.32b) is outside the actual focus domain, and the pronoun is in a syntactic argument position in the relative clause; therefore backward pronominalization is possible, just as in (5.28), because it meets the conditions in (5.29). In (5.32d) both the lexical NP and the pronoun are outside of the actual focus domain, which likewise satisfies (5.29).

What is the syntactic evidence that the preposed PP is in the precore slot in (5.31b, d) but in the left-detached position in (5.32b, d)? An important difference between the left-detached position and the precore slot in English involves the location of the respective positions inside or outside the clause and the behavioral properties that follow from these locations. The left-detached position is outside the clause and therefore does not interfere with the ability of either a yes–no question or a WH-question to appear in the following clause. A non-WH-NP in the precore slot, on the other hand, blocks the formation of questions, both WH and yes–no. This is because non-WH NPs appear in the precore slot only in assertions, never in in the precore slot and questions of any kind. Compare the following examples:

(5.35) a. In Sam's house, what did Jane do? LDP
b. *In Sam's house what did Jane put? PrCS
c. In Sam's house, did Jane have a good time? LDP
d. *In Sam's house did Jane put her stuff? PrCS

Given these contrasts, we predict that the structures in (5.32b, d) would readily cooccur with WH- and yes–no questions, whereas those in (5.31b, d) would not.

(5.36) a. Near the girl John was talking to, what did he see?
b. Near the girl John was talking to, did he see a snake?
c. (*)Near him what did John see?
d. (*)Near him did John see a snake?

The examples in (5.36a, b) are perfectly fine, as predicted. The ones in (5.36c, d) are more interesting. With no intonational break between *near him* and the rest of the clause, they are unacceptable. If, on the other hand, an intonational break is inserted after *near him*, analogous to the first two sentences, then they become readily acceptable, again as predicted.[14]

There is a second factor distinguishing the two types of phrase, namely, information content. Reinhart (1983) noted that when additional material is added to preposed phrases, their coreference properties change, just as we have seen. Why should this be so? The reason for this is that the more informational content there is in the initial phrase, the more difficult it is to interpret it as a focus. Focus expressions tend strongly to be very succinct, following the much noted tendency of speakers to introduce information into the discourse in small quantities (Chafe 1987, DuBois 1987, Lambrecht 1987). This is particularly true of clause-initial foci and is shown by the compactness of WH-expressions and the strangeness of complex, informationally rich WH-expressions like *Which guy that Mary talked to yesterday after the party about a new apartment did you see?* Left-detached phrases, on the other hand, are often quite complex, especially when they provide setting information; indeed preposed adverbial clauses like those in (5.28a, c) should be analyzed as being in the left-detached position. Comparing *near John/him* with *near the girl John was talking to*, we see that the latter is informationally much richer as it includes a restrictive relative clause containing presupposed information. Hence it is very difficult, if not impossible, to interpret it as a focal expression. It is, rather, more naturally interpreted as topical, and the pause following it indicates that it is in the left-detached position rather than the precore slot, which is not set off by a pause. Thus it appears that informationally rich expressions are interpreted as topical rather than as focal, and this is another factor reinforcing the focus interpretation of the initial PPs in (5.31).

Thus syntactic structure and focus structure interact to constrain the possible interpretation of coreference in sentence-internal pronominalization.

5.7 Intersentential pronominalization

Most communication does not take place using single sentences, but the principle that the form of the representation of a referent is associated with a certain degree of cognitive accessibility (as summarized in figure 5.2) still holds in longer segments of speech, and this principle is used in determining intersentential coreference (discourse anaphora) as well. As discussed above, a number of factors are involved in the determination of the form of the representation of a referent in a sentence. The major difference between intrasentential and intersentential pronominalization is that in texts there is often a greater distance between the first mention of a referent and its subsequent mention, and this distance can affect the form of the subsequent mention. The distance (in terms of clauses) between a referring element and the previous mention (including zero anaphors) of its referent is labeled **referential distance** in Givón (1983). Put simply, the more clauses that intervene between the mentions of a referent, the lower down the scale of accessibility the referent will be, and so the more explicit the later representation of the referent must be. Thus, a zero anaphor will normally have a very short referential distance, whereas overt elements, for example a full pronoun or a definite lexical NP, will have greater referential distances. But other factors are involved as well; one of these is thematic continuity.

For a chain of clauses to be considered a single cohesive text, there must be some common elements that run throughout the text. It may be that the text is about the actions of a particular referent, or it may be the clauses are all about a particular theme, a particular place or about a particular time. It is in fact the sameness of the referent(s), the location, the time or the action (or series of connected actions) that gives text its coherence. Here we are concerned with continuity of referents. If there is a particular referent or location that is salient throughout the text, then very often that referent will be the topic (in the sense we defined earlier) of every clause in the text. A sequence of clauses with a single topic is known as a topic chain. In languages that use zero anaphora regularly, the topic being spoken about will often be only mentioned once, with the rest of the clauses consisting of only the focus of the assertion. See, for example, the following passage from Mandarin Chinese (adapted from Chen 1984: 8); the zero anaphors will be represented as '*pro*'.

(5.37) a. Lǎo Qián$_i$ yǒu zhème ge píqì,
Old Qian have such CL disposition
'Old Qian has (just) such a disposition:

b. *pro*$_i$ wèn péngyǒu$_j$ yào shénme dōngxi$_k$,
ask friend want what/something thing
if (he) asks for something from (his) friend(s)

c. *pro*$_j$ lìkè jiù děi gěi *pro*$_i$ *pro*$_k$,
at-once then must give
(he/she/they) must give (it) (to him) at once;

d. *pro*$_j$ bù gěi *pro*$_i$ *pro*$_k$,
not give
if (he/she/they) don't give (it) (to him),

e. *pro*$_i$ jiù juéde *pro*$_j$ shì qiáo-bù-qǐ tā$_i$,
then feel COP look-down-on 3sg
(he) feels that (he/she/they) don't think much of him,

f. *pro*$_i$ jǐ tiān bù gāoxìng.
several day not pleased
(and) (he) would be displeased for a few days.'

Here we have a topic (Lao Qian) and a theme (Lao Qian's disposition) introduced in the first clause. As the theme is the same for the rest of the clauses, and the main topic of the entire thematic paragraph remains the same, there is no need to use anything other than a zero anaphor to refer to Lao Qian in most of the rest of the passage, even when a secondary topic (friend) appears in clause (b) and is the main topic of clause (c) and (d).

The fact that both the main and secondary topics can take the form of a zero anaphor in this passage is related to a second factor that affects referent identification, and that is the semantics of the predicate or other constituents. In clauses (c) and (d) the semantics of the predicates are incompatible with the assignment of Lao Qian as the main topic (as the text is about giving to Lao Qian, not Lao Qian giving to someone else), so the zero anaphor must refer to the only other possible agent, the friend mentioned in clause (b).

A third factor affecting the representation of a particular referent is the appearance or not of other semantically compatible referents in the intervening clauses. For example, Chafe (1976) mentions a novel where a letter is mentioned on page 13, and then not mentioned again until page 118, 105 pages later, yet on page 118 it is simply referred to as 'the letter'. This is only possible because no other letters were mentioned in the intervening 105 pages. The opposite situation would be, for example, the text in (5.38):

(5.38) Bob went to the store and Bill went to the movies. He will be back late.

Because of the existence of two possible antecedents for the pronoun, the pronoun could not be used successfully here, and so a form implying less accessibility or identifiability (the name *Bob* or *Bill*) must be used.

The distance between mentions of a referent is not always a straightforward measure of the number of clauses intervening, as the hierarchical structure of the discourse can also be involved in determining the accessibility of the referent. Consider the following example, again from Mandarin Chinese (Chang 1988: 2–3):

(5.39) a. Dīng lǎoshī$_i$ dài wǒmen$_j$ qù jiāoyóu,
Ding teacher lead 1pl go picnic
'Teacher Ding took us on a picnic,

b. *pro*$_{i+j}$ zǒu guò yī shān yòu yī shān,
go ASP one mountain also one mountain
(we – including Ding) passed mountain after mountain,

c. *pro*$_{i+j}$ kàn dào xǔdūo yěhuā.
see ASP many wildflowers
(and) saw many wildflowers.

d. Huā$_l$ wǒ$_k$ zuì xǐhuān [zǐsè de *pro*$_l$]$_m$,
flowers I most like purple NMZ
Flowers, I like purple ones best,

e. dàochù dōu shì *pro*$_m$,
everywhere all COP
(they) were everywhere.

f. *pro*$_k$ kàn *pro*$_m$ de *pro*$_k$ gāoxìng jíle.
see CD happy very
Seeing (them) made (me) very happy.

g. Tiān kuài hēi *pro*$_{i+j}$ cái húi jiā.
sky soon black then return home
It was almost dark when (we) returned home.'

In this example the entire first clause sets up the main theme for the rest of the passage, and contains the antecedents that control the zero anaphors in the second, third and last clauses. These four clauses are a narrative of an event, and form a topic chain. Clauses (d), (e) and (f) form a short evaluative (non-narrative, non-sequential) thematic paragraph themselves set in the middle of the main thematic paragraph. This subthematic paragraph is a backgrounded diversion from the main storyline. This structure can be diagrammed as follows (adapted from Cheng 1988: 5):

(5.40) *Thematic paragraph*
Clause 1 Teacher Ding took us on a picnic.
Clause 2 (We – including Ding) passed mountain after mountain.
Clause 3 (We) saw many wildflowers.
Subtheme {
Clause 1: Flowers, I like purple ones best.
Clause 2: (They) were everywhere.
Clause 3: Seeing (them) made (me) very happy.
}
Clause 4 It was almost dark when (we) returned home.

Even though several clauses (and another potential referent) intervene between clause 3 and clause 4 of the main topic chain, it is easy to recognize these intervening clauses as a backgrounded diversion from the main storyline, so they do not interfere with the continuity of the main thematic paragraph (topic chain). For this reason the topic in the last clause can still be represented by a zero anaphor

In chapter 6 we will discuss some of the grammatical means languages use to track referents in discourse.

5.8 Syntactic templates, linking and focus structure

At the end of chapter 2 we introduced the idea of syntactic templates for representing clause structure patterns, which are stored in what we called a 'syntactic inventory'. Some syntactic patterns cooccur with specific focus structure patterns, e.g. narrow focus on the WH-word in the precore slot in a WH-question in English and many other languages, and this correlation would be represented in the template for WH-questions in the syntactic inventory. Another example of a fixed correlation between focus structure and syntax is the 'inverted subject construction' used in presentational constructions, e.g. *Into the room ran a cat* or *Down the street lived an old man.* These patterns would be stored as in figure 5.7. Many templates are not associated with a specific focus structure construction, and their entry in the syntactic lexicon could not contain any focus structure information. Thus, forming the constituent and focus structure projections for a WH-question in English would involve the combination depicted in figure 5.8, which is a revision of figure 2.35.

Figure 5.8 has the lexical items in the sentence coming from the lexicon, but that is a serious oversimplification. It was pointed out in section 5.1 (see figure 5.2) that the form that an argument takes is a function of a number of factors, including its activation status (see figure 5.1). Thus the choice of referring expression involves the interaction of the lexicon and the speaker's model of the ongoing discourse, and this will affect whether the speaker chooses, for example, *he* vs. *Bill* vs. *the man* vs. *a man* vs. *this guy* vs. *someone* to fill a variable slot in a logical structure and to appear in the resulting sentence. We may, therefore, revise the basic linking example presented in chapter 4 (figure 4.10) to reflect this interaction between the lexicon and discourse pragmatics, as in figure 5.9. We will discuss the interaction of focus structure and linking in considerable detail in chapters 7 and 9. Figure 5.9 reflects only one aspect of the interaction, and we will see in the next chapter that these notions are also important for understanding the nature of grammatical relations cross-linguistically.

Further reading

For the general approach to cognition and communication that underlies the discussion of communication in the introduction to this chapter, see Sperber and Wilson (1986). Other like-minded approaches to information structure include those of the Prague School (see the relevant papers in Luelsdorf 1994, and also Firbas 1992 and Sgall, Hajičová and Panevová 1986), Chafe (1987, 1994), Prince (1981a, b) and Gundel (1976), Gundel, Hedberg and Zacharski (1993). See Fretheim and Gundel (1996) for discussion of referent accessibility and coding. For different taxonomies of focus, see Dik (1989) and Bearth (1992). For formal semantic work on focus, see

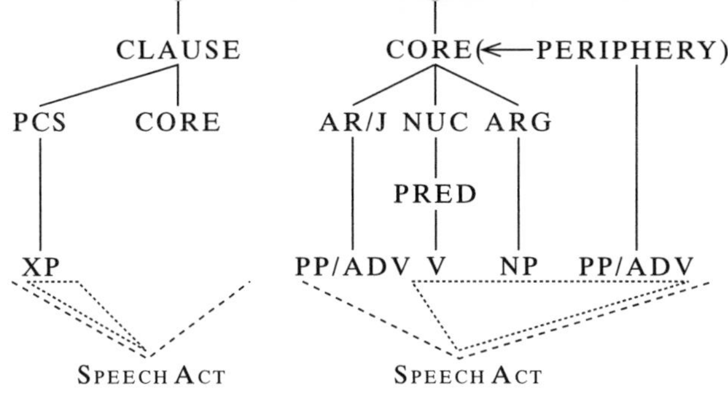

Figure 5.7 Syntactic templates for English WH-question and presentational constructions

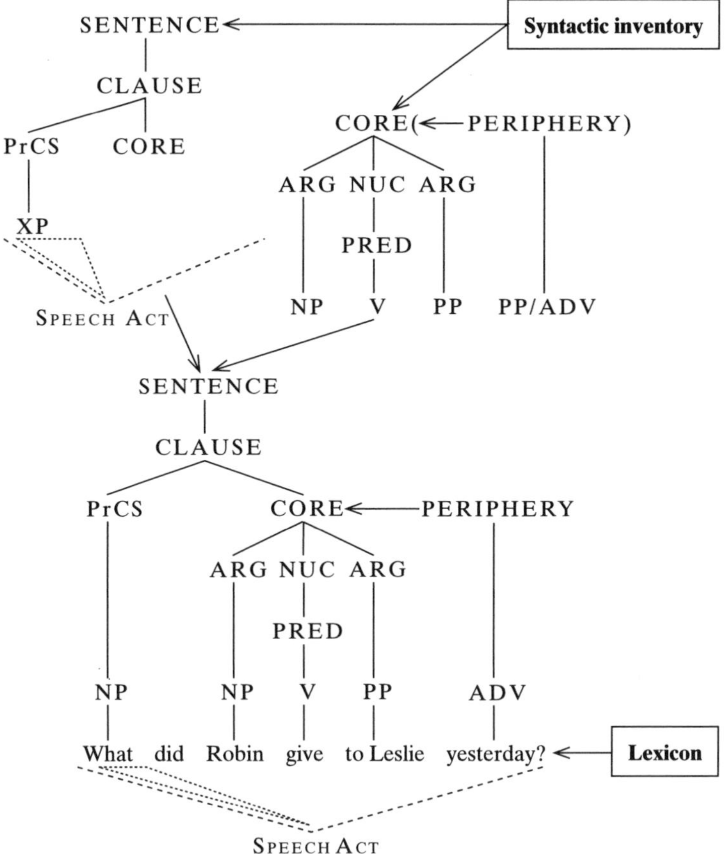

Figure 5.8 Combining templates (revised)

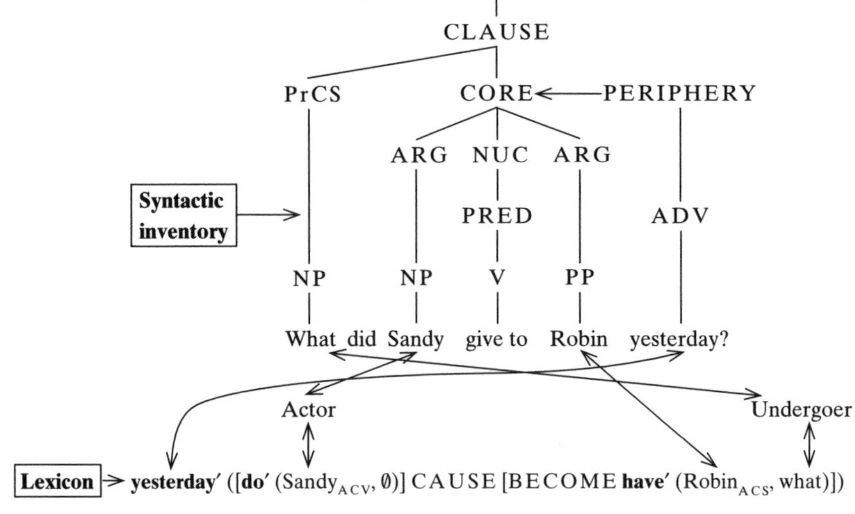

Figure 5.9 Linking from semantics to syntax in a simple English sentence

Rooth (1985), Partee (1991) and Krifka (1992). For rather different approaches to information structure, see Rochemont (1986), Rochemont and Culicover (1990) and É. Kiss (1994). For syntactic approaches to the analysis of quantifier scope, see May (1985), Clark (1985) and Aoun and Li (1993). See Ward (1990) for an analysis of the discourse function of VP-preposing in English. For a discussion of sentence-focus constructions in a number of languages, see Sasse (1987), Lambrecht (1989), Matras and Sasse (1995). For other pragmatically based accounts of pronominalization, see Levinson (1987, 1991), Huang (1994). For a CogG analysis of pronominalization, see van Hoek (1995), also Ariel (1990, 1995). For discussion of pronominalization in discourse, see Fox (1987); for syntactic approaches to pronominalization, see Chomsky (1981b, 1986a), Aoun (1985), Dalrymple (1993). For a hybrid approach to pronominalization, see Reinhart (1983). On text structure and cohesion, see Mann and Thompson (1992) and Halliday and Hasan (1976). For a discourse grammar of Biblical Hebrew using FG and RRG, see Winther-Nielsen (1995).

Exercises

1 Hungarian is often described as a 'free-word-order' language because of examples like (1), from É. Kiss (1987). Assuming these permutations are all core-internal, what can one conclude about how focus structure and syntax interact in Hungarian, based on (2)–(5)? In particular, is there a special focus position in the clause? How do focus structure constraints on syntax explain the ungrammatical examples in (3)–(5)? Keep in mind that the Hungarian examples are simple clauses, unlike the English translations in (2). **[section 5.3]**

(1) a. János tette a könyvet az asztalra. 'John put the book on the table.'
John put the book.ACC the table.on
b. János a könyvet tette az asztalra.
c. A könyvet János tette az asztalra.
d. Az asztalra János a könyvet tette.

(2) a. János a könyvet tette az asztalra. = (1b)
'As for John, it was the book that he put on the table.'
b. A könyvet János tette az asztalra. = (1c)
'As for the book, it was John who put it on the table'

(3) a. János mit tett az asztalra? 'What did John put on the table?'
b. Mit tett János az asztalra?
c. *Mit János tett az asztalra?
d. *János tett mit az asztalra?

(4) a. János nem a könyvet tette az asztalra. 'John did not put the book on the table.'
b. Nem a könyvet tette János az asztalra.
c. *János tette nem a könyvet az asztalra.
d. *János nem a könyvet az asztalra tette.

(5) a. János minden könyvet az asztalra tett. 'John put every book on the table.'
b. Minden könyvet János tett az asztalra.
c. *János minden könyvet tett az asztalra.
d. *Minden könyvet tett János az asztalra.

2 Consider the following data from Turkish (Erguvanlı 1984). How does focus structure interact with Turkish clause structure? In particular, is there any evidence for special topic and/or focus positions? (Some of the starred questions are acceptable if interpreted as an echo, rhetorical or exam question; however, they are not acceptable as a simple WH-question.) In the question–answer pairs in (3), '#' indicates that an answer is not appropriate for the question. [**section 5.3**]

(1) a. Murat kitap okuyor. 'Murat is reading a book.'
b. *Kitap Murat okuyor.
c. Murat kitabı okuyor. 'Murat is reading the book.'
d. Kitabı Murat okuyor.
e. Murat aceleyle kitab okuyor. 'Murat is hurriedly reading a book.'
f. *Murat kitab aceleyle okuyor.
g. Murat kitabı aceleyle okuyor. 'Murat is hurriedly reading the book.'
h. Murat aceleyle kitabı okuyor

Information structure

(2) a. Murat parayı (bankadan) çaldı. 'Murat stole the money (from the bank).'
b. Parayı (bankadan) kim çaldı? 'Who stole the money (from the bank)?'
b′. *Kim (bankadan) parayı çaldı?
b″. *Bankadan kim parayı çaldı? 'Who stole the money from the bank?'
c. Murat (bankadan) para çaldı. 'Murat stole (some) money (from the bank).'
c′. *Murat para bankadan çaldı.
d. (Bankadan) kim para çaldı? 'Who stole (some) money (from the bank)?'
d′. *(Bankadan) para kim çaldı?
d″. *Kim bankadan para çaldı?
e. Murat nereye gitti? 'Where did Murat go?'
e′. *Nereye Murat gitti?

(3) a. Q: Baba-n-a şarab-ı yeni bardak-la ver-di-n mi?
father-2sgGEN-DAT wine-ACC new glass-INST give-PAST-2sg Q
'Did you give the wine to your father in the new glass?
A: Hayır, eski bardak-la ver-di-m.
no old glass-INST give-PAST-1sg
'No, I gave (it to him) in the old glass.'
A′: #Hayır, amcana verdim.
'No, I gave (it) to my uncle.'
b. Q: şarabı yeni bardakla amcana verdin mi?
'Did you give the wine to your uncle in the new glass?'
A: #Hayır, eski bardakla verdim.
'No, I gave (it to him) in the old glass.'
A′: Hayır, babana verdim.
'No, I gave (it) to my father.'

(4) a. Ben makarna-yı hiç sev-mi-yor-um.
1sgNOM spaghetti-ACC at.all like-NEG-PROG-1sg
'I don't like spaghetti at all.'
a′. Makarnayı ben hiç sevmiyorum.
'I don't like spaghetti at all.'
b. Makarnayı ise ben hiç sevmiyorum.
'As for spaghetti, I don't like [it] at all.'
b′. *Ben makarnayı ise hiç sevmiyorum.
'I, as for spaghetti, don't like [it] at all.'
c. Murat ise parayı bir bankadan çaldı.
'As for Murat, [he] stole the money from a bank.'
c′. *Parayı Murat ise bir bankadan çaldı.
'The money, as for Murat, [he] stole from a bank.'

'As for the money, Murat stole [it] from a bank.'

d′. *Murat parayı ise bir bankadan çaldı.
'Murat, as for the money, stole [it] from a bank.'

3 Consider the following data from Toba Batak, an Austronesian language spoken in Indonesia (Schachter 1984a). How does focus structure interact with Toba Batak clause structure? In particular, is there any evidence for special topic and/or focus positions? [**section 5.3**]

(1) a. Manjaha buku guru i. 'The teacher read a book.'
a′. Manjaha buku guru. 'A (certain) teacher read a book.'
a″. ??Manjaha buku i guru i. 'The teacher read the book.'
a‴. ?*Manjaha buku i guru. 'A (certain) teacher read the book.'
b. Dijaha guru buku i. 'A teacher read the book.'
b′. Dijaha guru buku. 'A teacher read a (certain) book.'
b″. ??Dijaha guru i buku i. 'The teacher read the book.'
b‴. ?*Dijaha guru i buku. 'The teacher read a (certain) book.'

(2) a. Manjaha buku ise? 'Who read a book?'
b. Ise manjaha buku? 'Who read a book?'
c. Manjaha aha guru i? 'What did the teacher read?'
d. *Aha manjaha guru i?

(3) a. Dijaha guru aha? 'What did a teacher read?'
b. Aha dijaha guru? 'What did a teacher read?'
c. Dijaha ise buku i? 'Who read the book?'
d. *Ise dijaha buku i?

(4) a. Mangida imana do nasida? 'Do they see him?'
b. Olo, mangida imana do. 'Yes, [they] see him.'
c. *Olo, mangida nasida. 'Yes, they see [him].'

(5) a. Diida nasida do imana? 'Did they see him?'
b. Olo, diida nasida do. 'Yes, they saw [him].'
c. *Olo, diida imana. 'Yes, [they] saw him.'

4 Draw the constituent and focus structure projections for the following sentences: (2a) in exercise 1, (3a[Q]) in exercise 2, and (3c) in exercise 3. Be sure to specify both the potential and the actual focus domains in each representation. [**section 5.4**]

5 Based on the discussion of focus structure in Italian and Japanese in this chapter, how would you explain the following facts regarding quantifier scope interpretation in the two languages? ('⊃' means 'has wider scope than'.) [**section 5.5**]

(1) *Italian* (Melinger 1996)
a. Ogni ragazza ha baciato un ragazzo.
every girl has kissed a boy
'Every girl kissed a boy.' (unambiguous, *ogni* ⊃ *un*)

a boy is been kissed by every girl
'A boy was kissed by every girl.' (unambiguous, *un* ⊃ *ogni*)

(2) *Japanese* (K. Watanabe, p.c.)

a. Subete no hito ga dareka o aisiteiru.
every GEN person SUBJ someone OBJ loves
'Everyone loves someone.' (ambiguous)

b. Subete no hito wa dareka o aisiteiru.
every GEN person TOP someone OBJ loves
'Everyone loves someone.' (unambiguous, *subete* ⊃ *dareka*)

6 Based on the analysis of focus structure in Toba Batak in exercise 3, how would you explain the following facts regarding quantifier scope interpretation in the language? The data are from Clark (1985). How do the factors discussed by Ioup and Kuno interact with focus structure in these examples? Why is (1c) ungrammatical?

(1) a. Mangalean missel tu tolu soridadu ganup jeneral. (unambiguous, *ganup* ⊃ *tolu*)
'Each general is giving a missile to three soldiers.'
(i.e. 'each general is giving a missile to a different group of three soldiers')

b. Mangalean missel tu tolu soridadu angka jeneral. (ambiguous)
'Every general is giving a missile to three soldiers.'
(i.e. 'every general is giving a missile to a different group of three soldiers', or 'every general is giving a missile to the same group of three soldiers')

c. *Diilean ganup jeneral tu tolu soridadu missel.
'Each general gave a missile to three soldiers.'

d. Diilean angka jeneral tu tolu soridadu missel. (ambiguous)
'Every general gave a missile to three soldiers.'

(2) a. Tu tolu soridadu, mangalean missel ganup jeneral (ambiguous)
'To three soldiers, each general is giving a missile.'

b. Tu tolu soridadu, mangalean missel angka jeneral. (unambiguous, *tolu* ⊃ *angka*)
'To three soldiers, every general is giving a missile.'
(i.e. 'every general is giving a missile to the same group of three soldiers')

7 Explain why coreference is or is not possible in the following sentences. The asterisk means that the sentence is impossible on the coreference reading; it is of course grammatical if non-coreference is assumed. Focal stress is indicated by small capitals. **[section 5.6]**

b. *As for his$_i$ sister, she hasn't talked to LARRY$_i$ in three weeks.

(2) a. Larry$_i$ hasn't talked to his$_i$ SISTER in three weeks.
b. It is his$_i$ SISTER that Larry$_i$ hasn't talked to in three weeks.
c. It is Larry's$_i$ SISTER that he$_i$ hasn't talked to in three weeks.
c′. *It is LARRY's$_i$ sister that he$_i$ hasn't talked to in three weeks.
d. *It is LARRY$_i$ that his$_i$ sister hasn't talked to in three weeks.

6

Grammatical relations

6.0 Introduction

At the beginning of chapter 2 we stated that there are two types of structure, relational and non-relational. As the labels imply, relational structure deals with the relations that exist between one syntactic element and another, be they syntactic, semantic or pragmatic in nature, whereas non-relational structure expresses the hierarchical organization of phrases, clauses and sentences. Non-relational structure was the focus of chapter 2, while semantic and pragmatic relational structures were the topics of chapters 3–5. In this chapter we turn to syntactic relations, or, as they are better known, grammatical relations. We will begin by looking at some of the conceptions of grammatical relations that have been proposed by different linguistic theories and the implications for theory and analysis of each of the major conceptions, then we will discuss the cross-linguistic diversity of syntactic phenomena related to grammatical relations and propose an account of grammatical relations which deals with this diversity.

6.1 Conceptions of grammatical relations

Grammatical relations are a part of traditional grammar. They are important because if one thinks pretheoretically, or as pretheoretically as one can, it is obvious that there are a lot of syntactic phenomena that relate to grammatical relations. For example, if one considers what the *-s* is doing on the third person singular present tense verb in English, it is clear that it is agreeing with the subject. Notice that this innocuous statement presupposes a theory of grammatical relations of some kind. Take, for example, the passive construction, in which what would be the object in the active voice is now the subject, and what would be the subject in the active voice is either missing or the object of a preposition. This informal description makes crucial reference to notions of grammatical relations. Traditional grammar, furthermore, assumes a particular set of relations based on grammatical phenomena in Indo-European languages: **subject**, **direct object** and **indirect object**. These notions appear to be central to many grammatical phenomena, and many of them apparently are describable in these terms. These notions also seem important for many non-Indo-European languages, because subjects and direct objects appear to be elements in their grammars. One of the things to be investigated in this chapter is whether this is, in fact, true. One of the central questions of linguistic theory is 'How are languages different and how are they alike?', and one of the ways in which they could be alike is that they all employ notions of subject, object and indirect object. Therefore, if one is going to come up with a theory of universal grammar, one needs to determine whether these concepts should be assumed as part of the theory. There are theories that take them to be a crucial component and others that do not.

There are generally two ways in which grammatical relations can be handled within a theory which posits them. On the one hand, they can be treated as primitives (underived from anything else), while on the other they can be treated as derived from some other syntactic, semantic or pragmatic phenomenon (or some combination thereof). This is the fundamental contrast in the theoretical status of grammatical relations. Theories must make a choice here, for grammatical relations cannot be both primitive and derived.

6.1.1 Grammatical relations as primitives

What would it mean to say that grammatical relations are theoretical primitives? The primitive terms in the theory are those which do not admit of any further explication, for they are a part of the foundation of the theory and play a role in the formulation of the basic principles of the theory. As such, they form a crucial part of the explanatory basis of the theory. This is the case in a theory like RelG (e.g. Perlmutter 1978, 1980, 1982), which posits the basic grammatical relations as primitives. It is important to realize that it is not possible to argue against such an assumption directly. Theories are free to make any assumptions they wish, and it is the theoretical and empirical consequences of these assumptions which are open to challenge. In arguing against a particular assumption or set of assumptions, what one can do is show that a description based upon the assumption(s) in question will lead to a number of problems, such as inelegant descriptions, missed generalizations, *ad hoc* and unmotivated analyses, and incorrect empirical predictions (see section 1.2.1). It is not possible to say that there is or is not direct evidence that grammatical relations are primitive.

6.1.2 Grammatical relations as derived notions

If grammatical relations are derived, what are they derived from? We will give an overview of two general approaches: (1) deriving grammatical relations from constituent structure configurations, and (2) deriving them from other notions.

6.1.2.1 Configurational definitions of grammatical relations

In early transformational theory (Chomsky 1965), syntactic phrase structure was the accepted source for grammatical relations. Chomsky's early definition for subject was 'the NP which is immediately dominated by S' in the phrase structure tree,

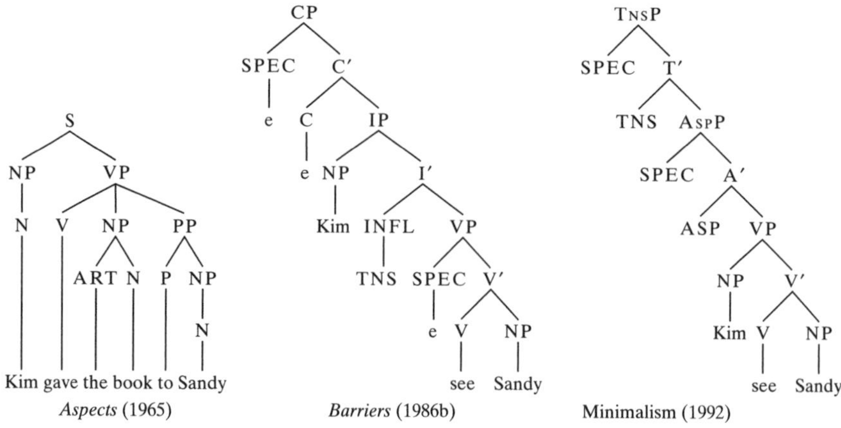

Figure 6.1 Configurational bases of grammatical relations in Chomskyan theory

while the definition of direct object was 'the NP immediately dominated by the VP'. This is represented in the leftmost tree in figure 6.1. There was no definition of indirect object; there was no structural notion of it, because indirect object in English is always a prepositional phrase. There is in fact nothing in Chomskyan theory that depends upon the concept of indirect object. The terms 'subject' and 'object' were later replaced by 'external argument' and 'internal argument', respectively. The external argument is defined as the syntactic argument external to the VP; in the *Barriers* tree in figure 6.1, the external argument *Kim* is external to the VP and is immediately dominated by IP (inflection phrase), which replaced 'S'.[1] The internal argument is the syntactic argument internal to the VP (*Sandy*); it is a sister to the verb and directly dominated by V-bar. The definition of external argument had to be changed with the development of the VP-internal subject hypothesis, as represented in the third (Minimalism) tree, because both arguments were within the VP initially. The internal argument is still a sister to the verb and directly dominated by V-bar, but the external argument is now the argument external to the V-bar, not the VP, and is directly dominated by VP, not IP (which has been split up into multiple functional categories). Despite these changes, the basic conception of subject (external argument) and object (internal argument) remains unchanged: the object is the sister to the verb within the phrase containing it and the verb, and the subject is external to this phrase.

What were the implications of these definitions? A very significant implication was that there has to be a VP in the structure.[2] As a configurational definition of grammatical relations was assumed, a VP was necessary in order to distinguish subject from direct object; if there were no VP, then there would be two NPs immediately dominated by the same node and the structure would fail to distinguish internal from external argument. Consequently, VP was by definition a linguistic universal, and all languages had to have a VP in their syntactic structure, given the type of configurational definition assumed.

While the configurational definition of grammatical relations did not require absolutely rigid word order, it did require that the verb and object be adjacent or at least not separated by non-VP elements. This restriction also encountered difficulties in languages with very free word order, as we argued in section 2.1.2. Consider the following examples from Warlpiri, an Australian Aboriginal language spoken in central Australia (Andrews 1985).

(6.1) a. Wajilipi-nyi ka maliki-∅ kurdu wita-ngku.
chase-NPST AUX dog-ABS child small-ERG
b. Maliki-∅ ka wajilipi-nyi kurdu wita-ngku.
c. Wajilipi-nyi ka kurdu wita-ngku maliki-∅.
d. Kurdu wita-ngku ka maliki-∅ wajilipi-nyi.
e. Kurdu wita-ngku ka wajilipi-nyi maliki-∅ .
f. Maliki-∅ ka kurdu wita-ngku wajilipi-nyi.
'The small child is chasing the dog.'

Since the verb and the object can appear in any position in the clause except second position, where the auxiliary must be, there is no overt evidence that the verb and the object form a phrase of any kind. There appears to be no evidence for the existence of a VP in Warlpiri. Again it is the kind of problem that the configurational approach, which was based on the analysis of fixed-word-order languages like English, was not well equipped to deal with. As we discussed in section 2.1.1, the obvious solution is to posit an abstract level of syntactic representation with a fixed order and a VP.

Thus, a number of problems arise in connection with the attempt to define grammatical relations in purely phrase structure terms. The solution proposed for these problems was to posit multiple levels of syntactic representation, namely one corresponding to the overt structure of the sentence and another one which is an abstract representation. The abstract level of representation is configurational, i.e. it always has a VP, and grammatical relations can be defined with reference to it. This approach then posited a rule schema which would derive the overt facts of the language. We discussed this approach with respect to the issue of clause structure in section 2.1 and pointed out that it is incompatible with the framework we are presenting in this book, since it involves abstract levels of representation and transformational rules linking them. Accordingly, we are forced to look for a different approach to grammatical relations, one which is compatible with the set of assumptions outlined in chapters 1 and 2.

6.1.2.2 Non-configurational definitions of grammatical relations

We now turn to non-configurational derivations of subject and object. We have already seen that attempting to derive grammatical relations from phrase structure configurations runs into significant problems. Possible alternatives would be deriving them from semantic relations or pragmatic relations. In this section we will present definitions of subject and object suggested by some of the major syntactic theories.

In FG (Dik 1978, 1980, 1989), different choices for subject and object are said to represent different 'perspectives' or 'vantage points' in the coding of a state of affairs. They are a level of organization of the presentation of the state of affairs over and above semantic roles and discourse-pragmatic-related notions, so cannot be defined simply as either of these. Subject is defined as 'that constituent which refers to the entity which is taken as a point of departure for the presentation of the state of affairs in which it participates' (Dik 1978: 87). Object choice (from among the semantic roles left over after subject assignment) represents a further specification of the perspective. The choice of what semantic roles can be specified as subject and object is governed by the hierarchy of semantic roles presented in (6.2) (Dik 1978: 76; cf. 1989: 226):

(6.2) *Semantic Function Hierarchy (SFH)*

	Agent	>	Goal	>	Recipient	>	Beneficiary	>	Instrument	>	Location	>	Time
Subject	×	>	×	>	×	>	×	>	×	>	×	>	×
Object			×	>	×	>	×	>	×	>	×	>	×

This hierarchy is said to be universal in languages that allow a choice. Languages differ as to what point in the hierarchy there is a cut-off, below which the roles do not have the possibility of being assigned to subject or object function. Some languages allow only Agent and Goal subjects, some allow Agent, Goal and Recipient subjects, and some allow other semantic functions to be assigned subject function. In terms of objects, some languages allow only Goal and Recipient objects, some allow Goal, Recipient and Beneficiary objects, and so on. The further to the right of the hierarchy the semantic function is, the more marked that type of subject or object will be. This markedness is said to be the result of 'tension' between the most natural perspective (Agent subject/Goal object) and the actual perspective taken in the sentence. Subject and object assignment are only relevant to languages where there is a possibility of differential assignment to Subject or Object function. Where there is no choice, no relations other than the semantic and pragmatic relations are necessary. A language may lack subject and object; if these functions exist, however, then assignment of semantic arguments to these functions follows general principles. Dik argues that a language with an ergative subject, such as Dyirbal (see below), may represent a 'nominative system with unmarked passive' (Dik 1980: 125; cf. Dik 1989: 242–5). That is, because of a markedness shift, the active transitive construction became a marked construction and the passive became the unmarked construction, and then the active construction became obsolete and so disappeared from the language. Dik also suggests that ergative systems may develop out of the frequent use of nominalizations (1989: 245–6).

grammatical relations. The subject/object distinction is seen as reflecting a more general trajector/landmark asymmetry, which is a linguistic instantiation of the even more general figure/ground contrast. In describing an event, such as a person moving past a tree, we take one part (substructure) of the scene as the focus of our attention, such that it is distinguished from the rest of the scene. In the case of our example, we will give special attention to the person doing the moving and see the tree and the rest of the scene as only a reference point for describing the movement of the person. The part given this special attention is the 'figure', while the background which provides the setting and reference point for the movement of the figure is the 'ground'. What is taken as the figure and what as the ground is a matter of perspective. This is most clear in relation predicates such as *look like*. We can say *Jim looks like Bill* or *Bill looks like Jim*, the difference being mainly one of perspective, a matter of which one we choose to be the figure and which one we choose to be the ground. The figure in such a relational predication is called the 'trajector' in CogG, while other entities in the relational predication are called 'landmarks'. Subject and object are then special cases of trajector and landmark respectively. In an unmarked transitive clause, there is an 'energy flow' between two participants, with subject being the head of the flow and object being the tail of the flow. The trajector and the head of the energy flow are the same participant. In a passive clause the tail of the energy flow is more salient and so is made trajector. There is then a conflict of alignment between the natural order of energy flow and the profiling of the tail of the energy flow as the trajector. This is said to be the reason for the marked nature of passive clauses.

For Givón (1979a, 1984b, 1990), subject and object are 'grammaticalized (i.e. "syntactically coded") pragmatic case roles' (1984b: 138). Subject is the 'primary clausal topic' and object is the 'secondary clausal topic'. They represent the simultaneous coding of the semantic and pragmatic functions of nominal participants in discourse. All languages are said to code the primary clausal topic in some way, though not all languages have a direct object distinct from the semantic role of patient. Again, similar to Dik's view (though Dik disagrees with the 'grammaticalized topic' view), there is a hierarchy for ranking the semantic roles according to the degree to which they are likely to be the subject or object of a simple active clause. This is called the 'topic accession hierarchy' or simply 'topic hierarchy' (1984b: 139). It is given in (6.3).

(6.3) Agent > Dative/ Benefactive > Patient > Locative > Instrument/Associative > Manner adverbs

The same hierarchy applies to access to both subject and object except that Agent is not available for access to object. Voice differences are seen as a basically pragmatic phenomenon, allowing different discourse-pragmatic perspectives. In the passive, semantic role, in accordance with the topic accession hierarchy (1990: 566).

In LFG, the assignment of grammatical relations is based on Lexical Mapping Theory (Bresnan and Kanerva 1989, Bresnan and Moshi 1990, Bresnan 1994). In this theory, grammatical relations are constituted of two primitive semantic features. One is the property of being restricted in terms of semantic role. Subject and object are seen as unrestricted ([–r]) in terms of what semantic roles can be associated with them; all other roles are restricted ([+r]) in this regard. The other property is that of being able to complement transitive predicators but not intransitive predicators ([+o]). Two types of object are said to have this property, those that are semantically restricted and those that are not. Oblique arguments are said to be restricted and to not have the property of complementing transitive predicators, though they can complement intransitive predicators ([+r, –o]). This then gives a four-way contrast based on the two properties, differentiating the four types of grammatical relation recognized in this theory (Bresnan and Moshi 1990: 167).

(6.4)

[–r] [–o]	SUBJ	[+r] [–o]	OBL_θ
[–r] [+o]	OBJ	[+r] [+o]	OBJ_θ

Based on these properties, grammatical relations can be grouped into four natural classes, with SUBJ and OBJ being [–r], OBJ and OBJ_θ being [+o], OBJ_θ and OBL_θ being [+r], and SUBJ and OBL_θ being [–o].

Assignment of grammatical relations through assignment of these properties is obligatory and universal. It is based on the thematic role hierarchy given in (6.5).

(6.5) agent > benefactive > goal > instrument > patient/theme > locative

This hierarchy determines the highest-ranking role associated with a particular predicate. If there is an agent, then agent is the highest role, if not, then benefactive is the highest role, etc. The highest thematic role is by default [–r], while all other roles are by default [+r]. Several intrinsic classifications are also assumed: agents are intrinsically [–o], themes/patients are intrinsically [–r] and locatives are intrinsically [–o]. It is also assumed (the 'well-formedness condition') that every verb form will have a subject, and that a single role will have one and only one grammatical function. An example of the derivation of grammatical relations using the verb *pěza* 'find' from Chicheŵa is given in (6.6) (Bresnan and Kanerva 1989: 29).

(6.6)

	pěza <	agent	theme	locative	> 'find'
intrinsic:		[–o]	[–r]	[–o]	
defaults:		[–r]		[+r]	
		S	O/S	OBL_{loc}	
well-formedness condition:		S	O	OBL_{loc}	

matic role, the agent is classified as [−r]. All other roles should then be classified as [+r], but as theme is intrinsically [−r], only the locative is classified as [+r]. The result is that the agent is the subject, the theme can either be subject or object, and the locative is an oblique locative. Given the well-formedness condition that only one role can fill a particular function, as the agent is already subject, the theme must then become the object.

It is also possible for morphosyntactic rules to intervene between the intrinsic and default classifications to change the result of the derivation. Following is an example of the passive verb *pezĕdpwa* 'be found' in Chichewa (Bresnan and Kanerva 1989: 30).

(6.7)		*pĕza*	<	agent	theme	locative	>	'find'
	intrinsic:			[−o]	[−r]	[−o]		
	passive	*-édw*		∅				
	defaults:					[+r]		
					O/S	OBL_{loc}		
	well-formedness condition:				S	OBL_{loc}		

In (6.7), the intrinsic classificatons are the same, but the passive rule suppresses the highest role on the thematic role hierarchy, here the agent, and so the default applies vacuously to the theme (which is now the highest-ranking role), and the locative is classified as [+r]. The theme is then the only unrestricted role available to be subject, and there is no other unrestricted or [+o] role that could be object. The locative then is still an oblique argument. (Other derivations are possible; see the references cited above.)

Of the theories discussed in this section, most agree that a hierarchy of thematic roles is involved in the assignment of subject and object, though the details of the hierarchies differ. All agree that agent is the highest role, and is unavailable for assignment to object. The first three theories presented above see voice as a matter of perspective, and acknowledge that not all languages have subjects and objects, while the LFG Lexical Mapping Theory is a formal account which assumes subject and object to be universal. Dik has attempted to deal with the problems posed by syntactically ergative languages, i.e. those in which the undergoer is the unmarked choice for 'subject', but his account is problematic, as it relies on the idea that the languages were once accusative and that the passive is the source of the ergative construction. There is no historical evidence for this for many syntactically ergative languages, and some of them, e.g. Jakaltek and Sama, have both ergative syntax and productive passive constructions. As we will see below, syntactically ergative languages raise profound problems for all theories of grammatical relations that assume that languages like English provide good models for a universal theory of grammatical relations.

In section 6.1.1 we said that empirical investigation of many languages is necessary to be able to determine if grammatical relations should be considered universal and/or primitives of linguistic theory. In this section we will investigate several languages from the point of view of the universality and comparability of grammatical relations.

6.2.1 Do all languages have grammatical relations?

The question here is quite straightforward: is it the case that in every language, one or more grammatical relations can be identified which cannot be reduced to any other type of relation, in particular to semantic or pragmatic relations? The answer, however, is not straightforward. The first crucial issue is how one could tell whether a given clause-internal syntagmatic relation is syntactic, semantic or pragmatic. That is, how can one tell if the constructions are organized as subject–object, actor–undergoer or topic–comment? There are criteria for deciding this question, based on the properties of grammatical relations.

Grammatical relations have two distinct and in principle independent types of properties, coding properties and behavioral properties, following the distinction proposed in Keenan (1976a). Coding properties refer to such things as case and the other morphological properties, such as verb agreement. Behavioral properties are those which define the role of the NP in grammatical constructions. We will talk about both types of properties. When we talk about grammatical relations, it should be kept in mind that subject is by far the most important grammatical relation, and consequently most of the discussion will be focused on it, although the same criteria must be met by any other grammatical relations.

An example of a coding property in English is verb agreement; it is illustrated in (6.8).

(6.8) a. 3rd person singular: The cat runs.
b. 3rd person plural: The cats run.

If the NP is singular, the verb takes the suffix *-s*; and if it is plural, the verb does not take *-s*. How can it be determined whether agreement is sensitive to semantic, pragmatic or syntactic relations? One could say that since the single argument of *run* is an actor, the verb is agreeing with the semantic actor and not the syntactic subject, or one could claim that the agreement is with the grammatical relation subject. How would one decide which of these two relations the verb is actually agreeing with? We could look for an instance where the subject is clearly not an actor and see if the verb still agrees with it; one possibility is *die*, since the single argument of this verb is not an actor.

(6.9) a. The dog dies.
b. The dogs die.

In this case the single argument is an undergoer, not an actor, yet the verb still agrees with it. A semantic analysis which claims that agreement is with a semantic relation like actor predicts that there should not be agreement in this instance, while the syntactic analysis predicts that agreement is with the syntactic relation 'subject' and therefore that there should be agreement. From this example, it would appear that the syntactic analysis is correct. Consider a sentence with a transitive verb like *kill*.

(6.10) a. John kills the ducklings.
b. The ducklings are killed by John.

In *John kills the ducklings*, *John* is the actor and *the ducklings* is the undergoer, and there is agreement here. One can also look at the passive form of the same sentence, which is *The ducklings are killed by John*. The active sentence shows agreement with the subject, an actor, while the passive sentence shows agreement with the subject, which is an undergoer. Therefore, agreement is with the syntactic relation of subject, and not with any particular semantic relation. This is a neutralization of the semantic opposition between actor and undergoer for (morpho)syntactic purposes, namely, verb agreement. Thus for the statement of verb agreement in English, it is irrelevant whether the subject NP is an actor or an undergoer. This contrast is neutralized and is therefore irrelevant to verb agreement. If there were different agreement patterns for every different semantic relation (if each were treated distinctly), then there would be no neutralization. In English, however, there is clearly such a neutralization. It is also a *restricted* neutralization, because the verb agrees with only the actor or the undergoer. If the verb agreed with any or all of its syntactic arguments, irrespective of their semantic role, then there would clearly be a neutralization of semantic oppositions for syntactic purposes, but it would not be restricted. We will see a clear instance of an unrestricted neutralization in English below. The type of restricted neutralization we have just seen is evidence that there is a syntactic syntagmatic relation (i.e. a grammatical relation) involved in this construction aside from the semantic relations actor and undergoer.

We have just argued that verb agreement is sensitive to syntactic rather than semantic relations, but no evidence has yet been presented against the possibility that the agreement is with the pragmatic relation of topic. It was noted earlier that subject in English is normally a topic, and therefore one could argue that the verb agrees with the pragmatic relation of topic rather than the syntactic relation of subject. The argument which must be made to resolve this issue is identical in structure to the one made above: it is necessary to find cases in which the subject is not a topic. In such a case, the pragmatic analysis predicts that there should be no agreement, while the syntactic analysis predicts that there should be agreement. Topics were characterized in chapter 5 as 'what is being talked about', and they contrast with the elements in the comment which often introduce new material into the discourse. An example of new information of this kind is the answer to a simple WH-question; the element in the answer corresponding to the WH-word in the question is in focus and not a topic. By looking at the answers to this kind of question, one can test the claim of the pragmatic analysis of verb agreement.

(6.11) Q: Who is winning the ball game?
A: The Giants are/*is/*be winning.

The Giants is the focus in the answer; it is not a topic. The pragmatic analysis predicts that the verb should not agree with this NP in (6.11), because it is not a topic, while the syntactic analysis predicts that there should be agreement. As (6.11) shows, the syntactic analysis makes the correct prediction. Thus verb agreement in English is sensitive to the syntactic relation of subject and not to the semantic relation of actor or the pragmatic relation of topic.

These arguments have concerned coding properties. The same kind of arguments can be made with respect to behavioral properties. Consider the constructions in (6.12) and (6.13).

(6.12) a. Susan$_i$ wants ___$_i$ to run in the park.
b. Susan$_i$ wants ___$_i$ to eat a hamburger.
c. Susan$_i$ wants ___$_i$ to be taller.
d. *Susan$_i$ doesn't want the police to arrest ___$_i$.
e. Susan$_i$ doesn't want ___$_i$ to be arrested by the police.

(6.13) a. Jack$_i$ seems ___$_i$ to be running in the park.
b. Jack$_i$ seems ___$_i$ to be eating a hamburger.
c. Jack$_i$ seems ___$_i$ to be taller.
d. *Jack$_i$ seems the police to have arrested ___$_i$.
e. Jack$_i$ seems ___$_i$ to have been arrested by the police.

In strictly syntactic terms, there is a missing NP in each of the dependent cores in (6.12); (6.12a) may be paraphrased as 'Susan wants + Susan run in the park', and the second occurrence of *Susan* is omitted. In (6.13) a semantic argument of the verb in the dependent core appears in the matrix core; that is, (6.13a) could be paraphrased by 'It seems that Jack is running in the park', and in this example *Jack* appears to replace *it* as the subject of *seem* in the matrix core. In both constructions there are restrictions on which NP can be omitted or matrix-coded, as the (d) examples show. The missing NP in the dependent clause in (6.12a, b) is an actor, in (6.12c, e) an undergoer, and similarly the matrix-coded NP is an actor in (6.13a, b) and an undergoer in (6.13c, e). In (6.12d) and (6.13d), the missing or matrix-coded NPs have the same semantic role as in the grammatical (e) examples, i.e. undergoer; this is crucial evidence that the restriction cannot be stated in semantic terms. What is the vital difference between the (d) and (e) sentences in each set? In both examples the omitted or matrix-coded NP is the undergoer, and the only difference between be the object, if it occurred overtly, whereas in (e) it would be the subject in a passive construction, if it occurred overtly. Hence the crucial deciding factor is not the semantic function of the NP, since it is undergoer in both sentences, but rather its syntactic function. There is thus a restricted neutralization like the one we saw with verb agreement with respect to the omitted NP in (6.12) and the matrix-coded NP in (6.13), as both actor and undergoer arguments can be omitted or matrix-coded. Therefore the relevant relation is the syntactic one of subject and not a semantic one like actor. In all of the grammatical sentences in (6.12), it is the subject of the dependent core that is omitted, while in (6.13) it is the subject of the dependent core which is matrix-coded, regardless of their semantic roles.

We have seen above two examples of a restricted neutralization of semantic roles for syntactic purposes in the behavior of grammatical relations in English. Not only was there a neutralization, but it was a restricted neutralization. The necessity of the notion of restrictiveness in discussing the behavior of grammatical relations can be seen clearly with respect to the following question about relativization in English. Does English relativization (with a finite relative clause) involve grammatical relations, akin to the situation found in (6.12) and (6.13)? In other words, is there a restricted neutralization with respect to the function the head (represented by the relative pronoun) can have in the relative clause? The relevant examples are presented in (6.14).

(6.14) Mary talked to the man
(a) who [AGENT] bought the house down the street.
(b) who [PATIENT] the dog bit.
(c) to whom [RECIPIENT] Bill sold the house.

Mary looked at the box
(d) in which [LOCATION] the jewelry was kept.
(e) out of which [SOURCE] the jewelry had been taken.

It is clear from these sentences that contrast among semantic roles is neutralized with respect to the function of the head in the relative clause. Hence there is definitely a neutralization of semantic roles for syntactic purposes here. But is it a *restricted* neutralization? The answer is 'no,' because the relative pronoun can have virtually any semantic role; the head can function as AGENT, PATIENT, RECIPIENT, LOCATION or SOURCE, among others. Consequently, this type of relativization in English provides no evidence regarding grammatical relations in the language, because it does not involve a restricted neutralization of semantic roles, only an unrestricted neutralization.

All of the examples we have looked at so far have been from English, a dependent-marking language. The same phenomena are found in head-marking languages, but, because they are head-marking, these tests are concerned primarily than the presence or absence of independent NPs. Consider the following examples from Enga, a Papuan language (Lang 1973, Li and Lang 1979).

(6.15) a. (Baa-mé) mená lóngó-∅ p-í-á.
3sg-ERG pig many-ABS hit-PAST-3sg
'He killed many pigs.'
a′. *(Baa-mé) mená lóngó-∅ p-í-amí.
3sg-ERG pig many-ABS hit-PAST-3pl
b. (Baá) ándá dokó-nyá ka-ly-á-mo.
3sg house DET-LOC be-PRES-3sg-DEC
'He is in the house.'
c. (Baá) pe-ly-á-mo.
3sg go-PRES-3sg-DEC
'He is going.'

Enga is what is known as a 'double-marking' language; that is, it has both NP case marking and bound arguments on the verb indicating the actor, etc. (see section 2.2.2.1). The independent pronouns are optional. What we are concerned with here is the suffix *-á* '3sg' on the verb. In (6.15a) it cross-references the actor *baa* 'he', not the plural undergoer *mená lóngó* 'many pigs', as (a′) clearly shows. In the following sentences it cross-references the undergoer of an intransitive verb in (b) and the actor of an intransitive verb in (c). This is exactly the same pattern we found in English verb agreement with intransitive verbs, and accordingly we have a restricted neutralization here as well. A strictly semantic analysis of the cross-reference pattern would make the wrong prediction about (6.15b), just as it did about (6.8)–(6.10) from English. Hence the cross-reference suffixes code the syntactic subject, not the actor or the undergoer. Turning to syntactic properties, we will examine 'want' constructions in Enga analogous to the English ones in (6.12), and in this case we are interested in whether the cross-referencing morpheme *-a* occurs on the verb in the dependent core or not. The relevant data are given in (6.16); the desiderative suffix *-nya* on the infinitive and the matrix verb *mási-* 'think' combine to produce the Enga equivalent of English *want* + infinitive.

(6.16) a. (Baa-mé) mená dóko-∅ pyá-la-nya mási-ly-a-mo.
3sg-ERG pig DET-ABS kill-INF-DES think-PRES-3sg-DEC
'He wants to kill the pig.'
a′. (Baa-mé) pyá-la-nya mási-ly-a-mo.
3sg-ERG kill-INF-DES think-PRES-3sg-DEC
*'He wants to be killed.'
b. (Baa-∅) akáli ká-lya-nya mási-ly-a-mo.
3sg-ABS man be-INF-DES think-PRES-3sg-DEC
'He wants to be a man.'

c. (Baá-∅) Wápaka pá-a-nya mási-ly-a-mo.
3sg-ABS Wabag go-INF-DES think-PRES-3sg-DEC
'He wants to go to Wabag.'

The linked verb does not carry the *-a* suffix which it did when it was the main verb in (6.15). Which semantic arguments can be omitted in the linked core? With a transitive verb, only the actor can be omitted, as (6.16a, a′) show; in other words, it is not possible to interprete the actor of *mási-* 'think' as the undergoer of *pyá-* 'kill'. Enga has no voice constructions of any kind, and accordingly the undergoer of a transitive verb cannot be omitted in this construction, unlike the English examples in (6.12e) and (6.13e). With respect to intransitive verbs, we find the same situation as in English: it is possible to omit the undergoer of an intransitive verb, as in (b), and the actor, as in (c). Thus, we have a restricted neutralization of semantic roles for syntactic purposes, because the omitted argument can be the actor of a transitive verb, the actor of an intransitive verb or the undergoer of an intransitive verb. The omitted argument is interpreted as the subject of the linked core; a semantic analysis that claimed that it is only the actor which can be omitted would wrongly predict the ungrammaticality of (b). While this is clearly a restricted neutralization of semantic roles for a syntactic purpose, it is also clear that this is not exactly the same restricted neutralization as in the English *want* construction in (6.12), a topic to which we will return in section 6.2.2.1.

We can use this type of behavioral test to determine whether or not grammatical relations are a significant part of the grammar of every language. Thus, there are purely syntactic grammatical relations in a language if there is at least one construction with a restricted neutralization of semantic and pragmatic relations for syntactic purposes. This is the case, as we have seen, in English and Enga. The converse of this is that if there are no constructions in a language in which there is a restricted neutralization of semantic and pragmatic relations for syntactic purposes, then there is no evidence of a syntactic predicate–argument relation in the language that could be called a grammatical relation. An example of a language in which there are no restricted neutralizations of semantic roles is Acehnese, an Austronesian language spoken at the northern end of the island of Sumatra in Indonesia. The data and analysis come from Durie (1985, 1987). We begin by looking at the coding property of verbal cross-reference; Acehnese is a head-marking language.

(6.17) (Gopnyan) geu-mat lôn
(3sg) 3-hold 1sg
'(S)he holds me.'

In this example the optional third-person pronoun *gopnyan* is unmarked for gender but does signal a certain social level, *mat* means 'hold,' and *lôn* is the first-person singular pronoun. There is also the *geu-* proclitic on *mat*, which cross-references *gopnyan*

(6.18) (Lôn) lôn-mat-geuh
(1sg) 1sg-hold-3
'I hold him/her.'

In this example, *lôn* is what we will provisionally call the subject pronoun and has the same form as the *lôn-* proclitic on the verb. The third-person clitic *geuh* appears after the verb and gets an *-h* at the end for phonological reasons; we will assume this indicates the object of the verb. The independent pronoun is optional, and consequently *lôn-mat-geuh* would be a complete sentence and have the same meaning as the example above. There is thus a proclitic on the verb to indicate the subject and an enclitic to indicate the object. Subject and object cross-references do not work in exactly the same way, however, since the subject proclitic occurs whether or not there is an independent NP functioning as subject, whereas the object enclitic appears only if there is no independent NP functioning as object.

In these two examples, the subject is also an actor and the object also an undergoer, and the same question that arose with respect to English verb agreement arises here: do the proclitics signal subject or actor, do the enclitics indicate object or undergoer? The two analyses make very different predictions with respect to intransitive verbs. The syntactic analysis predicts that the single argument of an intransitive verb should be cross-referenced in the same way as with the subject of a transitive verb, while the semantic account predicts that the cross-referencing should be the same only if the single argument of an intransitive verb is an actor. The single argument of *jak* 'go' in (6.19) is an actor, and the verb carries the same proclitic as with the subject of *mat* 'hold'.

(6.19) Geu-jak (gopnyan)
3-go (3sg)
'(S)he goes.'

This example does not provide any evidence for distinguishing between the two analyses, because the subject is an actor. The crucial case for deciding between them involves verbs whose single argument is not an actor, e.g. *rhët* 'fall'. Here the two accounts make different empirical predictions: the syntactic analysis predicts that the verb should take the same proclitic as *jak* 'go', because the NP is the subject, whereas the semantic account predicts that it should not take the proclitic but rather the enclitic, because the NP is not an actor. The crucial examples are in (6.20).

(6.20) a. Lôn rhët(-lôn).
1sg fall(-1sg)
'I fall.'
b. *Lôn lôn-rhët.
1sg 1sg-fall

The syntactic analysis predicts that (6.20b) is the correct form for 'I fall', while the semantic account predicts that the form should be (6.20a), and here the semantic account makes the correct prediction, not the syntactic one. This is in striking contrast to the situation in English and Enga, where the syntactic analysis was the correct one. With respect to the coding property of verb cross-reference in Acehnese, there is no neutralization of semantic relations for syntactic purposes and hence no evidence for grammatical relations. In order to interpret these facts in terms of grammatical relations, it would be necessary to say that verbs like *rhët* 'fall' have only an object without a subject, or that there is a subject, but it is really an object.[3] This is possible, but complicates the theory unnecessarily. The most straightforward account is to say simply that there is one kind of cross-reference for actors and another for undergoers. This is known as an 'active' system.

Acehnese has constructions like the English ones in (6.12) and (6.13), and they provide evidence regarding the behavioral properties tests for grammatical relations. The Acehnese equivalents of (6.12) are given in (6.21).

(6.21) a. Gopnyan geu-tém [(*geu-)jak]
3sg 3-want go
'(S)he wants to go.' (cf. (6.12a))

b. Geu-tém [(*geu-)taguen bu]
3-want cook rice
'(S)he wants to cook rice.' (cf. (6.12c))

c. *Gopnyan geu-tém [rhët]
3sg 3-want fall
'(S)he wants to fall.' (cf. (6.12b))

d. *Aneuk agam nyan ji-tém [geu-peuréksa lé dokto]
child male that 3-want 3-examine by doctor
'That child wants to be examined by the doctor.' (cf. (6.12d, e))

(The proclitic *ji-* in (d) is also third person, but it indicates a different level of social status than *geu-*. Despite the passive translation, the Acehnese construction is not a passive (Durie 1985, 1988a).) In Acehnese, as in English, the verb *tém* 'want' takes a dependent core which is missing an NP; the missing NP is interpreted as the subject of the complement clause in English, as we have seen. The omission of the NP in the Acehnese examples in (6.21a, b) is indicated not by the absence of the NP itself but rather by the absence of the proclitic on the verbs *jak* 'go' and *taguen* 'cook'; this omission is obligatory. There is likewise a restriction on the omitted argument in Acehnese, and the question is, how is this restriction to be characterized, syntactically or semantically? A syntactic analysis would predict that the subject of both transitive and intransitive verbs should be the omitted NP in the dependent clause; a semantic analysis, on the other hand, would state it in semantic terms, and in this case a reasonable hypothesis would be that only the actor can be omitted. This is the case in (6.21a) and (6.21b), and both analyses correctly predict the grammaticality of these sentences. Both of them also predict the ungrammaticality of (6.21d), since the NP in question is neither a subject nor an actor. The decisive example is (6.21c), in which the single argument is not an actor. Here the two approaches make opposite predictions, with the syntactic analysis predicting it to be grammatical (since the omitted NP is interpreted as the subject) and the semantic account predicting it to be ungrammatical (since it is not an actor), and the ungrammaticality of (6.21c) supports the semantic analysis over the syntactic one. As with verb agreement, there appears to be no neutralization of semantic relations for syntactic purposes and hence no evidence for grammatical relations.

A rather different pattern can be seen when 'possessor raising' is examined. In this construction, a possessed noun is compounded with the main predicate, and the possessor is treated as an independent syntactic argument of the verb. This is only possible if the possessive NP is the undergoer of the clause.

(6.22) a. Seunang até lôn.
happy liver 1sg
'I am happy.' (lit.: 'My liver is happy.')
b. Lôn seunang-até.
1sg happy-liver
'I am happy.'
c. Ka lôn-tët rumoh gopnyan.
ASP 1sgA-burn house 3sg
'I burned her house.'
d. Gopnyan ka lôn-tët-rumoh.
3sg ASP 1sgA-burn-house
'I burned her house', or 'She had her house burned by me.'
e. *Gopnyan ka aneuk-woe.
3sg ASP child-return
'His/her child returned.'

In (6.22) the possessive NP is the undergoer of the intransitive predicate *seunang* 'happy' in (a, b) and of the transitive predicate *tët* 'burn' in (c, d). In both cases the possessed noun can be compounded with the predicate and the possessor is treated as the undergoer of the clause. In (e), however, the possessive NP would be the actor, and in this instance 'possessor raising' is impossible. Here again we find a restriction (undergoer only) but no neutralization.

Acehnese, like English, has a matrix-coding construction in which a semantic argument of the verb in the dependent core appears in the main core. The Acehnese equivalents of the English constructions in (6.13) are given in (6.23).

(6.23) a. Gopnyan teuntèe [geu-woe]
3sg certain 3-return
'(S)he is certain to return.' (cf. (6.13a))

3sg certain win-3
'(S)he is certain to win.' (cf. (6.13b))

c. Gopnyan teuntèe [geu-beuet hikayat prang sabi]
3sg certain 3-recite epic
'He is certain to recite the Prang Sabi epic.' (cf. (6.13b))

d. Hikayat prang sabi teuntèe [geu-beuet].
epic certain 3-recite
'The Prang Sabi epic is certain to be recited by him.' (cf. (6.13d, e))

e. Gopnyan lôn-anggap [na neu-bi pèng baroe]
3sg 1sg-consider BE 2-give money yesterday
'I believe him to have been given money by you yesterday.'
(lit.: 'I consider him$_i$ [you gave money [to] ___$_i$ yesterday].')

The first four sentences could be paraphrased as 'it is certain that . . . ,' and in the actual sentence an NP from the dependent core replaces the 'it', just as in the English construction. The first two examples, (6.23a) and (6.23b), show that the situation with respect to this construction is very different from that of verb cross-reference or the 'want' construction; the single semantic argument of an intransitive verb can appear in the matrix core regardless of whether it is an actor, as in (6.23a), or an undergoer, as in (6.23b). This is clear evidence of a neutralization of semantic relations for syntactic purposes, and accordingly it appears that this construction may provide support for positing the existence of grammatical relations in Acehnese. Example (6.23c) supports this interpretation, as the subject–actor of a transitive verb occurs in the matrix core. However, the next two examples undermine this analysis thoroughly and demonstrate just how different Acehnese is from English. Acehnese lacks a passive construction (see Durie 1985, 1988a), and consequently the matrix-coded NP in (6.23d) is an undergoer. In English, as (6.13d, e) show, an undergoer can only occur in the matrix core if it is the subject of the passive dependent core, as in (6.13e); it cannot so occur if it is also the direct object in the dependent core, as in (6.13d). In Acehnese, on the other hand, there is no such restriction; either the actor or the undergoer of a transitive verb may appear in the matrix core. Moreover, *any semantic argument of the verb in the dependent core* may so appear; in (6.23e) the RECIPIENT with *bi* 'give' is located in the matrix core; it also would be possible to have the actor or the undergoer there as well. Thus, in this construction there is a neutralization of semantic relations for syntactic purposes, but it is not a *restricted* neutralization; 'any semantic argument of the verb' is not a grammatical relation in the sense that we are using the term here. The situation here is analogous to English relativization in (6.14), not to English matrix coding in (6.13). Hence this construction does not yield any evidence in support of the existence of grammatical relations in Acehnese. In the entire range of syntactic phenomena described in Durie (1985, 1987), there is either a restriction without any neutralization,

neutralization without any strong restrictions, as with the matrix-coding construction. Acehnese can therefore be said to be a language in which there is no motivation for postulating syntactic relations: grammatical constructions can be accounted for with two notions, semantic roles and 'semantic argument of the verb', neither of which are grammatical relations. This is extremely important with respect to the issue raised at the beginning of this section, for the facts from Acehnese suggest that there are good grounds for believing that syntactic relations like subject and object are not universal. Acehnese is also not the only language for which this has been claimed. Archi, a Caucasian language, also appears to lack grammatical relations (see Kibrik 1979a, b), as do Classical Tibetan (Andersen 1987), Kannada and Manipuri (Bhat 1991).

LaPolla (1990, 1993) argues that Mandarin Chinese also lacks grammatical relations, due to the non-existence of restricted neutralizations in the grammar, and that, in striking contrast to Acehnese, the relevant syntagmatic relations are pragmatic (topic–comment), rather than semantic (LaPolla 1995a). Mandarin does not have verb agreement or cross-referencing morphology, so we will look only at behavioral properties. We will first look at constraints on deletion and coreference in complex constructions.

In English, a semantic argument appearing in two conjoined active-voice transitive clauses can be represented by a zero pronoun in the second clause only if it is the actor in both clauses, as in (6.24a, b).

(6.24) a. The man$_i$ went downhill and *pro*$_i$ saw the dog.
b. *The dog$_i$ went downhill and the man saw *pro*$_i$.
c. The dog$_i$ went downhill and *pro*$_i$ was seen by the man.

It is not possible to have the representation of the actor of the first clause coreferring with a zero pronoun representing the undergoer of the second clause without using a passive construction, as shown in (6.24b). If the semantic argument the two clauses have in common is the undergoer of the second clause, then, in order for the two clauses to be conjoined, the realization of the argument (in this case, as a zero anaphor) must appear as the single direct core argument of a passive construction, as in (6.24c).

In Mandarin we do not find this type of restriction on cross-clause coreference. In Mandarin it is possible for the common semantic argument of a conjoined structure to appear as a zero pronoun regardless of its semantic role; there is no need for a passive construction:

(6.25) a. Xiǎo gǒu$_i$ zǒu dào shān dìxià, nèi ge rén jiù kànjiàn
little dog walk to mountain bottom that CL person then saw
le *pro*$_i$.
PRFV
'The little dog went downhill and was seen by the man.'
(lit.: 'The little dog$_i$ went downhill and the man saw *pro*$_i$.')

b. Nèi ge rén$_i$ zǒu dào shān dìxià, jiù *pro*$_i$ kànjiàn le xiǎo
that CL person walk to mountain bottom then saw PRFV little
gǒu.
dog
'The man went downhill and saw the little dog.'

There is then a neutralization of semantic roles in terms of cross-clause coreference, but it is unrestricted, and so provides no evidence for positing grammatical relations.

We saw that in English there is an unrestricted neutralization of semantic roles for (finite) relativization, but in some languages there is a restricted neutralization. In Malagasy, a western Austronesian language spoken in Madagascar, the head of the relative clause must function as the single argument of an intransitive clause or the actor of an active-voice transitive verb in the relative clause (Keenan 1976b: 265). Example (6.26) includes a simple clause and a Malagasy relative construction.

(6.26) a. Man-asa ny lamba amin'ity savony ity ny zazavavy.
ATV-wash DET clothes with-DEM soap DEM DET girl
'The girl is washing the clothes with this soap.'
b. ny zazavavy (izay) man-asa ny lamba
DET girl (that) ATV-wash DET clothes
'the girl who is washing the clothes'

If the head functions as the undergoer or INSTRUMENT of the transitive verb in the relative clause, then a special voice form must be used in the relative clause; passive is used in (6.27b, c), and what we may call the 'instrumental voice' is used in (6.27e, f). In all Malagasy relative clauses, the head noun must function as the subject of the relative clause.

(6.27) a. *ny lamba (izay) man-asa amin'ity savony ity ny zazavavy
DET clothes (that) ATV-wash with-DEM soap DEM DET girl
Intended: 'the clothes that the girl washed with this soap'
b. Sasa-n'ny zazavavy amin'ity savony ity ny lamba.
wash-PASS-DET girl with-DEM soap DEM DET clothes
'The clothes are washed with this soap by the girl.'
c. ny lamba (izay) sasa-n amin'ity savony ity ny zazavavy
DET clothes (that) wash-PASS with-DEM soap DEM DET girl
'the clothes that are washed with this soap by the girl'
d. *ity savony ity (izay) man-asa ny lamba amin ny zazavavy
DEM soap DEM (that) ATV-wash DET clothes with DET girl
Intended: 'the soap that the girl washed the clothes with'
e. An-asa-n'ny zazavavy ny lamba ity savony ity.
INST-wash-PASS-DET girl DET clothes DEM soap DEM
'The soap was washed the clothes with by the girl.'
f. ity savony ity (izay) an-asa-n'ny zazavavy ny lamba
DEM soap DEM (that) INST-wash-PASS-DET girl DET clothes
'the soap that was washed the clothes with by the girl'

This is an example of a restricted neutralization, because the head must have a specific syntactic relation within the relative clause, regardless of its semantic role.

In Mandarin, on the other hand, we find that an NP in any semantic role can be relativized upon. In (6.28) we give examples for actor and undergoer in both transitive and intransitive clauses (square brackets mark the relative clause):

(6.28) a. [Wǒ zài nèi ge shítáng chī fàn] de péngyǒu mǎi le shū.
1sg LOC that CL cafeteria eat rice REL friend buy PRFV book
'My friend who eats in that cafeteria bought some/a book(s).'

b. [Gāngcái pǎo jìn lái] de rén yòu zǒu le.
just.now run enter come REL person again go PRFV
'The person who ran in just now left again.'

c. [Gāngcái bù shūfu] de nèi ge rén zǒu le.
just.now not comfortable REL that CL person go PRFV
'The person who was not well just now left.'

d. Wǒ tǎoyàn [zài nèi ge shítáng chī] de fàn.
1sg dislike LOC that CL cafeteria eat REL rice
'I dislike the rice (I) ate in that cafeteria.'

Here we have a transitive actor, an intransitive actor, an intransitive undergoer, and a transitive undergoer, respectively, acting as head of the relative clause. Aside from being able to relativize on these roles, it is also possible to relativize on a LOCATIVE, a GOAL, a BENEFACTIVE, an INSTRUMENT, a possessor, either NP in a comparative structure, and a topic (regardless of whether it is a semantic argument of the verb or not) (see LaPolla 1993 for examples). Again we see a neutralization, but one that is quite unrestricted.

In (6.13) we saw that in English only the subject of an embedded clause can be matrix-coded as the subject of a verb such as *seem*. In Mandarin, though, we find no restriction, as the Mandarin analogs of (6.13b) and (d) are both perfectly acceptable:

(6.29) a. Hǎoxiàng Lǐsì mǎi le chēzi.
seem buy PRFV vehicle
'It seems Lisi bought the car.'

b. Lǐsì hǎoxiàng mǎi le chēzi.
seem buy PRFV vehicle
'Lisi seems to have bought the car.'

c. Chēzi hǎoxiàng Lǐsì mǎi le.
vehicle seem buy PRFV
'The car seems Lisi to have bought.'

As we can see from these examples, either of the referential constituents, or neither, can appear before *hǎoxiàng* 'seem' in Mandarin, no matter what the semantic role.[4] As there is no restriction on the semantic roles which can be involved in the matrix-coding construction, there is no evidence from this construction for identifying a subject in Mandarin.[5] No construction has been found in Mandarin that has such a restricted neutralization of semantic roles for syntactic purposes.

Thus, we may conclude that not all languages have grammatical relations, in the sense of syntactic paradigmatic relations that are independent of semantic and pragmatic relations and play a role in the grammar of the language. Most languages do have grammatical relations in this sense, but that is not sufficient for grammatical relations like 'subject' to be considered universally valid.

6.2.2 Are grammatical relations the same across languages?

Most languages have grammatical relations, and therefore it is reasonable to ask whether the grammatical relations they have are the same as the grammatical relations found in other languages. In other words, in every language which has grammatical relations, is the notion of 'subject' the same as that found in all the other languages with grammatical relations? The same question can be asked with respect to direct object. We will begin by investigating subjects, and then turn our attention to (direct) objects.

6.2.2.1 Subjects

We will explore this question with respect to subjects by investigating two ergative languages of Australia, Warlpiri (Andrews 1985) and Dyirbal (Dixon 1972). In characterizing ergativity, it is useful to distinguish S, the single argument of an intransitive verb, A, the actor of a transitive verb, and U, the undergoer of a transitive verb.[6] Grammatical relations are constituted of combinations of the functions. In English, the grammatical relation 'subject' includes both S and A, while the grammatical relation 'direct object' encompasses only U. This pattern (subject = [S, A], object = [U]) defines an *accusative* pattern. The name comes from the case-marking pattern in languages like German and Russian in which S and A receive nominative case and U receives accusative case. This is illustrated in (6.30) from Russian.

(6.30) a. Ženščin-a idë-t.
woman-FsgNOM go-3sgPRES
'The woman [S] is going.'

b. Ženščin-a vidi-t čelovek-a.
woman-FsgNOM see-3sgPRES man-MsgACC
'The woman [A] sees the man [U].'

c. Čelovek-∅ vidi-t ženščin-u.
man-MsgNOM see-3sgPRES woman-FsgACC
'The man [A] sees the woman [U].'

In an ergative language, the grouping of functions is different, at least for some grammatical phenomena. With respect to case marking, S and U are assigned absolutive case, while A receives ergative case. Thus in an ergative language, case

A	[U]	[A]	U
S		S	
Accusative pattern		Ergative pattern	

Figure 6.2 Accusative vs. ergative patterns

marking treats S and U alike and treats A differently. This is illustrated in (6.31) from Dyirbal.

(6.31) a. Ba-la-n ḍugumbil-∅ bani-ɲu.
DEIC-ABS-II woman-ABS come-TNS
'The woman [S] is coming.'
b. Ba-la-n ḍugumbil-∅ ba-ŋgu-l yaɽa-ŋgu buɽa-n.
DEIC-ABS-II woman-ABS DEIC-ERG-I man-ERG see-TNS
'The man [A] sees the woman [U].'
c. Ba-ŋgu-n ḍugumbi-ɽu ba-yi yaɽa-∅ buɽa-n.
DEIC-ERG-II woman-ERG DEIC-ABS.I man-ABS see-TNS
'The woman [A] sees the man [U].'

This contrast can be represented as in figure 6.2. The boxes indicate the functions which receive special morphological or syntactic treatment. Warlpiri and Dyirbal are both ergative systems with respect to non-pronominal NP case marking.

Andrews compares grammatical relations in English and Warlpiri by looking at participial constructions like the one in (6.32) in which the dependent clause lacks tense and is missing one NP.

(6.32) The student watched TV while eating pizza.
NP V (NP) while V-ing (NP)

The missing NP in the participial clause is always interpreted as the subject in English. In other words, the NP that is missing here always corresponds to the subject of the corresponding full clause, just as in (6.12) and (6.13). Andrews shows that it makes no difference whether the missing NP is actor or undergoer, only that it is subject.

(6.33) a. The student watched TV while eating pizza.
b. The student looked out the window while being questioned by the police.

In both sentences, it is the subject that is missing; in (a) it is an actor, while in (b) it is an undergoer. He also gives an analogous Warlpiri construction.

(6.34) a. Ngaju-rlu ∅-rna yankirri-∅ pantu-rnu, ngapa-∅ nga-rninyja-kurra
1sg-ERG AUX-1sg emu-ABS spear-PAST water-ABS drink-INF-while
'I speared the emu while [it] was drinking water.'

b. Nyampuju wati-∅ ka-rla nyi-na papardi-nyanu-∅ karnta-ku,
this man-ABS PRES-DAT sit-NPST brother-KIN-ABS woman-DAT
wangka-nja-kurra-ku.
talk-INF-while-DAT
'This man is the big brother to the woman [who is] talking.'

Andrews states that the missing NP in the *-kurra* construction is always interpreted as the subject of the non-finite clause, and this is the case in both sentences in (6.34). This sounds very similar to the situation in English in (6.32) and (6.33), but there is as yet no evidence that the restriction cannot be stated in terms of actor rather than subject. The evidence can be found in the following pair of sentences.

(6.35) a. Ngaju-∅ ka-rna-ngku mari-jarri-mi nyuntu-ku, murumuru
1sg-ABS PRES-1sg-2sg grief-being-NPST 2sg-DAT sick
nguna-nyja-kurra-(ku)
lie-INF-while-(DAT)
'I feel sorry for you while [you are] lying sick.'

b. Karli-∅ ∅-rna nya-ngu pirli-ngirli wanti-nyja-kurra
boomerang-ABS AUX-1sg see-PAST stone-ELATIVE fall-INF-while
'I saw the boomerang falling from the stone.'

In (6.35a) the verb is *nguna* 'lie' as part of the expression 'lie sick', which we assume is non-volitional since people do not volitionally lie sick, and in (6.35b) it is *wanti* 'fall' which does not take an actor for its subject, unlike the intransitive verb *wangka* 'talk' in (6.34b). These two verbs do not take actors as their single argument, and yet it is possible for the single argument to be omitted in this construction. This shows that the relevant notion is the grammatical relation of subject, not the semantic relation of actor. Therefore, with intransitives, there are examples of a restricted neutralization of semantic roles for syntactic purposes in English and Warlpiri (since only the one direct NP, and not the oblique NPs, can be deleted in the relevant constructions), and this shows that there is an identifiable grammatical relation in both languages.

Is there an analogous neutralization in sentences with transitive verbs? We have already seen in (6.33) that there is one in English. But is this also true for Warlpiri? In (6.34) the omitted NP in the non-finite clause is an actor; in order for the neutralization in Warlpiri to be the same as that in English, it must be possible for the undergoer of a transitive verb to function as subject in this construction, as in (6.33b). If subject in Warlpiri is comparable to that in English, then a sentence like 'I saw the emu being speared by a man' should be grammatical, but as (6.36) shows, this is not the case.

(6.36) *Yankirri-∅ ∅-rna nya-ngu ngarka-ngku pantu-nyja-kurra.
emu-ABS AUX-1sg see-PAST man-ERG spear-INF-while
'I saw the emu$_1$ while the man speared ___$_1$.'

It is impossible for the undergoer of a transitive verb in Warlpiri to function as subject, and this is a very different situation from the one in English. There is no passive construction which can assign subject status to the undergoer. Thus the restricted neutralization in English involves *both intransitive and transitive verbs*, while the one in Warlpiri includes *intransitive verbs only*. This means that with a transitive verb in Warlpiri, the subject is always the actor, and the actor is always the subject. In English either actor or undergoer can be the subject of the transitive verb, but in Warlpiri, while actors and undergoers can both be the subjects of intransitives (which is not the case in Acehnese), only actors can be the subjects of transitives.

This means that there are different neutralizations of semantic roles in these two languages. There is a subject notion which is independent of semantics in these two languages, but it is not exactly the same subject notion. In Warlpiri, with any transitive verb, the subject is the actor. In English, however, with any transitive verb, which semantic argument will be the subject cannot be predicted in advance, for there is more than one possibility. Therefore, the notions of subject are similar but not identical. There are restricted neutralizations in both languages, but the neutralizations are different.

Thus, Andrews is correct in saying that there is a subject-like grammatical relation in English and Warlpiri which is not reducible to semantic roles, but it is not the case that this grammatical relation is the same in both languages; they are not identical because the restricted neutralization which defines them is not identical. One could say that both English and Warlpiri have an S-A subject, which is absolutely true. But it is also misleading, because in Warlpiri, in terms of the role notions, the transitive subject is always the actor, and vice versa. What does not exist in Warlpiri are derived intransitive verbs with non-actor subjects. Warlpiri does not have any voice alternation, so verbs have only active voice. The same is true in Enga, as we saw in (6.16). By contrast, either actor or undergoer can function as subject with a transitive verb in English. Virtually all of the languages with a restricted neutralization with transitive verbs have a voice construction.[7]

We now turn our attention to another language of Australia, Dyirbal, which also has an ergative system of case marking. Examples of simple clauses with transitive and intransitive verbs are given in (6.37); all are taken from Dixon (1972).

(6.37) a. Ba-la-n d̪ugumbil-∅ ba-ŋgu-l yaɽa-ŋgu buɽa-n.
DEIC-ABS-II woman-ABS DEIC-ERG-I man-ERG see-TNS
'The man saw the woman.'
b. Ba-yi yaɽa-∅ ba-ŋgu-n d̪ugumbi-ɽu buɽa-n.
DEIC-ABS.I man-ABS DEIC-ERG-II woman-ERG see-TNS
'The woman saw the man.'
c. Ba-la-n d̪ugumbil-∅ wayɲd̪i-n.
DEIC-ABS-II woman-ABS go.uphill-TNS
'The woman went uphill.'

Table 6.1 *Systems of grammatical relations*

	Traditional grammatical relations	*Ergative grammatical relations*
[S, A]	Subject	d.n.a.
[S, U]	d.n.a.	Absolutive
[U]	Object	d.n.a.
[A]	d.n.a.	Ergative

d. Ba-la-n ḍugumbil-∅ / ba-yi yaṛa-∅ baḍi-ɲu.
DEIC-ABS-II woman-ABS / DEIC-ABS.I man-ABS fall.down-TNS
'The woman/the man fell down.'

Word order in Dyirbal is grammatically unconstrained ('free'), as we saw in chapter 2. With respect to case marking, there is a restricted neutralization of the kind found in English and Warlpiri. In (6.37a, b), with a transitive verb, the absolutive NP is an undergoer and the ergative NP is an actor; in the sentences with intransitive verbs, the S NP is an actor in (6.37c) and an undergoer in (6.37d), and in both sentences it is marked with absolutive case. Thus the contrast between actor and undergoer is neutralized with intransitive verbs with regard to case marking, and therefore case marking is sensitive to a grammatical relation rather than to the semantic relations of actor and undergoer. Following Dryer (1986), we may refer to these grammatical relations as 'absolutive' and 'ergative'. See table 6.1.

Having looked at a coding property, we now turn to behavioral properties. The construction involving a missing NP in a dependent clause to be investigated in Dyirbal is the purposive construction, and an example of it with an intransitive verb is given in (6.38).

(6.38) Ba-yi yaṛa-∅ walma-ɲu wayɲḍil-i.
DEIC-ABS.I man-ABS get.up-TNS go.uphill-PURP
'The man got up to go uphill.'

The structure of this sentence can be represented as [NP_1 V [$\_\__1$ V+PURP]], with the single argument (S) of the intransitive verb in the dependent clause omitted. If S and U are treated alike in this construction, then when a transitive verb appears in the dependent clause, it should be the U (absolutive NP) rather than the A (ergative NP) which is omitted. This is the case, as (6.39) shows.

(6.39) a. Ba-yi yaṛa-∅ walma-ɲu baŋgun ḍugumbi-ṛu buṛal-i.
DEIC-ABS.I man-ABS get.up-TNS DEIC-ERG-II woman-ERG see-PURP
[NP_S-ABS_1 V [$\_\__1$ NP_A-ERG V+PURP]]
'The man got up to be seen by the woman.'
(lit.: 'the man_1 got up for the woman to see $\_\__1$')

b. *Ba-yi yaɽa-∅ walma-ɲu ba-la-n ɖugumbil-∅ buɽal-i.
DEIC-ABS.I man-ABS get.up-TNS DEIC-ABS-II woman-ABS see-PURP
*[NP_S-ABS$_1$ V [NP_U-ABS __$_1$ V+PURP]]
'The man got up to see the woman.'

The dependent clause in (6.39a) is (6.37b), and in (6.39b) it is (6.37a). It is the U (undergoer) NP which must be omitted, not the A (actor) NP, as the ungrammaticality of (6.39b) proves. Since the missing NP is an actor in (6.38) and an undergoer in (6.39a), this rules out a purely semantic account of these facts. Thus these syntactic facts support the conclusion drawn from case marking that there is a restricted neutralization of semantic roles for syntactic purposes in Dyirbal, and hence there are grammatical relations in its grammar.

The crucial question now arises: can the other macrorole argument of a transitive verb be omitted in this construction? In other words, is the restricted neutralization in Dyirbal like the one in Warlpiri and Enga or the one in English? The answer is that it is like the one in English, in that either macrorole argument of a transitive verb can function as subject. Sentence (6.40) shows another way of saying 'the woman saw the man' (cf. (6.37b)) using the antipassive construction first introduced in section 4.1.

(6.40) Ba-la-n ɖugumbil-∅ ba-gu-l yaɽa-gu buɽal-ŋa-ɲu.
DEIC-ABS-II woman-ABS DEIC-DAT-I man-DAT see-ANTI-TNS
'The woman saw the man.'

Here *balan ɖugumbil* 'woman' is in the absolutive, *bagul yaɽa-gu* 'man' is in the dative, the verb stem for 'see', *buɽal-* bears a suffix *-ŋay*, the antipassive marker, followed by the tense suffix. If one compares (6.40) with (6.37b), one can see that in (6.37b) the undergoer (U) is in the absolutive, and the actor (A) is in the ergative with a simple verb form. But in (6.40) the actor is in the absolutive, and the undergoer is in the dative with the *-ŋay* marker on the verb. This is the ergative language equivalent of a passive, but the difference is that in a passive, the undergoer appears as subject, while in an antipassive, the actor is no longer ergative (as in the simple active) and appears as subject of a derived intransitive verb and receives absolutive case. In other words, the NP that would have the marked case form (which is accusative in English and ergative in Dyirbal) receives the unmarked case and appears as subject, while the formerly unmarked element is not subject and appears as an oblique, which in English means being the object of the preposition *by* and in Dyirbal occurring in the dative (or instrumental) case. The actor is now the absolutive NP in this form, and its function can be characterized as 'derived S' (d-S), that is, the single NP of an intransitive verb derived via voice from a transitive verb. Consequently, it can be used in a purposive construction to allow omission of the actor and to express the meaning intended for (6.39b).

Table 6.2 *Restricted neutralization of semantic roles*

	Intransitive Vs	*Transitive Vs*	*Grammatical relations*	*'Subject'*
Acehnese	no	no	no	d.n.a.
English	yes	yes	yes	[S, A, d-S]
Warlpiri, Enga	yes	no	yes	[S, A]
Dyirbal	yes	yes	yes	[S, U, d-S]

(6.41) Ba-yi yaɽa-∅ walma-ɲu ba-gu-n ḑugumbil-gu buɽal-ŋay-gu.
DEIC-ABS.I man-ABS get.up-TNS DEIC-DAT-II woman-DAT see-ANTI-PURP
[NP$_S$-ABS$_1$ V [___$_{1d\text{-}S}$ NP$_U$-DAT V+ANTI+PURP]]
'The man got up to see the woman.'

This example shows that Dyirbal allows either macrorole argument of a transitive verb to function as subject and be omitted in the dependent clause. Thus, the restricted neutralization in Dyirbal parallels the one in English, not the one in Warlpiri and Enga. This situation is summarized in table 6.2. The crucial difference in behavior among the three languages with grammatical relations is in the second column. It is this 'no' under the transitive verb column for Warlpiri and Enga that is the significant distinguishing factor. The grammatical relation subject in Warlpiri and Enga is not comparable to that in English or Dyirbal, because the restricted neutralization defining it is different; that is, in English and Dyirbal the restricted neutralization includes [d-S], while the one in Warlpiri and Enga does not.

Table 6.2 could give the impression that grammatical relations in English and Dyirbal are very similar, and indeed there are certain important similarities. Both languages have a grammatical relation 'subject' and have a voice alternation (passive in English, antipassive in Dyirbal) which permits semantic arguments other than the default choice to be subject. However, the difference between them derives from the nature of the default subject choice: in English it is actor, whereas in Dyirbal it is undergoer. In terms of grammatical functions, subject in English groups S and A together and U is treated differently (direct object); subject in Dyirbal encompasses S and U, and A is treated distinctly. The basic opposition in English is between subject (S, A, d-S) and direct object (U), whereas in Dyirbal it is between what we have been calling 'absolutive' (S, U, d-S) and 'ergative' (A).

We have already seen in (6.38) and (6.40) that the pattern of coreference in the two languages is different. This can be seen clearly in (6.42).

(6.42) a. Ba-yi yaɽa-∅ ba-ŋgu-n ḑugumbi-ɽu balga-n *pro*
DEIC-ABS.I man-ABS DEIC-ERG-II woman-ERG hit-TNS
baḑi-ɲu.
fall.down-TNS
'The woman hit the man and ___ fell down.'

b. Ba-gu-l yaɽa-gu ba-la-n ɖugumbil-∅ balgal-ŋa-ɲu *pro*
DEIC-DAT-I man-DAT DEIC-ABS-II woman-ABS hit-ANTI-TNS
baɖi-ɲu.
fall.down-TNS
'The woman hit the man and ___ fell down.'

Who fell down? In (6.42a) 'man' is in the absolutive, 'woman' is in the ergative, the verb 'hit' is transitive and in the active voice and the verb 'fall down' is intransitive. In this sentence it is the man who fell down. In (6.42b), 'man' is in the dative, 'woman' is in the absolutive and 'hit' is in the antipassive form. In this sentence, the woman hit the man and she was the one who fell down. In both cases, the woman hit the man, but in (6.42a) it is he who falls down, while in (6.42b) it is she who falls down. In the English equivalent of (6.42a), with an active-voice transitive verb in the first clause, the interpretation will be the opposite of that in Dyirbal. For this construction each language must use its marked voice form in order to express the meaning signaled by the use of the unmarked voice form in the other.

It would be appropriate to compare Warlpiri and Enga with Dyirbal. There is clear evidence for a notion of subject which is distinct from any particular semantic relations in all three languages, and yet there are substantial differences between Enga and Warlpiri, on the one hand, and Dyirbal, on the other. To begin with, subject in Warlpiri and Enga groups S and A together, like English; syntactically, S and A are treated alike (6.33)–(6.35), and the U is treated differently. Despite the similar case-marking morphology in the two languages, there are different syntactic alignments, as subject in Dyirbal groups S and U together. Moreover, there is another profound difference: there is no voice construction in Warlpiri or Enga. Thus there is no way to say 'I saw the kangaroo being speared by the man' in Warlpiri, using this type of construction. Instead, one would have to say 'I saw the man spearing the kangaroo.' Similarly, there is no way to say something like 'The man wants to be kissed by the woman' in Enga; rather, it would be necessary to say 'The man wants the woman to kiss him'. In Dyirbal, however, this is no problem. Both 'The man got up to see the woman' and 'The man got up to be seen by the woman' are possible in Dyirbal, but not in Warlpiri or Enga. With a given construction in these languages, there is only one possible subject. If the verb is transitive, then only the A can function as the subject in that clause. There is no construction in which a U is allowed to function as the subject of a transitive verb, i.e. there is no d-S function. We saw this contrast in the comparison of Warlpiri and Enga with English, and it is exactly the same contrast here, because English and Dyirbal are parallel in this respect: English and Dyirbal allow multiple semantic arguments of a transitive verb to function as subject, whereas Warlpiri and Enga do not.

6.2.2.2 Objects

The status of 'direct object' in accusative languages might be thought to be uncontroversial, but this is not the case. Dryer (1986) argues that in many languages the actual syntactic and morphological behavior of the accusative NP is not (or is not always) that of the traditional direct object. In a prototypical monotransitive clause with an AGENT and a PATIENT, the PATIENT is marked (or behaves syntactically) like the traditional direct object, but in a ditransitive clause it is the RECIPIENT argument (the traditional indirect object) which takes on the marking and behavior that is associated with the monotransitive direct object, while the THEME argument in a ditransitive clause (what would have the direct object marking in a true accusative system) remains unmarked and syntactically secondary. Following are examples from Lahu (Tibeto-Burman, Myanmar [Burma] and northern Thailand; Matisoff 1973: 156–7) and Huichol (Uto-Aztecan, Mexico; Comrie 1982: 99, 108) (Dryer's examples (20) and (15) respectively):

(6.43) a. ŋà thàʔ tâ dɔ̂ʔ. — Lahu
1sg OBJ NEG.IMP hit
'Don't hit me.'
b. Liʔ chi ŋà thàʔ pîʔ.
book that 1sg OBJ give
'Give me that book.'

(6.44) a. Uukaraawiciizi tɨɨri me-wa-zeiya. — Huichol
women children 3pl-3pl-see
'The women see the children.'
b. Nee uuki uukari ne-wa-puuzeiyastìa.
1sg girls man 1sg-3pl-show
'I showed the man to the girls.'

In the simple transitive (6.43a) the postposition *thàʔ* follows the THEME, while in the ditransitive (6.43b) the same form follows the RECIPIENT, and the THEME is unmarked. In the Huichol examples we are looking at the verb agreement, and we can see that in the monotransitive (6.44a) the agreement is with the THEME, while in (6.44b) the agreement is with the plural RECIPIENT, not with the THEME.

Dryer argues that this pattern of marking/behavior should be considered a separate set of grammatical relations distinct from subject and object. He calls the PATIENT/RECIPIENT role the 'primary object' (PO), and the PATIENT or THEME of a ditransitive (in that system) a 'secondary object' (SO). From this point of view, given a pair of corresponding English sentences such as in (6.45), (6.45b) would be taken as the basic form, with the core arguments both unmarked, rather than (6.45a), with the traditional indirect object being marked with a preposition.

(6.45) a. Mary gave a book to John.
b. Mary gave John a book.

Dryer calls the rule that relates these two sentences 'antidative', as it is the opposite of the traditional 'dative' rule. The antidative construction, as in (6.45a), is seen as parallel to the passive construction, as both constructions are seen as involving a difference in valence. That is, in the unmarked ditransitive clause, as in (6.45b), there are three direct core arguments (i.e. non-preposition-marked NPs), while in the passive (*John was given a book by Mary*) and antidative (example (6.45a)) there are only two direct core arguments, the RECIPIENT in the antidative and the actor in the passive being the objects of prepositions.

Dryer sees the PO/SO distinction as a grammatical relation on a par with subject, direct object and other grammatical relations, and so the nature of a language (or more accurately, a construction) as of the PO type is independent of whether it is also of the ergative or accusative type, therefore a language (construction) can be ergative and PO, ergative and DO, accusative and PO, or accusative and DO. Dryer argues that the function of PO marking is to distinguish a more topical object from a less topical object, 'thus the PO/SO distinction can be viewed as a grammaticalization of secondary topic vs. non-topic' (841). This parallels the subject/object distinction, which 'can be viewed as the grammaticalization of "more topical" vs. "less topical"' (841).

LaPolla (1992; see also LaPolla 1994) shows the prevalence of the PO type of marking among Tibeto-Burman languages, but argues that it does not constitute a grammatical relation in all languages that manifest it, as it has no syntactic consequences such as the antidative rule. He also argues that the development of the marking in the Tibeto-Burman languages he examined is based on a semantic actor vs. non-actor contrast, not on a pragmatic topical vs. non-topical object contrast. LaPolla argues that assuming the marking to be motivated by the need to distinguish topical from non-topical objects would not explain its use in monotransitive clauses, or why in many languages it can be used on question words and focal NPs, that is, on non-topical noun phrases, as in the following example from Chepang (Kiranti; Nepal; Caughley 1982: 248; *taŋʔ* functions to mark salient new information, and here follows the PO marker *kay*):

(6.46) ʔohaŋsykoʔ ʔal-taŋʔ-ʔaka-c lw ʔoʔ-nis ʔapa-caʔ-kay-taŋʔ
SEQ go-IIF-PAST-dl EXCL that-dl father-KIN-GOAL-IIF
krus-ʔa-tha-c.
meet-PAST-GOAL-dl
'Then they went and they met the father and child.'

In Chepang the PO marking 'has no necessary connection with definiteness' (Caughley 1982: 70), a corollary of topicality. PO marking can only indirectly be seen as related to the topicality and 'object' status of the noun phrase, as it is the animacy or overall saliency of the NP that is important to the use of this marking. In most of the languages discussed by LaPolla, the PO marking appears only with animate or human participants, and only when necessary for disambiguation, for example where the word order differs from the actor–recipient–theme order usual for those languages. That is, in most cases only non-actor NPs that could possibly be misconstrued as actors are marked as POs.[8] LaPolla's view, then, is that, at least in the Tibeto-Burman languages he discusses, ergative-marking and PO-marking systems are not as independent as assumed by Dryer, as both follow from the same motivation: the disambiguation of semantic role. For this reason LaPolla adopts the term 'anti-ergative' from Comrie (1975, 1978) for this type of marking. One consequence of this view is that while both the dative/antidative patterns and PO (anti-ergative) marking are influenced by certain pragmatic factors such as identifiability and the inherent lexical content of the NPs involved, they do not necessarily have the same motivations, and so should be considered separately in discussions of these phenomena.

6.2.3 Summary

The cross-linguistic diversity of grammatical relations appears to be so great that it is extremely problematic to assume that the traditional Indo-European-based notions of 'subject' and 'object' are features of the grammars of all languages. In Acehnese there does not seem to be any evidence that there is a restricted neutralization of semantic roles for syntactic purposes. Constructions are restricted to actors, or they are restricted to undergoers, or they are open to any semantic argument of the verb. In this last case, there is a neutralization, but not a restricted one. Thus the evidence from Acehnese suggests strongly that grammatical relations are not universal in the sense that they play a role in the grammar of every language. The data from Mandarin support this conclusion, albeit in a different way; Acehnese has both restrictions without neutralizations and neutralizations without restrictions, while Mandarin has only the latter. It might be suggested that in Acehnese, for example, actor and undergoer serve as the grammatical relations. On this view, grammatical relations are universal but may differ from language to language. The problem with this is that it uses the term 'grammatical relation' in a very different sense from the way it has been used in this chapter. No longer does it refer to restricted neutralizations of semantic roles for syntactic purposes; rather it refers to *any* syntagmatic relation that plays a role in grammar. In this discussion we have restricted the term 'grammatical relation' to *syntactic* relations only and rigorously distinguished them from semantic roles. This is consistent with the way the term has been used in theoretical discussions over the past three decades.

Even when we look at languages in which grammatical (syntactic) relations can be clearly motivated in terms of restricted neutralizations, we find that the neutralizations are not the same across languages. For instance, there is no neutralization of the actor and undergoer with a transitive verb in Warlpiri and Enga; there is neutralization of actor and undergoer only with intransitive verbs, whereas in English and Dyirbal there is neutralization of actor and undergoer with both transitive and intransitive verbs. Yet the neutralizations in these two languages are not the same, either. Even the traditional notion of direct object in accusative languages, long thought to be unproblematic, may in fact not be applicable to the 'primary object' languages discussed by Dryer. Thus, it appears that the traditional, Indo-European-based notions of 'subject' and 'direct object' will not stand up to the criterion of typological adequacy introduced in chapter 1, and we need to develop a rather different approach to dealing with grammatical relations cross-linguistically.

6.3 A theory of grammatical relations

In this section we will present an alternative view of grammatical relations. This view is unlike a very common view of grammatical relations, in that it does not recognize the three traditional grammatical relations subject, direct object and indirect object as primitive notions. It does not assume that grammatical relations must be manifested in the same way in each of the languages that has them, and, moreover, it is not claimed that all languages will have grammatical relations. Hence Acehnese and Mandarin are not problematic for this theory.

As discussed above, grammatical relations (syntactic relations) exist in a language only where the behavioral patterns of a language give evidence of a syntactic relation independent of semantic and pragmatic relations; that is, only where the behavior patterns are not reducible to semantic or pragmatic relations can we say there is evidence of syntactic relations. If there exists at least one construction in the language in which there is a restriction on the noun-phrase types functioning in the construction which involves a neutralization of semantic or pragmatic relations for syntactic purposes, then the language has grammatical relations. Thus, grammatical relations exist only where there is a *restricted neutralization* of semantic or pragmatic relations for syntactic purposes.

We have looked at two distinct types of morphosyntactic phenomena in this context. The first is core-internal phenomena like verb agreement or cross-reference, and the second is complex constructions such as the 'want' constructions in English and Enga and the matrix-coding construction in English. With respect to verb agreement, we investigated what the verb agrees with; is it a syntactic notion like subject or a semantic notion like actor? Another way of putting this is, what is the **controller** of verb agreement or cross-reference? In English and Enga, the controller is syntactic (because of the restricted neutralization), whereas in Acehnese it is semantic (because of the restriction without neutralization).

With regard to complex constructions we asked a different question: which argument in the linked or dependent core is omitted or occurs in the matrix core? In the English matrix-coding construction in (6.13), there is a restricted neutralization of the semantic arguments of the dependent core with respect to the possibility of occurrence in the matrix core. In the English *want* construction in (6.12) and its Enga equivalent in (6.16), there is a restricted neutralization with respect to which argument of the dependent core can be omitted. In the Dyirbal purposive construction in (6.39) and the Warlpiri *-kurra* construction in (6.34)–(6.35), there is a restricted neutralization with respect to which NP can be omitted in the linked core. In the Malagasy relative clauses in (6.26)–(6.27) there is a restricted neutralization as to which arguments can function as the head of the relative clause. This syntactic argument bears the privileged grammatical function in the construction, and we refer to it as the **pivot** of the construction.[9] Since it is defined by a restricted neutralization of semantic roles for syntactic purposes, it is a **syntactic pivot**. Accordingly, the omitted argument in the 'want' constructions in (6.12) in English and (6.16) in Enga is the syntactic pivot of the construction, as are the omitted arguments in the Dyirbal purposive construction in (6.39) and Warlpiri *-kurra* construction in (6.34)–(6.35). Similarly, the matrix-coded NP in the English matrix-coding construction in (6.13) is the syntactic pivot of the construction, and the head noun of a Malagasy relative clause in (6.26)–(6.27) must be the syntactic pivot in the relative clause. Because there are no restricted neutralizations in the comparable constructions in Acehnese or Mandarin, these constructions do not have syntactic pivots. Acehnese and Mandarin differ from each other in an important way: as noted earlier, most complex constructions in Acehnese have restrictions but no neutralizations, e.g. actors-only as in (6.21) or undergoers-only as in (6.22), whereas the Mandarin constructions discussed have neutralizations but no restrictions. Hence in the Acehnese constructions in (6.21) and (6.22) there is a privileged function, but it is semantic rather than syntactic. We will, therefore, refer to the actor in (6.21) and the undergoer in (6.22) as the **semantic pivot** of each of these constructions, just as they are the semantic controllers of cross-reference in (6.17)–(6.20). Constructions like English relativization in (6.14), Acehnese matrix coding in (6.23), and Mandarin relativization in (6.28) and matrix coding in (6.29) are pivotless, because none of them involves restrictions, only neutralizations. Thus, in order for a construction to have a pivot, there must be a restriction imposed on the semantic arguments that can participate in it. If the restriction is purely semantic, as in Acehnese, then the pivot is a semantic pivot. If, on the other hand, the restriction also involves a neutralization of semantic roles, as in the constructions in English, Dyirbal, Enga, Malagasy and Warlpiri, then the pivot is a syntactic pivot. Pivots are primarily a feature only of complex constructions, in particular constructions involving multiple cores or clauses; these are the topic of chapter 8.

A very important feature of the concepts of controller and pivot is that they exist only with reference to specific morphosyntactic phenomena, and each grammatical phenomenon may define one controller and /or one pivot. If a language has agreement, then there will be a controller for agreement. If there is a restricted neutralization associated with agreement, then the controller will be a syntactic controller. If there is a restriction but no neutralization, then the controller will be a semantic controller. Icelandic, for example, has both finite verb agreement and passive participle/predicate adjective agreement, and there are different controllers for each type of agreement. The controller for finite verb agreement is a syntactic controller, while the controller for passive participle/predicate adjective agreement is a semantic controller, as we will see in chapter 7. Pivots are construction-specific; there is a pivot for the matrix-coding construction in English, one for the purposive construction in Dyirbal, one for the 'want' construction in Enga, one for the *-kurra* construction in Warlpiri, and one for the 'possessor-raising' construction in Acehnese (see table 6.3 below). As we have seen, the first four are all syntactic pivots, while the last one is a semantic pivot. A complex construction may define both a controller and a pivot; this can be seen in the Dyirbal purposive and coordinate constructions in (6.38)–(6.42). In the simplest example, (6.38), there are two cores with intransitive verbs, with the second one marked with the purposive suffix in place of the tense suffix. The single argument of the verb bearing the purposive suffix is missing; this is the pivot of the construction. It must be interpreted as being the same as one of the core arguments in the first core; this argument is the controller. Since there is only a single core argument, it must be the controller. Thus the purposive construction in Dyirbal defines both a controller and a pivot. The same is true with respect to the coordinate construction in (6.42). The two share the same constraints on which is the controller and which is the pivot; if one replaces the purposive suffix by a tense suffix, then the constructions are coordinate rather than purposive. Compare (6.38), repeated in (6.47a) with its coordinate counterpart in (b).

(6.47) a. Ba-yi yaɽa-∅ walma-ɲu wayɲḑil-i.
DEIC-ABS.I man-ABS get.up-TNS go.uphill-PURP
'The man got up to go uphill.'

b. Ba-yi yaɽa-∅ walma-ɲu wayɲḑi-n.
DEIC-ABS.I man-ABS get.up-TNS go.uphill-TNS
'The man got up and went uphill.'

We will illustrate the syntactic nature of the controller and pivot with the coordinate (conjunction reduction) construction. The sentence in (6.47b) tells us very little, since the verbs are both intransitive and therefore there is only one candidate for controller and pivot. The syntactic nature of the controller is shown in (6.42), repeated below; the pivot is represented by *pro*.

(6.48) a. Ba-yi yaɽa-∅ ba-ŋgu-n ḑugumbi-ɽu balga-n *pro*
DEIC-ABS.I man-ABS DEIC-ERG-II woman-ERG hit-TNS
baḑi-ɲu.
fall.down-TNS
'The woman hit the man and ___ fell down.'

b. Ba-gu-l yaɽa-gu ba-la-n ḑugumbil-∅ balgal-ŋa-ɲu
DEIC-DAT-I man-DAT DEIC-ABS-II woman-ABS hit-ANTI-TNS
pro baḑi-ɲu.
fall.down-TNS
'The woman hit the man and ___ fell down.'

As discussed earlier, the controller in the first clause is the absolutive NP; accordingly, *bayi yaɽa* 'the man', the undergoer, is the controller in (a), while *balan ḍugumbil* 'the woman', the actor, is the controller in (b), in which the antipassive construction has been used to allow the actor to appear as the absolutive NP. Since either the actor or the undergoer with a transitive verb, if it is the absolutive NP, can be the controller, we have a restricted neutralization, and accordingly the controller is a syntactic, not a semantic, controller. The same variation can be seen in the choice of pivot in this construction, as (6.49) shows.

(6.49) a. Ba-yi yaɽa-Ø walma-ɲu *pro* baŋgun ḍugumbi-ɽu buɽa-n.
DEIC-ABS.I man-ABS get.up-TNS DEIC-ERG-II woman-ERG see-TNS
'The man got up and was seen by the woman.'
(Lit.: 'the man$_1$ got up and the woman saw ___$_1$')

b. Ba-yi yaɽa-Ø walma-ɲu *pro* ba-gu-n ḍugumbil-gu
DEIC-ABS.I man-ABS get.up-TNS DEIC-DAT-II woman-DAT
buɽal-ŋay-ɲu.
see-ANTI-TNS
'The man got up and saw the woman.'

In this pair of sentences, the controller is the single argument of the intransitive verb in the first clause, and the missing NP in the second clause, the pivot, is always the NP that would appear in the absolutive case if the second clause were an independent main clause. The omitted NP can be the undergoer, as in (a), or the actor, as in (b), in which again the antipassive construction is used. Since either the actor or the undergoer with a transitive verb can be the pivot, we have a restricted neutralization, and accordingly the pivot is a syntactic pivot. It is quite possible for the controller and the pivot in a complex construction to be of different types; in the English *want* construction in (6.12), the controller is a semantic controller (see section 9.1.3.1.1), while the pivot is a syntactic pivot.

Neither the concept of controller nor that of pivot is the same as the notion of subject in traditional grammar. Indeed, the prototypical subject subsumes both of them. In the English *want* construction in (6.12), for example, the subject of the matrix core is the controller and the subject of the linked or dependent core is the pivot. This statement blurs an important distinction which we just made: the controller in this construction is semantic in nature, while the pivot is syntactic. The traditional notion of subject does not make this distinction. Moreover, as we said above, controller and pivot are *construction-specific*. The usual notion of subject in syntactic theory, on the other hand, is not construction-specific but rather is a feature of the grammatical system as a whole. For this reason one does not talk about 'the subject of finite verb agreement' or 'the subject of the matrix-coding construction', since subject is not a construction-specific notion; rather, one can talk about 'subject in English' or 'subject in Malagasy', etc. Conversely, one does not speak of, for example, 'the pivot of English' or 'the controller of English', as there is no such concept. We can only speak in terms of the controllers and pivots of specific phenomena or constructions, such as 'the controller of finite verb agreement' and 'the pivot of the matrix-coding construction' in English.

What, then, is the 'subject' in traditional grammar? It first of all subsumes both controllers and pivots, and second of all, it assumes that the controller and/or pivot of each of the major grammatical phenomena in the language (or at least a majority of them) is the same. In terms of English this would mean that the controller and pivot of most major grammatical phenomena would be the actor of an active-voice transitive verb, the undergoer of a passive-voice transitive verb, and the single argument of an intransitive verb, i.e. [S, A, d-S] in terms of table 6.2. There are two immediate problems with the traditional notion of subject, in terms of this discussion. First, it is very important to distinguish syntactic controllers from semantic controllers and syntactic pivots from semantic pivots, both cross-linguistically and within individual languages, and the traditional notion of subject does not make this distinction. Second, it crucially assumes that languages are consistent in their choice of syntactic controller and pivot across constructions. But this, too, is problematic, as we shall see; there are languages which do not use the same controllers and pivots for all of their major grammatical phenomena, and even the alleged consistency of English turns out to be somewhat illusory, upon closer inspection. These problems are piled on top of the problems we raised for traditional grammatical relations in our discussion in section 6.2. We may summarize this discussion in table 6.3.[10] It is

Table 6.3 *Controllers and pivots*

Grammatical phenomenon	*Controller or pivot*	*Syntactic or semantic*	*Roles*
Acehnese cross-reference	Controller	Semantic	[A], [U]
Acehnese 'want' construction	Both	Controller = semantic	[A]
		Pivot = semantic	[A]
Acehnese 'possessor raising'	Pivot	Semantic	[U]
Dyirbal purposive construction	Both	Both syntactic	[S, U, d-S]
Dyirbal coordinate construction	Both	Both syntactic	[S, U, d-S]
Enga cross-reference	Controller	Syntactic	[S, A]
Enga 'want' construction	Both	Controller = semantic	[A]
		Pivot = syntactic	[S, A]
English verb agreement	Controller	Syntactic	[S, A, d-S]
English matrix-coding construction	Pivot	Syntactic	[S, A, d-S]
English *want* construction	Both	Controller = semantic	[A]
		Pivot = syntactic	[S, A, d-S]
Malagasy relativization	Pivot	Syntactic	[S, A, d-S]
Warlpiri -*kurra* construction	Pivot	Syntactic	[S, A]

important to realize that all of these phenomena (except 'possessor raising') have been attributed traditionally to subjects, and no candidate for a universally valid notion of subject emerges from this table.

The problem deciding what a subject is is compounded by the fact that more than one construction can cooccur in a single clause, and each of the constituent constructions may have a distinct controller or pivot. Consider the following examples from Sama, a syntactically ergative language of the Philippines (Walton 1986).

(6.50) a. B'lli d'nda daing ma di-na.
buy woman fish for REFL-3sg
'The woman bought the fish for herself.'
b. N-b'lli[11] d'nda daing ma di-na.
ANTI-buy woman fish for REFL-3sg
'The woman bought fish for herself.'
c. daing b'lli d'nda ma di-na
fish buy woman for REFL-3sg
'the fish that the woman bought for herself'
d. d'nda N-b'lli daing ma di-na
woman ANTI-buy fish for REFL-3sg
'the woman who bought fish for herself'
d′. d'nda b'lli daing ma di-na
woman buy fish for REFL-3sg
*'the woman who bought the fish for herself'
OK: 'the woman who the fish bought for itself'

Example (6.50a) is an active-voice form, while (b) is an antipassive form. As in Malagasy, the head of the relative clause must function as pivot within the relative clause, and therefore the only relative clause that can be formed from (a) is (c), with the head interpreted as the undergoer of the relative clause. Similarly, the only relative clause that can be formed from (b) is (d), in which the head noun is interpreted as the actor of the relative clause. If we combine the head noun *d'nda* 'woman' with an active-voice verb in the relative clause, as in (d′), the result is grammatical but nonsensical. Thus, with respect to the relative clause construction, the pivot is the undergoer with an active-voice verb in the relative clause and the actor with an antipassive voice verb. This is the same pattern we saw in the Dyirbal constructions above. Hence there is a restricted neutralization, and accordingly the pivot is a syntactic pivot. With respect to the reflexive construction, however, the controller is constant: it is the actor which controls or binds the reflexive anaphor, regardless of whether the verb is active or antipassive voice. Hence in (6.50c) there is a semantic controller of reflexivization (*d'nda* 'woman') and a syntactic pivot for relativization (*daing* 'fish'). In traditional terms, which NP is the subject of the sentence? This situation of having more than one possible subject in a clause is a well-known feature of Philippine languages (see Schachter 1976), and it highlights the difference between controllers and pivots, on the one hand, and subjects, on the other. There can be only one subject in a sentence, but these Sama examples in (c) and (d) contain two possible subjects, one for each of the two constructions in them: a syntactic pivot for relativization and a semantic controller for reflexivization.

In some of the more recent literature on grammatical relations, the concept of prototype categories has been brought to bear on the definition of subject (e.g. Bates and MacWhinney 1982, Lakoff 1987). The assumption is that like the macroroles actor and undergoer, which have the prototypes AGENT and PATIENT, respectively, and can each vary in terms of what other roles can be subsumed within them, subject can also be treated as a prototype category, with actor–topic being the prototype subject. Non-prototypical subjects would be, for example, the dummy subjects of English, or focal subjects, as in example (6.11). Languages then would be said to differ as to the degree to which, and in what way, subjects can stray from the prototype. These works differ as to whether they assume the prototype can *define* the grammatical relation, or whether it simply helps us understand the relative markedness of different semantic *values* for the relation. It seems clear that only the latter assumption is valid. The prototype approach can be useful for understanding the language-specific motivation behind the *selection* of a particular participant to be pivot in a particular clause or construction, but it cannot define the notions of pivot or controller (or that of subject). Syntactic controllers and pivots are grammatical phenomena. Prototype theory (as it applies to grammatical analysis) involves semantic universals, such as lexical categories (e.g. color terms) and semantic relation categories (e.g. transitivity). Prototypes are applicable to all languages. Syntactic pivot as a grammatical relation does not reflect any semantic prototype, unlike actor and undergoer, but is simply the grammaticalization of usage patterns that commonly have the actor and topic, or undergoer and topic, being represented by the same NP.

In our initial discussion of restricted neutralizations in section 6.2.1, we noted that the restricted neutralizations defining the syntactic pivots in the 'want' constructions in Enga and English are not identical; as tables 6.2 and 6.3 show, the neutralization in Enga is [S, A], while the neutralization in English is [S, A, d-S]. The same [S, A] pivot is found in the Warlpiri *-kurra* construction. In our discussion of subjects in section 6.2.2.1, we pointed out the implications of this contrast for the claim that Warlpiri and English or Enga and English have basically the same notion of subject (e.g. Anderson 1976, Li and Lang 1979). They do not, even though they are similar in many respects. The difference between the two types of restrictive neutralization, as table 6.2 makes clear, is that in the English-type there is a neutralization of actor and undergoer with both intransitive and transitive verbs, whereas in the Warlpiri/Enga-type, there is a neutralization of actor and undergoer only with intransitive verbs. There is a very important consequence of this second type of

Table 6.4 *Restricted neutralizations and pivot types*

Language	*Restricted neutralization*	*Pivot type*
Acehnese	None	Semantic pivot
Dyirbal	[S, U, d-S]	Variable syntactic pivot
Enga	[S, A]	Invariable syntactic pivot
English	[S, A, d-S]	Variable syntactic pivot
Malagasy	[S, A, d-S]	Variable syntactic pivot
Sama	[S, U, d-S]	Variable syntactic pivot
Warlpiri	[S, A]	Invariable syntactic pivot

neutralization: there is never any choice in the selection of the semantic argument to function as syntactic controller or pivot. Intransitive verbs have only a single direct argument, and it will always be the privileged core argument, when the controller or pivot is syntactic. With a transitive verb, on the other hand, because there is no restricted neutralization with them, there is always only one choice, namely the actor. Hence with transitive verbs the actor will always be the syntactic controller or syntactic pivot. We pointed this out explicitly in our discussion of Warlpiri and Enga in the earlier sections. In order to distinguish this type of restricted neutralization from the type found in Dyirbal, English, Sama and Malagasy, we will refer to the Warlpiri/Enga-type [S, A] pivots and controllers as **invariable syntactic pivots** and **invariable syntactic controllers**. Because there is in principle a choice of actor or undergoer to function as pivot or controller with transitive verbs in Dyirbal, English, Sama and Malagasy, we will refer to the pivots and controllers defined by the [S, A, d-S] and [S, U, d-S] neutralizations as **variable syntactic pivots** and **variable syntactic controllers**. Looking just at pivots for the moment, we may summarize the facts from all of the languages we have looked at in table 6.4. Syntactic controllers defined by the same restricted neutralizations would likewise be variable or invariable, just like the syntactic pivots in the table.

In our brief introductory discussion of linking in section 4.5, we stated that there are subject-selection principles which govern the selection of the subject with multi-argument verbs. In terms of our discussion in this chapter, we would need to rephrase this in terms of principles governing the selection of syntactic controllers and pivots with multi-argument verbs. Syntactic controllers and pivots are the privileged syntactic arguments in grammatical constructions, and henceforth when we mean both of them, we will use **privileged syntactic arguments** as a cover term for them. In section 4.5 we reinterpreted the Actor–Undergoer Hierarchy in figure 4.2 as a unidirectional hierarchy with 'argument of DO' (i.e. AGENT) as the highest-ranked argument and 'argument of **pred′** (x)' (i.e. PATIENT) as the lowest-ranked argument; the hierarchy in (4.51) is repeated in (6.51).

(6.51) *Privileged syntactic argument selection hierarchy*
arg. of DO > 1sg arg. of **do′** > 1st arg. of **pred′** (x, y) > 2nd arg. of **pred′** (x, y) > arg. of **pred′** (x)

If a verb takes actor and undergoer arguments, the actor will outrank the undergoer in terms of this hierarchy, since the actor will always code a higher argument than the undergoer, following the Actor–Undergoer Hierarchy. The basic selection principles for syntactically accusative constructions and syntactically ergative constructions are given in (6.52).

(6.52) *Privileged syntactic argument selection principles*
a. Syntactically accusative constructions: highest-ranking macrorole is default choice.
b. Syntactically ergative constructions: lowest-ranking macrorole is default choice.

Since we are talking about syntactic controllers and pivots here, we must restrict the principles to constructions only. If, for example, all of the grammatical constructions in a language followed an accusative pattern, then it would be appropriate to describe the language as syntactically accusative. We could make the same generalization for a language in which the majority of the constructions followed an ergative pattern.

We have already seen numerous examples of how the principles in (6.52) apply in constructions with variable syntactic controllers or pivots. The key to the variable pivots is the voice oppositions in the language. As we have seen repeatedly, in constructions with accusative syntactic pivots, it is passive constructions that allow a lower-ranking argument in terms of (6.51) to function as controller or pivot, e.g. (6.8)–(6.10) for English verb agreement (controller) and (6.26)–(6.27) for Malagasy relativization (pivot). Since the default choice in these constructions is actor, use of the passive makes it possible for the undergoer of a transitive verb to serve as the controller of verb agreement (English) or as the pivot for relativization (Malagasy). Similarly, in constructions with ergative syntactic pivots, e.g. Sama relativization in (6.50) or the Dyirbal purposive construction in (6.39)–(6.42), it is the antipassive construction which permits a higher-ranking argument in terms of (6.51) to function as pivot; that is, it allows the actor to function as syntactic pivot.

An excellent example of the role of voice constructions in variable syntactic pivots and of the reason for the necessity of talking in terms of constructions, rather than languages as a whole, is given by Tzutujil, a Mayan language. We are interested in two constructions; one is the focusing construction, in which an NP is in the precore slot and has marked narrow focus, and the second is the equivalent of the Dyirbal coordinate construction. The focusing construction is illustrated in (6.53), from Dayley (1981, 1985); it has the meaning of an *it*-cleft in English.

(6.53) a. X-Ø-uu-ch'ey jar aachi jar iixoq.
PAST-3ABS-3ERG-hit CL man CL woman
'The woman hit the man.'
b. Jar aachi x-Ø-uu-ch'ey jar iixoq.
CL man PAST-3ABS-3ERG-hit CL woman
'It was the man who the woman hit.' (*'It was the man who hit the woman.')
c. Jar iixoq x-Ø-ch'ey-ow-i jar aarchi.
CL woman PAST-3ABS-hit-ANTI-SUFF CL man
'It was the woman who hit the man.' (*'It was the woman who the man hit.')

The basic pattern with a transitive verb is given in (a); the actor is cross-referenced by the ergative marker on the verb, while the undergoer is cross-referenced by the absolutive affix. When an NP appears with narrow focus in the precore slot and the verb is in active voice, as in (b), then the focal NP in the precore slot must be interpreted as the undergoer, not as the actor. In order to have a focal actor occur in the precore slot, it is necessary to use an antipassive construction, as in (c). The single arguments of intransitive verbs can occur in the precore slot without any special marking, as one would expect, and therefore the restricted neutralization in this construction is [S, U, d-S], and it defines an ergative variable syntactic pivot. When we look at the coordinate construction, as in the text excerpt from Butler and Peck (1980) in (6.54), a very different pattern emerges. The story is about a thief; the elements referring to him are subscripted in both the Tzutujil original and in the English gloss and translation.

(6.54) a. Toq š-Ø$_1$-urqax-i Ø-Ø$_1$-koʔx-(i) pa čeʔ.
when PRFV-3ABS$_1$-arrive-SUFF PRFV-3ABS$_1$-put.PASS-(SUFF) in jail
'When he$_1$ arrived, he$_1$ was put in jail.'
b. Xa k'a či r-kab q'ix Ø-Ø$_1$-q'eʔt-(i) cix
CL next on 3ERG-second day PRFV-3ABS$_1$-cut.PASS-(SUFF) word
t-r-ix.
to-3ERG-back
'On the next day, he$_1$ was judged.'
c. In š-Ø-u$_1$-yaʔ t-r-ix či ni arxaʔ$_1$ wïʔ
and PRFV-3ABS-3ERG$_1$-give to-3ERG-back that INTS 3sg$_1$ INTS
n-Ø$_1$-alaq'a-n-i xa ẍal.
PRFV-3ABS$_1$-steal-ANTI-SUFF CL corn
'And he$_1$ admitted that he$_1$ was indeed the one$_1$ who was stealing the corn.'
d. Bueno, arxaʔ$_1$ Ø-Ø-lasa-š-i r$_1$-multa.
well 3sg$_1$ PRFV-3ABS-declare-PASS-SUFF 3ERG$_1$-fine.
'Well, he$_1$ was fined.' (lit.: 'well, he$_1$, his$_1$ fine was declared.')

e. K'ak'arïʔ pa xuu taq'aq'ix Ø-Ø-čomi-š-i xa xäl pa
then on one afternoon PRFV-3ABS-arrange-PASS-SUFF CL corn in
yaʔl Ø-$Ø_1$-r-izaq-i xa r-alaq'om_1.
net.bag PRFV-3ABS-3ERG_1-carry-SUFF CL 3ERG-$thief_1$
'Then, one afternoon, the corn was arranged in a net bag, and the $thief_1$ carried it.'

f. K'ak'arïʔ Ø-$Ø_1$-lasa-š-i pa taq bey
then PRFV-3ABS_1-take.out-PASS-SUFF in CL street
Ø-r_1-ixqa-n xa xäl.
3ABS-3ERG_1-carry-PRFV CL corn
'Then he_1 was taken out into the street, carrying the corn [to show he was a thief].'

If we represent this text in terms of the syntactic function of the primary topical participant, the thief, in each sentence, we get the following pattern.

(6.55) a. [S], [d-S (passive)]
b. [d-S (passive)]
c. [A], [d-S (antipassive)]
d. [d-S (passive)] (literally, LDP NP and possessor of d-S NP)
e. . . . , [A]
f. [d-S (passive)], [A]

When we generalize across the text, we get a [S, A, d-S] pattern, which is that of an accusative variable syntactic pivot. Thus in one language, Tzutujil, we find both types of variable syntactic pivots in different constructions. Note, by the way, that the restricted neutralization for cross-reference in these examples is [S, U, d-S]; the absolutive codes this pattern, and the ergative codes the [A], as well as possessors. There is thus an ergative variable syntactic controller for cross-reference in Tzutujil. This is why it is necessary to talk about construction-specific pivots and controllers rather than system-wide grammatical relations like subject. What is the subject in Tzutujil? There is no simple answer to this question, even if it could be given a meaningful answer at all. The situation is even more complex in Jakaltek, as argued in Van Valin (1981) based on data from Craig (1977); five different restricted neutralization patterns are realized in seven grammatical constructions in this language; the facts are summarized in table 6.5. The Tzutujil data in (6.53) and (6.54) correspond to (6) and (7) in this table. In our discussion of the traditional notion of subject, it was pointed out that it assumed great consistency on the part of grammatical systems, i.e. that all, or at the very least most, of the major grammatical constructions in the language would have the same restricted neutralization. While it is certainly true that there are many languages which exhibit the expected consistency, there are also languages like Jakaltek which do not. It seems clear that the notion of 'the subject in Jakaltek' is not a meaningful concept.

Table 6.5 *Syntactic pivots in Jakaltek*

Construction	*Pivot*
1 'Subject' [S, A]-triggered equi-NP-deletion	[S] only
2 'Object' [U]-triggered equi-NP-deletion	[S, d-S (passive)] only
3 Promotion ('subject' copying with verbs like *begin*)	Dialect 1: [S] only Dialect 2: [S, d-S (both)] only
4 Relativization	[S, U, d-S (antipassive)]
5 WH-question formation	[S, U, d-S (antipassive)]
6 Clefting	[S, U, d-S (antipassive)]
7 Cross-clause coreference (preferred)	[S, A, d-S (passive)]

As mentioned above, there is no need for any grammatical relations aside from the notions of controller and pivot. All phenomena traditionally dealt with by the concept 'direct object', such as dative shift, applicative constructions and passives, can be handled by the concepts undergoer and core argument. These phenomena will be analyzed in detail in chapter 7. We will also see in chapter 7 that rules for case marking and agreement do not involve reference to grammatical relations, either.

6.4 Discourse reference-tracking mechanisms and voice

One of the things which speakers and hearers must do is keep track of introduced referents in discourse, and syntactic pivots may play a central role in the grammatical means languages make available for this purpose. There are a number of different grammatical means which can serve this function, and some of them crucially involve syntactic pivots. In the next section, we will survey these reference-tracking systems, and in the following sections we will look at the implications of these systems for the notion of syntactic pivot and for our understanding of voice oppositions.

6.4.1 Reference-tracking systems

We begin our discussion of reference-tracking systems with the Tzutujil text in (6.54). In it, the primary topical participant, the thief, functions as the syntactic pivot in each of the clauses in which it occurs, as (6.55) makes clear. This structure is sometimes called a 'topic chain', following Dixon (1972) (see also section 5.7). When the primary topical participant does not function as actor in a particular clause, a passive construction is used, as in (a), (b), (d) and (f). In a Dyirbal topic chain, the primary topical participant would be pivot (in absolutive case), and then all of the subsequent clauses would have that participant as pivot in zero form. If that participant does not happen to be the undergoer in the clause, then it would be necessary to use an antipassive construction. We have already seen the basic pattern in (6.49), and it can be illustrated in the three-clause chain in (6.56).

(6.56) Ba-yi yaɽa-∅$_i$ walma-ɲu *pro*$_i$ wayɲɖi-n *pro*$_i$ ba-ŋgu-n
DEIC-ABS.I man-ABS get.up-TNS go.uphill-TNS DEIC-ERG-II
ɖugumbi-ɽu buɽa-n.
woman-ERG see-TNS
'The man$_i$ got up, *pro*$_i$ went uphill, and *pro*$_i$ was seen by the woman.'
(Lit.: 'the man$_i$ got up, *pro*$_i$ went uphill, [and] the woman saw *pro*$_i$.')

Since Dyirbal lacks a conjunction equivalent to *and* in English and true third-person pronouns, this is the only way such a construction can be formed. In English, as the translation of (6.56) shows, it is also possible to form a topic chain. This construction has an accusative variable pivot in English, and accordingly if the primary participant does not happen to be the actor in a clause, then it would be necessary to use a passive construction, as in the third clause of the translation of (6.56). The missing argument in the last clause is still the syntactic pivot, but the fact that it is passive tells us that *the man* is not an actor in that clause. Instead, it is an undergoer with that particular transitive verb. So this is one way of keeping track of the most important referent in the discourse and also the role of that referent in the series of clauses. An extended example of this same type of reference tracking from Tepehua (Watters 1986) is given in (6.57).

(6.57) 'Čun, wa k-tʔahun makča:-n', wa nahun ni haciʔi,
yes, FOC 1SUBJ-be.IMPF cook-INF FOC say.IMPF the girl
'Ka-tawl-čiy-ča', wa jun-kan ni šanati$_1$, mu:la:-ni-ka-ɬ *pro*$_1$
IRR-sit.down-here-already FOC tell-PASS the woman set-DAT-PASS-PRFV
ni ʔiš-t-a:nci, ʔeš wa tawla-ɬ-ča *pro*$_1$. Yu haciʔi$_2$ tʔahun makča:-n
the 3sg-chair then FOC sit-PRFV-already the girl be.IMPF make-INF
la kʔusi cʔa:lukʔu, maka:-y *pro*$_2$ šoqta yu la:ʔan laka:
very nice tortilla make-IMPF everything the take.IMPF to
kušta mu:la:-ta-ča *pro*$_2$ mu:la:-ta *pro*$_2$ mole, tʔahni. ʔeš tawaɬ
cornfield put.in-PERF-already put.in-PERF mole turkey and then
ʔaqtay-ɬ-ča *pro*$_2$ lakɬa-ni-kan, hun-kan-ča *pro*$_2$ čiwinti yu
begin-PRFV-already gossip-DAT-PASS tell-PASS-already words that
ha:ntu laqsawaɬ.
not true
'Yes, I'm cooking', says the girl. 'Sit down', the woman is told, was set a chair and then sat down. The girl was cooking real nice tortillas, [she] makes everything that [she] takes to the cornfield, put in [a basket]; [she] put in mole and turkey, and then [she] began to be gossiped to, is told words that are not true.'

In the first series of clauses, *ni šanati* 'the woman' is the primary topical participant. It is the pivot of two passive clauses, *junkan* 'be told' and *mu:la:nikan* 'be set [something]', and an intransitive verb, *tawla-* 'sit'. The morphology of the verb signals that the argument is the undergoer of 'tell' and 'set', and the actor of 'sit'. In the rest of the text, *ni haciʔi* 'the girl' is the primary topical participant and the pivot of all of the following clauses. It is the actor except in the last two clauses, as indicated by the active voice of the verbs, and then in the last two clauses the verbs are passive, marking a change in semantic function from actor to undergoer.

This type of reference tracking is called **switch-function**; the term was originally proposed in Foley and Van Valin (1984). This system tracks one primary participant which is always realized as the syntactic pivot, and the verbal system indicates its semantic role: a change in voice indicates a change in semantic function. Thus in Dyirbal, a change in voice indicates a change in the function of the primary participant being tracked in that stretch of discourse from an undergoer (the unmarked choice for pivot) to an actor. Conversely, in English, Tzutujil and Tepehua, a change in voice indicates the argument being tracked is now the undergoer instead of the actor, the latter being the unmarked case with transitive verbs.[12] The most important feature of these systems for this discussion is that, given a transitive verb with an actor and an undergoer, the choice of which one will function as syntactic pivot can be influenced by discourse-pragmatic factors; that is, in topic chains in languages like Tzutujil, Dyirbal, Tepehua and English, the primary topical participant is chosen as pivot, and 'primary topical participant' is clearly a discourse-pragmatic notion of the type we discussed in chapter 5.

An alternative reference-tracking system is **switch-reference**. Switch-reference is found mainly in verb-final languages, taking the form of a morpheme at the end of a clause which signals whether the subject of the next clause is the same referent as the subject of that clause. The example in (6.58) is from the Native American language Zuni (New Mexico; L. Nichols 1990, citing Bunzell 1933).

(6.58) An lelonal-kwin pro_i te'ci-nan lelo-nan pro_i kwato-p pro_j
his box-at arrive-SP box-inside enter-DfP
an-alt-u-nan pro_j iteh-k'aia-kae
indirective-be.closed-CAUSE-SP throw-river-PAST
'He$_i$ came to where the box was lying; he$_i$ entered the box and he$_j$ (the other) closed it for him$_i$ and pro_j threw it into the river.'

In this example, the verbal suffix *-nan*, glossed 'SP' ('same pivot') in, for example, the first clause marks the fact that the following clause has the same pivot as that clause, while the suffix *-p* in the second clause marks the fact that there is a difference in pivot between the second and third clauses.

In a switch-reference construction we have a series of linked clauses, just as in a switch-function topic chain, but the verb morphology signals whether the argument filling a particular syntactic function in clause *x* is the same as or different from the argument in the same syntactic function in the following clause. What the morphology tracks is not a single participant, as in switch-function, but rather a single syntactic function and signals a change in the reference of the argument with that function. The function monitored is the syntactic pivot. For instance, if we start out with *Bill* as the pivot, and then get the morpheme which indicates 'same' at the end of every clause, we then know that the pivot is still *Bill*. If, on the other hand, we get a morpheme which indicates 'different', then we know that the pivot is some other third person. And again, switch-reference is tracking a function and signaling whether the referent in that function is the same as the referent in that function in the following clause or not. Since we are tracking a function, we do not worry about whether the primary topical participant is in that same function. In other words, instead of tracking a participant and maintaining the same syntactic status for it across clauses, the system tracks a syntactic function (pivot) and indicates whether the argument bearing that function is the same or different.

Switch-reference and switch-function are not the only means languages employ for keeping track of referents in discourse. Another system involves increasing the number of possible distinct referring expressions, i.e. of making multiple distinctions among third-person referring expressions. One such system involves the marking of third-person NPs as obviative or proximate, and it is a well-known feature of Algonquian languages. Within a particular stretch of discourse that involves more than one third person referent, one of those referents will be assigned more topical status than the others, and so will be marked as proximate. Bloomfield (1962) describes the proximate argument as follows: 'The proximate third person represents the topic of discourse, the person nearest the speaker's point of view, or the person earlier spoken of and already known' (38). As generally only one participant can be marked as proximate, all other participants will be marked as obviative. The example in (6.59) is from Kutenai (southeastern British Columbia, Canada; Dryer 1992b: 157–8), which, while not an Algonquian language, has a very similar system of obviation.

(6.59) ʔat qak-iɬ-ni ka·kin-s k-ʔumi¢-ik-i ɬan'-[ʔ]is
habit say-TRANS-INDIC wolf-OBV SUB-break-REFL-INDIC moccasins-3GEN
k-qa-taɬ ɬaxam ɬaʔak'ɬak-s ʔat qa·nmiɬ hamat-ik¢-aps-i
SUB-NEG-can arrive different-OBV habit quickly give-IO-INV-INDIC
ɬan'-s
moccasin-OBV
'He$_i$ [prox] would tell Wolf$_j$ [obv] that he$_i$ [prox] wore out his$_i$ [prox] moccasins [(obv)], that he$_i$ [prox] couldn't make it there. He$_j$ [obv] would quickly hand$_{INV}$ him$_i$ [prox] different moccasins [obv].'

In this stretch of discourse, from a story 'Chickadee, Frog, and Wolf', Chickadee is the more topical participant, and assigned proximate status. Wolf is assigned obviative status. There is a verbal direct vs. indirect contrast that interacts with the proximate/obviate contrast, in that when the proximate referent is the pivot of the clause, the verb will be marked as direct (i.e. it will be unmarked), but when an obviative referent appears as pivot of the clause, as in the third line in this example, the verb is marked with the 'inverse' marker *-aps*. We will discuss inverse marking further in section 7.3.1.3.

Rather than assigning features, as in the three systems presented above, another way of keeping track of referents is by reference to inherent properties of the referents, such as gender marking. The simple case is like English, in which we can unambiguously refer to multiple third persons of opposite sexes by the gender marking alone. There are languages, however, which have a dozen or more gender classes. Actually, something like this is really a noun classification system. We call this gender marking only out of Indo-European bias, for in most of the world's languages it is based upon a classification system which has nothing to do with sex or gender. Therefore, every referring expression in the language is marked with a class indicator, and for two referring expressions to be coreferential, they must fall into the same class. An example of this type of language is Yateé Zapotec, which has a very simple class system consisting of four kinds of third persons as expressed by the following verb suffixes:

(6.60) *-eʔ* third person higher status or adult
-beʔ third person lower status or child
-baʔ animals
-n inanimates

In a Zapotec text, the two most important characters are assigned to the first two classes as a means of keeping them distinct. Although deciding who gets which marking can be arbitrary, there is a tendency for the protagonist to take *-eʔ*, while the secondary participants take *-beʔ*. For instance, if there is a man, a boy, a dog and a rock, then each of the participants is referred to by a distinct verb suffix. Other languages, especially Bantu languages in Africa and some languages of Australia, e.g. Nunggubuyu (Heath 1983) and Papua New Guinea, e.g. Alamblak (Bruce 1979), have much more elaborate noun class systems that can be used for discourse reference in the same way.

In switch-function languages, there is often a gender system which is normally used for non-pivot coreference; this is the case in English. So, the way in which we keep track of non-pivot NPs is by gender, while pivots may be tracked with zero anaphora. Dyirbal does exactly the same thing by means of noun markers which have noun class, case and deictic information, and these noun markers can substitute for the nouns of the sentence:

(6.61) Baŋgul yaɽaŋgu balan ɖugumbil buɽan. → Baŋgul balan buɽan.
'The man saw the woman.'

Tzutujil has noun classifiers, and, like the Dyirbal noun markers, they are used pronominally. For example, in the second sentence in (6.54e), the classifier *xa* refers back to the NP *xa xäl* 'the corn' in the preceding sentence; *xa* is the classifier for *xäl* 'corn'. Thus in both Dyirbal and Tzutujil, elements expressing noun class distinctions can function as pronouns in discourse.

6.4.2 Pragmatic pivots

We introduced two types of syntactic pivots in section 6.3, invariable syntactic pivots and variable syntactic pivots, and a striking fact about the two grammatical reference-tracking systems, switch-function and switch-reference, is that each is associated with one of these pivot types. All switch-function systems have variable syntactic pivots, and this follows from the very nature of the system. The voice oppositions signal changes in the semantic function of the pivot, and this is only possible with variable pivots. Virtually all switch-reference systems, on the other hand, have invariable syntactic pivots. While this is not a logical necessity, as in the case of switch-function and variable pivots, it is a natural cooccurrence, since the switch-reference system monitors a particular syntactic function and signals whether the syntactic argument with that function is the same as the one with that function in the following clause. Using a voice opposition to keep the same reference in the monitored function does not contribute to the system, which is concerned with signaling changes in the referent having the monitored syntactic function. If it were possible to always keep the same referent in the monitored function throughout an entire sequence of linked clauses, there would always be 'same pivot', in which case the information given by the switch-reference markers would cease to be significant. An exception to this appears to be Martuthinera, an Australian language (Dench 1988), which has a switch-reference system which monitors variable pivots rather than invariable pivots, but this type of switch-reference system is very rare.

An important question with respect to variable pivots is what factors influence which argument of a multi-argument verb will be selected to function as pivot. That is, given a verb which takes an actor argument and an undergoer argument, and given the fact that either choice for pivot is possible, what factors influence the choice? A very obvious factor is discourse topicality. We have seen in Tzutujil, Dyirbal, Tepehua and English that there is a very strong tendency to keep the primary topical participant in a discourse in the primary syntactic function, and this means that the relative topicality, or (as we discussed in chapter 5) levels of activation, of the referents of the actor NP and the undergoer NP can influence which is selected to function as pivot. This was amply illustrated in (6.54), (6.56) and (6.57).

In chapter 5, we saw that the activation status of a referent affects how it is coded, e.g. as a full NP vs. a pronoun, and activation status is also relevant to the linking between semantics and syntax in constructions with variable pivots. To illustrate this, let us consider a simple example involving the logical structure [**do′** (Mary, ∅)] CAUSE [INGR **surprised′** (Sally)], with *Mary* the actor and *Sally* the undergoer. Let us further suppose that in one possible context the referent of *Mary* is the

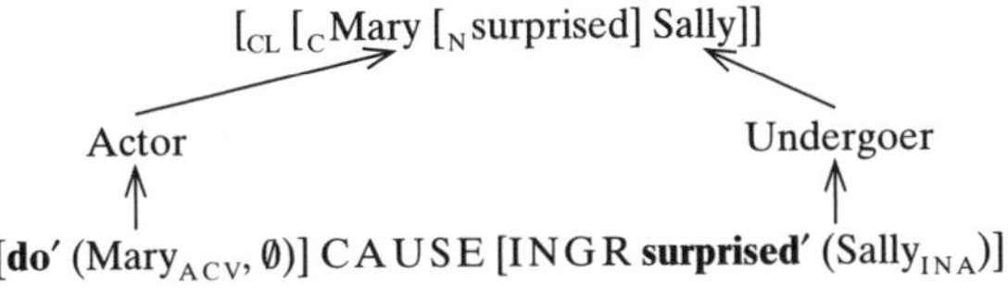

Figure 6.3 Active-voice linking

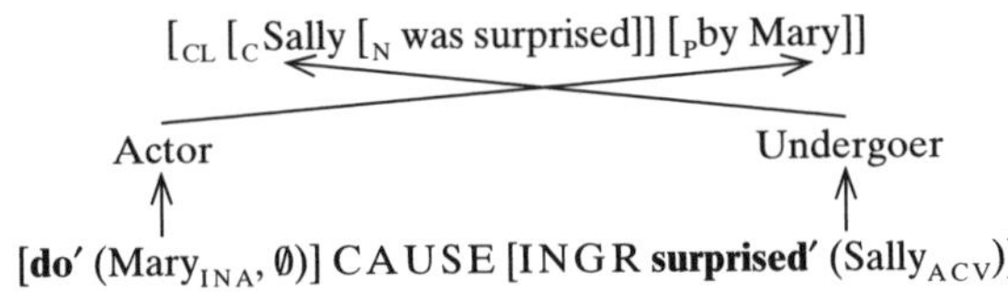

Figure 6.4 Passive-voice linking

primary topical participant and is therefore activated, while the referent of *Sally* is inactive. In such a context, *Mary* would most likely be realized as the pivot in an active-voice construction. This is illustrated in figure 6.3. The details of linking from semantics to syntax in simple sentences, including the role played by focus structure, will be presented in chapter 7. On the other hand, suppose that the referent of *Sally* is activated while that of *Mary* is inactive. In this case, *Sally* would refer to the primary topical participant, and therefore it is likely that a passive construction would be used, so that the undergoer *Sally* can be pivot. This is illustrated in figure 6.4. Hence, in languages like Tzutujil, Dyirbal, Tepehua and English, the choice of argument to serve as syntactic pivot can be influenced by discourse-pragmatic factors. It goes without saying that this applies only when there is more than one potential pivot argument; it does not apply to intransitive verbs, since there is only one potential pivot argument, nor does it apply to invariable syntactic pivots or to semantic pivots, by definition.

Variable syntactic pivots in switch-function systems correspond to what have been called **pragmatic pivots** in RRG. A pragmatic pivot is a variable syntactic pivot in which the selection of the argument to function as pivot of a transitive verb is not predictable from its semantic role and may be influenced by discourse-pragmatic considerations, in particular the topicality and activation status of its referent. The pivots in the topic chains in (6.54) from Tzutujil, (6.56) from Dyirbal and English, and (6.57) from Tepehua are all pragmatic pivots. The prototypical subject in English is a pragmatic pivot, an actor-pivot in a predicate–focus construction; the prototypical 'subject' in Dyirbal is also a pragmatic pivot. The choice of argument to serve as a variable syntactic controller can also be influenced by discourse-pragmatic considerations, e.g. the pragmatic pivot in a clause in a topic chain is the controller of the pragmatic pivot in the next clause (see also the Dyirbal examples in (6.42)). Hence there are 'pragmatic controllers' as well, but in RRG the term 'pragmatic pivot' has been used to refer to both variable syntactic pivots and controllers of this type. The notion of pragmatic pivot is useful for a couple of reasons. First, it ties focus structure into the linking between syntax and semantics in some constructions in some languages. That is, it is a grammatical relation which explicitly recognizes the intimate involvement of pragmatics in some grammatical systems. Second, because not all languages have pragmatic pivots, they are a useful concept in language typology. The grammatical systems of languages which have constructions with pragmatic pivots look very different from those of languages which lack pragmatic pivots altogether.[13] We have seen examples of this in this chapter. Acehnese, Enga and Warlpiri all lack constructions with pragmatic pivots, since they have only invariable syntactic pivots or semantic pivots. On the other hand, English, Dyirbal, Tepehua and Tzutujil, along with Malagasy and Sama, all have constructions with pragmatic pivots, and these constructions are among the most salient ones in their grammars. Furthermore, even if a language has constructions with variable syntactic pivots, this does not necessarily entail that the language has pragmatic pivots. As stated earlier, prototypical pragmatic pivots are variable syntactic pivots in the context of a switch-function reference-tracking system. If a language has variable syntactic pivots but uses a different primary reference-tracking system, then these pivots may not be pragmatic pivots. Many Bantu languages are of this type; they have constructions with variable syntactic pivots, but they use an elaborate noun class system for reference tracking; in particular, they do not appear to use voice constructions in their reference-tracking system, the hallmark of switch-function systems. However, to the extent that topicality affects the choice of argument to function as pivot in constructions with variable pivots, these pivots may be considered pragmatic pivots. If topicality has no effect on pivot selection with a variable pivot, then the pivot is not a pragmatic pivot.

We have mentioned several times that an important feature of syntactic pivots is that they are construction-specific, and accordingly it is possible for a language to have pragmatic pivots for some constructions and invariable syntactic pivots, semantic pivots or semantic controllers for others. In Dyirbal, for example, topic chains are formed on the basis of pragmatic pivots, but there is a semantic controller for imperative constructions (Dixon 1979). All languages which have constructions with pragmatic pivots also have constructions without them. The degree of pragmatic influence on pivot selection may vary across languages; in some, e.g. Sama, Dyirbal and Tepehua, it is very great, whereas in others, e.g. English, it is much less. This can be gauged in terms of (1) the balance between constructions which use pragmatic pivots and those which do not, and (2) whether the constructions with pragmatic pivots are obligatory or not. With respect to (1), we may compare the role of different pivot types in Dyirbal, Sama (Walton 1986) and English in table 6.6. Of the three languages with pragmatic pivots, they are much more important in the grammar of Dyirbal and Sama than they are in English, as they are a feature of

Table 6.6 *Role of pivot and controller types in different languages*

Construction	*Dyirbal*	*Sama*	*English*
WH-question	Pivotless	PrP	Pivotless
Relativization	PrP	PrP	Finite: pivotless Participial: VSP
Topicalization	d.n.a.	PrP	Pivotless
Topic chaining	PrP	PrP	PrP (optional)
Imperative	SmC	SmC	ISC
Reflexivization	d.n.a. (cf. section 7.5.1)	SmC	SmC (preferred)

more major constructions in those languages than in English. In order to form a topic chain in Dyirbal, which has a switch-function system, it is necessary for the clauses in the chain to have coreferential pragmatic pivots in zero form, as we saw in (6.56). As the English translation of (6.56) indicates, an analogous structure is possible in English, but it is not the only way to form a string of clauses about the same primary topical participant; it is also possible to use pronouns, as in *The man got up, he went uphill, and the woman saw him.* This is why in table 6.6 the use of the pragmatic pivot in the topic chain in English is listed as optional. With respect to relativization, Dyirbal, like Sama, relies on pragmatic pivots; that is, the head of the relative clause must always function as the pragmatic pivot inside the relative clause. This is not the case with finite relative clauses in English, as (6.14) showed. However, in non-finite, participial relatives in English, the head must be the pivot of the participle. Thus it is possible to have *the man running down the street*, *the woman talking to Sally* but not **the man the police arresting*; in this last example, the head noun (*the man*) does not function as subject (pivot) of the participle. In order to use this type of relative construction, it is necessary to use a passive construction, just as in the matrix-coding and 'equi' constructions in (6.12) and (6.13) discussed earlier, i.e. *the man being arrested by the police.* There is, however, an important difference between Dyirbal and English here: in Dyirbal the use of the construction with the pragmatic pivot is obligatory, as it is the only way to form a relative clause available in the grammar of Dyirbal, whereas the participial construction involving a pragmatic pivot in English is not obligatory, and there is another construction available which does not involve a syntactic pivot at all, let alone a pragmatic pivot. This brings up the second point mentioned above. Not only do Dyirbal and Sama have more constructions involving pragmatic pivots, but they are obligatory in the sense that they are the only constructions available for a particular function. The construction in (6.56) is the only way to form a multi-clause coordinate structure in Dyirbal, whereas there is more than one way to do that in English. Similarly, there is only one way to form a relative clause in Dyirbal, and again there is more than one way to do it in English. Hence pragmatic pivots play a more important role in the grammar of some languages because they are part of constructions which are the only option speakers have to express a particular semantic content.

As mentioned above, whether a pivot is a pragmatic pivot can only be ascertained by examining clauses with transitive verbs, since there is no option as to which argument will be pivot with an intransitive verb. It is vital to keep in mind that the issue with respect to whether a syntactic pivot is a pragmatic pivot or not is *not* whether the pivot itself is pragmatically salient or not; in the Tepehua topic chains in (6.57) the pivot is the primary topical participant, and in the Zuni switch-reference chain in (6.58) the invariable pivots are highly topical. Hence the pivots in both types of reference-tracking system are highly topical. Rather, the issue is whether these pragmatic considerations are a factor in the clause-internal process of selecting the semantic argument to function as pivot, and here Tepehua and Zuni differ dramatically: in Tepehua they may affect the selection of the pivot argument, while in Zuni they do not.

6.4.3 Types of voice constructions

In our discussion of syntactic pivots we have seen numerous examples of both passive and antipassive constructions, and we will now examine them more closely, in order to clarify the different roles they may play in grammatical systems. In the prototypical instances of both constructions, there are two distinct facets to the constructions. First, an argument which would not be selected as the privileged syntactic argument by the principles in (6.52) is selected as that argument; in a passive construction, it means that an argument lower on the hierarchy in (6.51) than the default choice is selected, while in an antipassive construction, it means that an argument higher on the hierarchy in (6.51) than the default choice is selected. Second, the argument that would be the default choice in terms of (6.52) either does not appear at all in the clause or appears as an oblique element of some kind; in this oblique status it no longer functions as a controller or pivot. Figures 6.3 and 6.4 illustrate this clearly for the English passive construction, and in (6.40)–(6.42) we saw how the *-ŋay* antipassive in Dyirbal changes the argument which can function as controller and as pivot; not only can a different argument function in this way, but the argument that would be the controller or pivot in the unmarked voice cannot have these functions.

While these two features of voice alternations cooccur in the prototypical constructions, they are logically independent of each other, and, as we shall see, they do not always occur together. We will, therefore, give each a separate label and description. The first will be called the **privileged syntactic argument** (PSA) **modulation voice**, since it specifically deals with allowing a non-default argument to function as syntactic pivot or controller. The second will be called the **argument**

modulation voice, since it involves the non-canonical status of a macrorole argument.[14] We can now break down the English passive and the Dyirbal *-ŋay* antipassive into their component parts, as in (6.62).

(6.62) a. *English passive construction*
1 PSA modulation: non-actor occurs as pivot/controller (default non-actor = undergoer).
2 Argument modulation: actor appears in periphery as object of *by* or is omitted.

b. *Dyirbal* -ŋay *antipassive construction*
1 PSA modulation: actor appears as syntactic pivot/controller.
2 Argument modulation: undergoer appears in dative or instrumental case.

There are many languages in which the voice constructions do not match these prototypes, and there are many instances in which a construction instantiates only one of the two facets of the prototypical passive or antipassive. The clearest example of how independent these two parts of the passive are comes from passives of intransitive verbs, which are found in a variety of languages, e.g. Icelandic, German, Latin and Turkish (Comrie 1977, Keenan 1985a). Since the verbs in these constructions have only one argument, they are by definition argument modulation only, since there is no second argument to function as the privileged syntactic argument. The following examples are from Icelandic (Van Valin 1991b).

(6.63) a. Það va-r dans-að.
3NEUTsg be.PAST-3sg dance-PSTP
'There was dancing.'

b. Það e-r mikið hóst-að í reykherberg-i-nu.
3NEUTsg be.PRES-3sg much coughed in smokingroom-DEF-DAT
'There is much coughing in the smoking room.'

The semantic argument that would normally be the single core argument of these verbs has been suppressed and cannot occur overtly, unlike the actor in a passive construction with a transitive verb in Icelandic (see (7.13b)). The two parts of the passive construction can also occur independently in constructions with transitive verbs in some languages. We begin by looking at passive constructions which involve only PSA modulation but no argument modulation, i.e. the actor remains a direct core argument. A very good example of this type of passive is found in Lango, a Nilo-Saharan language of East Africa (Noonan and Bavin-Woock 1978, Noonan 1992). The basic facts are given in (6.64).

(6.64) a. Rwòt ò-nèn-á (án).
king 3sg-see.PRFV-1sg (1sg)
'The king saw me.'

b. Án rwòt ò-nɛ̀n-á.
1sg king 3sg-see.PRFV-1sg
'I was seen by the king.'

c. Rwòt ò-mì-ɔ̀ dyàŋ bòtá.
king 3sg-give.PRFV-3sg cow to-1sg
'The king gave the cow to me.'

d. Án rwòt ò-mì-ɔ̀ dyàŋ bòtá.
1sg king 3sg-give.PRFV-3sg cow to-1sg
'I was given the cow by the king.'

e. Gwôk ò-bín-ô.
dog 3sg-come-PRFV
'The dog came.'

f. Gwôk ɔ-tɔ̀-ɔ̀.
dog 3sg-die-PRFV
'The dog died.'

The examples in (6.64a) and (c) are unmarked transitive and ditransitive clauses, respectively. In (6.64b) the undergoer *án* appears in the clause-initial pivot position; there is no morphological marker of this change in word order. In (6.64d) a RECIPIENT argument appears in pivot position, with a pronominal copy also appearing in the postverbal position. Simple intransitive sentences are given in (e) and (f). There is clearly a restricted neutralization with respect to the controller of the prefix agreement on the verb; it is an actor in (a)–(e) but an undergoer in (f). Note that in (b) and (d) the actor still controls the agreement prefix on the verb and the undergoer still controls the agreement suffix, just as in (a) and (c). This means that the neutralization is [S, A], yielding an invariable syntactic controller for the agreement prefix. Noonan (1992) refers to the construction in (b) and (d) as 'topicalization', whereas Noonan and Bavin-Woock (1978) refer to it as a 'passive analog', since the relevant NP must be an argument of the verb and takes on syntactic properties such as being controller of floated quantifiers and cross-clause coreference. Evidence that this is a core-internal construction rather than one involving the undergoer occurring in the precore slot ('topicalization') comes from the fact that this construction can be used in relative clauses; core-internal constructions like passive are fine in relative clauses, as we saw in the Malagasy examples in (6.27), but topicalization does not occur in relative clauses and indeed in most kinds of embedded clauses. Hence the initial NP in the sentences in (6.64) is core-initial, not in the precore slot. The following are examples of the initial NP controlling coreference in a complex sentence.

(6.65) a. Dákô ò-kòbbì lócə̀ nî ɛ̀-bínô dɔ̀k.
woman 3sg-tell man CMPL 3sg-go back
'The woman$_i$ told the man$_j$ that (s)he$_{i/*j}$ will go back.'

b. Lócə̀ dákô ò-kòbbɛ́ nî ɛ̀-bínô dɔ̀k.
man woman 3sg-tell CMPL 3sg-go back
'The man$_j$ was told by the woman$_i$ that (s)he$_{*i/j}$ will go back.'

In Lango, there is a special pronominal prefix which is used in complex constructions to indicate that the third-person argument in the linked or dependent clause is coreferential with the core-initial NP. In (6.65a) the *ɛ̀-* prefix refers back to *dákô* 'the woman', which is the core-initial NP and actor argument of the first clause. In the passive construction in (6.65b), on the other hand, the *ɛ̀-* prefix refers back to *lócə̀* 'the man', which is the core-initial NP and the undergoer of the first clause. This shows three things: first, the controller of the coreference is not semantically defined, and therefore there is a restricted neutralization with respect to the controller; second, the core-initial NP is a variable syntactic controller; and third, because the choice of the controller can be affected by discourse considerations, it is a pragmatic controller, on analogy with the pragmatic pivots discussed in the previous section. This can be seen clearly in (6.66), in which the core-initial controller controls coreference with pronominal elements in a subsequent linked or independent clause.

(6.66) a. Dákô lócə̀ ò-nɛ̀n-ò. ɛ̀-càmm-ò dɛ̀k.
woman man 3sg-see.PERF-3sg 3sg-eat.PROG-3sg stew
'The woman was seen by the man. She was eating stew.'
b. Dákô lócə̀ ò-nɛ̀n-ò t-ɛ̀ jwâtt-ò.
woman man 3sg-see.PERF-3sg and.then-3sg hit-3sg
'The woman was seen by the man, and then she hit him.'

Noonan (1992: 259) states that if *dákô* 'woman' did not appear in initial position in the first clause in each of these examples, *lócə̀* 'man' would then be interpreted as the actor of the second clause. While the core-initial NP in the passive construction takes on some control properties, the status of the actor does not change; it remains a direct core argument, it still controls prefix agreement on the verb, and it still controls reflexives and the missing argument in serial verb constructions (not illustrated here). An example of reflexive control is given in (6.67).

(6.67) a. Lócə̀ ò-kwæ-ò dákô pìr-ɛ́ kɛ̀nɛ̀.
man 3sg-ask-3sg woman about-3sg self.
'The man asked the woman about himself/*herself.'
b. Dákô lócə̀ ò-kwæ-ò pìr-ɛ́ kɛ̀nɛ̀.
woman man 3sg-ask-3sg about-3sg self
'The woman was asked by the man about himself/*herself.'

In both sentences the actor, *lócə̀* 'man', controls the reflexive, regardless of whether it is the core-initial privileged syntactic argument or not. The situation in Lango may be summarized as in (6.68).

(6.68)

Construction or pattern	*Controller*
Prefix agreement	Invariable syntactic controller [S, A]
Suffix agreement	Semantic controller [U]
Cross-clause coreference with -ɛ̀	Variable (pragmatic) syntactic controller
Floating quantifiers	Variable (pragmatic) syntactic controller
Reflexivization	Semantic controller [A]
Missing argument in serial V	Semantic controller [A]

If the actor is core-initial, as in (6.64a, c), (6.65a) and (6.67a), then all of the phenomena except suffix agreement have the same controller. If the undergoer is core-initial, as in (6.64b, d), (6.65b), (6.66) and (6.67b), then there is a split in the control properties: the controller for prefix agreement, reflexivization and serial verb constructions is the actor, while the core-initial undergoer controls coreference and floating quantifiers. What is important about the Lango construction is that it involves modulation of the syntactic controller with no modulation of the actor; it remains a core argument and controls a number of grammatical phenomena.

The opposite of this Lango construction would be one in which there is non-canonical coding of the actor but there is no occurrence of a non-actor as the privileged syntactic argument. Such a construction can be found in Ute (Uto-Aztecan; Givón 1981). In the Ute passive construction the actor is unexpressed in the clause, and no other argument serves as the privileged syntactic argument. The non-actor argument(s) of the clause take the same marking as in the active clause, and the unexpressed actor controls the number marking on the verb (Givón 1981: 171; 176).

(6.69) a. Ta'wá-c̱ 'u-∅ sivấãtu-ci 'u-wáy pa̱x̂á-qa.
man-NOM the-NOM goat-ACC the-ACC kill-ANT
'The man killed the goat.'
b. Sivấãtu-ci 'u-wáy pa̱x̂á-ta-x̂a.
goat-ACC the-ACC kill-PASS-ANT
'Someone killed the goat', or 'The goat was killed.'
c. Sivấãtu-ci 'u-wáy pa̱x̂á-x̂a̱-ta-x̂a.
goat-ACC the-ACC kill-pl-PASS-ANT
'The goat was killed (by a plural actor).'

The undergoer remains in the the accusative case, as in (c); it takes over no control or pivot properties. This type of passive construction is much more common than the Lango type, and its primary function is to suppress the expression of the actor argument in the clause. Passive constructions in syntactically ergative languages also have this function; they do not affect the choice of syntactic pivot or controller, as the undergoer has those properties in the non-antipassive voices. The Sama passive in (6.70), from Walton (1986), renders the actor oblique and optional but does not affect the syntactic status of the undergoer.

(6.70) a. B'lla d'nda kiyakan kami.
cook woman food our
'The woman cooked our food.'
a′. *B'lla kiyakan kami d'nda.
a″. *B'lla kiyakan kami.
b. B-i-'lla uk d'nda kiyakan kami.
PASS-cook by woman food our
'Our food was cooked by the woman.'
b′. Bi'lla kiyakan kami uk d'nda.
'Our food was cooked by the woman.'
b″. Bi'lla kiyakan kami.
'Our food was cooked.'

In the plain voice form in (a), the actor NP *d'nda* 'the woman' cannot be moved to the end of the clause, nor can it be omitted. In the passive construction (signaled by the infix *-i-*), on the other hand, the oblique actor can occur clause-finally and can be omitted. The function of this construction is argument modulation only; it has no effect on syntactic pivots or controllers.

Roberts (1995) proposes that passive morphology serves to signal the suppression of the actor as a core argument and that it is associated with argument modulation passives only. The data we have looked at support this hypothesis: in the impersonal passives of intransitive verbs in (6.63) from Icelandic and the Ute and Sama passives in (6.69) and (6.70) are purely argument modulation voice constructions, and they all have passive morphology, whereas the Lango construction in (6.64) involves PSA modulation only and lacks passive morphology.

We now turn to the discussion of antipassive constructions which instantiate pivot modulation and argument modulation voices separately. Just as it is possible to have a pivot modulation passive that does not at the same time affect the actor, as in Lango, it is also possible to have an antipassive construction that makes the actor a pivot or controller without affecting the undergoer. One such construction is found in Ingush (Caucasian; Nichols 1982).

(6.71) a. Suo:-na yz-∅ v-ie:z.
1sg-DAT 3sgM-NOM MASC-like.PRES
'I like him.'
b. Suo-∅ yz-∅ v-ie:z-až j-a.
1sg-NOM 3sgM-NOM MASC-like-NFIN FEM-be.3sgPRES
'I (fem.) like him.'
c. Cuo: cun-na bij-∅ b-iett.
3sgM-ERG 3sgM-DAT fist-NsgNOM NEUT-hit.PRES
'He hits him.'
d. Yz-∅ cun-na bij-∅ b-iett-až v-a.
3sgM-NOM 3sgM-DAT fist-NsgNOM NEUT-hit-NFIN MASC-be.3sgPRES
'He hits him.'

Examples (6.71a, c) are simple clauses; (6.71b, d) are antipassive clauses. In the antipassive clauses an otherwise dative or ergative argument appears in the nominative case, and can be an agreement controller. Agreement, marked by different initial consonants on the verb, is with nominative arguments only, 'him' in (6.71a), 'him' and also 'I (fem.)' in (6.71b), 'fist' in (6.71c), and 'fist' and 'he' in (6.71d). In discussing the use of the antipassive as opposed to the plain tense form (where case marking is the same as in simple sentences), Nichols (1982: 455) notes that 'the subject of the antipassive is more thematic than that of the plain tense, and consequently the antipassive is favored in chain-final or paragraph-final position or as an independent utterance'. There is no modulation of the undergoer in this construction, as it is still in the nominative case and controls verb agreement.

A given language may have different structures for the two types of antipassive. Jakaltek has three different antipassive forms, one for pivot modulation, two for argument modulation. In the pivot modulation antipassive, there is no ergative agreement marker on the verb and the suffix *-n(i)* appears affixed to the verb. This construction is used when an actor argument is questioned, clefted or serves as the head of a relative clause (see table 6.5). Tzutujil showed a similar pattern in (6.53). The following examples of Jakaltek relativization are from Craig (1977).

(6.72) a. X-∅-(y)-il naj winaj ix ix.
PAST-3ABS-3ERG-see CL man CL woman
'The man saw the woman.'
b. W-ohtaj ix ix x-∅-(y)-il naj winaj.
1sgERG-know CL woman PAST-3ABS-3ERG-see CL man
'I know the woman who the man saw.' (*'I know the woman who saw the man.')
c. W-ohtaj naj winaj x-∅-'il-ni ix ix.
1sgERG-know CL man PAST-3ABS-see-ANTI CL woman
'I know the man who saw the woman.' (*'I know the man who the woman saw.')

A basic transitive clause is given in (a). In (b) the head noun is interpreted as the undergoer of the relative clause, and there is no special marking on the verb. In (c), however, the head noun is interpreted as the actor of the relative clause, and the verb carries the antipassive suffix and is missing the ergative cross-reference marker. The status of the undergoer seems to be unchanged from (a); it is still a direct argument, and Craig argues that it is still cross-referenced on the verb. Hence there is a change of syntactic pivot, i.e. PSA modulation, with the default pivot choice, the undergoer, remaining a direct core argument, i.e. without argument modulation.

In one of the two Jakaltek argument modulation antipassives, the verb takes the antipassive marker *-w-*, no ergative marker appears on the verb, and the controller of the absolutive agreement is the actor, not the undergoer, which appears as an oblique (examples from Datz 1980).

(6.73) a. X-Ø-s-mak ix naj.
PAST-3ABS-3ERG-hit CL/she CL/he
'She hit him.'
b. X-Ø-mak-wa ix y-iñ naj.
PAST-3ABS-hit-ANTI CL/she 3ERG-on CL/he
'She hit (beat) on him.'

This construction is often used for disambiguating the actor from an undergoer by expressing the undergoer as the object of a preposition, i.e. as an oblique core argument rather than a direct core argument. It may also be left completely unexpressed. The other argument modulation antipassive results in the Jakaltek equivalent of an incorporated noun (see (2.26) from Greenlandic Eskimo and (2.27) from Lakhota in section 2.3.2).

(6.74) X-Ø-mak-wi naj ix.
PAST-3ABS-hit-ANTI CL/he CL/she
'She hits men (men-hits).'

The undergoer from the active form occurs immediately after the verb and cannot be modified in any way; it is normally interpreted as non-referential. This construction yields forms with the same interpretation as the activity verbs with non-referential objects discussed in section 3.2.3.3. This is quite common, in fact. In (3.49) from Kabardian, the plain form of the sentence has an active accomplishment interpretation, while the antipassive has an activity interpretation. The same is true in the following pair of Sama sentences; *na* is an aspectual adverb with no simple translation into English.

(6.75) a. B'lli na d'nda daing ma onde'.
buy woman fish OBL child
'The woman already bought the fish for the child.'
b. N-b'lli na d'nda daing ma onde'.
ANTI-buy woman fish OBL child
'The woman is now buying fish for the child.'

Daing 'fish' is interpreted as definite and referential in (a), and if (a) were to be used as a relative clause, for example, *daing* would be the pragmatic pivot (see (6.50c)). By contrast, in (b) it is interpreted as non-referential, and if (b) were to be used as a relative clause, as in (6.50d), *d'nda* 'woman' would be the pragmatic pivot. Hence (a) has a telic interpretation, while (b) does not; (b) is the form that is used to signal an activity interpretation with multiple argument verbs. Note that the only difference between the two sentences is the voice of the verb.

In these argument modulation antipassives the actor does become the potential pivot and controller in the clause, due to its being the only remaining direct macrorole argument. Why, then, should constructions like (6.73b) and (6.74) not be analyzed as a PSA modulation construction, like the one in (6.72c)? The answer lies in the constructions in which the voice form typically occurs. The antipassive in (6.72c) only occurs in cleft, WH-question and relativization constructions and only when it affects the choice of syntactic pivot; it cannot occur in a simple clause like the antipassives in (6.73) and (6.74). On the other hand, these two antipassives can occur in simple clauses and not as part of any construction with a variable syntactic pivot; they can occur in such a context, e.g. (6.54c) in Tzutujil is just such an example, but they need not. Dyirbal presents a similar situation. It has a second construction, called the 'false reflexive' construction in Dixon (1972), which is formally very similar to the -*ŋay* antipassive construction. It is illustrated in (6.76b).

(6.76) a. Ba-la-m wuḍu-∅ ba-ŋgu-l yaɽa-ŋgu ḍaŋga-ɲu.
DEIC-ABS-III fruit-ABS DEIC-ERG-I man-ERG eat-TNS
'The man is eating the fruit.'

b. Ba-yi yaɽa-∅ ḍaŋgay-mari-ɲu (ba-gu-m wuḍu-gu).
DEIC-ABS.I man-ABS eat-REFL-TNS DEIC-DAT-III fruit-DAT
'The man is eating (fruit).'

This parallels the -*ŋay* antipassive in (6.40) in that the actor is in the absolutive case and the argument corresponding to the undergoer in the plain form in (a) is in the dative case. Is this a pivot modulation antipassive like the -*ŋay* construction? The answer is 'no', for the following reason. Heath (1979) looked at a number of Dyirbal texts and found that the -*ŋay* construction is found almost exclusively in linked clauses in topic chains like (6.56) or purposive constructions like (6.41) and very rarely in simple, unlinked clauses. The false reflexive, on the other hand, is found primarily in unlinked, independent clauses and rarely in topic chains. Its function seems to be primarily related to allowing the undergoer argument to be omitted or to create activity uses of multiple argument verbs, as in (6.76b). Hence, it is an argument modulation antipassive, while the -*ŋay* construction is a PSA modulation antipassive.

In conclusion, we have shown that the prototypical voice construction, be it a passive or an antipassive, is actually an amalgam of two distinct, more basic voice constructions, which we have labelled 'PSA modulation voice' and 'argument modulation voice' constructions. Each of them may be given a general characterization as in (6.77).

(6.77) *General characterization of basic voice constructions*

a. PSA modulation voice: permits an argument other than the default argument in terms of (6.52) to function as the privileged syntactic argument.

b. Argument modulation voice: gives non-canonical realization to a macrorole argument.

We have seen examples of languages in which each of the basic voice types occurs on its own.

6.5 Some typological issues

In our discussion of grammatical relations in this chapter, we have argued that syntactic relations exist only when there is a restricted neutralization of semantic roles for syntactic purposes.[15] We have seen examples of three patterns of restricted neutralizations: [S, A], [S, A, d-S] and [S, U, d-S] (see tables 6.2 and 6.3). There is, however, a fourth possible pattern of neutralization, namely [S, U]. These patterns raise a number of important questions. First, why do only three of the four seem to occur? Are there any instances of [S, U]? Second, which are the most frequent patterns and why? Third, are there any asymmetries in the distribution of the three types? That is, do they all cooccur equally in grammatical systems?

While we have not encountered any [S, U] neutralizations in our discussion, they do exist, although true neutralizations of this kind are rare, and they are often difficult to distinguish from undergoer-only restrictions. An example of this neutralization can be found in the distribution of the partitive ('zerik') case in Basque (Levin 1989). The basic data are given in (6.78).

(6.78) a. Ez d-u-∅ gizon-ak ikusi ikaslea-∅.
NEG 3sgABS-AUX-3sgERG man-ERG see student-ABS
'The man didn't see a/the student.'
b. Ez d-u-∅ gizon-ak ikusi ikasle-rik.
NEG 3sgABS-AUX-3sgERG man-ERG see student-ZERIK
'The man didn't see any students/a (single) student.'
c. *Ez d-u-∅ gizon-ik ikusi liburua-∅.
NEG 3sgABS-AUX-3sgERG man-ZERIK see book-ABS
'Not a man saw the book.'
d. Ez d-a gizona-∅ etorri.
NEG 3sgABS-AUX man-ABS come
'A/the man didn't come.'
e. Ez d-a gizon-ik etorri.
NEG 3sgABS-AUX man-ZERIK come
'No men came.'

In negative sentences, the undergoer of a transitive, as in (b), and the single argument of an intransitive verb, as in (e), can take the partitive case; the actor of a transitive verb cannot, as (c) shows. We have illustrated only an actor-taking intransitive verb, *etorri* 'come', here, but intransitive undergoers also take the partitive case when negated (Levin 1989). This, then, appears to be an example of an [S, U] restricted neutralization. One of the reasons this is a rare pattern is that similar phenomena are usually restricted to undergoers only, rather than [S, U]. Levin compares the 'zerik' case distribution in Basque to the distribution of the genitive of negation in Russian, but the genitive of negation in Russian does not occur on all S arguments, only those which are undergoers, translating the GB analysis of Pesetsky (1982) into our terms. Hence the genitive of negation in Russian appears to be analogous to 'possessor raising' in Acehnese, in that it is restricted to undergoers rather than being constrained by a syntactic pivot or controller. Another example of this kind of pivot can be seen in Belhare, a Tibeto-Burman language of Nepal (Bickel 1996). In an internally headed relative clause, the head can be interpreted as the undergoer of a transitive verb, the non-macrorole direct core argument of a ditransitive verb, and the single argument of an intransitive verb; it cannot, however, be interpreted as the actor of a transitive verb. This is illustrated in (6.79), from Bickel (forthcoming).

(6.79) a. [Maʔi khiu-ʔ-na] misen niu-t-u-ga iʔ?
human quarrel-NPST-DET acquaintance know-NPST-3sgU-2sgA Q
'Do you know the person who is quarreling?'

b. [Kochu chomm-haiʔ-ŋa-ha] yuŋŋa, i-ne-e.
dog crazy-TEL-INTR.PERF-NMZ is DEIC-DEM-LOC
'There is a dog there who became crazy.'

c. [ŋka asen pepar in-u-ŋŋ-ha] mann-har-e.
1sg yesterday cigarettes buy-3sgU-1sgA-NMZ finish-TEL-PAST
'The cigarettes that I bought yesterday are used up.'

d. [Asenle paisa mai-khut-piu-sa-ha] n-chitt-he.
before money 1sgU-steal-BEN-TRANS.PERF-NMZ 3nsgA-find-PAST
'They found the money that he stole from me.'

e. [Tombhira-ŋa wa seiʔ-s-u-ha] chitt-he-m.
wild.cat-ERG chicken kill-TRANS.PERF-3sgU-NMZ find-PAST-1plA
'We found the chicken that the cat had killed.'
*'We found the cat that had killed the chicken.'

The first two examples involve intransitive verbs, the head being an actor in (a) and an undergoer in (b). In (c) the head is the undergoer of a transitive verb, while in (d) it is the non-macrorole direct core argument of a three-core-argument verb (Belhare is a primary-object language). The last example illustrates the restriction against interpreting the head as the actor of a transitive verb; *wa* 'chicken', the undergoer, must be interpreted as the head, not *tombhira* 'wild cat', the actor. Thus, the pivot for this construction can be characterized either as [S, U, DCA], 'DCA' being 'direct core argument' as in (d), or as [~A], i.e. direct core arguments except the actor of transitive verbs. This pattern of neutralization in internally headed relative clauses is not unique to Belhare; Tibetan also has internally headed relative clauses with an [S, U] pivot (Mazaudon 1978), and Korean internally headed relative clauses seem to have the related [S, U] pattern (Yang 1993). Given that restrictive neutralizations excluding the actor of transitive verbs exist, what could the motivation for them be? We return to this question below.

The two questions about the distribution of the types of neutralizations are distinct but closely related to each other. The most common restricted neutralization pattern cross-linguistically appears to be the [S, A] pattern. Virtually all languages have at least one construction which works with this pattern (Acehnese and Mandarin being obvious exceptions), and there are many languages in which this is the only pattern found, e.g. Enga, Kewa, Fore and many other Papuan languages, Choctaw, Cree, Zapotec, Sanuma and many other languages of North and South America, Mparntwe Arrernte, Warlpiri and many Australian languages. The next most common pattern is the [S, A, d-S] pattern of familiar accusative languages like English, Russian, German and Spanish, as well as Malagasy, Lango, Quechua and Tepehua. No language has only variable syntactic pivots and controllers; some phenomena, e.g. addressee of imperatives, have normally either invariable [S, A] controllers or semantic (actor) controllers. The controllers of 'want' constructions and related constructions are always semantic controllers, and the controllers in coordinate constructions like those in (6.42), (6.56) and (6.57) are always variable syntactic controllers; we will show in chapter 9 how this follows from the theory of complex sentences. The least common of the three most frequent patterns is the ergative syntactic pattern, [S, U, d-S]. It is found in a relatively small number of languages and is never the exclusive pivot or controller type.

The disparity in frequency among these three types needs an explanation, but what is also striking is the cooccurrence relations among them. It is not uncommon for a language to have [S, A] as the only pattern of neutralization defining syntactic pivots and controllers, whereas no languages appear to have [S, A, d-S] or [S, U, d-S] as the only pattern of neutralization. There is one more question: not only are [S, U] neutralizations rare, but there are no languages which have them exclusively, in stark contrast to the frequent monopoly of [S, A]. Why should these distributional patterns hold? Part of the answer lies in the importance of agency and animacy in language. Dixon (1979, 1994) argues that the only universally valid notion of subject is [S, A], and this stems from the fact that certain universal grammatical phenomena, e.g. forming imperatives, causative constructions and control of reflexivization, involve AGENT-like arguments primarily rather than PATIENT-like arguments. It has also long been noted by many observers that language users typically pay more attention to animate referents than to inanimate referents and talk about them more. This is reflected, for example, in the inherent lexical content hierarchy proposed in Silverstein (1976, 1981) (see (7.54)), which has the speech act participants and other humans at the top and inanimate and abstract entities at the bottom. These two sets of observations are not independent of each other, as AGENT-like arguments are normally animate or human, while PATIENT-like arguments may, but need not, be animate or human. We may represent this in (6.80).

(6.80) *Privileged syntactic argument selection hierarchy*

arg. of DO > 1sg arg. of **do′** > 1st arg. of **pred′** (x, y) > 2nd arg. of **pred′** (x, y) > arg. of **pred′** (x)

OBLIGATORILY ANIMATE > VERY LIKELY ANIMATE > NEED NOT BE ANIMATE

'Arg. of DO' is always animate, and the '1st arg. of **do′**', especially if it is an instigator, is almost always animate; it is non-instigator EFFECTORS which are inanimate (see section 3.2.3.2). Many of the classes of state **pred′** (x, y) verbs require the first argument to be animate, but none requires the second argument to be animate. Finally, there is no requirement on the single arguments of **pred′** (x) verbs that they be animate.

What are the implications of this for the four neutralization patterns? The grammatical system which reflects the hierarchy the most purely is Acehnese, since most constructions in the language have an actor semantic pivot or controller (Durie 1985, 1987). Among the four neutralization types, the [S, A] pattern has invariable syntactic pivots in which the more AGENT-like and almost certainly animate argument of a transitive verb is always selected as the privileged syntactic argument; the only deviation from the strong tendency toward animate, AGENT-like pivots and controllers would be the intransitive verbs which take undergoers as their single argument. Constructions with [S, A, d-S] pivots and controllers deviate more from the Acehnese 'ideal', since they permit the less AGENT-like and more likely inanimate argument of a transitive verb to function as the privileged syntactic argument, albeit as a derivative, marked option. Given this tendency, it is not surprising that there are comparatively few constructions that treat the less AGENT-like and more likely inanimate argument of a transitive verb as the default choice for pivot or controller and the more AGENT-like and almost certainly animate argument of a transitive verb as a derivative, marked option, i.e. have [S, U, d-S]. Finally, there are no languages which are the mirror image of Enga or Warlpiri which have [S, U] as the dominant or exclusive pattern of neutralization, for to do so would entail excluding the more AGENT-like and almost certainly animate argument of a transitive verb from ever being the privileged syntactic argument. This would preclude the usual patterns of imperative formation or control of reflexivization, for example. It is not surprising, then, that this type of language does not exist.

The importance of animate and AGENT-like arguments is a significant factor favoring [S, A] neutralizations. The wide occurrence of [S, A, d-S] and [S, U, d-S] neutralizations, however, suggests that there must be another factor at work which can override the animacy and agentiveness factors; the most obvious candidate for this second factor is discourse pragmatics. In our discussion of reference-tracking systems, we saw how these variable syntactic pivots may function in switch-function systems in connection with voice constructions to allow the primary topical participant in the discourse to appear as the privileged syntactic argument in a sequence of linked clauses. PSA modulation antipassive constructions allow actors of transitive verbs to function as the privileged syntactic argument in syntactically ergative constructions, and this is why [S, U, d-S] neutralizations are so much more common than [S, U] neutralizations. Moreover, this neutralization is most commonly found in so-called 'extraction' constructions, i.e. topicalization, relativization and WH-question formation, all of which have pragmatic conditions on their occurrence (see section 9.5). All of the languages we have discussed which have syntactically ergative constructions have this pattern for their extraction constructions. Because the primary topical participant in a text is normally animate and animates often function as undergoers, it is entirely possible for the primary topical participant to function as an undergoer. When this happens in syntactically accusative constructions, as we have seen, passive constructions allow the primary topical participant–undergoer to occur as the privileged syntactic argument. In this instance, discourse topicality and animacy outweigh agentiveness, and [S, A, d-S] neutralizations can be seen as reflections of the importance of the first two factors. Du Bois (1987) argues that information-flow factors, in particular, the introduction of new referents into the discourse, motivate the basic ergative pattern, because, he claims, (1) new referents are introduced primarily either as undergoers of transitives or the single argument of intransitives, and (2) actors of transitive verbs, on the other hand, tend strongly to be topical. Thus in terms of markedness as a focal NP, S and U group together in contrast to A, yielding the classic ergative pattern. While this claim is not uncontroversial (see e.g. Durie 1988b), we saw examples in chapter 5 from a number of languages in which the unmarked focus position corresponds to the normal position of undergoers in a transitive clause and the usual position of the actor of transitive verbs is a normally topical position. Moreover, the single argument of an intransitive verb can occur in either position.

We now have four interacting factors involved in these neutralization patterns: topic, focus, animacy and agentivity. Topic, animacy and agentivity converge in [S, A] and [S, A, d-S] patterns, and, not surprisingly, these are the most common cross-linguistically. Focus, animacy and agentivity coalesce in the [S, U, d-S] pattern; in particular, the 'd-S' component is a reflection of the importance of agentivity. Of these four factors only focus would seem to motivate the [S, U] pattern; there is, however, a semantic parameter potentially relevant here, namely affectedness. It is not surprising, then, that it is the least common pattern. The fact that [S, A, d-S] is much more common than [S, U, d-S] might seem to be somewhat puzzling; since both systems allow either macrorole argument of a transitive verb to function as the privileged syntactic argument, one might expect them to be equally common. The asymmetry between them stems from the fact that keeping track of referents in discourse is a more complex and demanding task than introducing new referents, and accordingly languages have typically devoted more grammatical machinery to the former task than to the latter. As we saw in section 6.4.1, there is a number of reference-tracking systems, and languages often employ more than one of them. In contrast, all a language needs for introducing new referents is a way of indicating focus, which they all have; some, but not all, have a special presentational construction for this purpose as well. Thus, it would appear that topic outranks focus as a factor, and this leads to the predominance of [S, A, d-S] over [S, U, d-S] patterns.

In closing, let us look again at the [S, U] neutralizations and the similar undergoer-only restrictions. We have seen three sets of phenomena here: possessor raising in Acehnese (undergoer-only), special case assignment under negation in Basque ([S, U]) and in Russian (undergoer-only), and internally headed relative clauses in Belhare, Tibetan and Korean ([S, U]). There seem to be two different factors at work in them, the semantic notion of affectedness and focus. The usual explanation for the restriction of possessor raising to possessors of undergoers is that in many cases the possessor is also affected by whatever affects the possessed undergoer. To take the Acehnese examples in (6.22c, d), if my house burns down, I am also affected, albeit in a different way from the house. On the other hand, if my child sings, for example, I am not singing or doing anything at all. Thus, an entity's undergoing a change of state or condition can also affect the possessor of the entity, especially if the relationship is one of kinship or inalienable possession. However, a participant's doing something does not imply anything about the possessor of the participant, hence the restriction to possessed undergoers. The explanation for the pattern of case assignment in Basque and Russian seems to be related to the distribution of focus and Du Bois' hypothesis about the information-flow motivation for ergativity. Recall from section 5.5 that the scope of negation in a sentence is normally the actual focus domain. The 'zerik' case in Basque and the genitive of negation in Russian are restricted to elements in the scope of negation, and therefore Du Bois' hypothesis that [S, U] are natural foci and [A] is not predicts their basic distribution; why the pattern is [S, U] in Basque and undergoer-only regardless of transitivity in Russian remains to be accounted for, but we have the basis for an independently motivated explanation of these case patterns. Finally, Yang (1993, 1994) argues that the internal head in a Korean internally headed relative clause is in fact focal and that this construction can be used to introduce new referents in a discourse; Bickel (1996) does not discuss the pragmatic properties of the Belhare construction. This again relates the ergative pattern to focus and information flow. Belhare, unlike Korean, does not have 'd-S' as part of the pattern; is this a potential deficit in expressiveness, not being able to have the internal head function as the actor of a transitive verb? The answer is 'no', because there is a second, externally headed relative clause construction in Belhare which is not subject to this restriction. Korean, too, has externally headed relatives as well which are not subject to the same restrictions. Therefore if a Belhare-speaker wishes to relativize on the actor of a transitive verb, it is always possible to do so, albeit with a different relative clause construction. We may predict, then, that if a language has constructions with an [S, U] pattern of neutralization, it will have an alternative, functionally overlapping construction which will include actor arguments of transitive verbs in its pattern of neutralization.

Further reading

For different theories of grammatical relations, see Bresnan (1982a), Bresnan and Kanerva (1989), Czepluch (1981), Dik (1989), Dziwirek, Farrell and Mejías Bikandi (1990), Marantz (1984), Palmer (1994), Perlmutter (1980, 1982), Williams (1984). For additional arguments against grammatical relations as universal, see Bhat (1991). For discussion of syntactic pivots, see Dixon (1979, 1994) and Palmer (1994). For more complete typologies of reference-tracking devices, see Van Valin (1987b), Kibrik (1991) and Comrie (1989a, 1994). See Keenan (1985a), Shibatani (1988), Siewierska (1984) and Klaiman (1991) for typologies of passives, and Cooreman (1994) for a typology of antipassives; Foley and Van Valin (1984, 1985) also present a typological survey of voice types. For discussions of ergativity, see Dixon (1979, 1987, 1994), Comrie (1978), Van Valin (1981, 1992b), Manning (1994), Kazenin (1994). See Schachter (1976, 1977) on Philippine languages. For a discussion of the interaction of animacy and agentivity, see Van Valin and Wilkins (1996).

Exercises

1 What is the syntactic pivot of the following English construction? Compare it to the syntactic pivot of other major constructions in English (*Hint*: the sentence-initial subject NP is not the pivot of the relevant construction.) [**section 6.2.2**]

(1) a. Pat brought the book to read.
b. *Pat brought the book to read it.
c. Pat brought the book for her sister to read.
d. *Pat brought the book for her sister to read it.

(2) a. John built a chest to put his clothes in.
b. *John built a chest to put his clothes in it.
c. John built a chest for his wife to put her clothes in.
d. *John built a chest for his wife to put her clothes in it.

(3) a. Sandy gave the book to Pat to read.
b. Sandy gave Pat the book to read.
c. *Sandy gave the book to Pat to read it.
d. *Sandy gave Pat the book to read it.
e. Sandy gave the book to Pat for her sister to read.
f. Sandy gave Pat the book for her sister to read.
g. *Sandy gave the book to Pat for her sister to read it.
h. *Sandy gave Pat the book for her to read it.

(4) a. Leslie brought a knife to carve the turkey with.
b. *Leslie brought a knife to carve the turkey with it.
c. Leslie brought a knife for Bruce to carve the turkey with.
d. *Leslie brought a knife for Bruce to carve the turkey with it.

(5) a. The book was bought by Sandy for Pat to read.
b. *The book was bought by Sandy for Pat to read it.
c. ??The book was bought by Sandy to read.
d. *The book was bought to read.
e. The book was bought for Pat to read.

(6) a. Chris brought the watch to be repaired by the jeweler.
b. *Chris brought the watch for it to be repaired by the jeweler.
c. The watch was brought to be repaired.
d. *The watch was brought for it to be repaired.

(7) a. The teacher sent the pupils away to study.
b. *The teacher sent the pupils away for them to study.
c. The pupils were sent away to study.
d. *The pupils were sent away for them to study.

(8) a. The terminally ill patients went to the hospice to die.
b. *The terminally ill patients went to the hospice for them to die.
c. The terminally ill patients were sent to the hospice to die.
d. *The terminally ill patients were sent to the hospice for them to die.

(9) a. The company supplied the team with uniforms to wear.
b. *The company supplied the team with uniforms to wear them.
c. The company supplied the team with uniforms for the players to wear.
d. *The company supplied the team with uniforms for the players to wear them.

2 Based on the data below and the data in (2)–(3) in exercise 3 in chapter 5, determine whether Toba Batak has grammatical relations or not. Follow the same procedures as used in section 6.2.1 in the discussion of English, Enga and Acehnese. If it does, characterize the restricted neutralization of each of the constructions illustrated in the data, and ascertain whether each pivot or controller is variable or invariable; if there is a variable syntactic pivot, is there any evidence as to whether it is a pragmatic pivot? What general patterns, if any, emerge regarding grammatical relations in this language? The data are from Schachter (1984b) and Shugamoto (1984). [**section 6.4.3**]

(1)	Mangantuk si Ria si Torus.	'Torus hit Ria.'
(2)	Manjaha buku guru i.	'The teacher read a book.'
(3)	Mate si Torus.	'Torus died.'
(4)	Diantuk si Torus si Ria.	'Torus hit Ria.'
(5)	Laho guru i.	'The teacher went/left.'
(6)	Ia si Torus mangantuk si Ria.	'[It was] Torus [who] hit Ria.' *'[It was] Torus [who] Ria hit.'
(7)	*Ia buku manjaha guru i.	'[It was] a book [that] the teacher read.'

(8)	Dijaha guru buku i.	'A teacher read the book.'
(9)	Ia si Torus diantuk si Ria.	'[It was] Torus [who] Ria hit.' *'[It was] Torus [who] hit Ria.'
(10)	Mangantuk si Torus si Ria.	'Ria hit Torus.'
(11)	Ia guru i manjaha buku.	'[It was] the teacher [who] read a book.'
(12)	Ia si Ria mate.	'[It was] Ria [who] died.'
(13)	Ia buku i dijaha guru.	'[It was] the book [that] a teacher read.'
(14)	Ia guru i laho.	'[It was] the teacher [who] left.'
(15)	guru [na manjaha buku] i	'the teacher who read a book'
(16)	*buku [na manjaha guru i]	'a book which the teacher read'
(17)	buku [na dijaha guru] i	'the book which a teacher read'
(18)	*guru [na dijaha buku i]	'a teacher who read the book'
(19)	guru [na mangida pangula] i	'the teacher who sees a farmer'/ *'the teacher who a farmer sees'
(20)	guru [na diida pangula] i	'the teacher who a farmer sees'/ *'the teacher who sees a farmer'
(21)	Mangida dirina si Torus.	'Torus sees himself.'
(22)	*Diida dirina si Torus.	*'Himself sees Torus.'
(23)	Diida si Torus dirina.	'Torus sees himself.'
(24)	*Mangida si Torus dirina.	*'Himself sees Torus.'
(25)	Mangantuk si Torus jala manipak guru si Ria.	'Ria hit Torus and kicked a teacher.'
(26)	Diantuk si Torus jala disipak guru si Ria.	'Ria was hit by Torus and was kicked by a teacher.'
(27)	Laho jala diantuk si Torus guru i.	'The teacher went and was hit by Torus.'
(28)	Mangantuk si Torus jala mate si Ria.	'Ria hit Torus and [Ria] died.'
(29)	Diantuk si Ria jala manipak guru si Torus.	'Torus was hit by Ria and kicked a teacher.'
(30)	Diantuk si Torus jala mate si Ria.	'Ria was hit by Torus and [Ria] died.'
(31)	Mangantuk guru jala disipak si Ria si Torus.	'Torus hit a teacher and was kicked by Ria.'
(32)	Laho jala manipak guru si Ria.	'Ria went and kicked a teacher.'

3 Based on the data below, determine whether Lakhota has grammatical relations or not. Follow the same procedures used in section 6.2.1 in the discussion of English, Enga and Acehnese. If it does, characterize the restricted neutralization of each of the constructions illustrated in the data, and ascertain whether each pivot or controller is variable or invariable; if there is a variable syntactic pivot, is there any evidence as to whether it is a pragmatic pivot? What general patterns, if any, emerge regarding grammatical relations in this language? [**section 6.4.3**]

(1)	Wahí/yahí/hí/hípi//blé/lé/yé/yápi	'I arrive'/'you arrive'/'(s)he arrives'/'they arrive'//'I go'/'you go'/'(s)he goes'/'they go'
(2)	Nawáxʔų/namáxʔų/nayáxʔų/namáyaxʔų/naníxʔų/naxʔų́/nawíčhaxʔų/nawíčhayaxʔų/nawíčhaxʔųpi	'I heard him/her/it'/'(s)he heard me'/'you heard him/her/it'/'you heard me'/'(s)he heard you'/'(s)he heard him/her/it'/'(s)he heard them'/'you heard them'/'they heard them'
(3)	Mištį́me/ništį́me/ištį́me/ištį́mapi	'I sleep'/'you sleep'/'(s)he sleeps'/'they sleep'
(4)	Makhúže/nikhúže/khúže/khúžapi//mat'é/nit'é/t'é/t'api	'I am sick'/'you are sick'/'(s)he is sick'/'they are sick'//'I die'/'you die'/'(s)he dies'/'they die'
(5)	Hokšíla ki ixʔé wą wąyą́ke.	'The boy saw a rock.'
(6)	Ixʔé ki lé/wą hokšíla ki wąyą́ke.	'The boy saw this/a rock.'
(7)	Hokšíla ki wį́yą ki wąyą́ke.	'The boy saw the woman.'
(8)	Wį́yą ki hokšíla ki wąyą́ke.	'The woman saw the boy.'/*'The boy saw the woman.'
(9)	Hokšíla ki táku/tuwá wąyą́ka he?	'What/who did the boy see?'
(10)	Tuwá wį́yą ki wąyą́ka he?	'Who saw the woman?'/*'Who did the woman see?'
(11)	Hokšíla wą wį́yą wą wąyą́ke ki le slolwáye.	'I know the boy who saw a woman.'/'I know the woman who a boy saw.'
(12)	Mathó wą hí čhąké wašíču ki hená ktépi.	'A bear came, and those whitemen killed it.'
(13)	Wašíču ki hená, mathó wą hí čhąké ktépi.	'Those whitemen, a bear came and they killed it.'
(14)	Wašíču ki hená hípi čhąké mathó ki wičhákte.	'Those whitemen arrived, and the bear killed them.'
(15)	Wašíču ki hená hípi ną mathó ki ktépi.	'Those whitemen arrived, and killed the bear.'
(16)	Mathó ki, wašíču ki hená hípi ną ktépi.	'The bear, those whitemen arrived and killed it.'
(17)	Mathó ki wašíču ki hená wąwíčhayąka čhąké ktépi.	'The bear saw those whitemen, and they killed it.'
(18)	Mathó ki wašíču ki hená wąwíčhayąkį ną wičhákte.	'The bear saw those whitemen and killed them.'
(19)	Mathó ki igmú ki aphá čha iyáye.	'The bear hit the cat$_i$, and so it$_i$ ran away.'
(20)	Mathó ki igmú ki aphį́ ną iyáye.	'The bear$_i$ hit the cat, and it$_i$ ran away.'
(21)	Mathó ki igmú ki aphá čha t'é.	'The bear hit the cat$_i$, and so it$_i$ died.'
(22)	Mathó ki igmú ki aphá čha yaxtáke.	'The bear$_i$ hit the cat$_j$, and so it$_j$ bit it$_i$.'
(23)	Mathó ki hí ną t'é.	'The bear came and died.'

(24)	Mathó ki hí ną iyáye.	'The bear came and ran away.'
(25)	Wašíču ki mathó ki wąyą́kį ną t'é.	'The whiteman saw the bear and died.'
(26)	Wašíču ki mathó ki wąyą́kį ną iyáye.	'The whiteman saw the bear and ran away.'
(27)	Mathó ki khúži ną t'é.	'The bear was sick and died.'
(28)	Mathó ki khúži ną iyáye.	'The bear was sick and ran away.'
(29)	Wówapi ki manú/*mawánu iblúthe.	'I tried to steal the book.'
(30)	Ištį́me/*mištį́me iblúthe.	'I tried to sleep.'
(31)	Iyáye/*iyáwaye iblúthe.	'I tried to run away.'
(32)	*Nayáxʔų iblúthe.	*'I tried for you to hear [me].' (intended meaning: 'I tried to be heard by you')
(33)	Ištį́me/ištį́mapi wąwíčhablake.	'I saw them sleeping.'
(34)	Hí(pi) wąwíčhablake.	'I saw them arrive.'
(35)	Hí(pi) nawíčhayaxʔų.	'You heard them arrive.'
(36)	Mathó ki kté(pi) wąwíčhablake.	'I saw them kill the bear.'/*'I saw the bear kill them.'
(37)	Mathó ki wičhákte wąbláke.	'I saw the bear kill them.'
(38)	*A (wíčha) waphe nawíčhayaxʔų.	*'You heard them-I hit [them].' (intended meaning: 'you heard them being hit by me')
(39)	Amáphaye!	'Hit me!'
(40)	Ištį́maye!	'Sleep!'
(41)	Iyáyaye!	'Go away!'

4 Discuss the results of the last two exercises in terms of the issues raised in this chapter regarding the diversity of grammatical relations systems cross-linguistically. Bring the data from Sama, Tzutujil and Jakaltek into the discussion. In particular, evaluate each of the proposals in section 6.1 as well as the theory of grammatical relations proposed in section 6.3 with respect to these phenomena. Do they support strong claims about the universality of grammatical relations? How do they bear on the issue of whether grammatical relations are primitives or are derived? [**section 6.4.3**]

5 It was mentioned in n. 7 that Barai, a language of Papua New Guinea (Olson 1978, 1981), neutralizes the actor–undergoer opposition with transitive verbs yet does not have a formal voice construction. Based on the Barai data below, explain how syntactic pivots work in Barai. Also, describe the Barai switch-reference system and specify the type of syntactic pivot that it is sensitive to. The switch-reference markers will be glossed 's/r', and you will need to determine which suffix marks 'same' and which signals 'different'. [**section 6.4.3**]

(1) a. Fu difuri. 'He is running.'
3sg run
b. E ije (fu) difuri. 'The man is running.'
person DEF 3sg run
b′. E be difuri. 'A (certain) man is running.'
[+SPEC]
b″. E-be difuri. 'Someone is running.'
[–SPEC]
c. Fu-ka difuri. 'He is really running.'
3sg-INTS run
d. E ije fu-ka difuri. 'The man is really running.'

(2) a. Fu visi. 'He is sick.'
3sg sick
b. E ije (fu) visi. 'The man is sick.'
c. Fu-ka visi. 'He is really sick.'
d. E ije fu-ka visi. 'The man is really sick.'

(3) a. Fu na kan-ie. 'He hit me.'
3sg 1sg hit-1sg
b. E ije (fu) na kan-ie. 'The man hit me.'
c. Fu-ka na kan-ie. 'He really hit me.'
c′. *Fu na-ka kan-ie.
d. E ije fu-ka na kan-ie. 'The man really hit me.'
d′. *E ije na-ka kan-ie.
e. Ame ije (fu) e ije kan-a. 'The child hit the man.'
e′. *Ame ije e ije fu kan-a.
f. Ame ije fu-ka e ije kan-a. 'The child really hit the man.'
f′. *Ame ije e ije fu-ka kan-a.

(4) a. Adame ije e n-one (bu) 'The disease sickened my people.'
disease 1sg-GEN 3pl
visinam-ia.
sicken-3pl
a′. *Adame ije (fu) e n-one visinam-ia.
b. Adame ije e n-one bu-ka visinam-ia. 'The disease really sickened my people.'
b′. *Adame ije fu-ka e n-one visinam-ia.
c. Ije na visinam-ie. 'It sickened me.'
d. Ije na-ka visinam-ie. 'It really sickened me.'
d′. *Ije-ka na visinam-ie.

(5) a. E ije fu-ka fanu ije kan-ia. 'The man really hit the animals.'
animal hit-3pl
b. Fanu ije bu-ka e-be kan-ia. 'Someone really hit the animals.'
b′. *E-be fu-ka fanu ije kan-ia.

	c.	*E-be fanu-be kan-ia.	'Someone hit some animals.'
	c′.	*Fanu-be e-be kan-ia.	'Someone hit some animals.'
	d.	Fanu be fu-ka e-be kan-a.	'Someone really hit a certain animal.'
	d′.	*E-be fu-ka fanu be kan-a.	
(6)	a.	Bara ije ame ije fu-ka mad-a. girl please-3sg	'The girls really pleased the child.'
	b.	E-be bara ije bu-ka mad-a.	'The girls really pleased someone.'
	b′.	*Bara ije e-be fu-ka ma-d-a.	
	c.	E-be ame ije fu-ka ma-d-a.	'Someone really pleased the child.'
(7)	a.	Ine are kan-a. tree house	'A/the tree hit a/the house.'
	b.	Are be ine kan-a.	'A/the tree hit a certain house.'
	c.	Are ije ine kan-a.	'A/the tree hit the house.'
	c′.	*Ine are be/ije kan-a.	
(8)	a.	Fu-ka e ij-iebe sa-e. NEW build-PAST	'THE MAN really built it.'
	a′.	*Ije-ka e ij-iebe sa-e.	'THE MAN really built it.'
	a″.	*E ij-iebe fu-ka ije sa-e.	
	b.	Ame ij-iebe bara ije bu-ka mad-a.	'The girls really please THE CHILD.'
	b′.	*Bara ije ame ij-iebe fu-ka mad-a.	
(9)	a.	Miane ije fu-ka ame ije sak-a. firestick bite-3sg	'The firestick really bit the child.'
	b.	Ame ije fu-ka miane sak-a.	'A firestick really bit the child.'
	b′.	*Miane ame ije sak-a.	'A firestick bit the child.'
	c.	Ine ije fu-ka na bij-ie. stick poke-1sg	'The stick really poked me.'
	d.	Na-ka ine bij-ie.	'A stick really poked me.'
	d′.	*Ine na bij-ie.	'A stick poked me.'
(10)	a.	Fu juae me-na fae kira. garden make-S/R fence tie	'He$_i$ made a garden and then $\emptyset_{i/*j}$ tied a fence.'
	a′.	Fu juae me-mo fu fae kira. -S/R	'He$_i$ made a garden and then he$_{*i/j}$ tied a fence.'
	b.	Ame ije fu ka na kan-ie-na ko. run.away	'The child$_i$ really hit me and then $\emptyset_i$ ran away.'
	b′.	Na-ka e-be kan-ie-mo fu ko.	'Someone$_i$ really hit me and then he$_i$ ran away.'
	b″.	Na-ka ame ij-iebe kan-ie-mo fu ko.	'THE CHILD$_i$ really hit me and then he$_i$ ran away.'

c.	Miane ije fu sak-i-mo fu barone. bite-3sg-S/R die	'The firestick bit him$_i$ and then he$_i$ died.'
c′.	Fu miane sak-i-na barone.	'A firestick bit him$_i$ and then he$_i$ died.'
d.	Na i me-na ine bij-ie. work do-S/R	'I was working and a stick poked me.'
e.	Adame ije ame ije visinam-a-na barone.	'The disease sickened the child$_i$ and it$_i$ died.'
f.	Bara ije ame ije mad-a-mo fu ko.	'The girl$_i$ pleased the child and she$_i$ ran away.'
f′.	Ame ij-iebe bara ije mad-a-na ko.	'The girl$_i$ pleased THE CHILD and she$_i$ ran away.'

7 Linking syntax and semantics in simple sentences

7.0 Introduction

In this chapter we address the details of the linking between syntax and semantics in simple sentences, that is, between the semantic representations introduced in chapters 3 and 4 and the syntactic representations introduced in chapter 2. This will involve syntactic pivots and controllers, as discussed in chapter 6. This will also involve focus structure, as we saw at the end of chapter 5. The system for linking syntax and semantics developed in chapters 3–6 is summarized in figure 7.1. The selection of privileged syntactic arguments, i.e. syntactic pivots and controllers, is based on the actor part of the Actor–Undergoer Hierarchy, as given in (7.1).

(7.1) *Privileged syntactic argument selection hierarchy*
arg. of DO > 1sg arg. of **do′** > 1st arg. of **pred′** (x, y) > 2nd arg. of **pred′** (x, y) > arg. of **pred′** (x)

In syntactically accusative constructions, the highest-ranking argument is the default choice to be the privileged syntactic argument (pivot or controller), whereas in syntactically ergative constructions, the lowest-ranking argument is the default choice. As we will see later in the chapter, languages vary as to whether the privileged syntactic argument must be a macrorole or not. PSA modulation voice constructions permit an alternative choice for pivot or controller. The basics of the linking for a simple sentence in English are illustrated in figure 7.2, repeated from chapter 5; the operator projection is omitted. The double-headed arrows in figures 7.1 and 7.2 indicate that the linking is bidirectional, that is, that linking goes from semantics to syntax and from syntax to semantics.

It is crucial to keep in mind that the relationship between the semantic representation and the syntactic representation is *not* derivational; that is, the syntactic representation is not derived from the semantic representation, and the semantic representation is not derived from the syntactic representation. Rather, the two independent representations are linked to each other, in the sense that argument variables in the semantic representation are associated with referring expressions in the syntactic representation, and vice versa. Accordingly, the relationship between the two representations is not the same as or analogous to the relationship between

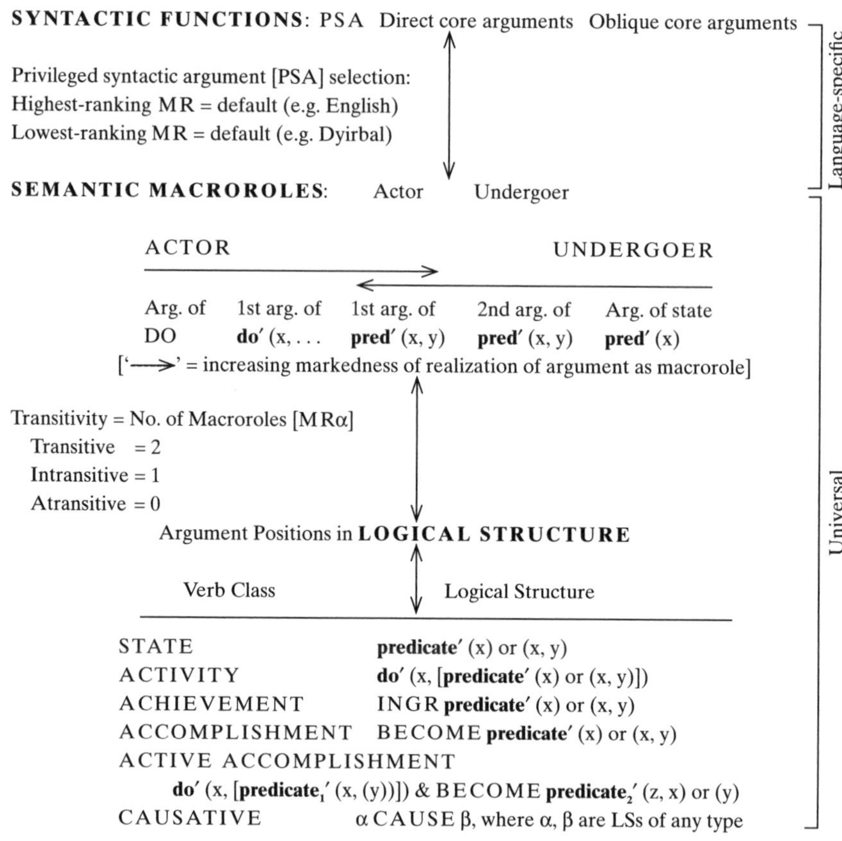

Figure 7.1 System linking semantic and syntactic representations

deep structure and surface structure in classical theories of transformational grammar or among D-structure, S-structure and logical form in GB/P&P. The arrows in diagrams like figure 7.2 merely represent the associations between argument positions in the semantic representations and referring expressions in the syntax. The macrorole labels do not constitute a distinct level of representation. Determining which argument is actor and which is undergoer does not produce a new level of representation; rather, it simply adds information to the semantic representation of the sentence. This is illustrated in the example in (7.2), which contains the logical structure for *Mary showed the photograph to Sam*/*Mary showed Sam the photograph*.

(7.2) a. [**do′** (Mary, ∅)] CAUSE [BECOME **see′** (Sam, photograph)]
b. [**do′** ($\text{Mary}_{\text{ACTOR}}$, ∅)] CAUSE [BECOME **see′** (Sam, $\text{photograph}_{\text{UNDERGOER}}$)]
c. [**do′** ($\text{Mary}_{\text{ACTOR}}$, ∅)] CAUSE [BECOME **see′** ($\text{Sam}_{\text{UNDERGOER}}$, photograph)]

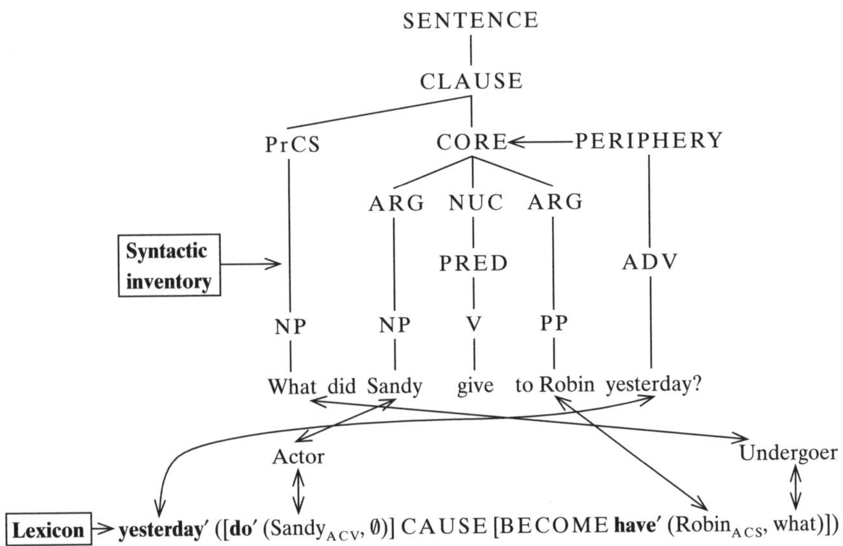

Figure 7.2 Linking syntax and semantics in a simple sentence in English

There are two possible macrorole assignments for the logical structure in (a). In both *Mary* is actor; in the default linking *photograph* is undergoer, but in the marked linking *Sam* is undergoer. The representations in (7.2b, c) show clearly that this is not a new level of representation but rather only an enrichment of the logical structure. These representations are in every way equivalent to the one in figure 7.2, which could give the misleading impression that actor and undergoer assignment create a new, intermediate level of representation between the semantic representation and the syntactic representation. There is no such intermediate level of representation. Given the amount of information which may need to be specified in the semantic representation of sentences, we will continue to represent the actor and undergoer assignments above the logical structure as in these figures in order to make them as clear as possible.

We will examine a wide range of grammatical phenomena: voice, case, agreement, reflexivization and WH-question formation. The discussion will proceed as follows. In the next section, we will briefly review the syntactic and semantic representations developed in chapters 2–5. In section 7.2 we lay out the algorithms for linking syntactic and semantic representations. A significant part of this discussion will concern the voice and undergoer alternations discussed in the previous chapter. In section 7.3 we will look at case marking and agreement and show how they can be captured in this system. In section 7.4 we will examine the two phases of the linking system. In section 7.5 we will focus on reflexivization, both as a type of anaphoric phenomenon as in languages like English, and as an operation on the argument structure of the verb, as in Slavic and Romance languages; this will lead to a discussion of middle constructions, since in many languages these constructions

Table 7.1 *Lexical representations for* Aktionsart *classes*

Verb class	*Logical structure*
State	**predicate′** (x) or (x, y)
Activity	**do′** (x, [**predicate′** (x) or (x, y)])
Achievement	INGR **predicate′** (x) or (x, y), or INGR **do′** (x, [**predicate′** (x) or (x, y)])
Accomplishment	BECOME **predicate′** (x) or (x, y), or BECOME **do′** (x, [**predicate′** (x) or (x, y)])
Active accomplishment	**do′** (x, [$\mathbf{predicate_1}$**′** (x, (y))]) & BECOME $\mathbf{predicate_2}$**′** (z, x) or (y)
Causative	α CAUSE β, where α, β are LSs of any type

bear what is traditionally considered to be reflexive morphology. In section 7.6, the topic will be the role of focus structure in linking. In the final section, we will discuss the nature of constructional templates and their role in the grammar.

7.1 Semantic and syntactic representations: a brief review

7.1.1 Constituting the semantic representation of a sentence

It would be useful here to briefly review how the semantic representation of a sentence is put together, based on the ideas developed in chapters 3, 4 and 5. The heart of it is the logical structure of the main predicating element in the sentence, usually a verb. The possible logical structures representing different verb types are presented in chapter 3 and are repeated in table 7.1.

Examples of lexical entries for some English verbs are given in (7.3), repeated from section 4.3.

(7.3)
a. *kill* [**do′** (x, ∅)] CAUSE [BECOME **dead′** (y)]
b. *receive* BECOME **have′** (x, y)
c. *own* **have′** (x, y)
d. *belong* (*to*) **have′** (x, y) [MR1]
e. *arrive* BECOME **be-at′** (x, y)
f. *go* **do′** (x, [**move.away.from.ref.point′** (x)]) & BECOME **be-LOC′** (y, x)
g. *seem* **seem′** (x, y) [MR0]
h. *see* **see′** (x, y)
i. *watch* **do′** (x, [**see′** (x, y)])
j. *show* [**do′** (w, ∅)] CAUSE [BECOME **see′** (x, y)]
k. *run* **do′** (x, [**run′** (x)])
l. *drink* **do′** (x, [**drink′** (x, y)])
m. *melt* BECOME **melted′** (x)
n. *afraid* **feel′** (x, [**afraid′** (y)])

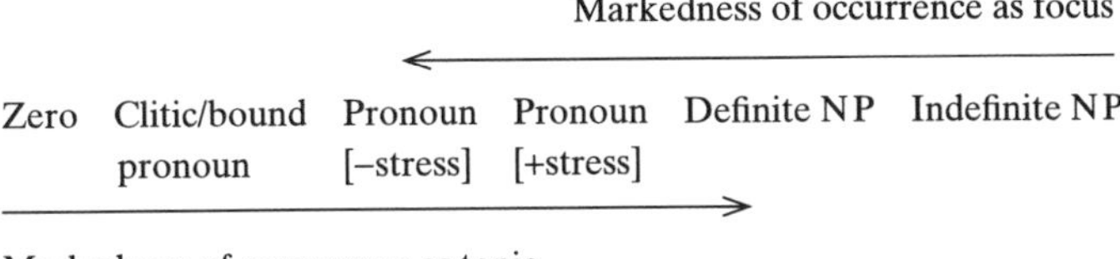

Figure 7.3 Coding of referents in terms of possible functions

Thus, the initial step in forming a semantic representation for a sentence is selecting the logical structure for the verb from the lexicon.

Predicative prepositions are also listed in the lexicon, and if they are to appear in the sentence as adjuncts, they too must be selected and added to the representation. The result would be a logical structure like **after′** (z, [**see′** (x, y)]). The variables in logical structure, if they are not marked as unspecified, must be filled in either by NPs or, in the case of complement-taking predicates, logical structures representing complements. The selection of the NP-type to fill the variable slot involves the interaction of the lexicon and focus structure. Nouns have lexical entries like verbs and adpositions; their semantic representation is in terms of qualia rather than a logical structure, as illustrated in (7.4), repeated from chapter 4.

(7.4) **door** (x $\vee$ y)
1 Const: **obstruction′** (x), **aperture′** (y)
2 Form: **physical-object′** (x), **frame′** (y)
3 Telic: BECOME **closed′/open′** (x), **do′** (z, [**go.through′** (z, y)])
4 Agentive: **artifact′** (x), **artifact′** (y)

The form of the NP filling a variable slot is a function, to a considerable degree, of discourse pragmatics, as we saw in chapter 5; this was summarized in figure 5.2, repeated here in figure 7.3. If the referent is highly activated, then it may be realized as a zero pronoun, clitic or unstressed pronoun. If it is unidentifiable, hence new, it is likely to be realized as an indefinite NP. In figure 7.2, this influence is depicted by the subscripts on the NPs indicating activation level. Anaphoric elements, both pronouns and reflexives/reciprocals, are present in the semantic representation of the sentence. The final aspect of the NP to be determined is its operators, and these reflect both lexical properties, e.g. nominal aspect (count vs. mass), and discourse properties, e.g. definiteness. Consider the following possessive NP, repeated from section 4.7.5.

(7.5) $\langle_{DEF}+\langle_{NEG}\emptyset\langle_{QNT}\exists\langle_{NUM}SG\langle_{NASP}COUNT\langle$**have′** (Larry, [**be′** (<u>house</u>, [**red′**])])$\rangle\rangle\rangle\rangle\rangle\rangle$

If the value of the definiteness operator is '+', then this would be instantiated as *Larry's red house*; whereas if it is '–', then it would appear as *a red house of Larry's*.

The remaining aspect of the representation to be determined is the operators for the sentence. The representation of *Has Joshua been singing?* is given in (7.6), repeated from section 4.4.2.

(7.6) ⟨$_{\text{IF}}$ *INT* ⟨$_{\text{TNS}}$ *PRES* ⟨$_{\text{ASP}}$ *PERF PROG* ⟨**do′** (Joshua, [**sing′** (Joshua)])⟩⟩⟩⟩

A complete semantic representation for the sentence *The big dog gently opened the green door in the kitchen yesterday*, including NP and clausal operators, is given in figure 7.4, repeated from section 4.8. Given the complexity of such a representation, we will specify only the information relevant to the issue under discussion in this chapter. So for many topics, for example, the internal structure of the NPs filling the variable positions in logical structure is not germane and therefore will not be specified. In the same vein, if the clausal operators are not at issue, they will not be represented.

7.1.2 Selecting the syntactic representation of the sentence

Having constituted a semantic representation akin to that in figure 7.4, we must now select the syntactic structure into which the elements of the semantic representation are to be mapped. At the end of chapter 2, we suggested that syntactic representations were best conceived of as *syntactic templates*, stored in what we have called the 'syntactic inventory'. Examples of templates from the syntactic inventory are given in figure 7.5. Moreover, at the end of chapter 5, we argued that some templates are stored with focus structure information, e.g. WH-questions, which always have narrow focus on the WH-word, or presentational constructions, which are always sentence focus. This is illustrated in figure 7.6, repeated from section 5.8. If one wanted to construct a WH-question, as in figure 7.2, then it would be necessary to combine the WH-question template in figure 7.6 with the appropriate core template from figure 7.5, in this case Core-2. The result is the template given in figure 7.7. In section 4.5 we discussed how the appropriate template is selected and proposed principles to account for this. They are given in (7.7) on page 324.

⟨IF *DCL* ⟨TNS *PAST* ⟨**yesterday′** ([**gentle′** (**do′** (x, ∅))] CAUSE [BECOME **open′** (y)])⟩⟩⟩

⟨DEF + ⟨QNT ∃ ⟨NUM *SG* ⟨NASP *COUNT* ⟨**be′** (**dog** (x), [**big′**])⟩⟩⟩⟩⟩

⟨DEF + ⟨QNT ∃ ⟨NUM *SG* ⟨NASP *COUNT* ⟨[**be-in′** (z, [**be′** (**door** (y), [**green′**])])]⟩⟩⟩⟩⟩

⟨DEF + ⟨QNT ∃ ⟨NUM *SG* ⟨NASP *COUNT* ⟨(**kitchen** (z))⟩⟩⟩⟩⟩

Figure 7.4 Semantic representation of *The big dog gently opened the green door in the kitchen yesterday*

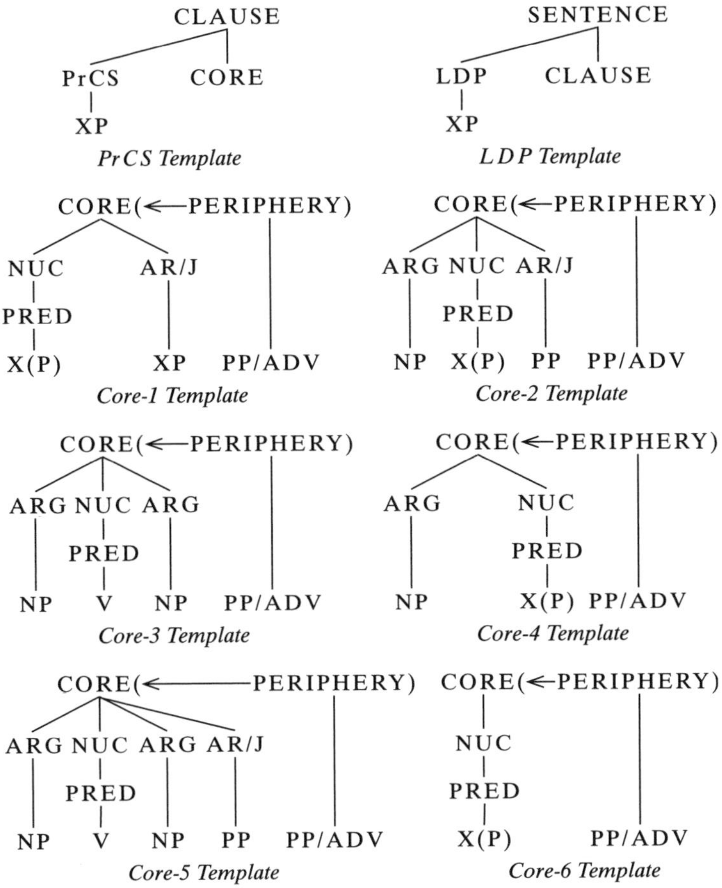

CLAUSE
PrCS CORE
XP
PrCS Template

SENTENCE
LDP CLAUSE
XP
LDP Template

CORE(←PERIPHERY)
NUC AR/J
PRED
X(P) XP PP/ADV
Core-1 Template

CORE(←PERIPHERY)
ARG NUC AR/J
PRED
NP X(P) PP PP/ADV
Core-2 Template

CORE(←PERIPHERY)
ARG NUC ARG
PRED
NP V NP PP/ADV
Core-3 Template

CORE(←PERIPHERY)
ARG NUC
PRED
NP X(P) PP/ADV
Core-4 Template

CORE(←PERIPHERY)
ARG NUC ARG AR/J
PRED
NP V NP PP PP/ADV
Core-5 Template

CORE(←PERIPHERY)
NUC
PRED
X(P) PP/ADV
Core-6 Template

Figure 7.5 Syntactic templates from the syntactic inventory

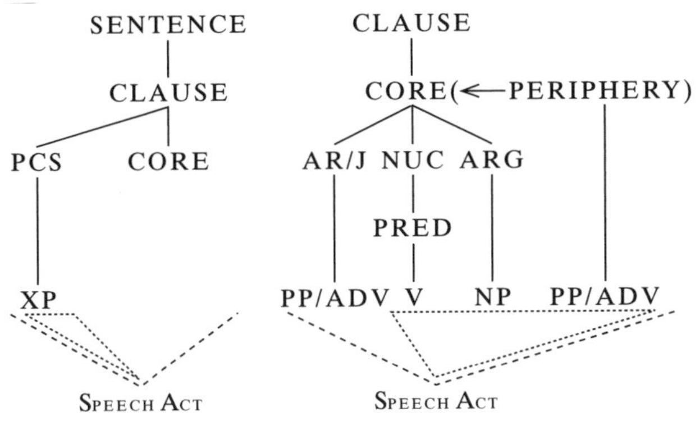

Figure 7.6 Syntactic templates for English WH-question and presentational constructions

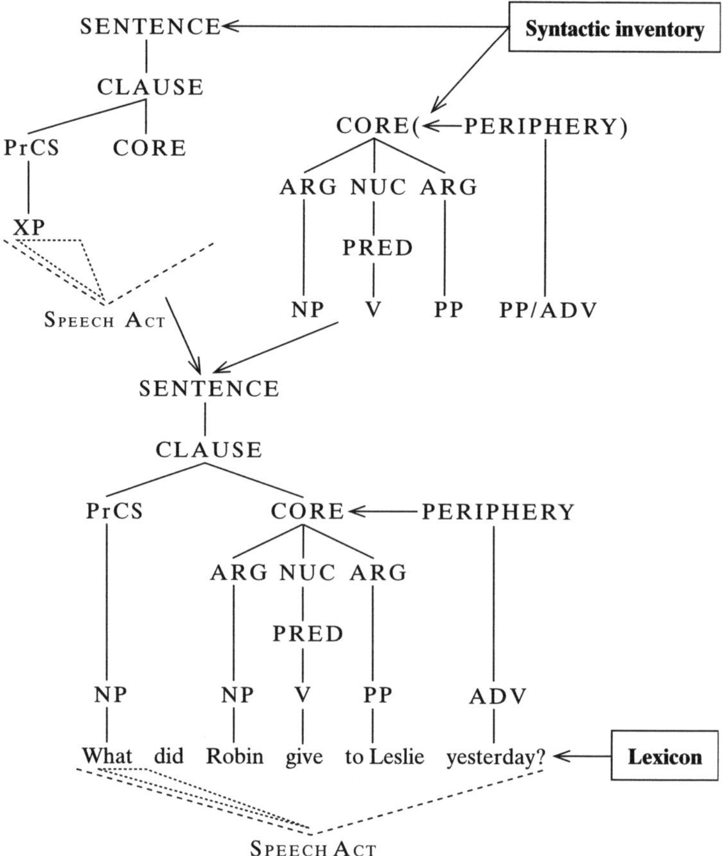

Figure 7.7 Combining templates to yield syntactic representation of a sentence

(7.7) a. *Syntactic template selection principle*
The number of syntactic slots for arguments and argument-adjuncts within the core is equal to the number of distinct specified argument positions in the semantic representation of the core.
b. *Language-specific qualifications of the principle in (a)*:
1 All cores in the language have a minimum syntactic valence of 1.
2 Passive constructions reduce the number of core slots by 1.
3 The occurrence of a syntactic argument in the pre-/postcore slot reduces the number of core slots by 1 (may override (1)).

These principles govern the selection of the appropriate syntactic template from the syntactic inventory for a given semantic representation.

7.2 The linking algorithms

An adequate theory of the relationship between syntax and semantics must be able to account for how semantic representations are mapped into syntactic representations and also how syntactic representations are mapped into semantic representations; the two processes are not identical. Before developing the linking algorithms that govern these mappings, it is necessary to first introduce a general principle constraining these algorithms.

7.2.1 The Completeness Constraint

The linking between syntax and semantics is governed by a very general constraint, called the *Completeness Constraint.* It is stated in (7.8).

(7.8) *Completeness Constraint*
All of the arguments explicitly specified in the semantic representation of a sentence must be realized syntactically in the sentence, and all of the referring expressions in the syntactic representation of a sentence must be linked to an argument position in a logical structure in the semantic representation of the sentence.

This is a common-sense condition which captures the basic intuitions that (1) in order for an element in the syntax to be interpreted, it must be tied to something in the semantic representation; and (2) all of the material in the semantic representation must be expressed in some way in the overt form of the sentence, otherwise the interpretation of the syntactic representation would not correspond to the meaning of the semantic representation to which it is linked. Two aspects of it need to be clarified. First, the phrase 'arguments explicitly specified in the semantic representation of a sentence' is very important. It is not always the case that all of the argument slots in a logical structure must be filled for a sentence to be grammatical. Consider the following sets of examples.

(7.9) a. Pat drank wine.
b. Pat drank.
c. **do′** (Pat, [**drink′** (Pat, wine)])
d. **do′** (Pat, [**drink′** (Pat, ∅)])

(7.10) a. Sandy loaded the truck with boxes.
b. Sandy loaded the truck.
c. [**do′** (Sandy, ∅)] CAUSE [BECOME **be-in′** (truck, boxes)]
d. [**do′** (Sandy, ∅)] CAUSE [BECOME **be-in′** (truck, ∅)]

The '∅' in the (d) logical structures indicates that the argument in question is unspecified; it cannot therefore be linked to any element in the syntax. In accordance with the Completeness Constraint, (7.9c) can be the logical structure for (7.9a) and (7.9d) for (7.9b), but not vice versa. That is, (7.9a) cannot be linked to (d), because the NP *wine* cannot be linked to the unspecified argument position; since it cannot be linked to a position in the logical structure, it cannot be interpreted. Similarly, (7.9c) cannot be the logical structure for (b), since the NP *wine* in the logical structure is not realized in the syntax. The same pairings of sentences and logical structures hold in (7.10): (a) with (c), (b) with (d), for the same reasons. The Completeness Constraint rules out the other possible linkings.[1]

The second aspect of (7.8) which needs clarification is the second part, 'all of the referring expressions in the syntactic representation of the sentence must be linked to an argument position in a logical structure'. 'Referring expressions in the syntactic representation of the sentence' refers to the NPs in the sentence, regardless of whether they are in the core, the periphery, a PP, the pre/postcore slot or a detached position.[2] It also includes the bound pronominal markers on the verb in head-marking languages. This means that non-core elements are subject to the Completeness Constraint, and that is why the wording is 'argument position in *a* logical structure'. This can be illustrated with the following example.

(7.11) a. Robin saw Pat after the concert.
b. **after′** (concert, [**see′** (Robin, Pat)])

As we saw in section 4.4.1.1, peripheral PPs like *after the concert* in (7.11a) are represented as higher predicates semantically; that is, *after* is a predicative proposition taking *the concert* and the whole logical structure for *Robin saw Pat* as its arguments. The NPs *Robin* and *Pat* are linked to the two argument positions in the logical structure for *see*, while *the concert* is linked to an argument position in the logical structure for *after*. Hence the Completeness Constraint is satisfied, even though the NPs in the sentence in (a) are linked to argument positions in different logical structures in (b).

7.2.2 Linking from semantics to syntax

The linking procedure for simple sentences is summarized in (7.12). It assumes that the semantic and syntactic representations have already been determined. The principles in (7.7) governing the selection of the appropriate syntactic template can only apply to a complete semantic representation.

(7.12) *Linking algorithm: semantics → syntax (preliminary formulation)*

1 Determine the actor and undergoer assignments, following the Actor–Undergoer Hierarchy in figure 7.1.
2 Assign specific morphosyntactic status to [–WH] arguments in logical structure (language-specific).
   a. Accusative privileged syntactic argument selection: default = Actor.
   b. Ergative privileged syntactic argument selection: default = Undergoer.
3 If there is a [+WH] XP, assign it to the precore slot (language-specific).
4 A non-WH XP may be assigned to the pre- or postcore slot, subject to focus structure restrictions (optional; language-specific).
5 Assign the core arguments the appropriate case markers/adpositions and assign the predicate in the nucleus the appropriate agreement marking (language-specific).
6 Assign arguments of logical structures other than that of the main verb to the periphery.

Case marking will be discussed in detail in section 7.3 below. Let us illustrate this with some very simple examples from Icelandic, a syntactically accusative language, and from Sama (Walton 1986), a syntactically ergative language. They are given in (7.13) and (7.14).

(7.13) a. Ólaf-ur sá Sigg-u.
Olaf-MsgNOM see.PAST Sigga-FsgACC
'Olaf saw Sigga.'
b. Sigg-a va-r séð af Ólaf-i.
Sigga-FsgNOM be.PAST-3sg see.PSTP.FsgNOM of Olaf-MsgDAT
'Sigga was seen by Olaf.'

(7.14) a. Nda' ku d'nda.
see 1sgERG woman
'I see the woman.'
b. N-nda' aku d'nda.
ANTI-see 1sgABS woman
'I see the woman.'

The nominative case NP is the privileged syntactic argument in the Icelandic examples. The situation is somewhat more complicated in Sama, which lacks case marking for NPs; pronouns, however, have absolutive and ergative forms, and in these examples *ku* is the first person singular ergative form and *aku* the first person singular absolutive form. Hence in (7.14a) *d'nda* 'woman' is the privileged syntactic argument, but in (b) *aku* '1sgABS' is. In Icelandic the actor argument is the default choice for privileged syntactic argument, and this is reflected by its clause-initial position, nominative case, agreement with the finite verb (which is not distinctive in this particular example) and lack of passive morphology on the verb. In Sama, on the other hand, the undergoer is the unmarked choice for privileged syntactic argument, and this is signaled by the ergative form of the actor pronoun and the lack of voice marking on the verb. If these sentences were used in the various types of complex sentences discussed in the last chapter, it would be clear that the nominative NP *Ólafur* in Icelandic and the NP *d'nda* 'woman' in Sama are pragmatic pivots (Walton 1986, Van Valin 1991b).

The logical structure of the verbs in all four sentences is **see′** (x, y). The semantic representations with lexical information only for each pair of sentences is given in (7.15).

(7.15) a. **see′** (Ólaf-, Sigg-)
b. **see′** (1sg, d'nda)[3]

Since both languages have pragmatic pivots, the discourse-pragmatic status of the arguments can influence the linking. Since Icelandic is a syntactically accusative language, the default linking of actor to privileged syntactic argument obtains, prototypically, in a predicate–focus construction, in which the actor is activated and

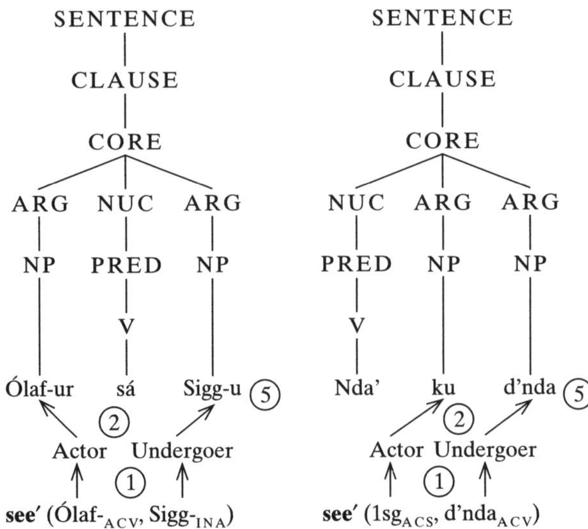

Figure 7.8 Active-voice linkings in Icelandic and Sama

the undergoer is inactive. The opposite situation would be found in the prototypical linking of undergoer to privileged syntactic argument in Sama: in a predicate–focus construction, the undergoer would have a higher activation status than the actor. Hence the more complete input semantic representations to the possible linkings in (7.13) and (7.14) would be those in (7.16); operators and NP properties are omitted.

(7.16) a. **see′** (Ólaf-$_{ACV}$, Sigg-$_{INA}$)
b. **see′** (1sg$_{ACS}$, d'nda$_{ACV}$)[4]

The active-voice linkings, those in the (a) sentences in (7.13)–(7.14), are diagrammed in figure 7.8. The numbers refer to the steps in (7.12). The first argument of **see′** would be the actor, the second the undergoer, following the Actor–Undergoer Hierarchy. Since Icelandic is an accusative language and *sjá* 'see' is a regular verb, the actor will receive nominative case and the undergoer accusative case (see section 7.3). In Sama, on the other hand, there is no NP case marking, but pronouns are distinguished on an ergative basis. Since the actor is not the choice for the privileged syntactic argument in the active-voice linking, the first-person pronoun would occur in the ergative form, *ku*. Actor normally precedes undergoer in the Sama clause (see (6.70)).

The alternative linking in (7.13b) and (7.14b) involves marked choices for the privileged syntactic argument, which would be undergoer for Icelandic and actor for Sama. These are represented in figure 7.9. What is perhaps most striking about these two examples is how little the Sama antipassive form differs from the active form, in contrast to the major differences between the Icelandic active and passive

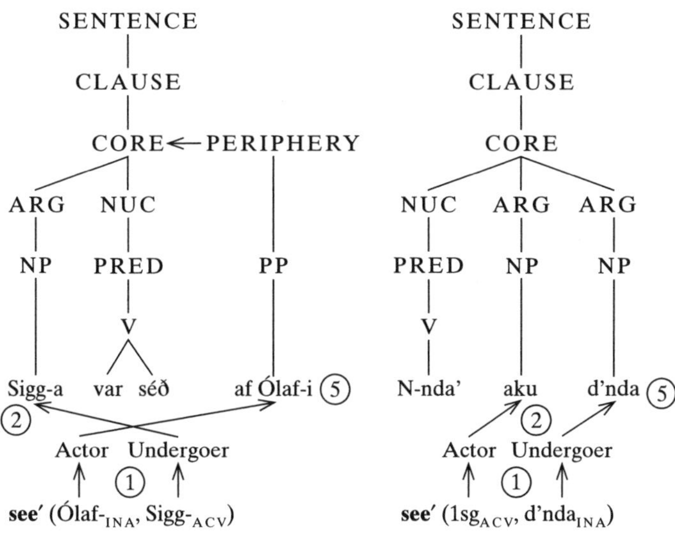

Figure 7.9 Passive- and antipassive-voice linkings in Icelandic and Sama

forms. The only changes in the clause are the form of the verb and the form of the actor pronoun; the arrangement of the arguments has not changed. In the Sama antipassive in (7.14b), the undergoer appears as a core argument, not as a peripheral oblique. In an agentless passive, e.g. *Sigga var séð* 'Sigga was seen', the argument position of the actor argument in the logical structure would be unspecified, leaving only the undergoer to be linked into the syntax.

An important thing to note in the syntactic representations in figures 7.8 and 7.9 is that there is no special marker, branch or label in the tree for the privileged syntactic argument, which is the core-initial NP in Icelandic and the core-medial or final NP in Sama in these examples. This is because the privileged syntactic argument (syntactic pivot or controller) is a construction-specific function, and therefore is not tied to a special position in the layered structure of the clause; contrast this with the configurational definition of 'subject' in section 6.1.2.1 (see especially figure 6.1). There are two reasons for the lack of a special representation for privileged syntactic arguments in the clause structures. First, there is no evidence that clause structure in languages with grammatical relations is different from clause structure in languages without them. Second, and more important, the same clause pattern can have different privileged arguments, depending upon constructional factors. We saw this with relativization and reflexivization from Sama in (6.50) in section 6.3. The examples, from Walton (1986), are repeated in (7.17).

(7.17) a. B'lli d'nda daing ma di-na.
buy woman fish for REFL-3sg
'The woman bought the fish for herself.'

b. N-b'lli d'nda daing ma di-na.
ANTI-buy woman fish for REFL-3sg
'The woman bought fish for herself.'

c. daing b'lli d'nda ma di-na
fish buy woman for REFL-3sg
'the fish that the woman bought for herself'

d. d'nda N-b'lli daing ma di-na
woman ANTI-buy fish for REFL-3sg
'the woman who bought fish for herself'

d′. d'nda b'lli daing ma di-na
woman buy fish for REFL-3sg
*'the woman who bought the fish for herself'
OK: 'the woman who the fish bought for itself'

In (7.17a), an active-voice form, *daing* 'fish' is the undergoer and the privileged syntactic argument; it has the same syntactic structure as the Sama sentence in figure 7.8. In (b), an antipassive form, the actor *d'nda* 'woman' is the privileged syntactic argument; it has the same structure as the Sama sentence in figure 7.9. Because the head of the relative clause must function as the syntactic pivot within the relative clause, the only relative clause that can be formed from (a) is (c). Similarly, the only relative clause that can be formed from (b) is (d). If the head noun *d'nda* 'woman' is combined with an active-voice verb in the relative clause, as in (d′), the result is grammatical but nonsensical. Thus, with respect to the relative clause construction, the syntactic pivot is the undergoer with an active voice verb in the relative clause and the actor with an antipassive voice verb. With respect to the reflexive construction, however, the controller is constant: the actor controls or binds the reflexive anaphor, regardless of whether the verb is active or antipassive voice. Hence in (7.17c) there are two distinct privileged arguments, a pragmatic pivot, *daing* 'fish', for relativization, and a semantic controller, *d'nda* 'woman', for reflexivization. There is no single position within the layered structure of the Sama clause which correlates with being the privileged argument, and therefore it would be pointless to try to represent the pivot or controller directly as a special branch, category or the like in the syntactic representation.

Both Icelandic and Sama are dependent-marking languages (see sections 2.1.2, 2.2.2), and accordingly the arguments mapped into the syntax occur as free forms. In head-marking languages, on the other hand, the core arguments appear as bound forms on the verb, and independent NPs appear within the clause but outside of the core. A Lakhota sentence with and without independent NPs is given in (7.18).

(7.18) a. Na-wíčha-ya-xʔų. (< *naxʔų́* 'hear')
stem-3plU-2sgA-hear
'You heard them.'

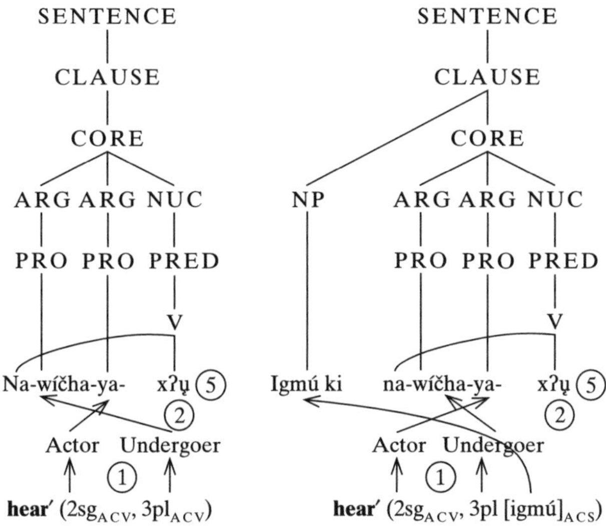

Figure 7.10 Linking in Lakhota, a head-marking language

b. Igmú ki na-wíčha-ya-xʔų.
cat the stem-3plU-2sgA-hear
'You heard the cats.'

A question that immediately arises is, if the bound pronominals on the verb are the true syntactic arguments, then how are the independent NPs represented semantically? It is clear that the logical structure for (a) would be **hear′** (2sg, 3pl). What is the semantic relationship between *igmú ki* 'the cat(s)' and *wičha-* '3plU'? They represent the same referent and function as the same argument, the undergoer, and accordingly they must fill the same argument position in the logical structure. Hence, the logical structure for (b) would be **hear′** (2sg, 3pl[igmú]), where '3pl[igmú]' represents the fact that the primary manifestation of the argument is the pronominal affix, with the full NP being an optional, secondary element. The linking in these two sentences is given in figure 7.10.

The different statuses of the bound morphemes on the finite verb in Lakhota and Icelandic represent the contrast between head-marking and dependent-marking languages: the bound morphemes count as the core arguments in Lakhota, but in Icelandic the independent NPs count as the core arguments, with the bound morphemes merely being agreement markers. There is, however, an intermediate situation, in which the independent NP counts as the core argument if present, but if it is absent, the bound marker on the verb functions as the argument, as we discussed in section 2.2.2.1. This is the situation in so-called 'pro-drop' languages like Spanish, Italian and Croatian. Bresnan and Mchombo (1987) argue that the 'subject' agreement prefix in Chicheŵa and other Bantu languages is also of this type; it is agreement, if the 'subject' NP is present, but otherwise it serves as the 'subject', just as in a head-marking language like Lakhota. Thus an Italian sentence like the one in (7.19) will have a slightly different semantic representation if there is no independent 'subject' NP.

(7.19) a. Maria ha aper-to la finestra.
have.3sgPRES open-PSTP the.Fsg window
'Maria opened the window.'
a′. [**do′** (Maria, ∅)] CAUSE [BECOME **open′** (finestra)]
b. Ha aper-to la finestra.
have.3sgPRES open-PSTP the.Fsg window
'(S)he opened the window.'
b′. [**do′** (3sg, ∅)] CAUSE [BECOME **open′** (finestra)]

When *Maria* (or an independent pronoun) is linked in (a), it will appear in an independent core argument position, as in a dependent-marking language, whereas when '3sg' is linked in (b), it will be realized as a bound suffix on the tensed verb or auxiliary, as in a head-marking language. There are finite verb agreement rules in Italian like those to be investigated in section 7.3.1.1, and they would not apply when a logical structure like (b′) is involved.

Step 4 in the linking algorithm in (7.12) refers to WH-questions in which the WH-word occurs in the precore slot. Examples of Icelandic and Sama WH-questions are given in (7.20).

(7.20) a. Hver-ja sá Ólaf-ur?
who-ACC see.PAST Olaf-MsgNOM
'Who did Olaf see?'
b. Say nda' d'nda?
who see woman
'Who did the woman see?' (*'Who saw the woman?')
b′. Say N-nda' d'nda?
who ANTI-see woman
'Who saw the woman?' (*'Who did the woman see?')

Sama, like many other western Austronesian languages, restricts WH-questions to pragmatic pivots; that is, only the privileged syntactic argument of the clause (as signaled by the voice of the verb) may be questioned in this construction. Hence the WH-word may only be interpreted as the undergoer with an active-voice verb and only as actor with an antipassive-voice verb, as in (7.20b, b′). The linkings in (7.20a) and (b) are given in figure 7.11. When we take up case marking and agreement in section 7.3, the accusative case on *hverja* 'who' in (7.20a) will be an important issue (see section 2.1.1). Step 4 is language-specific, because there are languages (1) in which WH-words appear in the same position that a non-WH-phrase would

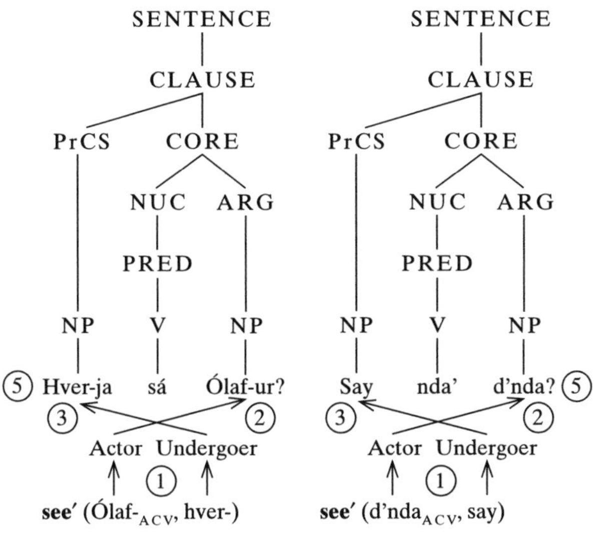

Figure 7.11 WH-question linking in Icelandic and Sama

appear in, e.g. Mandarin, and (2) in which WH-words appear in a core-internal focus position, e.g. Turkish. This is illustrated in (7.21). (Turkish examples from Underhill 1976.)

(7.21) a. Tā qiāo pò le yī ge fànwán. — Mandarin
3sg hit break ASP one CL ricebowl
'He broke (by hitting) a ricebowl.'
b. Tā qiāo pò le shénme?
3sg hit break ASP what
'What did he break?'
c. (Siz) Gazete-yi Halil-e ver-di-niz. — Turkish
2pl newspaper-ACC -DAT give-PAST-2pl
'You (pl) gave the newspaper to Halil.'
d. (Siz) Halil-e ne ver-di-niz?
2pl -DAT what give-PAST-2pl
'What did you (pl) give to Halil?'
d′. *(Siz) Ne Halil-e ver-di-niz?
2pl what -DAT give-PAST-2pl

The linking would be basically the same in the two Mandarin sentences, unlike in the two statement–question pairs in Icelandic and Sama. The Turkish sentences would have different linkings, because the WH-word normally appears in the immediately preverbal focus position in the core, as the data in exercise 2 in chapter 5 showed (Erguvanlı 1984); it does not, however, appear in a precore-slot position, unlike Icelandic and Sama.

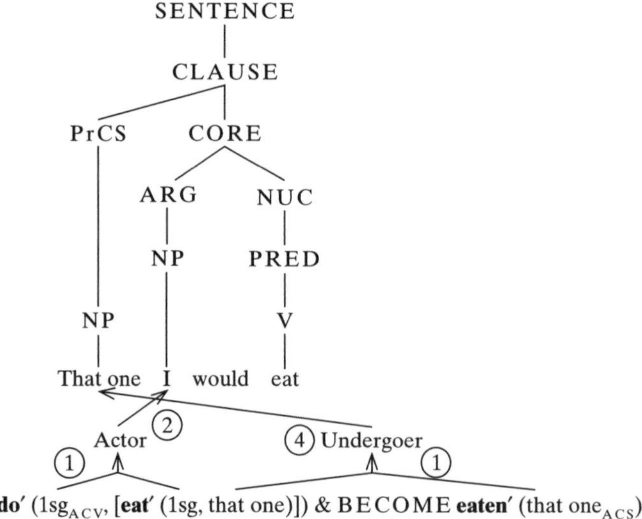

Figure 7.12 Semantics → syntax linking in English precore slot narrow-focus construction

The next step in (7.12) refers to the linking of non-WH-phrases to the precore slot or to the postcore slot. The linking in the English sentence *That one I would eat* is given in figure 7.12. Unlike English, Japanese has a postcore slot, and Shimojo (1995) shows that the element that occurs in the postcore slot is normally non-focal, the primary focus in the sentence being in the matrix core. The postcore slot element may be a secondary focus, in some contexts, but it is never the primary focal element in the sentence. Examples of this construction from chapter 2 are repeated below, and the linking in (7.22c) is given in figure 7.13.

(7.22) a. Hanako ga tosyokan de Ken ni hon o age-ta yo.
NOM library in DAT book ACC give-PAST PRT
'Hanako gave a book to Ken in the library.'
b. Hanako ga tosyokan de Ken ni age-ta yo hon o.
NOM library in DAT give-PAST PRT book ACC
b. Hanako ga tosyokan de hon o age-ta yo Ken ni.
NOM library in book ACC give-PAST PRT DAT

The last step in (7.12) refers to the linking of non-core elements. Given the logical structure in (7.11b), the linking would be as in figure 7.14. Peripheral adjuncts may also be linked to the left-detached position in many languages; this would yield *After the concert, Robin saw Pat.* In questions like *Where did Robin see Pat?* or *When did Robin see Pat?*, the source of the WH-word has to be from a logical structure like the one in (7.11b), and yet there is no predicative preposition to serve as a higher predicate. In such cases we must posit an abstract locative or temporal

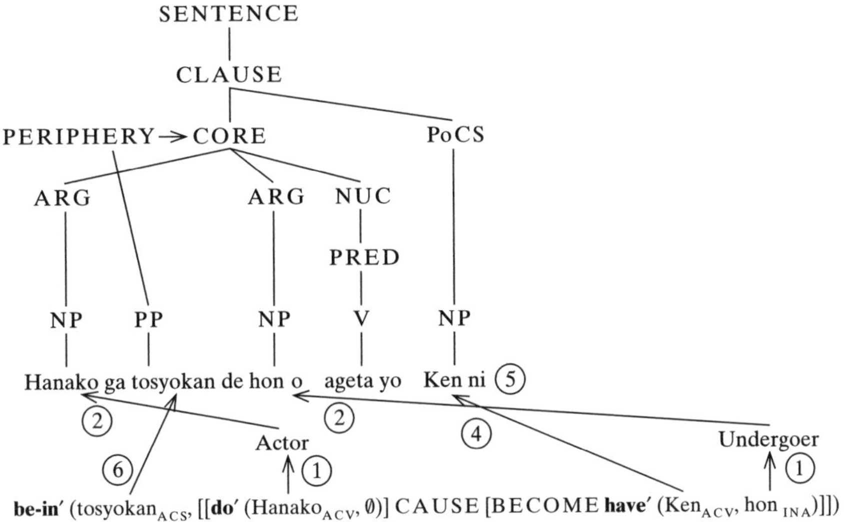

Figure 7.13 Semantic → syntax linking in Japanese postcore slot construction

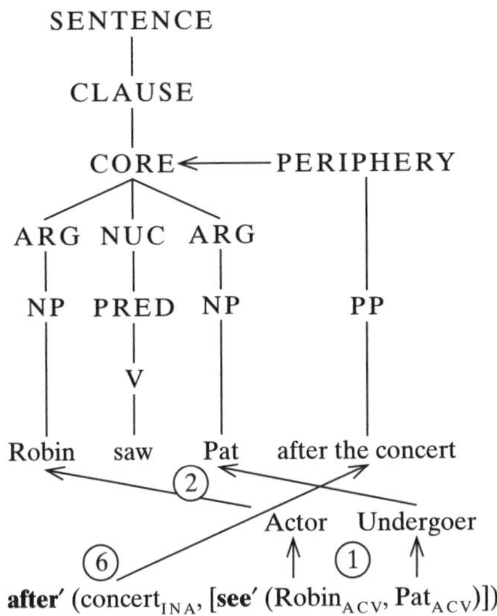

Figure 7.14 Linking of peripheral adjunct in English

higher predicate, i.e. **be-LOC′** or **be-TEMP′** (x, y), following a suggestion from Jurafsky (1992), in which the WH-word functions as the *x* argument and the logical structure of the core functions as the *y* argument. Hence the logical structure for *Where did Robin see Pat?* would be **be-LOC′** (where, [**see′** (Robin, Pat)]). The linking into the syntax would be the same as in figure 7.14, except that the WH-word would occur in the precore slot.

In section 4.1 we looked briefly at undergoer alternations, that is, variable linking of different arguments to undergoer. This can take a number of different forms in English and the other languages which allow it. The first are the 'dative shift' constructions, involving RECIPIENT and THEME arguments with verbs of transfer. These are exemplified in (7.23)–(7.25).

(7.23) *English*
give: [**do′** (Fred, ∅)] CAUSE [BECOME **have′** (Pamela, flowers)]
a. Fred$_{ACT}$ gave the flowers$_{UND}$ to Pamela$_{OCA}$.
b. Fred$_{ACT}$ gave Pamela$_{UND}$ the flowers$_{DCA}$.

(7.24) *Indonesian* -kan *construction* (Foley and Van Valin 1984)
-kirim 'send': [**do′** (Ali, ∅)] CAUSE [BECOME **have′** (Hasan, surat)]
a. Ali meng-kirim surat itu kepada Hasan.
ATV-send letter the to
'Ali$_{ACT}$ sent the letter$_{UND}$ to Hasan$_{OCA}$.
b. Ali meng-kirim-kan Hasan surat itu.
ATV-send-LOC letter the
'Ali$_{ACT}$ sent Hasan$_{UND}$ the letter$_{DCA}$.'

(7.25) *Dyirbal* (Dixon 1972)
wugal 'give': [**do′** (dyugumbil, ∅)] CAUSE [BECOME **have′** (yaɽa, miraɲ)]
a. Ba-la-m miraɲ-∅ ba-ŋgu-n ḑugumbi-ɽu
DEIC-ABS-III beans-ABS DEIC-ERG-II woman-ERG
wuga-n ba-gu-l yaɽa-gu.
give-TNS DEIC-DAT-I man-DAT
'The woman$_{ACT}$ gave beans$_{UND}$ to the man$_{DCA}$.'
b. Ba-yi yaɽa-∅ wuga-n ba-ŋgu-n ḑugumbi-ɽu baŋgum
DEIC-ABS.I man-ABS give-TNS DEIC-ERG-II woman-ERG DEIC-INST-III
miraɲ-ḑu.
beans-INST
'The woman$_{ACT}$ gave the man$_{UND}$ beans$_{OCA}$.'

In these linkings, either the second argument of the state predicate is linked to undergoer (the unmarked linking in terms of the Actor–Undergoer Hierarchy), or the first argument of the state predicate can be linked to undergoer (the marked linking). In English and Dyirbal there is no formal indicator on the verb of this alternation, but in Indonesian the verb must take the suffix *-kan*.

The second type of variable linking involves INSTRUMENT and LOCATIVE arguments, as in the following examples from English, German and Dyirbal.

(7.26) *English*
spray: [**do′** (Max, [**spray′** (Max, paint)])] CAUSE [BECOME **be-on′** (wall, paint)]
a. Max$_{ACT}$ sprayed the paint$_{UND}$ on the wall$_{OCA}$.
b. Max$_{ACT}$ sprayed the wall$_{UND}$ with the paint$_{OCA}$.

(7.27) *German* streichen/bestreichen *'spread'*
[**do′** (Max, [**spread′** (Max, Farbe)])] CAUSE [BECOME **be-on′** (Wand, Farbe)]
a. Max ha-t die Farbe an die Wand gestrichen.
have-3sgPRES the.FsgACC paint on the.FsgACC wall spread.PSTP
'Max$_{ACT}$ spread the paint$_{UND}$ on the wall$_{OCA}$.'
b. Max ha-t die Wand mit Farbe bestrichen.
have-3sgPRES the.FsgACC wall with paint spread.PSTP
'Max$_{ACT}$ spread the wall$_{UND}$ with paint$_{OCA}$.'

(7.28) *Dyirbal* -m(b)al *instrumentive construction*
a. Ba-la-∅ yugu-∅ ba-ŋgu-l yaɽa-ŋgu ba-ŋgu-∅ bari-ŋgu
DEIC-ABS-IV tree-ABS DEIC-ERG-I man-ERG DEIC-INST-IV axe-INST
nudi-n.
cut-TNS
'The man$_{ACT}$ cut the tree$_{UND}$ down with an axe$_{OCA}$.'
b. Ba-la-∅ bari-∅ baŋgul yaɽa-ŋgu nudil-ma-n ba-gu-∅
DEIC-ABS-IV axe-ABS DEIC-ERG-I man-ERG cut-INST-TNS DEIC-DAT-IV
yugu-gu.
tree-DAT
'The man$_{ACT}$ cut-down-with an axe$_{UND}$ the tree$_{DCA}$.'

As in the dative shift constructions, the THEME (*z*) argument is the default or unmarked linking to undergoer in the locative alternations in (7.26) and (7.27). In the Dyirbal instrumental construction in (7.28), the PATIENT is the default linking to undergoer, as in (a), but the instrument may occur as undergoer when the verb is marked with the *-m(b)al* affix. English does not have this alternation with *cut* but does with *hit*, e.g. *Pam hit the table with the stick* vs. *Pam hit the stick on the table.*

The final group of variable undergoer assignment constructions consists of applicative constructions; in these forms a non-argument of the verb is linked to undergoer, and it is the norm for this to be indicated morphologically on the verb (English is exceptional here).

(7.29) a. Larry$_{ACT}$ baked a cake$_{UND}$ for Sue.
b. Larry$_{ACT}$ baked Sue$_{UND}$ a cake$_{DCA}$.

(7.30) *Chicheŵa* (Baker 1988)
a. Mavuto a-na-umb-a mtsuko.
3sg-PST-mold-MOOD waterpot
'Mavuto$_{ACT}$ molded the waterpot$_{UND}$.'
b. Mavuto a-na-umb-ir-a mfumu mtsuko.
3sg-PST-mold-APL-MOOD chief waterpot
'Mavuto$_{ACT}$ molded the chief$_{UND}$ the waterpot$_{DCA}$.'

(7.31) *Indonesian* -kan *construction*

a. Ali mem-beli ayam itu untuk Hasan.
   ATV-buy chicken the for
   'Ali$_{\mathrm{ACT}}$ bought the chicken$_{\mathrm{UND}}$ for Hasan.'

b. Ali mem-beli-kan Hasan ayam itu.
   ATV-buy-LOC chicken the
   'Ali$_{\mathrm{ACT}}$ bought Hasan$_{\mathrm{UND}}$ the chicken$_{\mathrm{DCA}}$.'

(7.32) *Sama* -an *construction*

a. B'lli ku taumpa' ma si Andi.
   buy 1sgERG shoes OBL PNM Andy
   'I$_{\mathrm{ACT}}$ bought the shoes$_{\mathrm{UND}}$ for Andy.'

b. B'lli-an ku si Andi taumpa'.
   buy-LOC 1sgERG PNM Andy shoes
   'I$_{\mathrm{ACT}}$ bought Andy$_{\mathrm{UND}}$ some shoes$_{\mathrm{DCA}}$.'

(7.33) *Dyirbal* -m(b)al *comitative construction*

a. Ba-yi yaɽa-∅ yugu-ŋga ḍana-ɲu.
   DEIC-ABS.I man-ABS wood-LOC stand-TNS
   'The man$_{\mathrm{ACT}}$ is standing in/at/on some wood.'

b. Ba-la-∅ yugu-∅ ba-ŋgu-l yaɽa-ŋgu ḍanay-ma-n.
   DEIC-ABS-IV wood-ABS DEIC-ERG-I man-ERG stand-COM-TNS
   'The man$_{\mathrm{ACT}}$ is standing-on/with some wood$_{\mathrm{UND}}$.'

In each of these derived forms, a non-argument of the verb appears as undergoer, displacing the default choice for undergoer if the verb is transitive; in Dyirbal the comitative construction adds an undergoer to an intransitive verb, thereby transitivizing it.

The choice of undergoer is made at step 1 in (7.12). The two linkings in (7.23) from English are illustrated in the diagrams in figure 7.15. With verbs that allow variable linking to undergoer, the choice of which argument is to function as undergoer must be made at the outset of the mapping, as everything else depends upon the macrorole assignments either directly or indirectly.

A small minority of languages, English and French being prime examples, require an overt 'subject' for every clause, and therefore when atransitive verbs like *rain* or *pleuvoir* are used, an expletive pronoun, *it* in English or *il* in French, fills the subject slot in the clause. This element is not a privileged syntactic argument of any kind. Most languages do not require dummy fillers like this, and their atransitive verbs appear in argumentless clauses, e.g. Lakhota *magážu* 'it is raining'.

7.2.3 Linking from syntax to semantics

Of the two directions of linking, going from the syntactic representation to the semantic representation is the more difficult, because it involves interpreting the overt morphosyntactic form of a sentence and deducing the semantic functions of

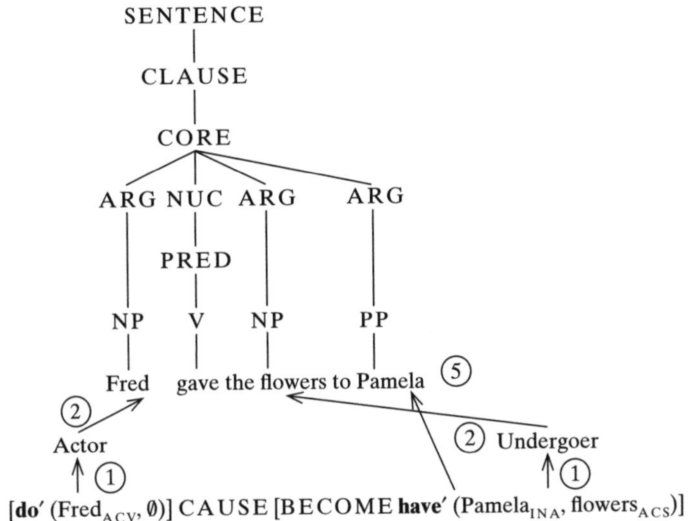

Figure 7.15a Semantics → syntax linking in English: unmarked linking to undergoer

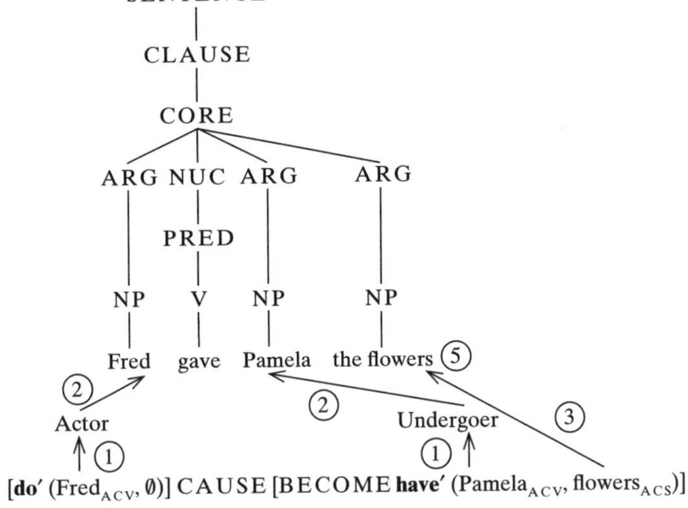

Figure 7.15b Semantics → syntax linking in English: marked linking to undergoer

the elements in the sentence from it. Accordingly, the linking rules must refer to the morphosyntactic features of the sentence. It might well be asked why a grammar should deal with linking from syntax to semantics. Isn't it enough to specify the possible realizations of a particular semantic representation, i.e. the possible linkings from semantics to syntax? The answer is 'no', for the following reason. In section

1.2.2 we introduced the criterion of psychological adequacy, and in particular we mentioned the point made by Kaplan and Bresnan (1982) that theories of linguistic structure should be directly relatable to testable theories of language production and comprehension. A theory which could describe the linking from semantics to syntax only could be part of a language production system, but it would not be adequate for a comprehension system. In such a system, the parser, we assume as an idealization, would take the input and produce a structured syntactic representation of it, identifying the elements of the layered structure of the clause and the cases, adpositions and other grammatically relevant elements in the sentence. It is then the grammar's job to map this structure into a semantic representation, as the first step in interpreting it, and this is where the syntax to semantics linking algorithm is required. The same syntactic and semantic representations are used in both linking algorithms.

The procedure for mapping from syntax to semantics is summarized in (7.34). It crucially presupposes the set of case-marking, adposition assignment and agreement rules in the grammar; these will be developed in section 7.3. Hence, for example, if privileged syntactic arguments receive nominative case in the language, for example, then the nominative NP will be taken as the privileged syntactic argument for step 1. In a language like English, on the other hand, the core-internal prenuclear direct NP will be interpreted as the privileged syntactic argument.

(7.34) *Linking algorithm: syntax → semantics (preliminary formulation)*

1 Determine the functions of the core arguments:

a. If the construction is syntactically accusative:
   (1) If it is the unmarked voice, the privileged syntactic argument is actor.
   (2) If it is passive, the privileged syntactic argument is not the actor of the predicate in the nucleus;
      (a) the actor may appear as a direct core argument (language-specific); or
      (b) the actor may appear in the periphery marked by an adposition or an oblique case (language-specific); or
      (c) if there is no actor in the core or the periphery, then replace the variable representing the highest-ranking argument in the logical structure with '∅'.

b. If the construction is syntactically ergative:
   (1) If it is the unmarked voice, the privileged syntactic argument is undergoer.[5]
   (2) If it is antipassive, the privileged syntactic argument is actor;
      (a) the undergoer may appear as an oblique element (language-specific);
      (b) if there is no undergoer in the core or the periphery, then replace the variable representing the lowest-ranking argument in the logical structure with '∅'.

   c. Assign macrorole status to the other direct core argument, if it is not dative or in an oblique case (language-specific).
   d. If the verb is intransitive, then assign the privileged syntactic argument either macrorole or direct core argument status (language-specific).
   e. If the language is head-marking and there are independent NPs in the clause, associate each NP with a bound argument marker (language-specific).
   f. If the language lacks variable syntactic pivots and controllers, determine the macroroles from case marking and/or word order (language-specific).

2 Retrieve from the lexicon the logical structure of the predicate in the nucleus of the clause and with respect to it execute step 1 from (7.12), subject to the following proviso:
   a. When there is more than one choice for undergoer, do not assign undergoer to an argument in the logical structure.[6]
   b. Assign actor to an argument in the logical structure, if the verb takes one.
   c. Determine the linking of the non-macrorole core argument:
      (1) if there is a state predicate in the logical structure and if there is a non-macrorole core argument marked by a locative adposition or dative or locative-type case, link the non-macrorole core argument with the first argument position in the state predicate in the logical structure; or
      (2) if it is not marked by a locative adposition or dative or a locative-type case, then link it with the second argument position in the state predicate.

3 Link the arguments determined in step 1 with the arguments determined in step 2 until all core arguments are linked.

4 If there is a predicative adpositional adjunct, then retrieve its logical structure from the lexicon, insert the logical structure of the core as the second argument in the logical structure and the object of the adposition in the periphery as the first argument.

5 If there is an element in the pre- or postcore slot (language-specific),
   a. assign it the remaining unlinked argument position in the semantic representation of the sentence;
   b. and if there are no unlinked argument positions in the sentence, then treat the WH-word like a predicative preposition and follow the procedure in step 4, linking the WH-word to the first argument position in the logical structure.

One of the main reasons there are so many steps in (7.34) is that it is intended to cover the whole cross-linguistic range of grammatical phenomena we have discussed; the linking algorithm for any particular language will, not surprisingly, contain only those steps that are relevant to that language.

There is a very fundamental problem that confronts syntax to semantics linking but not semantics to syntax linking, namely the split nature of some of the grammatical systems that we discussed in chapter 6. If pivots and controllers are construction-specific, and a language can, like Tzutujil, Jakaltek and Sama, for example, have an accusative pivot for one construction, an ergative pivot for another, and a semantic controller for yet another, then the syntax to semantic linking algorithm can only work if the construction is identified as having an ergative pivot, an accusative controller, etc., in advance of the operation of the algorithm. The grammar must know whether step 1a, 1b or 1f applies to the construction(s) it is dealing with. We will assume the following tentative solution. The parser will identify grammatical constructions, which will permit the grammar to access the constructional template for that construction, and the template, as we will discuss in section 7.7, contains a specification of the pivot type (if any) of the construction. It is on the basis of this information that steps 1a, 1b or 1f will be followed.

Step 1 involves deriving information about the semantic functions of NPs and other syntactic elements from the overt morphosyntactic form. We will begin by looking at Lakhota, a language which lacks variable syntactic pivots and controllers; this means that steps 1a and 1b do not apply to it. In sentences without independent NPs like (7.18a), the linking is very straightforward. All that is required is the identification of *-wíčha-* as the third plural animate undergoer marker and *-ya-* as the second-person (singular) actor marker. This, plus step 2, leads directly to the association of *-wičha-* with the *x* argument in the logical structure of *naxʔų́* 'hear' and of *-ya-* with the *y* argument, in step 3. The linking from syntax to semantics for (7.18a) is presented in the left diagram in figure 7.16. As before, the steps in the linking procedure in (7.34) are indicated by the numbers in the figure. The sentence with an independent NP in (7.18b) presents an additional complication, namely the interpretation of the independent NP. Step 1e requires that it be associated with a bound argument marker on the verb, and the way this is done will vary from language to language. In double-marking languages like Enga, case is a reliable clue; if the verb is transitive, then the person suffix cross-references an ergative case NP, whereas if the verb is intransitive, then it cross-references the absolutive case NP. In Jakaltek, linear order determines the interpretation; the first NP after a transitive verb is interpreted as being associated with the ergative marker, the second with the absolutive marker, in a simple clause. In order for an independent NP to be associated with a bound argument marker in Lakhota, the two must agree in person, number and animacy. If there are two independent NPs, both of which are compatible with both argument markers on the verb, then the default is that they are associated in terms of linear order: the first NP is associated with the actor marker, the second with the undergoer marker. In (7.18b), *igmú ki* 'the cat(s)' is animate, third person, and unspecified for number, and it is compatible with *-wičha-*, the third person plural animate undergoer affix, and not with *-ya-*, the

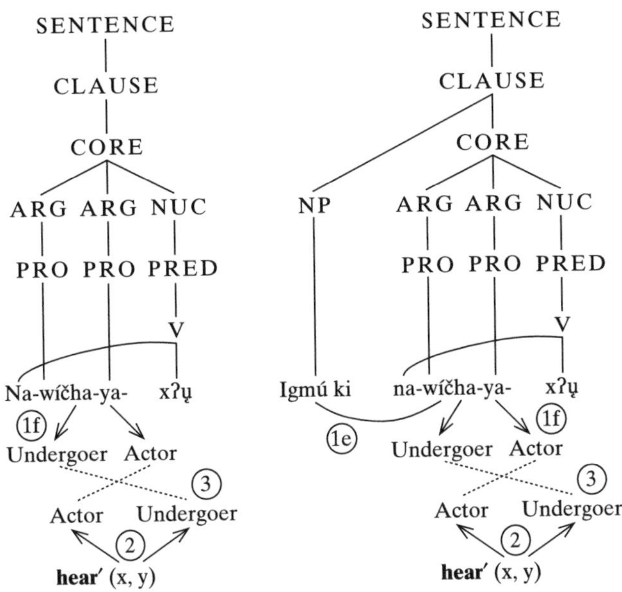

Figure 7.16 Syntax → semantics linking in Lakhota

second person singular actor affix. It will, therefore, receive the interpretation *-wičha-* receives, namely undergoer and the *y* argument of **hear′** (x, y).

The situation is more complex in languages like English, Malagasy and Dyirbal, since, as we have seen, these languages have variable syntactic pivots and controllers, and therefore more than one argument can function as syntactic pivot or controller with a transitive verb. Active voice with an M-transitive verb in a syntactically accusative construction signals that the privileged syntactic argument is the actor, whereas the unmarked voice in a syntactically ergative construction indicates that the privileged syntactic argument is the undergoer. It might be assumed that for English one could also conclude that the postnuclear direct NP is the undergoer, but this is in fact too strong, when we look across the range of both simple and complex constructions. Strictly speaking, one can conclude only that it is a non-actor direct core argument, and in almost all simple sentences involving a single core in a single clause, it will in fact be the undergoer (the one exception to this in English is discussed below). In Icelandic, on the other hand, one could conclude that it is the undergoer, if it is in the accusative case. But in certain types of complex constructions, e.g. *Olaf believed Sigga to have robbed the bank*, the non-actor direct core argument need not be the undergoer of the verb in the core (in this case, it is the actor of *rob*), and therefore we cannot draw the conclusion that it is an undergoer. Hence following step 1c, it can be assigned only 'macrorole' status in Icelandic or just 'direct core argument' status in English. This indeterminacy also affects the interpretation of passive constructions. The only thing that can be

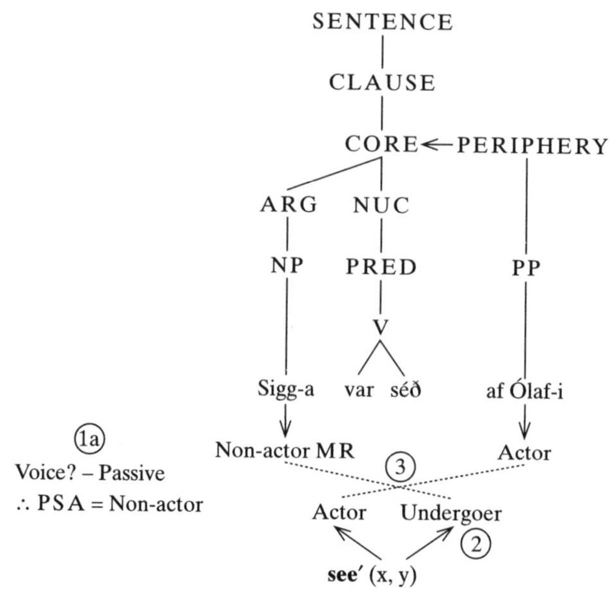

Figure 7.17 Syntax → semantics linking in Icelandic passive

definitively deduced from a passive construction is that the privileged syntactic argument is not the actor of the verb in the nucleus; strictly speaking, no general inference can be drawn as to the function of the argument serving as privileged syntactic argument, as this is an area of significant cross-linguistic variation. In English and German, for example, only undergoers can function as the privileged syntactic argument in passive constructions, but, as we will see in section 7.3.1.1, in Icelandic non-macrorole direct core arguments can so function in passive constructions. Accordingly, exactly what can be deduced from passive constructions will vary along language-specific lines. The same considerations do not hold for antipassive constructions in syntactically ergative languages, since it does seem always to be the case that the privileged syntactic argument in an antipassive construction is the actor of the antipassivized verb.

The linking in the Icelandic passive sentence in (7.13b) is presented in figure 7.17. Because the voice of the verb is passive, the privileged syntactic argument must be a non-actor, and the NP in the *af*-PP must be the actor. Because the privileged syntactic argument NP is nominative, it must be a macrorole, since only macrorole arguments receive nominative case (see section 7.3.1.1). From the logical structure of the verb, the *x* argument is the actor and the *y* argument the undergoer. Thus, the final associations are *Sigga* with the *y* argument and *Ólaf* with the *x* argument, which is the correct interpretation of the sentence. If the sentence were *Sigga var séð* 'Sigga was seen', then step 1a2c would come into play, assigning a '∅' to the *x* argument position in the logical structure for *sjá* 'see'.

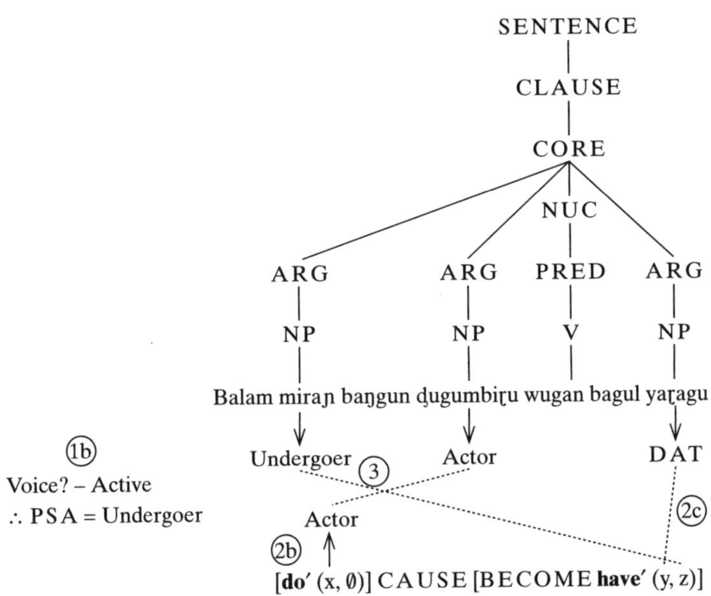

Figure 7.18 Syntax → semantics linking in Dyirbal (I)

A more complex situation arises with verbs with three core arguments which allow variable linking to undergoer. We will diagram the linking of the two Dyirbal sentences in (7.25) in figures 7.18 and 7.19; the example in (7.25a) reflects the default or unmarked linking in terms of the Actor–Undergoer Hierarchy. The first step is to check the voice of the verb, in order to ascertain the role of the privileged syntactic argument. Dyirbal is syntactically ergative, and therefore with an active voice verb, as in this sentence, the privileged syntactic argument is an undergoer. Ergative case marks the actor, and the remaining core argument is in the dative case.[7] From the lexicon the logical structure of *wugal* 'give' is retrieved, and it is necessary to do the macrorole assignments. However, since this verb allows variable linking to undergoer, only actor will be determined, following step 2b; it is the *x* argument. Crucial for the interpretation of the remaining NPs is the nature of the case marking the non-macrorole core argument, according to step 2c in (7.34): since it is the dative case, that NP must be linked to the first argument position in the state predicate in the logical structure. By step 3, actor is linked to actor, and the undergoer is linked to the remaining unlinked argument position, the *z* argument. This yields the correct interpretation of the sentence: *baŋgun ɖugumbiɽu* 'woman' is the actor and EFFECTOR, *balam miraɲ* 'beans' is the undergoer and THEME, and *bagul yaɽagu* 'man' is the RECIPIENT.

The linking in (7.25b) is diagrammed in figure 7.19. The first step is the same as before; the only difference in the outcome is the recognition that the non-macrorole argument in the clause is in the instrumental case, rather than the dative as in

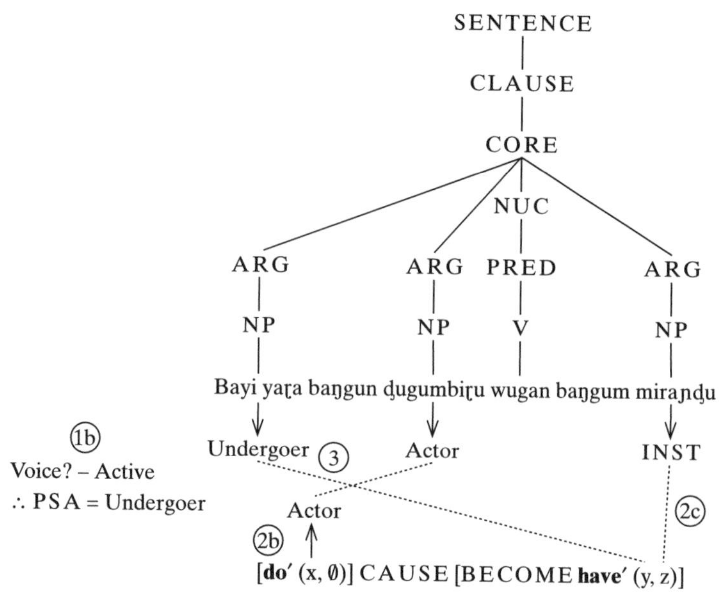

Figure 7.19 Syntax → semantics linking in Dyirbal (II)

(7.25a). As before, only actor can be assigned in step 2b. The crucial step is again 2c: because the third core argument is in the instrumental case, which is not the dative or a locative-type case, that NP must be linked to the second argument position in the state predicate in the logical structure, the *z* argument. Then, as in the above example, actor is linked with actor, and undergoer is linked to the remaining unlinked argument position, the *y* argument, and this yields the correct interpretation: *baŋgun ḑugumbiṛu* 'woman' is the actor and EFFECTOR, *bayi yaṛa* 'man' is the undergoer and RECIPIENT, and *baŋgum miraɲḑu* 'beans' is the THEME.

As these examples show, step 2c works for situations in which the two non-actor NPs are differentially case marked, either by having one direct and the other adpositionally marked, as in English, or having each with a distinct case, as in Dyirbal. It also works for English examples like *Sheila gave Bronwyn the book*, in which there are two direct arguments. Here the second postnuclear NP (*the book*), which is a non-macrorole core argument, is not marked by a locative preposition and therefore would be linked to the second argument position in the state predicate in the logical structure of *give*, i.e. the *z* argument in the logical structure in figure 7.19 (which has the same logical structure as English *give*). Problems arise, however, in a language in which both non-actor core arguments with verbs of giving take the same case; this is illustrated in (7.35) from Icelandic, involving the verb *skila* 'return, give back', which cooccurs with two case-marking patterns.

(7.35) a. Ég skila-ð-i pening-un-um til hennar.
1sgNOM return-PAST-1sg money-DEF-DAT to 3FsgGEN
'I returned the money to her.'

b. Ég skila-ð-i henni pening-un-um.
1sgNOM return-PAST-1sg 3FsgDAT money-DEF-DAT
'I returned her the money.'

The pattern in (7.35a) is no problem for (7.34): the third core argument is marked by a locative preposition, in this instance *til* 'to', and therefore its argument would be linked to the first argument position in the state predicate in the logical structure for *skila* (the *y* argument in a *give*-type logical structure). In the pattern in (7.35b), on the other hand, both non-actor core arguments are in the dative case, and in this situation step 2c fails, since according to it *both* NPs should be linked to the same argument position in logical structure, an impossible result. How can the two NPs be differentiated? One obvious difference between them is that *henni* '3FsgDAT' is an animate NP, while *peningunum* 'the money' is inanimate. Is this animacy contrast relevant to linking? If one looks back at the two-argument state predicates in table 3.5 and (3.52), it becomes immediately clear that if there are any animacy restrictions on the arguments of these predicates, it is always the *first* argument which is obligatorily animate, as we discussed in section 6.5. This is clearly true with perception, cognition, desire, propositional-attitude, emotion and internal-experience predicates, and it is usually true with alienable possession predicates. Hence, given two non-actor core arguments in a clause, one animate and the other inanimate, it will virtually always be the case that the animate one will be linked to the first argument position in the two-place state predicate in the logical structure and that the inanimate argument will be linked to the second argument position. This solves the problem in (7.35b), and it also solves a problem that arises in English. While a sentence like *Sheila gave Bronwyn the book* is no problem for step 2c, the WH-question *What did Sheila give Bronwyn?* is a problem, because there is no way to know how to link *Bronwyn* from the morphosyntactic properties of the clause alone; it is impossible to tell whether, for the purposes of step 2c, it counts as the second or third core argument. However, since it is animate and *give* is a three-argument verb with a two-place state predicate in its logical structure, we can use the fact that it is animate to link it to the first argument position in the state predicate (the *y* argument in the logical structure for *give*), which is the correct result. We will see in section 7.4.1 that animacy plays a crucial role in linking in what were called 'primary object' languages in section 6.2.2.2. When a noun is identified and its lexical entry called up, the fact that it is animate or inanimate will be represented in its qualia (see e.g. (7.4)). It is necessary, then, to reformulate step 2c in (7.34) to include information about animacy. This is given in (7.36).

(7.36) *Linking algorithm: syntax → semantics (revised formulation)*
1 Determine the functions of the core arguments:
a. If the construction is syntactically accusative:
(1) If it is the unmarked voice, the privileged syntactic argument is actor.

(2) If it is passive, the privileged syntactic argument is not the actor of the predicate in the nucleus;
   (a) the actor may appear as a direct core argument (language-specific); or
   (b) the actor may appear in the periphery marked by an adposition or an oblique case (language-specific); or
   (c) if there is no actor in the core or the periphery, then replace the variable representing the highest-ranking argument in the logical structure with '∅'.

b. If the construction is syntactically ergative:
   (1) If it is the unmarked voice, the privileged syntactic argument is undergoer.
   (2) If it is antipassive, the privileged syntactic argument is actor;
      (a) the undergoer may appear as an oblique element (language-specific);
      (b) if there is no undergoer in the core or the periphery, then replace the variable representing the lowest-ranking argument in the logical structure with '∅'.

c. Assign macrorole status to the other direct core argument, if it is not dative or in an oblique case (language-specific).

d. If the verb is intransitive, then assign the privileged syntactic argument either macrorole or direct core argument status (language-specific).

e. If the language is head-marking and there are independent NPs in the clause, associate each NP with a bound argument marker (language-specific).

f. If the language lacks voice oppositions, determine the macroroles from case marking and/or word order (language-specific).

2 Retrieve from the lexicon the logical structure of the predicate in the nucleus of the clause and with respect to it execute step 1 from (7.12), subject to the following proviso:

a. When there is more than one choice for undergoer, do not assign undergoer to an argument in the logical structure.

b. Assign actor to an argument in the logical structure, if the verb takes one.

c. Determine the linking of the non-macrorole core argument:
   (1) if there is a state predicate in the logical structure and if the non-macrorole core argument is marked by a locative adposition or dative or a locative-type case, then link it with the first argument position in the state predicate in the logical structure; or
   (2) if there is a state predicate in the logical structure and if it is not marked by a locative adposition or dative or a locative-type case, then link it with the second argument position in the state predicate;
   (3) otherwise, link the animate NP with the first argument position in the state predicate in the logical structure.

3 Link the arguments determined in step 1 with the arguments determined in step 2 until all core arguments are linked.
4 If there is a predicative adpositional adjunct, then retrieve its logical structure from the lexicon, insert the logical structure of the core as the second argument in the logical structure and the object of the adposition in the periphery as the first argument.
5 If there is an element in the pre- or postcore slot (language-specific),
   a. assign it the remaining unlinked argument position in the semantic representation of the sentence;
   b. and if there are no unlinked argument positions in the sentence, then treat the WH-word like a predicative preposition and follow the procedure in step 4, linking the WH-word to the first argument position in the logical structure.

Adjunct PPs in the periphery add extra complexity to the linking, which is handled in step 4 in (7.36). The mapping from syntax to semantics for (7.11) is given in figure 7.20. The linking of the core elements is straightforward. *After* is a predicative preposition in this sentence; it does not mark an oblique core argument, as all of the semantic arguments of the verb are linked to core arguments. Hence, following step 4, its logical structure must be retrieved from the lexicon, the object of *after* is linked to its first argument position and the logical structure of the verb in the nucleus is

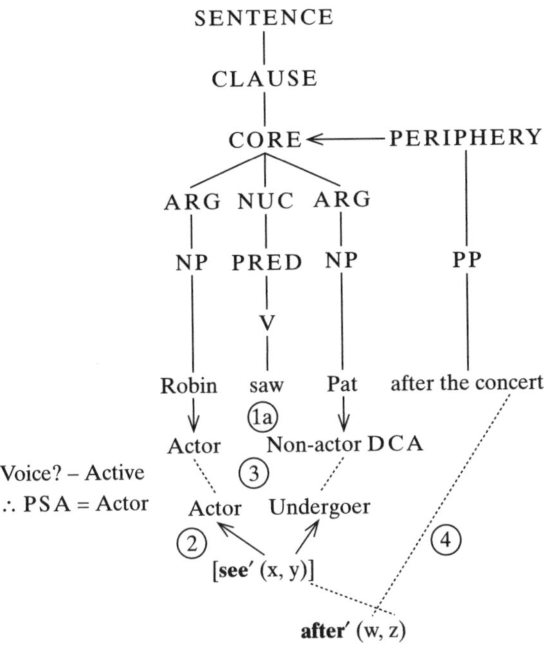

Figure 7.20 Syntax → semantics linking involving adjunct PP in English

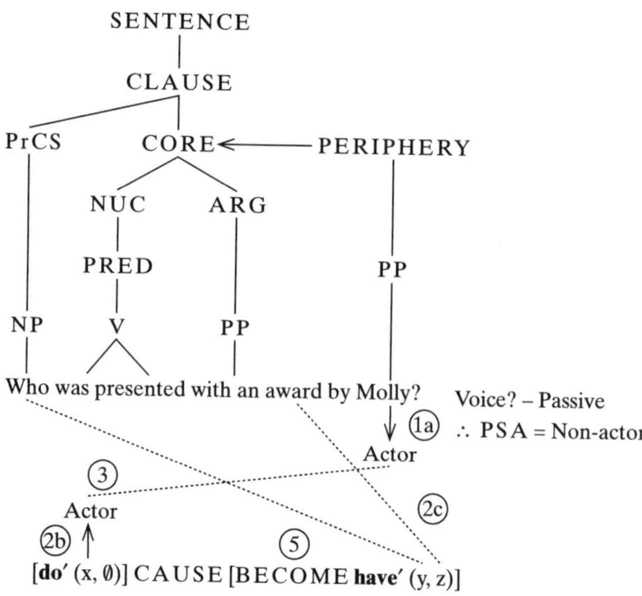

Figure 7.21 Syntax → semantics linking in an English WH-question

linked to its second argument position. This yields the correct interpretation, that in (7.11b).

WH-questions in a language like English present an interesting complication, because there may be nothing about the form of the WH-expression that gives any clue as to its function in the clause. For speakers who have lost the *who – whom* contrast (which is most of them), *who* can function as any of the core arguments, as in *Who did Mary talk to?*, *Who talked to Mary?* and *Who did Mary see?* The problem is less severe in Icelandic, where WH-words are case-marked, which provides an important indicator of their grammatical function, and there is no problem at all in Sama, where the WH-word always functions as syntactic pivot of the main clause and consequently its semantic role can always be deduced from the voice of the verb. Because English presents the most challenging case, we will diagram the linking of *Who was presented with an award by Molly?* in figure 7.21. In this particular example, step 1 is not as revealing as in the previous examples, because there is no structural privileged syntactic argument position in the core, i.e. there is no prenuclear NP within the core. It is possible to determine that the NP in the peripheral *by*-PP is the actor. Because the verb *present* allows variable linking to undergoer, only the actor can be determined from the logical structure. The next step involves the oblique core argument, *with an award*: since it is marked by a non-locative preposition, its object must be linked to the second argument position in the state predicate in the logical structure, the *z* argument. The NP in the precore slot is the only unlinked element in the syntax, and there is only one unlinked variable in

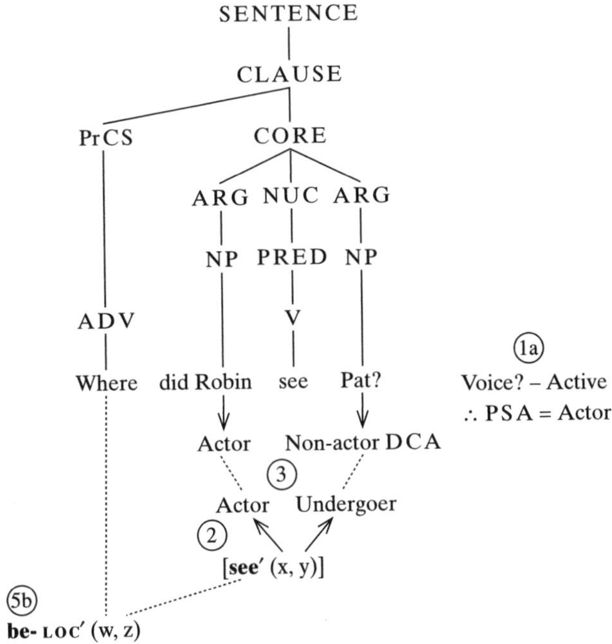

Figure 7.22 Syntax → semantics linking in an English adjunct WH-question

the logical structure, *y*. Linking *who* to *y* in step 5 yields the correct interpretation, namely that *who* refers to the RECIPIENT of *present*. The linking of WH-words in complex sentences poses important theoretical problems, and it will be investigated in detail in chapter 9. Step 5a also takes care of non-WH phrases in the precore slot in English, as in figure 7.12, and in the postcore slot in Japanese, as in (7.22b, c).

Step 5b in (7.36) deals with adjunct WH-words in sentences like *Where did Robin see Pat?* As in figure 7.20, all of the core-internal syntactic arguments would be linked to the argument positions in the logical structure of *see*, and there would be nothing to link *where* to. Since adjunct temporal and locative elements are modifiers of the logical structure of the core, as in (7.11) and figure 7.20, they must be linked to a higher locative or temporal predicate in the semantic representation of the sentence. We must assume, then, that in the lexicon *where* is associated with an abstract locative predicate, **be-**LOC′ (x, y), as discussed in section 7.2.2, and that when there is no argument position in the semantc representation for *where* to be linked to, then this logical structure must be retrieved from the lexicon; the logical structure of the core is linked to the *y* argument position, and *where* is linked to the *x* argument position, just as with non-WH peripheral adjuncts. This is summarized in figure 7.22.

Sentences containing a dummy *it* with an atransitive verb like *rain* in languages like English and French are technically not subject to the Completeness Constraint, because *it* is not an argument. Given a logical structure like **rain′**, there is no argument position to link the expletive pronoun to, but because it is not an argument of any kind, there is no requirement that it be linked. If a non-expletive appeared in that position, e.g. **Leslie rained*, there would be a Completeness Constraint violation, because the NP *Leslie* is not an expletive, dummy element and therefore would have to be linked to an argument position in a logical structure in the semantic representation.

7.3 Case marking, agreement and adposition assignment

In this section we will present the principles governing case marking, agreement and adposition assignment that are assumed in the linking algorithms. We begin by looking at case marking and agreement in the next section, and then in the following section we will explore preposition assignment in English.

7.3.1 Case marking and agreement

The discussion of case and agreement will be divided up in terms of the patterns of case and grammatical relations discussed in chapter 6: the first section will deal with languages with predominantly syntactically accusative constructions, the second with both syntactically ergative and morphologically ergative but syntactically accusative languages, and the third will look at active and inverse languages.

7.3.1.1 Case marking and agreement: accusative languages

Many accounts of case marking and agreement tie these phenomena to grammatical relations with statements like ‘the subject receives/appears in the nominative case’ or ‘the finite verb agrees with the subject’. Alternatively, some analyses have stated these phenomena in terms of structural positions in a phrase structure tree, e.g. ‘the external argument receives nominative case’, ‘the internal argument receives accusative case’ or ‘the finite verb agrees with the external argument’ (see section 6.1.2.1, esp. figure 6.1). Since the syntactic representations we are using do not make a structural internal argument–external argument distinction, the latter type of analysis is precluded. Following the first line of analysis, on the other hand, we could substitute ‘privileged syntactic argument’ for ‘subject’ and attempt a relationally oriented analysis. One difficulty that immediately arises is that there are no syntactic functions akin to ‘direct object’ or ‘indirect object’ in this system. In chapter 6 we argued that the primary phenomena associated with direct objects, appearing as subject in a passive construction and being the focus of applicative constructions, are actually properties of undergoer, and we discussed the linking in these constructions in section 7.2.2. Hence we will use the notion of ‘undergoer’ rather than ‘direct object’ in our case and agreement rules. Rather than ‘indirect object’ we will use ‘non-macrorole direct core argument’. This yields an odd set of relations, two of which are syntactic (privileged syntactic argument, direct core argument) and one of which is semantic (undergoer). It would be more desirable for the case and agreement rules to refer to a homogeneous group of relations.

We will begin by looking at case marking and agreement in German. A first approximation of the case assignment rules is given in (7.37).

(7.37) *Case assignment rules for German (preliminary formulation)*
 a. Assign nominative case to the privileged syntactic argument.
 b. Assign accusative case to the undergoer.
 c. Assign dative case to the direct core argument.

A first approximation of the finite verb agreement rule is given in (7.38).

(7.38) *Finite verb agreement in German (preliminary formulation)*
 The finite verb agrees with the privileged syntactic argument.

These can be illustrated with the following examples.

(7.39) a. Der Junge ha-t den Apfel gegessen.
 the.MsgNOM boy have-3sgPRES the.MsgACC apple eat.PSTP
 'The boy ate the apple.'
 b. Der Apfel wurde-∅ von dem Junge-n gegessen.
 the.MsgNOM apple become.PAST-3sg 'by' the.MsgDAT boy-DAT eat.PSTP
 'The apple was eaten by the boy.'
 c. Mein-∅ Freund ha-t mir ein-en Hut geschickt.
 my-MsgNOM friend have-3sgPRES 1sgDAT a-MsgACC hat sent.PSTP
 'My friend sent me a hat.'

The privileged syntactic argument is *der Junge* 'the boy' in (a), *der Apfel* 'the apple' in (b) and *mein Freund* 'my friend' in (c), and in each sentence the privileged syntactic argument NP bears nominative case. The undergoer in (a) and (c) is in the accusative case, *den Apfel* 'the apple' in (a) and *einen Hut* 'a hat' in (c). In (b) the undergoer is also the privileged syntactic argument, and it bears nominative, not accusative, case; hence if (7.37a) can apply, then it overrides (7.37b). The third core argument in (c), the RECIPIENT, receives dative case, following (7.37c). In all three of these sentences the finite verb agrees with the privileged syntactic argument.

Not all verbs in German work this way, however. The verbs *helfen* 'help' and *danken* 'thank' both take non-pivot core arguments in the dative rather than the accusative case. This is illustrated in (7.40).

(7.40) a. Die Frau ha-t den Männer-n geholfen.
 the.FsgNOM woman have-3sgPRES the.MplDAT men-DATpl help.PSTP
 'The woman helped the men.'
 a′. *Die Frau ha-t die Männer geholfen.
 the.FsgNOM woman have-3sgPRES the.MplACC men help.PSTP

b. Den Männer-n wurde-∅/*-n von der
the.MplDAT men-DATpl become.PAST-3sg/-3pl 'by' the.FsgDAT
Frau geholfen.
woman help.PSTP
'The men were helped by the woman.'

b′. *Die Männer wurde-n von der Frau
the.MplNOM men become.PAST-3pl 'by' the.FsgDAT woman
geholfen.
help.PSTP

In (a) the non-pivot core argument is in the dative rather than the accusative case, and in the passive construction in (b) the non-actor core argument is also in the dative, and the finite verb does not agree with it. These examples would appear to be exceptions to the rules in (7.37) and (7.38); how are we to account for them? There are at least two approaches we could take. The first would be to say that *helfen*, like *aufessen* 'eat up' or *sehen* 'see', is a transitive verb with an actor and an undergoer and that, unlike the other two verbs, *helfen* carries in its lexical entry a stipulation that its undergoer must appear in the dative case. This would account for the case marking, but it leaves a number of other questions unanswered. In German, as in many languages, only macrorole arguments may function as syntactic controller or pivot, i.e. as the privileged syntactic argument. This is clear in the examples in (7.41b, c), in which the dative RECIPIENT of verbs like *schicken* 'send' and *bringen* 'bring' cannot function as pragmatic pivot in German. The same is true with respect to the dative argument of *helfen*, as shown in (7.41d).

(7.41) a. Die Männer$_i$ sind in-s Geschäft gegangen
the.MplNOM men be.3plPRES into-the.NsgACC shop walk.PSTP
und *pro*$_i$ wurde-n von der Polizei verhaft-et.
and become.PAST-3pl 'by' the.FsgDAT police arrest-PSTP
'The men walked into the shop and were arrested by the police.'

b. *Mir$_i$ wurde-n viele Postkarte-n von mein-er Freund-in
1sg.DAT become.PAST-3pl much postcard-pl by my-FsgDAT friend-FEM
geschickt und sofort hab-e *pro*$_i$ sie verloren.
send.PSTP and immediately have-1sgPRES 3plACC lost.PSTP
'I was sent a lot of postcards by my girlfriend and immediately lost them.'

c. *Ich$_i$ bin um 8 Uhr aufgestanden und *pro*$_i$
1sg.NOM be.1sgPRES at o'clock get.up.PSTP and
wurde-∅ das Frühstück gebracht.
become.PAST-3sg the.NsgNOM breakfast bring.PSTP
'I got up at 8 o'clock and was brought breakfast.'

d. *Die Männer$_i$ sind in-s Geschäft gegangen
the.MplNOM men be.3plPRES into-the.NsgACC shop walk.PSTP
und *pro*$_i$ wurde-∅ von der Frau geholfen.
and become.PAST-3sg 'by' the.FsgDAT woman help.PSTP
'The men walked into the shop and were helped by the woman.'

The variable syntactic pivot of a German clause can be omitted under coreference with the variable syntactic controller of the previous clause in conjoined structures, as in (7.41a). In (7.41b) the dative core argument is in the first clause and cannot be the controller for a zero pivot in the second clause, whereas in (c) the omitted core argument in the second clause would be dative if it appeared overtly; the sentence is therefore ungrammatical. The ungrammaticality of (d) shows that the dative argument of *helfen* 'help' is not really the privileged syntactic argument in a passive construction like (7.40b), since it cannot be omitted in a conjoined structure. This is puzzling if the dative argument is truly an undergoer with an arbitrary case feature; why should such a feature keep the argument from functioning as syntactic pivot or controller? We would need to posit a further principle stating that macroroles bearing arbitrary case features cannot function as the privileged syntactic argument. This analysis thus requires two stipulations: the case feature and the principle just mentioned.

There is another approach to this problem. Recall from section 4.2 that M-transitivity in this framework is defined in terms of the number of macroroles a verb takes: an M-transitive verb takes two, an M-intransitive verb one, and an M-atransitive verb none. Let us suppose, then, that what is irregular about *helfen* is not the case it assigns to its non-actor direct core argument but rather its M-transitivity; that is, despite having two arguments in its logical structure, it is M-intransitive and therefore has only one macrorole argument. Following the macrorole assignment principles in (4.14b), the macrorole must be actor. This analysis correctly predicts all of the morphosyntactic properties of the non-actor core argument of *helfen* in (7.40)–(7.41). First, since it is a non-macrorole direct core argument, it should appear in the dative case, following (7.37c), which it does. Second, because it is not a macrorole argument, it cannot function as the privileged syntactic argument in a passive construction, which is correct. Furthermore, since it is a non-macrorole direct core argument, it should appear in the dative case in passive constructions, which it does. Third, since it is not a macrorole, it cannot function as either controller or pivot in coordinate constructions, which is correct. Finally, since it is not a macrorole argument and cannot function as pivot, the verb should not agree with it in passive constructions, which is also correct. Thus, all of the apparently exceptional properties of this argument fall out from the analysis of *helfen* as M-intransitive, and the only stipulation that would be required is the indication in its lexical entry that it takes only one macrorole; everything else follows without further specification. This stipulation is in fact not as arbitrary as it might appear; *helfen* is an activity verb, and we saw in section 4.2 that many activity verbs behave like intransitive verbs; hence we might expect *helfen* to be M-intransitive, especially given that it is difficult to use as an active accomplishment. This second analysis treats *helfen* and verbs like it as being exceptional in only one way, namely their (M-)transitivity, and it avoids positing arbitrary case features and an arbitrary principle dealing with just these arbitrary case features, as the first analysis does.

This discussion of the (M-)transitivity of *helfen* illustrates an important point. When we first introduced this notion in section 4.2, we gave no criteria based on semantic representations which could be used to determine exceptional transitivity. It is not clear that such criteria can in fact be given, since verbs with virtually the same meaning in different languages can differ in (M-)transitivity, e.g. Spanish *gustar* and Portuguese *gostar* are obviously cognates and mean 'please, like', but the Portuguese verb is M-transitive while its Spanish counterpart is M-intransitive. Differences in M-transitivity have definite morphosyntactic consequences, and accordingly, these consequences provide a means for testing competing analyses. Once we have established the principles governing case assignment and agreement for regular verbs, i.e. verbs whose M-transitivity follows the principles in (4.14), we are then in a position to evaluate competing analyses of problematic verbs like *helfen*. We considered two analyses: (1) it is M-transitive, i.e. it takes both macroroles, but it is necessary to stipulate its case-marking properties (dative rather than accusative undergoer) and the fact that a dative undergoer cannot function as a syntactic pivot or controller in a passive construction; or (2) it is M-intransitive, i.e. it takes only one macrorole, which must be specified in its lexical entry, but it is otherwise completely regular in all other properties, i.e. type of macrorole, case assignment and the failure of its second argument to function as a syntactic pivot or controller in a passive. Which analysis is to be preferred? In terms of the criteria discussed in chapter 1, the second analysis is to be preferred: only one stipulation is required, it is of a kind that is independently required, given the unpredictability of transitivity with many verbs, and the verb is then regular in its morphosyntactic behavior, whereas in the first account the verb is irregular in a number of respects and regular only in its transitivity. Hence, the second account maximizes the regularity of the morphosyntactic behavior of the verb and minimizes its irregularity, while the first account does the reverse. Thus, when dealing with verbs which are apparently irregular or exceptional in some respect, we can use their morphosyntactic properties in light of those of regular verbs to evaluate competing analyses of their M-transitivity and determine whether they are M-transitive or M-intransitive.

There is, however, a nagging problem with the case-marking and agreement rules in (7.37)–(7.38), one which we mentioned at the outset: the case rules in (7.37) refer to a mixed bag of relations, and it would be preferable to have an analysis which made reference to a homogeneous set of relations. In order to solve this problem we need to look at one of German's northern cousins, Icelandic. Icelandic has the same four cases as German (nominative, accusative, dative, genitive), and so as a first approximation we will assume that the case assignment and agreement rules in (7.37) and (7.38) apply in this language as well. This appears to work well for verbs like those discussed above. The following examples are from Zaenen, Maling and Thráinsson (1985).

(7.42) a. Lögregl-a-n tók Sigg-u fast-a.
police-FsgNOM-DEF take.PAST Sigga-FsgACC fast-FsgACC
'The police arrested Sigga.'

b. Sigg-a va-r tek-in föst af
Sigga-FsgNOM be.PAST-3sg take.PSTP-FsgNOM fast.FsgNOM by
lögregl-un-ni.
police-DEF-FsgDAT
'Sigga was arrested by the police.'

c. Ég sýn-d-i henni bíl-in-n.
1sgNOM show-PAST-1sg 3FsDAT car-DEF-MsgACC
'I showed her the car.'

d. Ég hjálpa-ð-i þeim.
1sgNOM help-PAST-1sg 3plDAT
'I helped them.'

e. Þeim va-r hjálp-að (af mér).
3plDAT be.PAST-3sg help-PSTP (by 1sgDAT)
'They were helped (by me).'

These examples parallel the ones we saw from German. In (a)–(d) the privileged syntactic argument is in the nominative case, the undergoer is in the accusative case and the non-macrorole direct core argument is in the dative case. The Icelandic equivalent of *helfen*, *hjálpa*, takes a dative second argument, which, like its German counterpart, appears in the dative in a passive construction and does not trigger finite-verb agreement.[8]

There are, however, some constructions in Icelandic which show that it is rather more different from German than the examples in (7.42) indicate.

(7.43) a. Þeim hef-ur alltaf þótt Ólaf-ur leiðinleg-ur.
3plDAT have-3sgPRES always think.PSTP Olaf-MsgNOM boring-MsgNOM
'They have always considered Olaf boring.'

b. Mér hafa/*hef alltaf þótt þeir leiðinleg-ir.
1sgDAT have.3pl/have.1sg always think.PSTP 3plNOM boring-MplNOM
'I have always considered them boring.'

c. Þeim virðist alltaf hafa þótt Ólaf-ur
3plDAT seem.3sgPRES always have.INF think.PSTP Olaf-MsgNOM
leiðinleg-ur.
boring-MsgNOM
'They always seem to have found Olaf boring.'

d. *Ólaf-ur virðist alltaf þeim hafa þótt
Olaf-MsgNOM seem.3sgPRES always 3plDAT have.INF think.PSTP
leiðinleg-ur.
boring-MsgNOM
(lit.) *'Olaf seems always them to have considered boring.'

While German also has 'dative subject' constructions like (7.43a), e.g. *mir gefäll-t das Buch* (1sgDAT please-3sgPRES the.NsgNOM book) 'I like the book', or 'The book pleases me', the important difference between the two languages is that dative case core arguments like *þeim* 'them' in (a) can function as syntactic pivots and controllers in Icelandic but not in German. This can be seen most clearly in the contrast in the (c) and (d) examples. Like English, but unlike German, Icelandic has productive matrix-coding constructions, and in the construction illustrated in (7.43c, d) it is the *dative* NP, not the nominative NP, which functions as pivot and occurs in the matrix core, as the grammaticality of (c) and the ungrammaticality of (d) show clearly. This contrast can be made even more striking when we compare dative NPs as controller or pivot in a conjunction reduction construction. The German examples in (7.41) show that a dative NP can function neither as pivot nor as controller in this construction. Contrast this with analogous constructions in Icelandic, taken from Rögnvaldsson (1982).

(7.44) a. Þeir$_i$ sjá stúlk-un-a og *pro*$_i$ finnst hún
3plNOM see.3plPRES girl-DEF-FsgACC and find.3sgPRES 3FsgNOM
álitleg-Ø.
attractive- FsgNOM
'They see the girl and find her attractive.'

b. Þeim$_i$ lík-ar matur-in-n og *pro*$_i$ borð-a mikið.
3plDAT like-3sgPRES food-DEF-MsgNOM and eat-3plPRES much
'They like the food and eat much.'

The verb in the second clause of (7.44a), *finnst*, takes a dative privileged syntactic argument, and therefore the omitted NP is the one that would appear in the dative case in a simple clause; note that the verb agrees with the nominative pronoun *hún* 'she'. The grammaticality of this sentence in Icelandic contrasts sharply with the ungrammaticality of (7.41b, d) in German. In (7.44b) the dative argument *þeim* 'them' in the first clause is the antecedent (controller) for the zero pivot in the second clause; the verb *borða* 'eat' takes a nominative subject. Again, there is a sharp contrast with the ungrammatical German examples in (7.41). It is clear, then, that dative core arguments can be syntactic (pragmatic) pivots and controllers in Icelandic but not in German. Because the dative NP is the syntactic pivot in the examples in (7.43a, b) and (7.44), the case-marking rules in (7.37) will not work for them. Note further, as highlighted in (b), the finite verb does not agree with the syntactic pivot; rather it agrees with the non-pivot nominative NP *þeir*. The word order in these examples is significant as well. Again like English and unlike German, Icelandic has relatively fixed word order, with the privileged syntactic argument being the initial NP within the core. The order in (7.43a, b) is the unmarked order; were the nominative NP to appear in initial position in the sentence, it would have to be in the precore slot and the privileged syntactic argument would follow the finite verb (cf. (2.16)–(2.17)). This is puzzling, since German, with a similar case system, has much more flexible word order, as least with respect to NPs. Why should Icelandic have such rigid word order, given its rich system of case marking? We will return to this question below.

It appears, then, that the case-marking rules for (7.43) are quite different from those for (7.42); in other words, the rules in (7.37) work for (7.42) but not for (7.43). The same holds true for finite-verb agreement: the rule in (7.38) works for (7.42) but not for (7.43). Is it possible to formulate a set of case-marking and finite-verb agreement rules which will work for all of these examples? The answer is 'yes', and to achieve this we need to make only one significant change in the rules as formulated. The case and agreement rules both refer to the notion of privileged syntactic argument, and, as we saw in chapter 6, there is a privileged syntactic argument selection hierarchy underlying the choice of argument to function as syntactic pivot or controller; it was given in (7.1). In these syntactically accusative languages the actor is the default choice for the privileged syntactic argument. So as a first move, we will replace 'privileged syntactic argument' in (7.37) and (7.38) by 'highest-ranking macrorole' in terms of (7.1). There is a second, minor, move we need to make, one which avoids a problem which came up earlier in the discussion of (7.39b). In a passive construction, the undergoer is the highest-ranking macrorole and is referenced by the rules in (a) and (b) in (7.37). We can eliminate this double reference by changing the (b) rule to 'Assign accusative case to the other macrorole'; in an active sentence, the 'other macrorole' is the undergoer, but in a passive there is no other macrorole in the core and therefore the rule cannot apply. We may now restate (7.37) and (7.38) as (7.45) and (7.46). We assume that these rules apply within the core (and the precore slot) to direct arguments only; they do not account for the case assigned by prepositions to their objects.

(7.45) *Case assignment rules for German and Icelandic*
a. Assign nominative case to the highest-ranking macrorole argument.
b. Assign accusative case to the other macrorole argument.
c. Assign dative case to non-macrorole arguments (default[9]).

(7.46) *Finite verb agreement in German and Icelandic*
The finite verb agrees with the highest-ranking macrorole argument.

The first thing to notice about these rules is that they solve the problem of the heterogeneity of relations invoked in the original rules in (7.37): they all refer to the status of an NP as a macrorole or not, and there is no mixing of syntactic and semantic relations as in (7.37). The regular case marking and agreement in (7.39) and (7.42a–c) can be accounted for straightforwardly. In each example, the highest-ranking macrorole is in the nominative case, and the finite verb agrees with it. In the passive constructions in the (b) examples, the undergoer is the highest-ranking macrorole, since it is the only core macrorole. The actor occurs in the periphery, is the object of a preposition and therefore is not affected by these rules. In the (a) and (c) sentences the other macrorole, the undergoer, appears in the accusative case, and in the (c) examples the non-macrorole core argument bears dative case. With respect to the other verbs, if we assume that the verb *þykja* 'think, consider' in (7.43) is M-intransitive, just like *helfen* and *hjálpa* 'help', then all of the case-marking and finite-verb agreement phenomena in (7.40) and (7.42d, e)–(7.43) are accounted for. The account proposed above for (7.41), which would also apply to (7.42d, e), could be carried over into this new analysis unchanged. Unlike *helfen* and *hjálpa*, which are activities, *þykja* is a state verb, and its single macrorole would be undergoer, following (4.14b). The crucial examples for this analysis are (7.43a, b). The logical structure for them would be **consider′** (x, [**be′** (y, [**boring′**])]). In them *y* (*Ólaf-* in (a), *þeir* 'they' in (b)) is undergoer, and because it is the only macrorole argument in the core, it receives nominative case and the finite verb agrees with it, as the (b) example makes clear. The *x* argument (*þeim* 'them' in (a) and *mér* 'me' in (b)) are non-macrorole direct core arguments, and accordingly they occur in the dative case and do not trigger finite-verb agreement.[10]

We have accounted for the case-marking and finite-verb agreement in (7.39)–(7.43) in German and Icelandic with a single set of rules covering both languages. How, then, do German and Icelandic differ? The difference lies not in the case-marking or agreement rules but rather in the privileged syntactic argument selection hierarchies in the two languages: in German the selection principle is 'actor = default', whereas in Icelandic it is 'highest-ranking direct core argument = default'; this is with reference to (7.1). The two principles appear to be the same with verbs of regular, predictable transitivity: given a verb with actor and undergoer arguments, both principles would rank the actor as the unmarked choice for the privileged syntactic argument. But when one of the arguments is a macrorole and the other a non-macrorole direct core argument, the two principles yield very different results. When *helfen* in German is passivized, the single dative NP does not function as syntactic pivot or controller; the result is a construction without a privileged syntactic argument. In Icelandic, on the other hand, the single dative NP of the passive form of *hjálpa* is the highest-ranking direct core argument and therefore is the privileged syntactic argument; it can, for example, occur in the matrix core in a matrix-coding construction analogous to (7.43c).

(7.47) Þeim virðist hafa ver-ið hjálp-að.
3plDAT seem.3sgPRES have.INF be-PSTP help-PSTP
'They seem to have been helped.'

With verbs like *gefallen* 'please, like' in German and *þykja* 'think, consider' in Icelandic, a similar contrast obtains. In both languages the verbs have a logical structure like **predicate′** (x, y) and are M-intransitive, and since they are states, the single macrorole is undergoer. The *y* argument would be the undergoer and the *x* argument a direct core argument. In German the *y* argument would be the syntactic pivot, since it is the only macrorole, whereas in Icelandic the *x* argument would be the syntactic pivot, since it is the highest-ranking direct core argument. We have already seen examples of the *x* argument as pragmatic pivot in Icelandic, e.g. (7.43c), and (7.48) illustrates the *y* undergoer argument as pivot in German.

(7.48) Das Buch$_i$ ist teuer aber *pro*$_i$ gefäll-t mir trotzdem.
the.NOM book is expensive but please-3sgPRES 1sgDAT nevertheless
'The book is expensive but I like it anyway' (lit.: '. . . but pleases me nevertheless.')

Thus, the major difference between German and Icelandic with respect to these phenomena is the nature of the privileged syntactic argument selection principles in the two languages: in German it is restricted to macroroles, whereas in Icelandic it is not.

We are now in a position to propose an answer to the question raised earlier regarding the contrast in flexibility of word order between the two languages: why should Icelandic have such rigid word order, given its rich system of case marking? Let us approach this question from the perspective of the algorithm for syntax → semantics linking. The starting point of this procedure is identifying the privileged syntactic argument in the clause and determining the semantic function of that NP. In German, nominative case is a reliable indicator of the privileged syntactic argument of the clause, but in Icelandic it is not; the nominative NP may, but need not, be the privileged syntactic argument. There are constructions in which both of the core arguments of the verb carry the same case, as illustrated in (7.49).

(7.49) a. Mig vant-ar pening-a.
1sgACC lack-3sgPRES money-ACC
'I lack money.'

b. Henni va-r skil-að pening-un-um.
3FsgDAT be.PAST-3sg return-PSTP money-DEF-DAT
'She was returned the money.'

In the (a) sentence, both NPs are accusative, while in (b) both are dative. Hence in sentences like these morphological case provides no clue as to the privileged syntactic argument of the clause. It makes sense, then, for Icelandic to require that the privileged syntactic argument be the core-initial NP, and given the privileged syntactic argument selection principle, that NP can be identified as the highest-ranking argument in the logical structure. No such requirement is needed in German, where nominative case on an NP always codes the privileged syntactic argument and the highest-ranking macrorole in the core.

We mentioned in note 8 that there is a second agreement rule in Icelandic involving passive participles and predicate adjectives; it has no analog in German. It can be seen in (7.42a, b) and in (7.43a–c), where *fast-* (in *taka fast* 'arrest' [lit. 'take/hold fast']) in (7.42) and *leiðinleg-* 'boring' in (7.43) are predicate adjectives and *tek-* 'taken' is a passive participle in (7.42b). The rule can be stated as in (7.50).

(7.50) *Passive participle and predicate adjective agreement in Icelandic*
Passive participles and predicate adjectives agree in gender, number and case with the undergoer of the predicate of which they are a part.

This is a clear example of a semantic controller for agreement, in contrast to the variable syntactic controller for finite-verb agreement. In (7.42a) in which the undergoer *Sigg-* is not the highest-ranking macrorole and therefore accusative, the predicate adjective *fast-* is in the singular feminine accusative form. In the (b) sentence, the construction is passive and therefore the undergoer is the highest-ranking direct core argument and the privileged syntactic argument; accordingly, the passive participle and the predicate adjective are in the singular feminine nominative form.

We now turn to a problem that we first raised at the beginning of chapter 2, namely case assignment involving non-local dependencies, e.g. WH-questions. It was pointed out in section 2.1.1 that one of the justifications given for positing multiple levels of syntactic representation and for transformational rules to link them was that these constructs allowed a simpler account of non-local case assignment and agreement. We have seen an example of non-local case assignment in Icelandic in (7.20a), repeated in (7.51a), and figure 7.11; in this sentence, a WH-word in the precore slot occurs in the accusative case. A similar sentence involving non-local agreement is (7.51b). The non-local agreement is between the predicate adjective and the WH-word in the precore slot.

(7.51) a. Hver-ja sá Ólaf-ur?
who-ACC see.PAST Olaf-MsgNOM
'Who did Olaf see?'
b. Hver-ja tók lögregl-a-n fast-a?
who-ACC take.PAST.3sg police-FsgNOM-DEF fast-FsgACC
'Who did the police arrest?'

Do the case and agreement rules proposed thus far handle these non-local constructions, or do we need special rules for them? The rules in (7.45) and (7.50) can handle these examples without any modification or extension. Consider the linking in (7.51a), represented in figure 7.11, repeated in figure 7.23, along with the linking for (7.51). All of the information needed for case marking and agreement is in figure 7.23.[11] For (7.51a), *Ólaf-* is the actor and accordingly will occur in the nominative case; the finite verb will agree with it. *Hver-* is the undergoer and therefore will occur in the accusative case; it makes no difference whether it is linked to a core-internal position or to the precore slot. The same is true with respect to (7.51b); *lögregl-* is the actor and will therefore occur in the nominative case, and the finite verb will agree with it. *Hver-* is the undergoer and consequently it will appear in the accusative case and the predicate adjective *fast-* will agree with it in

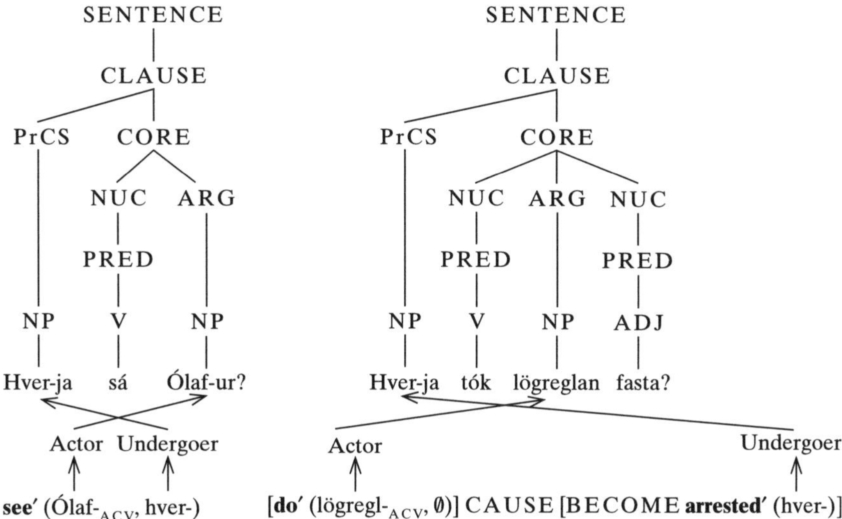

Figure 7.23 WH-question linking in Icelandic

gender, number and case. Again, it makes no difference whether it is a non-WH NP linked to a core-internal position or a WH-word linked to the precore slot; the crucial property for case marking and agreement is that it is the undergoer. Thus, the rules for case marking and agreement that we proposed in (7.45), (7.46) and (7.50) can handle non-local case and agreement without modification. Hence non-local dependencies of the type discussed in section 2.1.1 turn out not to be a problem at all for the syntactic theory we have presented, and it supports the position taken at the end of section 2.1.1 that multiple levels of syntactic representation are not necessary in linguistic theory.

7.3.1.2 Case marking and agreement: ergative languages

Ergative languages present a more complex picture with respect to case marking than accusative languages do, because most ergative languages have split case-marking systems; that is, there is more than one case-marking pattern manifested in the language. We will illustrate five different split systems, each with a different conditioning factor for the split.

The first split is between tensed and non-tensed clauses; in Jakaltek (Craig 1977), tensed clauses have an ergative pattern, whereas non-tensed clauses have an accusative pattern, as the following examples illustrate. The complements are italicized; the 'S, A, U' notation from chapter 6 is employed.

(7.52) a. Ch-in to an. ABS = S
TNS-1sgABS go 1p
'I go.'

b. Ch-in ha-mak an. ABS = U, ERG = A
TNS-1sgABS 2sgERG-hit 1p
'You hit me.'

c. X-∅-y-al naj *chubil xc-ach*
TNS-3ABS-3ERG-say he that TNS-2sgABS
y-il naj. ABS = U, ERG = A
3ERG-see he
'He said that he saw you.'

d. X-∅-aw-abe *tato ch-in to-j*
TNS-3ABS-2sgERG-hear that TNS-1sgABS go-FUT
hecal an. ABS = S
tomorrow 1p
'You heard that I will go tomorrow.'

e. Ch-∅-y-iptze naj ix *hach s-mak-ni.* ABS = U, ERG = A
TNS-3ABS-3ERG-force he her 2sgABS 3ERG-hit-SUFF
'He forces her to hit you.'

f. Xc-ach w-iptze *ha-to an.* ERG = S
TNS-2sgABS 1sgERG-force 2sgERG-go 1p
'I forced you to go.'

In the tensed clauses, the absolutive form marks the S or U, while the ergative form marks the A; this holds in both matrix and embedded tensed clauses. In the infinitives in (e) and (f), on the other hand, the absolutive pronoun indicates just the U, while the ergative prefix signals A and S, yielding an accusative pattern; contrast the marking of the S argument of *to* 'go' in the tensed clause in (a) and the infinitive in (f).

Hindi presents a common type of split, one based on aspect differences: in the imperfective aspect forms, case marking follows an accusative pattern, whereas in the perfective forms, it follows an ergative pattern. The following Hindi examples are from Bhat (1991).

(7.53) a. Raam sootaa hai.
[MASCsg] sleep is.MASCsg
'Ram [S] sleeps.'

b. Raam kitaab paṛhtaa hai.
book[FEMsg] read is.MASCsg
'Ram [A] reads the book [U].'

c. Raam sooyaa.
slept.MASCsg
'Ram [S] slept.'

d. Raam nee kitaab paṛhii.
ERG read.FEMsg
'Ram [A] read the book [U].'

In the imperfective examples in (a) and (b), there is no case marking on any of the NPs, and the verb agrees with the S or A. In the perfective examples in (c) and (d), the S and U NPs are not case-marked, and the verb agrees with them; the A NP in (d) bears the ergative marker *nee*, and the verb does not agree with it, in contrast to (b). Thus we have an accusative pattern in the imperfective but an ergative pattern in the perfective in Hindi.

As in Hindi, many ergative languages have both case marking on NPs and verb agreement, and it often happens that the two systems work on different patterns, with the NP case marking being ergative and the verb agreement or cross-reference being accusative. We saw this in the examples from Warlpiri and Enga in chapter 6, (6.15) for Enga and (6.34)–(6.35) for Warlpiri. We will discuss Warlpiri cross-reference in more detail below.

A very common type of split is based on what Silverstein (1976, 1981, 1993) calls the 'inherent lexical content' of NPs, which may be represented in terms of a hierarchy of NP types, as in (7.54).[12]

(7.54) 1st and 2nd > 3rd human > 3rd non-human animate > 3rd inanimate > others

Languages vary as to whether first or second person is ranked higher, but in every case the speech act participants are ranked higher than non-speech act participants. This hierarchy interacts with case marking in the following way: core arguments fall into one of the types on the hierarchy, and, as Silverstein (1976) showed, there is a point on the hierarchy (which varies from language to language) above which NPs are marked accusatively and below which NPs are marked ergatively. In Dyirbal (Dixon 1972), the division is between first- and second-person pronouns and all other NPs. It is illustrated in the following examples. All of the previous Dyirbal examples have involved third-person NPs only.

(7.55) a. ŋaḍa bani-ɲu.
1sgNOM come-TNS
'I [S] am coming.'
b. ŋaḍa ŋinuna buɽa-n.
1sgNOM 2sgACC see-TNS
'I [A] see you [U].'
c. ŋinda ŋayguna buɽa-n.
2sgNOM 1sgACC see-TNS
'You [A] see me [U].'

These pronouns follow a straightforward accusative pattern. In sentences in which one core argument is first or second person and the other core argument third person, each is marked according to the rules appropriate for its inherent lexical content; this yields sentences in which both NPs are in nominative or absolutive form, and others in which ergative and accusative case cooccur.

(7.56) a. ŋaḍa ba-yi yaɽa-∅ buɽa-n.
1sgNOM DEIC-ABS.I man-ABS see-TNS
'I see the man.'

b. ŋayguna ba-ŋgu-l yaɽa-ŋgu buɽa-n.
1sgACC DEIC-ERG-I man-ERG see-TNS
'The man sees me.'

In a system like this, the case of an NP is a function of its properties alone, without regard for the properties of the other core arguments. Tsova-Tush (Bats; Holisky 1987) exhibits a different split of this type: it has a split-intransitive or active system for first and second person, as illustrated in (3.39), and an ergative system for third person. Active systems will be discussed in section 7.3.1.3 below.

Silverstein (1976, 1981, 1993) calls the Dyirbal-type system a 'local' case-marking system, because the case marking an NP receives is a function of its properties alone. There are languages in which the case marking of one NP depends upon the inherent lexical content of another NP; Silverstein calls this a 'global' case-marking system. An example of this can be found in Kaluli, a Papuan language (Schieffelin 1985).

(7.57) a. Abi-yɔ siabulu-wɔ mɛnigab.
-ABS sweet.potato-ABS eat.3.TNS
'Abi is about to eat a sweet potato.'
b. Abi-yɛ Suela-yɔ sandab.
-ERG -ABS hit.3.TNS
'Abi hits Suela.'

Kaluli is a strict verb-final language with two possible word orders, AUV and UAV. In clauses with the unmarked AUV word order, both A and U normally receive what Schieffelin terms 'neutral' case marking (the citation form, the same as the absolutive), as in (7.57a). When A and U are *both* proper names or kinterms, the A receives ergative case and the U receives absolutive case, as in (b). S always receives absolutive marking. Thus, the case marking of the A depends upon the inherent lexical content of the U.

The final split to be discussed is conditioned by the focus structure of the clause, and again we turn to Kaluli for an example. In terms of focus structure, the immediately preverbal position is the focus position in the Kaluli clause. The initial position is topical, and the topic element is often not expressed. This is summarized schematically in (7.58).

(7.58) *Information structure of Kaluli clause*
(NP) NP V
(Topic) Focus

Of the two word-order possibilities, AUV is the unmarked order and UAV a special, restricted form. Hence the default situation is for the A to be topic and U to be focus; this is in fact the default situation in most languages, including English, as we saw in chapter 5. The examples in (7.57) are AUV, and it is only in this order with lexical NPs that the global case-marking system described there functions. Pronouns show no variation in form in AUV sentences; there is no case marking, and the verb agrees with the A.

(7.59) a. E ne sandab.
3sg 1sg hit.3.TNS
'He/she hits me.'
b. Ne e sondɔl.
1sg 3sg hit.1.TNS
'I hit him/her.'

The situation is strikingly different in UAV utterances. In them the A is focus, not topic, and with lexical NPs, deictics and demonstratives ergative case marking is obligatory; there is a special set of focus pronouns for the A of transitive verbs as well.[13] This is a local marking system, because the A is assigned ergative case regardless of the properties of the U. The conditioning factor for this case-marking pattern is whether the A is topic or focus, regardless of its place on the hierarchy in (7.54).

(7.60) a. Nodo-wɔ niba diɔl.
one.side-ABS 1sgCNTR take.1.TNS
'I (not you) take one side.'
b. Nodo-wɔ S-wɛ diab.
one.side-ABS S[name]-ERG take.3.TNS
'S takes one side.'

Note, by the way, that in all of these examples the verb agrees with the S or A. Thus Kaluli exhibits three of the splits we have discussed: inherent lexical content, NP case vs. verb agreement, and focus structure.

These five types of split ergative systems are summarized in table 7.2. Part of the complexity of these systems is that there can be more than one type of split within a language, as in Kaluli, Georgian (Harris 1981) and Mparntwe Arrernte (Wilkins 1989).

Table 7.2 *Split-ergative systems and their conditioning factors*

Conditioning factor	*Language*	*Example*
Tensed vs. non-tensed	Jakaltek	(7.52)
Tense–aspect	Hindi, Georgian	(7.53)
NP case vs. verb agreement	Enga, Kaluli, Warlpiri, Georgian, Mparntwe Arrernte	(7.57), (7.59), (7.60)
Inherent lexical content	Dyirbal, Kaluli, Mparntwe Arrernte, Tsova-Tush (Bats)	(7.55)–(7.57)
Focus structure	Kaluli, Mparntwe Arrernte	(7.60)

How are we to capture these systems? We could start off by proposing a set of case-marking rules for the ergative pattern, on the analogy of the rules for the accusative pattern proposed in (7.45). We assume the privileged syntactic argument hierarchy in (7.1).

(7.61) *Case assignment rules for ergative pattern*
  a. Assign absolutive case to the lowest-ranking macrorole argument.
  b. Assign ergative case to the other macrorole argument.
  c. Assign dative case to non-macrorole arguments (default).

As before, these rules apply to direct core arguments only; they do not account for case assigned by adpositions. The rules in (7.61) work for third-person NPs in Dyirbal, but not first or second person. They follow the rules in (7.62); the dative case rule is the same for all NP types.

(7.62) *Case assignment for first- and second-person arguments in Dyirbal*
  a. Assign nominative case to the highest-ranking macrorole argument.
  c. Assign accusative case to the other macrorole argument.

These rules differ from the rules in (7.61) in referring to the *highest*-ranking macrorole for nominative case. This is because, while Dyirbal is syntactically ergative, case marking for first- and second-person NPs follows an accusative pattern. Dyirbal is extremely unusual in combining ergative syntax with accusative case marking, even in this limited way, hence the need for two sets of rules. What is unusual from a cross-linguistic perspective, as we discussed in section 6.5, is the rules in (7.61), not those in (7.62).

We now turn our attention to Warlpiri as an example of a language that is syntactically accusative (as we saw in section 6.2.2.1) with ergative NP case marking and accusative agreement. The basic case and agreement patterns are illustrated in (7.63) from Hale (1973). There is no inherent lexical content split in Warlpiri, and accordingly, independent NPs and bound pronominals are marked consistently, regardless of person, number or animacy. ('I' and 'II' refer to the sets of agreement elements.)

(7.63) a. Ngaju-∅ ka-rna purla-mi.
  1sg-ABS PRES-1sgI shout-NONPAST
  'I am shouting.'
 b. Ngaju-rlu ka-rna-∅ wawiri-∅ pura-mi.
  1sg-ERG PRES-1sgI-3sgII kangaroo-ABS cook-NONPAST
  'I am cooking the kangaroo.'
 c. Ngaju-rlu ka-rna-ngku karli-∅ yi-nyi nyuntu-ku.
  1sg-ERG PRES-1sgI-2sgII boomerang-ABS give-NONPAST 2sg-DAT
  'I am giving you the boomerang.'

d. Ngaju-∅ ka-rna-ngku nyuntu-ku wangka-mi.
1sg-ABS PRES-1sgI-2sgII 2sg-DAT speak-NONPAST
'I am speaking to you.'

e. Ngaju-∅ ka-rna-ngku mari-jarri-mi nyuntu-ku. (cf. (6.44a))
1sg-ABS PRES-1sgI-2sgII grief-being-NONPAST 2sg-DAT
'I feel sorry for you.'

The actor of transitive verbs takes ergative case, as in (b) and (c), while the single macrorole of an intransitive verb and the undergoer with a transitive verb take absolutive case, as in (a)–(e). Non-macrorole direct core arguments take dative case, as in (c)–(e). The rules proposed in (7.61) work for Warlpiri as well as Dyirbal. Since there is only one macrorole argument in (a), (d) and (e), it is the lowest ranking by definition, as we mentioned earlier, and hence it would take absolutive case. In clauses with a transitive verb like (b) and (c), the undergoer is the lowest-ranking macrorole, actor being the highest ranked, and therefore it appears in the absolutive case. In these two-macrorole examples the actor is the other macrorole and occurs in the ergative case. The dative rule works as it has in the other languages we have looked at.[14]

The auxiliary element (*ka-* in (7.63)) always occurs in second position in the Warlpiri clause, and the agreement affixes are attached to it, not to the verb.[15] There are two sets, which we have labeled 'I' and 'II'. Set I cross-references the highest-ranking macrorole, which is the privileged syntactic argument in Warlpiri, as we saw in section 6.2.2.1. Set II is somewhat more complex, since it may cross-reference the undergoer, as in (b), the RECIPIENT in the dative case, not the undergoer, with a three-core-argument verb like *yi* 'give', as in (c), or a non-macrorole direct core argument in the dative case, as in (d) and (e). Particularly interesting is (c), which is reminiscent of the phenomena characteristic of the primary object languages discussed in section 6.2.2.2. These three instances can be unified in a single generalization, however: set II marks the second highest-ranking direct core argument in terms of (7.1). The two agreement rules are stated in (7.64).

(7.64) *Agreement rules for Warlpiri*
1 *Set I*: this form cross-references the highest-ranking direct core argument.
2 *Set II*: this form cross-references the second highest-ranking direct core argument.

We will not go into the other three types of splits in the same detail as we have with the inherent lexical content and case vs. agreement/cross-reference splits. The approach that would have to be taken should be clear, however. In both the tensed clause vs. infinitive and the tense–aspect splits, there would have to be distinct rules for the two primary cases (or cross-reference forms, as in Jakaltek) for each of the case-marking environments. Kaluli presents a somewhat different situation, since NPs appear in the same form, regardless of their function, except in two specific circumstances, and only the actor is affected. Hence what is needed is a rule specifying when the ergative case is used, and the formulation in (7.65) captures it; it is necessarily disjunctive, because there are two quite independent sets of conditions governing the use of the ergative case.

(7.65) *Ergative case marking in Kaluli*: assign ergative case to the actor NP *iff*
- a. it is a proper name or kinterm, and the co-argument undergoer is also a proper name or kinterm; or
- b. it functions as the focus in the clause.

Condition (a) expresses the global condition on the use of the ergative case, and condition (b) captures the local condition on it.

7.3.1.3 Case marking and agreement: active and inverse languages

Active and inverse languages are not as common as accusative and ergative languages, but they nevertheless raise important issues for theories of case and agreement. We will discuss active languages first.

We have already seen two active languages in some detail, Acehnese in section 6.2.1 and Lakhota in exercise 3 in chapter 6. Languages of this type tend overwhelmingly to be headmarking. Hence for head-marking active languages, the issue of case marking primarily concerns the form of the bound argument morphemes on the verb, and accordingly case marking and agreement/cross-reference are essentially the same phenomenon in these languages.

Because with single-argument verbs there is no neutralization of the case-marking contrasts found with transitive verbs, the case-marking rules might be assumed to be very simple, e.g. 'assign actor form "X" and undergoer form "Y"'. But this in fact overlooks a number of important complexities. To begin with, it is necessary to distinguish what Dixon (1979, 1994) calls 'split-S languages', i.e. languages in which the marking of single arguments is fixed and lexically determined, e.g. Lakhota, from what he calls 'fluid-S languages', i.e. languages in which the marking can vary, as in the Tsova-Tush example in (7.66), from Holisky (1987).

(7.66) a. (As) vuiž-n-as
(1sgERG) fall-TNS-1sgERG
'I fell down (on purpose).'

b. (So) vož-en-sO
(1sgABS) fall-TNS-1sgABS
'I fell down (accidentally).'

We will discuss split-S languages first, as they present the simpler situation.

With transitive verbs in Lakhota, as the data in exercise 3 in chapter 6 show, the actor takes the *wa-* class marker, and the undergoer takes the *ma-* class marker. The majority of single-argument verbs take the *ma-* class marker; that is, they inflect like transitive undergoers. The small class of single-argument verbs taking the *wa-* class marker can be characterized, following Boas and Deloria (1941: 23), as verbs of physical or mental activity which require an animate argument (there are five exceptional verbs which do not fit this characterization). These verbs do not require that the actor be agentive, only that it be animate. Hence included in this class are not only verbs like *lową́* 'sing', *wačhí* 'dance', *hí* 'arrive' and *nųwą́* 'swim', but also *pšá* 'sneeze', *blokáška* 'hiccough' and *gópa* 'snore'. For this language, then, single-argument activity verbs which require an animate actor take *wa-* marking, all others taking *ma-*. Other split-S languages show different semantic bases for their splits, as Merlan (1985) and Dixon (1994) discuss in some detail, and in those languages these semantic distinctions would underlie the assignment of case to the single arguments of intransitive verbs.

Fluid-S languages present a more complex problem, since the choice of case for the S NP can vary from sentence to sentence, depending upon the intended interpretation. Basically, the essential factor affecting case assignment with intransitive verbs in fluid-S languages is how agent-like the participant is or how much control they exert over their actions. Hence if the speaker wishes to code the participant as being very AGENT-like, the case used for the actors of transitive verbs is assigned, whereas if the speaker wishes to code the participant as not being AGENT-like (or as being more PATIENT-like), then the case used for the undergoers of transitive verbs is assigned. There are important complications involving markedness that appear when one looks at fluid-S languages in detail. We will take Tsova-Tush (Holisky 1987) as our example of a language of this type. Holisky shows that intransitive verbs in Tsova-Tush fall into five classes, which are listed in (7.67). This language has ergative marking in the third person, and therefore ergative is the case of transitive actors and nominative is the case of transitive undergoers.

(7.67) *Marking patterns of Tsova-Tush intransitive verbs* (Holisky 1987)
- a. Intransitives with only nominative marking, e.g. *maicdar* 'be hungry', *dah" ǧordar* 'freeze', *qerl' ar* 'be afraid'.
- b. Intransitives with variable marking:
  - 1 Nominative is the norm, and ergative is possible but unusual or rare, e.g. *dah" davar* 'die (pl)', *dah" dax:ar* 'drown, suffocate', *dah" maldalar* 'get tired'.
  - 2 Both nominative and ergative are possible, with no clear preference for either, e.g. *dah" daxar* 'get drunk', *ʕopdalar* 'hide, come to be hidden', *k'určdalar* 'go by rolling, roll', *dat'ar* 'lie around, be scattered', *dišdalar/det:dalar* 'bump into'.
  - 3 Ergative is the norm, and nominative is possible but unusual or rare, e.g. *ga=rek'a(da)dalar* 'run very fast', *deh" dalar* 'sneak up on', *dildalar* 'wash, get washed', *doldalar/debldalar* 'begin'.
- c. Intransitives with only ergative marking, e.g. *daǧar* 'come', *lalar* 'walk, wander', *lavar/levar* 'talk', *lap'c'ar* 'play'.

The verbs in group (a) are either states or accomplishments, and those in group (b1) are mostly accomplishments. Holisky comments with respect to *dah" davar* 'die (pl)' in (b1) that the 'use of nominative marking conveys nothing special about the situation, while using the ergative expresses an unusual state of affairs in which the referent of the subject wants to die' (110). The verbs in group (b2) are a mix of state, accomplishment and activity verbs. Accomplishment verbs 'with nominative marking . . . convey that the change takes place naturally, independently of the subject's will or control, while with ergative marking they convey that the subject has something to do with the change, perhaps by doing something to bring it about' (111). With respect to locational state verbs like *dat'ar* 'lie around, be scattered', 'nominative marking conveys the location merely as a fact, with no particular decision or intention on the part of the subject to be in that location. Ergative marking conveys that the subject is in that location because of her own will, because she wants to be there' (*ibid.*). Finally, the action denoted by the activity verbs is interpreted as being willfully done under the control of the referent of the subject if it is ergative but not if it is nominative. The verbs in group (b3) normally take ergative, and 'the rarer, nominative marking might be used to express an extremely odd situation in which the subject doesn't want or intend to perform the activity but nonetheless does so, perhaps mindlessly' (112). All of the verbs in (c) are verbs of mental or physical activity. Since this variable marking is restricted to first- and second-person arguments, they are all animate. The correlation of verb type and case marking should not come as a surprise, since the nominative-only and nominative-preferred verbs are states, achievements and accomplishments, all of which would have undergoer arguments, while the ergative-only and ergative-preferred verbs are primarily activity verbs, which would have actor arguments. The 'no-preference' group in (b2) has verbs of all types in it.

The fact that verbs in group (b1) can take undergoers in the ergative case and that the verbs in group (b3) can take actors in the nominative case shows clearly that ergative case is not uniquely associated with actors and that nominative case is not uniquely associated with undergoers. Moreover, Holisky also emphasizes that ergative is not necessarily associated with an agentive interpretation and nominative with a non-agentive interpretation. She characterizes the situation as follows:

> These facts follow naturally if nominative and ergative forms of intransitive verbs are analyzed as forming a privative opposition for the expression of agentivity. For a large number of verbs . . . the ergative is unmarked and can convey agentivity or non-agentivity. The form with nominative, as the marked member of the opposition, is always interpreted non-agentively.
>
> For a smaller number of verbs . . . however, the marking is reversed: the ergative is the marked member of the opposition and is used to

convey agentivity on the part of the subject. The nominative is neutral, expressing nothing in particular about agentivity.(116)

Following Holisky's RRG-based analysis, we may propose the following case assignment rules for first- and second-person S arguments; third-person NPs follow the same basic rules proposed for Dyirbal and Warlpiri in (7.61). They crucially presuppose the implicature account of agentivity proposed by Holisky and discussed in section 3.2.3.2.

(7.68) *Case marking rules for first- and second-person arguments of intransitive verbs in Tsova-Tush*

a. Defaults:
   1 Assign ergative case to actors.
   2 Assign nominative case to undergoers.
b. Utterance-specific options, applying to verbs in group (b) in (7.67):
   1 Assign nominative case to an actor to block the agentivity implicature.
   2 Assign ergative case to an undergoer to force the agentivity implicature.

Thus, assigning nominative case to an actor is analogous to adding an adverb like *accidentally* or *inadvertently* to a clause to signal overtly that the S NP is not to be interpreted as an AGENT, and similarly, assigning ergative case to an undergoer is analogous to adding an adverb like *intentionally* to a clause to indicate that the S NP should be interpreted as an AGENT. The rules in (b) reflect the privative semantic oppositions proposed by Holisky and account for the interpretation of the examples without positing unmotivated changes in the argument structure of the verbs. That is, an alternative analysis could claim that there are, for example, two verbs in the lexicon for each of those listed in the groups in (b) in (7.67), one which takes an actor and one which takes an undergoer, thereby eliminating the need for the rules in (7.68b). While this might seem simpler, since it requires fewer case-marking rules, it has at least two serious drawbacks. First, it requires duplicate lexical entries for the majority of intransitive verbs in the language; this is unusual, to be sure, and the wholesale positing of double lexical entries for verbs suggests strongly that an important generalization is being missed. Second, it requires the postulation of otherwise impossible macrorole + verb combinations, e.g. actor + *dah" davar* 'die (pl)' or undergoer + *ga=rek'a(da)dalar* 'run very fast'. This is a serious weakening of the theory, since it permits systematic violation of the macrorole assignment principles in (4.14b), principles which otherwise have few, if any, exceptions. Thus, the first approach, the one involving the rules in (7.68b), is to be preferred as simpler and better motivated within the theory. The use of case marking to block or force the agentivity implicature is not just a feature of fluid-S languages, as we will see in our discussion of case marking in causative constructions in chapter 9.

We briefly introduced an inverse language, Kutenai, in section 6.4.1. In an inverse language, case marking only indirectly indicates notions like actor, undergoer or privileged syntactic argument; what it directly signals is related to either the person of the core arguments or their discourse status. We will use Plains Cree, an Algonquian language (Wolfart 1973), as our example of an inverse language. To understand core argument marking in this type of language, we need two ideas we have talked about before. The first is a person hierarchy like the one in (7.54), and the second is the distinction between proximate and obviative third persons, which we discussed briefly in section 6.4.1 with reference to the Kutenai example in (6.59). The two may be combined to create an extended person hierarchy for Cree, which is given in (7.69).

(7.69) 2nd > 1st > 1st dual inclusive > 3rd PROX > 3rd OBV

Second-person core arguments are coded only by the prefix *ki*(*t*)-, while first-person core arguments may be coded by the prefix *ni*(*t*)- or the suffix *-n*. Third-person core arguments are always coded by suffixes, if coded on the verb. This is illustrated in the following examples.

(7.70) a. Ki-wāpam-i-n.
2sg-see-DCT-1sg
'You see me.'
b. Ki-wāpam-iti-n.
2sg-see-INV-1sg
'I see you.'

(7.71) a. Ni-wāpam-ā-w (nāpēw-∅).
1sg-see-DCT-3sg(man-PROX)
'I see him (the man).'
b. Ni-wāpam-ik (nāpēw-∅)
[< ni-wāpam-ekw-w]
1sg-see-INV-3sg (man-PROX)
'He (the man) sees me.'

The second-person core argument in (7.70) is coded by a prefix, regardless of whether it is actor or undergoer, and the first-person core argument is always a suffix, regardless of its function, if there is a second-person argument in the core. When, however, the core arguments are first and third person, as in (7.71), then the first-person argument is expressed by a prefix, regardless of its function. Thus the hierarchy in (7.69) governs which core argument will be coded by a prefix, if there is a first- or second-person argument in the clause.

If each core argument is coded the same way in both sentences in each pair, regardless of its function as actor or undergoer, then how does one tell who is doing the action to whom? The answer lies in the suffix coded 'DCT' for 'direct' or 'INV' for 'inverse': if the actor is higher on the hierarchy in (7.69) than the undergoer, then the direct suffix is used; if, on the other hand, the undergoer is higher on the hierarchy in (7.69) than the actor, then the inverse suffix is used. To express the logical structure **see′** (2sg, 1sg), the direct suffix must be used, because the actor is second person and the undergoer first person; the actor is higher on the hierarchy than the undergoer. To express the logical structure **see′** (1sg, 2sg), on the other hand, inverse coding must be used, because the actor is first person and the undergoer is second person; the undergoer is higher on the hierarchy than the actor. The same holds for the sentences in (7.71): when the actor is first person and the undergoer third person, as in (a), the actor is higher on the hierarchy than the undergoer, and accordingly the direct suffix occurs; when the actor is third person and the undergoer first person, as in (b), the undergoer is higher on the hierarchy, and therefore the inverse suffix occurs.

When there are two third-person core arguments, one must be proximate and the other obviative, and the lower end of the hierarchy applies.

(7.72) a. Wāpam-ē-w nāpēw-∅ atim-wa.
see-DCT-3sgPROX man-PROX dog-OBV
'The man sees the dog.'
b. Wāpam-ik nāpēw-∅ atim-wa.
[< wāpam-ekw-w]
see-INV-3PROX man-PROX dog-OBV
'The dog sees the man.'

The interpretation of these examples depends on the hierarchy, just like the others. Given the logical structure **see′** (nāpēw, atim) and the context-based determination that *nāpēw* 'man' is the proximate NP, then the direct suffix must be used, since the actor (*nāpēw* 'man') is higher on the hierarchy than the obviative undergoer (*atimwa* 'dog'). If the context were the same but the logical structure were **see′** (atim, nāpēw), then the inverse suffix would have to be used, because the obviative actor (*atimwa* 'dog') is lower on the hierarchy than the proximate undergoer (*nāpēw* 'man'). Suppose we now wish to express these two logical structures in contexts in which *atim* 'dog' is the proximate NP; the resulting sentences are given in (7.73).

(7.73) a. Wāpam-ik nāpēw-a atim-∅. (= (7.72a))
[< wāpam-ekw-w]
see-INV-3PROX man-OBV dog-PROX
'The man sees the dog.'
b. Wāpam-ē-w nāpēw-a atim-∅. (= (7.72b))
see-DCT-3sgPROX man-OBV dog-PROX
'The dog sees the man.'

Thus, in an inverse system the formal marking of a core argument is not related to its function as actor or undergoer at all; the pronominal affixes have the same form and position regardless of function, and proximate–obviative NP marking is likewise unrelated to function as actor or undergoer. This is very different from all of the other languages we have looked at, and it contrasts perhaps most strikingly with active languages, in which case marking is closely tied to function as actor or undergoer (for the most part). The direct and inverse suffixes on the verb are the real 'case markers', so to speak, since they, in combination with the person hierarchy in (7.69), determine the interpretation of the core arguments. Inherent lexical content hierarchies, like the person hierarchies in (7.54) and (7.69), play a central role in the case-marking systems of both split-ergative languages like Dyirbal and Kaluli and also in inverse languages like Plains Cree and Kutenai. Clearly, the linking algorithm for syntax → semantics for languages of this type must refer crucially to this suffix, in much the same way the linking algorithm in (7.36) refers crucially to the voice of the verb for languages like English and Dyirbal.

7.3.2 Adposition assignment

Many languages mark core arguments with adpositions, and accordingly there are rules governing their assignment just like those for morphological cases.[16] In section 4.3 we gave a brief sketch of how *to* and *from*, two of the prepositions that mark oblique core arguments in English, can be predicted from the logical structure of the verb in the clause, and in this section we will discuss *to*, *from*, *with* and *for* in English.

7.3.2.1 Argument-marking prepositions

We have already seen numerous instances of argument-marking prepositions; a few examples are given below.

(7.74) a. Sally gave/showed/sent/handed the box to Pat.
a′. Sally taught basketweaving to Pat.
b. Sandy took/stole/bought the keys from Kim.
b′. Pat drained the water from the pool.
b″. Kim escaped from the burning house.
c. Mary opened the drawer with a knife.
d. Pam filled the bag with presents.
e. Robin went to the concert with Pat.

If we look at the relevant parts of the logical structures in the sentences involving *to*, which are given in (7.75), a clear pattern emerges.

(7.75) a. . . . BECOME **have′** (Pat, box) = *give, hand, send*
b. . . . BECOME **see′** (Pat, box) = *show*
c. . . . BECOME **know′** (Pat, basketweaving) = *teach*

The NP marked by *to* is in every instance the first argument of a two-place state predicate embedded under a BECOME or INGR operator in the logical structure; it is also a non-macrorole core argument. The state predicate can be of various types; in these examples there are possession, perception, cognition and location predicates, and the arguments marked by *to* include POSSESSORS, PERCEIVERS, COGNIZERS and LOCATIONS. Hence it cannot be said that *to* marks a single type of thematic relation, but it does consistently mark the same argument type in terms of logical structure argument position. This is one more piece of evidence in favor of the basicness of logical structure argument positions and against the idea that thematic relations are basic (see chapter 3). We may propose the rule for assigning *to* given in (7.76), which is the same as (4.18a). This rule applies at step 5 in (7.12).

(7.76) *Rule assigning* to *in English*
Assign *to* to the non-macrorole *x* argument in the logical structure segment:
. . . BECOME/INGR **pred′** (x, y)

If we do a similar analysis of the sentences involving *from*, we likewise find a clear pattern.

(7.77) a. . . . BECOME NOT **have′** (Kim, keys) = *take, steal, buy*
b. . . . BECOME NOT **be-in′** (pool, water) = *drain*
c. . . . BECOME NOT **be-in′** (burning house, Kim) = *escape*

In each of these logical structures, *from* marks the first argument of the two-place state predicate which appears as a non-macrorole core argument. What is different about the logical structures in (7.77) from those in (7.75) is the occurrence of NOT; Gruber (1965) argued that *to* and *from* differ in just this way. The range of state predicates that occur in these logical structures appears to be more limited than that with *to*. Nevertheless, it is clear that *from* does not mark a single thematic relation. The rule for assigning *from* is given in (7.78).[17]

(7.78) *Rule assigning* from *in English*
Assign *from* to the non-macrorole *x* argument in the logical structure segment:
. . . BECOME/INGR NOT **pred′** (x, y)

With is perhaps the most intriguing preposition in English, because of its wide range of uses. Three are illustrated in (7.74c–e): the first is traditionally labeled 'instrumental'; the second does not easily fit traditional categories; and the third is called 'comitative'. It is the primary non-locative preposition in English, and it cannot be associated with a single thematic relation or argument position in logical structure. Indeed, it is possible to have five or more *with* PPs in a single English sentence, as (7.79) shows.

(7.79) The woman with strong arms loaded the truck with hay with a pitchfork with Bill with enthusiasm.

How should *with* be analyzed? One possibility would be to say simply that there are five or more homophonous prepositions *with* in English: one for INSTRUMENTS, one for attributes (*with strong arms*), one for THEMES (*with hay*), one for comitative and one for manner adverbials (*with enthusiasm*). This is really no analysis at all; it is, rather, just a labeling of the various uses. What we need to do is to examine each of these uses carefully to see what pattern emerges.

We begin with the instrumental use. In chapter 3 we argued for a particular logical structure configuration, repeated in (7.80a), as the definition of INSTRUMENT, and illustrated it with the logical structure for *Tom cut the bread with the knife*, repeated in (b).

(7.80) a. INSTRUMENT: IMPLEMENT 'y' argument in the logical structure configuration [**do′** (x, [. . . .])] CAUSE [[. . . **do′** (y, [. . .])] CAUSE [BECOME/ INGR **pred′** (. . .)]]

b. [**do′** (Tom, [**use′** (Tom, knife))] *CAUSE* [[**do′** (knife, [**cut′** (knife, bread])] CAUSE [BECOME **cut′** (bread)]]

There are two EFFECTORS in this logical structure, the animate NP *Tom* and the inanimate NP *knife*, which is also an IMPLEMENT, and both are potential actors in terms of the Actor–Undergoer Hierarchy. When there are two EFFECTORS, the first one in the causal chain becomes actor, as we argued in section 4.1. In (7.80b), *Tom* corresponds to the *x* argument in (a) and *knife* to *y*, and therefore *Tom* is the first argument in the causal chain and functions as actor. *Knife*, on the other hand, is not selected for undergoer either, as *bread* outranks it with respect to the undergoer end of the hierarchy, and accordingly it will be realized as a non-macrorole core argument and is marked by *with*. Thus, with respect to the instrumental use of *with*, we may say that *with* marks a potential actor which is not selected as actor.

The instrumental use of *with* requires a causal chain of the type represented in (7.80). In such a causal chain, the first EFFECTOR, the instigator, acts on the secondary IMPLEMENT–EFFECTOR, the INSTRUMENT, which in turn acts on the PATIENT or THEME, e.g. Tom acts on the knife, which comes into contact with the bread and acts on it, cutting it, as in (7.80b). In such cases the INSTRUMENT may occur as actor, as in *The knife cut the bread* or *The key opened the door*. As noted in section 3.2.3.2, there are apparently uses of *with* which do not involve a causal chain, and this is typically when they are used with activity verbs; in such cases, the argument marked by *with* cannot serve as actor with these verbs when there is no other potential actor argument. This is illustrated in (3.43), repeated in (7.81).

(7.81) a. Abdul ate the cereal with a spoon.

a′. *The spoon ate the cereal.

b. Tanisha looked at the comet with a telescope.

b′. *The telescope looked at the comet.

Like manner adverbs, these *with* PPs express an aspect of how the action is performed, and they primarily occur with activity predicates. The logical structures for these examples were given in (3.44), repeated in (7.82).

(7.82) a. **do′** (Abdul, [**eat′** (Abdul, cereal) ∧ **use′** (Abdul, spoon)])

b. **do′** (Tanisha, [**see′** (Tanisha, comet) ∧ **use′** (Tanisha, telescope)])

It might be argued that *pitchfork* in (7.79) is like *spoon* and *telescope* in (7.81) because of (7.83a), but this would in fact be the wrong conclusion to draw, as (7.83b) shows.

(7.83) a. *The pitchfork loaded the truck with hay.
b. The mechanized pitchfork loaded the truck with hay.

Example (7.83a) is not really ungrammatical; it is impossible in terms of our knowledge of how the world works. When we change *pitchfork* to *mechanized pitchfork*, the sentence immediately becomes plausible, even though the logical structures of the two are the same; in both, there is a causal chain involving *the woman* and *the pitchfork*, as in (7.84).

(7.84) [**do′** (woman, [**use′** (woman, pitchfork)]] *CAUSE* [[**do′** (pitchfork, [**load′** (pitchfork, hay)])] CAUSE [BECOME **be-on′** (truck, hay)]]

As in (7.80), *pitchfork* in (7.84) is outranked for actor by *woman* and outranked for undergoer by both *hay* and *truck*, since it is an IMPLEMENT–EFFECTOR. However, since the IMPLEMENT in (7.78) is not an argument of the verb but rather of **use′**, it will always be outranked for actor by the EFFECTOR of the primary activity predicate such as *eat* or *look at*.

The next use of *with* to be examined is its use with verbs like *load*, *spray*, *supply* and *present* in which it participates in the locative alternation discussed in section 7.2.2, e.g. *load the truck with (the) hay* vs. *load (the) hay on the truck*. The relevant part of the logical structure underlying this alternation is . . . CAUSE [BECOME **be-on′** (y, z)], with *y* being *the truck* and *z* being *(the) hay*. In the default linking in terms of the Actor–Undergoer Hierarchy, the *z* argument is undergoer and the *y* argument is marked by a locative preposition, as in *load (the) hay on the truck*. In the marked linking, the *y* argument is selected as undergoer, and the *z* argument is marked by *with*, yielding *load the truck with (the) hay*. Hence it appears that if a semantic argument which is the default choice for undergoer is not selected for undergoer, it is marked by *with*.[18]

The comitative use of *with* seems rather different from these first two, but, like the use of *with* with *load*, there is an alternation involved. It is illustrated in (7.85).

(7.85) a. Sandy and Kim loaded hay on the truck.
b. Sandy loaded hay on the truck with Kim.
c. Kim loaded hay on the truck with Sandy.

Let us assume that there is a single logical structure underlying these three sentences: [**do′** (Sandy, ∅) ∧ **do′** (Kim, ∅)] CAUSE [BECOME **be-on′** (truck, hay)]. If both *Sandy* and *Kim* are chosen as actor, then the result is (7.85a). It is also possible, however, to select only one of them as actor; if only *Sandy* is selected, the result is (b), and if only *Kim* is selected, the result is (c). Both *Sandy* and *Kim* are potential actors, as (a) shows, and when only one of them functions as actor, the other is marked by *with*, just as an EFFECTOR not selected as actor with a verb like *cut* or *open* is marked by *with*. But this is not restricted to potential actor arguments; it can also occur with potential undergoer arguments in some cases. Consider the examples in (7.86).

(7.86) a. Pat served wine and cheese.
b. Pat served wine with cheese.
c. Pat served cheese with wine.

Here again we have conjoined NPs alternating with *NP with NP*, and in this case we are dealing with potential undergoers rather than potential actors. But the generalization appears to be basically the same: if an argument which would otherwise appear as a macrorole does not, it is marked by *with*. Indeed, this generalization seems to cover the INSTRUMENT, THEME and comitative uses of *with* discussed so far. It may be formulated more precisely as in (7.87).

(7.87) *Rule for assigning* with *in English* (*preliminary formulation*)
If an argument of equal or lower rank on the Actor–Undergoer Hierarchy is selected as a macrorole argument instead of the argument under consideration, mark the non-macrorole argument with *with*.

This rule correctly predicts the use of *with* in the examples in (7.74). The important thing to note about this rule, as opposed to the rules for *to* and *from*, is that it does not refer to a specific argument position or positions in logical structures but rather to the macrorole assignment phase of the linking procedure. This is why it can mark NPs with such a range of semantic functions.

There are still two uses of *with* that we have not accounted for, the attributive and manner adverbial, and they would appear to be rather different from the first three, since they do not involve syntactic arguments. Let us first consider the attributive use. A phrase like *the woman with strong arms* involves possession, in this case inalienable possession. In section 4.7.3 we discussed the semantic representation for possessive NPs, and for this phrase it would be **have.as.part′** (woman, strong arms).[19] There are two possible realizations for this logical structure as an NP; if *strong arms* is taken as the head, the result is *the woman's strong arms*, whereas if *woman* is taken as the head, then the result is *the woman with strong arms*. It is reasonable to assume that the default realization of the POSSESSOR argument in this logical structure is as the possessor NP in the possessive NP, and therefore the default linking of **have.as.part′** (x, y) is with *y* (the POSSESSED argument) as the head of the NP, i.e. as *x's y*. When, on the other hand, the *x* argument is selected as head, the *y* argument is marked by *with*. While this does not involve macrorole assignment, as in the other cases of *with* assignment, it nevertheless concerns the failure of the default linking to obtain, and the NP which 'loses out', so to speak, gets marked by *with*. We saw this in section 4.7.3 in NPs containing modifying PPs. Given a logical structure like **be-in′** (bedroom, table), the default is for *table* to be selected as head of the NP, yielding *the table in the bedroom*. If, on the other hand, *bedroom* is the head of the NP, the result is *the bedroom with the table in it* (cf. (4.77)). What is of interest here is not only that the default choice for head is marked by *with*, as expected, but also that the preposition occurs with a pronominal copy of the head noun. This may seem odd, but given the choice of the LOCATION argument as head and the obligatory marking of the other argument with *with*, the only way for the preposition to occur is as a modifier and the only way to express the fact that the head is in fact semantically the LOCATION argument is to introduce a pronominal copy of it.

In order to unify this use of *with* with the argument-marking uses captured in (7.87), we need to generalize the principle to include linking within NPs as well as within cores.

(7.88) *Rule for assigning* with *in English*
Given two arguments, *x* and *y*, in a logical structure, with *x* lower than or equal to *y* on the Actor–Undergoer Hierarchy, and a specific grammatical status (macrorole, head of NP), assign *with* to the *y* argument iff it is not selected for that status.[20]

The two arguments in question have to be candidates for the same grammatical status; therefore in (7.80b), for example, only *Tom* and *knife* are candidates for actor, and *bread* is not.

The final use of *with* is in manner adverbials. Manner adverbs, as we saw in section 4.4.1.2, modify activity predicates, and they signal something about the way the actor performs the action. In a sense they are like the attributive constructions, in that they attribute a property to the actor's performance. Thus in *Bill loaded hay on the truck with enthusiasm*, we are asserting that Bill performed the task with great enthusiasm. It is possible to describe someone as 'having a lot of enthusiasm'. It is also possible to paraphrase this as *Bill enthusiastically loaded hay on the truck*, with an adverb rather than a PP. This suggests that the adverb and the PP are alternative realizations of the same semantic structure, much the same way *NP and NP* and *NP with NP* are alternative realizations of the same semantic structure. Hence we may represent the activity subpart of the logical structure as [**enthusiastic′** (**do′** (Bill, ∅))] CAUSE . . . This follows the treatment for manner adverbs outlined in section 4.4.1.2. The default realization of this is as a manner adverb, i.e. *Bill enthusiastically* . . . , but there is an alternative realization which involves it appearing as the corresponding noun *enthusiasm* in a PP. The preposition is *with*, at least in part because it is the primary non-locative preposition in English, and there is no locative relationship of any kind here. This use of *with* does not follow from (7.88) literally, but there is a sense in which this use is related to the ones captured in it.

The linkings which fall under (7.88) all involve non-default or marked realizations of the element in the logical structure, and this is the case here as well, since the default realization of **enthusiastic′** in this logical structure is as the manner adverb *enthusiastically*. Thus manner adverbials like *with enthusiasm* seem to follow the same general pattern for the use of *with* laid out in (7.88), even though this rule does not apply literally in this instance. This is a significant result, for it means that the INSTRUMENT, IMPLEMENT, THEME, comitative and attributive uses of *with* can be accounted for by a single principle, with the manner adverb use being a related case. The rule in (7.88) is very different from the previous preposition assignment rules, because it does not refer to specific logical structure configurations or argument positions but rather to the linking procedure itself. The complex logical structure for (7.79) is given in (7.89).

(7.89) [**enthusiastic′** (**do′** ([**have.as.part′** (woman, strong arms)], [**use′** (woman, pitchfork)]) ∧ **do′** (Bill, ∅)] *CAUSE* [[**do′** (pitchfork, [**load′** (pitchfork, hay)])] CAUSE [BECOME **be-on′** (truck, hay)]]

The woman would be chosen as actor and *the truck* would be undergoer. The modifier *strong arms* would be assigned *with* by the rule in (7.88), as would the INSTRUMENT *pitchfork*. Since *Bill* is not selected as actor and *hay* as undergoer, they would both be assigned *with* by the rule in (7.88). If **enthusiastic′** is not realized as a manner adverb, it appears as the corresponding noun in a PP headed by *with*. Because only *the woman with strong arms* functions as actor, the use of a pitchfork and having enthusiasm are attributed only to it, not to *Bill*. If the sentence were *Bill and the woman with strong arms loaded the truck with hay with pitchforks with enthusiasm*, then the logical structure would be as in (7.90), in which both arguments are modified by *with pitchforks* and *with enthusiasm*.

(7.90) [**enthusiastic′** (**do′** ([**have.as.part′** (woman, strong arms) ∧ Bill, [**use′** (woman ∧ Bill, pitchforks)])] *CAUSE* [[**do′** (pitchforks, [**load′**(pitchforks, hay)])] CAUSE [BECOME **be-on′** (truck, hay)]]

One of the surprising results of this analysis is that all of these uses of *with* except the manner adverb use are accounted for by the rule in (7.88), and the principle governing the manner adverb use seems to be a natural extension of it.

7.3.2.2 Argument-adjunct prepositions

These prepositions are predicates, but they introduce an argument rather than a modifier. Argument-adjunct prepositions with verbs like *run* and *put* were discussed in section 4.4.1.1.

For is a very complex and interesting preposition in English; it can have all three functions we have discussed.

(7.91) a. Lucy longs for a diamond ring. — Argument-marking
b. Robin baked a cake for Sandy. — Argument-adjunct
c. Rita sang for the students. — Adjunct

Jolly (1991, 1993) analyzes the basic meaning of *for* as being purposive, which may be characterized as one action being done with the intent of realizing another state of affairs. She gives the following semantic representation to capture the meaning of *for*.

(7.92) *Semantic representation of purposive* for
want′ (x, LS_2) ∧ DO (x, [LS_1 . . . CAUSE . . . LS_2])

This says that the participant denoted by *x* wants some state of affairs to obtain (LS_2) and intentionally does LS_1 in order to bring LS_2 about. The 'DO' is significant, because it is impossible for the action in LS_1 to be non-volitional, as the examples from Jolly (1993) in (7.93) show.

(7.93) a. *John knows Greek for mental exercise.
b. *Rita found a fifty-mark note for fun.

In the argument-marking use, as in (7.91a), only the first part of (7.92) is relevant. Only verbs of hope or desire take *for* as an argument marker. If one looks at them in detail, it becomes clear that the object of *for* is really a reduced proposition. That is, *Lucy longs for a diamond ring* means 'Lucy longs to have a diamond ring', and *Fred hopes for a BMW* means 'Fred hopes that he will get/have a BMW.' Thus the logical structures for these sentences is **want′** (Lucy, [**have′** (Lucy, diamond ring)]) and **hope′** (Fred, [BECOME **have′** (Fred, BMW)]), respectively. Thus the logical structure of these examples corresponds to the first part of the formula in (7.92).

The argument-adjunct use of *for* involves the whole logical structure in (7.92). If we give a full representation of (7.91b) in terms of this representation, the result is (7.94a); if we abbreviate (7.92) as 'PURP LS_2', the result is (7.94b).

(7.94) a. [**want′** (Robin, [BECOME **have′** (Sandy, cake)])] ∧ [[DO (Robin, [**do′** (Robin, ∅)] CAUSE [BECOME **baked′** (cake)]] CAUSE [BECOME **have′** (Sandy, cake)])]]
b. [[**do′** (Robin, ∅)] CAUSE [BECOME **baked′** (cake)]] PURP [BECOME **have′** (Sandy, cake)]

This is an argument-adjunct use of *for*, since the logical structure of *for* shares an argument, *cake*, with the logical structure of *bake*. The RECIPIENT argument *Sandy* can be linked to undergoer in a marked linking, as in *Robin baked Sandy a cake*. This thematic relation is commonly labeled 'benefactive' or 'beneficiary', but we did not introduce a thematic relation with either of these labels in chapter 3, because it is not a thematic relation which is part of a verb's logical structure. Rather, it arises either from a preposition like *for* or an applied verb form, as in the Chicheŵa examples in (7.30). There are at least three different senses of benefactive: (1) RECIPIENT benefactives, as in (7.94), (2) 'plain' beneficiaries, like *the students* in (7.91c), and (3) deputative beneficiaries, as in *Pat stood in line for Kim*, where the actor did the action in place of the beneficiary. Some languages use different markers for these types; in Lakhota, for example, *-ki-* marks plain and recipient beneficiaries, while *-kiči-* marks deputative beneficiaries (Boas and Deloria 1941, Van Valin 1977). In terms of (7.92), the LS_2 for plain beneficiaries would be something like 'the action of the actor provides them with amusement, enjoyment or other kind of benefit', while the LS_2 for deputative beneficiaries would be 'NOT LS_1', that is, the actor does LS_1 with the intention that the beneficiary not do the action. The plain beneficiary and deputative readings are not available when the beneficiary appears as undergoer, as in *Kim bought Pat a new book*; only the RECIPIENT reading is possible. The reason for this can be seen in the logical structures for these two readings in (7.95), using the 'PURP' abbreviation.

(7.95) a. Robin baked a cake for Sandy
a′. [to show her she could do it, to amuse her, etc.] Plain benefactive
a″. [so that she wouldn't have to] Deputative
b. **do′** (Robin, ∅)] CAUSE [BECOME **baked′** (cake)] PURP [BECOME **entertained′** (Sandy)] = (a′)
c. [**do′** (Robin, ∅)] CAUSE [BECOME **baked′** (cake)] PURP [NOT [**do′** (Sandy, ∅)] CAUSE [BECOME **baked′** (cake)]] = (a″)

The (b) logical structure represents the plain benefactive reading of (a), while the (c) logical structure represents the deputative reading. There is no shared argument between the two parts of the logical structure in (b), and therefore *for Sandy* is an adjunct. In the deputative logical structure in (b′), unlike the RECIPIENT benefactive logical structure in (7.94), *Sandy* is not a potential undergoer argument, since it is an EFFECTOR rather than a RECIPIENT, in contrast to (7.94).

This discussion of benefactives has highlighted again an important point from chapter 3, namely the importance of the logical structure representations over the thematic relations labels in accounting for the differential behavior of NPs. Just positing a BENEFACTIVE thematic relation label would not be adequate as an account for all of these uses of *for*.

7.4 The two phases of linking

Figure 7.1 summarizes the linking system, and it has two major phases: (1) mapping the arguments in logical structures into macroroles, and (2) mapping the macroroles and other arguments into the syntax. In terms of the semantics → syntax linking algorithm in (7.12), the first phase corresponds to step 1 and the second to steps

2–4. The two phases of the linking have important properties which will be investigated further in the next two sections.

7.4.1 Universal vs. language-specific aspects of linking

In figure 7.1 a distinction is made between universal and language-specific aspects of linking. The system of logical structures and the Actor–Undergoer Hierarchy for mapping argument positions into macroroles constitute the universal part, and the mapping of macroroles and other semantic arguments of the verb into the syntax, including case marking and the possible occurrence of WH-words in the precore slot, varies across languages. We have already seen many examples of this second type of cross-linguistic variation, and in this section we will explore the far more restricted variation which is manifested in the 'universal' part of the system.

The first important distinction to make is between variation in the properties of individual lexical items and variation in linking. To say, for example, that the system of lexical representation (logical structures) is universal is not to claim that verbs which appear to be translation equivalents of each other must have the same logical structure. We discussed this at the beginning of chapter 3, and it is worth mentioning again. A simple example of this concerns the verbs translated 'die' in Mandarin and English: in Mandarin it is an achievement, i.e. it is punctual, whereas in English it is an accomplishment, i.e. it is non-punctual. We also discussed there the difference between English and Lakhota verbs of breaking. Another type of lexical variation is in terms of M-transitivity: a given verb in one language, e.g. English *please* and Portuguese *gostar*, may be M-transitive, while its translation equivalents in other languages, e.g. German *gefallen*, Russian *nravitsja* or Spanish *gustar*, are M-intransitive. Nevertheless, the linking system into which these verbs enter is basically the same for all of these languages.

What kind of variation exists in the mapping between logical structure argument positions and macroroles? The primary factor which varies across languages is animacy; in other words, languages vary with respect to how much, if at all, animacy affects the assignment of semantic arguments to macroroles. With respect to actor, there are languages which restrict actors to animates or pseudo-animates, i.e. self-moving, effecting entities like storms, floods and tornados, as we discussed briefly in section 4.1. Lakhota is such a language. As we saw in (3.8b), repeated below, an inanimate INSTRUMENT like a rock cannot function as actor with a transitive verb.

(7.96) a. *Ixʔé wą ožą́žąglepi ki ka-bléčhe.
rock a window the by.striking-break
'A rock broke the window.'

b. Ixʔé wą ų ožą́žąglepi ki ∅-∅-ka-bléčha-pi.
rock a with window the INAN-3A-by.striking-break-pl
'They [unspecified] broke the window with a rock.'

It is possible to have a pseudo-animate like 'flood' function directly as actor, as in (7.97).

(7.97) Mníhiyaya-thąka ki thípi ki ∅-∅-wožúžu.
flood-big the house the INAN-3sgA-smash
'The big flood smashed (destroyed) the house.'

Actor is not restricted to simply AGENT or EFFECTOR arguments which are instigators, not INSTRUMENTS (see section 3.2.3.2), since the first arguments of verbs of perception, cognition and possession can all function as actor; they are all animate.

(7.98) a. Igmú ki na-∅-wá-xʔų̣.
cat the stem-3sgU-1sgA-hear
'I hear the cat.'
b. Wówapi wą ∅-l-uhá he?
book a INAN-2sgA-have Q
'Do you have a book?'
c. Slol-∅-wá-ye.
stem-INAN-1sgA-know
'I know it.'

Variation with respect to undergoer selection falls into two areas. The first is with respect to the possibility of marked linkings, as exemplified in the English examples in (7.23), (7.26) and (7.29) and the Dyirbal example in (7.25). Few languages allow such marked linkings without any overt morphological marking on the verb; the more common situation is that exemplified in the Indonesian, Sama, German, Dyirbal and Chicheŵa examples in (7.24)–(7.25), (7.27)–(7.28) and (7.30)–(7.33). There are, however, languages which permit either no or very few marked linkings to undergoer with a single verb, e.g. Romance and Slavic languages. In these languages, a RECIPIENT with a verb of giving or a beneficiary in a sentence like (7.99b) from Italian is either the object of the preposition *per* 'for' or a dative direct core argument; there is no alternative coding for these sentences in which the recipient or beneficiary appears as the undergoer in the accusative case.

(7.99) a. Maria mi ha da-to un libro.
1sgDAT have.3sgPRES give-PSTP a.Msg book
'Maria gave a book to me.'
b. Maria mi ha compra-to un libro.
1sgDAT have.3sgPRES buy-PSTP a.Msg book
'Maria bought a book for me.'
c. Maria ha compra-to un libro per Paolo.
have.3sgPRES buy-PSTP a.Msg book for
'Maria bought a book for Paolo.'

What these languages often have is pairs of verbs which lexicalize each of the possibilities. For example, *rob* and *steal* constitute such a lexicalized pair of verbs.

English examples of *rob* and *steal* are given in (7.100), while their Italian counterparts are given in (7.101).

(7.100) a. The thief$_x$ stole \$5,000$_z$ from the store$_y$.
a′. *The thief$_x$ stole the store$_y$ of \$5,000$_z$.
b. The thief$_x$ robbed the store$_y$ of \$5,000$_z$.
b′. *The thief$_x$ robbed \$5,000$_z$ from the store$_y$.
c. [**do′** (x, ∅)] CAUSE [BECOME NOT **have′** (y, z) & BECOME **have′** (x, z)]

(7.101) a. Mario ha ruba-to £5,000 dalla banca.
have.3sgPRES steal-PSTP from.the.Fsg bank
'Mario stole £5,000 from the bank.'
a′. *Mario ha rubato la banca (di £5,000).
b. Mario ha svaligia-to la banca (??di £5,000).
have.3sgPRES rob-PSTP the.Fsg bank of
'Mario robbed the bank (??of £5,000).'
b′. *Mario ha svaligiato £5,000 dalla banca.

Steal in English and *rubare* in Italian lexicalize the unmarked linking in terms of the Actor–Undergoer Hierarchy, while *rob* and *svaligiare* present the marked linking. The other linkings are not possible with either verb, as the (a′, b′) examples show.[21] English *rob* and Italian *svaligiare* differ, however, in that the Italian verb does not readily cooccur with an expression of the amount of money taken, whereas this is fine with its English counterpart. Thus, where a marked linking is not possible with a single verb, there may exist a different verb which realizes the other potential linking.

The second area of variation concerns the role of animacy in linking. In certain languages, if there are two arguments which could be linked to undergoer and one of them is animate, then that argument will be undergoer, regardless of which argument position it occupies in logical structure. The prototypical case of variable linking to undergoer involves transfer verbs, which all have '. . . BECOME **have′**(y, z)' as part of their logical structure, and normally the *y* argument is animate and the *z* argument inanimate. Hence in such languages the *y* argument, the RECIPIENT, would normally be undergoer with verbs of this type. Variation would only be possible if both *y* and *z* were animate, as would be possible with verbs like 'show' or 'give in marriage'. Recall from section 6.2.2.2 that Dryer (1986) argued that in what he called 'primary object languages' the RECIPIENT rather than the THEME serves as 'direct object'. Since undergoer is equivalent to 'direct object' in this case, we may conclude that primary object languages are in fact those languages in which animacy plays a determining role in linking to undergoer. Tepehua (Totonacan; Watters 1988) is an example of a primary object language. With a transfer verb like *štaq-* 'give' or *st'a:-* 'sell', the RECIPIENT must be the undergoer; this is signaled by the *-ni-* dative suffix. Consider the following examples involving *st'a:-* 'sell'. (Third person singular arguments are coded by ∅- affixes.)

(7.102) a. Ki-st'a:-ni-ɬ Kwan pa:n.
1sgU-sell-DAT-PRFV Juan bread
'Juan sold me bread.'
b. K-st'a:-ni-ka-ɬ pa:n.
1sgPrP-sell-DAT-PASS-PRFV bread
'I was sold bread.' (*'Bread was sold to me.')

In (a), the actor is *Kwan* 'Juan', the undergoer is coded by *ki-* '1sgU', and *pa:n* 'bread' is a direct core argument. In the passive in (b), only the first person argument can be interpreted as the undergoer and privileged syntactic argument. There is no way for *pa:n* 'bread' to be interpreted as the privileged syntactic argument, if there is an animate RECIPIENT in the argument structure (logical structure) of the verb. If *st'a:-* were used as a simple transitive verb, then *pa:n* could become the privileged syntactic argument in a passive.

(7.103) a. St'a:-ɬ Kwan pa:n.
sell-PFV Juan bread
'Juan sold bread.'
b. St'a:-ka-ɬ pa:n.
sell-PASS-PFV bread
'Bread was sold.'

Hence in Tepehua, as in other primary object languages, animacy plays a determining role in linking to undergoer; where there is more than one potential undergoer argument, one of which is animate, then the animate argument must function as undergoer.

Thus, we find very limited variation in the interaction between macroroles and logical structures in the linking system, and this variation is primarily related to the restrictiveness of the macrorole assignments. In some languages, only animates can function as actor, e.g. Lakhota, whereas in others, animates take priority over inanimates for undergoer, e.g. Tepehua. In addition, most languages do not allow variation in undergoer assignment without some kind of morphological indicator of a marked linking, and some languages do not permit even this, having pairs of verbs which lexicalize each of the linking possibilities instead.

In section 2.2.2.2 we noted with respect to the layered structure of the clause that the semantically motivated aspects of it are universal, while the pragmatically motivated aspects of it are not, and this same pattern is found with respect to the two phases of linking. As we have just discussed, there is only very restricted cross-linguistic variation with respect to the first phase of the linking, that between logical structure and macroroles, and this is clearly the more semantic phase of the linking.

The linking of macroroles and other arguments into the syntax, the second phase, is subject to a great deal of cross-linguistic variation, as shown in the previous chapter as well as this one. And one of the important factors in this variation is the role of discourse pragmatics, as we argued in sections 6.4.2 and 6.5; we will discuss this further in section 7.6. Thus here again we find that the more universal aspects of this area of grammar are semantically motivated and that the aspects of this area of grammar most subject to cross-linguistic variation are not semantically motivated and may involve discourse pragmatics.

7.4.2 Lexical vs. syntactic phenomena

Over the past two decades most grammatical theorists have recognized a distinction between lexical and syntactic phenomena, starting from the criteria proposed in Wasow (1977). A prime example of a lexical phenomenon is the variable linkings to undergoer discussed in section 7.2.2; they are subject to lexical variation, i.e. not all verbs which take three core arguments allow it (*put* does not, for example), they have semantic effects (e.g. affectedness as discussed in section 4.1), and they involve semantic notions only, i.e. argument positions in logical structure and macroroles. Recall that the lexical rules we discussed in section 4.6 affected the logical structure of a verb and therewith its argument structure. The best example of a syntactic phenomenon is the occurrence of WH-words in the precore slot in languages like English, Icelandic and Sama; in simple clauses, it is exceptionless and not subject to any kind of lexical variation; that is, it is always possible to form a WH-question, regardless of what the verb is, what the other core arguments are, etc. While the criteria for deciding the clear cases are generally agreed upon (e.g. lexical idiosyncrasies should be treated in the lexicon, processes which change the syntactic category of a lexical item should be in the lexicon, phenomena not or minimally subject to lexical government should be treated in the syntax), the criteria for distinguishing the two classes of phenomena are ultimately theory-internal.[22] In the framework we are presenting, the line between the two is clear-cut and falls out from the linking system in figure 7.1: lexical phenomena affect the logical structure of the predicate, its argument structure, and actor and undergoer assignment (step 1 in (7.12)), whereas syntactic phenomena deal with the morphosyntactic realization of the macroroles and other core arguments (step 2 in (7.12)).

Why is it important to make this distinction? The answer is that a lexical change can have very different grammatical consequences from a superficially similar syntactic change. Consider the following example from Japanese involving passivization and reflexivization. Japanese has two different passive constructions, which have often been called the 'adversative passive' and the 'plain passive'. The plain passive is much like passives in other languages; the undergoer appears as the privileged syntactic argument, and the actor is marked by the postposition *ni*. It is illustrated in (7.104).

(7.104) a. Hanako ga yakuza o korosi-ta.
NOM gangster ACC kill-PAST
'Hanako killed the gangster.'
b. Yakuza wa Hanako ni koros-(r)are-ta.
gangster TOP DAT kill-PASS-PAST
'The gangster was killed by Hanako.'

The adversative passive differs from the plain passive in that its privileged syntactic argument is not a semantic argument of the verb. It is illustrated in (7.105).

(7.105) a. Hanako ga nekom-da.
NOM become.bedridden-PAST
'Hanako became bedridden.'
a′. Taro wa Hanako ni nekom-(r)are-ta.
TOP DAT become.bedridden-PASS-PAST
'Taro was affected by Hanako's becoming bedridden.'
b. Hanako ga odot-ta.
NOM danced-PAST
'Hanako danced.'
b′. Taro wa Hanako ni odor-are-ta.
TOP DAT dance-PASS-PAST
'Taro was affected by Hanako's dancing.'

The so-called 'passive agent' is *Hanako ni* in (7.104b), (7.105a′) and (7.105b′). Reflexivization in Japanese involves the reflexive anaphor *zibun* 'self', and the antecedent of *zibun* must be a core argument (see section 7.5). In English, core arguments can antecede a reflexive pronoun, but peripheral adjuncts cannot; in particular, the actor in an adjunct *by*-PP in a passive construction cannot antecede a reflexive.

(7.106) a. Sally talked to Harry about herself/himself.
b. Sandy gave the flowers to herself.
c. *The flowers were given to herself by Sandy.
c′. *The flowers were given by Sandy to herself.

Is the same true in Japanese? Interestingly, the answer is 'yes' for the plain passive but 'no' for the adversative passive, according to Kuno (1973).[23]

(7.107) a. Yakuza wa Hanako ni zibun no uti de koros-(r)are-ta.
gangster TOP DAT self GEN house in kill-PASS-PAST
'The gangster$_i$ was killed by Hanako$_j$ in self$_{i/*j}$'s house.'
b. Taro wa Hanako ni zibun no uti de nekom-(r)are-ta.
TOP DAT self GEN house in become.bedridden-PASS-PAST
'Taro$_i$ was affected by Hanako$_j$'s becoming bedridden in self$_{i/j}$'s house.'
c. Taro wa Hanako ni zibun no uti de odor-are-ta.
TOP DAT self GEN house in dance-PASS-PAST
'Taro$_i$ was affected by Hanoko's$_j$ dancing in self$_{i/j}$'s house.'

Hanako ni cannot be interpreted as the antecedent of *zibun* in (a), but it can in (b) and (c). Why should this be so? The answer is that *Hanako ni* is a peripheral adjunct, just like its English counterpart, in the plain passive construction in (a), whereas it is still a core argument in (b) and (c). In the prototypical passive construction discussed in chapter 6, the undergoer functions as the privileged syntactic argument and the actor is treated as a peripheral adjunct, if it appears at all. This involves the assignment of actor and undergoer to particular morphosyntactic statuses in step 2 in (7.12). Hence it is a syntactic phenomenon. What happens in the adversative passive is very different; the argument which would be the privileged syntactic argument in the normal form in (7.105a, b) is not coded as the appropriate macrorole (undergoer in (a), actor in (b)) but rather as a non-macrorole direct core argument. Because it is a core argument, it can serve as the antecedent for *zibun*, unlike the NP in the adjunct *ni*-PP in the plain passive. This situation is not unique to adversative passive constructions; it also occurs in causative constructions, as in (7.108).

(7.108) a. Taro ga Hanako ni zibun no uti de hon o yom-(s)ase-ta.
NOM DAT self GEN house in book ACC read-CAUS-PAST
'Taro$_i$ made Hanako$_j$ read books in self$_{i,j}$'s house.'
b. [**do′** (x, ∅)] CAUSE [**do′** (y, [**read′** (y, z)])]

We will discuss linking and case marking in causative constructions in detail in chapter 9. The logical structure for the core of (a) is given in (b). In terms of step 1 in (7.12), the *x* argument is the actor, and the *z* argument is the undergoer, following the Actor–Undergoer Hierarchy.[24] This leaves the *y* argument as a non-macrorole core argument, and it is marked by *ni*, following the universal default rule in n. 9. Significantly, both *x* and *y* arguments can serve as an antecedent for *zibun* in this construction, and the ability of the *y* argument to be an antecedent parallels that of *Hanako ni* in (7.107b). Here it is clear that we are dealing with a lexical process, since it involves the assignment of arguments in logical structure to macroroles, not macroroles to syntactic functions as in the plain passive construction. Thus, by recognizing the distinction between the non-canonical assignment of the EFFECTOR of *yomu* 'read', the PATIENT of *nekomu* 'become bedridden', and the EFFECTOR of *odoru* 'dance' as non-macrorole core arguments in the causative and adversative passive constructions and the non-canonical syntactic assignment of actor and undergoer in the plain passive construction, we can explain the differential behavior of the NPs in the *ni*-PPs with respect to reflexivization.

Having made this distinction, we can look back at the passive and antipassive constructions discussed in chapter 6 and see that those argument modulation constructions which function primarily to suppress the actor or to derive an activity interpretation from a telic verb are really lexical in nature; that is, they involve an operation on the logical structure of the verb (such as changing its *Aktionsart* type from, for example, active accomplishment to activity, as in (6.76) from Dyirbal) or a change from the canonical linking of semantic arguments to macroroles (e.g. suppressing the semantic argument which would otherwise be linked to actor or undergoer, as in (6.69b) from Ute or (6.70) from Sama). As mentioned at the beginning of this section, the undergoer alternations discussed in section 7.2.2 are also lexical phenomena, since they involve variation in assignment of the argument to serve as undergoer.

7.5 Reflexivization

Reflexive constructions have been the focus of much interest within linguistic theory over the past three decades. We will examine three different reflexive constructions in this section; they will be termed (1) *lexical* reflexives, as in (7.109), (2) *coreference* reflexives, as in (7.110), and (3) *clitic* reflexives, as in (7.111).

(7.109) a. Ba-la-∅ yugu-∅ ba-ŋgu-l yaɽa-ŋgu buyba-n. Dyirbal
DEIC-ABS-IV stick-ABS DEIC-ERG-I man-ERG hide-TNS
'The man is hiding the stick.'
a′. Ba-yi yaɽa-∅ buyba-yiri-ɲu.
DEIC-ABS.I man-ABS hide-REFL-TNS
'The man is hiding himself.'
b. Na-ní-∅-xʔų. Lakhota
stem-2sgU-3sgA-hear
'She heard you.'
b′. Na-n-íč'i-xʔų.
stem-2-REFL-hear
'You heard yourself.'

(7.110) a. Maria ha taglia-to se stess-a. Italian
have.3sg cut-PSTP REFL-Fsg
'Maria cut herself.'
b. Petar-∅ je vidi-o sam seb-e. Croatian
Peter-MsgNOM be.3sg see-PAST.Msg only SELF-ACC
'Peter saw only himself.'

(7.111) a. Maria si è taglia-t-a. Italian
REFL be.3sgPRES cut-PSTP-Fsg
'Maria cut herself.'
b. Petar-∅ se vidi-o. Croatian
Peter-MsgNOM 3sgREFL see-PAST.Msg
'Peter saw himself.'

One of the questions we will be investigating is the proper analysis of the constructions in (7.111); are they best analyzed like the ones in (7.109) or the ones in (7.110), or do they require a distinct analysis from the other two types?

A few general points are in order before we proceed to the analysis of these constructions. First, we will limit ourselves to what are usually called 'clause-bound' reflexives; since we are dealing here with linking in simple sentences, we will postpone discussion of 'long-distance' reflexives until chapter 9. Second, we will limit our discussion to argument reflexives only, excluding possessor reflexives (found in many languages, e.g. Icelandic, Lakhota, Latin, Russian but not in English, which has only reciprocal possessors, e.g. *each other's addresses*) and picture reflexives (e.g. *Holly liked the picture of herself*). Pollard and Sag (1992) present a number of convincing arguments that these reflexives are subject to a variety of constraints, some grammatical and some discourse-based, and therefore operate rather differently from argument reflexives. Third, as we discussed in section 4.7.4 and section 7.2.2, referring expressions appear in logical structure in the form that they will appear in in the actually realized sentence, case marking aside. That is, if an argument is to be expressed by a pronoun in the syntactic representation, then the pronominal stem will occur in the appropriate variable slot in logical structure; the actual morphosyntactic form of the pronoun will be determined by the linking, including the case-marking rules of the language. In the same vein, if an argument is to be expressed by a reflexive element, as in (7.110a) for example, then it will likewise occur in a variable slot in logical structure. Hence the logical structure for a simple English sentence like *Molly saw herself* would be **see′** (Molly$_i$, herself$_i$). Coreferring pronouns will also be coindexed in the semantic representation, e.g. **see′** ([**have.as.kin′** (Molly$_i$, brother)], her$_i$) for *Molly$_i$'s brother saw her$_i$*. This does not hold for lexical reflexives, since there are no independent coreferring expressions in this type of construction. One of the most fundamental issues in the analysis of reflexives is how to rule out the ungrammatical **Herself saw Molly* (**see′** (herself$_i$, Molly$_i$)); is this best done at the syntactic level or at the semantic level? We will follow the proposal of Jackendoff (1992) that these restrictions are best captured at the *semantic* rather than the syntactic level; that is, the constraints on the interpretation of coreference in these two examples will be stated at the level of the semantic representation of the sentence, not at the level of the syntactic representation.

7.5.1 Lexical reflexives

Most syntactic theories have taken English-type reflexive constructions, like those in Italian and Croatian in (7.110), as the basic type of reflexive construction, with other types being analyzed as variants of it. In this view, all reflexive constructions involve a coreference relation between an antecedent and a pronominal element without independent reference. The constructions in Dyirbal and Lakhota in (7.109) present a serious problem for this view, since this construction does not have two distinct referring expressions. In the Dyirbal construction, a transitive verb carries the suffix *-yiriy-/-mariy-* and is detransitivized; an important question is, is the absolutive NP in (7.109a′) the actor or the undergoer? There is considerable evidence that it is the actor. This suffix is used in more than just reflexive constructions; it can also be used to detransitivize a transitive verb, and the argument that would be the undergoer with the transitive form may be omitted or it may appear as a direct core argument in the dative case. This is illustrated in (7.112), repeated from (6.76).

(7.112) a. Ba-la-m wuḍu-∅ ba-ŋgu-l yaɽa-ŋgu ḍaŋga-ɲu.
DEIC-ABS-III fruit-ABS DEIC-ERG-I man-ERG eat-TNS
'The man is eating the fruit.'
b. Ba-yi yaɽa-∅ ḍaŋgay-mari-ɲu.
DEIC-ABS.I man-ABS eat-REFL-TNS
'The man is eating.'
c. Ba-yi yaɽa-∅ ḍaŋgay-mari-ɲu ba-gu-m wuḍu-gu.
DEIC-ABS.I man-ABS eat-REFL-TNS DEIC-DAT-III fruit-DAT
'The man is eating fruit.'

Dixon (1972) labels the construction in (b) and (c) the 'false reflexive', since it has reflexive morphology but lacks reflexive meaning. This is a kind of antipassive construction, as the case pattern in (c) is exactly the same as that in the *-ŋay* antipassive, as we discussed in section 6.4.3. It is clear that the absolutive NP in this construction is the actor argument, especially in (c), in which the undergoer of (a) appears as a non-macrorole direct core argument in the dative case.

The sentence in (b) is technically ambiguous, although the false-reflexive reading is preferred, since people do not normally eat themselves. If a speaker wanted to make the reflexive reading unambiguous, in, say, a situation where someone is chewing on his finger as a 'contemplative accompaniment', as Dixon puts it, it is possible to add the suffix *-ḍilu* to the absolutive NP, as in *Bayi yaɽa-ḍilu ḍaŋgay-mariɲu* (lit.) 'The man is eating himself.' This suffix is not required for a reflexive interpretation, and it may occur in an NP without the reflexive suffix on the verb with a non-reflexive meaning. It is not, therefore, a type of reflexive pronominal analogous to English *himself* or *herself*.

What is the linking in this construction? In terms of the distinction introduced in section 7.4.2, the reflexive construction is a lexical construction; that is, the addition of the reflexive suffix to the verb reduces the M-transitivity of the verb from two macroroles to one, and the non-actor may either be unspecified or realized as a non-macrorole direct core argument. If the second semantic argument is unspecified, there are two interpretations, a reflexive and a non-reflexive one; the reflexive reading may be confirmed by the use of the nominal suffix *-ḍilu*. The absolutive case on the actor and the dative on the other core argument are predicted by the rules in (7.61). Dixon notes (1972: 90) that all transitive verbs can form both reflexive (if semantically plausible) and false-reflexive forms with this suffix, and thus the reflexive interpretation is an inference based on the form of the clause and the

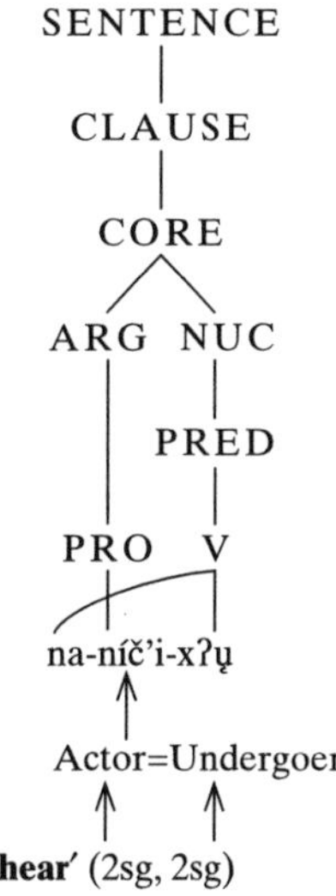

Figure 7.24 Reflexive linking in Lakhota

plausibility of a reflexive reading; with a verb like 'eat' it is disfavored, whereas with one like 'hide' it is favored.

In Lakhota, on the other hand, the reflexive interpretation is not an inference but is directly shown by the *-ič'i-* affix on the verb, as in (7.109b′). This affix has no function other than signaling that the actor and undergoer are the same participant. The person and number of the actor and undergoer are indicated by the affix: *-m-ič'i-* '1sg', *-n-ič'i-* '2sg', *-∅-ič'i-*'3sg', etc. There is no independent reflexive pronoun; there are only non-reflexive independent pronouns, e.g. *niyé* '2sg' as in *niye namáyaxʔų* 'YOU heard me' and *niyé naníč'ixʔų* 'YOU heard yourself' (emphatic) (cf. (7.109b)). Since (7.109b′) constitutes a complete reflexive construction, there is no possibility of analyzing it as involving coreference between two distinct referring expressions. Rather, it may be best analyzed as involving the linking of actor and undergoer to the same argument marker, in this case the reflexive *-nič'i-*.[25] It may be represented as in figure 7.24. There is a single bound marker on the verb in this construction, and it simultaneously indicates actor and undergoer. With a verb like *k'u* 'give' with three core arguments, the two animate arguments are interpreted as the same, as in (7.113).

(7.113) a. Wį́yą ki hokšíla ki wówapi wą ∅-∅-∅-k'ú.
woman the boy the book a INAN-3sgU-3sgA-give
'The woman gave the boy a book.'

b. Wį́yą ki wówapi wą ∅-∅-ič'í-č'u. (< *ič'i + k'u*)
woman the book a INAN-3-REFL-give
'The woman gave herself a book.'

Thus, in Lakhota we have another example of a lexical reflexive construction, one that involves linking actor and undergoer to the same marker, rather than coreference between independent elements. In both Dyirbal and Lakhota the reflexive constructions crucially refer to the linking from syntax to semantics, and hence could also be referred to as 'linking reflexives'.

7.5.2 Coreference reflexives

English, Italian, Croatian and many other languages have a coreference reflexive construction, and in it the antecedent and the reflexive pronominal are independent syntactic arguments, with the reflexive element interpreted as obligatorily referring to the antecedent. In the simple example mentioned in the introduction to this discussion, *Molly saw herself*, the logical structure is **see′** (Molly, herself), and the linking is trivial. This simplicity masks a host of important questions, the primary one being determining the range of possible relationships that the antecedent can bear to the reflexive. Why is **Herself saw Molly* ungrammatical? Why is **Molly's brother saw herself* also ungrammatical? Other languages have much more complex systems of reflexives than English, e.g. Norwegian, Icelandic and Marathi; the constraints on possible antecedents must also be captured for those systems. Finally, even though we are dealing with reflexives within simple sentences only in this section, the issue of the domain of reflexivization must be addressed. It is widely assumed that in English the clause is the syntactic domain in which reflexivization occurs, but it is necessary to distinguish the domain of possible reflexivization from the domain of obligatory reflexivization. In English, the clause is the domain of possible reflexivization but not the domain of obligatory reflexivization, as the following examples show.

(7.114) a. The $woman_i$ sent the book to $herself_i$/*her_i.
b. $Barbara_i$ saw a snake near her_i/*$herself_i$.
c. $Pamela_i$ got some spaghetti sauce on her_i/$herself_i$.

All of these are simple sentences, and yet reflexivization is obligatory in (a), impossible in (b) and apparently optional in (c). What is the nature of the contrast here? Is it syntactic or semantic?

These last three examples raise an important point. Reflexivization is often analyzed together with pronominalization, since pronouns and reflexives appear to be in complementary distribution in many grammatical environments. This complementarity is not perfect, as the sentences in (7.114) show. We have already discussed pronominalization in our discussion of information structure in chapter 5. We will not be positing an information-structure-based account of reflexivization; rather, we will propose that the answers to the questions raised above are best formulated with reference to the semantic representation of the sentence, rather than to the information structure or to the syntactic representation of the sentence.

The approach we will take is based largely on Jackendoff's (1972, 1992) work on reflexivization; he employs a somewhat different system of semantic representation, and accordingly his principles will have to be adapted to apply to the representations presented in chapters 3 and 4. In his 1972 book he proposed a thematic-relations-based constraint on reflexivization: the antecedent must be higher on the thematic relations hierarchy than the reflexive. The hierarchy he assumed was AGENT > LOCATION, SOURCE, GOAL > THEME. The obvious analog in our framework is the hierarchy in (7.1), which is the basic thematic relations hierarchy. However, there is another candidate: the hierarchy assumed in the privileged syntactic argument selection principles in a particular language. The one for German, we saw earlier, is restricted to macroroles only, while the one for Icelandic is not. Which is the correct hierarchy to use? The answer is, the second one, because the hierarchy governing reflexivization varies from language to language in one of the ways the privileged syntactic argument selection principles vary. That is, in some languages only a macrorole argument may function as the antecedent of a reflexive, whereas in other languages a non-macrorole direct core argument can be the antecedent. In languages of the first type, such as German, only a macrorole argument can function as the controller (or 'binder') of the reflexive, and therefore the macrorole hierarchy is the appropriate one. This is illustrated in (7.115); (b) is from Harbert (1977).

(7.115) a. Almuth$_i$ erzähl-te ihm$_j$ eine Geschichte über sich$_{i/*j}$.[26]
tell-3sgPAST 3MsgDAT a.ACC story about 3.SELF
'Almuth told him a story about herself/*himself.'

b. Ich hör-te ihn sich erschiessen.[27]
1sgNOM hear-PAST 3MsgACC 3.SELF shoot.to.death
'I heard him shoot himself.'

c. *Ihr$_i$ gefäll-t die Geschichte über sich$_i$.
3FsgDAT please-3sgPRES the.ACC story about 3.SELF
'She likes the story about herself.'

In German only a macrorole argument can antecede a reflexive; all speakers accept nominative NPs as controllers, as in (a). In causative and direct perception constructions accusative undergoers can be a controller, as in (b). However, a dative NP as in (c) is not possible antecedent. Hence in German the hierarchy in (7.1) is interpreted in terms of macrorole arguments only, just as in privileged syntactic argument selection. In languages of the second type, such as Icelandic, a non-macrorole direct core argument may bind a reflexive, and therefore (7.1) is interpreted in terms of direct core arguments, just as in privileged syntactic argument selection. This is illustrated in (7.116a), from Thráinsson (1979) and (c) from Zaenen, Maling and Thráinsson (1985).

(7.116) a. Jón-Ø$_i$ sýn-d-i Harald-i$_j$ föt á sig$_{i/j}$.
John-NOM show-PAST-3sg Harold-DAT clothes.NplACC for SELF
'John$_i$ showed Harold$_j$ clothes for himself$_{i/j}$.'

b. Harald-i vor-u sýn-d föt á sig$_i$.
Harold-DAT be.3plPAST show-PSTP.NplNOM clothes.NplACC for SELF
'Harold was shown clothes for himself.'

c. Henni þyk-ir bróð-ir sinn /*hennar
3FsgDAT think-3sgPRES brother-MsgNOM her[+REFL]/her[−REFL]
leiðingleg-ur.
boring-MsgNOM
'She finds her brother boring.'

In the (a) and (b) sentences *Haraldi* is a non-macrorole direct core argument in the dative case, and it is a possible antecedent for the reflexive *sig*, in sharp contrast to the German examples in (7.115a, c). In (c) the dative argument of *þykja* 'think, consider' is the antecedent for the reflexive possessor *sinn* 'her'; the use of the non-reflexive possessor *hennar* 'her' is ungrammatical. This contrast in possible antecedents for reflexives parallels the contrast discussed in section 7.2.1 regarding different privileged syntactic argument choices in the two languages. English is something of a mixed type; as it allows non-macrorole arguments to antecede a reflexive, as in *Mary talked to Bill about himself*, in this case (7.1) applies directly. Hence for English, the hierarchy is (7.1). We may reformulate Jackendoff's principle as in (7.117).

(7.117) *Role Hierarchy Condition on reflexivization*
The reflexive pronoun must not be higher on (7.1) (as applied to selection of privileged syntactic arguments in the language) than its antecedent.

For German, this means that only actors and undergoers can control reflexives, while for Icelandic, it means that the highest-ranking direct core argument, regardless of whether it is a macrorole or not, can control a reflexive. For English, this means that actors and undergoers are possible controllers, but it also means that non-macrorole core arguments can be as well. This is because there are constructions in English which can have non-macrorole core arguments as controllers or pivots. We saw examples of this in exercise 1 from chapter 6. This construction is illustrated in (7.118).

(7.118) a. John built a chest for his wife to put her clothes in.
b. The company supplied the coach with uniforms for her team to wear.

Example (7.118a) illustrates a non-macrorole pivot, namely the object of the preposition *in*, while (b) presents an oblique core argument controller, *with uniforms*. Because there are constructions with non-macrorole controllers and pivots in English, (7.117) permits syntactic arguments of this type to be a controller for reflexives as well.

The Role Hierarchy Condition in (7.117) is universal, in that the reflexive is never higher on the hierarchy than the antecedent; in other words, actors are always the antecedents for undergoers, never the other way around. We saw this in the examples in (6.50) from Sama, a syntactically ergative language; the actor is always the controller for reflexivization, regardless of whether it is the privileged syntactic argument or not. Hence the phrase in (7.117) 'as applied to the selection of privileged syntactic arguments in the language' refers exclusively to whether selection of the priviliged syntactic argument is restricted to macroroles only or not, or to direct core arguments only or not. In terms of what 'higher on (7.1)' means, it is the same for coreference reflexives in both syntactically ergative and syntactically accusative languages.

We can illustrate the operation of this principle with our simple examples introduced above, repeated in (7.119) with their logical structures.

(7.119) a. Molly saw herself.
a′. **see′** (Molly$_i$, herself$_i$)
b. *Herself saw Molly.
b′. **see′** (herself$_i$, Molly$_i$)
c. *Molly's brother saw herself.
c′. **see′** ([**have.as.kin′** (Molly$_i$, <u>brother</u>)], herself$_i$)

In (a) *Molly* is the actor and *herself* the undergoer, and the sentence is fine. In (b), on the other hand, *herself* is the actor and *Molly* the undergoer, which violates the condition in (7.117). In (c), *Molly* is neither actor nor undergoer; indeed, it is not an argument of *see* at all. Hence it is not a possible antecedent for *herself.* It would appear that there is an important unstated assumption in (7.117), namely, that both the antecedent and the reflexive must be semantic arguments of the verb. While this seems to work for (7.114a, b) and the examples in (7.119), it is too strong; in (7.114c), *herself* is not a semantic argument of *get*, and yet the sentence is clearly grammatical. This aspect of the relationship between the reflexive and its antecedent will be further clarified below. Jackendoff's second condition, presented in his 1992 paper, offers an alternative way of explaining the ungrammaticality of (7.119c). Since the system of semantic representation he employs differs from the one we are using, the condition will be reformulated in terms of logical structures. We will term the heads of the fillers of the variable positions in logical structure the *primary arguments* of the logical structure. In a simple logical structure like (7.119a′), both *Molly* and *herself* are primary arguments. In (c′), however, *brother* and *herself* are the primary arguments; *Molly* is not a primary argument, since *brother* is the head of the complex expression filling the *x* argument position in the logical structure. Similarly, in (7.89) *woman* is a primary argument, whereas *strong arms* is not. Jackendoff defines a notion which we will call *logical structure superiority* (or *LS-superiority*) as in (7.120a).[28]

(7.120) a. *Logical structure superiority* (*LS-superiority*)
A constituent P in logical structure is LS-superior to a constituent Q iff there is a constituent R in logical structure such that
(i) Q is a constituent of R, and
(ii) P and R are primary arguments of the same logical structure.
b. Superiority Condition on reflexivization
A bound variable may not be LS-superior to its binder.

Looking at (7.119c′) again, we see that *Molly* is a non-head constituent of **have. as. kin′** (Molly, brother), and therefore *herself* is LS-superior to *Molly*, since *herself* is a primary argument of the logical structure. Jackendoff proposes the condition on reflexivization given in (7.120b). That is, a reflexive pronoun may not be LS-superior to its antecedent in logical structure. This condition rules out (7.119c) but not (b), while the principle in (7.117) rules out (b) but not (c). Thus both principles are needed to account for the examples in (7.119a–c).

Are two semantic principles, (7.117) and (7.120b), really necessary here?[29] The answer is 'yes'. Consider the contrast between German and Icelandic discussed above, and let's look at the equivalents of 'She was told a story about herself' in the two languages. The sentences are given in (7.121a, b) and their common logical structure in (c). (See section 3.2.3.1 for a discussion of the logical structure of verbs of saying.)

(7.121) a. Henni var sögð sag-a um
3FsgDAT was.IMPER tell.PSTP.FsgNOM story-FsgNOM about
sig. Icelandic
SELF
'She was told a story about herself.'
b. *Ihr wurde eine Geschichte über German
3FsgDAT became.IMPER a.FsgNOM story about
sich erzähl-t.
3.SELF tell-PSTP
'She was told a story about herself.'
c. [**do′** (∅, [**express.**(α)**.to.**(β)**.in.language.**(γ)**′** (∅, her_i)])] CAUSE [BECOME **aware.of′** (her_i, [**be′** (story, [**about′** (herself_i)])])],
where α = *story about herself*, β = *her*[30]

The logical sructure in (c) meets the LS-Superiority Condition, as the antecedent *her* is LS-superior to the reflexive *herself*. It cannot, therefore, account for the ungrammaticality of the German example. That is explained by the difference in the Role Hierarchy Condition in the two languages. As noted earlier, German allows only macrorole arguments as privileged syntactic arguments, and therefore only macrorole arguments are possible antecedents for reflexives. Hence *ihr* '3FsgDAT', being a non-macrorole direct core argument, is not a possible antecedent for a reflexive, and consequently the sentence is ungrammatical. In Icelandic, on the other hand, the hierarchy in (7.1) refers to direct core arguments, and therefore the possibility of controlling a reflexive is not restricted to macroroles. Hence *henni* '3FsgDAT' is a possible antecedent, and because the reflexive is not higher on the hierarchy than its antecedent, the sentence is grammatical. Thus, the contrast in grammaticality between the German and Icelandic examples in (7.121) cannot be explained by the LS-superiority condition alone; rather, both principles are needed to explain this contrast.

The privileged syntactic argument selection principles in English include macrorole and non-macrorole core arguments, and, as mentioned above, this entails that both types of syntactic arguments can serve as reflexive controllers. This may be summarized as 'Actor > Undergoer > Other', and if both the controller and the reflexive fall into the 'other' category, then (7.1) applies to them directly. An example of an undergoer controller in English is a sentence like *Mary told Lloyd about himself*, where the undergoer *Lloyd* is the antecedent. When both actor and undergoer are potential antecedents, as in *Mary told Susan about herself*, the actor is always a possible antecedent, and for many speakers both are. It is also possible to have a non-macrorole argument as an antecedent, as in *Bob talked to Susan about herself.*

(7.122) **do′** (Bob, [**express.**(α)**.to.**(β)**.in.language.**(γ)′ (Bob, Susan_i)]) ∧ [**about′** (herself_i)],[31] where a = *about herself* and β =*Susan*.

In this logical structure, *Susan* is the second argument of a two-place predicate and therefore outranks *herself*, which is the argument of a one-place state predicate, on the Actor–Undergoer Hierarchy. Hence this logical structure meets both conditions governing reflexivization in English. Pollard and Sag (1992) present the two examples in (7.123) as counterexamples to Jackendoff's (1972) thematic hierarchy condition and as problems for any thematic-relations-based theory of reflexivization.

(7.123) a. I sold the slave to himself.
b. I sold the slave himself.

In (a) *the slave* is THEME and *himself* RECIPIENT (GOAL, in Jackendoff's terms), whereas in (b) *the slave* is RECIPIENT (GOAL) and *himself* THEME. Recall that Jackendoff's hierarchy is AGENT > LOCATION, SOURCE, GOAL > THEME, and while this predicts the grammaticality of (b), it incorrectly predicts the ungrammaticality of (a). It looks as if, in Jackendoff's terms, the hierarchy is different for different constructions, an unhappy result. But in terms of the Actor > Undergoer > Other hierarchy we are assuming, there is no problem, for in both sentences the undergoer is the antecedent and the reflexive is a non-macrorole core argument, which counts as 'other'. Thus, English reflexivization is governed by the formulation in (7.117), not the thematic relations hierarchy proposed by Jackendoff.

We stated at the beginning of section 7.5 that we are not going to deal with picture noun reflexives, but there is one construction involving them that has generated much discussion in the literature (e.g. Pesetsky 1987) which we will investigate. It is exemplified in the sentences in (7.124).

(7.124) a. The photo of himself in the newspaper upsets James.
a′. James is upset about the photo of himself in the newspaper.
b. The rumor about herself amuses Sally.
b′. Sally is amused by rumors about herself.

The sentences in (a) and (b) have long been thought to raise problems for syntactic theories of reflexivization, because a reflexive pronoun in the 'subject' NP is bound by an NP in 'object' position, which, as we saw in (7.119b), is normally impossible. Is it a problem for our semantic account? In order to answer this question, we must determine the logical structures for these two sentences. The first thing to note is that there are related sentences, those in (a′) and (b′), in which the relationship between the antecedent and the reflexive seems normal. Let us look at their logical structures first. The predicates are both stative, and their semantic representations are given in (7.125).

(7.125) a. **feel′** (James$_i$, [**upset.about′** (**be-in′** (newspaper, [**be′** (photo, [**of′** (himself$_i$)])]))])
b. **feel′** (Sally$_i$, [**amused.by′** (**be′** (rumor, [**about′** (herself$_i$)]))])

These logical structures meet both the Role Hierarchy and LS-Superiority Conditions on reflexivization proposed above: the antecedents are LS-superior to the reflexives, and they are higher on the English hierarchy than the reflexives. What, then, are the logical structures for the examples of interest? The most important fact about them is that they too are stative; they take the simple present tense and have a true present tense meaning, which is an important property of stative verbs in English. They have causative paraphrases, i.e. 'The photo in the newspaper causes John to be upset' and 'The rumor causes Sally to be amused'. Hence they are causative statives, and the second argument of CAUSE in the logical structure of each is the appropriate logical structure in (7.125).[32] What is the first argument? It must be the NP *the picture* or *the rumor*, and this means that the same logical structure subcomponent occurs twice in the entire logical structure.

(7.126) a. [**be-in′** (newspaper, [**be′** (photo, [**of′** (himself$_i$)])])] CAUSE [**feel′** (James$_i$, [**upset.about′** (**be-in′** (newspaper, [**be′** (photo, [**of′** (himself$_i$)])]))])]
b. [**be′** (rumor, [**about′** (herself$_i$)])] CAUSE [**feel′** (Sally$_i$, [**amused.by′** (**be′** (rumor, [**about′** (herself$_i$)]))])]

If we abstract away from the detail, we find that the basic logical structure is [. . . x . . .] CAUSE [**pred′** (y, [. . . x . . .])]. Chomsky (1970) and Koenig (1994) suggest

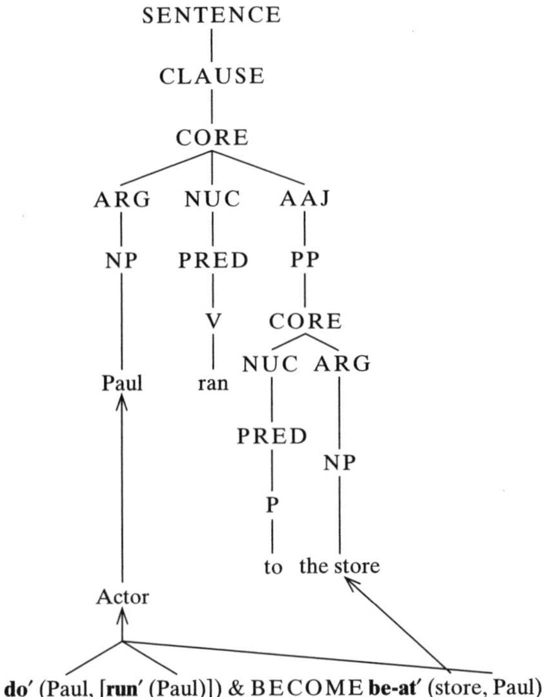

Figure 7.25 Linking involving multiple instances of same argument

similar analyses of these constructions. We have already seen several examples of logical structures in which the same argument occurs in more than one position, e.g. (4.12c′) for *Paul ran to the store* and (7.94) for *Robin baked a cake for Sandy.* In such a situation the two identical variables are linked to the same position in the syntax; the linking for *Paul ran to the store* is given in figure 7.25. The same holds in the linking of these logical structures; the identical subparts are mapped into the same argument position in the syntax. The linking of (7.126b) is presented in figure 7.26. With respect to the Role Hierarchy and LS-Superiority Conditions on reflexivization, the logical structures in (7.126) meet them, because they contain as a subpart the logical structures in (7.125), which, we have already seen, meet them. Thus, if an argument (or subpart of a logical structure) occurs more than once in the overall logical structure, and one of the occurrences meets the Role Hierarchy and LS-Superiority Conditions on reflexivization while none of them violates the conditions, then the whole logical structure is well formed with respect to them.[33] Hence at the semantic level these sentences are well formed, even though from the perspective of their syntactic forms they seem to violate the conventionally assumed syntactic conditions on reflexivization. These examples do not violate the principle in (7.117), because the reflexive is not in an argument position in the core; it is embedded within an NP.

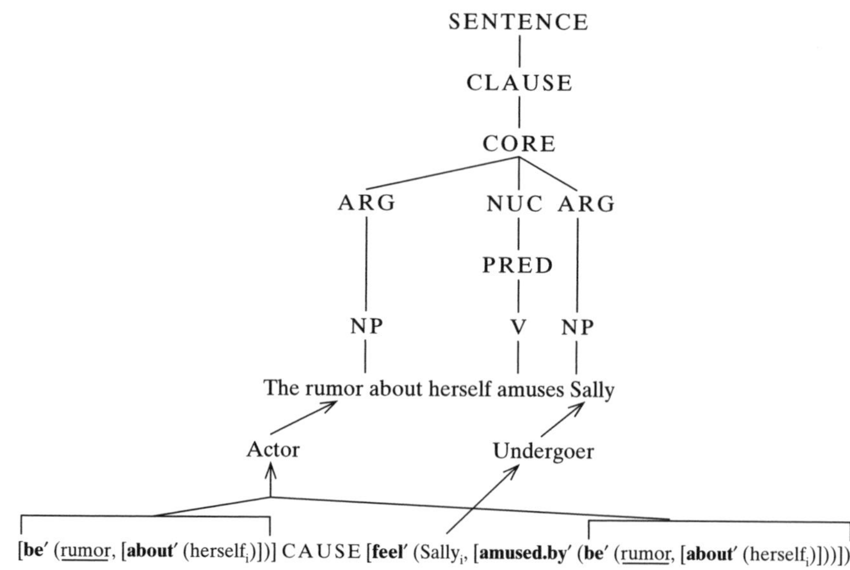

Figure 7.26 Linking in (7.124b)

We noted earlier that other languages have more complex reflexive systems than English, and Norwegian (Hellan 1988) is a good example of such a language. It has two reflexives that can be used in simple clauses, *seg selv* and *ham selv*. They are illustrated in (7.127).

(7.127) a. Jon fortal-te meg om seg selv.
tell-PAST 1sgACC about SELF
'John told me about himself.'

a′. *Vi fortal-te Jon om seg selv.
1plNOM tell-PAST about SELF
*'We told John about himself.'

b. Vi fortal-te Jon om ham selv.
1plNOM tell-PAST about SELF
'We told John about himself.'

b′. *Jon snakk-er om ham selv.
talk-PRES about SELF
'John talks about himself.'

Both reflexives must be bound within the core in which they occur, and they differ in that the antecedent of *seg selv* must always be the 'subject', while that of *ham selv* cannot be. How can this be captured in the framework we are developing? The item-specific conditions are given in (7.128).

(7.128) a. *Seg selv*: must be bound by the highest-ranking argument in the core (in terms of the privileged syntactic argument selection principles for Norwegian).

b. *Ham selv*: must not be bound by the highest-ranking argument in the core (in terms of the privileged syntactic argument selection principles for Norwegian).

Since Norwegian is a syntactically accusative language, the highest-ranking argument will be the privileged syntactic argument and hence the proper antecedent for *seg selv.* The principle in (b) interacts with those in (7.117) and (7.120) to give the right result for *ham selv*. The reflexive pronoun cannot be higher on the privileged syntactic argument selection hierarchy or LS-superior to its antecedent, and the antecedent of *ham selv* cannot be the highest-ranking argument in the core; in (7.128a) this leaves the undergoer NP *Jon* as the only possible antecedent.

At the beginning of this section we raised the question of the syntactic domain in which reflexivization occurs in English. It is usually assumed that the clause is the domain of reflexivization in English, but the examples in (7.114), repeated below, show that while the clause appears to be the domain of possible reflexivization in English, it is not the domain of obligatory reflexivization.

(7.114) a. The woman$_i$ sent the book to herself$_i$/*her$_i$.
b. Barbara$_i$ saw a snake near her$_i$/*herself$_i$.
c. Pamela$_i$ got some spaghetti sauce on her$_i$/herself$_i$.

If the clause were the domain of obligatory reflexivization, then all three sentences should have reflexive pronouns.[34] There is a domain of obligatory reflexivization, as (a) shows; what is it? First, the domain of possible reflexivization in English appears to be the *core*, not the clause, in simple sentences. All of these PPs are within the core. We will return to this issue in chapter 9 in our discussion of long-distance reflexivization. Second, reflexivization is obligatory among semantic co-arguments within the core; crucially, it is not obligatory when the coreferring element is in an argument-adjunct PP. In both (7.114b) and (c) the PPs are argument-adjuncts, whereas in (a) it is an argument PP, and as we stated at the outset, reflexivization is obligatory in (a) and only optional in (c). However, there are sentences like *Who injured herself?* which show that this constraint is too strong. In this sentence, the controller is a syntactic argument in the precore slot, which is outside of the core. In our initial discussion of the precore slot in section 2.2.2, we noted that both syntactic arguments as well as adjuncts can occur in the precore slot and syntactic arguments in the precore slot do not count as core arguments. Nevertheless, as this example shows, a syntactic argument in the precore slot can serve as the controller of a reflexive. Hence we must have the clause, not the core, as the proper domain. We may formulate this as the *Domain of Obligatory Reflexivization Constraint*, stated in (7.129).

(7.129) *Domain of Obligatory Reflexivization Constraint*
One of two coreferring semantic co-arguments within a simple clause must be realized as a reflexive, while one of two coreferring syntactic arguments (which are not semantic co-arguments) within a simple clause may be realized as a reflexive.

'Semantic co-arguments' are semantic arguments of the same logical structure and are realized as syntactic arguments. 'Within a simple clause' means a clause that contains a single core and possibly a precore slot; as we will see in chapter 9 in our discussion of long-distance reflexivization, the situation is rather different in clauses composed of multiple cores. 'Two coreferring syntactic arguments (which are not semantic co-arguments)' are syntactic arguments within the same simple clause which are not semantic arguments of the same logical structure; this is the case with the NP in argument-adjunct PPs, as it is the semantic argument of a predicative preposition and not directly a semantic argument of the logical structure of the verb (see section 4.4.1.1). We may illustrate the effect of this constraint, combined with the Role Hierarchy and LS-Superiority Conditions, on the logical structures in (7.130), which are for the examples in (7.114).

(7.130) a. [**do′** (woman$_i$, ∅)] CAUSE [BECOME **have′** (herself$_i$, book)]
a′. [**do′** (woman$_i$, ∅)] CAUSE [BECOME **have′** (her$_{*i/j}$, book)][35]
b. **see′** (Barbara$_i$, snake) ∧ **be-near′** (her$_i$/*herself$_i$, snake)
c. [**do′** (Pamela$_i$, ∅)] CAUSE [BECOME **have′** (Pamela, spaghetti sauce) ∧ BECOME **be-on′** (her$_i$/herself$_i$, spaghetti sauce)]

The logical structure in (7.130a) meets all three conditions: *woman* and *herself* are arguments of the same logical structure, *woman* (actor) is higher on the role hierarchy than *herself* (either undergoer or other, depending on the linking), and *herself* is not LS-superior to *woman*. In the logical structure in (a′), on the other hand, the Domain of Obligatory Reflexivization Constraint is violated, if the pronoun *her* is coindexed with *woman*, since they are semantic co-arguments. In both the (b) and (c) logical structures, the condition for optional reflexivization in (7.129) is met, and therefore in principle either a pronoun or a reflexive is possible; the other two conditions are also met.

What is the difference between these two, such that the reflexive is possible with (c) but not with (b) in (7.130)? Kuno (1987) suggests the difference lies in the degree of affectedness of the argument; the more affected the argument, the more acceptable the reflexive form is. The actor of *see* in (7.114a) is not affected by seeing a snake. On the other hand, Pamela is affected by getting spaghetti sauce on her clothes or body, and the choice of the plain form or the reflexive reflects the speaker's assessment of how affected she is. If we change the sentence to *Pamela got some spaghetti sauce all over herself/her*, the *all over* signals greater affectedness, and *herself* becomes the preferred form for many speakers. Argument-adjunct PPs are within the core, hence within the domain of possible reflexivization, and if the NP head of the PP is highly affected by the action of the verb, a reflexive may be used if the conditions in (7.117), (7.120) and (7.129) are met.

There is one more important example we must analyze; it is given in (7.131).

(7.131) *Herself was seen by Molly.

The first thing to note about this sentence is that it has the same logical structure as *Molly saw herself* in (7.119a), i.e. **see′** (Molly, herself), and therefore it meets the conditions in (7.117) and (7.120). It might be suggested that this is ungrammatical because 'backward reflexivization' is impossible, but this explanation is incorrect, as the sentences in (7.132) show.

(7.132) a. Molly bought nothing for herself.
a′. For HERSELF Molly bought nothing.
b. Jim likes himself; he can't stand other people.
b′. HIMSELF Jim likes; it's OTHER PEOPLE he can't stand.

Small capitals signal narrow (in this case, contrastive) focus in (7.132a′, b′). Both (a′) and (b′) involve backward reflexivization, and yet both are grammatical. Hence the ungrammaticality of (7.131) cannot be explained in terms of the impossibility of backward reflexivization. As in the (a) and (b) examples, both (a′) and (b′) meet the conditions in (7.117) and (7.120). Do (7.131) and (7.132) meet the condition in (7.129)? Examples (7.132a′, b′) do, because the reflexives are syntactic arguments in the precore slot, while (7.131) does not, because the controller is a peripheral adjunct. Hence (7.129) correctly accounts for the ungrammaticality of (7.131), because the controller is not a syntactic argument but rather is an adjunct in the periphery. Because this is a constraint on the syntactic domain of reflexivization, it applies to the syntactic representation and not to the semantic representation of the sentence.

Thus, in this section we have presented an analysis of coreference reflexives in simple clauses which refers to logical structure configurations for the determination of possible controllers, following the approach suggested in Jackendoff (1992). The constraint on the domain of obligatory reflexivization refers to the syntactic representation of the sentence, because the issue of the domain of reflexivization is syntactic by definition. We will extend this account to deal with long-distance coreference reflexives in Norwegian and other languages in chapter 9, after we have introduced the theory of complex sentence structure in chapter 8.

7.5.3 Clitic reflexives

The final type of reflexive construction to be considered involves clitic reflexive pronouns; the examples from Italian and Croatian given earlier are repeated below.

(7.111) a. Maria si è taglia-t-a. — Italian
REFL be.3sgPRES cut-PSTP-Fsg
'Maria cut herself.'
b. Petar-Ø se vidi-o. — Croatian
Peter-MsgNOM 3sgREFL see-PAST.Msg
'Peter saw himself.'

The first thing to note about these languages is that they often also have non-clitic coreference reflexive constructions of the type discussed in the previous section; the earlier examples are repeated below.

(7.110) a. Maria ha taglia-to se stess-a. Italian
have.3sg cut-PSTP REFL-Fsg
'Maria cut herself.'
b. Petar-∅ je vidi-o sam seb-e. Croatian
Peter-MsgNOM be.3sg see-PAST.Msg only SELF-ACC
'Peter saw only himself.'

A commonly proposed analysis of the constructions in (7.111), e.g. Kayne (1975), Burzio (1986), is that they are semantically equivalent to the constructions in (7.110) and that the only syntactic difference between them is that the reflexive is a clitic rather than a full pronoun. Translated into the analysis proposed in the previous section, it would mean that the logical structure for (7.111b), for example, would be **see′** (Petar, se), while that for (7.110b) would be **see′** (Petar, seb-), and in both sentences *Petar* is the actor and *se/sebe* the undergoer. However, Van Valin (1990) noted that these two constructions are *not* semantically equivalent in Italian; the controller in the *se stesso* construction must be interpreted agentively, whereas the controller in the *si* construction is neutral with respect to agency. The same contrast holds in Croatian.

(7.133) a. Maria ha taglia-to se stess-a di proposito/*per sbaglio.
have.3sg cut-PSTP REFL-Fsg on purpose /by mistake
'Maria cut herself on purpose/*accidentally.'
b. Maria si è taglia-t-a di proposito/per sbaglio.
REFL be.3sgPRES cut-PSTP-Fsg on purpose /by mistake
'Maria cut herself on purpose/accidentally.'

(7.134) a. Marij-a je samu seb-e poreza-l-a
-FsgNOM be.3sg only SELF-ACC cut-PAST-Fsg
namjerno/??slučajno
on.purpose/accidentally
'Maria cut herself on purpose/??accidentally.'
b. Marij-a se poreza-l-a namjerno/slučajno.
-FsgNOM 3sgREFL cut-PAST-Fsg on.purpose/accidentally
'Maria cut herself on purpose/accidentally.'

Why should such a contrast exist, if *Mari(j)a* is in every case the actor and the reflexive pronoun is in every case the undergoer? It appears that these two constructions are not as similar as the standard syntactic analyses portray them, and analyzing the clitic constructions as being the same as the coreference constructions, except for the form of the reflexive pronoun, does not predict this semantic difference. It appears, then, that a different analysis of the clitic constructions is called for.

It would be instructive to look at other constructions in which the clitic reflexive pronoun occurs. In both languages it plays an important role in another construction: deriving intransitive inchoative verbs (achievements or accomplishments) from transitive causative verbs (see section 3.2.1). This use is illustrated below.

(7.135) a. Maria ha aper-to la finestra.
have.3sgPRES open-PSTP the.Fsg window
'Maria opened the window.'
b. La finestra si è aper-t-a.
the.Fsg window REFL be.3sgPRES open-PSTP-Fsg
'The window opened.'
b′. La finestra è aper-t-a.
*'The window opened' but OK as 'The window is open.'

(7.136) a. Petar-∅ je otvori-o prozor-∅.
-MsgNOM be.3sg open-PAST.Msg window-MsgACC
'Peter opened the window.'
b. Prozor-∅ se otvori-o.
window-MsgNOM REFL.3sg open-PAST.Msg
'The window opened.'

The verbs in the (a) sentences are transitive (causative accomplishment) verbs, whereas the verbs in the (b) sentences are intransitive accomplishment verbs; the single NP in the (b) examples is an undergoer. Thus in this construction the privileged syntactic argument is an undergoer, not an actor.

Is this detransitivizing use of *si* related to its use in reflexive constructions? Working in a variety of theoretical frameworks, Grimshaw (1982, 1990), Manzini (1986), Wehrli (1986) and Farrell (1995), among others, have argued that a unified account can be given of the detransitivizing and reflexive functions of *si* in Italian and *se* in French. The first step in seeing whether a unified analysis can be given in our framework is to examine the alternation in (7.135) in order to ascertain exactly what *si* does to the logical structure of (a) to yield (b). Centineo (1996) compares pairs like (7.135) with those like the one in (7.137) in which *si* does not occur.

(7.137) a. Il capitano ha affonda-to la nave.
the.Msg captain have.3sgPRES sink-PSTP the.Fsg ship
'The captain sank the ship.'
b. La nave è affonda-t-a.
the.Fsg boat be. 3sgPRES sink-PSTP-Fsg
'The ship sank.'
b′. *La nave si è affonda-t-a.

Why is *si* required in (7.135b) but impossible in (7.137b)? Centineo shows that there is a number of systematic differences between the two intransitive forms, all of which point to the conclusion that *aprire* 'open' is basically a transitive verb of the causative accomplishment type, while *affondare* 'sink' is basically an intransitive accomplishment verb. One piece of evidence in support of this is the behavior of these verbs in causative constructions with *fare* 'do, make', as illustrated in (7.138).

(7.138) a. Maria fece aprire la porta.
make.3sgPAST open the.Fsg door
'Maria made someone open the door', or 'Maria got the door to open.'
b. Tonino fece affondare la barca.
make.3sgPAST sink the.Fsg boat
'Tonino made the boat sink', but not *'Tonino made someone sink the boat.'

Verbs like *aprire* can have two interpretations in this construction: as a transitive verb with an unspecified actor, or as an intransitive accomplishment verb. Verbs like *affondare*, on the other hand, have only one interpretation in this construction: as an intransitive accomplishment verb. This is predicted if *affondare* is an intransitive accomplishment, and not a transitive verb like *aprire*. Thus, Centineo proposes that the logical structure for *aprire* 'open' is the one given in (7.139a), while the logical structure for *affondare* 'sink' is the one given in (b).

(7.139) a. *aprire* 'open': [**do′** (x, ∅)] CAUSE [BECOME **open′** (y)]
b. *affondare* 'sink': BECOME **sunk′** (x)

Verbs like *affondare* may function as transitive causative accomplishments without any overt marker of the change, just like many verbs in English, e.g. *break*, *shatter*, *open*, *close*. With verbs like *aprire*, the reverse derivation, from transitive to intransitive, is marked by *si*.

Is the logical structure of *aprirsi* 'open' (intr.) the same as that of *affondare* in (7.139b), i.e. simply 'BECOME **open′** (x)'? Centineo presents some interesting data regarding manner adverbs that suggest that this is in fact not the case. Recall from section 4.4.1.2 that manner adverbs modify activity predicates; that is why they are given as a test for identifying activity predicates in logical structures in table 3.1. Given that there is no activity predicate in (7.139b), we predict that intransitive *affondare* and verbs like it should not cooccur with manner adverbs, and this seems to be the case. On the other hand, verbs like *aprirsi* and *chiudersi* 'close' (intr.) do cooccur with manner adverbs.

(7.140) a. La nave è affonda-t-a *violentemente/??facilemente.
the.Fsg boat be.3sgPRES sink-PSTP-Fsg violently/easily
'The boat sank violently/easily.'
b. La porta si è chius-a violentemente/facilemente.
the.Fsg door REFL be.3sgPRES close.PSTP-Fsg violently/easily
'The door closed violently/easily.'

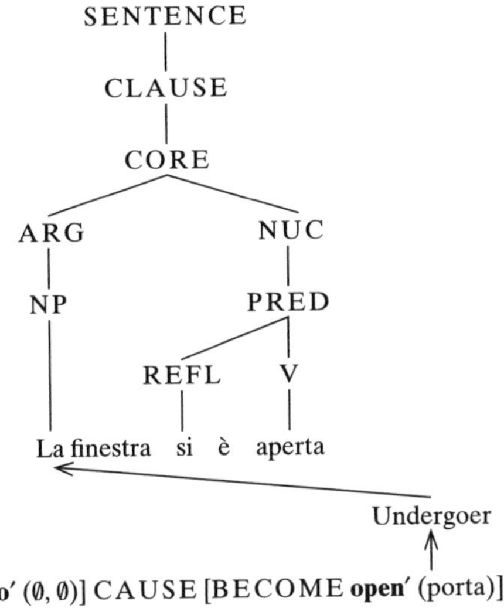

Figure 7.27 Linking in intransitive accomplishment construction in (7.135b)

The acceptability of (b) indicates clearly that there must an activity predicate in the logical structure of *chiudersi* 'close' (intr.) and verbs of this type, and therefore their logical structure cannot be the same as that of *affondare* in (7.139b). Rather, Centineo proposes that it must be as in (7.141), with the causing activity and its EFFECTOR (and therefore the actor) unspecified.

(7.141) a. *aprirsi* 'open': [**do′** (∅, ∅)] CAUSE [BECOME **open′** (y)]
b. *chiudersi* 'close': [**do′** (∅, ∅)] CAUSE [BECOME **closed′** (y)]

Thus, the linking in (7.135b) is that given in figure 7.27.

Let us assume that the linking is the same in the reflexive constructions as in these detransitivization constructions. The linking in (7.111a), 'Maria cut herself', would then be as in figure 7.28. This contrasts with the linking in the non-clitic reflexive construction in (7.110a). It is clear how the reflexive interpretation is generated in a sentence like (7.110a); it is not so clear how it follows from the linking in figure 7.28. Van Valin (1990) suggests that it arises as an inference in the following way. *Si* signals that the highest-ranking argument in the logical structure has been suppressed, and, given the Italian privileged syntactic argument selection principles, the undergoer will occur as the privileged syntactic argument. However, the verb is in active-voice form, which signals that the privileged syntactic argument is an actor, and, moreover, the NP is animate, which is a prototypical property of actors. This would appear to be a paradox, and it is resolved by interpreting the privileged syntactic argument as both actor and undergoer simultaneously, i.e. by giving it a reflexive interpretation. Such an interpretation cannot arise if the argument is inanimate, as in (7.135b), as this analysis would predict. In addition, the semantic contrast

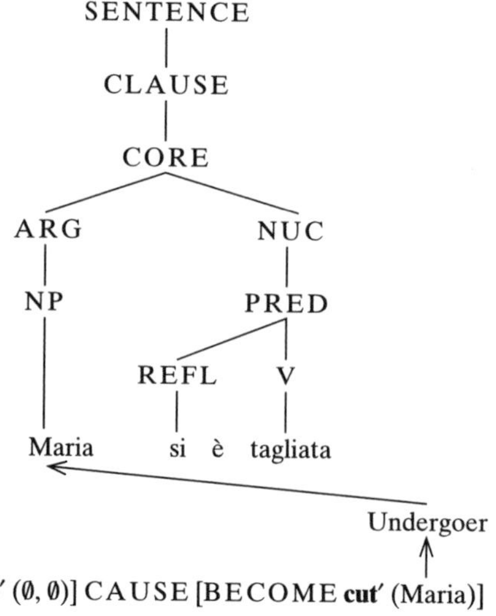

Figure 7.28 Linking in clitic reflexive construction in (7.111a)

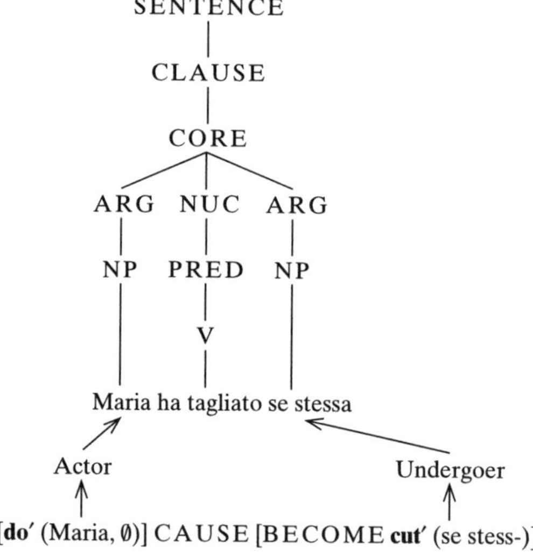

Figure 7.29 Linking in Italian coreference reflexive construction in (7.110a)

between (7.111) and (7.110) is to be expected, on this account. In the clitic reflexive, the actor–undergoer opposition is in effect neutralized, and therefore the sentence should be compatible with either an agentive or a non-agentive interpretation, as in (7.133b). In the *se stesso* construction, on the other hand, the controller is an animate actor, which, as we saw in chapter 3, is normally construed agentively. The agency implicature is strengthened by the opposition between the two constructions: since there is an alternative construction which is neutral with respect to the agentiveness of the privileged syntactic argument, the choice of the *se stesso* construction positively implicates the agentive reading. This explains the oddity of using *per sbaglio* 'by mistake' with this construction.

The same analysis can be given for the Croatian examples in (7.134) and (7.136). Croatian does, however, differ from Italian in two important ways. First, the transitive causative–intransitive accomplishment/achievement alternation is always mediated by the reflexive *se*; that is, there appear to be no verbs like *affondare* 'sink', and all verbs of this type pattern like *aprire* 'open'. Second, the two languages differ with respect to how benefactive reflexives are treated; both can use the non-clitic reflexive form, but only Italian can use the clitic reflexive.

(7.142) a. Maria ha compra-to gli libr-i per
have.3sgPRES buy-PSTP the.Mpl book-pl for
se stess-a. Italian
REFL-Fsg
'Maria bought the books for herself.'
b. Maria si è compra-t-a gli libr-i.
REFL be.3sgPRES buy-PSTP-Fsg the.Mpl book-pl
'Maria bought herself the books.'

(7.143) a. Marij-a je seb-i kupi-l-a knjig-u. Croatian
-FsgNOM be.3sg SELF-DAT buy-PAST-Fsg book-FsgACC
'Maria bought the book for herself.'
b. *Marij-a se kupi-l-a knjig-u.
-FsgNOM 3sgREFL buy-PAST-Fsg book-FsgACC
'Maria bought herself the book.'

The preposition *per* 'for' in (7.142a) is an argument-adjunct preposition like its English counterpart. *Sebi* 'self' is in dative case and codes the benefactive in (7.143a) in Croatian. We assume that all four sentences have basically the same logical structure, which is given in (7.144).

(7.144) [[**do′** (w, . . .)] CAUSE [BECOME **have′** (x, y)]] PURP [**have′** (z, y)], w = x

A couple of points are in order about this representation. First, '. . .' refers to the details of the representation of the buying activity, which have been omitted since they are not directly relevant to the point at hand. Second, 'w = x' indicates that the EFFECTOR is also the RECIPIENT. 'PURP [**have′** (z, y)]', where *z* is 'SELF' in the (a) sentences, is meant to represent the fact that Maria purchased the book with the intention of possessing it and using it in some way; nothing in the sentence is more specific than that. It does not tell us, for example, whether she intends to read the book or simply add it to her collection. This logical structure meets the Role Hierarchy and LS-Superiority Conditions discussed in the previous section. The linking in (7.143a) is presented in figure 7.30. The 'beneficiary' argument in the PURP part of the logical structure is treated as a non-macrorole direct core argument, and therefore takes dative case. There is no preposition in Croatian

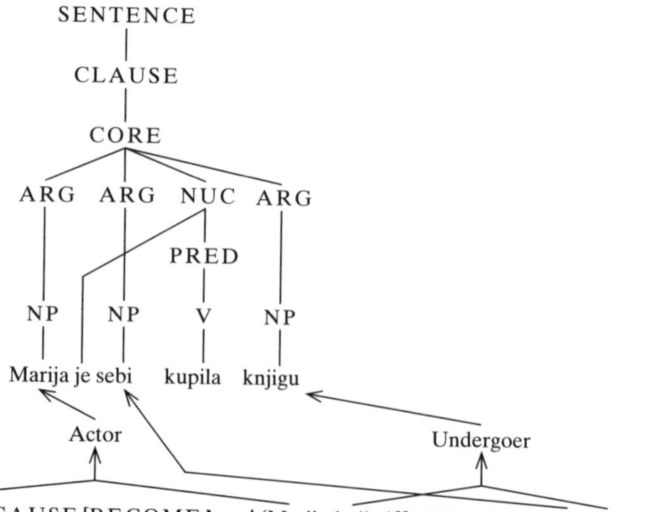

Figure 7.30 Linking in Croatian benefactive reflexive construction in (7.143a)

analogous to *per* in Italian. In the Italian sentence in (7.142a), the 'SELF' argument is realized as the object of the argument-adjunct preposition *per*.

In the Italian example in (7.142b) the *z* argument cannot be 'SELF', because on the analysis we are proposing *si* is a signal of the suppression of the highest-ranking argument in the logical structure and does not code an argument like *se stesso* or *sebe* does. Hence the *z* argument must be *Maria. Maria* cannot appear as the first argument of **do′** in the logical structure for *comprare* 'buy', because this argument is unspecified, as signaled by *si*; since the *w* argument is unspecified, then the *x* argument must be unspecified as well, because the lexical entry for *comprare* 'buy' specifies that 'w = x'. An important difference between this example and the earlier examples, e.g. (7.111a), is that the privileged syntactic argument cannot be the undergoer, because the undergoer is *gli libri* 'the books', which occurs postverbally. One piece of evidence that it is the undergoer comes from past participle agreement. In transitive clauses, the past participle normally agrees with the undergoer in number and gender only when it is a clitic pronoun, as in (7.145a), but it is often the case in spoken Italian that it agrees with a postverbal, NP undergoer, as in (b).

(7.145) a. Mario la ha taglia-t-a.
3FsgACC have.3sgPRES cut-PSTP-Fsg
'Mario cut it.'

b. Maria si è compra-t-i gli libr-i.
REFL be.3 buy-PSTP-Mpl the.Mpl book-pl
'Maria bought herself the books.'

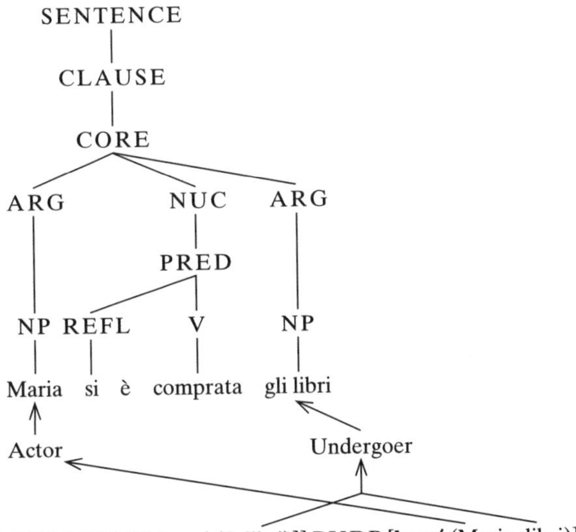

Figure 7.31 Linking in Italian benefactive clitic reflexive construction in (7.142b)

If *gli libri* 'the books' is the undergoer, what is *Maria*? An important fact is that Italian is like German, in that only macrorole arguments may function as the privileged syntactic argument and trigger finite-verb agreement. Given that *Maria* cannot be the undergoer and yet functions as the controller of finite-verb agreement, the only possible analysis is that it is the actor. The linking is given in figure 7.31.

The benefactive interpretation arises as follows. *Si* signals that the highest-ranking argument in the logical structure has been suppressed, and normally, given the Italian privileged syntactic argument selection principles, the undergoer should occur as the privileged syntactic argument. However, there is an overt undergoer in the clause, and therefore the privileged syntactic argument cannot be the undergoer. Given, as we stated above, that in Italian only macrorole arguments may function as the privileged syntactic argument and trigger finite-verb agreement, the privileged syntactic argument must therefore be interpreted as the actor. But *si* signals that the highest-ranking argument in the logical structure of *comprare* 'buy' has been suppressed; hence the EFFECTOR cannot function as actor. Again, a paradox seems to have arisen, and the only way to resolve it in this instance is to posit an additional benefactive component to the logical structure and to interpret the actor as the highest-ranking argument of the 'PURP . . .' component. This would have to be conventionalized, as not just any additional logical structure would be appropriate here. As in the other clitic reflexive constructions, this argument is also identified with the unspecified highest-ranking argument, in this case the 'buyer', yielding the correct benefactive reflexive interpretation. Positing an additional component of the logical structure in this case is in principle no different from what is required in the interpretation of adjunct WH-words in questions, as we saw with respect to figure 7.22 in section 7.2.3.

It might be suggested that the fact that the past participle agrees with the privileged syntactic argument in (7.142b) is evidence that it is not an actor, since in all of the other examples the agreement is with an undergoer, not an actor argument. However, there are other instances of past participle agreement with an actor argument in Italian. Consider the following two sentences from Centineo (1986).

(7.146) a. Luisa ha cor-so. — Activity
have.3sgPRES run-PSTP
'Luisa has run.'

b. Luisa è cor-s-a a casa. — Active accomplishment
be.3sgPRES run-PSTP-Fsg to house
'Luisa has run home.'

The verb *correre* 'run' is listed in the lexicon as an activity verb and therefore takes an actor as its single macrorole argument, following the macrorole assignment principles in chapter 4. Yet in the (b) sentence the past participle clearly agrees with it, and this shows that past participle agreement with an actor argument is indeed possible in Italian.

What, then, is the difference between Croatian and Italian that explains the ungrammaticality of (7.143b)? The simplest explanation is that Croatian disallows arguments from a logical structure other than that of the main predicate in the nucleus to function as a macrorole argument. Thus, given a logical structure like in figure 7.31, it would be impossible in Croatian for the argument in the 'PURP' component in the logical structure to serve as the actor in the core, after the highest-ranking argument in the logical structure of the verb has been suppressed. The result is that the clitic reflexive construction should only be possible with actor–undergoer reflexives, as in (7.111b) and (7.134b). Croatian also lacks the type of multi-verb monoclausal causative construction found in Italian and other Romance languages, which involves, as we will see in chapter 9, a semantic argument of the linked verb serving as undergoer in a core headed by the causative verb.

There is an additional construction to be considered here, the 'middle' construction. Examples from Italian and Croatian are given in (7.147).

(7.147) a. La porta si apre-Ø facilmente. — Italian
the.Fsg door REFL open-3sgPRES easily
'The door opens easily.'

b. Knjig-a se dobro čita-Ø. — Croatian
book-FsgNOM REFL good read-3sgPRES
'The book reads well.'

The clitic reflexive is obligatory in this construction, as is the adverb; it is very unusual for a modifier like an adverb to be obligatory in a verbal construction. How can this be captured? It would not be adequate to represent them the same way as when they are optional modifiers, as we did in chapter 4; if we did this, it would be necessary to add an *ad hoc* stipulation to the effect that they are obligatory, which is not explanatory. The meaning of these constructions gives an important clue to their logical structure: a plausible paraphrase of the meaning of the (a) sentence is 'Opening the door is easy.' This suggests that at the semantic level the adverb could be analyzed as a predicate in an attributive construction; these constructions are used to attribute a property to the 'subject', e.g. 'easy opening' or 'good reading'. Accordingly the logical structures for these two sentences are as in (7.148).

(7.148) a. **be′** ([[**do′** (∅, ∅)] CAUSE [BECOME **open′** (y)]], [**easy′**])
b. **be′** ([**do′** (∅, [**read′** (∅, y)])], [**good′**])

Since the predicate representing the manner adverbs is an obligatory part of these logical structures, the obligatoriness of the manner adverbs follows without stipulation. These representations have the added advantage that they capture the basically stative nature of middle constructions; in English, for example, verbs take the simple present in this construction, a hallmark of stative verbs, as the translations in (7.147) show. The linking is very simple. Since these are single-argument stative constructions, the single argument must be an undergoer. The only candidate for this is the *y* argument in the logical structure that fills the first variable slot of **be′** (x, [**pred′**]). The reflexive clitic signals the suppression of the highest ranking argument in the embedded logical structure. Hence the undergoer appears as the privileged syntactic argument, the verb of the embedded logical structure appears in the nucleus, and the attribute predicate appears as a manner adverb. This is illustrated for (7.147a) in figure 7.32.

Thus, analyzing the reflexive clitic as signaling the suppression of the highest-ranking argument in the logical structure of the verb makes possible an analysis in which the s*i* or *se* morpheme has the same function in reflexive, detransitived accomplishment/achievement and middle constructions in these languages. At the beginning of the discussion of reflexivization, we raised the question as to whether clitic reflexive constructions should be analyzed like lexical reflexives, coreference reflexives, or neither of them. The answer seems clearly to be that clitic reflexives have much more in common with lexical reflexives than with coreference reflexives; indeed, they seem to be a second type of 'linking' reflexive.

7.6 Focus structure, linearization and linking

In this chapter and the previous two, we have seen numerous examples of how information structure interacts with the mapping between syntactic and semantic representations, and we have seen that the nature of this interaction can vary from

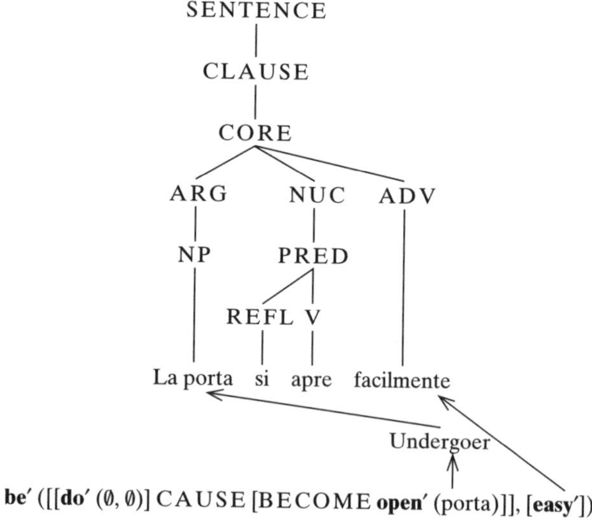

Figure 7.32 Linking in Italian 'middle' construction in (7.147a)

language to language. In this section we will concentrate on two aspects of this interaction, the linearization of the elements in a sentence and the input of focus structure into the linking algorithms.

7.6.1 Linearization

In section 2.5 we raised the issue of the principles governing linear precedence relations among the elements in a sentence, and we noted that languages vary substantially in this area. In languages with very fixed word order, focus structure has little or no direct effect on word order, although it may indirectly affect it via influence on privileged syntactic argument selection, as we will see in section 7.6.2. In languages with more flexible word order, however, the impact of focus structure can be very great. We have already seen examples of this in Italian, Hungarian and Turkish. In the Italian examples in (5.1)–(5.5), whether a sentence is NP–V or V–NP depends first and foremost on whether the NP is topical or focal. Because Italian does not allow prenuclear focal material within the core, a focal intransitive 'subject' must occur postverbally, either after the main verb or after the copula in a cleft construction, as in (5.3b), a sentence-focus construction, and (5.5b), narrow-focus constructions. If it is topical and appears overtly, it is preverbal, as in (5.1b). All are repeated below.

(7.149) a. What happened to your car?
(La mia macchina) si è ROT-T-A.
the.Fsg 1sgGEN.Fsg car REFL be.3sgPRES break.down-PSTP-Fsg
'My car/it broke DOWN.' (=(5.1b))

b. What happened?
Mi si è rot-t-a la MACCHINA.
1sgDAT REFL be.3sgPRES break.down-PSTP-Fsg the.Fsg car
'My CAR broke down.' (=(5.3b))

c. I heard your motorcycle broke down.
Si è rot-t-a la mia MACCHINA.
REFL be.3sgPRES break.down-PSTP-Fsg the.Fsg 1sgGEN. Fsg car
'My CAR broke down.' (=(5.5b))

c′. È la mia MACCHINA che si è
be.3sgPRES the.Fsg 1sgGEN.Fsg car which REFL be.3sgPRES
rot-t-a.
break.down-PSTP-Fsg
'It's my CAR that broke down.' (=(5.5b))

As we saw in exercises 1 and 2 in chapter 5, word order in Hungarian and Turkish is very flexible and very sensitive to focus structure. Turkish is the more rigid of the two, as the verb is normally clause-final; in Hungarian the verb is not restricted to a single position within the clause. This is illustrated in the following examples from É. Kiss (1987) and Erguvanlı (1984).

(7.150) a. János tette a könyvet az asztal-ra. Hungarian
put the book.ACC the table-on
b. János a könyvet tette az asztalra.
c. A könyvet János tette az asztalra.
d. Az asztalra János a könyvet tette.
'John put the book on the table.'

(7.151) a. Murat kitap ok-uyor. Turkish
book read-PROG
'Murat is reading a book.'
b. *Kitap Murat okuyor.
c. Murat kitab-ı okuyor.
book-ACC
c′. Kitabı Murat okuyor.
'Murat is reading the book.'

Only referentially specific (normally definite) undergoers receive accusative case in Turkish, and actor and undergoer may appear in either order only if both are definite, as in (7.151c, c′). Both languages have an immediately preverbal focus position in which WH-words appear.

(7.152) a. János mit tett az asztal-ra? Hungarian
what put the table-on
b. Mit tett János az asztalra?
c. *Mit János tett az asztalra?
d. *János tett mit az asztalra?
'What did John put on the table?'

(7.153) a. Murat para-yı çal-dı. Turkish
money-ACC steal-PAST
'Murat stole the money.'
b. Parayı kim çaldı?
'Who stole the money?'
b′. *Kim parayı çaldı?
c. Murat nere-ye git-ti?
what-ALL go-PAST
'Where did Murat go?'
c′. *Nereye Murat gitti?

As a final example of the influence of focus structure on linearization, we will look at Russian, often cited as a 'free-word-order language'. From the perspective of information distribution, however, Russian ordering is much less free: in statements the order topic–focus is strongly adhered to, while in WH-questions the focus is normally in clause-initial position, according to Comrie (1979, 1984a). He gives the following examples of questions and answers to illustrate these ordering constraints. Normally, the answer would be simply the focal element(s) and the topical elements would not be repeated. However, they are included here in order to better illustrate the focus structure constraints on word order.

(7.154) a. Q: [Kto-Ø] [zaščiščajet Viktor-a]? 'Who defends Victor?'
who-NOM defends Victor-ACC
FOCUS TOPIC
A: [Viktor-a zaščiščajet] [Maksim-Ø]. 'MAXIM defends Victor.'
Victor-ACC defends Maxim-NOM
TOPIC FOCUS
b. Q: [Kogo] [zaščiščajet Maksim-Ø]? 'Who(m) does Maxim defend?'
who-ACC defends Maxim-NOM
FOCUS TOPIC
A: [Maksim-Ø zaščiščajet] [Viktor-a]. 'Maxim defends VIKTOR.'
Maxim-NOM defends Victor-ACC
TOPIC FOCUS
c. Sp1: [Maksim-Ø] [ubivajet Aleksej-a]. 'Maxim KILLS ALEXEI.'
Maxim-NOM kills Alexei-ACC
TOPIC FOCUS
Sp2: [A Viktor-a]? 'And VIKTOR?' (i.e. 'What is happening to Victor?')
and Victor-ACC
FOCUS
Sp1: [Viktor-a Maksim-Ø] [zaščiščajet]. 'Maxim DEFENDS Victor.'
Victor-ACC Maxim-NOM defends
TOPIC FOCUS

WH-questions and their answers are narrow-focus constructions, and this is the case in (7.154a, b). Speaker 1's first utterance in (7.154c) is a predicate-focus construction, while speaker 2's question and 1's response are both narrow-focus constructions. In all of the declarative utterances in (7.154), topic precedes focus.

It is important to keep in mind that topic need not precede focus as the unmarked order in a language, even though this is the most common order cross-linguistically. Toba Batak, like other western Austronesian languages such as Malagasy (Keenan 1976a) and Tagalog, has comment–topic or focus–topic as its unmarked order. This is illustrated in (7.155), from Schachter (1984b).

(7.155) a. Man-jaha buku guru i.
ATV-read book teacher DEF
'The teacher is reading a book.'
a′. Manjaha buku guru.
'A (certain) teacher is reading a book.'
a″. ??Manjaha buku i guru i.
'The teacher is reading the book.'
a‴. ?*Manjaha buku i guru.
'A teacher is reading the book.'
b. Di-jaha guru buku i.
PASS-read teacher book DEF
'A teacher read the book.'
b′. Dijaha guru buku.
'A teacher read a (certain) book.'
b″. ??Dijaha guru i buku i.
'The teacher read the book.'
b‴. ?*Dijaha guru i buku.
'The teacher read a book.'

In certain respects Toba Batak is the mirror image of Turkish: it is verb-initial; it has a special focus position in the immediately postverbal position; and it is topic-final. As the data in exercise 3 in chapter 5 and exercise 2 in chapter 6 show, there are grammatical restrictions on where definite and indefinite NPs can occur, and this is tied in with the voice system and a number of grammatical constructions.

7.6.2 Linking

The Toba Batak phenomena in (7.155) and the exercises point to the important role that focus structure can play in grammatical constructions and therefore in linking in some languages. In this section we will investigate two of the most important interactions of focus structure and linking, namely privileged syntactic argument (pragmatic pivot) selection and WH-question formation.

As is well known, English shows a strong tendency to have topical 'subjects' and focal 'objects', but Toba Batak seems to be much stricter about this correlation, as the examples in (7.155) show. Schachter (1984b) states that 'the patient of [an active-voice] verb is normally non-individuated . . . [T]he class of individuated patients includes referential patients, zero-anaphor patients, and patients with

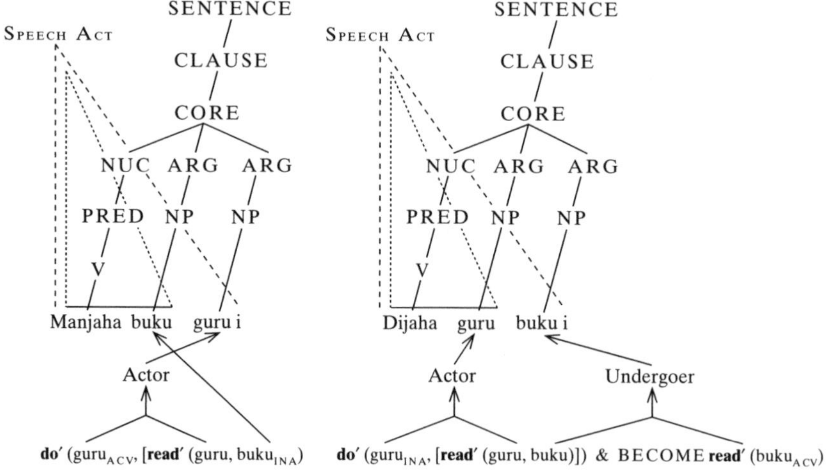

Figure 7.33 Focus structure and linking in Toba Batak (7.155a, b)

modifiers' (147). This is reminiscent of the discussion of the second argument of activity verbs in section 3.2.3.3, in which we saw that the second argument of activity verbs are often non-referential; the fact that the second argument with Toba Batak active-voice verbs is normally non-individuated seems to be the same phenomenon. The 'PATIENT' of an active-voice verb occurs in the immediately postverbal focus position, and this explains why (7.155a″, a‴) are so bad: both contain definite NPs in the focus position. The same is true in (7.155b″, b‴), in which the NP in the focus position is definite. The (a‴, b‴) are worse than the (a″, b″) examples because they also contain an indefinite NP as pragmatic pivot, which is also strongly disfavored. In order to maintain the correlation between privileged syntactic argument and topic, English may employ its passive construction, as exemplified in figures 6.3 and 6.4, but this is not obligatory. In Toba Batak, on the other hand, the active form in (a) is virtually obligatory when the actor is topical and the other core argument focal, and conversely, the passive form in (b) is likewise virtually obligatory when the actor is focal and the undergoer is topical. The difference between the two voice forms also correlates with *Aktionsart* differences, as the translations indicate. The active forms seem to have an activity reading, while the passive forms have an active accomplishment reading. This is similar to the situation in Sama illustrated in (6.75). The linkings in (7.155a) and (b) are illustrated in figure 7.33. These are not simple word-order variants, like (7.150a–d) in Hungarian, (7.151a–c′) in Turkish or (7.154a–c) in Russian; rather they involve different choices for the privileged syntactic argument, and these choices have important syntactic consequences, as is clear from the facts in the exercise in chapter 6.

This raises the question of where focus structure considerations come into the linking algorithm in (7.12). It is repeated below.

(7.12) *Linking algorithm: semantics → syntax (preliminary formulation)*

1 Determine the actor and undergoer assignments, following the Actor–Undergoer Hierarchy in figure 7.1.
2 Assign specific morphosyntactic status to [–WH] arguments in logical structure (language-specific).
   a. Accusative privileged syntactic argument selection: default = Actor.
   b. Ergative privileged syntactic argument selection: default = Undergoer.
3 If there is a [+WH] XP, assign it to the precore slot (language-specific).
4 A non-WH XP may be assigned to the pre- or postcore slot, subject to focus structure restrictions (optional; language-specific).
5 Assign the core arguments the appropriate case markers/adpositions and assign the predicate in the nucleus the appropriate agreement marking (language specific).
6 Assign arguments of logical structures other than that of the main verb to the periphery.

Focus structure considerations can actually affect all of these steps. With ditransitive verbs like *give* and *show* in English, the choice of argument to serve as undergoer (step 1) affects the linear order of the postnuclear core aguments, and Givón (1984a) and Erteschik-Shir (1979), among others, have argued that the more topical argument is chosen as 'object' (undergoer). This entails that the less topical, more focal argument will appear in the core-final position, which, we argued in section 5.2.3, is the unmarked focus position for non-WH-arguments in the English clause.

Step 2 involves privileged syntactic argument selection, and this is what is illustrated in figures 6.3 and 6.4 for English and in figure 7.33 for Toba Batak, languages with pragmatic pivots. Focus structure plays no role in privileged syntactic argument selection in languages like Lakhota, which lacks variable syntactic pivots and has only invariable pivots, as the data in exercise 3 in chapter 6 clearly show. There is no need to amend the formulation of step 2 to reflect the influence of focus structure in some languages but not in others, since it already states that there are important language-specific features to it. We argued in chapter 6 that 'privileged syntactic argument' is a construction-specific notion, and we have seen examples, e.g. relativization and reflexivization in Sama in (6.50) and (7.17), in which distinct constructions in the same sentence can have different privileged syntactic arguments. Hence focus structure involvement in this step in the linking is in fact a property of specific constructions, namely those with pragmatic pivots, and accordingly it will be captured in the representation of those constructions in constructional templates. We return to this issue in section 7.7 below.

The next step affected by focus structure is step 3, which involves WH-elements in WH-questions. There seem to be three possibilities regarding the placement of

WH-words in WH-questions. The simplest is found in Lakhota, in which WH-words occur in exactly the same position in the clause as the corresponding non-WH NP in a non-interrogative utterance. This is exemplified in (7.156).

(7.156) a. Šų́ka ki igmú wą ∅-∅-yaxtáke.
dog the cat a 3sgU-3sgA-bite
'The dog bit a cat.'
b. Šų́ka ki igmú wą yaxtáka he?
'Did the dog bite a cat?'
c. Šų́ka ki táku yaxtáke.
what/something
'The dog bit something.'
d. Šų́ka ki táku yaxtáka he?
'What did the dog bite?', or 'Did the dog bite something?'

Questions are formed in Lakhota by adding the question particle *he* to the end of the sentence; there is no other syntactic change in the sentence, as a comparison of (7.156a) and (b) readily reveals. Questions words in Lakhota also function as indefinite–specific pronouns; for example, *táku* can mean either 'what' or 'something'. If the sentence is non-interrogative, as in (c), then it can only mean 'something'. If the question particle occurs in a sentence with *táku*, as in (d), then the result is ambiguous: if the focus of the question is on *táku*, then it is interpreted as 'what' and the sentence is a WH-question; if, on the other hand, the focus of the question is on a different constituent, then *táku* is interpreted as an indefinite–specific pronoun and the sentence is a yes–no question, as the two alternative glosses for (d) indicate. Another way of putting this is that *táku* can only be interpreted as a WH-question word if it is in the actual focus domain; otherwise, it is interpreted as an indefinite–specific pronoun. The two readings for (d) are represented in figure 7.34. In the first diagram *táku* is in the actual focus domain, and therefore the sentence is interpreted as 'What did the dog bite?' In the second diagram, however, *šų́ka ki* 'the dog' is in the actual focus domain, and accordingly the sentence is a yes–no question with *táku* construed as an indefinite–specific pronoun.

The second situation is that found in English, Icelandic, Sama and many other languages, and it is captured in the current wording of step 3. It is illustrated in figures 7.2 and 7.11. The final situation is that found in Hungarian, Turkish and Sesotho, in which WH-words appear core-internally but not necessarily in the same position as the corresponding non-WH NP in a non-interrogative utterance. The basic Hungarian phenomena are presented in (7.151), and the basic Turkish data are in (7.152). The Sesotho examples were originally in (5.10); they are repeated below.

(7.157) a. *Mang o-pheh-ile lijo?
who 3sg-cook-PERF food
'Who cooked the food?'

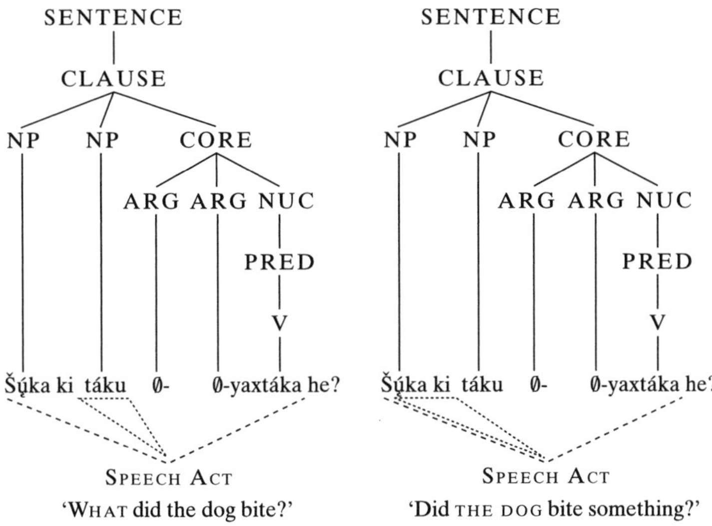

Figure 7.34 The actual focus domain in Lakhota questions

b. Lijo li-pheh-li-o-e ke mang?
food 3sg-cook-PERF-PASS-MOOD by who
'The food was cooked by who?' or 'Who cooked the food?'

c. Ea o-f-ile-ng ntja ke mang?
REL 3sg-give-PERF-REL dog COP who
'The one that gave you the dog is who?'

d. Ke mang ea o-f-ile-ng ntja?
COP who REL 3sg-give-PERF-REL dog
'It's who that gave you the dog?'

In all three of these languages the WH-word must occur within the potential focus domain of the clause, and the default is for it to occur in the unmarked focus position. We may revise step 3 to permit these three language-specific possibilities. Before doing this, however, we need to look at the interaction of focus structure considerations with steps 4 and 6.

Step 4 assigns non-WH-phrases to the precore slot or postcore slot, under specific focus structure constraints, as we discussed in sections 5.2.3, 5.6 and 7.2.2. The Turkish examples in (7.151) illustrate the interaction of discourse pragmatics with step 5. As mentioned there, only referentially specific (usually definite) undergoers receive accusative case; indefinite, newly introduced undergoers receive no case, as (7.151a) shows. Hence the accusative case assignment rule for Turkish is sensitive to the discourse-pragmatic properties of core arguments. Kaluli provides an example of the role of focus structure in an ergative case-marking system; recall that focal actors receive ergative case when they occur in the focus position in the clause (see section 7.3.1.2). Step 6 assigns temporal and locative modifiers of the core logical structure to the periphery, but this is in fact only the unmarked assignment. It is also possible for them to appear in the left-detached position or the precore slot. This is illustrated in the examples below.

(7.158) a. Dana went to Toronto yesterday.
b. Yesterday, Dana went to Toronto and did a lot of shopping.
c. Dana went to Toronto yesterday, and tomorrow she is going to Montreal.
d. When is Dana going to Montreal?
d′. Where is Dana going shopping tomorrow?

(7.159) a. Hún haf-ð-i unn-ið að brúarsmíði í sumar. — Icelandic
3FsgNOM have-PAST-3sg work-PSTP at bridge.building at summer
'She worked at bridge-building in the summer.'
b. Í sumar haf-ð-i hún unn-ið að brúarsmíði.
in summer have-PAST-3sg 3FsgNOM work-PSTP at bridge.building
'In the summer she worked at bridge-building.'
c. Hvenær haf-ð-i hún unn-ið að brúarsmíði?
when have-PAST-3sg 3FsgNOM work-PSTP at bridge.building
'When did she work at bridge-building?'

(7.160) a. Ben dün Bebek-te Ali-ye rastla-dı-m. — Turkish
1sg yesterday -LOC -DAT run.into-PAST-1sg
'I ran into Ali yesterday at Bebek.'
b. Dün Bebek-te ben Ali-ye rastla-dı-m.
'Yesterday at Bebek, I ran into Ali.'
c. Dün ben Ali-ye Bebek-te rastla-dı-m.
'Yesterday, at Bebek I ran into Ali', or 'Yesterday, I ran into Ali AT BEBEK.'
d. Bebek-te ben dün Ali-ye rastla-dı-m.
'At Bebek, I ran into Ali yesterday.'
e. Ben Bebek-te Ali-ye dün rastla-dı-m.
'Yesterday I ran into Ali at Bebek', or 'I ran into Ali at Bebek YESTERDAY.'

The Icelandic examples are repeated from (2.17); the Turkish examples are from Erguvanlı (1984). In the English example (7.158a), *yesterday* is in its default position in the periphery. In (b), on the other hand, it occurs in the left-detached position and modifies both of the subsequent conjoined clauses. In the second clause in (c), *tomorrow* appears in the precore slot and is interpreted as contrasting with *yesterday* in the previous clause. That an element from a higher temporal or locative predicate can occur in the precore slot is confirmed by (d, d′), in which the semantic argument of such a higher predicate appears as a WH-word in the precore slot (see figures 7.14, 7.22 and related discussion in sections 7.2.2, 7.2.3). The Icelandic sentence in (7.159a) illustrates the default position for a setting temporal PP in the periphery, and in (b) it occurs in the precore slot, as indicated by the occurrence of the privileged syntactic argument after the finite auxiliary verb, due to the verb-second constraint in Icelandic syntax (see section 2.2.2). As the (c) sentence shows, this is also the position that a temporal WH-word appears in. The Turkish example in (7.160a) represents the basic order in the Turkish clause; as in many verb-final languages, peripheral elements occur between the 'subject' and the remainder of the core (see figures 2.8, 2.10). In (b) the temporal adverbial and the locative PP both appear in the sentence-initial topic position, which we may take to be the left-detached position, since it is before the normal position of the 'subject' in (a). In (c) *dün* 'yesterday' is in the left-detached position and *Bebek-te* 'at Bebek' appears in the preverbal focus position. In (d) the situation is reversed, with the locative PP in the topical initial position and the temporal adverbial in focus position. Finally, in (e) the locative PP is in the unmarked position within the periphery, while *dün* 'yesterday' is in the focus position. There are, then, a number of linking possibilities for the semantic arguments of higher predicates conditioned by the focus structure of the sentence. This too needs to be expressed in the linking algorithm.

The revised algorithm is in (7.161).

(7.161) *Linking algorithm: semantics → syntax (revised)*

1 Determine the actor and undergoer assignments, following the Actor–Undergoer Hierarchy in figure 7.1.

2 Assign specific morphosyntactic status to [−WH] arguments in logical structure (language-specific).

  a. Accusative privileged syntactic argument selection: default = Actor.

  b. Ergative privileged syntactic argument selection: default = Undergoer.

3 If there is a [+WH] XP,

  a. assign it to the normal position of a non-WH XP with the same function (language-specific), or

  b. assign it to the precore slot (language-specific), or

  c. assign it to a position within the potential focus domain of the clause (default = the unmarked focus position) (language-specific).

4 A non-WH XP may be assigned to the pre- or post-core slot, subject to focus structure restrictions (optional; language-specific).

5 Assign the core arguments the appropriate case markers/adpositions and assign the predicate in the nucleus the appropriate agreement marking (language-specific).

6 For semantic arguments of logical structures other than that of the main verb,
   a. assign them to the periphery (default), or
   b. assign them to the precore slot or focus position (language-specific) if they are focal, or
   c. assign them to the left-detached position if they are highly topical.[36]

The primary function of focus structure in the linking from syntax to semantics is anaphora resolution, that is, in helping to determine possible coreference relations with respect to pronouns. The conditions on the interpretation of pronouns within a sentence in (5.29) refer to the focus structure of the sentence, and focus structure information is an important factor in the determination of possible coreference. Consider the following possible sentences in which the focus structure is indicated; it is derived from the prosodic properties of the sentence.

(7.162) a. $[_{\text{TOP}}$ Tom] $[_{\text{AFD}}$ saw $[_{\text{FOC}}$ his sister]]
b. $[_{\text{AFD}}$ $[_{\text{FOC}}$ Tom]] [saw $[_{\text{TOP}}$ his sister]]

Example (7.162a) represents a predicate-focus construction, while (b) exemplifies a marked narrow-focus construction with narrow focus on the privileged syntactic argument, *Tom*. In terms of (5.29), *Tom* and *his* can be interpreted as coreferential in (a) but not in (b), because in (b) clause (a) is not met. That is, in the context in which (7.162b) would be appropriate, the referent of *his* is already established as an activated discourse referent, and *Tom* is being introduced as new into the context; consequently, it cannot be the antecedent for *his*. Note that in (a) *his* need not refer to *Tom*; rather, coreference is merely possible. Hence the semantic representations that would be the output of the linking from syntax to semantics would include the logical structures in (7.163).

(7.163) a. **see′** (Tom$_i$, [**have.as.kin′** (his$_{i/j}$, sister)]) = (7.162a)
b. **see′** (Tom$_i$, [**have.as.kin′** (his$_j$, sister)]) = (7.162b)

Presumably, context would determine whether *his* actually refers to *Tom* or not in (7.162a), but the sentence is in principle ambiguous, in a way that (7.162b) is not.

Focus structure will also have a vital role to play in other areas of the grammar when we investigate linking in complex sentences in chapter 9.

7.6.3 The pervasive role of discourse pragmatics in grammar

We have been investigating syntax from the communication-and-cognition perspective outlined in chapter 1, and one of the things our inquiry has revealed is how discourse-pragmatics, often but not always in the guise of information structure, literally permeates grammar. That is, factors relating to information flow, the cognitive status of referents, and other aspects of discourse pragmatics can interact with and affect grammar at all levels. This is summarized in figure 7.35. We have seen examples of each of these influences in the last six chapters, and there are some

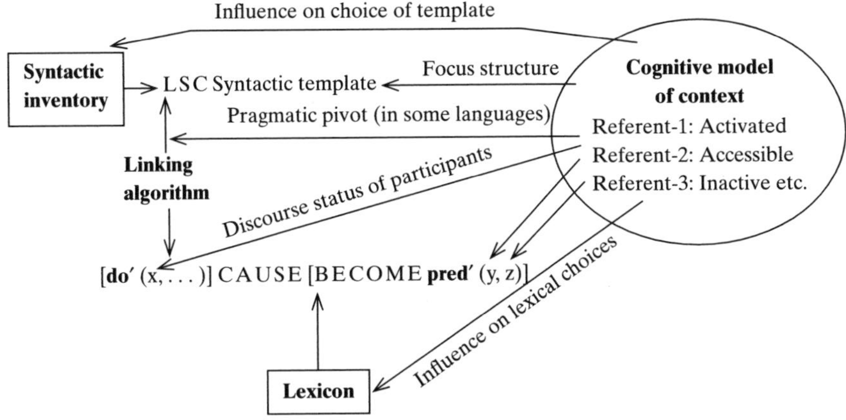

Figure 7.35 The pervasive role of discourse pragmatics in grammar

we have not discussed. For example, in a language with only invariable pivots and controllers or only semantic pivots or controllers, it is impossible to get by syntactic means the privileged syntactic argument choice effects that languages with voice constructions achieve routinely, e.g. keeping the primary topical participant functioning as the privileged syntactic argument in successive clauses. Their only option is alternative lexical choices; that is, rather than passivizing *give* in order to have the RECIPIENT–undergoer function as the privileged syntactic argument, an option not available in a language like Lakhota, a speaker can choose the verb *take* or *receive* instead of *give*, which will have the same effect. *Sell* can be selected instead of *buy*. These alternative lexical choices can potentially be influenced by context, in much the same way as syntactic options in linking can be influenced by context in languages which have them.

Another example of this can be seen in presentational constructions. We saw in figure 7.6 that presentational constructions have a specific combination of syntactic form and focus structure, which is reflected in the syntactic template for them. It is not the case that just any verb can occur in a presentational construction, as Kuno (1972a) and Lambrecht (1987), among others, have noted. Lambrecht comments on the types of verbs that occur in these sentence-focus constructions.

> Another argument in favor of the interpretation of [sentence-focus] structures as presentational in a broad sense can be seen in the constraints imposed in many languages on the kinds of predicates which [sentence-focus] structures may contain . . . [T]he predicates most commonly permitted in [sentence-focus] sentences involve 'presenting' verbs, i.e. intransitive verbs expressing appearance or disappearance of some referent in the internal or external discourse setting, or the beginning or end of some state involving the referent. (1987: 373)

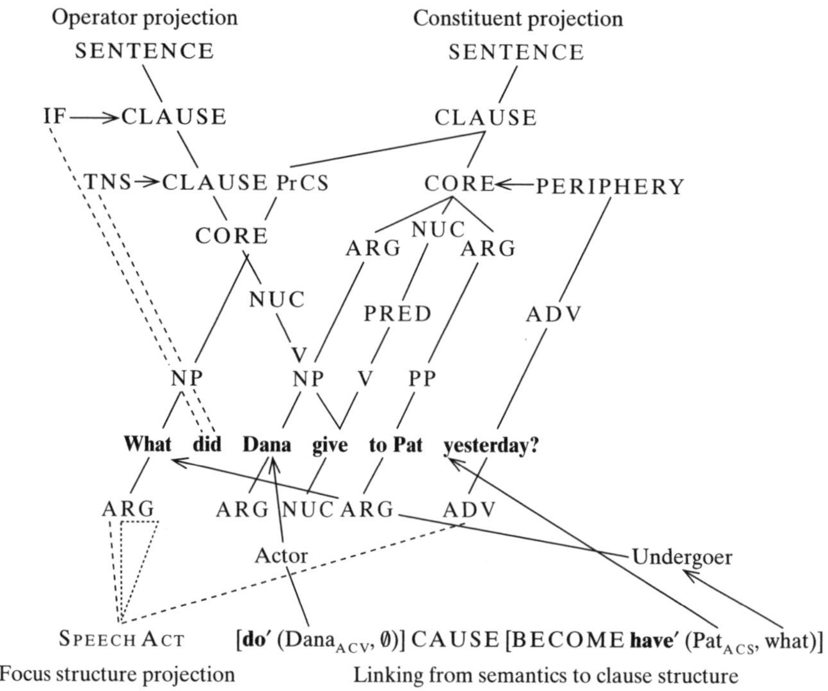

Figure 7.36 Interaction of the three projections of the clause with linking

These are typically achievement and accomplishment verbs, and accordingly we see that the focus structure of the construction (sentence focus) restricts lexical selection, in this instance the selection of the verb.

The interaction of all three projections of the syntactic representation with the linking from the semantic representation is presented in figure 7.36.

7.7 Templates, constructions and linking

In section 2.5 we introduced the idea of representing syntax in terms of constructional templates, following the approach of ConG. Each construction has a set of morphosyntactic, semantic and pragmatic properties, which are captured in the constructional template which characterizes it. In chapter 2 we developed the idea of syntactic templates to represent the layered structure of the clause, and in chapter 5 we augmented some of them with focus structure information (see figures 7.5, 7.6). In this chapter and the previous one we have developed the notion of privileged syntactic argument (syntactic pivot and controller) and explored the linking between syntax and semantics in simple sentences. We now have all of the components necessary for constituting templates for grammatical constructions in simple sentences.

Fillmore (1988) characterizes the notion of 'grammatical construction' as follows:

> By *grammatical construction* we mean any syntactic pattern which is assigned one or more conventional functions in a language, together with whatever is linguistically conventionalized about its contribution to the meaning or the use of structures containing it.
>
> On the level of syntax, we distinguish for any construction in a language its *external* and its *internal* properties. In speaking of the *external syntax* of a construction we refer to the properties of the construction as a whole, that is to say, anything speakers know about the construction that is relevant to the larger syntactic contexts in which it is welcome. By the *internal syntax* of a construction we have in mind a description of the construction's make-up. (36)

Fillmore, Kay and O'Connor (1988) note that 'constructions may specify, not only syntactic, but also lexical, semantic and pragmatic information' (501).[37] Thus the templates we propose for representing constructions must contain, at a minimum, syntactic, morphological, semantic and pragmatic information. ConG representations give full specifications of the morphological, syntactic and semantic properties of constructions, and where a number of constructions share a property which could be construed as a general property of the grammar, it is specified in a more general construction. Little cross-linguistic work has been done in ConG, and no significant generalizations about any cross-linguistic grammatical phenomena have yet been proposed. In the approach to grammatical constructions we are taking, the unique, idiosyncratic features of a construction are specified in its constructional template; the general principles developed in this and the past five chapters, e.g. the Actor–Undergoer Hierarchy, case marking and agreement principles, or the principle governing intrasentential pronominalization, would not be repeated on each template and would be assumed to apply where relevant, in the absence of any specification to the contrary in the template. Thus we are able to capture linguistically significant generalizations as well as specify the essential features of grammatical constructions in particular languages.

An important question is, what is the place of constructional templates in the theory of grammar we have developed? Before we can answer this question, we need to take a look at the overall structure of the theory, which is given in figure 7.37 (cf. figure 2.2). The two sources for the syntactic representation reflect one of the most important differences between semantics to syntax linking and syntax to semantics linking. As we discussed earlier in the chapter, in linking from semantics to syntax, the syntactic representation is constructed out of syntactic templates selected from the syntactic inventory. In syntax to semantics linking, however, the parser outputs a syntactic representation which the grammar must then map into a semantic representation as part of the process of interpreting the utterance (see section 7.2.3).

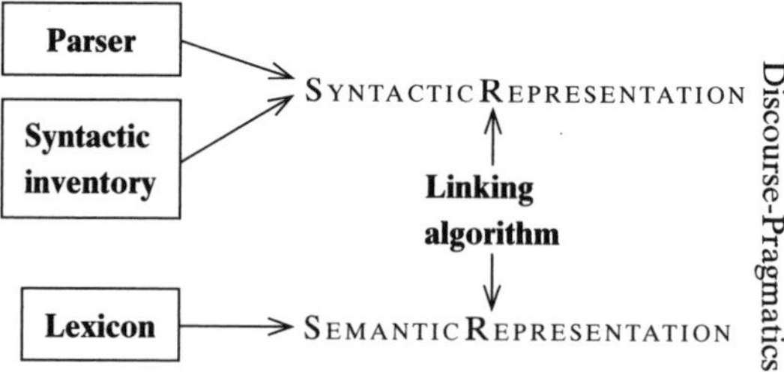

Figure 7.37 Organization of grammar

Now, returning to the question at the beginning of the paragraph, grammatical constructions are specific constellations of morphosyntactic, semantic and pragmatic properties, and accordingly the constructional templates representing them are in effect instructions to the grammar on how these properties should be combined in particular forms. With respect to the syntax of a construction, a constructional template gives construction-specific information about which syntactic templates are required, if the construction is exceptional with respect to the principles in (7.7), what the privileged syntactic argument is (if there is one), and whether the construction is ergative or accusative. Under morphology, the template states any construction-specific morphological information. Under semantics, it gives a general characterization of the meaning of the construction and any special semantic features or constraints. With respect to pragmatics, it presents information about the illocutionary force and focus structure properties of the construction. The primary constraint on the distribution of the construction comes from the type of syntactic template. If the template is a core template, then that construction can in principle occur in any other construction which has an open core slot in it, *ceteris paribus*. This was illustrated in figure 7.7, in which a core template is combined with a pre-core slot template to form the structure of a WH-question. There may, however, be semantic or pragmatic properties of the construction that render it incompatible with other constructions that it is syntactically compatible with.

The format we are using for constructional templates is very informal; it is intended to be a summary of the relevant types of information and not a formalism. Hence the characterizations of the various properties of the construction are not as formal as the syntactic, semantic and other representations they refer to; in particular, the specification of the general meaning of the construction is informal and is meant to express the semantic properties that would have to be captured by a more formal theory of constructional meaning. In order to exemplify our approach to constructional templates, two English and three Sama constructional templates will be presented. The constructional template for the English *be*-passive is given in table 7.3. Under syntax, 'Default core' means that the syntactic template is a core template, and the selection follows the principles in (7.7) as they exist in English

Table 7.3 *Constructional template for English passive (plain)*

CONSTRUCTION English passive (plain)
SYNTAX Template(s): Default core PSA: Pragmatic pivot (default) Linking: Actor ≠ pragmatic pivot; omitted or in peripheral *by*-PP Undergoer = pragmatic pivot (default)
MORPHOLOGY Verb: past participle Auxiliary: *be*
SEMANTICS PSA is not instigator of state of affairs but is affected by it (default)
PRAGMATICS Illocutionary force: Unspecified Focus structure: No restrictions; pragmatic pivot = topic (default)

grammar; all three of the qualifications in (7.7b) are applicable to English, and (b2) applies to this construction specifically. The privileged syntactic argument is a pragmatic pivot, and structurally it is the default pivot in English, i.e. the prenuclear direct core argument, the traditional 'subject'. If the construction were the purposive construction in exercise 1 in chapter 6, illustrated in (7.118), the privileged syntactic argument would not be the default and would have to be specified. The crucial features of the linking are specified: the actor is not the privileged syntactic argument and receives non-canonical coding as specified, while the undergoer is the default choice for the privileged syntactic argument. It is only the default choice, because, as we will see in chapter 9, there are constructions involving passive in which the argument functioning as privileged syntactic argument is not an argument of the predicate in the nucleus of the matrix core, e.g. *Tanisha was believed to have saved the child*. Under morphology, the form of the predicate is specified, in this case *be* + past participle. Under semantics, a general characterization of the meaning of the construction is given. Finally, under pragmatics, we see that there are no absolute pragmatic conditions on this construction and that it is not associated with any particular illocutionary force type. While there is in English a strong tendency to have the privileged syntactic argument be highly topical, this is merely the default situation and, as we saw in chapter 5, English does allow focal privileged syntactic arguments.

English WH-questions have a rather different constructional template from the passive construction; it is given in table 7.4. Under syntax, the precore-slot template

Table 7.4 *Constructional template for English WH-questions*

CONSTRUCTION English WH-questions
SYNTAX Template(s): PrCS PSA: None Linking: WH-XP to PrCS
MORPHOLOGY Default
SEMANTICS Contains an open proposition with a variable α, WH-XP = α
PRAGMATICS Illocutionary force: Interrogative Focus structure: Narrow focus on PrCS

in figure 7.6 is specified, but the core template is unspecified, subject to (7.7). This construction has no privileged syntactic argument, in the sense that WH-question formation in English does not involve a restricted neutralization. Hence there is no privileged syntactic argument specification. The situation with respect to linking is analogous to that regarding the templates: the WH XP must appear in the precore slot, but beyond that, the linking in the core is unspecified. This construction is compatible with either active or passive constructions, with either unmarked or marked linkings to undergoer, for example. There is no special morphology in this construction. The semantic properties are straightforward. The pragmatic information is crucial for the construction; narrow focus on the WH-word in the precore slot is one of its central features, and the fact that it has interrogative illocutionary force requires that the tensed verb or auxiliary will occur in core-initial position, since, as we saw in chapter 2, the position of the tense operator signals illocutionary force in English. This distinguishes the WH-question construction from the other precore-slot construction, namely topicalization as in *That book I wouldn't buy*. Because the illocutionary force is declarative in this construction, the tense operator appears in its normal, core-internal position.

It would be instructive to compare these English constructions with their counterparts in another language. We will look at three constructions in Sama, a language with a number of syntactically ergative constructions. The constructional template for the Sama antipassive construction is given in table 7.5. The antipassive construction affects the location and the identity of the argument functioning as the privileged syntactic argument. The activity–active accomplishment alternation in Sama verbs correlates with the active–antipassive distinction, as we saw in section

Table 7.5 *Constructional template for Sama antipassive*

CONSTRUCTION Sama antipassive
SYNTAX Template(s): Default PSA: Pragmatic pivot = immediate postverbal direct core argument Linking: Actor = pragmatic pivot Default choice for PSA = non-MR core argument
MORPHOLOGY Verb: *N*- + verb stem
SEMANTICS Pragmatic pivot is instigator of state of affairs *Aktionsart* = atelic (default)
PRAGMATICS Illocutionary force: Unspecified Focus structure: Non-MR core argument = non-specific Pragmatic pivot = topic (default)

6.4.3, (6.75). This is in turn related to the referential properties of the non-actor argument, as one would predict (see sections 3.2.2, 3.2.3.3).

Sama has both syntactic and semantic privileged arguments, as we saw in (7.17), and the following two constructions have a different privileged syntactic argument: WH-question formation has a pragmatic pivot (table 7.6), while reflexivization has a semantic controller (table 7.7). Because the WH-word must be the pragmatic pivot in Sama, it is necessary to combine the WH-question construction with the antipassive construction when the WH-word functions as actor. On the other hand, because the actor is the semantic controller for reflexivization, antipassive has no effect on reflexivization, as we saw in (7.17). However, the actor must be a direct core argument, which means that this construction is incompatible with the Sama passive in (6.78). The Sama template for WH-questions differs from its English counterpart also in that the WH-word is specified to be an NP in Sama, whereas in English it is an 'XP'. This is because the WH-word is always the pragmatic pivot in Sama, and therefore must be an NP. In English, on the other hand, the WH-element can be an NP (*who*), a PP (*in which room*) or an adverbial (*when*, *why*, *where*).

As these examples illustrate, constructional templates bring all aspects of the grammar together in the different aspects of each construction. Syntax, morphology, semantics and pragmatics all come together in them. The set of constructional templates, along with the linking algorithms developed in this chapter, constitute the heart of the grammar of a particular language. They impose language-particular restrictions on what are otherwise very general linking principles.

Table 7.6 *Constructional template for Sama WH-question formation*

CONSTRUCTION Sama WH-question formation
SYNTAX Template(s): PrCS PSA: WH-NP = Pragmatic Pivot Linking: WH-NP to PrCS Antipassive, if WH-NP ≠ default choice for PSA
MORPHOLOGY Verb: *N-* + verb stem if antipassive is required
SEMANTICS Contains an open proposition with variable α, WH-NP = α
PRAGMATICS Illocutionary force: Interrogative Focus structure: Narrow focus on PrCS

Table 7.7 *Constructional template for Sama reflexivization*

CONSTRUCTION Sama reflexivization
SYNTAX Template(s): Default PSA: Semantic controller = Actor Linking: Actor = direct core argument
MORPHOLOGY Reflexive: *di* + genitive pronoun (person, number)
SEMANTICS Actor and reflexive pronoun are obligatorily coreferential Subject to Role Hierarchy and LS-Superiority Conditions
PRAGMATICS Illocutionary force: Unspecified Focus structure: Unspecified

Further reading

For further discussion of this approach to case marking, see Silverstein (1976, 1981, 1993), Van Valin (1985, 1991b), Michaelis (1993), Holisky (1987), Schwartz (1986), Park (1995) and Roberts (1995); for rather different approaches to case marking, see Andrews (1982), Bittner and Hale (1996), Chomsky (1986a), Czepluch and Janßen (1984), Sag, Karttunen and Goldberg (1992), Yip, Maling and Jackendoff (1987), and Zaenen, Maling and Thráinsson (1985). For a comprehensive discussion of ergativity, see Dixon (1994). On split-S and fluid-S languages, see Merlan (1985), Mithun (1991), Dixon (1994) and Klimov (1977). For discussion of the syntax of inverse languages, see Dahlstrom (1986) on Plains Cree and Dryer (1996b) on Kutenai. On preposition assignment in English, see Jolly (1991, 1993) and Rudanko (1996). For typologies of reflexives, see Faltz (1985) and Geniusiene (1987). On Romance pronominal clitics, see Grimshaw (1982), Manzini (1986) and other papers in Borer (1986), Centineo (1996). For other approaches to reflexivization, see Chomsky (1981b), (1986a), Dalrymple (1993), Hellan (1988), Pollard and Sag (1992), Reinhart and Reuland (1993). For discussion of the semantic and pragmatic factors affecting reflexivization, see Kuno (1987). For discussion of applicative constructions in Bantu languages in terms of RRG, see Van Valin (1993b) and Roberts (1995); for other approaches, see Baker (1988), Bresnan and Moshi (1990), Marantz (1984). For discussion of focus structure and linearization, see Sgall, Hajičová and Panevová (1986), Hajičova and Sgall (1987), Downing and Noonan (1995), King (1995), Payne (1990), Reis (1993), Siewierska (1993). For a neurolinguistic model of language processing based on the linking system presented in this chapter, see Kemmerer (1996).

Exercises

1 Diagram the linking between the semantic representation and the syntactic representation for each of the following sentences. Start from the semantic representation and summarize each step of the process explicitly, following the linking algorithm in (7.12). For the syntactic structures, use only the constituent projection of the sentences; ignore the operator projection. **[section 7.2.2]**

(1) Leslie put the book on the table.
(2) Where did Marsha see Kevin?
(3) He showed his mother the picture.
(4) Who was injured by the bomb?

2 Diagram the linking between the syntactic representation and the semantic representation of each of the following sentences. Start from the syntactic structure and summarize each step of the process explicitly, following the linking algorithm in (7.36). For the syntactic structures, use only the constituent projection of the sentences; ignore the operator projection. **[section 7.2.3]**

(1) The pasta was eaten by Luigi.
(2) Celia wrote the letter in the library.
(3) What did Robin give to Kim?
(4) Pat taught Kelly Navajo.

3 Explain the ungrammaticality of (1) and (2). Why is (3b) not a possible logical structure for (a)? State which aspect of the linking algorithm is violated, and illustrate your answer with a diagram showing the linking. [**section 7.2.3**]

(1) *What did Juan put the bicycle in the garage?
(2) *The dog died the book.
(3) a. *Sally put the photograph.
  b. [**do′** (Sally, ∅)] CAUSE [BECOME **be-in′** (box, photograph)]

4 Diagram the linking between the semantic representation and the syntactic representation for each of the following sentences. Start from the semantic representation or syntactic representation, as specified, and summarize each step of the process explicitly, following the linking algorithms in (7.12) and (7.36). For the syntactic structures, use only the constituent projection of the sentences; ignore the operator projection. For the semantics to syntax linking, give an account of case marking and agreement/cross-reference. [**section 7.3.1.2**]

(1) *Jakaltek* (Craig 1977) [both semantics → syntax and syntax → semantics]
Mac x-∅-(y)-il naj winaj?
who PST-3ABS-3ERG-see CL man
'Who did the man see?'

(2) *Georgian* (Aronson 1991) [syntax → semantics only; treat the markers on the verb as agreement and Georgian as dependent marking]
P'ropesor-i st'udent'-s c'ign-s
professor-NOM student-DAT book-DAT
ga-∅-∅-u-gzavn-i-s.
PVB-3sgU-3sgDCA-PRV-send-FUT-3sgA
'The professor will send the a book to the student.'

(3) *Icelandic* [both semantics → syntax and syntax → semantics]
Þeim va-r hjálp-að af mér.
3plDAT be.PAST-3sg help-PSTP by 1sgDAT
'They were helped by me.'

5 Formulate a partial syntax → semantics linking algorithm for Plains Cree, based on the examples in (7.70)–(7.73). Give only those steps that would apply to these examples. If steps of a new type are needed, justify and explain them. How does the linking algorithm for this language differ from those for the other languages discussed in the text? [**section 7.3.1.3**]

6 Consider the Dyirbal comitative construction in (7.33), from Dixon (1972); is it a lexical or a syntactic phenomenon? Consider also the *-ŋay* antipassive construction discussed in chapter 6; an example is repeated in (1b) below. Given the interaction between these two constructions, illustrated in (2c), is the *-ŋay* antipassive a lexical

or a syntactic phenomenon? Give a brief, informal description of the semantics to syntax linking in (2c). Note: *-nay* in (2b, c) is an allomorph of *-ŋay*. Example (2c), despite the translation, is a single clause with a single verb in Dyirbal. [**section 7.4.2**]

(1) a. Ba-yi yaɽa-∅ ba-ŋgu-n d̪ugumbi-ɽu buɽa-n.
DEIC-ABS.I man-ABS DEIC-ERG-II woman-ERG see-TNS
'The woman saw the man.'
b. Ba-la-n d̪ugumbil-∅ ba-gu-l yaɽa-gu buɽal-ŋa-ɲu.
DEIC-ABS-II woman-ABS DEIC-DAT-I man-DAT see-ANTI-TNS
'The woman saw the man.'

(2) a. Ba-la-m d̪ubula-∅ ba-ŋgu-n d̪ugumbi-ɽu ɲuga-ɲu.
DEIC-ABS-III flour-ABS DEIC-ERG-II woman-ERG grind-TNS
'The woman is grinding wild flour.'
b. Ba-la-n d̪ugumbil-∅ ŋuga-na-ŋu ba-gu-m d̪ubula-gu.
DEIC-ABS-II woman-ABS grind-ANTI-TNS DEIC-DAT-III flour-DAT
'The woman is grinding wild flour.'
c. ba-yi ɲalŋga-∅ ba-ŋgu-n d̪ugumbi-ɽu ɲuga-nay-mba-n
DEIC-ABS.I boy-ABS DEIC-ERG-II woman-ERG grind-ANTI-COM-TNS
ba-gu-m d̪ubula-gu.
DEIC-DAT-III flour-DAT
'The woman is grinding wild flour with a boy [sitting next to her].'

7 Explain the ungrammaticality of the following sentences. [**section 7.5.2**]

(1) *Tanisha$_i$'s brother helped herself$_i$.
(2) *Herself$_i$ frightened Sally$_i$.
(3) *Sam asked herself$_i$ about Wendy$_i$.
(4) *Bill showed the picture of Karen$_i$ to herself$_i$.

8 Explain the constraints on reflexivization in Toba Batak; the data are from Shugamoto (1984). Build on the analysis of Toba Batak you did in exercise 2 in chapter 6. [**section 7.5.2**]

(1) a. Mang-ida diri-na si Torus.
ATV-see self-3sgGEN
'Torus sees himself.'
b. *Di-ida diri-na si Torus.
PASS-see self-3sgGEN
*'Himself sees Torus.'
c. Di-ida si Torus diri-na.
PASS-see self-3sgGEN
'Torus sees himself.'
d. *Mang-ida si Torus diri-na.
*'Himself sees Torus.'

(2) a. Mang-hatahon diri-na$_{i/*j}$ si Torus$_i$ tu si Ria$_j$.
ATV-talk.about self-3 to
'Torus$_i$ is talking about himself$_{i/*j}$ to Ria$_j$.'
b. Mang-hatahon diri-na$_{i/*j}$ tu si Ria$_j$ si Torus$_i$.
'Torus$_i$ is talking about himself$_{i/*j}$ to Ria$_j$.'
c. Di-hatahon si Torus$_i$ diri-na$_{i/*j}$ tu si Ria$_j$.
PASS-talk.about self-3 to
'Torus$_i$ talked about himself$_{i/*j}$ to Ria$_j$.'
d. Di-hatahon si Torus$_i$ tu si Ria$_j$ diri-na$_{i/*j}$.
'Torus$_i$ talked about himself$_{i/*j}$ to Ria$_j$.'

(3) a. Mang-hatahon si Ria$_j$ si Torus$_i$ tu diri-na$_{i/j}$.
ATV-talk.about to self-3
'Torus$_i$ talked about Ria$_j$ to himself$_{i/j}$.'
b. Mang-hatahon si Ria$_j$ tu diri-na$_{i/j}$ si Torus$_i$.
'Torus$_i$ talked about Ria$_j$ to himself$_{i/j}$.'
c. Di-hatahon si Torus$_i$ si Ria$_j$ tu diri-na$_{i/j}$.
PASS-talk.about to self-3
'Torus$_i$ talked about Ria$_j$ to himself$_{i/j}$.'
d. Di-hatahon si Torus$_i$ tu diri-na$_{i/j}$ si Ria$_j$.
'Torus$_i$ talked about Ria$_j$ to himself$_{i/j}$.'

8

Syntactic structure, II: complex sentences and noun phrases

8.0 Introduction

We now turn to the issue of the syntactic structure of complex sentences and complex NPs. The last six chapters have laid out the essential syntactic, semantic and pragmatic features of simple sentences, and in this chapter and the next we will investigate these aspects of complex sentences, starting with the layered structure of the clause in complex sentences.

8.1 Theoretical issues

There are two fundamental questions that every theory must answer about complex sentences; they are given in (8.1).

(8.1) a. What are the units involved in complex sentence constructions?
b. What are the relationships among the units in the constructions?

A great deal of controversy has surrounded the question of units in contemporary syntactic theory. In GB, all units in complex sentences contain a subject–predicate structure; the theory does not recognize any subclausal units in complex constructions.[1] In GPSG, HPSG, ConG and LFG, on the other hand, both clausal and subclausal (VP) units are posited in complex sentences. In our approach, the answer to (8.1a) is derived from the layered structure of the clause: the fundamental building blocks of complex sentences are the nucleus, core and clause. The traditional answer to (8.1b), the question about the structural relationships among units in a complex sentence, is summarized as follows:

> Complex sentences are divided into: (a) those in which the constituent clauses are grammatically **co-ordinate**, no one being dependent on the others, but all being . . . added together in sequence, with or without the so-called coordinating conjunctions . . . (*John talked to Mary, and they went to the store, and* . . .); and (b) those in which one of the clauses ('the main clause') is 'modified' by one or more **subordinate** clauses grammatically dependent upon it and generally introduced . . . by a subordinating conjunction. Subordinate clauses are subdivided by function as nominal, adjectival, adverbial, etc.; and further as temporal, conditional, relative, etc. (Lyons 1968: 178, emphasis in original)

The various types of subordinate clauses include sentential 'subjects' and 'objects', e.g. ***That it is raining*** *comes as no surprise* (clause as 'subject') and *Max regretted* ***that he had insulted Susan*** (clause as 'object'), and clauses used as sentential modifiers, e.g. *Sally talked to Bill* ***after she got home from work***. The theory of the units will henceforth be referred to as the theory of **juncture** and the theory of relations as the theory of **nexus**, following RRG. We will discuss each of these in the following sections, beginning with a discussion of juncture.

8.2 Levels of juncture

All theories agree that the clause is a possible unit in complex sentence formation. Where they differ, however, is in how to characterize the subclausal units. As stated above, we take the units in complex constructions to be those of the layered structure of the clause: nucleus, core and clause. In complex constructions, the following patterns emerge.

(8.2) a. [$_{\text{CORE}}$ ... [$_{\text{NUC}}$ PRED] ... + ... [$_{\text{NUC}}$ PRED] ...] Nuclear juncture
b. [$_{\text{CLAUSE}}$ ... [$_{\text{CORE}}$ ...] ... + ... [$_{\text{CORE}}$ ...] ...] Core juncture
c. [$_{\text{SENTENCE}}$ ... [$_{\text{CLAUSE}}$ ...] ... + ... [$_{\text{CLAUSE}}$ ...] ...] Clausal juncture

The unmarked linkage paradigm is for units of the same level to combine, i.e. nucleus with nucleus, core with core, and clause with clause. There is one striking instance of a marked, asymmetric linkage, clause with core, that we will discuss below.

Nuclear junctures involve a single core containing multiple nuclei; this is illustrated with examples from French, English and Mandarin in (8.3).

(8.3) a. Je fer-ai mang-er les gâteaux à Jean.[2]
1sg make-3sgFUT eat-INT the.Mpl cakes DAT John
'I will make John eat the cakes.'
b. John forced open the door.
b′. John forced the door open.
c. Tā qiāo pò le yī ge fànwǎn.
3sg hit break PRFV one CL bowl
'He broke (by hitting) a ricebowl.'

It has long been noted that the two French verbs in (8.3a), *faire* 'make, cause' and *manger* 'eat', are distinct nuclei which nevertheless act as a single complex predicate in this construction. Only certain adverbs may occur between the two verbs, e.g. *souvent* 'often' as in *Pierre fera souvent courir Marie* 'Pierre will make Marie run often.' In the English example, the two distinct predicates, *force* and *open*, each of which constitutes a distinct nucleus, may occur adjacent to each other, as in (b), or separated from each other by a core argument, the NP *the door*, as in (b′). Here too the two nuclei function as a single complex predicate. Mandarin offers the strictest case: nothing may intervene between the two verbs. As we saw in chapter 3, the semantic representation of these constructions parallels that of single clauses with a single lexical causative verb; they are repeated in (8.4).

(8.4) a. Bill pushed open the door.
a′. [**do′** (Bill, [**push′** (Bill, door)])] CAUSE [BECOME **open′** (door)]
b. Pierre fera courir Marie.
b′. [**do′** (Pierre, ∅)] CAUSE [**do′** (Marie, [**run′** (Marie)])]
c. Tā qiāo pò le yī ge fànwǎn.
c′. [**do′** (3sg, [**hit′** (3sg, fànwǎn)])] CAUSE [BECOME **broken′** (fànwǎn)]
d. Sally broke the vase.
d′. [**do′** (Sally, ∅)] CAUSE [BECOME **broken′** (vase)]

The constituent projections for the sentences in (8.3) are given in figure 8.1. In both cases, the two nuclei make up a complex nucleus which takes a single set of

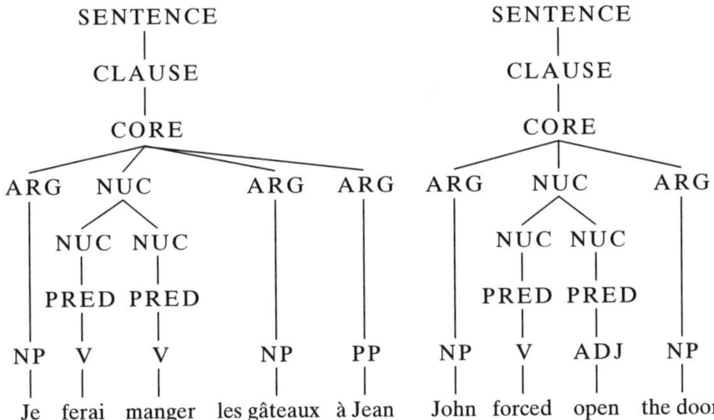

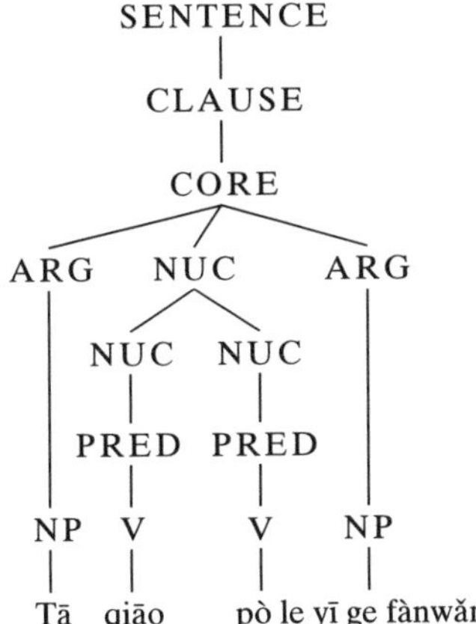

Figure 8.1 Nuclear junctures in French, English and Mandarin

arguments in the core. As we will see in section 8.4.1, this is only one of three possible patterns in nuclear junctures.

The abstract schema for **core junctures** is given in (8.2b). Here we have a single clause made up of multiple cores, and each core may itself be internally complex, i.e. may contain a nuclear juncture. Examples of core junctures from French, English and Mandarin are in (8.5).

(8.5) a. Je laisser-ai Jean mang-er les gâteaux.
1sg let-1sgFUT John eat-INF the.Mpl cakes
'I will let John eat the cakes.'
b. I ordered Fred to force the door open.
c. John forced the door to open.
d. Tā jiāo wǒ xǐe zì.
3sg teach 1sg write characters
'She teaches me to write characters.'

Each of the sentences is made up of two cores, each with its own nucleus: in (a) *Je laisserai Jean* and *Jean manger les gâteaux*, in (b) *I ordered Fred* and *Fred force the door open*, *John forced the door* and *the door open* in (c) and in (d) *Tā jiāo wǒ* and *wǒ xǐe zì*. In this type of core juncture, there is a core argument which is semantically an argument of the nucleus in each core (*Jean* in (a), *Fred* in (b), *door* in (c) and *wǒ* in (d)), and it occurs only once in the core carrying the clausal operators; this is the matrix core of the construction. The structures for these examples are given in figure 8.2. Note that the second core in the English sentence is itself complex, as it contains a nuclear juncture of the type discussed above. There are clear structural differences between the nuclear and core junctures in figures 8.1 and 8.2. In French, *Jean* occurs between the two verbs in the core juncture, something that would be impossible in a nuclear juncture. Furthermore, if the object is realized as a clitic pronoun, it occurs before the whole complex nucleus in a nuclear juncture, as in (8.6a), but it occurs cliticized to the nucleus of its core in a core juncture, as in (8.6b).

(8.6) a. Je les fer-ai mang-er à Jean.
1sg 3plACC make-1sgFUT eat-INF DAT John
'I will make John eat them.'
a′. *Je ferai les manger à Jean.
b. Je laisser-ai Jean les mang-er.
1sg let-1sgFUT John 3plACC eat-INF
'I will let John eat them.'
b′. *Je les laisserai Jean manger.

The structural differences between English core and nuclear junctures are reflected in several ways. First, core junctures may require a complementizer, in this

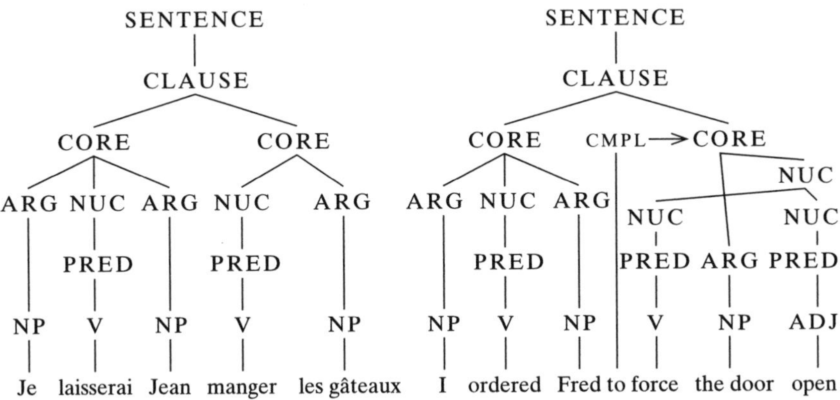

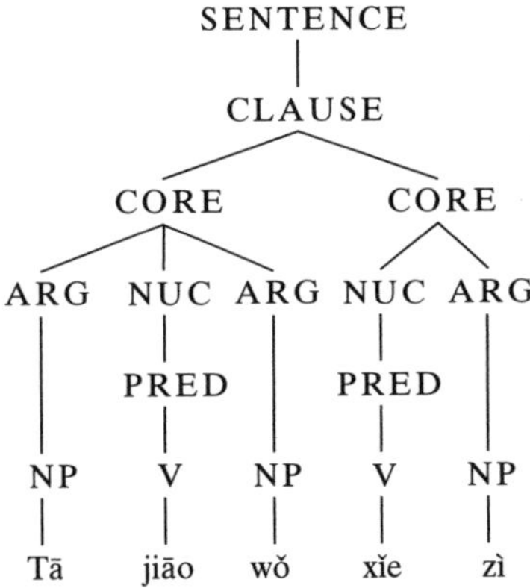

Figure 8.2 Core junctures in French, English and Mandarin

case *to* (see section 8.4.2), whereas nuclear junctures do not permit one. This can be seen most clearly when the second nucleus is a verb, as in (8.7).

(8.7) a. Mary persuaded Sally to leave.
a′. *Mary persuaded Sally leave.
b. Mary made Sally leave.
b′. *Mary made Sally to leave.

Second, the two nuclei may be adjacent in some nuclear junctures, e.g. (8.3b) or *Mary pushed open the window*, whereas this is impossible with a core juncture, as (8.8) shows.

(8.8) a. *John forced to open the door. (< John forced the door to open)
b. *Sam persuaded to leave Sally. (< Sam persuaded Sally to leave)

It should be noted that not all combinations in nuclear junctures permit this variable ordering, as the following examples illustrate. This variation is only possible when the second nucleus contains a state predicate, which may be adjectival or prepositional, and even when that condition is met, it is highly constrained. One factor is the 'heaviness of the NP': the heavier the NP, the more acceptable the examples with adjacent nuclei become.

(8.9) a. Bill pushed the door open. ~ Bill pushed open the door.
b. Bill pushed the door closed. ~ *Bill pushed closed the door.
b′. Bill pushed closed the heavy door that had just been repainted after the storm.
c. Bobby pushed the table over. ~ Bobby pushed over the table.
d. Kevin pushed the chair into the room. ~ *Kevin pushed into the room the chair.
d′. Kevin pushed into the room the old, overstuffed chair that his grandmother had left him.
e. Yvonne painted the table white. ~ *Yvonne painted white the table.

English nuclear junctures are much more limited than those in French or Mandarin. In particular, nuclear junctures are only possible in English if the predicate in the second nucleus is intransitive, i.e. is a verb, adjective or preposition taking a single argument. When the second nucleus contains a transitive verb, as in e.g. *Fred made Bill open the door*, the result is a core juncture. Evidence for this comes from reflexivization. In section 7.5.2 we saw that in English the antecedent and the reflexive pronoun must be syntactic co-arguments in a simple clause, i.e. a clause with a single core in it. Since there is only a single core in a nuclear juncture, the controller and the reflexive would be syntactic co-arguments within a single core, whereas in a core juncture, if they were in different cores, they would not be syntactic co-arguments and reflexivization would be impossible. When we contrast a clear case of a nuclear juncture with a clear case of a core juncture, this can be readily seen.

(8.10) a. $Sally_i$ made $herself_i$ sad.
b. $Fred_i$ told $himself_i$ to ask Pam out.
c. *$Fred_i$ asked Pam to help $himself_i$.
c′. $Fred_i$ asked Pam to help him_i.
d. *$Fred_i$ made Pam help $himself_i$.
d′. $Fred_i$ made Pam help him_i.

Example (8.10a) is a nuclear juncture, and as such, the two NPs are in the same core; hence the actor *Sally* can be the antecedent of the reflexive pronoun *herself*. The constructions in (8.10b, c) are core junctures, and if the actor of the first core is the antecedent, then the reflexive pronoun must be in the same core (see figure 8.2), which it is in (b) but not in (c), as the contrast between (c) and (c′) shows. When we

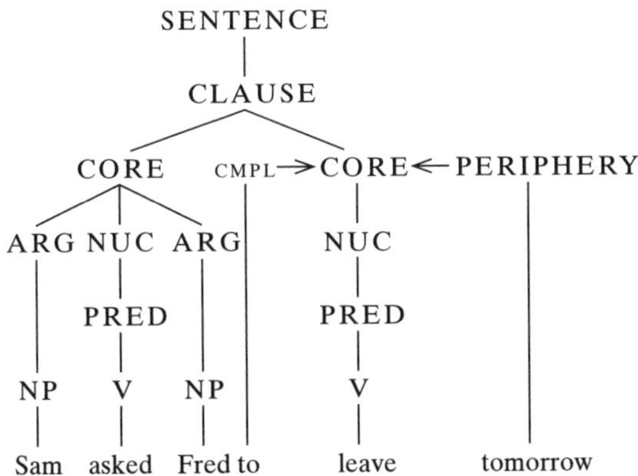

Figure 8.3 English core juncture with temporal adverb

create a juncture with *make* as the first nucleus and a transitive verb in the second, as in (d), the resulting construction patterns exactly like the core junctures in (c). Hence we must conclude that a juncture with *make* + transitive verb is a core juncture, not a nuclear juncture.

A somewhat surprising property of core junctures is that the dependent core can be modified by a temporal adverb independent of the matrix core. This was first mentioned in section 4.4.1.2. This is surprising, on the assumption that since tense is a clausal operator, temporal adverbs ought to be clausal modifiers as well. The following examples illustrate this from English and Turkish (Watters 1993).

(8.11) a. Sam asked Fred to leave tomorrow.
b. Akşam-lar-ı televizyon seyret-mek ist-iyor-um.
evening-pl-DAT television watch-INF want-PROG-1sg
'I want to watch television in the evenings.'

Tomorrow in (a) has to modify *leave* only; it is incompatible with the past tense of *ask*. Similarly, *akşamları* 'in the evenings' expresses when the speaker watches television, not the time of his desire. These are not a problem for the layered structure of the clause as we have developed it, for recall that peripheral adverbs such as these are modifiers of the core, not the clause, and therefore should be possible in this construction. The structure of (8.11a) is given in figure 8.3.

The schema in (8.2c) is for clausal junctures. The sentence in (8.12) contains all three juncture types.

(8.12) Mary called Fred yesterday, and she asked him to paint her room white.

The whole sentence is a clausal juncture, a single sentence made up of two clauses, *Mary called Fred yesterday* and *she asked him to paint her room white*. The second clause contains a core juncture, *she asked him to paint her room white*, and the

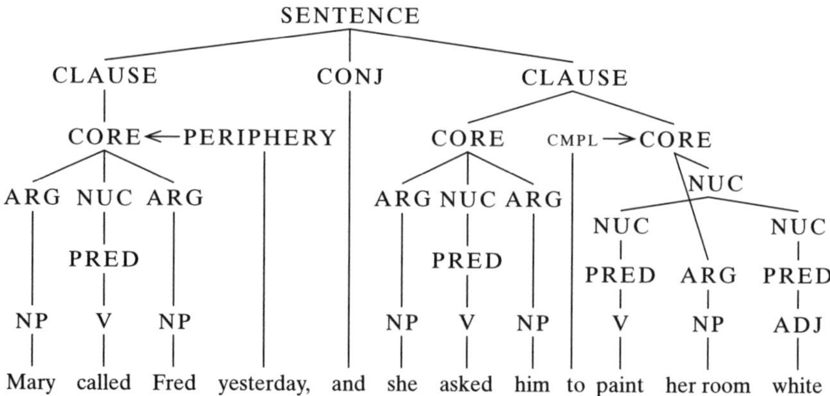

Figure 8.4 English sentence containing clausal, core and nuclear junctures

second core in the second clause contains a nuclear juncture, *paint her room white*. The structure of this sentence is given in figure 8.4.

To recap the juncture types, nuclear junctures are single cores containing more than one nucleus, and the multiple nuclei function as a single complex predicate taking a single set of core arguments. In a core juncture, on the other hand, there is a single clause containing more than one core. Each core may have its own core argument(s) not shared with the other core(s). In a clausal juncture, whole clauses are joined, and each clause may be fully independent of the others. These characterizations will require some refinement after we introduce the notion of nexus in the next section.

8.3 Nexus relations

The traditional contrast between subordination and coordination seems to be very clear cut for languages like English and its Indo-European brethren, but when one looks farther afield, constructions appear which do not lend themselves to this neat division. Papuan languages from Papua New Guinea, such as Chuave (Thurman 1975) and Fore (Scott 1978), present constructions which seem to have aspects of both nexus types. The examples in (8.13) are from Chuave, and those in (8.14) are from Fore.

(8.13) a. Yai kuba i-re kei si-re fu-m-e. — Chuave
man stick get-SEQ.SP dog hit-SEQ.SP go-3sg-INDIC
'The man got a stick, hit the dog, and went away.'

b. Yai kuba i-re kei su-n-goro fu-m-e.
man stick get-SEQ.SP dog hit-SEQ.DfP go-3sg-INDIC
'The man got a stick, hit the dog, and it went away.'

(8.14) a. Kanamagina agamagina máe'táye. Fore
kana-ma-ki-na a-ka-ma-ki-na máe-' tá-y-e
come-SEQ.SP-CONJ-3sg 3sg-see-SEQ.SP-CONJ get-PST-3sg-INDIC
'He came and saw it and got [it].'

b. Kanauwá:gana namogá
kana-uwá:-ki-na na-mu-ó-ki-á
come-1sgPST.DfP-CONJ-3sg 1sg-give-3sgPST.DfP-CONJ-1sg
máe'túwe.
máe-'tá-u-e
get-PST-1sg-INDIC
'I came, and he gave [it] to me, and I took [it].'

The Chuave construction in (8.13a) translates as *The man got a stick, hit the dog, and went away*, which looks like an ordinary English coordinate construction. But it is not an ordinary coordinate construction, because the first two clauses could not stand on their own as independent clauses. In a coordinate structure, every one of the clauses in it can stand on its own, outside of the chain. In a subordinate construction, on the other hand, this is not the case: *that he insulted Susan* and *after she got home from work* are not independent units and therefore cannot count as complete utterances. The same is true in (8.14a) from Fore; it looks like a coordinate construction, yet the non-final pieces in the chain do not have independent existence, as they cannot stand as independent utterances. In both languages the non-final clauses lack the expression of a crucial and obligatory grammatical category (in this case illocutionary force: the *-e* suffix on the final verbs labeled 'indicative'). Every independent utterance in Chuave and Fore ends with an illocutionary force morpheme; they cannot be an independent utterance without it. The first two clauses in the Chuave example lack this morpheme and also agreement with their privileged syntactic argument; agreement appears only on the final verb. So we have a construction which looks like a simple chain of clauses, yet there is a dependency relationship between the non-final units and the final unit.

It might be suggested that these are subordinate constructions, because of the dependency, but these languages have a subordinate clause construction which is distinct from this construction. In (8.15a) a true subordinate clause in Chuave is contrasted with the construction we have been discussing in (b).

(8.15) a. Yai kei su-n-g-a fu-m-e. Chuave
man dog hit-3sg-DEP-SEQ go-3sg-INDIC
'After the man hit the dog, he went away.'

b. Yai kei si-re fu-m-e.
man dog hit-SEQ.SP go-3sg-INDIC
'The man hit the dog and went away.'

In (8.15a) the clause meaning 'the man hit the dog' occurs with the special subordination suffix *-g-* and verb agreement. The result is a structurally different construction than the one in (b). Yet in both cases there are dependencies, and in both cases the units could not stand alone. It is possible to set up minimal triples of constructions in some languages, e.g. Kewa (Franklin 1971) in (8.16).

(8.16) a. Nipú ípu-la pare ní paalá na-pía. Kewa
3sg come-3sgPRES but 1sg afraid NEG-be.1sgPRES
'He is coming, but I am not afraid.'
b. (Ní) Épo lá-ri épa-wa.
1sg whistle say-SIM.SP come-1sgPAST
'I whistled while I came,' or 'I came whistling.'
c. (Ní) Épo lá-lo-pulu irikai épa-lia.
1sg whistle say-1sgPRES-CAUSAL dog come-3sgFUT
'Because I am whistling, the dog will come.'

The construction in (a) is a coordinate construction; each clause can be an independent utterance, and they are joined by a conjunction. The one in (c) is a subordinate construction; while the first clause cannot stand alone as an independent utterance, it carries agreement and tense. The construction in (b) fits neither category exactly; the first clause cannot stand on its own but is not marked for agreement and tense as in the subordinate construction. In all three of the languages we have looked at, this intermediate construction has a suffix which indicates whether the pivot of the first clause is the same as the pivot of the following clause; this is called 'switch-reference' marking (glossed 'SP' for 'same pivot' or 'DfP' for 'different pivot'), and was discussed from the point of view of referent tracking in chapter 6.

A further example of this three-way contrast can be found in Amele, another Papuan language (Roberts 1988). Roberts contrasts switch-reference constructions with coordinate and subordinate constructions. The basic Amele switch-reference construction is presented in (8.17).

(8.17) a. Ija hu-m-ig sab j-ig-a. Amele
1sg come-SP-1sg food eat-1sg-TPAST
'I came and ate the food.'
b. Ija ho-co-min sab ja-g-a.
1sg come-DfP-1sg food eat-2sg-TPAST
'I came and you ate the food.'

Like the Chuave, Fore and Kewa switch-reference constructions, the linked clause depends upon the final clause for the expression of an obligatory grammatical category (operator), in this case tense. Despite their coordinate translations, there is evidence against analyzing them as coordinate: unlike coordinate constructions, tense, mood (illocutionary force) and negation can be shared across conjuncts in the switch-reference constructions. This is illustrated in (8.18)–(8.20).

(8.18) a. Ho busale-ce-b dana age qo-ig-a. Tense
pig run.out-DfP-3sg man 3pl kill-3pl-TPAST
'The pig ran out and the men killed it.'

b. Ho busale-ce-b dana age qo-qag-an.
pig run.out-DfP-3sg man 3pl kill-3pl-FUT
'The pig will run out and the men will kill it.'

c. *Ho busale-ce-b-a dana age qo-qag-an.
pig run.out-DfP-3sg-TPAST man 3pl kill-3pl-FUT
'The pig ran out and the men will kill it.'

(8.19) a. Ho busale-ce-b dana age qo-ig-a fo? Mood
pig run.out-DfP-3sg man 3pl kill-3pl-TPAST Q
'Did the pig run out and did the men kill it?'
(*'The pig ran out and did the men kill it?')

b. *Ho busale-ce-b fo dana age qo-ig-a.
pig run.out-DfP-3sg Q man 3pl kill-3pl-TPAST
'Did the pig run out (?) and the men killed it.'

(8.20) a. Ho busale-ce-b dana age qee qo-l-oin. Negation
pig run.out-DfP-3sg man 3pl NEG kill-NEGPAST-3pl
'The pig ran out and the men did not kill it.'

b. Ho qee busale-ce-b dana age qo-l-oin.
pig NEG run.out-DfP-3sg man 3pl kill-NEGPAST-3pl
'The pig didn't run out and the men did not kill it.'

c. *Ho qee busale-ce-b dana age qo-ig-a.
pig NEG run.out-DfP-3sg man 3pl kill-3pl-TPAST
'The pig didn't run out and the men killed it.'

Both of the clauses in (8.18) must have the same tense, as indicated on the last verb in the sentence; the switch-reference marker occurs in the slot where tense would normally occur, and consequently there is no place for the tense marker in the linked verbs. Illocutionary force must also be shared; the interrogative illocutionary force marker *fo* can occur only at the end of the whole sentence and must be interpreted as having scope over the entire sentence, i.e. the whole sentence is interpreted as a question, not just the second clause. The situation with negation is somewhat more complex. If it occurs in the second clause, it can be interpreted as having scope just over that clause; if, on the other hand, it occurs in the initial clause, as in (8.20b), then it must be construed as negating both clauses, not just the first one. It appears that tense and illocutionary force have scope to the left, while negation has scope to the right, and therefore in this construction the scope of the tense and illocutionary force operators must be over everything in the sentence to their left and the scope of the negation operator must be over everything to the right of it.

These operators are not shared in Amele coordinate constructions; each operator is interpreted as modifying just the clause in which it occurs. This is exemplified in (8.21).

(8.21) a. Fred cum ho-i-an qa Bill uqadec h-ugi-an. Tense
yesterday come-3sg-YPAST but tomorrow come-3sg-FUT
'Fred came yesterday, but Bill will come tomorrow.'
b. Ho busale-i-a qa dana age qo-i-ga fo? Mood
pig run.away-3sg-TPAST but man 3pl hit-3pl-TPAST Q
'The pig ran away, but did the men kill it?'
c. Ho qee busale-l qa dana age qo-ig-a. Negation
pig NEG run.away-3sg.NEGPAST but man 3pl hit-3pl-TPAST
'The pig didn't run away, but the men killed it.'
d. Ho busale-i-a qa dana age qee qo-l-oin.
pig run.away-3sg-TPAST but man 3pl NEG hit-NEGPAST-3pl
'The pig ran away, but the men didn't kill it.'

These sentences differ strikingly from those in (8.18)–(8.20), in that the operators have scope only over the clause in which they occur, thus yielding sentences in which each clause differs in tense, illocutionary force or polarity from the other. Roberts also notes that the switch-reference constructions differ from subordinate constructions, in which independent specification of tense and negation is possible in the matrix and subordinate clauses.

Amele has three types of true subordinate clauses: complement clauses with verbs of cognition and saying, relative clauses, and adverbial clauses. The switch-reference constructions cannot be analyzed as complement clauses or relative clauses: they are clearly not relative clauses (they are not nominal modifiers), and they are not arguments, either syntactic or semantic, of the matrix verb; in addition, switch-reference marking is not found on complement or relative clauses. Hence the only possible analysis of them as subordinate is to classify them as adverbial clauses, and Roberts presents a number of arguments against this analysis, two of which will be presented here. First, it is possible for subordinate clauses to be postposed after the matrix clause; this is not possible with switch-reference or coordinate constructions, as the following examples demonstrate. The clauses at issue are italicized.

(8.22) a. *Ija ja hud-ig-a eu nu* uqa sab
1sg fire open-1sg-TPAST that for 3sg food
mane-i-a. Subordination
roast-3sg-TPAST
'Because I lit the fire, she cooked the food.'
b. Uqa sab mane-i-a *ija ja hud-ig-a*
3sg food roast-3sg-TPAST 1sg fire open-1sg-TPAST
eu nu.
that for
'She cooked the food because I lit the fire.'

(8.23) a. *Ija ja hud-ig-a qa* uqa sab mane-i-a. Coordination
1sg fire open-1sg-TPAST but 3sg food roast-3sg-TPAST
'I lit the fire but she cooked the food.'
b. *Uqa sab mane-i-a *ija ja hud-ig-a qa.*
3sg food roast-3sg-TPAST 1sg fire open-1sg-TPAST but

(8.24) *Dana age qo-ig-a *ho busale-ce-b.* Switch-reference
man 3pl hit-3pl-TPAST pig run.away-DfP-3sg (cf. (8.18a))

Thus, switch-reference constructions behave like coordinate constructions, not subordinate constructions, with respect to the possibility of occurring after the matrix clause. Second, a pronoun in an initial adverbial subordinate clause can be coreferential with a full NP in the subsequent matrix clause, but this is impossible in switch-reference and coordinate constructions.

(8.25) a. (Uqa$_i$) ja hud-i$_i$-a eu nu Mary$_i$ sab
(3sg) fire open-3sg-TPAST that for food
mane-i$_i$-a. Subordination
roast-3sg-TPAST
'Because she$_i$ lit the fire, Mary$_i$ cooked the food.'
b. *(Uqa$_i$) ho-i$_i$-a qa Fred$_i$ sab qee
(3sg) come-3sg-TPAST but food NEG
je-l-Ø$_i$. Coordination
eat-NEGPAST-3sg
*'He$_i$ came, but Fred$_i$ didn't eat the food.'
c. *(Uqa$_i$) bil-i-me-i$_i$ Fred$_i$ je-i$_i$-a. Switch-reference
(3sg) sit-PRED-SP-3sg eat-3sg-TPAST
*'He$_i$ sat and Fred$_i$ ate.'

With respect to these syntactic phenomena, Amele switch-reference constructions behave like coordinate constructions; yet with respect to operator scope, they behave quite differently from coordinate constructions. Hence we may conclude that they are neither coordinate nor subordinate and that the traditional dichotomy between subordination and coordination is inadequate as the basis of a universal theory of clause linkage.

How is the nexus type of the switch-reference constructions to be characterized? If we go back to Lyons' description of coordination and subordination in section 8.2, we find that the crucial feature of subordination is the '*modification*' of the main clause by the subordinate clause(s), whereas in coordination the linked clauses are not modifiers but are 'added together in sequence'. Not all subordinate clauses are modifiers; some are arguments, as in the examples of 'subject' and 'object' complements like ***That it is raining*** *comes as no surprise* (clause as 'subject') and *Max regretted* ***that he had insulted Susan*** (clause as 'object'). Looking at the switch-reference constructions, it seems clear that the clauses are 'added together in

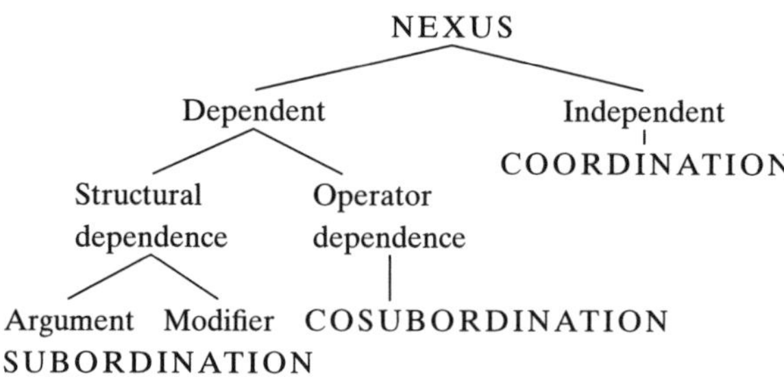

Figure 8.5 Nexus types

sequence' and that the linked clauses are neither modifiers nor arguments of the final clause. Moreover, with respect to the purely syntactic tests in Amele, the switch-reference constructions behave like coordinate, not subordinate, constructions, and therefore we may conclude that they are much more like coordinate than subordinate structures. On the other hand, they share with subordinate structures the important property of being dependent, albeit in a different way; switch-reference constructions exhibit operator dependence, e.g. shared tense and illocutionary force, whereas subordinate constructions are structurally dependent, i.e. they cannot occur independently, even though they may appear to be fully inflected for the obligatory operators. The nexus type of the switch-reference constructions will be called **cosubordination**, following Olson (1981). The three nexus types are summarized in figure 8.5. Subordination subsumes two distinct construction types: units functioning as core arguments (e.g. 'subject' and 'object' complement clauses), on the one hand, and modifiers (e.g. relative clauses, adverbial clauses), on the other.

Thus we will assume three nexus relations, rather than the traditional two, in our discussion of the structure of complex sentences.[3] This, then, is the answer to the second of the two questions in (8.1). With respect to coordination, the term refers to an abstract linkage relation involving a relationship of equivalence and independence at the level of juncture. It is distinct from conjunction, which is a construction type of the general form 'X conj Y', which may be one of the formal instantiations of coordinate or cosubordinate nexus. It is very important not to confuse coordination (an abstract syntactic relation between units in a juncture) with conjunction (a formal construction type).

8.4 The interaction of nexus and juncture

We have seen that there are three levels of juncture (nuclear, core and clausal), and three possible nexus relations among the units in the juncture (coordination, cosubordination, subordination). All three nexus types are possible at all three levels of juncture, and consequently there are nine possible juncture–nexus types in universal grammar. A language need not have all nine, and in fact most do not; for example, English exhibits seven juncture–nexus types, Nootka (Wakashan; North America) has six (Jacobsen 1993), and Korean appears to have all nine (Yang 1994). It is important to keep in mind that these juncture–nexus types are abstract linkage relations, not grammatical construction types; each juncture–nexus type may be realized by more than one grammatical construction type in a language. The juncture–nexus types found in English and some of their formal instantiations are given in (8.26).

(8.26) *English juncture–nexus combinations*

a.	Max made the woman leave. Vince wiped the table clean.	Nuclear cosubordination
b.	Ted tried to open the door. Sam sat playing the guitar.	Core cosubordination
c.	David regretted Amy's losing the race. That Amy lost the race shocked everyone.	Core subordination
d.	Louisa told Bob to close the window. Fred saw Harry leave the room.	Core coordination
e.	Harry ran down the hall laughing loudly. Paul drove to the store and bought some beer.	Clausal cosubordination
f.	John persuaded Leon that Amy had lost. Bill went to the party after he talked to Mary.	Clausal subordination
g.	Anna read for a few minutes, and then she went out.	Clausal coordination

These distinctions will be justified in the following section.

8.4.1 Operators in complex sentences

The distinguishing feature of cosubordination is operator dependence, i.e. obligatory sharing of operators across the units in the juncture. That is, the non-matrix unit(s) must be dependent upon the matrix unit for the expression of at least one operator *at the level of juncture*. What is crucial is that the sharing is *obligatory in the construction*. It is not enough that the operators happen to be the same or that they could be the same; rather, the construction must *require* that they be the same. In a nuclear juncture, the relevant operators are (nuclear) directionals, (nuclear) negation and aspect; in a core juncture, they are modality, (core) directionals, internal negation; and in a clausal juncture, they are any of the clausal operators, most often tense and illocutionary force. All operators above the level of juncture are shared equally by all units, e.g. in a core juncture all cores are equally within the scope of the clausal tense and illocutionary force operators. All operators below the level of juncture are free, subject to their compatibility with the semantics of the predicate; for example, if the nucleus in one of the cores in a core juncture contained a stative verb, it would not be able to take progressive aspect, a nuclear operator, not

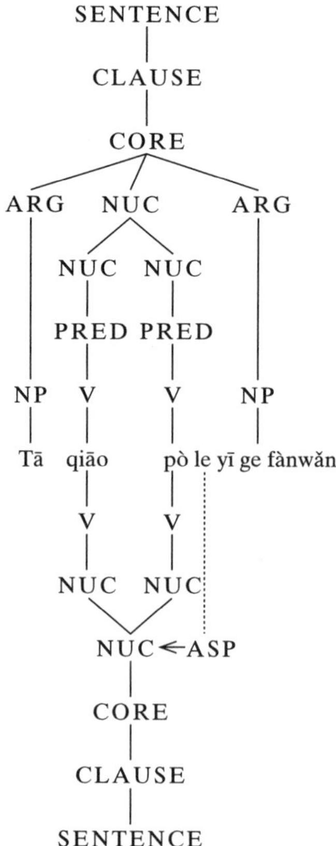

Figure 8.6 Operator sharing in Mandarin nuclear juncture

because of the restrictions imposed by the juncture–nexus type but because of the incompatibility of progressive aspect with stative verbs. We can illustrate this with the contrast between nuclear and core junctures in Mandarin. In (8.3c), repeated below in (8.27a), the postverbal perfective aspect marker *le* occurs after both verbs and has scope over both. It cannot occur between them, as shown in (b), and the two verbs cannot have distinct aspect operators, as (c) shows. The full representation of (8.27a) with operator and constituent projections is given in figure 8.6.

(8.27) a. Tā qiāo pò le yī ge fànwǎn.
3sg hit break PRFV one CL bowl
'He broke (by hitting) a ricebowl.'
b. *Tā qiāo le pò yī ge fànwǎn.
c. *Tā zhèngzài qiāo pò le yī ge fànwǎn.
3sg PROG hit break PRFV one CL bowl
'*He is hitting broke a ricebowl.'

Note that the operator and constituent projections mirror each other in the essential respects, especially the structure of the complex nucleus.

In a core juncture like (8.5d), repeated below, it is possible for there to be distinct aspect operators in each core, as in (8.28b), from Hansell (1993). It is also possible in some core junctures for there to be distinct modality operators, as in (8.28c) (also from Hansell 1993), but not in all, as in (8.28d′).

(8.28) a. Tā jiāo wǒ xǐe zì.
3sg teach 1sg write characters
'She teaches me to write characters.'
b. Wǒ zhèngzài zébèi tā méi bāngzhù nǐ.
1sg PROG reproach 3sg NEG.PERF help 2sg
'I am reproaching him for not having helped you.'
c. Lǐngdǎo kěyǐ mìnglìng nǐ bù kěyǐ chū-qù.
leader can/may order 2sg NEG can/may out-go
'The leader can order you to not be permitted to go out.'
d. Wǒ kěyǐ qù mǎi shū.
1sg can/may go buy book(s)
'I can go buy books.'
d′. *Wǒ kěyǐ qù néng mǎi shū.
1sg can/may go able buy book(s)
'I can go be able/permitted to buy books.'

These examples illustrate the importance of obligatorily shared operators at the level of juncture. In the nuclear juncture examples in (8.27), the obligatory scope of a single aspect operator defines the nexus type as cosubordination, but in core junctures like those in (8.28), aspect is irrelevant to determining the nexus type. Here modality is crucial, and the fact that the construction in (c) can have independent modality operators leads to the conclusion that it is core coordination, while the impossibility of independent modality operators in (d, d′) shows that this construction is core cosubordination.

Operator dependence is not significant for subordination; indeed, it is possible for the subordinate unit to be inflected for at least the operators at the relevant level of juncture. The one exception to this is that subordinate clauses may not have independent illocutionary force operators (see section 2.5). Subordinate clauses are either outside the domain of the illocutionary force operator of the clause, i.e. are presupposed, or have the same force as the main clause (see chapter 5). Hence operators play a crucial role in the analysis of complex sentences in this framework.

Operators in nuclear junctures are illustrated with the following pair of sentences from Barai (Olson 1981).

(8.29) a. Fu kai fu-one kume-fie va.
3sg friend 3sg-GEN call-listen continue
'He continued calling and listening for his friend.'

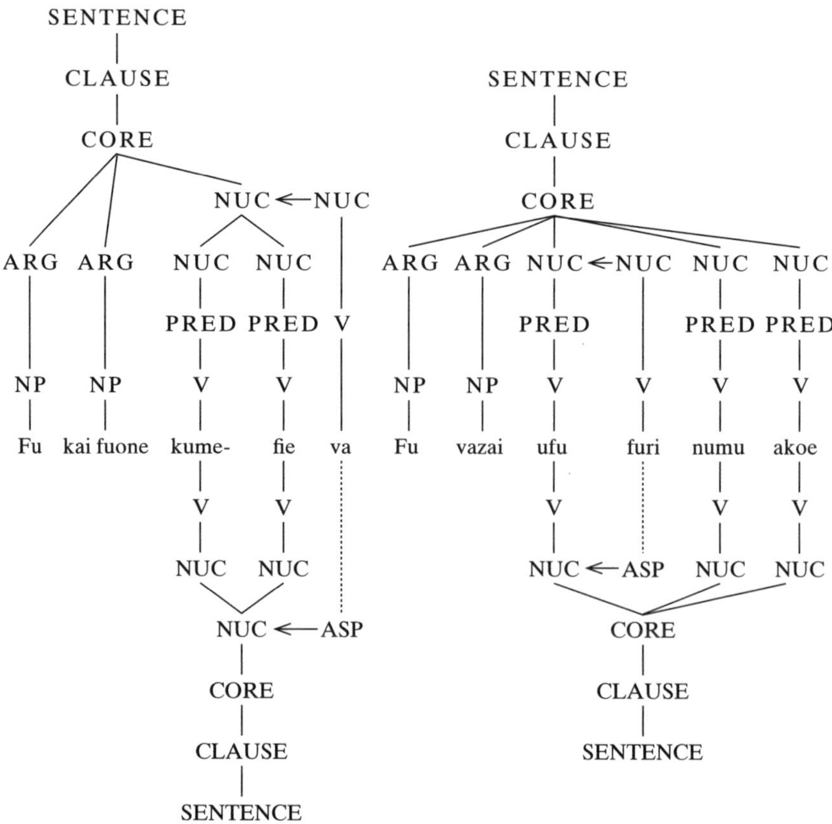

Figure 8.7 Barai nuclear junctures

b. Fu vazai ufu furi numu akoe.
3sg grass cut finish pile throw.away
'He finished cutting, piled and threw away the grass.'

In (a) both verbs, *kume* 'call' and *fie* 'listen', are in the scope of the progressive aspect marker, the verb *va* 'continue', and therefore both nuclei are under the scope of a single nuclear operator. In (b), on the other hand, *furi* 'finish', the perfective aspect marker, modifies only *ufu* 'cut' and not *numu* 'pile' and *akoe* 'throw away'; the aspect operator has scope only over one of the nuclei in the juncture but not all of them. Hence (a) is an example of nuclear cosubordination and (b) one of nuclear coordination. The structure of these sentences is presented in figure 8.7. All three nexus types at the nuclear level are illustrated in these two representations. The aspect operator *va* in (8.29a) has scope over both nuclei, and this is clearly indicated in the operator projection. In contrast, in (8.29b) the aspect operator *furi* modifies only *ufu* 'cut', with the other two nuclei being outside its scope; this too is signaled clearly in the operator projection. The use of verbs as aspect operators in serial verb constructions like these is the prime exemplar of nuclear subordination. The subordinate nuclei in these sentences are represented as a NUC node which dominates a verb which is not a predicate (hence no PRED label) but rather is a modifier. It is not a predicate because it does not contribute any arguments to the core; in other words, it is not part of the logical structure of the verb (predicate) of the nucleus in the core.[4] Because it functions as an aspectual modifier, it is also represented as an operator in the operator projection, just like other aspectual operators. This is the only juncture–nexus type in which a verb is represented as a constituent in one projection and as an operator in the other.

The contrast in operator projections in the two non-subordinate nexus types in core junctures is illustrated in the English examples in (8.30) and figure 8.8.

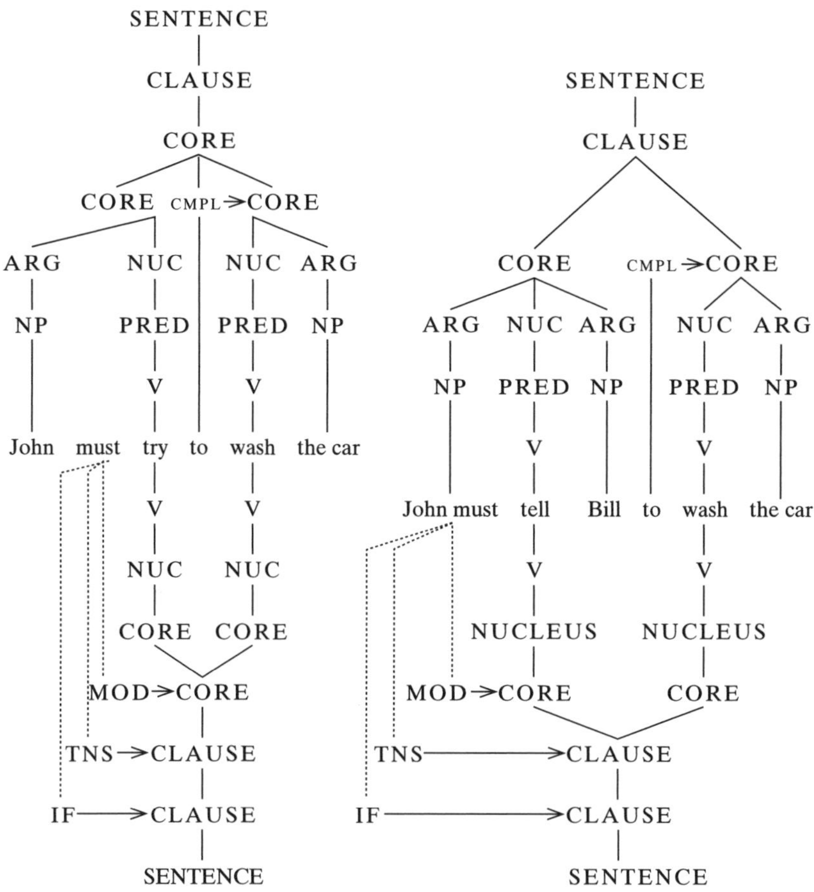

Figure 8.8 English core junctures

(8.30) a. John must try to wash the car.
b. John must tell Bill to wash the car.
c. John can promise Bill to wash the car.

In (8.30a), the deontic modal *must*, a core operator, has scope over both cores; what *John* is obliged to do is *try to wash the car*, not just *try*. In the (b) sentence, in contrast, *must* has scope only within the first core; *John* is obliged to *tell Bill*, but *Bill* is not obliged *to wash the car*. Hence (8.30a) is core cosubordination, (8.30b) coordination, because in (a) there is a shared core-level operator, modality, while in (b) there is no shared core-level operator. Again, the contrast is represented in both projections by the fact that the two cores in (8.30a) are dominated by a core node. In English, constructions with verbs like *want*, *try*, etc. have the privileged syntactic argument of the matrix verb being the controller of the missing argument, i.e. the pivot, in the linked core. With verbs like *tell*, *persuade* and *force*, on the other hand, the privileged syntactic argument of the matrix core is not the controller of the pivot in the linked core, when the verb in the matrix core is active voice. In English, constructions with *want*, *try*, etc. are always cosubordinate, whereas constructions with verbs like *tell*, *persuade*, *force*, etc. are always coordinate. This follows from the fact that a deontic modal operator can modify the relationship between one actor and a sequence of cores denoting actions by the same participant, whereas it cannot modify relationships between the actor and verb in distinct cores referring to actions by distinct participants, as the interpretation of the examples in figure 8.8 shows. Example (8.30c) presents a somewhat different situation. The actor of *promise* is also the controller of the missing pivot in the infinitival core,[5] and yet the ability expressed by deontic *can* seems to modify only the relationship between *John* and *promise* and not between *John* and *wash the car*; that is, (8.30c) asserts that John is able to make a promise, not that he is able to wash the car. In any case, it appears that this, like (8.30b), is an example of core coordination, again because the modality operator is not shared across both cores. Another example of core cosubordination in English is a sentence like *Carlos must wash the car and clean his room*, where the scope of *must* is over the two cores sharing the same actor. This example also emphasizes the point made earlier that it is always necessary to distinguish juncture–nexus type from formal construction type; this is an example of conjunction (construction type) but not of coordination (nexus type).

Further examples of same-pivot core coordinate constructions can be found in Turkish.[6] Watters (1993) shows that the same-pivot constructions in (8.31) have distinct nexus types due to the different interpretations of the scope of the core operators *-mEll-* 'ought' and *-Ebil-* 'able' in them. This difference is attributable to the different properties of the complementizers.

(8.31) a. Gid-ip gör-meli-yiz. Core cosubordination
go-CMPL see-MODAL-1pl
'We ought to go and see.'

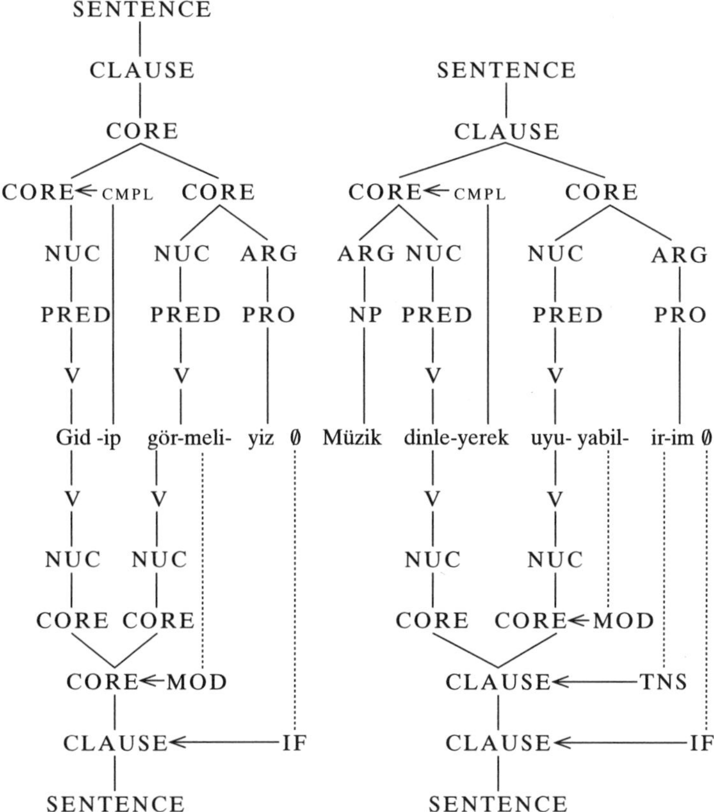

Figure 8.9 Turkish core junctures

b. Müzik dinle-yerek, uyu-yabil-ir-im.   Core coordination
music listen-CMPL sleep-MODAL-AOR-1sg
'Listening to music, I can sleep.'

The structures of these two sentences are presented in figure 8.9. Both cores share the same privileged syntactic argument in each example; the operator projection represents the fact that the modal operator has scope over both cores in (8.31a) but not in (b). Thus, it is the scope of the core-level operators that is crucial for distinguishing the two non-subordinate nexus types.

Over the past thirty years the usual analysis of the constructions in (8.30) has been that they involve subordination; i.e. the infinitives are embedded as object complements of the matrix verbs. There is, however, no syntactic evidence that they are subordinate. True subordination at the core level involves the subordinate unit serving as a core argument. Examples from English are given in (8.32).

(8.32) a. Fred's winning the race surprised Mary.
b. For Fred to win the race would be a shock to the experts.
c. Mary regretted Fred's losing the race.
d. Mary hoped for Fred to win the race.
e. That Fred won the race surprised Mary.

In the first four of these sentences a core, expressed as a gerund or infinitive, functions as a core argument. In the first two sentences the subordinate core functions as privileged syntactic argument of the sentence, while in the last two it functions as undergoer and a direct core argument. As core arguments, they may be clefted, and, depending upon the matrix verb, they may occur as privileged syntactic argument in a passive construction. This is exemplified in (8.33)–(8.34).

(8.33) a. It was Fred's losing the race that Mary regretted.
b. It was for Fred to win the race that Mary hoped.

(8.34) a. Fred's losing the race was regretted by Mary.
b. For Fred to win the race was hoped for by Mary.

This is not possible, however, with the infinitives in (8.30), as the following examples show.

(8.35) a. *It was to wash the car that Fred tried. (cf. It was the door that Fred tried.)
b. *It was to wash the car that John told Bill. (cf. It was the story that John told Bill.)

(8.36) a. *To wash the car was tried by Fred. (cf. The door was tried by Fred.)
b. *To wash the car was told Bill by John.[7]

The fact that these infinitives do not cleft or passivize, unlike simple NP objects and the gerundive or infinitival cores in (8.32), shows that they are not in fact core arguments of the matrix verbs and therefore are not in a subordinate relation to the matrix core. Hence they are not instances of core subordination and must be analyzed as non-subordinate core junctures. As we will see in chapter 9 when we look at the semantic representation of the constructions in (8.30) and (8.32a–d), the logical structure of the linked core is an argument in the logical structure of the matrix core, but argumenthood at the semantic level does not necessarily entail syntactic argumenthood in complex sentences.

All of the examples examined thus far conform to the unmarked linkage pattern summarized in (8.2): the joining of units of the same type. It is possible, however, for an asymmetrical linkage to occur, namely joining a larger unit, a clause, with a smaller unit, a core; this occurs in core subordination when a clause is used as a core argument, as in (8.32e). The simplified representations of the structures of (8.32a)

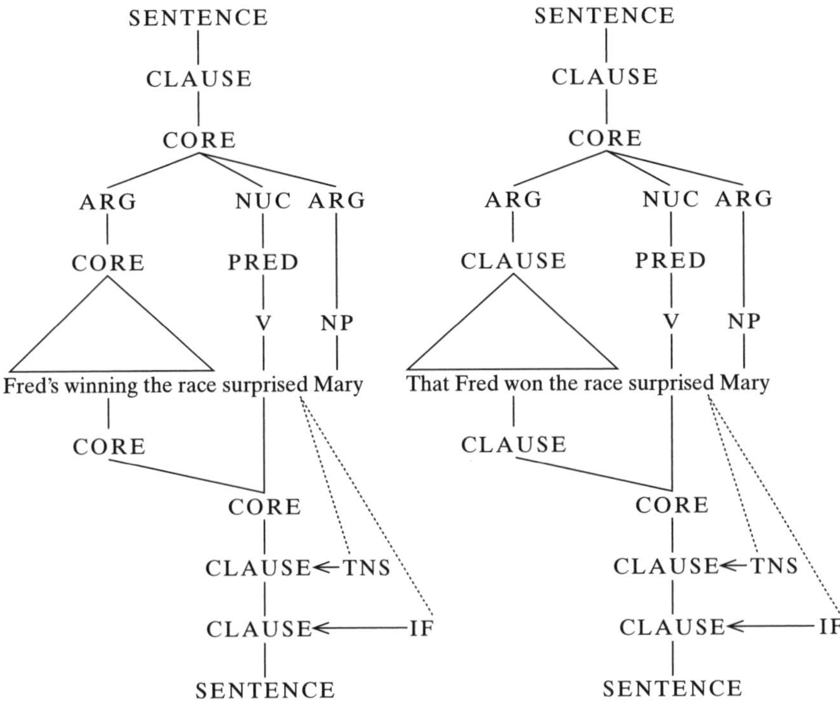

Figure 8.10 English core subordination

and (e) are presented in figure 8.10. In both instances the subordinate unit functions as a core argument; hence the linkage type is core subordination. Note again how the operator projection mirrors the constituent projection in terms of the main units.

Clausal junctures occur in all languages, and clausal coordination is unquestionably a universal juncture–nexus type. In clausal coordination, each clause is completely independent of the other in terms of operators, even to the point of having distinct illocutionary force, if need be. This is illustrated from English in (8.37); (8.21b) is a comparable example from Amele.

(8.37) a. Robin is known for liking big parties, but why did she invite the entire club?
b. Sit down and I'll fix you a drink.

In the first example the first clause is an assertion and the second a question, while in (b) the first clause is an imperative and the second is an assertion. The earlier English example of coordination in (8.12) and represented in figure 8.4 is repeated here with a full operator projection. Clausal cosubordination will be illustrated with the Amele example from (8.19a) in figure 8.12. The constituent and operator projections are

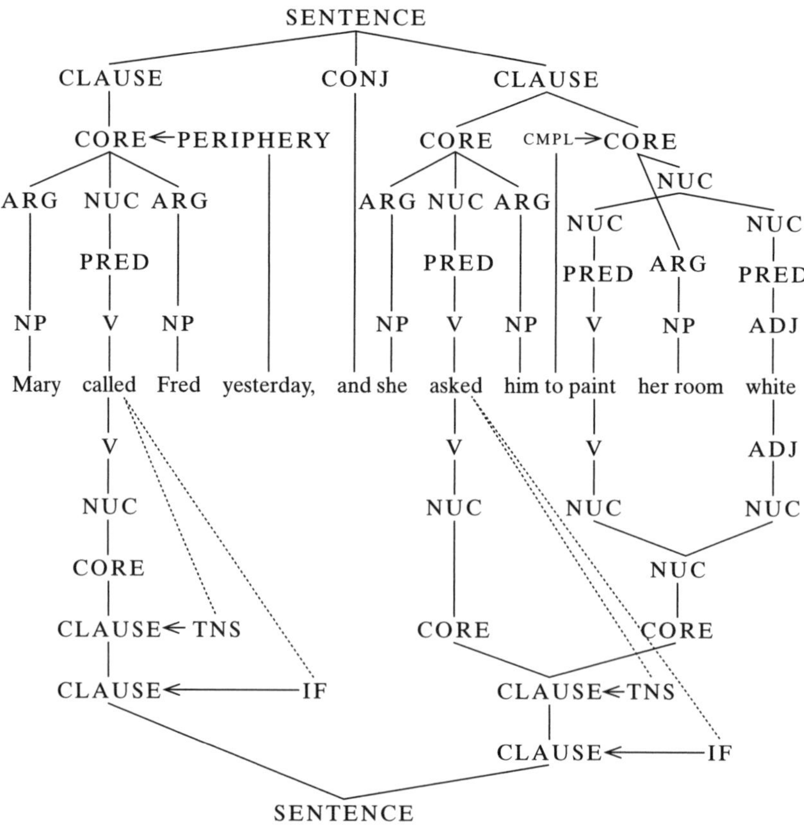

Figure 8.11 English clausal coordination (with core and nuclear junctures)

different from those figure 8.11; because tense and illocutionary force are obligatorily shared across both clauses, there are single clause nodes modified by tense and illocutionary force dominating both clauses, in sharp contrast to the independent tense and illocutionary force operators in figure 8.11. The two main types of clausal subordination in English, adverbial clauses and *that*-complement clauses, are presented in figures 8.13 and 8.14. In English adverbial clauses, subordinating conjunctions are treated as predicative prepositions taking a clausal argument and are part of the periphery of the clause. The subordinate clause is an adjunct modifier of the core, and this is represented in both projections.

The idea that a *that*-clause in English could be a clausal juncture may seem somewhat surprising, given that the clause is an argument in the semantic representation of the verb and therefore should be syntactically a core argument, hence core subordination. 'Subject' *that*-clauses are core arguments, as we saw in figure 8.10, but the situation is rather different with 'object' complement clauses. Even though they

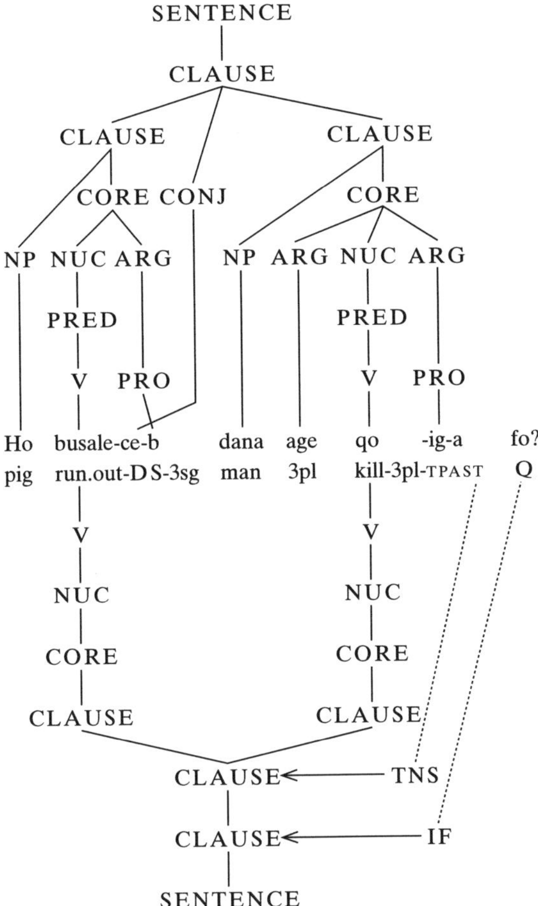

Figure 8.12 Amele clausal cosubordination

may occur right after the nucleus, it is not obvious whether they are in the core or outside of it. Evidence bearing on this concerns the placement of peripheral adverbials; they must follow all core elements in English, and yet the most natural placement of the *that*-clause with reference to peripheral elements is *after* them, not before them, as the sentences in (8.38) show.

(8.38) a. Kim ate the sandwich in the library.
a′. *Kim ate in the library the sandwich.
b. Kim introduced Sandy to Robin in the library.
b′. *Kim introduced Sandy in the library to Robin.
c. John decided [that he will go to the party] yesterday.
c′. John decided yesterday [that he will go to the party].

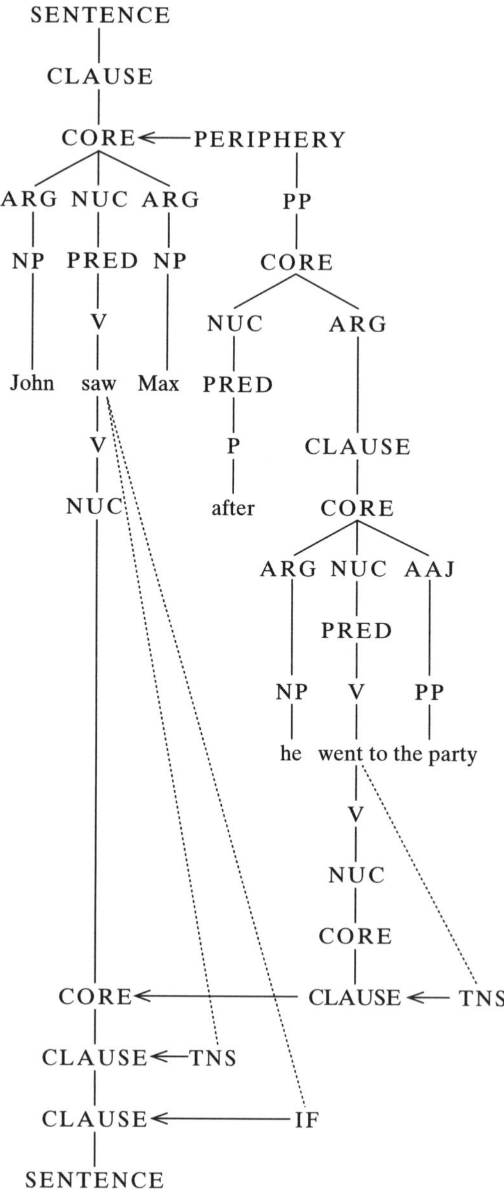

Figure 8.13 English clausal subordination (adverbial clause)

The example in (8.38c) with the clause inside of the matrix clause peripheral element is very odd and unnatural; whereas when the clause follows the peripheral element, the result is perfect. If peripheral elements intervene between the nucleus and the *that*-clause, then it cannot be within the core and must be analyzed as being a direct daughter of the higher clause node. Since it is always possible to insert peripheral material between the nucleus and the *that*-clause, these constructions must always be given this structure in English. Working in the framework of classical transformational grammar, Emonds (1976) comes to a similar conclusion. It might be suggested that the 'heaviness' of the clause is the real factor here; however, since the approach we are taking does not allow movement rules and the normal place for the peripheral material is before the *that*-clause, it is necessary to place the *that*-clause outside of the core. Note that placing it in this position also serves to disambiguate what the peripheral element modifies. A sentence like *Robin decided that Mary had behaved badly yesterday* is ambiguous as to whether *yesterday* modifies the matrix or embedded clause (although the clearly preferred interpretation associates the adverb with the embedded clause), whereas *Robin decided yesterday that Mary had behaved badly* is unambiguous. Placing the peripheral adverbs before the *that*-clause results in unambiguous structures which correspond to the speaker's default interpretations. The structure of (8.38c′) is given in figure 8.14.

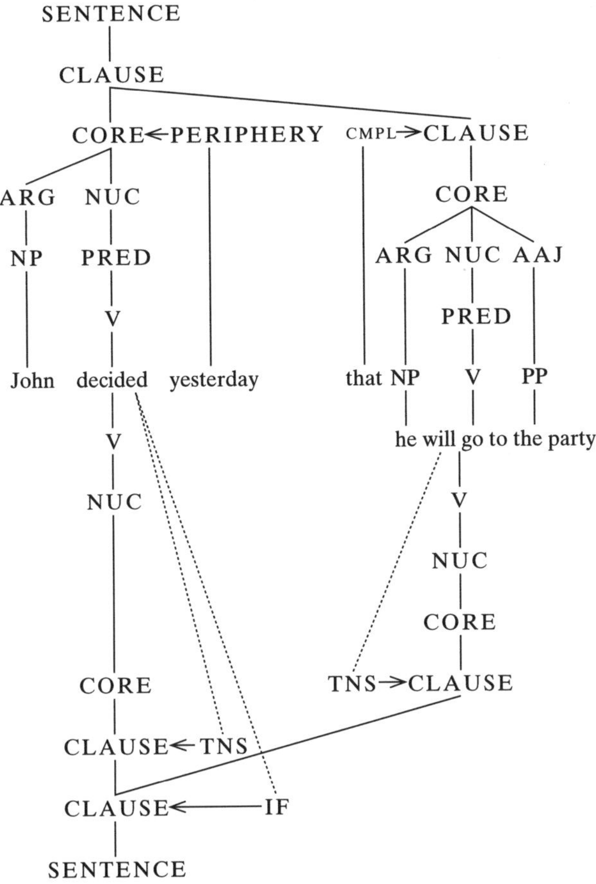

Figure 8.14 English clausal subordination (*that*-clause)

It was mentioned at the beginning of this section that there is no operator sharing with subordinate clauses, with the possible exception of illocutionary force; subordinate clauses may not have independent illocutionary force operators. They are either outside the domain of the illocutionary force operator of the clause, i.e. are presupposed, or they have the same force as the main clause (see chapter 5, also section 8.5).[8] Hence the subordinate clause in figure 8.14 is dominated by the clause node of the matrix clause which is modified by the illocutionary force operator. The difference between this structure and the one in figure 8.12 is meant to indicate that while the linked clause in figure 8.12 has a morphosyntactic form which in principle rules out the expression of independent illocutionary force, the subordinate clause in English is of a form which could stand alone as an independent assertion (minus the complementizer) but is blocked from being interpreted as an independent assertion by virtue of its occurrence in this structure, not by virtue of its form.

Operators, as we have seen, play a crucial role in distinguishing cosubordination from coordination at all levels of juncture, but they play no role at all in determining levels of juncture, which are defined purely structurally. In a nuclear juncture, multiple predicates or nuclei constitute what is in effect a single complex predicate with a single set of core arguments. In non-subordinate core junctures, the cores must share a core argument; as shown in section 8.3 and depicted in figure 8.2, one of the core arguments functions as a semantic argument in each core, in that it occurs syntactically in one core but is interpreted as a semantic argument of the linked core.[9] In subordinate core junctures, the linked unit functions syntactically as an argument of the nucleus in the matrix core. In clausal junctures, the core and peripheral constituents of the two clauses are independent; there is no argument sharing between the clauses. It is of course possible for there to be coreference between arguments in each clause, as in (8.12), where the 'subject' of the second clause, *she*, is normally construed as referring to the 'subject' of the first clause, *Mary*. Potential confusion in the analysis of level of juncture may arise when there is coreference between the pivot of one clause and that of another when the pivot of the linked clause is a zero anaphor in a topic chain, as in (8.39).

(8.39) Robin$_i$ drove out of Phoenix this morning and *pro*$_{i/*j}$ will arrive in Atlanta tomorrow.

The '*pro*' represents a zero or phonologically null pronoun;[10] it is one of the options for the coding of referring expressions given in figure 5.2 (repeated in figure 7.3). The pivot of the second clause is obligatorily interpreted as being the same as that of the first clause, but this is not a case of argument sharing as in core junctures; as we will see in chapter 9, argument sharing in the technical sense of the linking algorithm operates only between cores and not across clause boundaries. It is, rather, an instance of coreference between independent referring expressions. Some theories, e.g. GB, treat all argument identity as coreference and therefore claim that in, for example, (8.30a) *John* is coreferential with a zero element in the linked unit. This leads to a host of pseudo-problems whose solution leads to additional theoretical complexity. These issues simply do not arise in theories which posit VPs (e.g. GPSG, HPSG, LFG, ConG) or cores (RRG) as the linked units in this type of construction. The issue that all theories must deal with is how to interpret the missing argument in the linked unit, and this problem, known as the problem of control, will be discussed in chapter 9.

There is an additional linkage type which differs in important ways from those discussed thus far. It involves the linking of whole sentences, as in (8.40) with examples from English and Barai (Olson 1981).

(8.40) a. As for Sam, Mary saw him last week, and as for Paul, I saw him yesterday.
b. Fu vua kuae-ga siare ije, fu naebe ume.
3sg talk say-SP/DT betelnut DEF 3sg NEG chew
'He was talking, and as for betelnut, he did not chew it.'

In the English example there are two complete sentences, each with its own left-detached PP. The Barai example is particularly interesting, as the linking morpheme *-ga* signals that the pragmatic pivots of the two sentences are the same but that there is a change of topic in the second sentence; the new topic appears in the left-detached position of the second sentence. We will call this linkage **sentential juncture**, and it differs from other linkages in that there is only one nexus type possible at this level, namely, coordination. Cosubordination is ruled out, because there are no sentential-level operators which could be shared, and subordination is impossible, because sentential units cannot be embedded, only clause- and lower-level units can. The closest thing to 'sentential subordination' would be direct discourse constructions, e.g. *Amy said, 'As for Sam, I saw him last week'*, but there is in fact no evidence for claiming that the direct discourse sentence is in any way embedded in or dependent on the clause headed by the verb of saying. The English example in (8.40a) will be represented as in figure 8.15, with 'text' as the highest node dominating the two sentence nodes.

8.4.2 The status of complementizers

In the examples of complex constructions in this chapter, we have labeled elements like *to* and *that* in English and *-Ip* and *-yErEk* in Turkish as complementizers (CMPL), but this term is traditionally used primarily for elements like English *that* and *whether*, which mark the subordination of clausal complements (hence the name). English *to* has not been considered to be a complementizer in most theories, and in fact its status differs from theory to theory. In GB analyses, for example, it is considered to be a kind of defective auxiliary element which replaces the tense morpheme in INFL (Chomsky 1981b, 1986b; see section 2.4, figure 6.1 [middle tree] in section 6.1.2.1). In this section, we will first look at English *to*, in order to

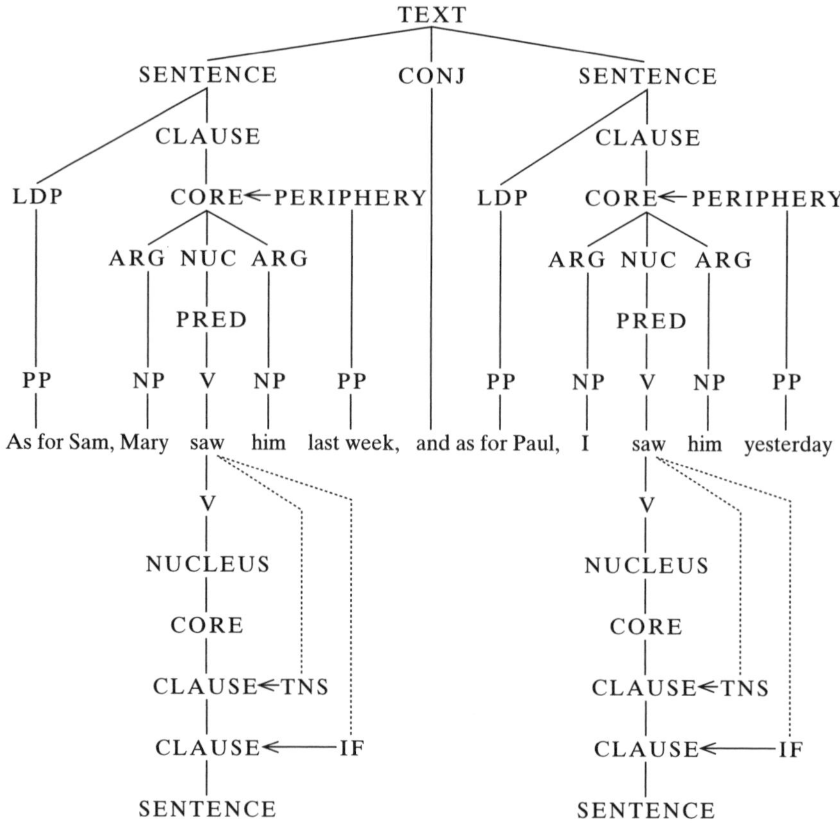

Figure 8.15 Sentential juncture in English

see if it is a defective element of a class like 'tense operator', and then we will look briefly at this class of elements in other languages and propose that they are all members of the class we will label 'clause-linkage markers'.

It seems reasonable to label an element a defective member of a class when there is only one element of this kind in the language, but if it turns out it is not in fact unique, then such an analysis becomes less plausible. Discussions of the status of non-finite 'complements' in general and of *to* in particular in English have concentrated on sentences like those in (8.41) and generally ignored sentences like those in (8.42).

(8.41) a. Sandy told Kim to go to the movies.
b. Robin asked Pat to apply for the job.

(8.42) a. Sandy stopped Kim from going to the movies.
b. Robin prevented Pat from applying for the job.

If *to* is a defective auxiliary here, then what is *from*? These sentences are quite parallel structurally; they are both instances of core coordination. Their acceptability (or lack of it) seems comparable with respect to clefting (cf. (8.33)–(8.35)).

(8.43) a. *It was to go to the movies that Sandy told Kim.
b. *It was from going to the movies that Sandy stopped Kim.
c. *It was to apply for the job that Robin asked Pat.
d. *It was from applying for the job that Robin prevented Pat.

It appears, then, that whatever analysis is given to *to* in (8.41) must also be given to *from* in (8.42), and consequently the class to which *to* belongs has at least one other member. It is no accident that *from* occurs with verbs that contain a negative component in their semantic structure; that is, *stop* and *prevent* both mean something like 'x cause y NOT to verb', and as we saw in sections 4.4.1.1 and 7.3.2.1, the semantic structure of *from* also contains NOT. Verbs with this 'negative causative' meaning, including *prohibit*, *dissuade* and *discourage*, all occur with *from* rather than *to*. The negative component of *from* can be seen clearly in the contrast in (8.44).

(8.44) a. Pam kept the dogs barking.
b. Pam kept the dogs from barking.

In (a) the actor is doing something which causes the dogs to bark continually, whereas in (b) the action causes the dogs not to bark, and the only difference between them is the presence or absence of *from*. Hence it must be *from* which is supplying the negative component of the negative causation in (b).

The contrast in (8.44) shows that the occurrence of an element like *from* can contribute to the meaning of the sentence, and this is also the case with *to*. Consider the following contrast, which has been discussed by Quirk *et al.* (1972), Bolinger (1975) and Dixon (1984, 1991); the examples are taken from Quirk *et al.* (1972).

(8.45) a. Will you help me clear the table?
b. This book helped me to see the truth.

They comment: '[T]he choice is conditioned by the subject's involvement . . . In the example with the bare infinitive, external help is called in; in the example with *to*-infinitive, assistance is outside the action proper' (841). That is, sentence (a) is interpreted as a request for both the speaker and the addressee to jointly clear the table, whereas in (b) only the speaker will see the truth. This is not simply a question of animacy. Consider the contrast in (8.46).

(8.46) a. Sam helped his neighbor build his new barn (by pouring the foundation/ ?by loaning him money).
b. Sam helped his neighbor to build his new barn (by pouring the foundation/ by loaning him money).

In (a) Sam actually participated in the labor, but in (b) he need not have; it is equally compatible with an interpretation whereby he loaned his neighbor money but did not participate in the actual building activities.[11] Another way of interpreting the contrast in the last two pairs of examples is that the clearing or building constitutes the help in the (a) examples, whereas the action of helping is a distinct action from that of seeing or building in the (b) examples. Interpreted temporally, this means that the action of the actor of *help* overlaps temporally with the action of the actor of the linked core in the (a) examples, whereas in the (b) examples it need not be and the actions may be viewed as non-overlapping or in sequence. Thus we may hypothesize that where it is possible for *to* to occur or not to occur, the construction without *to* is interpreted as involving temporally overlapping actions, whereas the one with *to* need not be so interpreted, with the preferred interpretation being that the actions are sequential.

Does *from* enter into the same opposition? It appears that it does, as (8.47) shows.

(8.47) a. Robin stopped Kim singing 'Advance Australia Fair'.
b. Robin stopped Kim from singing 'Advance Australia Fair'.

Example (8.47a) is marginal for many speakers, but nevertheless the contrast relevant to this discussion comes through clearly. In (a), Kim is singing the Australian national anthem and Robin stops her; since the singing has been going on at the time of the stopping action, the two overlap temporally. In (b), on the other hand, no singing ever occurred; that is, Robin acted to stop Kim before she even started to sing the song. Hence the stopping action and the singing are not simultaneous, i.e. there is no temporal overlap between them, as in (a). Thus it appears that there is a more general contrast here: given a contrast between *to* or *from* and its absence, the zero-marked construction necessarily involves temporally overlapping actions, while the *to-* or *from*-marked construction does not, and the default interpretation of the latter construction is as involving temporally non-overlapping (sequential) actions. This may be summarized as in (8.48).

(8.48) a. Constructions with zero marker on linked unit: [+temporal overlap]
b. Constructions with *to*/*from* marker on linked unit: [–temporal overlap][12]

This contrast can be seen in other constructions, where it is partially masked by other differences. With aspectual verbs like *start* and *begin*, the zero vs. *to* contrast is overlain by an opposition between the participial and infinitive forms of the verb in the linked core. This is illustrated in (8.49).

(8.49) a. Mary started to drive to work (but before she got in the car she changed her mind and took the bus).
b. Mary started driving to work (*but before she got in the car she changed her mind and took the bus).

The starting and the driving are distinct actions in (a), as the felicitous extension shows, whereas in (b) they are not distinct actions but rather overlap, as the unacceptability of the extension shows. This contrast has long been noted (see e.g. Quirk, *et al.* 1972), and it has usually been attributed to the participle (ongoing action) vs. infinitive (roughly, 'whole event') contrast, which is certainly an important factor in the interpretation of these constructions (see the discussion of perception verb complements below). However, the zero vs. *to* contrast complements and reinforces the aspectual opposition of the participle vs. infinitive contrast. This same contrast can be found in simultaneous action constructions like *Sally sat playing the guitar* and purpose clauses like *Sally sat down to play the piano*; in the first construction only zero can occur, as one would expect, and in the second, where the first action is done with the intention of doing the second action, there are two distinct actions in sequence, and *to* is obligatory. The semantics of the zero vs. *to/from* contrast can only be clearly seen in the few cases where it can be realized while the verb forms remain constant, thereby creating minimal pairs as in (8.46) and (8.47). There are many verbs which require *to* in all instances, e.g. *try*, *persuade* and *force*, and for them this contrast cannot arise.[13]

A significant predication which this analysis makes is that if there are constructions in which the actions in the component units must be interpreted as temporally overlapping, then the zero marker must be used. The best example of this would be direct perception constructions, since the act of perception is simultaneous with the acts being perceived. In such constructions, *to* cannot occur.

(8.50) a. Kim saw/heard Sandy leave early.
a′. *Kim saw/heard Sandy to leave early.
b. Kim saw/heard Sandy leaving early.

Kim's perceptual experience and Sandy's leaving are simultaneous, and there cannot be an overt linkage marker in the construction. In this case the semantic opposition between participle and infinitive is striking: the infinitive in (a) implies that Kim saw the entire event of Sandy's leaving, whereas the participle in (b) indicates that she saw Sandy in the process of leaving; that is, she glimpsed a moment of the ongoing event. Sentence (a), but not (b), implies that Sandy did in fact leave; this can be seen in (8.51).[14]

(8.51) a. Kim saw Sandy leaving early (and stopped her and asked her to stay a few minutes longer).
b. Kim saw Sandy leave early (and called her and asked her to come back/ *and stopped her and asked her to stay a few minutes longer).

A curious thing happens when these perception verbs are passivized, as in (8.52).

(8.52) a. Sandy was seen leaving early (by Kim).
b. Sandy was seen to leave early (by Kim).
b′. *Sandy was seen leave early (by Kim).

The (a) example with the participle appears to have the same basic meaning as its active counterpart. If the linked core has the non-participial form, as in (b), *to* is obligatory. This is striking, given that *to* is impossible in active-voice forms, as we saw in (8.50). Why should this be so? In order to give a partial answer to this question, we need to step back and briefly examine the contrast between direct and indirect perception meanings (see Kirsner and Thompson 1976). Perception verbs can express both meanings; the former has to do with unmediated apprehension through the senses of a state of affairs as it unfolds, whereas the latter refers to deductions from evidence regarding a state of affairs. The sentences in (8.50) are all direct perception; *that*-clauses are usually used for indirect perception, as in, for example, *Sam saw from the muddy footprints on the rug that the dog had run through the room after his walk*. In this case, Sam did not actually see the dog run through the room but deduced it from the footprints. Active-voice perception verbs, with the PERCEIVER as privileged syntactic argument, strongly favor direct perception interpretations, whereas passive-voice perception verbs, with the STIMULUS as 'subject' and the PERCEIVER as an optional peripheral oblique, favor indirect perception interpretations, since the coding emphasizes what is perceived and deemphasizes the perceiving participant. The combination of a passive perception verb with a participle can only yield a direct perception reading, due to the 'ongoing state of affairs' semantics of the participle, but the non-participial form carries no such meaning and therefore is compatible with both interpretations. The occurrence of *to*, then, correlates with the possibility of an indirect perception reading; as noted in n. 12, it is compatible with both temporal interpretations (simultaneous, for direct perception, or non-simultaneous, for indirect perception), whereas the zero form is compatible only with the simultaneous reading (direct perception). Evidence that (8.52b) is compatible with an indirect perception reading comes from the fact that the perfect aspect can be used in the infinitive, i.e. *Sandy was seen to have left early* (cf. **Kim saw Sandy have left early*). The use of the perfect signals that the leaving took place prior to the seeing. Hence, the fact that passive perception verbs require *to* in core junctures when the verb in the linked core is non-participial is not an arbitrary irregularity but rather is related to the semantics of the construction and to the semantics of the opposition between *to* and zero in core junctures. Thus, it appears that *to*, along with *from*, enters into an opposition with the lack of an overt marker in core junctures, with zero signaling temporally overlapping states of affairs and with *to* and *from* indicating the complementary range of temporal relations between states of affairs in core junctures.

English is not unique in having special markers for signaling temporal and other relations between the units in a juncture. Turkish, for example, has an extensive set of suffixes used to mark the linked unit in a juncture and indicate temporal, causal or other relationships between the units (Watters 1993). One of the forms of core coordination is zero marked and has a temporally overlapping actions interpretation, exactly like our English examples; two of the other suffixes have already been illustrated in (8.31), *-Ip* and *-yErEk*. There are suffixes with these functions in both core and clausal junctures in Turkish. In the same way, *-re* in Chuave in (8.13), *-ma-* in Fore in (8.14a), and *-ri* in Kewa in (8.16b) function to indicate temporal relations between clauses in clausal junctures, as well as 'same pivot' in the switch-reference system of the language. Nootka, a language of the Wakashan family spoken in British Columbia (Jacobsen 1993), has a suffix *-q(ḥ)* which indicates 'simultaneity of the action expressed by the predicate to which it is attached to another action' (245). This is illustrated in (8.53) from Jacobsen (1993).[15]

(8.53) a. Wa·ʔaƛweʔinƛa· čawaqƛḥʔaƛ.
say-FIN-QUOT-3-again spear.in-while-FIN-3
'[quotation] He said again, while the spear was stuck in him'

b. Kʷičiʔaƛweʔin nunu·kḥʔaƛ ʾa·tušm̓it.
file-MOM-FIN-QUOT-3 sing-while-FIN-3 Deer-son
'Deer began to file; meanwhile he was singing.'

c. Nunu·kḥčik̓aƛweʔin.
sing-while-travel-FIN-QUOT-3
'He sang while traveling along.'

There are additional suffixes such as *-ti·p* 'while' and *-taq* 'before'.

We now return to the issue raised at the outset of the section: what is the status of *to*? In particular, is it a kind of defective auxiliary element, as GB claims? If we assume, as GB does, that the linked unit is a clause and that INFL is the head of the clause, then there must be some element in the linked clause which fills the INFL node. Since there is no tense/agreement element in the clause, *to* is analyzed as occupying the INFL node. Given these assumptions, this seems reasonable from a paradigmatic point of view, i.e. *to* replaces tense in an obligatory position in the structure. However, such an analysis is highly implausible within the theory we are operating in. First, the linked unit in these constructions is a core, not a clause, and accordingly, there is no possibility of tense occurring in the linked core, since tense is a clausal operator. Second, the head of the clause is the nucleus, not an operator category like tense (see section 2.4). Hence there is no obligatory structural position for tense (i.e. INFL) left empty in the linked core that must be filled by something. There is thus no reason to associate *to* paradigmatically with tense, except for the fact that tense does not occur in linked cores in which *to* occurs. But this is equally true of the other clausal operators as well, including illocutionary force, the other obligatory clausal operator in independent clauses. Moreover, *to* is part of a set of semantically contrasting elements which also includes *from* and zero; it is not a solitary element that needs to be assigned to a larger class but in fact is a member of a class of elements with similar functions, none of which has auxiliary functions.

We have asked about the status of *to* from the point of view of English. Let us now turn the question around and ask it from the point of view of Turkish, Fore,

Kewa, Chauve and Nootka: how does English mark temporal sequencing relations among units in junctures, and what role, if any, does *to* play in the system? Looking at core junctures first, we see that there is a basic opposition between temporally overlapping states of affairs vs. non-temporally overlapping states of affairs, and this is coded by the opposition between a zero-marked linked core ([+temporal overlap]) and an overtly marked linked core ([–temporal overlap]). There are two markers, *to* and *from*, with different semantic properties, the differences being unrelated to temporal sequencing. At the clause level we find a much more complex system, with the bulk of the sequencing signaled by temporal prepositions used as subordinators with finite embedded clauses, e.g. *after*, *before*, *while* (see figure 8.13). There are, however, examples analogous to those at the core level, as illustrated in (8.54).[16]

(8.54)	a.	Running down the hall, Sandy waved to Sue.	Overlapping
	b.	After running down the hall, Sandy waved to Sue.	Non-overlapping
	c.	Before running down the hall, Sandy waved to Sue.	Non-overlapping
	d.	While running down the hall, Sandy waved to Sue.	Overlapping
	e.	Having run down the hall, Sandy waved to Sue.	Non-overlapping

As in core junctures, a zero-marked simple participial linked unit is interpreted as being simultaneous with the matrix unit, as in (a). The temporal relationship between the clauses may be made explicit by means of an overt temporal marker, as in (b)–(d). In (e), the use of the perfect aspect in the linked clause signals that the state of affairs was completed before the action of the finite clause took place, thereby indicating sequential states of affairs. It appears, then, that the simultaneous interpretation of the zero-marked clause is a default which can be overridden in clausal junctures. Thus, from this perspective, *to* appears to be one of a number of elements marking the linked units in complex constructions in English.

From the data in this section it is clear that languages have a category of what we will call **clause-linkage markers** which serve to express important aspects of the syntax and semantics of complex constructions. The elements which serve this function may be drawn from a variety of morphosyntactic categories, e.g. adpositions (as in English), determiners (e.g. the Lakhota complementizer *ki*, which is also the definite article), case markers (as in Mparntwe Arrernte; Wilkins 1989) and bound elements like the linking suffixes found in Nootka and the Papuan languages discussed above. Henceforth we will gloss these elements 'CLM' for 'clause-linkage marker' rather than 'CMPL' for 'complementizer', to reflect their more general functional class. The clause-linkage markers that are used in particular constructions are in part a function of the level of juncture; in English, for example, *to* and *from* mark only linked cores, while *that* marks only clausal units.

The distribution of these markers across juncture–nexus types follows an interesting pattern: nuclear junctures lack them altogether, there is usually a restricted number of them in core junctures in a language, and the greatest elaboration of them occurs in clausal junctures. A close examination of the examples discussed in this chapter up to this point illustrates this well. The reason for this distribution is two-fold. First, languages simply have the largest number of constructions instantiating clausal juncture, fewer at the core level and a very restricted number at the nuclear level. Second, as we will see in the next section, the possible semantic relations among the units in a nuclear juncture are very restricted; in languages that have nuclear junctures, there is usually only one kind of construction at this level of juncture, namely a causative construction. Hence no markers are necessary. At the core level, the semantics of the construction are to a considerable extent a function of the semantics of the matrix verb, and therefore there are only a few semantic contrasts independent of the matrix verb to be coded, primarily, as we have seen, with respect to temporal sequencing. Finally, at the clause level, the widest range of semantic relations between the units can be expressed, and since the units are largely independent of each other in terms of their semantic content, the burden of expressing the semantic relations among them falls on the clause-linkage markers. This raises the important question, 'what are the semantic relations that can hold among units in a complex construction?', which is the main topic of the next section.

8.4.3 The Interclausal Relations Hierarchy

It has long been noticed that the units in some complex sentence constructions seem very tightly bound to each other, whereas in other constructions they seem rather more loosely connected to each other. Looking back at the English examples in (8.26), for example, we see that *playing the guitar* is tightly linked to *Sam sat* in the core cosubordinate construction in (b), whereas the adverbial subordinate clause in (f) is more loosely linked to the main clause and may freely occur either before or after it. The nine possible juncture–nexus types may be organized into a hierarchy in which they are ranked in terms of the tightness of the syntactic link or bond between them. The resulting hierarchy will be termed the 'Interclausal Syntactic Relations Hierarchy' and is presented in figure 8.16. The linkage types at the top

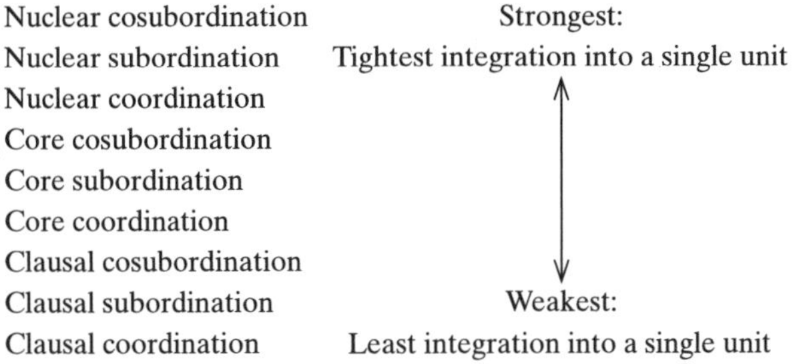

Figure 8.16 Interclausal Syntactic Relations Hierarchy

of the Interclausal Syntactic Relations Hierarchy all involve integrating the components of the juncture into a single subclausal or clausal unit, e.g. the nuclei in a nuclear juncture make up a single core with a single set of core arguments, and the cores in a core juncture are part of a single clause. At the bottom are combinations of whole clauses constituting sentences. As one goes up the hierarchy, the linked unit loses more and more features of an independent clause until it is reduced to a bare nucleus or predicate in nuclear cosubordination. The features being lost include both operators and coding of semantic arguments distinctly as core arguments of the predicate in the nucleus. In a clausal juncture, all operators are possible (depending upon the nexus type), and all arguments are coded morphosyntactically as syntactic arguments of a specific core. In a non-subordinate core juncture, this is true of all arguments except the one shared between or among the cores; as the tree for (8.30b) in figure 8.8 shows, *John* and *the car* are coded as core arguments of their respective nuclei, *tell* and *wash*, but *Bill* is formally coded only as a core argument of *tell*; hence the linked core lacks morphosyntactic coding for one of its semantic arguments, and it also lacks any coding of core or clausal operators. Finally, in nuclear junctures like those in figure 8.1, the linked unit is a single nucleus, and there is no formal indication of which predicate contributed which arguments to the construction; the arguments are pooled and treated as if they were all arguments of a single predicate in a simple core. The Interclausal Syntactic Relations Hierarchy thus makes it possible to make predictions about the form of the linked unit in a particular juncture–nexus type, given an account of the operators in a language.

One more thing needs to be mentioned about the Interclausal Syntactic Relations Hierarchy. It does not include relative clauses and other NP constructions, because it refers solely to predicate-based linkages. Relative clauses involve clause–NP linkages, and they will be dealt with separately in section 8.6. Given the structural analogies between the layered structure of the clause and the layered structure of the noun phrase, however, the concepts of juncture and nexus are applicable to NP constructions in various ways.

The juncture–nexus types of the Interclausal Syntactic Relations Hierarchy are purely syntactic, but they are used to express a wide variety of semantic relations between the units in the construction. As first argued by Silverstein (1976) and Givón (1980), such semantic relations themselves can be ranked in a continuum based on the degree of semantic cohesion between or among the units in the linkage, i.e. the extent to which a given construction expresses facets of a single event, action or state of affairs or discrete events, actions or states of affairs. A list of some of these relations is given in (8.55).

(8.55) *Interclausal semantic relations*

a. *Causative*: the bringing about of one state of affairs directly by another state of affairs, usually an event or action, e.g. (8.3a), (8.26a), *Harold pushed open the door*, *Velma let the bird go*.

b. *Aspectual*: a separate verb describes a facet of the temporal envelope of a state of affairs, specifically its onset, its termination or its continuation, e.g. *Chris started crying, Fred kept singing, Hari finished writing the chapter.*
c. *Psych-action*: a mental disposition regarding a possible action on the part of a participant in the state of affairs, e.g. *Max decided to leave, Sally forgot to open the window, Tanisha wants to go to the movies.*
d. *Purposive*: one action is done with the intent of realizing another state of affairs, e.g. *Juan went to the store to buy milk, Susan brought the book to read.*
e. *Jussive*: the expression of a command, request or demand (Lyons 1977), e.g. (8.30b), *Pat asked the student to leave, The king ordered the troops to attack the city.*
f. *Direct perception*: an unmediated apprehension of some act, event or situation through the senses, e.g. *Rex saw the child open the door, Yolanda heard the guests arrive.*
g. *Propositional attitude*: the expression of a participant's attitude, judgment or opinion regarding a state of affairs, e.g. *Carl believes that UFOs are a menace to the earth, Paul considers Carl to be a fool, Most fans want very much for their team to win.*
h. *Cognition*: an expression of knowledge or mental activity, e.g. *Aaron knows that the earth is round, George is thinking about Madeleine's refusal to go out with him.*
i. *Indirect discourse*: an expression of reported speech, e.g. *Frank said that his friends were corrupt* (vs. *Frank said, 'My friends are corrupt.'*)
j. *Conditional*: an expression of what consequence would hold, given the conditions in a particular state of affairs, e.g. *If it rains, we won't be able to have a picnic, Were Fred to leave now, he would look like a fool.*
k. *Simultaneous states of affairs*: one state of affairs is temporally coterminous with another, e.g. *Max danced while Susan played the piano, Kim had chicken pox at the same time as Leslie had the measles.*
l. *Sequential states of affairs*:
   1 Overlapping: one state of affairs partially overlaps temporally with another, e.g. *Before Juan had finished talking, Carlos entered the room.*
   2 Non-overlapping: one state of affairs begins immediately after another one ends, e.g. *As soon as Vidhu sat down, the band began to play.*
   3 Non-overlapping, with an interval: there is a temporal interval between the end of one state of affairs and the beginning of the next, e.g. *Five minutes after Sally settled into her hot bath, the phone rang.*
m. *Temporally unordered states of affairs*: the temporal relation between states of affairs is unexpressed, e.g. *Tyrone talked to Tanisha, and Yolanda chatted with Kareem.*

This list should not be taken as complete; rather, it represents major distinctions along a semantic continuum, much the same way the thematic relations discussed

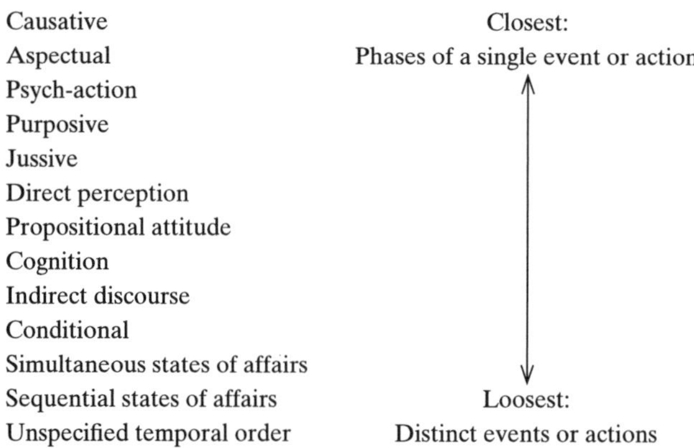

Figure 8.17 Interclausal Semantic Relations Hierarchy

in chapter 3 fall along a semantic continuum, and more distinctions are possible. These semantic relations can be ranked in a hierarchy in terms of how closely related the propositions in the linkage are (the notion of 'semantic cohesion' mentioned above). This hierarchy will be termed the Interclausal Semantic Relations Hierarchy, and it is given in figure 8.17. Thus, in causative and aspectual constructions, each unit expresses a phase of a single event, whereas from the psych-action relation on down, there are two distinct states of affairs; with psych-action, they are the mental disposition of the actor and the projected action, with purposive it is the initial action and the intended result or goal of the action, with jussive it is the expression of the command or request and the commanded or requested action, etc. In all of these cases the interpretation of the linked proposition is dependent upon the semantics of the matrix proposition. At the lower end of the Interclausal Semantic Relations Hierarchy are states of affairs which are related primarily through their temporal relations only.

Silverstein (1976) and Givón (1980) also argue that there is a fundamentally **iconic** relationship between the syntax and semantics of clause linkage: the closer the semantic relationship between two propositions is, the stronger the syntactic link joining them is. That is, the closeness of the semantic relationship between the units in a juncture is mirrored in the tightness of the syntactic relationship between them. This can be seen most clearly when we juxtapose the Interclausal Syntactic Relations and Interclausal Semantic Relations Hierarchies to create the Interclausal Relations Hierarchy in figure 8.18.

All languages can express the semantic relations in the Interclausal Semantic Relations Hierarchy part of the Interclausal Relations Hierarchy, and there are fewer juncture–nexus types in the Interclausal Syntactic Relations Hierarchy than distinct semantic relations in the Interclausal Semantic Relations Hierarchy; hence a language invariably has fewer syntactic juncture–nexus types than there are

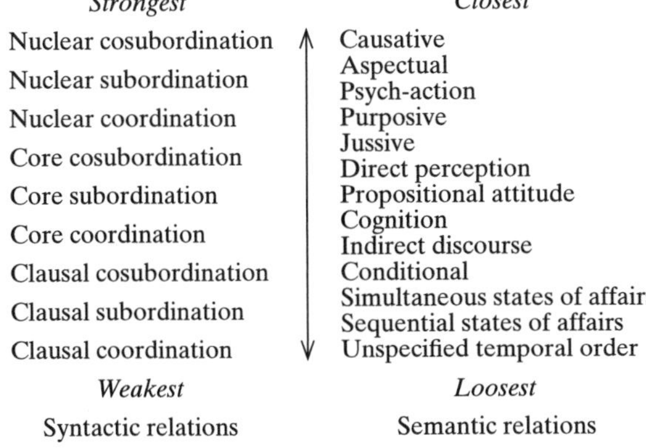

Figure 8.18 Interclausal Relations Hierarchy

semantic relations that need to be expressed. Consequently the mapping between the two sides of the Interclausal Relations Hierarchy is many-to-one. A given juncture–nexus type is normally used to express more than one interclausal semantic relation. In English, for example, core cosubordination instantiates aspectual, psych-action and purposive relations; core coordination is employed for jussive, direct perception and propositional attitude (as in *Paul considers Carl to be a fool*); and one type of clausal subordination, complement *that*-clauses (see figure 8.14), expresses propositional attitude, cognition and indirect discourse relations, while another type, adverbial clauses, is used for conditionals, simultaneous states of affairs and sequential states of affairs. This can be seen clearly if one takes the examples in (8.55) and plots their juncture–nexus types against the Interclausal Syntactic Relations Hierarchy. It is also the case that a given semantic relation can be conveyed by more than one juncture–nexus type. We mentioned above that propositional attitude can be realized by both core coordination and clausal subordination, and what is perhaps the most extreme case of multiple instantiation, causation, is presented in (8.56).

(8.56)
a. Harry shot Tom dead. — Nuclear cosubordination
b. Harry caused Tom to die. — Core coordination
c. Having been shot by Harry, Tom died. — Clausal cosubordination
d. Tom died, because Harry shot him. — Clausal subordination
e. After Harry shot him, Tom died. — Clausal subordination
f. Harry shot Tom, and he died. — Clausal coordination

Undoubtedly there are additional ways to express this state of affairs in English, but these examples illustrate the point well. Notice that the tighter the syntactic linkage, the more direct the causation is and that the looser the linkage, the more indirect the causation is, until it is really no more than an inference in the last two sentences; this is a reflection of the iconicity principle inherent in the Interclausal Relations Hierarchy.[17] Moreover, the higher a semantic relation is on the Interclausal Relations Hierarchy, the more likely it is that there will be multiple ways to realize it syntactically. That is, the higher the tightest linkage relation realizing a particular semantic relation is, the more looser linkage relations will be available for alternative codings of it, as illustrated in (8.56).

A given verb may take more than one juncture–nexus type in complex sentences. Some verbs can occur with as many as three juncture–nexus types, e.g. *be likely* and *remember*, as illustrated in (8.57) and (8.58).

(8.57) a. That Jim will win the race is likely. — Core subordination
b. It is likely that Jim will win the race. — Clausal subordination
c. Jim is likely to win the race. — Core cosubordination

(8.58) a. Morris remembered to apply the rule. — Core cosubordination
b. Morris remembered Abe applying the rule. — Core coordination
c. Morris remembered that Abe applied the rule. — Clausal subordination

This is related to the semantics of the construction, illustrated by the following examples with *persuade*.

(8.59) a. Felipe persuaded Manuel to leave. — Psych-action
b. Alicia persuaded Carlos that a quantum theory of gravity is possible. — Propositional attitude

Persuade has two basic senses, very roughly 'cause to want' and 'cause to believe', and this can be seen most clearly in the way *persuade* is translated into other languages. In Lakhota, for example, *persuade* is translated two ways; the first is *čhį́-khíya* [want-CAUSE] 'cause to want', and the second is *wičákhela-khiya* [believe (< *wičákhe-la* 'true-consider')-CAUSE] 'cause to believe'. These are reflected in the logical structures for these sentences in (8.60); **want′** entails a psych-action interclausal relation and **believe′** a propositional attitude or cognition interclausal semantic relation.

(8.60) a. *persuade* (psych-action): [**do′** (x, Ø)] CAUSE [**want′** (y, [. . .])]
b. *persuade* (propositional attitude/cognition): [**do′** (x, Ø)] CAUSE [**believe′** (y, [. . .])]

In terms of the choice of complement construction used with complement-taking predicates, it has been widely assumed that it is necessary to list the different complement forms a verb takes, yet *persuade* in its psych-action sense takes the same complement form as other psych-action verbs, such as *want*, i.e. a non-subordinate core juncture realized by an infinitive construction (*to* + infinitive), and this follows from the meaning of psych-action: the verb codes a mental disposition on the part of its actor to be involved in a state of affairs, and accordingly the actor must also

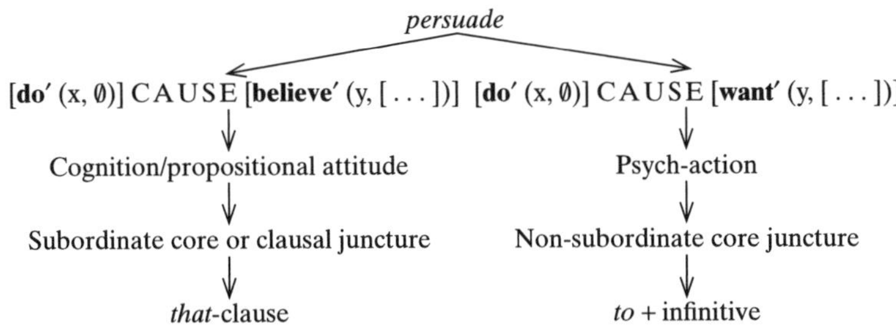

Figure 8.19 Analysis of English *persuade* complex sentence forms

be a semantic argument of the embedded logical structure, because the participant with the mental disposition must also be a participant in the state of affairs denoted by the embedded logical structure. Likewise, in its propositional attitude/cognition sense it takes the same complement form as other propositional attitude verbs such as *believe*, i.e. clausal subordination realized by a *that*-clause; the content of the belief is a proposition, and the canonical realization of a proposition is a clause, hence a *that*-construction for an embedded proposition. Thus, using the Interclausal Relations Hierarchy (figure 8.18) and the semantic representations for *persuade*, we can derive the appropriate complex sentence forms for this verb. This is summarized in figure 8.19.

This analysis makes clear that, given the framework presented in this chapter for the analysis of the syntax and semantics of complex sentences, the juncture–nexus type(s) and complement constructions that a verb takes can be derived from its semantic representation and need not be stipulated in its lexical entry. For the purposes of this discussion, it is sufficient to say that each of the two senses of *persuade* has a distinct but related logical structure. However, Van Valin and Wilkins (1993) argue that, with a more fine-grained decomposition than that presented in chapter 3, it is possible to give a single logical structure for verbs like *persuade* or *remember*, which occur with multiple juncture–nexus types in complex sentences.[18]

Thus, a given juncture–nexus type can express more than one semantic relation, and a given semantic relation can be expressed by more than one juncture–nexus type. Are there, then, any generalizations about the mapping between the two parts of the Interclausal Relations Hierarchy? The answer is 'yes': the tightest syntactic linkage realizing a particular semantic relation should be higher than or as high on the Interclausal Relations Hierarchy as the tightest syntactic linkage realizing semantic relations lower on the Interclausal Relations Hierarchy. Accordingly, the tightest linkage category in the grammar should always instantiate causation, the closest semantic relation on the Interclausal Relations Hierarchy. In English, the tightest instantiation of causation is nuclear cosubordination, the tightest juncture–nexus type, and the tightest realization of aspectual, psych-action and purposive relations is core cosubordination. This follows from this claim in two ways: first, the tightest expression of causation is realized by a linkage type higher on the Interclausal Relations Hierarchy than the tightest expression of the following three relations, and these three relations are realized by the next-tightest linkage type in English. What should not occur, according to this principle, is, for example, for causation through psych-action to be expressed by core cosubordination and for purposive to be expressed by some kind of nuclear juncture.[19]

There is one final complication that needs to be mentioned. In many languages it is the case that the semantic relations at the top of the Interclausal Relations Hierarchy, particularly causation, are not expressed through syntactic means but rather through derivational morphology, e.g. causation can be expressed in Lakhota by means of the bound causative suffixes *-ya* and *-khiya*, which, when added to a verb, create the semantic equivalent of syntactic junctures in other languages, e.g. *čhéya* 'cry' vs. *čheyá+ya* 'make cry, cause to cry', *čhį́* 'want' vs. *čhį́-khíya* 'cause to want, persuade'. We saw numerous examples of this in chapter 3. In this situation, the tightest syntactic linkage does not realize the closest semantic relation, but this is not a counterexample to the spirit of the Interclausal Relations Hierarchy. Indeed, the fact that it is the closest semantic relations that are grammaticalized into morphological constructions follows the basic claim of the Interclausal Relations Hierarchy: the stronger the semantic relation, the tighter the morphosyntactic bond between units, and the evolution from a tightly linked syntactic construction to an even more tightly linked morphological construction is a natural extension of the iconic relationship between form and meaning captured in the Interclausal Relations Hierarchy. It predicts, in fact, that grammaticalization should work from the closest semantic relations down; it should never be the case, for example, that psych-action relations are realized morphologically while causative and aspectual relations are conveyed only syntactically.

8.5 Focus structure in complex sentences

In chapter 5 we discussed focus structure in simple sentences, and in section 5.3 we introduced a distinction between the potential focus domain and the actual focus domain of a sentence. The potential focus domain is the syntactic domain in which the focus element(s) may occur. The actual focus domain, as the label implies, is the actual part of the sentence in focus. One of the most striking findings of that section was the fact that languages differ with respect to the extent of the potential focus domain in simple sentences: English allows any element within the clause to be focused; French, Italian and Mandarin restrict the potential focus domain for non-WH-words to postverbal position within the clause, and the only focused preverbal elements allowed are WH-words; and Sesotho and other Sotho languages are even stricter, restricting all focus elements to postverbal position within the clause, including WH-words in questions.

We now turn to the question of the potential focus domain in complex sentences. An important point to keep in mind is that the node anchoring the focus structure projection in the syntactic representation of a sentence, the speech act node (see figures 5.3–5.6), is closely related to the illocutionary force operator in the operator projection, because different speech acts have different illocutionary forces. We mentioned in section 8.4.1 that subordinate clauses may not have independent illocutionary force operators and that they are either outside the domain of the illocutionary force operator of the clause, i.e. are presupposed, or have the same force as the main clause. In general, certain types of construction, e.g. adverbial clauses, sentential 'subjects' and definite restrictive relative clauses, are virtually always presupposed and therefore outside of the potential focus domain, whereas others, most notably 'object' complements, may or may not be in the actual focus domain and may therefore be within the potential focus domain. Why should this be so? There is a very general structural principle governing the potential focus domain in complex sentences, which was originally proposed in Van Valin (1993b); it is stated in (8.61).

(8.61) *The potential focus domain in complex sentences*
A subordinate clause may be within the potential focus domain if it is a direct daughter of (a direct daughter of . . .) the clause node which is modified by the illocutionary force operator.

In principle there is no limit to the number of direct daughters involved, and therefore the specification in parentheses should be considered to be recursive. In terms of cross-linguistic variation, there appear to be only two possibilities: the potential focus domain is restricted to main clauses only, in which case (8.61) is irrelevant to the language, or the potential focus domain can extend to the deepest subordinate clause in any sentence, as long as the condition in (8.61) is met. There appear to be no languages that arbitrarily limit the potential focus domain to a specific depth of embedding; that is, languages with a restriction like 'only two clauses down and no more' do not exist.

We can illustrate the contrast in subordinate clause types by looking at the English examples in figures 8.13 and 8.14. In figure 8.14 the subordinate clause, a *that*-clause, is a direct daughter of the clause modified by the illocutionary force operator; this can be seen most clearly in the operator projection, even though it is represented in both projections. Hence it is within the potential focus domain. In figure 8.20 we replace the operator projection by the focus structure projection to depict this. As in the figures in chapter 5, the dotted line represents the potential focus domain, and the 'ARG', 'NUC', etc. indicate the basic information units. An important feature of this construction is that the subordinate clause as a whole may function as an information unit, since it can be replaced by a single WH-word, e.g. *What did John tell Mary*?, or the elements inside of it may also be interpreted as distinct information units, because the subordinate clause is in the potential focus

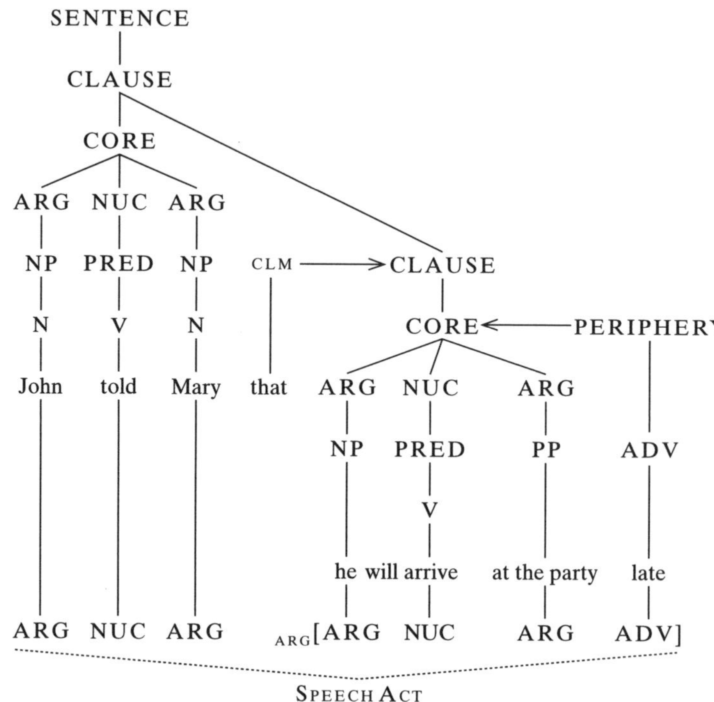

Figure 8.20 Potential focus domain in clausal subordination (*that*-complement)

domain. What evidence is there that it is in fact in the potential focus domain? As we saw in our discussion in section 5.3, in order to be the focus of a question, an element must be in the potential focus domain. Consider the following question–answer pair.[20]

(8.62) Q: Did John tell Mary that he will arrive at the party LATE?
A: No, EARLY.

It is possible for the focus of the yes–no question to fall on the subordinate clause peripheral adverb *late*, as the felicity of the response denying *late* and asserting *early* shows. Hence the subordinate clause must be in the potential focus domain, because in the question in (8.62) the actual focus domain is in the subordinate clause.

Now let us look at the example involving an adverbial subordinate clause in figure 8.13. The subordinate clause is not a direct daughter of the clause node modified by the illocutionary force operator; it is, rather, an adjunct modifier of the core. Hence the potential focus domain does not extend into the subordinate clause, but the clause as a whole is within the potential focus domain, as it is a constituent of the periphery of the main clause. This is illustrated in figure 8.21. The adverbial subordinate clause as a whole functions as a single information unit within the main clause and can be replaced by a WH-word, e.g. *When did Pat see Mary*?; its internal

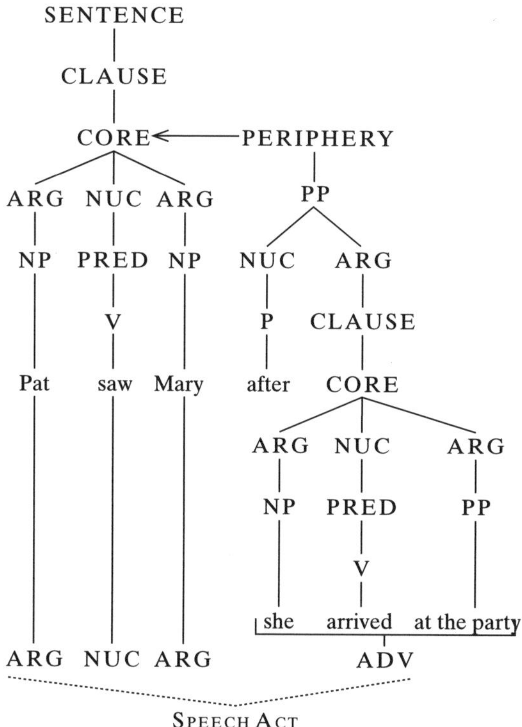

Figure 8.21 Potential focus domain in clausal subordination (adverbial clause)

constituents are not, however, within the potential focus domain. This can be seen in the question–answer pairs in (8.63).

(8.63) Q: Did Pat see Mary after she$_i$ arrived?
A: a. No, Sally.
b. No, before.
c. *No, she$_i$ left.[21]

The infelicitity of the (c) response, in sharp contrast to the answer in (8.62), shows that the constituents of the adverbial subordinate clause are outside of the potential focus domain. *After* can be the focus of a yes–no question, because it is part of the peripheral PP in the main clause. The principle in (8.61) correctly predicts that the *that*-clause in (8.62) is within the potential focus domain and that the adverbial clause in (8.63) is not.

What kind of evidence can be used to show that an embedded clause is in the potential focus domain or not? We have just seen one example, whether a constituent can be the focus of a yes–no question as indicated by the felicity of a single constituent response. Another type of evidence involves the distribution of focus-sensitive elements. For example, if a language has overt focus particles marking NPs in focus, then their distribution in embedded clauses would be a telling indicator of whether the potential focus domain extends into embedded clauses. If they can occur in a particular type of embedded clause with their focus-marking function, that is evidence that that clause type is within the potential focus domain. We will investigate one example of this from Lakhota.

The focus-sensitive element we are interested in in Lakhota is a set of indefinite articles which are non-referential (non-specific); they can occur in only three contexts: in the scope of the question particle *he*, in the scope of negation and in the scope of the 'future tense' morpheme *-kte* (Williamson 1984). We will use the question particle in our discussion; it occurs sentence-finally, as we saw in (7.156) in section 7.6.2. This is illustrated in (8.64).

(8.64) a. Hokšíla eyá thaló ki ma-Ø-Ø-nú-pi.[22]
boy some [+SPEC] meat the INAN-3A-steal-pl
a′. *Hokšíla etą́ thaló ki manúpi.
some [–SPEC]
'Some boys stole the meat.'
b. Hokšílá eyá thaló ki manúpi he?
some [+SPEC] Q
*'Did SOME BOYS steal the meat?', but OK: 'Did some boys STEAL the meat?' or 'Did some boys steal THE MEAT?'
b′. Hokšíla etą́ thaló ki manúpi he?
some [–SPEC]
'Did SOME BOYS steal the meat?', but *'Did some boys STEAL the meat?' or *'Did some boys steal THE MEAT?'

In the non-interrogative utterance in (a), only the indefinite–specific article *eyá* 'some' can occur; the non-specific indefinite article *etą́* is ungrammatical, as (a′) shows. In an interrogative utterance like (b), *eyá* is ungrammatical if its NP is the focus of the question; otherwise, it is grammatical. In (b′), on the other hand, *etą́* can only occur if its NP is the focus of the question; if the focus falls on a different constituent, the result is ungrammatical. The distribution of these two articles is evidence as to whether an NP can be the focus in a particular clause, and this in turn is evidence as to whether the clause is within the potential focus domain.

In the following sentences, NPs with *eyá* and *etą́* occur in three types of subordinate clauses: object complement in (8.65), definite restrictive relative clause in (8.66)[23] and adverbial clause in (8.67). Each sentence will have a question operator in the main clause, and if *etą́* can occur in the subordinate clause, then this shows that the focus of the yes–no question can be in the subordinate clause. Accordingly, the clause is in the potential focus domain.

(8.65) a. [Hokšíla etą́ thaló ki ma-Ø-Ø-nú-pi] i-Ø-Ø-yúkčą he?
boy some [–SPEC] meat the INAN-3A-steal-pl INAN-3sgA-think Q
'Does he think SOME BOYS stole the meat?'
b. *[Hokšíla etą́ thaló ki manúpi] iyúkčą.
'He thinks some boys stole the meat.'

(8.66) a. *Wičháša ki [[šų́ka wą igmú etą́ wičhá-∅-yaxtake] ki le]
man the [[dog a cat some [–SPEC] 3plU-3sgA-bite] the this]
wą-∅-∅-yą́ka he?
3sgU-3sgA-saw Q
'Did the man see the dog which bit some cats?'

b. *Wičháša ki [[šų́ka wą igmú etą́ wičháyaxtake] ki le] wąyą́ke.
'The man saw the dog which bit some cats.'

c. Wičháša ki [[šų́ka wą igmú eyá wičháyaxtake] ki le] wąyą́ke.
some [+SPEC]
'The man saw the dog which bit some cats.'

d. Wičháša ki [[šų́ka wą igmú eyá wičháyaxtake] ki le] wąyą́ka he?
'Did the man see the dog which bit some cats?'

(8.67) a. *Wičháša etą́ ∅-wóta-pi ečhúhą, wį́yą ki mní
man some [–SPEC] 3A-eat-pl while woman the water
i-∅-wíčha-∅-kičiču he?
INAN-3plU-3sgA-get.for Q
'While some men were eating, did the woman get them water?'

b. *Wičháša etą́ wótapi ečhúhą, wį́yą ki mní iwíčhakičiču.
'While some men were eating, the woman got them water.'

c. Wičháša eyá wótapi ečhúhą, wíyą ki mní iwíčhakičiču.
some [+SPEC]
'While some men were eating, the woman got them water.'

d. Wičháša eyá wótapi ečhúhą, wį́yą ki mní iwíčhakičiču he?
'While some men were eating, did the woman get them water?'

In (8.65a) *etą́* in the complement clause is grammatical, and this shows that the NP *hokšíla etą́* 'some boys' can be the focus of the yes–no question; hence, the complement clause is within the potential focus domain. In the relative clauses in (8.66), however, *etą́* is impossible, regardless of whether the sentence is a question or not, and only *eyá* is grammatical. Consequently, we may conclude that the restrictive relative clause is outside the potential focus domain. Finally, the same pattern is found in the adverbial subordinate clauses in (8.67) that is found in the relative clauses in (8.66): the occurrence of *etą́* in the embedded clause is ungrammatical and only *eyá* is possible, regardless of the illocutionary force of the sentence as a whole. Thus, the possibilities of occurrence of *etą́* and *eyá* in these embedded clauses leads to the conclusion that object complements are within the potential focus domain but definite restrictive relative clauses and adverbial subordinate clauses are not.

This conclusion is confirmed by looking at the range of possible felicitous answers to yes–no questions involving these same constructions, analogous to what we did with the English examples in (8.62) and (8.63). This is illustrated in (8.68).

(8.68) a. [Hokšíla etą́ thaló ki manúpi] iyúkčą he?
boy some [–SPEC] meat the steal think Q
'Does he think some boys stole the meat?'

– Hiyá, wičhį́čala eyá.
no girl some [+SPEC]
'No, some girls.'

b. Wičháša ki [[šų́ka wą igmú eyá wičháyaxtake] ki le]
man the dog a cat some [+SPEC] bite the this
wąyą́ka he?
see Q
'Did the man see the dog which bit some cats?'
– Hiyá, wąyą́kešni
no see.NEG
'No, he didn't see it.'
– Hiyá, wį́yą ki (wąyą́ke).
woman the (see)
'No, the woman (saw it).'
– Hiyá, mathó wą (wąyą́ke).
bear a (see)
'No, (he saw) a bear.'
– *Hiyá, magá eyá (wičháyaxtake).
duck some (bite)
*'No, (it bit) some ducks.'

c. [Wičháša ki wóte] ečhúhą, tha-wíču ki mní ikíčiču he?
man the eat while his-wife the water get.for Q
'While the man was eating, did his wife get him water?'
– Hiyá, Fred (mní ikíčiču/*wóte).
'No, Fred (got it for him)', or 'No, (she got it for) Fred.'
*'No, Fred was eating.'

In (a) the embedded clause is an object complement, and as the potentially appropriate response indicates, focus may fall within the embedded clause, since it is felicitous to deny the subject NP of the complement in the response. (Note the switch from *etą́* in the question to *eyá* in the answer.) This is further evidence in support of the conclusion reached above. In (b) the embedded clause is a definite restrictive relative clause. As always in this language, it is possible for the focus to fall on all of the matrix clause elements, including the NP interpreted as the head of the relative clause, but as the last response shows, it is impossible for an element within the relative clause to be the focus of the question. The final example involves an adverbial subordinate clause, and as the range of potential responses indicates, an element within the subordinate clause cannot be the focus of the question. Thus while the focus can fall on any major element of the matrix clause, it cannot fall within the embedded clause if it is a relative clause or adverbial subordinate clause, and this confirms the conclusion based on the distribution of the indefinite articles in these same constructions.

The potential focus domain in these Lakhota constructions is summarized in (8.69).

(8.69) *Summary of potential scope of* he: *Potential focus domain* (*in italics*)
a. [*Hokšíla etą́ thaló ki manúpi*] *iyúkčą* he?
b. *Wičháša ki* [[*šų́ka wą* igmú eyá wičháyaxtake] *ki le*] *wąyą́ka* he?
c. [Wičhaša ki wóte] *ečhúhą, tha-wíču ki mní ikíčiču* he?[24]

Does the principle in (8.61) predict this distribution of the potential focus domain in Lakhota? As can be seen from the simplified representations of these constructions in figure 8.22, the answer is 'yes'. The (a) diagram in this figure represents a complement clause like (8.69a), in which the embedded clause is a direct daughter of the clause node modified by the illocutionary force operator. As predicted, the potential focus domain extends into the embedded clause. The (b) diagram is a restrictive relative clause like (8.69b), and because the clause is embedded inside an NP, there is no relationship at all between the embedded clause and the clause node

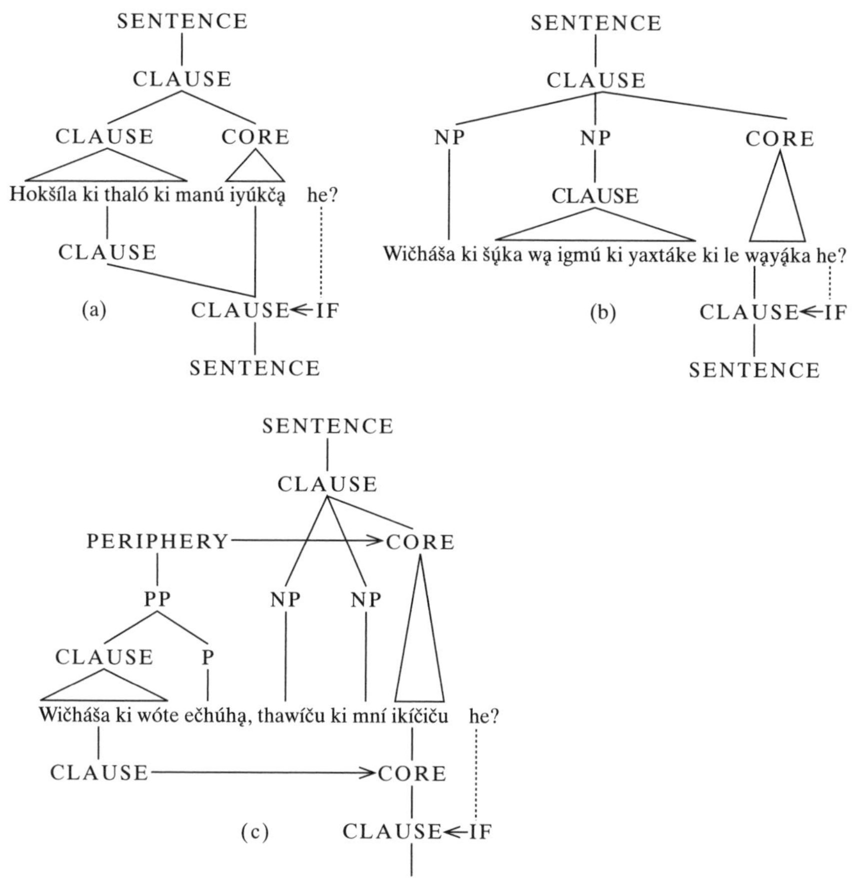

Figure 8.22 The structure of Lakhota complex sentences

modified by the illocutionary force operator. Accordingly, the principle in (8.61) correctly predicts that the embedded clause is outside of the potential focus domain. Finally the (c) diagram represents the adverbial subordinate clause in (8.69c), and as in the English adverbial clause discussed earlier, the embedded clause is an adjunct modifier of the core and not a direct daughter of the clause node modified by the illocutionary force operator. Hence, the principle in (8.61) correctly predicts that the embedded clause is outside the potential focus domain. Thus, the distribution of *eyá* and *etą́* in Lakhota, which must occur in the potential focus domain, is correctly predicted by the principle in (8.61).

We will return to the issue of the potential focus domain in complex sentences in our discussion of WH-question formation out of complex sentences in chapter 9. We will see that a variety of factors interact with the principle in (8.61) to determine the actual focus domain in particular constructions.

8.6 The structure of complex noun phrases

We introduced the layered structure of the NP in section 2.3.2, and in that section we discussed only 'simple' NPs, i.e. NPs containing only operators and NP or PP core_N arguments. We now turn our attention to NPs which have clauses and infinitives as constituents. The first question to ask is whether the layers of the layered structure of the noun phrase define levels of juncture in complex NPs in an analogous fashion to the layered structure of the clause in complex sentences. The answer appears to be 'yes'.

8.6.1 Juncture and nexus in complex NPs

NPs and sentences have similar but not identical layered structures, and this comes out most clearly in complex constructions. There are four layers in sentential units (sentence, clause, core and nucleus), whereas there are only three in NPs (NP, core_N, nucleus_N). Because there is only one level in NPs corresponding to two in sentences, the left-detached position–precore slot contrast is collapsed into a single position, the NP-initial position, in which arguments (e.g. ***the city's*** *destruction*), adjuncts (e.g. ***yesterday's*** *weather*) and WH-words (e.g. ***which*** *boy*) can appear. Hence the NP level is the analog to the clause level of juncture, and there are three distinct linkage types at the NP level which correspond to nexus differences in complex sentences. The simplest example of an NP-level linkage would be conjoined NPs, as in *the woman and the man*. Each constituent NP can have the full range of operators and arguments, e.g. ***The two tall sisters of my neighbor and the two short brothers of my best friend*** *are going out together*. Accordingly, this will be referred to as NP coordination. It is also possible to link two NPs which share a determiner, an NP-level operator (see table 2.3), but have all other operators independently, e.g. ***The three green cars and two red cars*** *were sold in an hour*. This is an example of NP cosubordination. Finally, it is possible to have a subordinate modifier at the NP level, a restrictive relative clause, e.g. *the two red cars which were* *sold yesterday*. Its relationship to the NP is analogous to that of an adverbial subordinate clause to the clause it modifies; indeed, it would seem appropriate to locate it in the periphery$_N$ of the NP, analogous to the location of an adverbial subordinate clause in the periphery of the clause (see figure 8.13). In both cases the subordinate clause serves to help the interlocutor locate the referent of the main clause (a state of affairs) or of the NP (an individual) in a temporal, spatial or other domain. The linkage type of NPs containing restrictive relative clauses will be referred to as NP subordination; it will be discussed in more detail in section 8.6.2 below. The structure of the first two types of linkage is presented in figures 8.23 and 8.24.

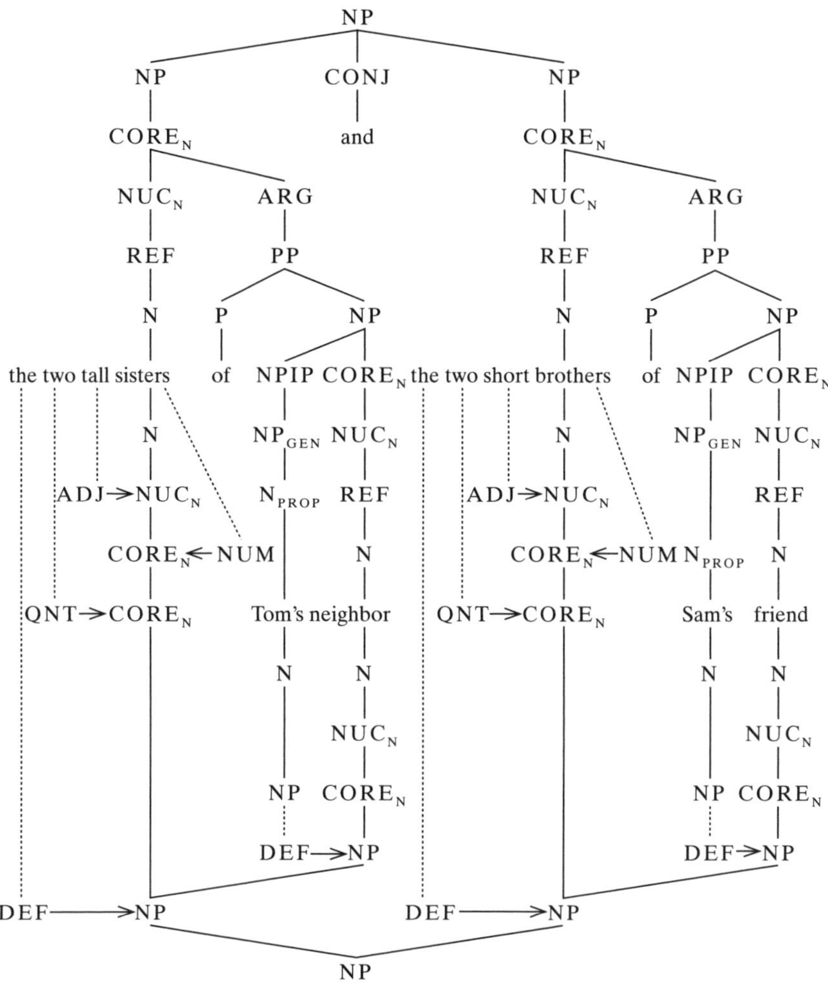

Figure 8.23 English NP coordination

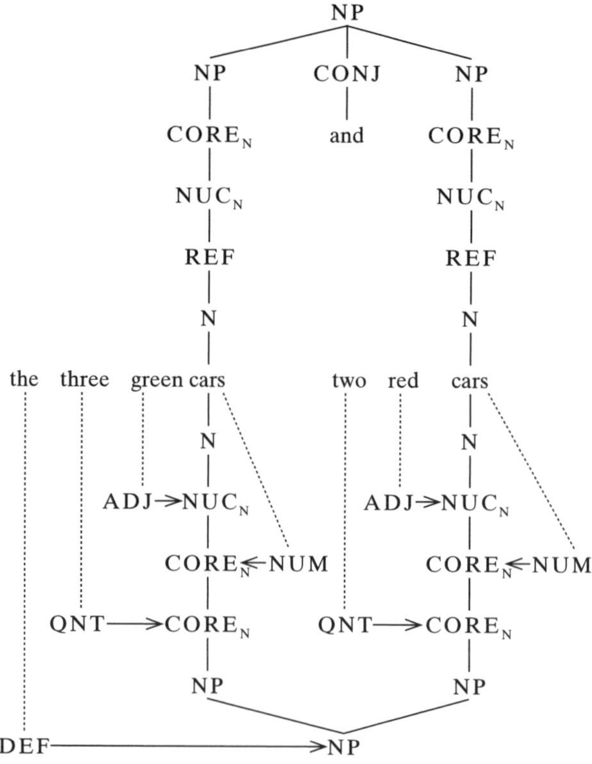

Figure 8.24 English NP cosubordination

There are at least two types of core$_N$ linkage. The first involves *that*-clauses serving as the core$_N$ argument of nouns like *story*, *rumor*, *belief*, *opinion*, etc., e.g. *Carl's belief that UFOs are a menace to the earth*, *the rumor that Fred saw a UFO*. The structure of core$_N$ subordination is given in figure 8.25. The other includes infinitival complements to nouns like *attempt*, *order*, *request* and *promise*, e.g. *the attempt by the prisoners to escape*, *the king's order to his troops to attack*, *Mary's request to leave* and *John's promise to wash the car tomorrow*. Similar constructions occur in Spanish, e.g. *el intento de los presos por escapar* 'the attempt by the prisoners to escape'. Like non-subordinate core junctures, there is a shared core$_N$ argument between the deverbal nominal and the infinitive. The primary core$_N$ operators, number and quantification, always have scope over both units in the linkage, e.g. *the seven attempts by the prisoners to escape*, *the king's many orders to his troops to attack*, *Mary's three futile requests to leave* and *John's many unfulfilled promises to wash the car*. Consequently there appears to be only one type of non-subordinate linkage at the core$_N$ level, and therefore we will posit core$_N$ subordination and core$_N$ cosubordination within complex NPs. The structure of core$_N$ cosubordination is illustrated in figure 8.26.

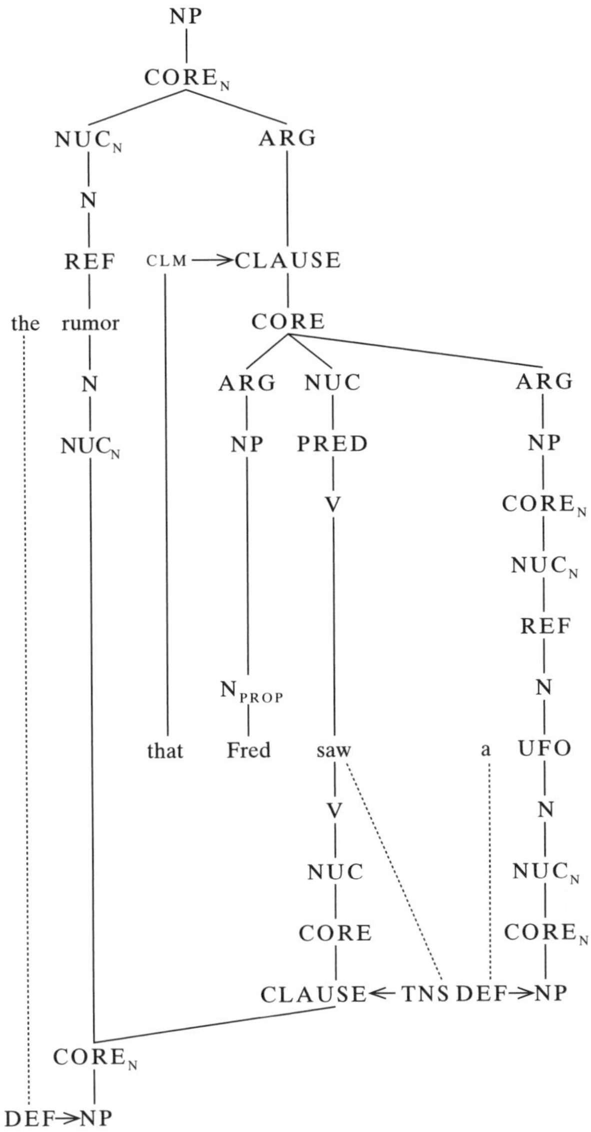

Figure 8.25 English core$_N$ subordination

We have already seen an example of a juncture at the nuclear$_N$ level within an NP: the Lakhota possessive form in which a reduced verb stem is incorporated into the head noun to produce a possessive construction in which the possessor is treated as a core$_N$ argument (see figure 2.27). Being a dependent-marking language, English has no analogous constructions; it does, however, have productive syntactic noun compounding, which would be a nuclear$_N$ juncture. An example of this would

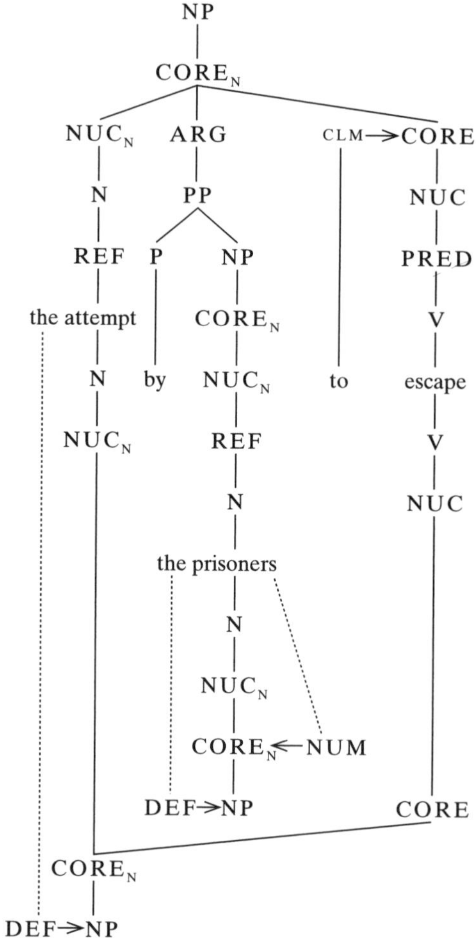

Figure 8.26 English core_N cosubordination

be the N + *hunter* pattern (which is itself an instance of the more general N + V-*er* pattern), as in *duck hunter*, *tiger hunter*, *lion hunter*, *deer hunter*, etc. The resulting compound nominal takes a single set of operators, all of which have scope over both components of the complex nucleus, e.g. *the two tall duck hunters*, *those three Dutch deer hunters*, etc. There appears to be only one nexus type at the nuclear_N level; in both the English and the Lakhota constructions, all operators would have scope over the derived nucleus_N, including all nuclear_N operators. The structure of these nuclear_N junctures is given in figure 8.27.

It appears that while there are juncture–nexus distinctions among complex NP constructions, they have a different distribution from that in complex sentence constructions. That is, while all three nexus types are possible at both the clausal and

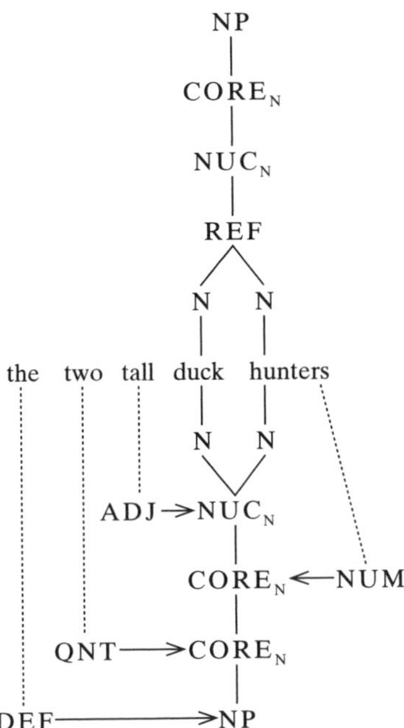

Figure 8.27 English nuclear$_N$ juncture

Table 8.1 *Juncture and nexus in the NP*

Level of juncture	*Nexus Type(s)*	*Example*
NP	Coordinate	Figure 8.23
	Cosubordinate	Figure 8.24
	Subordinate	Restrictive relative clause
Core$_N$	Cosubordinate	Figure 8.26
	Subordinate	Figure 8.25
Nuclear$_N$	No contrast	Figure 8.27

NP levels of juncture, only two nexus types are found at the core$_N$ level, subordination and cosubordination, and there appear to be no nexus contrasts at all at the nuclear$_N$ level. This is summarized in table 8.1.

8.6.2 Relative clauses

As mentioned in the previous section, the prime example of NP subordination is restrictive relative clauses. In such a construction, a clause is used as a restrictive modifier of an NP; it is part of the periphery$_N$ of the NP, since it is an optional modifier, not a core$_N$ argument. This description presupposes that there is a head noun which is outside of (external to) the relative clause. Such constructions are called *externally headed* relative clauses, and examples from English, German, Malagasy (Keenan 1985b) and Jakaltek (Craig 1977) are given in (8.70); the head noun is in boldface, and the relative clauses are in italics.

(8.70) a. the two red **cars** *which were sold yesterday*
b. die zwei rot-en **Auto-s** *die*
the.FEMplNOM two red-pl car-pl which.FEMplACC
ich gesehen habe
1sgNOM see.PSTP have.1sgPRES
'the two red cars which I saw' German
c. ny **vehivavy** (*izay*) *man-asa ny lamba*
the woman CLM ATV-wash the clothes
'the woman who is washing the clothes' Malagasy
c′. Man-asa ny lamba ny vehivavy.
ATV-wash the clothes the woman
'The woman is washing the clothes.'
d. te' **tx'at** *x-Ø-a-watx'e*
CL bed PAST-3ABS-2sgERG-make
'the bed you made' Jakaltek
d′. X-Ø-a-watx'e te' tx'at
PAST-3ABS-2sgERG-make CL bed
'You made the bed.'

In the English and German examples there are relative pronouns, *which* in English and *die* in German. In these languages relative pronouns occupy the same structural position in a clause as the WH-words in questions, the precore slot. This can be seen most clearly in English, in which the relative pronouns are formally the same as WH-pronouns.

(8.71) a. the man who(m) he saw
a′. Who(m) did he see?
b. the car which he bought
b′. Which did he buy?

In constructions with relative pronouns, the relative pronouns occur in the precore slot. The structures of the English and German examples are given in figures 8.28 and 8.29. These structures are analogous to those of clausal subordination with adverbial clauses (see figure 8.13); in both cases a clause is used as a modifier of the matrix unit. Hence clausal subordination involving adverbial clauses is structurally parallel to NP subordination involving restrictive relative clauses.

As in most languages, relative clauses in Malagasy and Jakaltek do not involve relative pronouns; the head noun is construed with a missing argument position in the relative clause. Malagasy has an optional invariable element *izay* marking the relative clause; it is analogous to the use of English *that* in relative clauses without

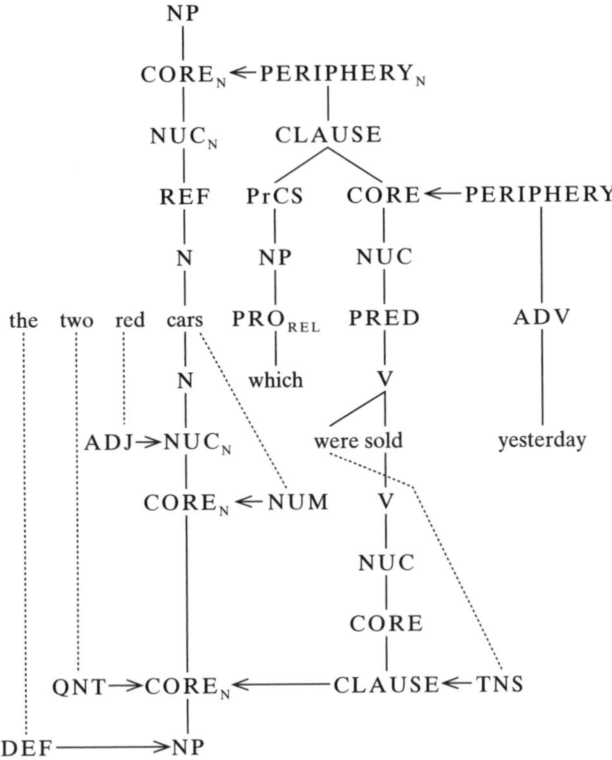

Figure 8.28 English restrictive relative clause with relative pronoun

a relative pronoun, e.g. *the* ***man*** (*that*) *Bill saw*. The structure of the Malagasy and Jakaltek examples is given in figures 8.30 and 8.31. The interpretation of relative clauses, including both that of the relative pronoun in the English–German type and that of the head noun with respect to the missing argument in the relative clause will be treated in the discussion of linking syntax and semantics in complex sentences in chapter 9.

Not all relative clause constructions have an external head noun, as we saw in the Belhare examples in section 6.5; in many languages, e.g. Belhare, Lakhota, Tibetan and Quechua, there are *internally headed* relative clause constructions. In this type of relative clause, the head occurs within the embedded clause and is simultaneously intepreted as an argument of the matrix clause.[25] Examples from Lakhota are given in (8.72); the head nouns are in italic.

(8.72) a. Wičháša ki [[šų́ka ki *igmú wą* Ø-Ø-yaxtáke] ki he] wą-Ø-Ø-yą́ke
man the dog the cat a 3sgU-3sgA-bite the that 3sgU-3sgA-see
yelo.
DEC
'The man saw the cat which the dog bit.'

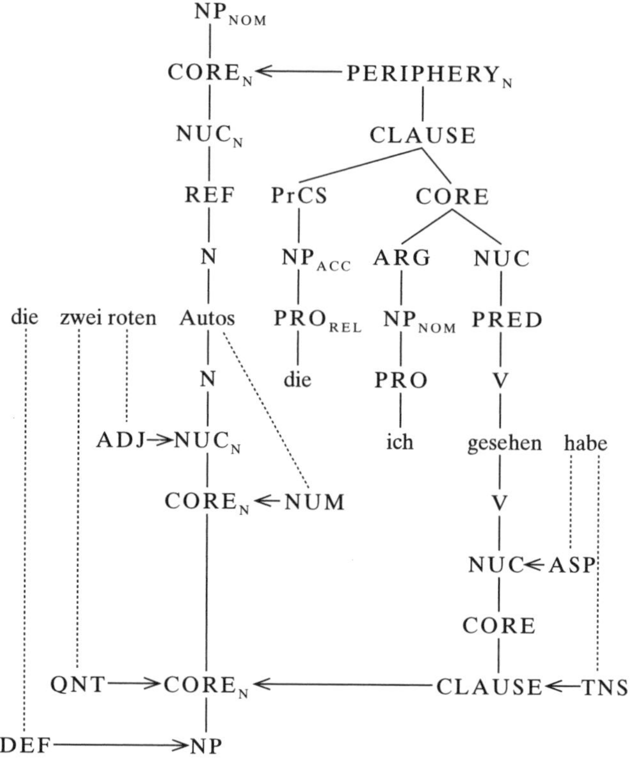

Figure 8.29 German restrictive relative clause

b. Wičháša ki [[*šųka wą* igmú óta wičhá-∅-yaxtake] ki he]
man the dog a cat many 3plU-3sgA-bite the that
wą-∅-∅-yą́ke yelo.
3sgU-3sgA-see DEC
'The man saw the dog which bit many cats.'

c. Wičháša ki [[šųka wą igmú wą ∅-∅-yaxtáke] ki he]
man the dog a cat a 3sgU-3sgA-bite the that
wą-∅-∅-yą́ke yelo.
3sgU-3sgA-see DEC
'The man saw the cat which a dog bit', or 'The man saw the dog which bit a cat.'

The relative clause is enclosed in brackets, and the head noun is in italics in (8.72a, b). In (8.72a) the NPs *wičháša ki* 'the man' and *igmú* 'cat', the head of the relative clause, are cross-referenced by the two zero third-person markers on the verb *wąyą́ke* 'see'. An important property of Lakhota relative clauses is that the head noun must be coded as indefinite within the relative clause; its true definiteness

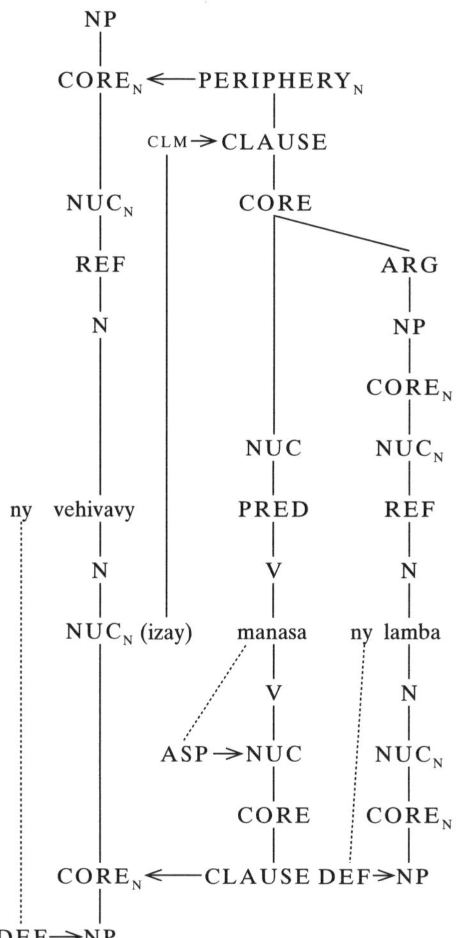

Figure 8.30 Malagasy restrictive relative clause

status is indicated by the article + demonstrative combination at the end of the relative clause. That these constructions are internally headed can be seen clearly in (8.72a), in which the head noun *igmú* 'cat' is surrounded by elements of the embedded clause. In (8.72b) the head is initial in the relative clause. If both NPs in the relative clause are marked indefinite, as in (8.72c), then the resulting construction is ambiguous, in that either NP may be interpreted as the head noun. The structure of (8.72a) is given in figure 8.32. Unlike a complement clause, the relative clause is dominated by an NP node in the constituent projection. The head noun is indicated explicitly in this representation in both projections. In the operator projection, the article + demonstrative combination marking the relative clause modifies the NP headed by *igmú wą* 'a cat', the head of the relative clause, signaling a definite

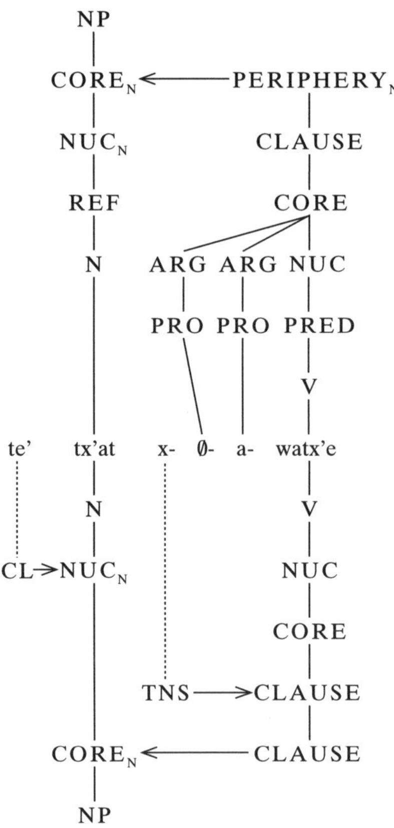

Figure 8.31 Jakaltek restrictive relative clause

interpretation for it. In the constituent projection, the head noun *igmú* 'cat' is coindexed with the matrix NP which also dominates the clause. With respect to the ambiguous sentence in (8.72c), it would be assigned two distinct structural representations; the reading with *igmú* 'cat' as head would have a representation analogous to that in figure 8.32, while the one with *šų̨ka* 'dog' as head would have *šų̨ka* 'dog' coindexed in the constituent projection, as *igmú* 'cat' is in figure 8.32, and in the operator projection the article + demonstrative definiteness operators modifying the NP consisting of its operator projection plus the operator projection of the clause. In externally headed relative clauses like those in Malagasy and Jakaltek, the interpretive problem is determining how to construe the head noun within the embedded clause; in internally headed relative clauses like (8.72c), on the other hand, the interpretive problem is determining which NP in the embedded clause should be construed as a matrix clause argument.

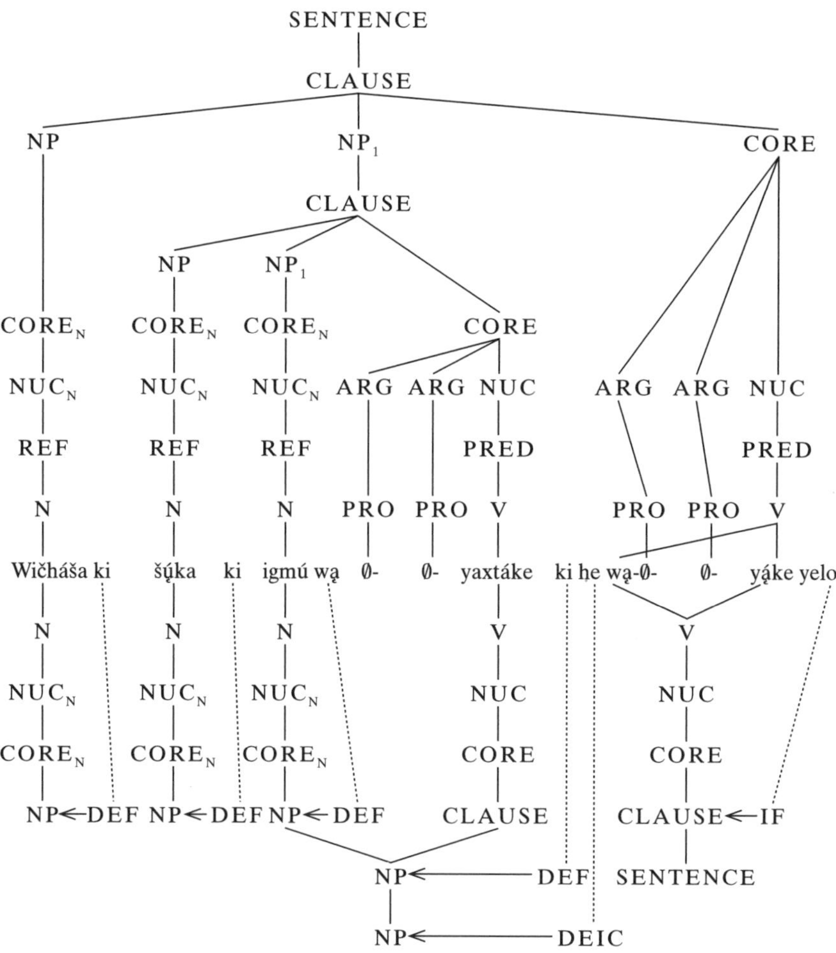

Figure 8.32 Lakhota internally headed relative clause in (8.72a)

8.6.3 Headless relative clauses and WH-complements

The final type of complex construction to be discussed is not really a type of complex NP, but it is nevertheless very similar to relative clauses; hence it is necessary to have talked about relative clauses before examining it. The constructions in question are exemplified in (8.73).

(8.73) a. I can't remember *who Jose saw*.
b. *What Mary bought* is a mystery to me.
c. Robin could not identify *who had talked to Kim at the party* to the police.

The italicized clauses in (a)–(c) have the same structure as the relative clause in figure 8.28, but they are not nominal modifiers, as there is no head noun. Hence they

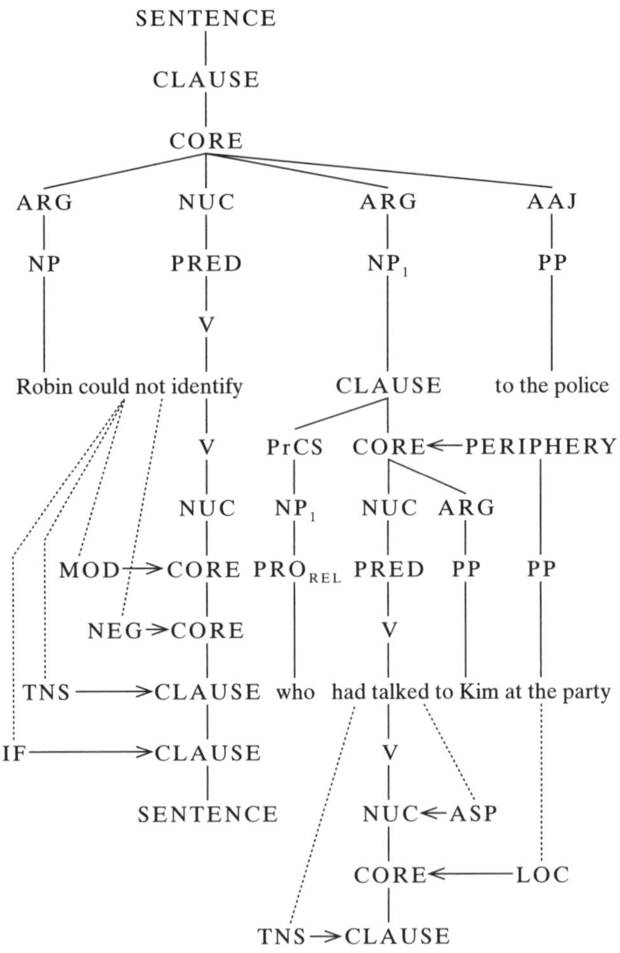

Figure 8.33 English headless relative clause in (8.73c)

are usually referred to as headless relative clauses. They constitute referring expressions in their own right, and accordingly they directly fill a core argument position in the matrix core; this can be seen most clearly in (b) and (c), in which the headless relatives function as privileged syntactic argument in the former and occur between the nucleus and a core PP in the latter. In terms of their structure, they are clauses, which form an NP without a layered structure. In this they are like pronouns, which lack a layered structure since they do not take any operators. The structure of (c) is given in figure 8.33.[26] The relative pronoun *who* is located in the precore slot, because first, in the non-subject headless relatives in (8.73a, b), the WH-word is clearly in that position, and second, in other constructions involving WH-words in English it occurs in the precore slot. Hence we posit a uniform position for the

WH-element in all of these constructions. As in internally headed relative clauses, the WH-head of the relative is coindexed with the NP dominated by the ARG node in the matrix core.

The WH-words in (8.73) are all core arguments, but it is also possible to have headless relative clauses with adjunct WH-words, as in (8.74). Since these refer not to individuals but to propositions, they are in many respects like complement clauses, and this is reflected in their possibilities of occurrence.

(8.74) a. Sandy could not explain *how/why she had opened the door* to the detective during the interview.
a′. Sandy could not explain to the detective during the interview *how/why she had opened the door.*
b. Sandy could not describe *where she had found the gun* to the detective during the interview.
b′. Sandy could not describe to the detective during the interview *where she had found the gun.*
c. Kim put the gun *where no one would find it* after the robbery.
c′. *Kim put the gun after the robbery *where no one would find it.*

In the (a) and (b) examples, the embedded clause can occur in a core-internal argument position and in a clearly postcore position after a peripheral PP. This seems to be related to the fact that the undergoers with *explain* and *describe* can be abstract and propositional. This is in striking contrast to the sentences in (c): here the headless relative realizes the third core argument of *put*, and because *put* takes entities (including places) rather than propositions as arguments, the headless relative cannot occur after a peripheral PP in the normal position for sentential complements, even when it is 'heavier' than the PP. It must appear in a core-internal position, unlike the embedded clauses in (a) and (b).

Finally, there are pure WH-complements, which in English are marked by the complementizer *whether*, as in *Robin doesn't know whether Pat will arrive or not.* The structure of sentences with *whether*-complements is basically the same as the structure for *that*-complements in figure 8.14. It typically occurs with interrogative complements and in place of *that*, which does not occur with this type of complement clause. Like *that*, *whether* will be considered the clause-linkage marker for this type of subordination.

8.7 Syntactic templates for complex sentences

In section 2.5 we introduced the notion of 'syntactic template' in our discussion of the syntax of simple sentences, and we now turn to applying it to the analysis of complex sentences. Certain complex constructions can be handled in terms of the templates introduced in chapter 2, whereas others require new templates specific to them. The constructions for which no special templates would be required involve core and clausal subordination. In core subordination, a core or a clause functions as a core argument, and in terms of the templates introduced in figure 2.34, all that needs to be stated is that an ARG node in a core can be filled by core or a clause, as in figure 8.10. Nothing special needs to be specified for clausal subordination involving adverbial clauses, as in figure 8.13. In this case there is a predicative preposition in the periphery which takes a clause rather than a simple NP as its argument; the basic template for the matrix clause is the same regardless of whether the argument of the preposition is an NP or a clause. Clausal subordination involving 'object complements' (e.g. *that*-clauses), as in figure 8.14, would require a specific template, which is given in figure 8.34. Optional peripheries will not be specified in the complex sentence templates, since they are represented in the simple clause templates which fill the slots in them. This template can iterate, with the whole template replacing the embedded clause node, producing a sequence of embedded complement clauses, as in *Fred says that Sam thinks that Mary knows that Sally claims that Robin denies . . .*

Nuclear subordination, as exemplified in figure 8.7, also requires a specific template, given in figure 8.35. There are two important criterial features of this template. The first is that the modified nucleus (NUC_1) is always dominated by a core node. This is because the subordinate nucleus (NUC_2) serves as an aspectual operator modifying NUC_1; if the nexus is cosubordinate, then NUC_1 is the superordinate nucleus node dominating the cosubordinate nuclei, as in the left tree in figure 8.7, and if the nexus is coordinate, then the modified nucleus is a direct daughter of the core node, as in the right tree in figure 8.7. If a single nucleus is being modified by another nucleus, as in Lakhota *lową́ + hą* (sing + stand[27]) 'be singing', the same structural relations hold. The second important point is that the modifying nucleus, NUC_2, does not predicate and therefore does not dominate a PRED node (see section 8.4.1). Unlike the template in figure 8.34, this one is not recursive, and this seems to be correct: we know of no examples where a single nucleus is modified aspectually by multiple subordinate nuclei. In none of these templates is it neces-

Figure 8.34 Template for clausal subordination (*that*-clauses)

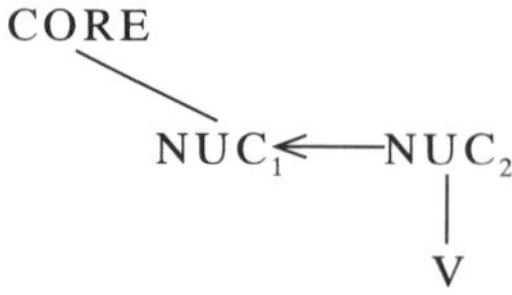

Figure 8.35 Template for nuclear subordination

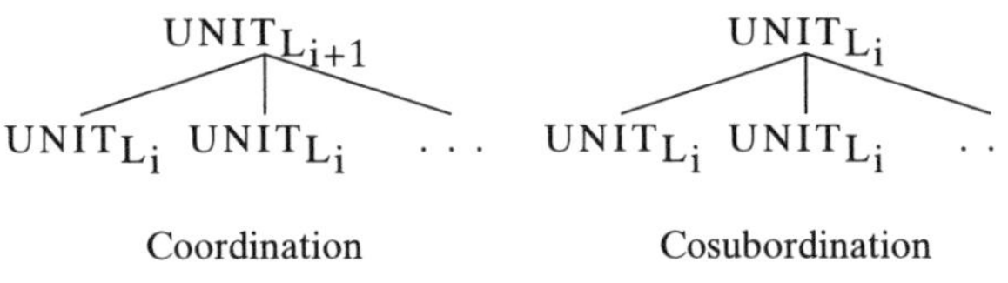

Figure 8.36 Templates for non-subordinate nexus types

sary to specify the structure of the operator projection, since it is in every case the mirror image of the constituent projection.

There are general templates for coordination and cosubordination, independent of the level of juncture. They are given in figure 8.36. The essential difference between the two templates is that in coordination the linked units are daughters of a node of the next-highest layer of the clause, whereas in cosubordination they are daughters of a node of the same layer of the clause. This is true at all levels of juncture, as can be seen by looking back at any of the relevant syntactic representations in this chapter. The two templates in figure 8.36 can be combined in a single complex construction. Examples of this are given in (8.75).

(8.75) a. Sandy tried to persuade Kim to visit Robin.
b. Pat asked Robin to try to visit Kim.

As we saw earlier, *try* + infinitive instantiates core cosubordination, while *ask* or *persuade* + infinitive realizes core coordination. The structures of these two sentences are given in figure 8.37. Recursion is not an issue with non-subordinate nexus; rather, the co(sub)ordinate structure may be extended, in principle indefinitely, by adding more linked units to the structure. There is a special requirement which applies to core junctures only: each non-matrix core lacks a core argument position. Which position is lacking is a function of the particular core-level construction and its linking properties; that is, the missing argument position is that of the syntactic pivot of the linked core. This is one of the main topics of the next chapter.

Finally, there is a general template for externally headed relative clauses; it is given in figure 8.38. The linear order is irrelevant; the periphery and therewith the relative clause could be prehead as well. The clause node can be filled out with clause templates containing a precore slot, as in English WH-relatives, or lacking one, as in the Malagasy, Jakaltek and English *that*-relatives.

Further Reading

For concrete examples of how juncture and nexus are realized in various languages, see Olson (1981), Tao (1986), Wilkins (1988), Hasegawa (1992, 1996), Ohori (1992), Jacobsen (1993), Bickel (1993), Hansell (1993), Yang (1994) and Watters (1993). For a more traditional view of complex structures, see Longacre (1985),

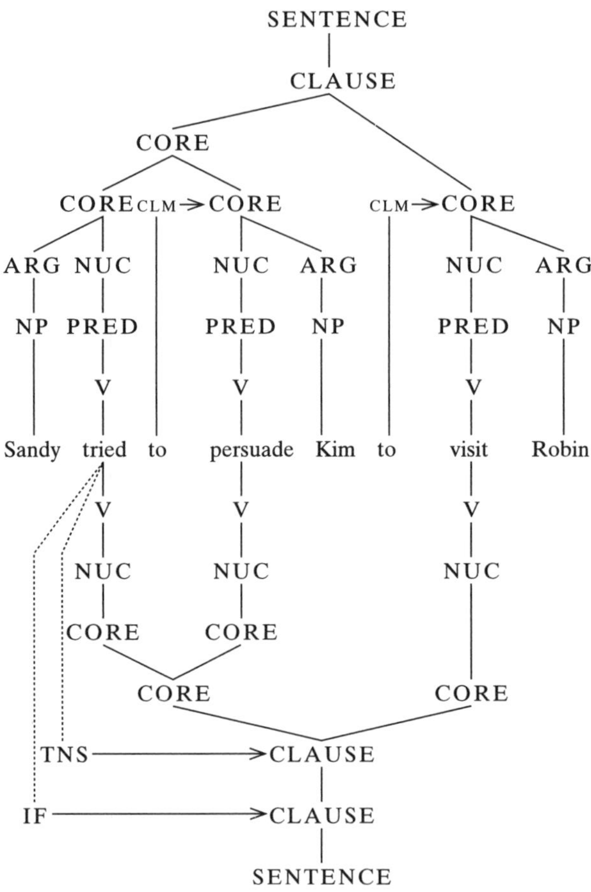

Figure 8.37a Syntactic structure of (8.75a)

Payne (1985b). For discourse-oriented views of complex structures, see the papers in Haiman and Thompson (1988) and Devriendt, Goosens and van der Auwera (1995). On the semantic relations hierarchy, see Silverstein (1976), Givón (1980), Van Valin (1984), Van Valin and Wilkins (1993). On the semantics of clause linkage, see Dixon (1984), Wierzbicka (1988), Ransom (1986) and Rudanko (1989, 1996). On complementation in general, see Noonan (1985). On the structure of complex NPs, see Payne (1985b); on relative clauses, see Keenan (1985b); and on adverbial clauses, see Thompson and Longacre (1985).

Exercises

1 Draw a tree diagram of the layered structure of each sentence below, giving both the constituent and operator projections. Don't worry about the internal structure

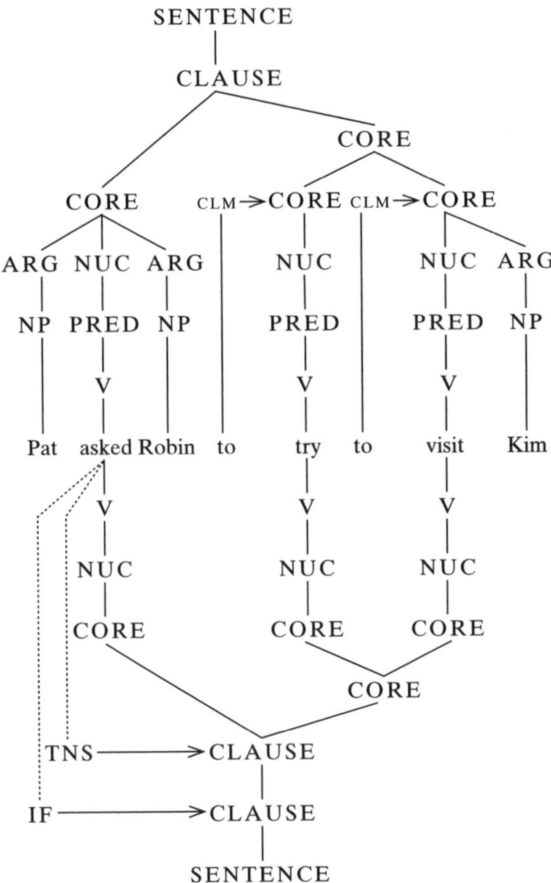

Figure 8.37b Structure of (8.75b)

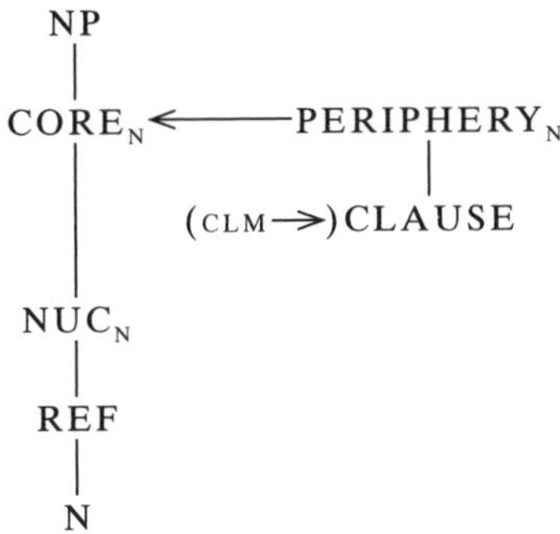

Figure 8.38 Syntactic template for externally headed relative clause

of NPs or PPs, unless the example contains a relative clause, noun complement or gerund. [**section 8.4.1**]

(1) Robin decided to go to the movies.
(2) Kim talked to Leslie yesterday, but they couldn't agree on anything.
(3) That Miguel won the lottery surprised his family.
(4) Kim will ask Pat to help during the party.
(5) Sam forgot that he had agreed to babysit for Robin.
(6) Sandy wanted to rest, after she solved the problem.

2 Consider the following sentences from Korean (Yang 1994). What is the juncture–nexus type of the construction, and what is the evidence that leads to that conclusion? Give the layered structure of (1b) and (2d), giving both the constituent and operator projections. [**section 8.4.1**]

(1) a. Emeni-ka atul-eykey nol-key hay-ss-ta.
mother-NOM son-DAT play-CLM do-PAST-DEC
'The mother made the son play.'
b. Emeni-ka atul-eykey nol-swuiss-key ha-lswueps-ess-ta.
mother-NOM son-DAT play-ABLE-CLM do-UNABLE-PAST-DEC
'The mother could not make the son be able to play.'
c. Emeni-nun nol-swuiss-key atul-eykey ha-lswueps-ess-ta.
mother-TOP play-ABLE-CLM son-DAT do-UNABLE-PAST-DEC
'The mother could not make the son be able to play.'

(2) a. Chelswu-ka Swunhi-eykey chayk-ul ilk-key hay-ss-ta.
-NOM -DAT book-ACC read-CLM do-PAST-DEC
'Chulsoo made Soonhi read the book.'
b. Chelswu-ka Swunhi-eykey chayk-ul ilk-ulswueps-key
-NOM -DAT book-ACC read-UNABLE-CLM
ha-lswuiss-ss-ta.
do-ABLE-PAST-DEC
'Chulsoo could make Soonhi be unable to read the book.'
c. Chelswu-ka Swunhi-eykey chayk-ul ilk-cimosha-key
-NOM -DAT book-ACC read-NEG-CLM
ha-lswuiss-ss-ta.
do-ABLE-PAST-DEC
'Chulsoo could make Soonhi not read the book.'
d. Chelswu-nun chayk-ul ilk-ulswueps-key Swunhi-eykey
-TOP book-ACC read-UNABLE-CLM -DAT
ha-lswuiss-ss-ta.
do-ABLE-PAST-DEC
'Chulsoo could make Soonhi be unable to read the book.'

e. Chelswu-nun chayk-ul ilk-cimosha-key Swunhi-eykey
-TOP book-ACC read-NEG-CLM -DAT
ha-lswuiss-ss-ta.
do-ABLE-PAST-DEC
'Chulsoo could make Soonhi not read the book.'

3 The Mandarin Chinese constructions in (1)–(4), from Tao (1986), instantiate the same juncture–nexus type, despite their formal differences. What juncture–nexus type is it, and what is the evidence that leads to that conclusion? Coreference across units is indicated in only the first example of a set of similar sentences; aspects of coreference in Mandarin were discussed in section 5.7.

In some of these sentences, there is an element *le* glossed simply as 'OP' for 'operator'. It is distinct from the perfective aspect operator *le*, which is glossed 'PRFV'. What can you conclude about the type of this operator? That is, is it a nuclear operator, a core operator or a clausal operator? Why? Example (8.5d) has been repeated in (5) below to provide additional data relevant to this question. **[section 8.4.1]**

(1) a. Tā$_i$ jìbù chōu yān, *pro*$_i$ yòubù hē jiǔ le.
3sg neither smoke cigarette nor drink liquor OP
'He neither smokes nor drinks now (he used to).'
a′. *Tā jìbù chōu yān le, yòubù hē jiǔ.
b. Tā$_i$ jì chōu yān, *pro*$_i$ yòu hē jiǔ ma?
either or
'Does he either smoke or drink?'
b′. *Tā jì chōu yān ma(?), yòu hē jiǔ.
'Does he smoke(?), or drinks.'

(2) a. Lǎo Zhāng$_i$ suīrán hěn máng, kě tā$_i$ haíshì qù le ba?
though very busy but he still go OP Q
'Did Lao Zhang still go even though he was busy?'
a′. *Lǎo Zhāng suīrán hěn máng ba, kě tā haíshì qù le ba?
'Though was Lao Zhang busy? But did he still go?'
b. Lǎo Zhāng suīrán hěn máng, kě tā haíshì qù le.
'Though Lao Zhang was busy, he still went.'
b′. *Lǎo Zhāng suīrán hěn máng le, kě tā haíshì qù.
b″. *Lǎo Zhāng suīrán hěn máng le, kě tā haíshì qù le.

(3) a. Tāmen$_i$ búshì chàng gē *pro*$_i$ jiùshì tiào wǔ.
3pl not.be sing song then jump dance
'They either sing or dance.'
b. Tāmen búshì chàng gē jiùshì tiào wǔ ma?
Q
'Did they either sing or dance?'

b′. *Tāmen búshì chàng gē ma, jiùshì tiào wǔ ma?
b″. *Tāmen búshì chàng gē ma, jiùshì tiào wǔ.
c. Tāmen$_i$ búshì chàng gē *pro*$_i$ jiùshì tiào wǔ le.
'They either sang or danced.'
c′. *Tāmen búshì chàng gē le jiùshì tiào wǔ le.
c″. *Tāmen búshì chàng gē le jiùshì tiào wǔ.

(4) a. Búshì tāmen chàng gē, jiùshì nǐmen tiào wǔ.
not.be 3pl sing song then 2pl jump dance
'Either they sing or you dance.'
b. Búshì tāmen chàng gē, jiùshì nǐmen tiào wǔ ma?
'Do either they sing or you dance?'
b′. *Búshì tāmen chàng gē ma, jiùshì nǐmen tiào wǔ.
c. Búshì tāmen chàng gē, jiùshì nǐmen tiào wǔ le.
'Either they sang or you danced.'
c′. *Búshì tāmen chàng gē le, jiùshì nǐmen tiào wǔ.
c″. *Búshì tāmen chàng gē le, jiùshì nǐmen tiào wǔ le.

(5) a. Tā jiāo wǒ xǐe zì.
3sg teach 1sg write characters
'She teaches me to write characters.'
b. Tā jiāo le wǒ xǐe zì.
PRFV
'She taught me to write characters.'
c. Tā jiāo wǒ xǐe zì le.
OP
'She taught me to write characters.'
c′. *Tā jiāo wǒ le xǐe zì.
OP

4 Analyze the following complex sentences in Jakaltek (Craig 1977). First, determine the juncture–nexus type of each of the constructions given below and present the evidence that led you to the analysis. There are all three nexus types at the clause level, two at the core level and one at the nuclear level. Sentences illustrating a particular juncture–nexus type are grouped together. Second, draw diagrams of the sentences in (4b), (5b), (6c) and (7a′); do not give the internal structure of NPs or PPs. [**section 8.4.1**]

(a) Some background information about Jakaltek: the basic case-marking patterns are given in (7.52), and a number of Jakaltek constructions were discussed in chapter 6. Examples of simple sentences, including a reflexive construction, are given in (1).

(1) a. X-Ø-to-pax heb naj winaj.
PST-3ABS-go-back pl CL man
'The men returned.'

b. X-∅-aw-il naj.
PST-3ABS-2sgERG-see CL/he
'You saw him.'

c. Ch-∅-s-lok-o' naj winaj no' txitam.
NPST-3ABS-3ERG-buy-FUT CL man CL pig
'The man will buy the pig.'

d. X-∅-a-mak ha-ba.
PST-3ABS-2sgERG 2sgERG-REFL
'You hit yourself.'

Jakaltek noun classifiers double as anaphoric pronouns. There is an optional particle *an* which signals the presence of a first-person argument; it is always in final position within a specific syntactic domain.

(2) a. Ch-in to (an).
NPST-1sgABS go 1p
'I go.'

b. Ch-in ha-mak (an).
NPST-1sgABS 2sgERG-hit 1p
'You hit me.'

A second, coreferential noun classifier must be deleted within a specific syntactic domain.

(3) a. X-∅-(y)-il naj_i [$_{NP}$ s_j-mam naj_j].
PST-3ABS-3ERG-see CL/he 3ERG-father CL/he
'He_i saw $his_{*i/j}$ father.'

b. X-∅-(y)-il naj_i [$_{NP}$ s_i-mam]
PST-3ABS-3ERG-see CL/he 3ERG-father
'He_i saw $his_{i/*j}$ father.'

(b) Complex sentence constructions

(4) a. X-∅-(y)-iche-coj ix_i x-∅-s-lah-ni y_i-unin
PST-3ABS-3ERG-start-on CL/she PST-3ABS-3ERG-finish-SUFF 3ERG-child
ix_i/*$∅_i$.
CL/she
'She started it, and her child finished it.'

b. Ch-in to hecal (an) yaj ch-ach can beti'.
NPST-1sgABS go tomorrow 1p but NPST-2sgABS stay here
'I will go tomorrow, but you stay here.'

b′. *Ch-in to hecal yaj ch-ach can beti' an.

c. Way-oj ab hon mach mac ay yoc j-in.
sleep-FUT EXH 1plABS NEG someone exist interest 1plERG-in
'Would that we sleep[!], nobody cares about us.'

(5) a. Xc-in to ∅ w-il-a' naj (an).
PST-1sgABS go 3ABS 1sgERG-see-INF CL/he 1p
'I went to see him.'
b. Xc-ach w-iptze ha-canalwi (an).
PST-2sgABS 1sgERG-force 2sgERG-dance 1p
'I forced you to dance.'
b′. *Xc-ach w-iptze an ha-canalwi.
c. Xc-ach to sajch-oj.
PST-2sgABS go play-INF
'You went to play.'
d. Ch-∅-(y)-iptze naj$_i$ ix$_j$ ∅ s-mak-ni ∅$_j$/*ix$_j$ ∅$_i$/*naj$_i$.
NPST-3ABS-3ERG-force CL/he CL/she 3ABS 3ERG-hit-SUFF CL/she CL/he
'He forces her to hit him.'
e. X-∅-to naj sajch-oj.
PST-3ABS-go CL/he play-INF
'He went to play.'
e′. *X-∅-to sajch-oj naj.

(6) a. Ch-in to hecal (an) cat ha-can beti'.
NPST-1sgABS go tomorrow 1p SEQ 2sgERG-stay here
'I will go tomorrow, and you will stay here.'
a′. *Ch-in to hecal cat ha-can beti' an.
b. Ch-∅-(y)-oche ix$_i$ ∅ s-tahtze-' te'$_j$ cenya cat ∅
NPST-3ABS-3ERG-like CL/she 3ABS 3ERG-cook-INF CL banana SEQ 3ABS
s-lo-ni-toj ix$_i$/*∅$_i$ te'$_j$/*∅$_j$.
3ERG-eat-SUFF-up CL/she CL/them
'She likes to cook the bananas and (then) she eats them.'
c. Peba te' pulta cat ∅ haw-a-ni-coj s-tel te'.
close CL door SEQ 3ABS 2sgERG-put-SUFF-on 3ERG-bar CL
'Close the door and put on the bar!'
(*'Close the door[!], and you put on the bar.')

(7) a. Ch-∅-(y)-a' ix xew-oj naj.
NPST-3ABS-3ERG-cause CL/she rest-INF CL/he
'She makes him rest.'
a′. Ch-∅-(y)-a' xew-oj ix naj.
b. X-in-(y)-a' naj mak-a' t-aw-et.
PST-1sgABS-3ERG-cause CL/he hit-INF AUG-2sgERG-to
'He made you hit me.'
b′. X-in-(y)-a' mak-a' naj t-aw-et.
c. X-∅-(y)-a' mak-a' s$_i$-ba naj$_i$ t-aw-et.
PST-3ABS-3ERG-cause hit-INF 3ERG-REFL CL/he AUG-2sgERG-to
'He$_i$ made you hit him$_i$.' (lit. 'He made you hit himself.')

(8) a. X-∅-(y)-al naj t-(y)-et anma y-ul parce ewi
PST-3ABS-3ERG-say CL/he AUG-3ERG-to people 3ERG-in park yesterday
chubil chi-m-∅-hul-uj naj presidente coñob.
that NPST-may-3ABS-come-FUT CL president village.
'He said to people yesterday in the park that the president may come to the village.'

b. Lañan ∅ hin-tx'ah-ni xil kape (an) yet xc-ach huli.
PROG 3ABS 1sgERG-wash-SUFF clothes 1p when PST-2sgABS come
'I was washing clothes when you came.'

b′. *Lañan ∅ hin-tx'ah-ni xil kape yet xc-ach huli an.

c. X-∅-'ayc'ay naj$_i$ bay x-∅-(y)-il naj$_i$/*∅$_i$ no' cheh.
PST-3ABS-fall CL/he where PST-3ABS-3ERG-see CL/he CL horse
'He fell where he saw the horse.'

d. X-∅-aw-abe tato ch-in to-j hecal (an).
PST-3ABS-2sgERG-hear that NPST-1sgABS go-FUT tomorrow 1p
'You heard that I will go tomorrow.'

(9) a. X-∅-w-il hach s-mak-ni ix (an).
PST-3ABS-1sgERG-see 2sgABS 3ERG-hit-SUFF CL/she 1p
'I saw her hit you.'

a′. *X-∅-w-il an hach s-mak-ni ix.

b. Ch-∅-(y)-oche naj$_i$ hin y-il-a' ∅$_i$/*naj$_i$ (an).
NPST-3ABS-3ERG-like CL/he 1sgABS 3ERG-see-INF CL/he 1p
'He likes to see me.'

c. X-∅-w-ilwe ∅ hin-watx'e-n kap camiẋe (an).
PST-3ABS-1sgERG-try 3ABS 1sgERG-make-SUFF CL shirt 1p
'I tried to make the shirt.'

d. X-∅-w-il s-to-j ix (an).
PST-3ABS-1sgERG-see 3ERG-go-INF CL/she 1p
'I saw her go.'

d′. *X-∅-w-il an s-to-j ix.

5 Toba Batak has a series of focus particles which mark individual constituents (Jackson 1984). One of them, *ma*, is illustrated in (1). What can be concluded regarding the potential focus domain in complex sentences in Toba Batak from the sentences in (2) and (3)? [**section 8.5**]

(1) a. Di-lean si Torus indahan i tu si Ria.
PASS-give rice DET to
'Torus gave the rice to Ria.'

b. Di-lean si Torus ma indahan i tu si Ria.
PASS-give FOC rice DET to
'TORUS gave the rice to Ria.'

c. Di-lean si Torus indahan i ma tu si Ria.
PASS-give rice DET FOC to
'Torus gave THE RICE to Ria.'

d. *Di-lean si Torus indahan i tu si Ria ma.
PASS-give rice DET to FOC
'Torus gave the rice to RIA.'

e. Tu si Ria ma di-lean si Torus indahan i.
To FOC PASS-give rice DET
'To RIA Torus gave the rice.'

(2) *pangula na mang-alean dengke ma tu huting i.
farmer CLM ATV-give fish FOC TO cat DET
'farmer that gives FISH to the cat'

(3) a. *Di-boto si Torus na pamangus ma si Ria.
PASS-know CLM crook FOC
'Torus knows that Ria is a CROOK.'

a′. Di-boto si Torus ma na pamangus si Ria.
'TORUS knows that Ria is a crook.'

b. *Di-boto si Torus na di-lean si Ria ma buku i tu guru i.
PASS-know PASS-give FOC book DET to teacher DET.
'Torus knows that RIA gave the book to the teacher.'

b′. Di-boto si Torus ma na di-lean si Ria buku i tu guru i.
'TORUS knows that Ria gave the book to the teacher.'

c. *Di-pabatohon si Ria tu guru i ise ma man-[t]uhor buku tu si Torus.
PASS-tell who FOC ATV-buy book for
'Ria told the teacher who bought a book for Torus.'

c′. Di-pabatohon si Ria ma tu guru i ise ma man-[t]uhor buku tu si Torus.
'RIA told the teacher who bought bought a book for Torus.'

6 Draw the layered structure of each of the complex NPs below, giving both the constituent and operator projections. [**section 8.6**]

(1) the order by the king to release the prisoners
(2) the controversial claim that global warming has already begun
(3) the two famous singers that Sally talked to yesterday
(4) the three tall buildings and two big hotels in Canberra

9

Linking syntax and semantics in complex sentences

9.0 Introduction

In this chapter we will investigate how semantic representations and syntactic representations are linked in complex sentences. We will start from the syntactic representations developed in chapter 8 and from the linking algorithms in chapter 7. An important question to be investigated is the extent to which the linking algorithms proposed in chapter 7 for simple sentences must be modified to deal with complex sentences. We will proceed as follows. In section 9.1 we look at linking in the different juncture–nexus types discussed in chapter 8. This includes discussion of a number of issues that have been important in theoretical debates over the past three decades: control constructions (a.k.a. 'equi-NP-deletion'), matrix-coding constructions (a.k.a. 'raising to subject', 'raising to object', 'exceptional case-marking') and causative constructions. We investigate case marking in complex constructions in section 9.2. The next section focuses on linking in complex NP constructions, primarily relative clause constructions. In section 9.4 we investigate reflexivization in complex constructions, and again the question arises as to the extent to which the principles proposed in section 7.5.2 will have to be modified to deal with these new phenomena. In section 9.5 we propose an account of the restrictions on so-called 'long-distance dependencies' involved in WH-question formation, topicalization and relativization. These restrictions, which fall under the principle known as 'subjacency' in the generative literature, are significant for linguistic theory, for theories of language acquisition and for related theories of cognitive organization (see section 1.3.1).

9.1 Linking in clausal, core and nuclear junctures

Most complex sentences pose no particular difficulties for the linking system we developed in chapter 7. Clausal junctures, for example, are composed of clauses, each of which links like an independent clause. Moreover, nuclear junctures act for linking purposes like simple clauses containing a complex predicate, and they basically follow the algorithms for simple sentences, as we will see. The real challenge comes from non-subordinate core junctures with their obligatory sharing of a core argument, as discussed in section 8.3. Accordingly, we will look at clausal and nuclear junctures first, before turning to the interesting and significant problems raised by core junctures.

We repeat the linking algorithms from chapter 7 below; the semantics to syntax algorithm in (7.161) is given in (9.1), and the syntax to semantics algorithm in (7.36) is given in (9.2).

(9.1) *Linking algorithm: semantics → syntax (revised)*

1 Determine the actor and undergoer assignments, following the Actor–Undergoer Hierarchy in figure 7.1.

2 Assign specific morphosyntactic status to [–WH] arguments in logical structure (language-specific).

a. Accusative privileged syntactic argument selection: default = Actor.

b. Ergative privileged syntactic argument selection: default = Undergoer.

3 If there is a [+WH] XP,

a. assign it to the normal position of a non-WH-XP with the same function (language-specific), or

b. assign it to the precore slot (language-specific), or

c. assign it to a position within the potential focus domain of the clause (default = the unmarked focus position) (language-specific).

4 A non-WH XP may be assigned to the pre- or post-core slot, subject to focus structure restrictions (optional; language-specific).

5 Assign the core arguments the appropriate case markers/adpositions and assign the predicate in the nucleus the appropriate agreement marking (language-specific).

6 For semantic arguments of logical structures other than that of the main verb,

a. assign them to the periphery (default), or

b. assign them to the precore slot or focus position (language-specific) if they are focal, or

c. assign them to the left-detached position if they are highly topical.

(9.2) *Linking algorithm: syntax → semantics (revised formulation)*

1 Determine the functions of the core arguments:

a. If the construction is syntactically accusative:

(1) If it is the unmarked voice, the privileged syntactic argument is actor.

(2) If it is passive, the privileged syntactic argument is not the actor of the predicate in the nucleus;

(a) the actor may appear as a direct core argument (language-specific); or

(b) the actor may appear in the periphery marked by an adposition or an oblique case (language-specific); or

(c) if there is no actor in the core or the periphery, then replace the variable representing the highest-ranking argument in the logical structure with '∅'.

b. If the construction is syntactically ergative:
   (1) If it is the unmarked voice, the privileged syntactic argument is undergoer.
   (2) If it is antipassive, the privileged syntactic argument is actor;
      (a) the undergoer may appear as an oblique element (language-specific);
      (b) if there is no undergoer in the core or the periphery, then replace the variable representing the lowest-ranking argument in the logical structure with '∅'.

c. Assign macrorole status to the other direct core argument, if it is not dative or in an oblique case (language-specific).

d. If the verb is intransitive, then assign the privileged syntactic argument either macrorole or direct core argument status (language-specific).

e. If the language is head-marking and there are independent NPs in the clause, associate each NP with a bound argument marker (language-specific).

f. If the language lacks voice oppositions, determine the macroroles from case marking and/or word order (language-specific).

2 Retrieve from the lexicon the logical structure of the predicate in the nucleus of the clause and with respect to it execute step 1 from (9.1), subject to the following proviso:

a. When there is more than one choice for undergoer, do not assign undergoer to an argument in the logical structure.

b. Assign actor to an argument in the logical structure, if the verb takes one.

c. Determine the linking of the non-macrorole core argument:
   (1) If there is a state predicate in the logical structure and if the non-macrorole core argument is marked by a locative adposition or dative or a locative-type case, then link it with the first argument position in the state predicate in the logical structure; or
   (2) If there is a state predicate in the logical structure and if it is not marked by a locative adposition or dative or a locative-type case, then link it with the second argument position in the state predicate;
   (3) otherwise, link the animate NP with the first argument position in the state predicate in the logical structure.

3 Link the arguments determined in step 1 with the arguments determined in step 2 until all core arguments are linked.

4 If there is a predicative adpositional adjunct, then retrieve its logical structure from the lexicon, insert the logical structure of the core as the second argument in the logical structure and the object of the adposition in the periphery as the first argument.

5 If there is an element in the pre- or postcore slot (language-specific),

a. assign it the remaining unlinked argument position in the semantic representation of the sentence;

b. and if there are no unlinked argument positions in the sentence, then treat the WH-word like a predicative preposition and follow the procedure in step 4, linking the WH-word to the first argument position in the logical structure.

9.1.1 Clausal junctures

Since clausal junctures are made up of clauses, their linking properties are for the most part determined by the linking properties of the constituent clauses. Consider the following two examples of clausal juncture.

(9.3) a. Dana walked to the store, and Kim waved to him.
b. Sandy worked on the school project, after Kelly brought it over.

In the first example, *Dana walked to the store* and *Kim waved to him* are distinct clauses, and each is linked independently of the other, just as if each were a simple sentence on its own. The fact that there is a pronoun in the second clause referring (possibly) to *Dana* in the first clause does not affect the linking. The same is true in the (b) example, in which each clause links separately. A simplified logical structure for (b) is given in (9.4).

(9.4) **after′** ([Kelly brought it over], [Sandy worked on the school project])

The first argument is the argument of *after*, while the second one is the logical structure of the matrix core, just as in the simple sentence in (7.10). Step 6 in the semantics → syntax linking algorithm in (9.1) handles the assignment of *after* + clause to the periphery.

An interesting issue is raised by sentences like (8.39), repeated in (9.5).

(9.5) Robin$_i$ drove out of Phoenix this morning and *pro*$_{i/*j}$ will arrive in Atlanta tomorrow.

Clausal junctures such as this are the English analog of the Dyirbal topic chains in (6.56) and the Tepehua switch-function chain in (6.57). The traditional name for them in the syntax literature is 'conjunction reduction'. The logical structure for (9.5) is given in (9.6).

(9.6) [**this morning′** [**do′** (Robin$_i$, [**drive′** (Robin$_i$, Ø)]) & BECOME NOT **be-in′** (Phoenix, Robin$_i$)]] **and′** [**tomorrow′** (BECOME **be-in′** (Atlanta, *pro*$_i$))][1]

Only highly topical elements can receive zero coding, and therefore from the point of view of focus structure, constructions like (9.5) involve conjoined predicate-focus or narrow-focus constructions in which the privileged syntactic arguments, which are pragmatic pivots, are topics. The juncture–nexus type of this construction is clausal cosubordination, because illocutionary force must be shared across all conjuncts. This is illustrated in (9.7).

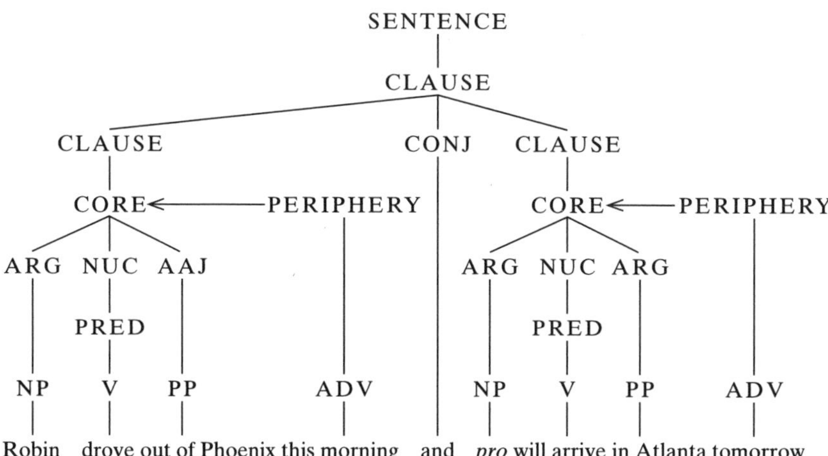

Figure 9.1 Constituent projection for (9.5)

(9.7) a. *Did Robin drive out of Phoenix this morning, and *pro* will arrive in Atlanta tomorrow?
b. *Robin drove out of Phoenix this morning, and will *pro* arrive in Atlanta tomorrow?

In the first example, only the first conjunct is questioned, and the result is ungrammatical, while in the second, only the second conjunct is questioned, which is likewise ungrammatical. The whole sentence must be interpreted either as an assertion or a question, and the most felicitous way to question it is *Is it the case that Robin drove out of Phoenix this morning and will arrive in Atlanta tomorrow?* The constituent structure representation of (9.5) is given in figure 9.1. The zero anaphor *pro* occupies an argument position in the second clause, just as a non-phonologically null pronoun would; accordingly, the constituent projection of the second clause of (9.5) is the same as for the second clause in *Robin drove out of Phoenix this morning, and she will arrive in Atlanta tomorrow.* This would also be true in the same-pivot switch-reference constructions discussed in section 8.3 from Chuave, Fore and Kewa; in the non-final clauses, there would be a zero anaphor representing the pivot in each clause in which it is not overt.

Since this is a clausal juncture, each of the clauses links separately, but the construction as a whole imposes a constraint on the linking in the non-initial conjuncts: the zero anaphor must occur as pragmatic pivot. This is captured in the constructional template for this construction, which is given in table 9.1. There is a number of new features in constructional templates for complex sentences. First, there are specifications of the juncture type and the nexus type. These would refer to the syntactic templates for complex sentences in figures 8.34–8.36. Second, there is a specification of the construction type, with an abstract representation of its criterial

Table 9.1 *Constructional template for English 'conjunction reduction'*

CONSTRUCTION English conjunction reduction
SYNTAX Juncture: Clausal Nexus: Cosubordination Construction type: Conjunction $[_{CL}[_{CORE}\mathrm{ARG}_i\,[_{NUC}\ldots]\ldots]\ldots]_1, [_{CL}[_{CORE}\,pro_i\,[_{NUC}\ldots]\ldots]\ldots]_2,\ldots$ $\mathrm{CLM}\,[_{CL}[_{CORE}\,pro_i\,[_{NUC}\ldots]\ldots]\ldots]_n$ Unit template(s): Default PSA: Clause 1: Variable syntactic controller = pragmatic controller Clause 1 + n: Variable syntactic pivot = pragmatic pivot Linking: *pro* = pragmatic pivot
MORPHOLOGY CLM: coordinating conjunction or disjunction
SEMANTICS Sequence of events sharing a common primary topical participant
PRAGMATICS Illocutionary force: Shared across all conjuncts Focus structure: Predicate focus in all conjuncts (default)

features. In this case it is the occurrence of *pro* in the non-initial conjuncts and the obligatory coreference with the initial pragmatic PSA, which follows from the semantics of the construction. This requires that the semantic representation of each non-initial clause contains a *pro* argument. 'Unit template(s)' refers to any special properties of the syntactic templates of the constituent clauses, and special linking requirements are also specified. 'CLM' stands for 'clause-linkage marker'.

There is one important requirement imposed on the linking in non-initial clauses, namely the requirement that *pro* be the pragmatic pivot. If *pro* is not the actor of the verb of the matrix core, or the single argument of an intransitive matrix predicate, then some special construction(s) must be used so that *pro* appears as the matrix pragmatic pivot. This could be a passive construction, as in (6.24c), which is repeated in (9.8a), it could be a simple 'raising to subject' construction, as in (9.8b), or even a combination of 'raising to object' plus passive, as in (9.8c).

(9.8) a. The dog_i ran downhill and pro_i was seen by the man.
b. Dana_i talked to the teacher_j and $pro_{i/*j}$ seems to have calmed $\text{him}_{*i/j}$ down.
c. The bank teller_i disappeared last week and pro_i is believed to be hiding in Mexico.

None of these possible combinations needs to be specified in this constructional template; they are simply some of the ways the grammar of English can satisfy the requirement that the zero anaphor be the pragmatic pivot of all of the non-initial clauses in the construction. For the linking from syntax to semantics, the template supplies the information that the missing pivots of the non-initial clauses should be interpreted as zero anaphors coreferential with the privileged syntactic argument of the initial clause. Otherwise, the linking in each clause is handled by (9.1) without any modifications.

The template in table 9.1 may appear to be too specific in many respects, but it is in fact very general and also represents the essential features of the analogous construction in Dyirbal in (6.56), in Tepehua in (6.57), in German in (7.41a) and in Icelandic in (7.44). Comrie (1988) discusses this construction in Slavic languages like Croatian, which, as we saw in chapters 2 and 7, is a so-called 'pro-drop language', and shows that for coreference purposes it behaves like the English, Tepehua, German and Icelandic constructions. Hence it would appear that this template would apply to these languages as well. The only thing that would have to be language-specific would be the lack of a specification for a coordinating conjunction in Dyirbal, since this construction lacks them in this language. Thus, the constructional template in table 9.1 can be taken to be the general template underlying switch-function 'topic chains' in languages that employ a switch-function reference-tracking system (see section 6.4.1).

In the construction in (9.5) and (9.8), the default focus structure is predicate focus, and the construction requires highly topical pragmatic pivots. There is another clausal cosubordinate construction in which the focus structure is just the opposite; that is, in this construction the pragmatic pivot in the second clause must be focal and the remainder of the second clause must be non-focal. It is exemplified in (9.9).

(9.9) a. Kim is eating an ice cream cone, and Sandy is, too.
b. Sam washed his car, and Bill did, too.
c. Leslie may go to the concert, and Pat may, too.
d. Donna has been interviewed by Channel 7, and Pedro will be, too.
d′. *Donna has been interviewed by Channel 7, and Pedro will, too.
e. Yolanda didn't see the UFO, and Vanessa didn't, either/*too.
f. Yolanda didn't see the UFO, but Vanessa did (*either/*too).

All of these sentences have focal stress on the NP in the second conjunct, which is the only element in the constituent projection of the second conjunct. The traditional name for this construction in the syntax literature is 'VP ellipsis'. The auxiliary configurations need not be identical in the two clauses, as (d) shows, but when they are different, all of the diverging auxiliary elements must be present in the second conjunct, as (d′) shows. If the two conjuncts both contain negative operators,

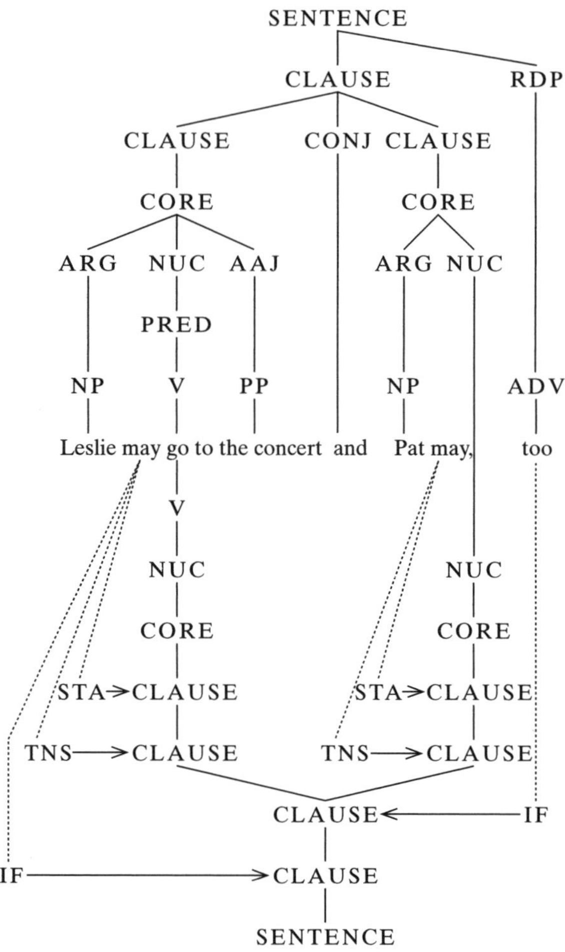

Figure 9.2 The syntactic representation of (9.9c)

as in (e), then *either* rather than *too* must be used. If the two clauses have different polarity, as in (f), then neither *either* nor *too* can be used. Even though the tense and other operators may be different, illocutionary force must be the same over the whole construction. This can be seen in (9.10).

(9.10) a. Did Sam wash his car, and did Bill, too?
b. *Did Sam wash his car, and Bill did, too?
c. *Sam washed his car, and did Bill, too?

Accordingly, the nexus type is cosubordination. The syntactic structure of (9.9c) is given in figure 9.2. *Too* is treated as a presuppositional adverb (Soames 1982), and consequently it must be a clausal modifier at the same level as the illocutionary force operator. The new feature of this representation is the constituent projection of the core of the second clause, since it contains only a single argument and the nucleus node dominates nothing and connects directly with its operator projection counterpart. Remember from chapters 2 and 8 that the constituent and operator projections are mirror images of each other, and accordingly there must be a full layered structure in each, due to the occurrence of a core argument in the constituent projection and at least one clausal operator (tense) in the operator projection.

The primary complexity in this construction lies in the linking between the syntactic and semantic representations. In the semantics to syntax linking, the elements in the semantic representation of the second clause which are identical to those in the semantic representation of the first clause are not mapped into the syntax. It might appear that this is technically a violation of the Completeness Constraint in (7.8), since elements in the semantic representation of a clause are not being mapped into the syntactic representation of that clause. It is not, however, as a close reading of the Completeness Constraint reveals. It is repeated in (9.11).

(9.11) *Completeness Constraint*
All of the arguments explicitly specified in the semantic representation of a sentence must be realized syntactically in the sentence, and all of the referring expressions in the syntactic representation of a sentence must be linked to an argument position in a logical structure in the semantic representation of the sentence.

The crucial phrase is 'must be realized syntactically *in the sentence*'; because the semantic information in the second clause is recoverable from the first clause, which is part of the same sentence, the constraint is satisfied.[2]

In the linking from syntax to semantics, the semantic representation of the second conjunct must be projected from the first conjunct. The semantic representation of the first clause in (9.9a) is given in (9.12).

(9.12) ⟨$_{IF}$*DEC*⟨$_{TNS}$*PRES*⟨$_{ASP}$*PROG*⟨[**do′** (Kim, [**eat′** (Kim, ice cream cone)])] & [BECOME **eaten′** (ice cream cone)]⟩⟩⟩⟩

This semantic representation is projected as the semantic representation for the second clause, with a variable replacing the argument corresponding to the privileged syntactic argument of the first clause; this yields (9.13).

(9.13) ⟨$_{IF}$*DEC*⟨$_{TNS}$*PRES*⟨$_{ASP}$*PROG*⟨[**do′** (x, [**eat′** (x, ice cream cone)])] & [BECOME **eaten′** (ice cream cone)]⟩⟩⟩⟩

Since there is only one element in the constituent projection of the second clause, it will be linked to the *x* argument in (9.13), thereby giving the correct interpretation. When the non-IF operators in the two clauses are different, as in (9.9d), then only the logical structure(s) will be projected, as the operators are represented overtly in the clause.

One final complication arises in examples like (9.9b) with respect to the interpretation of the pronoun *his*. It has long been noted that such sentences are ambiguous, because the second clause can be interpreted as meaning that Bill washed Sam's car, that Bill washed his own car or that they washed some third party's car, just as the full, unreduced sentence can. This follows from the fact that the pronoun *his*, unlike a reflexive, is not constrained to take a particular antecedent, and therefore can refer to any of the possible antecedents. We need to specify, then, that, when the semantic representation is projected from the first clause, no non-obligatory coindexing is projected. By 'non-obligatory coindexing' we mean coindexing not associated with reflexives, which require obligatory coindexing. Hence the semantic representation of the second clause of (9.9b) would be as in (9.14).

(9.14) $\langle_{\text{IF}}$*DEC*$\langle_{\text{TNS}}$*PAST*$\langle$**do′** (x, [**wash′** (x, [**have′** (3sgMASC, <u>car</u>)])]) &
BECOME **washed′** ([**have′** (3sgMASC, <u>car</u>)])$\rangle\rangle\rangle$

The 3sgMASC POSSESSOR can be construed as coreferential with *x*, with an NP in the previous clause or with a discourse antecedent. In the following examples, the coindexing would be projected into the second clause and adjusted to reflect the fact that there is a different privileged syntactic argument in the second clause.

(9.15) a. Dana saw herself, and Sally did, too.
b. Sam washed his own car, and Bill did, too.

Thus, if (9.16a) is the semantic representation for the first clause in (9.15a), then (9.16b) would be the projected semantic representation for the second clause.

(9.16) a. **see′** (Dana$_i$, herself$_i$)
b. **see′** (x$_j$, x-self$_j$)

The constructional template for English 'VP' ellipsis is given in table 9.2. These two constructions, 'VP' ellipsis and conjunction reduction, have been taken as evidence for the existence of a VP node in English clause structure, because the part of the clause left in the non-initial conjunct in conjunction approximates a VP and the part of the clause missing in the ellipsis construction also approximates a VP. We have, however, been able to account for these constructions in terms of the interaction of the layered structure of the clause and focus structure, following the proposal sketched in section 5.4.

There is one more construction relating to clausal juncture that deserves comment. It involves sentences like those in (9.17).

(9.17) a. I hate it that she arrived late.
a′. I hate that she arrived late.
b. It shocked everyone that she arrived late.
b′. That she arrived late shocked everyone.

Table 9.2 *Constructional template for English 'VP' ellipsis*

CONSTRUCTION
English 'VP' ellipsis

SYNTAX
Juncture: Clausal
Nexus: Cosubordination
Construction type: Conjunction
$[_{CL} [_{CORE} \ldots [_{NUC} \ldots] \ldots] \ldots]$ CLM $[_{CL} [_{CORE}$ NP $[_{NUC}]]]$ (RDP)
Unit template(s): Clause 1-Default
Clause 2-pivot only, remainder structurally empty
PSA: Clause 1: Pragmatic pivot
Clause 2: Pragmatic pivot
Linking: Voice must be the same in both conjuncts.

MORPHOLOGY
CLM: coordinating conjunction
Aux in Clause 2: Default
RDP: *too* (positive polarity)/*either* (negative polarity)

SEMANTICS
Semantic representation of second clause is projected from the first clause:
1 The PSA is replaced by a variable.
2 All non-IF operators are projected, except those overtly present in Clause 2.
3 Non-obligatory coindexing is not preserved.

PRAGMATICS
Illocutionary force: Shared across all conjuncts
Focus structure: Pragmatic pivots must be focal, remainder of clauses topical

The sentences in (a) and (b) illustrate the use of a pronoun *it* to occur in a core argument position which refers to a *that*-clause which is outside of the core. In the alternative forms in (a′) and (b′), the pronoun is not used and the *that*-clause occurs in either in the PSA position in (b′) or in its usual postverbal position in (a′). The *it* is not simply a dummy placeholder, as with verbs like *rain*; rather, the pronoun actually refers to the *that*-clause that follows and indicates its function, as actor or undergoer, in the core. Since it contributes to the semantic interpretation of the sentence, it must be part of the semantic representation, according to the Completeness Constraint. How is it to be represented? Since *it* has the same function as the *that*-clause, it would have to occupy the same argument position in the logical structure of the verb. While this might at first glance appear to be impossible, we have in fact already seen an example of this in chapter 7, namely the representation of independent NPs and the bound pronominal markers in a head-marking language in (7.18) and figure 7.10. The logical structures for the sentences in (9.17) are given in (9.18).

(9.18) a. **hate′** (1sg, [3sgNEUT, [**late′** (BECOME **be-at′** (∅, 3sgFEM))]])
a′. **hate′** (1sg, [**late′** (BECOME **be-at′** (∅, 3sgFEM))])
b. [3sgNEUT, [**late′** (BECOME **be-at′** (∅, 3sgFEM))]] CAUSE [INGR **feel′** (everyone, [**shocked′**])]
b′. [**late′** (BECOME **be-at′** (∅, 3sgFEM))] CAUSE [INGR **feel′** (everyone, [**shocked′**])]

In the (a) and (b) examples, the pronoun is linked to the appropriate core argument position, and the *that*-clause is linked to a core-external position. This is illustrated in figure 9.3, with simplified syntactic and semantic representations. The numbers

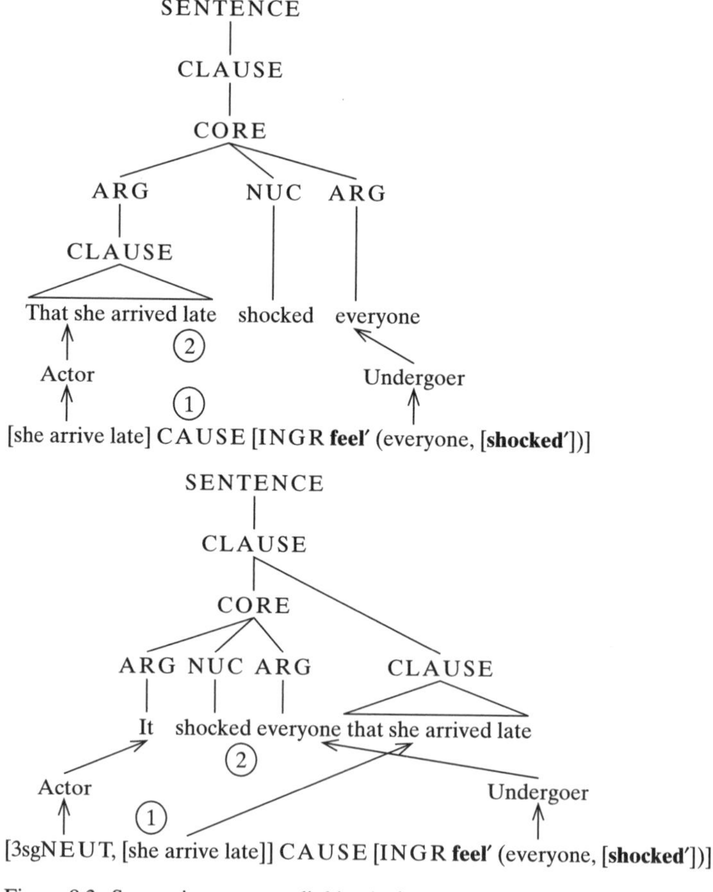

Figure 9.3 Semantics → syntax linking in (9.17b, b′)

refer to the steps in (9.1). The first linking looks like the typical English linking, whereas the second one looks a bit like the Lakhota linking in figure 7.10. For the linking from syntax to semantics, step (1e) in (9.2), which is designed for head-marking languages, can be adapted to deal with associating the *that*-clause with a compatible pronominal in an argument position. It then receives the interpretation that the pronoun receives when it is linked to the logical structure. Thus, the constructions in (9.17) require no modifications either to the types of logical structure representations the theory must allow or to the linking algorithms.

9.1.2 Nuclear junctures

Many nuclear junctures have logical structures very much like lexical causative accomplishment/achievement verbs and, not surprisingly, have very similar linking properties. Consider the English and Mandarin examples in (9.19), which are repeated from chapters 3 and 7.

(9.19) a. Max broke the window.
a′. [**do′** (Max, ∅)] CAUSE [BECOME **broken′** (window)]
b. Tā qiāo pò le yī ge fànwǎn. (= (8.27a))
3sg hit break PRFV one CL bowl
'She broke (by hitting) a ricebowl.'
b′. [**do′** (3sg, [**hit′** (3sg, fànwǎn)])] CAUSE [BECOME **broken′** (fànwǎn)][3]

In (9.19a′), *Max* would be the actor and *window* the undergoer, and they would follow the linking algorithms in (9.1) and (9.2). The nuclear juncture in (b) follows exactly the same pattern: *tā* '3sg' would be actor and *yī ge fànwǎn* 'a ricebowl' would be undergoer, and here again the linking would follow the two linking algorithms. The linking from semantics to syntax for these two sentences is given in figure 9.4.[4] The same situation holds in English nuclear junctures, as well.

(9.20) a. Kim pushed open the door.
a′. [**do′** (Kim, [**push′** (Kim, door)])] CAUSE [BECOME **open′** (door)]
b. John painted the table red.
b′. [**do′** (John, [**paint′** (John, table)])] CAUSE [BECOME **red′** (table)]

The linking from semantics to syntax in (9.20b) is presented in figure 9.5 on page 531; it is identical to that in figure 9.4 for the sentences in (9.19). The linking algorithms in (9.1) and (9.2) can handle all three of these cases without modification. The constructional template for the Mandarin nuclear juncture is given in table 9.3. The value for the 'unit template(s)' feature is 'none', because there are no special syntactic templates for nuclei. The value for 'privileged syntactic argument(s)' is 'does not apply', because, as we saw in chapter 6, Mandarin lacks syntactic pivots.

The prototypical nuclear juncture has causative semantics, like (9.19b) and (9.20), but there are nuclear junctures which simply represent the phases of a complex

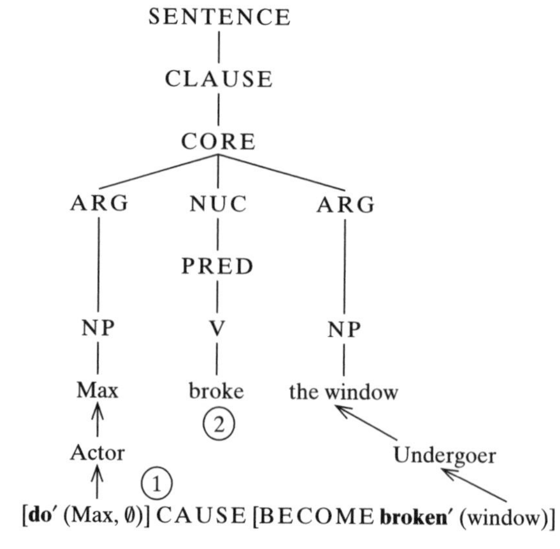

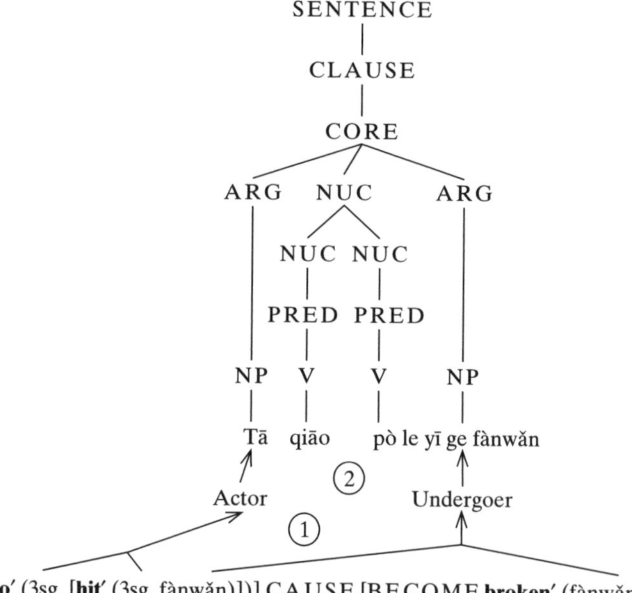

Figure 9.4 Linking from semantics to syntax in (9.19)

event. The Barai examples in (8.29), repeated below, are a good example of this type of nuclear juncture. The logical structure for each sentence is given as well.[5]

(9.21) a. Fu kai fu-one kume-fie va.
3sg friend 3sg-GEN call-listen continue
'He continued calling and listening for his friend.'

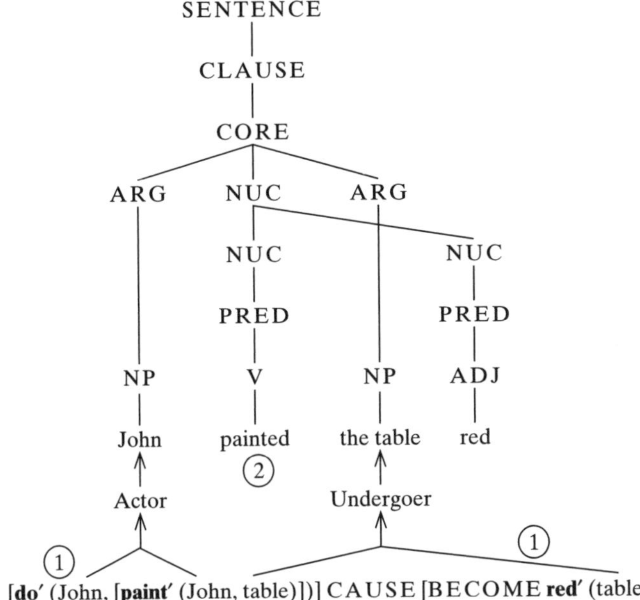

Figure 9.5 Linking from semantics to syntax in English nuclear juncture

Table 9.3 *Constructional template for Mandarin nuclear juncture in (9.19b)*

CONSTRUCTION
Mandarin Chinese resultative serial verb construction

SYNTAX
Juncture: Nuclear
Nexus: Consubordination
Construction type: Serial verb
[$_{\text{CL}}$ [$_{\text{CORE}}$ ARG [$_{\text{NUC}}$ [$_{\text{NUC}}$ . . .] [$_{\text{NUC}}$ . . .]] ARG]]
Unit template(s): None
PSA: d.n.a.
Linking: Default

MORPHOLOGY
None

SEMANTICS
[PRED$_{\text{NUC1}}$] CAUSE [PRED$_{\text{NUC2}}$]

PRAGMATICS
Illocutionary force: Unspecified
Focus structure: Unspecified

a′. **do′** (3sg, [**call′** (3sg, kai fuone)]) & **do′** (3sg, [**hear′** (3sg, kai fuone)])
b. Fu vazai ufu furi numu akoe.
3sg grass cut finish pile throw.away
'He finished cutting, piled and threw away the grass.'
b′. **do′** (3sg, [**cut′** (3sg, vazai)]) & **do′** (3sg, [**pile′** (3sg, vazai)]) & **do′** (3sg, [**throw.away′** (3sg, vazai)])

A couple of points need to be made about these representations. First, the verbs functioning as aspect operators (*va* in (a) and *furi* in (b)) are not in the logical structure, since they do not predicate and contribute to the semantic content of the representation; rather, they would be represented as aspect operators in a full semantic representation, analogous to aspect markers in other languages. Second, since these are nuclear junctures, there is only a single set of macroroles in the core, and therefore all of the EFFECTOR arguments will be the actor and all of the other arguments will be the undergoer. There is no need to stipulate that the '3sg' argument in the first logical structure is the same as that in the subsequent ones, or that the other arguments are the same across the string of logical structures, because the only way the Completeness Constraint could be satisfied is for there to be only two distinct arguments in the overall logical structure. If there were more than two, then one or more would not be linked to a syntactic realization, violating the constraint. Moreover, since there are only two syntactic arguments in the sentence, the only way the syntax to semantic linking can fulfill the constraint is if the actor argument in the syntax links to all three EFFECTOR arguments in the logical structure. The constructional template for this construction is given in table 9.4. The value for 'PSA' is 'none', because there is no privileged syntactic argument in the nuclear juncture itself; the core as a whole has a default privileged syntactic argument, but it is not a property of the nuclear juncture. The linking from syntax to semantics in (9.21a) is given in figure 9.6 on page 534. The numbers in the figure refer to the steps in the linking algorithm in (9.2). Since Barai has no voice construction but does have a pragmatic pivot, as the data in exercise 5 in chapter 6 show, step 1 would have to be reformulated in the grammar of Barai to take into account the factors determining the selection of the argument to function as PSA. Since *kume-* 'call' is a verb which would have the core-initial PSA position, and since *fu* '3sg' is a pronoun, we may conclude that this is the unmarked situation and therefore that *fu* is the actor. As mentioned above, the only way for the Completeness Constraint to be satisfied is for all of the actor arguments in the semantic representation to be linked to the single actor NP in the syntax, and similarly for all of the undergoer arguments in the semantics to be linked to the single undergoer NP in the syntax.

The linking in nuclear junctures becomes more complicated when the linked nucleus contains a transitive verb, as in (8.3a) from French, repeated below as (9.22a).

Table 9.4 *Constructional template for Barai nuclear junctures in (9.21)*

CONSTRUCTION
Barai nuclear serial verb constructions

SYNTAX
Juncture: Nuclear
Nexus: Coordination/Cosubordination
Construction type: Serial verb
Coordination: $[_{CL} [_{CORE}$ ARG ARG $[_{NUC} \ldots] [_{NUC} \ldots] \ldots]]$
Cosubordination: $[_{CL} [_{CORE}$ ARG ARG $[_{NUC} [_{NUC} \ldots] [_{NUC} \ldots]] \ldots]]$
Unit template(s): None
PSA: None
Linking: Default

MORPHOLOGY
None

SEMANTICS
Sequential phases of a complex event or process
$[\text{PRED}_{NUC1}]$ & $[\text{PRED}_{NUC2}]$ & . . . & $[\text{PRED}_{NUCn}]$

PRAGMATICS
Illocutionary force: Unspecified
Focus structure: Unspecified

(9.22)	a.	Je	fer-ai	mang-er	les	gâteaux	à	Jean.
		1sgNOM	make-1sgFUT	eat-INF	the.Mpl	cakes	DAT	John
		'I will make John eat the cakes.'						
	b.	Je	fer-ai	mang-er	les	gâteaux	par	Jean.
		1sgNOM	make-1sgFUT	eat-INF	the.Mpl	cakes	by	John
		'I will have John eat the cakes.'						
	c.	[**do′** (1sg, ∅)] CAUSE [**do′** (Jean, [**eat′** (Jean, gâteaux)]) & BECOME **eaten′** (gâteaux)]						

When the linked nucleus contains an intransitive verb, it will be the undergoer. When it contains a transitive verb, on the other hand, the question arises as to which argument will function as undergoer. Since this is a nuclear juncture, the logical structure in (c) maps into a single core. By the Actor–Undergoer Hierarchy, *je* '1sgNOM' would be actor, and of the remaining two arguments, the PATIENT *les gâteaux* is clearly the lowest-ranking argument with respect to the undergoer end of the hierarchy and therefore will be undergoer. That leaves the EFFECTOR *Jean* as a direct core argument, and assuming that French has the same basic case-marking rules as other accusative languages, it will be assigned dative case, which in French is

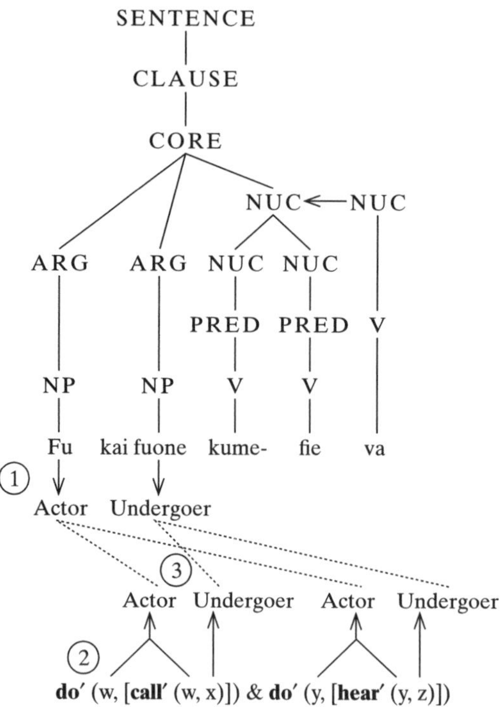

Figure 9.6 Linking from syntax to semantics in Barai nuclear cosubordination

realized by the preposition *à*. This accounts for (9.22a), and the linking from semantics to syntax is diagrammed in figure 9.7. This basic linking accounts for what Comrie (1976c) shows to be the predominant case-marking pattern found in this type of causative construction. There are other patterns, and we will discuss case marking in nuclear and core junctures in section 9.2 below.

There is a second linking possibility for the logical structure in (9.22c), and it yields (9.22b), in which *Jean*, the causee, is marked by *par*, the preposition which marks passive agents in French passive constructions. The difference between the (a) and (b) sentences in (9.22) is more than just the choice of preposition; as in a passive construction, the PP *par Jean* can be omitted, yielding *Je ferai manger les gâteaux* 'I will have the cakes eaten', or 'I will have someone eat the cakes', whereas the dative PP *à Jean* cannot be omitted. Hence *par Jean* acts like an adjunct in the periphery, whereas *à Jean* acts like an direct core argument. How can this be explained? Nuclear junctures have the logical structure of a transitive verb and therefore have actor and undergoer arguments. When the linked verb is intransitive, it contributes the argument that will function as undergoer. When it is transitive, it likewise contributes the argument that will function as undergoer, but it also

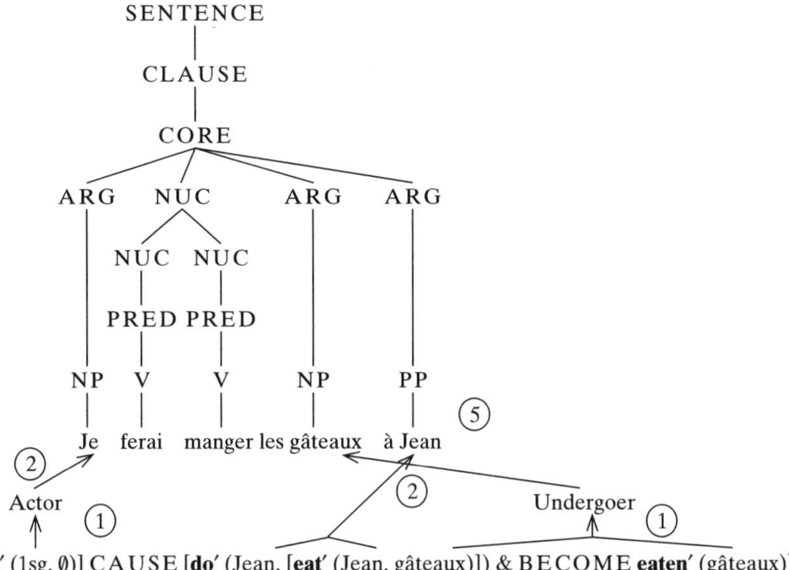

Figure 9.7 Semantics → syntax linking in the French nuclear juncture causative in (9.22a)

contributes another argument which is a potential actor; indeed, if the embedded logical structure were to occur on its own, that argument would be the actor in the clause. What French allows, and what most other languages with this construction do not, is for the embedded transitive logical structure to take two macroroles, just as if it were an independent logical structure. Since the EFFECTOR of *faire* 'make, cause' is also an actor, a problem arises: how can there be two actors in a single core? The answer is, there cannot be, and accordingly the actor which is not linked to the privileged syntactic argument appears in the periphery marked by *par*, just as in a passive construction, in which the actor is not a core argument. Which actor functions as the privileged syntactic argument? The actor of the matrix logical structure, that of *faire*, appears as the privileged syntactic argument. This follows from the fact that this actor is the first EFFECTOR in a causal sequence, and we argued in section 4.1 that the first EFFECTOR in a causal sequence has priority for actor; in the rare circumstance when there are two actors, as in (9.22b), this principle may be extended to give the actor of the first EFFECTOR in a causal sequence priority for privileged syntactic argument as well, since, in syntactically accusative languages, the norm is for the highest ranking argument in the logical structure to function as privileged syntactic argument. This linking is presented in figure 9.8. It should be clear that the linking from syntax to semantics in both (9.22a, b) can be handled by the linking algorithm in (9.2) without modification.

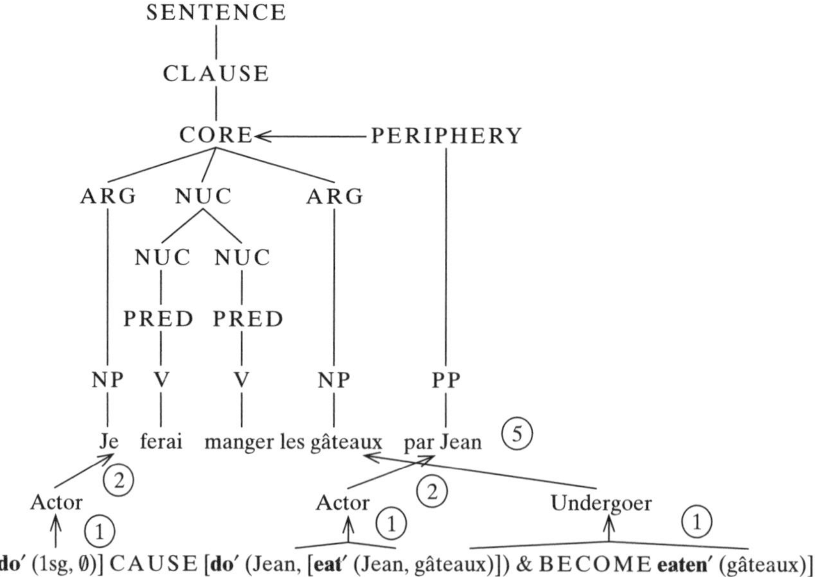

Figure 9.8 Semantics → syntax linking in the French nuclear juncture causative in (9.22b)

In addition to the syntactic difference regarding the causee in these two constructions, there is a semantic contrast as well, one which is captured somewhat in the English translations by means of the contrast between 'make' and 'have' as the gloss for *faire*. Hyman and Zimmer (1976) argue that in the construction in (9.22a) the causee may be interpreted as not acting volitionally, whereas in the construction in (b) the causee may be interpreted as acting volitionally. Another way of putting this is that the secondary EFFECTOR, the causee, can more easily be construed as an AGENT in (b) than in (a), in terms of the implicature theory of agency proposed in section 3.2.3.2. Thus, *par* encourages the AGENT implicature, while *à* is basically neutral with respect to it. This difference in interpretation is evidence that the PP which is omitted in a sentence like *Je ferai manger les gâteaux* is *par* NP, not *à* NP. The translation is 'I will *have* the cakes eaten' or 'I will *have* someone eat the cakes', not 'I will make the cakes be eaten' or 'I will make someone eat the cakes'; it is the interpretation of causatives with the causee marked by *par*, not by *à*. We will return to this issue in our discussion of case marking in nuclear junctures in section 9.2.2.

The constructional template for the French nuclear juncture causative is given in table 9.5. The case marking of the syntactic arguments, the priority of the actor of *faire* over that of the linked verb for privileged syntactic argument, and the occurrence of the secondary actor in the periphery like in a passive follow from both general principles (privileged syntactic argument selection principles, no more than

Table 9.5 *Template for French nuclear juncture causative construction in (9.22)*

CONSTRUCTION
French causative construction

SYNTAX
Juncture: Nuclear
Nexus: Cosubordination
Construction type: Serial verb
$[_{CL}\,[_{CORE}$ ARG $[_{NUC}\,[_{NUC} \ldots]\,[_{NUC} \ldots]]$ ARG . . .] . . .]
Unit template(s): None
PSA: None
Linking: Default; or
if verb in NUC_2 is transitive, then its logical structure may assign two MRs

MORPHOLOGY
None

SEMANTICS
$[PRED_{NUC1}]$ CAUSE $[PRED_{NUC2}]$

PRAGMATICS
Illocutionary force: Unspecified
Focus structure: Unspecified

two macroroles per core) and from language-specific ones (case-marking rules, treatment of non-core actor).

9.1.3 Core junctures

Neither clausal nor nuclear junctures have required any revision of the linking algorithms in (9.2) and (9.1), but some types of core junctures do, as we will see. There are two basic types of core junctures, subordinate and non-subordinate, each with rather different linking properties. Subordinate core junctures in English are illustrated in (9.23).

(9.23) a. Chris regretted Dana's painting the house red.
a′. **regret′** (Chris, [[**do′** (Dana, [**paint′** (Dana, house)])] CAUSE [BECOME **red′** (house)]])
b. That Dana painted the house red shocked everyone.
b′. [[**do′** (Dana, [**paint′** (Dana, house)] CAUSE [BECOME **red′** (house)])] CAUSE [**feel′** (everyone, [**shocked′**])]

The embedded logical structure links internally independently of the matrix logical structure, but as a whole unit it is part of the linking of the matrix logical structure,

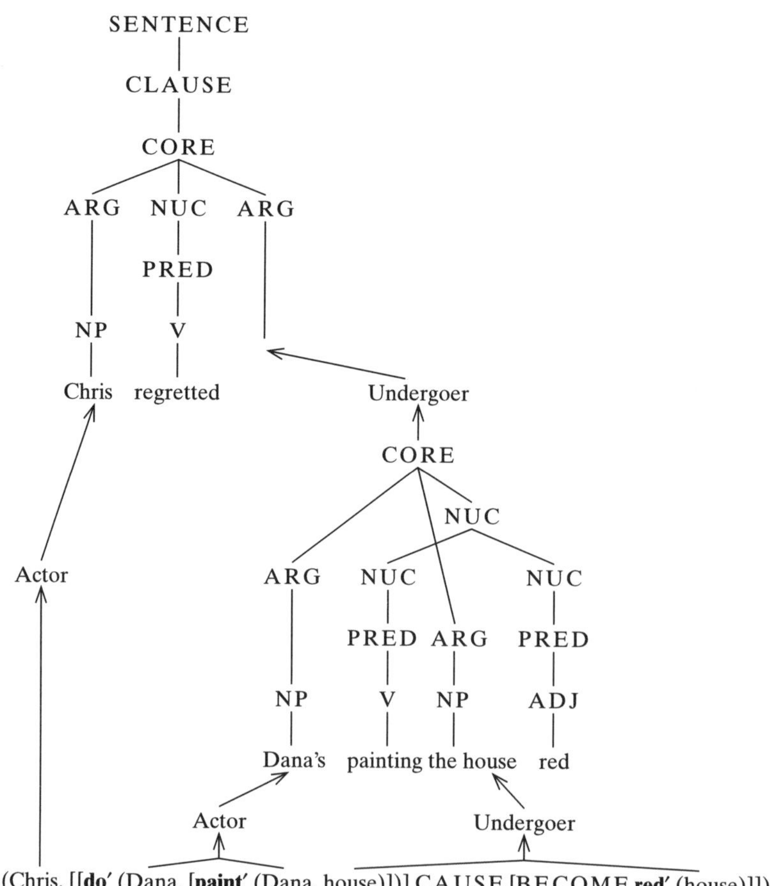

Figure 9.9 Linking from semantics to syntax in English core subordination in (9.23a)

because the embedded logical structure is an argument of the matrix logical structure in the semantics and a core argument of the matrix predicate in the syntax. The linking from semantics to syntax for (9.23a) is illustrated in figure 9.9.

The linking is presented in two parts, one for the embedded logical structure and one for the matrix logical structure. In the embedded logical structure *Dana* is the actor and *house* the undergoer, and they are mapped into their default positions in the core, which, not being part of a tensed clause, is formally a gerund. The embedded logical structure is an argument of the matrix logical structure and functions as its undergoer, while *Chris* functions as actor. Hence in the linking to the matrix clause, the gerundive core occupies the normal undergoer slot in the matrix core, and *Chris* occupies the normal actor slot. The primary differences between this example and (9.23b) are that the embedded logical structure is realized as a tensed clause, rather than a gerund, and that the embedded clause functions as actor rather than undergoer. In more complete semantic representations including operators, the difference between the logical structure which is realized as a tensed clause and one which is realized as a gerund would be readily apparent. This contrast is presented in (9.24).

(9.24) a. ⟨$_{\text{IF}}$*DEC*⟨$_{\text{TNS}}$*PAST*⟨**regret′** (Chris, [[**do′** (Dana, [**paint′** (Dana, house)])] CAUSE [BECOME **red′** (house)]])⟩⟩⟩
b. ⟨$_{\text{IF}}$*DEC*⟨$_{\text{TNS}}$*PAST*⟨[⟨$_{\text{TNS}}$*PAST*⟨[**do′** (Dana, [**paint′** (Dana, house)])] CAUSE [BECOME **red′** (house)]⟩⟩] CAUSE [**feel′** (everyone, [**shocked′**])]⟩⟩⟩

The initial illocutionary force and tense operators in both representations pertain to the matrix logical structure and therefore to the matrix clause; in (b) there is a tense operator modifying the embedded logical structure, and signaling that the logical structure will be realized as a tensed clause. The absence of any clausal operators modifying the embedded logical structure in (a) indicates that it will be realized as an infinitive (*for–to* construction) or gerundive core, depending on the overall semantics of the construction (see section 8.4.3).

In some languages the fact that a nominalized unit functions as undergoer would be indicated explicitly through case marking. In Huallaga Quechua (Weber 1983), for example, nominalized clauses take the accusative case suffix *-ta* after the nominalization suffix. This is illustrated in (9.25).

(9.25) a. Noqa-∅ musy-aa maqa-shu-sha-yki-ta.
1sgNOM know-1sg hit-2U-NMZ-2pl-ACC
'I know that he hits you (pl.).'
b. Qonqashk-aa aywa-shaa-ta.
forget-1sg go-NMZ.1sg-ACC
'I forgot that I had gone.'

If these are instances of core subordination, as in figure 9.9, then the occurrence of the accusative case on the nominalization is not surprising, since it is the undergoer.

The linking from semantics to syntax in (9.23) can be handled by the linking algorithm in (9.1) without modification. As far as linking from syntax to semantics is concerned, the linear order of the clauses is decisive: the linking starts with the first clause encountered, be it the matrix clause, a preposed adverbial clause, or a 'sentential subject', and goes from there. This is not surprising, given that linking from syntax to semantics is part of the comprehension process, which begins as soon as the sentence is encountered.

Thus, subordination at the core level requires no revision of the linking algorithms from chapter 7. This, however, is not the case for non-subordinate core junctures. In chapter 8 we showed that the criterial feature of non-subordinate core junctures is a shared semantic argument between or among the linked cores. This shared argument will require modification of both linking algorithms. We begin our discussion with control constructions (formerly known as 'equi-NP-deletion'), and then we will investigate matrix-coding (a.k.a. 'raising to subject', 'raising to object', 'exceptional case marking') constructions.

9.1.3.1 Control constructions

Examples of (obligatory) control constructions are given in (9.26).

(9.26) a. Leslie tried to open the door.
b. Kim persuaded Pat to go to the party.
c. Robin promised Sandy to clean the birdcage.[6]

These are called 'control' constructions, because there is a syntactic argument missing from the linked core which must be interpreted as being the same as one of the syntactic arguments of the matrix core; this is the shared semantic argument mentioned above. The matrix core argument interpreted as being the same as the missing syntactic argument in the linked core is the controller. (9.26a) exemplifies 'subject' control, since the controller is the 'subject' of the matrix core. The (b) sentence illustrates 'object' control, since the controller is the 'object' of the matrix core. Finally, the (c) example involves 'subject' control. Since 'subject' and 'object' have no theoretical status in this framework, we must find an alternative analysis using the appropriate theoretical terms, i.e. syntactic pivot or controller, actor or undergoer. These are *obligatory* control constructions, because there is no possibility of filling in the missing syntactic argument. They contrast with non-obligatory control constructions, in which all of the semantic arguments of the linked logical structure may optionally be realized in the syntax. This contrast is illustrated in (9.27).

(9.27) a. Tanisha brought the book in order to read it to the children.
a′. Tanisha brought the book in order for Chris to read it to the children.
b. *Leslie tried (for) Bill to open the door.
c. *Kim persuaded Pat (for) Sam to go to the party.
d. *Robin promised Sandy (for) Kim to watch the baby.

In (a) the actor of *read* is missing from the linked unit, and *Tanisha*, the actor of *bring*, is interpreted as the controller of the missing argument, i.e. *Tanisha* is construed as the actor of *read* as well. This appears to be analogous to (9.26a) with *try*, but in fact the two constructions are quite different: the construction in (a) permits an overt actor in the linked unit, as in (a′), whereas the *try* construction does not, as (b) shows. The same is true for the other obligatory control constructions, as the (c) and (d) examples demonstrate. Thus, obligatory control constructions involve the obligatory semantic argument sharing what we argued in chapter 8 to be the criterial feature of non-subordinate core junctures.

(a) The theory of obligatory control

The theory of obligatory control refers to hypotheses about how the controller of the missing syntactic argument in the linked unit is to be determined. There are two different albeit related syntactic approaches to this. The first is the solution originally proposed in Rosenbaum (1967) and adopted by Chomsky (1981b), which is called the 'minimal distance principle'. It says, in essence, that the NP higher up in the phrase structure tree which is closest to the embedded unit will be the controller. This correctly predicts the controller in sentences like (9.26a), since there is only one NP higher up in the tree, and also in sentences like (9.26b), since the 'object' (internal argument) is closer to the lower unit than the 'subject' (external argument). It does not, however, correctly predict the controller for (9.26c), and to deal with such cases Chomsky (1981b) argued that verbs like *promise* should be marked with a feature like [+SC] (for 'subject control') in their lexical entry. Bresnan (1982b) proposed an account of control based on grammatical functions in LFG. She posited a hierarchy of possible controllers in terms of grammatical functions, OBJ_{θ}[7] > OBJ > SUBJ, and then formulated a principle of control which says basically that the highest-ranking grammatical function in the matrix clause is the controller. As with the minimal distance principle, it correctly predicts the facts in (9.26a, b) but not in (c), and as with Chomsky's account, verbs like *promise* are marked as exceptions in the lexicon.

There are several problems with these approaches. The most glaring one is the control behavior of *promise*-type verbs, which virtually all syntactic accounts fail to predict correctly. Moreover, simply listing these verbs in the lexicon is thoroughly non-explanatory and leads to an empirically false prediction, as Radford (1981) points out.

> Firstly, arbitrary lists of properties associated with predicates have no predictive or explanatory value: ask the question 'How do you know this is a verb of subject control?', and you get the non-answer 'Because it's listed as a verb of subject control in the lexicon.' Secondly, treating *control* . . . as a *lexically governed* phenomenon implies that control properties are entirely arbitrary, and hence will vary in random fashion from dialect to dialect, or language to language: this would lead us to expect that the counterpart of [e.g. *John persuaded Bill to leave*] in some other dialect or language would have subject control rather than nonsubject control . . . But as far as we know, this is not the case. (p. 381)

The next problems concern the constructs in terms of which the analyses are framed, phrase structure constituency and grammatical relations. We argued in chapter 2 that the assumption that immediate-constituent representations are universally valid is untenable, given the constraints we imposed on universal theories of clause structure in section 2.1, and we gave examples from Dyirbal and Lakhota as examples of languages in which immediate-constituent representations were especially inappropriate. Yet the basic control facts in these languages are the same as in English, as the following examples illustrate; the Dyirbal examples are from Dixon (1972, 1994).

(9.28) a. Ba-yi yaɽa-Ø walma-ɲu wayɲḍi-li. Dyirbal
DEIC-ABS.I man-ABS get.up-TNS go.uphill-PURP
'The man got up to go uphill.'

b. Ba-la-n yabu-Ø ba-ŋgu-l ŋuma-ŋgu giga-n banagay-gu.
DEIC-ABS-II mother-ABS DEIC-ERG-I father-ERG tell-TNS return-PURP
'Father told mother to return.'

c. Wówapi ki Ø-yawá i-bl-úthe. Lakhota
book the INAN-read stem-1sgA-try
'I tried to read the book.'

d. Wówapi ki hená Ø-yawá-wičha-wa-ši.
book the those INAN-read-3plU-1sgA-tell
'I told them to read those books.'

Dyirbal does not express notions like 'want' or 'try' with complex sentence constructions, and accordingly a purpose construction is used to illustrate the first type of control construction. In Dyirbal and Lakhota, the control relations are analogous to those in the English examples in (9.26a, b), despite the major differences in immediate-constituent phrase structure among the three languages discussed in chapter 2.[8] Thus, structural position in a phrase structure tree cannot be the basis for explaining the fact that these three languages exhibit the same control phenomena.

The Dyirbal example also raises problems for the grammatical-relations-based account: given, as we saw in chapter 6, that Dyirbal is syntactically ergative and therefore the absolutive NP in (9.28) is the syntactic 'subject' (pragmatic pivot), the controller in (9.28b) is the 'subject', not the 'object'. The same is true in Sama, another syntactically ergative language; the examples are from C. Walton (personal communication); see also Walton (1986).

(9.29) a. Baya' aku N-b'lli tinapay. Sama
want 1sgABS ANTI-buy bread
'I want to buy some bread.'

b. Logos ku iya N-k'llo daing ma si ina'.
persuade 1sgERG 3sgABS ANTI-get fish OBL PNM mother
'I persuaded him to get fish for mother.'

c. Janji' ku iya bayad-an saung.
promise 1sgERG 3sgABS pay-LOC tomorrow
'I promised him to pay [him] tomorrow.'

The single NP in the matrix core in (a) is *aku*, the first singular absolutive pronominal form, and as the only NP it must be the controller of the missing argument in the linked core. The actor in the matrix core in the last two sentences is expressed by *ku*, which is the first singular ergative pronominal form, and the undergoer in the matrix core in both is expressed by *iya*, the third singular absolutive pronominal form. In (b) the matrix verb is *logos* 'persuade', and accordingly we expect there to be 'object' control; but because Sama is syntactically ergative, the controller *iya* is in fact the syntactic 'subject' (pragmatic pivot). In (c) the matrix verb is *janji'* 'promise', and accordingly, we expect 'subject' control. But again, because this is a syntactically ergative language, the controller is not in fact the subject; it is the non-'subject' actor, *ku*. In chapter 6 we also discussed languages like Acehnese (Durie 1985, 1987) and Mandarin Chinese (LaPolla 1990, 1993) which appear to lack grammatical relations (syntactic controllers and pivots) altogether. Yet the control facts in these two languages are just like those in all of the other languages we have looked at so far.

(9.30) a. Geu-tém [(*geu-)taguen bu]. — Acehnese
3-want (3A-) cook rice
'She wants to cook rice.'
b. Geu-yue lôn [(*lôn-)peugöt kuwéh].
3A-order 1sg (1sgA-)make cake
'(S)he ordered me to make a cake.'

(9.31) a. Wǒ yào chī fàn. — Mandarin Chinese
1sg want eat rice
'I want to eat (rice).'
b. Tā jiāo wǒ xǐe zì.
3sg teach 1sg write characters
'She teaches me to write characters.'

In these two languages, which, we have argued, lack grammatical relations in the usual sense, the control facts are exactly like those in English, Dyirbal, Lakhota and Sama. Thus, the basic control facts involving intransitive and transitive matrix verbs appear to be the same, regardless of whether the language has constituent structure in the GB sense or not, whether it has grammatical relations or not, or whether it is syntactically ergative or syntactically accusative.

Accounting for the controller in sentences in which there is only one possible controller, such as all of the (a) examples, is trivial. Is there any generalization that captures the control facts in the (b) examples? The answer should be obvious at this point: all of these sentences have *undergoer* control. That is, the undergoer of the matrix core is the controller of the missing syntactic argument in the linked core; it is the undergoer of the matrix core which is the shared argument with the linked core, the core argument which functions as a semantic argument in the logical structure of each core. Why should this be? Does it follow from anything? In Foley and Van Valin (1984) it was argued that this follows directly from the semantics of the verbs involved, and in particular from the semantics of causation, which we may represent roughly as in (9.32).

(9.32) Actor acts on undergoer (by verbal or non-verbal means) → Undergoer does action

In the prototypical case, the actor acts on the undergoer by either verbal or non-verbal means with the intention that the undergoer do some action or be involved in some process or other change. Verbs denoting states of affairs in which the actor acts on the undergoer by non-verbal means are usually called 'causative' verbs, e.g. *make*, *force* or *cause* in English, whereas if the actor uses verbal means, the verbs denoting these states of affairs are called 'jussive' verbs, e.g. *tell*, *order* or *persuade* in English (see (8.55)). The resulting theory of obligatory control, proposed originally in Foley and Van Valin (1984), is stated in (9.33).

(9.33) *Theory of obligatory control*
1 Causative and jussive verbs have undergoer control.
2 All other (M-)transitive verbs have actor control.

This theory applies to matrix verbs which are (M-)transitive; if the matrix verb is (M-)intransitive, then the single argument will be the controller by default. This semantically based theory has numerous advantages over syntactic approaches. First, it applies without modification to all of the languages we have discussed, regardless of their typological characteristics. That is, because it is stated in terms of macroroles, it applies equally to Sama and to Lakhota, to Acehnese and to Dyirbal, and to Mandarin and to English. Second, *it predicts that sentences like (9.25c) and (9.29c) should have actor control*; that is, verbs like *promise* are not exceptional in this theory. How does it make this prediction? Verbs like *promise* are what Searle (1975) calls *commissives*: 'Commissives . . . are those illocutionary acts whose point is to commit the speaker . . . to some future course of action' (Searle 1975: 356). The 'future course of action' is denoted by the infinitival core, and accordingly, the semantics of *promise* require that its actor be the controller. In terms of (9.33), commissives are neither causative nor jussive and therefore should have actor control. Third, because the control facts are a function of the semantics of the matrix verb, they also carry over into other constructions involving these verbs, as illustrated in (9.34).

(9.34) a. Tom promised Sam that he would wash the car.
b. Tom persuaded Sam that he should wash the car.

The pronoun *he* in the *that*-clause is technically free to refer to either of the NPs in the matrix core or even to a discourse referent, but the preferred interpretations of both of these sentences follows the predictions of the theory of obligatory control: *Tom* is the preferred antecedent for *he* in (a), and *Sam* is the preferred antecedent for *he* in (b). Fourth, because the choice of the controller is tied to the semantics of the verb, this analysis predicts that if a verb can be used alternatively as causative or non-causative or as jussive or non-jussive, then its control properties would change. This seems to be the case with a number of verbs of saying.

(9.35) a. Larry asked Sally to leave.
b. Larry made a polite request to Sally that she leave.
c. Larry requested permission from Sally so that he could leave.

For many English speakers (9.35a) is ambiguous, and the two interpretations are given in (b) and (c). *Ask* can be construed as either a jussive verb, as in (b), or a verb for requesting something, as in (c); when it has a jussive interpretation, there is undergoer control, as in (b), and when it is non-jussive, there is actor control, as in (c), exactly as predicted. Fifth, because control choices are characterized in terms of macroroles, rather than grammatical relations, the behavior of these verbs under passivization is predicted. Consider the examples in (9.36).

(9.36) a. Pat was persuaded (by Kim) to go to the party. (cf. (9.25b))
b. *Sandy was promised (by Robin) to help with the party. (cf. (9.25c))

Recall that the controller is the syntactic argument in the matrix core which also functions as a semantic argument in the linked core, and this entails that the controller must be a core argument in the matrix core. With a jussive verb like *tell* or *persuade*, the undergoer functions as privileged syntactic argument in a passive construction, and since it is a core argument, it continues to function as controller and the resulting sentence is fine, as (a) shows. As Cutrer (1987, 1993) points out, however, with a non-jussive verb like *promise*, the actor functions as an oblique peripheral constituent, not a core argument, in a passive construction, and consequently there is no core argument controller in the matrix core; the resulting sentence is therefore ungrammatical, as (b) shows. The fact that 'subject'-controlled complements cannot be passivized is known in the literature as 'Visser's generalization', and it follows directly from the account of passive in chapters 6 and 7 and the theory of obligatory control in (9.33). Thus, the semantic theory of obligatory control presented here is to be preferred over alternative syntactic accounts.

(*b*) *Linking in control constructions*

The theory of obligatory control in (9.33) and the Completeness Constraint in (9.11) play crucial roles in both phases of linking in these constructions. On the syntactic side, we showed in sections 8.2 and 8.4.1 that the linked core in a non-subordinate core juncture is missing a syntactic argument position, which is the syntactic pivot of the construction. In (7.7) we presented the syntactic template selection principles, which are keyed to the S-transitivity of the verb. They are repeated in (9.37).

(9.37) a. *Syntactic template selection principle*
The number of syntactic slots for arguments and argument-adjuncts within the core is equal to the number of distinct specified argument positions in the semantic representation of the core.

b. *Language-specific qualifications on the principle in* (*a*)
1 All cores in the language have a minimum syntactic valence of 1.
2 Passive constructions reduce the number of core slots by 1.
3 The occurrence of a syntactic argument in the pre-/postcore slot reduces the number of core slots by 1 (may override (1)).

In order to capture the fact that there is a syntactic argument slot missing in the linked core, we must add a universally valid qualification to (9.37), namely, the occurrence of the core as the linked core in a non-subordinate core juncture reduces the number of core slots by 1. The revised principles are given in (9.38).

(9.38) a. *Syntactic template selection principle* (*revised formulation*)
The number of syntactic slots for arguments and argument-adjuncts within the core is equal to the number of distinct specified argument positions in the semantic representation of the core.

b. *Universal qualification of the principle in* (*a*)
The occurrence of a core as the linked core in a non-subordinate core juncture reduces the number of core slots by 1.

c. *Language-specific qualifications of the principle in* (*a*)
1 All cores in the language have a minimum syntactic valence of 1.
2 Passive constructions reduce the number of core slots by 1.
3 The occurrence of a syntactic argument in the pre-/postcore slot reduces the number of core slots by 1 (may override (1)).

The statement in (b) does not specify which syntactic slot is missing, since that is a construction-specific feature. Since the obligatory control construction follows the overall pattern found in English, the pivot corresponds to the traditional 'subject', i.e. the prenuclear core argument slot in the core; this is not always the case in English, as (7.118) showed. The non-matrix core in the constructions in (9.26) will always be 'subjectless', and this is the central fact about these constructions that the linking system must accommodate.

We will begin with the linking in the simplest example, (9.26a); its logical structure is given in (9.39b).

(9.39) a. **do′** (x, [**try′** (x, [[**do′** (y, ∅)] CAUSE [BECOME **open′** (z)]])])

b. **do′** (Leslie$_i$, [**try′** (Leslie$_i$, [[**do′** (y$_i$, ∅)] CAUSE [BECOME **open′** (door)]])])

An important point needs to be repeated about this logical structure before we discuss linking. We argued in section 8.4.1 that the infinitives in these constructions do not function as *syntactic* arguments of the matrix verbs; that is, the facts in (8.32)–(8.36) show that these infinitives are not core arguments of the matrix verb the way gerunds and *for–to* infinitives are. Nevertheless, the logical structure of these infinitives is a *semantic* argument in the logical structure of the matrix verb, as in (9.39a). That is, the logical structure of *try* is **do′** (x, [**try′** (x, w)]), and the logical structure of *open* is [**do′** (y, Ø)] CAUSE [BECOME **open′** (z)]; the logical structure of *open* fills the *y* variable slot in the logical structure for *try*. Hence the logical structure of *open* is a semantic argument of *try*. Nevertheless, as (8.32)–(8.36) showed, *to open the door* is not a syntactic argument of *try* in *Leslie tried to open the door*. Thus, these constructions represent a mismatch between syntax and semantics; what is an argument in the semantics is not realized as an argument in the syntax.

Returning to the issue of linking, *try* takes a non-subordinate core juncture because it is a psych-action verb, in terms of the Interclausal Relations Hierarchy in figure 8.18; this follows from the meaning of psych-action: the verb codes a mental disposition on the part of its actor to be involved in a state of affairs, and accordingly the actor must also be a semantic argument of the embedded logical structure, because the participant with the mental disposition must also be a participant in the state of affairs denoted by the embedded logical structure (see figure 8.19). Thus the actor of *try* must control the missing argument in the linked core, i.e. it must also function as a semantic argument in the embedded logical structure. Hence *Leslie*, the only argument in the matrix core, is the controller. The crucial syntactic feature of non-subordinate core junctures is that the linked core lacks a syntactic argument position, following (9.38b). The missing argument is the syntactic pivot of the linked core, and in these constructions the pivot is the traditional 'subject'; therefore it is the prenuclear core argument position that is missing in the linked core. Because there is an obligatorily shared semantic argument in the construction, one of the arguments in the embedded logical structure is not filled by lexical material but is coindexed with the controller in the matrix logical structure. The result is the logical structure in (9.39b), and how it links into the syntax is presented in figure 9.10. Given the logical structure in (9.39b), the linking algorithm in (9.1) can handle this case without modification. Even though the *y* argument in the embedded logical structure is not directly linked to an expression in the syntax, it is coindexed with *Leslie*, which is linked to the syntax, thereby satisfying the Completeness Constraint.

The role of the Completeness Constraint can be seen more clearly when we look at more complex examples, such as (9.40).

(9.40) a. Chris tried to see Pat.
a′. **do′** (Chris_i, [**try′** (Chris_i, [**see′** (y_i, Pat)])])
b. *Chris_i tried [Pat] to see $\_\__i$.
b′. **do′** (Chris_i, [**try′** (Chris_i, [**see′** (Pat, z_i)])])

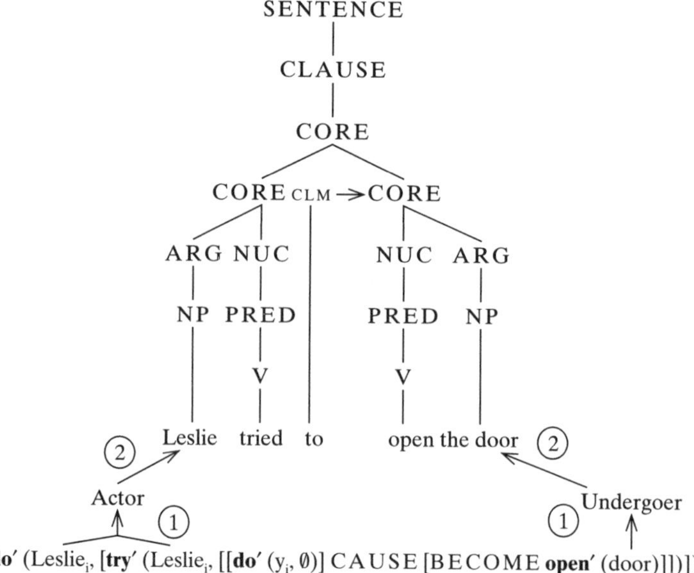

Figure 9.10 Linking from semantics to syntax in English control construction in (9.26a)

c. Chris tried to be seen by Pat.
c′. **do′** (Chris$_i$, [**try′** (Chris$_i$, [**see′** (Pat, z$_i$)])])
d. *Chris$_i$ tried [Pat] to be seen [by ___$_i$].
d′. **do′** (Chris$_i$, [**try′** (Chris$_i$, [**see′** (y$_i$, Pat)])])

In this logical structure, the single argument of *try* can be coindexed with either of the arguments of *see*; examples (a) and (d) have the same indexing, as do (b) and (c). For each of the possible coindexings, there is only one grammatical output. What rules out the impossible linkings? The answer is, the Completeness Constraint. Let's go through each of the possibilities to see how this works. The linking in (a) parallels that in figure 9.10, as *Chris* is the actor of *try* and *Pat* is the undergoer of *see*, and so requires no further comment. In (b), the actor of *try* is coindexed with the second argument of *see*. This means that *Chris* is the actor of *try* and *Pat* is the actor of *see*, and when these assignments are mapped into the syntactic structure in figure 9.10 a problem immediately arises: there is no syntactic position in the second core for an actor to appear in, since the second core has an active-voice verb. Hence *Pat* cannot be realized in the syntactic representation, and this violates the Completeness Constraint. This is given in figure 9.11. It is impossible to link an actor to the post-nuclear core argument slot, since actors may only be linked to the syntactic pivot position in an active-voice core in English. Hence

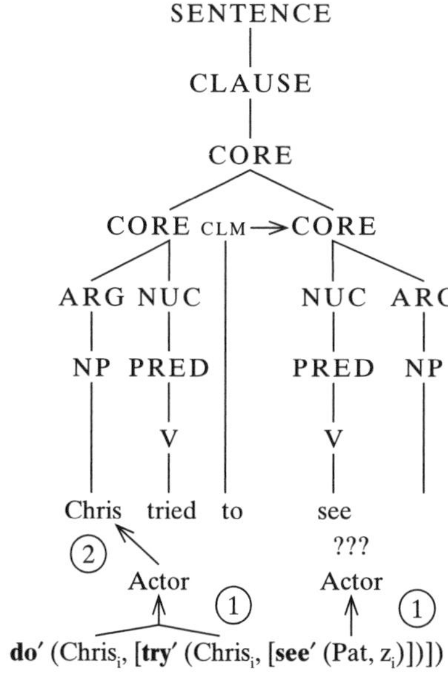

Figure 9.11 Failed linking from semantics to syntax in (9.40b)

no special constraints or principles are needed to explain the impossibility of this potential linking.

The other two sentences involve passive voice in the second core, and here too only one of the two possible linkings is permitted. The sentence in (9.40c) has the same logical structure as in figure 9.11, but the second core is passive. This makes possible a linking which does not violate the Completeness Constraint, as figure 9.12 shows. The final possible combination is the syntactic representation of figure 9.12 with the logical structure in (9.40a); this combination cannot be successfully linked, as figure 9.13 shows. The first thing to note here is that the sentence *Chris tried to be seen* is perfectly grammatical, but it is not a possible realization of the logical structure in (9.40a′). Its logical structure is **do′** (Chris$_i$, [**try′** (Chris$_i$, [**see′** (∅, z$_i$)])]), where the actor of the embedded logical structure is unspecified. The linking in figure 9.13 violates the Completeness Constraint, because the undergoer *Pat* cannot be realized overtly in this syntactic structure. An undergoer in English can only be realized as a core argument, either in its default postnuclear position or as syntactic pivot, and neither of these options is available in this structure. The only possible realization for this logical structure is as in figure 9.10, as noted above.

The four possibilities in (9.40) have been accounted for in terms of the linking algorithm in (9.1) and the Completeness Constraint; no special principles or constraints are required. In particular, it is not necessary to stipulate in the lexical entry for *try* that it must share an argument with its complement logical structure. Thus,

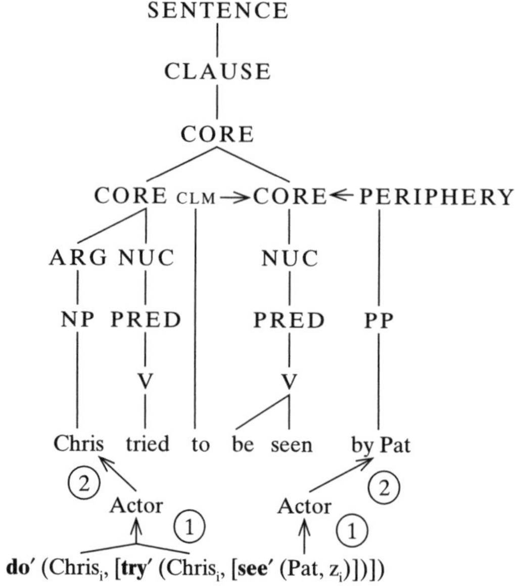

Figure 9.12 Linking from semantics to syntax in (9.40c)

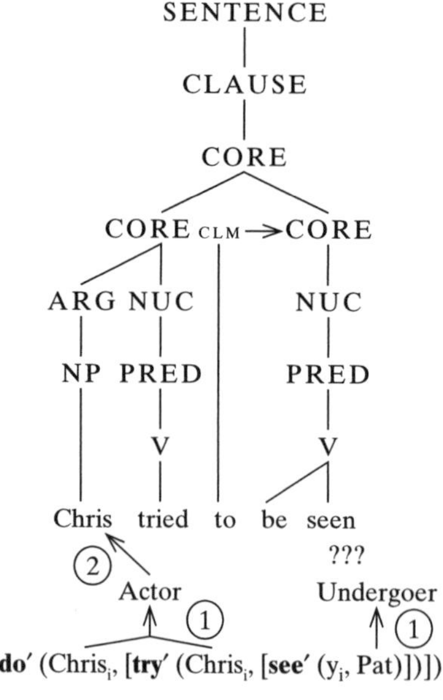

Figure 9.13 Failed linking from semantics to syntax in (9.40d)

there is no need to rule out via stipulation that **do′** (Chris, [**try′** (Chris, [**see′** (Dana, Pat)])]) is an impossible logical structure, since there is no possible linking between it and any of the syntactic structures in figures 9.9–9.12 that could satisfy the Completeness Constraint. Moreover, the same is true with respect to the more complex examples in (9.26b, c) and (9.28)–(9.31); they are handled in exactly the same way. We will not go through all of the possible combinations in detail the way we did with (9.40); we will, however, look at sentences like (9.26c) with *promise* in English and (9.29) from Sama.

With respect to sentences with *promise* in English, we have already noted that *promise* can also take a *that*-clause, as in (9.34a), and accordingly, the first question to ask is, what is the difference at the semantic level between sentences like (9.26c) and (9.34a)? We may make this more concrete by repeating (9.26c) and giving the alternative version in (9.41b).

(9.41) a. Robin promised Sandy to clean the birdcage.
b. Robin promised Sandy that he would clean the birdcage.

The answer may be somewhat surprising: these two sentences have the same logical structure but different semantic representations. A more complete logical structure for *promise* is given in (9.42a), and the abbreviated representation we will use for *promise* is given in (a′). The logical structure for the two sentences is given in (a″), and the semantic representation for (9.41a) is given in (9.42b) and that for (9.41b) in (c).

(9.42) a. [**do′** (w_i, [**express.(α).to.(β).in.language.(γ)′** (w_i, x)])] CAUSE [BECOME **obligated′** (w_i, . . .)], where α = second argument of **obligated′** (w_i, . . .), β = x.
a′. [**do′** (w_i, [**say′** (w_i, x)])] CAUSE [BECOME **obligated′** (w_i, . . .)]
a″. [**do′** (w_i, [**say′** (w_i, x)])] CAUSE [BECOME **obligated′** (w_i, [**do′** (y_i, ∅)] CAUSE [BECOME [**clean′** (z)]]
b. ⟨$_{IF}$*DEC*⟨$_{TNS}$*PAST*⟨[**do′** ($Robin_i$, [**say′** ($Robin_i$, Sandy)])] CAUSE [BECOME **obligated′** ($Robin_i$, [[**do′** (y_i, ∅)] CAUSE [BECOME **clean′** (birdcage)]])⟩⟩⟩
c. ⟨$_{IF}$*DEC*⟨$_{TNS}$*PAST*⟨[**do′** (Robin, [**say′** (Robin, Sandy)])] CAUSE [BECOME **obligated′** (Robin, [⟨$_{TNS}$*PAST*⟨$_{STA}$*PSBL*⟨[[**do′** (3sgM, ∅)] CAUSE [BECOME **clean′** (birdcage)]]⟩⟩⟩])⟩⟩⟩

The logical structure of *promise* in (a) states that the speaker (w) expresses an obligation (α) to someone (β) to do the action denoted by the logical structure filling the second argument of **obligated′** (w_i, . . .). We will, however, simplify the logical structure of control verbs of saying as in (a′), in order to avoid excessively complex representations. The logical structure in (a″) is the logical structure for *promise* in (a′) with the logical structure for *x clean y* filling the open variable slot in **obligated′** (w_i, . . .). The semantic representation in (b) is for the core juncture in

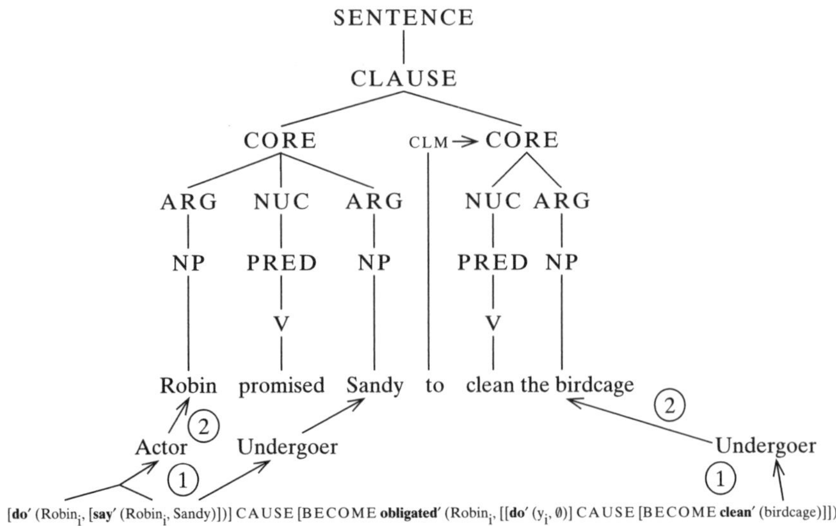

Figure 9.14 Linking from semantics to syntax in (9.41a)

(9.41a), and the fact that it must be realized as a core juncture follows from the lack of any clausal operators modifying the embedded logical structure, in particular the obligatory tense operator of finite clauses. Moreover, following the theory of obligatory control, one of the arguments in the embedded logical structure is not lexically filled and is coindexed with the actor of the matrix logical structure. In (c), however, the embedded logical structure has its own tense and status operators, indicating that it will be realized syntactically as a finite clause, i.e. as a *that*-clause. Moreover, because there is no shared argument, all argument variables in the embedded logical structure must be lexically filled (unless they are stipulated as unspecified arguments, as in the logical structure for *Chris tried to be seen* above; see section 7.2.1). In (c) the actor argument is filled by a third person singular masculine pronoun. Thus, the same logical structure can be the basis of two different semantic representations which can be realized by different juncture–nexus types and by correspondingly different formal constructions.

The semantic representation in (9.42b) is that of (9.41a), and the linking in this sentence is given in figure 9.14. By the theory of obligatory control in (9.33), the actor of *promise* is the controller of an argument in the embedded logical structure. *Robin* is the actor and *Sandy* the undergoer of *promise*, and *birdcage* is the undergoer of *clean*, and each links as per the algorithm in (9.1), satisfying the Completeness Constraint.

The Sama example in (9.29b) exemplifies an undergoer control construction, as *logos* 'persuade' is a jussive verb. As in English, the syntactic pivot of the second

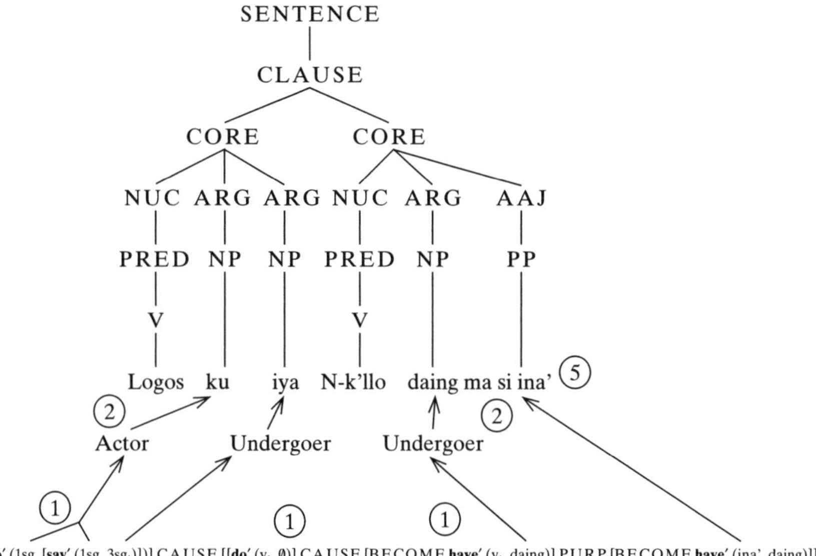

Figure 9.15 Linking from semantics to syntax in Sama control construction in (9.29b)

core is missing and is the shared semantic argument between the two cores. The example is repeated in (9.43) along with its logical structure in (c) and the logical structure of *logos* 'persuade' in (b).

(9.43) a. Logos ku iya N-k'llo daing ma si ina'.
persuade 1sgERG 3sgABS ANTI-get fish OBL PNM mother
'I persuaded him to get fish for mother.'
b. [**do′** (x, [**say′** (x, y)])] CAUSE [**want′** (y, z)]
c. [**do′** (1sg, [**say′** (1sg, 3sg$_i$)])] CAUSE [[**do′** (y_i, ∅)] CAUSE [BECOME **have′** (y_i, daing)] PURP [BECOME **have′** (ina', daing)]]

Since this is a jussive verb, it is the undergoer which will be the controller, following (9.33), and because this is a non-subordinate core juncture, one of the arguments in the embedded logical structure is left lexically unfilled and coindexed with the controlling argument in the matrix logical structure, as illustrated in (c). Because Sama is syntactically ergative and the shared semantic argument is the actor of the embedded logical structure, the second core must be in antipassive form in the syntax, so that the shared argument is interpreted as its missing syntactic pivot. The linking in (9.29) is illustrated in figure 9.15. Again the same problems arise as in the English examples when different coindexings and voice possibilities in the second core are tried, and the result is the same: there is only one possible coindexing with each voice option in the second core which satisfies the Completeness Constraint.

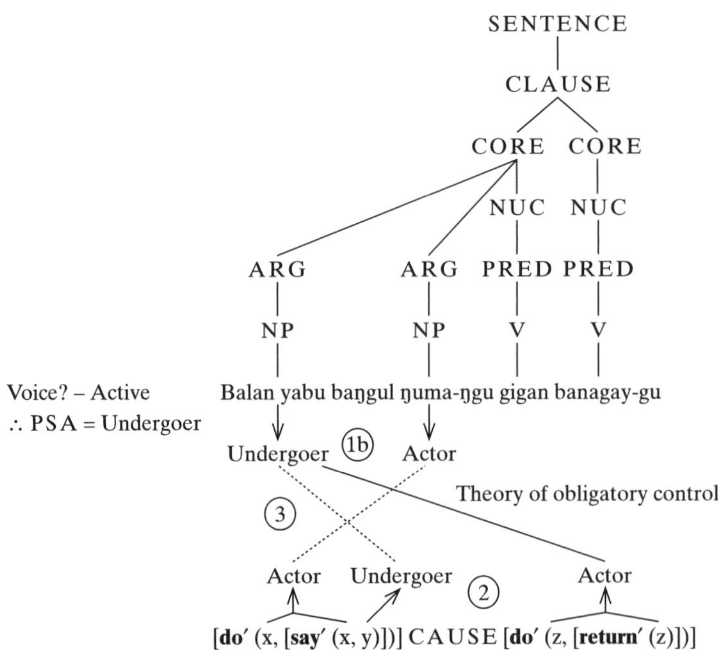

Figure 9.16 Linking from syntax to semantics in Dyirbal control construction in (9.44a)

We now turn to the problem of linking from syntax to semantics in these constructions. It is here that the problem of obligatory control is most acute, as the correct interpretation of the sentence depends upon the correct assignment of the controller in the matrix core. Since the issue of the controller is trivial in clauses with M-intransitive matrix verbs, we will focus our attention on clauses with M-transitive matrix verbs like *promise* and *persuade* in English, *yue* 'order' in Acehnese, *-ši* 'tell, order' in Lakhota, *gigal* 'tell' in Dyirbal, and *logos* 'persuade' and *janji'* 'promise' in Sama. The Dyirbal example in (9.28b) is repeated below, together with its logical structure.

(9.44) a. Ba-la-n yabu-∅ ba-ŋgu-l ŋuma-ŋgu giga-n banagay-gu.
DEIC-ABS-II mother-ABS DEIC-ERG-I father-ERG tell-TNS return-PURP
'Father told mother to return.'
b. [**do′** (x, [**say′** (x, y)])] CAUSE [**do′** (z, [**return′** (z)])]

The syntax to semantic linking in (9.44a), following the algorithm in (9.2), is presented in figure 9.16; the numbers refer to the steps in (9.2). The bulk of the linking is just as for the simple sentences discussed in chapter 7. Having determined the voice of the verb, the NPs functioning as actor and undergoer can be identified (step 1), and after accessing the lexical entries for the verbs in the lexicon and construct-

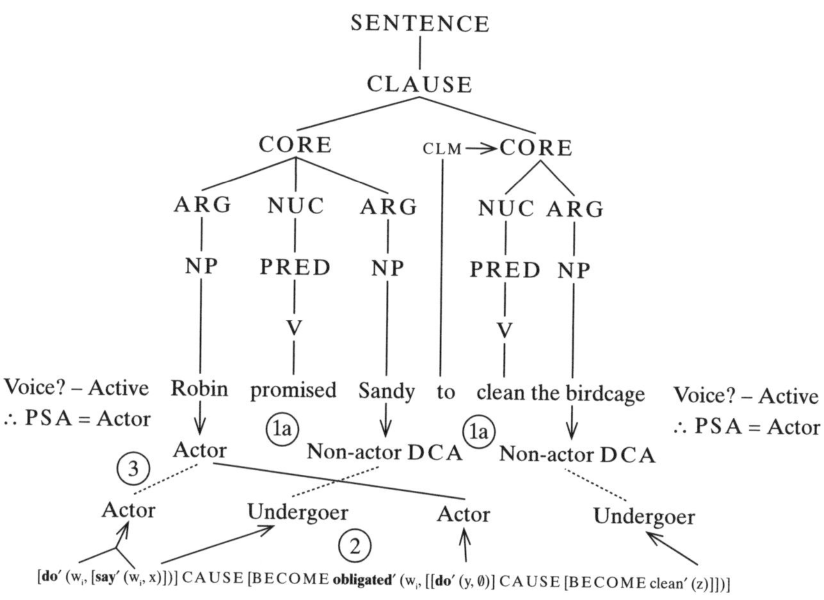

Figure 9.17 Linking from syntax to semantics in English control construction in (9.41a)

ing the composite logical structure for the whole sentence, the actor and undergoer assignments for the arguments in it can be determined (step 2). The third step is to match the actor and undergoer of *gigal* 'tell' in the syntax with the actor and undergoer of its logical structure. At this point, all of the relevant steps in (9.2) have been executed, and yet there is, crucially, an unlinked argument, the actor of *banagay* 'return'; the Completeness Constraint remains unsatisfied. This is where the theory of obligatory control in (9.33) comes into play: because *gigan* 'tell' is a jussive verb, its undergoer is the controller, and accordingly, the undergoer of *gigan* is linked to the actor of *banagay*, yielding the correct interpretation of the sentence and satisfying the Completeness Constraint. The obligatory control linking is represented by the solid black line.

The linking from syntax to semantics for (9.41a) with *promise* in English works exactly the same way; it is given in figure 9.17. There is a new feature in this linking that was absent in the previous one in Dyirbal. Because the verbs in both cores are M-transitive, step 1 must be done for both of them, since it gives information about the function of the core arguments in each core. Step 2 is as before, and again, at the end of step 3, there is an unlinked argument in the semantics, in this case the actor of *clean*. Because *promise* is neither jussive nor causative, the actor must be the controller, and therefore the actor of *promise* is linked with the actor of *clean*, yielding the correct interpretation and satisfying the Completeness Constraint.

It is clear that we need to add a step to the syntax to semantics linking algorithm to accommodate the crucial role that the theory of obligatory control plays. Before doing that, however, we need to investigate the interaction of these control constructions with a different one that also involves initially unlinked arguments in the logical structure, namely WH-questions. The relevant examples from English are given in (9.45).

(9.45) a. Who did Chris persuade Dana to visit?
b. Who did Chris persuade to visit Leslie?
c. *Who did Chris persuade Dana to visit Leslie?

The logical structure for *persuade* is given in (9.46a)[9] and the logical structure for these examples is given in (b).

(9.46) a. [**do′** (x, [**say′** (x, y)])] CAUSE [**want′** (y, z)]
b. [**do′** (w, [**say′** (w, x)])] CAUSE [**want′** (x, [**do′** (y, [**visit′** (y, z)])])]

The linking from syntax to semantics in terms of (9.2) for (9.45a–c) is summarized in (9.47).

(9.47) a. *Linking in (9.45a)*

1 *Step 1*: Voice in initial core is active, ∴ PSA = Actor
Voice in second core is active, ∴ PSA = Actor
Therefore, *Chris* is actor and *Dana* is non-actor direct core argument of *persuade.*

2 *Step 2*: Retrieve logical structures for verbs from lexicon and put together the logical structure in (9.46b).
(a) Assign actor to *w* argument and undergoer to *x* argument in logical structure of *persuade*; assign actor to *y* argument and undergoer to *z* argument in logical structure of *visit.*

3 *Step 3*: Link *Chris* with *w* argument of *persuade* and *Dana* with *x* argument of *persuade*. [Neither argument of *visit* is linked. Since this step states that the remaining core argument should be linked with the unlinked argument positions, the theory of control applies here.]

3′ *Step 3′*: Because *persuade* is a jussive verb, the undergoer will be the controller, following (9.33). Since the controlled argument is always the pivot of the second core, the fact that the voice of the verb in the second core is active indicates that the pivot is the actor (step 1); hence the undergoer of *persuade* is linked to the actor of *visit.*

4 Does not apply.

5 There is only one unlinked argument position in the semantic representation, the undergoer of *visit*, and therefore the WH-word is linked to the undergoer of *visit.*

b. *Linking in (9.45b)*

1 *Step 1*: Voice in initial core is active, ∴ PSA = Actor
Voice in second core is active, ∴ PSA = Actor

Therefore, *Chris* is actor of *persuade* and *Leslie* is non-actor direct core argument of *visit*.

2 *Step 2*: Retrieve logical structures for verbs from lexicon and put together the logical structure in (9.46b).

(a) Assign actor to *w* argument and undergoer to *x* argument in logical structure of *persuade*; assign actor to *y* argument and undergoer to *z* argument in logical structure of *visit*.

3 *Step 3*: Link *Chris* with *w* argument of *persuade* and *Leslie* with *z* argument of *visit*.

3′ *Step 3′*: Because *persuade* is a jussive verb, the undergoer will be the controller, following (9.33). Since the controlled argument is always the pivot of the second core, the fact that the voice of the verb in the second core is active indicates that the pivot is the actor (step 1); hence the undergoer of *persuade* is linked to the actor of *visit*.

4 Does not apply.

5 There is only one unlinked argument position in the semantic representation, the undergoer of *persuade*, and therefore the WH-word is linked to the undergoer of *persuade*.

c. *Linking in (9.45c)*

1 *Step 1*: Voice in initial core is active, ∴ PSA = Actor
Voice in second core is active, ∴ PSA = Actor

Therefore, *Chris* is actor and *Dana* a non-actor direct core argument of *persuade* and *Leslie* is a non-actor direct core argument of *visit*.

2 *Step 2*: Retrieve logical structures for verbs from lexicon and put together the logical structure in (9.46b).

(a) Assign actor to *w* argument and undergoer to *x* argument in logical structure of *persuade*; assign actor to *y* argument and undergoer to *z* argument in logical structure of *visit*.

3 *Step* 3: Link *Chris* with *w* argument of *persuade*, *Dana* with the *x* argument of *persuade*, and *Leslie* with *z* argument of *visit*.

3′ *Step* 3′: Because *persuade* is a jussive verb, the undergoer will be the controller, following (9.33). Since the controlled argument is always the pivot of the second core, the fact that the voice of the verb in the second core is active indicates that the pivot is the actor (step 1); hence the undergoer of *persuade* is linked to the actor of *visit*.

4 Does not apply.

5 There are no unlinked argument positions in the semantic representation, and therefore the WH-word in the precore slot cannot be linked to the semantic representation. Hence the Completeness Constraint is violated, and (9.45c) is ungrammatical.

In the syntax to semantics linking principles summarized in (9.2), all of the linking is done within the core before precore slot and peripheral elements are linked, and this may be extended naturally to these core junctures by requiring that all linking within and between cores be done before precore slot and peripheral elements are linked. This means that there is no direct interaction between the linking governed by the theory of obligatory control and that involving elements in the precore slot, since the linking of precore slot elements crucially involves an unlinked argument position in the semantic representation after all of the core-internal elements have been mapped into it. Accordingly, we may reformulate (9.2) as in (9.48), in which a step involving obligatory control is added; it is in italics.

(9.48) *Linking algorithm: syntax → semantics* (*revised formulation*)

1 Determine the functions of the core arguments:
- a. If the construction is syntactically accusative:
  - (1) If it is the unmarked voice, the privileged syntactic argument is actor.
  - (2) If it is passive, the privileged syntactic argument is not the actor of the predicate in the nucleus;
    - (a) the actor may appear as a direct core argument (language-specific); or
    - (b) the actor may appear in the periphery marked by an adposition or an oblique case (language-specific); or
    - (c) if there is no actor in the core or the periphery, then replace the variable representing the highest-ranking argument in the logical structure with '∅'.
- b. If the construction is syntactically ergative:
  - (1) If it is the unmarked voice, the privileged syntactic argument is undergoer.
  - (2) If it is antipassive, the privileged syntactic argument is actor;
    - (a) the undergoer may appear as an oblique element (language-specific);
    - (b) if there is no undergoer in the core or the periphery, then replace the variable representing the lowest-ranking argument in the logical structure with '∅'.
- c. Assign macrorole status to the other direct core argument, if it is not dative or in an oblique case.
- d. If the verb is intransitive, then assign the privileged syntactic argument either macrorole or direct core argument status (language-specific).
- e. If the language is head-marking and there are independent NPs in the clause, associate each NP with a bound argument marker (language-specific).
- f. If the language lacks voice oppositions, determine the macroroles from case marking and/or word order (language-specific).

2 Retrieve from the lexicon the logical structure of the predicate in the nucleus of the clause and with respect to it execute step 1 from (9.1), subject to the following proviso:

a. When there is more than one choice for undergoer, do not assign undergoer to an argument in the logical structure.
b. Assign actor to an argument in the logical structure, if the verb takes one.
c. Determine the linking of the non-macrorole core argument:
   (1) if there is a state predicate in the logical structure and if the non-macrorole core argument is marked by a locative adposition or dative or a locative-type case, then link it with the first argument position in the state predicate in the logical structure; or
   (2) if there is a state predicate in the logical structure and if it is not marked by a locative adposition or dative or a locative-type case, then link it with the second argument position in the state predicate;
   (3) otherwise, link the animate NP with the first argument position in the state predicate in the logical structure.

3 Link the arguments determined in step 1 with the arguments determined in step 2 until all core arguments are linked.
4 *In non-subordinate core junctures, one of the arguments of the matrix core must be linked to an argument position in the embedded logical structure, following* (*9.33*).
5 If there is a predicative adpositional adjunct, then retrieve its logical structure from the lexicon, insert the logical structure of the core as the second argument in the logical structure and the object of the adposition in the periphery as the first argument.
6 If there is an element in the pre- or postcore slot (language-specific),
   a. assign it the remaining unlinked argument position in the semantic representation of the sentence;
   b. and if there are no unlinked argument positions in the sentence, then treat the WH-word like a predicative preposition and follow the procedure in step 5, linking the WH-word to the first argument position in the logical structure.

The constructional template for the English control construction is given in table 9.6. Saying 'default' for Core-2 means that the template is chosen following the general principles in (9.38); because the juncture–nexus type is core coordination, (9.38b) applies. The template covers all of the constructions with *persuade*- and *promise*-type verbs discussed in this section. The controller is in Core-1 and is determined by (9.33). The pivot of the construction is in Core-2, not Core-1, and it is the highest-ranking core macrorole. The linking is specified as 'default', as it follows (9.48) without modification. The different possible clause linkage markers were discussed in section 8.4.2; the choice is a function of the semantics of the overall construction, as argued in that section.

In section 6.5 we mentioned that in conjunction reduction constructions like these the controller is always a syntactic controller (in these languages, a variable

Table 9.6 *Template for English control constructions in (9.26)*

CONSTRUCTION
English control construction
SYNTAX
Juncture: Core Nexus: Coordination Construction type: Serial verb [$_{CL}$ [$_{CORE}$ ARG [$_{NUC}$ . . .] (ARG)] CLM [$_{CORE}$ [$_{NUC}$ . . .] . . .] . . .] Unit template(s): Core 1: Default Core 2: Default PSA: Core 1: Controller = semantic controller, following (9.33) Core 2: Pivot = variable syntactic pivot Linking: Default
MORPHOLOGY
CLM *to*, *from* or Ø
SEMANTICS
Psych-action, causative/jussive; commissive, directive speech acts
PRAGMATICS
Illocutionary force: Unspecified Focus structure: Unspecified

syntactic controller), whereas in control constructions the controller is always a semantic controller. This follows from the different level of juncture of the constructions. The conjunction reduction constructions in section 9.1.1 are clausal junctures, and accordingly each clause is semantically independent of the other(s) to a considerable extent. The controller in the construction is the privileged syntactic argument of the first clause, which is determined syntactically and may be influenced by discourse pragmatics. It is not a function of the semantics of the verb in the first clause. As we have seen in this section, the determination of the controller in control constructions is entirely semantically determined with reference to the meaning of the matrix verb; hence in control constructions the controller is a semantic controller. With the exception of purpose clauses, the logical structure of the linked unit in a core juncture is virtually always an argument in the logical structure of the matrix verb or predicate and is therefore dependent upon the matrix logical structure semantically in a way that the independent logical structures in the clausal junctures are not dependent semantically on the logical structure of the first clause. Thus, the controllers in clausal junctures will always be syntactic controllers, while the controllers in core junctures will always be semantic.

9.1.3.2 Matrix-coding constructions

Matrix-coding constructions have gone by a number of names in the history of linguistics; the term 'matrix coding' is taken from Frajzynger (1995), who proposed it as a theory-neutral label. There are two basic types of matrix-coding constructions: what is called 'raising to subject' in the generative literature, as in (9.49a), and the construction in (b), which was known in traditional grammar as the 'accusative-plus-infinitive' construction,[10] was originally called 'raising to object' in transformational grammar but is known in the GB literature as the 'exceptional case marking' construction.

(9.49) a. Aisha seems to like her new computer.
a′. It seems that Aisha likes her new computer.
b. Tyrone believes Yolanda to have eaten his sandwich.
b′. Tyrone believes that Yolanda ate his sandwich.

Each of these constructions has an alternative form in which there is a finite *that*-clause complement, and in both the core argument which is the privileged syntactic argument of the finite embedded clause in the alternative construction appears as a core argument in the matrix core, as 'subject' in (a) or 'object' in (b), hence the names from transformational grammar.[11] As with the alternating constructions in (9.41), the two sentences in each pair have the same logical structure but different semantic representations. This is illustrated for (9.49b, b′) in (9.50), in which the logical structure for both sentences is given in (a) and abbreviated semantic representations for them are given in (b) and (c).

(9.50) a. **believe′** (Tyrone, [**do′** (Yolanda, [**eat′** (Yolanda, his sandwich)]) & BECOME **eaten′** (his sandwich)])
b. ⟨$_{\mathrm{IF}}$*DEC*⟨$_{\mathrm{TNS}}$*PRES*⟨**believe′** (Tyrone, [⟨$_{\mathrm{ASP}}$*PERF*⟨[**do′** (Yolanda, [**eat′** (Yolanda, his sandwich)]) & BECOME **eaten′** (his sandwich)]⟩⟩])⟩⟩⟩ (= (b))
c. ⟨$_{\mathrm{IF}}$*DEC*⟨$_{\mathrm{TNS}}$*PRES*⟨**believe′** (Tyrone, [⟨$_{\mathrm{TNS}}$*PAST*⟨[**do′** (Yolanda, [**eat′** (Yolanda, his sandwich]]) & BECOME **eaten′** (his sandwich)]⟩⟩])⟩⟩⟩ (= (b′))

The lack of the obligatory tense operator modifying the embedded logical structure in (b) entails that it will not be realized as a tensed clause, i.e. as a *that*-clause. Hence the semantic representation in (b) is for a core juncture. In (c), on the other hand, there is a tense operator modifying the embedded logical structure, and therefore it will be realized as a tensed clause. There are subtle differences in meaning between the two forms, which have been investigated in e.g. Borkin (1984) and Langacker (1995).

In the following sections, we will examine the linking in the two types of matrix-coding constructions separately. We will refer to the construction in (9.49a) as 'matrix coding as PSA' and to the one in (9.49b) as 'matrix coding as non-PSA'.

(*a*) *Matrix coding as PSA*

The matrix-coding as PSA construction is illustrated in (9.51) from Icelandic (Thráinsson 1979), Kinyarwanda (Bantu; Kimenyi 1980) and Nieuean (Polynesian; Seiter 1978); cf. also the examples from Acehnese in (6.31) and the Mandarin examples in (6.38).

(9.51) a. Harald-ur virðist haf-a far-ið heim. Icelandic
Harold-MsgNOM seem.3sgPRES have-INF go-PSTP home
'Harold seems to have gone home.'

b. Abá-nyéshuur ba-kwii-ye gu-some ibitabo. Kinyarwanda
2-student 2-essential-ASP INF-read 8-book
'Students must read the books.'

b′. Bi-rá-kwii-ye ko abá-nyéeshuûri ba-sóm-a
8-PRES-essential-ASP CLM 2-student 2-read-ASP
ibitabo.
8-book
'It is essential that students read the books.'

c. To maeke e ekekafo ke lagomatai e tama ē. Niuean
FUT PSBL ABS doctor SBJ help ABS child this
'The doctor could help this child.'

c′. To maeke ke lagomatai he ekefafo e tama ē.
FUT PSBL SBJ help ERG doctor ABS child this
'It is possible for the doctor to help this child.'

There is no Icelandic counterpart to (9.49a′) involving the verb *virðast* 'seem' plus a tensed complement. The counterparts to the Kinyarwanda and Niuean raising constructions are given in (b′) and (c′). The primary predicates which allow this construction in English are *seem*, *appear*, *be likely* and *be certain*, while only *virðast* 'seem' allows it in Icelandic, according to Thráinsson (1979). Kimenyi (1980) describes the verbs that occur in this construction in Kinyarwanda as 'modality impersonal verbs', e.g. *-shobok-* 'be possible', *-kwíi-* 'be essential' and *-bujijw-* 'be forbidden', and factitive verbs like *-babaj-* 'be sad' and *-taangaj-* 'be fascinating'. The matrix-coding verbs in Niuean are *maeke* 'be able, be possible', *kamata* 'begin', *faakai* 'emphatic negative', *mahani* 'be usual, customary' and *teitei* 'almost' (Seiter 1978).

The essential feature of the verbs in this construction is that they are either atransitive, like English *seem* and Icelandic *virðast*, or they are intransitive like English *be likely* and *be certain*. The logical structure for English *seem* and Icelandic *virðast* is **seem′** ((x), y) [MR0], where the *x* argument is an (optional) PERCEIVER which is realized in English by a *to* PP and in Icelandic by a dative NP, as illustrated by the Icelandic example in (9.52) and its English translation.

(9.52) Harald-ur virðist mér ver-a besti dreng-ur.
Harold-MsgNOM seem.3sgPRES 1sgDAT be-INF best boy-MsgNOM
'Harold seems to me to be a nice guy.'

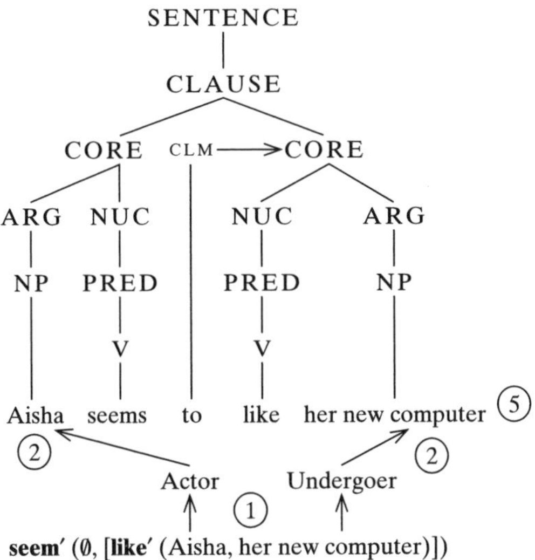

Figure 9.18 Linking from semantics to syntax in English matrix-coding construction in (9.49a)

The *y* argument is a proposition; hence it is filled by another logical structure. The occurrence of an argument from the embedded logical structure in the core headed by *seem* comes about as follows. There is a direct core argument slot in the matrix core, but the verb has no arguments which can fill it; moreover, since this is a core juncture, the second core is missing the prenuclear core argument position, following (9.38b). The semantic argument that would normally function as privileged syntactic argument in the second core cannot be realized in it, due to the absence of its syntactic slot, and this would normally lead to a Completeness Constraint violation, as we saw in, for example, figure 9.11. However, there is an open core argument position within the clause, namely the one in the matrix core. The argument may be linked to this position, thereby avoiding a Completeness Constraint violation. If the second core were passive voice, then the undergoer would appear as a core argument in the matrix core. The linking from semantics to syntax in (9.49a) is given in figure 9.18. *Aisha* is the actor of *like* but a core argument in the core headed by *seem*. The syntactic structure in figure 9.18 is similar to that in the control constructions with *try* in figure 9.10, but differs in terms of nexus. *Try*-constructions are cosubordinate, as we saw in (8.30), due to the shared deontic modality operator across the two cores. Sharing a core operator across the two cores is ruled out in principle in this construction, however, because the matrix predicate does not have an argument that can be modified by a deontic modal operator. Hence the nexus is coordinate. The essential difference between the two constructions lies not in the syntactic structure but rather in how the linking works, which is primarily a function of the semantic properties of the predicate in the matrix core.

Because *seem* and *appear* are atransitive and have no macrorole arguments, the propositional argument as a whole cannot function as a direct argument of these verbs. The situation is slightly different with the other two raising predicates, *be certain* and *be likely*, which have the logical structures **certain′** (x) and **likely′** (x) and are M-intransitive instead of atransitive. They allow their propositional argument to occur as undergoer of the matrix core, as in (9.53a, b).

(9.53) a. That Bill will lose the election is certain.
a′. It is certain that Bill will lose the election.
a″. Bill is certain to lose the election.
b. That Jorge will reject the analysis is very likely.
b′. It is very likely that Jorge will reject the analysis.
b″. Jorge is very likely to reject the analysis.

Seem and *appear* allow only the second two possibilities, and this difference can be attributed to the contrast in M-transitivity between the two groups of predicates.

The linking from syntax to semantics in this construction requires no substantial modification of the linking algorithm in (9.48). The linking for *What does Aisha seem to like?* is given in figure 9.19. As before, the numbers refer to the steps in the

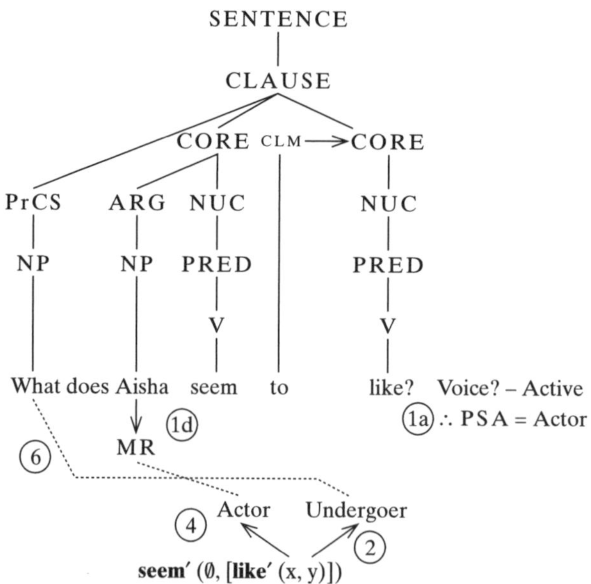

Figure 9.19 Linking from syntax to semantics in English matrix-coding construction

linking algorithm in (9.48). Step 1 applies in each core; since the first core is intransitive, the only conclusion that can be drawn is that *Aisha* is a macrorole argument; there is no evidence in the first core as to whether it is actor or undergoer. In the infinitival core the voice is active, and therefore the privileged syntactic argument would be the actor, if there were one in the core. Step 2 is straightforward. In order to execute step 3, the information from step 1 must be used. The core argument *Aisha* cannot be linked to an argument position in the logical structure of *seem*, because the first argument is unspecified and the second one is filled by a propositional logical structure. There are no core arguments in the second core to be linked to the embedded logical structure **like′** (x, y), and therefore *Aisha* can be linked to an argument position in the embedded logical structure; the question is, which one? As in the control constructions discussed above, the obligatorily missing argument in the linked core is the syntactic pivot, and since step 1 revealed that the pivot of the second core is the actor, *Aisha* must be linked to the actor argument in the semantic representation. Finally, the WH-word in the precore slot is linked to the remaining unlinked argument position, following step 6. The result is the correct linking, with *Aisha* interpreted as the actor of *like* and *what* as the undergoer.

The only modification of (9.48) that is required is to specify that in step 4, the theory of obligatory control in (9.33) applies only to control verbs. This may be stated as in (9.54); the modifications are in italic.

(9.54) *Linking algorithm: syntax → semantics (revised formulation)*

1 Determine the functions of the core arguments:

- a. If the construction is syntactically accusative:
  - (1) If it is the unmarked voice, the privileged syntactic argument is actor.
  - (2) If it is passive, the privileged syntactic argument is not the actor of the predicate in the nucleus;
    - (a) the actor may appear as a direct core argument (language-specific); or
    - (b) the actor may appear in the periphery marked by an adposition or an oblique case (language-specific); or
    - (c) if there is no actor in the core or the periphery, then replace the variable representing the highest-ranking argument in the logical structure with '∅'.
- b. If the construction is syntactically ergative:
  - (1) If it is the unmarked voice, the privileged syntactic argument is undergoer.
  - (2) If it is antipassive, the privileged syntactic argument is actor;
    - (a) the undergoer may appear as an oblique element (language-specific);
    - (b) if there is no undergoer in the core or the periphery, then replace the variable representing the lowest-ranking argument in the logical structure with '∅'.

c. Assign macrorole status to the other direct core argument, if it is not dative or in an oblique case.

d. If the verb is intransitive, then assign the privileged syntactic argument either macrorole or direct core argument status (language-specific).

e. If the language is head-marking and there are independent NPs in the clause, associate each NP with a bound argument marker (language-specific).

f. If the language lacks voice oppositions, determine the macroroles from case marking and/or word order (language-specific).

2 Retrieve from the lexicon the logical structure of the predicate in the nucleus of the clause and with respect to it execute step 1 from (9.1), subject to the following proviso:

a. When there is more than one choice for undergoer, do not assign undergoer to an argument in the logical structure.

b. Assign actor to an argument in the logical structure, if the verb takes one.

c. Determine the linking of the non-macrorole core argument:

(1) if there is a state predicate in the logical structure and if the non-macrorole core argument is marked by a locative adposition or dative or a locative-type case, then link it with the first argument position in the state predicate in the logical structure; or

(2) if there is a state predicate in the logical structure and if it is not marked by a locative adposition or dative or a locative-type case, then link it with the second argument position in the state predicate;

(3) otherwise, link the animate NP with the first argument position in the state predicate in the logical structure.

3 Link the arguments determined in step 1 with the arguments determined in step 2 until all core arguments are linked.

4 In non-subordinate core junctures, one of the arguments of the matrix core must be linked to an argument position in the embedded logical structure:

a. *if the matrix predicate is a control verb, this follows (9.33); otherwise,*

b. *if the matrix predicate is not a control verb, then link the unlinked syntactic argument in the matrix core to the logical structure argument position of the pivot of the linked core.*

5 If there is a predicative adpositional adjunct, then retrieve its logical structure from the lexicon, insert the logical structure of the core as the second argument in the logical structure and the object of the adposition in the periphery as the first argument.

6 If there is an element in the pre- or postcore slot (language-specific),

a. assign it the remaining unlinked argument position in the semantic representation of the sentence;

b. and if there are no unlinked argument positions in the sentence, then treat the WH-word like a predicative preposition and follow the procedure in step 5, linking the WH-word to the first argument position in the logical structure.

We will return to the Icelandic example in (9.52) after we have looked at the other matrix-coding construction.

(*b*) *Matrix coding as non-PSA*

While there has been a great deal of agreement among syntacticians over the past three decades about the properties of the construction in (9.49a), the construction in (9.49b), *Tyrone believes Yolanda to have eaten his sandwich*, has been the subject of great controversy. It was originally analyzed as a 'raising' construction in Rosenbaum (1967), and the conventional wisdom in transformational grammar was that the NP *Yolanda* originated in the embedded clause and was moved to the direct object position in the matrix clause. Chomsky (1973) argued that there was no rule of raising to object and that in this construction the NP *Yolanda* is the subject of the embedded infinitive clause. Postal (1974) was devoted to arguing against Chomsky's new analysis and for the existence of a raising rule and the structure in (9.55a) below.

(9.55) a. Surface structure assumed in traditional transformational analysis:
[$_S$ Tyrone [$_{VP}$ believed Yolanda [$_{VP}$ to have eaten his sandwich]]]
b. Chomsky's (1973) reanalysis:
[$_S$ Tyrone [$_{VP}$ believed [$_S$ Yolanda to have eaten his sandwich]]]

The structure in (b) is assumed in GB theory (Chomsky 1981b, 1986a, b) and has been vigorously defended. The accusative case on the external argument in the embedded clause (e.g. *Tyrone believed her to have eaten his sandwich*) was argued to be due to 'exceptional case marking' by the matrix verb across a clause boundary, hence the GB name for the construction. Other generative theories, e.g. LFG, RelG, GPSG, and HPSG, take the structure to be as in (a), *mutatis mutandum*. There is, then, considerable agreement that (a) is the correct structure. In terms of the layered structure of the clause, it means that *Yolanda* is a core argument in the core headed by *believe* and that this matrix-coding construction has the same syntactic structure as control constructions with *promise* and *persuade*, which, as we showed in sections 8.4.1–8.4.2, involves core coordination. The linking is different in the two constructions, however.

One of the standard arguments for the (a) structure over the (b) structure involves reflexivization. Consider the contrast in (9.56).

(9.56) a. Bob$_i$ believed that he$_i$/*him$_i$/*himself$_i$ was very sick.
b. Bob$_i$ believed *he$_i$/*him$_i$/himself$_i$ to be very sick.

When *believe* takes a finite complement, as in (a), only a nominative pronoun is permitted in the privileged syntactic argument position in the embedded clause. When the 'raising construction' occurs, as in (b), this same semantic argument can be expressed only by a reflexive, if it is coreferential with the actor of *believe*. In our discussion of reflexivization in English in section 7.5.2, we found that the controller and the reflexive must be cosyntactic arguments within a core, and since reflexivization is obligatory here, if the two NPs are coreferential, it follows that both *Bob* and *himself* must be within the same core. We will return to the issue of reflexivization in complex sentences in section 9.4.2 below.

Examples of this matrix-coding construction from Icelandic (Thráinsson 1979) and Malagasy (Keenan 1976b) are given in (9.57) and (9.58).

(9.57) a. Jón-Ø tel-ur í barnaskap sínum — Icelandic
John-MsgNOM believe-3sgPRES in foolishness his
að Harald-ur haf-i tek-ið
CLM Harold-MsgNOM have.SBJ-3sgPRES take-PSTP
bók-in-a.
book-DEF-FsgACC
'John believes in his foolishness that Harold has taken the book.'

b. Jón-Ø tel-ur Harald-Ø í barnaskap
John-MsgNOM believe-3sgPRES Harold-MsgACC in foolishness
sínum haf-a tek-ið bók-in-a.
his have-INF take-PSTP book-DEF-FsgACC
'John believes in his foolishness Harold to have taken the book.'

(9.58) a. Nan-antena fa nan-asa ny zaza Rasoa Rabe. — Malagasy
ATV-hope CLM ATV-wash DET child Rasoa Rabe
'Rabe hoped that Rasoa washed the child.'

b. Nan-antena an-dRasoa ho nan-asa ny zaza Rabe.
ATV-hope ACC-Rasoa CLM ATV-wash DET child Rabe
'Rabe hoped Rasoa to have washed the child.'

The (a) sentences involve a finite complement and no matrix coding, whereas the (b) forms show the construction in question. In the Icelandic examples the adverbial phrase *í barnaskap sínum* 'in his foolishness' modifies *Jón telur* 'John believes' and hence is a constituent of the matrix core. The fact that the accusative NP *Harald* 'Harold' occurs between it and *telur* 'believes' shows that *Harald* is in fact a constituent of the matrix core in (b). The change in the position of the NP in question in the Malagasy examples is much more dramatic, given the VOS basic order in the language. In (a), *Rasoa* is the actor and privileged syntactic argument in the embedded clause, which is marked by the complementizer *fa*; it is the final constituent in the embedded clause. In (b), on the other hand, it occurs after the matrix verb and before the embedded clause, and in addition it is marked for accusative case. It is clear, then, that in the (b) examples in (9.57)–(9.58) the accusative NP in the matrix core is a semantic argument of the verb in the linked core.

As in the construction discussed in the previous section, there must be a core argument position in the matrix core which cannot be filled by a semantic argument from the logical structure of the matrix predicate. Since these verbs are obviously not (M-)atransitive like *seem*, the explanation for this open syntactic slot must lie elsewhere. In (9.38) we presented the principles governing the relationship between the number of argument positions in the logical structure of the predicate and the number of core argument positions in the syntactic template of the core that is appropriate for it. In Foley and Van Valin (1984) it was noted that there is a systematic relationship between the S-transitivity of a verb when it takes NP or clausal syntactic arguments and when it functions as a complement-taking predicate in a core juncture; namely, its S-transitivity is reduced by 1 in complex constructions. This follows from (9.38) and is illustrated in (9.59).

(9.59) a. *Three core arguments → two*
Phil told Dana a story / Phil told Dana that . . . [3] → Phil told Dana to . . . [2]
Kim promised Sandy a picture of Chris / Kim promised Sandy that . . . [3] → Kim promised Sandy to . . . [2]
b. *Two core arguments → one*
Eileen remembered her purse / Eileen remembered that . . . [2] → Eileen remembered to . . . [1]
Beckie wants a new Porsche [2] → Beckie wants to . . . [1]

It appears, then, that not only is the S-transitivity of the linked core reduced by 1 but that of the matrix core is as well. We must, therefore, amend (9.38) to reflect this. The revised template selection principles are given in (9.60).

(9.60) a. *Syntactic template selection principle* (*revised formulation*)
The number of syntactic slots for arguments and argument-adjuncts within the core is equal to the number of distinct specified argument positions in the semantic representation of the core.
b. *Universal qualification of the principle in* (*a*)
The occurrence of a core as either the matrix or linked core in a non-subordinate core juncture reduces the number of core slots by 1.
c. *Language-specific qualifications of the principle in* (*a*)
1 All cores in the language have a minimum syntactic valence of 1.
2 Passive constructions reduce the number of core slots by 1.
3 The occurrence of a syntactic argument in the pre-/postcore slot reduces the number of core slots by 1 (may override (1)).

What happens with *believe*? If it followed the pattern in (9.59) and (9.60b), then we should have *Juan believed the story* [2] → **Juan believed to* . . . [1] as the only two patterns with this verb. But this is not the case, as we have seen. Rather, with *believe* we have *Juan believed the story* [2] → *Juan believed Carlos to* . . . [2]. This is also true for the other verbs which license the construction in (9.49b), e.g. *expect, consider* and *find*. Hence the crucial property of the verbs in this construction is that they are exceptions to the general pattern in (9.59) and therefore to (9.60b) and have one more syntactic argument position in the core than they should.

The actual linking in this construction is the same as that in the other matrix-coding construction, and it is illustrated for the Icelandic example in (9.57b) in figure 9.20; the adverbial phrase *í barnaskap sínum* 'in his foolishness' is omitted. If the linking in the second core had been passive, then the undergoer *bók-* 'book'

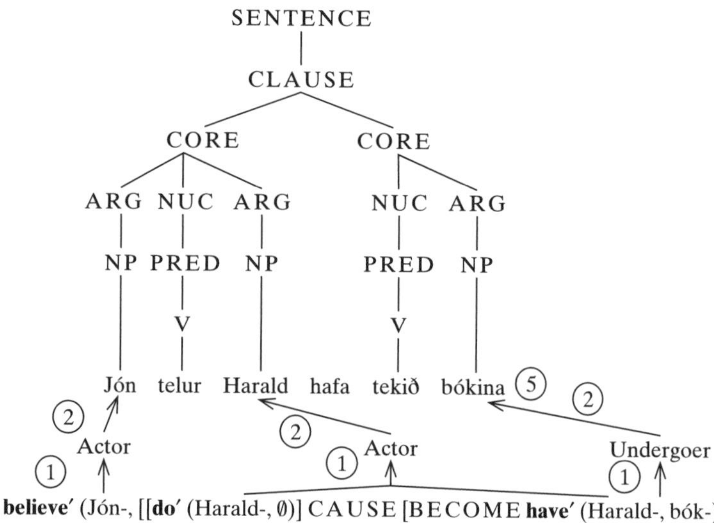

Figure 9.20 Linking from semantics to syntax in the Icelandic construction in (9.57b)

would have appeared in the open matrix core slot, yielding the Icelandic equivalent of 'John believes the book to have been taken by Harold', *Jón telur bókina hafa verið tekið af Haraldi.*

In section 9.1.3.2 we said that the subordinate (*that*-clause) and non-subordinate (infinitive) constructions have the same logical structure but different semantic representations, due to the different patterns of operators in the two representations (see (9.50)). This assumption, together with the linking pattern illustrated in figure 9.20, leads to the conclusion that the class of verbs which can occur in this matrix-coding construction is considerably greater than previously thought. In particular, perception verbs like *see* and *hear* can now be analyzed as occurring in this construction. Consider the following Icelandic examples from Thráinsson (1979) and their English translations.

(9.61) a. Ég sá lögregl-un-a tak-a Marí-u fast-a.
1sgNOM see.PAST police-DEF-FsgACC take-INF Mary-FsgACC fast-FsgACC
'I saw the police arrest Mary.'

b. Ég sá Marí-u ver-a tek-na fast-a
1sgNOM see.PAST Mary-FsgACC be.INF take-PSTP.FsgACC fast-FsgACC
af lögregl-un-ni.
by police-DEF-FsgDAT
'I saw Mary being arrested by the police.'

Chomsky (1965) proposed the standard test for distinguishing between control and matrix-coding constructions: whether the meaning changes when the infinitive is passivized. It does in control constructions but not in matrix-coding constructions. This is illustrated in (9.62).

(9.62) a. Bill persuaded the doctor to examine Sally.
a′. Bill persuaded Sally to be examined by the doctor.
b. Bill expected the doctor to examine Sally.
b′. Bill expected Sally to be examined by the doctor.

The first two sentences differ in meaning: in (a) Bill talks to the doctor with respect to Sally, whereas in (a′) Bill talks to Sally with respect to the doctor. In the two (b) sentences, however, Bill has an expectation, namely, that the doctor will examine Sally, and that is true of both versions. Now, if we compare the English and Icelandic sentences in (9.61) with the sentences in (9.62), it seems clear that they pattern with (b, b′) rather than (a, a′); as Thráinsson (1979) notes, if one sees Mary being arrested by the police, one also sees the police arresting Mary. Hence the core junctures with perception verbs in (9.61) must have the same general linking properties as the matrix-coding constructions with *believe* and not those of control constructions with *persuade*. The core coordination pattern with perception verbs correlates with a direct perception interpretation, while a clausal subordination (*that*-clause) pattern correlates with an indirect perception interpretation, as has long been noted (Kirsner and Thompson 1976; see section 8.4.2). Borkin (1984), in her study of the semantics of matrix-coding constructions with *believe*, *consider* and *find*, argues that the core coordinate pattern implies that the actor of the matrix verbs has more direct knowledge of or more direct contact with the referent of the matrix-coded NP than in the alternative subordinate (finite complement) pattern, and this parallels the semantic contrast between the two constructions with perception verbs.

The close connection between the two types of matrix-coding constructions can be seen most clearly when the matrix verb in a matrix-coding as non-PSA construction is passivized; the result is the equivalent of a matrix-coding as PSA construction, as in (9.63) from English and Icelandic (Thráinsson 1979).

(9.63) a. Yolanda was believed by Tyrone to have eaten his sandwich.
b. Bill was expected to lose the election.
c. Jón-∅ er tal-inn ver-a besti
John-MsgNOM be.3sgPRES believe-PSTP.MsgNOM be-INF best
dreng-ur.
boy-MsgNOM
'John is believed to be a nice guy.'

Because the actor of the matrix verb appears in a peripheral PP, there is only one direct core argument position in the core, and there is no semantic argument in the logical structure of the matrix verb that can fill this position. Hence a semantic argument from the embedded logical structure occurs in the matrix privileged syntactic

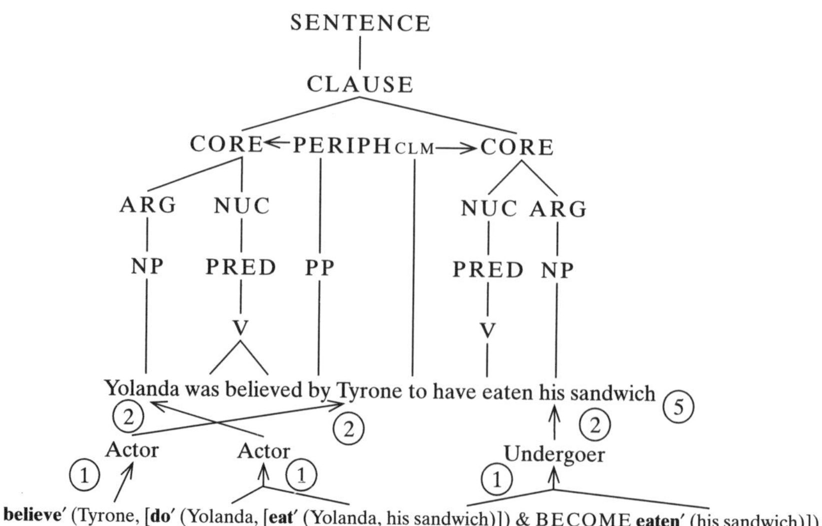

Figure 9.21 Linking from semantics to syntax in (9.63a)

argument position, just as in a matrix-coding as PSA construction. The linking from semantics to syntax in (9.63a) is given in figure 9.21.

Further evidence that making a rigid distinction between the two types of matrix-coding construction is problematic comes from a reconsideration of the Icelandic example in (9.52), repeated below in (9.64a).

(9.64) a. Harald-ur virðist mér ver-a besti dreng-ur.
Harold-MsgNOM seem.3sgPRES 1sgDAT be-INF best boy-MsgNOM
'Harold seems to me to be a nice guy.'
a′. Haraldur virðist mér í barnaskap mínum vera besti drengur.
'Harold seems to me in my foolishness to be a nice guy.'
b. Mér virðist Haraldur vera besti drengur.
'Harold seems to me to be a nice guy.'
b′. Mér virðist Haraldur í barnaskap mínum vera besti drengur.
'Harold seems to me in my foolishness to be a nice guy.'

The two sentences in (9.64) reflect the two possible word orders in the matrix core, and the position of the NPs with respect to the matrix core adverbial *í barnaskap mínum* 'in my foolishness' shows that they are in the matrix core. In our discussion of Icelandic in section 7.3.1.1, we noted that Icelandic, despite its rich case system for NPs, has relatively rigid word order, and in particular that the privileged syntactic argument is always the initial NP in the core. Moreover, we showed that the privileged syntactic argument selection principle for Icelandic is that the highest-ranking direct core argument (with respect to (7.1)) is the privileged syntactic argument, regardless of whether it is a macrorole or not. Since *mér* '1sgDAT' is the only argument of *virðist* 'seem' in the matrix core, it must be the highest ranking, and therefore it must be the privileged syntactic argument, not *Haraldur*. Thus, (9.64b) reflects the basic word order, and (a) is a topicalization construction with *Haraldur* in the pre-core slot. The fact that *mér* and not *Haraldur* is the privileged syntactic argument is confirmed when we combine the sentences in (9.64) with *telja* 'believe' to form a matrix-coding as non-PSA construction, as in (9.65).

(9.65) a. *Jón-∅ tel-ur Harald-∅ virðast mér
John-MsgNOM believe-3sgPRES Harold-MsgACC seem.INF 1sgDAT
haf-a ger-t þetta vel.
have-INF do-PSTP this.ACC well
'John believes Harold to seem to me to have done this well.'

b. Jón-∅ tel-ur mér virðast Harald-ur
John-MsgNOM believe-3sgPRES 1sgDAT seem.INF Harold-MsgNOM
haf-a ger-t þetta vel.
have-INF do-PSTP this.ACC well
'John believes [to] me Harold to seem to have done this well.' (literal)

c. Jón telur mér í barnaskap sínum virðast Haraldur hafa gert þetta vel.
'John believes [to] me in his foolishness Harold to seem to have done this well.' (literal)

The analysis of Icelandic grammatical relations in section 7.3.1.1 predicts that only (9.64b) could be the basis of a matrix-coding construction, and this is correct, as the ungrammaticality of (9.65a) and the grammaticality of (9.65b, c) show. Thus, the unmarked form in (9.64) is the (b, b′) example, in which *mér* '1sgDAT' is the privileged syntactic argument and *Haraldur* 'Harold-NOM' is a direct core argument in the matrix core. But this is exactly the same pattern as in (9.57b), in which *Jón-∅* 'John-NOM' is the privileged syntactic argument and *Harald-∅* 'Harold-ACC' is a direct core argument in the matrix core. Hence both *virðast* 'seem' and *telja* 'believe' occur as the matrix verb in matrix-coding as non-PSA constructions. *Virðast* 'seem' and *telja* 'believe' have similar logical structures, **seem′** (x, y) [MR0] and **believe′** (x, y), and in both the *x* argument becomes the privileged syntactic argument and the *y* argument is filled by another logical structure. When this logical structure is mapped into a core coordinate syntactic structure, the *x* argument is the privileged syntactic argument in the matrix core and the would-be privileged syntactic argument of the embedded logical structure occupies the open core argument position in the matrix core.

One last peculiarity of English and a handful of other languages needs to be mentioned before we investigate linking from syntax to semantics in these constructions. The expletive pronoun *it* may occur in the open core argument position, if there is no semantic argument from any of the logical structures to fill it. Hence the argumentless logical structures in (9.66a, b) would necessitate the occurrence of *it*, as would the one in (c).

(9.66) a. **seem′** (∅, [**rain′**])
a′. It seems to be raining.
b. **believe′** (∅, [**rain′**])
b′. It is believed to be raining.
c. **believe′** (Ali, [**rain′**])
c′. Ali believes it to be raining.

The syntax to semantics linking algorithm in (9.54) applies to matrix-coding constructions with *believe/telja*, *expect*, etc. in exactly the same way as in the ones with *seem/virðast* discussed in the previous section. This should come as no surprise, since we have seen that the two constructions are basically the same in terms of linking. The linking from syntax to semantics for (9.63a) is given in figure 9.22. As before, the numbers refer to the steps in (9.54). Each core contains an M-transitive verb, and therefore step 1 applies to both. Because the verb in the first core is passive, and because only macrorole arguments can function as pivot in English, we can conclude that *Yolanda* is a macrorole argument and is not the actor of *believe*; the actor of *believe*, *Tyrone*, is in the periphery marked by the preposition *by*. In the second core, the verb is active, and therefore we can conclude that its privileged syntactic argument is an actor and that *his sandwich* is a non-actor direct core argument. We cannot conclude that *his sandwich* is a macrorole argument, because it is possible for direct arguments after the verb to be non-macrorole arguments, as in *Bronwyn was given the book by Sheila* (see section 7.2.3). Step 2 is straightforward, and in step 3 it is possible to link *Tyrone* with the actor of *believe* and *his*

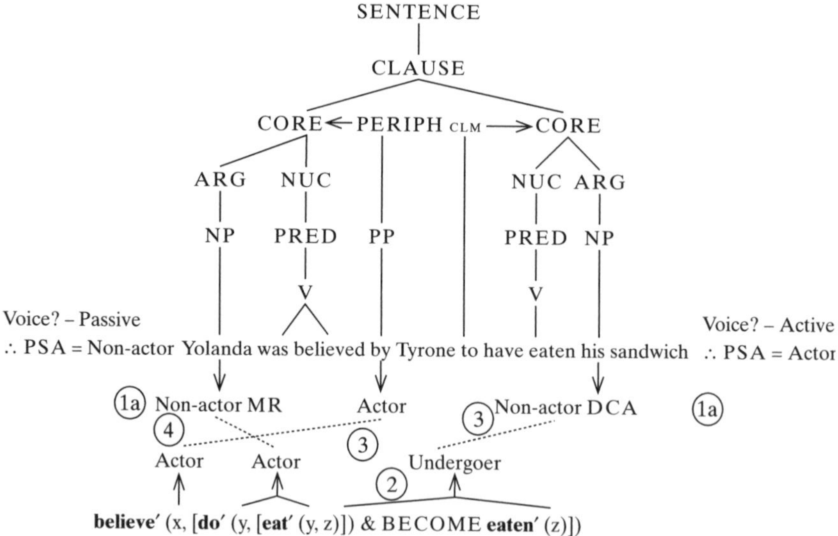

Figure 9.22 Linking from syntax to semantics in English matrix-coding construction

sandwich with the undergoer of *eat*. There was no argument position available for *Yolanda* in the logical structure of *believe*, and therefore step 4 comes into play. The actor of *eat* is the only unlinked argument position in the logical structure, and it is the argument that would be the pivot of *eat*, were it to occur as the main verb in a simple clause. By step 4 *Yolanda* may be linked to the actor of *eat*, which yields the correct interpretation of the sentence and satisfies the Completeness Constraint. Note that the label 'non-actor MR' under *Yolanda* in figure 9.22 means, as we stated above, that *Yolanda* is not the actor of *believe*; it does not mean that the NP cannot be interpreted as the actor of a different verb.

The constructional templates for the English matrix-coding constructions are given in table 9.7. There are two templates here, as the crucial feature of the second construction is the violation of (9.60b); the first construction follows it. As in control constructions, the syntactic pivot is in core 2, not core 1, and it is, following the hierarchy for English, the highest ranking core macrorole. The linking is specified as 'default', since it follows (9.54) without modification. The choice of the different clause linkage markers is a function of the semantics of the construction, as discussed in section 8.4.2. These templates would also work for the Icelandic constructions we have examined, with the exception that there is no clause linkage marker in the Icelandic matrix-coding constructions.

9.2 Case marking in complex sentences

We developed a theory of case marking for simple sentences in chapter 7, and in this section we will address the issues that the syntax of complex sentences raises for it. We will focus on two main topics, the questions of case marking in core junctures and the proper domain of case assignment in section 9.2.1 and the issue of case marking in nuclear-juncture causative constructions in section 9.2.2.

9.2.1 Core junctures and the domain of case assignment

The two types of non-subordinate core junctures we have discussed, control and matrix-coding constructions, interact with the case-marking rules proposed in chapter 7 in different ways. We will look at case marking in the matrix core first, and then examine case marking in the linked core as part of the investigation of the domain of case assignment.

There is no real problem with case marking in the matrix core of control constructions. The basic rules for accusative and ergative case assignment from chapter 7 are repeated in (9.67).

(9.67) a. *Case assignment rules for accusative constructions*
1 Assign nominative case to the highest-ranking macrorole argument.
2 Assign accusative case to the other macrorole argument.
3 Assign dative case to non-macrorole arguments (default).

Table 9.7 *Constructional templates for English matrix-coding constructions*

CONSTRUCTION
English matrix-coding as PSA construction
SYNTAX
Juncture: Core Nexus: Coordination Construction type: Serial verb $[_{CL}\ [_{CORE}\ \text{ARG}\ [_{NUC} \ldots]\ (\text{ARG})]\ \text{CLM}\ [_{CORE}\ [_{NUC} \ldots] \ldots] \ldots]$ Unit template(s): Core 1: Default Core 2: Default PSA: Syntactic pivot of Core 2 Linking: Default
MORPHOLOGY
CLM *to*
SEMANTICS
Propositional attitude, perception, evidential
PRAGMATICS
Illocutionary force: Unspecified Focus structure: Unspecified

CONSTRUCTION
English matrix-coding as non-PSA construction
SYNTAX
Juncture: Core Nexus: Coordination Construction type: Serial verb $[_{CL}\ [_{CORE}\ \text{ARG}\ [_{NUC} \ldots]\ \text{ARG}]\ \text{CLM}\ [_{CORE}\ [_{NUC} \ldots] \ldots] \ldots]$ Unit template(s): Core 1: Violates (9.60b) Core 2: Default PSA: Syntactic pivot of Core 2 Linking: Default
MORPHOLOGY
CLM *to*
SEMANTICS
Propositional attitude, perception, cognition
PRAGMATICS
Illocutionary force: Unspecified Focus structure: Unspecified

b. *Case assignment for ergative constructions*
   1 Assign absolutive case to the lowest-ranking macrorole argument.
   2 Assign ergative case to the other macrorole argument.
   3 Assign dative case to non-macrorole arguments (default).

English, of course, lacks the dative rule in (9.67a3). In a sentence like *They persuaded us to go to the party*, the third person plural actor is the highest-ranking macrorole and therefore nominative, and the first person plural undergoer is the other macrorole and therefore accusative. Similarly, in the Dyirbal example in (9.28a), *bayi ŋuma* 'father' is the actor in the matrix core and appears in the ergative case (*baŋgul numaŋgu*), and *balan yabu* 'mother' is the undergoer and occurs in the absolutive case. The interesting examples are those involving matrix coding, such as the Icelandic example in (9.57) and its English equivalent, *John believes Harold to have taken the book*. In Icelandic, *Jón* 'John' is nominative and *Harald* 'Harold' is accusative, and the same pattern holds in English if we replace the proper nouns with pronouns, i.e. *He believes him to have taken the book*. *Jón* and *he* are the actor arguments of *telja* and *believe*, but *Harald* and *him* are the actor arguments of *taka* and *take*. Thus the matrix core contains two actor arguments; how is their case to be decided? The logical structure of these sentences is given in (9.68).

(9.68) **believe′** (x, [[**do′** (y, ∅)] CAUSE [BECOME **have′** (y, z)]])

Jón or *he* is the *x* argument, and *Harald* or *him* is the *y* argument. There is a very simple solution to the problem at hand: only *Jón* and *he* are arguments of *telja* or *believe*, while *Harald* and *him* are not, and therefore *Jón* and *he* are the highest-ranking arguments of *telja* and *believe* and receive nominative case, following (9.67a1). *Harald* and *him* are the other macrorole arguments and therefore receive accusative case. Note that we would have run into a serious problem if (9.67a2) had been 'assign accusative case to the undergoer', since the accusative NPs in these examples are not undergoers. In sentences like (9.49a), (9.51a) and (9.63b), the only macrorole in the matrix core is a semantic argument of the predicate in the linked core; since it is the only macrorole in the core, it counts as the highest ranking and gets nominative case. Thus, the case assignment rules proposed in chapter 7 for simple sentences can account for case marking in the matrix cores in these examples.

In the discussion of accusative case marking in section 7.3.1.1, we stated that the case-marking rules in (7.45) apply to direct syntactic arguments within the core or in the pre/postcore slot, and since we were dealing only with simple sentences there, this was the only possible domain they could apply in, since they did not apply to NPs in PPs in the periphery. However, in core junctures there is more than one core in a clause, and so the question arises, do the case-marking rules apply to each individual core separately, or do they apply to all of the cores jointly within the clause? In other words, is the domain of case assignment the core or the clause? If it is the core, then the case assignment rules would apply in each core independently in a complex sentence, whereas if it is the clause, then they would apply to all of the cores in each clause jointly but would apply independently in each clause. It turns out that languages vary with respect to the domain of case assignment: in some it is the clause, while in others it is the core.

Icelandic presents the clearest example of a language in which the core is the domain of case marking. The case assignment rules for Icelandic are repeated in (9.67). That the core is the domain of case assignment in Icelandic can be seen most readily in sentences like (9.69).

(9.69) Jón-Ø tel-ur mér (í barnaskap sínum) haf-a alltaf
John-MsgNOM believe-3sgPRES 1sgDAT (in foolishness his) have-INF always
þótt Ólaf-ur leiðinleg-ur.
think.PSTP Olaf-MsgNOM boring-MsgNOM
'John believes me (in his foolishness) to have always considered Olaf boring.'

What is crucial about this example is the occurrence of two nominative NPs, one in each core. If the core is the domain for the application of the case-marking rules in (9.67), then the case pattern in (9.69) is accounted for, because *Jón* is the highest-ranking macrorole in the matrix core and *Ólafur* is the highest-ranking macrorole in the second, linked core. If the clause were the domain, then only one nominative NP would be possible, namely the highest-ranking macrorole in the matrix core, *Jón*; all other macrorole arguments would be assigned accusative case, which they are not.

One more thing needs to be said about case marking in Icelandic. In a sentence like (9.57b), the undergoer is the only macrorole actually occurring in the second core, and yet it is accusative instead of nominative, unlike the single macrorole in the linked core in (9.69). What is the difference? The answer lies in the M-transitivity of the two verbs; *taka* 'take' in (9.57b) is M-transitive and therefore takes two macroroles, while *þykja* 'think, consider' is M-intransitive and takes only one. When the case assignment rules apply to a core containing *þykja*, the single macrorole in it is the only possible one and is therefore the highest ranking; hence it gets nominative case. When they apply to a core containing *taka* in the active voice, which has only a single macrorole (undergoer), due to the other macrorole occurring in the matrix core, as in (9.57b), this is only one of the two macroroles that *taka* takes, and it is not the highest ranking. Hence it should get accusative case rather than nominative.

In English, on the other hand, because the clause is the domain of case assignment only the highest-ranking macrorole in the matrix core can be nominative; all other macroroles are accusative.[12] This is illustrated in (9.70).

(9.70) a. Pat believed her to have told him to ask us to help them.
b. For her to hire them would shock us.

The (b) example is particularly interesting, because it contains no nominative NP at all. This is because the highest-ranking macrorole argument, the actor, is realized by an infinitival core, *for her to hire them*, and cores functioning as arguments do not carry case in English and many other languages. There are languages, however, in which cores, even ones which are not syntactic arguments, carry case, e.g. Quechua. This is not so surprising in cases of core subordination in Huallaga Quechua (Weber 1983), as in (9.25), but it also occurs in non-subordinate core junctures, as in (9.71), also from Huallaga Quechua.

(9.71) a. Hwan-Ø wasi-ta rika-n.
Juan-NOM house-ACC see-3sg
'Juan sees the house.'
a′. Wasi-Ø rika-ka-n.
house-NOM see-PASS-3sg
'The house is seen.'
b. Wasin-chaw ka-shan-ta maya-ra-n. Core subordination
house-LOC be-NMZ.3sg-ACC perceive-PAST-3sg
'He$_i$ perceived that he$_j$ was in his$_j$ house.'
b′. Wasin-chaw ka-shan maya-ka-ra-n.
house-LOC be-NMZ.3sg perceive-PASS-PAST-3sg
'It is known that he was at his house.'
c. Maqa-ma-y-ta muna-n. Core cosubordination
hit-1sgU-INF-ACC want-3sg
'He wants to hit me.'
c′. *Maqwa-ma-y muna-ka:-n.
hit-1sgU-INF want-PASS-3sg
*'To him me was wanted (by someone).'

The Huallaga Quechua passive construction is illustrated in (9.71a′). The example in (b) is like the earlier one, and the nominalized core functions as undergoer and as a direct core argument. Like the simple NP undergoer in (a), it can appear as the privileged syntactic argument in a passive construction, as (b′) shows. But in (c), it is not clear that infinitive *maqamayta* 'to hit me' is a syntactic argument; unlike the cores and clauses that function as syntactic arguments, e.g. *wasinchaw kashanta* 'that he was in his house' in (b), the infinitive does not carry a nominalization suffix. Like its English counterpart, it fails to appear as the privileged syntactic argument in a passive construction, as (c′) shows. If it is not a core argument, why does it get accusative case in (c)? The answer seems to be that in this variety of Quechua case is tied primarily to the semantic role properties of a phrase. *Muna-* 'want', like *rika-* 'see' and *maya-* 'perceive', is M-transitive and therefore assigns two macroroles. The logical structure for *muna-* is **want′** (x, y), and the *x* argument functions as actor and the *y* argument as undergoer. The logical structure (simplified) for (c) is **want′** (3sg$_i$, [**do′** (x$_i$, [**hit′** (x$_i$, 1sg)])]), and the embedded logical structure is the undergoer of *muna-* 'want'. Hence the infinitive realizing it receives accusative case, following (9.67a2), despite the fact that it is not realized as a core argument of *muna-* but rather as the linked core in a non-subordinate core juncture. Thus Huallaga Quechua M-transitive verbs assign two macroroles and therefore accusative case, even if the embedded logical structure is not realized as a core argument. We have here an interesting mismatch between semantics and morphosyntax: the accusative case on the infinitive is a function of the fact that it is the undergoer of the matrix verb, but the lack of a nominalization suffix and its syntactic behavior is a function of the fact that it is not a syntactic argument of the matrix verb.

Two very interesting examples of languages which take the clause as their case-marking domain are Newari (Tibeto-Burman, Nepal; Genetti 1986) and Enga (Papua New Guinea; Li and Lang 1979). They are both morphologically ergative languages, and in a core juncture the semantics of the shared semantic argument in the linked core can affect whether the actor in the matrix core receives ergative case or not. This is illustrated in the following examples.

(9.72) Wɔ̃-ɔ̃ ɔitobar khɔpe-e wɔn-a-a parsi nyat-ɔ. Newari
3sg-ERG Sunday Bhaktapur-LOC go-PART-CLM sari buy-PAST.EVID
'On Sunday he went to Bhaktapur and bought saris.'

(9.73) a. Baá-∅ Wápaka pe-ly-á-mo. Enga
3sg-ABS Wabag go-PRES-3sg-DEC
'He is going to Wabag.'
b. Baa-((mé)) mená méndé nya-la pe-ly-á-mo.
3sg-((ERG)) pig DET get-INF go-PRES-3sg-DEC
'He is going (somewhere) to get a pig.'
c. Baa-(mé) mená dóko pyá-la pe-ly-á-mo.
3sg-(ERG) pig DEF kill-INF go-PRES-3sg-DEC
'He is going (somewhere) to kill the pig.'

(9.74) a. Baa-((mé)) akáli ká-lya-nya mási-ly-a-mo.
3sg-((ERG)) man be-INF-DES think-PRES-3sg-DEC
'He wants to be a man.'
b. Baa-(mé) mená méndé nyá-la-nya mási-ly-a-mo.
3sg-(ERG) pig DET get-INF-DES think-PRES-3sg-DEC
'He wants [to get] a pig.'
c. Baa-mé mená dóko pyá-la-nya mási-ly-a-mo.
3sg-ERG pig DEF kill-INF-DES think-PRES-3sg-DEC
'He wants to kill the pig.'

These are all non-subordinate core junctures, except for (9.73a), which is a simple clause. In the Enga examples, '(*mé*)' indicates that the presence of the ergative marker is preferred, while '((*mé*))' indicates that it is neutral or disfavored; no parentheses means that it is obligatory. The verb in the matrix core in the Newari example in (9.72) and the Enga examples in (9.73) is 'go', which, being intransitive, would take an absolutive rather than an ergative actor, as (9.73a) shows. However, when the verb in the second core is transitive, then the ergative case may be obligatory, as in (9.72), or it may be optional but preferred, as in (9.73c). The logical structures for (9.73b, c) are given in (9.75a, b), respectively; the logical structure for 'go' is simplified for ease of presentation.

(9.75) a. **do′** (3sg$_i$, [**go′** (3sg$_i$, ∅)]) PURP [BECOME **have′** (x$_i$, mená)]
b. **do′** (3sg$_i$, [**go′** (3sg$_i$, ∅)]) PURP [[**do′** (x$_i$, ∅)] CAUSE [BECOME **dead′** (mená)]]

The second logical structure, in (b), represents a more dynamic action with greater effect on its second argument than the one in (a), and this is reflected in the disfavoring of the ergative marker in (9.73b) and the preference for it in (9.73c). The case-marking rules in (9.67b) apply in Enga. If each core were linked completely independently of the other, then there is no obvious way for the properties of the second core to affect the case marking in the first core. Since there is only one macrorole in the first core, it should be absolutive case, but in fact this is not what these examples show. Rather, the case assignment rules take the clause as a whole as its domain. In Newari, the occurrence of an undergoer in the linked core triggers the assignment of ergative case to the actor in the matrix core. In Enga, on the other hand, just how close the event denoted by the linked core is to the prototypical transitive event with a highly efficacious actor and a strongly affected undergoer (Hopper and Thompson 1980) plays a role in determining whether the ergative case is appropriate or not; in order for the ergative case to be possible, there must be two macrorole arguments in the clause, and the overall semantics of the construction determines its appropriateness. This is also the case in the sentences in (9.74), in which the matrix verb is *masa-* 'think' and the linked cores take the desiderative suffix *-nya*, yielding the equivalent of a 'want' construction in English and other languages. The ergative case on the matrix actor is strongly disfavored when the linked core is stative but is obligatory when it is close to the transitive prototype.

Thus, languages vary with respect to the domain of case assignment: in Icelandic the rules apply independently in each core, while in English, Enga and Newari, they apply to all of the cores in a clause jointly.

9.2.2 Case marking in causative constructions

The case-marking rules proposed in chapter 7 apply in simple sentences. Since the causative constructions in (9.19)–(9.22) involve either lexical derivation or a syntactic nuclear juncture, the resulting construction is a simple sentence with a single clause containing a single core, and therefore we should expect that the rules from chapter 7 should apply to these constructions. As our discussion of the French examples in (9.22) showed, they do work for this type of construction. However, as these French examples also showed, there can be variation in the treatment of causee, and this variation has been much discussed in the literature (e.g. Comrie

1976c, 1989b, Cole 1983, Polinsky 1995). The issue is, when an additional argument, the causer, is added to a core, how does this affect the coding of the other arguments? Comrie (1976c, 1989b) showed that the most common patterns are those shown in (9.76a), and he proposed an explanation for them in terms of the grammatical relations hierarchy in (b). The function of the arguments in the base forms is given in square brackets.

(9.76) a. *Changes in grammatical relations in causative constructions* (*most frequent pattern*)
1 Intransitive base verb: NP_{SUBJ} V → Derived transitive verb: NP_{SUBJ} $NP_{DO[SUBJ]}$ V
2 Transitive base verb: NP_{SUBJ} NP_{DO} V → Derived ditransitive verb: NP_{SUBJ} $NP_{IO[SUBJ]}$ $NP_{DO[DO]}$ V
3 Ditransitive base verb: NP_{SUBJ} NP_{IO} NP_{DO} V → Ditransitive + passive agent adjunct NP_{SUBJ} $NP_{IO[IO]}$ $NP_{DO[DO]}$ $PP_{OBL[SUBJ]}$ V

b. *Grammatical relations hierarchy*
SUBJ > DOBJ > IOBJ > OBL

The first thing to note is that it is the 'subject' of the base verb, the causee, which undergoes a change in its syntactic status; the 'direct object' of the base verb and the 'indirect object' with ditransitives are not affected. The causer, the actor of the causative verb or morpheme, functions as the 'subject' of the derived verb. Comrie proposes that when the base verb is causativized and the causer argument added, the causee takes over the highest open grammatical relation in the clause. If the base verb is intransitive, then the causee becomes the 'direct object' of the derived verb, as in (a1). If it is transitive, then the causee becomes the 'indirect object', as in (a2). If it is ditransitive, then the causee receives the same treatment as the actor in a passive construction, as in (a3). We had an example from French of (a1) in (3.25b) and of (a2) in (9.22a). They are repeated in (9.77) along with an example of (a3), from Comrie (1989b).

(9.77) a. Pierre fer-a cour-ir Marie.
make-3sgFUT run-INF
'Pierre will make Marie run.'

b. Je fer-ai mang-er les gâteaux à Jean.
1sgNOM make-1sgFUT eat-INF the.Mpl cakes DAT John
'I will make John eat the cakes.'

c. Je fer-ai expédi-er une lettre au
1sgNOM make-1sgFUT send-INF a.Fsg letter the.MsgDAT
directeur par Paul.
director by Paul
'I will make Paul send a letter to the director.'

d. Je lui fer-ai expédi-er une lettre au directeur.
1sgNOM 3sgDAT make-3sgFUT send-INF a.Fsg letter the.MsgDAT director
'I will make him send a letter to the director.'

Why should the pattern in (9.76a) be the most frequent pattern cross-linguistically? The answer is, this is the pattern that the semantics to syntax linking algorithm in (9.1) yields. To see this, let's look at the logical structures of these examples.

(9.78) a. [**do′** (Pierre, ∅)] CAUSE [**do′** (Marie, [**run′** (Marie)])]
b. [**do′** (1sg, ∅)] CAUSE [**do′** (Jean, [**eat′** (Jean, gâteaux)]) & BECOME **eaten′** (gâteaux)]
c. [**do′** (1sg, ∅)] CAUSE [[**do′** (Jean, ∅)] CAUSE [BECOME **have′** (directeur, lettre)]]

We assume that *faire* 'make, cause' has one macrorole when it occurs in these constructions and that the complement verb has one or two, depending upon its transitivity. Since there can be no more than two macroroles per core, the status of the 'extra' argument must be addressed. In the linking between (9.78a) and (9.77a), *Pierre*, as the EFFECTOR of *faire*, will be the actor (see section 4.1), and *Marie* is the only candidate for undergoer. Hence *Marie* will be undergoer, which yields the pattern in (9.76a1). The linking between (9.78b) and (9.77b) is presented in figure 9.7. Given this logical structure, *je*, the EFFECTOR of *faire*, will be the actor, and of the remaining two arguments, *les gâteaux* 'the cakes' outranks *Jean* for undergoer on the Actor–Undergoer Hierarchy; hence *les gâteaux* will be undergoer and *Jean* a direct core argument in the dative, following (9.67a3). We mentioned in section 9.1.2 that there is a second possible linking of (9.78b), which is represented in figure 9.8. In it *Jean* is treated as an actor, yielding three macroroles in the core. Since there can be only two macroroles in a core, one of them must occur as a non-core element. As before, the actor of *faire* will be the privileged syntactic argument in the sentence, and the undergoer will also occur as a core argument. The only coding possibility for the second actor, *Jean*, is as a peripheral oblique as in passive constructions, and this is the result in (9.22b), repeated below.

(9.79) Je fer-ai manger les gâteaux par Jean.
1sgNOM make-1sgFUT eat-INF the.Mpl cakes by John
'I will have John eat the cakes.'

This is the same treatment that the causee gets in (9.77c). There is also a second coding possible for (9.78c), namely (9.77d). While it is impossible to have two *à NP* phrases in a single French core, it is possible to have the causee realized as a dative clitic, as in (9.77d). Turkish also has two options for realizing a logical structure like (9.78c), one with the causee marked by the passive agent marker, and the other with the causee and the 'indirect object' both in the dative. The following examples are from Comrie (1989a).

(9.80) a. Dişçi-∅ Hasan-a mektub-u müdür tarafından göster-t-ti.
dentist-NOM Hasan-DAT letter-ACC director by show-CAUS-PAST
'The dentist got the director to show the letter to Hasan.'

b. Dişçi-∅ müdür-e mektub-u Hasan-a göster-t-ti.
dentist-NOM director-DAT letter-ACC Hasan-DAT show-CAUS-PAST
'The dentist got the director to show the letter to Hasan.'

In both languages, the 'double-dative' linking would be the result of the causee and the RECIPIENT being treated as non-macrorole direct core arguments, while the 'passive agent' linking would involve two actors, the subordinate one being treated as an adjunct in a passive.

Another example of variable linking in a causative construction can be found in Chicheŵa (Alsina 1992). The relevant examples are given in (9.81).

(9.81) a. Chatsalĩra a-ku-nám-íts-á mwã́na.
1-PRES-lie-CAUS-IND 1.child
'Chatsalira is making the child tell lies.'
b. Nŭngu i-na-phík-íts-a maûngu kwá kádzīdzi.
9.porcupine 9-PAST-cook-CAUS-IND 6.pumpkins to 1a.owl
'The porcupine had the pumpkins cooked by the owl.'
c. Nŭngu i-na-phík-íts-a kadzidzi maûngu.
9.porcupine 9-PAST-cook-CAUS-IND 1a.owl 6.pumpkins
'The porcupine made the owl cook the pumpkins.'

When an intransitive verb like *-nám-* 'tell lies' is causativized as in (a), the causee appears as the undergoer, just as in the French example. When a transitive verb like *-phík-* 'cook' is causativized, there are two possible linkings. The linking in (b) is exactly parallel to that in (9.77b) in French (see figure 9.7): the second argument of the base verb appears as the undergoer of the derived verb, and the causee appears in a PP marked by *kwá* 'to'.[13] This is the unmarked linking. In the alternative linking in (c), the causee is the undergoer of the derived verb, and the second argument of the base verb appears as a direct core argument. The PP *kwá kádzīdzi* 'to owl' can be omitted from (b), but the NP *maûngu* 'pumpkins' cannot be omitted from (c). These two linking possibilities parallel exactly the two possibilities with verbs like *give* in English (see section 7.2.2), and the omissibility of the third core argument is also parallel, as (9.82) shows.

(9.82) a. Chris gave flowers to Dana.
a′. Chris gave flowers.
b. Chris gave Dana flowers.
b′. Chris gave Dana.

Omitting *to Dana*, as in (a′), does not change the basic interpretation of the sentence, whereas omitting *flowers* as in (b′), does change the meaning of the sentence; in (b′) *Dana* cannot be interpreted as the RECIPIENT but must be construed as the THEME, just like *flowers* in (a′). The reason for this is that the only overt cue to whether the linking to undergoer is the unmarked one, as in (a), or the marked one, as in (b), is the coding of the third core argument. This is why the coding of the third core argument plays such a prominent role in the syntax to semantics linking algorithm developed in section 7.2.3. If that cue is missing, then the undergoer NP is interpreted as if the unmarked linking had taken place; with this verb it means that the undergoer must be interpreted as a THEME. Exactly the same is true in the Chicheŵa examples in (9.81b, c); the only cue that a marked linking has occurred is the coding of the third core argument, and if it is missing, then the undergoer is interpreted as if the unmarked linking had taken place. This means that if *maûngu* 'pumpkins' is omitted from (9.81c), then the sentence must be interpreted as 'The porcupine had the owl cooked.' Hence the status of *kwá NP* is exactly analogous to that of the *to NP* with a ditransitive verb in English.

These examples of variable linking of the causee have involved transitive and ditransitive verbs to this point; it is also possible with intransitive verbs in some languages. Two examples of this which are often discussed in the literature come from Hungarian (Hetzron 1976) and Japanese (Shibatani 1973, Kuno 1973).

(9.83) a. Köhög-tet-tem a gyerek-et. — Hungarian
cough-CAUS-1sgPAST DET boy-ACC
'I made the boy cough.'
b. Köhög-tet-tem a gyerek-kel.
cough-CAUS-1sgPAST DET boy-INST
'I had the boy cough.'
c. Level-et ír-at-tam a gyerek-kel/*gyerek-et.
letter-ACC write-CAUS-1sgPAST DET boy-INST/boy-ACC
'I made the boy write the letter.'

(9.84) a. Taroo ga Ziroo o ik-ase-ta. — Japanese
NOM ACC go-CAUS-PAST
'Taroo made Ziroo go.'
b. Taroo ga Ziroo ni ik-ase-ta.
NOM DAT go-CAUS-PAST
'Taroo let/had Ziroo go', or 'Taroo got Ziroo to go.'
c. Taroo ga Ziroo ni/*o hon o yom-ase-ta.
NOM DAT/ACC book ACC read-CAUS-PAST
'Taroo made Ziroo read the book.'

The default linkings are represented by the (a) sentences; they follow the same pattern as the French example in (9.77a) and the Chicheŵa example in (9.81a); in languages which permit only one pattern with causativized intransitive verbs, it is virtually always the (a) pattern which occurs, the (a) pattern corresponding to (9.76a1). In the (b) patterns, the causees are non-macrororole core arguments, and the derived verbs are M-intransitive. In both languages this pattern is possible only if the base verb is an activity verb, and given the discussion in section 4.2 about the strong tendency of activity verbs to behave like intransitive verbs, even if they have two arguments, this variation is perhaps not so surprising. The Japanese example in (9.84b) follows the case assignment rules in (7.45), with the non-macrorole direct core argument receiving dative case, whereas in the Hungarian example in (9.83b) the default is overridden and the non-macrorole direct core argument is in the instrumental case (see chapter 7, n. 9).[14] There is no alternation when the base verb is transitive in either language; the causee must be in the instrumental case in Hungarian, as in (9.83c), and in the dative in Japanese, as in (9.84c).

All of the examples discussed so far have been from accusative languages, but the same patterns of linking and case assignment are found in ergative languages as well. Examples from Jakaltek (Craig 1977), Georgian (Hewitt 1995, Harris 1981), Sanuma (Borgman 1989) and Sama (Walton 1986) are given below.

(9.85) a. Ch-∅-(y)-a' xew-oj ix naj. — Jakaltek
NPST-3ABS-3ERG-cause rest-INF CL/she CL/he
'She makes him rest.'
b. X-in-(y)-a' mak-a' naj t-aw-et.
PST-1sgABS-3ERG-cause hit-INF CL/he AUG-2sgERG-to
'He made you hit me.'

(9.86) a. Ektan-ma avadmaq'op-i
nurse-ERG sick.person-NOM
da-∅-∅-a-c'v-in-a. — Georgian
PVB-3sgU-3sgDCA-PRV-lie.down-CAUS-3sgA
'The nurse made the sick person lie down.'
b. Geno-m mi-∅-∅-a-t'an-in-a
Geno-ERG PVB-3sgU-3sgDCA-PRV-take-CAUS-3sgA
Rezo-s c'igneb-i tav-is-tan.
Rezo-DAT books-NOM self-GEN-at
'Geno$_i$ got Rezo$_j$ to take the books to his$_{i,j}$ place.'

(9.87) a. Ipa hepala a wani-nö
1sgGEN older.brother 3sg DEPR-ERG
pusopö-∅ tiki-ma kölö. — Sanuma
wife-ABS sit.off.ground-CAUS there
'My older brother makes his wife sit (in the tree) down there.'
b. Pata töpö-nö pole niha wale-∅ kökö se-ma-nö ke.
old 3pl-ERG dog LOC peccary-ABS 3dl kill-CAUS-GOAL IMM
'The old people made the dogs kill the peccary.'

(9.88) a. Pa-lahi ku na onde' di'aw. — Sama
CAUS-flee 1sgERG already child yesterday
'I sent the child away yesterday.'
b. Pa-inum ku iya kahawa.
CAUS-drink 1sgERG 3sgABS coffee
'I had him drink coffee.'

In each pair of sentences, the base verb in (a) is intransitive and in (b) is transitive. In all four languages the causee is the undergoer in the (a) pattern; it appears in the absolutive case in Georgian and Sanuma, is cross-referenced by the absolutive form in Jakaltek, and is the absolutive NP in Sama. The (b) sentences follow the unmarked linking pattern in Jakaltek, Georgian and Sanuma but the marked pattern in Sama. In the first three languages, the causer is in the ergative, the undergoer of the base verb in the absolutive, and the causee is coded the same way as the third argument of a ditransitive verb; it is the object of the postposition *-et* 'to' in Jakaltek, in the dative in Georgian, and the object of the locative postposition *niha* in Sanuma. This is exactly as predicted by the case assignment rules for ergative languages proposed in section 7.3.1.2. Sama presents a marked linking analogous to (9.81c) in Chicheŵa; the causee is the undergoer. This is shown by the fact that it is expressed by the absolutive form of the third person singular pronoun with the verb in the unmarked voice; since Sama is syntactically ergative, this means that the absolutive NP is the undergoer. Thus, we find the same basic patterns of linking and case marking in causative constructions across languages, regardless of whether they are morphologically ergative or accusative or syntactically ergative or accusative.

Since the primary function of language is communication, we assume that formal alternations of the kind illustrated in (9.77b) vs. (9.79) and in (9.81b, c), (9.83) and (9.84) are not random and meaningless but rather serve to signal some semantic or other meaningful contrast. The alert reader will have noticed that the translations of the contrasting sentences in each pair are not the same, and the semantic contrast in each case revolves around the degree of independent action, volition and control that can be attributed to the causee. We discussed this briefly with respect to the French examples in section 9.1.2. The contrast between (9.77b) and (9.79) revolves around the volitionality of the causee. As noted earlier, Hyman and Zimmer (1976) argue that in the construction in (9.77b) the causee may be interpreted as not acting volitionally, whereas in the construction in (9.79) the causee may be interpreted as acting volitionally. In other words, the secondary EFFECTOR, the causee, can more easily be construed as an AGENT in (9.79) than in (9.77b), in terms of the implicature theory of agency proposed in section 3.2.3.2. Thus, *par* encourages the AGENT implicature, while *à* is basically neutral with respect to it. When we look at the translations of the pairs of Chicheŵa, Hungarian and Japanese examples, we find the same semantic contrast: one form seems to favor a volitional interpretation of the causee (the *kwá* [dative] form in Chicheŵa, the dative in Japanese, and the instrumental in Hungarian), whereas an opposing form (the accusative in all three languages) does not favor it. We argued that in these three languages the accusative form reflects the linking of the causee to the undergoer of the derived causative verb, and given the semantics of undergoer (see section 4.1), an undergoer–causee should be impossible to construe as agentive. In the contrasting forms, the causee is not an undergoer but a non-macrorole core argument, and therefore the form of the

NP does not block the agent implicature; with respect to the Hungarian instrumental, it could, like the passive agent coding in French, be interpreted as favoring the agentive implicature.

There are languages in which alternative coding of the causee does not appear to involve any variation in the linking itself but rather in the case assigned to the non-macrorole core argument; actor and undergoer assignments are constant across the various forms. The languages we will look at are Bolivian Quechua (Bills, Vallejo and Troike 1969) and Kannada (Sridhar 1976). In Bolivian Quechua, causees of intransitive base verbs are always accusative, but the causees of transitive base verbs may be accusative or instrumental, as shown in (9.89).

(9.89) a. Nuqa-∅ warmi-ta asi-či-ni.
1sgNOM woman-ACC laugh-CAUS-1sg
'I make the woman laugh.'
b. Nuqa-∅ Fan-ta rumi-ta apa-či-ni.
1sgNOM Juan-ACC rock-ACC carry-CAUS-1sg
'I make Juan carry the rock.'
c. Nuqa-∅ Fan-wan rumi-ta apa-či-ni.
1sgNOM Juan-INST rock-ACC carry-CAUS-1sg
'I had Juan carry the rock.'

The undergoer of *apa-či-* 'cause to carry', *rumi-* 'rock', is in the accusative case in both sentences, and therefore there is no question of there being an alternative linking to undergoer in these examples. Rather, there are two possible cases that can be assigned to the causee, a non-macrorole core argument, accusative and instrumental, and the choice of case affects the viability of the AGENT implicature for the causee. Not surprisingly, accusative, the normal case for undergoers, strongly disfavors the AGENT implicature, whereas instrumental seems to favor it, as the translations indicate. This parallels the situation in Hungarian. In Kannada the variable marking on the causee involves a contrast between dative and instrumental, as illustrated in (9.90).

(9.90) a. Avanu-∅ nana-ge bisket-annu tinn-is-id-anu.
3sg-NOM 1sg-DAT biscuit-ACC eat-CAUS-PAST-3sgMASC
'He fed me a biscuit.'
a′. Avanu-∅ nann-inda bisket-annu tinn-is-id-anu.
3sg-NOM 1sg-INST biscuit-ACC eat-CAUS-PAST-3sgMASC
'He had me eat a biscuit.'
b. Avanu-∅ nana-ge tīy-annu kud-is-id-anu.
3sg-NOM 1sg-DAT tea-ACC drink-CAUS-PAST-3sgMASC
'He made me drink tea.'
b′. Avanu-∅ nann-inda tīy-annu kud-is-id-anu.
3sg-NOM 1sg-INST tea-ACC drink-CAUS-PAST-3sgMASC
'He had me drink tea.'

Table 9.8 *Case alternations in causee marking in causative constructions*

Language	*Case: neutral or disfavoring* AGENT *implicature*	*Case: favoring* AGENT *implicature*	*Marked linking*	*Base verb: intransitive, transitive or both?*
French	Dative	Instrumental (*par*)	Yes	Transitive
Chicheŵa	Accusative	Dative (*kwá*)	Yes	Transitive
Hungarian	Accusative	Instrumental	Yes	Intransitive
Japanese	Accusative	Dative	Yes	Intransitive
Bolivian Quechua	Accusative	Instrumental	No	Transitive
Kannada	Dative	Instrumental	No	Transitive

The instrumental case on the causee is compatible with the AGENT implicature, as in Hungarian and Bolivian Quechua, whereas the dative case disfavors it. Again, the undergoer is in the accusative case throughout, and accordingly this alternation does not involve a marked linking to undergoer. Rather, it involves assignment of the instrumental case instead of the default dative to the non-macrorole core argument.

The facts we have looked at regarding variable causee case marking and its interpretation are summarized in table 9.8. It is not surprising that accusative shows up consistently as the case neutral to or disfavoring the AGENT implicature, given that it is associated normally with undergoers; nor is it surprising that instrumental shows up consistently as the case favoring the AGENT implicature, since it is associated normally with secondary EFFECTORS that may under certain circumstances function as actors and in some of the languages marks the adjunct actor in a passive construction. What is perhaps surprising is that the dative case shows up in both columns, with contrasting interpretations, depending upon which case it is in opposition to. If it is in opposition to the instrumental, it disfavors the AGENT implicature, whereas if it is in opposition to the accusative, it favors the AGENT implicature. Comrie (1989b) expresses this in terms of a case hierarchy of instrumental > dative > accusative, where the higher-ranking case in the opposition correlates with a more agentive interpretation of the causee and the lower-ranking case with a less or non-agentive interpretation. This is, however, to be expected if the dative is the default case for (non-macrorole) core arguments, as argued in chapter 7. As the default case, it is not associated with any particular semantic content, unlike the cases normally associated with actor, undergoer, INSTRUMENT, etc., and its particular interpretation is a function of the opposition it enters into with a case which is consistently associated with some semantic content.

The idea of the dative as a default case seems to fly in the face of the intuition of many linguists that there is some kind of inherent meaning associated with the dative, namely 'experiencer' (see e.g. Wierzbicka 1980b, 1988), and the RRG approach to case marking has been explicitly criticized on this point (e.g. Haspelmath 1995b). However, such claims are difficult to maintain when all of the uses of the dative cross-linguistically are considered. The facts in table 9.8 certainly do not support such an interpretation of the dative, and the occurrence of multiple dative arguments in a single clause, each with a different interpretation (often having nothing to do with 'experiencer'), argues strongly against this idea. In the Icelandic double-dative construction in (7.35b), dative marks both THEME and RECIPIENT, as it does in the Georgian example in exercise 4 in chapter 7. Indeed, in Georgian the range of semantic arguments coded in the dative in different constructions covers virtually the entire Actor–Undergoer Hierarchy (see Van Valin 1990). In the French example in (9.77d) and the Turkish example in (9.80b), both the RECIPIENT and the causee are in the dative case. LaPolla (1995b) surveyed over 150 Tibeto-Burman languages and found that dative was normally used for GOAL/RECIPIENT and for direction of motion but rarely for EXPERIENCER. There are, of course, many examples in which dative does mark an 'experiencer'-type argument, e.g. (9.69) from Icelandic, but the cross-linguistic data do not support an analysis in which this particular use is taken as basic or prototypical.

9.3 Linking in complex noun phrases

The primary issue regarding linking in complex NPs concerns relative clauses, in particular, the linking of the head noun to both the matrix clause and to the relative clause, since it functions in both. There are two main types of relative clause, head-external and head-internal, and each presents a different linking problem: with head-external relatives, the problem is determining the function of the head inside the relative clause, whereas with head-internal relatives, the problem is determining which argument or adjunct in the relative clause also functions in the matrix clause. Within head-external relatives, the two main types are those which have a relative pronoun, such as in English relative clauses with *who* or *which*, and those which have no relative pronoun and a gap in the relative clause, as exemplified by the Malagasy and Jakaltek examples in (8.70) and by English sentences like *The man (that) I saw is a spy*. We will discuss how the linking works in each of the three types. We begin with the most common type cross-linguistically, externally headed relative clauses with no relative pronoun.

Both English and Malagasy have this type of relative clause, but Malagasy has an extra twist: the head noun must always function as the privileged syntactic argument (pragmatic pivot) of the relative clause (see (6.26)–(6.27)) (Keenan 1976b), while English lacks this restriction.

(9.91) a. Na-hita ny vehivavy (izay) nan-asa ny zaza Rakoto.[15]
PRFV.ATV-see DET woman CLM PRFV.ATV-wash DET child Rakoto
'Rakoto saw the woman that washed the child.'
*'Rakoto saw the woman that the child washed.'

a′. Na-hita ny zaza (izay) nan-asa ny vehivavy Rakoto.
PRFV.ATV-see DET child CLM PRFV.ATV-wash DET woman Rakoto
'Rakoto saw the child that washed the woman.'
*'Rakoto saw the child that the woman washed.'

a″. Na-hita ny zaza (izay) sas-an'ny vehivavy Rakoto.
PRFV.ATV-see DET child (CLM) wash-PASS-DET woman Rakoto
'Rakoto saw the child that was washed by the woman.'

b. Trevor talked to the woman (that) Colin introduced him to.

b′. Trevor talked to the woman *(that) introduced Colin to him.

In the first two of the Malagasy examples, the head noun, which precedes the relative clause, can only be interpreted as the privileged syntactic argument of the relative clause; since Malagasy is an accusative language and the voice of the verb is active, it is always interpreted as the actor. In the third example it is interpreted as the undergoer, because the voice of the verb in the relative clause is passive. The only restriction that English has on this construction is that if the head noun is the privileged syntactic argument of the relative clause, as in (b′), then the complementizer *that* is obligatory; otherwise it is optional.

The logical structure for (9.91a) is given in (9.92a), while the one for (9.91a″) is given in (9.92b).

(9.92) a. **see′** (Rakoto, [**be′** ($\underline{\text{vehivavy}}_i$, [**do′** ($x_i$, [**wash′** ($x_i$, zaza)])])])
b. **see′** (Rakoto, [**be′** ($\underline{\text{zaza}}_i$, [**do′** (vehivavy, [**wash′** (vehivavy, y_i)])])])

Following the convention introduced in section 4.7.3, the head noun in the complex nominal logical structure is indicated by underlining. The underlining indicates that *vehivavy* 'woman' will be interpreted as the argument of *-hita* 'see', not the entire logical structure, in (a); the same holds for *zaza* 'child' in (b). Restrictive relative clauses are modifiers like adjectives, and in section 4.7.5 we represented adjectival modifiers in an attributive logical structure, **be′** (x, [**pred′**]) (see (4.83)). Accordingly, we will use the same representation for restrictive relative clauses, with the logical structure of the relative clause filling the '**pred′**' slot in the attributive logical structure. While this is not a control construction, we may use the same mechanism for representing the function of the head noun within the logical structure of the relative clause; the head noun is coindexed with a lexically unfilled variable in the logical structure. In the linking from semantics to syntax, the head of the relative clause must be the privileged syntactic argument of the relative clause in Malagasy, and therefore if the head noun had been coindexed with a variable that would function

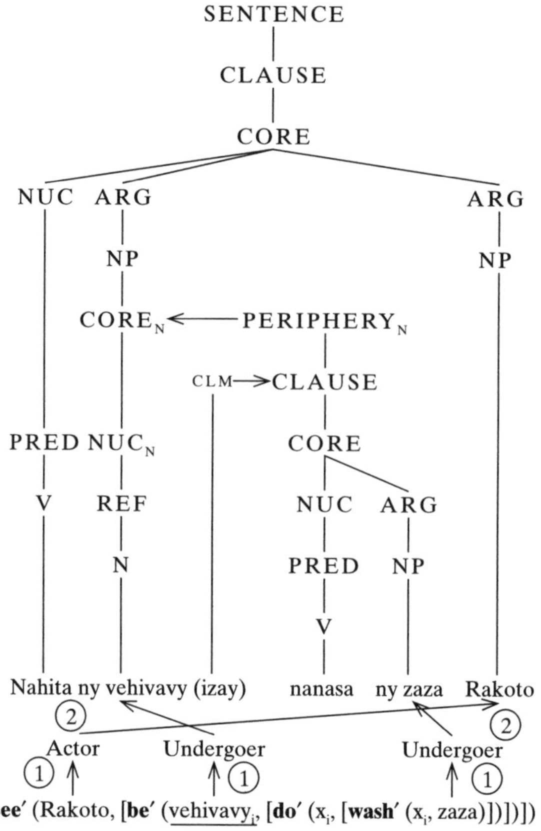

Figure 9.23 Linking from semantics to syntax in Malagasy relative clause in (9.91a)

as a non-actor, then passive or one of the other Malagasy voices would be necessary, as in (9.91a″) and (6.27). The linking from semantics to syntax in (9.91a) is illustrated in figure 9.23. The core template in the relative clause is missing a core argument position, one corresponding to the head noun, and so we must revise (9.60) to handle this. It already refers to syntactic arguments occurring in the precore slot, and this would account for relative clauses with relative pronouns. For other types of externally headed relative clause, however, there is no element in the precore slot, and therefore technically (9.60c3) does not apply to them. Since it is a universal feature of externally headed relative clauses that the core is missing an argument position when the head noun is a semantic argument of the verb or predicate in the relative clause, we should add the relative clause provision to (b), rather than (c) in (9.60). Nothing needs to be said regarding cases in which the head noun is not an argument of the verb in the relative clause, because peripheral constituents are always optional in the syntactic templates. The revised version is given in (9.93).

(9.93) a. *Syntactic template selection principle (revised formulation)*
The number of syntactic slots for arguments and argument-adjuncts within the core is equal to the number of distinct specified argument positions in the semantic representation of the core.

b. *Universal qualifications of the principle in (a)*
1 The occurrence of a core as either the matrix or linked core in a non-subordinate core juncture reduces the number of core slots by 1.
2 The occurrence of a core in an externally headed relative clause construction in which the head noun is a semantic argument of the predicate in the core reduces the number of core slots by 1.

c. *Language-specific qualifications of the principle in (a)*
1 All cores in the language have a minimum syntactic valence of 1.
2 Passive constructions reduce the number of core slots by 1.
3 The occurrence of a syntactic argument in the pre-/postcore slot reduces the number of core slots by 1 (may override (1)).

The main complication which relative clauses introduce to the linking from syntax to semantics is that when the relative clause is recognized, an attributive logical structure must be introduced into the argument position occupied by the head noun, with the head noun functioning as the first argument of it, and the logical structure of the verb in the relative clause filling the '**pred′**' slot in it. Since there will be an unlinked argument position in the semantics after all of the NPs in the clause are linked, the head must be linked to this position, in order to satisfy the Completeness Constraint. Hence it will be necessary to add a construction-specific condition to the linking specification in the constructional template for relative clauses to deal with these additional complexities; this would be a general condition which all constructional templates for relative clauses would have. It can be formulated as in (9.94).

(9.94) *Conditions governing linking from syntax to semantics in externally headed relative clauses*
a. Retrieve from the lexicon an attributive logical structure and substitute the logical structure of the verb in the relative clause for the *y* argument.
b. If there is no pre-/postcore slot element in the relative clause, then treat the head noun as if it were in the pre-/postcore slot for linking purposes; if there is an element in the pre-/postcore slot in the relative clause, coindex the head noun with it.
c. Coindex the *x* argument in the attributive logical structure with the argument in the relative clause logical structure linked to the head noun in (b).

The linking from syntax to semantics in (9.91a″) is given in figure 9.24. Since Malagasy has a rich voice system, the first step is to determine the voice of the verb in the main clause; since it is active, we may conclude that the privileged syntactic argument is the actor and that the NP immediately following the nucleus is the

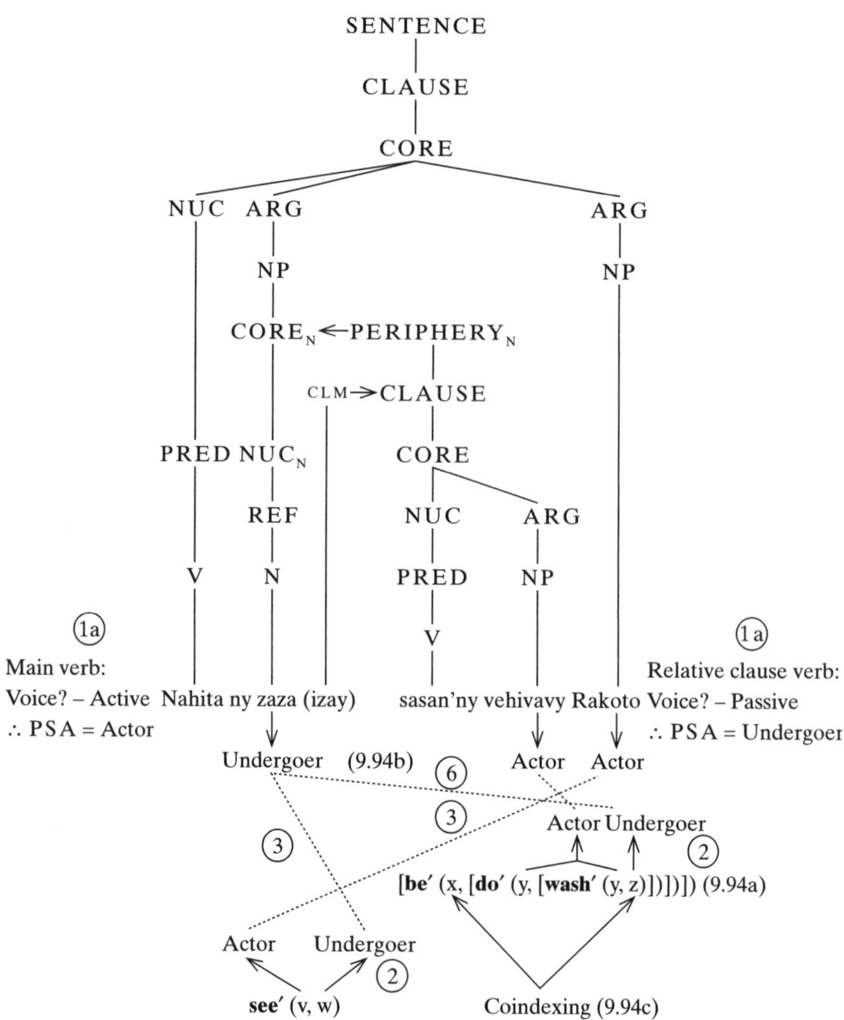

Figure 9.24 Linking from syntax to semantics in Malagasy relative clause in (9.91a″)

undergoer. With respect to the relative clause, the voice is passive, which means that the privileged syntactic argument is the undergoer and that the NP immediately following the nucleus is the actor. The head noun, *ny zaza* 'the child', is linked both to the second argument position in the logical structure of the matrix verb *-hita* 'see' and to the second argument position in the logical structure of the relative clause; this follows from the fact that Malagasy has a 'pivot-only' constraint on the function of the head noun and that, as we just noted, the voice of the verb indicates that the pivot is the undergoer. The two logical structures are related only indirectly through the common linking to the head noun. It would be a simple further step to replace the *w* variable in the matrix logical structure with the attributive logical structure after the coindexing mandated by (9.94c), yielding the logical structure in (9.92b). The use of step 6 in the linking algorithm to relate the head noun to the empty argument position in the relative clause logical structure is justified by the fact that in languages with this type of relative clause construction, there is a strong structural similarity, sometimes virtual identity, between WH-question, topicalization/cleft and relative clause constructions. This is illustrated for Malagasy in (9.95) and for Jakaltek in (9.96) (Craig 1977).

(9.95) a. Iza no nan-asa ny zaza?   Malagasy
who PRT ATV-wash DET child
'Who washed the child?'

b. Ny zaza no sas-an'ny vehivavy.
DET child PRT wash-PASS-DET woman
'It is the child who was washed by the woman.'

(9.96) a. W-ohtaj [ix ix x-Ø-(y)-il naj winaj].   Jakaltek
1sgERG-know CL woman PST-3ABS-3ERG-see CL man
'I know the woman the man saw.'

b. Mac x-Ø-(y)-il naj winaj?
who PST-3ABS-3ERG-see CL man
'Whom did the man see?'

c. Ha' ix ix x-Ø-(y)-il naj winaj.
CL woman PST-3ABS-3ERG-see CL man
'It is the woman the man saw.'

With the exception of the occurrence of the particle *no* in WH-questions and clefts, the structure of the three constructions in Malagasy is virtually the same. The identity is complete in the three constructions in Jakaltek. The head noun + relative clause is in square brackets in (9.96a), so that this sequence can be compared with the sentences in (b) and (c). In both languages, the three constructions are subject to the same 'syntactic-pivot only' linking constraint, and accordingly, it is entirely reasonable to use the linking step that handles clefts/topicalizations (which seem to be the same construction in these languages) and WH-questions for handling the head nouns of relative clauses.

The constructional template for Malagasy relative clauses is given in table 9.9. The externally headed relative clause template was given in figure 8.38.

The logical structure of relative clauses with relative pronouns differs from those discussed above only in that instead of the logical structure of the verb in the relative clause containing a lexically unfilled variable, the WH-word fills that position

Table 9.9 *Constructional template for Malagasy relative clause constructions*

CONSTRUCTION

Malagasy relative clause construction

SYNTAX

Juncture: NP
Nexus: Subordination
Construction type: Clausal modifier
Unit template(s): Main clause: Default
Relative clause template: External head
Relative clause: Default, [–PrCS]
PSA: Head noun = variable syntactic pivot of relative clause
Linking: Semantics → syntax – If actor ≠ syntactic pivot, then marked voice
Syntax → semantics – (9.94)

MORPHOLOGY

CLM *izay* (optional)

SEMANTICS

Restrictive modifier; **be′** (x_i, [**pred′** (. . . y_i . . .)]), where *y* is lexically unfilled

PRAGMATICS

Illocutionary force: None (outside of potential focus domain)
Focus structure: All elements are non-focal

and is coindexed with the head. An example of this type of relative clause from English and its logical structure are given in (9.97).

(9.97) a. I liked the cars which were destroyed yesterday.
b. **like′** (1sg, [**be′** (cars$_i$, [**yesterday′** ([**do′** (∅, ∅)] CAUSE [BECOME **destroyed′** (which$_i$)])])])

The linking from semantics to syntax follows the linking algorithm in (9.1), and the relative pronoun is linked to the precore slot, just as a WH-word is in a WH-question. The linking for (9.97a) is given in figure 9.25. The linking from syntax to semantics parallels that for the Malagasy example, with the exception that instead of linking the head noun directly with the logical structure of the relative clause, it is coindexed with the WH-word in the precore slot, which is linked to the logical structure of the relative clause. This is given in figure 9.26. The relationship between the two main logical structures is expressed by the coindexing required by (9.94b). In order to integrate the two logical structures, the *x* argument in the attributive logical structure must be coindexed with the argument in the embedded logical structure which is coindexed as required by (9.94b), following (9.94c). The whole

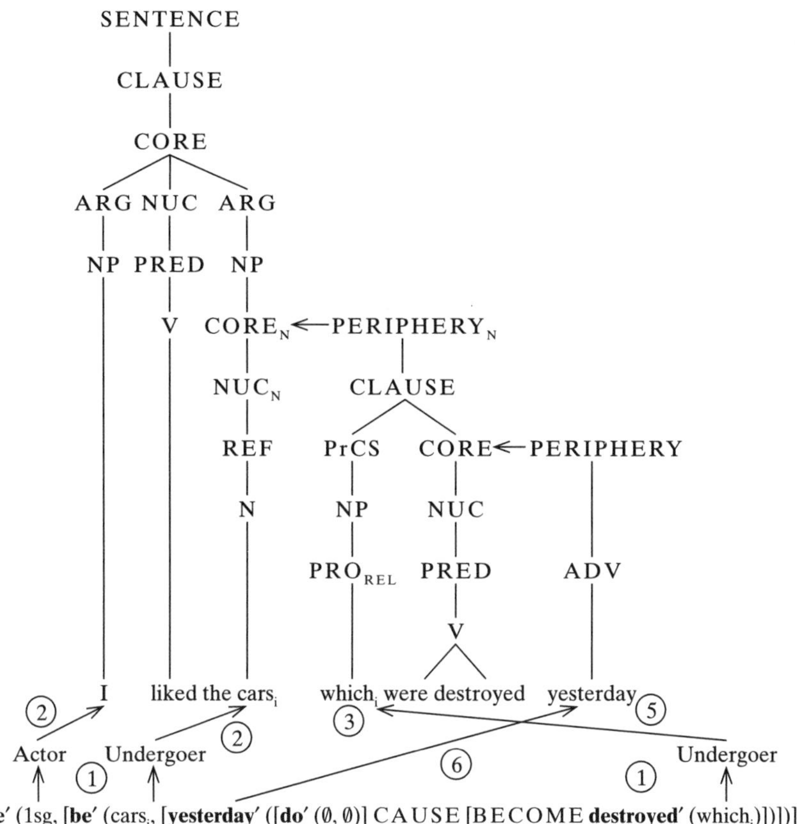

Figure 9.25 Linking from semantics to syntax in English relative clause in (9.97a)

attributive logical structure then fills the matrix verb logical structure argument variable which was coindexed with the relative pronoun by (9.94b). The particular example contains the added complication of the peripheral adverbial *yesterday*, which requires retrieving its logical structure from the lexicon and integrating it with the logical structure of the verb in the relative clause, following step 5. The result of the linking, when all of the logical structures are integrated, is (9.97b). Several crucial steps in the linking are supplied by the construction-specific linking requirements in (9.94), which are stated in the constructional templates for English relative clauses given in table 9.10 on page 599. There is obviously a great deal of overlap between the two templates, but each type of relative clause has enough distinct features to warrant its own template. Aside from the lack of a pivot for relativization in English, the template for the non-relative pronoun construction is otherwise basically the same as its Malagasy counterpart.

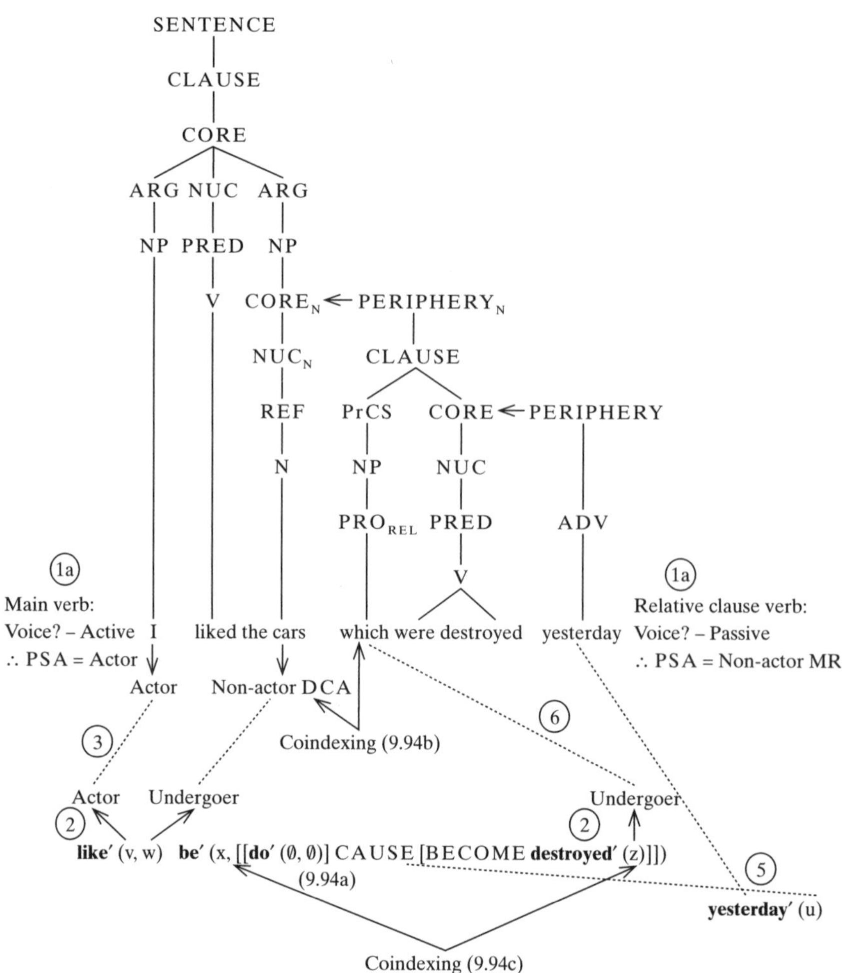

Figure 9.26 Linking from syntax to semantics in English WH-relative clause in (9.97)

We now turn to internally headed relative clauses. They present a very different linking problem from externally headed relatives. In this construction there is no problem determining the function of the head within the relative clause, since it occurs overtly in it; rather, the problem is determining which NP inside the relative clause is the head. Examples of internally headed relative clauses from Lakhota and Bambara (Bird 1968) are given below; the head nouns are in italics.

(9.98) a. Wičháša ki [[šų́ka ki *igmú eyá* wičhá-∅-yaxtake] ki hená]
man the dog the cat some 3plU-3sgA-bite the those
wą-wíčha-∅-yąke yelo.
3plU-3sgA-see DEC
'The man saw the cats which the dog bit.'

Table 9.10 *Constructional templates for English relative clause constructions*

CONSTRUCTION
English relative clause construction (without relative pronoun)

SYNTAX
Juncture: NP
Nexus: Subordination
Construction type: Clausal modifier
Unit template(s): Main clause: Default
Relative clause template: External head
Relative clause: Default, [–PrCS]
PSA: None
Linking: Syntax → semantics – (9.94)

MORPHOLOGY
CLM *that* (required if head noun = PSA of subordinate clause; otherwise optional)

SEMANTICS
Restrictive modifier; **be′** (x_i, [**pred′** (. . . y_i . . .)]), where *y* is lexically unfilled

PRAGMATICS
Illocutionary force: None (outside of potential focus domain)
Focus structure: All elements are non-focal

CONSTRUCTION
English relative clause construction (without relative pronoun)

SYNTAX
Juncture: NP
Nexus: Subordination
Construction type: Clausal modifier
Unit template(s): Main clause: Default
Relative clause template: External head
Relative clause: Default, [+PrCS]
PSA: None
Linking: Syntax → semantics – (9.94)

MORPHOLOGY
WH-relative pronouns

SEMANTICS
Restrictive modifier; **be′** (x_i, [**pred′** (. . . y_i . . .)]), where *y* is relative pronoun

PRAGMATICS
Illocutionary force: None (outside of potential focus domain)
Focus structure: All elements are non-focal

b. Wičháša ki [[*šų́ka wą* igmú óta wičhá-∅-yaxtake] ki he]
man the dog a cat many 3plU-3sgA-bite the that
wą-∅-∅-yą́ke yelo.
3sgU-3sgA-see DEC
'The man saw the dog which bit many cats.'

c. Wičháša ki [[šų́ka wą igmú wą ∅-∅-yaxtáke] ki he] wą-∅-∅-yą́ke
man the dog a cat a 3sgU-3sgA-bite the that 3sgU-3sgA-see
yelo.
DEC
'The man saw the cat which a dog bit', or 'The man saw the dog which bit a cat.'

(9.99) a. Ne ye so ye. Bambara
1sg PAST horse see
'I saw a horse.'

b. [Ne ye *so* min ye] tye ye san.
1sg PAST horse REL see man PAST buy
'The man bought the horse that I saw.'

In the Lakhota construction, the NP interpreted as the head noun is cross-referenced on the matrix verb, indicating its status as a core argument in the matrix core, and it is obligatorily indefinite within the relative clause, its true definiteness status being indicated by the article + demonstrative following the verb at the end of the relative clause. In (9.98a, b) the actor in the relative clause is singular and the undergoer plural, and therefore the head is clear both from the form of the cross-referencing pronominal on the matrix verb and also from the form of the demonstrative at the end of the relative clause. If, however, both NPs in the relative clause are singular and indefinite, as in (c), then the resulting construction is ambiguous, since in principle either NP within the relative clause can be interpreted as the head. In the Bambara construction in (9.99b), the relative marker *min* follows the head noun within the relative clause.

The logical structures for internally-headed relative clauses are basically the same as their counterparts for externally-headed relative clauses, i.e. [. . . (x, [**be′** (y_i, [**pred′** (. . . y_i . . .) . . .])] . . .], but instead of lexically filling the first *y* argument and leaving the second one either unfilled or filled by a relative pronoun, the first *y* argument is left unfilled and the second one is lexically filled; the coindexing is the same in both types of relative clauses. The logical structure for (9.99b) is given in (9.100).

(9.100) [**do′** (tye, ∅)] CAUSE [BECOME **have′** (tye, [**be′** (y_i, [**see′** (1sg, $\underline{so_i}$)])])]

The lexically unfilled *y* argument will not be linked to a core argument position in the matrix core, whereas both arguments of *ye* 'see' will be linked into the core of the relative clause, and this clause will then be linked into the open core argument

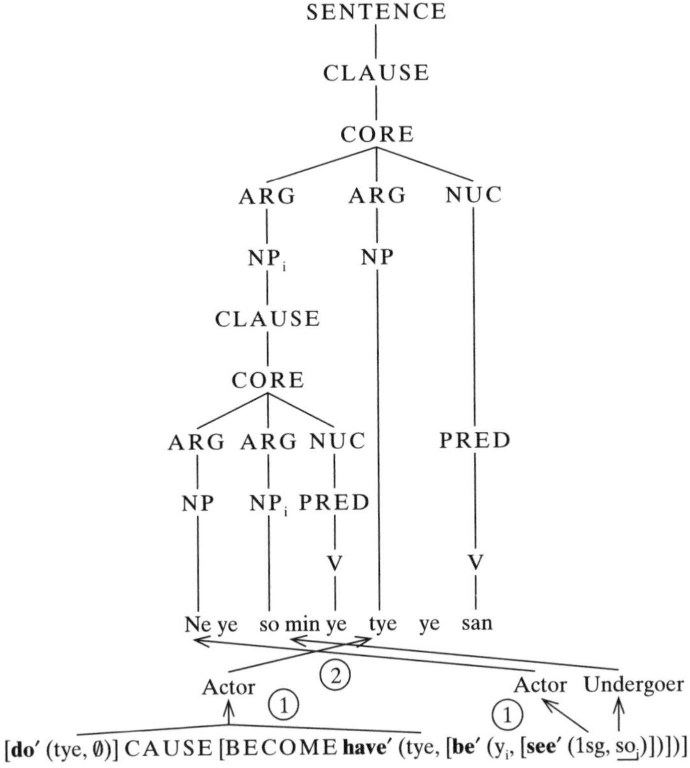

Figure 9.27 Linking from semantics to syntax in Bambara internally headed relative clause

slot in the matrix clause. This is illustrated in figure 9.27. The coindexing of the matrix core argument NP node with the core argument NP node inside the relative clause mirrors the coindexing in the logical structure.

The Lakhota examples present a more complex linking problem, because it is a head-marking language. As we argued in chapter 7, each argument position in a logical structure is obligatorily filled by a pronominal element and may also be optionally filled by a full NP as well; the pronominal will link to the verb and be realized as a bound marker, while the NP will appear in a clause-internal but core-external position. Given the full complement of NPs in the examples in (9.98), all of the argument positions will be doubly filled in the logical structure. In addition, it is necessary to represent the NP operators for the head noun, since they are an obligatory part of its coding. A partial semantic representation for (9.98a) is given in (9.101).

(9.101) **see′** (3sg[wičháša], ⟨$_{\text{DEF}}$+ ⟨$_{\text{DEIC}}$ *DIST* ⟨$_{\text{NUM}}$ *PL* [**be′** (3_i[x_i], [**do′** (3sg[šų́ka], [**bite′** (3sg[šų́ka], ⟨$_{\text{DEF}}$u ⟨$_{\text{NUM}}$ *PL* (3_i[<u>igmú$_i$</u>])⟩⟩)])])]⟩⟩⟩)

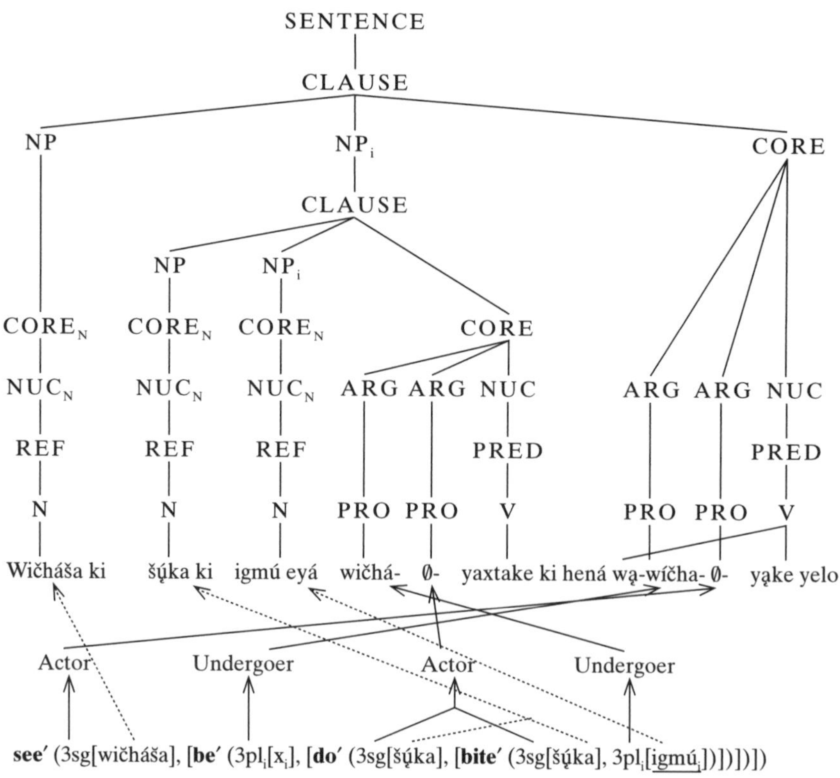

Figure 9.28 Linking from semantics to syntax in Lakhota internally headed relative clause

In the case of a head-marking language, leaving the first argument in the attributive logical structure lexically unfilled means that no full NP is possible, but the pronominal argument must be there, as it is coded on the verb in the matrix clause. NP operators are represented only for the head noun; hence for it the pronominal is designated '3' with no number specification, since that is signalled by the number operator, whereas the other pronominals are coded as '3sg'. The definiteness operator is crucial, since, as noted above, the head noun must be coded as indefinite internally to the relative clause with its true definiteness value signaled externally. In the semantic representation of (9.98a), the definiteness value of the NP is coded in the NP operators which modify the attributive logical structure containing the representation of the relative clause; for the head noun itself, its definiteness value is left unspecified ('u'), which is formally realized by an indefinite-specific article. The linking from semantics to syntax in (9.98a) is given in figure 9.28; the dashed lines indicate the linking of the full NPs to their core-external positions, while the non-dashed lines indicate the linking of the pronominal arguments to the verbs. The logical structure has been simplified for ease of interpretation. Again, the coindexing on the NP nodes in the constituent projection mirrors the coindexing within the logical structure. It should be noted that if there were no overt NPs in the sentence, as in *Wičháyaxtake ki hená wąwíčhayake*, it would mean 'I saw the ones that he/she/it bit.'

The linking from syntax to semantics for internally headed relative clauses does not follow all of the conditions in (9.94); (a) still applies, (c) must be modified slightly, but (b), which refers specifically to the external head, is inapplicable. It must be replaced by a specification that the NP functioning as head inside the relative clause should be linked to the open argument position in the matrix verb's logical structure. The head is normally readily identifiable: in Lakhota it must be indefinite, while in Bambara it is marked by the relativizer *min*. The constraints on the linking from syntax to semantics in internally headed relative clauses are given in (9.102).

(9.102) *Conditions governing linking from syntax to semantics in internally headed relative clauses*

a. Retrieve from the lexicon an attributive logical structure and substitute the logical structure of the verb in the relative clause for the *y* argument.
b. Link the NP marked as the head noun within the relative clause with the open argument position in the logical structure of the matrix core (including adjuncts).
c. Coindex the *x* argument in the attributive logical structure with the argument in the relative clause logical structure identified as the head noun in (b).

The linking from syntax to semantics in (9.99b) is given in figure 9.29. Bambara has no voice oppositions, and therefore the interpretation of the arguments can be determined directly from their position in the clause in step 1f. Because *so* 'horse' is marked by *min*, the relative marker, it is interpreted as the head noun and linked to the open argument position in the matrix verbs's logical structure, following (9.102b). The two logical structures are now indirectly connected via the double linking of the head noun *so* 'horse'. If the two logical structures are integrated by substituting the attributive logical structure for the *w* variable in the matrix logical structure, the result is the logical structure in (9.100).

The constructional templates for internally headed relative clauses in Lakhota and Bambara are given in table 9.11 on p. 605. No special syntactic template for these internally headed relative clauses is required, because they involve an NP dominating a clause.

The new feature which linking in relative clauses has introduced is construction-specific constraints on the linking algorithms, specifically the syntax to semantics algorithm. Since they are construction-specific, they need not be part of the general algorithms and need only be stated once and referred to then by the constructional templates for relative clauses.

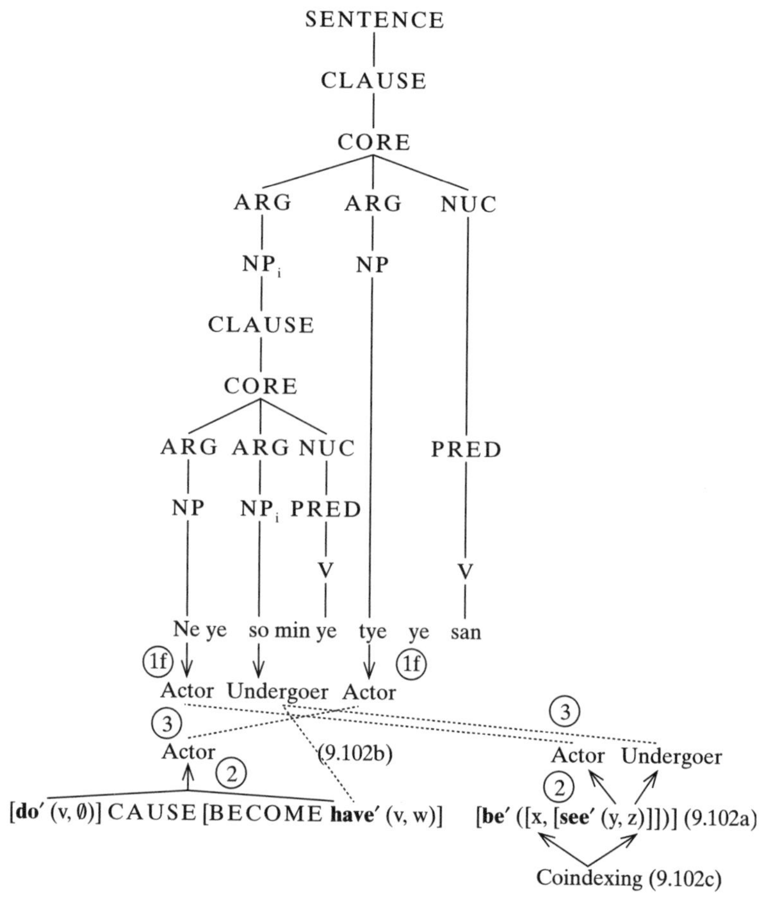

Figure 9.29 Linking from syntax to semantics in Bambara internally headed relative clause

9.4 Reflexivization in complex sentences

In section 7.5 we presented a set of principles which govern reflexivization in simple sentences, i.e. constructions with a single nucleus in a single core in a single clause. They are repeated in (9.103).

(9.103) a. *Role Hierarchy Condition on reflexivization*
The reflexive pronoun must not be higher on (7.1) (as applied to selection of privileged syntactic arguments in the language) than its antecedent. (= (7.117))

b. *Logical structure superiority (LS-superiority)*
A constituent P in logical structure is LS-superior to a constituent Q iff there is a constituent R in logical structure such that

Table 9.11 *Constructional templates for Bambara and Lakhota internally headed relative clauses*

CONSTRUCTION
Bambara relative clause construction (internally headed)

SYNTAX
Juncture: NP
Nexus: Subordination
Construction type: Clausal NP
Unit template(s): Main clause: Default
Relative clause template: None
Relative clause: Default
PSA: None
Linking: Syntax → semantics – (9.102)

MORPHOLOGY
Head marked by *min*

SEMANTICS
Restrictive modifier; **be′** (x_i, [**pred′** (. . . y_i . . .)]), where *y* is lexically unfilled

PRAGMATICS
Illocutionary force: None (outside of potential focus domain)
Focus structure: All elements are non-focal

CONSTRUCTION
Lakhota relative clause construction (internally headed; definite restrictive)

SYNTAX
Juncture: NP
Nexus: Subordination
Construction type: Clausal NP
Unit template(s): Main clause: Default
Relative clause template: None
Relative clause: Default
PSA: None
Linking: Syntax → semantics – (9.102)

MORPHOLOGY
Head must be marked indefinite-specific
Clause nominalized by determiners realizing definiteness and deictic operators of head noun

SEMANTICS
Restrictive modifier; **be′** (x_i, [**pred′** (. . . y_i . . .)]), where *x* is lexically unfilled

PRAGMATICS
Illocutionary force: None (outside of potential focus domain)
Focus structure: All elements are non-focal

(i.) Q is a constituent of R, and
(ii.) P and R are primary arguments of the same logical structure.

c. *Superiority Condition on reflexivization*
A bound variable may not be LS-superior to its binder. (= (7.120))

d. *Domain of Obligatory Reflexivization Constraint*
One of two coreferring semantic co-arguments within a simple clause must be realized as a reflexive, while one of two coreferring syntactic arguments (which are not semantic co-arguments) within a simple clause may be realized as a reflexive. (= (7.129))

These constraints were intended to handle examples like those in (9.104), repeated from (7.114).

(9.104) a. The woman$_i$ sent the book to herself$_i$/*her$_i$.
b. Barbara$_i$ saw a snake near her$_i$/*herself$_i$.
c. Pamela$_i$ got some spaghetti sauce on her$_i$/herself$_i$.

These constraints govern what is an acceptable antecedent (Role Hierarchy and Superiority Conditions) and what the domain of reflexivization is (Obligatory Reflexivization Constraint). The formulation of the latter constraint also has implications for the acceptability of potential antecedents; since it refers to coreferring arguments within a clause, it requires that both the antecedent and the reflexive be syntactic arguments either in the core or the precore slot. Complex sentences present challenges to both of these issues. With respect to the first issue, nuclear junctures create composite logical structures; do all of the arguments in the derived logical structures behave like those in the logical structures of simple verbs? Matrix-coding constructions treat semantic arguments from different verbs as syntactic co-arguments; is reflexivization obligatory or optional in this instance? With respect to the second, it is well known that some languages allow what is known as 'long-distance reflexivization', as illustrated in the following Icelandic example (Thráinsson 1991).

(9.105) Jón-Ø$_i$ sag-ð-i að ég hef-ð-i
John-MsgNOM say-PAST-3sg CLM 1sgNOM have.SBJ-PAST-1sg
svik-ið sig$_i$.
betray-PSTP SELF
'John$_i$ said that I had betrayed himself$_i$.'

The ungrammaticality of the English translation indicates that this construction is not found in English. In the following two sections, we will address the problems raised by nuclear junctures and non-subordinate core junctures (section 9.4.1) and then those raised by long-distance reflexives (section 9.4.2).

9.4.1 Reflexivization in nuclear and core junctures

Nuclear junctures raise the issue of just exactly what counts as a semantic co-argument in a derived, composite logical structure. Examples of reflexives in nuclear junctures from French, German and Jakaltek, along with their (in some cases simplified) logical structures, are given in (9.106).

(9.106) a. Marie se fer-a aid-er par Pierre. — French
REFL make-3sgFUT help-INF by
'Marie will make Pierre help her.'

a′. [**do′** (∅, ∅)] CAUSE [**do′** (Pierre, [**help′** (Pierre, Marie)])]

a″. *Marie se fer-a aid-er à Pierre.
REFL make-3sgFUT help-INF DAT

b. Maria ließ sich von Peter küss-en. — German
make.PAST REFL by kiss-INF
'Maria made/let Peter kiss her.'

b′. [**do′** (Maria$_i$, ∅)] CAUSE [**do′** (Peter, [**kiss′** (Peter, SELF$_i$)])]

b″. *Maria ließ sich Peter küss-en.
make.PAST REFL kiss-INF

b‴. Marie ließ Peter sich küssen.
'Marie made/let Peter kiss himself.' /*'Maria made/let Peter kiss her.'

c. X-∅-w-a' maka-' hin-ba t-aw-et. — Jakaltek
PAST-3ABS-1sgERG-make hit-INF 1sgERG-self AUG-2sgERG-to
'I made you hit me.' (lit. 'I made you hit myself')

c′. [**do′** (1sg$_i$, ∅)] CAUSE [**do′** (2sg, [**hit′** (2sg, SELF$_i$)])]

In the Jakaltek example, the reflexive NP *hin-ba* 'my-self' is cross-referenced by the third-person absolutive marker on the verb. Reflexivization is obligatory in all of these constructions; replacing the reflexive by a non-reflexive pronoun results in an obligatory disjoint reference interpretation, i.e. the pronoun cannot be interpreted as referring to the actor. In the coreference reflexives in German and Jakaltek, the antecedent and the reflexive are technically semantic arguments of distinct logical structures. The binder is the actor of the causative verb, which has the logical structure [**do′** (x, ∅)] CAUSE [. . .], while the reflexive is an argument of the complement logical structure. However, the resulting composite logical structure is exactly like the logical structure of many causative accomplishment, achievement or activity verbs, and accordingly it does count as a single logical structure with a single set of arguments for the purposes of the constraint in (9.103d). Supporting this is the fact that the antecedent is in every case the actor of the core and the reflexive is the undergoer; hence, they are semantic co-arguments also with respect to macrorolehood. Nuclear junctures, then, necessitate no revision of the principles in (9.103).

In both French and German, it is possible to code the causee of a base transitive verb in one of two ways, either in the dative or as a passive agent adjunct in French, or either in the accusative or as a passive agent adjunct in German. In the examples in (9.106), however, only the passive agent adjunct coding is possible. Why should this be the case? The answer is different for the two languages, because the German construction is a coreference reflexive, while the French one is a clitic reflexive. An important clue to the answer for the German example comes when we look at the alternative causee codings, as in the (b″) example. It is ungrammatical, at least with the intended meaning, and native speakers report that they can give it an odd interpretation with the causee as a possible but strongly disfavored controller; in fact, it seems to be confused with (b‴) which has a very different meaning. Hence it appears that the motivation for treating the causee as an adjunct is to eliminate it as a possible controller of the reflexive, thereby preventing ambiguity from arising in a potentially ambiguous construction.

The situation with the French clitic construction is somewhat different. As we argued in section 7.5.3, *se* signals the suppression of the highest-ranking argument in the logical structure, and this is represented in (9.106a′). There is, however, another potential actor, *Pierre*, the EFFECTOR of *aider*. If, however, it were actor and linked to pivot, the sentence would get the wrong interpretation, namely that *Pierre* is the actor of *faire*. In order to ensure the correct interpretation, the actor of the embedded verb must be treated as an adjunct. The undergoer of *aider* appears as the privileged syntactic argument, and as we argued in section 7.5.3, it is interpreted as actor and undergoer simultaneously; since *Pierre* is explicitly marked as the actor of *aider*, the sentence can only be interpreted as Marie making Pierre help her, which is the correct interpretation.

Core junctures do raise a number of important questions, however. As we have seen, English does not appear to allow reflexivization across a core boundary within a clause containing a core juncture, but other languages do, as the following example from Icelandic (Maling 1986) illustrates.

(9.107) Harald-ur$_i$ skipa-ð-i mér að rak-a sig$_i$.
Harold-MsgNOM order-PAST-3sg 1sgDAT CLM shave-INF SELF
'Harold$_i$ ordered me to shave himself$_i$.'

We will deal with the issues raised by these constructions in the next section on long-distance reflexivization. Control constructions in English and other languages of the type illustrated in (9.108) pose no problems for (9.103).

(9.108) a. Max persuaded himself to call Dana.
b. Sally persuaded Tom to perjure himself.

The undergoer of *persuade* is a semantic argument of both verbs, and therefore it is a semantic co-argument of *Max* in (a) and of *himself* in (b). Hence both of these sentences meet the condition in (9.103d). A construction which does present a problem for (9.103d) is reflexivization in the matrix-coding construction, as illustrated in (9.109).

(9.109) a. $Laura_i$ believed $herself_i$/*her_i to have been elected treasurer.
b. $Miguel_i$ believes $himself_i$/*him_i to be the heir to the Spanish throne.

Because *Laura* and *herself* are arguments of different logical structures, the Role Hierarchy Condition as formulated in (9.103a) does not apply to them, since it refers to the arguments of a single logical structure. However, **Herself believed Laura to have been elected treasurer* is ruled out by the Superiority Condition in (b); since *herself* in this sentence is an argument of the matrix logical structure and *Laura* is an argument in the embedded logical structure, the reflexive is LS-superior to its binder, which violates this condition. On the other hand, reflexivization is obligatory in this construction, and yet the antecedent and the reflexive are not semantic co-arguments; *Laura* and *Miguel* are semantic arguments of *believe*, and the reflexive is a semantic argument of the embedded logical structure, as we discussed in section 9.1.3.2. Accordingly the problem lies with (9.103d). Replacing 'semantic co-arguments within a core' with 'syntactic co-arguments within a core', for example, would work fine for the sentences in (9.109) and (9.108a), but it would not work for (9.108b), since *Tom* and *himself* are in different cores, or for the sentences in (9.110), in which the antecedent and the reflexive are also in different cores.

(9.110) a. $Tanisha_i$ seems to have injured $herself_i$/*her_i.
b. $Hamid_i$ was believed to have recognized $himself_i$/*him_i in the picture.

If we were to change the restriction to 'syntactic co-arguments within a clause', which would cover all of these cases, we would then have no explanation for the ungrammaticality of the English equivalent to (9.107), **Harold ordered me to shave himself.* The primary difference between this sentence and the ones in (9.108b) and (9.110) is that the antecedent and the reflexive are not semantic co-arguments in **Harold ordered me to shave himself*, while they are semantic co-arguments in (9.108b) and (9.110). This strongly suggests that in English the domain restriction on the reflexivization of semantic co-arguments is different from the domain restriction on the reflexivization of co-referring syntactic arguments which are not semantic co-arguments. Thus, the domain restrictions seem to be as in (9.111).

(9.111) *Domain restrictions on obligatory reflexivization in English*
a. Co-referring semantic co-arguments: can be in different cores within a clause.
b. Co-referring syntactic co-arguments which are not semantic co-arguments: cannot be in different cores within a clause (one may be in PrCS with co-argument in adjacent core).

This contrast falls out from the linking algorithms for complex sentences we have developed, in particular the syntax to semantics linking algorithm in (9.54).

Semantic co-arguments are by definition part of the same logical structure in the semantic representation of the sentence, and therefore it is possible to recover their cosemantic argumenthood across core boundaries in non-subordinate core junctures but not across clause boundaries, since clauses link independently of each other. In matrix-coding constructions like (9.109), the controller in the matrix core is linked to an argument position in the same logical structure as the reflexive; hence, even if they are in different cores, the controller and the reflexive will be linked to argument positions in the same logical structure. In control constructions like (9.108b), in which the controller and the reflexive are in different cores, the theory of control in (9.33) links the controller in the matrix core to an argument position in the same logical structure as the reflexive. This is not the case in **Harold ordered me to shave himself*, however; *Harold* is a semantic argument of *order* and *himself* of *shave*. They are not semantic co-arguments and are not in the same core, and therefore the sentence is ungrammatical. Because the obligatory sharing of a semantic argument in non-subordinate core junctures is the basis of the semantic co-argumenthood across a core boundary, this analysis predicts that reflexivization across core boundaries should not be possible in core subordination, due to the lack of any argument sharing, and this is correct, as (9.112) shows.

(9.112) a. *Dana$_i$ regretted Bob's kissing herself$_i$.
b. *Debra$_i$ wanted very much for Sam to kiss herself$_i$.

We may predict, moreover, that the clause will universally be the syntactic domain for obligatory reflexivization of semantic co-arguments. On the other hand, there is nothing in the linking system that would constrain the interpretation of syntactic (co-)arguments which are not semantic co-arguments, and therefore we would predict that languages will vary quite substantially with respect to the treatment of syntactic arguments of this type. This is exactly what we see in (9.107): in Icelandic coreferring syntactic co-arguments which are not semantic co-arguments can have a domain larger than a core, while in English they cannot. Indeed, Icelandic reflexivization is not even restricted by clause boundaries in some cases, as (9.105) shows.

We must, then, reformulate the Domain of Obligatory Reflexivization Constraint for English in (9.103d) as in (9.113).

(9.113) *Obligatory Reflexivization Constraint in English*
a. For semantic co-arguments, the domain of obligatory reflexivization is the clause: one of two coreferring core arguments which are semantic co-arguments must be realized as a reflexive.
b. For co-referring syntactic co-arguments that are not semantic co-arguments, the domain of possible reflexivization is the core (and the precore slot):
1 if they are both direct arguments, then one of them must be realized as a reflexive;

2 if the lower-ranking one in terms of (9.103a) is an argument-adjunct, then it may optionally be realized as a reflexive, subject to semantic conditions.

The condition in (a) accounts for the sentences in (9.104a), (9.108) and (9.110); the condition in (b1) accounts for the obligatory reflexives in (9.109), while the one in (b2) accounts for the possibility of reflexivization in (9.104b, c). The semantic condition of affectedness, proposed by Kuno and discussed in section 7.5.2, accounts for the impossibility of the reflexive in (b) and its possibility in (c). Thus, it appears that English does in fact have a type of long-distance reflexivization, namely reflexivization involving semantic co-arguments across a core boundary. It does not, however, have long-distance reflexivization involving syntactic arguments which are not semantic co-arguments, unlike Icelandic and many other languages.

9.4.2 Long-distance reflexivization

The phenomena which fall under the heading of 'long-distance reflexivization' are varied indeed, ranging from grammatically-controlled constructions like (9.107) to essentially discourse uses of reflexives (cf. e.g. Zribi-Hertz 1989, Zubin, Chun and Li 1990). As discussed in section 7.5, we will limit our discussion to argument reflexives and will not discuss reflexive possessors or picture reflexives, and we will further restrict ourselves to grammatically controlled argument reflexives, following Pollard and Sag (1992). As with local reflexivization, the two primary issues are (1) delimiting the domain in which reflexivization can occur and (2) determining the constraints on possible antecedents. Ideally, there should be one set of constraints which govern both local and long-distance reflexivization, with languages varying in terms of which constraints are in effect in them. With respect to possible binders, there will again be a set of very general constraints, those in (9.103a, c), and some constraints specific to particular reflexive morphemes, such as the conditions on the Norwegian reflexives presented in (7.128) and repeated below.

(9.114) a. *Seg selv*: must be bound by the highest-ranking argument in the clause (in terms of the privileged syntactic argument selection principles for Norwegian).
b. *Ham selv*: must not be bound by the highest-ranking argument in the clause (in terms of the privileged syntactic argument selection principles for Norwegian).

These will need to be revised as we develop the general framework for the analysis of reflexivization, but they illustrate two very common item-specific restrictions on reflexives: a requirement that a reflexive be bound by a 'subject', as in (a), and one that it be bound by a 'non-subject' in (b).

Our purpose here is not to present a comprehensive overview of long-distance reflexivization phenomena; Koster and Reuland (1991) and Dalrymple (1993) present

Table 9.12 *Syntactic domains for reflexivization, from Dalrymple (1993)*

Syntactic domain	*Definition in LFG*	*Definition in terms of LSC*
Co-argument domain	Arguments of syntactic PRED	Core [–argument-adjuncts]
Minimal complete nucleus	Minimal domain with a SUBJ	Core [+argument-adjuncts]
Minimal finite domain	Minimal domain with TENSE	Clause
Root S	Entire sentence	Sentence

such surveys. Rather, our interest is in arriving at a set of principles which constrain linking in complex sentences. Dalrymple (1993) formulates such a set in LFG terms, and we will adopt her approach and adapt it into our framework. She argues that there are four possible syntactic domains for grammatically controlled reflexivization. They are presented in table 9.12, in which the equivalents in terms of the layered structure of the clause and our linking theory are given. What is perhaps surprising about this table is that we have already seen and discussed all of these domains. The sentence as a reflexivization domain is illustrated in the Icelandic example in (9.105), and the clause as a possible domain is exemplified in (9.107)–(9.110). The contrast between 'co-argument domain' and 'minimal complete nucleus' is illustrated in (9.104); in (a), the PP *to herself* is in the co-argument domain, since it is an oblique core argument, whereas the PPs *near her* and *on her/herself* in (b) and (c), being argument-adjuncts and not oblique core arguments, are outside the co-argument domain but within the minimal complete nucleus. We have already seen that these two types of PP have different properties with respect to reflexivization in English, as it is obligatory for oblique core arguments but optional for argument-adjuncts. Dalrymple cites the following Norwegian examples from Hellan (1988) to illustrate this contrast.

(9.115) a. *Hun kast-et meg fra seg selv.
3FsgNOM throw-PAST 1sgACC from SELF
'She$_i$ threw me away from herself$_i$.'

b. De kast-et meg til og fra hverandre.
3plNOM throw-PAST 1sgACC to and from each.other
'They threw me to and from each other.'

Dalrymple argues that this contrast motivates the distinction between 'co-argument domain' and 'minimal complete nucleus'; *seg selv* 'him/herself' must be a co-argument of its antecedent, whereas *hverandre* 'each other' need only be within the 'minimal complete nucleus'. In our terms, this means that *seg selv* must be a co-core argument (which in simple clauses means a semantic co-argument) of its antecedent; hence it must be a direct or oblique core argument in the core. *Hverandre*, on the other hand, can be an argument-adjunct, as in (b), and therefore it need not be a semantic co-argument of its antecedent. Both reflexives must, however, occur within the same core as their antecedent.

It should be noted that other factors may interact with the domain conditions to constrain reflexivization. Three will be mentioned briefly here. First, reflexivization across clause boundaries is often affected by the mood of the subordinate clause. The embedded finite clause in the Icelandic example in (9.105) is in the subjunctive mood; were it in the indicative, as in (9.116) from Thráinsson (1991), then reflexivization would be blocked.

(9.116) Jón-Ø$_i$ heyr-ð-i að ég hef-ð-i
John-MsgNOM hear-PAST-3sg CLM 1sgNOM have.SBJ-PAST-1sg
/*haf-ð-i svik-ið sig$_i$.
/have.IND-PAST-1sg betray-PSTP SELF
'John$_i$ heard that I had betrayed himself$_i$.'

The identity of the matrix verb is another important factor; long-distance reflexivization seems to be preferred when the matrix predicates are verbs of saying or believing.[16] Thus, in addition to the basic domain constraints, there may be additional language-specific constraints which affect the possibility of long-distance reflexivization.

We now turn to the question of the constraints on possible antecedents. Dalrymple argues that there are both positive and negative conditions on the possible binders, which have to do with whether an anaphor must or must not be bound by a 'subject' or whether one must or must not be bound by a syntactic co-argument. There is a third reflexive in Norwegian, which illustrates the interaction of these conditions with the domain conditions. It is *seg*, which, like *seg selv*, must be bound by a 'subject' but which must not be bound by a co-argument of any kind; moreover, its domain is the minimal finite domain, i.e. the clause. This is illustrated in the following examples from Hellan (1988).

(9.117) a. Jon$_i$ snakk-et om seg selv$_i$/*seg$_i$.
John talk-PAST about SELF
'John$_i$ talked about himself$_i$.'
b. Jon$_i$ fortal-te Ola$_j$ om seg selv$_{i/*j}$/ham self$_{*i/j}$/*seg$_{i/j}$.
John tell-PAST Ola about SELF
'John$_i$ told Ola$_j$ about himself$_i$/herself$_j$.'
c. Jon$_i$ lik-te din artikkel om seg$_i$.
John like-PAST 2sgGEN article about SELF
'John$_i$ liked your article about himself$_i$.'
d. Jon$_i$ hør-te oss snakk-e om seg$_i$/*seg selv$_i$.
John hear-PAST 1sgACC talk-INF about SELF
'John$_i$ heard us talk about himself$_i$.'

e. *Jeg lov-et Jon$_i$ å snakk-e pent om seg$_i$.
1sgNOM promise-PAST John CLM talk-INF nicely about himself
'I promised John$_i$ to talk nicely about himself$_i$.'

f. *Jon$_i$ war ikke klar over at vi had-de snakk-et
John be.PAST NOT clear about CLM 1plNOM have-PAST talk-PSTP
om seg$_i$.
about SELF
*'John$_i$ was not clear that we had talked about himself$_i$.'

The sentences in (a) and (b) show that *seg* cannot have a co-core argument as an antecedent, regardless of its grammatical function, while (c) shows that if it is a non-argument, it can have a controller within the same core. The examples in (d)–(f) illustrate long-distance reflexivization with *seg*; (d) and (e) involve non-subordinate core junctures, while (e) is subordination with a tensed complement clause. Only (d) is grammatical, as in (e) its antecedent is a 'non-subject' and in (f) its antecedent is outside of the clause. The conditions on the antecedents for the three Norwegian reflexives and the reciprocal *hverandre* 'each other' are given in (9.118).

(9.118) *Conditions on possible antecedents for Norwegian anaphors*

a. *Seg selv*: must be bound by the highest-ranking semantic co-argument in the core in which *seg selv* occurs (in terms of the privileged syntactic argument selection principles for Norwegian).

b. *Ham selv*: its antecedent must not be the highest-ranking semantic argument in the core in which *ham selv* occurs (in terms of the privileged syntactic argument selection principles for Norwegian).

c. *Seg*: its antecedent must be the highest-ranking semantic argument in the core in which the antecedent occurs in the clause in which *seg* occurs (in terms of the privileged syntactic argument selection principles for Norwegian); the controller and *seg* cannot be co-core arguments.

d. *Hverandre*: its antecedent must be a syntactic co-argument within the core in which *hverandre* occurs.

These conditions would be stated in the lexical entries of the anaphors, and the different domain restrictions they refer to would be statable with respect to the semantic representations of the sentences, where the Role Hierarchy and LS-Superiority Conditions apply. The contrast between core arguments and argument-adjuncts was originally proposed in section 4.4.1.1 on the basis of differences in their logical structure representations. The contrast between core and clause is signalled by the presence or absence of the obligatory clausal operator tense in the semantic representation, as we saw in (9.24), (9.41), and (9.50), and any coreference relationship involving a reflexive crossing a tense operator would be one with the sentence as its domain. The semantic representation of operators is also important for depicting the constraint on long-distance reflexivization in Icelandic which is tied to the mood of the subordinate clause; having the status operator with the value 'irrealis' modifying the embedded logical structure would represent subjunctive, while the value 'realis' would represent indicative.

9.5 Constraints on linking in WH-questions and related constructions

In our discussion of linking in WH-questions in chapter 7, we discussed how the WH-word can be mapped into the syntactic representation in one of three ways: into the precore slot, as in English, into the normal position for an argument or adjunct, as in Lakhota, or into the core-internal focus position, as in Turkish. We did not discuss any restrictions on the linking from syntax to semantics, because there seem to be few if any of them in simple sentences. The picture is very different in complex sentences. Chomsky (1964) first noted some restrictions in this area, but it was Ross (1967) who first explored this aspect of syntax and laid the foundations for all subsequent work on this topic. Ross noticed that it is not possible to form a WH-question out of all syntactic configurations in a language. Consider the following examples involving complex NPs.

(9.119) a. Mulder believes that Scully hid the files.
a′. What does Mulder believe that Scully hid?
b. Mulder believes the rumor that Scully hid the files.
b′. *What does Mulder believe the rumor that Scully hid?
c. Scully interviewed the witness who saw the alien spacecraft.
c′. *What did Scully interview the witness who saw?

It is grammatical in English to form a WH-question with the question word functioning as the undergoer of the embedded clause, when the embedded clause is an object complement, as in (a′). When the embedded clause is a noun phrase complement, as in (b), or a relative clause, as in (c), the result is very different, as (b′) and (c′) clearly show. Ross argued that NP complements and relative clauses share a common structural feature, namely, the subordinate clause is embedded within a complex NP with a lexical head noun, and it is this property which blocks question formation. It also blocks the formation of related constructions, namely topicalization and relativization, as illustrated in (9.120).

(9.120) a. Those files Mulder believes Scully hid.
a′. *Those files Mulder believes the rumor that Scully hid.
a″. *The alien spacecraft Scully interviewed the witness who saw.
b. The files which Mulder believes that Scully hid were actually in the trunk of his car.
b′. *The files which Mulder believes the rumor that Scully hid were actually in the trunk of his car.
b″. *The alien spacecraft which Scully interviewed the witness who saw is stored in an abandoned missile silo in North Dakota.

Ross suggested that embedded clauses in complex NPs are like islands, in that there is no way for the NP to escape from the embedded clause in them, and he proposed

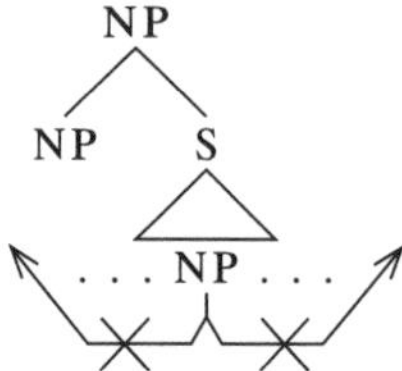

Figure 9.30 Complex NP Constraint (Ross 1967)

the Complex NP Constraint to account for the facts in (9.119) and (9.120). It states, roughly, that an element cannot be moved out of a clause which is embedded under a lexical head noun. The relevant structural configuration is represented in figure 9.30. The constraints Ross proposed for 'extraction constructions', i.e. WH-question formation, topicalization and relativization, came to be known as 'island constraints' or 'Ross constraints'. Among them, the Complex NP Constraint, the Sentential Subject Constraint (blocking extraction out of sentential subjects), the WH-island Constraint (blocking extraction out of complements with WH-complementizers) and the Coordinate Structure Constraint (blocking extraction out of coordinate structures) were the most important.

The constraints proposed by Ross described but did not explain the phenomena, as they were not derived from any more general theoretical principles. The first major attempt to unify them theoretically was Chomsky (1973 [1977]), which subsumed them all under the general principle of *subjacency*. This principle has undergone a number of reformulations over the past two decades, but the basic idea is still that movement transformations (in GB, WH-movement and NP-movement) cannot move an element across more than one bounding node in a single move. In English the bounding nodes are NP and S (IP).

The idea that subjacency violations like those in (9.119b′, c′) and (9.120a′, a″, b′, b″) are caused by a syntactic rule moving an element across more than one bounding node runs into difficulties in languages like Lakhota in which question words do not appear in the precore slot but rather occur in the normal core-internal position for a corresponding non-WH element, i.e. *in situ*. This might lead one to expect that there would be no subjacency violations in such a language, but this is incorrect, as the following Lakhota examples show.

(9.121) a. Wičháša ki [[šų́ka wą igmú ki ∅-∅-yaxtáke] ki le]
man the dog a cat the 3sgU-3sgA-bite the this
wą-∅-∅-yą́ke yelo.
3sgU-3sgA-see DEC
'The man saw the dog which bit the cat.'

b. Wičháša ki [[šų́ka wą táku ∅-∅-yaxtáke] ki le] wą-∅-∅-yą́ke yelo.
man the dog a 3sgU-3sgA-bite the this 3sgU-3sgA-see DEC
'The man saw the dog which bit something.'

c. Wičháša ki [[šųka wą táku ∅-∅-yaxtáke] ki le] wą-∅-∅-yąka he?
man the dog a 3sgU-3sgA-bite the this 3sgU-3sgA-see Q
'Did the man see the dog which bit something?'
*'What did the man see the dog which bit?'

The sentence in (a) is very similar to the Lakhota relative examples in (9.98) discussed in section 9.3. In (b) the undergoer of the relative clause has been replaced by *táku* 'what, something (specific)', and the result is a sentence with an indefinite–specific undergoer. In (c), the crucial example, the sentence has the question particle *he* and must be interpreted as a question. In section 7.6.2 it was mentioned that simple Lakhota sentences with *táku* and the question particle *he* are ambiguous between WH-question and yes–no question interpretations, as (7.156d) showed; it is repeated below.

(9.122) Šų́ka ki táku ∅-∅-yaxtáka he?
dog the 3sgU-3sgA-bite Q
'What did the dog bite?', or 'Did the dog bite something?'

What is striking about (9.121c) is that it is *unambiguous*, even though it might be expected to be ambiguous just like (9.122). It cannot have the WH-question interpretation, unlike (9.122); it can only have the yes–no question reading. Put another way, *táku* cannot be interpreted as a question word in (9.121c); it can only be interpreted as an indefinite–specific pronoun. This is a subjacency effect, just as in (9.119c′) in English; in both examples, it is impossible to form a WH-question if the WH-word functions as (in these cases) a semantic argument in the relative clause. Thus, it appears that the Complex NP Constraint or subjacency is operative in the grammar of Lakhota, even though the formation of WH-questions does not involve question words occurring in the precore slot.

This is a very important fact. Chomsky's account of subjacency crucially refers to the movement of WH-words and other elements across certain phrase-structure configurations; the result of this movement is a long-distance dependency between the WH-word and a syntactic 'gap' in an embedded clause which spans these configurations. English, which has been analyzed as having syntactic movement rules due to the displacement of the WH-word to the precore slot from the position in which the corresponding non-WH-word would occur, shows subjacency effects, as demonstrated in (9.119) and (9.120). Lakhota, which presents no *prima facie* evidence for the existence of any movement rules in its grammar, also shows subjacency effects, as in (9.121c). Hence languages with 'movement' show subjacency effects, and languages without 'movement' also show subjacency effects. We may, therefore, conclude that 'movement', i.e. the displacement of the WH-word to the precore slot and the creation of a long-distance dependency, is *irrelevant* to the explanation of these subjacency effects. We must look for some other feature common to the grammars of both types of languages for the explanation.[17]

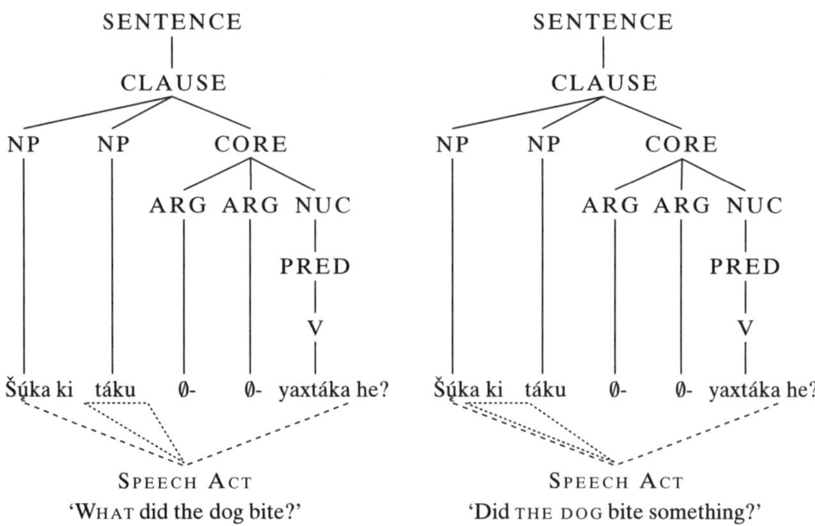

Figure 9.31 The actual focus domain in Lakhota questions in simple sentences

An important clue to what this feature could be comes from the Lakhota sentence in (9.122). In section 7.6.2, we argued that the two interpretations of this sentence result from different construals of what the focus of the question is. That is, if the focus of the question is on *táku*, then it is interpreted as a question word, yielding the meaning 'What did the dog bite?' If, on the other hand, the focus is on another constituent, then *táku* must be construed as an indefinite–specific pronoun, resulting in the reading 'Did the dog bite something?' This was represented in figure 7.34, which is repeated in figure 9.31. If the question word being the focus of the question is the crucial precondition for the WH-question interpretation, then it follows that the reason (9.121c) is not ambiguous is that it is impossible to interpret *táku* as the focus of the question, leaving only the yes–no question reading possible. Why should it be impossible to interpret *táku* as the focus of the question? The most plausible answer is that it is in some way related to the syntactic structure, in particular, that it is the result of *táku* functioning in a definite restrictive relative clause. In section 5.3 we introduced the notion of the *potential focus domain*, the part of the sentence in which focal elements can occur; the actual focus domain, where focal elements actually occur in a particular utterance, must be within the potential focus domain. With respect to (9.121c), if *táku* cannot be the focus of the question, then there is no possible utterance in which it is in the actual focus domain, and from this it follows that it must be outside the potential focus domain of the sentence. Note that in (9.122) *táku* is within the potential focus domain, as figure 9.31 shows clearly.

The idea that a definite restrictive relative clause is outside the potential focus domain is one we encountered originally in section 8.5 in our discussion of focus structure in complex sentences. In that section we introduced a general principle governing the extent of the potential focus domain in complex sentences in (8.61), taken from Van Valin (1993b, 1995b); it is repeated in (9.123).

(9.123) *The potential focus domain in complex sentences*
A subordinate clause may be within the potential focus domain if it is a direct daughter of (a direct daughter of . . .) the clause node which is modified by the illocutionary force operator.

As discussed in section 8.5, there is no limit in principle to the number of direct daughters involved, and accordingly the specification in parentheses should be considered to be recursive. In terms of cross-linguistic variation, there appear to be only two possibilities: the potential focus domain is restricted to main clauses only, in which case (9.123) is irrelevant to the language, or the potential focus domain can extend to the deepest subordinate clause in any sentence, as long as the condition is not violated.

Looking back at the structure of the Lakhota relative clause in figure 9.28, which is the same structure as in (9.121), we see that the embedded clause is not a direct daughter of the matrix clause, the clause modified by the illocutionary force operator. Hence the principle in (9.123) predicts correctly that this relative clause is outside the potential focus domain, and this in turn predicts correctly that *táku* could not be interpreted as a question word in this structure. We independently arrived at this conclusion about Lakhota definite restrictive relative clauses in section 8.5 by looking at the distribution of the indefinite–non-specific articles and at the possible felicitous responses to yes–no questions (see (8.64)–(8.68)). We investigated these phenomena in three complex constructions (the other two being object complements and adverbial clauses) and concluded that the potential focus domain in them is as in (9.124), repeated from (8.69).

(9.124) *Summary of potential scope of* he: *potential focus domain* (*in italics*)
a. [*Hokšíla etą́ thaló ki manúpi*] *iyúkčą* he?
boys some meat the steal think Q
'Does he think some boys stole the meat?'
b. *Wičháša ki* [[*šų́ka wą* igmú eyá wičháyaxtake] *ki le*] *wąyą́ka* he?
man the dog a cat some bite the this see Q
'Did the man see the dog which bit some cats?'
c. [Wičháša ki wóte] *ečhúhą, tha-wíču ki mní ikíčiču* he?
man the eat while his-wife the water get.for Q
'While the man was eating, did his wife get him water?'

These potential focus domains follow from the principle in (9.123), as figure 8.22, repeated in figure 9.32, shows. In (a), the embedded clause is a direct daughter

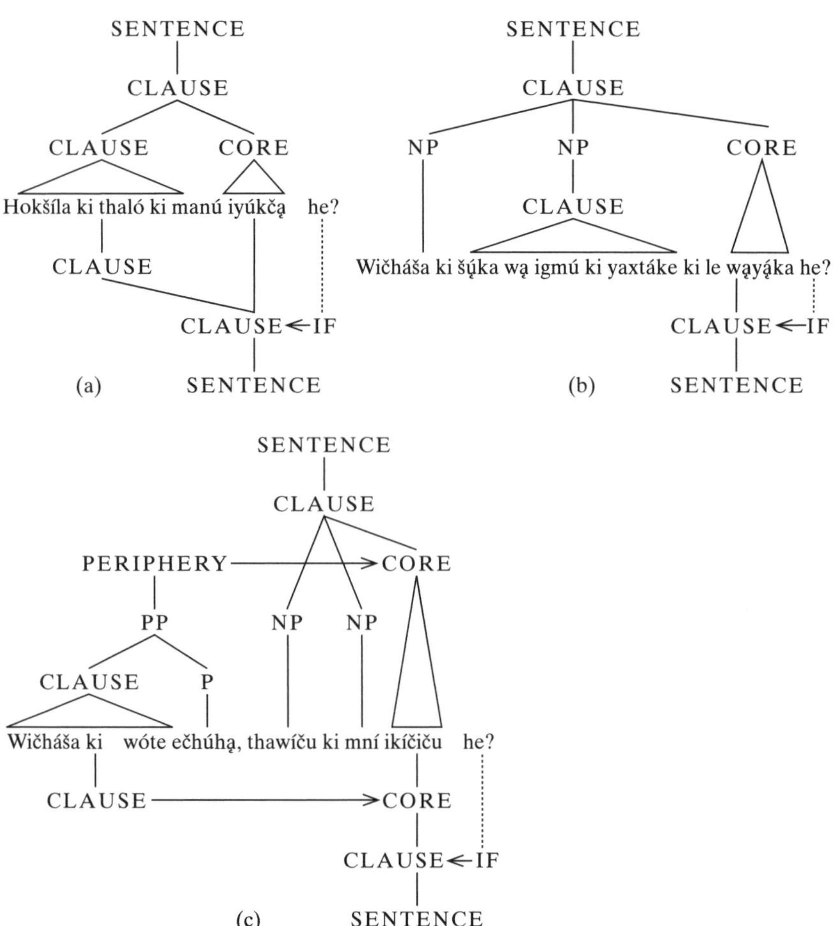

Figure 9.32 The structure of Lakhota complex sentences

of the clause modified by the illocutionary force operator, and consequently, the embedded clause is within the potential focus domain, as in (9.124a). In (b) and (c), on the other hand, the embedded clause is not a direct daughter of the clause modified by the illocutionary force operator, and therefore the embedded clauses are outside the potential focus domain, as in (9.124b, c).

Our explanation for the impossibility of the WH-question interpretation of *táku* when it is in a definite restrictive relative clause makes a specific prediction about object complements and adverbial clauses: words like *táku* should be construable as question words in object complements but not in adverbial clauses. That is, if *táku*, *tuwá* 'who, someone' or one of the other Lakhota words of this class were to occur in the embedded clause in a construction like (a) in figure 9.32, the resulting sentence should be ambiguous between WH-question and yes–no question readings, just like (9.122), whereas if they were to occur in an adverbial subordinate clause like (c), then the resulting sentence should be unambiguous and have only the yes–no question reading. These predictions are correct, as (9.125) shows.

(9.125) a. [Tuwá thaló ki manú] iyúkčą he?
who meat the steal think Q
'Who does he think stole the meat?', or 'Does he think someone stole the meat?'

b. [Wičháša ki táku yúte] ečhúhą, tha-wíču ki mní ikíčiču he?
man the eat while his-wife the water get.for Q
'While the man was eating something, did his wife get him water?'
*'What did his wife get him water, while the man was eating ___ ?'

It is clear, then, that in order for *táku*, *tuwá* or one of the other question words/indefinite–specific pronouns in Lakhota to be interpreted as a question word, it must occur in the potential focus domain of the sentence. We may express this in a preliminary fashion as the constraint on question formation in (9.126).

(9.126) *Constraint on question formation* (*preliminary formulation*)
The element questioned (the question word in a simple, direct WH-question[18] or the focal NP in a simple, direct yes–no question) must function in a clause which is within the potential focus domain of the sentence.

We saw in section 8.5 that the possible interpretation of the focus in a yes–no question is affected by the constraint in (9.123), and therefore the restriction in (9.126) applies to both types of questions. Thus, the principles in (9.123) and (9.126) provide an explanation for the observed subjacency effects in Lakhota.

The crucial question now is, can this analysis be applied to languages like English, Icelandic and Sama, in which questions words do not occur *in situ* but rather in the precore slot? The first thing to note is that in languages of this type, the position of the WH-word in the question is not relevant to explaining the subjacency effects, because in all questions of this kind the WH-word occurs in the precore slot, regardless of the grammaticality of the question. Rather, what is relevant is whether the clause in which the question word functions semantically is in the potential focus domain or not. Applying the principle in (9.123) to English in section 8.5, we found that object complements are in the potential focus domain (see figure 8.20) and that adverbial subordinate clauses are not (see figure 8.21). If we apply it to the English relative clauses in figures 9.24 and 9.25, we see that the embedded clause is not a direct daughter of the clause modified by the illocutionary force operator, and therefore relative clauses in English, as in Lakhota, are outside of the potential focus domain. Finally, if we look at the structure of the noun complement clause in figure 8.25, we see that the embedded clause is within an NP and therefore could not be a direct daughter of the clause modified by the illocutionary force operator; accordingly, it too is outside the potential focus domain. We may summarize these results

Table 9.13 *Potential focus domain in English complex sentence constructions*

Construction	*Structure represented*	*Direct daughter?*	*In potential focus domain?*
Object complement	Figure 8.20	Yes	Yes
Adverbial clause	Figure 8.21	No	No
Relative clause (restrictive)	Figures 9.25, 9.26	No	No
Noun complement	Figure 8.25	No	No

in table 9.13. Looking back at the examples in (9.119), we can see that the results in table 9.13 together with the principle in (9.126) account for the grammaticality or ungrammaticality of all of the sentences. Forming a question in which the WH-word functions in an object complement, as in (9.119a′) is grammatical, as predicted, whereas forming a question in which the WH-word functions in a relative clause or noun complement clause, as in (c′) and (b′), respectively, is ungrammatical, again as predicted. It also explains the ungrammaticality of the English translation of the Lakhota example in (9.125b), where the WH-word functions in an adverbial subordinate clause. A particularly striking example of the explanatory potential of this account can be found in the contrast among the sentences in (9.127).

(9.127) a. That Fred won the race surprised Mary.
a′. It surprised Mary that Fred won the race.
b. *What did that Fred won surprise Mary?
b′. What did it surprise Mary that Fred won?

In (9.127a) there is a 'sentential subject', *that Fred won the race*, and forming a WH-question out of it, as in (b), is quite ungrammatical; ruling such sentences out was the motivation for Ross' Sentential Subject Constraint (1967). There is, however, an alternative way to code the same lexical material, namely as in (a′), in which the embedded clause appears in an extraposed position and the pronoun *it* fills the empty 'subject' position. The structural contrast between (a) and (b) is represented in figure 9.33. If we now evaluate these two structures with respect to the principle in (9.123), we see that the *that*-clause is not a direct daughter of the matrix clause in (a) but is a direct daughter of the matrix clause in (a′), and accordingly, it is not in the potential focus domain of the sentence in (a) but is in the potential focus domain of the sentence in (a′) (see Huck and Na 1990). The constraint in (9.126) therefore predicts that WH-question formation with the WH-word functioning in the *that*-clause should not be possible in the structure in (a) but should be grammatical in the structure in (a′), and this is correct, as the ungrammaticality of (b) and the grammaticality of (b′) clearly show.

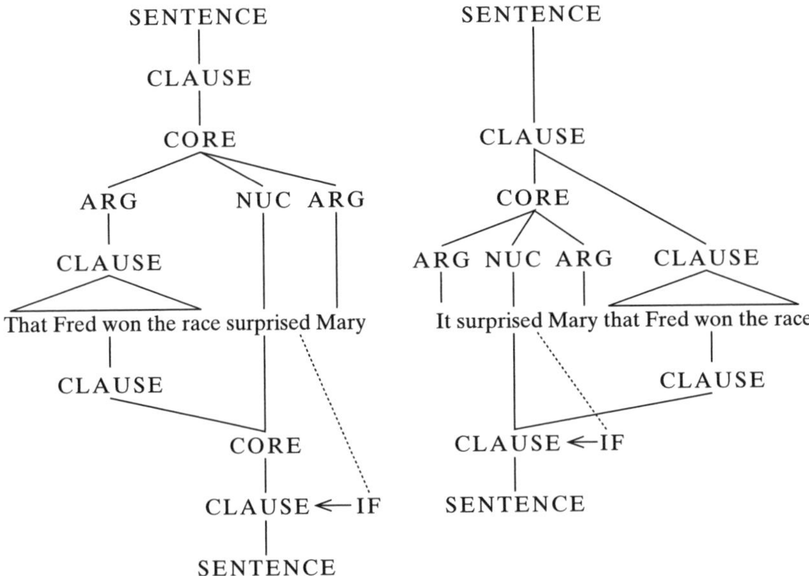

Figure 9.33 English *that*-clause as 'sentential subject' and in extraposed position

We have, thus, provided an explanation for the subjacency effects in both English and Lakhota which does not require the existence of a long-distance dependency between a WH-word in the precore slot and a syntactic 'gap' in an embedded clause.[19] Rather, what is common to the two languages is the crucial role of the potential focus domain in constraining question formation. This is captured in the principles in (9.123) and (9.126), which apply equally to both languages, despite their manifest syntactic differences. The principle in (9.126) can be integrated naturally into the linking algorithms. In order to block the generation of sentences like (9.119b′), we need to modify step 3 of the semantics to syntax algorithm as in (9.128); the modification is in italics.

(9.128) *Linking algorithm: semantics → syntax (revised)*

1 Determine the actor and undergoer assignments, following the Actor–Undergoer Hierarchy in figure 7.1.

2 Assign specific morphosyntactic status to [–WH] arguments in logical structure (language-specific).

  a. Accusative privileged syntactic argument selection: default = Actor.

  b. Ergative privileged syntactic argument selection: default = Undergoer.

3 If there is a [+WH] XP *in the logical structure of a clause in the potential focus domain*,

  a. assign it to the normal position of a non-WH-XP with the same function (language-specific), or

b. assign it to the precore slot (language-specific), or
c. assign it to a position within the potential focus domain of the clause (default = the unmarked focus position in its clause) (language-specific).

4 A non-WH XP may be assigned to the pre- or post-core slot, subject to focus structure restrictions (optional; language-specific).

5 Assign the core arguments the appropriate case markers/adpositions and assign the predicate in the nucleus the appropriate agreement marking (language-specific).

6 For semantic arguments of logical structures other than that of the main verb,
a. assign them to the periphery (default), or
b. assign them to the precore slot or focus position (language-specific) if they are focal, or
c. assign them to the left-detached position if they are highly topical.

The addition of the requirement 'in the logical structure of a clause in the potential focus domain' makes it impossible to link a WH-word to any position in the syntactic representation if this condition is not met, resulting in a Completeness Constraint violation. In order to constrain the linking from syntax to semantics, we need to modify steps 3 and 6 in (9.54) as follows.

(9.129) *Linking algorithm: syntax → semantics* (*revised formulation*)

1 Determine the functions of the core arguments:
a. If the construction is syntactically accusative:
(1) If it is the unmarked voice, the privileged syntactic argument is actor.
(2) If it is passive, the privileged syntactic argument is not the actor of the predicate in the nucleus;
(a) the actor may appear as a direct core argument (language-specific); or
(b) the actor may appear in the periphery marked by an adposition or an oblique case (language-specific); or
(c) if there is no actor in the core or the periphery, then replace the variable representing the highest-ranking argument in the logical structure with '∅'.
b. If the construction is syntactically ergative:
(1) If it is the unmarked voice, the privileged syntactic argument is undergoer.
(2) If it is antipassive, the privileged syntactic argument is actor;
(a) the undergoer may appear as an oblique element (language-specific);
(b) if there is no undergoer in the core or the periphery, then replace the variable representing the lowest-ranking argument in the logical structure with '∅'.

c. Assign macrorole status to the other direct core argument, if it is not dative or in an oblique case.
d. If the verb is intransitive, then assign the privileged syntactic argument either macrorole or direct core argument status (language-specific).
e. If the language is head-marking and there are independent NPs in the clause, associate each NP with a bound argument marker (language-specific).
f. If the language lacks voice oppositions, determine the macroroles from case marking and/or word order (language-specific).

2 Retrieve from the lexicon the logical structure of the predicate in the nucleus of the clause and with respect to it execute step 1 from (9.128), subject to the following proviso:
a. When there is more than one choice for undergoer, do not assign undergoer to an argument in the logical structure.
b. Assign actor to an argument in the logical structure, if the verb takes one.
c. Determine the linking of the non-macrorole core argument:
(1) if there is a state predicate in the logical structure and if the non-macrorole core argument is marked by a locative adposition or dative or a locative-type case, then link it with the first argument position in the state predicate in the logical structure; or
(2) if there is a state predicate in the logical structure and if it is not marked by a locative adposition or dative or a locative-type case, then link it with the second argument position in the state predicate;
(3) otherwise, link the animate NP with the first argument position in the state predicate in the logical structure.

3 Link the [-WH] arguments determined in step 1 with the arguments determined in step 2 until all [-WH] core arguments are linked.

4 In non-subordinate core junctures, one of the arguments of the matrix core must be linked to an argument position in the embedded logical structure:
a. If the matrix predicate is a control verb, this follows (9.33); otherwise,
b. If the matrix predicate is not a control verb, then link it to the logical structure argument position of the pivot of the second core.

5 If there is a predicative adpositional adjunct, then retrieve its logical structure from the lexicon, insert the logical structure of the core as the second argument in the logical structure and the object of the adposition in the periphery as the first argument.

6 *If there is an element in the pre- or postcore slot (language-specific), or a WH-word* in situ *or in the unmarked focus position (language-specific),*
a. *assign it the remaining unlinked argument position in the semantic representation of the sentence, provided that the logical structure to which it is linked is for a clause in the potential focus domain.*
b. *if there are no unlinked argument positions in the sentence, then treat the WH-word like a predicative preposition and follow the procedure in*

step 5, linking the WH-word to the first argument position in the logical structure.

(1) *treat the entire logical structure of the sentence as the second argument of the predicative preposition* (*default*); *or*

(2) *if the embedded clause is within the potential focus domain, then treat only the logical structure of the embedded clause as the second argument of the predicative preposition* (*optional*).

The constraint in step 6a prevents a WH-word from being linked to the semantic representation unless the condition in (9.126) is met. In a language like English it would leave the WH-word stranded in the precore slot, resulting in a Completeness Constraint violation. In a language like Lakhota, on the other hand, it would block the linking if *táku* is construed as a question word, likewise resulting in a Completeness Constraint violation. But there is another option in Lakhota; *táku* can also be interpreted as an indefinite–specific pronoun, and on this interpretation the condition in (9.126) does not apply, thereby allowing the linking of *táku* to a variable in the logical structure, satisfying the Completeness Constraint, and yielding the yes–no question reading.

The reformulation of step 6b makes it possible to capture well-known constraints on the interpretation of adjunct WH-questions, as exemplified in (9.130).

(9.130) a. When did Skinner say that Krycek would be at the missile silo?
b. When did Scully interview the witness who saw the alien spacecraft in the silo?

The sentence in (a) is ambiguous; it can be a question about when something was said or about when someone would be somewhere. The sentence in (b), however, is not ambiguous; it can only be a question about when the interview took place, not about when someone saw something. The issue here is again what can be questioned, more specifically, what can be questioned with respect to the time of its occurrence. We would expect, then, that the potential focus domain would play a key role in constraining the interpretation of the question, and this seems to be the case. Example (9.130a) involves a structure which is compatible with the embedded clause being in the potential focus domain, and accordingly it is ambiguous with respect to the interpretation of the scope of *when*. The structure in (b), however, does not meet the condition in (9.123), as we have seen (see table 9.13), and therefore the embedded clause is not in the potential focus domain; hence it cannot be the focus of the question, and *when* must be interpreted as modifying the matrix clause.

We have concentrated our discussion thus far on WH-question formation, but as we showed in (9.120), topicalization and restrictive relativization are also subject to the same constraints. In many languages these constructions are syntactically very similar, but functionally they are not so similar in terms of the discourse function of

Table 9.14 *Discourse functions of 'extracted' element in 'extraction' constructions*

Construction	*Function of 'extracted' element*
WH-question	Focus
Topicalization	Focus or Topic
Relativization	Topic

the WH-word in a question, the non-WH NP in the precore slot in a topicalization construction and the head of a relative clause. This is summarized in table 9.14.

There is an obvious connection between WH-elements, which are always focal, and focal non-WH elements in the precore slot, on the one hand, and the potential focus domain, on the other, and this is the basis for the provisions in the linking algorithms that we introduced in (9.128) and (9.129). Why should topicalization and restrictive relativization also be constrained by the potential focal domain, given that the NP in the precore slot in a topicalization construction can be topical and that the head noun is always topical with respect to the relative clause? The essential feature that these two constructions share is that the clause in which the displaced NP functions is always *about* the referent of the NP (Maling and Zaenen 1982, Kuno 1987). The central notion, then, is *pragmatic* aboutness; the restrictive relative clause must be interpretable as being about its head, and the sentence fragment following a topical element in the precore slot must likewise be interpretable as being about the precore slot element. We may formulate this condition as in (9.131); Kuno (1987) presents a similar constraint.

(9.131) *Pragmatic-aboutness condition on topicalization and relativization*
The sentence fragment following a topical element in the precore slot or a restrictive relative clause must be pragmatically interpretable as being about the precore slot element or the head noun.

Reinhart (1981) presents an analysis of pragmatic aboutness. She argues that in order for a sentence to be about the referent of an NP, it must be possible to form an alternative sentence (with the same essential structure) in such a way that the NP at issue functions as the focus of a possible assertion that the sentence can be used to make. To illustrate what she means here, let us look again at (9.120a), *Those files Mulder believes Scully hid*. Reinhart's analysis requires that, in order for the sentence fragment *Mulder believes Scully hid* to be construable as pragmatically about the precore slot NP *those files*, there must be an alternative form of this sentence in which the NP *those files* serves as the focus of an assertion. The sentence in (9.119a), *Mulder believes that Scully hid those files*, is such a sentence; how can we show that *those files* can serve as the focus of (9.119a)? As we saw in section 5.5, only the asserted part of an utterance can be interpreted as being negated or denied, and accordingly, if the constituent can be negated in a conversational exchange, then it is a possible focus. This is illustrated in (9.132).

(9.132) Speaker 1: Mulder believes that Scully hid those files.
Speaker 2: No, the keys to his car.

The fact that this is a felicitous exchange shows that *those files* can be negated and therefore is a possible focus in (9.119a). We have met Reinhart's criterion for pragmatic aboutness, and consequently we may conclude that the sentence fragment *Mulder believes Scully hid* is interpretable as being about the NP *those files* in (9.120a). Hence the construction in (9.120a) meets the condition in (9.131) and is predicted to be grammatical, which it is. Her criterion makes crucial reference to the constituent serving as the focus of a possible assertion that the sentence can be used to make, and here is where the potential focus domain comes in: in order for a constituent to be the focus of a possible assertion that a sentence can be used to make, it must be in potential focus domain, as we saw in chapter 5.

Let's compare (9.120a) with (9.120a″), **The alien spacecraft Scully interviewed the witness who saw*. In order to determine whether the sentence fragment *Scully interviewed the witness who saw* can be interpreted pragmatically as being about the NP *the alien spacecraft*, we need to take an alternative form of the sentence and ascertain if *the alien spacecraft* is a possible focus in it. The alternative sentence is (9.119c), *Scully interviewed the witness who saw the alien spacecraft*; we must now place it in the same type of context as in (9.132) to see if this NP can be negated.

(9.133) a. Speaker 1: Scully interviewed the witness who saw the alien spacecraft.
Speaker 2: *No, some lights in the sky.
b. Speaker 1: Scully interviewed the witness who saw the alien spacecraft.
Speaker 2: No, Skinner. (= 'Skinner interviewed the witness', = 'Scully interviewed Skinner', but not = 'the witness who saw Skinner')

The results are very different from (9.132). In both interchanges it is impossible to deny *the alien spacecraft*, and this means that it cannot be interpreted as the focus of a possible assertion that (9.119c) can be used to make. If that is the case, then the sentence fragment *Scully interviewed the witness who saw* cannot be interpreted pragmatically as being about *the alien spacecraft*, and therefore the condition in (9.131) is not met, and the topicalization construction in (9.120a″) is predicted to be ungrammatical, which it is.

In order for a constituent to be negatable (deniable) as in (9.132), i.e. without repeating the whole previous utterance, it must be interpretable as the focus of the question, and, as we have seen, this requires it to be in the potential focus domain. Restrictive relativization and the occurrence of topical elements in the precore slot are constrained by the condition in (9.131), which crucially builds on Reinhart's analysis of pragmatic aboutness. In her analysis, in order for a sentence fragment or relative clause to be about the referent of an NP, it must be possible to form an alternative sentence (with the same essential structure) in such a way that the constituent at issue functions as the focus of a possible assertion that the sentence can be used to make. This requires the constituent to be in the potential focus domain, as we saw in chapter 5. Thus, even if the displaced NP is a topic, the interpretation of the construction is still constrained by the potential focus domain. If it is focal, then the interaction with the potential focus domain is the same as for WH-questions. Thus, all of the constructions in table 9.14 are constrained by the potential focus domain, and therefore the provisions in the linking algorithms regarding the potential focus domain will work for them, too.

There is still one puzzle remaining regarding relative clauses. While it makes sense to talk about the sentence asserting something about the topic NP in the precore slot in a construction like (9.120a), for example, we cannot say the same thing about (9.120b), in which *the files* is the head noun and *which Mulder believes that Scully hid* is the relative clause. Restrictive relative clauses do not assert anything; as restrictive modifiers, they are presupposed (see section 5.1). Why, then, should the potential focus domain restrict the interpretation of constructions which are by definition not asserted? A plausible answer lies in the connection between assertion and predication. Cattell (1984) and Kluender (1992) argue that the constraints we have been investigating are derived from restrictions on the formation of complex predication structures, and it has long been recognized that the subject–predicate opposition is fundamentally one of topic and comment, with the predicate being an assertion about the topic (see the discussion of predicate focus in section 5.2.1). If this is the case, then limits on what can be construed as an assertion about a topic are also limits on what can be construed as a possible predication about a 'subject'. Restrictive relative clauses are complex predications modifying an NP; note that the logical structure of a head noun + relative clause is the same as that of an attributive construction (see section 9.3). Thus the predication relationship between *The boy* and *is tall* in *The boy is tall* is analogous to that between *the files* and *which Mulder believes that Scully hid* in *the files which Mulder believes that Scully hid* in (9.120b). It is uncontroversial that the predicate *is tall* asserts something about *the boy* in *The boy is tall*, and there it is clear that predication and 'assertion about' are fundamentally related notions. If this is the case, then the application of constraints on 'assertion about' to predication follows naturally. Hence, the head noun must be related to the relative clause in such a way that if the relative clause were an independent sentence and the head noun a topic, the relative clause could be construed as an assertion about that topic. And the precondition for this is that the NP serving as the head noun must function within the relative clause in such a way that if the relative clause were an independent assertion containing the NP, the NP would be in the potential focus domain. Thus, despite the different functions of the displaced elements in these three constructions, they are all ultimately constrained by whether the embedded clause in question can be in potential focus domain, and this follows from (9.123).

The constraint in (9.123) represents the default distribution of the potential focus domain in complex sentences. There are a number of other factors which interact with it to reduce or extend the potential focus domain. In particular, lexical semantic factors may also influence the potential focus domain, both in terms of preventing a position in the potential focus domain from being the actual focus domain and of overriding the principle in (9.123) and permitting the actual focus domain to be in structural configurations where it would otherwise be impossible. These two possibilities can be illustrated in English. The principle in (9.123) predicts that WH-question formation etc. should be possible out of object complements, but this is not always true. It has long been noted that while it is very easy to form a question out of the complement of *say*, it is highly odd to do this out of the complements of verbs of manner of speaking, e.g. ??*What did Fred murmur/chortle/lisp that Mary had bought?* There is a straightforward Gricean explanation for this (Grice 1975). The focus of an utterance is the most informationally rich part, and the selection of *say*, the most semantically neutral verb of saying, together with an unmarked intonation pattern, indicates that the primary information content of the utterance is the substance of the communication, which is syntactically expressed in the complement clause. Hence the focus can fall in the *that*-clause, making question formation etc. possible. The choice of a verb which highlights the way in which something is said rather than what is said, such as *murmur*, *chortle* and *lisp*, causes the focus to shift to the verb in the main clause, because of the maxim of relevance: the speaker's choice of an informationally richer expression (*murmur*) over another, more neutral possibility (*say*) only makes sense in terms of the Cooperative Principle if the manner of expression is in fact highly relevant to the main point of the utterance. Hence the focus must fall on the matrix verb, keeping the complement from being the actual focus domain despite the fact that the structure as a whole meets the condition in (9.123). The same thing occurs in 'extraction' out of NPs: when the main verb is not informationally distinctive, as in *Who did you read a book about ___?*, forming a question out of the PP in the undergoer NP is fine; however, when the verb is informationally rich, it naturally draws the focus for the same Gricean reason as above, precluding the possibility of the object NP being the actual focus domain, e.g. **Who did you deface/lose/destroy a book about ___?* The second type of lexical semantic effect is exemplified with complex NPs like *make the claim* or *hold the belief*. The structure of a sentence like *Fred made the claim that Mary stole the money* does not meet the condition in (9.123), because the subordinate clause is part of an NP and is not a direct daughter of the matrix clause node, as we have seen; hence it should be outside the potential focus domain and question formation out of it should be impossible. However, it has long been known that question formation is in fact possible for at least some speakers, e.g. *What did Fred make the claim that Mary stole?*, and it has usually been argued that this question is acceptable because *make the claim that X* is virtually synonymous with *claim that X*, an expression whose structure meets the principle in (9.123). When there is no simple object complement paraphrase, as in e.g. **What did Fred investigate the claim that Mary stole?*, then the question is ungrammatical as predicted. Here lexical semantic factors have overridden the principle in (9.123) to permit an otherwise excluded structure to fall within the actual focus domain. Finally, discourse considerations may also affect the interpretation of the focus domains, as Kuno (1987) has argued. For example, the odd extraction-from-NP question above can be made rather more acceptable if it is part of an exchange like the one in (9.134), from Kuno (1987).

(9.134) A: Right after Chairman Mao died, they started taking pictures of Committee members off the walls.
B: Who did they destroy more pictures of, Chairman Mao or Jiang Qing?

It has also been long known that these constructions are strongly affected by the definiteness of the head noun, as the examples in (9.135) show.

(9.135) a. Who did you read a book about?
b. ?*Who did you read the book about?
c. *Who did you read the green book about?
d. *Who did you read Hakeem's book about?

The only difference among these four sentences is the definiteness and the restrictive modification of the head noun; the basic syntactic structure of the four is the same. Hence whatever rules out (b)–(d) cannot be syntactic in nature. Relative clauses in some languages can be affected by the definiteness and semantic content of the head noun. In Danish, for example, it is possible to form a question out of a relative clause if the main clause is relatively empty semantically and the head noun is non-specific or generic, according to Erteschik-Shir (1973) and Erteschik-Shir and Lappin (1979); they show that the Danish equivalent of *What are there many who like?* is perfectly acceptable, whereas a sentence like *What did the man see the dog which bit?* is just as bad in Danish as it is in English and Lakhota.[20] These facts show that restrictions on WH-question formation and related constructions cannot be treated as a purely structural phenomenon but rather must be seen as involving the interaction of syntactic structure, pragmatic functions and lexical semantics. Indeed, the fact that the same syntactic configuration may permit WH-question formation in one context or with one main verb but not allow it in a different context or with a different main verb is strong evidence that the restrictions are not purely syntactic in nature.

An important example of a structure which meets the condition in (9.123) but which is nevertheless incompatible with question formation etc. is illustrated in (9.136).

(9.136) a. Scully said (that) Mulder interviewed the suspect.
b. Who did Scully say interviewed the suspect?
c. *Who did Scully say that interviewed the suspect?
d. Who did Scully say (that) Mulder interviewed?

The basic sentence, given in (a), meets the condition in (9.123), and as expected WH-question formation is possible out of it, as in (b) and (d). The embedded clause is in the potential focus domain. What is surprising is the ungrammaticality of (c); the only difference between (b) and (c) is the presence of the complementizer *that* in (c). The presence or absence of *that* has no effect on questions in which the WH-word is related to a postverbal position; it is relevant only when the WH-word is interpreted as the privileged syntactic argument of the clause.[21] This phenomenon is not universal, by any means. In Lakhota, for example, the presence or absence of an overt complementizer has no effect on WH-question formation in object complements (Van Valin 1993b).

If we compare (c) with (d), we find a pattern of question formation possibilities that we have seen before, namely the pattern in Sesotho and other southern Bantu languages illustrated in (5.10) and (7.157). In these languages, marked narrow focus on the preverbal 'subject' is impossible, and therefore passive or some other device must be used to ensure that a 'subject' WH-word occurs in a postverbal position. Why does the possibility of marked narrow focus in a clause matter? As we have seen, a WH-word is narrow focus, and, as figure 9.31 shows clearly, in a language in which WH-words occur *in situ*, the position in the clause where the WH-word occurs must be a possible position for narrow focus. In a language like English in which the WH-word occurs in the precore slot, the corresponding requirement is that the position the WH-word is interpreted as filling in the clause must be a possible position for narrow focus. We saw in (9.132) that the 'object' position in a *that*-clause is a possible focus position; what about core-initial position? We can use the same test as in (9.132) to find out.

(9.137) a. Speaker 1: Scully said Mulder talked to the detective.
Speaker 2: No, Skinner. (= 'Skinner said . . .', = 'Scully said Skinner talked . . .', = 'Mulder talked to Skinner')
b. Speaker 1: Scully said that Mulder talked to the detective.
Speaker 2: No, Skinner. (= 'Skinner said . . .', = 'Mulder talked to Skinner', but ?? = 'Scully said Skinner talked . . .')

In (a), it seems relatively easy to interpret *Skinner* as replacing any of the three NPs in speaker 1's utterance. In (b), on the other hand, while it is easy to construe *Skinner* as replacing *Scully* or *the detective* in speaker 1's utterance, it is more difficult than in (a) to interpret it as replacing *Mulder*. This means that it is more difficult to interpret *Mulder* as the focus of speaker 1's utterance in (b) than in (a), and this correlates with the presence or absence of *that*. It is easiest to interpret *Mulder* as the focus in (b) if *that* is destressed and *Mulder* is stressed. This seems to parallel the fact that many native speakers find (9.136c) more acceptable if *that* is destressed and pronounced [ðət] rather than [ðæt].

It appears, then, that for reasons that are not well understood, the occurrence of an overt complementizer blocks marked narrow focus on the preverbal privileged syntactic argument position, and if narrow focus is not possible in a position in a clause, then it is not possible to form a WH-question with the WH-word interpreted as having the function associated with that position. This is not an issue of the potential focus domain; that the embedded clause is in the potential focus domain is shown by the grammaticality of the WH-questions in (9.136d). Thus it appears that while unmarked narrow focus is possible in the embedded clause in (9.136d) when a complementizer is present, marked narrow focus on the privileged syntactic argument is not. Note that when the complementizer is absent, the privileged syntactic argument of the embedded clause immediately follows the matrix verb, a position which is often a focus position, as we have seen in several non-verb-final languages, and in this form marked narrow focus on the privileged syntactic argument of the embedded clause is indeed possible, as the grammaticality of (a) shows.

If we were to try to form a topic construction with (9.136d), the result is predictably ungrammatical, **Mulder Scully said that interviewed the suspect*. Because this sentence does not pass the negation test in (9.137b), it fails to meet Reinhart's pragmatic aboutness criterion and therefore fails to meet the condition on topic constructions in (9.131). The issues raised above in the discussion of pragmatic aboutness apply to (9.136c) as well, and the failure to meet Reinhart's criterion has the same consequences. Thus, the occurrence of an overt complementizer renders the privileged syntactic argument of the embedded clause pragmatically and syntactically inert with respect to 'extraction' constructions.

We have shown in this section that the much discussed and theoretically very important restrictions on WH-question formation and related constructions are the result primarily of the complex interaction of syntactic structure and focus structure; they are neither purely syntactic, nor are they purely pragmatic.[22] As is well known, languages vary with respect to the restrictions placed on question formation, and the approach presented here makes it possible to identify the parameters along which languages will vary. There are two major ones: (1) how 'deep' into the sentence does (9.123) apply, and (2) how much can lexical semantic and other factors override (9.123)? As mentioned in chapter 8, some languages restrict the potential focus domain to matrix clauses only, and accordingly no extraction out of any kind of embedded clauses is possible. We have already seen examples of how lexical semantic and other factors can interact with (9.123) to lead to variation in acceptability of question formation etc. within a single language and across languages.

The account presented here has important implications for the issue of language acquisition raised in chapter 1, and we return to it in the epilog.

Further reading

For alternative semantic theories of control, see Jackendoff (1972), Bach (1979), Růžička (1983), Chierchia (1984), Comrie (1984b) and Sag and Pollard (1991). Cutrer (1987) presents detailed critiques of syntactic theories of control as well as semantic theories based primarily on thematic relations; Cutrer (1987, 1993) extends the RRG account in Foley and Van Valin (1984) to account for cases of non-obligatory control and arbitrary control. For alternative accounts of matrix-coding constructions, see Chomsky (1981b, 1986a), Bresnan (1982b), Pollard and Sag (1994), Langacker (1995) and Frajzynger (1995). See Koster and Reuland (1991) and Dalrymple (1993) for discussion of long-distance reflexivization. See Erteschik-Shir (1973), Erteschik-Shir and Lappin (1979), Cattell (1984), Deane (1991), Kluender (1992) and Kuno and Takami (1993) for related analyses of island phenomena. For purely syntactic, non-movement accounts of these phenomena, see Gazdar *et al.* (1985), Kaplan and Zaenen (1989) and Pollard and Sag (1994).

Exercises

1 Diagram the linking from semantics to syntax for the German sentence in (7.41a), the Dyirbal sentence in (6.49b), and the Yateé Zapotec sentence in (1) below (tones are omitted from the Zapotec example). Give the constituent projection only for each sentence and logical structure for each clause. Where relevant, indicate the application of the appropriate case assignment and agreement rules. [**section 9.1.1**]

(1)	W-zaʔa	ş̌kwidenoʔole	naʔa	b-leʔele-beʔ	bidobio.
	PAST-walk	girl	and	PAST-see-3sgA	boy

‘The girl was walking and saw the boy.’

2 Does the theory of obligatory control in (9.33) correctly predict the controller selection in the following French sentences? Explain your answer for each example. [**section 9.1.3.1.1**]

(1)	Marc	a	promis	d’y	all-er.
		have.3sgPRES	promise.PSTP	of-there	go-INF

‘Marc promised to go there.’

(2)	Susanne	veu-t	part-ir.
		want-3sgPRES	leave-INF

‘Susanne wants to leave.’

(3) Michel a persuad-é Pierre d'y all-er.
have.3sgPRES persuade-PSTP of-there go-INF
'Michel persuaded Pierre to go there.'

(4) Caroline di-t être fatigu-é-e.
say-3sgPRES be.INF tired-PSTP-3sg
'Caroline says she is tired.'

(5) Jean croi-t être au-dessus de la loi.
believe3sgPRES be.INF above of the.Fsg law
'Jean believes he is above the law.'

(6) Marthe prétend ne pas comprend-re l'anglais
claim.3sgPRES NEG understand-INF the English
'Martha claims she does not understand English.'

3 How does the voice system in Toba Batak interact with the theory of obligatory control in the following examples? The data are from Schachter (1984b). Is the controller semantically determined, and if so, does it follow (9.33)? What kind of pivot is there in the linked core? [**section 9.1.3.1.2**]

(1) a. Man-[s]uba man-[t]uhor biang si Torus.
ATV-try ATV-buy dog
'Torus is trying to buy a dog.'
b. Di-suba si Torus man-[t]uhor biang.
PASS-try ATV-buy dog
'Torus tried to buy a dog.'

(2) a. Mang-elek si Torus si Ria man-uhor biang.
ATV-persuade ATV-buy dog
'Ria is persuading Torus to buy a dog.'
b. Mang-elek si Torus si Ria di-pareso doktor.
ATV-persuade PASS-examine doctor
'Ria is persuading Torus to be examined by a doctor.'

(3) a. Di-elek si Ria si Torus man-uhor biang.
PASS-persuade ATV-buy dog
'Ria persuaded Torus to buy a dog.'
b. Di-elek si Ria si Torus di-pareso doktor.
'Ria persuaded Torus to be examined by a doctor.'

(4) a. Mar-janji si Torus (tu si Ria) man-[t]uhor biang.
INTR-promise to ATV-buy dog
'Torus promised (Ria) to buy a dog.'

b. Mar-janji si Torus (tu si Ria) di-pareso doktor.
INTR-promise to PASS-examine doctor
'Torus promised (Ria) to be examined by a doctor.'

4 Diagram the linking from syntax to semantics for the Lakhota sentence in (9.28c), the Acehnese sentence in (9.30b), and the English sentence in (9.36a). Give the constituent projection only for each sentence and logical structure of the sentence. [**section 9.1.3.1.2**]

5 Diagram the linking from semantics to syntax for the Malagasy sentence in (9.58b) and the linking from syntax to semantics for the Icelandic sentence in (9.61b). Give the constituent projection only for each sentence and logical structure for the sentence. [**section 9.1.3.2.2**]

6 Based on the data presented below, give the following information:

(a) the logical structure for each sentence in (1);
(b) the interclausal semantic relations that each predicate (*eager* vs. *easy*) expresses;
(c) the relationship between (i) the different logical structures and different interclausal semantic relations and (ii) the different permutations possible with each predicate (i.e. how do the different syntactic possibilities in (2)–(5) follow from the logical structure of and interclausal semantic relation expressed by each predicate?) (see section 8.4.3);
(d) the linking from semantics to syntax for each sentence in (1); give the constituent projection only (omit the operator and focus structure projections). [**section 9.1.3.2**]

(1) a. Pat is eager to please.
b. Pat is easy to please.

(2) a. Pat is eager to please Chris.
b. *Pat is easy to please Chris.

(3) a. *It is eager to please Chris.
a′. *It is eager for Pat to please Chris.
b. It is easy to please Chris.
b′. It is easy for Pat to please Chris.

(4) a. *To please Chris is eager.
a′. *For Pat to please Chris is eager.
b. To please Chris is easy.
b′. For Pat to please Chris is easy.

(5) a. *Chris is eager for Pat to please.
a′. Chris is eager for Pat to please her.

b. Chris is easy for Pat to please.
b′. *Chris is easy for Pat to please her.

7 Describe the juncture–nexus type of the construction from Ancash Quechua (Cole 1984) in (1) and state how it differs from the constructions in (2), based on the data below. The data in (3)–(5) are relevant to determining the type of linkage. Describe the linking from semantics to syntax for (1a′), and give a constructional template for the construction. [**section 9.1.3.2**]

(1) a. Noqa-∅ muna-a libru-ta lei-y-ta.
1sg-NOM want-1sg book-ACC read-INF-ACC
'I want to read the book.'
a′. Noqa-∅ libru-ta muna-a lei-y-ta.
1sg-NOM book-ACC want-1sg read-INF-ACC
'I want to read the book.'
b. Qalla-rqo-o-mi libru-ta lei-r.
begin-REC-1sg-EVID book-ACC read-INF
'I began to read the book.'
b′. Libru-ta qalla-rqo-o-mi lei-r.
book-ACC begin-REC-1sg-EVID read-INF
'I began to read the book.'
c. Noqa-∅ Huaraz-chaw muna-a wayi-ta rura-y-ta.
1sg-NOM -LOC want-1sg house-ACC make-INF-ACC
'I want to make a house in Huaraz.'
d. Noqa-∅ qam-ta waray las sesi-m muna-q
1sgNOM 2sg-ACC tomorrow the six-EVID want-1sg → 2sg
rika-y-niki-ta.
see-INF-2sgU-ACC
'I want to see you tomorrow at six.'

(2) a. Noqa-∅ malisya-a Fwan-∅ qellay-ta suwa-nqa-n-ta.
1sg-NOM suspect-1sg Juan-NOM money-ACC steal-NMZ-3sg-ACC
'I suspect (that) Juan stole the money.'
a′. *Noqa-∅ qellay-ta malisya-a Fwan-∅ suwa-nqa-n-ta.
1sg-NOM money-ACC suspect-1sg Juan-NOM steal-NMZ-3sg-ACC
'I suspect (that) Juan stole the money.'
b. Mama-∅ muna-n wawa-n-∅ aytsa-ta miku-na-n-paq.
mother-NOM want-3sg child-3sg-NOM meat-ACC eat-NMZ-3sg-SBJ
'Mother wants her child to eat meat.'
b′. *Mama-∅ aytsa-ta muna-n wawa-n-∅ miku-na-n-paq.
mother-NOM meat-ACC want-3sg child-3sg-NOM eat-NMZ-3sg-SBJ
'Mother wants her child to eat meat.'

(3) a. Noqa-∅-m musya-a Fuan-∅ María-ta kuya-shqa-n-ta.
1sg-NOM-EVID know-1sg Juan-NOM Maria-ACC love-NMZ-3sg-ACC
'I know that Juan loves Maria.'

a′. Noqa-∅ musya-a-mi Fuan-∅ María-ta kuya-shqa-n-ta.
1sg-NOM know-1sg-EVID Juan-NOM Maria-ACC love-NMZ-3sg-ACC
'I know that Juan loves Maria.'

a″. Noqa-∅ musya-a Fuan-∅ María-ta kuya-shqa-n-ta-m.
1sg-NOM know-1sg Juan-NOM Maria-ACC love-NMZ-3sg-ACC-EVID
'I know that Juan loves Maria.'

b. *Noqa-∅ musya-a Fuan-∅-mi María-ta kuya-shqa-n-ta.
1sg-NOM know-1sg Juan-NOM-EVID Maria-ACC love-NMZ-3sg-ACC
'I know that Juan loves Maria.'

b′. *Noqa-∅ musya-a Fuan-∅ María-ta-m kuya-shqa-n-ta.
1sg-NOM know-1sg Juan-NOM Maria-ACC-EVID love-NMZ-3sg-ACC
'I know that Juan loves Maria.'

(4) a. Noqa-∅ muna-a libru-ta-m lei-y-ta.
1sg-NOM want-1sg book-ACC-EVID read-INF-ACC
'I want to read the book.'

a′. Noqa-∅ libru-ta-m muna-a lei-y-ta.
1sg-NOM book-ACC-EVID want-1sg read-INF-ACC
'I want to read the book.'

b. Qalla-rqo-o kechwa-ta-m yachatsi-r.
begin-REC-1sg Quechua-ACC-EVID teach-INF
'I began to teach Quechu.'

b′. Kechwa-ta-m qalla-rqo-o yachatsi-r.
Quechua-ACC-EVID begin-REC-1sg teach-INF
'I began to teach Quechua.'

(5) a. *Noqa-∅ malisya-a Fwan-∅ qellay-ta-m suwa-nqa-n-ta.
1sg-NOM suspect-1sg Juan-NOM money-ACC-EVID steal-NMZ-3sg-ACC
'I suspect (that) Juan stole the money.'

b. *Mama-∅ muna-n wawa-n-∅ aytsa-ta-m miku-na-n-paq.
mother-NOM want-3sg child-3sg-NOM meat-ACC-EVID eat-NMZ-3sg-SBJ
'Mother wants her child to eat meat.'

8 Diagram the linking from semantics to syntax and from syntax to semantics in the externally headed Korean relative clause in (1a) (Yang 1994) and the internally headed Belhare relative clause in (1b) (=(6.79e)). For the purposes of this exercise, treat Belhare as dependent-making with verb agreement, like Croatian. Give the constituent projection only and logical structure for each sentence. **[section 9.3]**

(1) a. Chelswu ka kocangna-n khempwuthe-lul kochi-ess-ta.
NOM broken-REL computer-ACC fix-PAST-DEC
'Chelsoo fixed the computer that was broken.'

b. Tombhira-ŋa wa seiʔ-s-u-ha chitt-he-m.
wild.cat-ERG chicken kill-TRANS.PERF-3sgU-NMZ find-PAST-1plA
'We found the chicken that the cat had killed.'
*'We found the cat that had killed the chicken.'

9 (*Note*: this last problem is only for students who have a background in GB theory.) **[section 9.5]**

Sentences like those in (1) have posed a problem for GB theory, as they seem to involve a conflict between the demands of bounding theory (subjacency), on the one hand, and those of binding and case theory, on the other. Are sentences like this a problem for theory presented in this chapter? Explain.

(1) a. Who does Pat seem to like?
    b. What does Chris expect Kim to buy?
    c. Who was believed to have stolen the money?

EPILOG
The goals of linguistic theory revisited

The task in this book was to present a theory of syntax from the communication-and-cognition perspective. As stated in section 1.4, the general skeleton of the theory is drawn from RRG, and many parts of the theory are elaborations on basic RRG concepts, e.g. the layered structure of the clause, semantic macroroles, potential focus domain, pragmatic pivots, juncture and nexus. But the content of many of the analyses integrate ideas from a variety of theories and individuals, e.g. Rijkhoff's theory of noun phrase structure from FG, the notion of constructional template adapted from ConG, Lambrecht's theory of information structure, Pustejovsky's theory of nominal qualia, the pragmatic analysis of pronominalization of Kuno, Bolinger and Bickerton, and Jackendoff's ideas about reflexivization, to name a few.

Of the issues raised in chapter 1, one of the most important issues, and for some linguists, *the* most important issue, is language acquisition. In section 1.3.2 we briefly mentioned work by a number of linguists, psycholinguists and psychologists on this topic from the communication-and-cognition perspective, and in this final section, we will look at the implications of the syntactic analyses we have presented for theoretical questions in acquisition and child language.

The first step is to clarify the foundational issue, namely, assumptions about the nature of the human cognitive endowment regarding language. Chomsky has always been very clear that for him the essential features of the grammars of human languages are part of a species-specific, genetically determined biological organ of language; indeed, he now claims (Chomsky 1995) that the basic syntax of all languages is the same and that all cross-linguistic variation is due to lexical differences. This position is usually paraphrased as a claim that 'language is innate', but this paraphrase is very misleading, for two reasons. First, Chomsky has always maintained that innateness is not the issue; the question is not whether language is innate, but rather *how* it is innate (see Chomsky 1975: 13, 33). That is, it is uncontroversial that human beings are endowed with the cognitive faculties to learn and use language; the issue is, rather, what is the nature of this endowment? In particular, are the cognitive mechanisms that enable humans to learn language unique to language, or are they involved in the acquisition of other knowledge and capacities? Thus, the central issue for Chomsky is the *autonomy* of the language faculty. He maintains that the language acquisition device (LAD) discussed in section 1.3.1 is an autonomous mental organ which is independent of other human cognitive capacities. Second, as we discussed in section 1.3.1, Chomsky is concerned with grammar, not language in the usual sense, and even then it is restricted to what he calls 'core grammar'.

Researchers investigating language acquisition and development from the communication-and-cognition perspective do not assume that the cognitive endowment that enables children to learn language is autonomous. Rather, they take the question of unique cognitive structures for language learning to be an open question to be decided by empirical research and not by theoretical fiat. Hence, as we discuss the implications for acquisition of the different aspects of the syntactic theory we have proposed, the primary issues to be addressed are (1) what distinctions must be learned in order to acquire the category or concept, (2) what kind of evidence is available to the child in the input from caregivers and from the situation in which utterances are used, and (3) to what extent is the concept or category related either to the child's innate non-linguistic cognitive capacities or to other non-linguistic capacities or knowledge.

If children do not bring a Chomskyan LAD to the task of acquiring a first language, what do they bring? There are many proposals in this area, e.g. Slobin (1973, 1985), Schlesinger (1982), Bruner (1983), Karmiloff-Smith (1992) and Braine (1992, 1994). Braine (1992, 1994) argues for the following preconditions to language learning (1992: 80).

(1) a. A cognitive architecture for an initial learning mechanism for concepts and relations.
    b. An account of the kinds of input delivered by sensory systems to the learning mechanism.
    c. 'Kantian-type framework categories', e.g. 'ontological categories' such as object, place and event, 'predicate' which comprises concepts (including properties) and relations, and 'argument' which refers to instances of concepts or entities related by relations.

The first two points refer to general cognitive processes; it is the third point which is most relevant to this discussion. Braine argues that there must be a system of mental representation which human beings have in which notions like 'object', 'place' and 'event' are represented and manipulated; this is sometimes called a 'language of thought' (e.g. Fodor 1975). Despite this potentially misleading label, this representational system is not linguistic; it is, according to Braine, part of the initial cognitive endowment and is used in cognitive processes in many domains. Of particular importance is the idea that objects and their properties and objects and the relations among them are represented in terms of predicates (properties, relations) and arguments (objects). Braine (1990, 1993) calls this a 'natural logic' and argues that it is a fundamental component of human cognitive processes in many domains.

Braine, Bruner, Slobin and others portray the initial cognitive endowment of human beings as very rich and structured.[1] Bruner (1983) emphasizes that human infants are capable of highly focused analysis and reasoning in abstract domains and are also strongly predisposed to goal-directed activity, including communicative social interaction with other humans. Braine (1990, 1993) provides some of the details about the 'natural logic' humans are born with and the representational system it employs. Neither of them posits a Chomsky-type autonomous LAD, and so the crucial question is, can a plausible account of the acquisition of syntax be built on the foundations that Braine and others have laid? If so, then that is evidence that an autonomous LAD is unnecessary.[2] A detailed account of the acquisition of syntax is manifestly impossible in this short chapter; rather, we will address the three questions given above with respect to the major topics in the previous chapters, in order to see whether such a detailed account is at least plausible, based on what is known in each of the areas.

The first issue is the acquisition of clause structure, specifically, the acquisition of the layered structure of the clause. What distinctions must be learned to acquire clause structure? As we argued in chapter 2, the universal aspects of the layered structure are based on two oppositions: first, between predicating vs. non-predicating elements, and second, between those NPs or PPs which are semantic arguments of the predicate vs. those which are not. The first distinction underlies the notion of nucleus vs. other, and the second distinguishes core arguments from peripheral adjuncts. These distinctions are coded overtly in every language, and in every theory of acquisition the child must learn these distinctions based on input from caregivers; even if one assumes an innate syntactic schema for clauses, the child would still have to learn these distinctions in order to know how to map lexical items into the innate schema. It is not necessary to posit the innate syntactic schema, however. The central concepts of the layered structure of the clause can be constructed on the basis of these two oppositions and the notions of predicate and argument in the 'natural logic' discussed by Braine. He gives an explicit account of how basic clause structure could be developed on the basis of these notions. He begins by specifying the (innate) developmental primitives he assumes (1992: 90).

(2) *Developmental primitives*
- a. A learning mechanism that uses the 'old-rules-analyze-new-material' principle.
- b. Semantic categories such as 'argument' and 'predicate', including ontological categories, for example 'object', 'place', 'action' and 'event'.
- c. A tendency to classify words and phrases, not already classified, as referring to instances of the categories in (b).

The semantic categories of 'argument' and 'predicate' are derivative of the 'natural logic' categories mentioned in (1c). Neither of the primitives in (2a) or (2b) is unique to language. The learning process posited by Braine (1992) is summarized in (3).

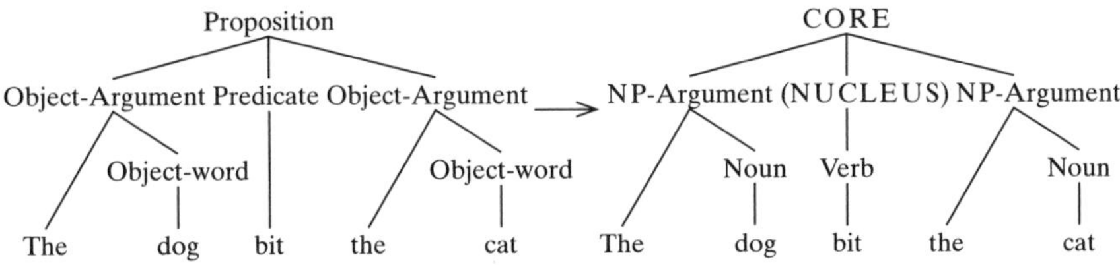

Figure E1 Transition from analysis in terms of ontological categories to syntactic categories, adapted from Braine (1992)

(3) *Learning process*

a. Child begins to parse sentences based on the semantic categories in (2b) yielding (for English) a parse tree like the one on the left in figure E1.
b. Encountering new sentences which do not fit the semantic prototypes, e.g. *The situation justified the measures*, the child applies the principles in (2a) and (2c) and assimilates such propositions to the patterns arrived at by principle (2b).
c. Syntactic categories are generalized from semantic ones: Noun from 'object', Verb from 'predicate', Adjective from 'property', etc.
d. Result is a semantically based yet syntactic representation of clause structure, as in the right tree structure in figure E1.

The syntactic structure is represented in terms of the layered structure of the clause. The core expresses a proposition, and the arrow represents the generalizations in (3b, c) made during development on the basis of experience. The result of the learning process as discussed by Braine is very close to the layered structure of the clause, and it is very plausible to assume that this process, together with the mastering of the contrasts between predicates vs. non-predicates and arguments vs. non-arguments, leads to the constituent projection of the layered structure of the clause as presented in chapter 2. The language-specific features of clause structure, e.g. precore slot, right-detached position, are readily learned on the basis of positive evidence in the input. It should be noted that in languages without variable syntactic pivots or controllers and *in situ* WH-words in questions, e.g. Lakhota, the units of the layered structure of the clause will be virtually isomorphic with the semantic notions that motivate them. This is a very common language type, if not the most common.

The other aspect of clause structure discussed in chapter 2 is the operator projection, and the acquisition of operators, which are modifiers of the different layers of the clause, would be tied to the acquisition of the central distinctions in clause structure sketched above. There are striking cross-linguistic patterns in the acquisition of tense and aspect (Weist 1986), modality (Stephany 1986) and negation, e.g. aspectual distinctions appear either before or simultaneous with tense distinctions in child language but tense does not appear prior to aspect. Van Valin (1991a) presents an analysis of the acquisition of tense, aspect, modality and negation and shows how the observed cross-linguistic patterns can be accounted for in terms of the theory we have presented. Thus, there is a plausible account of the acquisition of the constituent and operator projections of the layered structure of the clause, based on the initial cognitive endowment posited by Braine and others.

The three projections of the clause in the projection grammar representations include focus structure, and much less work has been done on the acquisition of information structure than any of the other areas covered in the book, though there has been work on the acquisition of pragmatics in general, e.g. Bates (1976), Ochs and Schieffelin (1979), Karmiloff-Smith (1979), and on phenomena related to focus structure, e.g. Greenfield (1978), Greenfield and Goldring-Zukow (1978), Clancy (1993) and Greenfield and Dent (1995). Children readily acquire the distinctions between topic and focus and do this on the basis of information in the input from their interactions with caregivers.

Verbs and their arguments are the subject of chapters 3 and 4, and there has been extensive research done on the acquisition of verbs and argument structure, e.g. Bowerman (1974, 1982), Pinker (1989), Tomasello (1992) and Tomasello and Merriman (1995). The crucial distinctions for the *Aktionsart* classes are static vs. non-static, punctual vs. non-punctual, telic vs. non-telic and causative vs. non-causative. An important question is, what are the kinds of cues children can use to identify the verbs in the language that express these distinctions? In a series of papers on the acquisition of verbs in English and Japanese (1987, 1989, 1990, 1991a, 1992, 1995), Rispoli has shown that there are many cues in the input which the child can use to determine whether a verb is punctual or not, telic or not, etc. and assign it to the appropriate class. Research by Bowerman, Pinker, Tomasello and many others has shown that the verb classes discussed in chapter 3 are readily learned by children. Turning to argument structure, it might be thought that children learn the argument structure of verbs by simply attending to the NPs and PPs that accompany verbs in the input from caretakers. While this is clearly an important source of information, it is in many cases insufficient, due to the ability of speakers of some languages, e.g. Japanese, to omit NPs and pronouns in the appropriate discourse context. In the papers mentioned above, Rispoli shows how Japanese children learn the argument structure of Japanese verbs, even in contexts in which there are very high rates of ellipsis in the input. Rispoli's work was done in RRG, from which the framework that we presented in chapters 3 and 4 is taken. With respect to the nature of the arguments themselves, Braine and Hardy (1982) show that children operate with a semantic role they call actor which is more general than AGENT and is close to the notion of the semantic macrorole actor. It appears, then, that there is evidence for semantic macroroles as being important in early grammar.

A major issue in acquisition studies is the nature of grammatical relations in early child language: are they syntactic or semantic? Bowerman (1973) and Braine (1976) argued that they are basically semantic in nature; Braine and Hardy (1982) argued that there are no grounds for positing a syntactic relation of subject independent of the semantic relation of actor in the early stages of the acquisition of English, and Matthei (1987) provides additional experimental support for this view. English children operate for a long time on the thesis that the only relations in a transitive clause are actor (preverbal NP) and undergoer (postverbal NP), as indicated by the well-known failure of children to comprehend passives correctly for a considerable period of time. Hyams (1986), on the other hand, argued that they are syntactic, based on the fact that intransitive verbs in Italian agree with their single argument regardless of its thematic relation, and that this proves that 'grammatical agreement is a strictly formal process which holds between what is traditionally referred to as "subject" and "verb"' (138). Given the discussion in chapter 6 about restricted neutralizations, it should be clear that both sides in this debate are in a sense correct. Bowerman, Braine and Matthei are correct in saying that children do not use the same grammatical relations as adults, and Hyams is correct in pointing out that the fact that Italian children treat actors and undergoers with intransitive verbs alike is evidence that the child's grammatical relations are not purely semantic; that is, their system is not like the one in Acehnese discussed in chapter 6. Weist (1990) presents an analysis of early grammatical relations in Polish, showing that Polish-speaking children, like Italian- and English-speaking children, neutralize actor and undergoer with intransitive verbs. However, he draws the correct conclusion that children learning English, Polish and Italian use an [S, A] pivot in their early grammar, and this is neither a purely semantic system like in Acehnese, nor is it the system used by adults in any of the three languages. It is, however, the system used in Enga, Lakhota, Warlpiri and Zapotec, and we argued in section 6.5 that it is in fact the most common pivot type found in human languages. It is probably no accident that the system children construct initially is also the cross-linguistically most common one, not because it is innate or the like, but because it is the one which balances the demands discussed in section 6.5 most efficiently. The adult grammatical relations in English, Polish and Italian involve pragmatic pivots, and this means that children have to factor focus structure distinctions into the mix. Rispoli (1991b, 1994) has shown how children piece together the different factors that go into constituting the privileged syntactic argument types in their language; he looks at this issue in Turkish, Georgian, Hebrew, Kaluli, Hungarian and Italian. Thus, the account of grammatical relations in chapter 6 is not only able to handle the diversity of grammatical relations systems across languages but also provides an explanatory framework for the analysis of the acquisition of grammatical relations.

The heart of the grammar is the linking algorithms governing the mapping between semantic representation and syntactic representations. Are the linking rules learned? Pinker (1984), for example, posits an innate set of linking rules. Bowerman (1990) investigates this question and concludes that there is no evidence in her data that would support the postulation of any innate preferences in linking. Rather, children seem to go through the same stages that children do when learning other rules. For example, the Actor–Undergoer Hierarchy specifies that with verbs which have . . . **predicate′** (y, z) in their logical structure, e.g. *give*, *show*, *load*, etc., the second argument is the unmarked choice for undergoer and the first argument is the marked choice. Some verbs which have this as part of their logical structure do not allow the expected alternation, e.g. *donate*, and in other cases pairs of verbs lexicalize the alternation, e.g. for most speakers, *rob* lexicalizes the LOCATIVE as undergoer and *steal* the THEME. If the acquisition of these alternations follows the same pattern as, for instance, the learning of the English plural or past tense, then the following sequence is predicted: (1) the patterns associated with individual verbs are learned; (2) the child discovers a generalization about the alternations, namely the second argument (THEME) is the unmarked choice, and applies it across the board, producing overgeneralizations akin to **goed* and **mouses*; and (3) the marked assignments are learned as exceptions to the 'rule'. This is almost exactly the sequence which Bowerman (1982) reports with respect to the acquisition of these alternations; crucially, children overwhelmingly overgeneralize the THEME as the unmarked choice, not the LOCATIVE, e.g. *Can I fill some salt* [THEME] *into the bear?* [LOCATIVE] (1982: 338), and this is in accord with the Actor–Undergoer Hierarchy. Thus there is evidence that the lexical part of the linking (macrorole assignment) is learned.

What about the linking between macroroles and grammatical relations? It should be clear that this could not possibly be innate, given the construction-by-construction variation we found both within languages and across languages in chapter 6; Van Valin (1992b) makes the same argument based on data from ergative languages alone. Evidence that the learning of this phase is strongly influenced by the input to the child comes from a comparison of the emergence of the passive construction in English vs. Sesotho (Demuth 1989, 1990), as discussed in chapter 5. We saw there that the potential focus domain in Sesotho excludes preverbal elements, with the consequence that WH-words in questions must occur postverbally. Hence, in order for a Sesotho caregiver to ask a crying child 'Who hit you?', a passive must be used, i.e. 'You were hit by who?', and Demuth reports that there is a much more frequent occurrence of the passive in caretaker speech to children in Sesotho than in English. One of the striking consequences of this is that children as young as 2.8 years are productively using full passives with agent phrases, something which their English-learning counterparts appear to do at a much later age, and Demuth attributes this to its high frequency in the input. Thus, Sesotho children master the marked linking between macroroles and grammatical relations earlier than their English counterparts due to differences in the input the children receive.

The acquisition of complex sentences has not received nearly as much attention as the acquisition of syntactic phenomena in simple sentences, unfortunately.

One prediction that could be made about the acquisition of complex sentences is the following: assuming that simpler structures are acquired before more complex structures, and assuming further that subordinate constructions are more complex structures than non-subordinate constructions, we may predict that the first complex sentences to emerge will be non-subordinate rather than subordinate. Limber (1973) and Bowerman (1979) assert that the first complex sentences to appear in English-learning children's speech are 'object complements' like *I wanna read book*. If 'object complements' are truly the first complex structures to appear, then this prediction is definitely incorrect. But note that these are the very constructions that were argued to be *non*-subordinate in chapter 8, contrary to the conventional analysis of them; they are, rather, examples of core cosubordination, and therefore the prediction is correct, at least for English. Since RRG, the theory from which the notion of core cosubordination is taken, is the only theory that treats these constructions as not involving subordination, it is the only one that makes a correct prediction here. This suggests that the theory of clause linkage presented in chapter 8 could be fruitfully applied to the analysis of the complex sentences in child language.

The restrictions on WH-question formation, topicalization and relativization discussed in section 9.5 have played a very important role in discussions of innateness, autonomy and the LAD. They are often presented as the paradigm case of the argument from the poverty of the stimulus in (1.7) and the strongest argument for an innate, autonomous LAD. If one considers the GB analysis of these restrictions as applied to languages like Lakhota, summarized in n. 17 in chapter 9, the conclusion that the principle of subjacency must be a part of an autonomous LAD seems inescapable; how could children acquiring Lakhota learn a constraint on NP-movement applying at the abstract level of Logical Form, when the language gives no overt evidence of any movement rules in the first place? However, the analysis presented in section 9.5 has very different implications for language acquisition, as argued in Van Valin (1991a, 1994). What a Lakhota child has to learn on this account is (1) the rule that in order for a word like *táku* 'what, something' to be interpreted as a question word, it must be the focus of the question operator *he*, and (2) the restriction on the potential focus domain in complex sentences in (9.123). The combination gives all of the restrictions found in Lakhota. A child acquiring English, on the other hand, must learn (1) that a WH-word in the precore slot can only be properly interpreted if it functions as a semantic argument in the logical structure of a clause in the potential focus domain, and (2) the restriction on the potential focus domain in (9.123). This accounts for all of the basic restrictions, as we saw in section 9.5. What kind of evidence could a child use to learn the restrictions on the potential focus domain?

It is commonly claimed that there is no evidence available to the child concerning constraints on WH-question formation and related constructions, but there is in fact abundant evidence available to children with respect to the range of possible interpretations of yes–no questions from their own interactions with caretakers and peers and from observing the verbal interactions of others. We showed in section 8.5 that the focus of yes–no questions must be within the potential focus domain, and thus these questions are subject to the same constraints as WH-questions and related constructions. It has never been suggested that the source of a child's knowledge of the principles governing the interpretation of yes–no questions is anything other than the verbal interactions in which the child is involved. The restrictions on yes–no questions so acquired are naturally extended to other types of questions, in particular, WH-questions. Thus the child's knowledge of restrictions on WH-question formation has its origin in the learned restrictions on yes–no questions. Is there any evidence that such a transfer of syntactico-pragmatic restrictions could occur? A clear example of this extension of restrictions can be seen in Wilson and Peters' (1988) study of a three-year-old blind child's production of WH-questions which apparently violate extraction constraints; some of his deviant WH-questions are given in (4).

(4) a. What are you cookin' on a hot ___? [Answer: 'stove']
b. What are we gonna go at [to] Auntie and ___?
c. What are we gonna look for some ___ with Johnnie?

Wilson and Peters demonstrate that the constructions have their source in a questioning routine that the child engaged in with his primary caregiver. Examples are given in (5).

(5) a. CAREGIVER: What did you eat? Eggs and . . .
CHILD: Mbacon.
b. CAREGIVER: Oh, that's a . . .
CHILD: Aleph.
CAREGIVER: That's a aleph.

In this routine the caregiver leaves a gap in his utterance which the child is expected to fill in. The child mastered the routine, and then the restrictions on question formation derived from it were incorrectly assumed to apply to 'movement' WH-questions as well; when the child learned to make WH-questions in which the WH-word occurs in the precore slot, he applied these restrictions to them, leading to the questions in (4). The account of these questions that Wilson and Peters present gives evidence that children do in fact transfer the restrictions learned for one type of question to other types.

Thus, we have sketched a plausible account of how children learning Lakhota or English could learn the constraints on the potential focus domain that are the basis for the restrictions on WH-question formation and related constructions. We have addressed two of the three relevant questions, those dealing with the distinctions to be learned and the kind of evidence needed. The third question concerns the extent to which the concepts involved are related to non-linguistic cognitive processes. In Van Valin (1986b) it is shown how the crucial notions in this account can be derived from Grice's (1975) pragmatic theory. The definitions of 'presupposition' and 'assertion' (and therewith 'focus') are derived from Kempson's (1975) reformulation of Grice's maxim of quantity. The Gricean foundation for these principles is absolutely crucial. Kasher (1976) argues that Grice's principles can be derived from general principles of rational action, and Grice himself maintained that they apply to both linguistic and non-linguistic behavior. The point here is not about whether Grice's principles are innate or not; rather, it is that they are not autonomous linguistic principles. Hence the principles underlying the concepts introduced in chapter 5, which form the basis of the account of subjacency phenomena we have given, are ultimately grounded in Grice's general principles of rational human behavior.[3]

This brief survey of issues in language acquisition has shown that the theory of syntax presented in the book can serve as an explanatory framework for the analysis of language acquisition and child language. Moreover, at no point did it become necessary to invoke an autonomous LAD to account for the acquisition of these phenomena. On the contrary, we found considerable evidence that the grammatical phenomena are learned on the basis of the initial cognitive endowment posited by Braine, Slobin, Bruner and others, together with the input that the children receive from caregivers. To the extent that this conclusion holds up in light of future research, it stands as a powerful argument against Chomsky's theory of an autonomous LAD and in favor of the communication-and-cognition approach to language and language acquisition.

NOTES

1 The goals of linguistic theory

1 As this example illustrates, the operation of normal science involves both induction and deduction; that is, hypotheses to be tested normally arise from observations of the phenomena under consideration.

2 This is not the only prediction that could be derived; it is merely being chosen as an illustration.

3 It should be noted that there are many followers of Chomsky who do psycholinguistic research and study child language. The point here is that it is not a necessary part of the study of language acquisition, in Chomsky's conception of the issue.

2 Syntactic structure, I: simple clauses and noun phrases

1 These trees are not intended as accurate representations of the structures that would be assigned by e.g. GB theory; rather they are intended to represent the relevant aspects of structure only.

2 Strictly speaking, in recent models neither of the two syntactic levels, D-structure or S-structure, corresponds to the actual form of the sentence. Both of these are still abstract, although S-structure is closer to the surface form than D-structure, and the surface structure, the actual form of the sentence, is the output of the phonology. We return to the question of non-local dependencies involving case assignment and agreement in section 7.3.1.

3 While the details of phrase-structure trees have changed over the years, it remains true that, for Chomsky, the 'direct object' is the NP that is sister to the V and the 'subject' is the sister to the node dominating the V node and the 'direct object', be it the VP or the V′, depending on the theory. See section 6.1.2.1 for detailed discussion.

4 The noun markers like *balan* and *baŋgul* in Dyirbal express three pieces of information. The stem, *ba*-, is a deictic element that expresses how far the referent is from the speaker and whether it is visible or not; *ba*- signals 'visible and not far away'. The next part is a case marker, and the final part is an indicator of the class of the noun. There are four classes in Dyirbal: class I includes males, kangaroos, the moon, boomerangs, etc.; class II includes females, dogs, the sun, fire, scorpions, etc. (the 'women, fire and dangerous things' referred to in the title of Lakoff 1987); class III includes trees with edible fruit; and class IV is the residual class. See Dixon (1972) for more discussion.

5 This characterization of these NPs as 'subject' and 'object' are meant only for expository purposes; the nature of grammatical relations in Dyirbal will be discussed in chapter 6.

6 The representation may be abstract with respect to phonology or morphophonology, e.g. the output could be in terms of abstract morphophonological units rather than concrete phonetic ones. We will not be concerned with the issue of (morpho)phonological representation.

7 There is a weaker sense of 'universal': the concept or relation is part of the universal inventory from which the grammars of particular languages are constituted. It is in this sense that features in phonology are universal; they make up the universal inventory from which languages draw, but some features are not found in the phonology of every language. Universals of this type were called 'substantive universals' in Chomsky (1965).

8 In many European linguistic theories, the term 'actant' is used for syntactic arguments and 'circonstant' for adjuncts (cf. Abraham 1978, Kibrik 1987); 'argument' is used for semantic arguments only.

9 Bare NP adverbials like *yesterday* or *tomorrow*, as in *He arrived yesterday* or *She will leave tomorrow*, are obvious exceptions to this generalization.

10 Our use of the term 'direct argument' is broader than that in traditional grammar, where it refers to NPs in the nominative and accusative cases only.

11 In Dyirbal, all NPs are case-marked, and there are no adpositions; consequently there is no coding contrast between core and peripheral NPs. They can be clearly distinguished on syntactic grounds, however. Direct core arguments take absolutive, ergative and dative cases; these cases code the primary grammatical functions/relations. What distinguishes the oblique core arguments in the instrumental and (some uses of the) locative case from the peripheral NPs in the allative and ablative cases is the ability of NPs in the instrumental and locative case (if they are part of the semantic representation of the verb) to appear as direct core arguments in the absolutive case; this is never possible with locative NPs which are not represented in the semantic representation of the verb, such as allative NPs and ablative NPs. Thus it is possible to establish the distinctions among direct core argument, oblique core argument and peripheral NP even if all receive the same type of coding. See section 3.3.3 in Foley and Van Valin (1984) for detailed discussion.

12 An example of this is applicative constructions in Bantu languages; see section 7.2.2.

13 The Lakhota verb *wąyą́ke* 'see' takes its subject and object markers as infixes; hence in the glosses 'stem' refers to the part of the stem that occurs before the infixes.

14 The source of VPs in languages which have them will be discussed in chapter 5.

15 This idea has a long history; von Humboldt (1836) argued that this was the case for Classical Aztec, and Boas (1911) made the same argument for Chinook.

16 This spelling of the language's name reflects current practice by both Mayanists and the Mayan-speaking communities in Central America. It was formerly spelled 'Jacaltec'.

17 It might be expected that honorifics, as in Japanese, Korean and many other languages, would be considered to be an operator. But there are good reasons to doubt that they are; the primary one is that honorific vs. non-honorific forms involve different lexical choices, rather than differently inflected forms of the same word. In Japanese, for

example, the different honorific possibilities for the verb 'give', for example, involve different lexical items, not inflected forms of the same basic verb. Even for Korean, where there is less lexicalization of honorific distinctions, Yang (1994) argues convincingly that honorifics should not be treated as part of the operator system.

18 This type of structural representation, called a 'projection grammar', was first proposed in Johnson (1987).

19 It should be emphasized that the term 'constituent' is not being used here in the same sense as in 'immediate constituent'. It refers here to the main constituents of the layered structure of the clause, the nucleus (containing the predicate), the arguments of the predicate (NPs, PPs), the core and the periphery (PPs, adverbials).

20 For readers familiar with GB Theory, this representational system bears some resemblance to representations of clause structure involving a VP-internal subject and extended functional projections. A VP containing the subject corresponds roughly to the core (see section 6.1.2.1), and the higher functional projections correspond roughly to the operator projection. This may be represented as follows:

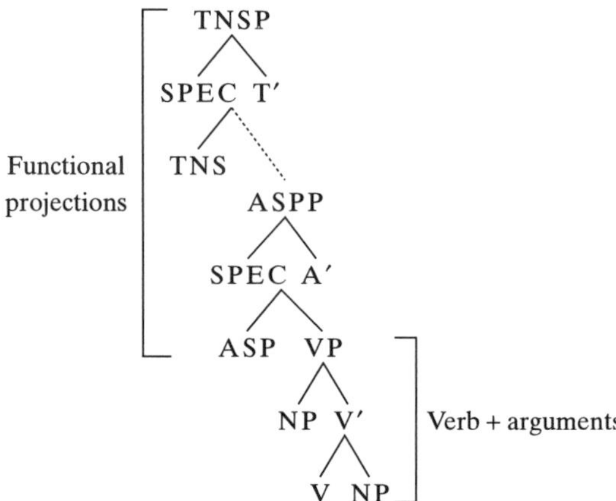

Despite these similarities, there are fundamental and important differences between the two types of syntactic representations. First, GB includes verb agreement morphemes among the functional projections, whereas these are not considered to be operators in RRG. Second, NPs and the verb move from their VP-internal initial positions up the tree to get case, check agreement, etc. in GB, whereas in RRG the elements of the constituent projection interact with the elements of the operator projection only in linearization. Agreement and case assignment, as we will see in chapter 7, are handled in the linking between the semantic representation and the constituent projection; the operator projection plays no direct role of any kind in the account of these phenomena. Third, there is no principled motivation within GB Theory for the hierarchical arrangement of functional categories; that is, there is no principled explanation for why TenseP should be higher in the tree than AspectP. In contrast, we have seen that there is a clear semantic explanation for the hierarchical arrangement of the operators in the operator projection within RRG. Finally, for a purely historical point, the distinct operator projection in clause structure was first proposed in Johnson (1987) and thus antedates the development of this type of clause representation in GB.

21 Originally put forth in Foley and Van Valin (1984), this claim has been supported strongly by the results of a cross-linguistic study of morphology in Bybee (1985). Interestingly, Tesnière (1939) proposed basically a similar universal order of verbal affixes.

22 This is certainly true for English and Icelandic, for example. There are instances where a prepositionally marked argument functions like a direct core argument; such a case would be the so-called 'prepositional objects' in Spanish.

(i) a. Ve-o a María. / *Veo María.
see-1sgPRES to Maria
'I see Maria.'
b. Ve-o la casa. / *Veo a la casa.
see-1sgPRES the.F house
'I see the house.'

When the 'direct object' is human and specific it is marked by *a*, the preposition meaning 'to' which marks, among other things, 'indirect objects' with verbs of giving. Despite this superficial oblique marking, animate direct objects behave exactly like non-prepositionally marked direct objects, therefore *a María* in (a) should be considered a direct core argument, not an oblique core argument.

23 The prepositions with particle verbs in English, e.g. *rely on*, *decide on*, *look at*, *listen to*, do not function as argument markers but rather are part of the nucleus; their 'object' is in fact the argument of the whole complex nucleus, and it behaves like the argument of a simple nucleus with respect to grammatical processes like passivization or topicalization.

24 These semantic functions will be discussed in detail in chapter 3.

25 These notions will be discussed in more detail in chapter 5.

26 For a different non-derivational analysis of this phenomenon, see Sadock (1991).

27 See Payne (1993) for arguments in favor of the traditional analysis of the noun as head of the NP.

28 Saussure contrasted radically arbitrary linguistic elements like *cat* and *tree* with relatively motivated elements like *farmer* and *singer*. While *farm*, *sing* and *-er* are themselves radically arbitrary, the combinations *farm* + *-er* and *sing* + *-er* are not, since their meaning is derivable from the meanings of the constituent elements plus the V + *-er* rule in English. Presented with a form **glarfer*, an English-speaker could at least understand it as meaning 'one who glarfs'. This is not possible with radically arbitrary forms like *dog* and **glarf*. See also Lakoff (1987) for discussion of the difference between reduction and motivation.

29 See the references at the end of chapter 1 for such a presentation.

30 In these rules, ',' indicates that the elements are unordered and '( )' indicates that an element is optional, '{ }' indicates that the element is optional in the sense that a language need not have the category in question, * (called a 'Kleene star') signals that there can be from zero to an unspecified number of the elements, and '/' means 'or'.

31 Branching direction is even clearer in complex sentences, where subordinate clauses follow the matrix clause or core in English and precede it in Japanese.

32 Dik (1978) argues for what he calls a 'language-independent preferred order of constituents', which is based on the size of the constituents; it is, roughly, Clitics > Pronouns > NPs > PPs > Cores > Clauses.

33 Some terminological clarification is in order. In ConG, the term 'construction' is used for the abstract representation of the properties of the grammatical form, and the term 'construct' is used for the grammatical form itself. In HPSG (Pollard and Sag 1994), which shares many features with ConG, constructions in this sense are called 'signs'. We are using the term 'construction' for the grammatical form and 'constructional template' for the abstract representation of the properties of the form. Hence our 'constructional template' is equivalent to ConG's 'construction' and HPSG's 'sign'.

34 Such processes have been formalized in Tree-Adjoining Grammars (Joshi 1985, Kroch and Joshi 1987); these systems are formalizations for linguistic theories and not theories in their own right.

3 Semantic representation, I: verbs and arguments

1 This could be broken down into subactions, e.g. the knife coming into contact with the rope, Juan manipulating the knife in a sawing motion, and the knife passing through the rope.

2 It is also true that they would not all be equally informative answers to the question 'what happened?' But we are concerned with the relationship between sentences and states of affairs and not with conversational cooperation.

3 This is true for older speakers of the language; some younger speakers accept sentences like (3.8b) (D. Rood, personal communication).

4 This observation goes back to the beginning of modern linguistics; see Saussure (1917 [1959]), Boas (1911), Sapir (1921, 1924 [1951]).

5 Lexical decomposition is not uncontroversial; see Fodor (1970) for a critique and Jackendoff (1990: 37–41) for a convincing rejoinder.

6 It is important to keep in mind that semantic representations, even informal ones, like 'cause to die', are not equivalent to the English sentence *X caused Y to die*. Rather, the claim is that the semantic representation of *kill* involves causation, a change of state and a result state.

7 *Receive* may be paraphrased as '*x* comes to have *y*' and *give* as '*w* causes [*x* come to have *y*]'.

8 Some of these tests are taken from Dowty (1979), in which additional tests are proposed.

9 In applying this test in a language, it is crucial to make sure that the form in question is a true progressive, and not a form which may be called 'continuative', which indicates that a state of affairs continues in time without any implication that there is any action involved, unlike a true progressive. In Lakhota, for example, there is a suffix *-hą* which, when combined with a verb like *lową́* 'sing', yields *lową́hą* 'be singing', which looks like a progressive. But this suffix can equally well occur with many stative verbs, e.g. *bléča* 'to be shattered', giving *blečahą* 'it is shattered'. If one assumed that *-hą* is simply a progressive morpheme, one would wrongly conclude that verbs like *blečha* 'be shattered' are not states. The same considerations hold for the Japanese *-te i-* and Korean

-ko-iss constructions, neither of which is a true progressive (Hasegawa 1992, Yang 1994). Therefore it is important to ensure that one is dealing with a form which is a true progressive, and not one with the meaning 'state of affairs continues'.

10 There is an additional complexity with the progressive test. Some stative predicates, such as *sit*, *stand* and *lie*, may occur with the progressive under certain circumstances, as in (i).

(i) a. The book is lying on the table.
  b. The city lies/*is lying at the base of the mountains.

Carlson (1977) calls the statives in (i a) *stage-level* predicates, because they depict a situation which is not necessarily permanent. When the situation is necessarily permanent, as in (i b), the progressive is impossible.

11 Languages vary in terms of how many verbs can undergo this alternation (see Talmy 1985, 1991). In Italian and other Romance languages, for example, verbs like 'walk' and 'swim' typically cannot occur as active accomplishments. Rather, in order to say 'walk to the park' or 'swim to the island', one must use the verb *go* plus a participle, yielding 'go to the park walking' or 'go to the island swimming'.

12 This term is taken from Dowty (1979), who proposes a different interpretation of the Vendler categories and a different decomposition system from the one presented here, although this system has many features in common with Dowty's proposal.

13 For the task of distinguishing achievements from accomplishments, the ability of a verb to have an imperfective form can be interpreted as being equivalent to taking the progressive in test 1 in table 3.2.

14 Phrasal inceptive constructions like English *start to sing* or *begin to rain* are not punctual, as it is possible to say *He is starting to sing* or *It is beginning to rain.* Hence their logical structure would contain BECOME rather than INGR.

15 There are some complications involving causality that we will not go into in detail. First, there is a contrast among three basic types of causality: (i) *Pam made Sally go* [Direct (Coercive)]; (ii) *Pam had Sally go* [Indirect (Non-coercive)]; and (iii) *Pam let Sally go* [Permissive]. Both direct and indirect causality will be represented by 'CAUSE', and permissive causality will be represented by 'LET' in logical structure. English verbs like *let*, *drop* and *release* would have LET instead of CAUSE in their logical structure. Virtually all the examples to be discussed involve direct or indirect causality. Second, there is an important contrast between implicative and non-implicative causality; that is, the difference revolves around whether the resulting state of affairs is necessarily entailed or not. In English, lexical causatives and direct causality are implicative, whereas permissive is not: **Pam broke the dish, but it didn't break*; **Pam made Sally go, but she did not go*; *Pam let Sally go, but she did not go*.

Third, in some languages, e.g. Korean (Park 1993), lexical and direct causatives are not implicative.

(i) a. Chelswu-nun mwul-ul el-li-ess-una, mwul-i an
  -TOP water-ACC freeze-CAUS-PAST-but water-NOM NEG
  el-ess-ta.
  freeze-PAST-DEC
  'Chelswu froze the water, but the water did not freeze.'

b. Congi-lul thay-wu-ess-una, ku congi-ka an tha-ess-ta.
paper-ACC burn-CAUS-PAST-but the paper-NOM NEG burn-PAST-DEC
'I burned the paper, but the paper didn't burn.'

In order to make them implicative, the verb *noh* 'put' must be serialized with them, and this creates a contradiction within the sentence frame of (i).

(ii) a. *Chelswu-nun mwul-ul el-li-e-noh-ess-una, mwul-i an
-TOP water-ACC freeze-CAUS-LNK-put-PAST-but water-NOM NEG
el-ess-ta.
freeze-PAST-DEC
'Chelswu froze the water, but the water did not freeze.'

b. *Congi-lul thay-wu-e-noh-ess-una, ku congi-ka an
paper-ACC burn-CAUS-LNK-put-PAST but the paper-NOM NEG
tha-ess-ta.
burn-PAST-DEC
'I burned the paper, but the paper didn't burn.'

See Talmy (1991) for examples of similar phenomena from Tamil and Mandarin and Talmy (1976, 1988) for discussion of the different types of causation in language. We will have nothing further to say about this contrast, as it has little impact on the syntactic issues to be addressed in this and subsequent chapters.

16 This representation for *hit* is highly oversimplified; in fact, *hit* involves induced contact in a complex causal structure, i.e. [**do′** (x, ∅)] CAUSE [INGR **be-at′** (y, z)]; that is, it involves induced contact between *y* and *z*, as in *The boy hit the chair with a stick* ([**do′** (boy, ∅)] CAUSE [INGR **be-at′** (chair, stick)].

17 The ordering of arguments in logical structure will be discussed in the next section.

18 While '∧' is formally identical to the logical operator 'and', it is being used here as a conjunction for joining the component logical structures referring to substates-of-affairs that make up the macro-state-of-affairs denoted by the entire logical structure.

19 They in fact go by a variety of labels: semantic roles, case roles, semantic case roles, thematic roles and θ-roles, to name the most common ones.

20 That is, it is simpler to say 'EXPERIENCER' now and then than 'the first argument of a two-place state predicate of internal experience' every time.

21 This occurs in the first and second person only; it will be discussed in more detail in section 7.3.1.3.

22 The difference in the vowels in the stems reflects morphophonemic processes in the language; there are not two different verb stems.

4 Semantic representation, II: macroroles, the lexicon and noun phrases

1 The notion of 'semantic macroroles' was originally proposed in Van Valin (1977) and further elaborated in Van Valin and Foley (1980) and Foley and Van Valin (1984). A. E. Kibrik (1985, 1987) argues for a different set of generalized semantic roles which he terms 'hyperroles', 'motivated fusions of roles having their own generalized meanings' (1985: 272). He proposes two: ACTOR, 'the actant designating the chief participant,

the protagonist, of the situation' (*ibid.*), and FACTITIVE, 'the actant designating the immediate, closest, most affected participant in the situation' (*ibid.*). These are rather different from semantic macroroles, because they are tied to the ergative–accusative language opposition and they include the single argument of intransitive verbs. That is, Kibrik argues that in accusative languages like English his notion of actor is the dominant hyperrole, covering the actor of transitive verbs and the single argument of intransitive verbs and being in opposition to the notion of PATIENT. In ergative languages like Dyirbal on the other hand, factitive is the dominant hyperrole, subsuming the undergoer of transitive verbs and the single argument of intransitives and being in opposition to AGENT. Hence his notions of actor and factitive do not map directly onto the notions of actor and undergoer. Dowty (1991) proposed a different version of macroroles, which he called 'proto-roles'. He argued that unlike the notions of actor and undergoer in RRG, proto-roles are not discrete but rather gradient categories with fuzzy boundaries. Subsequent research has shown this idea of non-discrete generalized semantic roles to be untenable. Jackendoff (1990) proposed an 'action tier' containing the notions of 'agent' and 'patient' in his system of semantic representation, and they are similar in some respects to actor and undergoer.

2 Interestingly, some speakers do get both possibilities with *rob*: *Bill robbed the bank of $500* vs. *Bill robbed $500 from the bank*. They apparently do not get both possibilities with *steal*, however; **Bill stole the bank of $500* is bad for these speakers as well.

3 English is particularly rich in location–theme-type alternations; many languages do not allow them at all, except in lexicalized pairs like *rob* and *steal* or *fill* and *pour*, e.g. *I filled the bottle with the milk* vs. *I poured the milk into the bottle*. In some languages, e.g. German and Indonesian, these alternations are marked by derivational morphology; see section 7.2.2. See Foley and Van Valin (1985) for a survey of languages that allow the English-style alternations.

4 The English translation, *Spaghetti was eaten by Anna for five minutes*, is ungrammatical for some English-speakers but is only semantically odd for others. English seems to be more tolerant of this type of passive than Italian is. There seems to be a continuum of acceptability with the passive of activity verbs. The best examples involve generic subjects and passive agents with no time interval specified, e.g. *Spaghetti is eaten by Italians.* Generic NPs refer to sets rather than individuals, and they should be more acceptable than non-specific NPs in this construction. Some languages have a different passive form for activity verbs (Keenan 1985a), e.g. in Russian the *be* + past participle passive is used with *postroit'* 'build' (active accomplishment) and the reflexive passive is used with *stroit'* 'build' (activity).

(i) Dač-a by-l-a postro-en-a raboč-im-i.
dacha-NOM be-PAST-Fsg build-PPP-Fsg worker-INST-pl
'The dacha was built by the workers.'

(ii) *Dača byla stroena rabočimi.

(iii) Dač-a stroit-sja (raboč-im-i)
dacha-NOM build-REFL (worker-INST-pl)
'The dacha is (being) built (by the workers).'

5 Dummy subjects will be discussed in chapter 7.

6 The verb *go* has a similar logical structure, as it is an active accomplishment. In place of **run′**, the logical structure would have a general verb of motion together with a specification that the motion is away from the relevant reference point, usually, but not always, the speaker, e.g. **move.away.from.ref.point′**.

7 It should be noted that many verbs of directed perception take an oblique core argument for their optional second argument in English, e.g. *I'm looking* vs. *I'm looking at it*, and *I'm listening* vs. *I'm listening to the radio.* It is also interesting that in Latin activity verbs of use and enjoyment behave intransitively rather than transitively and mark their second argument with the ablative rather than the accusative case (Michaelis 1993). These facts support the claim that transitive activity verbs are quite exceptional.

8 In *Harry seems to me to be winning the race*, *Harry* is an actor, but of the verb *win* in the propositional *y* argument; it is therefore not a macrorole argument of *seem*. These 'raising' constructions will be investigated in detail in chapter 9.

9 It was mentioned in n. 2 that some speakers get *Bill robbed $500 from the bank*, but no speakers get **Bill stole the bank of $500.* This asymmetry can be explained in terms of the markedness relations in the Actor–Undergoer Hierarchy. *Rob* lexicalizes the marked linking to undergoer, namely the first argument of **have′** (POSSESSOR/RECIPIENT) over the second (POSSESSED), while *steal* lexicalizes the unmarked linking. The extension of *rob* from the marked linking only to both marked and unmarked linkings is more natural than the reverse extension from unmarked to marked, and this is reflected in the change in *rob* but not *steal*.

10 Possessive *have* presents a number of interesting problems. It is usually analyzed as a transitive verb, yet it behaves very differently from M-transitive state verbs, e.g. *own*, *believe* and *see*, in that it does not passivize, e.g. *This house was owned for many years by the local Mafia boss* vs. **This house was had for many years by the local Mafia boss.* In this respect it behaves much more like verbs such as *weigh* and *cost*, which are S-transitive but do not passivize. These verbs express attributive logical structures, e.g. **weigh′** (fish, [**five pounds′**]) or **cost′** (book, [**seven dollars′**]); note that if a shop assistant is weighing something or looking up a price for something, one can ask 'How much is it?' and get the felicitous response 'It's five pounds/seven dollars.' Many uses of *have* are also of this type as well, e.g. *Pat has great ambition* vs. *Pat is very ambitious*. While this deserves more investigation, it is not unreasonable to draw these parallels between basic possessive *have* constructions and attributive constructions. When we look at other languages, these parallels emerge even stronger. In many Australian Aboriginal languages (Dixon 1976), for example, basic possessive as well as attributive constructions are expressed by a verbless construction in which the POSSESSOR or ATTRIBUTANT is the undergoer and subject and the POSSESSED or ATTRIBUTE is a nominal or other element in what is usually called the 'proprietive' case; the following examples are from Mparntwe Arrernte (Wilkins 1989), in which the suffix *-kerte* signals the proprietive case.

(i) Lyete re Kwementyaye-kenhe mwetekaye-kerte.
now 3sgSUBJ -GEN car-PRPR
'Today he has Kwementyaye's car.'

(ii) arlwerte-arlwerte-kerte-kwenye, arlpentye-kerte-rle
curls-curls-PRPR-NEG long-PRPR-FOC
'not the curly-haired one, the long-haired one'

On the other hand, its case-marking properties are those of a regular (M-)transitive verb, and the verbs derived from it, e.g. *receive*, *give*, behave like canonically (M-)transitive verbs. *Receive* is particularly significant in this regard, as the addition of 'BECOME' to the logical structure does not normally affect the argument structure of the base verb in any way; yet *receive* does passivize, e.g. *The letter was received by Mary*. Given these complexities, we will leave the detailed analysis of possessive *have* to future research and continue to assume that it has the same basic logical structure as *own* and *belong to* and that it is (M-)transitive.

11 Van Valin and Wilkins (1993) presents a richer decomposition for *remember* in English and its equivalents in Mparntwe Arrernte.

12 The terminology used here differs somewhat from Jolly's but the distinctions are the same. The term 'argument-adjunct' comes from Grimshaw (1990) but is not being used in exactly the same sense. Whaley (1993) uses the term 'oblique complement' for what we are calling argument-adjuncts.

13 See Nuyts (1994) for detailed analysis of the conditions under which one form or the other is used.

14 In the operator projection in these figures, the two-part English aspect morphemes, *be -ing* 'progressive' and *have -en* 'perfect' are represented only once, with the bound part of the pair being represented. This is for ease of representation and interpretation.

15 The logical structure notation presented in chapter 3 has been used in place of the verb notation used in the original.

16 These qualia are based on those of Pustejovsky (1991, 1995), but are not identical to his analysis.

17 '{ . . . }' represents qualia which are not specified for the example. The LS for *begin* would be BECOME **do′** (x, y), where the logical structure of the complement verb fills the *y* variable slot.

18 See Pustejovsky (1991, 1995) for a formal semantic account of this composition.

19 The genitive pronoun *čems* '1sg' in the Georgian derived nominal is genitive due to its being the object of the postposition *mier* 'by'; the genitive NP corresponding to the *of*-NP in English is *c'erilis* 'letter'.

20 There do not appear to be any deverbal nominals derived from causative state verbs in English; rather, only the nominal corresponding to the state verb is possible, e.g. ??*the angering of the children by the babysitter* (< *The babysitter angered the children*) but *the anger of the children at the babysitter.*

21 Qualia will not be included in these representations, for ease of presentation.

22 There is cross-linguistic and cross-cultural variation as to the parameters of what can count as inalienably possessed; for example, in Tongan, fishing nets are treated as inalienably possessed (Churchward 1953), and in Cree snowshoes are considered to be inalienably possessed (Wolfart 1973).

23 This logical structure is different from the one for *Mary's tall sister* in the previous

section, and this is due to the difference between alienable possession and kin possession, as illustrated in the contrast between (i) and (ii)–(iii).

(i) I've seen Larry's blue car, but I haven't seen the/his red one.
(ii) I've met Larry's tall sister, but I haven't met the/*his short one.
(iii) I've fixed the car's left fender, but I haven't fixed the/??its right one.

It appears that the kin possessor in (ii), like the inalienable possessor in (iii), is a primary element in the semantic representation of the NP in a way that the alienable possessor in (i) is not; hence *one* includes the kin and inalienable possessors but not the alienable possessor. This is not surprising, because inalienable and kin possession are necessary, inherent relationships, whereas alienable possession is non-essential and adventitious.

24 This language is known by a variety of names: Maninka, Mandingo, Bamanakan, Bambara, Marka, Marka-Dafin, Dyula and Wangara. We have referred to it as 'Bambara', as this is the name which is best known in the linguistics literature.

5 Information structure

1 Hereafter, 'speaker' will be shorthand for 'speaker/writer', and includes anyone producing a message with communicative intent; 'sentence' will include many types of communicative utterance. Following the practice that has become the standard, we will use 'she'/'her' for the speaker and 'he'/'him' for the addressee.

2 While there are languages, e.g. verb-initial languages such as Tagalog, where the unmarked order is comment–topic, and comment–topic is also a marked word-order possibility in otherwise topic–comment languages, the discussion here is valid, *mutatis mutandis*, for both word orders.

3 Compare Kuno's two types of information: 'the concept applied to lexical items, on the one hand, and the concept applied to the particular semantic relations which lexical items enter into in the given sentence' (1972a: 272).

4 What we are interested in here is identifiability, not definiteness. The former is a universal *pragmatic* category related to referents, while the latter is a language-specific *grammatical* category related to the linguistic representation of referents. A discussion of this issue is beyond the scope of this chapter; see Lambrecht (1994, ch. 3) and DuBois (1980) for extended discussion.

5 Compare the definition of focus given by Halliday (1967: 204f.):

> Information focus is one kind of emphasis, that whereby the speaker marks out a part (which may be the whole) of a message block as that which he wishes to be interpreted as informative. What is focal is 'new' information; not in the sense that it cannot have been previously mentioned, although it is often the case that it has not been, but in the sense that the speaker presents it as not being recoverable from the preceding discourse . . . The focus of the message, it is suggested, is that which is represented by the speaker as being new, textually (and situationally) non-derivable information.

6 Note, however, that if the question is *Did you put it in or on the box?*, then *On* is a felicitous answer. The reason for this seems to be the following. Having established

P_1 *or* P_2 *NP* in the immediately preceding discourse, it is possible to reply immediately with just P_1 or P_2, with the NP understood from the immediately preceding context. This makes them a type of definite zero anaphora, and therefore the responses are really '$[_{PP}$ in $[_{NP}\ \emptyset]]$' or '$[_{PP}$ on $[_{NP}\ \emptyset]]$'. Hence these examples are not a problem for the claim that the minimal information unit corresponds to the minimal phrasal category in syntax. As we will see below, the focus domain may include topical or non-focal material.

7 See Reinhart (1981) for a formal account of the notion of pragmatic 'aboutness'. Lambrecht (1994: 193) calls the examples in (5.2b–d) 'unlinked topic constructions'. Example (5.2c) is adapted from Matsumoto (1991). The Mandarin example in (d) is from Li and Thompson (1976). Example (5.2a) is a 'linked topic construction', because there is a resumptive pronoun in the clause referring to the topic NP in the left-detached position.

8 In his most recent writings Lambrecht has begun using 'argument focus' for what he formerly called 'narrow focus', but as narrow focus is not limited to arguments of the verb (e.g. includes adverbs and adjuncts), we have continued to use the term 'narrow focus' to avoid confusion with the use of 'argument' elsewhere in this book.

9 In the construction exemplified by (5.10b), the object NP (here *lijo*) can appear either in sentence-initial position or immediately following the passivized verb (before the 'by'-phrase). In spoken French the same type of cleft construction as in (5.10d) is used for questions. The French equivalent of (5.10a) would not be ungrammatical, but it is generally avoided and replaced by the cleft construction: *C'est qui qui a préparé la nourriture?* (Knud Lambrecht, personal communication); see also Demuth (1990) and Lambrecht (1987).

10 The notion of 'topic' as a part of the structural organization of sentences was introduced in Chao (1955) with reference to Chinese and further developed in the approach to syntax laid out in Hockett (1958), where it was applied to English and other languages. The first proposal for simultaneous representation of constituent structure and information structure was Hockett (1958), in which Hockett proposed overlaying box-diagram representations of immediate-constituent structure with topic–comment distinctions.

11 Note that Sesotho is a head-marking language; hence the subject NP is not part of the core.

12 See section 7.5.3 for a discussion of the role of the reflexive *si* in this construction. The dative clitic pronoun *mi* '1sg' is a kind of malefactive argument-adjunct (see section 7.3.2. for the logical structure of benefactives and other argument-adjuncts). A translation better reflecting this meaning would be 'The car broke down on me', where the possession of the car by the speaker is an inference from the dative argument-adjunct.

13 For the purposes of this constraint, a sentence is a construction in which the sentence node dominates a single clause node modified by a single illocutionary force operator, thereby creating a single focus domain. The clause node may dominate other clause nodes, either directly or indirectly. This characterization excludes sentences like *Pat called Chris, and they are still talking*, in which the sentence node dominates two clause nodes, each of which has its own illocutionary force operator and therefore its own focus domain. (See chapter 8 for discussion of the structure of complex sentences.)

14 Interestingly, there are some speakers of English for whom (5.31d) is fully grammatical on the coreference reading, and these speakers seem to require a pause after the preposed PP. This suggests that these speakers interpret the PPs as being in the left-detached position rather than in the precore slot, and this predicts that they should find questions like (5.36c, d) perfectly grammatical, which they do. This interpretation may be forced on them by the fact that the precore slot cannot be doubly filled with two focal constituents that would then have to have the same intonation.

6 Grammatical relations

1 'SPEC' stands for 'specifier', 'C' for 'complementizer', 'CP' for 'complementizer phrase', and 'e' represents an empty node. As can be seen from the *Barriers* tree, INFL is the head of the clause, as we discussed in section 2.4.

2 Even though the latest structures involve V-bar rather than VP for distinguishing internal from external argument, we will use VP in the discussion to refer to the relevant node.

3 One could claim that there are multiple levels at which grammatic relations are represented and that at the abstract level the single argument with verbs like *rhët* is an object in a clause without a subject but that while it is a subject in the overt structure, the verb agrees with it as if it is still an object. This proposal, known as the 'Unaccusative Hypothesis', was originally put forward in Perlmutter (1978) and a number of other works; see Van Valin (1990) and Kishimoto (1996) for detailed critiques from the perspective of RRG.

4 See Tsao (1990: 378ff.) for other examples of matrix coding in Mandarin showing the possibility of all arguments being matrix-coded.

5 It is often assumed that word order distinguishes subject from object in Mandarin, that is, that a NP V NP structure is unambiguously actor–verb–undergoer, yet this is not always the case. Although the NP representing the actor of a transitive verb must appear before the verb when it appears, it often does not appear overtly in the sentence. This fact, plus the fact that any argument can be made the sentence-initial topic, means it is the semantics of the referents and the total discourse context that determine the interpretation of the arguments, not word order. See, for example, the ambiguous sentence in (i).

(i) Zhèxiē xúeshēng dōu méi gěi chéngjī.
these students all not give grades
a. 'These students all did not give grades.'
b. 'These students were all not given grades.'

It is also possible in Mandarin for the NPs representing the actor and undergoer to both be preverbal, and here also only real-world semantics and the pragmatics of the discourse situation disambiguate the utterance. See, for example, the following ambiguous example, from Chao (1968: 32):

(ii) Zhè ge rén shéi dōu bù rènde.
this CL man who all not know
a. 'Nobody knows this man.'
b. 'This man doesn't know anybody.'

Word order then also cannot be used to define grammatical relations in Mandarin. As argued in LaPolla (1995a), the main function of word order is to mark relative topicality.

6 Dixon (1972) introduced this three-way contrast, using 'O' for 'object' of transitive verb.

7 Barai is an example of a language which has no formal voice opposition but nevertheless neutralizes the actor–undergoer contrast with transitive verbs; see Olson (1978, 1981), Foley and Van Valin (1984: 346–51). It may well be unique in this regard.

8 See, for example, Matisoff (1976: 425–6), where the PO marker in Lahu (*thàʔ*) is characterized as an 'efficacy depressant' which indicates that 'the accompanying noun is a receiver of the action in spite of the fact that it might well be, under other circumstances, the initiator of the action'.

9 The term 'pivot' goes back at least to Chao (1968), in which it is used for the NP shared by both verbs in a Mandarin 'pivotal construction', e.g. (8.5d). Heath (1975) used the term 'pivot', together with 'controller', in the analysis of 'want' constructions in exactly the same sense they are being used here. Dixon (1979) used the term in place of 'subject' or 'topic' in his analysis of ergativity.

10 There is a controller in the Warlpiri *-kurra* construction, but we have not discussed it; see Andrews (1985).

11 The antipassive marker is a nasal prefix which assimilates to the place of articulation of the initial consonant of the verb stem; the initial consonant is dropped. Hence in this case, because the initial consonant is /b/, the nasal becomes /m/. The assimilation may be summarized as *N + b'lli > m'lli*.

12 It should be emphasized that this is but one of a range of functions that voice constructions may have in these languages. It is never the case that voice constructions function exclusively in switch-function systems; rather, it seems that this type of reference-tracking system appropriates the voice construction. Languages with voice constructions need not have switch-function systems.

13 In Van Valin (1980), Van Valin and Foley (1980) and Foley and Van Valin (1984) this was described in terms of typological contrast between *reference-dominated languages* (languages with pragmatic pivots) and *role-dominated languages* (languages without pragmatic pivots).

14 In the RelG literature, PSA modulation is referred to as 'promotion' and argument modulation as 'demotion'. In Foley and Van Valin (1984, 1985), the former is labeled 'foregrounding' and the latter 'backgrounding'.

15 We stated too that there also has to be a restricted neutralization of pragmatic relations like topic or focus. Since no languages treat topic as a grammatical relation (in the sense we have been using the term), we have not argued against this possibility throughout this discussion and instead have concentrated on neutralizations of semantic roles. It is well known that in some languages, e.g. Mandarin and Japanese, topic NPs can exhibit certain syntactic properties, e.g. control reflexivization. But it is never the case that only topics can have such a property, as at least some core-internal arguments can also have the property in question; hence there is no restricted neutralization involving topics, and therefore 'topic' is not a grammatical relation.

7 Linking syntax and semantics in simple sentences

1 Jean-Pierre Koenig (personal communication) has pointed out another kind of apparent exception to the Completeness Constraint; it involves definite zero anaphora, as in the following exchange: A: *Did you know that Mary went out with Sam?* B: *I know.* The second argument of *know* in B's utterance is not overtly realized, yet it is clear that it is *that Mary went out with Sam.* This is a case of a discourse referent satisfying an argument requirement of a verb. We will discuss this and other, related phenomena in chapter 9 in our discussion of linking in complex sentences. See also n. 6 in chapter 5.

2 An NP in a detached position must have a resumptive pronoun within the following clause, e.g. *As for Tom, Mary hadn't seen him in two weeks.* The pronoun *him* would occur in the logical structure of *see* in the semantic representation, and because *Tom* binds *him*, it can be interpreted, thereby satisfying the Completeness Constraint.

3 Because case-marking rules in most languages refer to aspects of the linking and not to the logical structure status of arguments (languages like Acehnese are the exceptional ones), the nouns in NPs filling argument positions will be represented as stems, to which the case-marking affixes will be added as part of the linking. Hence in the logical structure of the Icelandic examples the two NP arguments will be represented as *Ólaf-* and *Sigg-*, to which the appropriate case features are added, which will be realized as appropriate in their phonological representations. In a situation where the forms in a paradigm are not analyzable as 'stem + affix', as is often the case with pronouns, the logical structure representation of the arguments will be in terms of their common lexical properties, e.g. '1sgMASC' or '3plFEM'. This is the case in Sama, as *aku* '1sgABS' and *ku* '1sgERG', despite the obvious similarity in form, are not part of a general paradigm which is analyzable as 'stem + affix'; cf. the contrast between the second and third person singular forms: *ka'u* '2sgABS' vs. *nu* '2sgERG', *iya* '3sgABS' vs. *na* '3sgERG'. Hence they will be represented in terms of their common lexical properties, in this instance '1sg', and the appropriate form of the pronoun will be determined in the same way as the appropriate case is determined for the Icelandic NPs.

4 The speaker could not be truly inactive, since he/she is obviously present in the environment of the speech act. Hence it is treated as accessible rather than inactive; see section 5.0.

5 We will henceforth use the term 'active' for the unmarked voice in both ergative and accusative systems; we will *not* be using it in the more restricted sense of the 'actor as pivot' form in opposition to the passive voice in accusative systems only.

6 This step would be rather easier in languages like German, Sama and Indonesian, in which the verb carries an overt marker indicating a marked linking to undergoer. In these cases, the marker indicates that the undergoer in the syntax should be linked to the first argument in the state predicate in the logical structure.

7 Given the discussion regarding the interpretation of the accusative NP in active clauses, one might wonder why it is legitimate to draw the strong conclusion that the ergative NP is in fact the actor rather than the weaker conclusion that it is simply a macrorole argument. The reason for this is that ergative case does in fact correlate with actor in active (unmarked) voice constructions in ergative languages; the kind of variation in interpretation mentioned above does not occur with ergative NPs. Hence this is an appropriate conclusion to draw.

8 As in German, the verb is in the third person singular form and will be glossed as such. There is also agreement in case, gender and number involving the passive participle and the predicate adjective in (a) and (b); we return to this below.

9 The idea of dative case as the default case for non-macrorole direct core arguments in languages with morphological case systems is derived from Silverstein (1976, 1981, 1993). Dative is the default case for non-macrorole direct core arguments, and as a default case it may be overridden with certain verbs. In German, for example, *bedürfen* 'need' takes a genitive object rather than a dative object, whereas in Icelandic there is a large number of verbs which substitute genitive (with transitive verbs), e.g. *vitja* 'visit', and accusative or genitive (with intransitive verbs) for dative, e.g. *langa* 'want, desire' (accusative), *gæta* 'notice, take heed of' (genitive; see Andrews 1982). In Latin (Michaelis 1993) verbs of remembering (e.g. *memini* 'remember') substitute genitive for dative, while verbs of use (e.g. *utor* 'use'), lack (e.g. *indigeo* 'need') and abundance (e.g. *abundo* 'abound') replace dative by ablative and, less commonly, genitive. In the Dyirbal example in (7.25b) the non-macrorole direct core argument receives instrumental rather than dative case.

10 We argued in section 4.2 that the non-referential second argument in activity predications like *Pat drank milk* is not an undergoer but a non-macrorole direct core argument. In languages like German, Icelandic and Russian, the rules in (7.45) predict that the second argument should be dative; it is, however, accusative rather than dative. Note, however, that these verbs also have an active accomplishment use in which the second argument would be an undergoer, hence accusative by (7.45b). We know of no languages in which the activity–active accomplishment is signaled by an accusative–dative alternation of this kind. There are languages in which the second argument is marked by the partitive with activity verbs and the accusative with active accomplishment verbs, e.g. French and Finnish (Kiparsky 1995), as illustrated below. (*Du* in French is a contraction of *de* 'of' plus *le* 'the.Msg'.)

(i)	a.	Il	a	mang-é	du	pain.	Activity
		3sgNOM	have.3sgPRES	eat-PSTP	PRTV	bread	
		'He ate bread.'					
	b.	Il	a	mang-é	le	pain.	Active accomplishment
		3sgNOM	have.3sgPRES	eat-PSTP	the.Msg	bread	
		'He ate the bread.'					

(ii)	a.	Matti-Ø	luk-i	kirjo-j-a	(tunni-n)	Activity
		Matti-NOMsg	read-3sgPAST	book-pl-PRTV	(hour-ACC)	
		'Matti read books (for an hour).'				
	b.	Matti-Ø	luk-i	kirja-t	(tunni-ssa)	Active accomplishment
		Matti-NOMsg	read-3sgPAST	book-ACCpl	(hour-INES)	
		'Matti read the books (in an hour).'				

It appears that there are two options that languages take: one is simply to case-mark verbs which enter into the activity–active accomplishment alternation as if they are always active accomplishments, and the other is to make a distinction between partitive (activity) and accusative (active accomplishment).

11 Two points need to be made about the linking diagram for (7.51b). First, the structure with two nuclei represented here is called a 'nuclear juncture' and will be discussed in detail in chapter 8. Second, the logical structure for *taka fast* 'arrest' is given as if it were a simplex verb like its English counterpart for ease of presentation; what is most relevant here is the determination of actor and undergoer, and it is clear that regardless of how the logical structure is set up, the first argument in the logical structure would be the actor and the second argument the undergoer.

12 This hierarchy is sometimes misleadingly called an 'animacy' hierarchy or an 'agentivity' hierarchy. The first term is very confusing, as it is difficult to imagine in what sense the referent of a first- or second-person pronoun is more *animate* than the referent of a third-person human pronoun or NP. The second label derives from the fact that the referents of highly agentive NPs are almost always animate, as we discussed in section 6.5, but this correlation does not entail that the person hierarchy is itself an agentivity hierarchy.

13 There are a number of complexities here. First, there are five different focused pronoun forms, and they are subject to varying restrictions. For example, only one of the forms can be used with S arguments; all others are restricted to arguments of transitive verbs. Second, three of them can only occur in the past tense. Third, none of them can be used to express the experiencer of verbs of affect or internal state. See Schieffelin (1985) for detailed discussion.

14 There are two exceptions that should be mentioned. First, according to Hale (1973), there is one verb, *wari* 'seek, look for', which takes an ergative actor and a dative second core argument; the predicted pattern for such a verb would be that in (7.63d), and therefore the ergative case on the actor would have to be specified in its lexical entry. Second, in order to signal that an action did not have the intended affect or result, it is possible to put what would otherwise be the undergoer in the dative, as in (i).

(i) a. Nyuntulu-rlu Ø-npa-ju nantu-rnu ngaju-Ø.
2sg-ERG PAST-2sgI-1sgII spear-PAST 1sg-ABS
'You speared me.'

b. Nyuntulu-rlu Ø-npa-ju-rla nantu-rnu ngaju-ku.
2sg-ERG PAST-2sgI-1sgII-DAT spear-PAST 1sg-DAT
'You speared at me.'

Here too the actor appears in the ergative case, despite the dative coding of the second argument. We may capture this by positing a special, semantically motivated linking option in which with verbs like *nantu* 'spear' the second argument may be linked as a direct core argument rather than as undergoer, in order to avoid the implication of affectedness associated with undergoerhood but which does not affect the linking or case marking of the actor.

15 Unlike agreement elements in English, German or French, the Warlpiri agreement markers are more like the bound pronominals in head-marking languages like Lakhota. All nominal and pronominal elements can be omitted, and the result is a full sentence, e.g. *purla-mi ka-rna* 'I'm shouting', *yi-nyi ka-rna-ngku* 'I gave it to you.' Hence Warlpiri, like Enga and Choctaw, is a double-marking language: it has head marking for verbal

arguments but in addition has case on independent NPs cross-referenced by the markers on (in this language) the auxiliary.

16 Adpositions may assign case themselves, as they do in many Indo-European and other languages. We will not discuss case assignment by adpositions.

17 This does not cover all of the uses of *from* in English; see Jolly (1991, 1993) for discussion of the other uses, many of which can be derived from this basic logical structure pattern.

18 This does not apply with the 'dative shift' verbs like *give*, *show* and *send*; the outranked *z* argument appears simply as a non-macrorole direct core argument, as in *Robin showed Sandy the picture.*

19 We ignore the semantic representation of the adjective *strong*, since it is tangential to the discussion.

20 For constructions like those in (7.85) and (7.86), since [**do′** (Sandy, ∅) ∧ **do′** (Kim, ∅)] is logically equivalent to [**do′** (Kim, ∅) ∧ **do′** (Sandy, ∅)], this rule will permit either argument to be the *y* argument for the purposes of this rule.

21 As noted in n. 2 in chapter 4, there are some speakers who get (7.100b′); even for those speakers, however, it is still the case that *steal* and *rob* lexicalize both linking possibilities, but the marked linking with *rob* is equivalent to the only linking possible with *steal*. See also n. 9 in chapter 4.

22 It is crucial to recognize the distinction between lexical and syntactic *phenomena*, on the one hand, and lexical and syntactic *rules*, on the other. These are independent distinctions, and we are concerned with differentiating lexical from syntactic phenomena. At different points in the history of generative grammar, it has been argued that all grammatical phenomena, both lexical and syntactic, can or should be handled by the same kind of rule. In early generative grammar, when the only descriptive devices were phrase structure rules and transformations, all phenomena, including word formation, were handled syntactically. In the last two decades theories have been proposed, e.g. LFG and HPSG, which attempt to handle all lexical and as many syntactic phenomena as possible by means of lexical rules. RelG, on the other hand, treats many processes which other theories recognize as lexical by means of syntactic rules.

23 Native speakers seem to agree that plain passive agents cannot control a reflexive, but they differ with respect to their judgments regarding adversative passives. In particular, while they all agreed that some examples are grammatical, they often disagreed as to which ones are grammatical. The ones presented here were acceptable to all of the speakers we consulted.

24 In a logical structure with two EFFECTORS, the first one in the causal chain counts as the highest ranking; see sections 3.2.3.2, 4.1.

25 This is similar to the idea of 'multi-attachment' proposed by Perlmutter (1980) in RelG to handle these constructions. He claims that the single reflexive affix is simultaneously subject and direct object; in our analysis, it signals actor and undergoer simultaneously.

26 Huber (1980), cited in McKay (1985), gives examples similar to these as possible. However, all of the German-speakers we consulted rejected them.

27 It should be noted that while this is a single clause, it is a construction containing two nuclei; such constructions will be discussed in detail in chapter 8.

28 Jackendoff refers to primary arguments as 'direct arguments'; since we are already using this term in a different sense, we have chosen to use 'primary arguments' instead. His term 'conceptual structure superiority' (cs-superiority) is the model for our term 'LS-superiority'.

29 It seems clear from the discussion in Jackendoff (1992) that he intends the cs-superiority condition to replace the 1972 thematic hierarchy condition. His semantic representations have each argument position embedded with respect to the next-higher one, and given his definitions of thematic relations in terms of these positions, the thematic hierarchy condition falls out from the cs-superiority condition. Because logical structures do not have the same type of embedding relationships among argument positions, the two cannot be collapsed in our framework.

30 *Story about X* is represented semantically as **be′** (story, [**about′** (X)]), because this would be the logical structure for the attributive construction *The story is about X.* The difference between the two is that *story* is the undergoer 'subject' of the clause in the one construction and the head of the NP in the other.

31 It might appear that *about herself* should be analyzed as an argument-adjunct PP, since the logical structure resembles that in (7.114b). However, **about′** (herself) is an argument PP, not an argument-adjunct, because it is the optional realization of the α-variable in the logical structure of *talk*. Cf. the discussion of the logical structure of verbs of saying in section 3.2.3.1.

32 It has been argued that these verbs are not in fact causative (e.g. Bouchard 1995), but there is strong evidence in favor of the causative analysis. First, as noted in the text, they pass the causative paraphrase test from chapter 3. Second, as pointed out in chapter 3, in many languages the translation equivalents of these psych-verbs are overtly causative, i.e. they bear a causative morpheme. In chapter 3 we gave examples of the explicit derivation of transitive psych-verbs from intransitive state psych-verbs via causativization from Japanese, Lakhota and Barai in section 3.2.1 and from Sanuma in exercise 6.

33 Note that the ungrammatical **Himself amuses Sam* would be ruled out by the Role Hierarchy Condition. In grammatical sentences like *Pictures of herself amuse Sally*, the actor is *pictures of herself*, with *pictures* as head and *of herself* a modifier of it, and the reflexive is not in a syntactic argument position within the core.

34 In view of this, Kuno (1987), among others, has claimed that *her* in these examples is [+REFL]. This preserves the claim that the clause is the domain of reflexivization, but it is circular, since there is no independent evidence, other than the fact that *her* is bound clause-internally, that it is [+REFL].

35 If the logical structure were [**do′** (she_i, ∅)] CAUSE [BECOME **have′** ($woman_i$, book)] for **she_i gave the book to the $woman_i$*, this would be ruled out by condition (b) in (5.29), the principle governing intrasentential anaphora.

36 This highlights a difference in the linking properties of elements which occur in the logical structure of the main verb and those of higher predicates. Semantic arguments of the main verb may not be linked directly to the left-detached position; rather, they are linked as pronouns to the core, reflecting the fact that when the element in the left-detached position is not a setting modifier but rather interpretable as an semantic argument of the verb, there must be a resumptive pronoun referring to it in the core. Setting

locative and temporal adverbials and PPs do not require resumptive elements, since they are not arguments of the verb, semantically or syntactically, and therefore they may be linked directly to the left-detached position.

37 It is important to recall that what Fillmore and other advocates of ConG call 'constructions' we are calling 'constructional templates'; see chapter 2, n. 33. The following terminological equivalences obtain:

Theory	*Form in language being described*	*Theoretical description of form*
ConG	construct	construction
RRG	construction	constructional template

8 Syntactic structure, II: complex sentences and noun phrases

1 Even what GB calls 'small clauses', as in *Harry considers* [$_{sc}$ *Sam a fool*], contain a subject (*Sam*) and predicate (*a fool*), on a GB analysis.

2 Case marking in causative constructions will be discussed in section 9.2.2.

3 Yang (1994) reports that Choi (1929 [1989]) classified Korean complex sentences into three types which parallel the distinctions proposed here. Bearth (1969) also proposed a three-way distinction among linkage relations, based on the analysis of the Mande language Toura, which is spoken in the Ivory Coast (Africa).

4 As we saw in section 4.4.2, operators receive a different semantic representation from argument-taking predicates.

5 The question of the interpretation of the subject of the infinitive in sentences like those in (8.30) is the problem of control, and it will be addressed in section 9.1.3.1.

6 Haspelmath (1995a) refers to the linked verb in this type of clause-linkage construction as a 'converb'.

7 The second object NP with a verb like *tell* cannot readily function as subject in a passive, e.g. ??*The story was told Bill by Sam.* However odd this example is, (8.36b) is quite impossible.

8 Sentences from Japanese containing a question particle in a subordinate clause appear superficially to be a counterexample to this, but they are not. An example is given in (i).

(i) Taroo ga dare to kekkon suru (no) ka shir-anai.
NOM who COM marry do (NMZ) Q know-NEG
'I don't know who(m) Taro is going to marry.'

The function of the particle is to indicate that the clause is an interrogative complement, analogous to an English example like *I don't know whether he has left.* As in the English indirect question complement, the subordinate clause does not constitute a question independent of the main clause; rather, the whole sentence has the illocutionary force of the main clause. Contrast this with examples involving clausal coordination like (8.37) and (8.21b), in which each clause has distinct illocutionary force. The choice of a subordinate clause with or without a question particle in Japanese is analogous to the choice of *that* vs. *whether* as a complementizer for English complement clauses.

9 'Sharing a core argument' will be characterized formally in terms of the linking between syntactic and semantic representations in complex sentences in chapter 9. As mentioned

in chapter 6, this is the original sense of the term 'pivot' as used in Chao (1968). We now use the term in a broader sense, but it still subsumes the pivot in this construction.

10 This zero pronoun is not equivalent to any of the empty categories posited in GB theory, as argued in Van Valin (1986a). However, some cases of the zero pronoun are equivalent to the empty pronominal *pro* in GB, e.g. in the Mandarin examples in (5.37). As should be clear from the analysis of linking in WH-questions presented in chapter 7, there is nothing equivalent to NP-trace or WH-trace in this theory, and as we will see in the discussion of control constructions in section 9.1.3.1, there is nothing equivalent to PRO, either.

11 Some native speakers of English appear to have lost this distinction, using *help* uniformly without *to*.

12 Just as with the opposition between punctual and non-punctual verbs discussed in chapter 3, the unmarked member of the opposition, in this case the [–temporal overlap] constructions with *to* or *from*, can range in interpretation from clearly sequential to nearly simultaneous, whereas the marked member, the [+temporal overlap] constructions marked by zero, must always be interpreted as temporally overlapping.

13 *To* also occurs together with *for* to mark subordinate cores in constructions like *For Hamid to leave now would be a mistake* or *The Dutch want very much for their team to win the European Championship*. Note that if the adverb *very much* is omitted from the second example, the *for* disappears as well, i.e. *The Dutch want (*for) their team to win the European Championship*. It appears that *for–to* is a discontinuous complementizer, with there being complex conditions on its occurrence. While it might seem odd to talk about a discontinuous complementizer, keep in mind that English and other languages have grammatical elements that are discontinuous, e.g. the progressive (*be* + *-ing*) and the perfect (*have* + *-en*), French *ne* + *pas*, *ne* + *personne*.

14 This contrast in perception verb complements provides evidence in support of the distinction made in chapter 3 between punctual (achievement) and non-punctual verbs. There are punctual perception verbs like *notice*, *find* and *glimpse*, and because they are punctual, the actor could not take in an entire action, event or process; rather, only a short temporal segment could be observed. Accordingly, we predict that punctual perception verbs would take only participles in this construction, and that is correct, e.g. *Robin noticed Kim reading/*read, Sandy found Pat talking to Sam/*talk to Sam.*

15 All of Jacobsen's examples are taken from Sapir and Swadesh (1939); because of the complex morphophonemics of the language, the words are not broken down morpheme-by-morpheme as are the other examples we use. The relevant part of the word in each example is in boldface.

16 These are clausal junctures, as there is no obligatory shared argument as in core junctures. The missing pivot is a zero anaphor coreferential with the privileged syntactic argument of the finite clause. Tense and illocutionary force are obligatorily shared, and therefore the nexus is cosubordinate. Examples with overt subjects in the non-finite clause are given in (i)–(ii).

(i) Mary having finished doing the dishes, Pat and Neil could start their next project in the kitchen.

(ii) With Sam going to the store for beer and pretzels, the other guys could get the surprise party ready.

17 This brings up a point made in note 6 in chapter 3, namely, that *kill* is not equivalent to *cause to die*. *Cause to die* is a core juncture, and consequently the causality is much less direct than in a nuclear juncture causative or in a lexical causative like *kill*. There are many instances in which one could be used and the other could not, as critics of lexical decomposition like Fodor (1970) have pointed out. But this is not an argument against lexical decomposition; rather, it is a demonstration of the validity of the iconicity principle inherent in the Interclausal Relations Hierachy. The logical structure for the English verb *cause* is [**do′** (x, ∅)] CAUSE [**undergo′** (y, z)], where the logical structure of the complement verb fills the *z* variable. Hence the logical structure for (8.56b) would be [**do′** (Harry ∅)] CAUSE [**undergo′** (Tom, [BECOME **dead′** (Tom)], which is clearly different from the logical structure for *Harry killed Tom*, [**do′** (Harry ∅)] CAUSE [BECOME **dead′** (Tom)]. See Wierzbicka (1980a) for further discussion.

18 Dik and Hengeveld (1991) present an analysis of perception verb complements in FG and argue that differences in the semantic representations correlate with the different possible complement forms. They do not use decompositional semantic representations of the kind employed herein, but their general line of analysis and argumentation parallels that in Van Valin and Wilkins (1993).

19 There is an interesting apparent exception to the hierarchy found in French involving perception verbs. Kayne (1975) gives the following minimal pair of sentences.

(i) J'ai vu Jean faire des bêtises.
1sg-have.1sg see.PP do some stupidities
(ii) J'ai vu faire des bêtises à Jean.
1sg-have.1sg see.PP do some stupidities to
'I have seen Jean do foolish things.'

The sentence in (i) is a core juncture, paralleling (8.5a) in structure, whereas (ii) is a nuclear juncture, paralleling (8.3a) in structure. Since the main verb, *voir* 'see', is a perception verb, this seems to be an important exception to the claim regarding the interaction of the semantic and syntactic sides of the Interclausal Relations Hierarchy. Kayne notes that the two are not synonymous; he comments, 'the first . . . appears to involve a stronger sense of actual visual perception of *Jean* than does the second' (1975: 232). That is, (i) has a strong direct perception interpretation, and this is in line with the predictions of the Hierarchy. Native speakers we have talked to do not have strong intuitions about the meaning of (ii) but agree that it has a much weaker sense of direct perception than (i). Achard (1996) shows that the construction in (i) is the unmarked direct perception construction and that (ii) is very restricted, being subject to a number of semantic conditions. Many combinations which are unproblematic in (i), e.g. *J'ai vu Marie cuisiner* 'I saw Mary cook' are questionable in (ii), e.g. ?*J'ai vu cuisiner Marie*. The fact that the construction in (i) is the unmarked direct perception construction follows from the Interclausal Relations Hierarchy, but the construction in (ii) remains, nevertheless, a problem for the Interclausal Relations Hierarchy. Moreover, German seems to have a similar construction, as exemplified in (7.115b).

20 This test involves question–answer pairs in which the answer consists of 'No' plus a single constituent representing a single information unit. This single constituent is the focus in the answer and corresponds to the focus constituent in the question.

21 The (c) response becomes felicitous if the entire clause is repeated, as in *No, after she left*. In this case, the entire subordinate clause is being treated as questioned, which is appropriate, since the clause as a whole is a constituent of the main clause and therefore in the potential focus domain. The response in (c) becomes truly impossible as a reply to the content of the adverbial clause if it occurs sentence initially, as in *After she$_i$ arrived, did Pat see Mary?*

22 The Lakhota verbs *manú* 'steal', *wąyą́ke* 'see', *iyúkčą* 'think' and *ikíčiču* 'get for' in (8.64)–(8.67) take their actor and undergoer markers as infixes.

23 The structure of Lakhota relative clauses will be discussed in section 8.6.2 below.

24 The reason *ečhúhą* 'while' is in the potential focus domain is that [$_{PP}$ CLAUSE + *ečhúhą*] is a matrix clause peripheral constituent and therefore can be questioned, as in a question like 'When did his wife get him water?' Its individual constituents cannot be questioned, however, as we have seen.

25 Japanese and Korean also have internally headed relative clauses, but their occurrence is heavily restricted. Both languages also have externally headed relative clauses, which are the most used type. In Lakhota, by contrast, the internally headed type is the only kind of relative clause construction in the language. See Yang (1994) for an analysis of internally headed relative clauses in Korean within RRG.

26 The linear order of the two core operators in the matrix clause does not reflect their scope, hence the crossing lines in the operator projection. If the sentence were *Robin was not able to indentify who had talked to Kim at the party to the police*, then the linear order would have corresponded to their scope relations.

27 This construction is used to express 'continuative' aspect; see chapter 3, n. 9. This verb is used only with inanimate arguments such as trees or poles; there is a different verb *nažį́* 'stand' which is used with animate arguments.

9 Linking syntax and semantics in complex sentences

1 **'and'**' represents coordinating conjunctions which may (as in English) or may not (as in Dyirbal) correspond to an overt lexeme; it should be distinguished from the logical structure-internal connective '∧', which is part of semantic representations only, e.g. the logical structure of active accomplishments.

2 There also seems to be discourse 'VP' ellipsis, as in (i).

(i) Speaker 1: Kim is eating an ice cream cone.
Speaker 2: Sandy is, too.

In this instance the Completeness Constraint would be violated, since speaker 2's utterance is a different sentence from speaker 1's. While a complete solution to this problem is beyond the scope of this discussion, we can sketch an approach for dealing with it. If there were an explicit representation of the context in which the two utterances in (i) occurred of the kind provided by Discourse Representation Theory (Kamp and Reyle 1993), then the Completeness Constraint could be modified to permit elements in the discourse representation to satisfy it, under the appropriate circumstances.

3 We are using a simplified representation of the logical structure of *hit* here, since it is not the semantic structure of *hit* which is important here; rather, it is the compositional semantics of the nuclear juncture.

4 Indications of the discourse-pragmatic status of the referring expressions in the logical structures will only be indicated when relevant.

5 Here again since the main point is the overall pattern of the logical structure, we have used simplified representations for *his friend* and several of the constituent verbs.

6 It should be noted that there are major dialects of English in which this sentence is ungrammatical, a good example being Australian English. In this dialect, *promise* + infinitive can only be used without a second argument, e.g. *Robin promised to clean the birdcage*. In order to convey the meaning of (9.26c), a tensed complement clause must be used, i.e. *Robin promised Sandy that he would clean the birdcage*.

7 This grammatical function, called 'OBJ2' in earlier work in LFG, is the non-macrorole direct core argument in a dative shift construction, i.e. *the book* in *Sandy gave Kim the book*.

8 See Van Valin (1992a) for discussion of the difficulties the Dyirbal control structures raise for certain claims in GB theory.

9 As pointed out in the discussion of *persuade* in section 8.4.3, this logical structure is just an approximation of its meaning, but it does correspond to one of the ways that this verb is expressed in some languages.

10 The Latin constructions from which the name is derived actually have quite different properties; see Bolkestein (1979) for a comparison of the Latin accusative-plus-infinitive construction with this English construction.

11 It should be kept in mind that 'matrix' here refers to the core to which is linked the core containing the predicate of which the matrix-coded NP is a semantic argument; it does not entail that this core is always the 'main' core in the sentence. It is perfectly possible to embed a matrix-coding construction, as in *Dana said that Pat believes Kim to have left the party early*. In this sentence, *Pat believes Kim* is the matrix core with reference to the linked core *to have left the party early* in which the verb *leave* takes *Kim* as a semantic but not a syntactic argument, and this whole construction is in a subordinate relationship to the 'main' core *Dana said*. *Pat believes Kim* is thus the matrix core in the construction but not the matrix core in the clause.

12 The case-marking rules in (9.67a) refer to macrorole status, and therefore would not apply to the *it* in (9.66c′), *Ali believes it to be raining*. While this might seem to be a problem at first glance, it is not in reality, because *it* does not have distinct nominative–accusative forms; therefore there is no evidence that it in fact has case at all in this construction. Since *it* is not an argument, it cannot be replaced by a masculine or feminine form which would show case distinctions. When *it* occurs and can be replaced by a case-bearing pronoun, it is always a semantic argument of the predicate, and therefore the rules in (9.67a) would apply to *it* or any other pronoun occurring in the same position.

13 Despite the translation of the sentence as 'The porcupine had the pumpkins cooked *by* the owl', *kwá* is not the passive agent marker, which is *ndi* 'by'. This preposition is used to mark RECIPIENTS with verbs of giving and directional phrases with verbs of motion.

14 Example (9.83b) is apparently grammatical only for some Hungarian-speakers. The three native speakers we consulted uniformly rejected this sentence as impossible. See also Comrie (1989b: 184).

15 The active voice is signaled by the prefix *man-* (perfective *nan-*) for most verbs; with some stative verbs, e.g. *-hita* 'see', *-fana* 'be hot', the prefix is *ma-* (perfective *na-*). In the case of the verb 'wash', *sasa-*, since the initial consonant is voiceless, it is dropped before the prefix. The passive voice is signaled by the addition of the suffix *-ana*, whose final vowel drops if there is an agent phrase following.

16 This phenomenon is known as 'logophoricity'; see Clements (1975), Hyman and Comrie (1981), Sells (1987), Kuno (1987).

17 Readers familiar with GB theory will be aware that GB draws a very different conclusion from this contrast between Lakhota and English. Since subjacency violations are caused by movement across bounding nodes, the existence of subjacency effects in a language is taken as evidence that the language does have syntactic movement rules, regardless of the overt patterns. Huang (1981) argued that the movement is covert and occurs in the mapping between S-structure and L(ogical) F(orm). This is illustrated in the figure below; 'Move α' is the general movement rule subsuming WH-movement and NP-movement.

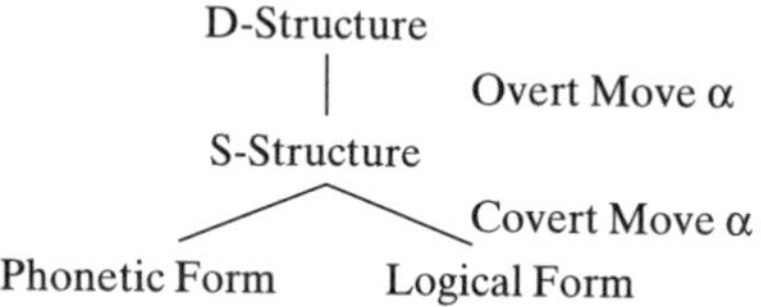

Chomsky (1986a) argued that the primary difference between languages like English and languages like Lakhota is that subjacency holds overtly in the syntax (i.e. in the mapping between D-structure and S-structure) in languages like English and holds covertly at LF in languages like Lakhota.

18 This constraint does not apply to echo questions, rhetorical questions or to metalinguistic questions.

19 This is important, because some of the other non-transformational accounts of subjacency, e.g. the GPSG account in Gazdar *et al.* (1985), do require the positing of a long-distance dependency between the WH-word and a syntactic 'gap' in an embedded clause. Such a long-distance dependency cannot be motivated for Lakhota and other languages like it.

20 Williamson (1984) claims that Lakhota sentences like (9.121c) are grammatical if the head noun is indefinite. However, none of the native speakers of Lakhota that the first author has worked with accept such sentences. If there are speakers who find such sentences grammatical, then those speakers, like Danish-speakers, are allowing pragmatic factors to override syntactic ones in the determination of the potential focus domain in these constructions.

21 In GB, the ungrammaticality of (9.136c) is not explained in terms of subjacency but rather in terms of the empty category principle (Chomsky 1981b, 1986a).

22 In GB theory, the level of Logical Form handles a number of different phenomena, in particular, quantifier scope, binding of pronouns and reflexives, and covert WH-movement together with subjacency. It is striking that quantifier scope, pronominalization and subjacency are all handled in terms of focus structure in this theory.

Recognizing focus structure as part of grammar eliminates the need for positing an abstract level like Logical Form to handle these phenomena.

Epilog

1 But see Slobin (forthcoming) for some cautionary points regarding these claims.

2 Two points need to be made here. First, the only way empirically to test the claim that there is an autonomous LAD is to assume that grammar can be learned without one and to try to show how this could be done; if the attempt does not succeed, then this can be taken as an empirical argument in favor of Chomsky's position. If one assumes from the outset that there is an autonomous LAD, then there is no possible fact that could disprove its existence, because even if one could show that some aspect of grammar could plausibly be learned, it could be argued that the reason it can be learned is that there is an autonomous LAD. Second, the argument given in (1.7) in section 1.3.1 in favor of the LAD is not an empirical argument and is logically invalid, for the following reason. It crucially presupposes that there is only one account of the adult grammatical competence, but if there are multiple accounts, each with different implications for acquisition, then the conclusion that some construct or concept must be part of the LAD simply does not follow. We will see a clear example of this at the end of this chapter when we look at the analysis of extraction restrictions presented in chapter 9.

3 This makes the point of the previous note. The analysis of subjacency phenomena presented in chapter 9 has radically different implications for acquisition from the GB account, and therefore if we were to invoke (1.7) in the context of this analysis, we would conclude that a principle like subjacency is *not* part of the initial endowment of the child. Hence as long as there are competing analyses of the relevant linguistic phenomena (and there always will be), then the conclusions reached in terms of (1.7) are meaningless. See Van Valin (1994) for more detailed argumentation on this point.

REFERENCES

Abbreviations

BLS *Proceedings of the Nth Annual Meeting of the Berkeley Linguistics Society* (Berkeley: University of Calfornia).

CLS *Papers from the Nth Regional Meeting of the Chicago Linguistic Society* (University of Chicago).

DWPIL *Davis Working Papers in Linguistics* (Davis: University of California).

Abdoulaye, M. L. 1992. Aspects of Hausa morphosyntax in Role and Reference Grammar. PhD dissertation, SUNY at Buffalo.

Abney, Stephen. 1987. The English noun phrase in its sentential aspect. PhD dissertation, MIT.

Abraham, Werner, ed. 1978. *Valence, semantic case, and grammatical relations*. Amsterdam and Philadelphia: John Benjamins.

Achard, Michel. 1996. Structure and grammatical coding of a conceptual category: the complements of perception verbs in French. Presented at the Second Conference on Conceptual Structure, Discourse and Language, SUNY at Buffalo; to appear in the proceedings.

Allerton, D. J. 1982. *Valency and the English verb*. London: Academic Press.

Alsina, Alex. 1992. On the argument structure of causatives. *Linguistic Inquiry* 23: 517–56.

Andersen, Paul Kent. 1987. Zero-anaphora and related phenomena in Classical Tibetan. *Studies in Language* 11.2: 279–312.

Anderson, Stephen R. 1976. On the notion of subject in ergative languages. In Li, ed., 1–23.

Anderson, Stephen R. and Paul Kiparsky, eds. 1973. *A festschrift for Morris Halle*. New York: Holt, Rinehart and Winston.

Andrews, Avery D. 1982. The representation of case in modern Icelandic. In Bresnan, ed., 427–503.

1985. The major functions of the noun phrase. In Shopen, ed., vol. I, 62–154.

Aoun, Joseph. 1985. *The grammar of anaphora*. Cambridge, MA: MIT Press.

Aoun, Joseph and Yen-hui Audrey Li. 1993. *The syntax of scope*. Cambridge, MA: MIT Press.

Ariel, Mira. 1990. *Accessing noun-phrase antecedents*. London and New York: Routledge.

1995. Interpreting anaphoric expressions: a cognitive vs. a pragmatic approach. *Journal of Linguistics* 30: 3–42.

Aronson, Howard. 1991. Modern Georgian. In Alice C. Harris, ed., *The indigenous languages of the Caucasus*, vol. I: *The Kartvelian languages*, 219–312. Delmar, NY: Caravan.

Austin, J. L. 1962. *How to do things with words*. Cambridge, MA: Harvard University Press.

Bach, Emmon. 1979. Control in Montague Grammar. *Linguistic Inquiry* 10.3: 515–51.

Baker, Mark. 1988. *Incorporation*. University of Chicago Press.

Bates, Elizabeth. 1976. *Language and context: the acquisition of pragmatics*. New York: Academic Press.

Bates, Elizabeth and Brian MacWhinney. 1982. Functionalist approaches to grammar. In Wanner and Gleitman, eds., 173–218.

Bearth, Thomas. 1969. Phrase et discours en Toura. *Cahiers Ferdinand de Saussure* 25: 29–45.

1992. Constituent structure, natural focus hierarchy and focus types in Toura. *Folia Linguistica* 26: 75–94.

Beaugrande, Robert de. 1985. Text linguistics in discourse studies. In Djik, ed., 41–70.

Bennett, David C. 1975. *Spatial and temporal uses of English prepositions: an essay in stratificational semantics*. London: Longman.

Berman, Ruth A. 1978. *Modern Hebrew structure*. Tel Aviv: University Publishing.

Bhat, D. N. S. 1991. *Grammatical relations: the evidence against their necessity and universality*. London and New York: Routledge.

Bickel, Balthasar. 1993. Belhare subordination and the theory of topic. *Arbeiten des Seminars für Sprachwissenschaft* 12: 23–55. Zurich.

1995. *Aspect, mood and time in Belhare: studies in the semantics–pragmatics interface of a Himalayan language*. Zurich: University Press.

forthcoming. Hidden syntax in Belhare. In G. Van Driem, ed., *Himalayan Linguistics*. Berlin: Mouton de Gruyter.

Bickerton, Derek. 1975. Some assertions about presuppositions and pronominalization. *CLS* 11, *Parasession on functionalism*, 580–609.

Bills, Garland, Bernardo C. Vallejo and Rudolph Troike. 1969. *An introduction to spoken Bolivian Quechua*. Austin: University of Texas Press.

Bird, Charles. 1968. Relative clauses in Bambara. *Journal of West African Languages* 5: 35–47.

Bird, Charles and Timothy Shopen. 1979. Maninka. In Shopen, ed., 59–111.

Bittner, Maria and Kenneth Hale. 1996. The structural determination of case and agreement. *Linguistic Inquiry* 27: 1–68.

Bloomfield, Leonard. 1933. *Language*. New York: Holt.

1962. *The Menomini language*. New Haven, CT: Yale University Press.

Boas, Franz. 1911. Introduction. In F. Boas, ed., *Handbook of American Indian languages*, vol. I. Washington: Bureau of American Ethnology.

Boas, Franz and Ella Deloria. 1941. *Dakota grammar*. Memoirs of the National Academy of Sciences, vol. 23, no. 2.

Bolinger, Dwight. 1975. Concept and percept: two infinitive constructions and their vicissitudes. In *World papers in phonetics: festschrift for Dr. Onishi's Kiju*, 65–91. Tokyo: Phonetic Society of Japan.

1979. Pronouns in discourse. In Givón, ed., 289–310.

Bolkestein, A. Machtelt. 1979. Subject-to-object raising in Latin? *Lingua* 48: 15–34.

Bondarko, Alexander V. 1991. *Functional grammar: a field approach*. Amsterdam and Philadelphia: John Benjamins.

Borer, Hagit, ed. 1986. *Syntax and Semantics*, vol. XIX: *The syntax of pronominal clitics*. Orlando, FL: Academic Press.

Borgman, Donald M. 1989. Sanuma. In Derbyshire and Pullum, eds., 15–248.

Borkin, Ann. 1984. *Problems in form and function*. Norwood, NJ: Ablex.

Bouchard, Denis. 1995. *The semantics of syntax*. University of Chicago Press.

Boutin, Michael E. 1994. Aspect in Bonggi. PhD dissertation, University of Florida.

Bowerman, Melissa. 1973. *Early Syntactic Development*. Cambridge University Press.

1974. Learning the structure of causative verbs: a study in the relationship of cognitive, semantic and syntactic development. *Papers and Reports on Child Language Development* 8: 142–78.

1979. The acquisition of complex sentences. In P. Fletcher and M. Garman, eds., *Language acquisition* (1st edn.), 285–306. Cambridge University Press.

1982. Reorganizational processes in lexical and syntactic development. In Wanner and Gleitman, eds., 316–46.

1990. Mapping semantic roles onto syntactic functions: are children helped by innate linking rules? *Linguistics* 28: 1253–89.

Braine, Martin D. S. 1976. *Children's first word combinations*. Monographs of the Society for Research in Child Development.

1990. The 'natural logic' approach to reasoning. In W. F. Overton, ed., *Reasoning, necessity and logic*. Hillsdale, NJ: LEA.

1992. What sort of innate structure is needed to 'bootstrap' into syntax? *Cognition* 45: 77–100.

1993. The mental logic and how to discover it. In J. Macnamara and G. Reyes, eds., *The logical foundations of cognition*, 241–63. Oxford University Press.

1994. Is nativism sufficient? *Journal of Child Language* 21: 9–31.

Braine, Martin D. S. and Julia Hardy. 1982. On what case categories there are, why they are, and how they develop: an amalgam of *a priori* considerations, speculation, and evidence from children. In Wanner and Gleitman, eds., 219–39.

Bresnan, Joan. 1978. A realistic transformational grammar. In M. Halle, J. Bresnan and G. Miller, eds., *Linguistic theory and psychological reality*, 1–59. Cambridge, MA: MIT Press.

ed. 1982a. *The mental representation of grammatical relations*. Cambridge, MA: MIT Press.

1982b. Control and complementation. In Bresnan, ed., 282–390.

1994. Locative inversion and the architecture of universal grammar. *Language* 70.1: 72–131.

Bresnan, Joan and Jonni H. Kanerva. 1989. Locative inversion in Chicheŵa: A case study of factorization in grammar. *Linguistic Inquiry* 20: 1–50.

Bresnan, Joan and Sam A. Mchombo. 1987. Topic, pronoun and agreement in Chicheŵa. *Language* 63: 741–82.

Bresnan, Joan and Lioba Moshi. 1990. Object asymmetries in comparative Bantu syntax. *Linguistic Inquiry* 21: 147–85.

Breu, Walter. 1994. Interactions between lexical, temporal and aspectual meanings. *Studies in Language* 18: 23–44.

Bruce, Les. 1979. A grammar of Alamblak (Papua New Guinea). PhD dissertation, Australian National University.

Bruner, Jerome. 1983. *Child's talk: learning to use language*. New York: Norton.

Buechel, Eugene J. 1939. *A grammar of Lakota*. Pine Ridge, SD: Red Cloud Indian School.

Bunzell, Ruth. 1933. *Zuni texts* (Publications of the American Ethnological Society 15). New York: G. E. Stechert.

Burzio, L. 1986. *Italian syntax*. Hingham, MA: Kluwer.

Butler, Christopher S. 1995. Layering in functional grammars: a comparative survey. In Devriendt, Goossens and van der Auwera, eds., 1–27.

Butler, James and Charles Peck. 1980. The use of passive, antipassive, and absolutive verbs in Tzutujil of San Pedro la Laguna. *Journal of Mayan Linguistics* 2.1: 40–52.

Bybee, Joan. 1985. *Morphology*. Amsterdam and Philadelphia: John Benjamins.

Carden, Guy. 1982. Backwards anaphora in discourse context. *Journal of Linguistics* 18: 361–87.

Carlson, Greg N. 1977. Reference to kinds in English. PhD dissertation, University of Massachusetts.

Catford, Ian. 1975. Ergativity in Caucasian languages. *North Eastern Linguistics Society Papers* 6: 37–48.

Cattell, Ray. 1984. *Composite predicates in English*. Orlando, FL: Academic Press.

Caughley, Ross. 1982. *The syntax and morphology of the verb in Chepang* (Pacific Linguistics Series B, no. 84). Canberra: Australian National University.

Centineo, Giulia. 1986. A lexical theory of auxiliary selection in Italian. *DWPIL* 1: 1–35.

1996. The distribution of *si* in Italian transitive/inchoative pairs. In Mandy Simmons and Theresa Galloway, eds. *Proceedings of SALT V*, 54–71. Ithaca, NY: Cornel University Press.

Chafe, Wallace L. 1976. Givenness, contrastiveness, definiteness, subjects, topics, and point of view. In Li, ed., 27–55.

1987. Cognitive constraints on information flow. In Tomlin, ed., 21–52.

1994. *Discourse, consciousness, and time: the flow and displacement of conscious experience in speaking and writing*. University of Chicago Press.

Chafe, Wallace and Johanna Nichols, eds. 1986. *Evidentiality: the linguistic encoding of epistemology*. Norwood, NJ: Ablex.

Chao, Yuen Ren. 1955. Notes on Chinese grammar and logic. *Philosophy East and West* 5: 13–31.

1968. *A grammar of spoken Chinese*. Berkeley: University of California Press.

Chen Ping. 1984. *A discourse analysis of third person zero anaphora in Chinese*. Bloomington: Indiana University Linguistics Club.

Cheng, Chin-chuan. 1988. Hùatí běnwèi Hànyǔ piànzhāng yǔfǎ [A discourse-topic based grammar of Chinese]. Paper presented to the Seventh Workshop on Chinese Linguistics, Project on Linguistic Analysis, University of California, Berkeley, March 24–25.

Chierchia, Gennaro. 1984. Topics in the syntax and semantics of infinitives and gerunds. PhD dissertation, University of Massachusetts.

Choi, Hyon-Bae. 1929[1989]. *Uli mal pon* [Our grammar]. Seoul: Chong Um Sa.

Chomsky, Noam. 1957. *Syntactic structures* (*Janua Linguarum* no. 4). Gravenhage: Mouton.

1964. *Current issues in linguistic theory*. The Hague: Mouton.

1965. *Aspects of the theory of syntax*. Cambridge, MA: MIT Press.

1970. Remarks on nominalization. In Roderick Jacobs and Peter Rosenbaum, eds., *Readings in English transformational grammar*, 184–221. Waltham, MA: Ginn.

1973[1977]. Conditions on transformations. In Anderson and Kiparsky, eds., 232–86. [Reprinted in Chomsky 1977, 81–160.]

1975. *Reflections on language*. New York: Pantheon.

1977. *Essays on form and interpretation*. New York: North-Holland.

1980. *Rules and representations*. New York: Columbia University Press.

1981a. On the representation of form and function. *The Linguistics Review* 1: 3–40.

1981b. *Lectures on government and binding*. Dordrecht: Foris.

1982. *Some concepts and consequences of the theory of government and binding*. Cambridge, MA: MIT Press.

1986a. *Knowledge of language: its nature, origin, and use*. New York: Praeger.

1986b. *Barriers*. Cambridge, MA: MIT Press.

1992. A minimalist program for linguistic theory. *MIT Occasional Papers in Linguistics*, no. 1. Cambridge, MA: MIT.

1994. Bare phrase structure. In G. Webelhuth, ed., *Government and binding theory and the minimalist program*, 383–439. Cambridge, MA: Blackwell.

1995. *The minimalist program*. Cambridge, MA: MIT Press.

Chung, Sandra. 1978. *Case marking and grammatical relations in Polynesian*. Austin: Texas Press.

Churchward, C. Maxwell. 1953. *Tongan grammar*. London: Oxford University Press.

Clancy, Patricia. 1993. Preferred argument structure in Korean acquisition. In E. V. Clark, ed., *Proceedings of the twenty-fifth annual Child Language Acquisition Research Forum*, 307–14. Stanford: CSLI.

Clark, Robin. 1985. The syntactic nature of logical form: evidence from Toba Batak. *Linguistic Inquiry* 16: 663–69.

Clark, Ross. 1973. Transitivity and case in Eastern Oceanic languages. *Oceanic Linguistics* 12: 559–605.

Clements, George N. 1975. The logophoric pronoun in Ewe: its role in discourse. *Journal of West African Languages* 10: 141–77.

Cole, Peter. 1983. The grammatical role of the causee in universal grammar. *International Journal of American Linguistics* 49: 115–33.

1984. Clause reduction in Ancash Quechua. In Cook and Gerdts, eds., 105–21.

Cole, Peter and J. M. Sadock, eds. 1977. *Syntax and semantics*, vol. VIII: *Grammatical relations*. New York: Academic Press.

Comrie, Bernard. 1975. Antiergative. *CLS* 11: 112–21.

1976a. The syntax of action nominals – a cross-language survey. *Lingua* 40: 177–201.

1976b. *Aspect*. Cambridge University Press.

1976c. The syntax of causative constructions: cross-language similarities and divergences. In Shibatani, ed., 261–312.

1977. In defense of spontaneous demotion: the impersonal passive. In Cole and Sadock, eds., 47–58.

1978. Ergativity. In Winfred P. Lehmann, ed., *Syntactic typology*, 329–94. Austin: University of Texas Press.

1979. Russian. In Timothy Shopen, ed., *Languages and their status*, 91–150. Cambridge, MA: Winthrop.

1982. Grammatical relations in Huichol. In P. J. Hopper and S. A. Thompson, eds., *Syntax and semantics*, vol. XV: *Studies in transitivity*, 95–115. New York: Academic Press.

1984a. Russian. In W. S. Chisolm, Jr., ed., *Interrogativity*, 7–46. Amsterdam and Philadelphia: John Benjamins.

1984b. Subject and object control: syntax, semantics, pragmatics. *BLS* 10: 450–64.

1985a. *Tense*. Cambridge University Press.

1985b. Causative verb formation and other verb-deriving morphology. In Shopen, ed., vol. III, 309–98.

1988. Conjunction reduction in pro-drop languages: some evidence. In Manfred Bierwisch, Wolfgang Motsch and Ilse Zimmermann (eds.), *Syntax, Semantik und Lexikon* (Studia Grammatica 29), 83–87. Berlin: Akademie-Verlag.

1989a. Some general properties of reference-tracking systems. In Doug Arnold, Martin Atkinson, Jacques Durand, Clair Grover and Louisa Sadler, eds., *Essays on grammatical theory and universal grammar*, 37–51. Oxford: Clarendon.

1989b. *Language universals and linguistic typology* (2nd edn.). University of Chicago Press.

1994. Towards a typology of reference-tracking devices. Paper presented to the International Symposium on Language Typology, University of Tsukuba, January.

Comrie, Bernard and Sandra A. Thompson. 1985. Complex nominalizations. In Shopen, ed., vol. III, 349–98.

Cook, Eung-Do and Donna B. Gerdts, eds. 1984. *Syntax and semantics*, vol. XVI: *The syntax of Native American languages*. Orlando, FL: Academic Press.

Cooreman, Ann. 1994. A functional typology of anti-passives. In Barbara Fox and Paul Hopper, eds., *Voice: form and fuction*, 49–88. Amsterdam and Philadelphia: John Benjamins.

Corbett, Greville G., Norman M. Fraser and Scott McGlashan, eds. 1993. *Heads in grammatical theory*. Cambridge University Press.

Cowper, Elizabeth. 1992. *A concise introduction to syntactic theory*. University of Chicago Press.

Craig, Colette G. 1977. *The structure of Jacaltec*. Austin and London: Texas Press.

1979. Jacaltec: field work in Guatemala. In Shopen, ed., 2–57.

Cresswell, M. 1978. Prepositions and point of view. *Linguistics and Philosophy* 2: 1–41.

1979. Adverbs of space and time. In F. Güenther and S. Schmidt, eds., *Formal semantics and pragmatics for natural languages*, 171–200. Dordrecht: Reidel.

Croft, William. 1990. *Typology and universals*. Cambridge University Press.

1991. *Syntactic categories and grammatical relations*. Chicago and London: University of Chicago Press.

1993. Case marking and the semantics of mental verbs. In J. Pustejovsky, ed., *Semantics and the lexicon*, 55–72. Dordrecht: Kluwer.

Crystal, David. 1982. *Linguistic controversies*. London: Edward Arnold.

Cutrer, L. Michelle. 1987. Theories of obligatory control. *DWPIL* 2: 6–37.

1993. Semantic and syntactic factors in control. In Van Valin, ed., 167–95.

Czepluch, Hartmut. 1981. *Syntaktische Funktionen im Englischen: Elemente einer 'funktionalen autonomen Syntax'*. Tübingen: Gunter Narr.

Czepluch, Hartmut and Hero Janßen, eds. 1984. *Syntaktische Struktur und Kasusrelation*. Tübingen: Gunter Narr.

Dahl, Östen. 1981. On the definition of the telic–atelic (bounded–nonbounded) distinction. In Tedeschi and Zaenen, eds., 79–90.

Dahlstrom, Amy. 1986. Plains Cree morphosyntax. PhD dissertation, University of California, Berkeley.

Dalrymple, Mary. 1993. *The syntax of anaphoric binding*. Stanford: CSLI.

Datz, M. 1980. Jacaltec syntactic structures and the demands of discourse. PhD dissertation, University of Colarado.

Davies, William D. 1984. Choctaw switch-reference and levels of syntactic representation. In Cook and Gerdts, eds., 123–47.

Dayley, Jon. 1981. Voice and ergativity in Mayan languages. *Journal of Mayan Lingusitics* 2.2: 3–81.

Dayley, Jon. 1985. Voice in Tzutujil. In Nichols and Woodbury, eds., 192–226.

Deane, Paul. 1991. Limits to attention: a cognitive theory of island phenomena. *Cognitive Linguistics* 2: 1–63.

Demuth, Katherine. 1989. Maturation and the acquisition of the Sesotho passive. *Language* 65: 56–80.

1990. Subject, topic and the Sesotho passive. *Journal of Child Language* 17: 67–84.

Dench, Alan. 1988. Complex sentences in Martuthunira. In P. Austin, ed., *Complex sentence constructions in Australian languages*, 97–140. Amsterdam and Philadelphia: John Benjamins.

Derbyshire, Desmond. 1985. *Hixkaryana and universal grammar*. Arlington, TX: Summer Institute of Linguistics.

Derbyshire, Desmond and Geoffrey K. Pullum, eds. 1986. *Handbook of Amazonian languages*, vol. I. Berlin: Mouton de Gruyter.

eds. 1989. *Handbook of Amazonian languages*, vol. II. Berlin: Mouton de Gruyter.

DeReuse, Willem. 1994. Noun incorporation in Lakota Siouan. *International Journal of American Linguistics* 60: 199–260.

Devriendt, Betty, Louis Goossens and Johan van der Auwera, eds. 1995. *Complex structures: a functionalist perspective*. Berlin: Mouton de Gruyter.

Dijk, Teun A. van, ed. 1985. *Handbook of discourse analysis*, vol. I. London: Academic Press.

Dik, Simon C. 1978. *Functional Grammar*. Amsterdam: North-Holland.

1980. *Studies in Functional Grammar*. London and New York: Academic Press.

1989. *The theory of Functional Grammar, part 1*. Dordrecht: Foris.

1991. Functional Grammar. In Droste and Joseph, eds., 247–74.

Dik, Simon C. and Kees Hengeveld. 1991. The hierarchical structure of the clause and the typology of perception-verb complements. *Linguistics* 29: 231–59.

Dinneen, Francis P. and E. F. Konrad Koerner, eds. 1990. *North American contributions to the history of linguistics* (Amsterdam Studies in the Theory and History of Linguistic Science. Series III, Studies in the History of the Language Sciences 58). Amsterdam and Philadelphia: John Benjamins.

Dixon, R. M. W. 1972. *The Dyirbal language of North Queensland*. Cambridge University Press.

ed. 1976. *Grammatical categories in Australian languages*. Canberra: Australian Institute of Aboriginal Studies.

1977. *A grammar of Yidiɲ*. Cambridge University Press.

1979. Ergativity. *Language* 55.1: 59–138.

1984. The semantic basis of syntactic properties. *BLS* 10: 583–95.

ed. 1987. *Studies in ergativity*. Amsterdam: North-Holland.

1988. *A grammar of Boumaa Fijian*. University of Chicago Press.

1991. *A new approach to English grammar, on semantic principles*. Oxford University Press.

1994. *Ergativity*. Cambridge University Press.

Downing, Pamela and Michael Noonan. 1995. *Word order in discourse*. Amsterdam and Philadelphia: John Benjamins.

Dowty, David. 1979. *Word meaning and Montague Grammar*. Dordrecht: Reidel.

1991. Thematic proto-roles and argument selection. *Language* 67.3: 547–619.

Droste, Fred and John Joseph, eds. 1991. *Linguistic theory and grammatical description*. Amsterdam and Philadelphia: John Benjamins.

Dryer, Matthew S. 1986. Primary objects, secondary objects, and antidative. *Language* 62: 808–45.

1992a. The Greenbergian word order correlations. *Language* 68.1: 81–138.

1992b. A comparison of the obviation systems of Kutenai and Algonquian. In William Cowan, ed., *Papers from the twenty-third annual Algonquian Conference*, 119–63. Ottawa: Carleton University.

1996a. Focus, pragmatic presupposition and activated propositions. *Journal of Pragmatics* 26: 475–523.

1996b. *Grammatical relations in Kutenai*. Winnipeg: Voices of Rupert's Land.

Du Bois, John W. 1980. Beyond definiteness: the trace of identity in discourse. In Wallace Chafe, ed., *The pear stories*, 203–74. Norwood, NJ: Ablex.

1987. The discourse basis of ergativity. *Language* 63: 805–55.

Durie, Mark. 1985. *A grammar of Acehnese*. Dordrecht: Foris.

1987. Grammatical relations in Acehnese. *Studies in Language* 11: 365–99.

1988a. The so-called passive of Acehnese. *Language* 64: 104–13.

1988b. Preferred argument structure in an active language. *Lingua* 74: 1–25.

Dziwirek, Katarzyna, Patrick Farrell and Errapel Mejías Bikandi, eds. 1990. *Grammatical relations: a cross-theoretical perspective*. Stanford: CSLI.

Emonds, Joseph. 1976. *A transformational approach to English syntax*. New York: Academic Press.

Erguvanlı, Eser. 1984. *The function of word order in Turkish grammar* (University of California publications in linguistics 106). Berkeley and Los Angeles: University of California Press.

Erteschik-Shir, Nomi. 1973. On the nature of island constraints. PhD dissertation, MIT.

1979. Discourse constraints on dative movement. In Givón ed., 441–67.

Erteschik-Shir, Nomi and Shalom Lappin. 1979. Dominance and the functional explanation of island phenomena. *Theoretical Linguistics* 6: 41–85.

Everett, Daniel. 1986. Pirahã. In Derbyshire and Pullum, eds., 200–325.

Faltz, Leonard. 1985. *Reflexivization: a study in universal syntax*. New York: Garland.

Farrell, Patrick. 1995. Lexical binding. *Linguistics* 33: 939–80.

Farrell, Patrick, Stephen A. Marlett and David M. Perlmutter. 1991. Notions of subjecthood and switch reference: evidence from Seri. *Linguistic Inquiry* 22: 421–56.

Fillmore, Charles J. 1968. The case for case. In Emmon Bach and Robert Harms, eds., *Universals in linguistic theory*, 1–88. New York: Holt, Reinhart and Winston.

1986. Pragmatically controlled zero anaphora. *BLS* 12: 95–107.

1988. The mechanisms of 'Construction Grammar'. *BLS* 14: 35–55.

Fillmore, Charles J., Paul Kay and Mary Catherine O'Connor. 1988. Regularity and idiomaticity in grammatical constructions: the case of *let alone*. *Language* 64: 501–38.

Firbas, Jan. 1964. On defining the theme in Functional Sentence Perspective. *Travaux linguistiques de Prague* 1: 267–80.

1966. Nonthematic subjects in contemporary English. *Travaux linguistiques de Prague* 2: 239–56.

1992. *Functional sentence perspective in written and spoken communication*. Cambridge University Press.

Fletcher, Paul and Michael Garman, eds. 1986. *Language acquisition* (2nd edn.). Cambridge University Press.

Fodor, Jerry. 1970. Three reasons for not deriving 'kill' from 'cause to die'. *Linguistic Inquiry* 1: 429–38.

1975. *The language of thought*. Cambridge, MA: Harvard University Press.

Foley, William A. and Robert D. Van Valin, Jr. 1984. *Functional syntax and universal grammar*. Cambridge University Press.

1985. Information packaging in the clause. In Shopen, ed., vol. I, 282–364.

Fox, Barbara. 1987. *Discourse structure and anaphora: written and conversational English*. Cambridge University Press.

Frajzynger, Zygmunt. 1995. A functional theory of matrix coding. Paper presented at the conference on Functional Approaches to Grammar, Albuquerque, NM.

Franklin, Karl. 1971. *A grammar of Kewa, New Guinea* (Pacific Linguistics C-16). Canberra: Australian National University.

Fretheim, Thorstein and Jeanette Gundel, eds. 1996. *Reference and referent accessibility*. Amsterdam and Philadelphia: John Benjamins.

Gawron, Jean Mark. 1986. Situations and prepositions. *Linguistics and Philosophy* 9: 327–82.

Gazdar, Gerald. 1982. Phrase structure grammar. In Jacobson and Pullum, eds., 131–86.

Gazdar, Gerald, Ewan Klein, Geoffrey Pullum and Ivan A. Sag. 1985. *Generalized Phrase Structure Grammar*. Cambridge, MA: Harvard University Press.

Genetti, Carol. 1986. Juncture, nexus, operators, and the Newari non-final construction. In S. Delancey and R. Tomlin, eds., *Proceedings of the second annual meeting of the Pacific Linguistics Conference*, 173–86. Eugene, OR: University of Oregon.

Geniusiene, Emma. 1987. *The typology of reflexives*. Berlin: Mouton de Gruyter.

Givón, Talmy. 1979a. *On understanding grammar*. New York, San Francisco and London: Academic Press.

ed. 1979b. *Syntax and semantics*, vol. XII: *Discourse and syntax*. New York: Academic Press.

1980. The binding hierarchy and the typology of complements. *Studies in Language* 4: 333–77.

1981. Typology and functional domains. *Studies in Language* 5.2: 163–93.

1983. Topic continuity in discourse: an introduction. In Talmy Givón, ed., *Topic continuity in discourse: a quantitative cross-language study*, 1–42. Amsterdam and Philadelphia: John Benjamins.

1984a. Direct object and dative shifting: semantic and pragmatic case. In Plank, ed., 151–82.

1984b. *Syntax: a functional–typological introduction*, vol. I. Amsterdam and Philadelphia: John Benjamins.

1989. *Mind, code and context: essays in pragmatics*. Hillsdale, NJ: Lawrence Erlbaum Associates.

1990. *Syntax: a functional–typological introduction*, vol. II. Amsterdam and Philadelphia: John Benjamins.

Greenberg, Joseph H. 1966. Some universals of grammar with particular reference to the order of meaningful elements. In J. H. Greenberg, ed., *Universals of language*, 73–113. Cambridge, MA: MIT Press.

Greenfield, Patricia M. 1978. Informativeness, presupposition, and semantic choice in single-word utterances. In N. Waterson and C. Snow, eds., *The development of communication*. New York: John Wiley.

Greenfield, Patricia M. and C. H. Dent. 1995. A developmental study of the communication of meaning: the role of uncertainty and information. In P. French, ed., *The development of meaning*. Tokyo: Oonka Hyoron Press.

Greenfield, Patricia M. and P. Goldring Zukow. 1978. Why do children say what they say when they say it? An approach to the psychogenesis of presupposition. In Katherine Nelson, ed., *Children's language*, vol. I. New York: Gardner Press.

Grice, H. Paul. 1975. Logic and conversation. In Peter Cole and Jerry Morgan, eds., *Syntax and semantics*, vol. III: *Speech acts*, 41–58. New York: Academic Press.

Grimshaw, Jane. 1982. On the lexical representation of Romance reflexives. In Bresnan, ed., 87–148.

1990. *Argument structure*. Cambridge, MA: MIT Press.

Gruber, Jeffrey. 1965. Studies in lexical relations. PhD dissertation, MIT.

Gundel, Jeanette K. 1976. *The role of topic and comment in linguistic theory*. Distributed by the Indiana University Linguistics Club, Bloomington, Indiana.

Gundel, Jeanette K., Nancy Hedberg and Ron Zacharski. 1993. Cognitive status and the form of referring expressions in discourse. *Language* 69.2: 274–307.

Haegeman, Liliane M. V. 1994. *Introduction to government and binding theory* (2nd edn.). Oxford, UK and Cambridge, MA: Basil Blackwell.

Haiman, John, and Sandra A. Thompson, eds. 1988. *Clause combining in grammar and discourse*. Amsterdam and Philadelphia: John Benjamins.

Hajičová, Eva and Petr Sgall. 1987. The ordering principle. *Journal of Pragmatics* 11: 435–54.

Hale, Kenneth. 1973. Person marking in Warlbiri. In Anderson and Kiparsky, eds., 308–44.

Halliday, Michael A. K. 1967. Notes on transitivity and theme in English. *Journal of Linguistics* 3: 37–81 (pt. I), 199–244 (pt. II).

1975. *Learning how to mean*. London: Edward Arnold.

1985. *An introduction to Functional Grammar*. Baltimore: University Park Press.

1994. *An introduction to Functional Grammar* (2nd edn.). London: Edward Arnold.

Halliday, Michael A. K. and Ruquia Hasan. 1976. *Cohesion in English*. London: Longman.

Hansell, Mark. 1993. Serial verbs and complement constructions in Mandarin: a clause linkage analysis. In Van Valin, ed., 197–233.

Harbert, Wayne. 1977. Clause union and German accusative plus infinitive constructions. In Cole and Sadock, eds., 121–49.

Harris, Alice. 1981. *Georgian syntax*. Cambridge University Press.

1982. Georgian and the unaccusative hypothesis. *Language* 58: 290–306.

Harris, Randy A. 1993. *The linguistics wars*. New York: Oxford University Press.

Harris, Zellig. 1946. From morpheme to utterance. *Language* 22: 161–83.

1957. Cooccurrence and transformation in linguistic structure. *Language* 33: 283–340.

Hasegawa, Yoko. 1992. Syntax, semantics, and pragmatics of TE-linkage. PhD dissertation, University of California, Berkeley.

1995. Metaphors and multiple thematic relations in case marking: a RRG analysis of Japanese ablative *kara*. Ms., University of California, Berkeley.

1996. *A study of Japanese clause linkage: the connective* TE *in Japanese*. Stanford: CSLI.

Haspelmath, Martin. 1995a. The converb as a cross-linguistically valid category. In M. Haspelmath and E. König, eds., *Converbs in cross-linguistic perspective: structural and semantic aspects of adverbial verbs forms*, 1–55. Berlin: Mouton de Gruyter.

1995b. Review of Van Valin 1993a. *Lingua* 97: 287–92.

Hawkins, Bruce W. 1985. The semantics of English spatial prepositions. PhD dissertation, University of California, San Diego; distributed by LAUT, Trier.

Hawkins, John A. 1983. *Word order universals*. New York: Academic Press.

ed. 1988. *Explaining language universals*. Basil Blackwell.

1994. *A performance theory of order and constituency*. Cambridge University Press.

Heath, Jeffrey. 1975. Some functional relationships in grammar. *Language* 51: 89–104.

1977. Choctaw cases. *BLS* 3: 204–13.

1979. Is Dyirbal ergative? *Linguistics* 17: 401–63.

1983. Reference-tracking in Nunggubuyu. In John Haiman and Pamela Munro, eds., *Switch-reference and universal grammar*, 129–49. Amsterdam and Philadelphia: John Benjamins.

Hellen, Lars. 1988. *Anaphora in Norwegian and the theory of grammar*. Dordrecht: Foris.
Hengeveld, Kees. 1989. Layers and operators in Functional Grammar. *Journal of Linguistics* 25: 127–57.
Hewitt, B. G. 1979. *Abkhaz* (Lingua Descriptive Series 2). Amsterdam: North-Holland.
1995. *Georgian: a structural reference grammar*. Amsterdam and Philadelphia: John Benjamins.
Hetzron, Robert. 1976. On the Hungarian causative verb and its syntax. In Shibatani, ed., 371–98.
Hockett, Charles. 1958. *A course in modern linguistics*. New York: Macmillan.
Holisky, Dee A. 1981a. On derived inceptives in Georgian. In Bernard Comrie, ed., *Studies of the languages of the USSR*, 148–71. Edmonton: Linguistic Research.
1981b. Aspect theory and Georgian aspect. In Tedeschi and Zaenen, eds., 127–44.
1987. The case of the intransitive subject in Tsova-Tush (Batsbi). *Lingua* 71: 103–32.
Hopper, Paul. 1987. Emergent grammar. *BLS* 13: 139–57.
Hopper, Paul J. and Sandra A. Thompson. 1980. Transitivity in grammar and discourse. *Language* 56: 251–99.
1984. The discourse basis for lexical categories in universal grammar. *Language* 60.4: 703–52.
1993. Language universals, discourse pragmatics, and semantics. In P. W. Davis, ed., *Language and its cognitive interpretation*, special issue of *Language Sciences* 15.4: 357–76.
Huang, C.-T. James. 1981. Move WH in a language without WH movement. *The Linguistic Review* 1: 369–416.
1982. Logical relations in Chinese and the theory of grammar. PhD dissertation, MIT.
Huang, Yan. 1994. *The syntax and pragmatics of anaphora*. Cambridge University Press.
Huber, W. 1980. Infinitivkomplemente im Deutschen. Transformationsgrammatische Untersuchungen zum Verb 'lassen'. PhD dissertation, Berlin.
Huck, Geoffrey J. and Younghee Na. 1990. Extraposition and focus. *Language* 66: 78–105.
Hudson, Richard. 1984. *Word Grammar*. Oxford: Blackwell.
1987. Zwicky on heads. *Journal of Linguistics* 23: 109–32.
1993. So-called 'double objects' and grammatical relations. *Language* 68: 251–76.
Humboldt, Wilhelm von. 1836. *Über die Verschiedenheit des menschlichen Sprachbaues und ihren Einfluss aft die geistige Entwicklung des Menschengeschlects*. Berlin: Dümmler.
Hyams, Nina. 1986. *Language acquisition and the theory of parameters*. Dordrecht: Reidel.
Hyman, Larry M. and Karl Zimmer. 1976. Embedded topic in French. In Li, ed., 189–211.
Hyman, Larry M. and Bernard Comrie. 1981. Logophoric reference in Gokana. *Journal of African Languages and Linguistics* 3: 19–37.
Hymes, Dell. 1974. *Directions in sociolinguistics*. Philadelphia: University of Pennsylvania Press.
Hymes, Dell and John Fought. 1981. *American structuralism*. Berlin: Mouton de Gruyter.
Ioup, G. 1975. Some universals for quantifier scope. In J. Kimball, ed., *Syntax and semantics*, vol. IV, 37–58. New York: Academic Press.
Jackendoff, Ray S. 1972. *Semantic interpretation in generative grammar*. Cambridge, MA: MIT Press.

1975. Morphological and semantic regularities in the lexicon. *Language* 51: 639–71.

1976. Toward an explanatory semantic representation. *Linguistic Inquiry* 7.1: 89–150.

1977. *X-bar syntax*. Cambridge, MA: MIT Press.

1990. *Semantic structures*. Cambridge, MA: MIT Press.

1992. Madame Tussaud meets the Binding Theory. *Natural Language and Linguistic Theory* 10: 1–31.

1997. *The architecture of the language faculty*. Cambridge, MA: MIT Press.

Jackson, Catherine A. 1984. Focus particles in Toba Batak. In Schachter, ed., 80–99.

Jacobsen, William H. 1979. The noun and verb in Nootkan. In Barbara S. Efrat, ed., *The Victoria Conference on Northwestern Languages* (British Columbia Provincial Museum Heratige Record 4), 83–155. Victoria: British Columbia Provincial Museum.

1993. Subordination and cosubordination in Nootka: clause combining in a polysynthetic verb-initial language. In Van Valin, ed., 235–74.

Jacobson, Pauline and Geoffrey Pullum, eds. 1982. *The nature of syntactic representation*. Dordrecht: Reidel.

Jakobson, Roman. 1957[1971]. Shifters, verbal categories, and the Russian verb. Published by the Dept. of Slavic Languages and Literatures, Harvard. [Reprinted in *Selected writings*, vol. II, 130–47. The Hague: Mouton.]

Johnson, Mark. 1987. A new approach to clause structure in Role and Reference Grammar. *DWPIL* 2: 55–9.

Jolly, Julia. 1991. *Prepositional analysis within the framework of Role and Reference Grammar*. New York: Peter Lang.

1993. Preposition assignment in English. In Van Valin, ed., 275–310.

Joshi, Aravind K. 1985. Tree-adjoining grammars: how much context-sensitivity is required to provide reasonable structural descriptions? In D. Dowty, L. Karttunen and A. Zwicky, eds., *Natural language parsing*, 206–50. Cambridge University Press.

Jurafsky, Dan. 1992. An on-line model of human sentence interpretation: a theory of the representation and use of linguistic knowledge. PhD dissertation, University of California, Berkeley.

Kamp, Hanse and Uwe Reyle. 1993. *From discourse to logic*. Hingham, MA: Kluwer.

Kaplan, Ronald and Joan Bresnan. 1982. Lexical–Functional Grammar: a formal system for grammatical representation. In Bresnan, ed., 173–281.

Kaplan, Ronald and Annie Zaenen. 1989. Long-distance dependencies, constituent structure, and functional uncertainty. In Mark Baltin and Anthony Kroch, eds., *Alternative conceptions of phrase structure*, 17–42. University of Chicago Press.

Karmiloff-Smith, Annette. 1979. *A functional approach to child language*. Cambridge University Press.

1992. *Beyond modularity*. Cambridge, MA: MIT Press.

Kasher, A. 1976. Conversational maxims and rationality. In A. Kasher ed., *Language in focus: foundations, methods and systems. Essays in memory of Yehushua Bar-Hillel*, 197–216. Dordrecht: Reidel.

Kayne, Richard. 1975. *French syntax: the transformational cycle.* Cambridge, MA: MIT Press.

1994. *The antisymmetry of syntax*. Cambridge, MA: MIT Press.

Kazenin, Konstantin I. 1994. Split syntactic ergativity: toward an implicational hierarchy. *Sprachtypologie und Universalienforschung* 47: 78–98.

Keenan, Edward L. 1976a. Towards a universal definition of 'subject.' In Li, ed., 305–33.

1976b. Remarkable subjects in Malagasy. In Li, ed., 247–301.

1985a. Passive in the world's languages. In Shopen, ed., vol. I, 243–81.

1985b. Relative clauses. In Shopen, ed., vol. II, 141–70.

Kemmerer, David. 1996. An investigation of syntactic comprehension deficits in Parkinson's Disease. PhD dissertation, SUNY at Buffalo.

Kempson, Ruth. 1975. *Presuppositon and the delimitation of semantics*. Cambridge University Press.

Kibrik, A. A. 1991. Maintenance of reference in sentence and discourse. In W. P. Lehmann and Helen-Jo Jakusz Hewitt, eds., *Language typology 1988*, 57–84. Amsterdam and Philadelphia: John Benjamins.

Kibrik, A. E. 1979a. Cannonical ergativity and Daghestan languages. In Plank, ed., 61–78.

1979b. Materialy k tipologii èrgativnosti. In *IRJaANSSSR, Problemnaja gruppa po èksperimental'noj i prikladnoj lingvistiki, Predvaritel'nye publikacii*, 126–7. Moscow: IRJaANSSSR.

1985. Toward a typology of ergativty. In Nichols and Woodbury, eds., 268–323.

1987. Constructions with clause actants in Daghestanian languages. *Lingua* 71: 133–78.

Kim, Alan H. O. 1988. Preverbal focusing and type XXIII languages. In M. Hammond, E. Moravcsik and J. Wirth, eds., *Studies in syntactic typology*, 147–72. Amsterdam and Philadelphia: John Benjamins.

Kimenyi, Alexandre. 1980. *A relational grammar of Kinyarwanda* (University of California publications in linguistics 91). Berkeley: University of California Press.

King, Tracy H. 1995. *Configuring topic and focus in Russian*. Stanford: CSLI.

Kiparsky, Paul. 1995. Partitive case and aspect. Paper presented at the Conference on Lexical Structures, University of Wuppertal.

Kirsner, Robert S. and Sandra A. Thompson. 1976. The role of pragmatic inference in semantics: a study of sensory verb complements in English. *Glossa* 10: 200–40.

Kishimoto, Hideki. 1996. Split intransitivity in Japanese and the unaccusative hypothesis. *Language* 72: 248–86.

É. Kiss, Katalin. 1987. *Configurationality in Hungarian*. Dordrecht: Reidel.

ed. 1994. *Discourse configurational languages*. Oxford Univesity Press.

Klaiman, M. H. 1991. *Grammatical voice*. Cambridge University Press.

Klimov, G. A. 1977. *Tipologija jazykov aktivnogo stroja*. Moscow: Nauka.

Kluender, Robert. 1992. Deriving island constraints from principles of predication. In Helen Goodluck and Michael Rochmont, eds., *Island constraints*, 223–58. Dordrecht: Kluwer.

Koenig, Jean-Pierre. 1994. Lexical underspecification and the syntax/semantics interface. PhD dissertation, University of California, Berkeley.

Koerner, E. F. K., ed. 1978. *Western histories of linguistic thought: an annotated chronological bibliography 1822–1976*. Amsterdam and Philadelphia: John Benjamins.

Koerner, E. F. K. and R. E. Asher, eds. 1995. *Concise history of the language sciences: from the Sumerians to the cognitivists*. Oxford: Pergamon.

Koster, Jan and Robert May, eds. 1981. *Levels of syntactic representation*. Dordrecht: Foris.

Koster, Jan and Eric Reuland, eds. 1991. *Long-distance anaphora*. Cambridge University Press.

Krifka, Manfred. 1992. A framework for focus-sensitive quantification. In C. Barker and D. Dowty, eds., *Proceedings of SALT II*, 215–36. Columbus: Ohio State Working Papers in Linguistics, no. 10.

Kroch, Anthony and Aravind K. Joshi. 1987. Analyzing extraposition in a tree adjoining grammar. In G. Huck and A. Ojeda, eds., *Syntax and semantics*, vol. XX: *Discontinuous constituency*, 107–49. New York: Academic Press.

Kuno, Susumu. 1972a. Functional Sentence Perspective: a case study from Japanese and English. *Linguistic Inquiry* 3: 269–320.

1972b. Pronominalization, reflexivization, and direct discourse. *Linguistic Inquiry* 3: 161–96.

1973. *The structure of the Japanese language*. Cambridge, MA: MIT Press.

1975. Three perspectives in the functional approach to syntax. *CLS Parasession on functionalism*, 276–336.

1976. Subject, theme, and the speaker's empathy. In Li, ed., 417–44.

1987. *Functional syntax: anaphora, discourse, and empathy*. University of Chicago Press.

1991. Remarks on quantifier scope. In H. Nakajima, ed., *Current English linguistics in Japan*, 261–87. Berlin and New York: Mouton de Gruyter.

Kuno, Susumu and Ken-Ichi Takami. 1993. *Grammar and discourse principles: functional syntax and GB theory*. University of Chicago Press.

Lakoff, George. 1987. *Women, fire, and dangerous things*. University of Chicago Press.

Lambrecht, Knud. 1986. Topic, focus, and the grammar of spoken French. PhD dissertation, University of California Berkeley.

1987. Sentence focus, information structure, and the thetic-categorial distinction. *BLS* 13: 366–82.

1989. When subjects behave like objects: a markedness analysis of sentence focus constructions across languages. Ms. (revised and expanded version of 1987 LSA paper), Austin.

1994. *Information structure and sentence form*. Cambridge University Press.

Lang, Rainer. 1973. Grammatical sketch. In A. Lang, *Enga dictionary*, xviii–lvii. Series C, no. 20. Canberra: Pacific Linguistics.

Langacker, Ronald W. 1987. *Foundations of Cognitive Grammar*, vol. I: *Theoretical prerequisites*. Stanford University Press.

1990. Settings, participants, and grammatical relations. In Savas L. Tsohatzidis, ed., *Meaning and prototypes: studies in linguistic categorization*. London and New York: Routledge.

1991. *Foundations of Cognitive Grammar*, vol. II. Stanford University Press.

1995. Raising and transparency. *Language* 71: 1–62.

LaPolla, Randy J. 1990. Grammatical relations in Chinese: synchronic and diachronic considerations. PhD dissertation, University of California, Berkeley.

1992. 'Anti-ergative' marking in Tibeto-Burman. *Linguistics of the Tibeto-Burman Area* 15.1: 1–9.

1993. Arguments against 'subject' and 'direct object' as viable concepts in Chinese. *Bulletin of the Institute of History and Philology* 63.4: 759–813.

1994. Parallel grammaticalizations in Tibeto-Burman: evidence of Sapir's 'drift.' *Linguistics of the Tibeto-Burman Area* 17.1: 61–80.

1995a. Pragmatic relations and word order in Chinese. In Pamela Downing and Michael Noonan, eds., *Word order in discourse*, 297–329. Amsterdam and Philadelphia: John Benjamins.

1995b. On the utility of the concepts of markedness and prototypes in understanding the development of morphological systems. *Bulletin of the Institute of History and Philology* 66.4: 1149–86.

Levin, Beth. 1989. The Basque verbal inventory and configurationality. In L. Marácz and P. Muysken, eds., *Configurationality: the typology of asymmetries*, 39–62. Dordrecht: Foris.

1993. *English verb classes and alternations*. University of Chicago Press.

Levinson, Stephen C. 1987. Pragmatics and the grammar of anaphora: a partial pragmatic reduction of binding and control phenomena. *Journal of Linguistics* 23: 379–434.

1991. Pragmatic reduction of the binding conditions revisited. *Journal of Linguistics* 27: 107–61.

Li, Charles N., ed. 1976. *Subject and topic*. New York: Academic Press.

Li, Charles N. and Rainer Lang. 1979. The syntactic irrelevance of an ergative case in Enga and other Papuan languages. In Plank, ed., 307–24.

Li, Charles N. and Sandra A. Thompson. 1976. Subject and topic: a new typology of language. In Li, ed., 459–89.

1981. *Mandarin Chinese: a functional reference grammar*. Berkeley: University of California Press.

Limber, John. 1973. The genesis of complex sentences. In T. Moore, ed., *Cognitive development and the acquisition of language*, 169–86. New York: Academic Press.

LoCasio, V. 1986. Interaction between verbal tenses and temporal adverbs in complex sentences. In V. LoCasio and C. Rohrer, eds., *Temporal structure in sentence and discourse*, 229–50. Dordrecht: Foris.

Longacre, Robert E. 1985. Sentences as combinations of clauses. In Shopen, ed., vol. II, 235–86.

Luelsdorf, Philip A. 1994. *The Prague School of structural and functional linguistics*. Amsterdam and Philadelphia: John Benjamins.

Lyons, John. 1968. *Introduction to theoretical linguistics*. Cambridge University Press.

1977. *Semantics*. Cambridge University Press.

Maling, Joan. 1986. Clause-bounded reflexives in Modern Icelandic. In L. Hellan and K. Christensen eds., *Topics in Scandinavian syntax*, 53–64. Dordrecht: Reidel.

Maling, Joan and Annie Zaenen. 1981. Germanic word order and the format of surface filters. In Frank Heny, eds., *Binding and filtering*, 255–78. Cambridge, MA: MIT Press.

1982. A phrase structure account of Scandinavian extraction phenomena. In Jacobson and Pullum, eds., 229–82.

Mann, William C. and Sandra A. Thompson. 1992. *Discourse description*. Amsterdam and Philadelphia: John Benjamins.

Manning, Christopher. 1994. Ergativity: argument structure and grammatical relations. PhD dissertation, Stanford University.

Manzini, Maria Rita. 1986. On Italian *si*. In Borer, ed., 241–62.

Marantz, Alec. 1984. *On the nature of grammatical relations*. Cambridge, MA: MIT Press.

Martinet, André. 1962. *A functional view of language*. Oxford: Clarendon Press.

1975. *Studies in functional syntax*. Munich: W. Fink.

Mathesius, Vilém. 1928[1964]. On linguistic characterology with illustrations from modern English. *Actes du Premier Congrès international de linguistes à la Haye*, 56–63. [Reprinted in J. Vachek, ed., 59–67.]

1929[1983]. Functional linguistics. In J. Vachek, ed., 121–42.

Matisoff, James A. 1973. *The grammar of Lahu* (University of California publications in linguistics 75). Berkeley and Los Angeles: University of California Press.

1976. Lahu causative constructions: case hierarchies and the morphology/syntax cycle in a Tibeto-Burman perspective. In Shibatani, ed., 413–42.

Matras, Yaron and Hans-Jürgen Sasse, eds. 1995. Verb–subject order and theticity in European languages. *Sprachtypologie und Universalien Forschung* 48, no. 1–2.

Matsumoto, Yoshiko. 1991. Is it really a topic that is relativized? Arguments from Japanese. *CLS* 27: 388–402.

Matthei, E. H. 1987. Subject and agent in emerging grammars: evidence for a change in children's biases. *Journal of Child Language* 14: 295–308.

Matthews, P. H. 1982. *Syntax*. Cambridge University Press.

1993. *Grammatical theory in the United States from Bloomfield to Chomsky*. Cambridge University Press.

Matthiessen, Christian. 1995. *Lexicogrammatical cartography: English systems*. Tokyo: International Language Sciences Publishers.

Matthiessen, Christian and Sandra A. Thompson. 1988. The structure of discourse and 'subordination'. In Haiman and Thompson, eds., 275–329.

May, Robert. 1985. *Logical form: its structure and derivation*. Cambridge, MA: MIT Press.

Mazaudon, Martine. 1978. La formation des propositions relatives en tibétain. *Bulletin de la Société de Linguistique de Paris* 73: 401–14.

McCawley, James D. 1979. *Adverbs, vowels and other objects of wonder*. University of Chicago Press.

McConnell-Ginet. 1982. Adverbs and logical form. *Language* 58: 144–84.

McKay, Terence. 1985. *Infinitival complements in German*. Cambridge University Press.

Mel'chuk, Igor. 1979. *Studies in dependency syntax*. Ann Arbor, MI: Karoma.

1987. *Dependency syntax: theory and practice*. Albany, NY: SUNY Press.

Mel'chuk, Igor and Nikolai V. Pertsov. 1986. *Surface syntax of English: a formal model within the Meaning–Text framework*. Amsterdam and Philadelphia: John Benjamins.

Melinger, Alissa. 1996. Quantifier scope in Italian: a syntactic comparison. In Eve Ng and Corinne Grimm, eds., *Proceedings from the second Buffalo–Toronto Student Conference in Linguistics*, 160–78. Buffalo: SUNY Buffalo Linguistics Dept.

Merlan, Francesca. 1985. Split intransitivity: functional oppositions in intransitive inflection. In Nichols and Woodbury, eds., 324–62.

Michaelis, Laura. 1993. On deviant case marking in Latin. In Van Valin, ed., 311–73.

Mithun, Marianne. 1991. Active/agentive case marking and its motivations. *Language* 67: 510–46.

Moortgaat, Michael. 1991. Generalized categorial grammar: the Lambek calculus. In Droste and Joseph, eds., 137–78.

Moravcsik, Edith A. and Jessica R. Wirth. 1980. *Syntax and semantics*, vol. XIII: *Current approaches to syntax*. New York: Academic Press.

Mourelatos, Alexander P. D. 1981. Events, processes and states. In Tedeschi and Zaenen, eds., 191–212.

Napoli, Donna Jo. 1993. *Syntax: theory and problems*. Oxford University Press.

Narasimhan, B. 1995. A lexical semantic explanation for 'quirky' case marking in Hindi. Paper presented at the annual meeting of the Linguistic Society of America.

Newmeyer, Frederick J., ed. 1980. *Linguistic theory in America: the first quarter-century of transformational generative grammar*. New York: Academic Press. (2nd edn. Orlando: Academic Press, 1986).

1986. *The politics of linguistics*. University of Chicago Press.

ed. 1988a. *Linguistic theory: foundations*. Cambridge University Press.

ed. 1988b. *Linguistic theory: extensions and implications*. Cambridge University Press.

Nichols, Johanna. 1982. Ingush transitivization and detransitivization. *BLS* 8: 445–62.

1984. Functional theories of grammar. *Annual Review of Anthropology* 13: 97–117.

1986. Head-marking and dependent-marking grammar. *Language* 62: 56–119.

Nichols, Johanna and Anthony Woodbury, eds. 1985. *Grammar inside and outside the clause*. Cambridge University Press.

Nichols, Lynn. 1990. Direct quotaion and switch reference in Zuni. *BLS* 16s, *Special session on general topics in American Indian linguistics*, 91–100.

Noonan, Michael. 1985. Complementation. In Shopen, ed., vol. II, 42–140.

1992. *A grammar of Lango*. Berlin and New York: Mouton de Gruyter.

Noonan, Michael and Edith Bavin Woock. 1978. The passive analog in Lango. *BLS* 4: 128–39.

Nunes, Mary L. 1993. Argument linking in English derived nominals. In Van Valin, ed., 375–432.

Nuyts, Jan. 1993. Epistemic modal adverbs and adjectives and the layered representation of conceptual and linguistic structure. *Linguistics* 31: 933–69.

1994. *Epistemic modal qualifications: on their linguistic and conceptual structure* (Antwerp Papers in Linguistics 81). University of Antwerp.

Nuyts, Jan, A. Machtelt Bolkestein and Co Vet, eds. 1990. *Layers and levels of representation in language theory: a functional view*. Amsterdam and Philadelphia: John Benjamins.

Ochs, Elinor and Bambi Schieffelin, eds. 1979. *Developmental pragmatics*. New York: Academic Press.

Ohori, Toshio. 1992. Diachrony in clause linkage and related issues. PhD dissertation, University of California, Berkeley.

Olson, Michael L. 1978. Switch-reference in Barai. *BLS* 4: 140–57.

1981. Barai clause junctures: toward a functional theory of inter-clausal relations. PhD dissertation, Australian National University.

Palmer, Frank R. 1986. *Mood and modality*. Cambridge University Press.
1994. *Grammatical roles and relations*. Cambridge University Press.
Park, Ki-seong. 1993. Korean causatives in Role and Reference Grammar. MA thesis, SUNY at Buffalo.
1995. The semantics and pragmatics of case marking in Korean: a Role and Reference Grammar account. PhD dissertation, SUNY at Buffalo.
Partee, Barbara. 1991. Topic, focus and quantification. In *Proceedings of SALT I*. Ithaca, NY: Cornell Working Papers in Linguistics, no. 10.
Payne, Doris L. 1990. *The pragmatics of word order: typological dimensions of verb-initial languages*. Berlin: Mouton de Gruyter.
Payne, Doris L. and Thomas E. Payne. 1989. Yagua. In Derbyshire and Pullum, eds., 249–474.
Payne, John R. 1985a. Negation. In Shopen, ed., vol. I, 197–242.
1985b. Complex phrases and complex sentences. In Shopen, ed., vol. II, 3–41.
1993. The headedness of noun phrases: slaying the nominal hydra. In Corbett, Fraser and McGlashan, eds., 114–39.
Perlmutter, David M. 1978. Impersonal passives and the unaccusative hypothesis. *BLS* 4: 157–89.
1980. Relational Grammar. In Moravcsik and Wirth, eds., 195–229.
1982. Syntactic representation, syntactic levels and the notion of subject. In Jacobson and Pullum, eds., 283–340.
Pesetsky, David. 1982. Paths and categories. PhD dissertation, MIT.
1987. Binding problems with experiencer verbs. *Linguistic Inquiry* 18.1: 126–40.
Pike, Kenneth. 1982. *Linguistic concepts: an introduction to Tagmemics*. Lincoln: University of Nebraska Press.
Pinker, Stephen. 1984. *Language learnability and language development*. Cambridge, MA: Harvard University Press.
1989. *Learnability and cognition*. Cambridge, MA: MIT Press.
Plank, Frans, ed. 1979. *Ergativity: toward a theory of grammatical relations*. London: Academic Press.
Polinsky, Maria. 1995. Double objects in causatives: towards a study of coding conflict. *Studies in Language* 19: 129–221.
Pollard, Carl and Ivan A. Sag. 1992. Anaphors in English and the scope of binding theory. *Linguistic Inquiry* 23.2: 261–304.
1994. *Head-driven Phrase Structure Grammar*. University of Chicago Press.
Postal, Paul. 1974. *On raising*. Cambridge, MA: MIT Press.
Prince, Ellen F. 1981a. Topicalization, focus movement and Yiddish movement: a pragmatic differentiation. *BLS* 7: 249–64.
1981b. Toward a taxonomy of given-new information. In Peter Cole, ed., *Radical pragmatics*, 223–55. New York and London: Academic Press.
Pustejovsky, James J. 1991. The generative lexicon. *Computational Linguistics* 17: 409–41.
1995. *The generative lexicon*. Cambridge, MA: MIT Press.
Quirk, Randolph, Sidney Greenbaum, Geoffrey Leech and Jan Svartvik. 1972. *A grammar of contemporary English*. New York: Seminar Press.

Radford, Andrew. 1981. *Transformational syntax*. Cambridge University Press.

1988. *Transformational grammar: a first course*. Cambridge University Press.

Ransom, Evelyn N. 1986. *Complementation: its meanings and forms*. Amsterdam and Philadelphia: John Benjamins.

Rauh, Gisa, ed. 1991. *Approaches to prepositions*. Tübingen: Gunter Narr.

Reinhart, Tanya. 1981. Pragmatics and linguistics: an analysis of sentence topics. *Philosophica* 27: 53–94.

1983. *Anaphora and semantic interpretation*. University of Chicago Press.

Reinhart, Tanya and Eric Reuland. 1993. Reflexivity. *Linguistic Inquiry* 24: 657–720.

Reis, Marga, ed. 1993. *Wortstellung und Informationsstruktur*. Tübingen: M. Niemeyer.

Riemsdijk, Henk van. 1982. Derivational vs. representational grammar. *Linguistics in the morning calm: selected papers from SICOL 1989*, 211–32. Seoul: Hanshin.

Riemsdijk, Henk van and Edwin Williams. 1981. NP-structure. *The Linguistic Review* 1: 171–217.

Rijkhoff, Jan. 1990. Explaining word order in the noun phrase. *Linguistics* 28: 5–42.

1992. The noun phrase: a typological study of its form and structure. PhD dissertation, University of Amsterdam.

Rispoli, Matthew. 1987. The acquisition of transitive and intransitive action verb categories in Japanese. *First Language* 7: 183–200.

1989. Encounters with Japanese verbs. *First Language* 9: 57–80.

1990. Lexical assignability and perspective switch: the acquisition of verb subcategorization for aspectual inflections. *Journal of Child Language* 17: 375–92.

1991a. The acquisition of verb subcategorization in a functionalist framework. *First Language* 11: 41–63.

1991b. The mosaic acquisition of grammatical relations. *Journal of Child Language* 18: 517–52.

1992. Discourse and the acquisition of *eat*. *Journal of Child Language* 19: 581–95.

1994. Structural dependency and the acquisition of grammatical relations. In Y. Levy, ed., *Other children, other languages: issues in the theory of language acquisition*, 265–301. Hillsdale, NJ: Lawrence Erlbaum Associates.

1995. Missing arguments and the acquisition of predicate meaning. In Tomasello and Merriman, eds., 331–52.

Roberts, John. 1988. Amele switch-reference and the theory of grammar. *Linguistic Inquiry* 19.1: 45–64.

Roberts, Linda. 1995. Pivots, voice and macroroles: from Germanic to universal grammar. *Australian Journal of Linguistics* 15: 157–214.

Rochemont, Michael S. 1986. *Focus in generative grammar*. Amsterdam and Philadelphia: John Benjamins.

Rochemont, Michael S. and Peter W. Culicover. 1990. *English focus constructions and the theory of grammar*. Cambridge University Press.

Rögnvaldsson, Eiríkur. 1982. We need (some kind of a) rule of conjunction reduction. *Linguistic Inquiry* 13.3: 557–61.

Rooth, Mats. 1985. Association with focus. PhD dissertation, University of Massachusetts, Amherst.

Rosen, Carol. 1984. The interface between semantic roles and initial grammatical relations. In David Perlmutter and Carol Rosen, eds., *Studies in Relational Grammar*, vol. II, 38–77. University of Chicago Press.

Rosenbaum, Peter. 1967. *The grammar of English predicate complement constructions.* Cambridge, MA: MIT Press.

Ross, John Robert. 1967[1986]. Constraints on variables in syntax. PhD dissertation, MIT. [Published as *Infinite syntax*, Norwood, NJ: Ablex, 1986.]

1972. Act. In D. Davidson and G. Harman, eds., *Semantics of natural language*, 70–126. Dordrecht: Reidel.

Rudanko, Juhani. 1989. *Complementation and case grammar: a syntactic and semantic study of selected patterns of complementation in present-day English.* Albany, NY: SUNY Press.

1996. *Prepositions and complement clauses: a syntactic and semantic study of verbs governing prepositions and complement clauses in present-day English.* Albany, NY: SUNY Press.

Russell, Bertrand. 1905. On denoting. *Mind* n.s. 14: 479–93.

Růžička, Rudolph. 1983. Remarks on control. *Linguistic Inquiry* 14: 309–24.

Sadock, Jerrold. 1991. *Autolexical syntax.* University of Chicago Press.

1995. An optimality-like account of English word order. Unpublished ms., University of Chicago.

Sadock, Jerrold and Arnold Zwicky. 1985. Speech act distinctions in syntax. In Shopen, ed., vol. I, 155–95.

Sag, Ivan A., Lauri Karttunen and Jeffrey Goldberg. 1992. A lexical analysis of Icelandic case. In Ivan Sag and Anna Szabolcsi, eds., *Lexical matters*, 301–18. Stanford: CSLI.

Sag, Ivan A. and Carl Pollard. 1991. An integrated theory of complement control. *Language* 67: 63–113.

Sampson, Geoffrey. 1980. *Schools of linguistics.* Stanford University Press.

Sapir, Edward. 1921. *Language.* New York: Henry Holt.

1924[1951]. The grammarian and his language. *American Mercury* 1: 149–55. [Reprinted in D. Mandelbaum, ed., *Selected writings of Edward Sapir in language, culture and personality*, 150–9. Berkeley: University of California Press.]

Sapir, Edward and Morris Swadesh. 1939. *Nootka texts: tales and ethnological narratives with grammatical notes and lexical materials.* Philadelphia, PA: Linguistic Society of America.

Sasse, Hans-Jürgen. 1987. The thetic/categorial distinction revisited. *Linguistics* 25: 511–80.

1991a. Aspect and aktionsart: a reconciliation. In Carl Vetters and Willy Vandeweghe, eds., *Perspectives on aspect and Aktionsart*, 31–45. *Belgian Journal of Linguistics* 6.

1991b. Aspekttheorie. In H.-J. Sasse, ed., *Aspectsysteme* (Arbeitspapier no. 14), 1–35. Institut für Sprachwissenschaft, Universität Köln.

Saussure, Ferdinand de. 1917[1959]. *Course in general linguistics*, ed. by Charles Bally and Albert Sechehaye, with Albert Riedlinger. New York: McGraw-Hill.

Schachter, Paul. 1976. The subject in Philippine languages: actor, topic, actor–topic, or none of the above. In Li, ed., 491–518.

1977. Reference-related and role-related properties of subjects. In Cole and Morgan, eds., 279–306.

ed. 1984a. *Studies in the stucture of Toba Batak* (UCLA Occasional Papers in Linguistics 5). UCLA Department of Linguistics.

1984b. Semantic-role-based syntax in Toba Batak. In Schachter, ed., 122–49.

1985. Parts-of-speech systems. In Shopen, ed., vol. I, 1–61.

Schieffelin, Bambi. 1985. The acquisition of Kaluli. In Dan I. Slobin, ed., *The cross-linguistic study of language acquisition*, 525–93. Hillsdale, NJ: Lawrence Erlbaum.

Schlesinger, I. M. 1982. *Steps to language: toward a theory of language acquisition*. Hillsdale, NJ: LEA.

Schwartz, Linda. 1986. Levels of grammatical relations and Russian reflexive controllers. *BLS* 12: 235–45.

1993. On the syntactic and semantic alignment of attributive and identificational constructions. In Van Valin, ed., 433–63.

Scott, Graham. 1978. *The Fore language of Papua New Guinea* (Pacific Languages B-47). Canberra: Australian National University.

Searle, John R. 1969. *Speech acts: an essay in the philosophy of language*. Cambridge University Press.

1975. A taxonomy of illocutionary acts. In K. Gunderson, ed., *Language, mind, and knowledge*, 344–69. Minneapolis: University of Minnesota Press.

Seiler, Hansjakob and Waldfried Premper, eds. 1991. *Partizipation: das sprachliche Erfassen von Sachverhalten*. Tübingen: Gunter Narr.

Seiter, William. 1978. Subject/direct object raising in Niuean. *BLS* 4: 211–22.

Selkirk, Elizabeth. 1984. *Phonology and syntax*. Cambridge, MA: MIT Press.

Sells, Peter. 1987. Aspects of logophoricity. *Linguistics Inquiry* 18: 445–79.

Sgall, Petr, Eva Hajičová and Jarmila Panevová. 1986. *The meaning of the sentence in its semantic and pragmatic aspects*, ed. by Jacob L. Mey. Dordrecht and Boston: D. Reidel.

Shibatani, Masayoshi. 1973. Semantics of Japanese causativization. *Foundations of Language* 9: 327–73.

ed. 1976. *Syntax and semantics*, vol. VI: *The grammar of causative constructions*. New York: Academic Press.

ed. 1988. *Passives and voice* (Typological studies in language 16). Amsterdam and Philadelphia: John Benjamins.

Shibatani, Masayoshi and Sandra A. Thompson, eds. 1996. *Grammatical constructions*. Oxford University Press.

Shimojo, Mitsuaki. 1995. Focus structure and morphosyntax in Japanese: *wa* and *ga*, and word order flexibility. PhD dissertation, State University of New York at Buffalo.

Shopen, Timothy, ed. 1979. *Languages and their speakers*. Cambridge, MA: Winthrop.

ed. 1985. *Language, typology and syntactic description* (3 vols.). Cambridge University Press.

Shugamoto, Nobuko. 1984. Reflexives in Toba Batak. In Schachter, ed., 150–71.

Siewierska, Anna. 1984. *The passive: a comparative linguistic analysis*. London: Croom Helm.

1993. Syntactic weight vs. information structure and word order variation in Polish. *Journal of Linguistics* 29: 233–66.

Silverstein, Michael. 1976. Hierarchy of features and ergativity. In Dixon, ed., 112–71.

1977. Cultural prerequisites to grammatical analysis. In M. Saville-Troike, ed., *Linguistics and anthropology*, 139–51. Washington: Georgetown University Press.

1981. Case marking and the nature of language. *Australian Journal of Linguistics* 1: 227–46.

1987. The three faces of 'function': preliminaries to a psychology of language. In M. Hickman, ed., *Social and functional approaches to language and thought*, 17–38. Orlando: Academic Press.

1993. Of nominatives and datives: universal grammar from the bottom up. In Van Valin, ed., 465–98.

Slobin, Dan I. 1973. Cognitive prerequisites for the development of grammar. In C. Ferguson and D. Slobin, eds., *Studies of child language development*, 175–208. New York: Holt, Rinehart and Winston.

1985. Cross-linguistic evidence for the language-making capacity. In Dan Slobin, ed., *The crosslinguistic study of language acquisition*, vol. II, 1157–256. Hillsdale, NJ: Lawrence Erlbaum Associates.

forthcoming. The origins of grammaticizable notions: beyond the individual mind. In Dan Slobin, ed., *The crosslinguistic study of language acquisition*, vol. V. Hillsdale, NJ: Lawrence Erlbaum Associates.

Soames, Scott. 1982. How presuppositions are inherited: a solution to the projection problem. *Linguistic Inquiry* 13: 483–545.

Sperber, Dan and Dierdre Wilson. 1986. *Relevance: communication and cognition.* Cambridge, MA: Harvard University Press.

Sridhar, S. N. 1976. Dative subjects. *CLS* 12: 582–93.

Steedman, Mark. 1991. Structure and intonation. *Language* 67.2: 260–96.

Stephany, Ursula. 1986. Modality. In Fletcher and Garman, eds., 375–400.

Talmy, Leonard. 1976. Semantic causative types. In Shibatani, ed., 43–116.

1978. The relation of grammar to cognition – a synopsis. In D. Waltz, ed., *Theoretical issues in natural language processing*, vol. II. New York: Association for Computing Machinery.

1985. Lexicalization patterns: semantic structure in lexical form. In Shopen, ed., vol. III, 57–149.

1988. Force dynamics in language and cognition. *Cognitive Science* 12: 49–100.

1991. Path to realization – via aspect and result. *BLS* 17: 480–519.

Tao, Liang. 1986. Clause linkage and zero anaphora in Mandarin Chinese. *DWPIL* 1: 36–102.

Tedeschi, Philip J. and Annie Zaenen, eds. 1981. *Syntax and semantics*, vol. XIV: *Tense and aspect.* New York: Academic Press.

Tesnière, Lucien. 1939. Théorie structurale des temps composés. *Mélanges Bally*, 153–83. Geneva: Georg.

1953. *Equisse d'une syntaxe structurale*. Paris: Klinksieck.

1959. *Eléments de syntaxe structurale*. Paris: Klinksieck.

Thompson, Sandra A. 1987. The passive in English: a discourse perspective. In Robert Channon and Linda Shockey, eds., *In honor of Ilse Lehiste: Ilse Lehiste puhendusteos*, 497–511. Dordrecht: Foris.

1988. A discourse approach to the cross-linguistic category 'adjective.' In Hawkins, ed., 167–85.

to appear. Discourse motivations for the core-oblique distinction as a language universal. In Akio Kamio, ed., *Functionalism in linguistics*. Berlin: Mouton de Gruyter.

Thompson, Sandra A. and Robert E. Longacre. 1985. Adverbial clauses. In Shopen, ed., vol. II, 171–234.

Thráinsson, Höskuldur. 1979. *On complementation in Icelandic*. New York: Garland.

1991. Long-distance reflexives and the typology of NPs. In Koster and Reuland, eds., 49–75.

Thurman, Robert. 1975. Chuave medial verbs. *Anthropological Linguistics* 17.7: 342–52.

Toman, Jindrich. 1995. *The magic of a common language: Jakobson, Mathesius, Trubetzkoy, and the Prague Linguistic Circle*. Cambridge, MA: MIT Press.

Tomasello, Michael. 1992. *First verbs: a case study in early grammatical development*. Cambridge University Press.

Tomasello, Michael and William E. Merriman, eds. 1995. *Beyond names for things: children's acquisition of verbs*. Hillsdale, NJ: LEA.

Tomlin, Russell S. 1986. *Basic word order: functional principles*. London: Croom Helm.

ed. 1987. *Coherence and grounding in discourse* (Typological studies in language 11). Amsterdam and Philadelphia: John Benjamins.

Tsao, Feng-fu. 1990. *Sentence and clause structure in Chinese: a functional perspective*. Taipei: Student Book Company.

Underhill, Robert. 1976. *Turkish grammar*. Cambridge, MA: MIT Press.

Vachek, J., ed. 1964. *A Prague School reader in linguistics*. Bloomington and London: Indiana University Press.

ed. 1983. *Praguiana*. Amsterdam and Philadelphia: John Benjamins.

van Hoek, Karen. 1995. Conceptual reference points: a cognitive grammar account of pronominal anaphora constraints. *Language* 71: 310–40.

Van Valin, Robert D., Jr. 1977. Aspects of Lakhota syntax. PhD dissertation, University of California, Berkeley.

1980. On the distribution of passive and antipassive constructions in universal grammar. *Lingua* 50: 303–27.

1981. Grammatical relations in ergative languages. *Studies in Language* 5: 361–94.

1984. A typology of syntactic relations in clause linkage. *BLS* 10: 542–58.

1985. Case marking and the structure of the Lakhota clause. In Nichols and Woodbury, eds., 363–413.

1986a. An empty category as the subject of a tensed S in English. *Linguistic Inquiry* 17: 581–86.

1986b. Pragmatics, island phenomena, and linguistic competence. *CLS* 22.2: *Papers from the parasession on Pragmatics and Grammatical Theory*, 223–33.

1987a. The role of government in the grammar of head-marking languages. *International Journal of American Linguistics* 53: 371–97.

1987b. Aspects of the interaction of syntax and pragmatics: discourse coreference mechanisms and the typology of grammatical systems. In Jef Verschueren and Marcella Bertuccelli-Papi, eds., *The pragmatic perspective: selected papers from the*

1985 International Pragmatics Conference (Pragmatics and Beyond Companion Series 5), 513–31. Amsterdam and Philadelphia: John Benjamins.

1990. Semantic parameters of split intransitivity. *Language* 66.2: 221–60.

1991a. Functionalist linguistic theory and language acquisition. *First Language* 11: 7–40.

1991b. Another look at Icelandic case marking and grammatical relations. *Natural Language and Linguistic Theory* 9: 145–94.

1992a. Incorporation in universal grammar: a case study in theoretical reductionism. *Journal of Linguistics* 28: 199–220.

1992b. An overview of ergative phenomena and their implications for language acquisition. In D. Slobin, ed., *The cross-linguistic study of language acquisition*, vol. III, 15–37. Hillsdale, NJ: LEA.

ed. 1993a. *Advances in Role and Reference Grammar*. Amsterdam and Philadelphia: John Benjamins.

1993b. A synopsis of Role and Reference Grammar. In Van Valin, ed., 1–164.

1994. Extraction restrictions, competing theories and the argument from the poverty of the stimulus. In Susan Lima, Roberta L. Corrigan and Gregory K. Iverson, eds., *The reality of linguistic rules*, 243–59. Amsterdam and Philadelphia: John Benjamins.

1995a. Role and Reference Grammar. In J. Verschueren, J.-O. Östman and J. Blommaert, eds., *Handbook of pragmatics: manual*, 461–8. Amsterdam and Philadelphia: John Benjamins.

1995b. Toward a functionalist account of so-called extraction constraints. In Devriendt, Goosens and van der Auwera, eds., 29–60.

Van Valin, Robert D., Jr. and William A. Foley. 1980. Role and Reference Grammar. In Moravcsik and Wirth, eds., 329–52.

Van Valin, Robert D., Jr. and David P. Wilkins. 1993. Predicting syntactic structure from semantic representations: *remember* in English and Mparntwe Arrernte. In Van Valin, ed., 499–534.

1996. The case for 'effector': case roles, agents and agency revisited. In Shibatani and Thompson, eds., 289–322.

Vendler, Zeno. 1957[1967]. *Linguistics in philosophy*. Ithaca: Cornell University Press.

Verkuyl, Henk J. 1993. *A theory of aspectuality*. Cambridge University Press.

Vincent, Nigel. 1993. Head-versus dependent-marking: the case of the clause. In Corbett, Fraser and McGlashan, eds., 140–63.

Voorst, Jan van. 1988. *Event structure*. Amsterdam and Philadelphia: John Benjamins.

Walton, Charles. 1986. *Sama verbal semantics: classification, derivation and inflection*. Manila: Linguistic Society of the Philippines.

Wanner, Eric. and Lila. Gleitman, eds. 1982. *Language acquisition: the state of the art*. Cambridge University Press.

Ward, Gregory L. 1990. The discourse functions of VP preposing. *Language* 66: 742–63.

Wasow, Thomas. 1977. Transformations and the lexicon. In Peter Culicover, Thomas Wasow and Adrian Akmajian, eds., *Formal syntax*, 327–60. New York: Academic Press.

Watters, James K. 1986. Notes on Tepehua verbal semantics. *DWPIL* 1: 118–44.

1988. Topics in the Tepehua grammar. PhD dissertation, University of California, Berkeley.

1993. An investigation of Turkish clause linkage. In Van Valin, ed., 535–60.

1996. The interpretation of deverbal nominals in Tepehua. In Shibatani and Thompson, eds., 333–9.

Weber, David J. 1983. *Relativization and nominalized clauses in Huallaga (Huanuco) Quechua* (University of California Publications in Linguistics 103). Berkeley: University of California Press.

1989. *A grammar of Huallaga (Huanuco) Quechua* (University of California Publications in Linguistics 112). Berkeley: University of California Press.

Wehrli, Eric. 1986. On some properties of French clitic *se*. In Borer, ed., 263–83.

Weist, Richard M. 1986. Tense and aspect. In Fletcher and Garman, eds., 356–74.

1990. Neutralization and the concept of subject in child Polish. *Linguistics* 28.1331–49.

Whaley, Lindsay J. 1993. The status of obliques in linguistic theory. PhD dissertation, State University of New York at Buffalo.

Wierzbicka, Anna. 1972. *Semantic primitives*. Frankfurt: Atheneum.

1980a. *Lingua mentalis*. Sydney: Academic Press.

1980b. *The case for surface case*. Ann Arbor, MI: Karoma.

1987. *English speech act verbs: a semantic dictionary*. Sydney: Academic Press.

1988. *The semantics of grammar*. Amsterdam and Philadelphia: John Benjamins.

1992. *Semantics, culture, and cognition: universal human concepts in culture-specific configurations*. New York: Oxford University Press.

Wilkins, David P. 1988. Switch-reference in Mparntwe Arrernte (Aranda): form, function, and problems of identity. In Peter Austin, ed., *Complex sentences in Australian languages*, 141–76. Amsterdam and Philadelphia: John Benjamins.

1989. Mparntwe Arrernte (Aranda): studies in the structure and semantics of grammar. PhD dissertation, Australian National University.

Williams, Edwin. 1984. Grammatical relations. *Linguistics Inquiry* 15: 639–73.

1994. *Thematic structure in syntax*. Cambridge, MA: MIT Press.

Williamson, Janice. 1984. Studies in Lakhota grammar. PhD dissertation, University of California, San Diego.

Wilson, Bob and Ann Peters. 1988. What are you cookin' on a hot? A three-year-old blind child's violation of universal constraints on constituent movement. *Language* 64: 249–73.

Winther-Nielsen, Nicolai. 1995. *A functional discourse grammar of Joshua*. Stockholm: Almquist and Wiksell International.

Wölck, Wolfgang. 1987. *Pequeño Breviario Quechua*. Lima: IEP.

Wolfart, H. C. 1973. *Plains Cree: a grammatical study* (Transactions of the American Philosophical Society 63, pt. 5). Philadelphia: American Philosophical Society.

Yang, Byong-seon. 1993. Clause structure and NP accessibility of Korean internally headed relative clause in Role and Reference Grammar. In S. Kuno, ed., *Harvard Studies in Korean Linguistics*, vol. V, 230–8. Seoul: Hanshin.

1994. Morphosyntactic phenomena of Korean in Role and Reference Grammar: psych-verb constructions, inflectional verb morphemes, complex sentences, and relative clauses. PhD dissertation, State University of New York at Buffalo. [Published by Hankuk, Seoul, 1994.]

Yip, Moira, Joan Maling and Ray Jackendoff. 1987. Case in tiers. *Language* 63: 217–50.

Zaenen, Annie, Joan Maling and Höskuldur Thráinsson. 1985. Case and grammatical functions: the Icelandic passive. *Natural Language and Linguistic Theory* 3: 441–83.

Zribi-Hertz, Anne. 1989. Anaphor binding and narrative point of view: English reflexive pronouns in sentence and discourse. *Language* 65: 695–727.

Zubin, David, Soon Ae Chun, and Naicong Li. 1990. Misbehaving reflexives in Korean and Mandarin. *B L S* 16: 338–54.

Zwicky, Arnold. 1985. Heads. *Journal of Linguistics* 21: 1–29.

INDEX OF LANGUAGES

SUBJECT INDEX